Government Support Index

HANDBOOK

2020

Government

Support Index

HANDBOOK

2020

OMNIGRAPHICS

615 Griswold St., Suite 520
Detroit, MI 48226

Omnigraphics

Angela L. Williams, *Managing Editor*

Copyright © 2020 Omnigraphics

ISBN 978-0-7808-1747-0
Printed in the United States of America

615 Griswold St., Suite 520
Detroit, MI 48226
www.omnigraphics.com

Table of Contents

Disclaimer

We have endeavored to compile and present information in this book simply and accurately. The programs described intend to provide a basic understanding of the programs' benefits intended by their federal agencies.

Federal agency offices, contact details, and programs are subject to change over time. As a result, there may be unintended errors, inaccuracies, or omissions despite every effort being made to avoid such inaccuracies.

The information in this publication was compiled from the Catalog of Federal Domestic Assistance (CFDA), Federal Assistance Listings maintained by the General Services Administration (GSA) and other government-funding data made available from USAspending.gov. While these sources are considered reliable and every effort has been made to ensure the reliability of this content, the publisher will not assume liability for damages caused by inaccuracies, and makes no warranty, express or implied, on the accuracy of the information contained herein.

GOVERNMENT SUPPORT INDEX HANDBOOK users may share their comments about the book with the editor. Suggestions are welcome in order to improve upon any aspect of the book and are appreciated.

Editor
Omnigraphics
615 Griswold St., Suite 520
Detroit, MI 48226
www.omnigraphics.com
editorial@omnigraphics.com

Introduction

The Government Support Index Handbook provides a basic description of all domestic programs that offer financial and nonfinancial assistance from federal agencies, and helps readers distinguish between programs administered to the public via local offices and those administered from the federal agency headquarters.

This book includes 2,255 federal programs that are summarized from data contained in the Catalog of Federal Domestic Assistance (CFDA), maintained by the General Services Administration. It provides a basic profile of each program that condenses over 3,000 pages in the CFDA to just the essential details.

This book includes new programs that are created through federal authorization, including USC, ACT, Statute, Public Law, and Executive Order, to meet the new needs of the American public. While it's rare that programs are terminated, it is more common for programs to be replaced. Over time, the number of programs has grown from 989 in 1984 to 2,255 today.

When available, the following information is provided for each program:

- Agency abbreviation and program number (shown graphically)
- Program name and Popular name, when applicable
- Award type(s)
- Purpose and objectives
- Applicant and Beneficiary eligibility rules
- Award range and average values awarded applicable to financial awards
- Funding values of recent awards by fiscal year
- Headquarter office address and contact

Each program is given an identifying graphic block. It shows each program by its agency abbreviation, such as HHS (which refers to HEALTH AND HUMAN SERVICES, DEPARTMENT OF), as provided in the Agency Index. It also identifies its five-digit Program number. The first two digits identify and coordinate to the administrative entity responsible for the program. The last three digits identify the program.

The arrangement of programs is organized into two sections. The first is programs administered by federal headquarters where contacts, pre-qualifications, application, and administration are handled from the federal agency directly. In this section, the sequence of programs is alphabetical by Program name. The second section contains programs administered by regional, state, and local offices that are first points of contact when both headquarters and regional offices are applicable. This section of programs is arranged by the administering agency and the programs are sequenced by Program number numerically. The program office locations and contact details appear before the program entries to which they apply.

Timeliness of Information

Currently, there are 54 federal agencies, departments, independent offices, and commissions that manage programs through their headquarter office, or through their 174 sub-agencies, or through regional, state, and local offices. Agencies may update programs, contacts, office, email, and website addresses. At the time of printing, the information provided in this book is accurate and has a 90 percent likelihood of remaining so over the course of one year based on a sampling of similar published directories.

However, in order to provide more timely updates, a companion website, *GOVERNMENT SUPPORT INDEX*, is made available with this book. This website provides updates or corrections to data with ongoing and regular frequency. The website includes annual updates to existing programs, and adds new programs as a result of agency updates and annual government fiscal-year funding. Likewise, programs without annual updates for Fiscal Year 2020 are provided in the website, but do not appear in the book. It is recommended that users contact the agency with questions about the program's status. The government fiscal year runs from October 1 to September 30 of the current year. For example, Fiscal Year 2019 covers October 1, 2018 through September 30, 2019. Annual program updates appear in the website after the government's fiscal-year end.

Federal Award Types

Programs are identified by 15 award types of federal domestic assistance that are either financial or nonfinancial.

The financial award types are:

1. Direct loans—loan of federal funds for a specific term, with or without interest, with repayment expected.

2. Direct payments/specified use—funds for a specified purpose, with no repayment expected.

3. Direct payments/unrestricted use—funds for use at will by the recipient, with no repayment expected.

4. Formula grants—funds are distributed to states or other recipients according to a formula (often population-based) for continuing activities not restricted to a specific project. No repayment is expected.

5. Guaranteed/insured loans—guarantee or insurance against loan defaults for private or public lending institutions, covering all or a portion of the amount borrowed.

6. Insurance—coverage for reimbursement of losses under specified conditions such as coverage from a federal agency directly or through a private company subject to program specifics.

7. Project grants—federal funds awarded for specific projects or services such as construction, research, planning, and technical assistance. Funds may cover whole or part of project costs. Some project grants include cooperative agreements with local or state governments or organizations with federal granting agency to fulfill project's performance. No repayment is expected.

The nonfinancial award types are:

8. Advisory services/counseling—federal subject-matter experts offering conferences, workshops, personal contact, or publications for advice or consultation.

9. Federal employment—federal-government jobs offered through the U.S. Office of Personnel Management (OPM) for the recruiting and hiring of civilian personnel. Ongoing federal-agency employment activities are not considered a domestic-assistance program.

10. Investigation of complaints—federal agencies examine or investigate claims of violations of federal law, policy, or regulation. Claims must originate outside the federal government.

11. Sale, exchange, or donation of property and goods—transfer of federally owned real estate or personal property, commodities and goods such as equipment, supplies, food, or drugs.

12. Specialized services—federal personnel who provide expertise as specific services for communities or individuals.

13. Technical information—prepared, published, and distributed technical information made available through libraries and community centers.

14. Training—federal subject-matter expertise provided to the general public and those who are not employed by the federal government.

15. Use of property, facilities, and equipment—temporary access and use of federally owned resources with or without cost to the recipient.

Block grants are excluded from the list of award types as they typically act as formula grants or project grants. Also excluded from this list of award types is the cooperative agreement, which is an arrangement used in the administration of programs where mentioned.

Other forms of government assistance are part of ongoing government operations and not considered domestic programs. These are: procurement contracts, government foreign activities, federal-employee recruitment programs, programs to benefit federal employees or military personnel, ongoing agency information services, and basic government functions.

Many programs offer more than a single award type. In these programs, a combination of financial and nonfinancial benefits, such as a program that includes project grant, specialized service, advisory services/counseling, and technical information, are granted.

Who May Obtain Government Support

The program Purpose is provided to describe the objective, intent, and use of the awarded fund or service. Assistance programs benefit the American public in various sectors of society, such as public organizations like libraries, that offer publications and technical information through their facilities and community outreach. Based on the program, because of laws or regulations governing its administration, assistance is awarded based on certain categories of applicants—e.g., farmers, states, small businesses or Native American status. Moreover, only specified categories of prospective recipients may apply.

Other programs may directly benefit only certain industries—e.g., shipbuilding or agriculture, or certain demographic groups such as the elderly, or teenagers, or immigrants from specific countries.

Yet, under other federal programs, both eligible applicants and beneficiaries are the same —e.g., certain veteran, small business, and student programs.

The distinction between programs offering assistance specifically to eligible applicants, eligible beneficiaries, and eligible applicants/beneficiaries is identified by descriptions of Applicant Eligibility and Beneficiary Eligibility.

This distinction between eligible applicants and eligible beneficiaries is important to those seeking assistance and being awarded assistance, or not. And members of the public may be ineligible to apply to certain programs, but may still be able to benefit from those programs.

Finding More Information

The *GOVERNMENT SUPPORT INDEX* website provides a searchable menu of programs. It is recommended that readers of this book augment their program search by using the website. Users can discover programs and agency contacts by federal agency, award types, applicant/beneficiary eligibility, and subject of need. It also includes a keyword-driven search box that complements this book. Additional program details are provided for each program and organized in a thoughtful and procedural way as to guide the user through the search and evaluation of programs, eligibility, and application procedures. More informational resources will be added to continually improve access to and discovery of appropriate programs.

PROGRAMS ADMINISTERED BY FEDERAL HEADQUARTERS

Programs Administered by Federal Headquarters

HHS93.423 | 1332 STATE INNOVATION WAIVERS
"1332 Waiver Program"

Award: Cooperative Agreements
Purpose: To receive approval, the state must demonstrate that a proposed waiver will provide access to quality healthcarethat is at least as comprehensive and affordable as would be provided without the waiver, will provide coverage to at least a comparable number of residents of the state as would be provided coverage without a waiver, and will not increase the federal deficit.
Applicant Eligibility: This funding opportunity is only open to US States, Territories and Possessions.
Beneficiary Eligibility: N/A
Award Range/Average: To Be Determined.
Funding: (Cooperative Agreements) FY 18 $244,619,917.00; FY 19 est $939,201,611; FY 20 est Estimate Not Available
HQ: 7501 Wisconsin Avenue, Bethesda, MD 21244
   Phone: 301-492-4225 | Email: michelle.koltov@cms.hhs.gov
   https://www.cms.gov/CCIIO/Programs-and-Initiatives/State-Innovation-Waivers/Section_1332_State_Innovation_Waivers-.html

USDA10.513 | 1890 FACILITIES GRANTS PROGRAM
"1890 FGP"

Award: Project Grants
Purpose: To assist in improving agricultural and food sciences institutions with equipment and other essential requirements.
Applicant Eligibility: Eligible applicants under this Program are the 1890 land-grant Institutions, including Central State University, Tuskegee University, and West Virginia State University. The detailed listing of eligible applicants follows: Alabama A&M University, Tuskegee University, University of Arkansas-Pine Bluff, Delaware State University, Florida A&M University, Fort Valley State University, Kentucky State University, Southern University, University of Maryland-Eastern Shore, Lincoln University, Alcorn State University, North Carolina A&T State University, Langston University, South Carolina State University, Tennessee State University, Prairie View A&M University, Virginia State University, West Virginia State University, and Central State University. SPECIAL NOTE: Please refer to the Competitive Request for Applications (RFAs) for further specific and pertinent details. The most current RFA is available via: https://nifa. usda.gov/funding-opportunity/1890-facilities-grants-Program -renewals. RFAs for new and/or renewal applications are generally released annually. The RFAs provide the most current and accurate information available. Any specific instructions in the Competitive RFAs supersede the general information provided in the CFDA database.
Beneficiary Eligibility: Extension Programs at the State and county level are available to the general public.
Award Range/Average: If minimum or maximum amounts of funding per competitive and/or capacity project grant, or cooperative agreement are established, these amounts will be announced in the annual Competitive Request for Application (RFA). The most current RFA is available via: https://nifa.usda.gov/funding-opportunity/1890-facilities-grants-program-renewals.
Funding: (Project Grants (with Formula Distribution)) FY 17 $0.00; FY 18 est $0.00; FY 19 $18,904,653
HQ: 1400 Independence Avenue SW, PO Box 2250, Washington, DC 20250-2250
   Phone: 202-720-5305 | Email: edwin.lewis@nifa.usda.gov
   https://nifa.usda.gov/program/1890-land-grant-institutions-programs

USDA10.216 | 1890 INSTITUTION CAPACITY BUILDING GRANTS
"1890 Capacity (CBG)"

Award: Project Grants
Purpose: Conducting cooperative programs with Federal and nonfederal entities and build the research and teaching capacities of the 1890 land-grant institutions and Tuskegee University.
Applicant Eligibility: The 1890 land-grant Institutions and Tuskegee University. The 1890 land-Grant Institutions are: Alabama A&M University; Alcorn State University; University of Arkansas-Pine Bluff; Delaware State University; Florida A&M University; Fort Valley State University; Kentucky State University; Lincoln University (MO); Langston University; University of Maryland-Eastern Shore; North Carolina A&T State University; Prairie View A&M University; South Carolina State University; Southern University and A&M College; Tennessee State University; Virginia State University; and West Virginia State College.

Beneficiary Eligibility: The seventeen 1890 land-grant institutions and Tuskegee University, non-1890 academic institutions, private industry, and the Department of Agriculture.

Award Range/Average: If minimum or maximum amounts of funding per competitive and/or capacity project grant, or cooperative agreement are established, these amounts will be announced in the annual Competitive Request for Application (RFA).

Funding: (Project Grants) FY 18 est $18,275,686.00; FY 19 est $18,232,059.00; FY 20 est $0.00

HQ: 1400 Independence Avenue SW, PO Box 2250, Washington, DC 20250-2250

Phone: 202-720-2324 | Email: edwin.lewis@nifa.usda.gov

http://nifa.usda.gov/program/1890-land-grant-institutions-programs

USDA10.227 | 1994 INSTITUTIONS RESEARCH PROGRAM
"Tribal Colleges Research Grants Program (TCRGP)"

Award: Project Grants

Purpose: To provide support for agricultural research projects and investigative studies on food and agriscience.

Applicant Eligibility: Bay Mills Community College, Blackfeet Community College, Cankdeska Cikana Community College, Cheyenne River Community College, Dine Community College, D-Q University, Dullknife Memorial College, Fond Du Lac Community College, Fort Belknap Community College, Fort Berthold Community College, Fort Peck Community College, LacCourte Orielles Ojibwa Community College, Little Big Horn Community College, Nebraska Indian Community College, Northwest Indian College, Oglala Lakota College, Salish Kootenai College, Sinte Gleska University, Sisseton Wahpeton Community College, Sitting Bull College, Stonechild Community College, Turtle Mountain Community College, United Tribes Technical College, Southwest Indian Polytechnic Institute, Institute of American Indian Arts, Crown point Institute of Technology, Haskell Indian National University, Leech Lake Tribal College, College of the Menominee Nation, and Little Priest Tribal College.

Beneficiary Eligibility: Current Listing of 1994 Land-Grant Institutions (aka Tribal Colleges):Aaniiih Nakoda College; Bay Mills Community College; Blackfeet Community College; Cankdeska Cikana Community College; Chief Dull Knife College; College of Menominee Nation; College of the Muscogee Nation; Dine' College; Fond du Lac Tribal and Community College; Fort Peck Community College; Haskell Indian Nations University; Ilisagvik College; Institute of American Indian Arts; Keweenaw Bay Ojibwa Community College; Lac Courte Oreilles Ojibwa Community College; Leech Lake Tribal College; Little Big Horn College; Little Priest Tribal College; Navajo Technical University; Nebraska Indian Community College; Nueta, Hidatsa and Sahnish College; Northwest Indian College; Oglala Lakota College; Saginaw Chippewa Tribal College; Salish Kootenai College; Sinte Gleska University; Sisseton Wahpeton College; Sitting Bull College; Southwestern Indian Polytechnic Institute; Stone Child College; Tohono O'odham Community College; Turtle Mountain Community College; United Tribes Technical College; and White Earth Tribal and Community College.

Award Range/Average: If minimum or maximum amounts of funding per competitive and/or capacity project grant, or cooperative agreement are established, these amounts will be announced in the annual Competitive Request for Application (RFA).The most current RFA is available via: https://nifa.usda.gov/funding-opportunity/tribal-colleges-research-grants-program-tcrgp

Funding: (Project Grants (Cooperative Agreements)) FY 17 $1,670,933.00; FY 18 est $3,513,893.00; FY 19 est $1,665,845.00

HQ: 1400 Independence Avenue SW, PO Box 2250, Washington, DC 20250-2250

Phone: 202-720-2324 | Email: erin.riley@nifa.usda.gov

http://nifa.usda.gov/program/tribal-college-research-grant-program

EAC90.404 | 2018 HAVA ELECTION SECURITY GRANTS

Award: Formula Grants

Purpose: To improve the administration of elections for Federal office, including to enhance election technology and make election security improvements.

Applicant Eligibility: Assistance is to be used to improve the administration of elections for federal office, including enhancing election technology and making election security improvements.

Beneficiary Eligibility: States, the District of Columbia, Puerto Rico, the Virgin Islands, Guam and American Samoa.

Award Range/Average: $600,000 - $34,560,000

Funding: (Formula Grants) FY 17 $0.00; FY 18 est $380,000,000.00; FY 19 Estimate Not Available

HQ: 1335 E W Highway, Suite 4300, Silver Spring, MD 20910

Phone: 202-566-2166 | Email: mabbott@eac.gov

http://www.eac.gov

Programs Administered by Federal Headquarters

DOI15.154 | 21ST CENTURY CONSERVATION SERVICE CORPS
Award: Cooperative Agreements
Purpose: Through this program, work and training opportunities are offered to young people and veterans in order to help the next generation of lifelong conservation stewards and protect, restore and enhance America's Great Outdoors.
Applicant Eligibility: N/A
Beneficiary Eligibility: N/A
Award Range/Average: Smallest: $25,000 Largest: $1,800,000.
HQ: 1849 C Street NW, Room 4257, Washington, DC 20240
　　Phone: 202-513-0692 | Email: megan_olsen@ios.doi.gov
　　http://www.doi.gov/youth/index.cfm

HHS93.353 | 21ST CENTURY CURES ACT-BEAU BIDEN CANCER MOONSHOT
Award: Project Grants
Purpose: To provide support for initiatives funded under the 21st Century Cures Act to support cancer research, such as the development of cancer vaccines, the development of more sensitive diagnostic tests for cancer, immunotherapy and the development of combination therapies, and research that has the potential to transform the scientific field.
Applicant Eligibility: The awardee will be a University, college, hospital, public agency, nonprofit research institution or for-profit Organization that applies and receives a grant for support of research by a named principal investigator. To be eligible for funding, a grant application must be approved for scientific merit and Program relevance by a scientific review group and a national advisory council.
Beneficiary Eligibility: Any nonprofit or for-profit organization, company, or institution engaged in biomedical research.
Award Range/Average: Range: $169,560 to $4,864,165 Average $1,875
Funding: (Cooperative Agreements) FY 18 $86,243,000.00; FY 19 est $143,995,000.00; FY 20 est $76,437,000.00
HQ: 9609 Medical Center Drive, Suite 7W532, Rockville, MD 20850
　　Phone: 240-276-6443 | Email: battistc@mail.nih.gov
　　http://www.cancer.gov/research/key-initiatives/moonshot-cancer-initiative

HHS93.372 | 21ST CENTURY CURES ACT-BRAIN RESEARCH THROUGH ADVANCING INNOVATIVE NEUROTECHNOLOGIES
"The BRAIN Initiative"
Award: Project Grants
Purpose: To provide support for initiatives funded under the 21st Century Cures Act.
Applicant Eligibility: The awardee will be a University, college, hospital, public agency, nonprofit research institution or for-profit Organization that applies and receives a grant for support of research by a named principal investigator. To be eligible for funding, a grant application must be approved for scientific merit and Program relevance by a scientific review group and a national advisory council.
Beneficiary Eligibility: Any nonprofit or for-profit organization, company, or institution engaged in biomedical research.
Funding: (Project Grants (Cooperative Agreements)) FY 17 $10,000,000.00; FY 18 est $86,000,000.00; FY 19 est $115,000,000.00
HQ: 31 Center Drive, Room 8A52, Rockville, MD 20892
　　Phone: 301-496-3167 | Email: koroshetzw@nih.gov
　　http://www.braininitiative.nih.gov

HHS93.368 | 21ST CENTURY CURES ACT-PRECISION MEDICINE INITIATIVE
"All of U.S. Research Program"
Award: Cooperative Agreements
Purpose: To provide support for initiatives funded under the 21st Century Cures Act, the All of Us Research Program will gather data from one million or more diverse people living in the United States to accelerate research and improve health.
Applicant Eligibility: The awardee will be a University, college, hospital, public agency, nonprofit research institution or for-profit Organization that applies and receives an award for support of research by a named principal investigator. To be eligible for funding, a grant application must be approved for scientific merit and Program relevance by a scientific review group and a national advisory council.

Beneficiary Eligibility: Any nonprofit or for-profit organization, company, or institution engaged in biomedical research.
Funding: (Project Grants (Cooperative Agreements)) FY 17 $40,000,000.00; FY 18 est $100,000,000.00; FY 19 est $186,000,000.00
HQ: 6011 Executive Boulevard, Suite 214, Rockville, MD 20852
    Phone: 301-594-0651 | Email: justin.hentges@nih.gov
    http://allofus.nih.gov

HHS93.370 | 21ST CENTURY CURES ACT: REGENERATIVE MEDICINE INITIATIVE
"Regenerative Medicine Initiative"

Award: Project Grants
Purpose: To provide support for initiatives funded under the 21st Century Cures Act to support the BRAIN Initiative's aim of revolutionizing our understanding of the human brain.
Applicant Eligibility: The awardee will be a University, college, hospital, public agency, nonprofit research institution or for-profit Organization that applies and receives a grant for support of research by a named principal investigator. To be eligible for funding, a grant application must be approved for scientific merit and Program relevance by a scientific review group and a national advisory council.
Beneficiary Eligibility: Any nonprofit or for-profit organization, company, or institution engaged in biomedical research.
Funding: (Project Grants (Cooperative Agreements)) FY 17 $2,000,000.00; FY 18 est $10,000,000.00; FY 19 est $10,000,000.00
HQ: 6701 Rockledge Drive, Room 7176, Bethesda, MD 20832
    Phone: 301-827-7968 | Email: pharesda@nhlbi.nih.gov

SBA59.041 | 504 CERTIFIED DEVELOPMENT LOANS
"504 Loans"

Award: Guaranteed/insured Loans
Purpose: To assist small business concerns by providing long-term, fixed-rate financing for fixed assets.
Applicant Eligibility: Certified Development Companies (CDCs) package, close, and service these SBA-guaranteed loans to small businesses. A CDC must be incorporated under general State corporation statute, on a nonprofit basis, for the purpose of promoting economic growth in a particular area.
Beneficiary Eligibility: Small businesses must be independently owned and operated for profit. The small business applicant and its affiliates (affiliation defined at 13 CFR 121.103) must have: a) A Tangible net worth of $15 million or less and b) Average net income after Federal income taxes (excluding any carry-over losses) for the preceding two completed fiscal years of $5 million or less.
Funding: (Guaranteed/Insured Loans) FY 17 $271,000,000.00; FY 18 est $7,500,000,000.00; FY 19 est $1,000,000,000.00
HQ: 409 3rd Street SW, 8th Floor, Washington, DC 20416
    Phone: 202-205-9949 | Email: linda.reilly@sba.gov
    http://www.sba.gov

SBA59.054 | 7(A) EXPORT LOAN GUARANTEES

Award: Guaranteed/insured Loans
Purpose: To aid and assist small-business to increase their ability to compete in international markets by enhancing their ability to export.
Applicant Eligibility: A small business is eligible, which is independently owned and operated and not dominant in its field. They also need to meet the SBA size standards.
Beneficiary Eligibility: Small businesses, including those owned by low-income and handicapped individuals located in high unemployment areas.
Award Range/Average: Additional information available on SBA's website at www.sba.gov.
HQ: 409 3rd Street SW, 6th Floor, Washington, DC 20416
    Phone: 202-205-7654 | Email: robert.carpenter@sba.gov
    http://www.sba.gov

Programs Administered by Federal Headquarters

SBA59.012 | 7(A) LOAN GUARANTEES
"Regular Business Loans 7(a) Loans"

Award: Guaranteed/insured Loans

Purpose: To provide guaranteed loans from lenders to small businesses which are unable to obtain financing in the private credit marketplace but can demonstrate an ability to repay loans if granted, in a timely manner.

Applicant Eligibility: N/A

Beneficiary Eligibility: Small businesses that meet the size and eligibility standards.

Award Range/Average: Additional information is available on SBA's website at www.sba.gov

Funding: (Guaranteed/Insured Loans) FY 18 $25,400,000,000.00; FY 19 est $30,000,000,000.00; FY 20 est $30,000,000,000.00

HQ: 409 3rd Street SW, 8th Floor, Washington, DC 20416
   Phone: 202-205-7654 | Email: robert.carpenter@sba.gov
   http://www.sba.gov/7a-loan-program

SBA59.007 | 7(J) TECHNICAL ASSISTANCE

Award: Project Grants

Purpose: The purpose of the program is to provide Business Development Assistance for Small Disadvantaged Businesses.

Applicant Eligibility: Educational Institutions, public or private Organizations and businesses, individuals, State and local Governments, Indian Tribes and lending and financial Institutions and sureties that have the capability to provide the required business development assistance.

Beneficiary Eligibility: 8(a) program certified firms, small disadvantaged businesses, businesses operating in areas of low-income or high-unemployment, and firms owned by low-income individuals like Economically Disadvantaged Women Owned Businesses.

Funding: (Project Grants) FY 17 $1,796,000.00; FY 18 est $2,800,000.00; FY 19 est $2,800,000.00

HQ: 409 3rd Street SW, 6th Floor, Washington, DC 20416
   Phone: 202-205-1904 | Email: ajoy.sinha@sba.gov
   http://www.sba.gov

SBA59.006 | 8(A) BUSINESS DEVELOPMENT PROGRAM
"Section 8(a) Program"

Award: Provision of Specialized Services

Purpose: To foster business ownership by individuals who are both socially and economically disadvantaged; and to promote the competitive viability of such firms by providing business development and mentoring assistance.

Applicant Eligibility: Firms applying for 8(a) Program participation must meet certain requirements which include, but are not limited to: (a) Status as a small business; (b) at least 51 percent unconditional ownership, control and management of the business by an American citizen(s) determined by SBA to be socially and economically disadvantaged, or by an economically disadvantaged Indian Tribe, Alaska Native Corporation, or Native Hawaiian Organization; and (c) demonstrated potential for success; and (d) possess good character. Absent evidence to the contrary, the following individuals are presumed to be socially disadvantaged: African Americans, Hispanic Americans, Native Americans, Asian Pacific Americans and Subcontinent Asian Americans. Individuals who are not members of the named groups may establish their social disadvantage on the basis of a preponderance of evidence of personal disadvantage stemming from color, national origin, gender, physical handicap, long-term residence in an environment isolated from the American society, or other similar cause beyond the individual's control. Economic disadvantage must be demonstrated on a case-by-case basis.

Beneficiary Eligibility: Socially and economically disadvantaged individuals and small businesses owned and operated by such individuals; economically disadvantaged Indian tribes including Alaskan Native Corporations and economically disadvantaged Native Hawaiian organizations.

Award Range/Average: Additional information available on SBA's website at www.sba.gov.

HQ: 409 3rd Street SW, 8th Floor, Washington, DC 20416
   Phone: 202-205-1904 | Email: ajoy.sinha@sba.gov
   http://www.sba.gov

DOI15.430 | 8(G) STATE COASTAL ZONE

Award: Direct Payments With Unrestricted Use

Purpose: Shares 27 percent of mineral leasing revenue derived from any lease issued after September 18, 1978, of any Federal tract which lies wholly or partially within 3 nautical miles of the Seaward boundary of any coastal state.

Applicant Eligibility: Revenue from qualified leasing will trigger automatic payment distribution computed in accordance with the law.

Beneficiary Eligibility: Leased Outer Continental Shelf Lands must be located within the 8(g) zone of a coastal state.

Award Range/Average: Not Applicable.

Funding: (Direct Payments with Unrestricted Use) FY 17 $10,322,000.00; FY 18 est $12,717,000.00; FY 19 est $12,908,000.00

HQ: 1849 C Street NW, PO Box 4211, Washington, DC 20240

Phone: 202-513-0600

http://www.ONRR.gov

HHS93.762 | A COMPREHENSIVE APPROACH TO GOOD HEALTH AND WELLNESS IN INDIAN COUNTY-FINANCED SOLELY BY PREVENTION AND PUBLIC HEALTH
"Tribal Wellness"

Award: Cooperative Agreements

Purpose: The five-year funding opportunity offers support to prevent heart disease, diabetes and associated risk factors in American Indian and Alaska Native communities through a holistic approach to population health and wellness.

Applicant Eligibility: Federally recognized American Indian Tribes and Alaska Native Villages and Corporations which meet the definition set forth in 25 U.S.C. Section 1603. Tribal Organizations, as set forth in 25 U.S.C. Section 1603. Urban Indian Organizations that meet the definition set forth in 25 U.S.C., section 1603. Tribal college or University as set forth in section 1059c (b) of title 20. Tribal epidemiology Centers as set forth in 25 U.S.C. Section 1621m.

Beneficiary Eligibility: Federally recognized Indian Tribal Government, Individual/Family, Native American Organization, Pre-school, infant, Child, Youth, Senior Citizen, unemployed, welfare recipient, pension recipient, moderate income, low income, rural.

Award Range/Average: Anticipated amounts are: FY2014: $13-15 million; $14-15m per year with $65075 million over the five years; average annual award $500,000, range $300,000- $800,000

Funding: (Cooperative Agreements) FY 18 $15,449,829.00; FY 19 est $32,971,184.00; FY 20 est $32,971,184.00

HQ: 4770 Buford Highway NE, PO Box F80, Atlanta, GA 30341

Phone: 770-488-6045

http://www.cdc.gov

HHS93.506 | ACA NATIONWIDE PROGRAM FOR NATIONAL AND STATE BACKGROUND CHECKS FOR DIRECT PATIENT ACCESS EMPLOYEES OF LONG TERM CARE FACILITIES AND PROVIDERS

Award: Project Grants

Purpose: To establish a nationwide program to identify efficient, effective, and economical procedures for long term care facilities and providers to conduct background checks on a statewide basis on all prospective direct patient access employees.

Applicant Eligibility: CMS is inviting proposals from all States and U.S. territories to be considered for inclusion in this National Background Check Program. Federal matching funds are available to all States and U.S. territories.

Beneficiary Eligibility: These facilities and providers include skilled nursing facilities, nursing facilities, home health agencies, hospice care providers, long-term care hospitals, personal care service providers, adult day care providers, residential care providers, assisted living facilities, intermediate care facilities for the mentally retarded (ICFs/MR) and other entities that provide long-term care services, as specified by each participating State.

Award Range/Average: $1.5 million to $3 million

Funding: (Project Grants) FY 18 $5,015,348.00; FY 19 est $0.00; FY 20 est $0.00

HQ: 7500 Security Boulevard, Baltimore, MD 21244

Phone: 410-786-3270 | Email: melissa.rice@cms.hhs.gov

Programs Administered by Federal Headquarters

HHS93.624 | ACA-STATE INNOVATION MODELS: FUNDING FOR MODEL DESIGN AND MODEL TESTING ASSISTANCE
"State Innovation Models (SIM)"

Award: Cooperative Agreements

Purpose: The State Innovation Models program is based on the premise that state innovation with broad stakeholder input and engagement, including multi-payer models, will accelerate delivery system transformation to provide better care at lower costs.

Applicant Eligibility: CMS invites the 50 state Governor's Offices, United States Territories Governors Offices (American Samoa, Guam, Northern Mariana Islands, Puerto Rico, and the Virgin islands), and the Mayor's Office of the District of Columbia to apply. Only one application from a Governor per state is permitted for either a Model Design or a Model Test award (assuming the state applied and was not selected for funding under the first round of Model Test awards). A state cannot receive multiple Round 2 Model Design or Model Test awards. A state cannot receive both a Round 2 Model Design award and a Round 2 Model Test award. Each application must include a letter from the Governor (or the Mayor, if from the District of Columbia) officially endorsing the application for a Model Design award or for a Model Test award. States currently engaged in a Model Test award with CMS are NOT eligible to apply for funding under Round 2. A state may propose that an outside Organization focused on quality and state delivery system transformation, such as a non-profit affiliated with the State Department of Health or a public-private partnership supported by the Governor's Office, receive and administer funds through a Model Design or Model Test award. The Governor's Office must submit such requests in writing to CMS with its Letter of Intent and include a justification for the request and an attestation that the state will actively participate in all activities described in its proposal. Approval of such requests will be at the sole discretion of CMS. Only one such request supported by the Governor will be allowed per state. A state pursuing this approach will still be expected to address all of the required areas described in this FOA. Eligibility Threshold Criteria: All applicants must have submitted a required letter of intent to the Programmatic point of contact in Section VI. Agency Contacts by June 6, 2014. If a letter of intent has not been submitted by the required due date, any subsequent application submitted by the entity will be ineligible. See Section IV. 2. A, Letter of Intent to Apply, for more information. Application deadline: Applications not received by the application deadline (TBD) through www.grants.gov will not be reviewed. Application requirements: Applications will be considered for funding only if the application meets the requirements outlined in Section III, Eligibility Information and Section IV, Application and Submission Information. Page limits: Model Test applications shall not be more than 55 pages in length. Model Design applications shall not be more than 27 pages in length. Both types of applications must be limited to the page maximums, sequence of sections, and section content specified in Section IV. 2 Content and Form of Application Submission, parts C & D. In addition, applications should include attestations of support from key stakeholders. The letters of support will not be included in the page limits for applications. The letters should attest to stakeholders active engagement in the model and must contain specific information about how the stakeholders will contribute to the SIM process. The standard forms, project abstract, Governor's endorsement, and curriculum vitae are also not included in these page limits. States are strongly encouraged to review the criteria information provided in Section V of the FOA, Application Review Information, to help ensure that the proposal adequately addresses all the criteria that will be used in evaluating applications and determining appropriate funding levels for each award.

Beneficiary Eligibility: The emphasis is on targeting Medicare, Medicaid, and CHIP populations. Proposals will describe the target populations, geographic areas, or communities that will be the focus of service delivery and payment model testing, the current quality and beneficiary experience outcomes including current health population status, and the specific improvement targets expected from the model.

Award Range/Average: Model Test: 11 Model Test cooperative agreements were awarded under this State Innovation Models initiative. Awards for Model Test states range from $20-100 million per state, based on the size of the state population and the scope of the proposal. The amount awarded will include any state cost of testing the model and meeting state and federal evaluation requirements as specified in Section V.3 below. While the Innovation Center is responsible for the evaluation of each Model Test, states must also develop their own model evaluation process, under the guidance of the Innovation Center. The state evaluations should include an examination of the models impact on the entire state population. In general, CMS expects that Model Test awards will cover only costs that are not normally part of a states operational cost, data collection cost, or administrative cost.

Funding: (Formula Grants) FY 18 $116,930,300.00; FY 19 $64,233,356.00; FY 20 $0

HQ: 7205 Windsor Boulevard, Baltimore, MD 21244

Phone: 410-786-9726 | Email: Allison.Pompey@cms.hhs.gov

http://www.innovations.cms.gov

HHS93.638 | ACA-TRANSFORMING CLINICAL PRACTICE INITIATIVE: PRACTICE TRANSFORMATION NETWORKS (PTNS)
"TCPI"

Award: Cooperative Agreements

Purpose: The Transforming Clinical Practice Initiative model will test whether a three-pronged approach to national technical assistance will enable large scale transformation of thousands of clinician practices to deliver better care and result in better health outcomes at lower costs.

Applicant Eligibility: Interstate; Intrastate; Local; Sponsored Organizations; Federally Recognized Indian Tribal Government; Private Nonprofit Institution/Organization; Quasi-public Nonprofit Institution/Organization; Other private Institution/Organization; Native American Organization; Specialty group; Small Business; Profit Organization; Other public Institution/Organization; Public Nonprofit Institution/Organization; Other public Institution/Organization *Clinicians receiving other CMMI support (e.g. CPCI) and those already participating in alternate payment Programs (e.g. Medicare Shared Savings Program) are not eligible for participation in TCPI.

Beneficiary Eligibility: The Beneficiary eligibility includes the list as noted above with the exception of: Federal, Interstate, Intrastate, Student/Trainee and Graduate Students, Artist/Humanist, Engineer/Architect, Builder/Contractor/Developer, Farmer/Rancher/Agriculture Producer, Industrialist/Business Person; Small Business Person, Homeowner, Property Owner; Anyone/General public.

Award Range/Average: This will be a new service delivery model. Therefore, no funds ($0) have been requested for past or current fiscal years.

Funding: (Cooperative Agreements) FY 18 $120,567,781.00; FY 19 est $0.00; FY 20 est $0.00

HQ: LT 7500 Security Boulevard, Baltimore, MD 21244

  Phone: 410-786-5239 | Email: fred.butler@cms.hhs.gov

  http://www.innovation.cms.gov

HHS93.639 | ACA-TRANSFORMING CLINICAL PRACTICE INITIATIVE: SUPPORT AND ALIGNMENT NETWORKS (SANS)
"TCPI"

Award: Cooperative Agreements

Purpose: The Transforming Clinical Practice Initiative model will test whether a three-pronged approach to national technical assistance will enable large scale transformation of thousands of clinician practices to deliver better care and result in better health outcomes at lower costs. Support Alignment Networks formed by group practices, healthcaresystems, and others that join together to serve as trusted partners to provide clinician practices with quality improvement expertise, best practices, coaching and help as they prepare and begin clinical and operational practice transformation.

Applicant Eligibility: CMS anticipates that SANs will include but not be limited to Organizations like: Public Nonprofit Institution/Organizations pecialized group Profit Organization Private Nonprofit Institution/Organization Quasi-public Nonprofit Institution/Organization Other private institution/Organization *Clinicians receiving other CMMI support (e.g. CPCI) and those already participating in alternate payment Programs (e.g. Medicare Shared Savings Program) are not eligible for participation in TCPI.

Beneficiary Eligibility: The Beneficiary eligibility includes the list as noted above with the exception of: Federal, Interstate; Intrastate; Student/Trainee and Graduate Students; Artist/Humanist; Engineer/Architect, Builder/Contractor/Developer; Farmer/Rancher/Agriculture Producer; Industrialist/Business Person; Small Business Person; Homeowner; Property Owner; Anyone/General public.

Award Range/Average: This will be a new service delivery model. Therefore, no funds ($0) have been requested for past or current fiscal years.

Funding: (Cooperative Agreements) FY 18 $7,104,814.00; FY 19 est $0.00; FY 20 est $0.00

HQ: LT 7500 Security Boulevard, Baltimore, MD 21244

  Phone: 410-786-5239 | Email: fred.butler@cms.hhs.gov

  http://www.innovation.cms.gov

Programs Administered by Federal Headquarters

DOS19.432 | ACADEMIC EXCHANGE PROGRAMS-EDUCATIONAL ADVISING AND STUDENT SERVICES

Award: Cooperative Agreements

Purpose: The Department of State's Bureau of International Information Programs awards grants to cooperating organizations with experience in international exchanges for the administration of projects that enable U.S. experts to present lectures, serve as consultants, or conduct workshops and seminars for professional audiences worldwide.

Applicant Eligibility: Pursuant to the Mutual educational and Cultural Exchange Act of 1961, as amended (Fulbright-Hays Act) the Bureau of educational and Cultural Affairs of the U.S. Department of State awards grants and cooperative agreements to educational and cultural public or private nonprofit foundations or Institutions. Applications may be submitted by public and private non-profit Organizations meeting the provisions described in Internal Revenue Code section 26 USC 501(c)(3). Organizations must have nonprofit status with the IRS at the time of application. Please refer to the Grants.gov or the U.S. Department of State's SAMS Domestic announcement for further eligibility criteria.

Beneficiary Eligibility: Beneficiaries include recipient organizations, educational institutions, other non-government organizations (NGOs) that meet the provisions described in Internal Revenue Code section 26 USC 501(c)(3), as well as sponsored participants, and the American people and the people of participating countries who interact with the international participants.

Award Range/Average: $500,000 to $5,499,999.

Funding: (Cooperative Agreements) FY 17 $7,734,949.00; FY 18 est $7,734,949.00; FY 19 est $7,734,949.00

HQ: 2200 C Street NW SA-05, Room 04W12, Washington, DC 20037

Phone: 202-632-6353 | Email: bollam@state.gov

http://educationusa.state.gov

DOS19.421 | ACADEMIC EXCHANGE PROGRAMS-ENGLISH LANGUAGE PROGRAMS

"English Language Programs include the English Access Microscholarship Program, the English Language Fellow and Specialist Program, and the American English E-Teacher Program"

Award: Cooperative Agreements

Purpose: The Bureau of Educational and Cultural Affairs (ECA) seeks to increase mutual understanding between the people of the United States and the people of other countries by means of educational and cultural exchange programs. ECA programs foster engagement and encourage dialogue with citizens around the world.

Applicant Eligibility: Pursuant to the Mutual educational and Cultural Exchange Act of 1961, as amended (Fulbright-Hays Act) the Bureau of educational and Cultural Affairs of the U.S. Department of State awards grants and cooperative agreements to educational and cultural public or private nonprofit foundations or Institutions. Applications may be submitted by public and private non-profit Organizations meeting the provisions described in Internal Revenue Code section 26 USC 501(c)(3). Organizations must have nonprofit status with the IRS at the time of application. Please refer to the Grants.gov or the U.S. Department of State's SAMS Domestic announcement for further eligibility criteria.

Beneficiary Eligibility: Beneficiaries include recipient organizations, educational institutions, other non-government organizations (NGOs) that meet the provisions described in Internal Revenue Code section 26 USC 501(c)(3), as well as sponsored participants, and the American people and the people of participating countries who interact with the international participants.

Award Range/Average: $4,250,000 to $27,100,000.

Funding: (Cooperative Agreements) FY 17 $37,950,000.00; FY 18 est $37,950,000.00; FY 19 est $37,950,000.00

HQ: Office of English Language Programs English Language Fellow Program 2200 C Street NW SA-05, Room 4B15, Washington, DC 20037

Phone: 202-632-9412 | Email: danzcb@state.gov

http://americanenglish.state.gov

DOS19.400 | ACADEMIC EXCHANGE PROGRAMS-GRADUATE STUDENTS

Award: Project Grants

Purpose: Seeks to increase mutual understanding between the people of the United States and the people of other countries by means of educational and cultural exchange programs, including the exchange of scholars, researchers, professionals, students, and educators.

Applicant Eligibility: Pursuant to the Mutual educational and Cultural Exchange Act of 1961, as amended (Fulbright-Hays Act) the Bureau of educational and Cultural Affairs of the U.S. Department of State awards grants and cooperative agreements to educational and cultural public or private nonprofit foundations or Institutions. Applications may be submitted by public and private non-profit Organizations meeting the provisions described in Internal Revenue Code section 26 USC 501(c)(3). Organizations must have nonprofit status with the IRS at the time of application. Please refer to the Grants.gov or the U.S. Department of State's SAMS Domestic announcement for further eligibility criteria.

Beneficiary Eligibility: Beneficiaries include recipient organizations, educational institutions, other non-government organizations (NGOs) that meet the provisions described in Internal Revenue Code section 26 USC 501(c)(3), as well as sponsored participants, and the American people and the people of participating countries who interact with the international participants.

Award Range/Average: $7,991,733 to $81,216,212.

Funding: (Project Grants (Cooperative Agreements)) FY 17 $89,207,945.00; FY 18 est $89,207,945.00; FY 19 est $89,207,945.00

HQ: 2200 C Street NW SA-05, Room 4N6 4th Floor, Washington, DC 20037
Phone: 202-632-6067 | Email: meieraw2@state.gov
http://exchanges.state.gov

DOS19.010 | ACADEMIC EXCHANGE PROGRAMS-HUBERT H. HUMPHREY FELLOWSHIP PROGRAM

"Hubert H. Humphrey Fellowship Program"

Award: Cooperative Agreements

Purpose: Seeks to increase mutual understanding between the people of the United States and the people of other countries by means of educational and cultural exchange programs. The Humphrey Program brings young and mid-career professionals from developing countries to the United States for a year of non-degree graduate-level study, leadership development, and professional collaboration with U.S. counterparts.

Applicant Eligibility: N/A

Beneficiary Eligibility: N/A

Award Range/Average: Not Applicable.

Funding: (Cooperative Agreements) FY 17 $11,438,615.00; FY 18 est $11,438,615.00; FY 19 est $11,438,615.00

HQ: Humphrey and Institutional Linkages Branch 2200 C Street NW SA-05, Room 4CC14, Washington, DC 20037
Phone: 202-632-6343 | Email: gibsonjm@state.gov
http://www.exchanges.state.gov/non-us/program/hubert-h-humphrey-fellowship-program

DOS19.401 | ACADEMIC EXCHANGE PROGRAMS-SCHOLARS

Award: Project Grants

Purpose: Seeks to increase mutual understanding between the people of the United States and the people of other countries by means of educational and cultural exchange programs, including the exchange of scholars, researchers, professionals, students, and educators.

Applicant Eligibility: Pursuant to the Mutual educational and Cultural Exchange Act of 1961, as amended (Fulbright-Hays Act) the Bureau of educational and Cultural Affairs of the U.S. Department of State awards grants and cooperative agreements to educational and cultural public or private nonprofit foundations or Institutions. Applications may be submitted by public and private non-profit Organizations meeting the provisions described in Internal Revenue Code section 26 USC 501(c)(3). Organizations must have nonprofit status with the IRS at the time of application. Please refer to the Grants.gov or the U.S. Department of State's SAMS Domestic announcement for further eligibility criteria.

Beneficiary Eligibility: Beneficiaries include recipient organizations, educational institutions, other non-government organizations (NGOs) that meet the provisions described in Internal Revenue Code section 26 USC 501(c)(3), as well as sponsored participants, and the American people and the people of participating countries who interact with the international participants.

Programs Administered by Federal Headquarters

Award Range/Average: $239,990 to $32,331,958.
Funding: (Cooperative Agreements) FY 17 $38,629,738.00; FY 18 est $38,629,738.00; FY 19 est $38,629,738.00
HQ: 2200 C Street NW SA-05, Room 4N6 4th Floor, Washington, DC 20037
    Phone: 202-632-6067 | Email: meieraw2@state.gov
    http://eca.state.gov/about-bureau-0/organizational-structure/office-academic-exchanges

DOS19.011 | ACADEMIC EXCHANGE PROGRAMS-SPECIAL ACADEMIC EXCHANGE PROGRAMS

Award: Cooperative Agreements; Project Grants
Purpose: Seeks to increase mutual understanding between the people of the United States and the people of other countries by means of educational and cultural exchange programs. The purpose of Special Academic Exchange Programs is to provide targeted support for U.S. and foreign students and others who may not otherwise have the resources to pursue international exchange opportunities or who are in fields directly relevant to identified needs in their countries.
Applicant Eligibility: Pursuant to the Mutual educational and Cultural Exchange Act of 1961, as amended (Fulbright-Hays Act) the Bureau of educational and Cultural Affairs of the U.S. Department of State awards grants and cooperative agreements to educational and cultural public or private nonprofit foundations or Institutions. Applications may be submitted by public and private non-profit Organizations meeting the provisions described in Internal Revenue Code section 26 USC 501(c)(3). Organizations must have nonprofit status with the IRS at the time of application. Please refer to the Grants.gov or the U.S. Department of State's SAMS Domestic announcement for further eligibility criteria.
Beneficiary Eligibility: Beneficiaries include recipient organizations, educational institutions, other non-government organizations (NGOs) that meet the provisions described in Internal Revenue Code section 26 USC 501(c)(3), as well as sponsored participants, and the American people and the people of participating countries who interact with the international participants.
Award Range/Average: $350,000 to $14,090,000.
Funding: (Cooperative Agreements) FY 17 $19,925,000.00; FY 18 est $19,925,000.00; FY 19 est $19,925,000.00
HQ: 2200 C Street NW SA-05, Room 4CC16 4th Floor, Washington, DC 20037
    Phone: 202-632-9265
    http://exchanges.state.gov

DOS19.408 | ACADEMIC EXCHANGE PROGRAMS-TEACHERS

Award: Cooperative Agreements
Purpose: Seeks to increase mutual understanding between the people of the United States and the people of other countries by means of educational and cultural exchange programs, including the exchange of scholars, researchers, professionals, students, and educators.
Applicant Eligibility: Pursuant to the Mutual educational and Cultural Exchange Act of 1961, as amended (Fulbright-Hays Act) the Bureau of educational and Cultural Affairs of the U.S. Department of State awards grants and cooperative agreements to educational and cultural public or private nonprofit foundations or Institutions. Applications may be submitted by public and private non-profit Organizations meeting the provisions described in Internal Revenue Code section 26 USC 501(c)(3). Organizations must have nonprofit status with the IRS at the time of application. Please refer to the Grants.gov or U.S. Department of State's SAMS Domestic announcement for further eligibility criteria.
Beneficiary Eligibility: Beneficiaries include recipient organizations, educational institutions, other non-government organizations (NGOs) that meet the provisions described in Internal Revenue Code section 26 USC 501(c)(3), as well as sponsored participants, and the American people and the people of participating countries who interact with the international participants.
Award Range/Average: $1,250,000 to $6,900,000.
Funding: (Cooperative Agreements) FY 17 $12,731,249.00; FY 18 est $12,731,249.00; FY 19 est $12,731,249.00
HQ: Teacher Exchange Branch 2200 C Street NW SA-05, Room 4S17, Washington, DC 20037
    Phone: 202-632-6346 | Email: kubanmm@state.gov
    http://exchanges.state.gov

DOS19.009 | ACADEMIC EXCHANGE PROGRAMS-UNDERGRADUATE PROGRAMS

Award: Cooperative Agreements

Purpose: Seeks to increase mutual understanding between the people of the United States and the people of other countries by means of educational and cultural exchange programs. The main objective of the Undergraduate Programs is to provide targeted support for American students to pursue intensive language study abroad and for foreign students to gain a better understanding of the United States, while developing new generations of world leaders.

Applicant Eligibility: Pursuant to the Mutual educational and Cultural Exchange Act of 1961, as amended (Fulbright-Hays Act) the Bureau of educational and Cultural Affairs of the U.S. Department of State awards grants and cooperative agreements to educational and cultural public or private nonprofit foundations or Institutions. Applications may be submitted by public and private non-profit Organizations meeting the provisions described in Internal Revenue Code section 26 USC 501(c)(3). Organizations must have nonprofit status with the IRS at the time of application. Please refer to the Grants.gov or the U.S. Department of State's SAMS Domestic announcement for further eligibility criteria.

Beneficiary Eligibility: Beneficiaries include recipient organizations, educational institutions, other non-government organizations (NGOs) that meet the provisions described in Internal Revenue Code section 26 USC 501(c)(3), as well as sponsored participants, and the American people and the people of participating countries who interact with the international participants.

Award Range/Average: $238,857 to $12,200000.

Funding: (Cooperative Agreements) FY 17 $52,288,777.00; FY 18 est $52,288,777.00; FY 19 est $52,288,777.00

HQ: 2200 C Street NW SA-05, Room 4CC16 4th Floor, Washington, DC 20037

  Phone: 202-632-9265

  http://exchanges.state.gov

HHS93.650 | ACCOUNTABLE HEALTH COMMUNITIES
"AHC"

Award: Formula Grants

Purpose: Assesses whether systematically identifying the health-related social needs of community- dwelling Medicare and Medicaid beneficiaries, including those who are dually eligible, and addressing their identified needs impacts those beneficiaries' total healthcare costs and their inpatient and outpatient utilization.

Applicant Eligibility: -Community based Organizations -Individual and group provider practices-Hospitals and health systems-Institutions of Higher education -Local government entities and tribal Organization from all 50 states, United States territories, and the District of Columbia.

Beneficiary Eligibility: Potential applicants are limited to the eligible entities described in the sections above. Successful applicants will provide intervention services to community-dwelling Medicare and Medicaid beneficiaries, including dually eligible beneficiaries. Community-dwelling beneficiaries include beneficiaries not residing in a correctional facility or long-term care institution (e.g., long stay nursing homes) when accessing clinical care at a participating clinical delivery site. The application will describe the target populations, geographic areas, and communities that will be the focus of the AHC intervention, the current quality and beneficiary experience outcomes, including current needs assessments of health-related social needs, and specific targets to be impacted by the AHC intervention.

Award Range/Average: The anticipated total funding per award, per budget period is $500,000 - $900,000. The total amount of federal funds available is up to $30.84 million to 12 award recipients to implement the Assistance Track Intervention and $90.20 million to 20 award recipients to implement the Alignment Track Intervention.

Funding: (Formula Grants) FY 18 $24,851,501.00; FY 19 est $18,235,451.00; FY 20 est $18,113,824.00

HQ: 7500 Security Boulevard, Baltimore, MD 21244

  Phone: 410-786-2142 | Email: rivka.friedman@cms.hhs.gov

  http://www.innovation.cms.gov

HHS93.464 | ACL ASSISTIVE TECHNOLOGY
"State AT Grants"

Award: Project Grants

Purpose: To improve the provision of assistive technology to individuals with disabilities through comprehensive statewide programs of technology-related assistance, for individuals with disabilities of all ages.

Programs Administered by Federal Headquarters

Applicant Eligibility: States, including the District of Columbia, Puerto Rico, and outlying areas may apply. Applicants are designated by Governors.

Beneficiary Eligibility: Individuals with disabilities, States, and community-based organizations providing services to individuals with disabilities will benefit.

Award Range/Average: To Be Determined.

Funding: (Formula Grants) FY 17 $26,470,517.00; FY 18 est $28,165,621.00; FY 19 est $28,170,000.00

HQ: 330 C Street SW, Room 1317B, Washington, DC 20201

  Phone: 202-795-7356 | Email: robert.groenendaal@acl.hhs.gov

  https://www.acl.gov/node/411

HHS93.843 | ACL ASSISTIVE TECHNOLOGY STATE GRANTS FOR PROTECTION AND ADVOCACY

Award: Formula Grants

Purpose: To provide protection and advocacy services under the Developmental Disabilities Assistance and Bill of Rights Act for the purpose of assisting in the acquisition, utilization, or maintenance of assistive technology for individuals with disabilities.

Applicant Eligibility: Designated protection and advocacy agencies in States and outlying areas only.

Beneficiary Eligibility: Persons with disabilities who may benefit from assistive technology services and devices.

Funding: (Formula Grants) FY 17 $4,450,000.00; FY 18 est $4,800,000.00; FY 19 est Estimate Not Available

HQ: 330 C Street SW, Suite 1139-A, Washington, DC 20201

  Phone: 202-795-7360 | Email: ladeva.harris@acl.hhs.gov

  http://www.acl.gov

HHS93.844 | ACL CENTERS FOR INDEPENDENT LIVING RECOVERY ACT

Award: Project Grants

Purpose: To provide independent living services to individuals with significant disabilities to assist them to function more independently in family and community settings, by developing and supporting a statewide network of centers for independent living.

Applicant Eligibility: N/A

Beneficiary Eligibility: N/A

HQ: 330 C Street SW, Washington, DC 20201

  Phone: 202-495-7453 | Email: roslyn.thompson@acl.hhs.gov

HHS93.432 | ACL CENTERS FOR INDEPENDENT LIVING
"CILs"

Award: Project Grants

Purpose: To support a Statewide network of centers for independent living (centers or CILs) and provide financial assistance to centers that comply with the standards and assurances in section 725(b) and (c) of the Rehabilitation Act of 1973, as amended (Rehabilitation Act) consistent with the design included in the State Plan for Independent Living for establishing a statewide network of centers.

Applicant Eligibility: Private non-profit Organizations. An eligible agency under the CIL Program is a consumer-controlled, community-based, cross-disability, nonresidential, private nonprofit agency or a state agency in states in which no eligible private non-profit Organization applies for a grant. A State's allotment for IL Part C funds is determined according to a population-based formula. To the extent funds are available, the Rehabilitation Act requires the Administrator to make awards based on a statutory order of priorities to the extent funds are available: (1) The Administrator shall support existing centers for independent living, as described in subsection (c), that comply with the standards and assurances set forth in section 725, at the level of funding for the previous year. (2) The Administrator shall provide for a cost-of-living increase for such existing centers for independent living. (3) The Administrator shall fund new centers for independent living, as described in subsection (d), that comply with the standards and assurances set forth in section 725.

Beneficiary Eligibility: Individuals with significant disabilities as defined in section 7(21)(B) of the Rehabilitation Act. This refers to an individual with a severe physical or mental impairment whose ability to function independently in the family or community or whose ability to obtain, maintain, or advance in employment is substantially limited and for whom the delivery of independent living services will improve the ability to function, continue functioning, or move toward functioning independently in the family or community or to continue in employment, respectively.

Funding: (Project Grants (Discretionary)) FY 17 $78,305,000.00; FY 18 est $88,305,000.00; FY 19 est Estimate Not Available
HQ: 330 C Street SW, Washington, DC 20201
   Phone: 202-795-7446 | Email: corinna.stiles@acl.hhs.gov
   http://www.acl.gov/programs/aging-and-disability-networks/centers-independent-living

HHS93.369 | ACL INDEPENDENT LIVING STATE GRANTS
"Independent Living Services"

Award: Formula Grants
Purpose: To provide financial assistance to States for expanding and improving the provision of independent living (IL) services to individuals with significant disabilities.
Applicant Eligibility: Any designated State Entity (DSE) in a State with an approved State Plan for Independent Living (SPIL) may apply for assistance under this Program. The DSE is the State entity of such State as the agency that, on behalf of the State, receives, accounts for and disburses funds received under this chapter based on the SPIL. DSEs in the 50 States and the District of Columbia and the territories (Commonwealth of Puerto Rico and Virgin Islands) and the outlying areas (Guam, American Samoa, and the Commonwealth of the Northern Mariana Islands) are eligible to apply.
Beneficiary Eligibility: Individuals with significant disabilities as defined in section 7(21)(B) of the Rehabilitation Act, as amended. This refers to an individual with a severe physical or mental impairment whose ability to function independently in the family or community or whose ability to obtain, maintain, or advance in employment is substantially limited and for whom the delivery of independent living services will improve the ability to function, continue functioning, or move toward functioning independently in the family or community or to continue in employment, respectively.
Funding: (Formula Grants) FY 17 $22,878,000.00; FY 18 est $24,878,000.00; FY 19 est Estimate Not Available
HQ: 330 C Street SW, Washington, DC 20201
   Phone: 202-795-7446 | Email: corinna.stiles@acl.hhs.gov
   http://www.acl.gov

HHS93.433 | ACL NATIONAL INSTITUTE ON DISABILITY, INDEPENDENT LIVING, AND REHABILITATION RESEARCH
"NIDILRR"

Award: Cooperative Agreements
Purpose: To support and coordinate research and its utilization in order to improve the lives of people of all ages with physical and mental disabilities, especially persons with severe disabilities, through identifying and eliminating causes and consequences of disability.
Applicant Eligibility: States, public, private, or nonprofit agencies and Organizations, Institutions of higher education, and Indian Tribes and tribal Organizations are eligible for research projects and specialized research activities related to the rehabilitation of individuals with disabilities; fellowships may be awarded to individuals.
Beneficiary Eligibility: Individuals with disabilities may benefit directly or indirectly from research and other activities conducted by grantees, such as technical assistance and dissemination.
Award Range/Average: The range and average vary greatly according to the competition.
Funding: (Cooperative Agreements) FY 18 $105,320,800.00; FY 19 est Estimate Not Available; FY 20 est Estimate Not Available
HQ: 330 C Street SW, Washington, DC 20201
   Phone: 202-795-7305 | Email: phillip.beatty@acl.hhs.gov

HHS93.118 | ACQUIRED IMMUNODEFICIENCY SYNDROME (AIDS) ACTIVITY

Award: Cooperative Agreements
Purpose: Develops and implements HIV prevention programs of public information and education.
Applicant Eligibility: Public and private Organizations, both nonprofit and for-profit (universities, colleges, research Institutions and other public and private Organizations); State and local Governments, U.S. Territories and possessions; including American Indian/Alaska Native tribal Governments or tribal Organizations located wholly or in part within their boundaries, small and minority businesses, and businesses owned by women.
Beneficiary Eligibility: Official health and education agencies, as well as individuals subject to AIDS.
Funding: (Cooperative Agreements) FY 18 $5,562,453.00; FY 19 est $7,470,000.00; FY 20 est $8,670,000.00

Programs Administered by Federal Headquarters

HQ: 1600 Clifton Road NE, PO Box E07, Atlanta, GA 30333
  Phone: 404-639-1877 | Email: lrw3@cdc.gov
  http://www.cdc.gov/hiv

HHS93.391 | ACTIVITIES TO SUPPORT STATE, TRIBAL, LOCAL AND TERRITORIAL (STLT) HEALTH DEPARTMENT RESPONSE TO PUBLIC HEALTH OR HEALTHCARE CRISES
"CDC Partner Crisis Response NOFO"

Award: Cooperative Agreements
Purpose: To establish a pool of organizations capable of rapidly providing essential expertise to governmental public health entities involved in a response.
Applicant Eligibility: Eligible applicants are limited to the following: 1. Nonprofits having a 501(c)(3) or 501(c)(6) status with the IRS, other than Institutions of higher education. 2. Public and private Institutions of higher education. 3. Native American tribal Organizations (other than Federally-recognized tribal Governments).
Beneficiary Eligibility: Direct awards will be made to the non-governmental organizations described in the eligible applicant section. Beneficiaries of the support provided by those non-governmental organizations will include state health departments; tribal health organizations; local health departments; the District of Columbia; U.S. Territories; and other components of the public health system. The general public will also serve as beneficiaries.
Award Range/Average: Due to the nature of the issues that would trigger CDC to activate this NOFO as designed, it is difficult to project the total funding amount that would be made available. When and if CDC activates this NOFO, it is expected to be only for the time necessary to respond to the emergency at hand, and that long-term recovery needs (and/or emergencies that shift from an epidemic to an endemic nature) would be addressed by other NOFOs as appropriate.
HQ: 1600 Clifton Road NE, PO Box K90, Atlanta, GA 30329-1602
  Phone: 770-488-1602 | Email: rnielson@cdc.gov

HUD14.175 | ADJUSTABLE RATE MORTGAGES
"ARMS"

Award: Guaranteed/insured Loans
Purpose: To provide mortgage insurance for an adjustable rate mortgage that offers lower than market interest rate initially. The interest rate may then change annually for the remainder of the mortgage term.
Applicant Eligibility: All persons intending to occupy the property are eligible to apply.
Beneficiary Eligibility: Individuals/families.
HQ: 451 7th Street SW, Washington, DC 20410
  Phone: 800-225-5342
  http://portal.hud.gov/hudportal/hud?src=/program_offices/housing/sfh/ins/203armt

HHS93.603 | ADOPTION AND LEGAL GUARDIANSHIP INCENTIVE PAYMENTS

Award: Formula Grants
Purpose: Provides incentive to States and eligible Tribes to increase the number of children in foster care who find permanent homes through adoption or legal guardianship.
Applicant Eligibility: Applications are not required. States (including the District of Columbia, Puerto Rico, the U.S. Virgin Islands, Guam and American Samoa) and Tribes that have an approved title IV-E plan and that submit data to the Adoption and Foster Care Analysis and Reporting System (AFCARS) are eligible to receive payments. The Children's Bureau (CB) shall determine an agency's eligibility for funding based on foster care, adoption and guardianship data reported to AFCARS. AFCARS data must be reported and accepted by CB no later than May 15 of the fiscal year subsequent to the fiscal year in which the adoptions or guardianships were finalized (i.e., the "earning year").
Beneficiary Eligibility: Beneficiaries are those children and families eligible under Title IV-B and Title IV-E of the Social Security Act, as amended.
Award Range/Average: FY 2017 earning year,52 States earned incentive payments that ranged from $11,850 to $4,076,960, with an average award amount of $727,403.
Funding: (Formula Grants) FY 18 $75,000,000.00; FY 19 est $74,742,000.00; FY 20 est $37,943,000.00

HQ: 330 C Street SW, Room 3512, Washington, DC 20201
    Phone: 202-205-8552 | Email: gail.collins@acf.hhs.gov
    http://www.acf.hhs.gov/programs/cb

HHS93.659 | ADOPTION ASSISTANCE

Award: Formula Grants

Purpose: Provides Federal Financial Participation to states, Indian tribes, tribal organizations and tribal consortia in adoption subsidy costs for the adoption of children with special needs who cannot be reunited with their families and who meet certain eligibility tests. This assistance is intended to prevent inappropriately long stays in foster care and to promote the healthy development of children through increased safety, permanency and well-being.

Applicant Eligibility: Funds are available to states (including the District of Columbia, Puerto Rico, the U.S. Virgin Islands, Guam and American Samoa) and to Tribes with approved title IV-E plans.

Beneficiary Eligibility: Eligible beneficiaries include certain children who are legally freed for adoption where an adoption assistance agreement has been entered into prior to the finalization of an adoption. These children must: (1) have been determined by the state or tribe to be special needs, e.g., a special factor or condition which makes it reasonable to conclude that they cannot be adopted without adoption assistance; a state or tribe determination that the child cannot or should not be returned home; and a reasonable effort has been made to place the child without providing financial or medical assistance and (2) meet one of the relevant statutory categorical eligibility criteria. These criteria differ during the phase-in period (federal fiscal years (FFYs) 2010 through June 30, 2024) based on the FFY in which the adoption assistance agreement was entered into and the child's circumstances at that time. See section 473 of the Act for additional details on program eligibility requirements. FFP is available from the time of placement for adoption in accordance with state, local or tribal law or final adoption decree to age 18 (21 if the state/tribe finds that a disability means aid should continue or where provided for in an adoption assistance agreement that was entered for a child that had attained at least 16 years of age before the agreement became effective) as long as the parent supports the child. No child adopted prior to the approval of the state or tribal title IV-E plan is eligible for FFP. No means test applies to adopting parents, but the amount of subsidy is agreed to by agency and parents and may be readjusted by joint agreement.

Award Range/Average: FY 2017 Grants to states ranged from: $788,754 to $575,653,089 with an average of $53,451,923.

Funding: (Formula Grants) FY 18 $2,784,978,934.00; FY 19 est $2,841,686,682.00; FY 20 est $2,942,000,000.00

HQ: 330 C Street SW, Room 3509B, Washington, DC 20201
    Phone: 202-205-8438 | Email: eileen.west@acf.hhs.gov
    http://www.acf.hhs.gov/programs/cb

HHS93.652 | ADOPTION OPPORTUNITIES

Award: Project Grants

Purpose: To eliminate barriers, to adoption and to provide permanent, loving home environments for children who would benefit from adoption, particularly children with special needs.

Applicant Eligibility: Grants or Contracts: State, local government entities, public or private licensed child welfare or adoption agencies or community based Organizations.

Beneficiary Eligibility: Children who are in foster care with the goal of adoption, especially children with special needs, that is, children who are older, minority children and infants and toddlers with disabilities who have a life-threatening condition.

Award Range/Average: FY 2017: $300,000 to $5,170,000 with an average of $1,053,919

Funding: (Project Grants (Discretionary)) FY 18 $24,097,720.00; FY 19 est $17,946,939.00; FY 20 est $17,804,511.00

HQ: 330 C Street SW, Room 3503, Washington, DC 20201
    Phone: 202-205-8172 | Email: jan.shafer@acf.hhs.gov
    http://www.acf.hhs.gov/programs/cb

ED84.002 | ADULT EDUCATION-BASIC GRANTS TO STATES

Award: Formula Grants

Purpose: To fund local programs like adult education and literacy services, including workplace literacy services, family literacy services, and English literacy and integrated English literacy-civics education programs.

Applicant Eligibility: Formula grants are made to designated eligible State agencies that under State law are responsible for administering or supervising statewide policy for adult education and literacy, including such entities as State educational agencies (SEAs), postsecondary agencies, or workforce agencies. State agencies must provide direct and equitable access to: local educational agencies; public or private nonprofit agencies; community-based Organizations of demonstrated effectiveness; Institutions of higher education; volunteer literacy Organizations of demonstrated effectiveness; libraries; public housing authorities; nonprofit Institutions not described above that have the ability to provide literacy services to adults and families; and consortia of the entities described above.

Beneficiary Eligibility: Adults and out-of-school youths who are 16 years of age and older, who are not enrolled or required to be enrolled in secondary school under State law, and who lack sufficient mastery of basic educational skills to enable them to function effectively in society or do not have a secondary school diploma or its recognized equivalent, and have not achieved an equivalent level of education, or are unable to speak, read, or write the English language.

Award Range/Average: FY18: $12,158- $100,012,921; $10,637,155 average. FY19: $10,942- $103,037,992; $11,068,190 average. FY20: $9,848- $77,509,220; $8,376,707 average.

Funding: (Formula Grants) FY 18 est $616,955,000.00; FY 19 est $641,955,000.00; FY 20 $485,849,000.00

HQ: 550 12th Street SW, Washington, DC 20024

Phone: 202-245-6836 | Email: cheryl.keenan@ed.gov

http://www2.ed.gov/about/offices/list/ovae/pi/adulted/index.html

ED84.191 | ADULT EDUCATION NATIONAL LEADERSHIP ACTIVITIES

Award: Cooperative Agreements; Project Grants; Direct Payments for Specified Use

Purpose: To support applied research, development, demonstration, dissemination, evaluation, and related activities that contribute towards the improvement of adult education and literacy activities nationally.

Applicant Eligibility: Postsecondary education Institutions, public or private agencies or Organizations, or consortia of these Institutions, agencies, or Organizations are eligible.

Beneficiary Eligibility: Basic education and literacy programs for adults seeking to obtain an education at the primary or secondary levels will benefit through national evaluation, research, leadership, and/or technical assistance efforts.

Award Range/Average: For Fiscal Year 2018: Range: $625,458 - $2,600,000; Average: $1,244,273. For Fiscal Year 2019: Range: $650,000 - $4,100,000; Average: $1,371,200.

Funding: (Project Grants (Contracts)) FY 18 $13,712,000.00; FY 19 est $13,712,000.00; FY 20 est $73,712,000.00

HQ: Potomac Center Plaza 550 12th Street SW, Washington, DC 20024

Phone: 202-245-7717 | Email: christopher.coro@ed.gov

http://www2.ed.gov/programs/aenla/index.html

HHS93.719 | ADVANCE INTEROPERABLE HEALTH INFORMATION TECHNOLOGY SERVICES TO SUPPORT HEALTH INFORMATION EXCHANGE

Award: Cooperative Agreements

Purpose: The Advance Interoperable Health IT Services to Support Health Information Exchange Cooperative Agreement Program will leverage investments and lessons learned from the previous State Health Information Exchange Cooperative Agreement Program to rapidly build capacity for the interoperable exchange of health information across the entire care continuum both within and across states while moving toward nationwide interoperability.

Applicant Eligibility: Either a State, Territory, or State Designated Entity was eligible to apply.

Beneficiary Eligibility: N/A

Award Range/Average: Average of each award is estimated at $2.47M.

HQ: 330 C Street SW, Suite 7033A, Washington, DC 20201

Phone: 202-720-2861 | Email: larry.jessup@hhs.gov

http://www.healthit.gov

HHS93.247 | ADVANCED NURSING EDUCATION WORKFORCE GRANT PROGRAM

"Advanced Nursing Education Workforce (ANEW), Advanced Nurse Education-Sexual Assault Nurse Examiner (ANE-SANE)"

Award: Project Grants

Purpose: To support innovative academic-practice partnerships to prepare advanced practice registered nursing students to practice in rural and underserved settings through academic and clinical training.

Applicant Eligibility: ANEW: Eligible applicants are collegiate schools of nursing, nursing centers, academic health centers, State or local Governments, and other public or private nonprofit entities accredited by a national nurse education accrediting agency recognized by the Secretary of the U.S. Department of education. In addition to the 50 states, only the District of Columbia, Guam, the Commonwealth of Puerto Rico, the Northern Mariana Islands, American Samoa, the U.S. Virgin Islands, the Federated States of Micronesia, the Republic of the Marshall Islands, and the Republic of Palau are eligible to apply. Federally Recognized Indian Tribal Government and Native American Organizations may apply if they are otherwise eligible. ANE SANE: Eligible applicants include accredited schools of nursing, nursing centers, nurse-managed health clinics, academic health centers, State or local health departments, Community Health Centers, Rural Health Clinics, public or non-profit Hospitals, other emergency healthcare service providers, Federally Qualified Health Centers, Clinics receiving funding under Title X and other relevant public or private non-profit entities. Federally recognized Indian Tribal Government and Native American Organizations, as well as nonprofit (Internal Revenue Service (IRS) 501(c)(3) status) community-based and faith-based Organizations may apply if they are otherwise eligible. The eligible state government entities include the 50 states, and the District of Columbia, Guam, the Commonwealth of Puerto Rico, the Northern Mariana Islands, American Samoa, the U.S. Virgin Islands, the Federated States of Micronesia, the Republic of the Marshall Islands, and the Republic of Palau. ANE-NPR: Eligible applicants are schools of nursing, nurse managed health clinics/centers, academic health centers, state or local Governments and other private or public nonprofit entities determined appropriate by the Secretary. Consortiums may apply for these funds, if otherwise eligible. hrsa will make one award per consortium to a lead entity for the consortium provided it is an eligible entity and has the legal authority to apply for and to receive the award on behalf of the other consortium members. Domestic faith-based and community-based Organizations, Tribes, and tribal Organizations may apply for these funds, if otherwise eligible. In addition to the 50 states, only eligible applicants in the District of Columbia, Guam, the Commonwealth of Puerto Rico, the Northern Mariana Islands, American Samoa, the U.S. Virgin Islands, the Federated States of Micronesia, the Republic of the Marshall Islands, and the Republic of Palau may apply. Individuals and foreign entities are not eligible under ANEW, ANE-SANE or ANE-NPR.

Beneficiary Eligibility: ANEW: Accredited schools of nursing, nursing centers, academic health centers, state or local governments, and other public or private nonprofit entities determined appropriate by the Secretary. ANE SANE: An eligible participant must be a citizen of the United States, a non-citizen national, or a foreign national who possesses a visa permitting permanent residence in the United States (i.e., individuals on temporary or student visas are not eligible to receive SANE support). Award recipients may use this funding to support the following beneficiaries: (1) Currently practicing generalist Registered Nurses; (2) Students in Advanced Nursing Education Programs including Advanced Practice Registered Nursing and Forensic Nursing Programs; and (3) Currently practicing Advanced Practice Registered Nurses and Forensic Nurses. ANE-NPR: To be eligible for the ANE-NPR Program the Nurse Practitioner (NP) or Nurse Midwife (NM) must meet all of the following: (1) Be a licensed RN within 18 months of graduate school completion from a Primary Care NP or NM Program and NP or NM certification; (2) Be a citizen of the United States, a non-citizen national, or a foreign national who possesses a visa permitting permanent residence in the United States (i.e., individuals on temporary or student visas are not eligible to receive ANE-NPR Program support); and (3) Agree to be a full-time participant in the ANE-NPR Program.

Award Range/Average: ANEW: FY 18 Range: $257,513 to $700,000; Average - $629,667. FY 19 est. $34,839,914 Range - $275,284,00 - $700,000 Average - $657,357; FY 20 est, $0 ANE-SANE: FY 18 Range: $213,611 to $500,000, Average: $405,878.5 FY 19: est. Range: $229,383 to $500,000; Average: $407,896 FY 20: est. 0 ANE-NPR Data Pending

Funding: (Project Grants) FY 18 $42,119,578.00; FY 19 est $62,997,848.00; FY 20 est $0.00

HQ: 5600 Fishers Lane, Room 11N94C, Rockville, MD 20857

Phone: 301-443-0856 | Email: mmccalla@hrsa.gov

http://www.hrsa.gov

DOC11.612 | ADVANCED TECHNOLOGY PROGRAM
"ATP"

Award: Project Grants

Purpose: To promote partnership for the development of technologies that offer significant economic benefits.

Applicant Eligibility: U.S. businesses and U.S. joint research and development ventures. Foreign-owned businesses are eligible for funding, provided they meet the requirements of Public Law 102-245, Sec. 201(c)(6-7). universities, government laboratories (excluding any NIST laboratory), independent research Organizations, and/or nonprofit Organizations, may participate as a member of a joint venture that includes at least two separately owned for-profit companies, both of which are substantially involved in the R&D and both contributing towards the matching-fund requirement.

Beneficiary Eligibility: U.S. businesses and U.S. joint ventures; and foreign-owned businesses that meet the requirements of Public Law 102-245, Section 201(c)(6-7).

HQ: 100 Bureau Drive, Gaithersburg, MD 20899

Phone: 301-975-4429 | Email: heather.mayton@nist.gov

http://www.nist.gov

Programs Administered by Federal Headquarters

HHS93.088 | ADVANCING SYSTEM IMPROVEMENTS FOR KEY ISSUES IN WOMEN'S HEALTH
"Improving Health of Women and Girls"

Award: Cooperative Agreements

Purpose: To promote program and systems innovation, policy and performance management and strategic communications that will advance improvement for key issues in women's health.

Applicant Eligibility: Nonprofit Organizations must provide evidence of tax-exempt status. When projects involve the collaborative efforts of more than one Organization or require the use of services or facilities not under the direct control of the applicant, written assurances of specific support or agreements must be submitted by the affected parties.

Beneficiary Eligibility: All women and girls, adults and children, including those underserved and minority populations, usually residing in the U.S., including Bone Fide territories, cities and islands.

Award Range/Average: $500,000 - $2,200,000 for 1 - 3 grants; $200,000 - $300,000 for up to 5 grants

Funding: (Cooperative Agreements)FY 16 $5,926,431.00; FY 17 est $9,534,078.00; FY 18 est $5,859,960.00

HQ: 1101 Wootton Parkway, Suite 550 Tower Building, Rockville, MD 20852

Phone: 240-453-8822 | Email: eric.west@hhs.gov

http://www.womenshealth.gov

DOS19.900 | AEECA/ESF PD PROGRAMS
"Assistance for Europe, Eurasia, and Central Asia (AEECA) & Economic Support Fund (ESF) Public Diplomacy Programs (EUR/PD and SCA/PPD)"

Award: Project Grants

Purpose: To provide civil society and democracy building public diplomacy programs within Europe, Eurasia and Central Asia.

Applicant Eligibility: See individual federal assistance announcements on U.S. Embassy web sites in: Albania, Armenia, Azerbaijan, Belarus, Bosnia & Herzegovina, Georgia, Kazakhstan, Kosovo, Kyrgyzstan, Macedonia, Moldova, Montenegro, Russia, Serbia, Tajikistan, Turkmenistan, Ukraine, or Uzbekistan for details.

Beneficiary Eligibility: Only applicants NGO's from Albania, Armenia, Azerbaijan, Belarus, Bosnia & Herzegovina, Georgia, Kazakhstan, Kosovo, Kyrgyzstan, Macedonia, Moldova, Montenegro, Russia, Serbia, Tajikistan, Turkmenistan, Ukraine, or Uzbekistan are eligible for this program.

Funding: (Project Grants) FY 16 Actual Not Available; FY 17 est $23,000,000.00; FY 18 est Estimate Not Available

HQ: 2201 C Street NW, Room 3249, Washington, DC 20520

Phone: 202-647-8519 | Email: langem2@state.gov

NASA43.002 | AERONAUTICS

Award: Cooperative Agreements; Project Grants; Dissemination of Technical Information

Purpose: To offer basic research, educational outreach, or training opportunities in the area of science.

Applicant Eligibility: Basic Research, educational Outreach, or Training Opportunities in the area of Aeronautics. Review funding opportunity announcement for additional information.

Beneficiary Eligibility: Same as Applicant Eligibility.

Funding: (Salaries and Expenses) FY 18 $37,226,670.65; FY 19 est $38,583,420.86; Fy 20 est Estimate Not Available

HQ: 300 E Street SW, Washington, DC 20546

Phone: 202-358-0848 | Email: tony.springer@nasa.gov

http://www.nasa.gov

NASA43.004 | AERONAUTICS RECOVERY ACT

Award: Project Grants

Purpose: To provide a stimulus to the U.S. economy, and among other provisions, it provides funds to Federal agencies for use on contracts, grants, cooperative agreements, and other financial assistance arrangements.

Applicant Eligibility: Generally, it is anticipated that Recovery Act funds will be used to fund grants or cooperative agreements with Institutions of higher education and/or other non-profit Institutions.

Beneficiary Eligibility: Same as Applicant Eligibility.

Award Range/Average: No new programs will be awarded off of this CFDA no.

Funding: (Salaries and Expenses) FY 18 $294,581.38; FY 19 est $74,921.29; FY 20 est Estimate Not Available
HQ: 300 E Street SW, Washington, DC 20546-0001
　　Phone: 202-358-4683 | Email: antanese.n.crank@nasa.gov

HHS93.535 | AFFORDABLE CARE ACT (ACA) CHILDHOOD OBESITY RESEARCH DEMONSTRATION
"Childhood Obesity Research Demonstration"

Award: Cooperative Agreements
Purpose: To determine whether an integrated model of primary care and public health approaches in the community, such as policy, systems, and environmental supports for nutrition and physical activity, can improve underserved children's risk factors for obesity.
Applicant Eligibility: Initial applicants are identified above. FY14 is the final year of the 5 year agreement, as such only grantees already awarded under FOA DP11-1107 are currently eligible.
Beneficiary Eligibility: The general public will benefit from the objectives of this program, with a specific focus on low income children eligible for services under titles XIX and XXI of the Social Security Act; children and their families living at least 150% or higher federal poverty level; or catchment areas where 50% of students are in schools eligible for the National School Lunch Program.
Award Range/Average: Awards range was $1,750,000 for the initial 12 month period and $2,500,000 for the 16 month period - 2 awards total.
HQ: Extramural Research Program Office 1600 Clifton Road NE, Atlanta, GA 30333
　　Phone: 770-488-8390

HHS93.093 | AFFORDABLE CARE ACT (ACA) HEALTH PROFESSION OPPORTUNITY GRANTS
"HPOG"

Award: Cooperative Agreements
Purpose: To provide education and training to Temporary Assistance for Needy Families (TANF) recipients and other low-income individuals for occupations in the healthcarefield.
Applicant Eligibility: An eligible applicant is a State, an Indian tribe or tribal Organization, an institution of higher education, a local workforce investment board established under section 117 of the Workforce Investment Act of 1998, a sponsor of an apprenticeship Program registered under the National Apprenticeship Act or a community-based Organization.
Beneficiary Eligibility: Eligible individual beneficiaries are individuals receiving assistance under the State TANF program; or other low-income individuals described by the eligible entity in its application for a grant under this section.
Award Range/Average: The range is $889,896 - $3,000,000. The average is 2,247,500.
Funding: (Cooperative Agreements (Discretionary Grants)) FY 18 $71,920,000.00; FY 19 est $69,846,538.00; FY 20 est $71,920,000.00; (Training) FY 18 $1,140,089.00; FY 19 est $1,160,000.00; FY 20 est $1,529,000.00; (Salaries and Expenses) FY 18 $973,775.00; FY 19 est $986,000.00; FY 20 est $991,000.00
HQ: 330 C Street SW, Suite 3026, Washington, DC 20201
　　Phone: 816-426-2225 | Email: kim.stupica-dobbs@acf.hhs.gov
　　http://www.acf.hhs.gov/ofa/programs/hpog

HHS93.621 | AFFORDABLE CARE ACT INITIATIVE TO REDUCE AVOIDABLE HOSPITALIZATIONS AMONG NURSING FACILITY RESIDENTS
"Nursing Facility Initiative"

Award: Project Grants
Purpose: The Centers for Medicare & Medicaid Services selected eligible organizations to test a series of evidence-based clinical interventions. Eligible organizations will partner with long-term care facilities and practitioners to implement and test a new payment model with the goal of improving the health and healthcare among LTC facility residents and ultimately reducing avoidable hospital admissions.

Programs Administered by Federal Headquarters

Applicant Eligibility: Applicants eligible to be enhanced care & coordination providers included, but were not limited to: Organizations that provide care coordination, case management, or related services; Medical care providers, such as physician practices; Health plans (although this initiative will not be capitated managed care); Public or not-for-profit Organizations, such as Aging and Disability Resource Centers, Area Agencies on Aging, Behavioral Health Organizations, Centers for Independent Living, universities, or others; Integrated delivery networks, if they will extend their networks to include unaffiliated nursing facilities. Nursing facilities, entities controlled by nursing facilities, or entities for which the primary line of business is the delivery of nursing facility/skilled nursing facility services were excluded from serving as enhanced care & coordination providers under this cooperative agreement. Legal Status: To be eligible, an Organization must have been recognized as a single legal entity by the State where it is incorporated, and must have had a unique Tax Identification Number (TIN) designated to receive payment. The Organization must have had a governing body capable of entering into a cooperative agreement with CMS on behalf of its members.

Beneficiary Eligibility: The primary target population for the clinical interventions is fee-for-service Medicare-Medicaid enrollees in nursing facilities, but fee-for-service long-stay residents who are not yet Medicare-Medicaid enrollees will also benefit (i.e., Medicare beneficiaries not yet eligible for Medicaid, or Medicaid beneficiaries not yet eligible for Medicare but who represent similar opportunities for inpatient reductions).

Award Range/Average: The six (6) organizations which received funding are: Alabama Quality Assurance Foundation - Alabama, Comagine Health - Nevada, Indiana University - Indiana, The Curators of the University of Missouri - Missouri, The Greater New York Hospital Foundation, Inc. - New York City, and UPMC Community Provider Services - Pennsylvania. The awards ranged from: $5 million to $25 million to cover a four-year period of performance.

Funding: (Cooperative Agreements) FY 18 $27,614,601.00; FY 19 est $28,092,794.00; FY 20 est $28,004,625.00

HQ: 7500 Security Boulevard, Baltimore, MD 21214

Phone: 410-786-8786 | Email: nicole.perry@cms.hhs.gov

HHS93.505 | AFFORDABLE CARE ACT (ACA) MATERNAL, INFANT, AND EARLY CHILDHOOD HOME VISITING PROGRAM
"MIECHV Program"

Award: Formula Grants

Purpose: To strengthen and improve the programs and activities carried out under Title V.

Applicant Eligibility: Eligibility for funding is limited to a single application from each State, the District of Columbia, Puerto Rico, Guam, the Virgin Islands, the Northern Mariana Islands, and American Samoa. The Governor has the responsibility and authority to designate which entity or group of entities will apply for and administer home visiting Program funds on behalf of the State or US Territory. Regardless of the entity or entities designated by the Governor, this application must contain the concurrence and signatures of the: Director of the State's Title V agency; Director of the State's agency for Title II of the Child Abuse Prevention and Treatment Act (CAPTA); The State's child welfare agency (Title IV-E and IV-B), if this agency is not also administering Title II of CAPTA: Director of the State's Single State Agency for Substance Abuse Services; The State's childcare and Development Fund (CCDF) Administrator; Director of the State's Head Start State Collaboration Office, and The State's Advisory Council on Early Childhood education and Care authorized by 642B(b)(1)(A)(i) of the Head Start Act. For those states that have elected not to participate in MIECHV, nonprofit Organizations with an established record of providing early childhood home visiting Programs or initiatives in a state or several states are eligible to apply to carry out Programs in those states.

Beneficiary Eligibility: Eligible families residing in communities in need of such services, as identified in a State needs assessment; Low-income eligible families; Eligible families who are pregnant women under age 21; Eligible families with a history of child abuse or neglect or have had interactions with child welfare services; Eligible families with a history of substance abuse or need substance abuse treatment; Eligible families that have users of tobacco products in the home; Eligible families that are or have children with low student achievement; Eligible families with children with developmental delays or disabilities; Eligible families who, or that include individuals serving or formerly serving in the Armed Forces, including those with members who have had multiple deployments outside the U.S. Eligible family: A woman who is pregnant, and the father of the child if available, or A parent or primary caregiver of the child, including grandparents or other relatives and foster parents serving as the child's primary caregiver from birth until kindergarten entry, including a noncustodial parent with an ongoing relationship with, and at times provides physical care for the child.

Award Range/Average: Formula (2013): $1,000,000 - $11,234,549 Formula (2014): $1,000,000 - $11,923,154 Formula (2015) actual: $1,000,000 - $13,201,834 Competitive (2013): A Expansion - $1,428,900 - $8,949,070.B. Nonprofit - $589,685 - $5,479,908.Competitive (2014):A Expansion - $961,615 - $8,751,850B Nonprofit - $1,000,000 - $5,801,252 Competitive (2015) actual:A Expansion - $2,344,479- $9,400,000B Nonprofit - $1,000,000 - $6,402,965

HQ: Division of Home Visiting and Early 5600 Fishers Lane, Room 18N-150, Rockville, MD 20857
   Phone: 301-594-4149 | Email: mbezuneh@hrsa.gov
   http://mchb.hrsa.gov/programs/homevisiting

HHS93.538 | AFFORDABLE CARE ACT-NATIONAL ENVIRONMENTAL PUBLIC HEALTH TRACKING PROGRAM-NETWORK IMPLEMENTATION
"National Center for Environmental Health, Division of Environmental Hazards and Health Effects, Environmental Health Tracking Branch"

Award: Cooperative Agreements
Purpose: To establish and maintain a nationwide tracking network to obtain integrated health and environmental data and use it to provide information in support of actions that improve the health of communities.
Applicant Eligibility: Consistent with appropriation legislative history which began the Tracking initiative in FY 2002, states and local government health departments or their Bona Fide Agents.
Beneficiary Eligibility: The general public will benefit from the objectives of this program.
Award Range/Average: Approximate Average Award is $700,000. This amount is for the first 12-month budget period, and includes both direct and indirect costs. Floor of Individual Award Range is $ 500,000. Ceiling of Individual Award Range is $1,100,000.
HQ: 4770 Buford Highway NE, Atlanta, GA 30341-3717
   Phone: 770-488-0711
   http://www.cdc.gov/ephtracking

HHS93.092 | AFFORDABLE CARE ACT (ACA) PERSONAL RESPONSIBILITY EDUCATION PROGRAM
"PREP"

Award: Formula Grants; Project Grants
Purpose: To educate adolescents and young adults on both abstinence and contraception for the prevention of pregnancy and sexually transmitted infections, including HIV/AIDS.
Applicant Eligibility: There is $55,250,000 appropriated annually to fund 59 States and Territories to enable them to carry out Personal Responsibility education Programs (PREP). Eligible applicants include the 50 United States, the District of Columbia, Puerto Rico, Virgin Islands, Guam, American Samoa, Northern Mariana Islands, Federated States of Micronesia, the Republic of the Marshall Islands, and the Republic of Palau. States or Territories that did not apply for funding in FY 2016 or 2017, are no longer eligible to apply for this Program for the five year project period and their allotments will be made available as Competitive PREP grants to community-based Organizations for the same State or territory. The annual award for the first cohort of Competitive PREP in FY2012 was $18,856,405. The award for the second cohort of Competitive PREP grants awarded in FY2015 was $11,049,699. With the Bipartisan Budget Act of 2018 extension of Competitive PREP through FY2019, the estimated annual continuation award amount in FY 2018 and FY2019 is $11,000,000. Funds ($10,000,000) shall be reserved to award PREP Innovative Strategies (PREIS) grants to entities to implement innovative youth pregnancy prevention strategies and target services to high-risk, vulnerable, and culturally under-represented youth populations. Funds ($3,250,000) shall be reserved for Tribal PREP grants to Indian Tribes and tribal Organizations. Funds ($6,500,000) shall be reserved for Program support that may be provided directly or through a competitive award process. Program support includes research, training and technical assistance, providing consultation and resources on a broad array of teen pregnancy prevention strategies, and developing materials to support grant activities. Funds shall also be reserved to evaluate PREP Programs and activities.
Beneficiary Eligibility: PREP shall provide services to adolescents and young adults. Applicants are encouraged to serve youth populations that are the most high-risk or vulnerable for pregnancies or otherwise have special circumstances, including youth in and aging of out foster care, homeless youth, youth with HIV/AIDS, victims of human trafficking, pregnant youth who are under 21 years of age, mothers who are under 21 years of age, and youth residing in areas with high birth rates for youth. Applicants must include the most recent pregnancy data for the State for youth ages 10 to 14 and youth ages 15-19, the most recent birth rates among the same age groups, and trends in those rates for the most recently preceding 5-year period for which data are available.
Award Range/Average: Each State or Territory shall be allotted at least $250,000 or an amount determined by a formula, using the number of individuals who have attained age 10 but not attained age 19 in the State or Territory to the total number of

such individuals in the entire U.S. based on the most recent Census data, whichever is greater. Applicants for which Census data are not available will be eligible for the minimum allocation of $250,000. The range for State PREP awards to 51 states and territories is $250,000 to $5,860,140.The range for the awards to 13 PREP Innovative Strategies grantees is $478,919 to $852,022. The range for the awards to 8 Tribal PREP grantees is $316,782 to $598,227. The range for the awards to the 21 Competitive PREP grantees is $250,000 to $794,240.

Funding: (Formula Grants) FY 18 $43,726,481.00; FY 19 est $43,620,627.00; FY 20 est $43,620,627.00; (Project Grants (Discretionary)) FY 18 $23,611,032.00; FY 19 est $23,233,373.00; FY 20 est $23,233,373.00

HQ: 330 C Street SW, Washington, DC 20021

    Phone: 202-205-9605 | Email: lebretia.white@acf.hhs.gov

HHS93.606 | AFFORDABLE CARE ACT-PREPAREDNESS AND EMERGENCY RESPONSE LEARNING CENTERS

"Preparedness and Emergency Response Learning Centers (PERLC)"

Award: Cooperative Agreements

Purpose: The program addresses legislative requirements, as stated in section 319F(d) of the Public Health Service, as part of a plan to improve the nation's public health and medical preparedness and response capabilities for emergencies, whether deliberate, accidental, or natural.

Applicant Eligibility: Eligible applicants for this project are accredited Schools of Public Health, as required by section 319F-2(d) of the Public Health Service Act. Only schools accredited by the Council on education for Public Health are eligible.

Beneficiary Eligibility: The general public, and federal state, local, and tribal public health preparedness programs that protect the public from all-hazards will benefit from the objectives of this program.

Award Range/Average: FY 2011 Actual: $714,286 to $714,286 Avg - $714,286

HQ: OPHPR N 1600 Clifton Road NE, PO Box D29, Atlanta, GA 30029-4018

    Phone: 404-639-5276 | Email: vbk5@cdc.gov

    http://www.cdc.gov

HHS93.534 | AFFORDABLE CARE ACT PROGRAM FOR EARLY DETECTION OF CERTAIN MEDICAL CONDITIONS RELATED TO ENVIRONMENTAL HEALTH HAZARDS

"Agency for Toxic Disease Registry, Division of Health Studies"

Award: Project Grants

Purpose: Goal of this program are for Early Detection of Certain Medical Conditions Related to Environmental Health Hazards.

Applicant Eligibility: Eligibility as defined by the authorizing legislation. A hospital or community health center. A Federally qualified health center. A facility of the Indian Health Service. A National Cancer Institute-designated cancer center. An agency of any State or local government. A nonprofit Organization.

Beneficiary Eligibility: Same as Applicant Eligibility.

Award Range/Average: Expected: $2,000,000 - 3,000,000

Funding: (Cooperative Agreements) FY 16 $2,499,995.00; FY 17 est $2,499,999.00; FY 18 est $2,499,999.00

HQ: 4770 Buford Highway NE, PO Box F45, Atlanta, GA 30341

    Phone: 770-488-0563

HHS93.540 | AFFORDABLE CARE ACT STREAMLINED SURVEILLANCE FOR VENTILATOR-ASSOCIATED PNEUMONIA: REDUCING BURDEN AND DEMONSTRATING PREVENTABILITY; AND PREVENTION AND PUBLIC HEALTH FUND

Award: Cooperative Agreements

Purpose: To facilitate a study to demonstrate the utility and relevance of sVAP and promote acceptance of sVAP within the critical care community.

Applicant Eligibility: Eligible applicants include recipients funded under the CDC Prevention Epicenters Program (CI11-001): a. Chicago Prevention Epicenter b. Duke University Prevention Epicenter c. Harvard/Irvine Prevention Epicenter d. University of Pennsylvania Prevention Epicenter e. Washington University Prevention Epicenter.

Beneficiary Eligibility: State and local health departments, U.S. Territories, and the general public.

Award Range/Average: Approximately $1,544,309 in FY 2011 was awarded fund 1 application. The award period was 24 months. An applicant may request a project period up to 24 months for a total of $1,544,309 including direct and indirect costs.

HQ: 1600 Clifton Road NE, PO Box A16, Atlanta, GA 30329
Phone: 404-639-7093

HUD14.878 | AFFORDABLE HOUSING DEVELOPMENT IN MAIN STREET REJUVENATION PROJECTS
"Main Street"

Award: Project Grants

Purpose: To redevelop main street areas, preserve historic or traditional architecture in main street areas, enhance economic development efforts in main street areas, and to provide affordable housing in main street areas.

Applicant Eligibility: Eligible applicants include, and are limited to, Units of Local Government ("Local Government") that are subdivisions of State Governments, and other Governments listed in Section 102 of the Housing and Community Development Act of 1974. The jurisdiction of the Local Government must contain a population of no more than 50,000. The Local Government must either have no Public Housing Agency (PHA) or a PHA that administers no more than 100 public housing units.

Beneficiary Eligibility: The beneficiaries are low-income families that occupy the newly developed affordable housing, and the local community that is benefiting from the Main Street rejuvenation project.

Award Range/Average: The grant amount was $500,000

HQ: 451 7th Street SW, Room 4130, Washington, DC 20410
Phone: 202-401-8812 | Email: lawrence.gnessin@hud.gov
http://www.hud.gov/mainstreet

HHS93.866 | AGING RESEARCH
"Aging"

Award: Project Grants

Purpose: To encourage biomedical, social, and behavioral research and research training directed toward greater understanding of the aging process and the diseases, special problems, and needs of people as they age. The National Institute on Aging has established programs to pursue these goals.

Applicant Eligibility: Grants: universities, colleges, medical, dental and nursing schools, schools of public health, laboratories, hospitals, State and local health departments, other public or private Institutions (both for-profit and nonprofit), and individuals. National Research Service Award: Individual NRSAs may be made for postdoctoral training to applicants who hold a professional or scientific degree (M.D., Ph.D., D.D.S., D.O., D.V.M., Sc.D., D.Eng., or equivalent domestic or foreign degree) or for predoctoral training to applicants registered for doctoral research training. Institutional NRSAs may be made for both predoctoral and postdoctoral research training. Predoctoral awardees must have a baccalaureate degree. Applicants must be citizens of the United States or admitted for permanent residency. Individual NRSA awardees must be nominated and sponsored by a public or private nonprofit institution having staff and facilities suitable to the proposed research training. Nonprofit domestic Organizations may apply for the Institutional NRSA. SBIR grants can be awarded only to domestic small businesses (entities that are independently owned and operated for profit, are not dominant in the field in which research is proposed, and have no more than 500 employees). Primary employment (more than one-half time) of the principal investigator must be with the small business at the time of award and during the conduct of the proposed project. In both Phase I and Phase II, the research must be performed in the U.S. or its possessions. STTR grants can be awarded only to domestic small business concerns (entities that are independently owned and operated for profit, are not dominant in the field in which research is proposed and have no more than 500 employees) which "partner" with a research institution in cooperative research and development. At least 40 percent of the project is to be performed by the small business concern and at least 30 percent by the research institution. In both Phase I and Phase II, the research must be performed in the U.S. and its possessions. To be eligible for funding, a grant application other than a fellowship must be assessed for scientific merit by a scientific review group and receive approval from a national advisory council. Individual funding opportunity announcements published in the NIH Guide provide more detail on eligibility.

Beneficiary Eligibility: Any nonprofit or for-profit organization, company, or institution engaged in biomedical research. Students pursuing doctoral research training.

Award Range/Average: Awards vary in range depending on the particular activity codes. Individual fellowships range from $23,376 to $57,504 and average about $46,000. Research grants have much larger ranges - from $75,000 to several million dollars. Average costs of research grants are around $400,000. All costs are shown on a single year basis. Awards may be for up to five years.

Funding: (Project Grants) FY 18 $2,253,600,000.00; FY 19 est $2,627,325,000.00; FY 20 est $2,230,601,000.00

HQ: National Institute on Aging 7201 Wisconsin Avenue, Room 2C218, Bethesda, MD 20892

    Phone: 301-402-7715 | Email: barrr@mail.nih.gov

    http://www.nia.nih.gov

USDA10.291 | AGRICULTURAL AND FOOD POLICY RESEARCH CENTERS

Award: Cooperative Agreements

Purpose: To conduct research on public policies and trade agreements such as farm and agricultural sectors, environment, rural economies, food and nutrition.

Applicant Eligibility: Applicants must have substantial experience in the field of research for which they are applying, including a history of providing (1) unbiased, nonpartisan economic analysis to Congress on the farm and agricultural sectors (including commodities, livestock, dairy, and specialty crops), the environment, rural families, households, and economies, and consumers, food, and nutrition; or (2) objective, scientific information to Federal agencies and the public to support and enhance efficient, accurate implementation of Federal drought preparedness and drought response Programs, including inter agency thresholds used to determine eligibility for mitigation or emergency assistance.

Beneficiary Eligibility: Funds are awarded directly to the ultimate beneficiary. This is not a pass-through program.

Award Range/Average: 2016 range: $3,800,000 - $3,800,0002016 average: $3,800,0002017 range: $3,800,000 - $3,800,0002017 average: $3,800,0002018 range: $3,800,000 - $3,800,0002018 average: $3,800,000

Funding: (Cooperative Agreements) FY 17 $3,800,000.00; FY 18 est $3,800,000.00; FY 19 est $0.00

HQ: 1400 Independence Avenue SW, Room 4434-S, Washington, DC 20250-3812

    Phone: 202-690-2477 | Email: hcolby@oce.usda.gov

    http://www.usda.gov/oce

USDA10.250 | AGRICULTURAL AND RURAL ECONOMIC RESEARCH, COOPERATIVE AGREEMENTS AND COLLABORATIONS

Award: Cooperative Agreements; Project Grants; Dissemination of Technical Information

Purpose: ERS provides help for development, administration, and evaluation of agricultural and rural policies.

Applicant Eligibility: Any individual or Organization in the U.S. and U.S. Territories is eligible to receive the popular or technical research publications that convey the research results, although there may be a fee.

Beneficiary Eligibility: Same as Applicant Eligibility.

Funding: (Project Grants) FY 17 $200,000.00; FY 18 est $400,000.00; FY 19 est $0.00; (Cooperative Agreements) FY 17 $1,500,000.00; FY 18 est $1,500,000.00; FY 19 est $0.00

HQ: 355 E Street SW, Room 5-254, Washington, DC 20024-3231

    Phone: 202-694-5008 | Email: nthomas@ers.usda.gov

USDA10.290 | AGRICULTURAL MARKET AND ECONOMIC RESEARCH

Award: Cooperative Agreements

Purpose: To conduct research on public policies and trade agreements such as farm and agricultural sectors, environment, rural economies, food and nutrition.

Applicant Eligibility: Applicants must have substantial experience in the field of research for which they are applying.

Beneficiary Eligibility: Funds are awarded directly to the ultimate beneficiary. This is not a pass-through program.

Award Range/Average: For FY17, the range of Financial Assistance was $15,000 to $365,000, with an average award of $124,713.

Funding: (Cooperative Agreements) FY 17 $1,572,000.00; FY 18 est $2,776,000.00; FY 19 est $400,000.00

HQ: 1400 Independence Avenue SW, Room 4434-S, Washington, DC 20250-3812

    Phone: 202-690-2477 | Email: hcolby@oce.usda.gov

    http://www.usda.gov/oce

USDA10.618 | AGRICULTURAL TRADE PROMOTION PROGRAM
"ATP"

Award: Formula Grants

Purpose: The Agricultural Trade Promotion Program assists the U.S. agricultural industries to promote U.S. agricultural commodities in foreign markets.

Applicant Eligibility: To be approved, applicants must be: (1) A nonprofit U.S. agricultural trade Organization; (2) a nonprofit state regional trade group; (3) a U.S. agricultural cooperative; or (4) a state agency.

Beneficiary Eligibility: CCC will enter into ATP agreements only where the eligible agricultural commodity is comprised of at least 50 percent U.S. origin content by weight, exclusive of added water.

Funding: (Formula Grants) FY 18 $0.00 FY 19 est $300,000,000 FY 20 est $0.00

HQ: 1400 Independence Avenue SW, Washington, DC 20250

　　Phone: 202-720-4327 | Email: curt.alt@fas.usda.gov

USDA10.310 | AGRICULTURE AND FOOD RESEARCH INITIATIVE (AFRI)
"AFRI"

Award: Project Grants

Purpose: To provide standard funds for research and education.

Applicant Eligibility: This initiative supports integrated and non-integrated Programs. Please refer to Part III, A of the current Agriculture and Food Research Initiative (AFRI) Request for Applications for the complete eligibility requirements.

Beneficiary Eligibility: This initiative supports integrated and non-integrated programs. Please refer to Part III, A of the current Agriculture and Food Research Initiative (AFRI) Request for Applications (RFA) for the complete eligibility requirements.

Award Range/Average: If minimum or maximum amounts of funding per competitive and/or capacity project grant, or cooperative agreement are established, these amounts will be announced in the annual Competitive Request for Application (RFA). The most current RFAs are available as follows: AFRI: Agricultural and Natural Resources Science for Climate Variability and Change: https://nifa.usda.gov/funding-opportunity/agriculture-and-food-research-initiative-agriculture-and-natural-resources AFRI: Food Safety: https://nifa.usda.gov/funding-opportunity/agriculture-and-food-research-initiative-food-safety-challenge-area AFRI: Sustainable Bioenergy: https://nifa.usda.gov/funding-opportunity/afri-foundational-bioenergy-natural-resources-and-environment AFRI: Food, Agriculture, Natural Resources and Human Sciences Education and Literacy Initiative (ELI): https://nifa.usda.gov/funding-opportunity/agriculture-and-food-research-initiative-food-agriculture-natural-resources AFRI: Childhood Obesity Prevention: https://nifa.usda.gov/funding-opportunity/agriculture-and-food-research-initiative-childhood-obesity-prevention-challenge AFRI: Foundational Program: https://nifa.usda.gov/funding-opportunity/agriculture-and-food-research-initiative-foundational-program https://nifa.usda.gov/funding-opportunity/afri-foundational-exploratory-research Joint Plant Feedstock: https://nifa.usda.gov/funding-opportunity/plant-feedstock-genomics-bioenergy-joint-research-solicitation-usda-doe AFRI: Water (for Agriculture): https://nifa.usda.gov/funding-opportunity/agriculture-and-food-research-initiative-water-agriculture-challenge-area Innovation at the Nexus of Food, Energy, and Water Systems (INFEWS): https://nifa.usda.gov/funding-opportunity/innovations-nexus-food-energy-and-water RFAs are generally released annually. Hence, the RFAs provide the most current and accurate information available. Any specific instructions in the Competitive RFAs supersede the general information provided in the CFDA database.

Funding: (Project Grants) FY 18 $365,236,233.00; FY 19 est $378,828,821.00; FY 20 est $457,613,568.00

HQ: 1400 Independence Avenue SW, PO Box 2240, Washington, DC 20250

　　Phone: 202-401-6134

　　http://nifa.usda.gov/grants

USDA10.512 | AGRICULTURE EXTENSION AT 1890 LAND-GRANT INSTITUTIONS
"1890 LGIs - Section 1444 Extension"

Award: Formula Grants

Purpose: To support forest and agricultural extension activities.

Applicant Eligibility: Applications may only be submitted by 1890 Land-Grant universities that conduct agricultural extension activities in accordance with NARETPA section 1444(a)(1): Alabama A&M University; Tuskegee University; University of Arkansas - Pine Bluff; Delaware State University; Florida A&M University; Fort Valley State University; Kentucky State University; Southern University; University of Maryland - Eastern Shore; Alcorn State University; Lincoln University; North Carolina A & T State University; Central State University, Langston University; South Carolina State University; Tennessee State University; Prairie View A&M University; Virginia State University; and West Virginia State University.

Programs Administered by Federal Headquarters

Beneficiary Eligibility: Same as Applicant Eligibility.

Award Range/Average: If minimum or maximum amounts of funding per competitive and/or capacity project grant, or cooperative agreement are established, these amounts will be announced in the annual Capacity Request for Application (RFA).The most current RFA is available via: https://nifa.usda.gov/sites/default/files/resources/FY%202017%20 Agricultural%20Extension%20at%201890_revised.pdf

Funding: (Formula Grants) FY 17 $0.00; FY 18 est $0.00; FY 19 est $45,533,000.00

HQ: National Program Leader Institute of Youth Family and Community Division of Community and Education 1400 Independence Avenue SW, PO Box 2250, Washington, DC 20250-2250

　　Phone: 202-720-5305 | Email: wesley.dean@nifa.usda.gov

USDA10.113 | AGRICULTURE RISK COVERAGE PROGRAM
"ARC"

Award: Direct Payments for Specified Use

Purpose: The ARC compensates for the eligible producers of covered commodities.

Applicant Eligibility: An eligible producer is eligible to enter into a contract if 1) the owner of the farm has an ownership of a crop and assumes all or a part of the risk producing a crop that is commensurate with that claimed ownership of the crop; 2) a producer, other than the owner, on a farm with a share-rent lease for such farm, regardless of the length of the lease, if the owner of the farm enters into the same contract; 3) a producer, other than an owner, on a farm who rents such farm under a lease expiring on or after September 30 of the year of the contract in which case the owner is not required to enter into the contract; 4) a producer, other than an owner, on a farm who cash rents such farm under a leasing expiring before September 30 of the year of the contract; 5)An owner of an eligible farm who cash rents such farm and the lease expires before September 30 of the year of the contract, if the tenant declines to enter into a contract for the applicable year.

Beneficiary Eligibility: ARC provides payments to eligible producers on farms enrolled for the 2014 through 2018 crop years.

Funding: (Direct Payments with Unrestricted Use) FY 18 $673,000,000.00; FY 19 est $104,000,000.00; FY 20 est $106,000,000.00

HQ: 1400 Independence Avenue SW, Room 4759-S, Washington, DC 20250

　　Phone: 202-720-7641 | Email: brent.orr@wdc.usda.gov

　　http://www.fsa.usda.gov/programs-and-services/arcplc_program/index

USDA10.520 | AGRICULTURE RISK MANAGEMENT EDUCATION PARTNERSHIPS COMPETITIVE GRANTS PROGRAM
"ARME"

Award: Project Grants

Purpose: This grants program provides education for agricultural producers on risk management activities such as agricultural trade options, crop insurance, cash forward contracting, debt reduction, etc. Further, NIFA also provides risk management strategies for farmers and ranchers on various purposes and disciplines.

Applicant Eligibility: Qualified public and private entities (including land grant colleges, cooperative extension services, and colleges or universities) may use funds for the purpose of educating agricultural producers about the full range of risk management activities, including futures, options, agricultural trade options, crop insurance, cash forward contracting, debt reduction, production diversification, farm resources risk reduction, and other risk management strategies.

Beneficiary Eligibility: Applications may be submitted by qualified public and private entities. This includes all colleges and universities, Federal, State, and local agencies, nonprofit and for-profit private organizations or corporations, and other entities. Award recipients may subcontract to organizations not eligible to apply provided such organizations are necessary for the conduct of the project.

Award Range/Average: If minimum or maximum amounts of funding per competitive and/or capacity project grant, or cooperative agreement are established, these amounts will be announced in the annual Competitive Request for Application (RFA).The most current RFA is available via: https://nifa.usda.gov/funding-opportunity/agriculture-risk-management-education-partnerships-arme-competitive-grants.

Funding: (Project Grants (Discretionary)) FY 17 $0.00; FY 18 est $0.00; FY 19 est $4,800,000.00

HQ: 1400 Independence Avenue SW, Room 4434, Washington, DC 20250

　　Phone: 202-690-3468 | Email: toija.riggins@nifa.usda.gov

　　https://nifa.usda.gov/funding-opportunity/agriculture-risk-management-education-partnerships-arme-competitive-grants

USDA10.616 | AGRICULTURE WOOL APPAREL MANUFACTURERS TRUST FUND

Award: Direct Payments With Unrestricted Use

Purpose: The Agriculture Wool Apparel Manufacturers Trust compensates for accidents to the domestic manufacturers resulting from tariffs on wool fabric.

Applicant Eligibility: Payments to reduce the injury to domestic manufacturers resulting from tariffs on wool fabric that are higher than tariffs on certain apparel articles made of wool fabric.

Beneficiary Eligibility: Beneficiaries limited to: each eligible manufacturer under paragraph (3) of section 4002(c) of the Wool Suit and Textile Trade Extension Act of 2004 (Public Law 108-429; 118 Stat. 2600), as amended by section 1633(c) of the Miscellaneous Trade and Technical Corrections Act of 2006 (Public Law 109-280; 120 Stat. 1166) and section 325(b) of the Tax Extenders and Alternative Minimum Tax Relief Act of 2008 (division C of Public Law 110-343; 122 Stat. 3875), and any successor-in-interest to such a manufacturer as provided for under paragraph (4) of such section 4002(c).

Award Range/Average: Benefits Range from approximately $14,000 to $5 million.

Funding: (Direct Payments with Unrestricted Use) FY 17 $30,000,000.00; FY 18 est $30,000,000.00; FY 19 est $30,000,000.00

HQ: 1400 Independence Avenue SW, Washington, DC 20250

Phone: 202-720-3538 | Email: amy.harding@fas.usda.gov

http://www.fas.usda.gov

DOD12.801 | AIR FORCE ACADEMY ATHLETIC PROGRAMS

Award: Cooperative Agreements

Purpose: Operates and supports the United States Air Force Academy athletic program.

Applicant Eligibility: Per 10 U.S.C. 9362, the Secretary of the Air Force may, in accordance with the laws of the State of Incorporation, establish a corporation to support the athletic Programs of the Academy. There is only 1 eligible entity, the Air Force Academy Athletic Corporation, a 501(c)(3) nonprofit, incorporated in the state of Colorado, and per 10 USC 9362 the Secretary of the Air Force may enter into cooperative agreements with the corporation for the purposes related to the athletic Programs of the Academy.

Beneficiary Eligibility: N/A

Award Range/Average: Not Available.

Funding: (Cooperative Agreements) FY 18 $10,379,732.00; FY 19 est $11,300,000.00; FY 20 est $12,000,000.00

HQ: 1060 Air Force Pentagon 4C149, Washington, DC 20330

Phone: 571-256-2422 | Email: venton.j.lamont.civ@mail.mil

http://www.airforce.com

DOD12.800 | AIR FORCE DEFENSE RESEARCH SCIENCES PROGRAM

Award: Project Grants

Purpose: To maintain technological superiority in the scientific areas relevant to Air Force needs.

Applicant Eligibility: Private/public educational Institutions; other private/public nonprofit Organizations which are operated primarily for scientific, educational, or similar purposes in the public interest, and commercial concerns.

Beneficiary Eligibility: Same as Applicant Eligibility.

Award Range/Average: The range for Federal Assistance is $4,314 to $2,501,710.

Funding: (Project Grants (Cooperative Agreements)) FY 18 $319,100,000.00; FY 19 est $317,000,000.00; FY 20 est $209,000,000.00

HQ: 1060 Air Force Pentagon 4C149, Washington, DC 20330

Phone: 571-256-2422 | Email: venton.j.lamont.civ@mail.mil

http://www.airforce.com

DOD12.810 | AIR FORCE MEDICAL RESEARCH AND DEVELOPMENT

Award: Cooperative Agreements; Project Grants

Purpose: To enhance the health, safety, readiness, and performance of Air Force personnel through applied medical research and advanced development.

Applicant Eligibility: Applicants must be an institution/Organization. Applications will not be accepted from individuals.

Beneficiary Eligibility: Same as Applicant Eligibility.

Award Range/Average: Projects from $50,000.00 to $5,000,000.00. Average award is $750,000.00

Funding: (Project Grants (Cooperative Agreements or Contracts)) FY 18 $1,926,460.00; FY 19 est $1,359,000.00; FY 20 est $2,200,000

Programs Administered by Federal Headquarters

HQ: SAF/AQC 1060 Air Force Pentagon 4C149, Washington, DC 20330
   Phone: 571-256-2422 | Email: venton.j.lamont.civ@mail.mil
   http://www.af.mil

DOI15.421 | ALASKA COASTAL MARINE INSTITUTE
"ALASKA CMI"

Award: Cooperative Agreements
Purpose: The Bureau of Ocean Energy Management oversees the exploration and development of oil, natural gas and other minerals and renewable energy alternatives on the Nations outer continental shelf. The purpose of the Alaska Coastal Marine Institute is to use highly qualified scientific expertise at local levels to collect and disseminate environmental information needed for OCS oil and gas and marine minerals decisions; address local and regional OCS-related environmental and resource issues of mutual interest; and strengthen the BOEM-State partnership in addressing OCS oil and gas and marine minerals information needs.
Applicant Eligibility: University of Alaska may make application for support by a named principal investigator. Non-UA scientists may participate in collaboration with a UA principal investigator.
Beneficiary Eligibility: Research scientists, Federal, State and local decision-makers, Native American Organizations, and the general public will ultimately benefit from the program.
Award Range/Average: Range is $12,000 to $360,000; Average $170,000.
Funding: (Cooperative Agreements) FY 17 $684,800.00; FY 18 est Estimate Not Available; FY 19 est Estimate Not Available
HQ: 381 Elden Street HM 3115, Herndon, VA 20170
   Phone: 703-787-1087 | Email: rodney.cluck@boem.gov
   http://www.boem.gov

ED84.356 | ALASKA NATIVE EDUCATIONAL PROGRAMS

Award: Project Grants
Purpose: To support projects that recognize and address the unique educational needs of Alaska Native students.
Applicant Eligibility: Alaska Native Organizations with experience operating Alaska Native education Programs; Alaska Native Organizations that do not have experience operating Alaska Native education Programs, but that apply in partnership with: a State educational agency (SEA) or an Alaska Native Organization that operates an Alaska Native education Program; or an entity located in Alaska and predominantly governed by Alaska Natives that has experience operating Alaska Native Programs and is granted an official charter or sanction from at least one Alaska Native tribe or Alaska Native Organization to carry out such Programs.
Beneficiary Eligibility: Alaska Natives as defined in the Alaska Native Claims Settlement Act.
Award Range/Average: Range of new awards: $200,000- $1,000,000; Average new award: $550,000
Funding: (Project Grants) FY 18 $35,453,000.00; FY 19 est $35,453,000.00; FY 20 est $0.00
HQ: Department of Education OESE School Improvement Programs 400 Maryland Avenue SW, Washington, DC 20202
   Phone: 202-260-1979 | Email: almita.reed@ed.gov
   http://www.ed.gov/programs/alaskanative/index.html

DOI15.442 | ALASKA NATIVE SCIENCE AND ENGINEERING
"ANSEP"

Award: Cooperative Agreements
Purpose: Alaska Native Science and Engineering Program (ANSEP) provides an opportunity to further engage Alaska's Native professionals and develop the future scientific and engineering employment pool required to support the BSEE mission. The overall objective is to expand the professional science employment preparedness of ANSEP students and to develop a more diversified pool of highly educated professionals with the BSEE workforce to reflect the rich diversity of the Nation.
Applicant Eligibility: N/A
Beneficiary Eligibility: Research scientists, Federal, State and local decision-makers, the youth participants, BSEE, and the general public will ultimately benefit from the program.
Award Range/Average: Range is $50,000 to $250,000; Average $300,000
Funding: (Cooperative Agreements) FY 17 $50,000.00; FY 18 est $50,000.00; FY 19 est Estimate Not Available
HQ: 45600 Woodlawn Road HE 2126, Sterling, VA 20166
   Phone: 703-787-1630 | Email: eric.turner@bsee.gov
   http://www.bsee.gov

USDA10.228 | ALASKA NATIVE SERVING AND NATIVE HAWAIIAN SERVING INSTITUTIONS EDUCATION GRANTS
"ANNH Grants Program"

Award: Project Grants

Purpose: To promote education, research, agricultural sciences, and community development.

Applicant Eligibility: Individual public or private, non-profit Alaska Native-Serving and Native Hawaiian-Serving Institutions of higher education that meet the definitions of Alaska Native-Serving Institution or Native Hawaiian Serving Institution established in Title III, Part A of the Higher education Act of 1965, as amended (20 U.S.C. 1059d.) are eligible Institutions under this Program.

Beneficiary Eligibility: Alaska Native Serving Institutions and Native Hawaiian Serving Institutions.

Award Range/Average: If minimum or maximum amounts of funding per competitive and/or capacity project grant, or cooperative agreement are established, these amounts will be announced in the annual Competitive Request for Application (RFA).The most current RFA is available via: https://nifa.usda.gov/funding-opportunity/alaska-native-serving-and-native-hawaiian-serving-institutions-education

Funding: (Project Grants) FY 18 $3,060,121.00; FY 19 est $3,066,240.00; FY 20 est $0.00

HQ: National Program Leader Institute of Youth Family and Community Division of Community and Education 1400 Independence Avenue SW, PO Box 2250, Washington, DC 20250-2250

    Phone: 202-720-2324

    http://nifa.usda.gov/program/alaska-native-serving-and-native-hawaiian-serving-institutions-education-competitive-grants

DOI15.431 | ALASKA SETTLEMENT AGREEMENT

Award: Direct Payments With Unrestricted Use

Purpose: Shares 100 percent with the State of Alaska to be paid monthly subject to late disbursement interest for contracts, leases, permits, rights-of-way, or easements under Section 6(h) of the Alaska Statehood Act.

Applicant Eligibility: Revenue from effected leases will trigger automatic payment distribution computed in accordance with the law.

Beneficiary Eligibility: Limited to Leases A-028056, A-028063, A-028135, A-028143, A-028103, A-028140, A-19230, A028055, and A-028047.

Award Range/Average: Not Applicable.

Funding: (Direct Payments for Specified Use) FY 17 $23,000.00; FY 18 est $28,000.00; FY 19 est $31,000.00

HQ: Office of Natural Resources Revenue 1849 C Street NW, PO Box 4211, Washington, DC 20240

    Phone: 202-513-0600

    http://www.ONRR.gov

HHS93.273 | ALCOHOL RESEARCH PROGRAMS

Award: Project Grants

Purpose: To develop a sound fundamental knowledge base which can be applied to the development of improved methods of treatment and more effective strategies for preventing alcoholism and alcohol-related problems.

Applicant Eligibility: Public or private profit and nonprofit agencies, including State, local, or regional government agencies, universities, colleges, hospitals, academic or research Institutions may apply for research grants. SBIR grants can be awarded only to domestic small businesses (entities that are independently owned and operated for profit, are not dominant in the field in which research is proposed, and have no more than 500 employees). Primary employment (more than one-half time) of the principal investigator must be with the small business at the time of award and during the conduct of the proposed project. In both Phase I and Phase II, the research must be performed in the U.S. and its possessions. To be eligible for funding, a grant application must be approved for scientific merit and Program relevance by a scientific review group and a national advisory council. STTR grants can be awarded only to domestic small business concerns (entities that are independently owned and operated for profit, are not dominant in the field in which research is proposed and have no more than 500 employees) which "partner" with a research institution in cooperative research and development. At least 40 percent of the project is to be performed by the small business concern and at least 30 percent by the research institution. In both Phase I and Phase II, the research must be performed in the U.S. and its possessions. To be eligible for funding, a grant application must be approved for scientific merit and Program relevance by a scientific review group and a national advisory council.

Beneficiary Eligibility: Public, profit and nonprofit private organizations.

Funding: (Project Grants) FY 18 $386,602,000.00; FY 19 est $399,597,000.00; FY 20 est $334,666,000.00

Programs Administered by Federal Headquarters

HQ: 6700B Rockledge Dr, Rockville, MD 20817
   Phone: 301-451-2067 | Email: srinivar@mail.nih.gov
   http://www.nih.gov

USDA10.330 | ALFALFA AND FORAGE RESEARCH PROGRAM "AFRP"

Award: Project Grants
Purpose: To protect crops, reduce pest, improve seed production, and increase harvest production.
Applicant Eligibility: (1) State agricultural experiment stations; (2) colleges and universities; (3) University research foundations; (4) other research Institutions and Organizations; (5) Federal agencies, (6) national laboratories; (7) private Organizations or corporations; (8) individuals who are U.S. citizens or permanent residents; and (9) any group consisting of 2 or more entities identified in (1) through (8).
Beneficiary Eligibility: Same as Applicant Eligibility.
Award Range/Average: If minimum or maximum amounts of funding per competitive and/or capacity project grant, or cooperative agreement are established, these amounts will be announced in the annual Competitive Request for Application (RFA).
Funding: (Project Grants) FY 17 $2,083,825.00; FY 18 est $2,084,967.00; FY 19 est $0.00
HQ: Institute of Food Production and Sustainability (IFPS) Division of Plant Systems - Production 1400 Independence Avenue SW, PO Box 2250, Washington, DC 20250-2250
   Phone: 202-401-5024
   http://nifa.usda.gov/program/agronomic-forage-crops-program

VA64.124 | ALL-VOLUNTEER FORCE EDUCATIONAL ASSISTANCE "Montgomery GI-Bill Active Duty (MGIB) - Chapter 30"

Award: Direct Payments With Unrestricted Use
Purpose: To help servicepersons readjust to civilian life after their separation from military service.
Applicant Eligibility: What follows is not a complete list of eligibility requirements. For more information on the newest MGIB Program changes go to the VA web-site address listed below. A high school diploma or equivalency certificate is always required for eligibility to the MGIB as is an honorable discharge from the qualifying period of service unless the individual is currently on active duty. (1) Individuals initially entering military service on or after July 1, 1985 may be eligible unless they specifically elect not to participate in the MGIB Program. Service members can use the MGIB benefit after completing two continuous years of service. Veterans whose initial obligation was 3 years or more may use the MGIB benefit after completing three continuous years of active duty, or less time if discharged early for an acceptable reason. Veterans whose initial obligation was less than 3 years may use the MGIB benefits after serving two years of active duty, or less time if discharged early for an acceptable reason or if they sign up for 4 years in the Selected Reserve. Any period of active duty may be used to meet these requirements, but generally, periods of active duty cannot be combined. (2) Individuals who were eligible for the Old (Vietnam-Era) GI Bill benefits as of December 31, 1989, and served on continuous active duty for 3 years after June 30, 1985, may be eligible for the MGIB. (3) Persons involuntarily separated from the military for certain reasons may be eligible for the MGIB. Likewise, persons who received voluntary separation incentives may be eligible for the MGIB. (4) Persons who converted from VEAP (Veterans educational Assistance Program) to the MGIB during open seasons from October 9, 1996 through July 8, 1997, or from November 1, 2000 to October 31, 2001, may be eligible for the MGIB. Likewise, certain persons serving full-tome under title 32 in the National Guard during the period from July 1, 1985 to November 28, 1989 with no previous active duty and who elected the MGIB during the open season from October 9, 1996 through July 8, 1997, may be eligible for the MGIB. In addition, in very limited circumstances, dependents of veteran or service member may be eligible for the MGIB if the veteran or service member transferred entitlement to those dependents.
Beneficiary Eligibility: As stated above under Applicant Eligibility.
Award Range/Average: Currently, the full-time monthly benefit range from $1,509 to over $3,000 depending on the length of the service obligation, military incentives, military career field, branch of service and voluntary contributions. In most cases, benefits last for 36 (48 months when combined with other VBA education benefits) calendar months of full-time training. The work-study allowance is limited to the higher of the Federal minimum wage, or the State minimum wage where work is performed. Tutorial assistance can be up to a maximum of $1,200.
HQ: Department of Veterans Affairs 810 Vermont Avenue NW, Washington, DC 20420
   Phone: 202-461-9800
   http://www.benefits.va.gov/gibill

HHS93.855 | ALLERGY AND INFECTIOUS DISEASES RESEARCH

Award: Project Grants

Purpose: To assist public and private nonprofit institutions and individuals to establish, expand and improve biomedical research and research training in infectious diseases and related areas; to conduct developmental research, to produce and test research materials.

Applicant Eligibility: Universities, colleges, hospitals, laboratories, and other public or private nonprofit domestic Institutions, including State and local units of government, and individuals are eligible to make application for grant support of research by a named principal investigator or a research career development candidate. For-profit Organizations are also eligible, with the exception of NRSA. Individual NRSA awardees must be nominated and sponsored by a public or nonprofit private institution having staff and facilities appropriate to the proposed research training Program. All NRSA awardees must be citizens or have been admitted to the United States for permanent residence. To be eligible, predoctoral candidates must have completed the baccalaureate degree, and postdoctoral awardees must have a professional or scientific degree (M.D., Ph.D., D.D.S., D.O., D.V.M., Sc.D., D.Eng., or equivalent domestic or foreign degree). SBIR grants can be awarded only to domestic small businesses (entities that are independently owned and operated for profit, are not dominant in the field in which research is being proposed and have no more than 500 employees). Primary employment (more than one-half time) of the principal investigator must be with the small business at the time of award and during the conduct of the proposed project. In both Phase I and Phase II, the research must be performed in the U.S. or its possessions. STTR grants can be awarded only to domestic small business concerns (entities that are independently owned and operated for profit, are not dominant in the field in which researches proposed and have no more than 500 employees) which "partner" with a research institution in cooperative research and development. At least 40 percent of the project is to be performed by the small business concern and at least 30 percent by the research institution. In both Phase I and Phase II, the research must be performed in the U.S. and its possessions. To be eligible for funding, a grant application must be approved for scientific merit and Program relevance by a scientific review group and a national advisory council.

Beneficiary Eligibility: Any nonprofit or for-profit organization, company, or institution engaged in biomedical research.

Award Range/Average: from $2,500 to $6,395,901 and the average $426,165.

Funding: (Project Grants) FY 18 $3,326,210,000.00; FY 19 est $3,514,732,000.00; FY 20 est $2,977,136,000.00

HQ: 5601 Fishers Lane, Suite 5E39, Rockville, MD 20852

Phone: 301-761-7870 | Email: kevin.richardson@nih.gov

http://www.niaid.nih.gov

HHS93.051 | ALZHEIMER'S DISEASE DEMONSTRATION GRANTS TO STATES
"Alzheimer's Disease Supportive Services Program"

Award: Cooperative Agreements

Purpose: To expand the availability of diagnostic and support services for persons with Alzheimer's Disease and Related Dementias (ADRD), their families, and their caregivers.

Applicant Eligibility: State government agencies are eligible for grant awards; the applicant agency is encouraged to have the support and active involvement of the Single State Agency on Aging. Only one application per State will be funded, however, multiple state and local agencies are encouraged to collaborate in planning and carrying out the project.

Beneficiary Eligibility: (1) Individuals with Alzheimer's disease and related disorders; (2) families of those individuals; and (3) care providers of those individuals.

Award Range/Average: 5 grants were awarded for a total of $2,294,892 in FY15. The average was $458,978 per award.

Funding: (Cooperative Agreements) FY 17 $4,800,000.00; FY 18 est $4,799,998.00; FY 19 est Estimate Not Available

HQ: 330 C Street SW, Washington, DC 20201

Phone: 202-795-7389 | Email: erin.long@acl.hhs.gov

http://www.acl.gov

HHS93.763 | ALZHEIMER'S DISEASE INITIATIVE: SPECIALIZED SUPPORTIVE SERVICES PROJECT (ADI-SSS) THRU PREVENTION AND PUBLIC HEALTH FUNDS (PPHF)
"Alzheimer's Initiative"

Award: Project Grants

Purpose: Purpose of Alzheimer's Disease Initiative: Specialized Supportive Services project is to fill gaps in long term services and supports for persons living with Alzheimer's disease and related dementias and their caregivers by expanding the availability of specialized services and supports.

Programs Administered by Federal Headquarters

Applicant Eligibility: Funding eligibility is limited to public and/or private entities that are able to 1) demonstrate the existence of a dementia capable system dedicated to the population that they serve, and 2) articulate opportunities and additional services that would enhance and strengthen the existing system. Organizations that have not received previous awards through this Program, individuals, foreign entities and sole proprietorship Organizations are not eligible to compete for, or receive awards under this announcement.

Beneficiary Eligibility: Public and/or private entities that are able to 1) demonstrate the existence of a dementia capable system dedicated to the population that they serve, and 2) articulate opportunities and additional services that would enhance and strengthen the existing system. Eligible consumers of eligible applicants are the beneficiaries of this program.

Award Range/Average: As many as 10 grants forward funded for a period of 36 months with an award ceiling of $1,000,000 and a floor of $800,000.

Funding: (Project Grants) FY 17 $10,500,000.00; FY 18 est $10,500,000.00; FY 19 Estimate Not Available

HQ: U.S. Department of Health and Human Services 330 C Street SW, Washington, DC 20201
Phone: 202-795-7389 | Email: erin.long@acl.hhs.gov
http://www.acl.gov

HHS93.470 | ALZHEIMER'S DISEASE PROGRAM INITIATIVE (ADPI) "ADPI"

Award: Cooperative Agreements

Purpose: To work at state and community levels to develop and expand the availability of dementia-capable supports and services for persons with Alzheimer's disease and related dementias (ADRD), their families, and their caregivers.

Applicant Eligibility: Funding eligibility is limited to public and/or private entities that are able to 1) demonstrate the existence of and their operation within a dementia-capable home and community-based system dedicated to the population that they serve, and 2) articulate opportunities and additional services that would enhance and strengthen the existing system. Community Program applicants are not eligible to apply for or receive more than one grant through the ADPI Program. States may only hold a single grant at any one time. Individuals, foreign entities and sole proprietorship Organizations are not eligible to compete for, or receive awards under this announcement.

Beneficiary Eligibility: Eligible consumers of eligible applicants are the beneficiaries of this program, including (1) Individuals with Alzheimer's disease and related disorders; (2) families of those individuals; and (3) care providers of those individuals.

Award Range/Average: As many as 20 grants forward funded for a period of 36 months with an award ceiling of $1,200,000 and a floor of $800,000.

Funding: (Cooperative Agreements (Discretionary Grants)) FY 17 Actual Not Available; FY 18 est $23,500,000.00; FY 19 est $19,490,000.00

HQ: 330 C Street SW, Washington, DC 20201
Phone: 202-795-7389 | Email: erin.long@aoa.hhs.gov
http://www.acl.gov

ED84.274 | AMERICAN OVERSEAS RESEARCH CENTERS

Award: Project Grants

Purpose: To enable American overseas research centers to promote postgraduate research, exchanges, and area studies.

Applicant Eligibility: The Secretary shall only award grants to centers that: (1) receive more than 50 percent of their funding from public or private United States sources; (2) have a permanent presence in the country in which the center is located; and (3) are Organizations described in Section 501(c)(3) of the Internal Revenue Code of 1986 which are exempt from taxation under Section 501(a) of the Code.

Beneficiary Eligibility: Consortia of institutions of higher education that (1) receive more than 50 percent of their funding from public or private United States sources; (2) have a permanent presence in the country in which the center is located; and (3) are organizations described in Section 501(c)(3) of the Internal Revenue Code of 1986 which are exempt from taxation under Section 501(a) of the Code will benefit.

Award Range/Average: FY 2018: Average award was $65,000 per year; Awards ranged from $48,000- $65,000 per year.

Funding: (Project Grants) FY 18 $650,000.00; FY 19 est $650,000.00; FY 20 est $0.00

HQ: International and Foreign Language Education Department of Education 400 Maryland Avenue SW, Washington, DC 20202
Phone: 202-453-5690 | Email: cheryl.gibbs@ed.gov
http://www.ed.gov/programs/iegpsaorc

CNCS94.027 | AMERICORPS VISTA RECRUITMENT SUPPORT

Award: Salaries and Expenses

Purpose: Builds support relationships with higher education institutions to improve the public response and recognition of AmeriCorps VISTA service opportunities within their campus and community.

Applicant Eligibility: Institutions of higher education (2 CFR 200. 55), both four-year and two-year, with at least 5,000 undergraduate students, that have DUNS numbers that are active and are registered in System for Award Management (SAM). Under Section 132A(b) of the National and Community Service Act of 1990, as amended, Organizations that have been convicted of a federal crime may not receive assistance described in this Notice. Applications that propose to engage in activities that are prohibited under CNCS's statutes, regulations, or the terms and conditions of its awards are not eligible to receive CNCS funding. If CNCS is aware that any corporation has any unpaid federal tax liability that has been assessed for which all judicial and administrative remedies have been exhausted or have lapsed that is not being paid in a timely manner pursuant to an agreement with the authority responsible for collecting the tax liability then that corporation is not eligible for an award under this Notice. However, this exclusion will not apply to a corporation which a federal agency has considered for suspension or debarment and has made a determination that suspension or debarment is not necessary to protect the interests of the federal government. Pursuant to the Lobbying Disclosure Act of 1995, an Organization described in the Internal Revenue Code of 1986, 26 U.S.C. 501 (c)(4) that engages in lobbying activities is not eligible to apply for CNCS funding.

Beneficiary Eligibility: N/A

Award Range/Average: CNCS anticipates approximately $200,000 for AmeriCorps VISTA Campus Recruitment Services 2019 awards. Award amounts will vary, as determined by the scope of the projects. CNCS expects to make awards in the range of $15,000 to $20,000.

Funding: (Salaries and Expenses) FY 18 Actual Not Available; FY 19 est $200,000.00; FY 20 est Estimate Not Available

HQ: 250 E Street SW, 3rd Floor, Washington, DC 20525

Phone: 202-606-7572 | Email: bbinkley@cns.gov

https://www.nationalservice.gov/grants-funding/funding-resources

CNCS94.006 | AMERICORPS
"AmeriCorps State and National"

Award: Project Grants

Purpose: AmeriCorps is a grant program that recruits, trains and manages volunteer members to help address community needs that are still unmet.

Applicant Eligibility: Use of assistance must be consistent with the funded approved grant application. See Program's Notice of Funding.

Beneficiary Eligibility: Beneficiaries must be identified within application for assistance.

Award Range/Average: See Notice of Federal Funding.

Funding: (Project Grants) FY 16 $229,068,630; FY 17 est $228,723,609.00; FY 18 est Estimate Not Available

HQ: 250 E Street SW, Washington, DC 20525

Phone: 202-606-6905 | Email: jgraham@cns.gov

http://www.nationalservice.gov/programs/americorps/americorps-programs/americorps-state-and-national

HHS93.341 | ANALYSES, RESEARCH AND STUDIES TO ADDRESS THE IMPACT OF CMS PROGRAMS ON AMERICAN INDIAN/ALASKA NATIVE (AI/AN) BENEFICIARIES AND THE HEALTH CARE SYSTEM SERVING THESE BENEFICIARIES

Award: Cooperative Agreements

Purpose: To providing high quality healthcareto the American Indian/Alaska Native (AI/AN) community by providing research and analysis to increase the understanding of, access to, and impact of CMS' programs in Indian Country.

Applicant Eligibility: Eligibility is limited to the National Indian Health Board, and this single source award was approved by the Chief Grants Management Officer. NIHB meets the definition of tribal Organization under the Indian healthcare Improvement Act (IHCIA) 25 USC Section 1603(26), with significant historical experience in providing outreach and education and the provision of healthcare information for Indian Tribes and Tribal Organizations. NIHB is a legally established Organization controlled and governed by Indians and includes the maximum participation of Indians in all phases if its activities. NIHB has 100 percent appointed or elected officers that comprise the Board of Directors. NIHB acts in a

Programs Administered by Federal Headquarters

supportive role to ensure the dissemination of healthcare education and information to Tribes. NIHB must submit a copy of the 501(c) (3) Non-profit Certification as proof of non-profit status. Applicant must have an Employer Identification Number (EIN), otherwise known as a Taxpayer Identification Number (TIN), to apply. Applicant must have a Dun and Bradstreet (D&B) Data Universal Numbering System (DUNS) number. The DUNS number is a nine-digit identification number that uniquely identifies business entities. To obtain a DUNS number, access the following website: http://www.dnb. com/ or call -866-705-5711. This number should be entered in the block 8c (on the Form SF-424, Application for Federal Assistance). The Organization name and addressed entered in block 8a and 8c should be exactly as given for the DUNS number. Applicant should obtain this DUNS number immediately to ensure all registration steps are completed in time. Applicant must also register in the Central Contractor Registration (CCR) database in order to be able to submit the application. Applicant should begin the CCR registration process immediately to ensure that it does not impair ability to meet required submission deadlines.

Beneficiary Eligibility: The primary beneficiaries of this effort are American Indians and Alaska Natives who are eligible for CMS' programs to get them educated about and enrolled in CMS' programs, as appropriate, ensure that Indian health care providers can participate and are enrolled in CMS programs, and to reduce health disparities in tribal communities. By enrolling in CMS' programs, AI/ANs benefit by having greater access to services that may not be provided by their local Indian health care providers, and tribal communities benefit through increased resources to their Indian health care programs. The Federal government will benefit by obtaining information to help make more informed policies which will improve administration of CMS' programs in tribal communities and thereby provide AI/ANs access to quality health care. Federally Recognized Indian Tribal Governments and Native American Organizations would benefit because they can provide information and insight to help CMS understand the tribal provider and tribal beneficiary perspective so that CMS can make informed policies decisions that would permit CMS' programs to be administered and operate effectively and efficiently in tribal communities and not conflict with legislative/regulatory authority under which the Indian Health Service programs operates.

Award Range/Average: FY 2014 - $635,000 FY 2015 - $635,000 FY 2016 - $860,000 Approximate average award - $800,000.

Funding: (Cooperative Agreements (Discretionary Grants)) FY 18 est $800,000.00; FY 19 est $800,000.00; FY 20 est $ 800,000.00

HQ: 7501 Security Boulevard, PO Box B3-30-03, Baltimore, MD 21244
Phone: 410-786-9954 | Email: linda.gmeiner@cms.hhs.gov
http://www.nihb.org

USDA10.207 | ANIMAL HEALTH AND DISEASE RESEARCH "AHDR"

Award: Formula Grants

Purpose: To provide funds for safeguard of domestic animal health and prevention of diseases.

Applicant Eligibility: Eligibility is restricted to the following public nonprofit Institutions having demonstrable capacity in animal disease research: (1) Schools and Colleges of Veterinary Medicine; and (2) State Agricultural Experiment Stations. Funds are appropriated by Congress for distribution to States and eligible State Institutions according to the statutory formula stated in the Act. Applications may be submitted by accredited State veterinary schools or colleges or agricultural experiment stations that conduct animal health and disease research in accordance with NARETPA section 1433(c): Auburn University, Agricultural Experiment Station; Auburn University, School of Veterinary Medicine; Tuskegee University, School of Veterinary Medicine; University of Alaska, Agricultural Experiment Station; University of Arizona, Agricultural Experiment Station; University of Arkansas, Agricultural Experiment Station; University of California-Oakland, Agricultural Experiment Station; University of California-Davis, School of Veterinary Medicine; Colorado State University, Agricultural Experiment Station and College of Veterinary Medicine; University of Connecticut-Storrs, Agricultural Experiment Station; University of Delaware, Agricultural Experiment Station; University of Florida, Agricultural Experiment Station; University of Florida, College of Veterinary Medicine; University of Georgia, Agricultural Experiment Station; University of Georgia, College of Veterinary Medicine; University of Hawaii, Agricultural Experiment Station; University of Idaho, Agricultural Experiment Station; University of Illinois, Agricultural Experiment Station and College of Veterinary Medicine; Purdue University, Agricultural Experiment Station and College of Veterinary Medicine; Iowa State University, Agricultural and Home Economics Experiment Station; Iowa State University, College of Veterinary Medicine; Kansas State University, Agricultural Experiment Station and College of Veterinary Medicine; University of Kentucky, Agricultural Experiment Station; Louisiana State University, Agricultural Experiment Station; Louisiana State University, College of Veterinary Medicine; University of Maine, Agricultural Experiment Station; University of Maryland, Agricultural Experiment Station; University of Massachusetts, Agricultural Experiment Station; Tufts University, School of Veterinary Medicine; Michigan State University, Agricultural Experiment Station and College of Veterinary Medicine; University of Minnesota, Agricultural

Experiment Station; University of Minnesota, College of Veterinary Medicine; Mississippi State University, Agricultural and Forestry Experiment Station and College of Veterinary Medicine; University of Missouri, Agricultural Experiment Station; University of Missouri, College of Veterinary Medicine; Montana State University, Agricultural Experiment Station; University of Nebraska, Agricultural Experiment Station; University of Nevada, Agricultural Experiment Station; University of New Hampshire, Agricultural Experiment Station; Rutgers University, Agricultural Experiment Station; New Mexico State University, Agricultural Experiment Station; Cornell University, Agricultural Experiment Station; Cornell University, College of Veterinary Medicine; North Carolina State University, Agricultural Experiment Station; North Carolina State University, College of Veterinary Medicine; North Dakota State University, Agricultural Experiment Station; Ohio State University, Ohio Agricultural Research & Development Center; Ohio State University, College of Veterinary Medicine; Oklahoma State University, Agricultural Experiment Station and College of Veterinary Medicine; Oregon State University, Agricultural Experiment Station; Pennsylvania State University, Agricultural Experiment Station; University of Pennsylvania, College of Veterinary Medicine; University of Puerto Rico, Agricultural Experiment Station; University of Rhode Island, Agricultural Experiment Station; Clemson University, Agricultural Experiment Station; South Dakota State University, Agricultural Experiment Station; University of Tennessee, Agricultural Experiment Station; University of Tennessee, College of Veterinary Medicine; Texas A&M University, Agricultural Experiment Station and College of Veterinary Medicine; Utah State University, Agricultural Experiment Station; University of Vermont, Agricultural Experiment Station; Virginia Polytechnic Institute and State University, Agricultural Experiment Station and College of Veterinary Medicine; Washington State University, Agricultural Experiment Station and College of Veterinary Medicine; West Virginia University, Agricultural and Forestry Experiment Station; University of Wisconsin, Agricultural Experiment Station and College of Veterinary Medicine; and University of Wyoming, Agricultural Experiment Station. Award recipients may subcontract to Organizations not eligible to apply for funding provided that such arrangements are necessary to complete the project or activity.

Beneficiary Eligibility: Eligibility is restricted to the following public nonprofit institutions having demonstrable capacity in animal disease research: (1) Schools and Colleges of Veterinary Medicine; and (2) State Agricultural Experiment Stations. Funds are appropriated by Congress for distribution to States and eligible State institutions according to the statutory formula stated in the Act.

Award Range/Average: If minimum or maximum amounts of funding per Capacity, Competitive, and/or Non-Competitive project grant, or cooperative agreement are established, these amounts will be announced in the annual Capacity, Competitive, and/or Non-Competitive Request for Application (RFA).The most current RFA is available via: https://nifa.usda.gov/program/animal-health-and-disease-research-program

Funding: (Formula Grants (Apportionments)) FY 17 $3,696,260.00; FY 18 est $2,717,120.00; FY 19 est $0.00

HQ: Institute of Food Production and Sustainability Division of Animal System 1400 Independence Avenue SW, PO Box 2240, Washington, DC 20250-2240

Phone: 202-401-4952

http://nifa.usda.gov/program/animal-health-research-and-disease-program

EOP95.004 | ANTI-DOPING ACTIVITIES

Award: Project Grants

Purpose: The program provides support to anti-doping efforts of the Office of National Drug Control Policy to educate athletes on the dangers and thereby eliminate the use of drugs in athletic competitions. It also provides support for legal efforts to adjudicate athletes appeals involving doping.

Applicant Eligibility: Anti-doping activities.

Beneficiary Eligibility: Same as Applicant Eligibility.

Funding: (Project Grants) FY 18 $9,500,000.00; FY 19 est $9,500,000.00; FY 20 est Not Separately Identifiable

HQ: 1800 G Street NW, Washington, DC 20503

Phone: 202-395-6739 | Email: phuong_desear@ondcp.eop.gov

http://www.whitehouse.gov/ondcp/grants-programs

HHS93.876 | ANTIMICROBIAL RESISTANCE SURVEILLANCE IN RETAIL FOOD SPECIMENS
"NARMS Retail Food Surveillance"

Award: Cooperative Agreements

Purpose: The chief goal of the National Antimicrobial Resistance Monitoring System retail food surveillance program is to improve the detection of and surveillance for antimicrobial resistance among enteric bacteria in raw retail food commodities,

Programs Administered by Federal Headquarters

particularly fresh retail meat. The NARMS program is looking to collaborate with institutions or organizations to enhance and strengthen antibiotic resistance surveillance in retail food specimens.

Applicant Eligibility: Applicants should review the individual funding opportunity announcement issued under this CFDA Program to see which applicant Organizations are eligible to apply.

Beneficiary Eligibility: Improving antimicrobial resistance surveillance, food safety, and antimicrobial drug approvals for animals and humans.

Award Range/Average: Estimated $2,500,000 available for anticipated 30 awards.

Funding: (Cooperative Agreements) FY 18 $2,500,000.00; FY 19 est $2,348,277.00; FY 20 est $1,981,627.00

HQ: National Antimicrobial Resistance Monitoring System 8401 Muirkirk Road, Laurel, MD 20708

 Phone: 240-402-0891 | Email: patrick.mcdermott@fda.hhs.gov

 http://www.fda.gov

DOS19.030 | ANTITERRORISM ASSISTANCE-DOMESTIC TRAINING PROGRAMS

Award: Cooperative Agreements

Purpose: The Bureau of Diplomatic Security (DS) aims to build counterterrorism capacity, enhance bilateral relationships and increase respect for human rights through its Office of Antiterrorism Assistance (ATA) Program. The purpose of ATA programs is to develop the capacity of key partner nations to combat terrorism, establish security relationships between U.S. and foreign officials to strengthen cooperative antiterrorism efforts, and share modern, humane, and effective antiterrorism techniques.

Applicant Eligibility: Please refer to the specific announcement on www.Grants.gov.

Beneficiary Eligibility: Foreign law enforcement and security personnel from Partner Nations lacking resources needed to maintain an effective antiterrorism program and infrastructure.

Award Range/Average: Anti-Terrorism Executive ForumSenior Crisis Management Seminar (SCMS)

Funding: (Salaries and Expenses) FY 12 Actual Not Available; FY 14 est $1,500,000.00; FY 13 est $1,500,000.00

HQ: 1800 N Kent Street, Arlington, VA 22209

 Phone: 703-875-6998 | Email: colantoniomj@state.gov

DOJ16.321 | ANTITERRORISM EMERGENCY RESERVE

Award: Project Grants

Purpose: To support eligible victims of criminal mass violence and terrorism with appropriate services and/or reimburse eligible victims for expenses related to their victimization, encompassing two programs for victims of terrorism and/or mass violence. The Antiterrorism and Emergency Assistance Program (AEAP) provides assistance and compensation services for victims of domestic terrorism and intentional mass criminal violence and assistance for victims of international terrorism. The International Terrorism Victim Expense Reimbursement Program (ITVERP) provides reimbursement for victims of acts of international terrorism that occur outside the United States for expenses associated with that victimization.

Applicant Eligibility: AEAP: Criteria will vary depending on the grant. For terrorism or mass violence occurring within or outside the U.S., eligible applicants for funding under VOCA, Title II, 42 U.S.C. 10603b, 1404B, include states, victim service Organizations, and public agencies (including federal, State and local Governments) and non-governmental Organizations that provide assistance to victims of crime. With the exception of ITVERP, OVC does not provide funding directly to individual crime victims. ITVERP: For an applicant to be eligible to receive reimbursement under ITVERP as authorized under VOCA, Title II, 42 U.S.C. 10603c, 1404C, an individual must be a national of the United States or an officer or employee of the U.S. government, as of the date on which the act of terrorism occurred. In addition, the individual must have suffered direct physical or emotional injury or death as a result of an act of international terrorism occurring on or after October 23, 1983, with respect to which an investigation or prosecution was ongoing after April 24, 1996.

Beneficiary Eligibility: AEAP: Public and private nonprofit victim assistance agencies; victims of domestic and international terrorism. Eligibility depends on the nature of the grant. ITVERP: The law requires that the individual victim must have suffered direct physical or emotional injury or death as a result of an act of international terrorism occurring on or after October 23, 1983, with respect to which an investigation or prosecution was ongoing or was commenced after April 24, 1996. In the case of a victim who is a minor, incompetent, incapacitated, or is killed, a family member or legally designated representative of the victim may receive expense reimbursement on behalf of the victim. In addition to the victim, claimants may include the following: Spouse of the victim, Parents of the victim, Children of the victim, Siblings of the victim, Legally designated victim representative.

Award Range/Average: Varies depending on terrorism/mass violence event and specific need(s).

Funding: (Project Grants (Contracts)) FY 18 $7,287,574; FY 19 est $50,000,000.00; FY 20 est $50,000,000

HQ: Department of Justice 810 7th Street NW, Washington, DC 20531

 Phone: 202-305-2117 | Email: allison.turkel@ojp.usdoj.gov

 http://www.ovc.gov

HUD14.270 | APPALACHIA ECONOMIC DEVELOPMENT INITIATIVE

Award: Project Grants

Purpose: To increase access to capital for business lending and development in the chronically under-served and -capitalized Appalachian region. It will also provide direct investment and technical assistance to community development lending and investing institutions that suffer from a lack of capacity to support business development.

Applicant Eligibility: Applicants that are eligible to participate in this initiative are State community and/or economic development agencies that apply on behalf of local rural nonprofit Organizations in the Appalachia Region. Applicants may serve markets other than Appalachia residents and communities, using other sources of financing.

Beneficiary Eligibility: Eligible target markets for use of AEDI funds include geographic areas and/or populations, as described below. Geographic areas include the 420 counties in 13 states that make up the Appalachia Region, as defined by the Appalachian Regional Commission. Appalachian Regional Commission (ARC) is a federal-state partnership working to stimulate economic development. The ARC is composed of the governors of the 13 Appalachian states and a federal co-chair, who is appointed by the president. Local participation is provided through multi-county local development districts. The thirteen states that are included in the region are: Alabama, Georgia, Kentucky, Maryland, Mississippi, New York, North Carolina, Ohio, Pennsylvania, South Carolina, Tennessee, West Virginia, and Virginia.

Award Range/Average: Up to $1,000,000

HQ: U.S. Department of Housing and Urban Development Office of Rural Housing and Economic Development 451 7th Street SW, Room 7137, Washington, DC 20410

  Phone: 877-787-2526 | Email: thann.young@hud.gov

ARC23.002 | APPALACHIAN AREA DEVELOPMENT
"Supplemental and Direct Grants"

Award: Project Grants

Purpose: To help the regional economy become more competitive by putting in place the building blocks for self-sustaining economic development, while continuing to provide special assistance to the Region's most distressed counties and areas.

Applicant Eligibility: States, their subdivisions and instrumentalities and private nonprofit agencies.

Beneficiary Eligibility: State, local and not for profit organizations.

Funding: (Project Grants) FY 16 $84,529,632.00; FY 17 Estimate Not Available; FY 18 Estimate Not Available

HQ: 1666 Connecticut Avenue NW, Suite 600, Washington, DC 20009

  Phone: 202-884-7668 | Email: jwilmoth@arc.gov

  http://www.arc.gov

ARC23.003 | APPALACHIAN DEVELOPMENT HIGHWAY SYSTEM
"Appalachian Corridors"

Award: Project Grants

Purpose: To provide a highway system which, in conjunction with other federally-aided highways, will open up areas with development potential within Appalachia.

Applicant Eligibility: State Governments only are eligible for development highways within their Appalachian portions.

Beneficiary Eligibility: N/A

Funding: (Project Grants) FY 16 $271,200,000.00; FY 17 Estimate Not Available; FY 18 Estimate Not Available

HQ: 1666 Connecticut Avenue NW, Suite 600, Washington, DC 20009

  Phone: 202-884-7668 | Email: jwilmoth@arc.gov

  http://www.arc.gov

ARC23.009 | APPALACHIAN LOCAL DEVELOPMENT DISTRICT ASSISTANCE
"LDD"

Award: Project Grants

Purpose: To provide planning and development resources in multicounty areas; to help develop the technical competence essential to sound development assistance; and to meet the objectives stated under the program entitled Appalachian Regional Development.

Applicant Eligibility: Multicounty Organizations certified by the State.

Programs Administered by Federal Headquarters

Beneficiary Eligibility: Multicounty organizations.
Funding: (Project Grants) FY 18 est Estimate Not Available FY 17 est $7,000,000.00; FY 16 $7,264,543.00
HQ: 1666 Connecticut Avenue NW, Suite 600, Washington, DC 20009
    Phone: 202-884-7668 | Email: jwilmoth@arc.gov
    http://www.arc.gov

ARC23.001 | APPALACHIAN REGIONAL DEVELOPMENT (SEE INDIVIDUAL APPALACHIAN PROGRAMS)
"Appalachian Program"

Award: Project Grants
Purpose: To help the regional economy become more competitive by putting in place the building blocks for self-sustaining economic development, while continuing to provide special assistance to the Region's most distressed counties and areas.
Applicant Eligibility: States, and through the States, public bodies and private nonprofit Organizations. All proposed projects must meet the requirements of the State Appalachian plan and the annual State strategy statement, both of which must be approved annually by the Commission.
Beneficiary Eligibility: General public.
Award Range/Average: See Individual programs
Funding: (Project Grants) FY 16 $95,080,282.00; FY 17 Estimate Not Available; FY 18 Estimate Not Available
HQ: 1666 Connecticut Avenue NW, Suite 600, Washington, DC 20009
    Phone: 202-884-7668 | Email: jwilmoth@arc.gov
    http://www.arc.gov

ARC23.011 | APPALACHIAN RESEARCH, TECHNICAL ASSISTANCE, AND DEMONSTRATION PROJECTS
"State Research"

Award: Project Grants
Purpose: To expand the knowledge of the region to the fullest extent possible by means of research in order to assist the Commission in accomplishing the objectives of the Act, and implementation of the ARC strategic plan.
Applicant Eligibility: Qualified candidates with subject matter experience who respond to Commission issued requests for proposals that are advertised on the Appalachian Regional Commission website (www.arc.gov).
Beneficiary Eligibility: States and local public bodies.
Funding: (Project Grants) FY 16 $1,064,328.00; FY 17 est $1,000,000.00; FY 18 est Estimate Not Available
HQ: 1666 Connecticut Avenue NW, Suite 600, Washington, DC 20009
    Phone: 202-884-7668 | Email: jwilmoth@arc.gov
    http://www.arc.gov

USDA10.782 | APPROPRIATE TECHNOLOGY TRANSFER FOR RURAL AREAS
Award: Cooperative Agreements
Purpose: To provide educational resources on sustainable agriculture to farmers, agriculture-related businesses, and community food organizations across the U.S.
Applicant Eligibility: Applicants are not eligible if they have been debarred or suspended or otherwise excluded from participation in Federal assistance Programs under Executive Order 12549, Debarment and Suspension. Applicants are not eligible if they have an outstanding judgement obtained by the U.S. in a Federal Court (other than U.S. Tax Court), are delinquent on the payment of Federal income taxes, or are delinquent on a Federal debt. Any corporation that has been convicted of a felony criminal violation under any Federal law within the past 24 months or that has any unpaid Federal tax liability that has been assessed, for which all judicial and administrative remedies have been exhausted or have lapsed, and that is not being paid in a timely manner pursuant to an agreement with the authority responsible for collecting the tax liability, is not eligible for funding.
Beneficiary Eligibility: N/A
Award Range/Average: Average = 1,500,000 Range = 611,000 to 2,500,000
Funding: (Cooperative Agreements) FY 18 $2,750,000.00; FY 19 est $2,750,000.00; FY 20 est Estimate Not Available

HQ: Cooperative Programs Grants Division 1400 Independence Avenue SW Room 4208-S, PO Box 3253, Washington, DC 20250
   Phone: 202-690-1374 | Email: christopher.mclean@wdc.usda.gov
   http://www.atra.ncat.org

DOD12.100 | AQUATIC PLANT CONTROL
Award: Provision of Specialized Services; Dissemination of Technical Information
Purpose: To provide for the Army Corps of Engineers with State agencies in the control of obnoxious aquatic plants.
Applicant Eligibility: States and their political subdivisions or instrumentalities.
Beneficiary Eligibility: Same as Applicant Eligibility.

HHS93.107 | AREA HEALTH EDUCATION CENTERS
"AHEC"

Award: Project Grants
Purpose: To enhance access to high quality, culturally competent healthcarethrough academic-community partnerships.
Applicant Eligibility: Entities eligible to apply for AHEC Infrastructure Development awards under 751(a)(1) are public or nonprofit private accredited schools of allopathic medicine and osteopathic medicine and incorporated consortia made up of such schools, or the parent Institutions of such schools. In states and territories in which no AHEC Program is in operation, an accredited school of nursing is an eligible applicant. An entity eligible to apply for AHEC Point of Service Maintenance and Enhancement awards under section 751 (a) (2) means an entity has received funds under this section (751), is operating an area health education center Program, including an area health education center or centers, and has a center or centers that are no longer eligible to receive financial assistance under subsection (a)(1). Eligible entities are accredited public or nonprofit schools of allopathic medicine or osteopathic medicine, the parent institution on behalf of such schools, and accredited schools of nursing, which have received funds under section 751 to operate an AHEC Program. Federally Recognized Indian Tribal Government and Native American Organizations may apply if they are otherwise eligible.
Beneficiary Eligibility: Beneficiaries include a full range of trainees: high school students from underrepresented minority populations or from disadvantaged or rural backgrounds, health professions students, and practicing health professionals.
Award Range/Average: FY 2018 actual $255,605- $1,912,000; Average Award: $735,056. FY 2019 Est $249,967- $1,793,760; Average Award: $738,980. FY 2020 Est. $0; Average Award: $0
Funding: (Cooperative Agreements) FY 18 $36,017,749.00; FY 19 est $36,210,000.00; FY 20 est $0.00
HQ: Department of Health and Human Services 5600 Fishers Lane, Parklawn Building, Rockville, MD 20857
   Phone: 301-945-9383 | Email: lbrayboy@hrsa.gov
   https://bhw.hrsa.gov/grants/healthcareers

HHS93.714 | ARRA-EMERGENCY CONTINGENCY FUND FOR TEMPORARY ASSISTANCE FOR NEEDY FAMILIES (TANF) STATE PROGRAM
"TANF Emergency Fund, Recovery Act"

Award: Formula Grants
Purpose: Provides economic stimulus to the nation while furthering the ACF mission to promote the economic and social well-being of children, youth, families, and communities. This Emergency Fund was in addition to the TANF Contingency Fund in section 403(b) of the Act that gives money to qualifying States during an economic downturn.
Applicant Eligibility: N/A
Beneficiary Eligibility: N/A
Award Range/Average: The range for ARRA actual allocations for FY 2014 was $608,842 to $3,328,006 with an average of $1,857,757.
HQ: 330 C Street SW, Washington, DC 20201
   Phone: 202-401-9275 | Email: susan.golonka@acf.hhs.gov
   http://www.acf.hhs.gov/programs/ofa

Programs Administered by Federal Headquarters

HHS93.721 | ARRA-HEALTH INFORMATION TECHNOLOGY PROFESSIONALS IN HEALTH CARE
"Health Information Technology Education (HITE)"

Award: Cooperative Agreements; Project Grants

Purpose: PHSA 3016, as added by the Recovery Act, directs the Secretary to provide assistance to institutions of higher education to establish or expand health informatics education programs, including certification, undergraduate, and masters degree programs, for both healthcare and information technology students and incumbent healthcare workers to ensure the rapid and effective utilization and development of health information technologies.

Applicant Eligibility: Financial assistance to Institutions of higher education, or consortia thereof, to rapidly develop and sustain a health information technology workforce.

Beneficiary Eligibility: Same as Applicant Eligibility.

Award Range/Average: Awards made to 7 organizations in the amount of $966,436 each.

HQ: Office of the National Coordinator for Health Information Technology 330 C Street SW, Washington, DC 20201
Phone: 202-720-2919 | Email: carmel.halloun@hhs.gov
http://healthit.gov

HHS93.728 | ARRA-STRATEGIC HEALTH IT ADVANCED RESEARCH PROJECTS (SHARP)
"SHARP"

Award: Cooperative Agreements

Purpose: To competitively-award cooperative agreements to establish Strategic Health IT Advanced Research Projects, wherein the awardees will conduct research focusing on where breakthrough advances are needed to address well-documented problems that have impeded adoption of health IT and to accelerate progress towards achieving nationwide meaningful use of health IT in support of a high-performing, learning healthcare system.

Applicant Eligibility: Any entity submitting an application for this award must be a U.S. -based: public or private institution of higher education; or other public or private institution or Organization with a research mission.

Beneficiary Eligibility: This Funding Opportunity Announcement (FOA) will result in new competitively-awarded cooperative agreements to establish Strategic Health IT Advanced Research Projects (SHARP). The awardees will conduct research focusing on where breakthrough advances are needed to address well-documented problems that have impeded adoption of health IT and to accelerate progress towards achieving nationwide meaningful use of health IT in support of a high-performing, learning health care system.

Award Range/Average: Awards may range from $10,000,000 - $18,000,000. Four awards each $15,000,000 were awarded in FY 2010.

HQ: 200 Independence Avenue SW, Washington, DC 20201
Phone: 202-690-7151 | Email: avinash.shanbhag@hhs.gov
http://healthit.gov/policy-researchers-implementers/strategic-health-it-advanced-research-projects-sharp

DOC11.619 | ARRANGEMENTS FOR INTERDISCIPLINARY RESEARCH INFRASTRUCTURE
"Not applicable"

Award: Cooperative Agreements

Purpose: To establish interdisciplinary research infrastructure for federal researchers for innovations in measurement science, standards, and technology.

Applicant Eligibility: Public and private Institutions of higher education, public and private hospitals, and other quasi-public and private non-profit Organizations such as, but not limited to, community action agencies, research institutes, educational associations, and health centers. The term may include commercial Organizations, foreign or international Organizations (such as agencies of the United Nations) which are recipients, subrecipients, or contractors or subcontractors of recipients or subrecipients at the discretion of the DoC. The term does not include government-owned contractor-operated facilities or research centers providing continued support for mission-oriented, large-scale Programs that are government-owned or controlled, or are designated as federally-funded research and development centers.

Beneficiary Eligibility: Public and private institutions of higher education, public and private hospitals, and other quasi-public and private non-profit organizations such as, but not limited to, community action agencies, research institutes, educational associations, and health centers. The term may include commercial organizations, foreign or international organizations (such as agencies of the United Nations) which are recipients, subrecipients, or contractors or subcontractors of recipients or subrecipients at the discretion of the DoC. The term does not include government-owned contractor-operated facilities or research centers providing continued support for mission-oriented, large-scale programs that are government-owned or controlled, or are designated as federally-funded research and development centers. institutions of research and/or education, professional institutes and associations, non-profit organizations, state and local governments, and commercial organizations.
Award Range/Average: Dependent upon nature and type of grant
Funding: (Cooperative Agreements) FY 18 $23,745,000.00; FY 19 est $23,539,000.00; FY 20 est $23,539,000.00
HQ: 100 Bureau Drive, Gaithersburg, MD 20899
   Phone: 301-975-4350 | Email: margaret.phillips@nist.gov
   http://www.nist.gov

HHS93.846 | ARTHRITIS, MUSCULOSKELETAL AND SKIN DISEASES RESEARCH

Award: Project Grants
Purpose: To support research relevant to arthritis, musculoskeletal and skin diseases, the National Institute of Arthritis and Musculoskeletal and Skin Diseases supports research training and basic and clinical investigations including epidemiology and clinical trials in the areas of skin and rheumatic diseases and musculoskeletal diseases. The Division of Extramural Research promotes and supports basic, epidemiological, and clinical studies of skin and rheumatic and related diseases.
Applicant Eligibility: Research Grants: Individuals and public and private Institutions, both nonprofit and for-profit, who propose to establish, expand, and improve research activities in health sciences and related fields. National Research Service Awards: Individuals must be nominated and sponsored by a public or private, for-profit or nonprofit institution having staff and facilities appropriate to the proposed research training Program. All awardees must be citizens or have been admitted to the United States for permanent residence. To be eligible, predoctoral awardees must have completed the baccalaureate degree and postdoctoral awardees must have a professional or scientific degree (M.D., Ph.D., D.D.S., D.O., D.V.M., Sc.D., D.Eng., or equivalent domestic or foreign degree). Nonprofit domestic Organizations may apply for the Institutional National Research Service grant. Small Business Innovation Research grants can be awarded only to domestic small businesses (entities that are independently owned and operated for profit, are not dominant in the field in which research is proposed, and have no more than 500 employees). Primary employment (more than one-half time) of the principal investigator must be with the small business at the time of award and during the conduct of the proposed project. In both Phase I and Phase II, the research must be performed in the U.S. or its possessions. To be eligible for funding, a grant application must be approved for scientific merit and Program relevance by a scientific review group and a national advisory council. STTR grants can be awarded only to domestic small business concerns (entities that are independently owned and operated for profit, are not dominant in the field in which research is proposed and have no more than 500 employees) which partner with a research institution in cooperative research and development. At least 40 percent of the project is to be performed by the small business concern and at least 30 percent by the research institution. In both Phase I and Phase II, the research must be performed in the U.S. and its possessions. To be eligible for funding, a grant application must be approved for scientific merit and Program relevance by a scientific review group and a national advisory council.
Beneficiary Eligibility: Research Grants: Although no degree of education is either specified or required, nearly all successful applicants have doctoral degrees in one of the sciences or professions. National Research Service Awards: Predoctoral awardees must have completed the baccalaureate degree and postdoctoral awardees must have a professional or scientific degree.
Award Range/Average: Research Grants: $632 to $2,646,510; $300,930. National Research Service Awards: $49,209 to $606,558; $239,254. SBIR: Phase 1 awards - approximately $211,685; Phase II awards -approximately $584,849. STTR: Phase 1 awards - approximately $123,874; Phase II awards -approximately $774,350.
Funding: (Project Grants) FY 18 $476,478,975.00; FY 19 est $489,603,424.00; FY 20 est $416,750,000.00
HQ: Office of Extramural Operations 6701 Democracy Boulevard, Suite 800, Bethesda, MD 20892
   Phone: 301-435-5278 | Email: melinda.nelson@nih.gov
   http://www.niams.nih.gov

NFAH45.201 | ARTS AND ARTIFACTS INDEMNITY

Award: Insurance
Purpose: To provide for indemnification against loss or damage for eligible art works, artifacts, and objects.
Applicant Eligibility: Federal, State, and local government entities, and nonprofit agencies and Institutions may apply.

Programs Administered by Federal Headquarters

Beneficiary Eligibility: Federal, State, and local government entities, and nonprofit agencies and institutions will benefit. Audiences of indemnified exhibitions will also benefit.

Award Range/Average: Not Applicable.

HQ: National Endowment for the Arts 400 7th Street SW, Washington, DC 20506
    Phone: 202-682-5541 | Email: loikop@arts.gov
    http://www.arts.gov

HHS93.081 | ASPR SCIENCE PREPAREDNESS AND RESPONSE GRANTS

Award: Cooperative Agreements; Project Grants

Purpose: Conducts preparedness and response research that will inform the ongoing response to, and recovery from disasters.

Applicant Eligibility: Research on environmental exposure: such as health risk from mold, toxic exposure, flooding of hospitals. Research on resilience factors Surveys regarding decision making during response and recovery. How can social media be or is being used for response and recovery activities for preparedness and response activities?.

Beneficiary Eligibility: Domestic, foreign and international public or private non-profit entities including state and local governments, Indian tribal governments and organizations (American Indian/Alaskan Native/Native American), faith-based organizations, community-based organizations, hospitals, and institutions of higher education.

Funding: (Cooperative Agreements) FY 18 $0.00; FY 19 est $0.00; FY 20 est $100,000.00

HQ: HHS Headquarters 200 C Street SW, Washington, DC 20024
    Phone: 202-260-0400 | Email: virginia.simmons@hhs.gov
    http://www.phe.gov

HHS93.602 | ASSETS FOR INDEPENDENCE DEMONSTRATION PROGRAM "AFI Program"

Award: Project Grants

Purpose: The program is to demonstrate and evaluate the effectiveness of asset-building projects that assist low-income people in becoming economically self-sufficient by teaching them about economic and consumer issues and enabling them to establish matched savings accounts called individual development accounts.

Applicant Eligibility: This Program supports innovative projects administered by national, State-wide, regional and community-based Organizations. Eligible applicants are: [(1) Private nonprofit Organizations that are tax exempt under Section 501(c) (3) of the Internal Revenue Code;] (2) State or local Governments or agencies or Tribal Governments submitting applications jointly with; (3) credit unions designated as low-income credit unions by the National Credit Union Administration; or an Organization designated as a Community Development Financial Institution by the Secretary of the Treasury.

Beneficiary Eligibility: The Assets for Independence Act limits eligibility for participation in AFI-funded projects to individuals and families with the following characteristics: 1) Individuals who are members of households that are eligible to receive support under the Federal Temporary Assistance for Needy Families program; 2) Individuals whose adjusted gross household income is less than twice the Federal poverty line, taking into consideration the number of household members, and whose household net worth as of the end of the prior calendar year was less than $10,000; and 3) Individuals whose adjusted gross household income enables them to qualify for the Federal Earned Income Tax Credit, taking into consideration the number of household members, and whose household net worth as of the end of the prior calendar year was less than $10,000. When determining the net worth of the household, a household's assets shall not be considered to include the primary dwelling unit and one motor vehicle owned by a member of the household.

Award Range/Average: The Office of Community Services (OCS) awards grants for this program ranging up to $1,000,000. The average grant is approximately $350,000. Eligible entities may apply for new grants up to the statutory limit of $1,000,000 for 5-year project periods.

HQ: 330 C Street SW, 5th Floor W, Washington, DC 20201
    Phone: 202-401-9365 | Email: lynda.perez@acf.hhs.gov
    http://www.acf.hhs.gov/programs/ocs/afi

HHS93.875 | ASSISTANCE FOR ORAL DISEASE PREVENTION AND CONTROL

Award: Cooperative Agreements

Purpose: To strengthen state oral health programs and public health core capacity to reduce inequalities in the oral health of targeted populations by establishing oral health leadership and program guidance and implementing science-based programs (including dental sealants and community water fluoridation) to improve oral and physical health.

Applicant Eligibility: Eligible applicants are the official State and territorial health agencies of the United States, the District of Columbia, tribal Organizations, the Commonwealth of Puerto Rico, the Virgin Islands, Guam, the Northern Mariana Islands, the Federated States of Micronesia, the Republic of the Marshall Islands, the Republic of Palau, and American Samoa, or their Bona Fide Agents. For specific funding announcements, eligible applicants may be more limited, for example, State Governments, including the District of Columbia, or their Bona Fide Agents.

Beneficiary Eligibility: States, political subdivisions of States, local health authorities, and individuals or organizations with specialized health interests will benefit.

Award Range/Average: This is a new program no data range or average award available.

HQ: 4770 Buford Highway NE, PO Box F80, Atlanta, GA 30341

    Phone: 770-488-6075

    http://www.cdc.gov

HHS93.604 | ASSISTANCE FOR TORTURE VICTIMS
"Services for Survivors of Torture"

Award: Project Grants; Direct Payments for Specified Use

Purpose: The Office of Refugee Resettlement provides funding and technical support to domestic survivors of torture programs. The Services for Survivors of Torture program assists persons who have suffered torture in a foreign country to regain their health and independence and build productive lives in the U.S.

Applicant Eligibility: Eligible applicants are public or private non-profit agencies.

Beneficiary Eligibility: The Services for Survivors of Torture program serves individuals and families, regardless of immigration status, who have suffered torture in a foreign country and are currently residing in the U.S.

Award Range/Average: Grant awards range from $172,900 to $444,600. The average award was $297,800.

Funding: (Salaries and Expenses) FY 18 $308,580.00; FY 19 est $535,000.00; FY 20 est $535,000.00; (Project Grants) FY 18 $10,400,000.00; FY 19 est $13,465,000.00; FY 20 est $13,465,000.00

HQ: Division of Refugee Health 330 C Street SW, Mary E Switzer Building, Washington, DC 20201

    Phone: 202-401-5585 | Email: curi.kim@acf.hhs.gov

    http://www.acf.hhs.gov/programs/orr

HHS93.945 | ASSISTANCE PROGRAMS FOR CHRONIC DISEASE PREVENTION AND CONTROL

Award: Cooperative Agreements

Purpose: The purpose of the program is to engage American Indian and Alaska Native communities in identifying and sharing healthy traditional ways of eating, being active, and communicating health information and support for diabetes prevention and wellness.

Applicant Eligibility: Eligible applicants are the official State and territorial health agencies of the United States, the District of Columbia, tribal Organizations, the Commonwealth of Puerto Rico, the Virgin Islands, Guam, the Northern Mariana Islands, the Federated States of Micronesia, the Republic of the Marshall Islands, the Republic of Palau, and American Samoa. Other public and private nonprofit community based Organizations are also eligible (see REACH).

Beneficiary Eligibility: State health agencies and community based organizations will benefit.

Funding: (Cooperative Agreements) FY 18 $3,753,491.00; FY 19 est $3,969,485.00; FY 20 est $3,969,485.00

HQ: DPH 4770 Buford Highway NE, Atlanta, GA 30341

    Phone: 770-488-1371

    http://www.cdc.gov

DHS97.044 | ASSISTANCE TO FIREFIGHTERS GRANT
"Fire Grants"

Award: Project Grants

Purpose: AFG program provides financial assistance to fire departments, fire training academies and other EMS organizations to equip and train emergency personnel in fire and fire-related hazards.

Applicant Eligibility: Eligible applicants for AFG are limited to fire departments, nonaffiliated EMS Organizations, and State Fire Training Academies. These Organizations operating in any of the 50 States plus the District of Columbia, the Commonwealth of the Northern Mariana Islands, the Virgin Islands, Guam, American Samoa, and Puerto Rico are eligible

Programs Administered by Federal Headquarters

for funding. A "fire department" is defined as an agency or Organization that has a formally recognized arrangement with a State, territory, local, or tribal authority (city, county, parish, fire district, township, town, or other governing body) to provide fire suppression to a population within a fixed geographical area on a first-due basis. A "nonaffiliated EMS Organization " is defined as a public or private nonprofit emergency medical services Organization that provides direct emergency medical services, including medical transport, to a specific geographic area on a first-due basis but is not affiliated with a hospital and does not serve a geographic area where emergency medical services are adequately provided by a fire department. A State Fire Training Academy is defined as the primary state fire training academy, agency, or institution, for each state; which provides entity-wide delivery of fire training (and EMS training if applicable) as specified by legislative authorization, by general statutory authorization or charter, or is ad-hoc in nature with the general acceptance of the fire service. A listing of eligible State Fire Training Academy Organizations and Institutions can be found at: http://www.usfa. fema.gov/fireservice/. Fire departments; and national, regional, state, local, federally recognized tribal, and non-profit Organizations that are recognized for their experience and expertise in fire prevention and safety Programs and activities. Both private and public non-profit Organizations are eligible to apply for funding in the Fire Prevention and Safety Grant Program.

Beneficiary Eligibility: The ultimate beneficiaries of this program are the local or tribal communities serviced by the applicants, including, but not limited to, local businesses, homeowners and property owners. Additionally, children under 16 years of age, senior citizens, and firefighters would be the beneficiaries since these groups are the targeted "risk groups" for the fire prevention program.

Award Range/Average: Refer to program guidance.

Funding: (Project Grants) FY 18 $350,000,000.00; FY 19 est $350,000,000.00; FY 20 est $350,000,000.00

HQ: DHS/FEMA/Grant Programs Directorate Assistance to Firefighters Grant Program 400 C Street SW 3N, Washington, DC 20472-3635

    Phone: 866-274-0960

    http://www.fema.gov

USDA10.859 | ASSISTANCE TO HIGH ENERGY COST RURAL COMMUNITIES "High Energy Cost Grants"

Award: Project Grants

Purpose: To assist the rural communities with high energy costs.

Applicant Eligibility: Eligible applicants include States, political subdivisions of States, for-profit and non-profit businesses, cooperatives, associations, Organizations, and other entities organized under the laws of States, Indian Tribes, tribal entities, and individuals. The Governments and entities located in any U.S. Territory/possession or other area authorized by law to receive the services and Programs of the Rural Utilities Service or the Rural Electrification Act of 1936, as amended, are also eligible.

Beneficiary Eligibility: Projects must serve rural communities in which the annual average residential expenditure for home energy is at least 275 percent of the national average. Energy cost eligibility benchmarks are included in the published Notice of Funding Availability.

Award Range/Average: Minimum award is $50,000 and maximum is $3,000,000.

Funding: (Project Grants) FY 18 $21,793,415.00; FY 19 est $10,000,000.00; FY 20 est $0.00

HQ: 1400 Independence Avenue, PO Box 1560, Washington, DC 20250

    Phone: 202-720-9545 | Email: christopher.mclean@wdc.usda.gov

    http://www.rd.usda.gov/programs-services/high-energy-cost-grants

DOT20.910 | ASSISTANCE TO SMALL AND DISADVANTAGED BUSINESSES

Award: Cooperative Agreements

Purpose: To enter into successful partnerships between OSDBU and chambers of commerce, community-based organizations, colleges and universities, community colleges, or trade associations, to establish regional Small Business Transportation Resource Centers (SBTRCs) to provide business assessment, technical assistance, technical assistance referrals, business training, and the dissemination of information regarding DOT and DOT funded contracting opportunities.

Applicant Eligibility: Established 501 c (6) tax-exempt Chambers of Commerce, Trade Associations and 501 c (3) nonprofit Organization, community colleges, minority educational Institutions, tribal colleges and universities that have the documented experience and capacity necessary to successfully operate and administer a coordinated, Small Business Transportation Resource Center (SBTRC) within their regions.

Beneficiary Eligibility: For the purpose of this program, the term small businesses refers to: 8 (a), small disadvantaged business (SDB), disadvantaged business enterprises (DBE), women-owned small business (WOB), Hub Zone, service- disabled veteran-owned business, and veteran owned small business.

Award Range/Average: Average of $200,000
Funding: (Salaries and Expenses) FY 18 $1,900,000.00; FY 19 est $2,400,000.00; FY 20 $2,400,000.00
HQ: Office of Small and Disadvantaged Business Utilization S-40 1200 New Jersey Avenue SE, Washington, DC 20590
Phone: 202-366-2253 | Email: michelle.harris@dot.gov
http://www.transportation.gov/osdbu

HUD14.314 | ASSISTED LIVING CONVERSION FOR ELIGIBLE MULTIFAMILY HOUSING PROJECTS
"ALCP"

Award: Project Grants
Purpose: To promote aging in place and prevent premature institutionalization of the target people.
Applicant Eligibility: Only private nonprofit owners of eligible multifamily assisted housing developments specified in Section 683(2)(B), (C), (D), (E), and (F) (Section 202 projects for the elderly, Rural Housing Section 515 projects receiving Section 8 rental assistance, projects receiving project-based rental assistance under Section 8, projects financed by a below-market interest rate loan or mortgage insured under Section 221(d)(3) of the Housing Act, or housing financed under Section 236 of the National Housing Act) that have been in occupancy for at least five years are eligible for funding. To be eligible, owners must meet the following criteria: (1) Must be in compliance with Loan Agreement, Capital Advance Agreement, Regulatory Agreement, Housing Assistance Payment Contract, Project Rental Assistance Contract, Rent Supplement or LMSA Contract, or any other HUD grant or contract document; (2) Must be in compliance with all fair housing and civil rights laws, statutes, regulations, and executive orders as enumerated in 24 CFR 5. 105(a).
Beneficiary Eligibility: Eligible residents who meet the admissions/discharge requirements as established for assisted living by State and local licensing, or HUD frailty requirements under 24 CFR 891.205 if more stringent. The residents must be able to live independently but may need assistance with activities of daily living (that is, assistance with eating, bathing, grooming, dressing and home management activities).Service-Enriched Housing is designed to accommodate elderly persons and people with disabilities with a functional limitation, meaning residents who are unable to perform at least one activity of daily living.
Award Range/Average: $2-6 million; average $4 million
Funding: (Project Grants) FY 15 $16,000,000.00; FY 16 est $0.00; FY 17 est $0.00
HQ: 451 7th Street SW, Room 6152, Washington, DC 20410
Phone: 202-708-3000 | Email: katina.x.washington@hud.gov
http://www.hud.gov/offices/hsg/mfh/progdesc/alcp.cfm

HHS93.997 | ASSISTED OUTPATIENT TREATMENT
"Assisted Outpatient Treatment Grant Program for Individuals with Serious Mental Illness (Short title: Assisted Outpatient Treatment [AOT])"

Award: Project Grants
Purpose: The Assisted Outpatient Treatment program which was passed as a pilot project under the Protecting Access to Medicare Act of 2014 provides grants for patient volunteers with serious medical illnesses. The program helps to improve the patient's health outcomes and reduce homelessness by providing referrals to medical and social service provides based on the volunteer's needs.
Applicant Eligibility: States, counties, cities mental health systems (including state mental health authorities), mental health courts, or any other entity with authority under the law of the state in which the applicant grantee is located to implement, monitor, and oversee AOT Programs.
Beneficiary Eligibility: Same as Applicant Eligibility.
Award Range/Average: Up to $1,000,000.
Funding: (Project Grants (Discretionary)) FY 18 $13,263,515.00; FY 19 est $.0013,515,424.00; FY 20 est $2,849,389
HQ: 5600 Fishers Lane, Rockville, MD 20857
Phone: 240-276-1418 | Email: roger.george@samhsa.hhs.gov
http://www.samhsa.gov

Programs Administered by Federal Headquarters

HHS93.469 | ASSISTIVE TECHNOLOGY ALTERNATIVE FINANCING PROGRAM "AT AFP"

Award: Project Grants

Purpose: To support programs that provide for the purchase of AT devices and services, such as low-interest loan fund, an interest buy-down program, a revolving loan fund, and a loan guarantee program.

Applicant Eligibility: State agencies and community-based disability Organizations that are directed by and operated for individuals with disabilities shall be eligible to compete.

Beneficiary Eligibility: The purpose of the Assistive Technology (AT) Alternative Financing Program (AFP) is to support programs that provide for the purchase of AT devices and services, such as low-interest loan fund, an interest buy-down program, a revolving loan fund, and a loan guarantee program. Successful applicants must emphasize consumer choice and control and build programs that will provide financing for the full array of AT devices and services and ensure that all people with disabilities, regardless of type of disability or health condition, age, level of income and residence have access tot the program.

Award Range/Average: The average award amount for three grants issued in FY 2017 is $664,670 for a total of $1,994,009. The estimate average award amount for three grants issued in FY 2018 is $661,512 for a total of $1,984,537.

Funding: (Project Grants (Discretionary)) FY 17 $1,994,009.00; FY 18 est $1,894,932.00; FY 19 est $1,990,000.00

HQ: 330 C Street SW, Room 1317B, Washington, DC 20201
Phone: 202-795-7356 | Email: robert.groenendaal@acl.hhs.gov
https://www.acl.gov/programs/assistive-technology/assivtive-technology

HHS93.362 | ASSISTIVE TECHNOLOGY NATIONAL ACTIVITIES "AT National Activities"

Award: Cooperative Agreements (discretionary Grants)

Purpose: To support activities to improve the administration of the AT Act in the following areas: national public awareness; state training and technical assistance; data collection and reporting; and research and development of assistive technology.

Applicant Eligibility: N/A

Beneficiary Eligibility: N/A

Award Range/Average: FY 2017 Range for Grants is $309,983 - $573,681 FY 2018 Range for Grants is $320,194 - $575,000

Funding: (Cooperative Agreements (Discretionary Grants)) FY 17 $883,664.00; FY 18 est $895,194.00; FY 19 est $895,194.00

HQ: 330 C Street SW, Room 1317B, Washington, DC 20201
Phone: 202-795-7356 | Email: robert.groenendaal@acl.hhs.gov

HUD14.914 | ASTHMA INTERVENTIONS IN PUBLIC AND ASSISTED MULTIFAMILY HOUSING

Award: Cooperative Agreements

Purpose: To develop and implement interventions and protocols for controlling asthma among residents and to create sustainable programs and policies for reducing exposure to asthma triggers in the indoor environment.

Applicant Eligibility: Residents of federally assisted multi-family housing.

Beneficiary Eligibility: Academic, not-for-profit and for-profit institutions located in the U.S. (for-profit firms are not allowed to profit from the project), state and local governments, and Federally recognized Native American tribes are eligible under all existing authorizations. Federal agencies and federal employees are not eligible to submit applications. The General Section of the Super NOFA provides additional eligibility requirements.

Award Range/Average: Range and Average of Financial Assistance: The total amount to be awarded is approximately $2.6 million. The anticipated amounts and/or numbers of individual awards will be approximately 5 to 8 cooperative agreements, with each not to exceed $600,000.

HQ: 451 7th Street SW, Room 8236, Washington, DC 20410-3000
Phone: 202-402-7696 | Email: j.kofi.berko@hud.gov
http://www.hud.gov/Grants

DOC11.474 | ATLANTIC COASTAL FISHERIES COOPERATIVE MANAGEMENT ACT
Award: Project Grants
Purpose: To assist States and Marine Fisheries Commission to implement effective interstate conservation and management of Atlantic Coastal resources.
Applicant Eligibility: Eligible applicants for assistance are the Atlantic States Marine Fisheries Commission (ASMFC), the Atlantic Coast State Governments which are Maine, New Hampshire, Massachusetts, Rhode Island, Connecticut, New York, New Jersey, Pennsylvania, Delaware, Maryland, Virginia, North Carolina, South Carolina, Georgia, Florida, the Potomac River Fisheries Commission, and the District of Columbia.
Beneficiary Eligibility: This program benefits State, and interstate marine resource conservation agencies, the marine fishing industries and the general public.
Award Range/Average: $38,000 to $1,900,000. Average: $330,000
Funding: (Cooperative Agreements) FY 16 $11,382,892.00; FY 17 est $11,382,892.00; FY 18 Estimate Not Available
HQ: National Marine Fisheries Service 1315 E W Highway, Silver Spring, MD 20910
Phone: 301-713-2334
http://www.nmfs.noaa.gov

HHS93.998 | AUTISM AND OTHER DEVELOPMENTAL DISABILITIES, SURVEILLANCE, RESEARCH, AND PREVENTION
"Autism and Other Developmental Disabilities"
Award: Cooperative Agreements
Purpose: The program funds the health agencies that work on planning, implementing and evaluating programs related to infant and child health, especially to autism and its developmental outcomes.
Applicant Eligibility: N/A
Beneficiary Eligibility: State; Consumer; Local; Public nonprofit institution/organization; Federally Recognized Indian Tribal Governments; Private nonprofit institution/organizations and others.
Award Range/Average: FY17/18 range is depended upon funding availability. Award amount range is $75,000- $800,000.
Funding: (Cooperative Agreements) FY 17 $5,099,939.00; FY 18 est $5,099,939.00; FY 19 est $4,200,000.00
HQ: 4770 Buford Highway NE, PO Box E86, Atlanta, GA 30341
Phone: 404-639-1938

HHS93.877 | AUTISM COLLABORATION, ACCOUNTABILITY, RESEARCH, EDUCATION, AND SUPPORT
"Autism CARES"
Award: Project Grants
Purpose: The Program supports activities to provide information and education on autism spectrum disorder and other developmental disabilities to increase public awareness; and promote research into the development and validation of reliable screening tools and interventions for autism spectrum disorder and other developmental disabilities.
Applicant Eligibility: For training grants: eligible applicants include public or nonprofit agencies, including Institutions of higher education. For research grants: eligible applicants include any public or private nonprofit entity, including research centers or networks. Faith-based and community-based Organizations, Tribes, and tribal Organizations are eligible to apply. Any public or private entity is eligible for other project grants.
Beneficiary Eligibility: For training grants: (1) Trainees in the health professions related to MCH; and (2) mothers and children who receive services through training programs. For research grants: public or private nonprofit entities, including research centers or networks. For other projects: (1) Public or private agencies, organizations and institutions; and (2) mothers and children, and persons who receive services through the programs.
Award Range/Average: (Project Grants) FY 18: $293,497 to $420,000; $378,916 FY 19: $98,338 to $420,000; $259,318 FY 20: $100,000 to $420,000; $190,667 (Cooperative Agreements) FY 18: $275,000 to $500,000; 424,988 FY 19: $275,000 to $500,000; 424,988 FY 20: $275,000 to $500,000; 425,000
Funding: (Project Grants) FY 18 $2,273,497.00; FY 19 est $2,852,499.00; FY 20 est $2,860,000.00; (Cooperative Agreements Total) FY 18 $1,274,964.00; FY 19 est $1,274,993.00; FY 20 est $1,275,000.00
HQ: 5600 Fishers Lane, Rockville, MD 20857
Phone: 301-443-2170 | Email: lkavanagh@hrsa.gov
http://hrsa.gov

Programs Administered by Federal Headquarters

VA64.100 | AUTOMOBILES AND ADAPTIVE EQUIPMENT FOR CERTAIN DISABLED VETERANS AND MEMBERS OF THE ARMED FORCES

Award: Direct Payments for Specified Use

Purpose: To provide financial assistance to certain disabled servicepersons and veterans toward the purchase price of an automobile or other conveyance and an additional amount for adaptive equipment deemed necessary to insure the eligible person will be able to operate or make use of the automobile or other conveyance.

Applicant Eligibility: Veterans with honorable service and servicepersons on active duty having a service-connected disability due to loss or permanent loss of use of one or both feet, one or both hands, or a permanent impairment of vision of both eyes to a prescribed degree. For adaptive equipment only, eligibility also exists if there is service-connected ankylosis of one or both knees or one or both hips. Servicepersons on active duty also qualify under the same criteria as veterans.

Beneficiary Eligibility: Disabled servicepersons and veterans.

Funding: (Direct Payments for Specified Use) FY 07 $53,443,000.00; FY 08 est $57,300,000.00; FY 09 est $61,600,000.00

HQ: Department of Veterans Affairs 810 Vermont Avenue NW, Washington, DC 20420

  Phone: 202-461-9700

  http://www.va.gov

TREAS21.021 | BANK ENTERPRISE AWARD PROGRAM
"BEA Program"

Award: Project Grants

Purpose: To encourage insured depository institutions to increase their level of community development activities in the form of loans, investments, services, and technical assistance.

Applicant Eligibility: For Profit Organizations and Other Private Institution/Organizations in the form of FDIC-insured depository Institutions.

Beneficiary Eligibility: Distressed communities as defined in 12 C.F.R. 1806.

Award Range/Average: FY 2016 Range of awards $12,500 to 227,282; Average Award $182,599; FY 2017 Range of awards $15,000 to $233,387; Average Award $201,657. FY 2018 Range of awards $14,700 to $233,244; Average Award $209,887.

Funding: (Project Grants) FY 18 $24,766,663.00; FY 19 est $25,000,000.00; FY 20 est $25,000,000.00

HQ: 1500 Pennsylvania Avenue NW, Washington, DC 20036

  Phone: 202-653-0300

  http://www.cdfifund.gov

BGSF85.200 | BARRY M. GOLDWATER SCHOLARSHIP PROGRAM
"Barry Goldwater Scholarship Foundation"

Award: Direct Payments for Specified Use

Purpose: To honor former Senator Barry Goldwater through the operation of an education scholarship program.

Applicant Eligibility: Undergraduate sophomore and junior level students, at two and four year colleges and universities accredited by the Department of education, must be nominated by the institution's Goldwater Campus Representative.

Beneficiary Eligibility: U.S. citizens or nationals, resident aliens (must provide additional documentation), college sophomores and juniors will benefit.

Award Range/Average: $0- $7,500

Funding: (Direct Payments for Specified Use) FY 16 $2,000,000.00; FY 17 est $2,000,000.00; FY 18 est Estimate Not Available

HQ: 6225 Brandon Avenue, Suite 315, Springfield, VA 22150

  Phone: 703-756-6012

  http://goldwater.scholarsapply.org

DOD12.300 | BASIC AND APPLIED SCIENTIFIC RESEARCH

Award: Cooperative Agreements; Project Grants

Purpose: To support and stimulate basic and applied research and technology at educational institutions, non-profits and other research organizations, which have potential for superiority in the improvement of naval operations.

Applicant Eligibility: Office of Naval Research (ONR) headquarters Grants and Agreements cannot be awarded to individuals or families. ONR Global Grants and Agreements can be awarded to individuals.

Beneficiary Eligibility: N/A

Award Range/Average: $5,000 - $20,000,000; mean= $500,000; median= $300,000
Funding: (Project Grants) FY 18 $123,381,832.00; FY 19 est $125,000,000.00; FY 20 est Estimate Not Available
HQ: 875 N Randolph Street, Arlington, VA 22203
    Phone: 703-696-4601 | Email: susan.sutherland@navy.mil
    http://www.onr.navy.mil

HHS93.623 | BASIC CENTER GRANT
"Basic Center Program (BCP)"

Award: Project Grants
Purpose: Establishes or strengthens locally controlled community-based programs that address the immediate needs of runaway and homeless youth and their families.
Applicant Eligibility: States, localities, private entities, and coordinated networks of such entities are eligible to apply for a Basic Center Program grant unless they are part of the law enforcement structure or the juvenile justice system. Federally recognized Indian Organizations are also eligible to apply for grants as private, non-profit agencies.
Beneficiary Eligibility: Runaway and homeless youth and their families are the beneficiaries. Services can be provided to youth up to the age of 18.
Award Range/Average: $100,000 to $200,000 per budget period. Average $168,535
Funding: (Project Grants (Discretionary)) FY 18 $54,434,142.00; FY 19 est $54,230,350.00; FY 20 est $48,218,848.00
HQ: 330 C Street SW, Washington, DC 20201
    Phone: 202-205-9560 | Email: christopher.holloway@acf.hhs.gov
    http://www.acf.hhs.gov/programs/fysb

HHS93.640 | BASIC HEALTH PROGRAM (AFFORDABLE CARE ACT)
"BHP"

Award: Insurance
Purpose: Section 1331 of the Affordable Care Act gives states the option of creating a Basic Health Program, a health benefits coverage program for low-income residents who would otherwise be eligible to purchase coverage through the Health Insurance Marketplace.
Applicant Eligibility: Any State that submits a BHP Blueprint may be considered for certification by the Secretary of HHS.
Beneficiary Eligibility: The program is for specified individuals who do not qualify for Medicaid but whose income does not exceed 200 percent of the federal poverty level (FPL).
Award Range/Average: Based on formula of state-specific data.
Funding: (Formula Grants) FY 18 $4,767,350,945.00; FY 19 est $5,372,550,988.00; FY 20 est $5,686,754,253.00
HQ: 7500 Security Boulevard, Baltimore, MD 21244
    Phone: 410-786-0719 | Email: kelly.whitener@cms.hhs.gov

DOD12.431 | BASIC SCIENTIFIC RESEARCH
Award: Project Grants
Purpose: To support basic research related to or has potential for leading to the improvement of Army programs or operations.
Applicant Eligibility: See specific broad agency announcements or similar announcements resulting from this CFDA number for eligibility requirements. Awards will not be made to individuals.
Beneficiary Eligibility: Investigators and resulting awardees.
Award Range/Average: Range: $1,374,000.00- $1,500,000.00 and Average Award: $1,457,744.00
Funding: (Project Grants (Cooperative Agreements or Contracts)) FY 18 $441,684,853.00; FY 19 est $485,000,000.00; FY 20 est $490,000,000.00
HQ: U.S. Army Research Office/ ACC-APG-RTP Division, PO Box 12211, Research Triangle Park, NC 27709-2211
    Phone: 919-541-4691 | Email: julia.b.wertleyrotenberry.civ@mail.mil
    https://beta.sam.gov/fal/47a2a2a6b7e298da288add74a5ed54cf/view

Programs Administered by Federal Headquarters

DOD12.630 | BASIC, APPLIED, AND ADVANCED RESEARCH IN SCIENCE AND ENGINEERING

Award: Cooperative Agreements; Project Grants

Purpose: To support basic, applied, or advanced research in mathematical, physical, engineering, environmental, and life sciences, and other fields with good, long-term potential for contributing to technology for Department of Defense missions.

Applicant Eligibility: The eligibility for applicants will be in accordance with the individual Program announcements, BAAs, or other notices of funding opportunity. Generally, competitions are open to private and public educational Institutions that carry out science and engineering research and/or related science and engineering education; however, competition may be limited to a class of such Institutions, such as Historically Black Colleges and universities or other minority Institutions (HBCUs/MIs). Some competitions may allow eligibility to other types of Organizations, such as for-profit applicants. However, awards are not made to individuals.

Beneficiary Eligibility: Beneficiaries may include individual graduate and undergraduate students (e.g., recipients of fellowships or research traineeships) in science and engineering disciplines important to defense, as well as organizations described under "Applicant Eligibility.".

Award Range/Average: See individual BAAs for expected range of award accounts (generally vary from $50,000 to $3,000,000 over 1 to 5 year periods of performance).

Funding: (Project Grants) FY 18 est $251,441,997.00; FY 19 est $250,000,000.00; FY 20 est Estimate Not Available

HQ: Arlington, VA 22203 | Email: barbara.j.orlando.civ@mail.mil

DOD12.101 | BEACH EROSION CONTROL PROJECTS
"Small Beach Erosion Control Projects"

Award: Provision of Specialized Services

Purpose: To control beach and shore erosion through projects.

Applicant Eligibility: States, political subdivisions of States or other responsible local agencies established under State law with full authority and ability to undertake necessary legal and financial responsibilities.

Beneficiary Eligibility: Same as Applicant Eligibility.

HHS93.727 | BEACON COMMUNITIES-COMMUNITY HEALTH PEER LEARNING PROGRAM

Award: Cooperative Agreements

Purpose: The Community Health Peer Learning Program will provide funding to an awardee to leverage and build upon healthcare delivery and practice transformation programs introduced through the Beacon Community Program and engage 15 communities addressing health challenges at the population level through a community-based collaborative approach.

Applicant Eligibility: The lead applicant must be a US-based non-profit Organization or state, local, tribal or territorial government entity. Private providers and insurers will be encouraged to participate in the consortia.

Beneficiary Eligibility: The identification and dissemination of best practices and lessons learned will directly benefit organizations and communities advancing health information technology and exchange. The knowledge attained by these awarded communities will, in turn, benefit the nation's communities as a whole.

Award Range/Average: Award in the amount of $2,226,818 to a single Community Health Peer Learning Program awardee granted in Fiscal Year 2015.

HQ: 330 C Street SW, Washington, DC 20201

Phone: 202-720-2919 | Email: carmel.halloun@hhs.gov

http://healthit.gov

USDA10.311 | BEGINNING FARMER AND RANCHER DEVELOPMENT PROGRAM
"BFRDP"

Award: Project Grants

Purpose: To assist beginning farmers by providing regional training and technical assistance to address their needs.

Applicant Eligibility: The recipient must be a collaborative, State, tribal, local, or regionally-based network or partnership of public or private entities, which may include: state cooperative extension service; community-based and nongovernmental Organization; college or University (including Institutions awarding associate degrees); or any other appropriate partner.

Others may be eligible to apply. Please refer to Part III of the current BFRDP Request for Applications for complete eligibility requirements.

Beneficiary Eligibility: Same as Applicant Eligibility.

Award Range/Average: If minimum or maximum amounts of funding per competitive and/or capacity project grant, or cooperative agreement are established, these amounts will be announced in the annual Competitive Request for Application (RFA).The most current RFA is available via: https://nifa.usda.gov/funding-opportunity/beginning-farmer-and-rancher-development-program-bfrdp

Funding: (Cooperative Agreements) FY 17 $17,758,724.00; FY 18 est $17,792,373.00; FY 19 est $19,083,524.00

HQ: Institute of Food Production and Sustainability Division of Agricultural Systems 1400 Independence Avenue SW, PO Box 2240, Washington, DC 20250-2240

Phone: 202-401-0151

http://nifa.usda.gov/program/beginning-farmer-and-rancher-development-program

HHS93.336 | BEHAVIORAL RISK FACTOR SURVEILLANCE SYSTEM

Award: Cooperative Agreements

Purpose: To provide assistance to State and Territorial Health Departments to maintain and expand specific health surveillance on the behaviors of the general adult population that contribute to the occurrences and prevention of chronic diseases, injuries, and other public health threats through the Behavioral Risk Factor Surveillance System (BRFSS).

Applicant Eligibility: Eligible applicants are US State Health Departments and US Territories that have been funded under SO11-1101 and SO11-1102.

Beneficiary Eligibility: BRFSS data is published on the CDC website and all of the above entities can access it.

Funding: (Cooperative Agreements) FY 18 $17,278,605.00; FY 19 est $21,892,778.00; FY 20 est $0.00

HQ: 4770 Buford Highway NE, Atlanta, GA 30341

Phone: 404-498-0514

http://www.cdc.gov

DHS97.122 | BIO-PREPAREDNESS COLLABORATORY

Award: Cooperative Agreements

Purpose: The program helps to identity and respond to biological and other health hazardous threats and helps create a safer environment for better health protection.

Applicant Eligibility: Specific information on applicant eligibility is identified in the funding opportunity announcement and Program guidance.

Beneficiary Eligibility: Refer to the program guidance for further information.

Funding: (Salaries and Expenses) FY 18 $850,000.00; FY 19 est $0.00; FY 20 est $0.00

HQ: Bio-Preparedness Collaboratory Office of Health Affairs 1120 Vermont Avenue NW Office 6-180, Washington, DC 20528

Phone: 202-254-2433 | Email: reajul.mojumder@hq.dhs.gov

http://www.dhs.gov

USDA10.306 | BIODIESEL
"Biodiesel Fuel Education Program"

Award: Project Grants

Purpose: To promote biodiesel conservation and educate on the advantages of biodiesel and fuel safety.

Applicant Eligibility: Eligibility is restricted to nonprofit Organizations or institution of higher education (as defined in section 101 of the Higher education Act of 1965 (20 U.S.C. 1001)).

Beneficiary Eligibility: Nonprofit organizations or institutions of higher education (as defined in section 101 of the Higher Education Act of 1965 (20 U.S.C. 1001)).

Award Range/Average: If minimum or maximum amounts of funding per competitive and/or capacity project grant, or cooperative agreement are established, these amounts will be announced in the annual Competitive Request for Application (RFA).The most current RFA is available via: https://nifa.usda.gov/funding-opportunity/biodiesel-fuel-education

Funding: (Project Grants) FY 17 $893,760.00; FY 18 est $896,640.00; FY 19 est $960,000.00

HQ: Institute of Bioenergy Climate and Environment Division of Bioenergy 1400 Independence Avenue SW, PO Box 2210, Washington, DC 20250-2210

Phone: 202-401-5244

http://nifa.usda.gov/funding-opportunity/biodiesel-fuel-education

Programs Administered by Federal Headquarters

USDA10.867 | BIOENERGY PROGRAM FOR ADVANCED BIOFUELS
"Advanced Biofuel Payments Program"

Award: Direct Payments With Unrestricted Use

Purpose: To support and expand production of advanced biofuels by providing payments to eligible advanced biofuel producers.

Applicant Eligibility: Advance Biofuel Producer - an individual, corporation, company, foundation, association, labor Organization, firm, partnership, society, joint stock company, group of Organizations, or non-profit entity that produces and sells an advanced biofuel. An individual, corporation, company, foundation, association, labor company, group of Organizations, or non-profit entity that blends or otherwise combines advanced biofuels into a blended biofuel is not considered an advanced biofuel producer under this Program.

Beneficiary Eligibility: The Advanced Biofuel Producer must produce a biofuel that meets the definition of advanced biofuel, be a solid, liquid, or gaseous advanced biofuel, be a final product. Fuel must be derived from renewable biomass other than corn kernel starch.

Award Range/Average: Awards are based on requests received and production for each producer. Budget has not been approved as of the update of this information, contact the office listed below for more information.

Funding: (Salaries and Expenses) FY 18 Actual Not Available; FY 19 est 7,000,000.00; FY 20 est Estimate Not Available

HQ: U.S. Department of Agriculture Rural Development Energy Division 511 W 7th Street, Atlantic, IA 50022
Phone: 712-243-2107 | Email: lisa.noty@wdc.usda.gov

USDA10.117 | BIOFUEL INFRASTRUCTURE PARTNERSHIP
"BIP"

Award: Project Grants

Purpose: To provide innovative ways for expanding and conserving renewable fuels.

Applicant Eligibility: Additional information is provided in the Notice of Funds Availability (NOFA) published on June 16, 2015.

Beneficiary Eligibility: Same as Applicant Eligibility.

Funding: (Project Grants) FY 18 $24,432,239.00; FY 19 est $0.00; FY 20 est $0.00

HQ: 1400 Independence Avenue SW, Washington, DC 20250
Phone: 202-720-3175 | Email: katina.hanson@wdc.usda.gov
http://origin2.www.fsa.usda.gov/programs-and-services/energy-programs/index

NSF47.074 | BIOLOGICAL SCIENCES
"BIO"

Award: Project Grants

Purpose: To promote the progress of the biological sciences and thereby strengthen the Nation's scientific enterprise; to increase scientific knowledge and enhance understanding of major problems confronting the Nation.

Applicant Eligibility: Except where a Program solicitation establishes more restrictive eligibility criteria, individuals and Organizations in the following categories may submit proposals: universities and colleges; Non-profit, non-academic Organizations; For-profit Organizations; State and local Governments; and unaffiliated individuals. See the NSF Grant Proposal Guide, Chapter i.e., for a full description of eligibility requirements: http://www.nsf.gov/publications/pubsumm. jsp?odskey=gpg.

Beneficiary Eligibility: N/A

Award Range/Average: Range Low $5,000 Range High $14,999,752 Average $244,366.

Funding: (Project Grants) FY 18 $756,600,000.00; FY 19 est $783,690,000.00; FY 20 est $683,360,000.00

HQ: 2415 Eisenhower Avenue, Alexandria, VA 22314
Phone: 703-292-7770 | Email: erchiang@nsf.gov
http://nsf.gov/dir/index.jsp?org=bio

USDA10.312 | BIOMASS RESEARCH AND DEVELOPMENT INITIATIVE COMPETITIVE GRANTS PROGRAM (BRDI) "BRDI"

Award: Project Grants

Purpose: To promote research, methods, and technologies for the production of biofuels and biobased products.

Applicant Eligibility: Eligible entities include: (A) an institution of higher education; (B) a National Laboratory; (C) a Federal research agency; (D) a State research agency; (E) a private sector entity; (F) a nonprofit Organization; or (G) a consortium of 2 or more entities described in subparagraphs (A) through (F).

Beneficiary Eligibility: Same as Applicant Eligibility.

Award Range/Average: If minimum or maximum amounts of funding per competitive and/or capacity project grant, or cooperative agreement are established, these amounts will be announced in the annual Competitive Request for Application (RFA).The most current RFA is available via: https://nifa.usda.gov/funding-opportunity/biomass-research-and-development-initiative-brdi

Funding: (Project Grants) FY 17 $2,506,479.00; FY 18 est $0.00; FY 19 est $0.00

HQ: Institute of Bioenergy Climate and Environment Division of Bioenergy 1400 Independence Avenue SW, PO Box 2210, Washington, DC 20250-2210

    Phone: 202-401-5244

    http://nifa.usda.gov/program/biobased-products-processing-programs

HHS93.360 | BIOMEDICAL ADVANCED RESEARCH AND DEVELOPMENT AUTHORITY (BARDA), BIODEFENSE MEDICAL COUNTERMEASURE DEVELOPMENT

Award: Cooperative Agreements; Project Grants

Purpose: To coordinate the acceleration of countermeasure and product advanced research and development by-(A) facilitating collaboration between the Department of Health and Human Services and other Federal agencies, relevant industries, academia, and other persons.

Applicant Eligibility: All types of entities are eligible, including highly qualified foreign nationals outside the United States either alone or in collaboration with American participants when such transactions may inure to the benefit of the American people. Applicants should review the individual funding opportunity announcements issued under this CFDA Program.

Beneficiary Eligibility: All individuals including at-risk individuals such as children, pregnant women, elderly, and others at-risk who may be given special priority.

Award Range/Average: $30,000,000 to $55,000,000

Funding: (Project Grants (Cooperative Agreements)) FY 17 $55,000,000.00; FY 18 est $55,000,000.00; FY 20 est $55,000,000.00

HQ: 330 Independence Avenue SW, Room G-640, Washington, DC 20201

    Phone: 202-260-8535 | Email: rick.bright@hhs.gov

    https://www.medicalcountermeasures.gov

HHS93.859 | BIOMEDICAL RESEARCH AND RESEARCH TRAINING

Award: Project Grants

Purpose: The National Institute of General Medical Sciences supports basic research that increases our understanding of biological processes and lays the foundation for advances in disease diagnosis, treatment, and prevention. It also provides leadership in training the next generation of scientists, in enhancing the diversity of the scientific workforce, and in developing research capacity throughout the country.

Applicant Eligibility: NIGMS trainees must be U.S. citizens, non-citizen nationals, or permanent residents.

Beneficiary Eligibility: Any nonprofit or for-profit organization, company or institution engaged in biomedical research.

Award Range/Average: $20,000 to $10,000,000.

Funding: (Project Grants) FY 18 $2,675,446,000.00; FY 19 est $2,763,693,000.00; FY 20 est $2,375,898,000.00

HQ: 45 Center Drive, PO Box C6200, Bethesda, MD 20892

    Phone: 301-496-7301 | Email: atheys@nigms.nih.gov

    http://www.nigms.nih.gov

Programs Administered by Federal Headquarters

HHS93.062 | BIOMONITORING PROGRAMS FOR STATE PUBLIC HEALTH LABORATORIES

Award: Cooperative Agreements
Purpose: To support the development or expansion of state-based biomonitoring programs, including necessary infrastructure, that will increase the capability and capacity of state public health laboratories.
Applicant Eligibility: No additional information.
Beneficiary Eligibility: N/A
Funding: (Cooperative Agreements) FY 18 $0.00; FY 19 est $25,000,000.00; FY 20 est $25,000,000.00
HQ: 4770 Buford Highway NE, PO Box F45, Atlanta, GA 30341
    Phone: 770-488-0563
    http://www.cdc.gov

USDA10.865 | BIOREFINERY ASSISTANCE
"Section 9003 - Biorefinery, Renewable Chemical, and Biobased Manufacturing Assistance Program"

Award: Guaranteed/insured Loans
Purpose: To provide guarantees for the development, construction, and bio based product manufacturing facilities.
Applicant Eligibility: Eligible entities under the Program include: individuals, entities, Indian Tribes, or units of State or local government, corporations, farm cooperatives, farmer cooperative Organizations, associations of agricultural producers, National Laboratories, Institutions of higher education, rural electric cooperatives, public power entities, or consortia of any of those entities.
Beneficiary Eligibility: N/A
Award Range/Average: Maximum loan guarantee cannot exceed $250 million.
Funding: (Direct Payments for Specified Use) FY 18 $180,004,000.00; FY 19 est $1,647,384,763.00; FY 20 est Estimate Not Available
HQ: U.S. Department of Agriculture Rural Development Business Programs Energy Branch 1400 Independence Avenue SW, Washington, DC 20250
    Phone: 202-690-2516 | Email: aaron.morris@wdc.usda.gov
    http://www.rd.usda.gov/programs-services/biorefinery-renewable-chemical-and-biobased-product-manufacturing-assistance

USDA10.219 | BIOTECHNOLOGY RISK ASSESSMENT RESEARCH
"BRAG"

Award: Project Grants
Purpose: To assist Federal regulatory agencies in making science-based decisions about the effects of introducing into the environment genetically engineered organisms. The BRAG program provides Federal regulatory agencies with scientific information relevant to regulatory considerations derived from the risk assessment research that the program funds.
Applicant Eligibility: Any public or private research or educational institution or Organization.
Beneficiary Eligibility: Same as Applicant Eligibility.
Award Range/Average: If minimum or maximum amounts of funding per competitive and/or capacity project grant, or cooperative agreement are established, these amounts will be announced in the annual Competitive Request for Application (RFA).The most current RFA is available via: https://nifa.usda.gov/funding-opportunity/biotechnology-risk-assessment-research-grants-program-brag
Funding: (Project Grants) FY 17 $3,926,101.00; FY 18 est $4,213,797.00; FY 19 est $3,833,002.00
HQ: Institute of Food Production and Sustainability Division of Plant Systems-Production 1400 Independence Avenue SW, PO Box 2240, Washington, DC 20250-2240
    Phone: 202-401-4202
    http://nifa.usda.gov/program/biotechnology-risk-assessment-research-grants-program

HHS93.073 | BIRTH DEFECTS AND DEVELOPMENTAL DISABILITIES-PREVENTION AND SURVEILLANCE

Award: Cooperative Agreements

Purpose: To work with State health agencies, universities, and public and private nonprofit organizations in planning, implementing coordinating or evaluating programs, research or surveillance activities related to improved birth outcomes, prevention of birth defects, and the improvement of infant and child health and developmental outcomes.

Applicant Eligibility: N/A

Beneficiary Eligibility: State; Consumer; Local; Public nonprofit institution/organization; Federally Recognized Indian Tribal Governments; Individual/Family; Private nonprofit institution/organizations and others.

Award Range/Average: FY19/20 range is dependent upon funding availability. Award Amounts range from $5,000 to $1,500,000.

Funding: (Cooperative Agreements) FY 18 $32,696,630.00; FY 19 est $37,735,571.00; FY 20 est $32,505,000.00

HQ: 1600 Clifton Road NE, PO Box E86, Atlanta, GA 30333

Phone: 404-498-2416

http://www.cdc.gov/ncbddd

HHS93.839 | BLOOD DISEASES AND RESOURCES RESEARCH
"Division of Blood Diseases and Resources (DBDR)"

Award: Project Grants

Purpose: The Division of Blood Diseases and Resources supports research and research training on the pathophysiology, diagnosis, treatment, and prevention of non-malignant blood diseases, including anemias, sickle cell disease, thalassemia; leukocyte biology, pre-malignant processes such as myelodysplasia and myeloproliferative disorders; hemophilia and other abnormalities of hemostasis and thrombosis; and immune dysfunction.

Applicant Eligibility: Any nonprofit Organization engaged in biomedical research and Institutions or companies organized for profit may apply for almost any kind of grant. Only domestic, non-profit, private or public Institutions may apply for NRSA Institutional Research Training Grants. An individual may apply for an NRSA or, in some cases, for a research grant if adequate facilities to perform the research are available. SBIR grants can be awarded only to United States small business concerns (entities that are independently owned and operated for profit, or owned by another small business that itself is independently owned and operated for profit, are not dominant in the field in which research is proposed, and have no more than 500 employees including affiliates). Primary employment (more than one-half time) of the principal investigator must be with the small business at the time of award and during the conduct of the proposed project. In both Phase I and Phase II, the research must be performed in the U.S. or its possessions. To be eligible for funding, a grant application must be approved for scientific merit and Program relevance by a scientific review group and a national advisory council. SBIR projects are generally performed at least 67% by the applicant small business in Phase I and at least 50% of the Project in Phase II. STTR grants can be awarded only to United States small business concerns (entities that are independently owned and operated for profit and have no more than 500 employees) that formally collaborate with a University or other non-profit research institution in cooperative research and development. The principal investigator of an STTR award may be employed with either the small business concern or collaborating non-profit research institution as long as s/he has a formal appointment with or commitment to the applicant small business concern. At least 40% of the project is to be performed by the small business concern and at least 30% by the non-profit research institution. In both Phase I and Phase II, the research must be performed in the U.S. and its possessions.

Beneficiary Eligibility: Any nonprofit or for-profit organization, company or institution engaged in biomedical research. Only domestic for-profit small business firms may apply for SBIR and STTR programs.

Award Range/Average: Grants: $8,557 to $4,697,455; $443,566. SBIR Phase I- $150,000, Phase II- $1,000,000; STTR Phase I- $150,000, Phase II- $1,000,000.

Funding: (Project Grants) FY 18 $371,540,656.00; FY 19 est $376,723,040.00; FY 20 est $376,723,040.00

HQ: 6701 Rockledge Drive, Room 7176, Bethesda, MD 20892

Phone: 301-827-7968 | Email: pharesda@nhlbi.nih.gov

https://www.nhlbi.nih.gov/about/scientific-divisions/division-blood-diseases-and-resources

Programs Administered by Federal Headquarters

HHS93.080 | BLOOD DISORDER PROGRAM: PREVENTION, SURVEILLANCE, AND RESEARCH
"Division of Blood Disorders - Prevention, Surveillance and Research"

Award: Cooperative Agreements
Purpose: To work with State health agencies and other public, private, and nonprofit organizations in planning, development, implementation, coordination, or evaluation of programs or other activities related to improved blood disorders.
Applicant Eligibility: N/A
Beneficiary Eligibility: N/A
Award Range/Average: FY19/20 Financial Assistance is dependent upon funding availability. Award amounts range from $5,000 to $4,300,000.
Funding: (Cooperative Agreements) FY 18 $6,960,136.00; FY 19 est $7,143,879.00; FY 20 est $7,143,879.00
HQ: 1600 Clifton Road NE, PO Box E64, Atlanta, GA 30333
   Phone: 404-498-3950 | Email: kra0@cdc.gov
   http://www.cdc.gov/ncbddd

DHS97.012 | BOATING SAFETY FINANCIAL ASSISTANCE
"RBS Program"

Award: Formula Grants; Project Grants
Purpose: The U.S. Coast Guard funds grant programs that encourage participation in boating safety and thereby reducing the number of accidents and injuries on waterways. It also assists local and State governments in developing and carrying out recreational boating safety programs.
Applicant Eligibility: States & Territories: States and Territories must have a Coast Guard-approved boating safety Program as described by 46 U.S.C. 131: Recreational Boating Safety. Nonprofits: Organizations do not have to be boating-related, but it must be a nongovernmental Organization that has been accorded tax exempt status which is defined as having, or being capable of obtaining an IRS tax exempt classification (26 U.S.C. 501(c)(3)). Boating Safety Survey Grant: Institutions of higher education or other public nonprofit institution/Organization, quasi-public nonprofit institution/Organization, or other private institution/Organization that can sufficiently demonstrate through their application significant experience in their ability to design, manage, and complete a nationwide statistical survey for the Federal Government.
Beneficiary Eligibility: Please see the Notice of Funding Opportunity for program-specific information.
Award Range/Average: Please see our website for previous and current awards: http://www.uscgboating.org/grants/grant-archives.php. State and Territory grants are determined by a three-part formula mandated by statute.The 2018 nonprofit grants range from $50,000 to $550,000. The average award amount is approximately $160,000.
Funding: (Project Grants) FY 18 $108,811,049.00; FY 19 est $110,134,520.00; FY 20 $108,344,671.00
HQ: 2703 Martin Luther King Jr Avenue SE, Washington, DC 20593
   Phone: 202-372-1055 | Email: pavlo.oborski@uscg.mil
   http://www.uscgboating.org

DOJ16.835 | BODY WORN CAMERA POLICY AND IMPLEMENTATION
"BWCPIP"

Award: Formula Grants; Cooperative Agreements; Project Grants; Use of Property, Facilities, and Equipment; Provision of Specialized Services; Advisory Services and Counseling; Dissemination of Technical Information; Training; Investigation of Complaints
Purpose: BJA helps law enforcement agencies in identifying effective methods for deploying technology and provides reliable digital media evidence for internal law enforcement.
Applicant Eligibility: Eligible applicants to be funded to deploy BWC Programs are limited to public agencies of state government, units of local government, and federally recognized Indian tribal Governments that perform law enforcement functions (as determined by the Secretary of the Interior); or any department, agency, or instrumentality of the foregoing that performs criminal justice functions (including combinations of the preceding, one of which is designated as the primary applicant). Additionally, training and technical assistance services require applicants be national or regional public and private entities, including for-profit (commercial) and nonprofit Organizations (including tribal nonprofit or for-profit Organizations), faith-based and community Organizations, and Institutions of higher education (including tribal Institutions of higher

education) that support initiatives to improve the functioning of the criminal justice system. For-profit Organizations must agree to forgo any profit or management fee.

Beneficiary Eligibility: Beneficiaries are the criminal justice agencies involved in a BWC program deployment and the communities involved.

Funding: (Project Grants) FY 17 $17,984,097.00; FY 18 est $22,500,000.00; FY 19 est $22,500,000.00

HQ: U.S. Department of Justice Bureau of Justice Assistance 810 7th Street NW, Washington, DC 20531

Phone: 202-616-3785 | Email: john.markovic2@usdoj.gov

http://www.bja.gov

HUD14.266 | BORDER COMMUNITY CAPITAL INITIATIVE

Award: Project Grants

Purpose: To increase community facilities in the acutely under-served and -capitalized U.S./Mexico border region. It will also provide direct investment and technical assistance to focus on affordable housing, small business and community facilities to benefit the residents of colonias.

Applicant Eligibility: Applicants that are eligible to participate in this initiative are community development lenders and investors, which may be local rural non-profit Organizations or federally recognized Tribes. Applicants do not need to be certified as Community Development Financial Institutions by the CDFI Fund at the time of application. Applicants may serve other markets than colonias residents and communities, using other sources of financing.

Beneficiary Eligibility: Eligible target markets for use of Border Initiative funds include geographic areas defined as colonias by The Cranston-Gonzalez National Afford Housing Act of 1990 (Pub. L. 101-625, Nov. 28, 1990) (the Act) and the Appropriations Act of 1997 (Pub L. 104-204, Sept. 26, 1996, 110 Stat. 2887).

Award Range/Average: Up to $2,000,000

HQ: U.S. Department of Housing and Urban Development Office of Rural Housing and Economic Development 451 7th Street SW, Room 7137, Washington, DC 20410

Phone: 202-402-4464 | Email: thann.young@hud.gov

DOC11.557 | BROADBAND TECHNOLOGY OPPORTUNITIES PROGRAM (BTOP) "BTOP"

Award: Project Grants

Purpose: The Broadband Technology Opportunities Program accelerates broadband deployment in unserved and underserved areas to ensure they have broadband connections.

Applicant Eligibility: INACTIVE - Funding for the BTOP Program has ended.

Beneficiary Eligibility: Same as Applicant Eligibility.

Award Range/Average: Program is currently inactive.

HQ: 1401 Constitution Avenue NW, Room 4887, Washington, DC 20230

Phone: 202-482-3590 | Email: pbeasley-timpson@ntia.doc.gov

https://www.ntia.doc.gov/legacy/broadbandgrants/projects.html

HHS93.466 | BUILDING CAPACITY OF THE PUBLIC HEALTH SYSTEM TO ADDRESS EBOLA THROUGH NATIONAL NONPROFIT ORGANIZATIONS
"Strengthening the Public Health System in U.S.-affiliated Pacific Islands"

Award: Cooperative Agreements

Purpose: To ensure provision of capacity building assistance (CBA) to address Ebola-related needs.

Applicant Eligibility: N/A

Beneficiary Eligibility: N/A

Award Range/Average: 1 award at approximate average award of $2,000,000

HQ: 2920 Brandywine Road, PO Box K98, Atlanta, GA 30341

Phone: 770-488-2756 | Email: lbrowning@cdc.gov

http://www.cdc.gov

Programs Administered by Federal Headquarters

HHS93.524 | BUILDING CAPACITY OF THE PUBLIC HEALTH SYSTEM TO IMPROVE POPULATION HEALTH THROUGH NATIONAL, NON-PROFIT ORGANIZATIONS-FINANCED IN PART BY PREVENTION AND PUBLIC HEALTH FUNDS (PPHF)
"CBA to Strengthen Public Health Infrastructure and Performance"

Award: Cooperative Agreements

Purpose: Cover projects under two funding initiatives specific capacity building activities (CBA) under PPHF; and CBA activities under an umbrella cooperative agreement for unique target populations.

Applicant Eligibility: 1. Eligible Applicants: Organizations with nonprofit 501(c)(3) or nonprofit 501(c)(6) IRS status (other than Institutions of higher education). 2. Special Eligibility Requirements: The applicant Organization must provide evidence of national scope of work and of public health charge or mission. 3. Justification for Less than Maximum Competition: The Program leadership in the Office of State, Tribal, Local and Territorial Support (OSTLTS) determined that in order to achieve its strategic priorities for strengthening the public health infrastructure and advancing the quality of public health decision making, OSTLTS will need to expand its capacity building assistance (CBA) efforts through national, non-profit Organizations with experience and expertise providing capacity building assistance to governmental and non-governmental components of the public health system. Eligible applicants are limited to national, non-profit professional public health mission Organizations with experience and expertise providing capacity building assistance (CBA) to governmental and non-governmental components of the public health system. The CDC is requesting the provision of capacity building assistance (CBA) to public health agencies and other public health entities across the United States and its territories in order to strengthen public health practice to improve health for all populations. These national public health mission Organizations are the only entities positioned to effectively and efficiently execute on the expected capacity building outcomes, outputs, and activities outlined in the FOA. The characteristics that position these Organizations are: 1) designated mission and experience working nationally, 2) demonstrated infrastructure, experience and expertise providing CBA, and 3) relationship to the public health system workforce across the United States and Territories. Therefore, eligibility is limited to the above specified types of applicants/Organizations that are expected to demonstrate significant experience and expertise providing capacity building assistance (CBA) to the target populations described in the attached OT13-1302 FOA. This expertise is necessary for the grantee to effectively and efficiently complete the related activities and achieve the Program outcomes described in the funding opportunity announcement. Additionally the following capacities will facilitate the completion of projects in the specified timeframe: Infrastructure to organize, conduct work and disseminate key outcomes. Communicate key information to Organization members, stakeholders and the public health community on a regular basis. Leverage a wide array of resources among Organization members and the public health community to expeditiously achieve results in a cost-effective manner. Interact with other public health Organizations; act as a networking hub to build the capacity of governmental and non-governmental components of the public health system.

Beneficiary Eligibility: Beneficiaries include state health departments; tribal health organizations; local health departments; the District of Columbia; U.S. Territories; and other components of the public health system. The general public will also serve as beneficiaries.

Award Range/Average: The floor of individual award range is $4 million for Category A, $1 million for Category B and $100,000 for Category C. The approximate average award ranges for the 12-month budget period are up to $9 million for Category A, up to $2.5 million for Category B and up to $1 million for Category C.

HQ: 1825 Century Boulevard NE, PO Box V18-1, Atlanta, GA 30345

    Phone: 770-488-1522

    http://www.cdc.gov/stltpublichealth/funding/rfaot13.html

DOJ16.607 | BULLETPROOF VEST PARTNERSHIP PROGRAM
"BVP"

Award: Direct Payments for Specified Use

Purpose: To provide up to 50% of the cost of armored vests for state, local, and tribal jurisdictions.

Applicant Eligibility: Only chief executives of jurisdictions (or their designees) may apply for funds. Jurisdictions are defined as general purpose units of local government (e.g., cities, towns, townships, boroughs, counties, etc.), Federally-recognized Indian Tribes, the 50 State Governments, the District of Columbia, the Commonwealth of Puerto Rico, the U.S. Virgin Islands, American Samoa, Guam, and the Northern Mariana Islands. The chief executive of the jurisdiction registers on-line, submits the jurisdiction application, and requests payment for completed vest orders.

Beneficiary Eligibility: Only law enforcement officers may receive vests through this program. According to the Act, "law enforcement officer" means any officer, agent, or employee of a State, unit of local government, or an Indian tribe authorized by law or by a government agency to engage in or supervise the prevention, detection, or investigation of any violation of criminal law, or authorized by law to supervise sentenced criminal offenders. Eligible officers may be full-time, part-time, paid or volunteer. In order to receive BVP funds, jurisdictions must certify, during the application process, that all law enforcement agencies benefitting from the BVP Program have a written "mandatory wear" policy in effect. FAQ: https://ojp. gov/bvpbasi/docs/FAQsBVPMandatoryWearPolicy.pdfThe BVP Reauthorization Act of 2015 included a provision that states that BJA may give preferential consideration to BVP recipients that provide armor vests to law enforcement officers that are uniquely fitted for such officers, including vests uniquely fitted to individual female law enforcement officers. A certification section has been added to the 2017 application (in the BVP system) stating the jurisdictions and law enforcement agency are aware of and will comply with this requirement.

Award Range/Average: Not Applicable.

Funding: (Direct Payments for Specified Use) FY 18 $30,054,064.00; FY 19 est $22,500,000.00; FY 20 est $22,500,000.00

HQ: U.S. Department of Justice Bureau of Justice Assistance 810 7th Street NW, Washington, DC 20531

    Phone: 877-758-3787

    http://ojp.gov/bvpbasi/home.html

DOS19.600 | BUREAU OF NEAR EASTERN AFFAIRS

Award: Cooperative Agreements; Project Grants

Purpose: Supports the foreign assistance goals and objectives of the Department of State, Bureau of Near Eastern Affairs, as delineated in the FY Bureau Strategic and Resource Plan. This program is for all grant awards for the entire fiscal year funded through State/NEA/AC.

Applicant Eligibility: U.S. or foreign non-profit Organizations; for-profit Organizations; private Institutions of higher education, public or state Institutions of higher education; public international Organizations; and small businesses with functional and regional experience. Each solicitation outlines who is eligible and what types of experience are needed to apply for funding.

Beneficiary Eligibility: U.S. or foreign non-profit organizations; for-profit organizations; private institutions of higher education, public or state institutions of higher education; public international organizations; and small businesses with functional and regional experience. Each solicitation outlines who is eligible and what types of experience are needed to apply for funding. Any award made using State/NEA funds requires the full complement of standard federal forms and budget documents, CVs of main program staff, as dictated by the U.S. Department of State, Bureau of Administration, and the relevant OMB circulars. See www.grants.gov for specific announcement. OMB Circular No. A-87 applies to this program. See www.grants.gov for specific announcement.

Award Range/Average: Depends on specifc grant award. See www.grants.gov for specific announcement.

HQ: 2430 E Street NW, Washington, DC 20037

    Phone: 202-776-8691 | Email: curleysl@state.gov

    http://www.state.gov/p/nea

DOI15.423 | BUREAU OF OCEAN ENERGY MANAGEMENT (BOEM) ENVIRONMENTAL STUDIES (ES)
"ESP"

Award: Cooperative Agreements

Purpose: The Bureau of Ocean Energy Management provides major economic and energy benefits and also oversees the exploration and development of oil, natural gas and other minerals and renewable energy alternatives on the nations outer continental shelf. The purpose of the Environmental Studies Program is to obtain the information needed for the assessment and the management of environmental impacts; to predict impacts on marine biota; and to monitor the human, marine, and coastal environments to provide time series and data trend information.

Applicant Eligibility: State agencies, public universities, and non-profits in affected states may apply. More than one institution may collaborate in the preparation of an application for assistance. Scientists from other Institutions may participate in collaboration with a principal investigator from a State agency or public University.

Beneficiary Eligibility: Research scientists, Federal, State and local decision-makers, Native American Organizations, and the general public will ultimately benefit from the program.

Award Range/Average: Range is $150,000 to $1,200,000; Average $350,000.

Funding: (Cooperative Agreements) FY 17 $7,600,000.00; FY 18 Estimate Not Available; FY 19 Estimate Not Available

Programs Administered by Federal Headquarters

HQ: 45600 Woodland Road, Sterling, VA 20166
Phone: 703-787-1087 | Email: rodney.cluck@boem.gov
http://www.boem.gov

DOI15.408 | BUREAU OF OCEAN ENERGY MANAGEMENT RENEWABLE ENERGY
"Renewable Energy Program"

Award: Cooperative Agreements
Purpose: Oversees the leasing of areas on the outer continental shelf for development of renewable energy facilities. The program not only supports decisions made within the Department of the Interior, but also provides coastal states and local governments with the information necessary to ensure that all stages of offshore renewable energy projects are conducted in a manner to protect both the human and natural environments.
Applicant Eligibility: State agencies and public universities may apply. More than one institution may collaborate in the preparation of an application for assistance.
Beneficiary Eligibility: Research scientists, Federal, state and local decision makers, Native American Organizations, and the general public will ultimately benefit from the program.
Award Range/Average: Range is $100,000 to $1,000,000; Average $500,000.
Funding: (Cooperative Agreements) FY 17 $700,000.00; FY 18 est Estimate Not Available; FY 19 est Estimate Not Available; - (FY 18 Exp: 0, FY 19 Exp: 0)
HQ: 381 Elden Street HM 3115, Herndon, VA 20170
Phone: 703-787-1662 | Email: mary.boatman@boem.gov
http://www.boem.gov

DOS19.750 | BUREAU OF WESTERN HEMISPHERE AFFAIRS (WHA) GRANT PROGRAMS (INCLUDING ENERGY AND CLIMATE PARTNERSHIP FOR THE AMERICAS)
"Bureau of Western Hemisphere Affairs WHA"

Award: Project Grants
Purpose: To support the foreign assistance goals and objectives of the Department of State, Bureau of Western Hemisphere Affairs (WHA), as delineated in the FY Bureau Strategic and Resource Plan and other strategic planning documents.
Applicant Eligibility: Uses of assistance vary according to the individual award. Please see www.grants.gov for specific announcement.
Beneficiary Eligibility: U.S. Department of State, WHA Bureau, issues grants to domestic entities that implement programs in WHA countries. Primary beneficiaries are residents of any community abroad where program activities are taking place. See www.grants.gov for specific announcement. See www.grants.gov for individual application.
Award Range/Average: Grants can range from small amounts (thousands of dollars) up to $2-3 million. The average federal share of expenditures for WHA grants is around $1M. See www.grants.gov for specific announcement.
Funding: (Project Grants) FY 10 $10,000,000.00; FY 11 est $15,000,000.00; FY 12 est $15,000,000.00
HQ: 2201 C Street NW, Room 6913 Harry S Truman Building, Washington, DC 20520
Phone: 202-647-5506 | Email: raoas@state.gov

VA64.101 | BURIAL EXPENSES ALLOWANCE FOR VETERANS

Award: Direct Payments for Specified Use
Purpose: To provide a monetary allowance not to exceed $747, or that amount authorized under 38 U.S.C. 2303 whichever is greater, toward the plot or interment expense for certain Veterans not buried in a national cemetery.
Applicant Eligibility: Eligible surviving spouses of record or added to the record at the time the death is reported are paid burial and plot allowances automatically upon notification of a Veteran's death, without the need to submit a claim. VA may grant additional benefits, including the internment and transportation allowance, if VA receives a claim for these benefits. If the burial benefit has not been automatically paid to the surviving spouse, VA will pay the first living person to file a claim of those listed below: The Veteran's surviving spouse, OR The survivor of a legal union between the deceased Veteran and the survivor, OR The Veteran's children, regardless of age, OR The Veteran's parents or surviving parent, OR The executor or administrator of the estate of the deceased Veteran. If no one has been appointed, then VA may pay someone acting in such a capacity for the estate. The next of kin, friend or associate of the deceased Veteran is eligible for the flag.

Beneficiary Eligibility: The Veteran's surviving spouse, the survivor of a legal union between the deceased Veteran and the survivor, the Veteran's children, regardless of age, the Veteran's parents or surviving parent, or the executor or administrator of the estate of the deceased Veteran who paid the Veteran's burial expenses. If no one has been appointed as executor or administrator of the estate, then VA may pay someone acting in such a capacity for the estate. A funeral director may be eligible if the Veteran's remains are unclaimed.

Award Range/Average: Up to $747 for plot or interment expenses. Up to $300 for burial allowance if death is not service-connected. Up to $2,000 if death is service-connected. Reasonable transportation charges may be covered in certain cases. A reasonable transportation expense is an expense that is usual and customary in the context of burial transportation, with a corresponding charge that is the usual and customary charge made to the general public for the same or similar services.

Funding: (Direct Payments with Unrestricted Use) FY 16 $225,269,000.00; FY 17 est $231,669,000.00; FY 18 est Estimate Not Available

HQ: Department of Veterans Affairs 810 Vermont Avenue NW, Washington, DC 20420
  Phone: 202-461-9700
  http://www.va.gov

USDA10.768 | BUSINESS AND INDUSTRY LOANS
"B&I Guaranteed Loan Program"

Award: Guaranteed/insured Loans

Purpose: The B&I Guaranteed Loan Program is to develop business, industry, and employment to improve the economic condition in rural communities.

Applicant Eligibility: A borrower may be a cooperative Organization, corporation, partnership, or other legal entity organized and operated on a profit or nonprofit basis; an Indian tribe on a Federal or State reservation or other Federally recognized tribal group; a public body; or an individual.

Beneficiary Eligibility: N/A

Funding: (Guaranteed/Insured Loans) FY 18 $1,200,000,000.00; FY 19 est $1,400,000,000.00; FY 20 Estimate Not Available no approved President budget as of today

HQ: B and I Processing Branch U.S. Department of Agriculture 1400 Independence Avenue SW, PO Box 3224, Washington, DC 20250-3224
  Phone: 202-690-4103 | Email: brenda.griffin@wdc.usda.gov
  http://www.rd.usda.gov/programs-services/business-industry-loan-guarantees

DOC11.601 | CALIBRATION PROGRAM

Award: Provision of Specialized Services

Purpose: To assist with a system of physical measurement in the U.S.

Applicant Eligibility: Calibrations and tests are provided on a fee basis to state and local Governments, academic Institutions, scientific laboratories, industrial firms, corporations, and individuals.

Beneficiary Eligibility: N/A

Funding: (Sale, Exchange, or Donation of Property and Goods) FY 18 $7,014,454.00; FY 19 est $6,915,100.00; FY 20 est $6,800,000.00

HQ: 100 Bureau Drive, Room B-266 Building 221, Gaithersburg, MD 20899
  Phone: 301-975-2356 | Email: martin.wilson@nist.gov
  http://www.nist.gov/calibrations

DOI15.432 | CALIFORNIA REFUGE ACCOUNT

Award: Direct Payments With Unrestricted Use

Purpose: Shares 40.87 percent with the State of California.

Applicant Eligibility: Revenue from effected land leasing will trigger automatic payment distribution computed in accordance with the Authorization.

Beneficiary Eligibility: The State shares 38 percent of well production attributable to the portion of the well within 500 feet of the State/Federal boundary, 62 percent outside the 500 feet. Consequently, the total State share of the revenue equals 40.87 percent.

Award Range/Average: Not Applicable.

Funding: (Direct Payments for Specified Use) FY 17 $1,000.00; FY 18 est $1,000.00; FY 19 est $1,000.00

Programs Administered by Federal Headquarters

HQ: Office of Natural Resources Revenue 1849 C Street NW, PO Box 4211, Washington, DC 20240
Phone: 202-513-0600
http://www.ONRR.gov

HHS93.396 | CANCER BIOLOGY RESEARCH

Award: Cooperative Agreements; Project Grants
Purpose: To provide fundamental information on the cause and nature of cancer in people, with the expectation that this will result in better methods of prevention, detection and diagnosis, and treatment of neoplastic diseases.
Applicant Eligibility: The awardee will be a University, college, hospital, public agency, nonprofit research institution or for-profit Organization that submits an application and receives a grant for support of research by a named principal investigator. To be eligible for funding, a grant application must be approved for scientific merit and Program relevance by a scientific review group and a national advisory council.
Beneficiary Eligibility: Any nonprofit or for-profit organization, company, or institution engaged in biomedical research.
Award Range/Average: Range: $28,104 to $4,537,433 Average: $424,815
Funding: (Salaries and Expenses) FY 18 $475,693,000.00; FY 19 est Estimate Not Available; FY 20 est Estimate Not Available; Cancer Biology Research GrantsFY2016 act. $510,555,000 - SBIR/STTR $3,905,000 - Other Research $8,839,000 FY2017 est. $539,414,000 - SBIR/STTR $4,260,000 - Other Research $25,902,000 FY2018 est. $451,368,000 - SBIR/STTR $3,291,000 Other Research $21,034,000; (Project Grants (Cooperative Agreements)) FY 18 $555,658,000.00; FY 19 est $574,944,271.00; FY 20 est $533,921,447.00
HQ: ORRPC DEA NCI 9609 Medical Center Drive 7th Floor W Tower 7W530, PO Box 9750, Rockville, MD 20850
Phone: 240-276-6442 | Email: shamala@mail.nih.gov
http://dcb.nci.nih.gov

HHS93.393 | CANCER CAUSE AND PREVENTION RESEARCH

Award: Cooperative Agreements; Project Grants
Purpose: To identify cancer risks and risk reduction strategies, to identify factors that cause cancer in man, and to discover and develop mechanisms for cancer prevention in man.
Applicant Eligibility: The awardee will be a University, college, hospital, public agency, nonprofit research institution or for-profit Organization that submits an application and receives a grant or cooperative agreement for support of research by a named principal investigator. SBIR grants can be awarded only to domestic small businesses (entities that are independently owned and operated for profit, are not dominant in the field in which research is proposed, and have no more than 500 employees). Primary employment (more than one- half time) of the principal investigator must be with the small business at the time of award and during the conduct of the proposed project. In both Phase I and Phase II, the research must be performed in the U.S. and its possessions. To be eligible for funding, a grant application must be approved for scientific merit and Program relevance by a scientific review group and a national advisory council. STTR grants can be awarded only to domestic small business concern (entities that are independently owned and operated for profit, are not dominant in the field in which research is proposed and have no more than 500 employees) which "partner" with a research institution in cooperative research and development. At least 40 percent of the project is to be performed by the small business concern and at least 30 percent by the research institution. In both Phase I and Phase II, the research must be performed in the U.S. and its possessions. To be eligible for funding, a grant application must be approved for scientific merit and Program relevance by a scientific review group and a national advisory council.
Beneficiary Eligibility: Any nonprofit or for-profit organization, company, or institution engaged in biomedical research on cancer.
Award Range/Average: Range: $3,203 to $3,475,469 Average: $521,572
Funding: (Cooperative Agreements) FY 18 $630,581,000.00; FY 19 est $652,483,024.00; FY 20 est $605,920,749.00
HQ: ORRPC DEA NCI 9609 Medical Center Drive 7th Floor W Tower 7W530, PO Box 9750, Rockville, MD 20850
Phone: 240-276-6442 | Email: shamala@mail.nih.gov
http://www.cancer.gov

HHS93.397 | CANCER CENTERS SUPPORT GRANTS
"Cancer Centers"

Award: Cooperative Agreements; Project Grants
Purpose: To provide an organizational focus and stimulus for the highest quality cancer research that effectively promotes interdisciplinary cancer research aimed toward the ultimate goal of reducing cancer incidence, mortality and morbidity.

Applicant Eligibility: Any nonprofit institution within the United States with a peer-reviewed cancer research base of 4. 0 million dollars in direct costs may apply for a Cancer Center Support Grant.

Beneficiary Eligibility: University, college, public agency or research institution in the U.S.

Award Range/Average: Range: $144,556 to $12,352,942 Average: $2,486,304

Funding: (Project Grants) FY 18 $564,391,000.00; FY 19 est 559,003,000.00; FY 20 est $373,259,000.00

HQ: 9609 Medical Center Drive 7th Floor W Tower 7W530, PO Box 9750, Rockville, MD 20850

Phone: 240-276-6442 | Email: shamala@mail.nih.gov

http://cancercenters.cancer.gov

HHS93.399 | CANCER CONTROL
"Cancer Control Grants"

Award: Project Grants

Purpose: To reduce cancer risk, incidence, morbidity, and mortality and enhance quality of life in cancer survivors through an orderly sequence from research on interventions and their impact in defined populations to the broad, systematic application of the research results through dissemination and diffusion strategies.

Applicant Eligibility: The awardee will be a University, college, hospital, public agency, nonprofit research institution or for-profit Organization that submits an application and receives a grant or cooperative agreement for support of research by a named principal investigator. SBIR grants can be awarded only to domestic small businesses (entities that are independently owned and operated for profit, are not dominant in the field in which research is proposed, and have no more than 500 employees). Primary employment (more than one- half time) of the principal investigator must be with the small business at the time of award and for the duration of the project period. In both Phase I and Phase II, the research must be performed in the U.S. and its possessions. To be eligible for funding, a grant application must be approved for scientific merit, technical merit, and Program relevance by a scientific review group and a national advisory council. STTR grants can be awarded only to domestic small business concern (entities that are independently owned and operated for profit, are not dominant in the field in which research is proposed and have no more than 500 employees) which "partner" with a research institution in cooperative research and development. At least 40 percent of the project is to be performed by the small business concern and at least 30 percent by the research institution. The Principal Investigator may be primarily employed by either the small business concern or the collaborating research institution at the time of award and for the duration of the project period. In both Phase I and Phase II, the research must be performed in the U.S. and its possessions. To be eligible for funding, a grant application must be approved for scientific merit, technical merit and Program relevance by a scientific review group and a national advisory council.

Beneficiary Eligibility: University, college, hospital, public agency, nonprofit research institutions or for-profit organizations will benefit.

Award Range/Average: Range 0 to 0 Average: 0

HQ: 9609 Medical Center Drive 7th Floor W Tower 7W532, PO Box 9750, Rockville, MD 20850

Phone: 240-276-6443 | Email: battistc@mail.nih.gov

http://cancercontrol.cancer.gov

HHS93.394 | CANCER DETECTION AND DIAGNOSIS RESEARCH

Award: Cooperative Agreements; Project Grants

Purpose: To improve screening and early detection strategies and to develop accurate diagnostic techniques and methods for predicting the course of disease in cancer patients.

Applicant Eligibility: The awardee will be a University, college, hospital, public agency, nonprofit research institution or Organization, unit of tribal government, or a for-profit Organization that submits an application and receives a grant or cooperative agreement for support of research by a named principal investigator. SBIR grants can be awarded only to domestic small businesses (entities that are independently owned and operated for profit, are not dominant in the field in which research is proposed, and have no more than 500 employees). Primary employment (more than one-half time) of the principal investigator must be with the small business at the time of award and during the conduct of the proposed project. In both Phase I and Phase II, the research must be performed in the U.S. and its possessions. To be eligible for funding, a grant application must be approved for scientific merit and Program relevance by a scientific review group and a national advisory council. STTR grants can be awarded only to domestic small business concerns (entities that are independently owned and operated for profit, are not dominant in the field in which research is proposed and have no more than 500 employees) which "partner" with a research institution in cooperative research and development. At least 40 percent of the project is to be performed by the small business concern and at least 30 percent by the research institution. In both Phase I and Phase II, the

Programs Administered by Federal Headquarters

research must be performed in the U.S. and its possessions. To be eligible for funding, a grant application must be approved for scientific merit and Program relevance by a scientific review group and a national advisory council.

Beneficiary Eligibility: Any nonprofit or for-profit organization, company, or institution engaged in biomedical research.

Award Range/Average: Range: $40,682 to $2,413,205 Average: 487,839

Funding: (Project Grants(Cooperative Agreements)) FY 18 $376,612,000.00; FY 19 est $389,525,327.00; FY 20 est $361,804,844.00

HQ: ORRPC DEA NCI 9609 Medical Center Drive 7th Floor W Tower 7W530, PO Box 9750, Rockville, MD 20850
  Phone: 240-276-6442 | Email: shamala@mail.nih.gov
  http://prevention.cancer.gov

HHS93.752 | CANCER PREVENTION AND CONTROL PROGRAMS FOR STATE, TERRITORIAL AND TRIBAL ORGANIZATIONS FINANCED IN PART BY PREVENTION AND PUBLIC HEALTH FUNDS
"National Breast and Cervical Cancer Early Detection Program (NBCCEDP) - PPHF"

Award: Cooperative Agreements

Purpose: Works with official State and territorial health agencies or their designees, in developing comprehensive breast and cervical cancer early detection programs.

Applicant Eligibility: Eligible applicants are the official State health agencies of the United States.

Beneficiary Eligibility: Eligible applicants are the official State health agencies of the United States, the District of Columbia, the Commonwealth of Puerto Rico, the Virgin Islands, Guam, the Northern Mariana Islands, the Federated States of Micronesia, the Republic of the Marshall Islands, American Samoa, American Indian and Alaska Native tribes and tribal organizations as defined in Section 4 of the Indian Self-Determination and Education Assistance Act.

Award Range/Average: No PPHF Funds used in FY16. This co-op ended 6/29/2017.

HQ: 4770 Buford Highway NE, PO Box F76, Atlanta, GA 30341
  Phone: 770-488-1074
  http://www.cdc.gov

HHS93.898 | CANCER PREVENTION AND CONTROL PROGRAMS FOR STATE, TERRITORIAL AND TRIBAL ORGANIZATIONS

Award: Cooperative Agreements

Purpose: FOA's purpose is to transition a highly-functional public health infrastructure for cancer prevention and control into new roles and functions to anticipate the nation's needs over the next decade by developing organized screening programs and offer evidence-based, scalable interventions that already exist and can be broadly implemented.

Applicant Eligibility: Program 1; State Governments or their bona fide agents (includes the District of Columbia); Territorial Governments or their bona fide agents in the Commonwealth of Puerto Rico, the Virgin Islands, the Commonwealth of the Northern Marianna Islands, American Samoa, Guam, the Federated States of Micronesia, the Republic of the Marshall Islands, and the Republic of Palau.; American Indian or Alaska Native tribal Governments (federally recognized or state-recognized); Native American tribal Governments (Federally recognized); Native American tribal Organizations (other than Federally recognized tribal Governments); American Indian or Alaska native tribally designated Organizations; Program 2 - Limited Competition Justification has been submitted Program 3; State Governments or their bona fide agents (includes the District of Columbia); Territorial Governments or their bona fide agents in the Commonwealth of Puerto Rico, the Virgin Islands, the Commonwealth of the Northern Marianna Islands, American Samoa, Guam, the Federated States of Micronesia.

Beneficiary Eligibility: Same as Applicant Eligibility.

Award Range/Average: 250K - 750K

Funding: (Cooperative Agreements) FY 18 $214,043,344.00; FY 19 est $215,284,167.00; FY 20 est $215,284,167.00

HQ: 4770 Buford Highway NE, PO Box F76, Atlanta, GA 30341
  Phone: 770-488-4378
  http://www.cdc.gov

HHS93.398 | CANCER RESEARCH MANPOWER
"Cancer Manpower Grants"

Award: Project Grants

Purpose: To make available support to nonprofit and for-profit institutions interested in providing biomedical training opportunities for individuals interested in careers in basic, clinical, and prevention research.

Applicant Eligibility: University, college, hospital, public agency, or nonprofit research institution for institutional grants and individuals for fellowships. The applicant institution must be able to provide the staff and facilities and be responsible for the selection of trainees and overall direction of the training. Selected awardees must be citizens of the United States or be admitted to the United States for permanent residency. Career and Cancer education awards may be given to for-profit Institutions.

Beneficiary Eligibility: University, college, hospital, public agency, nonprofit research institution or for-profit institution.

Award Range/Average: Range: $4,200 to $1,097,811 Average: $144,391

Funding: (Project Grants) FY 18 $175,322,000.00; FY 19 est $204,675,000.00; FY 20 est $184,822,000.00

HQ: 9609 Medical Center Drive 7th Floor West Tower, PO Box 9750, Rockville, MD 20850

Phone: 240-276-6442 | Email: shamala@mail.nih.gov

http://www.cancer.gov/researchandfunding/training

HHS93.395 | CANCER TREATMENT RESEARCH

Award: Cooperative Agreements; Project Grants

Purpose: To develop the means to cure as many cancer patients as possible and to control the disease in those patients who are not cured.

Applicant Eligibility: The awardee will be a University, college, hospital, public agency, nonprofit research institution, or for-profit Organization that submits an application and receives a grant or cooperative agreement for support of research by a named principal investigator. SBIR grants can be awarded only to domestic small businesses (entities that are independently owned, and operated for profit, are not dominant in the field in which research is proposed and have no more than 500 employees). Primary employment (more than one-half time) of the principal investigator must be with the small business at the time of award and during the conduct of the proposed project. In both Phase I and Phase II, the research must be performed in the U.S. and its possessions. To be eligible for funding, a grant application must be approved for scientific merit and Program relevance by a scientific review group and a national advisory council. STTR grants can be awarded only to domestic small business concerns (entities that are independently owned and operated for profit, are not dominant in the field in which research is proposed and have no more than 500 employees) which "partner" with a research institution in cooperative research and development. At least 40 percent of the project is to be performed by the small business concern and at least 30 percent by the research institution. In both Phase I and Phase II, the research must be performed in the U.S. and its possessions. To be eligible for funding, a grant application must be approved for scientific merit and Program relevance by a scientific review group and a national advisory council.

Beneficiary Eligibility: Any nonprofit or for-profit organization, company, or institution engaged in biomedical research.

Award Range/Average: Range: $25,595 to $23,766,226 Average: $493,164

Funding: (Cooperative Agreements) FY 18 $574,536,000.00; FY 19 est $593,700,377.00; FY 20 est $551,694,959.00

HQ: ORRPC DEA NCI 9609 Medical Center Drive 7th Floor W Tower 7W530, PO Box 9750, Rockville, MD 20850

Phone: 240-276-6442 | Email: shamala@mail.nih.gov

http://www.cancer.gov/cancertopics/treatment

HHS93.834 | CAPACITY BUILDING ASSISTANCE (CBA) FOR HIGH-IMPACT HIV PREVENTION
"CBA for High-Impact HIV Prevention"

Award: Cooperative Agreements

Purpose: To reduce morbidity and mortality by preventing cases and complications of HIV and other sexually transmitted diseases by building the capacity of healthcare organizations, community based organizations, and State and local health departments. The grants and cooperative agreements may be for training, technical assistance, or information dissemination; HIV testing and diagnosis; interventions and strategies that support targeted HIV prevention and the HIV care continuum; and use of data for program quality improvement.

Programs Administered by Federal Headquarters

Applicant Eligibility: Any State, and, in consultation with the appropriate State Health Authority, any political subdivision of a State, including American Indian/Alaska Native tribal Governments or tribal Organizations located wholly or in part within their boundaries.

Beneficiary Eligibility: Official public health agencies of State and local governments, including the District of Columbia, the Commonwealth of Puerto Rico, the Virgin Islands, Guam, the Northern Mariana Islands, the Federated States of Micronesia, the Republic of the Marshall Islands, the Republic of Palau, and American Samoa.

Funding: (Cooperative Agreements) FY 18 $0.00; FY 19 est $29,049,992.00; FY 20 est $24,049,992.00

HQ: 1600 Clifton Road NE, PO Box E07, Atlanta, GA 30333

Phone: 404-639-1877 | Email: lrw3@cdc.gov

http://www.cdc.gov

HHS93.733 | CAPACITY BUILDING ASSISTANCE TO STRENGTHEN PUBLIC HEALTH IMMUNIZATION INFRASTRUCTURE AND PERFORMANCE-FINANCED IN PART BY THE PREVENTION AND PUBLIC HEALTH FUND (PPHF)
"Immunization Program - 2012 Prevention and Public Health Fund and Other Capacity-Building Activities"

Award: Cooperative Agreements

Purpose: The program improves the efficiency, effectiveness, and/or quality of immunization practices by strengthening the immunization information technology infrastructure, building capacity for public health department insurance billing, and expanding immunization delivery partnerships so that more children, adolescents, and adults are protected against vaccine-preventable diseases.

Applicant Eligibility: Eligibility is limited to the current 64 CDC Immunization Program grantees and some Program areas have more specific criteria. Private individuals; private, nonprofit agencies; and Indian Tribes are not eligible.

Beneficiary Eligibility: Any U.S. state, political subdivision and U.S. territories (as described above), and other public entities will benefit.

Award Range/Average: Awards will range from approximately $25,000 to $900,000 with an average of approximately $300,000.

Funding: (Cooperative Agreements) FY 18 $2,673,010.00; FY 19 est $0.00; FY 20 est Estimate Not Available

HQ: 1600 Clifton Road NE, PO Box 19, Atlanta, GA 30333

Phone: 404-639-7824 | Email: ibr0@cdc.gov

http://www.cdc.gov

USDA10.326 | CAPACITY BUILDING FOR NON-LAND GRANT COLLEGES OF AGRICULTURE (NLGCA)

Award: Project Grants

Purpose: To encourage the NLGCA institutions to instruct on education, research, agriculture, and renewable resources.

Applicant Eligibility: Only a non-land-grant public college or University (NLGCA) offering a baccalaureate or higher degree in the study of agriculture or forestry. The terms "NLGCA Institution" and "non-land-grant college of agriculture" do not include - (i) Hispanic-serving agricultural colleges and universities; or (ii) any institution designated under - (I) the Act of July 2, 1862 (commonly known as the "First Morrill Act"; 7 U.S.C. 301 et seq.); (II) the Act of August 30, 1890 (commonly known as the "Second Morrill Act") (7 U.S.C. 321 et seq.); (III) the Equity in educational Land-Grant Status Act of 1994 (Public Law 103-382; 7 U.S.C. 301 note); or (IV) Public Law 87-788 (commonly known as the "McIntire-Stennis Cooperative Forestry Act") (16 U.S.C. 582a et seq.).

Beneficiary Eligibility: A non-land-grant public college or university offering a baccalaureate or higher degree in the study of agriculture or forestry, faculty of NLGCA, students engaged in the study of agriculture or forestry, the public, interested members of the agriculture, renewable resources, and other relevant and interested communities.

Award Range/Average: If minimum or maximum amounts of funding per competitive and/or capacity project grant, or cooperative agreement are established, these amounts will be announced in the annual Competitive Request for Application (RFA).The most current RFA is available via: https://nifa.usda.gov/funding-opportunity/capacity-building-grants-non-land-grant-colleges-agriculture-program-nlgca

Funding: (Project Grants (Cooperative Agreements)) FY 17 $4,790,100.00; FY 18 est $4,736,100.00; FY 19 est $0.00

HQ: Institute of Youth Family and Community 1400 Independence Avenue SW, PO Box 2250, Washington, DC 20250-2250
  Phone: 202-720-1973 | Email: edwin.lewis@nifa.usda.gov
  http://nifa.usda.gov/program/capacity-building-grants-non-land-grant-colleges-agriculture-program

DOJ16.746 | CAPITAL CASE LITIGATION INITIATIVE
"CCLI"

Award: Project Grants
Purpose: The Capital Case Litigation Initiative provides assistance to prosecutors in litigation capital cases. The Wrongful Conviction Review Program prevents wrongful convictions.
Applicant Eligibility: Capital Case Litigation Initiative: Applicants are limited to state agencies in states that authorize capital punishment and that conduct, or will conduct prosecutions in which capital punishment is sought. For the state agency to be eligible, its state must have an effective system for providing competent legal representation for indigent defendants in capital cases. An effective system is defined in 42 U.S.C. 14163(e) as a system that invests the responsibility for appointing qualified attorneys to represent indigent defendants in capital cases either: (A) In a public defender Program that relies on staff attorneys, members of the private bar, or both, to provide representation in capital cases; (B) In an entity established by statute or by the highest state court with jurisdiction in criminal cases, which is composed of individuals with demonstrated knowledge and expertise in capital cases, except for individuals employed as prosecutors; or (C) Pursuant to a statutory procedure enacted before the date of the enactment of the CCLI Act [October 30, 2002] under which the trial judge is required to appoint qualified attorneys from a roster maintained by a state or regional selection committee or similar entity. Wrongful Conviction Review Program - Eligible applicants are limited to Institutions of higher education, non-profit Organizations with missions dedicated (in whole or in part) to exonerating the innocent, to state or local public defender offices, as well as to public and nonprofit Organizations that have experience and expertise in providing representation to wrongfully convicted defendants in post-conviction claims of innocence cases.
Beneficiary Eligibility: Capital Case Litigation Initiative: Defense counsel, prosecutors and judges in the States, the District of Columbia, the Commonwealth of Puerto Rico, the Virgin Islands, America Samoa, Guam, and the Northern Mariana Islands that currently enforce their death penalty statutes. Wrongful Conviction Review Program: State or local government public defenders and non-profit organizations dedicated to exonerating the innocent.
Award Range/Average: See the current fiscal year's solicitation available at www.bja.gov.
Funding: (Project Grants) FY 18 $2,684,411.00; FY 19 est $5,000,000.00; FY 20 est $3,000,000.00
HQ: U.S. Department of Justice Bureau of Justice Assistance 810 7th Street NW, Washington, DC 20531
  Phone: 202-616-6500
  https://www.bja.gov/ProgramDetails.aspx?Program_ID=52

TREAS21.011 | CAPITAL MAGNET FUND
"CMF"

Award: Project Grants
Purpose: To attract financing for and increase investment in affordable housing for low-income, very low-income, and extremely low-income people.
Applicant Eligibility: Applicants must be (1) a Treasury certified CDFI; or (2) a nonprofit Organization having as one of its principal purposes the development or management of affordable housing.
Beneficiary Eligibility: Low income, very low-income, and extremely low-income people as set forth in 12 C.F.R. Part 1807.
Award Range/Average: FY 2018 Range of CMF Awards was from $562,500 to $7,500,000. The average FY 2018 Award was $3,760,963. The maximum allowable award by statute is 15% of the annual available funding.
Funding: (Project Grants) FY 18 $1,429,916,610.00; FY 19 est $131,000,000.00; FY 20 est $110,000,000.00
HQ: Capital Magnet Fund 1500 Pennsylvania Avenue NW, Washington, DC 20220
  Phone: 202-653-0300
  http://www.cdfifund.gov

Programs Administered by Federal Headquarters

HHS93.799 | CARA ACT-COMPREHENSIVE ADDICTION AND RECOVERY ACT OF 2016
"CARA"

Award: Project Grants

Purpose: Prevents and reduces the abuse of opioids or methamphetamines and the abuse of prescription medications among youth ages 12-18 in communities throughout the United States. Grants awarded through the CARA Act are intended as an enhancement to current or formerly funded Drug-Free Communities Support Program grant award recipients as established community-based youth substance use prevention coalitions capable of effecting community-level change.

Applicant Eligibility: The statutory authority for this Program, 42 USC 1536 of the Comprehensive Addiction and Recovery Act, limits eligibility to domestic public and private nonprofit entities that are current or former Drug-Free Communities (DFC) Support Program recipients. Eligible applicants are community-based coalitions addressing local youth opioid, methamphetamine, and/or prescription medication abuse. The purpose of this Program is to prevent and reduce the abuse of opioids or methamphetamines and the abuse of prescription medications among youth ages 12-18 in communities throughout the United States.

Beneficiary Eligibility: The purpose of this program is to prevent and reduce the abuse of opioids or methamphetamines and the abuse of prescription medications among youth ages 12-18 in communities throughout the United States*For the purposes of this FOA, "youth" is defined as individuals 18 years of age and younger.

Award Range/Average: Anticipated Total Available Funding: $2,750,000 Estimated Award Amount:Up to $50,000

Funding: (Salaries and Expenses) FY 18 est $2,744,145.00; FY 19 est $2,744,145.00; FY 20 est $2,744,145.00

HQ: Formula Grants Branch 5600 Fishers Lane, Rockville, MD 20857

Phone: 240-276-1078 | Email: odessa.crocker@samhsa.hhs.gov

http://www.samhsa.gov

HHS93.837 | CARDIOVASCULAR DISEASES RESEARCH

Award: Project Grants

Purpose: To foster heart and vascular research in the basic, translational, clinical and population sciences, and to foster training to build talented young investigators in these areas.

Applicant Eligibility: Any nonprofit Organization engaged in biomedical research and Institutions or companies organized for profit may apply for almost any kind of grant. Only domestic, non-profit, private or public Institutions may apply for NRSA Institutional Research Training Grants. An individual may apply for an NRSA or, in some cases, for a research grant if adequate facilities to perform the research are available. SBIR grants can be awarded only to United States small business concerns (entities that are independently owned and operated for profit or owned by another small business that itself is independently owned and operated for profit, are not dominant in the field in which research is proposed and have no more than 500 employees including affiliates). Primary employment (more than one-half time) of the principal investigator must be with the small business at the time of award and during the conduct of the proposed project. In both Phase I and Phase II, the research must be performed in the U.S. or its possessions. To be eligible for funding, a grant application must be approved for scientific merit and Program relevance by a scientific review group and a national advisory council. SBIR projects must be performed at least 67% by the applicant small business in Phase I and at least 50% of the Project in Phase II. STTR grants can be awarded only to United States small business concerns (entities that are independently owned and operated for profit and have no more than 500 employees) that formally collaborate with a University or other non-profit research institution in cooperative research and development. The principal investigator of an STTR award may be employed with either the small business concern or collaborating non-profit research institution as long as s/he has a formal appointment with or commitment to the applicant small business concern. At least 40% of the project is to be performed by the small business concern and at least 30% by the non-profit research institution. In both Phase I and Phase II, the research must be performed in the U.S. and its possessions.

Beneficiary Eligibility: Any nonprofit or for-profit organization, company or institution engaged in biomedical research. Only domestic for-profit small business firms may apply for SBIR and STTR programs.

Award Range/Average: Grants: $2,710 to $18,967,704; $448,135. SBIR Phase I - $150,000; Phase II - up to $1,000,000; STTR Phase I - $100,000, Phase II - $750,000.

Funding: (Project Grants) FY 18 $1,478,233,004.00; FY 19 est $1,498,851,933.00; FY 20 est $1,498,851,933.00

HQ: 6701 Rockledge Drive, Room 7176, Bethesda, MD 20892

Phone: 301-827-7968 | Email: pharesda@nhlbi.nih.gov

http://www.nhlbi.nih.gov/about/scientific-divisions/division-cardiovascular-sciences

ED84.048 | CAREER AND TECHNICAL EDUCATION-BASIC GRANTS TO STATES

Award: Formula Grants

Purpose: To develop academic, career, and technical skills for secondary and postsecondary students who enroll in career and technical education programs.

Applicant Eligibility: The Department of education makes formula grants to State boards for career and technical education or the agency responsible for overseeing career and technical education in States. Eligible recipients for subgrants include local educational agencies and postsecondary Institutions.

Beneficiary Eligibility: A wide range of individuals pursuing career and technical education will benefit.

Award Range/Average: The range or awards in FY 2019 was $5,037,372 to $127,058,834.

Funding: (Formula Grants) FY 18 $1,173,158,653.00; FY 19 est $1,242,017,053.00; FY 20 est $1,242,017,053.00

HQ: Department of Education OCTAE Division of High School Postsecondary and Career Education 400 Maryland Avenue SW, Washington, DC 20202

Phone: 202-245-7846 | Email: sharon.miller@ed.gov

http://cte.ed.gov

ED84.051 | CAREER AND TECHNICAL EDUCATION-NATIONAL PROGRAMS

Award: Project Grants

Purpose: To support directly or through grants, contracts, or cooperative agreements, for research, development, demonstration, dissemination, evaluation, assessment, capacity-building, and technical assistance activities to improve the quality and effectiveness of career and technical education (CTE) programs authorized under the Perkins Act IV.

Applicant Eligibility: Depending on the activity to be funded, eligible applicants may include Institutions of higher education or consortia of Institutions of higher education, public or private nonprofit Organizations, or consortia thereof, and State boards designated as the sole State agencies for the administration of State career and technical education, or consortia thereof.

Beneficiary Eligibility: CTE sole State agencies; local educational agencies; CTE providers, and CTE students.

Award Range/Average: Varies by program competition.

Funding: (Project Grants) FY 18 est $7,421,000.00; FY 19 $7,421,000.00; FY 20 est $20,000,000.00

HQ: Department of Education OCTAE Division of Academic and Technical Education 400 Maryland Avenue SW, Washington, DC 20202

Phone: 202-245-7767 | Email: robin.utz@ed.gov

http://www2.ed.gov/programs/venp/index.html

ED84.101 | CAREER AND TECHNICAL EDUCATION-GRANTS TO NATIVE AMERICANS AND ALASKA NATIVES

Award: Project Grants

Purpose: To make grants, cooperative agreements, or enter into contracts with Indian tribes, tribal organizations, Alaska Native entities, plan, conduct, and administer programs or authorized programs by and consistent with the Carl D. Perkins Career and Technical Education Act of 2006.

Applicant Eligibility: Federally recognized Indian Tribes, tribal Organizations, Alaska Native entities, and consortia of any of these entities may apply. Additionally, Bureau-funded schools proposing to use their award to assist secondary schools operated and supported by the U.S. Department of the Interior to carry out career and technical education Programs may apply.

Beneficiary Eligibility: Federally recognized Indian tribes, tribal organizations, and Alaska Natives, and Bureau-funded schools except for Bureau-funded schools proposing to use their grants to support secondary school CTE programs.

Award Range/Average: Range: $300,000- $600,000 Average award: $450,000

Funding: (Project Grants) FY 18 $14,907,475.00; FY 19 est $15,782,475.00; FY 20 est $15,782,475.00

HQ: Department of Education OCTAE Division of Academic and Technical Education 400 Maryland Avenue SW, Washington, DC 20202-7241

Phone: 202-245-7792 | Email: linda.mayo@ed.gov

http://cte.ed.gov/grants/discretionary-grants

Programs Administered by Federal Headquarters

HHS93.456 | CDC UNDERGRADUATE PUBLIC HEALTH SCHOLARS PROGRAM (CUPS): A PUBLIC HEALTH EXPERIENCE TO EXPOSE UNDERGRADUATES INTERESTED IN MINORITY HEALTH TO PUBLIC HEALTH AND THE PUBLIC HEALTH PROFESSIONS

Award: Cooperative Agreements

Purpose: To implement a national summer training program to introduce undergraduate and graduate students, including but not limited to those from under-represented and underserved racial and ethnic minority populations, to public health and biomedical sciences.

Applicant Eligibility: Funds are to be used for recruitment, orientation, placement, mentorship and follow-up tracking of undergraduate and graduate students.

Beneficiary Eligibility: OMHHE will collaborate with educational institutions, including those serving minority populations, to increase the knowledge, diversity, and skills of students in public health through internship and fellowship programs.

Award Range/Average: $2,745,067 to $3,000,000.

Funding: (Cooperative Agreements) FY 18 $6,865,888.00; FY 19 est $7,100,051.00; FY 20 est $7,200,000.00

HQ: 2900 Woodcock Boulevard, Atlanta, GA 30013

   Phone: 770-488-1387

   http://www.cdc.gov

HHS93.967 | CDC'S COLLABORATION WITH ACADEMIA TO STRENGTHEN PUBLIC HEALTH

Award: Cooperative Agreements

Purpose: The Funding Opportunity Announcement seeks to catalyze innovative efforts to provide public health professionals, students, and faculty with the competencies and knowledge to reduce the leading causes of death and illness and build workforce capacity to transform the health system and improve population health.

Applicant Eligibility: Open Competition Eligible applicants are groups and Organizations that are: A national voice and representative Organization for their respective accredited academic constituency member schools or Programs; Able to demonstrate evidence of existing and prior collaboration with all or the majority of Council on education for Public Health (CEPH)-accredited schools or Programs of public health, Liaison Committee on Medical education (LCME)-accredited medical colleges; and, Committee on Collegiate Nursing education (CCNE)-accredited colleges of nursing at the baccalaureate or higher level; National in scope in order to ensure the broadest coverage; Engaged in established liaison relationships with related accreditation agency for their respective professional target audience; Experienced in implementing community-based activities to improve health; Experienced in convening deans or representative faculty of respective academic constituency schools; Experienced with influencing curriculum standards or requirements of membership schools; Experienced in working across disciplines at the national, regional, state, and/or community level to improve health; and Possess the Organizational and administrative capacity, skill, and expertise to perform the stated activities contained in the funding announcement.

Beneficiary Eligibility: State, local, Non-profits.

Award Range/Average: Total Project Funding $1,698,035,000 Average One Year Award Funding: $200,000 per awardee

Funding: (Cooperative Agreements (Discretionary Grants)) FY 18 $2,227,464.00; FY 19 est $2,200,000.00; FY 20 est $2,499,999.00

HQ: 1600 Clifton Road NE, PO Box 24-6, Atlanta, GA 30345

   Phone: 404-498-0518 | Email: smccarthy@cdc.gov

   http://www.cdc.gov

DOC11.478 | CENTER FOR SPONSORED COASTAL OCEAN RESEARCH COASTAL OCEAN PROGRAM
"CSCOR/COP"

Award: Cooperative Agreements; Project Grants

Purpose: NOAA's Coastal Ocean Program assists in managing coastal ecosystems. CSCOR/COP supports high-priority research and detects harmful algal blooms and hypoxia. CSCOR/COP supports research on critical issues and Gulf of Mexico ecosystem for its fish stocks, wildlife, and fishing industries.

Applicant Eligibility: Institutions of higher education, not-for- profit Institutions, State, local and Indian tribal Governments, commercial Organizations and Federal agencies. Foreign researchers may apply as subawards through an eligible US entity. All applicants will be treated equally in the competitive process.

Beneficiary Eligibility: Organizations and individuals utilizing science in effectively managing the Nation's coastal resources.

Funding: (Cooperative Agreements) FY 16 $7,728,299.00; FY 17 est $9,000,000.00; FY 18 est $9,000,000.00

HQ: 1305 E W Highway SSMC4 Station 8307, Silver Spring, MD 20910

Phone: 301-713-3338

http://coastalscience.noaa.gov/about/centers/cscor

DOD12.598 | CENTERS FOR ACADEMIC EXCELLENCE
"Intelligence Community Centers for Academic Excellence"

Award: Project Grants

Purpose: To enhance the recruitment and retention of an ethnically and culturally diverse intelligence community workforce with capabilities critical to the national security interests.

Applicant Eligibility: N/A

Beneficiary Eligibility: N/A

Award Range/Average: $250,000 - $300,000 per year

Funding: (Salaries and Expenses) FY 18 $14,015,447.00; FY 19 est $2,892,361.00; FY 20 est 0.00

HQ: ADI4A 200 MacDill Boulevard Joint Base Bolling Anacostia, Washington, DC 20340

Phone: 202-231-4457 | Email: tonia.smith@dodiis.mil

HHS93.425 | CENTERS FOR DISEASE CONTROL AND PREVENTION-RESIDENT POSTDOCTORAL PROGRAM IN MICROBIOLOGY
"CDC Resident Postdoctoral Program in Microbiology"

Award: Cooperative Agreements

Purpose: To conduct a resident postdoctoral fellowship program in microbiology in infectious diseases laboratories at the Centers for Disease Control and Prevention (CDC).

Applicant Eligibility: Eligible applicants must have experience and demonstrated success in administering training Programs in public health laboratory/microbiology research or other life sciences.

Beneficiary Eligibility: This program contributes to developing a public health laboratory workforce for the diagnosis, prevention and control of infectious diseases in the United States and abroad. The nation's public is the ultimate recipient of benefits from this program.

Award Range/Average: Awards have ranged from $500k - $1.3M for FY2012-FY2018.

HQ: 1600 Clifton Road NE, PO Box C18, Atlanta, GA 30329

Phone: 404-639-7722 | Email: aslaughter@cdc.gov

http://www.cdc.gov

HHS93.283 | CENTERS FOR DISEASE CONTROL AND PREVENTION INVESTIGATIONS AND TECHNICAL ASSISTANCE
"CDC, Technical Assistance, Vital Statistics"

Award: Cooperative Agreements

Purpose: To assist State and local health authorities and other health related organizations in controlling communicable diseases, chronic diseases and disorders, and other preventable health conditions.

Applicant Eligibility: States, political subdivisions of States, local health authorities, Federally recognized or state recognized American Indian/Alaska Native tribal Governments and Organizations with specialized health interests may apply. Colleges, universities, private nonprofit and public nonprofit domestic Organizations, research Institutions, faith-based Organizations, and managed care Organizations for some specific Programs such as Diabetes.

Beneficiary Eligibility: States, political subdivisions of States, local health authorities, and individuals or organizations with specialized health interests will benefit. Colleges, universities, private non-profit and public nonprofit domestic organizations, research institutions, faith-based organizations, and managed care organizations for some specific programs such as Diabetes.

Programs Administered by Federal Headquarters

Funding: (Cooperative Agreements) FY 18 $6,564,572.00; FY 19 Not Separately Identifiable; FY 20 $0.00; Because this is a CDC-wide CFDA# this is to identify the HHS/CDC CSELS/DHIS portion/update for: FY14 ($6,695,957), FY15 ($6,565,572) and FY16 ($6564572) and FY17 (6564572) above NCCDPHP funding for this NOFO FY16($5,455,639), FY17($5,782,651), FY18($5,481,262) these programs will end FY19.

HQ: 4770 Buford Highway NE, Atlanta, GA 30341

Phone: 770-488-5314 | Email: ehill@cdc.gov

http://www.cdc.gov

DHS97.061 | CENTERS FOR HOMELAND SECURITY
"COE"

Award: Cooperative Agreements; Project Grants

Purpose: The program funds homeland-security led research and education work at U.S. colleges and universities.

Applicant Eligibility: Eligible applicants are accredited U.S. Institutions of higher education.

Beneficiary Eligibility: Public and private colleges and universities.

Funding: (Salaries and Expenses) FY 18 est $24,731,500.00; FY 19 est $25,550,000.00; FY 20 est $14,250,000.00

HQ: Department of Homeland Security University Programs S and T 245 Murray Lane Building 410, PO Box 0205, Washington, DC 20523

Phone: 202-254-8680 | Email: matthew.coats@hq.dhs.gov

http://www.hsuniversityprograms.org

ED84.220 | CENTERS FOR INTERNATIONAL BUSINESS EDUCATION

Award: Project Grants

Purpose: To provide a comprehensive university approach to improve the teaching of international business and to engage in research to promote the international competitiveness of U.S. business.

Applicant Eligibility: Accredited public and nonprofit private Institutions of higher education, or consortia of such Institutions, that establish a center advisory council before the date Federal assistance is received may apply. This council will conduct extensive planning concerning the scope of the center's activities and the design of its Program prior to establishing the center.

Beneficiary Eligibility: Students and faculty of accredited institutions of higher education will benefit.

Award Range/Average: FY 2018: Average award was $285,712; Awards ranged from $265,000- $305,000.

Funding: (Project Grants) FY 18 $4,571,000.00; FY 19 est $4,571,000.00; FY 20est $0.00

HQ: International and Foreign Language Education Department of Education 400 Maryland Avenue SW, Washington, DC 20202

Phone: 202-453-7521 | Email: timothy.duvall@ed.gov

http://www.ed.gov/programs/iegpscibe

HHS93.779 | CENTERS FOR MEDICARE AND MEDICAID SERVICES (CMS) RESEARCH, DEMONSTRATIONS AND EVALUATIONS
"CMS Research"

Award: Project Grants

Purpose: The Centers for Medicare & Medicaid Services conducts research, demonstrations, and evaluations in support of CMS' key role as a beneficiary-centered purchaser of high-quality healthcare at a reasonable cost.

Applicant Eligibility: Grants or cooperative agreements may be made to private, or public agencies or Organizations, including State agencies that administer the Medicaid Program. Private profit Organizations may apply.

Beneficiary Eligibility: All Medicare and Medicaid beneficiaries are eligible.

Award Range/Average: Not determined at this time.

Funding: (Cooperative Agreements) FY 18 $500,000.00; FY 19 est $500,000.00; FY 20 est $500,000.00

HQ: Office of Research Center for Strategic Planning 7500 Security Boulevard, Baltimore, MD 21244

Phone: 800-633-4277

http://www.cms.hhs.gov/contracts

HHS93.135 | CENTERS FOR RESEARCH AND DEMONSTRATION FOR HEALTH PROMOTION AND DISEASE PREVENTION
"Prevention Research Centers"

Award: Cooperative Agreements

Purpose: To establish, maintain, and operate multi-disciplinary academic-based centers that conduct high-quality applied health promotion and disease prevention research.

Applicant Eligibility: Eligible applicants are accredited schools of medicine, schools of osteopathy, and schools of public health as defined in Section 701 (4) of Public Health Service Act.

Beneficiary Eligibility: Academic health centers, scientist/researchers, operational public health programs, targeted high risk groups, selected demonstration areas, and the general public.

Funding: (Cooperative Agreements) FY 18 $38,168,000.00; FY 19 est $0.00; FY 20 est $0.00

HQ: 4770 Buford Highway NE, Atlanta, GA 30341

　　Phone: 770-488-6384

　　http://www.cdc.gov/prc

USDA10.523 | CENTERS OF EXCELLENCE AT 1890 INSTITUTIONS
"1890 COES"

Award: Project Grants (discretionary)

Purpose: Aims to fund for the three federally-funded Centers of Excellence, and thereby improve the prosperity of underserved rural farming communities.

Applicant Eligibility: Applications may only be submitted by 1890 Land-grant Institutions and Tuskegee University.

Beneficiary Eligibility: N/A

Award Range/Average: If minimum or maximum amounts of funding per competitive and/or capacity project grant, or cooperative agreement are established, these amounts will be announced in the annual Request for Applications (RFA). The most current RFA is available via: (NOTE: Insert hyperlink for Program's funding opportunity here.)

Funding: (Project Grants (Discretionary)) Fy 18 $0; FY 19 est $4,800,000; FY 20 est $0

HQ: 1400 Independence Avenue SW, PO Box 2250, Washington, DC 20250-2250

　　Phone: 202-720-5305 | Email: edwin.lewis@nifa.usda.gov

HHS93.157 | CENTERS OF EXCELLENCE
"COE"

Award: Project Grants

Purpose: To assist eligible schools in supporting programs of excellence in health professions education for underrepresented minority (URM) individuals.

Applicant Eligibility: Eligible applicants include designated HBCUs and health professions schools that are accredited schools of allopathic medicine; osteopathic medicine; dentistry; pharmacy; or a graduate Program in behavioral or mental health; or other public and nonprofit health or educational entities that meet the required conditions regarding: underrepresented minorities as described in Section 736 of the Public Health Service Act. Native American Centers of Excellence are eligible, as specified in statute. Eligible applicants must also have: (1) a significant number of underrepresented minority individuals enrolled in the schools; (2) been effective in assisting underrepresented minority students of the schools to complete the Program of education and receive the degree involved; (3) been effective in recruiting underrepresented minority individuals to enroll in and graduate from the school, including providing scholarships and other financial assistance to such individuals and encouraging underrepresented minority students from all levels of the educational pipeline to pursue health professions careers; and(4) made significant recruitment efforts to increase the number of underrepresented minority individuals serving in faculty or administrative positions at the school.

Beneficiary Eligibility: Designated HBCUs and eligible health professions schools must recruit and train a significant number of underrepresented minority students in medicine, dentistry, and pharmacy; recruit, train, and retain underrepresented minority faculty recruitment; and facilitate faculty and student research activities.

Award Range/Average: HBCUs: FY 2016 actual: $2,339,598 to $3,498,237; Average: $3,000,000 FY 2017actual: $2,502,475 to $3,499,317; Average: $3,000,000 FY 2018 est.: $2,753,488 to $3,177,641; Average: $3,000,000 Non-HBCUs: FY 2016 actual: $620,509 to $700,000: Average: $676,427 FY 2017 est.: $ 606,099 to $693,000: Average: $660,250 FY 2018 est.: $ 666,526 to $700,000; Average: $692,192

Programs Administered by Federal Headquarters

Funding: (Project Grants) FY 18 $22,385,267.00; FY 19 est $22,415,585.00; FY 20 est $0.00
HQ: Department of Health and Human Services 5600 Fishers Lane, Room 15N-62C, Rockville, MD 20857
    Phone: 301-443-0550 | Email: dsellers-mccarthy@hrsa.gov
    http://bhw.hrsa.gov/grants/healthcareers

HHS93.355 | CERTIFIED HEALTH IT SURVEILLANCE CAPACITY AND INFRASTRUCTURE IMPROVEMENT COOPERATIVE AGREEMENT PROGRAM
"Surveillance Capacity Cooperative Agreement"
Award: Cooperative Agreements
Purpose: To implement and use the most advanced health information technology (health IT) and the electronic exchange of health information.
Applicant Eligibility: The purpose of these cooperative agreements is to support ONC's mission to improving the surveillance capacity and infrastructure that exists for health IT certified under the ONC Health IT Certification Program, with a particular focus on capabilities that are directly related to interoperability.
Beneficiary Eligibility: The purpose of this cooperative agreement is to advance the market's ability to electronically exchange health information through the use of certified health IT and to ensure that the products function in the production environment in the form and manner they are certified to. While the beneficiaries are ultimately the broader public at-large, the direct beneficiaries include those who work directly with certified health IT products.
Award Range/Average: There has been $1,250,000 allocated for FFY17-18 for this award. We estimate that we will award one (1) to three (3) awards total; the award amounts will range between $400,000 - $1,250,000 and may not exceed $1,250,000 in total. The award amount will be determined upon the documentation, scope, and strength the awardee's proposal.
Funding: (Cooperative Agreements) FY 16 Estimate Not Available; FY 17 est $1,250,000.00; FY 18 est Estimate Not Available
HQ: 330 C Street SW, Washington, DC 20201
    Phone: 202-720-2919 | Email: carmel.halloun@hhs.gov
    http://www.healthit.gov/certification

HHS93.599 | CHAFEE EDUCATION AND TRAINING VOUCHERS PROGRAM (ETV)
Award: Formula Grants
Purpose: Provides resources to states and eligible Indian tribes to make available vouchers for postsecondary training and education to youth who have experienced foster care at age 14 or older, who have aged of foster care, or who have been adopted or left for kinship guardianship from the public foster care system after age 16.
Applicant Eligibility: State Governments, including the 50 states, the District of Columbia, Puerto Rico, and U.S. Virgin Islands (hereafter "states"), Guam and American Samoa, and eligible Indian Tribes, Indian tribal Organizations, or Indian tribal consortia (hereafter "Tribes ") with an approved plan.
Beneficiary Eligibility: Youth and young adults who have experienced foster care at age 14 or older, youth who exited foster care or kinship guardianship at age 16 or older, and youth who aged out of foster care. Youth otherwise eligible for the John H. Chafee Foster Care Program for Successful Transition to Adulthood (Chafee program) may receive vouchers. Eligible youth may receive vouchers up until their 26th birthday, provided they are making satisfactory progress toward completing their course of study or training, but may receive vouchers for no more than five years.
Award Range/Average: FY 2017 States: $69,550 to $5,556,457 with an average of $816,208 per stateFY 2017 Tribes: $4,012 to $14,043 with an average of $7,083 per tribe
Funding: (Formula Grants) FY 18 $42,608,145.00; FY 19 est $42,461,573.00; FY 20 est $42,608,145.00
HQ: 330 C Street SW, Room 3508B, Washington, DC 20201
    Phone: 202-690-7888 | Email: catherine.heath@acf.hhs.gov
    http://www.acf.hhs.gov/programs/cb

VA64.039 | CHAMPVA
"USASpending.gov"
Award: Direct Payments for Specified Use
Purpose: To account for Veterans healthcarespending and display the spending by the beneficiary residence.
Applicant Eligibility: Dependents of Veterans are eligible for services under Title 38 USC 1781.
Beneficiary Eligibility: Same as Applicant Eligibility.

Award Range/Average: According to the cost of the services
HQ: 100 Grandview Road, Suite 114, Braintree, MA 02184
Phone: 781-849-1837 | Email: michelle.staton@va.gov
http://www.va.gov

DOS19.020 | CHARLES B. RANGEL INTERNATIONAL AFFAIRS PROGRAM
"Rangel Program"

Award: Cooperative Agreements; Project Grants
Purpose: Program develops a source of trained men and women, from academic fields representing the skill needs of the Department who are dedicated to representing America's interests abroad. It encourages the application of members of minority groups historically underrepresented in the Foreign Service, women and those with financial need. It develops a source of trained men and women, from academic fields representing the skill needs of the Department who are dedicated to representing America's interests abroad.
Applicant Eligibility: Assistance supports activities and financial obligations such as tuition costs, student travel, Program administration costs and other costs as they relate to the administration of the Charles B. Rangel international Affairs Program.
Beneficiary Eligibility: Applications may be submitted by public and private non-profit organizations. Please refer to Grant.gov for further eligibility criteria. OMB Circular No. A-87 applies to this program.
Award Range/Average: Please see obligations
HQ: HR/REE 2401 E Street NW SA-01, Room H-518, Washington, DC 20522
Phone: 202-261-8892 | Email: georgecm@state.gov

DHS97.040 | CHEMICAL STOCKPILE EMERGENCY PREPAREDNESS PROGRAM
"CSEPP"

Award: Cooperative Agreements
Purpose: The program assists local and State communities to plan ahead and respond to accidents that involve chemical weaponry.
Applicant Eligibility: Applications are accepted only from the State of Colorado and the Commonwealth of Kentucky. These eligible States house the U.S. Army stockpiles unitary chemical warfare agent as bulk chemicals and munitions. Local Governments are eligible to participate as subrecipients under their State's application.
Beneficiary Eligibility: State, local and tribal governments, and general public.
Award Range/Average: Refer to program guidance.
Funding: (Project Grants) FY 18 $40,786,923.00; FY 19 est $21,153,456.00; FY 20 est $27,485,272
HQ: FEMA 400 C Street SW, Washington, DC 20472-3025
Phone: 202-212-7961 | Email: terry.hobbs@fema.dhs.gov
http://www.fema.gov/technological-hazards-division-contacts

DOC11.457 | CHESAPEAKE BAY STUDIES

Award: Project Grants
Purpose: To compensate for research and development projects to acquire information on the living marine resources of Chesapeake Bay. The B-WET Program supports organizations that provide environment-based education to students and communities throughout the Chesapeake Bay watershed.
Applicant Eligibility: Eligible applicants are Institutions of higher education, hospitals, other nonprofits, commercial Organizations, foreign Governments, Organizations under the jurisdiction of foreign Governments, international Organizations, State, local and Indian tribal Governments.
Beneficiary Eligibility: Federal, State and local governments, universities, independent school divisions, nonprofit organizations, and the general public.
Funding: (Cooperative Agreements) FY 16 $3,406,725.00; FY 17 $3,406,725.00; FY 18 est Estimate Not Available
HQ: 1305 E W Highway, Silver Spring, MD 20910
Phone: 301-427-8771 | Email: jeffrey.kulnis@noaa.gov
http://noaa.chesapeakebay.net

Programs Administered by Federal Headquarters

HHS93.670 | CHILD ABUSE AND NEGLECT DISCRETIONARY ACTIVITIES

Award: Project Grants

Purpose: Improves the national, state, and community activities for the prevention, assessment, identification, and treatment of child abuse and neglect through research, demonstration, evaluation of best practices, dissemination of information, and technical assistance.

Applicant Eligibility: Grants: States, local Governments, Tribes, public agencies or private agencies or Organizations (or combinations of such agencies or Organizations) engaged in activities related to the prevention, identification, and treatment of child abuse and neglect. Contracts: Public and private agencies.

Beneficiary Eligibility: Children that have been abused or neglected, or that are at-risk for abuse or neglect, and their families.

Award Range/Average: FY 2017 grants ranged between $103,663 to $3,000,000 with an average award of $779,313.

Funding: (Project Grants (Discretionary)) FY 18 $18,437,969.00; FY 19 est $15,247,727.00; FY 20 est $12,243,259

HQ: 330 C Street SW, Room 3503, Washington, DC 20201

Phone: 202-205-8172 | Email: jan.shafer@acf.hhs.gov

http://www.acf.hhs.gov/programs/cb

HHS93.669 | CHILD ABUSE AND NEGLECT STATE GRANTS
"CAPTA state grants"

Award: Formula Grants

Purpose: Assists States in the support and improvement of their child protective services systems.

Applicant Eligibility: This includes States, the District of Columbia, Puerto Rico, Guam, the U.S. Virgin Islands, American Samoa, and the Commonwealth of the Northern Mariana Islands.

Beneficiary Eligibility: There are no eligibility requirements associated with the beneficiaries of these funds (abused and neglected children and their families).

Award Range/Average: In FY 2017 grants ranged from $55,163 to $2,795,812 with an average award of $450,511.

Funding: (Formula Grants) FY 18 $85,285,000.00; FY 19 est $85,000,000.00; FY 20 est $84,185,000.00

HQ: 330 C Street SW, Room 3512, Washington, DC 20201

Phone: 202-205-8552 | Email: gail.collins@acf.hhs.gov

http://www.acf.dhhs.gov/programs/cb

ED84.335 | CHILD CARE ACCESS MEANS PARENTS IN SCHOOL

Award: Project Grants

Purpose: Supports the participation of low-income parents in postsecondary education through the provision of campus-based childcare services.

Applicant Eligibility: An institution of higher education is eligible to apply if the total amount of all Federal Pell Grant funds awarded to students enrolled at the institution of higher education for the preceding fiscal year equals or exceeds $350,000.

Beneficiary Eligibility: Low-income student parents enrolled in postsecondary programs will benefit.

Award Range/Average: $10,000 - $300,000

Funding: (Project Grants) FY 18 $50,000,000.00; FY 19 est $50,000,000.00; FY 20 est $15,134,000.00

HQ: Department of Education Higher Education Programs 400 Maryland Avenue SW, Washington, DC 20202

Phone: 202-453-5649 | Email: antionette.edwards@ed.gov

http://www.ed.gov/programs/campisp

HHS93.596 | CHILD CARE MANDATORY AND MATCHING FUNDS OF THE CHILD CARE AND DEVELOPMENT FUND
"Child Care and Development Fund (CCDF)"

Award: Formula Grants

Purpose: The childcare and Development Fund is the primary federal funding source to help certain low-income families access childcare and to improve the quality of childcare for all children.

Applicant Eligibility: All 50 States, the District of Columbia, and Federally recognized Tribal Governments, including Alaskan Native Corporations.

Beneficiary Eligibility: Children under age 13 (or, at the option of the grantee, up to age 19, if physically or mentally incapable of self-care or under court supervision), who (1) reside with a family whose income does not exceed 85 percent of the State median income for a family of the same size, and (2) who reside with a parent (or parents) who is working or attending job training or educational program, who or are in need of, or are receiving protective services. A Lead Agency shall re-determine a child's eligibility for child care services no sooner than 12 months following the initial determination or most recent re-determination. Once determined eligible, children are expected to receive a minimum of 12 months of child care services, unless family income rises above 85% SMI or, at Lead Agency option, the family experiences a non-temporary cessation of work, education, or training.

Award Range/Average: For States, including DC, the range of grants in FY 2018 is: $ 9,254,429 to $ 515,678,905; the average grant is $ 90,158,455. For 243 Tribal grantees, the range of grants in FY 2018 is: $4,444 to $6,892,551; the average grant is $240,082. These figures are not inclusive of funds received through CFDA 93.575.

Funding: (Formula Grants) FY 18 $2,946,142,984.00; FY 19 est $2,887,830,000.00; FY 20 est $3,179,880,000.00

HQ: 330 C Street SW, Washington, DC 20201

Phone: 202-401-2113 | Email: abdihakin.abdi@acf.hhs.gov

http://www.acf.hhs.gov/programs/occ

HHS93.312 | CHILD DEVELOPMENT AND SURVEILLANCE, RESEARCH AND PREVENTION

Award: Cooperative Agreements

Purpose: Supports State health agencies, universities, and public and private nonprofit organizations in planning, implementing, coordinating, or evaluating programs related to promoting optimal child health.

Applicant Eligibility: N/A

Beneficiary Eligibility: In addition to the eligible applicants, other groups who will receive benefits from the program include persons with or at-risk for developmental delays, developmental disabilities, mental disorders, or neurobehavioural disorders such as Attention-Deficit/Hyperactivity Disorder, Tourette syndrome and the conditions that co-occur with them; family members of persons with or at-risk for developmental delays, developmental disabilities, mental disorders, or neurobehavioural disorders such as Attention-Deficit/Hyperactivity Disorder, Tourette syndrome and the conditions that co-occur with them; minority populations, including Spanish speaking populations, infants, children, youth, adults; Federally Recognized Indian Tribal Governments; individual and families; educators, health care professionals, Private nonprofit institution/organizations and others.

Award Range/Average: The FY19/20 range is dependent upon funding availability. Awards amounts may range from $200,000 to $1,000,000.

Funding: (Cooperative Agreements) FY 18 $1,750,000.00; FY 19 est $1,750,000.00; FY 20 est $1,750,000.00

HQ: 1600 Clifton Road NE, PO Box 88, Atlanta, GA 30033

Phone: 404-498-4159

HHS93.865 | CHILD HEALTH AND HUMAN DEVELOPMENT EXTRAMURAL RESEARCH

"Child Health and Human Development"

Award: Project Grants

Purpose: To conduct and support laboratory research, clinical trials, and studies with people that explore health processes by examining the impact of disabilities, diseases, and defects on the lives of individuals. With this information, the NICHD hopes to restore, increase, and maximize the capabilities of people affected by disease and injury.

Applicant Eligibility: Universities, colleges, medical, dental and nursing schools, schools of public health, laboratories, hospitals, State and local health departments, other public or private Institutions, both nonprofit and for-profit, and individuals. National Research Service Award: Support is provided for academic and research training only, in health and health-related areas that are periodically specified by the National Institutes of Health. Individuals with a professional or scientific degree are eligible (M.D., Ph.D., D.D.S., D.O., D.V.M., Sc.D., D.Eng., or equivalent domestic or foreign degree). Predoctoral research training grants to Institutions are also supported. Proposed study must result in biomedical or behavioral research training in a specified shortage area and which may offer opportunity to research health scientists, research clinicians, etc., to broaden their scientific background or to extend their potential for research in health-related areas. Applicants must be citizens of the United States or be admitted to the United States for permanent residency; they also must be nominated and sponsored by a public or private institution having staff and facilities suitable to the proposed research training. Domestic nonprofit Organizations may apply for the institutional NRS grant. SBIR: SBIR grants can be awarded only to domestic small businesses (entities that are independently owned and operated for profit, are not dominant in the field in which research is proposed, and have no more than 500 employees). Primary employment (more than one- half time) of the principal investigator must be with the small business at the time of award and during the conduct of the proposed project. In both Phase I and Phase II, the research must be performed in the U.S. or its possessions. To be eligible for funding, a grant application must be approved for scientific merit and Program relevance by a scientific review group and a national advisory council. STTR grants can be awarded only to domestic small business concerns (entities that are independently owned and operated for profit, are not dominant in the field in which research is proposed and have no more than 500 employees) which "partner" with a research institution in cooperative research and development. At least 40 percent of the project is to be performed by the small business concern and at least 30 percent by the research institution. In both Phase I and Phase II, the research must be performed in the U.S. and its possessions. To be eligible for funding, a grant application must be approved for scientific merit and Program relevance by a scientific review group and a national advisory council.

Beneficiary Eligibility: Any nonprofit or for-profit organization, company, or institution engaged in biomedical or biobehavioural research.

Award Range/Average: For research project grants, fiscal year 2019, range is $50,000 to $5,000,000; average is $462,704. Individual research fellowship awards: Basic stipend (first year beyond the doctoral degree) of approximately $45,000. The sponsoring institution will be provided, on application, with an allowance of up to approximately $8,000 per year to help defray the cost of training. No dependency allowances. SBIR: Average Phase I awards are for approximately $225,000 (grant activity R43 - for up to six months); Phase II awards may be made for amounts up to $1,500,000 (grant activity R44 - for up to two years).

Funding: (Project Grants) FY 18 $1,040,649,876.00; FY 19 est $1,083,139,000.00; FY 20 est $916,805,000.00

HQ: 6710-B Rockledge Drive, Room 2216, Bethesda, MD 20892-7510

    Phone: 301-435-6856 | Email: ehayunga@mail.nih.gov

    http://www.nichd.nih.gov/pages/index.aspx

HHS93.753 | CHILD LEAD POISONING PREVENTION SURVEILLANCE FINANCED IN PART BY PREVENTION AND PUBLIC HEALTH (PPHF) PROGRAM

"Preventive and Public Health Fund (PPHF) - Childhood Lead Poisoning Prevention Surveillance"

Award: Cooperative Agreements

Purpose: Supports and enhances surveillance capacity at the state and city level to prevent and eliminate childhood lead poisoning.

Applicant Eligibility: Applicants should review the individual CDC Funding Opportunity Announcement document issued under this CFDA Program for any required proof or certifications that must be submitted prior to, or simultaneous with, submission of an application package.

Beneficiary Eligibility: Others who will receive benefits from the program include infants and children from six months to six years of age who are screened for lead poisoning and family members who care for lead-poisoned children. Lead poisoning potentially affects all children, but disproportionately affects minority children and children of low-income families. Since the side effects of lead poisoning can be long lasting, benefits of the program can also affect youth and adults, persons at all educational and income levels, and urban, suburban and rural populations.

Award Range/Average: The estimated annual average range of an award is $250,000 to $500,000.

Funding: (Cooperative Agreements) FY 18 $9,451,814.00; FY 19 est $14,995,342.00; FY 20 est $14,995,342

HQ: 4770 Buford Highway NE, PO Box F45, Atlanta, GA 30341

    Phone: 770-488-0563

    http://www.cdc.gov/nceh/lead

HHS93.563 | CHILD SUPPORT ENFORCEMENT

Award: Formula Grants

Purpose: To enforce the support obligations owed by absent parents to their children.

Applicant Eligibility: All States, the District of Columbia, Puerto Rico, Virgin Islands, and Guam. Each of these jurisdictions is required to establish or designate a single and separate State Child Support Enforcement Agency. Tribes are eligible and we currently have fifty-nine tribal child support Programs and four in the start-up phase.

Beneficiary Eligibility: The State must provide support enforcement services to: (1) All applicants for, or recipients of TANF, Foster Care Maintenance Payments, and Medicaid, for whom an assignment to the State of support rights has been made and who are in need of such services; (2) all individuals who cease to receive TANF; (3) individuals who provide authorization to the IV-D agency to continue support enforcement services; and (4) any other individual who is in need of such services and who has applied for them.

Award Range/Average: FY 2017, from $3,796,650 to $500,224,386; Average Award Amount $65,291,622, and FY 2018, from $3,893,572 to $512,994,207; Average Award Amount 66,958,399, and FY 2019, from $3,903,852 to $514,348,645; Average Award Amount $67,135,187.

Funding: (Formula Grants) FY 18 $3,602,848,401.00; FY 19 est $3,702,300,000.00; FY 20 est $3,782,700,000

HQ: 330 C Street SW, 5th Floor, Washington, DC 20201

Phone: 202-401-5101 | Email: rjackson@acf.hhs.gov

http://www.acf.dhhs.gov/programs/cse

HHS93.564 | CHILD SUPPORT ENFORCEMENT RESEARCH

Award: Project Grants

Purpose: To provide federal funds for experimental, pilot, or demonstration projects that are likely to assist in promoting the objectives of Part D of Title IV.

Applicant Eligibility: Section 1115 grants may be made only to State or Tribal Child Support Enforcement agencies or their umbrella agencies.

Beneficiary Eligibility: Only Title IV-D Child Support Agencies or Tribal Child Support Program operating a comprehensive program.

Award Range/Average: $150,000 to $800,000. Average changes each fiscal year.

Funding: (Project Grants) FY 18 $3,652,428.00; FY 19 est $4,000,000.00; FY 20 est $4,000,000.00

HQ: 330 C Street SW, Washington, DC 20201

Phone: 202-401-4578 | Email: michelle.jadczak@acf.hhs.gov

http://www.acf.hhs.gov/programs/cse

HHS93.648 | CHILD WELFARE RESEARCH TRAINING OR DEMONSTRATION

Award: Project Grants

Purpose: Supports research and demonstration projects which are of national or regional significance and special projects for the demonstration of new methods which show promise of substantial contribution to the advancement of child welfare.

Applicant Eligibility: Eligible applicants include public or other nonprofit Institutions of higher learning, public or other nonprofit agencies or Organizations engaged in research on child welfare activities; and state or local public agencies responsible for administering, or supervising the administration of the title IV-B plan.

Beneficiary Eligibility: Grants are made to accredited public or other nonprofit institutions of higher learning, public or other nonprofit agencies and/or organizations and to state or local child welfare agencies for specific projects for training prospective and current personnel for work in the field of child welfare, including trainee-ships with stipends; child welfare demonstration projects of national or regional significance; and for utilization of child welfare research to encourage experimental and special types of welfare services.

Award Range/Average: FY 2017 grants ranged from $432,742 to $4,240,690 with the average of $1,061,856.

Funding: (Project Grants (Discretionary)) FY 18 $9,270,284.00; FY 19 est $10,648,480.00; FY 20 est $10,650,174.00

HQ: 330 C Street SW, Room 3504, Washington, DC 20201

Phone: 202-205-8807 | Email: jane.morgan@acf.hhs.gov

http://www.acf.hhs.gov/programs/cb

HHS93.197 | CHILDHOOD LEAD POISONING PREVENTION PROJECTS, STATE AND LOCAL CHILDHOOD LEAD POISONING PREVENTION AND SURVEILLANCE OF BLOOD LEAD LEVELS IN CHILDREN
"Childhood Lead Poisoning Prevention Program (CLPPP)"

Award: Project Grants

Purpose: To develop and/or enhance a surveillance system that monitors all blood lead levels.

Applicant Eligibility: Assistance will be provided to State health departments or their bonafide agents and the health departments of the following five local jurisdictions (or their bonafide agents)that have the highest estimated number of children with elevated blood lead levels: New York, NY; Chicago, IL; Detroit, MI; Los Angeles County, CA, and Philadelphia, PA, or their bona fide agents. Also eligible are health departments or other official Organizational authorities of the District of Columbia, the Commonwealth of Puerto Rico, the Virgin Islands, the Commonwealth of the Northern Mariana

Islands, American Samoa, Guam, the Federated States of Micronesia, the Republic of the Marshall Islands, the Republic of Palau, and federally recognized Indian tribal Governments. Competition is limited by authorizing legislation.

Beneficiary Eligibility: In addition to the eligible applicants, others who receive benefits from the program include infants and children from six months to six years of age who are screened for lead poisoning and family members who care for lead-poisoned children. Lead poisoning potentially affects all children, but disproportionately affects minority children and children of low-income families. Since the effects of lead poisoning can be long lasting, benefits of the program can also affect youth and adults, persons at all educational and income levels, and urban, suburban, and rural populations.

Funding: (Cooperative Agreements) FY 18 $6,444,358.00; FY 19 est $6,444,358.00; FY 20 est $6,444,358.00

HQ: 4770 Buford Highway NE, PO Box F45, Atlanta, GA 30341

Phone: 770-488-0563

http://www.cdc.gov

DOJ16.818 | CHILDREN EXPOSED TO VIOLENCE
"Defending Childhood"

Award: Project Grants

Purpose: Children Exposed to Violence Program reduces the frequency and severity of violence in homes and schools, assists children exposed to violence, and promotes safety and well-being of children.

Applicant Eligibility: N/A

Beneficiary Eligibility: N/A

Award Range/Average: Awards may range up to $2.5 million.

Funding: (Project Grants (Discretionary)) FY 17 Not Separately Identifiable; FY 18 est Not Separately Identifiable; FY 19 est $8,000,000.00

HQ: 810 7th Street NW 2136, Washington, DC 20531

Phone: 202-307-9963 | Email: robin.delany-shabazz@usdoj.gov

http://ojjdp.ncjrs.org

DOJ16.832 | CHILDREN OF INCARCERATED PARENTS WEB PORTAL
"COIP Web Portal"

Award: Project Grants

Purpose: To promote government initiatives to support children of incarcerated parents and their caregivers.

Applicant Eligibility: Funds may be used for an array of activities designed to develop a new or enhance and existing web site that would accomplish the goals of the Program.

Beneficiary Eligibility: The beneficiaries of this program are youth, families, and specialized service providers who can provide services to youth, incarcerated parents, and the communities.

Award Range/Average: Award amounts vary according to the appropriation amount

Funding: (Project Grants (Cooperative Agreements)) FY 18 $905,970.00; FY 19 est $500,000.00; FY 20 est $500,000.00

HQ: Office of Juvenile Justice and Delinquency Prevention 810 7th Street NW, Washington, DC 20531

Phone: 202-307-5911 | Email: james.antal@usdoj.gov

http://www.ojjdp.gov

DOJ16.831 | CHILDREN OF INCARCERATED PARENTS
"Children of Incarcerated Parents Demonstration"

Award: Project Grants

Purpose: To develop strategies to strengthen the relationships between parents and children and provisions that will enhance youth development and innovative approaches to communication.

Applicant Eligibility: The target population for this Program is incarcerated parents who have minor children younger than 18.

Beneficiary Eligibility: N/A

Award Range/Average: award amounts vary according to solicitaiton

Funding: (Salaries and Expenses) FY 17 $4,176,332.00; FY 18 est $5,000,000.00; FY 19 est $5,000,000.00

HQ: Office of Juvenile Justice and Delinquency Prevention 810 7th Street NW, Washington, DC 20531

Phone: 202-616-5176 | Email: kathy.mitchell@usdoj.gov

http://www.ojjdp.gov

USDA10.521 | CHILDREN, YOUTH AND FAMILIES AT-RISK
"CYFAR, CYFAR-SCP and CYFAR-PDTA"

Award: Project Grants

Purpose: The Land-grant Institutions and Cooperative Extension Systems in collaboration provide education for youth, professional development, and military skills to contribute for lives. The CYFAR program provides educational resources and technological skills for youth.

Applicant Eligibility: Applications may only be submitted by Cooperative Extension at 1890 Land-grant Institutions, including Tuskegee University, Central State University, and West Virginia State University; 1862 Land-grant Colleges and universities; and the University of the District of Columbia.

Beneficiary Eligibility: Same as Applicant Eligibility.

Award Range/Average: If minimum or maximum amounts of funding per competitive and/or capacity project grant, or cooperative agreement are established, these amounts will be announced in the annual Competitive Request for Application (RFA).

Funding: (Project Grants) FY 17 $0.00; FY 18 est $0.00; FY 19 est $8,037,990.00

HQ: Institute of Youth Family and Community (IYFC) Division of Youth and 4-H 1400 Independence Avenue SW, PO Box 2250, Washington, DC 20250-2250

Phone: 202-720-5305 | Email: edwin.lewis@nifa.usda.gov

https://nifa.usda.gov/program/children-youth-and-families-risk-cyfar

HHS93.767 | CHILDREN'S HEALTH INSURANCE PROGRAM
"CHIP"

Award: Formula Grants

Purpose: Provides funds to States to enable them to maintain and expand child health assistance to uninsured, low-income children, low-income pregnant women and legal immigrants.

Applicant Eligibility: The following entities are eligible to apply for this Program funding: State (includes District of Columbia, public Institutions of higher education and hospitals), Local (includes State-designated Indian Tribes, excludes Institutions of higher education and hospitals, U.S. Territories and possessions (includes Institutions of higher education and hospitals), Native American Organizations (includes Indian groups, cooperatives, corporations, partnerships, associations) States with an approved child health plan under this title [42 U.S.C. Section1397aa et seq.]; local Governments; Indian Tribes or tribal consortium, tribal Organizations, urban Indian Organizations receiving funds under title V of the Indian healthcare Improvement Act (25 U.S.C. 1651 et seq.), or Indian Health Service providers; federal health safety net Organizations; national, state, local, or community-based public or nonprofit private Organizations, including Organizations that use community health workers or community-based doula Programs; faith-based Organizations or consortia, to the extent that a cooperative agreement awarded to such an entity is consistent with the requirements of Section 1955 of the Public Health Service Act (42 U.S.C. 300x-65) relating to a grant award to nongovernmental entities; and/or elementary or secondary schools may apply. For eligibility requirements the Connecting Kids to Coverage project grants, refer to the website https://www.InsureKidsNow.gov under the Campaign Information tab for more information about each funding opportunity announcement.

Beneficiary Eligibility: Targeted low-income children will benefit. These children are defined (for the purposes of Title XXI) as children who have been determined eligible by the State for child health assistance under their State plan; are low-income children as defined by each state and are not found to be covered under a group health plan or under other health insurance coverage.

Award Range/Average: For the Connecting Kids to Coverage Cooperative Agreements, the projected awards will range from ($250,000 up to $1,000,000). FY 2018, the range is from $3,072,998 (American Samoa) to $2,825,935,404 (California).

Funding: (Formula Grants (Apportionments)) FY 18 $17,309,197,911.00; FY 19 est $17,415,604,629.00; FY 20 est $18,366,180,998.00

HQ: 7500 Security Boulevard, Baltimore, MD 21244

Phone: 410-786-5780 | Email: grace.ponte@cms.hhs.gov

http://www.cms.gov

Programs Administered by Federal Headquarters

HHS93.255 | CHILDREN'S HOSPITALS GRADUATE MEDICAL EDUCATION PAYMENT PROGRAM
"CHGME Payment Program"

Award: Direct Payments for Specified Use

Purpose: To provide funds to freestanding children's teaching hospitals to support the training of pediatric and other residents in graduate medical education (GME) programs.

Applicant Eligibility: A children's hospital is eligible to apply for CHGME Payment Program funding if it participates in an approved GME Program; has a Medicare Provider Agreement; is excluded from the Medicare Inpatient Prospective Payment System (IPPS); and operates as a freestanding children's teaching hospital. A freestanding children's teaching hospital does not operate under a Medicare hospital provider number assigned to a larger healthcare entity that receives Medicare GME payments. A hospital remains eligible for payments as long as it trains residents as a freestanding children's hospital during the federal fiscal year that HRSA makes CHGME Program payments.

Beneficiary Eligibility: Any public or private nonprofit and profit freestanding children's teaching hospital with an accredited residency training program which meets all eligibility requirements may apply.

Award Range/Average: FY 18 Range: $32,294- $21,826,749; Average $5,161,757 in combined DME and IME payments. FY 19 Range est: $27,269- $21,538,999; Average $5,172,414 in combined DME and IME payments. FY 20 Range est: $0; Average $0

Funding: (Direct Payments for Specified Use) FY 18 $300,000,000.00; FY 19 est $300,000,000.00; FY 20 est $0.00

HQ: 5600 Fishers Lane, Room 15N190A, Rockville, MD 20857

Phone: 301-443-0365 | Email: aflach-fulcher@hrsa.gov

http://bhw.hrsa.gov/grants/medicine/chgme

DOJ16.583 | CHILDREN'S JUSTICE ACT PARTNERSHIPS FOR INDIAN COMMUNITIES
"CJA"

Award: Project Grants; Direct Payments for Specified Use

Purpose: To provide funding, technical assistance, and training to help American Indian and Alaska Native communities develop, establish, and operate programs designed to improve the investigation, prosecution, and handling of cases of child abuse and neglect.

Applicant Eligibility: Federally recognized Indian tribal Governments and nonprofit Indian Organizations that provide services to American Indians and Alaska Natives. Specific criteria will vary depending on the grant.

Beneficiary Eligibility: American Indian and Alaskan Native youth who are victims of child abuse and/or child sexual abuse.

Funding: (Project Grants) FY 17 $2,946,093.00; FY 18 est $3,000,000.00; FY 19 est $3,000,000.00

HQ: Office of Victims of Crime Department of Justice 810 7th Street NW, Washington, DC 20531

Phone: 202-307-5983 | Email: yolanda.c.gibson@ojp.usdoj.gov

http://www.justice.gov

HHS93.643 | CHILDREN'S JUSTICE GRANTS TO STATES

Award: Formula Grants

Purpose: Encourages states to enact reforms which are designed to improve the assessment and investigation of suspected child abuse and neglect cases, including cases of suspected child sexual abuse and exploitation, in a manner that limits additional trauma to the child and the child's family.

Applicant Eligibility: States (including Puerto Rico and the District of Columbia), Virgin Islands, Guam, American Samoa, and the Commonwealth of the Northern Marianas.

Beneficiary Eligibility: Beneficiaries include state governments and victims of child abuse and neglect, particularly child sexual abuse and exploitation.

Award Range/Average: FY 2017: $53,269 to $1,788,425 with an average grant of $303,571.

Funding: (Formula Grants) FY 17 $17,000,000.00; FY 18 est $15,974,483.00; FY 19 est $17,000,000.00

HQ: Office on Child Abuse and Neglect 330 C Street SW, Room 3420C, Washington, DC 20201

Phone: 202-205-4539 | Email: lauren.fischman@acf.hhs.gov

http://www.acf.dhhs.gov/programs/cb

HUD14.889 | CHOICE NEIGHBORHOODS IMPLEMENTATION GRANTS
Award: Project Grants
Purpose: To transform neighborhoods of poverty into feasible mixed-income neighborhoods with access to economic activities.
Applicant Eligibility: For Choice Neighborhoods Implementation Grants, Public Housing Agencies (PHAs), local Governments, non-profits, and for-profit developers that apply jointly with a public entity.
Beneficiary Eligibility: For Choice Neighbourhoods Implementation Grants, the ultimate beneficiaries are residents of the severely distressed public and/or assisted housing projects and residents of the surrounding community these grants aim to transform.
Award Range/Average: Range is $24,214,284 to $30,000,000. Average is $29,035,714
Funding: (Project Grants) FY 17 $132,280,927.00; FY 18 est $145,000,000.00; FY 19 est $0.00
HQ: 451 7th Street SW, Room 4130, Washington, DC 20410
    Phone: 202-402-5461
    http://www.hud.gov/cn

HUD14.892 | CHOICE NEIGHBORHOODS PLANNING GRANTS
Award: Project Grants
Purpose: To support the development of comprehensive neighborhood Transformation Plans that integrate effective strategies to implement public and/or assisted housing revitalization, coordination, and design of supportive services.
Applicant Eligibility: Choice Neighborhoods Planning Grants will support the development of comprehensive neighborhood Transformation Plans. The Transformation Plan should integrate effective strategies to implement public and/or assisted housing revitalization, the coordination and design of supportive services, including educational opportunities for children, and neighborhood-level planning to improve a range of neighborhood assets. The Transformation Plan should be created as part of a collaborative planning process that involves neighborhood stakeholders and local governmental entities to build the necessary support to successfully implement the plan.
Beneficiary Eligibility: For Choice Neighbourhoods Planning Grants, the ultimate beneficiaries are residents of the severely distressed public and/or assisted housing unit and residents of the surrounding community these grants aim to engage in the creation of the community drafted Transformation Plan.
Award Range/Average: Grants ranged from $350,000 to $1,300,000; Average: $825,000 (FY17) and $808,333 (FY18)
Funding: (Project Grants) FY 17 $2,155,727.00; FY 18 est $5,000,000.00; FY 19 est $0.00
HQ: 451 7th Street SW, Room 4130, Washington, DC 20410
    Phone: 202-402-5461
    http://www.hud.gov/cn

HHS93.068 | CHRONIC DISEASES: RESEARCH, CONTROL, AND PREVENTION
"Research, Control, and Prevention"
Award: Cooperative Agreements
Purpose: To assist State and local health agencies, health related organizations, and other public and private organizations in their efforts to prevent and control chronic diseases and disorders through research, development, capacity building, and intervention.
Applicant Eligibility: Applications may be submitted by State or local Governments or their Bona Fide Agents (this includes the District of Columbia, the Commonwealth of Puerto Rico, the Virgin Islands, the Commonwealth of the Northern Marianna Islands, American Samoa, Guam, the Federated States of Micronesia, the Republic of the Marshall Islands, and the Republic of Palau). Eligible applicants also include public and private nonprofit Organizations, for profit Organizations, small, minority, women-owned businesses, universities, colleges, research Institutions, hospitals, community-based Organizations, faith-based Organizations, Federally recognized Indian tribal Governments, Indian Tribes, and Indian tribal Organizations. Foreign Institutions may be eligible for some specific Programs.
Beneficiary Eligibility: The general public will benefit from the objectives of this program.
Award Range/Average: N/A
Funding: (Cooperative Agreements) FY 18 $5,440,119.00; FY 19 est $5,457,929.00; FY 20 est $2,784,929.00
HQ: 4770 Buford Highway NE, Atlanta, GA 30341
    Phone: 770-488-1371
    http://www.cdc.gov

Programs Administered by Federal Headquarters

DHS97.010 | CITIZENSHIP EDUCATION AND TRAINING
Award: Cooperative Agreements; Project Grants
Purpose: The Citizenship and Integration Grant Program ensures the availability of high-quality citizenship preparation services for low-income and underserved permanent residents in communities across the nation.
Applicant Eligibility: Community-and faith-based Organizations, public libraries, as well other nonprofit Institutions / Organizations that conduct citizenship education classes for permanent residents, are eligible. Restrictions on the type of Organization eligible to apply for a specific funding opportunity will be identified in the announcement.
Beneficiary Eligibility: Immigrant Service Providers; Refugee/Alien.
Award Range/Average: Not applicable for dissemination of technical information projects.
Funding: (Project Grants (Contracts)) FY 18 $9,425,000.00; FY 19 est $10,000,000.00; FY 20 est $0.00
HQ: USCIS 245 Murray Lane SW Building 410, PO Box 0115, Washington, DC 20528
　　Phone: 202-357-7927 | Email: stephen.t.mchale@uscis.dhs.gov
　　http://www.uscis.gov/grants

DOD12.840 | CIVIL AIR PATROL PROGRAM
Award: Cooperative Agreements
Purpose: To encourage and aid citizens of the United States in contributing their efforts, services, and resources in developing aviation and in maintaining air supremacy.
Applicant Eligibility: Any awards under this Program will be made on a noncompetitive basis to the Civil Air Patrol, a nonprofit corporation that is federally chartered under 10 U.S.C. 9491-9498.
Beneficiary Eligibility: Beneficiary identified in statute.
Funding: (Cooperative Agreements) FY 18 $59,885,018; FY 19 est $60,000,000; FY 20 est $60,000,000
HQ: 1060 Air Force Pentagon 4C149, Washington, DC 20330
　　Phone: 571-256-2422

HHS93.001 | CIVIL RIGHTS AND PRIVACY RULE COMPLIANCE ACTIVITIES
"Office for Civil Rights"
Award: Advisory Services and Counseling; Investigation of Complaints
Purpose: Investigates complaints, enforces rights, and promulgates regulations, develops policy and provides technical assistance and public education to ensure understanding of and compliance with non-discrimination and health information privacy laws.
Applicant Eligibility: Anyone who believes he or she has been discriminated against in the manner outlined, seeks information concerning civil rights, and recipients of Federal financial assistance who desire technical assistance and information for the purpose of assuring their compliance with nondiscrimination laws. Regarding the HIPAA Privacy and Security Rules, anyone who believes that the Privacy and/or Security Rules have been violated in the manner outlined or who seeks information about these Rules; consumers that need to know their rights under the Privacy Rule; and entities that need technical assistance and information for the purpose of assuring compliance with the Privacy and Security Rules.
Beneficiary Eligibility: Individuals subject to discrimination and recipients who require technical assistance and information. Regarding the HIPAA Privacy Rule, individuals subject to violation of their health information privacy, covered entities, and others needing or seeking technical assistance and information concerning the Rule.
Award Range/Average: Not Applicable.
Funding: (Investigation of Complaints) FY 16 $$38,798,000.00; FY 17 est $38,798,000.00; FY 18 est $32,530,000.00

ED84.004 | CIVIL RIGHTS TRAINING AND ADVISORY SERVICES (ALSO KNOWN AS EQUITY ASSISTANCE CENTERS)
Award: Project Grants
Purpose: To provide technical assistance and training services to school districts and governmental agencies to cope with educational problems occasioned by race, sex, religion, and national origin desegregation.
Applicant Eligibility: Any private, nonprofit Organization or any public agency (other than a State educational agency or school board) may apply.
Beneficiary Eligibility: Educational personnel and elementary and secondary students in local school districts benefit.
Award Range/Average: In FY 18, $1,634,250 average. In FY 19, $1,633,500 average. In FY 20, $1,633,500 average.
Funding: (Project Grants) FY 18 $6,575,000.00; FY 19 est $6,575,000.00; FY 20 est $6,575,000.00

HQ: Department of Education 400 Maryland Avenue SW, Room 3E206 LBJ Building, Washington, DC 20202
   Phone: 202-453-5990 | Email: david.cantrell@ed.gov
   http://www.ed.gov/programs/equitycenters/index.html

DOC11.431 | CLIMATE AND ATMOSPHERIC RESEARCH

Award: Project Grants
Purpose: To analyze and implement a predictive mechanism for short and long-term climate changes.
Applicant Eligibility: Institutions of higher education, other nonprofits, commercial Organizations, international Organizations, state, local and Indian tribal Governments.
Beneficiary Eligibility: Organizations and individuals with interests in meteorology, oceanography, and climate research and prediction.
Funding: (Project Grants) FY 16 $44,040,094.00; FY 17 est $45,134,708.00; FY 18 est $36,000,000.00
HQ: 1315 E W Highway, Suite 12860, Silver Spring, MD 20910
   Phone: 301-734-1263 | Email: wayne.higgins@noaa.gov
   http://cpo.noaa.gov

HHS93.220 | CLINICAL RESEARCH LOAN REPAYMENT PROGRAM FOR INDIVIDUALS FROM DISADVANTAGED BACKGROUNDS
"NIH Clinical Research Loan Repayment Program; CR LRP"

Award: Direct Payments for Specified Use
Purpose: To recruit and retain health professionals from disadvantaged backgrounds to conduct clinical research at the National Institutes of Health (NIH) by providing for the repayment of educational loans.
Applicant Eligibility: Eligible applicants must: (1) Be a citizen, national, or permanent resident of the United States; (2) possess a M.D., Ph.D., D.O., D.D.S., D.M.D., D.V.M., D.P.M., A.D.N., B.S.N., or equivalent degree; or hold the position of Physician Assistant; (3) come from a disadvantaged background as determined by the Secretary of Health and Human Services; (4) have qualified educational debt, which results from governmental or commercial loans obtained to support their undergraduate and/or graduate education, in excess of 20 percent of their annual NIH salary on the Program eligibility date; (5) be appointed under any temporary or permanent employment mechanism in the Intramural Research Program of the NIH, so long as their employment has the potential to last a minimum of 2 years; (6) are not eligible to participate in the CR-LRP if they have an existing service obligation to Federal, State, or other entities, until such obligation is discharged or unless it is deferred during the period of Program service; (7) submit an application to participate in the CR-LRP; and (8) sign and submit to the Secretary of Health and Human Services, at the time of agreeing to accept repayment of educational loans, a contract agreeing to engage in clinical research as an employee of the NIH for a minimum of 2 years.
Beneficiary Eligibility: Clinical researchers from disadvantaged backgrounds who have unpaid educational loans will benefit from this program.
Award Range/Average: For initial 2-year contracts, loan repayments range from $4,000 to $70,000, Tax reimbursements range from $1,977 to $34,598. The average contract cost which includes loan and tax reimbursement is $68,454.
Funding: (Project Grants) FY 17 $0.00; FY 18 est $31,882.00; FY 19 est $102,550.00
HQ: U.S. Department of Health and Human Services 2 Center Drive, Room 2E18 Building 2, Bethesda, MD 20892-0230
   Phone: 301-402-1283 | Email: colep@mail.nih.gov
   http://www.lrp.nih.gov

HHS93.826 | CLOSING THE GAP BETWEEN STANDARDS DEVELOPMENT AND IMPLEMENTATION

Award: Cooperative Agreements
Purpose: To establish a mechanism for ongoing long-term collaborative engagement with Health Level 7 International in order to support advancements in the technical standards necessary to achieve interoperability among health IT systems.
Applicant Eligibility: Sole source award to Health Level 7 International.
Beneficiary Eligibility: The beneficiaries will include all health care organizations and patients using electronic health records.
Funding: (Cooperative Agreements) FY 18 $1,360,000.00; FY 19 est $1,360,000.00; FY 20 est Estimate Not Available
HQ: 330 C Street SW, Suite 726-G, Washington, DC 20201
   Phone: 202-691-2132 | Email: matthew.rahn@hhs.gov
   http://www.healthit.gov

Programs Administered by Federal Headquarters

DOL17.307 | COAL MINE WORKERS' COMPENSATION
"Black Lung"

Award: Direct Payments With Unrestricted Use

Purpose: Provides benefits to coal miners who have become totally disabled due to coal workers' pneumoconiosis (CWP), and to widows and other surviving dependents of miners who have died of this disease.

Applicant Eligibility: The miner (including some workers involved in coal transportation in and around mines and coal mine construction workers) must have worked in the Nation's coal mines or a coal preparation facility and become "totally disabled" (as defined in the Act) from pneumoconiosis. The applicant may be able to work in areas other than coal mines and still be eligible for benefits. Benefits to miner shall be reduced on account of excess earnings as determined under sections 203(b) through (1) of the Social Security Act for claims filed on or after January 1, 1982. Widows and other surviving dependents of coal miners whose death resulted from coal workers' pneumoconiosis are also eligible for benefits with earnings offsets applicable to certain classes of dependents. Applicants can reside anywhere in the world at the time they apply.

Beneficiary Eligibility: Disabled coal miners, widows and other surviving dependents of the deceased.

Award Range/Average: On January 1,2019 new monthly rates went into effect for Black Lung. The rates are as follows: PART B MONTHLY BENEFITS RATES (claims approved by the Social Security Administration - payments received around the 3rd of each month): Primary beneficiary: $669.30, Primary beneficiary and one dependent: $1,004.00, Primary beneficiary and two dependents: $1,171.30, Primary beneficiary and three or more dependents: $1,338.60. PART C BLACK LUNG MONTHLY BENEFIT RATES (claims approved by the Department of Labor - payments received around the 15th of each month): Primary beneficiary: $669.00, Primary beneficiary and one dependent: $1,004.00, Primary beneficiary and two dependents: $1,171.00, Primary beneficiary and three or more dependents: $1,339.00. Benefits rates are set accordance with Section 412(a)(1) of the Federal Coal Mine Health and Safety Act, which specifies that the rate for an individual Black Lung beneficiary is 37.5% of the base salary of a Federal employee at level GS-2, Step 1.

Funding: (Direct Payments with Unrestricted Use) FY 18 $249,862,000.00; FY 19 est $236,909,000.00; FY 20 $235,254,000.00

HQ: Division of Coal Mine Workers Compensation 200 Constitution Avenue NW, Washington, DC 20210

   Phone: 202-693-0046

   http://www.dol.gov/owcp/dcmwc

HHS93.965 | COAL MINERS RESPIRATORY IMPAIRMENT TREATMENT CLINICS AND SERVICES
"Black Lung Clinics Program (BLCP) and the Black Lung Center of Excellence (BLCE)"

Award: Cooperative Agreements

Purpose: The Black Lung Clinics Program aims to reduce the morbidity and mortality associated with occupationally-related coal mine dust lung disease through the provision of medical, outreach, educational, and benefits counseling services to coal miners and their families.

Applicant Eligibility: The BLCP is open to any state or public or private entity that meets the requirements of the Program. This includes faith-based and community-based Organizations as well as federally-recognized Tribes and Tribal Organizations. The requirements may be met by a state, a single entity in a state, or a newly-formed consortium within a state. In addition to the 50 states and the District of Columbia, applicants can be located in the Commonwealth of Puerto Rico, the Commonwealth of the Northern Mariana Islands, the Territories of the Virgin Islands, Guam, American Samoa, the Compact Free Association Jurisdictions of the Republic of the Marshall Islands, the Republic of Palau, and the Federated States of Micronesia, if they meet eligibility requirements. Foreign entities are not eligible for HRSA awards, unless the authorizing legislation specifically authorizes awards to foreign entities or the award is for research. This exception does not extend to research training awards or construction of research facilities. The BLCE is open to BLCP recipients awarded funding under the HRSA-17-023/Black Lung Clinics Program notice of funding opportunity and that are involved in the operation of fixed-site and or mobile clinic facilities for the analysis, examination and treatment of respiratory and pulmonary impairments in active and inactive coal miners, assuming they meet the requirements of the BLCE.

Beneficiary Eligibility: Per 42 CFR Part55a, a "coal miner" is defined as: Any individual who works or has worked in or around a coal mine or coal preparation facility in the extraction or preparation of coal. The term also includes an individual who works or has worked in coal mine construction or transportation in and around a coal mine, to the extent that the individual was exposed to coal dust as a result of employment.

Funding: (Cooperative Agreements) FY 18 $120,000.00; FY 19 est $125,000.00; FY 20 est $125,000.00; (Project Grants) FY 18 $9,770,410.00; FY 19 est $10,680,746.00; FY 20 est $11,500,000.00

HQ: 5600 Fishers Lane, PO Box 17W59D, Rockville, MD 20857
   Phone: 301-443-0491 | Email: kmastel@hrsa.gov
   http://www.hrsa.gov/ruralhealth

DOC11.419 | COASTAL ZONE MANAGEMENT ADMINISTRATION AWARDS

"Agency: Department of Commerce Office: National Oceanic and Atmospheric Administration (NOAA)"

Award: Formula Grants; Project Grants
Purpose: To assist in implementing Coastal Zone Management programs.
Applicant Eligibility: Any coastal State, including those that border the Great Lakes, and including Puerto Rico, the U.S. Virgin Islands, Guam, American Samoa, the Commonwealth of the Northern Mariana Islands, and the Freely Associated States of the Pacific whose Coastal Zone Management Program has been approved by the Secretary of Commerce. The Governor shall designate the State agency or entity that is to be the applicant.
Beneficiary Eligibility: Institutions of higher educations, hospitals, other nonprofits, commercial organizations, foreign governments, organizations under the jurisdiction of foreign governments, international organizations, and state, local and Indian tribal governments.
Award Range/Average: $795,000 to $2,300,000 (average $2,000,000)
Funding: (Cooperative Agreements) FY 16 $82,978,692.00; FY 17 est $72,143,911.00; FY 18 est $72,143,911.00
HQ: Department of Commerce 1305 E W Highway, Silver Spring, MD 20910
   Phone: 240-533-0908 | Email: russell.callendar@noaa.gov
   http://coastalmanagement.noaa.gov/programs/czm.html

DOC11.420 | COASTAL ZONE MANAGEMENT ESTUARINE RESEARCH RESERVES

Award: Project Grants
Purpose: To assist States in monitoring, research, education, operation, and facilities construction to educate people about the human processes occurring within the estuaries of the coastal zone.
Applicant Eligibility: Land acquisition, development, operation, and facilities construction grants are available to any coastal State and, in some cases, public or private person, including those bordering the Great Lakes. For the purposes of the Coastal Zone Management Act, the coastal State also applies to Puerto Rico, the U.S. Virgin Islands, Guam, American Samoa, and the Commonwealth of the Northern Mariana Islands. The Governor shall designate the State agency or entity to be the applicant. Competitive research grants are available to any coastal State or qualified public or private person. education grants are available to any coastal State entity.
Beneficiary Eligibility: Any coastal State including those bordering the Great Lakes, as well as Puerto Rico, the U.S. Virgin Islands, Guam, American Samoa, and the Commonwealth of the Northern Mariana Islands are eligible for reserve operation, land acquisition, or construction awards where a reserve has been designated and for development awards for designating new reserves. Also qualified students are eligible to apply for research fellowship grants.
Award Range/Average: $20,000 to $600,000 (average $250,000)
Funding: (Project Grants) FY 16 $24,146,039.00; FY 17 est $22,938,262.00; FY 18 est $22,938,262.00
HQ: 1305 E W Highway N/ORM5, 10th Floor, Silver Spring, MD 20910
   Phone: 240-533-0908 | Email: russell.callendar@noaa.gov
   http://www.nerrs.noaa.gov

USDA10.962 | COCHRAN FELLOWSHIP PROGRAM-INTERNATIONAL TRAINING-FOREIGN PARTICIPANT

"Cochran Fellowship Program"

Award: Project Grants; Direct Payments for Specified Use
Purpose: To deliver quality training in meeting the food security needs and strengthen agricultural businesses in the United States.
Applicant Eligibility: The Cochran Program solicits proposals for training from U.S. Institutions of higher education, nonprofit Organizations, U.S. agricultural trade and market development associations, and private agribusinesses.
Beneficiary Eligibility: Technical assistance provided through these agreements benefits foreign governments and agricultural institutions in their countries.
Award Range/Average: Training activities last approximately two weeks. Average cost of each project is $60,000.

Programs Administered by Federal Headquarters

Funding: (Direct Payments for Specified Use) FY 18 $2,888,703.00; FY 19 est $3,000,000.00; FY 20 est $3,500,000.00
HQ: 1400 Independence Avenue SW, Washington, DC 20250
    Phone: 202-690-0947 | Email: desiree.thomas@usda.gov
    https://www.fas.usda.gov/programs/cochran-fellowship-program

HHS93.099 | COLLABORATION WITH THE WORLD HEALTH ORGANIZATION AND ITS REGIONAL OFFICES FOR GLOBAL HEALTH SECURITY AND THE INTERNATIONAL HEALTH REGULATIONS (IHR 2005)

Award: Cooperative Agreements
Purpose: To help WHO Member States strengthen their capabilities to support the International Health Regulations (IHR), an international agreement that requires Member States to prevent and respond to acute public health risks that have the potential to cross borders.
Applicant Eligibility: Only the World Health Organization and its regional offices are eligible to apply. For purposes of this document, the term WHO includes its regional offices (e.g., PAHO, EMRO, AFRO, SEARO, etc). WHO is the only international and intergovernmental agency qualified to conduct activities under this cooperative agreement because: WHO is an international public health agency that works to improve health and living standards globally. WHO is part of the United Nations system. As such, WHO has a unique position among the world's health agencies as the lead technical agency for health globally. For additional information, please see http://www.who. org WHO and its Regional Offices are at the apex of global public health Organizations and thus have an exclusive status as the United States government's key partners for global public health. On September 19, 2011, the Government of the United States of America and the World Health Organization signed a memorandum of understanding (MOU) to help developing nations strengthen their capabilities to support the International Health Regulations (IHR). The IHR (2005) is an international agreement that requires WHO Member States to prevent and respond to acute public health risks that have the potential to cross borders and threaten people worldwide. The U.S. government and WHO share a commitment to strengthen cooperation in the area of global health security to ensure that the international community effectively manages public health risks. Improving the ability of all nations to detect, report, and respond to infectious diseases quickly and accurately lies at the heart of the global community's ability to address all infectious disease threats, as reflected in the IHR. The MOU establishes a framework for collaboration in line with the provisions set forth in the IHR, which provides a construct for coordinating the management of actions in the event of a public health emergency of international concern. The MOU was signed by Secretary Kathleen Sebelius, Department of Health and Human Services, and Director-General Margaret Chan, World Health Organization, and subsequently by Ambassador Betty E. King, United States Permanent Representative to the United Nations in Geneva. The full text of the MOU can be accessed at: http://www.globalhealth.gov/global-health-topics/health-diplomacy/agreements-and-regulations/20110922-mem. html. The MOU includes the following specific statements that support sole-source consideration of WHO and its regional offices (including PAHO) for funding activities that fall under the scope of the MOU: Section 8. a.: The United States Department of Health and Human Services (DHHS) continues to serve as the primary substantive interface with WHO on global health and health security. DHHS plans to ensure coordination with other U.S. government departments, agencies, and entities that collaborate on health matters within the scope of this Memorandum to enhance the effectiveness of such activities. The U.S. government agencies intend to develop Programs and provide funds through mechanisms that may be determined jointly by the U.S. government agency and WHO. Section 8. b.: Specific funding mechanisms are intended to be developed and U.S. government agencies intend to collaborate with WHO to define specific work to be undertaken by the Participants and the division of responsibilities. .
Beneficiary Eligibility: The World Health Organization and its regional offices work will benefit individuals worldwide, including in the U.S., through collaboration with National Ministries of Health and other organizations/institutions. The purpose is to support WHO to reduce the global disease burden through improved international capacity to detect and respond to emerging infectious diseases and other threats.
Award Range/Average: Varies.
Funding: (Cooperative Agreements) FY 18 $49,378,834.00; FY 19 est $63,744,471.00; FY 20 $63,744,471.00
HQ: 1600 Clifton Road NE, Atlanta, GA 30333
    Phone: 404-718-6503
    http://www.cdc.gov

DOD12.114 | COLLABORATIVE RESEARCH AND DEVELOPMENT
"Construction Productivity Advancement Research (CPAR) Program"

Award: Project Grants
Purpose: To facilitate productivity by improving research and development and application of advanced construction technologies through collaborative research and development.
Applicant Eligibility: Any U.S. private firm, including corporations, partnerships, limited partnerships and industrial development Organizations; public and private foundations; nonprofit Organizations; units of State and local Governments; academic Institutions; and others who have interest in and the capability to address CPAR objectives.
Beneficiary Eligibility: Beneficiaries of CPAR products will include the U.S. construction industry (builder/contractor/ developer, engineer/architect, construction equipment/material suppliers) profit and nonprofit business organizations, the general public, and Federal, State and local government agencies.
Funding: (Salary or Expense) FY 07 $6,000,000.00; FY 08 Estimate Not Available FY 09 Estimate Not Available; (Cooperative Agreement) FY 07 $6,000,000; FY 08 est not reported; and FY 09 est not reported. Note: No current information provided by Agency.
HQ: U.S. Army Corps of Engineers Attention: CERD-C 20 Massachusetts Avenue NW, Washington, DC 20314-1000
Phone: 202-272-1846
http://www.usace.army.mil/business.html

DOI15.568 | COLORADO RIVER PILOT SYSTEM CONSERVATION
"Pilot System Conservation Program (PSCP)"

Award: Cooperative Agreements
Purpose: Conservation projects that creates "system water" through voluntary compensated reductions in water use. All water conserved as a result of the SCPP becomes system water with the sole purpose of increasing storage levels in Lakes Powell and Mead and does not accrue to the benefit of any individual user.
Applicant Eligibility: Eligibility of the Upper Colorado River Commission established through PL 113-235.
Beneficiary Eligibility: Pursuant to PL 113-235, participation in the Pilot Program is limited to Entitlement Holders in the Lower Colorado Division States and Colorado River Water Users in the Upper Colorado River Basin.
Award Range/Average: Range: $1,065,000 Average: $1,065,000
Funding: (Cooperative Agreements) FY 17 $1,065,000.00; FY 18 est $1,065,000.00; FY 19 est $1,065,000.00
HQ: Upper Colorado Regional Office, Salt Lake City, CO 84138

DOC11.436 | COLUMBIA RIVER FISHERIES DEVELOPMENT PROGRAM

Award: Project Grants
Purpose: To protect and enhance the salmon and steelhead resources in the Columbia River Basin.
Applicant Eligibility: State Governments and quasi-public nonprofit institution/Organizations.
Beneficiary Eligibility: Federal, Interstate, State, and Quasi- public nonprofit entities.
Funding: (Cooperative Agreements) FY 16 $14,287,632.00; FY 17 est $14,287,632.00; FY 18 est Estimate Not Available
HQ: 1305 E W Highway, Silver Spring, MD 20910
Phone: 301-427-8771 | Email: jeffrey.kulnis@noaa.gov
http://www.nmfs.noaa.gov

DOJ16.844 | COMBATTING CONTRABAND CELL PHONE USE IN PRISONS
"Combat Cell Phone Contraband"

Award: Project Grants
Purpose: Aims at implementing the technological solutions on comprehensive contraband interdiction systems for state and local governments. To implement technologies that prevent and limit cell phone contraband. It also provides technical assistance on reviewing policies, procedures, and technology implementation by conducting case studies.
Applicant Eligibility: Eligible applicants are limited to nonprofit Organizations, for-profit Organizations (including tribal nonprofit or for-profit Organizations), Institutions of higher education (including tribal Institutions of higher education), faith-based Organizations, and consortiums with demonstrated experience in providing training and technical assistance on a national level in the identified subject areas. All recipients and subrecipients (including any for-profit Organization) must

Programs Administered by Federal Headquarters

forgo any profit or management fee. BJA welcomes applications under which two or more entities would carry out the federal award; however, only one entity may be the applicant. Any others must be proposed as subrecipients (subgrantees). The applicant must be the entity that would have primary responsibility for carrying out the award, including administering the funding and managing the entire Program. Only one application per lead applicant will be considered; however, an applicant may be proposed as a subrecipient (subgrantee) in multiple proposals.

Beneficiary Eligibility: N/A
Funding: (Project Grants) FY 18 Actual Not Available; FY 19 est $2,000,000.00; FY 20 est Estimate Not Available
HQ: 810 7th Street NW, Washington, DC 20531
    Phone: 202-353-0583 | Email: andre.bethea@usdoj.gov
    https://www.bja.gov

DOJ16.307 | COMBINED DNA INDEX SYSTEM
"CODIS"

Award: Project Grants
Purpose: To develop/improve forensic DNA analysis capabilities in State and local crime laboratories. The Combined DNA Index Systems (CODIS) allows State and local crime laboratories to store and match DNA records.
Applicant Eligibility: To receive CODIS software and technical assistance, participants must be publicly funded forensic laboratories performing DNA analysis, or private forensic laboratories performing DNA analysis under contract with crime laboratories.
Beneficiary Eligibility: To be eligible for DNA grants, participants must be publicly funded State or local forensic laboratories performing DNA analysis.
Funding: (Project Grants) FY 16 $12,305,252.00; FY 17 est $11,741,382.00; FY 18 est $11,635,962.00
HQ: 935 Pennsylvania Avenue Finance Division, Room 6712, Washington, DC 20535
    Phone: 202-324-0495 | Email: michael.tyler@ic.fbi.gov
    http://www.fbi.gov

DOD12.225 | COMMERCIAL TECHNOLOGIES FOR MAINTENANCE ACTIVITIES PROGRAM
"CTMA"

Award: Cooperative Agreements
Purpose: To advance the development, integration, and use of commercial sustainment technologies and processes.
Applicant Eligibility: N/A
Beneficiary Eligibility: N/A
Award Range/Average: The projected range of financial assistance to be applied to CTMA annually is historically in the range of $10M- $25M. The average expected financial assistance is $15M annually.
Funding: (Cooperative Agreements) FY 17 $27,503,485.00; FY 18 est $42,801,277.00; FY 19 est $42,801,277.00
HQ: 1225 S Clark Street, Suite 910, Arlington, VA 22202
    Phone: 703-545-3559 | Email: jonathan.e.bertsch.civ@mail.mil

CNCS94.008 | COMMISSION INVESTMENT FUND
"TTA Commission Investment Funds"

Award: Project Grants
Purpose: The Training and Technical Assistance Commission Investment Funds supports Corporation for National and Community Service's approach to help the State Service Commissions to expand their capacities (knowledge, resources and skills) and implement their duties as amended.
Applicant Eligibility: See Program's Notice of Funding Opportunity.
Beneficiary Eligibility: States will benefit.
Funding: (Project Grants (Discretionary)) FY 16 $5,784,993.00; FY 17 est $7,301,255.00; FY 18 est Estimate Not Available
HQ: 250 E Street SW, Washington, DC 20525
    Phone: 202-606-3915 | Email: rlampi@cns.gov
    http://www.nationalservice.gov

USDA10.051 | COMMODITY LOANS AND LOAN DEFICIENCY PAYMENTS
"Marketing Assistance Loans (MAL's) and Loan Deficiency Payments (LDP's)"

Award: Direct Payments With Unrestricted Use; Direct Loans

Purpose: To assist farmers in receiving stabilized income through proper marketing of their crops.

Applicant Eligibility: Owner, landlord, tenant, or sharecropper on an eligible farm that has produced the eligible commodities or, in the case of sugar, a processor or refiner who meets Program requirements as announced by the Secretary.

Beneficiary Eligibility: Owner, landlord, tenant, or sharecropper on a farm that has produced the eligible commodities, meets program requirements as announced by the Secretary, and maintains beneficial interest in the commodity. State and County governments may be eligible for MAL's and LDP's when they have a share in produced and harvested eligible commodities on land they own, if the benefits or payments are used to support public schools.

Funding: (Direct Loans) FY 18 $3,145,610,000.00; FY 19 est $3,205,858,000.00; FY 20 est $3,159,314,000.00; (Direct Payments with Unrestricted Use) FY 18 $72,000.00; FY 19 est $33,451,000.00; FY 20 est $65,467,000.00

HQ: 1400 Independence Avenue SW, PO Box 0510, Washington, DC 20250-0510

   Phone: 202-720-9889 | Email: deann.allen@wdc.usda.gov

   http://www.fsa.usda.gov/programs-and-services/price-support/index

HHS93.590 | COMMUNITY-BASED CHILD ABUSE PREVENTION GRANTS

Award: Formula Grants

Purpose: Supports community-based efforts to develop, operate, expand, and enhance, and coordinate initiatives, programs, and activities to prevent child abuse and neglect and to support the coordination of resources and activities to better strengthen and support families to reduce the likelihood of child abuse and neglect.

Applicant Eligibility: States, the District of Columbia, Puerto Rico, the U.S. Virgin Islands, Guam, American Samoa, the Commonwealth of the Northern Mariana Islands are eligible. Before a state can apply, the Governor must designate a lead entity to administer the funds for the implementation of community-based child abuse and neglect prevention Programs and activities. Tribes may participate through application for grants made available by a 1% (of the entire CBCAP apportionment, of both mandatory and discretionary funds) annual funds set aside, legislated for Tribes, tribal Organizations and migrant Programs. These are discretionary competitive grants, awarded every five years. Complete information regarding these grants may be found on the Federal website, www.grants.gov.

Beneficiary Eligibility: There are no eligibility requirements. Beneficiaries, which include children and their families, organizations providing community-based, prevention focused programs and activities designed to prevent child abuse and neglect.

Award Range/Average: In FY 2018 for states the range of financial assistance was from $200,000 to $3,220,669 with an average of $673,620. In FY 2018 for tribes the range of financial assistance was from $128,374 to $132,546 with an average of $131,097.

Funding: (Formula Grants) FY 18 $37,722,708.00; FY 19 est $37,540,168.00; FY 20 est $37,722,545.00; (Project Grants (Discretionary)) FY 18 $393,292.00; FY 19 est $393,044.00; FY 20 est $392,455.00

HQ: Office on Child Abuse and Neglect 330 C Street SW, Room 3403, Washington, DC 20201

   Phone: 202-205-8879 | Email: julie.fliss@acf.hhs.gov

   http://www.acf.hhs.gov/cb/resource/cbcap-state-grants

DOJ16.123 | COMMUNITY-BASED VIOLENCE PREVENTION PROGRAM

Award: Project Grants

Purpose: To support a coordinated and multidisciplinary approach to community youth gun and gang violence through prevention, intervention, suppression, and reentry in targeted communities. This Program will work with community-based organizations to develop and implement strategies to reduce and prevent violence, particularly shootings, and killings.

Applicant Eligibility: Eligible applicants are limited to states (including territories), units of local government, federally recognized tribal Governments as determined by the Secretary of the Interior, nonprofit Organizations, and for-profit Organizations (including tribal nonprofit and for-profit Organizations), as well as Institutions of higher education (including tribal Institutions of higher education). For-profit Organizations (as well as other recipients) must agree to forgo any profit or management fee.

Beneficiary Eligibility: N/A

Award Range/Average: Not Applicable.

Funding: (Project Grants) FY 18 $1,043,332.00; FY 19 est $8,000,000.00; FY 20 est Estimate Not Available

Programs Administered by Federal Headquarters

HQ: Office of Juvenile Justice and Delinquency Prevention 810 7th Street NW, Washington, DC 20531
Phone: 202-598-9391 | Email: cynthia.pappas@usdoj.gov
http://ojjdp.gov

DHS97.023 | COMMUNITY ASSISTANCE PROGRAM STATE SUPPORT SERVICES ELEMENT (CAP-SSSE)
"CAP-SSSE"

Award: Cooperative Agreements
Purpose: The program provides technical assistance to the flood insurance program to evaluate the National Flood Insurance Program and build the State and community floodplain management expertise and capacity.
Applicant Eligibility: The Cooperative Agreement is only available to the state or territorial agency so designated by the Governor, as the state or territorial National Flood Insurance Program state Coordinating Agency. The CAP-SSSE is administered through the Mitigation Division of each FEMA Regional Office. FEMA's Regional Offices will contact eligible States to negotiate a mutually acceptable grant agreement. Funding is made available when the grant agreement is negotiated and agreed upon. Continued participation in the CAP-SSSE is dependent upon completing activities described in the grant agreement. The CAP-SSSE is designed to utilize the floodplain management capabilities of individual States in a cost effective cooperative agreement with FEMA. A State's participation in the CAP-SSSE is voluntary and is contingent upon need and skill level capability.
Beneficiary Eligibility: The direct beneficiary of the CAP-SSSE is the individual State receiving financial assistance. In addition, participating NFIP communities and local governments which receive flood plain management and flood loss reduction assistance provided by the State are also (indirect) beneficiaries as a consequence of the services they receive.
Award Range/Average: $10,400,000 Total Funding for all 50 states and U.S. Territories.
Funding: (Cooperative Agreements) FY 18 $10,400,000.00; FY 19 est $10,400,000.00; FY 20 est $10,400,000.00
HQ: Community Assistance Program - State Support Services FEMA 400 C Street SW, Washington, DC 20472
Phone: 202-212-3460 | Email: julie.grauer@fema.dhs.gov
http://www.fema.gov

HUD14.259 | COMMUNITY COMPASS TECHNICAL ASSISTANCE AND CAPACITY BUILDING
"Community Compass TA"

Award: Cooperative Agreements
Purpose: To help HUD's customers navigate complex housing and community development challenges by equipping them with the knowledge, skills, tools, capacity, and systems to implement HUD programs and policies successfully and be more effective stewards of HUD funding. The goal is to empower communities by providing effective technical assistance and capacity building so that successful program implementation is sustained over the long term.
Applicant Eligibility: Awardees tasked to provide technical assistance to PHAs must have at least one staff, subcontractor, or consultant that has at least five years of demonstrated Public Housing Programs experience, including agency operations, voucher Programs, property management operations, and capital investment Programs including capital improvements and various methods of housing development. In addition, awardees tasked to provide technical assistance to PHAs must have at least one staff, subcontractor, or consultant that has at least two years of demonstrated finance and underwriting experience related to RAD conversions. Funds may only be used to assist Organizations to improve their ability to manage HUD funds. Funds may not be used to assist individuals or families.
Beneficiary Eligibility: Selected providers will be deployed as HUD deems most necessary across the country to assist organizations receiving HUD funds to improve performance and management of HUD funds.
Award Range/Average: The Range is between $250,000 and $20,000,000. The applicant awarded funding for Native Hawaiian Housing Block Grant Program TA may receive less than the minimum award amount. The maximum award amount is an estimate based on the amount of funding available and the expected number of awards.
Funding: (Cooperative Agreements) FY 18 $68,520,790.00; FY 19 $56,218,000.00; est FY 20 est $56,000,000.00
HQ: 7th Street SW Room 7218, PO Box 451, Washington, DC 20147
Phone: 202-708-3176 | Email: stephanie.v.stone@hud.gov
http://portal.hud.gov/hudportal/hud?src=/program_offices/comm_planning/about/cpdta

USDA10.863 | COMMUNITY CONNECT GRANT PROGRAM
"Community Connect"

Award: Project Grants
Purpose: To provide grants to eligible rural communities to provide facilities such as schools, education centers, hospitals, law enforcement agencies, public safety organizations, etc.
Applicant Eligibility: To be eligible for a grant, the applicant must: (a) be legally organized as an incorporated Organization, an Indian tribe or tribal Organization, a state or local unit of government, or other legal entity, including cooperatives or private corporations or limited liability companies organized on a for profit or not-for profit basis, and (b) have the legal capacity and authority to own and operate the broadband facilities as proposed in its application, to enter into contracts and to otherwise comply with applicable federal statutes and regulations.
Beneficiary Eligibility: The people living in rural areas and to improve rural opportunities through the availability of access to high speed broadband networks.
Funding: (Project Grants) FY 18 $30,000,000.00; FY 19 est $30,000,000.00; FY 20 est $30,000,000.00
HQ: 1400 Independence Avenue SW, PO Box 1590, Washington, DC 20250
   Phone: 202-720-9554 | Email: chad.parker@wdc.usda.gov
   http://www.rd.usda.gov/programs-services/community-connect-grants

HUD14.248 | COMMUNITY DEVELOPMENT BLOCK GRANTS SECTION 108 LOAN GUARANTEES
"Section 108"

Award: Guaranteed/insured Loans
Purpose: To provide communities with a source of funding for economic development, housing rehabilitation, public facilities, and large-scale development projects.
Applicant Eligibility: Eligible Applicants include: metropolitan cities and urban counties, i.e., CDBG entitlement recipients; non entitlement communities that are assisted in their submission of applications by States that administer the CDBG Program; non entitlement communities eligible to receive CDBG funds under the HUD-Administered Small Cities CDBG Program; and Insular Areas (American Samoa, Guam, Northern Mariana Islands, and the Virgin Islands). The public entity may be the borrower or it may designate a public agency to be the borrower. Furthermore, HUD's FY 2017 appropriations act continues HUD's authority to provide loan guarantees to States borrowing on behalf of local Governments in non entitlement areas.
Beneficiary Eligibility: The principal beneficiaries are low and moderate income persons.
Award Range/Average: In FY 2016 commitments were issued in amounts ranging from $694,000 to $20,000,000. The average commitment amount was $7,727,545.
Funding: (Guaranteed/Insured Loans) FY 16 $85,003,000.00; FY 17 est $250,000,000.00; FY 18 est $0.00
HQ: 451 7th Street SW, Room 7180, Washington, DC 20410
   Phone: 202-402-4563 | Email: paul.webster@hud.gov
   http://www.hudexchange.info/programs/section-108

TREAS21.014 | COMMUNITY DEVELOPMENT FINANCIAL INSTITUTIONS BOND GUARANTEE PROGRAM
"BGP"

Award: Guaranteed/insured Loans
Purpose: To support community development lending and investment by providing a new source of long-term capital to certified Community Development Financial Institutions (CDFIs).
Applicant Eligibility: The Act defines Eligible CDFIs and authorizes the CDFI Fund to determine which entities may serve as Qualified Issuers.
Beneficiary Eligibility: Eligible CDFIs must use the Bond Proceeds for Eligible Community and Economic Development Purposes. This may include, but is not limited to, lending activities in low-income communities and underserved rural areas such as: owner-occupied home mortgages, charter schools, and municipal and community entity lending, among others.
Funding: (Guaranteed/Insured Loans) FY 18 $150,000,000.00; FY 19 est $500,000,000.00; FY 20 est $500,000,000.00

Programs Administered by Federal Headquarters

HQ: 1500 Pennsylvania Avenue NW, Washington, DC 20220
   Phone: 202-653-0300
   http://www.cdfifund.gov

TREAS21.020 | COMMUNITY DEVELOPMENT FINANCIAL INSTITUTIONS PROGRAM
"CDFI Program"

Award: Project Grants
Purpose: To promote economic revitalization and community development through investment and assistance to Community Development Financial Institutions (CDFIs).
Applicant Eligibility: Only certified CDFIs are eligible to apply for Financial Assistance awards. Certified CDFIs and entities seeking to become certified CDFIs may apply for Technical Assistance awards. No awards may be issued to Federal Government agencies, departments or instrumentalities, State Governments local Governments or any agency or instrumentality thereof.
Beneficiary Eligibility: Investment Areas and Targeted Populations, as defined in 12 C.F.R. 1805.
Award Range/Average: FY 2018 Range of Financial Assistance Awards was $125,000 to $1,525,000; FY 2018 Small and/or Emerging CDFI Assistance (SECA) Average Financial Assistance Awards were $394,680; FY 2018 Core Average Financial Assistance Award was $837,194, which included Base-FA, Persistent Poverty Counties-FA and Disability Funds-FA awards. FY 2018 Range of Technical Assistance Awards was $59,550 - $125,000; FY 2018 Average Technical Assistance Awards were $118,776. FY 2018 Range of Healthy Food Financing Initiative (HFFI) Assistance Awards was $500,000 - $3,000,000; FY 2018 Average HFFI Assistance Awards were $1,571,429.
Funding: (Project Grants) FY 18 $187,741,119.00; FY 19 est $182,000,000.00; FY 20 est $182,000,000.00
HQ: 1500 Pennsylvania Avenue NW, Washington, DC 20220
   Phone: 202-653-0300
   http://www.cdfifund.gov

NCUA44.002 | COMMUNITY DEVELOPMENT REVOLVING LOAN FUND PROGRAM FOR CREDIT UNIONS
"Loan Program for Low-Income Designated Credit Unions Grant Program for Low-Income Designated Credit Unions Office of Small Credit Union Initiatives Grant and Loan Program (CDRLF) (CDCU)"

Award: Direct Payments for Specified Use; Direct Loans
Purpose: To stimulate economic development in low income communities served by credit unions.
Applicant Eligibility: Federal and state chartered credit unions that have a low-income designation from the NCUA and/ or appropriate state regulator pursuant to NCUA Rules and Regulation at 701. 34(a)(1) or 741. 204. In the case of a non-federally insured, state-chartered credit union, a low-income designation from a state regulator, made under appropriate state standards with the concurrence of NCUA. Services to low-income members must include, at a minimum, offering share accounts and loans.
Beneficiary Eligibility: A credit union wishing to participate must serve a field of membership which is comprised primarily of low-income individuals. To participate in the CDRLF Program, a federally chartered credit union must be currently designated as a "low-income" credit union as set forth in NCUA's Rules and Regulations. A state-chartered credit union must have the equivalent low-income designation from its respective state supervisory authority and concurrence from NCUA. 12 CFR 701.34 A low-income designated credit union is one in which more than half of its members meet the NCUA definition for a "low-income member." Low-income members are those who earn 80 percent or less than the median family income for the metropolitan area where they live, or the national metropolitan area, whichever is greater. Low-income designated credit unions have offices and serve members throughout the United States, Puerto Rico, Guam, and the U.S. Virgin Islands, and on military bases around the world. Depending on the charter type, these credit unions serve occupational groups, associations and communities.
Award Range/Average: Smallest FY16 grant award - $200 Largest FY16 grant award - $15,000 Average FY16 grant award - $8,085 Smallest FY17 grant award - $1,500 Largest FY17 grant award - $25,000 Average FY17 grant award - $8,719 Smallest FY18 grant award - $1,300 Largest FY18 grant award - $20,000 Average FY18 grant award - $9,852

Funding: (Project Grants (Special)) FY 18 $2,000,000.00; FY 19 est $2,000,000.00; FY 20 est $2,000,000.00; (Direct Loans) FY 18 $1,500,000.00; FY 19 est $2,000,000.00; FY 20 est $2,000,000.00
HQ: 1775 Duke Street, Alexandria, VA 22314
   Phone: 703-518-6645 | Email: gvaliyil@ncua.gov
   https://www.ncua.gov/services/Pages/resources-expansion.aspx

DHS97.030 | COMMUNITY DISASTER LOANS
Award: Direct Loans
Purpose: The program provides loans to a local government that has suffered a substantial loss of revenues in a disaster-designated area to help communities to recover effectively in accordance with PPD-8.
Applicant Eligibility: Local (includes State-designated Indian Tribes, excludes Institutions of higher education and some hospitals) Applicants must be in a designated major disaster area and must demonstrate that they meet the specific conditions of FEMA Disaster Assistance Regulations 44 CFR Part 206, Subpart K, Community Disaster Loans. To be eligible, the applicant must demonstrate: 1) a substantial loss of revenues as a result of a major disaster; 2) a need for financial assistance to perform its governmental functions. During the 2017 hurricane season, a supplemental provided funding and new guidance specific to Hurricanes Harvey, Irma, and Maria. Public Law 115-72 and Public Law 115-123 provides additional supplemental appropriations and eligibility criteria for disaster relief requirements for the fiscal year ending September 30, 2018.
Beneficiary Eligibility: Local governments in a designated disaster area.
Award Range/Average: Not Available.
Funding: (Direct Loans) FY 18 $622,420,310.00; FY 19 est $58,000,000.00; FY 20 est $45,000,000.00
HQ: 500 C Street SW, PO Box 3163, Washington, DC 20472
   Phone: 202-646-5761 | Email: martha.polanco.2@fema.dhs.gov
   http://www.dhs.gov

DOD12.614 | COMMUNITY ECONOMIC ADJUSTMENT ASSISTANCE FOR ADVANCE PLANNING AND ECONOMIC DIVERSIFICATION
Award: Project Grants
Purpose: To assist State and local governments to lessen an area's dependence on defense expenditures by preparing economic diversification strategies, and contingency strategies and schematic land use plans for the potential redevelopment of a military installation prior to closure or realignment decisions.
Applicant Eligibility: Applicants for this assistance are to contact the Office of Economic Adjustment and a Project Manager will be assigned to work with the applicant to determine eligibility for assistance under this Program. States, counties, municipalities, other political subdivisions of a State, special purpose units of a State or local government, and tribal nations are eligible for this assistance if a substantial portion of the economic activity or population of the applicant's geographic area is dependent on defense expenditures. The Office of Economic Adjustment must determine, in consultation with the affected state or community, that a substantial portion of the economic activity or population of the geographic area subject to the planning under this Program is dependent on Department of Defense (Defense) expenditures. For purposes of eligibility determination, an area is considered Defense-dependent if it can demonstrate: (1) Direct military and civilian employment totals at least one and a half times the national level of Defense employment as a percent of the total U.S. labor force or (2) Defense-related expenditures comprise at least one and a half times the Defense percent of gross domestic product. The National Defense Budget Estimates for FY2016 states that the 2014 Defense employment as a percent of total labor force is 1. 4% and the 2014 Defense share of gross domestic product is 3. 4%. One and half times the Defense employment as a percent of the total labor force is 2. 1%, and one and half times the Defense percent of gross domestic product is 6. 0%. Technical and financial assistance is structured through an assigned Project Manager working with a defense-dependent State and/or local government.
Beneficiary Eligibility: States and communities, including workers, businesses, and other community interests, that could be affected by Defense budget reductions and base closures/realignments.
Award Range/Average: $1,000,000 - $4,000,000; $2,000,000
Funding: (Project Grants) FY 18 $4,734,728.00; FY 19 est $3,087,127.00; FY 20 est $3,000,000.00
HQ: 2231 Crystal Drive, Suite 520, Arlington, VA 22202-3711
   Phone: 703-697-2161 | Email: karen.e.bass-mcfadden.civ@mail.mil
   http://www.oea.gov/grants

Programs Administered by Federal Headquarters

DOD12.610 | COMMUNITY ECONOMIC ADJUSTMENT ASSISTANCE FOR COMPATIBLE USE AND JOINT LAND USE STUDIES

Award: Project Grants

Purpose: To assist State and local governments to mitigate or prevent incompatible civilian land use/activity that is likely to impair the continued operational utility of a Department of Defense (DoD) military installation.

Applicant Eligibility: Applicants for this assistance are to contact the Office of Economic Adjustment and a Project Manager will be assigned to work with the applicant to determine eligibility for assistance under this Program. States, counties, municipalities, other political subdivisions of a State, and special purpose units of a State or local government are eligible for this assistance if the Director, Office of Economic Adjustment determines that the encroachment of the civilian community is likely to impair the continued operational utility of the military installation.

Beneficiary Eligibility: States and communities, including local property owners, as well as the local military installation.

Award Range/Average: $50,000 - $750,000; $250,000

Funding: (Project Grants) FY 18 est $4,315,687.00; FY 19 $5,016,095.00; FY 20 est $4,500,000.00

HQ: 2231 Crystal Drive, Suite 520, Arlington, VA 22202-3711

    Phone: 703-697-2130
    http://www.oea.gov

DOD12.618 | COMMUNITY ECONOMIC ADJUSTMENT ASSISTANCE FOR ESTABLISHMENT OR EXPANSION OF A MILITARY INSTALLATION

Award: Cooperative Agreements; Project Grants

Purpose: To plan and carry out local adjustments in local public services and facilities, workforce training programs, and other community economic development activities in response to the proposed or actual expansion, establishment, or growth of a military installation by the Department of Defense (DoD).

Applicant Eligibility: Applicants for this assistance are to contact the Office of Economic Adjustment and a Project Manager will be assigned to work with the applicant to determine eligibility for assistance under this Program. U.S. States and Territories, counties, municipalities, other political subdivisions of a State, special purpose units of a State or local government, and tribal nations are eligible for this assistance if: 1) community impact assistance is not otherwise available; 2) the expansion, establishment, or growth involves the assignment to the installation of (i) more than 2,000 military, civilian, and contractor Department of Defense personnel, or (ii) more military, civilian, and contractor DoD personnel than the number equal to ten percent of the number of persons employed in counties or municipalities within fifteen miles of the installation, whichever is lesser; and, 3) The Secretary, through the Office of Economic Adjustment, determines the action is likely to have a direct and significant adverse consequence on the affected community. Where multiple jurisdictions may be affected, one Program of assistance will be available and the affected jurisdictions will need to combine their efforts into one responsive Program.

Beneficiary Eligibility: States, Territories and communities, including workers, businesses and other community interests that are affected by Department of Defense installation establishment or expansion actions.

Award Range/Average: The range of assistance is projected to be from $300,000 to $1 million.

Funding: (Salaries and Expenses) FY 18 $2,252,916.00; FY 19 est $2,738,887.00; FY 20 est $2,000,000.00

HQ: 2231 Crystal Drive, Suite 520, Arlington, VA 22202-3711

    Phone: 703-697-2130 | Email: karen.e.bass-mcfadden.civ@mail.mil
    http://www.oea.gov

DOD12.607 | COMMUNITY ECONOMIC ADJUSTMENT ASSISTANCE FOR REALIGNMENT OR CLOSURE OF A MILITARY INSTALLATION

Award: Project Grants

Purpose: To plan and carry out adjustment strategies; engage the private sector in order to plan and undertake community economic development and base redevelopment; and, partner with the Military Departments in response to the proposed or actual expansion, establishment, realignment or closure of a military installation by the Department of Defense (DoD).

Applicant Eligibility: Applicants for this assistance are to contact the Office of Economic Adjustment and a Project Manager will be assigned to work with the applicant to determine eligibility for assistance under this Program. States, counties, municipalities, other political subdivisions of a State, special purpose units of a State or local government, and tribal nations are eligible for this assistance if there is a proposed or actual realignment or closure of a military installation that is likely to have a direct and significant adverse consequence on the affected community. In the case of the establishment or expansion of a military installation, assistance may be made only if community impact assistance is not otherwise available and if the establishment or expansion involves the assignment to the installation of: (1) more than 2,000 military, civilian, and contractor Department of Defense personnel or (2) more military, civilian, and contractor DoD personnel than the number equal to ten percent of the number of persons employed in counties or municipalities within fifteen miles of the installation, whichever is lesser. Where multiple jurisdictions may be affected, one Program of assistance will be available and the affected jurisdictions will need to combine their efforts into one responsive Program.

Beneficiary Eligibility: States and communities, including workers, businesses, and other community interests that are affected by Department of Defense base closures and realignments.

Award Range/Average: Range: $79,560 - $2,331,240 Average grant: $648,093

Funding: (Project Grants) FY 18 $5,465,034.00; FY 19 est $2,784,625.00 FY 20 est $2,500,000.00

HQ: 2231 Crystal Drive, Suite 520, Arlington, VA 22202-3711

Phone: 703-697-2130

http://www.oea.gov

DOD12.611 | COMMUNITY ECONOMIC ADJUSTMENT ASSISTANCE FOR REDUCTIONS IN DEFENSE INDUSTRY EMPLOYMENT

Award: Project Grants

Purpose: To assist States and local governments to plan and carry out community adjustment and economic diversification activities in response to reductions in defense industry employment.

Applicant Eligibility: Applicants for this assistance are to contact the Office of Economic Adjustment and a Project Manager will be assigned to work with the applicant to determine eligibility for assistance under this Program. States, counties, municipalities, other political subdivisions of a State, special purpose units of a State or local government, and tribal nations are eligible for this assistance if there is: a publicly announced planned major reduction in Department of Defense (DoD) spending; the closure or significantly reduced operations of a defense facility as the result of the merger, acquisition, or consolidation of the defense contractor operating the defense facility; the cancellation or termination of a DoD contract; or the failure to proceed with an approved major weapon system Program if these actions will have a direct and significant adverse impact on a community or its residents. The local action must result in the loss of: 2, 500 or more employee positions, in the case of a Metropolitan Statistical Area; 1,000 of more employee positions, in the case of a labor market area outside of a Metropolitan Statistical Area; or one percent of the total number of civilian jobs in that area to be considered for this assistance.

Beneficiary Eligibility: States and communities, including workers, businesses, and other community interests, that may be affected by Defense actions.

Award Range/Average: $250,000 - $1,500,000; $500,000

Funding: (Project Grants) FY 18 $2,466,536.00; FY 19 est $1,000,000.00; FY 20 est $1,000,000.00

HQ: 2231 Crystal Drive, Suite 520, Arlington, VA 22202-3711

Phone: 703-697-2161 | Email: karen.e.bass-mcfadden.civ@mail.mil

http://www.oea.gov/grants

DOD12.604 | COMMUNITY ECONOMIC ADJUSTMENT ASSISTANCE FOR REDUCTIONS IN DEFENSE SPENDING

Award: Cooperative Agreements; Project Grants; Dissemination of Technical Information

Purpose: Provides assistance to State and local governments affected by qualifying Department of Defense actions.

Applicant Eligibility: Applicants for this assistance are to contact the Office of Economic Adjustment and a Project Manager will be assigned to work with the applicant to determine eligibility for assistance under this Program. States, counties, municipalities, other political subdivisions of a State, special purpose units of a State or local government, and tribal nations are eligible for this assistance if there are reductions in Defense spending resulting in a proposed or actual military and/or civilian personnel reduction resulting from a reduction in spending. Personnel reductions must result in the loss of not less than: 2,000 military, civilian, and contractor personnel in an urban labor market area, or 1,000 military, civilian, and contractor personnel in the case of a non-urban labor market area. The Director, Office of Economic Adjustment must also determine whether the loss results is a direct and significant adverse impact on a community and its residents. Where multiple jurisdictions may be affected by reduced spending and personnel reductions, one Program of assistance will be available and the affected jurisdictions will need to combine their efforts into one responsive Program.

Beneficiary Eligibility: States and communities, including workers, businesses, and other community interests that are affected by a qualifying Department of Defense action.

Programs Administered by Federal Headquarters

Award Range/Average: $300,000 - $400,000
Funding: (Project Grants) FY 18 $1,290,246.00; FY 19 est $0.00; FY 20 est $0.00
HQ: 2231 Crystal Drive, Suite 520, Arlington, VA 22202-3711
  Phone: 703-697-2130
  http://www.oea.gov

DOD12.003 | COMMUNITY ECONOMIC ADJUSTMENT ASSISTANCE FOR RESPONDING TO THREATS TO THE RESILIENCE OF A MILITARY INSTALLATION
"Community Economic Adjustment Assistance for Military Installation Resilience"

Award: Project Grants
Purpose: Assist State and local governments to provide planning and technical assistance to communities to perform a military installation resilience review and develop strategies to minimize the effect of, adapt to, and recover from extreme weather events.
Applicant Eligibility: Interstate, Intrastate, State (includes District of Columbia, public Institutions of higher education and hospitals), Local (includes State-designated Indian Tribes, excludes Institutions of higher education and hospitals).
Beneficiary Eligibility: Applicants for this assistance are to contact the Office of Economic Adjustment and a Project Manager will be assigned to work with the applicant to determine eligibility for assistance under this program. States, counties, municipalities, other political subdivisions of a State, and special purpose units of a State or local government are eligible for this assistance if the Director, Office of Economic Adjustment determines that the capability of a military installation to avoid, prepare for, minimize the effect of, adapt to, and recover from extreme weather events, or from anticipated or unanticipated changes in environmental conditions is at risk due to lack of necessary resources outside the military installation.
Award Range/Average: $50,000 - $500,000
Funding: (Project Grants) FY 18 Actual Not Available; FY 19 est Estimate Not Available; FY 20 est $500,000.00
HQ: 2231 Crystal Drive, Suite 520, Arlington, VA 22202
  Phone: 703-697-2161 | Email: karen.e.bass-mcfadden.civ@mail.mil

USDA10.766 | COMMUNITY FACILITIES LOANS AND GRANTS

Award: Project Grants; Direct Loans; Guaranteed/insured Loans
Purpose: To maximize community facilities by providing essential services to rural residents.
Applicant Eligibility: City, county, and State agencies; political and quasi-political subdivisions of States and associations, including corporations, Indian Tribes on Federal and State reservations and other federally recognized Indian Tribes; and existing private corporations which: (1) are operated on a not-for-profit basis; (2) have or will have the legal authority necessary for constructing, operating, and maintaining the proposed facility or service and for obtaining, giving security for, and repaying the loan; and (3) are unable to finance the proposed project from its own resources or through commercial credit at reasonable rates and terms. Assistance is authorized for eligible applicants in rural areas of the States, Puerto Rico, the Virgin Islands, Guam, American Samoa, the commonwealth of the Northern Mariana Islands, the Marshall Islands, the Republic of Palaw, and the Federated States of Micronesia.
Beneficiary Eligibility: Loans for essential community facilities are made to eligible entities who provide essential community services to the population living within the service area of the facility or being served by the facility. Beneficiaries include farmers, ranchers, rural residents, rural businesses, and other users of such public facilities in eligible applicant areas as set out above.
Award Range/Average: 2017 Direct Loan ranged from $1,800 to $113,000,000. Average: $3,677,066. Guaranteed Loan ranged from $500,000 to $16,500,000. Average: $4,417,853. Grants ranged from $1,200- $238,000. Average $31,043.
Funding: (Project Grants) FY 17 $23,600,000.00; FY 18 est $24,700,000.00; FY 19 est $25,000,000.00; (Direct Loans) FY 17 $2,366,000,000.00; FY 18 est $2,520,000,000.00; FY 19 est $2,500,000,000.00; (Guaranteed/Insured Loans) FY 17 $141,300,000.00; FY 18 est $148,287,000.00; FY 19 est $148,000,000.00
HQ: 1400 Independence Avenue SW, Washington, DC 20250
  Phone: 202-720-1498 | Email: geoffrey.armes@wdc.usda.gov
  http://www.rd.usda.gov

USDA10.225 | COMMUNITY FOOD PROJECTS
"Community Foods"

Award: Project Grants
Purpose: To support and develop food projects designed to meet the food needs of low-income people; increase the self-reliance of communities; and promote comprehensive responses to local food, farm, and nutrition issues.
Applicant Eligibility: Proposals may be submitted by private nonprofit entities. Because projects must promote comprehensive responses to local food, farm, and nutrition issues, applicants are encouraged to seek and create partnership among public, private nonprofit and private for-profit Organizations or firms. To be further eligible for a grant, a private nonprofit applicant must meet three mandatory requirements: 1. Have experience in the area of: (a) community food work, particularly concerning small and medium-sized farms, including the provision of food to people in low-income communities and the development of new markets in low-income communities for agricultural producers; or (b) job training and business development activities in low-income communities; 2. demonstrate competency to implement a project, provide fiscal accountability and oversight, collect data, and prepare reports and other appropriate documentation; and 3. demonstrate a willingness to share information with researchers, practitioners, and other interested parties.
Beneficiary Eligibility: Low income people.
Award Range/Average: If minimum or maximum amounts of funding per competitive and/or capacity project grant, or cooperative agreement are established, these amounts will be announced in the annual Competitive Request for Application (RFA).The most current RFA is available via: https://nifa.usda.gov/funding-opportunity/community-food-projects-cfp-competitive-grants-program
Funding: (Project Grants) FY 18 $8,640,000.00; FY 19 est $3,840,000.00; FY 20 est $4,800,000.00
HQ: Division of Nutrition 1400 Independence Avenue SW, PO Box 2225, Washington, DC 20250-2225
    Phone: 202-401-2138
    http://nifa.usda.gov/program/community-food-projects-competitive-grant-program-cfpcgp

DOD12.600 | COMMUNITY INVESTMENT

Award: Cooperative Agreements; Project Grants; Dissemination of Technical Information
Purpose: Provides assistance authorized by statute.
Applicant Eligibility: Applicant eligibility for this Program may be directed or restricted by statute and Department of Defense policy. Applicants for this assistance are to contact the Office of Economic Adjustment and a Project Manager will be assigned to work with the applicant to determine eligibility for assistance under this Program. Unsolicited applications will not be accepted.
Beneficiary Eligibility: Beneficiaries under this program may be directed or restricted by statute and/or Department of Defense policy.
Award Range/Average: Average: $20,260,000
Funding: (Direct Payments for Specified Use) FY 18 $21,738,047.00; FY 19 est $53,770,314.00; FY 20 est $10,000,000.00
HQ: 2231 Crystal Drive, Suite 520, Arlington, VA 22202-3711
    Phone: 703-697-2130 | Email: karen.e.bass-mcfadden.civ@mail.mil
    http://www.oea.gov

DOD12.561 | COMMUNITY PARTNERS IN SUICIDE PREVENTION
"Community Partners in Suicide Prevention Outreach and Education"

Award: Project Grants
Purpose: To conduct outreach and education efforts around mental health, substance use disorders, traumatic brain injury, and suicide prevention.
Applicant Eligibility: N/A
Beneficiary Eligibility: N/A
Award Range/Average: Grants range from $500,000 to $2,500,000.
HQ: 4800 Mark Center Drive, Suite 05J25, Arlington, VA 22350
    Phone: 703-614-8833 | Email: malcolm.k.hawkins.civ@mail.mil

Programs Administered by Federal Headquarters

HHS93.137 | COMMUNITY PROGRAMS TO IMPROVE MINORITY HEALTH GRANT PROGRAM

Award: Project Grants

Purpose: To facilitate the improvement of minority health and eliminate health disparities through the development of partnerships with state, tribal, and local governments and nongovernmental organizations.

Applicant Eligibility: State and local Governments or their Bona Fide Agents (this includes the District of Columbia, the Commonwealth of Puerto Rico, the Virgin Islands, the Commonwealth of the Northern Mariana Islands, American Samoa, Guam, the Federated States of Micronesia, the Republic of the Marshall Islands, and the Republic of Palau); Nonprofit with 501(c)(3) IRS status (other than institution of higher education); Nonprofit without 501(c)(3) IRS status (other than institution of higher education); For-profit Organizations (other than small business); for profit Organizations must agree to forgo any profit or management fee.; Small, minority, and women-owned business; universities; Colleges; Research Institutions; Hospitals; Community-based Organizations; Faith-based Organizations; Federally recognized or state-recognized American Indian/Alaska Native Tribal Governments; American Indian/Alaska Native tribally designated Organizations; Alaska Native health Organizations; Urban Indian health Organizations; Tribal epidemiology centers; Political subdivisions of states (in consultation with states).

Beneficiary Eligibility: Target populations: American Indian or Alaska Natives; Asians; Blacks or African Americans; Hispanics or Latinos; Native Hawaiians or other Pacific Islanders; economically and/or environmentally disadvantaged; and limited English proficient populations. However, services may not be denied to any otherwise eligible persons.

Award Range/Average: Range from $275,000 to $500,000

Funding: (Project Grants) FY 16 $19,424,704.00; FY 17 est $22,552,878.00; FY 18 est $22,552,878.00

HQ: 1101 Wootton Parkway, Suite 550 Tower Building, Rockville, MD 20852

　　Phone: 240-453-8822 | Email: eric.west@hhs.gov

　　http://www.hhs.gov

ED84.368 | COMPETITIVE GRANTS FOR STATE ASSESSMENTS (FORMERLY GRANTS FOR ENHANCED ASSESSMENT INSTRUMENTS)

Award: Project Grants

Purpose: To improve the quality, validity, and reliability of State academic assessments; and to measure student academic achievement through the use of multiple measures from multiple sources.

Applicant Eligibility: State educational agencies (SEAs) and/or consortia of SEAs are eligible to receive grants.

Beneficiary Eligibility: State educational agencies (SEAs) and/or consortia of SEAs, local educational agencies and local schools will benefit.

Award Range/Average: The average award is $4,545,709.

Funding: (Project Grants) FY 18 $8,948,000.00; FY 19 est $8,900,000.00; FY 20 est $8,900,000.00

HQ: Department of Education 400 Maryland Avenue SW, Washington, DC 20202

　　Phone: 202-453-7982 | Email: donald.peasley@ed.gov

　　http://www.2.ed.gov/programs/eag/index.html

DOD12.556 | COMPETITIVE GRANTS: PROMOTING K-12 STUDENT ACHIEVEMENT AT MILITARY-CONNECTED SCHOOLS
"The Department of Defense Education Activity (DoDEA) Educational Partnership Grant Program"

Award: Project Grants

Purpose: The DoDEA Educational Partnership Grant Program provide resources for local education agencies [LEAs] to meet the academic, social and emotional needs of the highly mobile military-connected students in their community.

Applicant Eligibility: Awards will be made to local educational agencies (LEAs) on behalf of their eligible school(s). To qualify all participating schools must have a 15 percent or greater military dependent student enrollment.

Beneficiary Eligibility: K-12 students are the primary beneficiaries, although the grants may also fund teacher professional development.

Award Range/Average: In FY16, DoDEA awarded 56 grants that ranged from $250,000 to $1,500,000. These awards are implemented over a 5 year cycle.

Funding: (Project Grants (Discretionary)) FY 17 Actual Not Available; FY 18 est $16,350,000.00; FY 19 est Estimate Not Available

HQ: 4800 Mark Center Drive, Alexandria, VA 22350

Phone: 571-372-6026

http://www.dodea.edu/partnership/grants.cfm

HHS93.269 | COMPLEX HUMANITARIAN EMERGENCY AND WAR-RELATED INJURY PUBLIC HEALTH ACTIVITIES

Award: Project Grants

Purpose: To bring public health and epidemiologic principles to the aid of populations affected by complex humanitarian emergencies.

Applicant Eligibility: The general public will benefit from the objectives of this Program.

Beneficiary Eligibility: Same as Applicant Eligibility.

Award Range/Average: N/A

Funding: (Project Grants (Cooperative Agreements)) FY 18 $10,940,076.00; FY 19 est $226,264.00; FY 20 est $226,265.00

HQ: 1600 Clifton Road NE, PO Box H21-9, Atlanta, GA 30333

Phone: 404-718-6503

http://www.cdc.gov

ED84.283 | COMPREHENSIVE CENTERS

Award: Project Grants

Purpose: To support comprehensive centers that provide training, professional development, and technical assistance to State educational agencies, local educational agencies, regional educational agencies, and schools in the region where the center is located.

Applicant Eligibility: Research Organizations, Institutions, agencies, Institutions of higher education (IHEs), or partnerships among such entities, or individuals with the demonstrated ability or capacity to carry out the required activities, including providing training to States, school districts, and schools, may apply.

Beneficiary Eligibility: Agencies supporting or providing elementary and secondary education will benefit, including State and local educational agencies, regional educational agencies, the Bureau of Indian Education, Indian tribes, community-based organizations, and other recipients of funds under the ESEA.

Award Range/Average: The Department held a competition for new awards in FY 2019. Applications were due by May 24,2019; awards will be made by September 30,2019. The Department plans to make 5-year awards for 19 regional centers and one national center; awards will range from $1.0 to $6.5 million. In addition, the Department supports a 5-year award made in FY 2016 for a center that focuses on students at risk of not attaining full literacy skills due to a disability; this center receives $1.5 million per year. For additional information, see https://www2.ed.gov/programs/newccp/applicant.html.

Funding: (Project Grants) FY 18 $52,000,000.00; FY 19 est $52,000,000.00; FY 20 est $0.00

HQ: Office of Elementary and Secondary Education Department of Education 400 Maryland Avenue SW, LBJ Building Room 3E108, Washington, DC 20202

Phone: 202-453-5546 | Email: danielle.smith@ed.gov

http://www.ed.gov/programs/newccp/index.html

HHS93.104 | COMPREHENSIVE COMMUNITY MENTAL HEALTH SERVICES FOR CHILDREN WITH SERIOUS EMOTIONAL DISTURBANCES (SED)
"CMHS Child Mental Health Service Initiative"

Award: Project Grants

Purpose: To provide community-based systems of care for children and adolescents with a serious emotional disturbance and their families.

Applicant Eligibility: States, political subdivisions of a State, such as county or local Governments, and Federally Recognized Indian Tribal Governments.

Beneficiary Eligibility: Children under age 22 with a diagnosed serious emotional disturbance, serious behavioural disorder, or serious mental disorder.

Award Range/Average: $376,096 to $2,000,000; $1,329,454

Programs Administered by Federal Headquarters

Funding: (Project Grants (Discretionary)) FY 18 $96,854,583.00; FY 19 est $64,099,899.00; FY 20 est $27,167,122.00
HQ: 5600 Fishers Lane, Rockville, MD 20857
Phone: 240-276-1418 | Email: roger.george@samhsa.hhs.gov
http://www.samhsa.gov

ED84.371 | COMPREHENSIVE LITERACY DEVELOPMENT

Award: Project Grants
Purpose: To advance literacy skills, including pre-literacy skills, reading and writing for students from birth through grade 12, including English learner and students with disabilities.
Applicant Eligibility: State educational agencies are eligible applicants.
Beneficiary Eligibility: The Comprehensive Literacy Development program benefits children and youth from birth through 12th grade.
Award Range/Average: Not Available.
Funding: (Project Grants) FY 18 $190,000,000.00; FY 19 est $190,000,000.00; FY 20 est $0.00
HQ: 400 Maryland Avenue SW, Washington, DC 20202
Phone: 202-260-2551 | Email: sylvia.lyles@ed.gov
http://www.ed.gov/programs/strivingreaders/index.html

DOJ16.838 | COMPREHENSIVE OPIOID ABUSE SITE-BASED PROGRAM "COAP"

Award: Cooperative Agreements; Project Grants
Purpose: The Comprehensive Opioid Abuse Site-based Program reduces opioid misuse fatalities. It also supports the clinical decision-making and prevents the misuse.
Applicant Eligibility: For TTA - eligible applicants are limited to for-profit (commercial) Organizations, nonprofit Organizations (including tribal nonprofit and for-profit Organizations), and Institutions of higher education (including tribal Institutions of higher education) that have experience delivering training and technical assistance nationwide. For-profit Organizations must agree to forgo any profit or management fee. Applicants are encouraged to submit an application that demonstrates a thorough understanding of the diverse training and technical assistance needs of communities and states attempting to plan and implement comprehensive strategies in response to the growing opioid epidemic.
Beneficiary Eligibility: Program aims to plan and implement comprehensive strategies in response to the growing national opioid epidemic.
Award Range/Average: For specifics, please see the current fiscal year's solicitation available at the Office of Justice Programs web site https://ojp.gov/funding/Explore/CurrentFundingOpportunities.htm.
Funding: (Cooperative Agreements) FY 17 $11,743,182.00; FY 18 est $145,000,000.00; FY 19 est $20,000,000.00
HQ: U.S. Department of Justice Bureau of Justice Assistance 810 7th Street NW, Washington, DC 20531
Phone: 202-616-6500
http://www.OJP.gov

NSF47.070 | COMPUTER AND INFORMATION SCIENCE AND ENGINEERING "CISE"

Award: Project Grants
Purpose: To support investigator-initiated research and education in all areas of computer and information science and engineering; advance the development and use of cyberinfrastructure across the science and engineering enterprise; and contribute to the education and training.
Applicant Eligibility: Except where a Program solicitation establishes more restrictive eligibility criteria, individuals and Organizations in the following categories may submit proposals: universities and colleges; Non-profit, non-academic Organizations; For-profit Organizations; State and local Governments; and unaffiliated individuals. See the NSF Grant Proposal Guide, Chapter i.e., for a full description of eligibility requirements: http://www.nsf.gov/publications/pub_summ.jsp?ods_key=gpg.
Beneficiary Eligibility: N/A
Award Range/Average: Range Low $5,000 Range High $17,529,856 Average $172,469
Funding: (Project Grants) FY 18 $960,800,000; FY 19 est $980,740,000.00; FY 20 est $883,040,000

HQ: 2415 Eisenhower Avenue, Alexandria, VA 22314
Phone: 703-292-8900 | Email: cwhitson@nsf.gov
http://nsf.gov/dir/index.jsp?org=cise

DOS19.121 | CONFLICT AND STABILIZATION OPERATIONS "CSO"

Award: Cooperative Agreements; Project Grants
Purpose: To strengthen U.S. national security by breaking cycles of violent conflict and mitigating crisis in priority countries.
Applicant Eligibility: CSO recommends applicants view the open application on www.grants.gov for more information.
Beneficiary Eligibility: Same as Applicant Eligibility.
Award Range/Average: CSO recommends applicants view the open application on www.grants.gov for more information.
Funding: (Project Grants) FY 16 $17,500,000.00; FY 17 est $6,650,000.00; FY 18 est Estimate Not Available
HQ: 2121 Virginia Avenue NW, Suite 7100, Washington, DC 20037
Phone: 202-663-0316 | Email: perrinao@state.gov
http://www.state.gov/j/cso/index.htm

DOD12.599 | CONGRESSIONALLY DIRECTED ASSISTANCE "Annual Congressionally Directed Assistance"

Award: Cooperative Agreements; Project Grants
Purpose: To implement Congressionally directed assistance for the purposes identified in the Department of Defense ("DoD") annual appropriations act.
Applicant Eligibility: Types of Organizations that may apply vary with the statutory requirements and appropriate sources of supporting information. Examples of Organizations that have received assistance include nonprofit Organizations, educational Institutions, memorial Organizations, local Governments and cultural Organizations. Merit-based or competitive processes are followed when applicable.
Beneficiary Eligibility: Eligible beneficiaries are determined in accordance with the applicable statutory authorization.
Award Range/Average: Dependent on the language and direction found in the annual Defense Appropriations Act.
Funding: (Project Grants) FY 17 Actual Not Available FY 18 est Estimate Not Available FY 19 est $44,000,000.00
HQ: 1155 Defense Pentagon, Washington, DC 20301
Phone: 703-545-1046 | Email: karen.rooney@whs.mil

DOC11.469 | CONGRESSIONALLY IDENTIFIED AWARDS AND PROJECTS

Award: Project Grants
Purpose: The program funds research and development of marine and atmospheric science for the construction of suitable facilities.
Applicant Eligibility: Eligible applicants include State and local Governments, including their universities and colleges, quasi-governmental agencies, private universities and colleges, and private profit and nonprofit Organizations and/or individuals. Typically those specifically identified by Congress in agency appropriations legislation.
Beneficiary Eligibility: Through the awarding of financial assistance to facilitate education, research and development in the fields of marine and atmospheric science, and for the construction of educational, research and development facilities, this program benefits Federal, State, local governments, public and private universities and colleges, profit and nonprofit organizations, and the general public.
Funding: (Cooperative Agreements) FY 16 $1,796,658.00; FY 17 est $1,796,658.00; FY 18 est Estimate Not Available
HQ: 1325 E W Highway, Silver Spring, MD 20910
Phone: 301-713-0926
http://www.nmfs.noaa.gov

Programs Administered by Federal Headquarters

DOD12.005 | CONSERVATION AND REHABILITATION OF NATURAL RESOURCES ON MILITARY INSTALLATIONS
"Sikes Act"

Award: Cooperative Agreements
Purpose: Deals with protecting and enhancing fish, fauna, and other natural resources on and associated with U.S. military lands.
Applicant Eligibility: Federal and State agencies having responsibility for the conservation or management of fish and wildlife. Centers for natural lands management, universities, etc.
Beneficiary Eligibility: Public in general.
Funding: (Cooperative Agreements) FY 18 $500,000.00; FY 19 est $500,000.00; FY 20 est $500,000.00
HQ: 2219 Infantry Post Road, Fort Sam Houston, TX 78234
    Phone: 210-466-2485 | Email: yamileth.e.moneymaker.civ@mail.mil
    https://www.fws.gov/fisheries/sikes_act

DOJ16.888 | CONSOLIDATED AND TECHNICAL ASSISTANCE GRANT PROGRAM TO ADDRESS CHILDREN AND YOUTH EXPERIENCING DOMESTIC AND SEXUAL VIOLENCE AND ENGAGE MEN AND BOYS AS ALLIES

Award: Project Grants
Purpose: The Consolidated and Technical Assistance Grant Program prevent sexual assault, domestic violence, dating violence, and responds to violence targeting children and youth. The program supports prevention strategies.
Applicant Eligibility: Applicants for grant funding are limited to: Nonprofit, nongovernmental entities with the demonstrated primary goal of providing services to children or youth exposed to or victims of domestic violence, dating violence, sexual assault, or stalking; Non-profit, nongovernmental entities with demonstrated histories of providing comprehensive services to children or youth exposed to or victims of domestic violence, dating violence, sexual assault, or stalking; Nonprofit, nongovernmental entities with demonstrated histories of creating effective public education and/or community organizing campaigns to encourage men and boys to work as allies with women and girls to prevent sexual assault, domestic violence, dating violence, and stalking; Indian Tribes or tribal nonprofit Organizations that provides services to tribal children and youth exposed to or are of domestic violence, dating violence, sexual assault, or stalking; or Territorial, Tribal or unit of local government entities.
Beneficiary Eligibility: Other nonprofit, nongovernmental organizations including community and faith-based organizations.
Award Range/Average: $340,000- $750,000
Funding: (Project Grants) FY 16 $8,379,218.00; FY 17 est $8,525,945.00; FY 18 est $8,500,000.00
HQ: 145 N Street NE, Suite 10W121, Washington, DC 20530
    Phone: 202-305-1177 | Email: tia.farmer@usdoj.gov
    http://www.justice.gov/ovw

ED84.403 | CONSOLIDATED GRANT TO THE OUTLYING AREAS

Award: Formula Grants
Purpose: To make an annual consolidated grant to assist an Insular Area in carrying out one or more State-administered formula grant programs of the Department.
Applicant Eligibility: Virgin Islands, Guam, American Samoa and the Commonwealth of the Northern Mariana Islands.
Beneficiary Eligibility: Contact Program Office.
Award Range/Average: Estimated FY 2019 awards range from approximately $15.6 million to $31.4 million.
Funding: (Formula Grants) FY 18 $90,085,800.00; FY 19 est $91,305,134.00; FY 20 est $0.00
HQ: 400 Maryland Avenue SW, LBJ Building Room 3E228, Washington, DC 20202
    Phone: 202-205-0940 | Email: tiffany.forrester@ed.gov
    http://www.ed.gov/about/offices/list/oese/sst/index.html

HHS93.759 | CONSORTIUM FOR TOBACCO USE CESSATION TECHNICAL ASSISTANCE FINANCED SOLELY BY PREVENTION AND PUBLIC HEALTH FUNDS
"Consortium for Tobacco Use Cessation Technical Assistance"
Award: Cooperative Agreements
Purpose: Provide technical assistance to state tobacco control programs and national and state partners.
Applicant Eligibility: A Bona Fide Agent is an agency/Organization identified by the state as eligible to submit an application under the state eligibility in lieu of a state application. If applying as a bona fide agent of a state or local government, a legal, binding agreement from the state or local government as documentation of the status is required.
Beneficiary Eligibility: The general public will benefit from the objectives of this program.
Funding: (Cooperative Agreements) FY 18 $450,000.00; FY 19 est $0.00; FY 20 est $0.00
HQ: NCCDPHP 4770 Buford Highway NE MSK50, Atlanta, GA 30341
Phone: 770-488-1172 | Email: sbabb@cdc.gov

NASA43.010 | CONSTRUCTION & ENVIRONMENTAL COMPLIANCE & REMEDIATION
Award: Cooperative Agreements; Project Grants
Purpose: To review funding opportunity announcement for additional information.
Applicant Eligibility: Construction & Environmental Compliance & Remediation. Review funding opportunity announcement for additional information.
Beneficiary Eligibility: Review funding opportunity announcement for additional information.
Funding: (Salaries and Expenses) FY 16 $395,332.00; FY 17 est $0.00; FY 18 Estimate Not Available
HQ: 300 E Street SW, PO Box LH010, Washington, DC 20546
Phone: 202-358-0047 | Email: jennifer.l.richards@nasa.gov
http://www.nasa.gov

HHS93.352 | CONSTRUCTION SUPPORT
"Extramural Construction"
Award: Project Grants
Purpose: To renovate existing research facilities and build new research facilities to meet basic and clinical space requirements, laboratory safety, biohazard containment, and animal care standards.
Applicant Eligibility: Construction.
Beneficiary Eligibility: Public nonprofit institution/organization.
Funding: (Project Grants) FY 18 Actual Not Available; FY 19 est $50,000,000.00; FY 20 est Estimate Not Available
HQ: 6701 Democracy Boulevard Room 957, PO Box 4874, Bethesda, MD 20892-4874
Phone: 301-435-0864 | Email: pnewman@mail.nih.gov
http://dpcpsi.nih.gov/orip/index

USDA10.253 | CONSUMER DATA AND NUTRITION RESEARCH
Award: Cooperative Agreements; Project Grants; Dissemination of Technical Information
Purpose: ERS provides help for development, administration, and evaluation of agricultural and rural policies.
Applicant Eligibility: Any individual or Organization in the U.S. and U.S. Territories is eligible to receive the popular or technical research publications that convey the research results, although there may be a fee.
Beneficiary Eligibility: Same as Applicant Eligibility.
Funding: (Cooperative Agreements) FY 17 $1,100,000.00; FY 18 est $1,100,000.00; FY 19 est $0.00; (Project Grants) FY 17 $2,700,000.00; FY 18 est $2,700,000.00; FY 19 est $0.00
HQ: 355 E Street SW, Room 5-254, Washington, DC 20024-3231
Phone: 202-694-5008 | Email: nthomas@ers.usda.gov
http://www.ers.usda.gov

Programs Administered by Federal Headquarters

HHS93.545 | CONSUMER OPERATED AND ORIENTED PLAN [CO-OP] PROGRAM

Award: Direct Loans

Purpose: To provide assistance to applicants for activities related to establishing and maintaining a Consumer Operated and Oriented (CO-OP), nonprofit health insurance issuer.

Applicant Eligibility: To be eligible to apply for a loan under the CO-OP Program, an applicant must: 1. Intend to become a CO-OP; 2. Have formed a private nonprofit member Organization (see Section IV. B of the FOA for acceptable evidence of certified nonprofit status).; 3. Submit in its loan application an Eligibility Affidavit and Application Certification signed by the applicant's Chief Executive Officer, Chief Financial Officer, or an officer of the applicant's Board of Directors, certifying the accuracy, completeness, and truthfulness of all information contained in the loan application; and certifying that, if the applicant Organization is awarded loan(s) under this FOA, it will repay them according to the terms laid out in this FOA, finalized in 45 CFR part 156 subpart F, and in the Loan Agreement issued when the award is announced. The signatory must be legally authorized to bind the CO-OP. For a description of the Eligibility Affidavit and Application Certification, see Section IV. B. 10. 4. Commit to offering a CO-OP qualified health plan at the silver and gold benefit levels in every individual market Exchange that serves the geographic regions in which it is licensed and intends to provide healthcare coverage; and5. If choosing to offer at least one plan in the small group market outside the Exchange, commit to offering a CO-OP qualified health plan at both the silver and gold benefit levels in each Small Business Health Options Program (SHOP) that serves the geographic regions in which the Organization offers coverage in the small group market; and 6. Commit that at least two-thirds of the contracts issued by the CO-OP will be CO-OP qualified health plans offered in the individual market or individual and small group markets of the States in which the CO-OP is licensed.

Beneficiary Eligibility: N/A

Award Range/Average: Loan Range: $56,656,900 to $265,133,000 Average Loan Size: $ $106,278,338.

HQ: 200 Independence Avenue SW, Room 739H, Washington, DC 20201

Phone: 301-492-4127 | Email: reed.cleary@cms.hhs.gov

http://www.cms.gov

HUD14.267 | CONTINUUM OF CARE PROGRAM

Award: Project Grants; Direct Payments for Specified Use

Purpose: To encourage community-wide commitment to end homelessness, provide funding for efforts, promote access to and effective utilization of mainstream programs by homeless individuals and families, and optimize self-sufficiency among individuals and families experiencing this condition.

Applicant Eligibility: States, local Governments, other governmental entities and nonprofit Organizations.

Beneficiary Eligibility: Homeless individuals and families with children; Recipients in Continuums of Care that have been designated by HUD as High Performing Communities (HPC) may serve persons determined to be at-risk of homelessness, based on criteria established through the present year Notice of Funding Availability (NOFA).

Award Range/Average: HUD imposes the following limitations: Funding of up to 75 percent for acquisition, new construction, rehabilitation, supportive services, operating, and HMIS costs; funding for up to 10 percent for project administration costs; and indirect costs may be allocated to each eligible activity as long as that allocation is consistent with an indirect cost rate proposal developed in accordance with 2 CFR 200, as applicable.

Funding: (Project Grants (Discretionary)) FY 18 $2,122,333,866.00; FY 19 est $2,200,000,000.00; FY 20 est $2,200,000,000.00

HQ: Community Planning and Development Office of Special Needs Assistance Programs 451 7th Street SW, Room 7270, Washington, DC 20410

Phone: 202-402-5697 | Email: tonya.proctor@hud.gov

http://www.hudexchange.info/coc

HHS93.209 | CONTRACEPTION AND INFERTILITY RESEARCH LOAN REPAYMENT PROGRAM
"CIR LRP"

Award: Direct Payments for Specified Use

Purpose: To provide an incentive for health professionals to work in areas of reproductive extramural contraception and/or infertility research.

Applicant Eligibility: Applicants must be a U.S. citizen (or U.S. national or permanent resident) and a physician, Ph.D. level scientist, nurse, physician's assistant, graduate student, or postgraduate research fellow training in the health professions. You must commit to conduct contraception and infertility research for 50% of your time (at least 20 hours weekly based on a 40 hour week) for two years and it must be funded by a domestic nonprofit or U.S. government (Federal, state or local) entity. Also, the research must not be prohibited by Federal law or NIH policy. Complete eligibility information is available at https://grants. nih.gov/grants/guide/notice-files/NOT-OD-17-079. html.

Beneficiary Eligibility: Assistance in the form of loan repayments will be made to qualified health professionals (including graduate students) who are participants in the CIR-LRP.

Award Range/Average: In fiscal year 2018 the range of financial assistance was between $10,839 and $97,300. The average contract cost was $72,549.

Funding: (Direct Payments for Specified Use) FY 18 $1,088,000.00; FY 19 est $1,037,000.00; FY 20 est $974,000.00

HQ: 6710-B Rockledge Drive, Room 2421C, Bethesda, MD 20817

    Phone: 301-496-8363 | Email: kaufmans@mail.nih.gov

    http://www.lrp.nih.gov

DOS19.515 | CONTRIBUTIONS TO INTERNATIONAL ORGANIZATIONS FOR OVERSEAS ASSISTANCE

Award: Project Grants; Direct Payments for Specified Use

Purpose: Provides voluntary and assessed contributions to Public International Organizations to carry out humanitarian assistance activities overseas benefitrefugees, victims of conflict, and other persons of concern.

Applicant Eligibility: Voluntary and assessed contributions to Public International Organizations to provide assistance to refugees and victims of conflict overseas.

Beneficiary Eligibility: Refugees, victims of conflict, and other persons of concern requiring protection and assistance.

Funding: (Direct Payments for Specified Use) FY 16 $2,585,558,782.00; FY 17 est $2,600,000,000.00; FY 18 est $2,600,000,000.00

HQ: 2025 E Street NW, Washington, DC 20522-0908

    Phone: 202-453-9239 | Email: hembreeel@state.gov

    http://www.state.gov/j/prm/index.htm

DHS97.045 | COOPERATING TECHNICAL PARTNERS
"CTP"

Award: Cooperative Agreements

Purpose: The CTP program's objective is to deliver data for creating public awareness on flood hazards and steps to take that can reduce risk to life and property.

Applicant Eligibility: Only qualified CTPs are eligible for federal assistance awards through this Program. Eligible recipients generally include entities who already perform certain functions in flood risk analysis, flood hazard identification, flood risk communication and mitigation processes in States and local communities to reduce flood losses and protect life and property from the risk of future flood damage. Specifically, eligible CTPs include three main groups: (1) NFIP-participating communities, as defined in 44 CFR 59 (typically this includes State, Tribal and local Governments), who are in good standing with the NFIP (i.e., not on probation or suspended); (2) State, local and regional governmental agencies, such as water management districts, river authorities, municipal utility districts, State universities, etc., whose activities support floodplain management and flood mitigation actions within the NFIP communities they serve; and (3) non-profit Organizations whose primary mission is to support the ability of NFIP communities to more effectively understand and manage their flood risk. In accordance with Section 1361 of the National Flood Insurance Act of 1968 (42 U.S.C. 4102), these entities and Organizations must have existing facilities and services to carry out studies and investigations with respect to land management and use, flood control, flood zoning and flood damage prevention in flood-prone areas, floodways, building codes and permits, and associated laws, regulations and ordinances. For additional information, see the Eligibility Criteria in the Funding Opportunity Announcement.

Beneficiary Eligibility: State, local, specialized group, small business, general public.

Award Range/Average: Range: $4,000 to $14,105,950 Average: approximately $1.4M

Funding: (Cooperative Agreements) FY 18 $116,472,041.00; FY 19 est $110,000,000.00; FY 20 est $110,000,000.00

HQ: 400 C Street SW, Washington, DC 20024

    Phone: 202-212-1054 | Email: laura.alego@fema.dhs.gov

    http://fema.gov

Programs Administered by Federal Headquarters

HHS93.332 | COOPERATIVE AGREEMENT TO SUPPORT NAVIGATORS IN FEDERALLY-FACILITATED EXCHANGES
"Navigator Grants"

Award: Cooperative Agreements

Purpose: To develop and implement a Navigator grant program. Navigators will serve consumers in States with an FFM, including State Partnership Marketplaces.

Applicant Eligibility: Under section 1311(i)(2)(B) of the PPACA, eligible entities may include, but are not limited to, trade, industry and professional associations; commercial fishing industry Organizations; ranching and farming Organizations; community and consumer-focused nonprofit groups; and other entities capable of meeting Program requirements. Eligible applicants may choose to partner with other entities and/or individuals to form a consortium of subrecipients in order to target a larger total portion of the left behind population. Funding through the cooperative agreement is open to individuals and private and public entities capable of carrying out the Navigator duties and other Program requirements in a FFE, as outlined in statute, regulations, and this announcement, including community and consumer-focused nonprofit groups; faith-based Organizations; trade, industry and professional associations; commercial fishing industry Organizations; ranching and farming Organizations; chambers of commerce; unions; resource partners of the Small Business Administration; licensed insurance agents and brokers; and other public or private entities. Other entities may include, but are not limited to, Indian Tribes, tribal Organizations, urban Indian Organizations, and State or local human services.

Beneficiary Eligibility: The following list, includes but is not limited to, the varying types of beneficiaries served under this cooperative agreement: Individual/Family, Minority group, Specialized group (e.g., LGBT, health professionals, students, veterans), Small business, Anyone/general public, Small Business Person, Black, American Indian, Spanish Origin, Other Non-White, Migrant, Immigrants, U.S. Citizen, Women, Disabled (e.g. Deaf, Blind, Physically Disabled), Physically Afflicted (e.g. TB, Arthritis, Heart Disease), Mentally Disabled, Unemployed, Low Income, Major Metropolis (over 250,000), Other Urban, Suburban, Rural.

Award Range/Average: Current Fiscal Year: 2018 Projection: up to $10,000,000

Funding: (Cooperative Agreements) FY 18 $10,000,000.00; FY 19 est $10,000,000.00; FY 20 est $10,000,000.00

HQ: 7501 Wisconsin Avenue, Bethesda, MD 20814

    Phone: 301-492-4319

    http://www.cms.gov/cciio/programs-and-initiatives/health-insurance-marketplaces/assistance.html

HHS93.919 | COOPERATIVE AGREEMENTS FOR STATE-BASED COMPREHENSIVE BREAST AND CERVICAL CANCER EARLY DETECTION PROGRAMS
"National Breast and Cervical Cancer Early Detection Program (NBCCEDP)"

Award: Cooperative Agreements

Purpose: To work with State and territorial health agencies or their designees, and tribal health agencies in developing comprehensive breast and cervical cancer early detection programs.

Applicant Eligibility: Eligible applicants are the official State health agencies of the United States, the District of Columbia, the Commonwealth of Puerto Rico, the Virgin Islands, Guam, the Northern Mariana Islands, the Federated States of Micronesia, the Republic of the Marshall Islands, American Samoa, American Indian and Alaska Native Tribes and tribal Organizations as defined in Section 4 of the Indian Self-Determination and education Assistance Act.

Beneficiary Eligibility: Official State and Territorial health agencies, women especially low-income women.

Award Range/Average: 96,735 to 9,692,758; $2,234,163

HQ: 4770 Buford Highway NE, PO Box F76, Atlanta, GA 30341

    Phone: 770-488-4880 | Email: fwong@cdc.gov

    http://www.cdc.gov/cancer

HHS93.988 | COOPERATIVE AGREEMENTS FOR STATE-BASED DIABETES CONTROL PROGRAMS AND EVALUATION OF SURVEILLANCE SYSTEMS
"DPCPs Behavioral Risk Factor Surveillance System BRFSS"

Award: Cooperative Agreements

Purpose: The Diabetes Prevention and Control Programs are funded to prevent diabetes, reduce or prevent the complications associated with the disease and eliminate health disparities related to diabetes. The program achieves its goals by partnering with state-wide diabetes communities.

Applicant Eligibility: Eligible applicants are the official State and territorial health agencies of the United States, the District of Columbia, the Commonwealth of Puerto Rico, the Virgin Islands, Guam, the Northern Mariana Islands, the Federated States of Micronesia, the Republic of the Marshall Islands, the Republic of Palau, and American Samoa.

Beneficiary Eligibility: State health agencies will benefit.

HQ: 2877 Brandywine Road, Williams Building, Atlanta, GA 30341
Phone: 770-488-1094 | Email: bpark@cdc.gov
http://www.cdc.gov

HHS93.004 | COOPERATIVE AGREEMENTS TO IMPROVE THE HEALTH STATUS OF MINORITY POPULATIONS

Award: Cooperative Agreements

Purpose: To provide support for activities which have the potential to improve the health status and/or quality of life of racial/ethnic minorities.

Applicant Eligibility: Public and private nonprofit entities may apply. Faith based Organizations are eligible to apply.

Beneficiary Eligibility: Members of the minority and disadvantaged groups: Blacks; Hispanics; American Indians; Alaska Natives; Asian/American Pacific Islanders; or subgroups of these.

Award Range/Average: Grant program ended in 2015

HQ: 1101 Wootton Parkway, Suite 550 Tower Building, Rockville, MD 20852
Phone: 240-453-8822 | Email: eric.west@hhs.gov
https://minorityhealth.hhs.gov

HHS93.079 | COOPERATIVE AGREEMENTS TO PROMOTE ADOLESCENT HEALTH THROUGH SCHOOL-BASED HIV/STD PREVENTION AND SCHOOL-BASED SURVEILLANCE

Award: Cooperative Agreements

Purpose: To improve the health and well-being of our nation's youth by working with education and health agencies, and other organizations to reduce HIV, STD, teen pregnancy, and related risk behaviors among middle and high school students.

Applicant Eligibility: Component 1 eligible applicants are limited to: State Governments or their Bona Fide Agents (includes the District of Columbia); Local Governments or their Bona Fide Agents; Territorial Governments or their Bona Fide Agents in the Commonwealth of Puerto Rico, the Virgin Islands, the Commonwealth of the Northern Mariana Islands, American Samoa, Guam, the Federated States of Micronesia, the Republic of the Marshall Islands, and the Republic of Palau Governments; American Indian or Alaska Native tribal Governments (federally recognized or state-recognized); and, American Indian or Alaska native tribally designated Organizations. If an education agency declines to apply for funding, the health agency in its jurisdiction or the health agency's Bona Fide Agent may apply on its behalf. To obtain and then maintain funding for Component 2, local education agencies are required to apply for and meet the additional requirements of Component 1. While agencies are encouraged to apply for funding for both YRBS and Profiles, education or health agencies in jurisdictions that are not applying for Component 2 funding are permitted to apply for a reduced amount of funding under Component 1 for a single survey (either YRBS or Profiles). Component 2 eligible applicants are limited to local education agencies (LEA) only. An LEA must demonstrate an ability to reach a minimum of 10,000 students in priority schools (high schools, or a combination of middle and high schools) with the proposed work plan in order for the application to be eligible for review. LEA with an enrollment of less than 10,000 students may combine with other geographically contiguous districts to create a consortium application. In doing so, the consortium must designate a single LEA to submit the application and, if funded, administer the Program. This designated LEA will become the fiscal agent and responsible agency for all activities under this cooperative agreement. Existing regional structures such as Boards of Cooperative educational Services (BOCES)

Programs Administered by Federal Headquarters

or their equivalent may also apply. Component 2 applicants are also required to apply for and meet the requirements of Component 1. Component 3 eligibility is open to all applicants.

Beneficiary Eligibility: Official state education agencies in states and territories in the United States (including the District of Columbia, the Commonwealth of Puerto Rico, American Samoa, Commonwealth of the Northern Mariana Islands, Federated States of Micronesia, Guam, the Republic of the Marshall Islands, the Republic of Palau, and the U.S. Virgin Islands); local education agencies; public and private non-profit organizations that serve education organizations; school-aged youth; and school personnel including, but not limited to, teachers, school nurses, paraprofessionals, and school administrators.

Award Range/Average: Awards will range from approximately $20,000 to $450,000 (subject to the availability of funds), with an average of approximately $200,000, depending on the specific components funded.

Funding: (Cooperative Agreements) FY 18 $16,850,000.00; FY 19 est $16,900,000.00; FY 20 est $16,900,000.00

HQ: CDC NCHHSTP DASH 1600 Clifton Road NE US8-1, Atlanta, GA 30333

Phone: 404-718-8333

http://www.cdc.gov/healthyyouth

HHS93.130 | COOPERATIVE AGREEMENTS TO STATES/TERRITORIES FOR THE COORDINATION AND DEVELOPMENT OF PRIMARY CARE OFFICES
"State Primary Care Offices (PCO)"

Award: Cooperative Agreements

Purpose: To coordinate local, State, and Federal resources contributing to primary care service delivery and workforce issues in the State.

Applicant Eligibility: States or territories, political subdivisions of States, agencies of States, or other public entities that operate solely within one State or represent multiple territories where appropriate. These entities must provide statewide coverage for primary healthcare issues and represent or have relationships with the broad range of primary healthcare delivery systems and Programs in the State.

Beneficiary Eligibility: Health Professional Shortage Areas and Medically Underserved Areas/Populations within States and Territories will benefit from this program. Primary Care Offices (PCO) submit applications for designation status, which are reviewed and processed by the Division of Policy and Shortage Designation.

Award Range/Average: For FY 2016, awards ranged from $152,056 to $444,379; Average award per recipient $203,509.For FY 2017, awards ranged from $152,056 to $444,379; Average award per recipient $203,509.For FY 2018, est awards ranged from $152,056 to $444,379; Average award per recipient $203,509.

Funding: (Cooperative Agreements) FY 18 $10,899,000.00; FY 19 est $10,899,000.00; FY 20 est $10,899,000.00

HQ: Shortage Designation Branch Division of Policy and Shortage Designation Bureau of Health Workforce 5600 Fishers Lane, Room 11W16, Rockville, MD 20852

Phone: 301-594-4454 | Email: msalaga@hrsa.gov

http://www.hrsa.gov

HHS93.938 | COOPERATIVE AGREEMENTS TO SUPPORT COMPREHENSIVE SCHOOL HEALTH PROGRAMS TO PREVENT THE SPREAD OF HIV AND OTHER IMPORTANT HEALTH PROBLEMS
"SHEPSA"

Award: Project Grants

Purpose: To improve a youth's well-being and prepare them for a healthy future.

Applicant Eligibility: Eligible applicants are official States (including the District of Columbia, the Commonwealth of Puerto Rico, American Samoa, Commonwealth of the Northern Marina Islands, Federated States of Micronesia, Guam, the Republic of the Marshall Islands, the Republic of Palau, and the U.S. Virgin Islands), Tribal Governments, large urban school districts (with the highest number of reported AIDS cases, high levels of poverty, and student enrollment greater than 75,000 students), and national non-governmental Organizations.

Beneficiary Eligibility: Official State education agencies in states and territories in the United States (including the District of Columbia, the Commonwealth of Puerto Rico, American Samoa, Commonwealth of the Northern Marina Islands, Federated States of Micronesia, Guam, the Republic of the Marshall Islands, the Republic of Palau, and the U.S. Virgin Islands); local education agencies; national private sector organizations and their constituents; universities and colleges; school-age youth, including minority youth, youth in high-risk situations, and youth with special education needs; college-age youth; and school personnel, including teachers, school nurses, paraprofessionals, and school administrators.

Award Range/Average: $1,000 to $678,000; $283,600

HHS93.946 | COOPERATIVE AGREEMENTS TO SUPPORT STATE-BASED SAFE MOTHERHOOD AND INFANT HEALTH INITIATIVE PROGRAMS
"Safe Motherhood and Infant Health (Reproductive Health)"

Award: Cooperative Agreements

Purpose: To promote optimal and equitable health in women and infants and to identify and address male and female reproductive issues and infant health issues by providing technical assistance, consultation and training.

Applicant Eligibility: Official State and Territorial public health agencies. City of New York public health agency and District of Columbia. Applications may be submitted by public and private nonprofit and for-profit Organizations and by Governments and their agencies; that is, universities, colleges, research Institutions, hospitals, other public and private nonprofit and for-profit Organizations, State and local Governments or their bona fide agents, including the District of Columbia, the Commonwealth of Puerto Rico, the Virgin Islands, the Commonwealth of the Northern Mariana Islands, American Samoa, Guam, the Federated States of Micronesia, the Republic of the Marshall Islands, and the Republic of Palau, federally recognized Indian tribal Governments, Indian Tribes, or Indian tribal Organizations, and small, minority, women-owned businesses.

Beneficiary Eligibility: Same as Applicant Eligibility.

Funding: (Cooperative Agreements) FY 18 $7,677,560.00; FY 19 est $15,634,393.00; FY 20 est $15,634,393.00

HQ: DRH 4770 Buford Highway NE, Atlanta, GA 30341

   Phone: 770-488-6245

   http://www.cdc.gov

USAID98.002 | COOPERATIVE DEVELOPMENT PROGRAM (CDP)

Award: Project Grants

Purpose: Helps to find financial and human support for CDOs to improve the quality of its members and their communities.

Applicant Eligibility: Applicants eligible are U.S. cooperatives and recognized cooperative development Organizations (CDOs) that are organically-linked to cooperatives and groups of cooperatives and whose demonstrated capabilities are broadly consistent with USAID's strategic objectives.

Beneficiary Eligibility: Cooperatives and their members in USAID eligible countries.

HQ: 301 4th Street SW, Washington, DC 20547

   Phone: 202-567-4688 | Email: rwillis@usaid.gov

   http://www.usaid.gov/hum_response/pvc/coop.html

USDA10.500 | COOPERATIVE EXTENSION SERVICE
"CES"

Award: Formula Grants; Project Grants

Purpose: The program deals with funds and other requirements to develop agriculture, extension works, and awareness on various disciplines such as; (a) Formula funds to conduct agriculture and other extension works. (b) Funds for special needs is provided to maximize agricultural and other extension works. (c) The extension special needs program is to strengthen families and communities to self-sustain during disasters. (d) The cooperative extension program creates awareness for disaster preparedness, response, and remediation. (e) To provide awareness, education, and other technical information for various purposes. (d) The CSRS and FERS provide information on retirement contribution and other assistance. (e) To expand food and nutrition, developing agriculture through modern ways, and education on farming. (f) To provide funds for conserving renewable resources. (g) To assist youth with various development programs and much more.

Applicant Eligibility: SPECIAL NOTE: Please refer to the Competitive, Non-Competitive and/or Capacity Requests for Applications (RFAs) for further specific and pertinent details. RFAs are generally released annually. Hence, the RFAs provide the most current and accurate information available. Any specific instructions in the Competitive and/or Capacity RFAs supersede the general information provided in the CFDA database. 1. SMITH-LEVER 3(b) & (c): (a) Cooperative Extension Programs at 1862 Land-Grant Institutions 3b & c Capacity (formerly known as formula) Grants: Applications may be submitted by the following 1862 Land-grant Institutions: Auburn University, University of Alaska-Fairbanks, American

Programs Administered by Federal Headquarters

Samoa Community College, University of Arizona, University of Arkansas, University of California, Colorado State University, University of Connecticut, University of Delaware, University of Florida, University of Georgia, University of Guam, University of Hawaii, University of Idaho, University of Illinois, Purdue University, Iowa State University, Kansas State University, University of Kentucky, Louisiana State University, University of Maine, University of Maryland-College Park, University of Massachusetts, Michigan State University, College of Micronesia, University of Minnesota, Mississippi State University, University of Missouri, Montana State University, University of Nebraska, University of Nevada-Reno, University of New Hampshire, Rutgers University, New Mexico State University, Cornell University, North Carolina State University, North Dakota State University, Northern Marianas College, Ohio State University, Oklahoma State University, Oregon State University, Pennsylvania State University, University of Puerto Rico, University of Rhode Island, Clemson University, South Dakota State University, University of Tennessee, Texas A & M University, Utah State University, University of Vermont, Virginia Polytechnic Institute & State University, University of the Virgin Islands, Washington State University, West Virginia University, University of Wisconsin, and University of Wyoming. Award recipients may subcontract to Organizations not eligible to apply for funding provided that such arrangements are necessary to complete the project. (b) Cooperative Extension Programs at 1862 Land-Grant Institutions (Special Needs): Applications may be submitted by the following 1862 Land-grant Institutions: University of Alaska-Fairbanks, University of Arizona, Colorado State University, University of Idaho, Kansas State University, Montana State University, University of Nebraska, University of Nevada-Reno, New Mexico State University, North Dakota State University, Oregon State University, South Dakota State University, Texas A & M University, Utah State University, University of Vermont, and University of Wyoming. Award recipients may subcontract to Organizations not eligible to apply for funding provided that such arrangements are necessary to complete the project. (c) Smith-Lever Special Needs Program Applications may be submitted with the approval of Extension Directors of 1862 Land-grant Institutions in the 50 states, American Samoa, Guam, Micronesia, Northern Marianas, Puerto Rico, and the U.S. Virgin Islands. Award recipients may subcontract to Organizations not eligible to apply provided such Organizations are necessary for the conduct of the project. An applicant's failure to meet an eligibility criterion by the time of an application deadline will result in NIFA not accepting the application or, even though an application may be reviewed, will preclude NIFA from making an award. (d) CSRS Retirement Contributions Program (aka ERET CSRS Retirement): This Program is no longer funded by NIFA. The deadline for the FY 2015 Request for Applications (RFA) was October 15, 2014. (e) FERS Retirement Contributions Program (aka ERET FERS Retirement): This Program is no longer funded by NIFA. The deadline for the FY 2016 RFA was July 20, 2015. (f) District of Columbia Public Postsecondary education Re Organization Act Program (Cooperative Extension Programs) aka EUDC The University of the District of Columbia, as the 1862 Land-Grant Institution, is the only applicant eligible for funding under the DCPPERA. The award recipient may subcontract to Organizations not eligible to apply for funding provided that such arrangements are necessary to complete the project. 2. Agricultural Extension at 1890 Land-Grant Institutions, Including Tuskegee University and West Virginia State University (Section 1444): A. Eligible Applicants: Applications may be submitted by 1890 Land-Grant universities, including Tuskegee University and West Virginia State University, that conduct agricultural extension activities in accordance with NARETPA section 1444(a)(1): Alabama A&M University; Tuskegee University; University of Arkansas - Pine Bluff; Delaware State University; Florida A&M University; Fort Valley State University; Kentucky State University; Southern University; University of Maryland - Eastern Shore; Alcorn State University; Lincoln University; North Carolina A & T State University; Langston University; South Carolina State University; Tennessee State University; Prairie View A&M University; Virginia State University; and West Virginia State University. Further, in accordance with Section 7129 of the Agricultural Act of 2014 (House Conference Report 113-333, to accompany H. R. 2642), Central State University has the Designation as 1890 Institution. Institutions may subcontract to Organizations not eligible to apply for funding provided that such arrangements are necessary to complete the project or activity. 3. SMITH-LEVER 3(d): (a) Expanded Food and Nutrition (EFNEP) (ENUT Nutrition education): Applications may be submitted by State colleges and universities in accordance with Section 3(d) of the Smith-Lever Act: Auburn University; Alabama A & M University; Tuskegee University; University of Alaska; American Samoa Community College; University of Arizona; University of Arkansas; University of Arkansas - Pine Bluff; University of California; Colorado State University; University of Connecticut; University of Delaware; Delaware State University; University of the District of Columbia; University of Florida; Florida A & M University; University of Georgia; Fort Valley State University; University of Guam; University of Hawaii; University of Idaho; University of Illinois; Purdue University; Iowa State University; Kansas State University; University of Kentucky; Kentucky State University; Louisiana State University; Southern University; University of Maine; University of Maryland (College Park); University of Maryland (Eastern Shore); University of Massachusetts; Michigan State University; College of Micronesia; University of Minnesota; Mississippi State University; Alcorn State University; University of Missouri; Lincoln University; Montana State University; University of Nebraska; University of Nevada; University of New Hampshire; Rutgers University; New Mexico State University; Cornell University; North Carolina State University; North Carolina A & T University; North Dakota State University; Northern Marianas College; Ohio State University; Oklahoma State University; Langston University; Oregon State University; Pennsylvania State University; University of Puerto Rico; University of Rhode Island; Clemson University;

Programs Administered by Federal Headquarters

South Carolina State University; South Dakota State University; University of Tennessee; Tennessee State University; Texas A&M University; Prairie View A & M University; Utah State University; University of Vermont; University of the Virgin Islands; Virginia Polytechnic Institute and State University; Virginia State University; Washington State University; West Virginia University; West Virginia State University; University of Wisconsin; and University of Wyoming. Award recipients may subcontract to Organizations not eligible to apply for funding provided that such arrangements are necessary to complete the project. (b) Children, Youth, and Families at Risk (CYFAR) Pertinent details will be provided at a future date. (c) Improve Rural Quality of Life Pertinent details will be provided at a future date. (d) Farm Safety NOTE: Effective FY 2012, the following Programs were consolidated: ¢ Youth Farm Safety; ¢ Farm Safety and Youth Safety education and Certification; and ¢ Assistive Technology Program for Farmers with Disabilities: National AgrAbility Project. Pertinent details will be provided at a future date. (e) New Technologies at Ag Extension Pertinent details will be provided at a future date. (f) Pest Management Pertinent details will be provided at a future date. (g) Sustainable Agriculture (SARE-PD) NOTES: (1) Effective Fiscal Year 2014, Programs under Sustainable Agriculture (research, education and extension) were merged into a single Program under the research account. (2) See CFDA Number 10. 215 for all pertinent details. (h) Federally Recognized Tribes Pertinent details will be provided at a future date. (i) Youth Farm Safety education & Certification NOTE: Effective FY 2012, the following Programs were consolidated: ¢ Youth Farm Safety; ¢ Farm Safety and Youth Safety education and Certification; and ¢ Assistive Technology Program for Farmers with Disabilities: National AgrAbility Project. Pertinent details will be provided at a future date. (j) EIPM Support Pertinent details will be provided at a future date. (k) EIPM Coordination Pertinent details will be provided at a future date. 4. OTHER EXTENSION ACTIVITIES: (a) Renewable Resources Extension Act (RREA)Applications may be submitted by 1862 and 1890 land-grant Institutions. Award recipients may subcontract to Organizations not eligible to apply provided such Organizations are necessary for the conduct of the project. An applicant's failure to meet an eligibility criterion by the time of an application deadline will preclude NIFA from making an award. (b) Rural Health and Safety (RHSE)Land-grant colleges and universities that are eligible to receive funds under the Act of July 2, 1862 (7 U.S.C. 301 et seq.), and the Act of August 30, 1890 (7 U.S.C. 321 et seq.), including Tuskegee University, West Virginia State University and the University of the District of Columbia. Applications may be submitted by any of the Tribal colleges and universities designated as 1994 Land-Grant Institutions under the educational Land-Grant Status Act of 1994, as amended. Award recipients may subward to other Organizations provided such Organizations are necessary for the conduct of the project. Failure to meet an eligibility criterion by the application deadline will disqualify an applicant from consideration and will result in NIFA returning the application without review or, even though an application may be reviewed, will preclude NIFA from reviewing the application and making an award. (c) Extension Services at the 1994 Institutions Applications may be submitted by any of the Tribal colleges and universities designated as 1994 Land-Grant Institutions under the educational Land-Grant Status Act of 1994, as amended. Award recipients may subcontract to Organizations not eligible to apply provided such Organizations are necessary for the conduct of project goals and objectives. An applicant's failure to meet an eligibility criterion by the time of an application deadline will result in NIFA returning the application without review or, even though an application may be reviewed, will preclude NIFA from making an award. (d) Grants to Youth Serving Institutions (RYD) Pursuant to 7 U.S.C. Section 7630, only the Girl Scouts of the United States of America, the National 4-H Council, the Boy Scouts of America, and the National FFA Organization are eligible to apply. NIFA will accept only one application from each Organization. The application must be developed and submitted by the national office of each respective Organization. Rural Youth Development awards will be distributed to each of the four (4) eligible Organizations that submits an application in accordance with RFA requirements, if the application is found to be worthy of support through the peer review process. The amount awarded to each Organization will be determined based on review and recommendations of a peer review panel. Award recipients may subcontract to Organizations not eligible to apply provided such Organizations are necessary for the conduct of the project. If an applicant fails to meet an eligibility criterion by the time of the application deadline, the application will be at risk of being excluded from NIFA review and will preclude NIFA from making an award. (e) Food Animal Residue Avoidance Database Program (FARAD) The Secretary shall offer to enter into a contract, grant, or cooperative agreement with 1 or more appropriate colleges and universities to operate the FARAD Program. (f) Federal Administration (DIRECT APPROPRIATION) Pertinent details will be provided at a future date. (g) 1890 Facilities (Section 1447) Eligible applicants under this RFA are the 1890 land-grant Institutions, including Tuskegee University and West Virginia State University. They are: Alabama A&M University, Tuskegee University, University of Arkansas-Pine Bluff, Delaware State University, Florida A&M University, Fort Valley State University, Kentucky State University, Southern University, University of Maryland-Eastern Shore, Lincoln University, Alcorn State University, North Carolina A&T State University, Langston University, South Carolina State University, Tennessee State University, Prairie View A&M University, Virginia State University, and West Virginia State University. Further, in accordance with Section 7129 of the Agricultural Act of 2014 (House Conference Report 113-333, to accompany H. R. 2642), Central State University has the Designation as 1890 Institution.

Beneficiary Eligibility: Extension Programs at the State and county level are available to the general public.

Award Range/Average: If minimum or maximum amounts of funding per the Capacity, Competitive, and/or Non-Competitive

Programs Administered by Federal Headquarters

project grant, or cooperative agreement are established, these amounts will be announced in the annual Capacity, Competitive, and/or Non-Competitive Request for Application (RFA). The most current RFAs are available as follows: JOINT PROGRAM: Cooperative Extension Programs at 1862 Land-grant Institutions and District of Columbia Public Postsecondary Education Reorganization Act Program (DCPPERA) (Capacity): https://nifa.usda.gov/program/smith-lever-act-capacity-grant Cooperative Extension Programs at 1862 Land-grant Institutions - (Special Needs) (Capacity): https://nifa.usda.gov/sites/default/files/resources/FY18-CES-SLSN-Modification-882017.pdf Smith-Lever Special Needs Competitive Grants Program: https://nifa.usda.gov/program/smith-lever-act-sections-3b-and-3c-special-needs-capacity-grant 1890 LGI's and Tuskegee, West Virginia & Central State: https://nifa.usda.gov/program/agricultural-extension-programs-1890-institutions Expanded Food and Nutrition Education Program (EFNEP): https://nifa.usda.gov/resource/fy2017-efnep-rfa https://nifa.usda.gov/funding-opportunity/expanded-food-and-nutrition-education-program-webneers Farm Safety and Youth Safety Education and Certification https://nifa.usda.gov/funding-opportunity/youth-farm-safety-education-and-certification-program New Technologies at Ag Extension (NTAE) https://nifa.usda.gov/funding-opportunity/new-technologies-ag-extension-ntae Children, Youth, and Families At- Risk (CYFAR); Sustainable Community Projects (CYFAR-SCP) and Professional Development Technology Assistance (CYFAR-PDTA): Sustainable Community Projects (SCP): https://nifa.usda.gov/funding-opportunity/children-youth-and-families-risk-cyfar-sustainable-community-projects Military: https://nifa.usda.gov/funding-opportunity/archive-children-youth-and-families-risk-military https://nifa.usda.gov/funding-opportunity/cyfar-4-h-military-partnership-professional-development-and-technical-assistance Professional and Technical Assistance (PDTA): https://nifa.usda.gov/funding-opportunity/archive-children-youth-and-families-risk-professional-development-and-technical Federally-Recognized Tribes Extension Program (aka FRTEP): https://nifa.usda.gov/funding-opportunity/federally-recognized-tribes-extension-program-frtep-formerly-extension-indian Extension Services at the 1994 Institutions (aka Tribal Colleges Extension Program) (TCEP) and Special Emphasis (TCEP-SE): https://nifa.usda.gov/funding-opportunity/tribal-colleges-extension-services-program-capacity-tcep https://nifa.usda.gov/funding-opportunity/tribal-colleges-extension-program-special-emphasis-tcep-se Renewable Resources Extension Act Program - (RREA) and National Focus Fund Projects (RREA-NFF): https://nifa.usda.gov/program/renewable-resources-extension-act-capacity-grant https://nifa.usda.gov/funding-opportunity/renewable-resources-extension-act-national-focus-fund-projects-rrea-nff Rural Health and Safety (aka Rural Health & Safety Education): https://nifa.usda.gov/funding-opportunity/rural-health-and-safety-education-competitive-grants-program-rhse 1890 Facilities Grant Program (and Renewals): https://nifa.usda.gov/funding-opportunity/1890-facilities-grants-program-renewals Food Animal Residue Avoidance Database Program (FARAD) http://www.farad.org/ Agriculture Risk Management Education Program (aka RME Program): https://nifa.usda.gov/funding-opportunity/agriculture-risk-management-education-partnerships-arme-competitive-grants Assistive Technology Program for Farmers with Disabilities: National AgrAbility Project: https://nifa.usda.gov/funding-opportunity/agrability-assistive-technology-program-farmers-disabilities Healthy Homes Partnership: https://nifa.usda.gov/funding-opportunity/healthy-homes-partnership RFAs are generally released annually. Hence, the RFAs provide the most current and accurate information available. Any specific instructions in the Capacity, Competitive, and/or Non-Competitive RFAs supersede the general information provided in the CFDA database.
Funding: (Project Grants) FY 17 $455,489,177.00; FY 18 est $458,054,144.00; FY 19 est $0.00
HQ: 1400 Independence Avenue SW, PO Box 2240, Washington, DC 20250
Phone: 202-401-4939
http://nifa.usda.gov/grants

DOC11.434 | COOPERATIVE FISHERY STATISTICS
Award: Project Grants
Purpose: To maintain State and Federal partnership and to support fishery management in the States' Territorial Sea.
Applicant Eligibility: Eligible applicants are the Marine Fisheries Conservation agencies of the States of Alabama, Florida, Georgia, Louisiana, Mississippi, North Carolina, South Carolina, Texas, Puerto Rico, U.S. Virgin Islands and the Gulf States Marine Fisheries Commission.
Beneficiary Eligibility: This program benefits Federal, State and interstate marine resource conservation and management agencies; U.S. and foreign commercial and recreational fishing industries; conservation organizations; academic institutions; international and Indian Tribal treaties; private and public research groups; consumers; and the general public.
Funding: (Cooperative Agreements) FY 16 $12,542,204.00; FY 17 est $12,542,204.00; FY 18 est Estimate Not Available
HQ: 1305 E W Highway, Silver Spring, MD 20910
Phone: 301-427-8771 | Email: jeffrey.kulnis@noaa.gov
http://sero.nmfs.noaa.gov/grants/csp.htm

USDA10.202 | COOPERATIVE FORESTRY RESEARCH
"McIntire-Stennis Cooperative Forestry Research Act (M/S) Program"

Award: Formula Grants
Purpose: To compensate for the protection of forestland, forestry research, advancement of technological, and ecosystems.
Applicant Eligibility: Funds are appropriated by Congress for distribution to State Institutions certified as eligible by a State representative designated by the Governor of each State. Funds are apportioned among States by the Secretary of Agriculture after consultation with a National Advisory Council representing the State- certified forestry schools and other groups concerned with forestry research. This Program is also available to Guam, Puerto Rico, the Virgin Islands, American Samoa, Northern Mariana Islands, and Micronesia.
Beneficiary Eligibility: Funds are appropriated by Congress for distribution to State institutions certified as eligible by a State representative designated by the Governor of each State. Funds are apportioned among States by the Secretary of Agriculture after consultation with a National Advisory Council representing the State- certified forestry schools and other groups concerned with forestry research. This program is also available in Guam, Puerto Rico, the Virgin Islands, American Samoa, Northern Mariana, and Micronesia.
Award Range/Average: If minimum or maximum amounts of funding per the Capacity, Competitive, and/or Non-Competitive project grant, or cooperative agreement are established, these amounts will be announced in the annual Capacity, Competitive, and/or Non-Competitive Request for Application (RFA).The most current RFA is available via: https://nifa.usda.gov/program/mcintire-stennis-capacity-grant
Funding: (Formula Grants (Apportionments)) FY 18 $31,888,021.00; FY 19 est $33,802,560.00; FY 20 est $27,104,958.00
HQ: 1400 Independence Avenue SW, PO Box 2210, Washington, DC 20250-2210
   Phone: 202-720-5229
   http://nifa.usda.gov/program/mcintire-stennis-capacity-grant

DOC11.455 | COOPERATIVE SCIENCE AND EDUCATION PROGRAM

Award: Project Grants
Purpose: To compensate for cooperative science and education on marine issues to develop innovative approaches and methods for marine and estuarine science and education.
Applicant Eligibility: Eligible applicants for assistance are State, U.S. territorial, and private Institutions of higher learning and education, especially universities and colleges, with which the National Marine Fisheries Service or the National Oceanic and Atmospheric Administration has entered into, or may enter into, an enduring partnership for purposes of research and education on the marine environment. Also included are private and public research Organizations affiliated with Institutions of higher learning, and national and international Organizations and Programs dedicated to marine and estuarine research, education, and outreach.
Beneficiary Eligibility: This program benefits Federal, State, and interstate marine resource conversation and management agencies; U.S. and foreign commercial and recreational fishing industries; conservation organizations, academic institutions; international and Indian Tribal treaties; private and public research groups; consumers; and the general public.
Funding: (Cooperative Agreements) FY 16 $263,771.00; FY 17 est $263,771.00; FY 18 est Estimate Not Available
HQ: 1305 E W Highway, Silver Spring, MD 20910
   Phone: 301-427-8771 | Email: jeffrey.kulnis@noaa.gov
   http://www.woodsholediversity.org/pep

HHS93.153 | COORDINATED SERVICES AND ACCESS TO RESEARCH FOR WOMEN, INFANTS, CHILDREN, AND YOUTH
"Ryan White HIV/AIDS Program (RWHAP) Part D Women, Infants, Children and Youth (WICY) Program"

Award: Project Grants
Purpose: To provide family-centered care in the outpatient or ambulatory care setting (directly or through contracts or MOU) to low income, uninsured, and medically underserved women (25 years and older) living with HIV, infants (up to two years of age) exposed to or living with HIV, children (ages two to 12) living with HIV, and youth (ages 13 to 24) living with HIV and additional support services to affected family members.

Programs Administered by Federal Headquarters

Applicant Eligibility: Public and nonprofit private entities (including a health facility operated by or pursuant to a contract with the Indian Health Service) that provide family-centered care involving outpatient or ambulatory care (directly or through contracts or memoranda of understanding (MOUs) for WICY with HIV/AIDS.

Beneficiary Eligibility: Women, infants, children, and youth living with HIV and their affected family members.

Award Range/Average: $113,823 - $2,185,691;Average $583,894.Supplemental grants are limited to $150,000.

Funding: (Project Grants) FY 18 $70,265,154.00; FY 19 est $69,397,778.00; FY 20 est $70,147,778.00

HQ: 5600 Fishers Lane, Room 9N18, Rockville, MD 20857

Phone: 301-443-3944 | Email: mhitch@hrsa.gov

http://www.hrsa.gov

DOC11.482 | CORAL REEF CONSERVATION PROGRAM

Award: Cooperative Agreements

Purpose: To support projects that preserve, sustain, and restore U.S. and international coral reef ecosystems.

Applicant Eligibility: Institutions of higher education, non-profit Organizations, commercial Organizations, local and Indian tribal government agencies, foreign Governments, relevant Regional Fishery Management Councils (i.e., Caribbean Fishery Management Council, the Gulf of Mexico Fishery Management Council, the South Atlantic Fishery Management Council, and the Western Pacific Regional Fishery Management Council), and State, Territorial and Commonwealth resource management agencies that were appointed by their respective Governors to serve as the primary point of contact agencies for coral reef conservation activities in each of the jurisdictions of American Samoa, Florida, the Commonwealth of the Northern Mariana Islands, Guam, Hawaii, Puerto Rico, and the U.S. Virgin Islands. Eligible international applicants are Institutions of higher education, non-profit Organizations, non-U.S. government natural resource management agencies, foreign public entities and foreign Organizations, and for-profit Organizations.

Beneficiary Eligibility: Organizations and individuals with professional expertise in managing and conserving coral reef ecosystems in the U.S. and internationally.

Award Range/Average: Range is approximately $35,000 to $850,000; average is $259,000.

Funding: (Salaries and Expenses) FY 16 $8,097,097.00; FY 17 est $7,264,862.00; FY 18 est $7,264,862.00

HQ: 1305 E W Highway SSCMC4-N/ORM1, Silver Spring, MD 20910

Phone: 240-533-0908 | Email: russell.callendar@noaa.gov

http://coralreef.noaa.gov

DOJ16.602 | CORRECTIONS RESEARCH AND EVALUATION AND POLICY FORMULATION

Award: Project Grants; Provision of Specialized Services; Dissemination of Technical Information

Purpose: To conduct, encourage, and coordinate research relating to corrections including the causes, prevention, diagnosis, and treatment of criminal offenders.

Applicant Eligibility: States, general units of local government, public and private agencies, educational Institutions, Organizations and individuals involved in the development, implementation or operation of correctional Programs and services.

Beneficiary Eligibility: States, general units of local government involved in the development, implementation or operation of correctional programs and services.

Funding: (Cooperative Agreements) FY 15 $147,500.00; FY 16 est $200,000.00; FY 17 est $450,000.00

HQ: 500 1 Saint Street NW, Washington, DC 20534

Phone: 202-307-6687 | Email: hfenstermaker@bop.gov

http://www.usdoj.gov

DOJ16.603 | CORRECTIONS TECHNICAL ASSISTANCE/CLEARINGHOUSE

Award: Project Grants; Provision of Specialized Services; Dissemination of Technical Information

Purpose: To encourage and assist Federal, State, and local government programs and services, and programs and services of other public and private agencies, institutions, and organizations in their efforts to develop and implement improved corrections programs.

Applicant Eligibility: States, general units of local government, public and private agencies, educational Institutions, Organizations, and individuals involved in the development, implementation or operation of correctional Programs and services.

Beneficiary Eligibility: States, general units of local government involved in the development, implementation or operation of correctional programs and services.
Funding: (Cooperative Agreements) FY 15 $625,000.00; FY 16 est $800,000.00; FY 17 est $800,000.00
HQ: 500 1 Saint Street NW, Washington, DC 20534
   Phone: 202-307-6687 | Email: hfenstermaker@bop.gov
   http://www.usdoj.gov

DOJ16.601 | CORRECTIONS TRAINING AND STAFF DEVELOPMENT
Award: Project Grants; Provision of Specialized Services; Dissemination of Technical Information; Training
Purpose: To devise and conduct in various geographical locations, seminars, workshops, and training programs for law enforcement officers, judges and judicial personnel, probation and parole personnel, correctional personnel, welfare workers and other personnel.
Applicant Eligibility: States, general units of local government, as well as public and private agencies, educational Institutions, Organizations, and individuals involved in the development, implementation or operation of correctional Programs and services.
Beneficiary Eligibility: States, general units of local government involved in the development, implementation or operation of correctional programs and services.
Funding: (Training) FY 15 $495,852.00; FY 16 est $750,000.00; FY 17 est $750,000.00
HQ: 500 1 Saint Street NW, Washington, DC 20534
   Phone: 202-307-6687 | Email: hfenstermaker@bop.gov
   http://www.usdoj.gov

USDA10.118 | COTTON GINNING COST SHARE PROGRAM
"CGCS"
Award: Direct Payments With Unrestricted Use
Purpose: To provide one-time cost-share payment for the cotton crop producers.
Applicant Eligibility: 1. Eligible applicants are individuals and legal entities with a share in the 2015 cotton crop reported as planted, including failed acres. 2. Use of the assistance is not restricted. 3. Cotton producers must comply with all USDA provisions on fraud (including the Federal Crop Insurance Corporation), conservation compliance, controlled substance, determined to be actively engaged in n farming, and the adjusted gross non-farm income cannot exceed $900,000.
Beneficiary Eligibility: The beneficiary or estate of a deceased producer may submit a CGCS payment application provided the deceased producer or the estate meets all of the eligibility requirements required for a CGCS payment.
Funding: (Direct Payments with Unrestricted Use) FY 18 $215,832,098.00; FY 19 est $0.00; FY 20 est $0.00
HQ: 1400 Independence Avenue SW, PO Box 0512, Washington, DC 20250-0512
   Phone: 202-720-0448 | Email: kelly.hereth@wdc.usda.gov
   http://www.fsa.usda.gov/cgcs

DOS19.704 | COUNTER NARCOTICS
"Counter Narcotics, Interdiction, Demand Reduction"
Award: Cooperative Agreements; Project Grants
Purpose: To disrupt the overseas production and trafficking of illicit drugs through targeted counter-narcotics and institution-building assistance and coordination with foreign nations and international organizations.
Applicant Eligibility: Please see announcements in www.grants.gov.
Beneficiary Eligibility: Same as Applicant Eligibility.
Award Range/Average: Range varies widely. Please see announcments in www.grants.gov.
HQ: 2430 E Street NW, Washington, DC 20037
   Phone: 202-776-8774 | Email: steinlf@state.gov
   http://www.state.gov/j/inl

Programs Administered by Federal Headquarters

DOJ16.756 | COURT APPOINTED SPECIAL ADVOCATES "CASA"

Award: Cooperative Agreements

Purpose: The CASA program fosters care system for children and provides advocacy for abused and neglected children.

Applicant Eligibility: As set forth in the authorizing language in 42 U.S.C. Section 13013, the successful applicant shall be: (1) a national Organization that has broad membership among court-appointed special advocate Programs (OJJDP defines as having a network of volunteers representing the interests of abused and neglected children operating in a minimum of 40 of the Nation's 56 states and territories) and in providing training and technical assistance to court-appointed special advocate Programs; or (2) a local public or not-for-profit agency that has demonstrated the willingness to initiate, sustain, and expand a court-appointed special advocate Program.

Beneficiary Eligibility: N/A

Funding: (Cooperative Agreements) FY 18 $10,935,128.00; FY 19 est $12,000,000.00; FY 20 est $9,000,000.00

HQ: U.S. Department of Justice Office of Juvenile Justice and Delinquency Prevention 810 7th Street NW, Washington, DC 20735
Phone: 202-616-3750 | Email: darian.hanrahan@usdoj.gov
http://www.ojjdp.gov

DOJ16.582 | CRIME VICTIM ASSISTANCE/DISCRETIONARY GRANTS

Award: Project Grants; Direct Payments for Specified Use

Purpose: To improve the overall quality of services delivered to crime victims through the provision of training and technical assistance to providers.

Applicant Eligibility: Criteria will vary depending on the grant or grant Program. Generally, eligible applicants may include American Indian/Alaska Native Tribes and tribal Organizations, States, United States Attorneys' offices, universities and colleges, eligible public agencies that provide victim services and private nonprofit agencies. Applicants for Tribal Victim Assistance grants must be an Indian Tribe, Tribal Organization, partnership or nonprofit Organization that provides direct services to victims of crime in Indian Country.

Beneficiary Eligibility: Eligible victim assistance agencies. Eligibility depends on the nature of the grant but may include a wide variety of public and private nonprofit agencies.

Award Range/Average: OVC anticipates awarding grants ranging from $35,000 to $2.4 million, with an average award amount of $250,000.

Funding: (Project Grants) FY 17 $103,802,946.00; FY 18 est $0.00; FY 19 Estimate Not Available

HQ: Office for Victims of Crime 810 7th Street NW, Washington, DC 20531
Phone: 202-307-5983 | Email: zoe.french@usdoj.gov
http://www.ovc.gov

DOJ16.575 | CRIME VICTIM ASSISTANCE

Award: Formula Grants

Purpose: Providing an annual grant from the Crime Victims Fund to each State and eligible territory for the financial support of services to crime victims by eligible crime victim assistance programs.

Applicant Eligibility: All states, the District of Columbia, the Puerto Rico, the U.S. Virgin Islands, American Samoa, Guam, and the Northern Mariana Islands are eligible to receive an annual VOCA victim assistance formula grant. Eligible agencies that receive VOCA victim assistance formula grant funds must meet the eligibility requirements specified in the Victims of Crime Act (VOCA), 34 U.S.C. 20103 (a) and (b).

Beneficiary Eligibility: Eligible crime victim assistance programs.

Award Range/Average: Base of $500,000 to each State, Commonwealth, and the District of Columbia. Territories of Northern Mariana Islands, Guam, and American Samoa receive a base of $200,000. Remaining dollars will be divided based on population.

Funding: (Formula Grants) FY 18 $3,328,058,070.00; FY 19 est $1,305,958,825.00; FY 20 est Not Separately Identifiable

HQ: Domestic and International Victim Assistance Division Office for Victims of Crime Department of Justice 810 7th Street NW, Washington, DC 20531
Phone: 202-395-1508 | Email: kathrina.peterson@usdoj.gov
http://www.ojp.usdoj.gov/ovc

DOJ16.576 | CRIME VICTIM COMPENSATION

Award: Formula Grants

Purpose: Awarding grants to each state, the District of Columbia, the U.S. Virgin Islands, and the Commonwealth of Puerto Rico to support state crime victim compensation programs.

Applicant Eligibility: States, the District of Columbia, the Commonwealth of Puerto Rico, the U.S. Virgin Islands, Guam, and any other possession or territory of the United States who have an established eligible crime victim compensation Program, and who meet the eligibility requirements discussed above.

Beneficiary Eligibility: Victims of crime that results in death or physical or personal injury and are determined eligible under the State victim compensation statute. State compensation statutes either declare that coverage extends generally to any crime resulting in physical or personal injury, or they list all specific crimes that can be covered.

Award Range/Average: Each State receives 60 percent of its prior year payout of State compensation funds

Funding: (Formula Grants) FY 18 $128,685,000.00; FY 19 est $128,685,000.00; FY 20 est $128,658,000.00

HQ: U.S. Department of Justice Office for Victims of Crime State Compensation and Assistance Division 810 7th Street NW, Washington, DC 20531

Phone: 202-307-5983 | Email: kathrina.peterson@usdoj.gov

http://www.ovc.gov

DOJ16.745 | CRIMINAL AND JUVENILE JUSTICE AND MENTAL HEALTH COLLABORATION PROGRAM
"JMHCP"

Award: Project Grants

Purpose: To increase public safety through collaboration for individuals with mental illness, to maintain jail capacity for violent offenders, to increase public safety and reduce recidivism, and to support law enforcement.

Applicant Eligibility: Applicants are limited to States, units of local government, Indian Tribes, and tribal Organizations. BJA will only accept joint applications; each application must include a mental health agency as well as a unit of government with responsibility for criminal justice activities.

Beneficiary Eligibility: General Public.

Award Range/Average: In amounts consistent with the applicant's proposed project and the BJA's plans, priorities and levels of financing. For additional information, please see the current fiscal year's solicitation available at the Office of Justice Programs web site (http://www.ojp.gov/funding/solicitations.htm).and/or www.bja.gov.

Funding: (Project Grants) FY 17 $10,963,114.00; FY 18 est $30,000,000.00; FY 19 est $10,000,000.00

HQ: U.S. Department of Justice Office for Victims of Crime State Compensation and Assistance Division 810 7th Street NW, Washington, DC 20531

Phone: 202-616-6500 | Email: maria.fryer@usdoj.gov

https://www.bja.gov/ProgramDetails.aspx?Program_ID=66

DOJ16.562 | CRIMINAL JUSTICE RESEARCH AND DEVELOPMENT GRADUATE RESEARCH FELLOWSHIPS
"Graduate Research Fellowship Program"

Award: Project Grants

Purpose: Providing awards to accredited universities for the support of doctoral students engaged in research relevant to ensuring public safety, preventing and controlling crime, and ensuring the fair and impartial administration of criminal justice in the United States.

Applicant Eligibility: Degree-granting academic Institutions in the United States. The institution must be fully accredited by one of the regional institutional accreditation agencies recognized by the U.S. Secretary of education.

Beneficiary Eligibility: The ultimate beneficiaries of this program are graduate students engaged in research relevant to criminal justice, forensic science, and public safety.

Award Range/Average: Maximum award amounts: $32,000 for GRF-SBS; $50,000/yr. for GRF-STEM. See current solicitation for current award maximum.

Funding: (Project Grants) FY 17 est Not Separately Identifiable FY 18 est Not Separately Identifiable

HQ: National Institute of Justice 810 7th Street NW, Washington, DC 20531

Phone: 202-307-2942 | Email: eric.d.martin@ojp.usdoj.gov

http://www.nij.gov

Programs Administered by Federal Headquarters

DOS19.703 | CRIMINAL JUSTICE SYSTEMS
"Rule of Law, Justice Systems"

Award: Cooperative Agreements; Project Grants

Purpose: Develops and expands criminal justice systems to strengthen partner country law enforcement and judicial effectiveness, foster cooperation in legal affairs, and advance respect for human rights.

Applicant Eligibility: Please see announcements in www.grants.gov.

Beneficiary Eligibility: Same as Applicant Eligibility.

Award Range/Average: Range varies widely. Please see announcements in www.grants.gov.

HQ: 2430 E Street NW, Washington, DC 20037

    Phone: 202-776-8774 | Email: steinlf@state.gov

    http://www.state.gov/p/inl

DHS97.032 | CRISIS COUNSELING
"CCP"

Award: Project Grants

Purpose: The Crisis Counseling Assistance and Training Program provides support to individuals and communities in recovering from the challenging effects of natural and human-caused disasters through the provision of community-based outreach and psycho-educational services.

Applicant Eligibility: States are eligible for grants. If the Governor determines, during an assessment of the need for crisis counseling services, that because of unusual circumstances or serious conditions within the State or local mental health network, the State cannot carry out the crisis counseling Program, he/she may identify a public or private mental health agency or Organization to carry out the Program or request the Department of Homeland Security's Federal Emergency Management Agency (FEMA) Regional Director to identify, with assistance of such an agency or Organization.

Beneficiary Eligibility: In order to be eligible for services under this program, an individual must be a resident of the designated disaster area or must have been in the designated area at the time the disaster occurred.

Award Range/Average: Not Applicable.

Funding: (Project Grants) FY 18 est $26,996,637.00; FY 19 est $26,841,295.00; FY 20 $27,500,000.00

HQ: Individual Assistance Department of Homeland Security 500 C Street SW, 6th Floor, Washington, DC 20472-3100

    Phone: 202-212-1117

    http://www.samhsa.gov

USDA10.329 | CROP PROTECTION AND PEST MANAGEMENT COMPETITIVE GRANTS PROGRAM
"CPPM"

Award: Project Grants

Purpose: The CPPM compensates for the regional and national pest management. It supports national research efforts on food security and other implementations.

Applicant Eligibility: Colleges and universities (as defined in section 1404 of NARETPA) (7 U.S.C. 3103) are eligible to submit applications for the CPPM Program. Section 1404 of NARETPA was amended by section 7101 of the Food, Conservation, and Energy Act of 2008 (FCEA) to define Hispanic-serving Agricultural Colleges and universities (HSACUs), and to include research foundations maintained by eligible colleges or universities. For the purposes of this Program, the terms college and University mean an educational institution in any state which (1) admits as regular students only persons having a certificate of graduation from a school providing secondary education, or the recognized equivalent of such a certificate; (2) is legally authorized within such state to provide a Program of education beyond secondary education; (3) provides an educational Program for which a bachelor's degree or any other higher degree is awarded; (4) is a public or other nonprofit institution; and (5) is accredited by a nationally recognized accrediting agency or association. Applications also may be submitted by 1994 Land-Grant Institutions (see Part VIII, E), HSACUs, and research foundations maintained by eligible colleges or universities. Section 7206 of the Farm Security and Rural Investment Act of 2002 amended section 406(b) of AREERA to add the 1994 Land-Grant Institutions as eligible to apply for grants under this authority.

Beneficiary Eligibility: Same as Applicant Eligibility.

Award Range/Average: If minimum or maximum amounts of funding per competitive and/or capacity project grant, or cooperative agreement are established, these amounts will be announced in the annual Competitive Request for Application

(RFA).The most current RFA is available via: https://nifa.usda.gov/funding-opportunity/crop-protection-and-pest-management

Funding: (Project Grants (Discretionary)) FY 17 $18,862,054.00; FY 18 est $19,021,619.00; FY 19 est $0.00
HQ: 1400 Independence Avenue SW, PO Box 2240, Washington, DC 20024

    Phone: 202-401-1761

    http://nifa.usda.gov/program/crop-protection-and-pest-management-competitive-grants-program

NASA43.009 | CROSS AGENCY SUPPORT

Award: Cooperative Agreements; Project Grants
Purpose: Provides basic research, educational outreach, or training opportunities in the area of Cross Agency Support (CAS).
Applicant Eligibility: Review funding opportunity announcement for additional information.
Beneficiary Eligibility: Same as Applicant Eligibility.
Funding: (Salaries and Expenses) FY 18 $12,215,052.1; FY 19 est $10,021,463.5; FY 20 est Estimate Not Available
HQ: 300 E Street SW, Washington, DC 20546

    Phone: 202-358-3125 | Email: daniel.j.tenney@nasa.gov

    http://www.nasa.gov

HHS93.322 | CSELS PARTNERSHIP: STRENGTHENING PUBLIC HEALTH LABORATORIES

"Laboratory Leadership, Workforce Training and Management Development"

Award: Cooperative Agreements
Purpose: To enhance and strengthen the work and functionality of public health laboratories both domestically and abroad.
Applicant Eligibility: Applicants must have experience with enhancing and strengthening the work and functionality of public health laboratories both domestically and abroad. The overarching goal is to improve several aspects of public health laboratories.
Beneficiary Eligibility: Applicants must have experience with enhancing and strengthening the work and functionality of public health laboratories both domestically and abroad. The overarching goal is to improve several aspects of public health laboratories. The nation's public is the ultimate recipient of benefits from this program.
Award Range/Average: Subject to avail funds.Approximate Average Award: $27 MFloor Award Amount: $7 MCeiling Award Amount: $30 Anticipated Award Date: July 1,2015 Budget Period Length: 12 monthsProject Period Length: 5 years
Funding: (Cooperative Agreements) FY 18 $27,552,526.00; FY 19 est $20,645,594.00; FY 20 est $0.00
HQ: 2400 Century Center Boulevard, Atlanta, GA 30345

    Phone: 404-639-3008

    http://www.cdc.gov

DHS97.009 | CUBAN/HAITIAN ENTRANT PROGRAM

Award: Cooperative Agreements
Purpose: The program offers resettlement services to people especially Cubans and Haitians, who have been paroled into the country by the Department of Homeland Security.
Applicant Eligibility: Public or Private, nonprofit Organizations or agencies, and under certain conditions for-profit Organizations, agencies, or Institutions.
Beneficiary Eligibility: Cuban and Haitian nationals who meet the definition of entrant set forth in Title V, Section 501(e) of Public Law 96-422.
Award Range/Average: Refer to program guidance.
Funding: (Cooperative Agreements) FY 18 $4,886,000.00; FY 19 est $0.00; FY 20 est $0.00
HQ: DHS/USCIS/IO/HAB 999 North Capitol Street NE, 3rd Floor, Washington, DC 20529

    Phone: 202-245-2111 | Email: john.w.bird@uscis.dhs.gov

    https://www.uscis.gov/humanitarian/humanitarian-parole/cuban-haitian-entrant-program-chep

Programs Administered by Federal Headquarters

DOS19.015 | CULTURAL, TECHNICAL AND EDUCATIONAL CENTERS

Award: Cooperative Agreements

Purpose: Assists various organizations identified by Congress to achieve objectives specified by Congress. The Bureau of Educational and Cultural Affairs (ECA) seeks to increase mutual understanding between the people of the United States and the people of other countries by means of educational and cultural exchange programs. It is premised on the knowledge that mutual understanding, the development of future leaders, and the benefits of education programs.

Applicant Eligibility: Organizations specifically identified by Congress in agency appropriations legislation.

Beneficiary Eligibility: Beneficiaries are those served by the organizations receiving awards.

Award Range/Average: $774,683 to $16,700,000.

Funding: (Cooperative Agreements) FY 17 $17,474,863.00; FY 18 est $17,474,863.00; FY 19 est $17,474,863.00

HQ: Office of Academic Exchanges 2200 C Street NW SA-05, Room 4N6, Washington, DC 20037

　　Phone: 202-632-6067 | Email: meieraw2@state.gov

　　http://exchanges.state.gov

DOJ16.016 | CULTURALLY AND LINGUISTICALLY SPECIFIC SERVICES PROGRAM
"Culturally Specific Services Program"

Award: Project Grants

Purpose: To enhance culturally-specific services for the victims of domestic violence, dating violence, sexual assault, and stalking.

Applicant Eligibility: Community-based Programs whose primary purpose is providing culturally specific services to victims of domestic violence, dating violence, sexual assault, and stalking; and community-based Programs whose primary purpose is providing culturally specific services who can partner with a Program having demonstrated expertise in serving victims of domestic violence, dating violence, sexual assault, and stalking.

Beneficiary Eligibility: Community and faith-based programs.

Award Range/Average: Range: $200,000- $300,000

Funding: (Project Grants) FY 16 $5,910,000.00; FY 17 est $6,168,114.00; FY 18 $6,000,000.00

HQ: 145 N Street NE, Suite 10W121, Washington, DC 20530

　　Phone: 202-305-1177 | Email: tia.farmer@usdoj.gov

　　http://www.justice.gov/ovw

DOS19.035 | CYBER CAPACITY BUILDING

Award: Cooperative Agreements; Project Grants

Purpose: Enhances global cybersecurity.

Applicant Eligibility: See www.grants.gov for specific application.

Beneficiary Eligibility: Same as Applicant Eligibility.

Award Range/Average: See www.grants.gov for specific application

HQ: 2201 C street NW, Washington, DC 20520

　　Phone: 202-647-3918 | Email: lahaiejmc@state.gov

DOD12.905 | CYBERSECURITY CORE CURRICULUM

Award: Project Grants

Purpose: To develop Cybersecurity Core Curriculum that will ensure cybersecurity graduates who wish to join the Federal Government have the requisite knowledge and skills.

Applicant Eligibility: Must be a U.S. college or University, a public or private school or school system, or a not-for-profit educational institution. The principal investigator and Program staff must be U.S. citizens or permanent residents of the United States. Program eligibility will be determined by NSA's College of Cyber.

Beneficiary Eligibility: Same as Applicant Eligibility.

Award Range/Average: Estimated range is $40,000 to $1,000,000. This is the first year so no average is available

Funding: (Salaries and Expenses) FY 17 $6,396,954.00; FY 18 est $6,396,954.00; FY 19 est Estimate Not Available

HQ: 9800 Savage Road, Fort George G. Meade, MD 20755

　　Phone: 443-479-4327 | Email: dlberr1@nsa.gov

　　http://www.nsa.gov

DHS97.127 | CYBERSECURITY EDUCATION AND TRAINING ASSISTANCE PROGRAM (CETAP)
"CETAP"

Award: Project Grants
Purpose: The program helps the Department of Homeland Security to secure civilian government computer systems to analyze and reduce cyber threats.
Applicant Eligibility: Specific information on applicant eligibility is identified in the funding opportunity announcements.
Beneficiary Eligibility: Refer to program guidance.
Award Range/Average: Refer to the funding opportunity announcements.
Funding: (Project Grants) FY 18 $4,000,000.00; FY 19 est $4,300,000.00; FY 20 Estimate Not Available
HQ: DHS 245 Murray Lane SW, Building 410, Washington, DC 20528
    Phone: 703-705-6672
    http://www.dhs.gov

DHS97.076 | CYBERTIPLINE
"ICE/HSI"

Award: Project Grants
Purpose: The funding program creates an awareness on using CyberTipline to report abductions, abuse and/or sexual exploitation of children and thereby assist the global law enforcement in their recovery.
Applicant Eligibility: Non-profits with 501(3) IRS status, other than institution of higher education Non-profits without 501(3) IRS status, other than institution of higher education For-profit Organizations other than small businesses Small businesses.
Beneficiary Eligibility: General public.
Award Range/Average: Amount may vary.
Funding: (Project Grants) FY 18 $305,000.00; FY 19 est $305,000.00; FY 20 est $0.00
HQ: 11320 Random Hills Rd, Suite 400, Fairfax, VA 22030
    Phone: 703-293-9207 | Email: margie.m.jones@ice.dhs.gov
    http://www.dhs.gov

USDA10.176 | DAIRY BUSINESS INNOVATION INITIATIVES
"DBI Initiatives"

Award: Project Grants
Purpose: To diversify dairy product markets to develop higher-value uses for dairy products and promote business development that increases farmer income through processing and marketing innovation. It also focuses on encouraging the use of regional milk production.
Applicant Eligibility: Eligible entities include: State departments of agriculture or other state entities, cooperative extension services, Institutions of higher education, and nonprofit Organizations. Entities must have the capacity to provide consultation and expertise necessary to advance the purpose and activities of the DBI Initiatives, and expertise in grant distribution and tracking to be considered eligible for this Program. Dairy Promotion Programs are ineligible to host an initiative.
Beneficiary Eligibility: Producers, processors, growers, state agencies, beginning and socially disadvantaged farmers, and general public.
Award Range/Average: As provided for in the applicable Request for Applications (RFA).
Funding: (Project Grants) FY 18 Actual Not Available; FY 19 est $1,500,000.00; FY 20 est Estimate Not Available
HQ: 1400 Independence Avenue SW, Washington, DC 20250
    Phone: 202-720-1403
    https://www.ams.usda.gov/services/grants

Programs Administered by Federal Headquarters

USDA10.127 | DAIRY MARGIN COVERAGE
"DMC"

Award: Direct Payments for Specified Use
Purpose: To provide a protection plan for dairy operators when the price difference between milk and average feed cost for cattle falls below a certain value set by the producers.
Applicant Eligibility: N/A
Beneficiary Eligibility: The ultimate benefit of the DMC-Dairy program will help protect farm equity and reduce financial losses that occur during times of low margins.
Funding: (Direct Payments for Specified Use Total) FY 18 $0; FY 19 est $779,000,000.00; FY 20 est $583,000,000.00
HQ: 1400 Independence Avenue SW, Washington, DC 20250-0512
   Phone: 202-720-9011 | Email: douglas.e.kilgore@usda.gov
   https://www.fsa.usda.gov/programs-and-services/dairy-margin-coverage-program/index

DOD12.777 | DEFENSE PRODUCTION ACT TITLE III (DPA TITLE III)
"DPA Title III"

Award: Cooperative Agreements; Project Grants; Direct Loans
Purpose: Creates, maintains, protects, expands, or restores domestic industrial base capabilities essential for the national defense.
Applicant Eligibility: The Title III Office makes the determination of applicant eligibility and assistance types based on the criticality of the national defense need and availability of funds.
Beneficiary Eligibility: The Title III Office makes the determination for beneficiary eligibility based on the criticality of need and availability of funds.
Award Range/Average: Individual award amounts vary, according to the project need.
HQ: ACC-NJ-ET 1 Buffington Street Benet Laboratories, Building 40, Watervliet, NY 12189
   Phone: 518-266-5100 | Email: travis.t.clemons.civ@mail.mil
   http://www.businessdefense.gov/programs/dpa-title-iii

DRA90.201 | DELTA AREA ECONOMIC DEVELOPMENT
"Supplemental and Direct Grants"

Award: Project Grants
Purpose: To develop the transportation infrastructure of the region for the purpose of facilitating economic development in the region.
Applicant Eligibility: State, their subdivisions and instrumentalities and private nonprofit agencies.
Beneficiary Eligibility: General public.
Funding: (Formula Grants) FY 07 $8,015,805.00; FY 08 Estimate Not Available; FY 09 est $8,000,000.00
HQ: 236 Sharkey Avenue, Suite 400, Clarksdale, MS 38614
   Phone: 662-624-8600 | Email: akangelos@dra.gov
   http://www.dra.gov

HUD14.271 | DELTA COMMUNITY CAPITAL INITIATIVE
"DCCI"

Award: Project Grants
Purpose: To increase access to capital for business lending and development in the chronically under-served and -capitalized Lower Mississippi Delta region. It will also provide direct investment and technical assistance to community development lending and investing institutions so that funding opportunities will be more effective to the under-served residents of Lower Mississippi Delta Region.
Applicant Eligibility: Applicants that are eligible to participate in this initiative are community development lenders and investors, which may be local rural non-profit Organizations or federally recognized Tribes. Applicants do not need to be certified as Community Development Financial Institutions by the CDFI Fund at the time of application. If applicants propose to become certified as a CDFI, they should lay out milestones and time frames toward the CDFI certification process in their application. Applicants may serve other markets than Delta residents and communities, using other sources of financing.

Beneficiary Eligibility: Eligible target markets for use of DCCI funds include businesses owned by or serving low income residents of the Lower Mississippi Delta Region. The Delta region includes the 252 counties and parishes in eight states that make up the Lower Mississippi Delta Region, as defined by the Delta Regional Authority. The Delta Regional Authority (DRA) is a federal-state partnership working to stimulate economic development and governed by the Delta Regional Authority Board, comprised of the Federal Co-Chairman, appointed by the President and confirmed by the U.S. Senate, and the governors of the eight states. The eight states that are included in the region are: Alabama, Arkansas, Illinois, Kentucky, Louisiana, Mississippi, Missouri, and Tennessee.

Award Range/Average: Original projection was $1,000,000. Actual amount of funds made available was $1,478,040.

HQ: U.S. Department of Housing and Urban Development Office of Rural Housing and Economic Development 451 7th Street SW, Room 7137, Washington, DC 20410

Phone: 877-787-2526 | Email: thann.young@hud.gov

DRA90.203 | DELTA CREATIVE PLACE-MAKING PILOT INITIATIVE

Award: Project Grants

Purpose: Serves 252 counties and parishes in an eight-state region: Alabama, Arkansas, Illinois, Kentucky, Louisiana, Mississippi, Missouri, and Tennessee.

Applicant Eligibility: The Delta Creative Place-making Initiative is designed to help communities enhance the quality of place and quality of life by investing in the distinctive local character of Delta places, for positive economic and community outcomes.

Beneficiary Eligibility: For more information, please visit the Delta Regional Authority website at www.dra.gov.

Award Range/Average: DRA funding and technical assistance provided for DCPI projects will commence on September 1,2017, for a period of up to 24 months. Applicants should allow sufficient time for asset mapping, partnership dialogue and collaboration building, planning, execution, internal evaluation, and project completion/close-out.

Funding: (Project Grants) FY 16 Actual Not Available; FY 17 est $30,900.00; FY 18 est Estimate Not Available

HQ: 236 Sharkey Avenue, Suite 400, Clarksdale, MS 38614

Phone: 662-483-8212 | Email: shoskins@dra.gov

http://www.dra.gov

USDA10.874 | DELTA HEALTH CARE SERVICES GRANT PROGRAM

Award: Project Grants

Purpose: To assist the Delta Region through cooperation among healthcareprofessionals, institutions of higher education, research institutions, and other organizations in the Delta Region.

Applicant Eligibility: Eligible applicants are consortiums of the following: regional Institutions of higher education, academic health and research institutes, and/or economic development entities located within the Delta Region. Applicants are not eligible if they have been debarred or suspended or otherwise excluded from participation in Federal assistance Programs under Executive Order 12549, Debarment and Suspension. Applicants are not eligible if they have an outstanding judgement obtained by the U.S. in a Federal Court (other than U.S. Tax Court), are delinquent on the payment of Federal income taxes, or are delinquent on a Federal debt. Any corporation that has been convicted of a felony criminal violation under any Federal law within the past 24 months or that has any unpaid Federal tax liability that has been assessed, for which all judicial and administrative remedies have been exhausted or have lapsed, and that is not being paid in a timely manner pursuant to an agreement with the authority responsible for collecting the tax liability, is not eligible for funding.

Beneficiary Eligibility: Ultimate beneficiaries must be located in rural areas in the Delta Region.

Award Range/Average: Average = $N/ARange = $50,000 (minimum) to $500,000 (maximum)

Funding: (Project Grants (Discretionary)) FY 18 $3,000,000.00; FY 19 est $3,000,000.33.00; FY 20 Estimate Not Available

HQ: Cooperative Programs Grants Division 1400 Independence Avenue SW Room 4208-S, PO Box 3253, Washington, DC 20250-1550

Phone: 202-690-1374

http://www.rd.usda.gov/programs-services/delta-health-care-services-grants

DRA90.202 | DELTA LOCAL DEVELOPMENT DISTRICT ASSISTANCE "LDD"

Award: Project Grants

Purpose: To provide planning and development resources in multicounty areas.

Programs Administered by Federal Headquarters

Applicant Eligibility: Multicounty Organizations certified by the State.
Beneficiary Eligibility: Multicounty organizations.
Funding: (Salary or Expense) FY 07 $396,000.00; FY 08 est Estimate Not Available; FY 09 est $396,000.00; FY 07 $396,000;
FY 08 $396,000; and FY 09 est $396,000
HQ: 236 Sharkey Avenue, Suite 400, Clarksdale, MS 38614
Phone: 662-624-8600
http://www.dra.gov

DRA90.200 | DELTA REGIONAL DEVELOPMENT
"Delta Program"

Award: Project Grants
Purpose: A federal-state partnership serving a 240-county/parish area in an eight-state region.
Applicant Eligibility: The Authority may approve grants to States and public and nonprofit entities. All proposed projects must
meet the clarification notes as part of the pre-application and the requirements of the State Delta plan which must be approved
annually by the Authority.
Beneficiary Eligibility: General public.
HQ: 236 Sharkey Avenue, Suite 400, Clarksdale, MS 38614 | Email: akangelos@dra.gov
http://www.dra.gov

HUD14.866 | DEMOLITION AND REVITALIZATION OF SEVERELY DISTRESSED PUBLIC HOUSING
"HOPE VI"

Award: Project Grants
Purpose: To improve the living environment for public housing residents of severely distressed public housing projects; revitalize
the sites on which gravely distressed public housing projects are located; lessen alienation and reduce the denseness of low-
income families; build sustainable mixed-income communities; and provide well-coordinated.
Applicant Eligibility: For HOPE VI Revitalization Grants, Public Housing Agencies (PHAs) operating public housing units are
eligible to apply. Indian Housing Authorities and PHAs that only administer the Section 8 Program are not eligible to apply.
Beneficiary Eligibility: For HOPE VI Revitalization Grants, the ultimate beneficiaries are residents of the severely distressed
public housing and residents of the revitalized development.
Award Range/Average: N/A
HQ: 451 7th Street SW, Room 4130, Washington, DC 20410
Phone: 202-402-5788 | Email: leigh.e.vanrij@hud.gov
http://www.hud.gov/offices/pih/programs/ph/hope6

HHS93.327 | DEMONSTRATION GRANTS FOR DOMESTIC VICTIMS OF HUMAN TRAFFICKING
"Domestic Victims of Human Trafficking Program"

Award: Cooperative Agreements; Project Grants
Purpose: To conduct community assessments with the goal to build capacity, create partnerships, and deliver comprehensive,
quality services to domestic victims.
Applicant Eligibility: Eligible Organizations includes: state Governments, Tribes, units of local government, and non-profit,
non-governmental victim service Organizations. Victim service Organizations include those who by nature of their current
operations serve victims of sexual assault, sexual violence, domestic violence, human trafficking, and youth homelessness.
Victim services Organizations may also include faith-based Organizations that are addressing human trafficking in their
services. Individuals (including sole proprietorships) and foreign entities are not eligible.
Beneficiary Eligibility: Eligible recipients for DVHT program services include United States citizens and lawful permanent
residents.
Award Range/Average: $150,000 to $300,000 per grant per budget period for the three-year project period. The average grant
award per budget period is $263,000.
Funding: (Project Grants) FY 18 $2,898,525.00; FY 19 est $3,198,525.00; FY 20 est $4,000,000.00

HQ: 330 C Street SW, 4th Floor, Washington, DC 20201
    Phone: 202-401-9372 | Email: katherine.chon@acf.hhs.gov
    http://www.acf.hhs.gov/programs/otip

HHS93.933 | DEMONSTRATION PROJECTS FOR INDIAN HEALTH

Award: Cooperative Agreements; Project Grants
Purpose: To promote improved healthcareamong American Indians and Alaska Natives by addressing issues in women's health care, tribal dental clinical and preventive support centers, public health nursing, methamphetamine and suicide prevention program, national HIV program and healthy lifestyles in youth.
Applicant Eligibility: Federally recognized Indian Tribes; tribal Organizations; nonprofit inter-tribal Organizations; nonprofit urban Indian Organizations contracting with the Indian Health Service under Title V of the Indian healthcare Improvement Act; public or private nonprofit health and education entities; and State and local government health agencies.
Beneficiary Eligibility: American Indians/Alaska Natives will be the ultimate beneficiaries of the funded projects either directly or indirectly depending upon the nature of the project. For example, those individuals who participate in research studies and receive services will be direct beneficiaries while those impacted by policy changes resulting from analyses of Indian health care issues will be indirect beneficiaries.
Funding: (Cooperative Agreements) FY 18 $7,615,628.00; FY 19 est $6,854,883.00; FY 20 est $6,854,883.00; - (Project Grants) FY 18 $42,630,790.00; FY 19 est $41,510,790.00; FY 20 est $41,962,000.00
HQ: 5600 Fishers Lane, PO Box 09E70, Rockville, MD 20857
    Phone: 301-443-5204
    http://www.ihs.gov

USDA10.858 | DENALI COMMISSION GRANTS AND LOANS
"RUS - Denali Commission Grants"

Award: Project Grants
Purpose: To provide loans to the Denali Commission for the benefit of rural communities in Alaska.
Applicant Eligibility: The Denali Commission, a Federal Agency, is the only eligible applicant.
Beneficiary Eligibility: Beneficiaries are residents of rural communities in Alaska with extremely high energy costs. Eligible beneficiary communities must apply for assistance directly to the Denali Commission and eligible projects must be on Denali Commission Annual Approved Work Plan.
Award Range/Average: Grant awards have ranged from $2,310,686 to $18,500,000.
Funding: (Project Grants) FY 18 $1,000,000.00; FY 19 est $0.00; FY 20 est $0.00
HQ: 1400 Independence Avenue SW, PO Box 1560, Washington, DC 20250
    Phone: 202-720-9545 | Email: christopher.mclean@wdc.usda.gov
    http://www.denali.gov

DC90.100 | DENALI COMMISSION PROGRAM
"Denali Commission"

Award: Project Grants
Purpose: To provide funding and partner coordination for critical utilities and infrastructure projects throughout Alaska, particularly in distressed communities.
Applicant Eligibility: Awards are available to State and local Governments, private, public, profit, nonprofit Organizations and Institutions.
Beneficiary Eligibility: General public, particularly distressed communities.
Award Range/Average: Varies.
Funding: (Project Grants (Discretionary)) FY 16 Not Separately Identifiable; FY 17 est $15,000,000.00; FY 18 est $15,000,000.00
HQ: 510 L Street, Suite 410, Anchorage, AK 99501
    Phone: 907-271-1414 | Email: ceilo@denali.gov
    http://www.denali.gov

Programs Administered by Federal Headquarters

USAID98.010 | DENTON PROGRAM

Award: Provision of Specialized Services

Purpose: Provides military transportation for private citizens at low or no cost on humanitarian grounds.

Applicant Eligibility: Applicants must be an U.S. based private voluntary Organization (PVOs), non-governmental Organization (NGOs) or small Organization.

Beneficiary Eligibility: PVOs, NGOs and International Organizations (IOs) in eligible countries.

Funding: (Project Grants) FY 16 est Not Separately Identifiable; FY 17 est Not Separately Identifiable

HQ: 301 4th Street SW, Washington, DC 20547

　　Phone: 202-567-4688 | Email: rwillis@usaid.gov

　　http://www.usaid.gov

DOD12.116 | DEPARTMENT OF DEFENSE APPROPRIATION ACT OF 2003 "Section 8044"

Award: Provision of Specialized Services

Purpose: For developing a system for prioritization of mitigation and cost to complete estimates for mitigation, on Indian lands resulting from Department of Defense activities.

Applicant Eligibility: The 50 States, the District of Columbia, Guam, American Samoa, the Commonwealth of the Northern Marinas, Palau Island, the Commonwealth of Puerto Rico, the Virgin Islands, and Federally recognized Indian Tribes.

Beneficiary Eligibility: Same as Applicant Eligibility.

Funding: (Provision of Specialized Services) FY 14 $6,055,500.00; FY 15 est $185,160.00; FY 16 est $4,000,000.00

HQ: 441 G Street NW, Washington, DC 20314

　　Phone: 202-761-1504 | Email: donnie.l.tew@usace.army.mil

DOD12.350 | DEPARTMENT OF DEFENSE HIV/AIDS PREVENTION PROGRAM

Award: Cooperative Agreements; Project Grants

Purpose: To train and assist selected foreign militaries in establishing and implementing HIV/AIDS prevention, care, and treatment programs.

Applicant Eligibility: Generally any type of applicant may apply. Grants cannot be awarded to individuals.

Beneficiary Eligibility: Beneficiaries are primarily foreign Governments.

Award Range/Average: $50,000 to $5,000,000

Funding: (Project Grants) FY 16 $47,000,000.00; FY 17 est $47,000,000.00; FY 18 Estimate Not Available

HQ: c/o Naval Health Research Center 140 Sylvester Road, San Diego, CA 92103

　　Phone: 619-553-8415

DOD12.558 | DEPARTMENT OF DEFENSE IMPACT AID (SUPPLEMENT, CWSD, BRAC) "DoD Impact Aid"

Award: Direct Payments With Unrestricted Use

Purpose: To reimburse local educational agencies (LEAs) for education related costs for military dependent children enrolled in the LEA during the specified school year.

Applicant Eligibility: Only LEAs eligible for Federal Impact Aid pursuant to Section 7703 of Title 20, U.S.C. may be eligible for one or more of the three independent DoD Impact Aid Programs.

Beneficiary Eligibility: Please see the DoD Impact Aid web site for detailed eligibility information: http://www.dodea.edu/partnership/impact.cfm.

Award Range/Average: Not Applicable.

Funding: (Direct Payments with Unrestricted Use) FY 17 $35,000,000.00; FY 18 Estimate Not Available; FY 19 est $35,000,000.00

HQ: 4800 Mark Center Drive, Alexandria, VA 22350-1400

　　Phone: 571-372-5870 | Email: marilyn.hall@ed.gov

　　http://www.dodea.edu/partnership/impact.cfm

DOL17.791 | DEPARTMENT OF LABOR CHIEF EVALUATION OFFICE
"Department of Labor Evaluation Grants"

Award: Project Grants

Purpose: Examines the impact of the agencies' programs and policies is by conducting rigorous research and evaluation studies that allow DOL to learn systematically about and improve the effectiveness of programs and services.

Applicant Eligibility: The following Organizations are eligible to apply: Public/State Controlled Institution of Higher education Alaska Native and Native Hawaiian Serving Institutions Asian American and Native American Pacific Islander-Serving Institutions Indian/Native American Tribal Government (Federally Recognized)Indian/Native American Tribal Government (Other than Federally Recognized)Indian/Native American Tribally Designated Organization Private Institution of Higher education Hispanic-serving Institution Historically Black Colleges and universities (HBCUs)Tribally Controlled Colleges and universities (TCCUs).

Beneficiary Eligibility: N/A

Funding: (Project Grants (Discretionary)) FY 17 $1,968,946.00; FY 18 est $0.00; FY 19 est $0.00

HQ: U.S. Department of Labor 200 Constitution Avenue NW, Room S2312 Frances Perkins Building, Washington, DC 20210
Phone: 202-693-5087 | Email: lohmann.jessica@dol.gov

HHS93.223 | DEVELOPMENT AND COORDINATION OF RURAL HEALTH SERVICES
"Rural Assistance Center Program"

Award: Cooperative Agreements

Purpose: For the development and coordination of rural health services.

Applicant Eligibility: Public or private entities with a service commitment to and experience with rural issues at a national level. Applicant must directly employ a project director with a professional record in national rural health and/or social services policy issues, and directly employ staff for the Information Center, with exceptions only through written agreement with ORHP.

Beneficiary Eligibility: The rural health information clearinghouse is a gateway to information on rural health and social services for residents in rural areas of the United States and for all others interested in these issues.

Award Range/Average: Average award is $2,100,000.

Funding: (Project Grants) FY 18 $2,100,000.00; FY 19 est $2,100,000.00; FY 20 est Estimate Not Available

HQ: 5600 Fishers Lane, Room 17W41D, Rockville, MD 20857
Phone: 301-443-0835 | Email: shirsch@hrsa.gov
http://www.hrsa.gov/ruralhealth

HHS93.630 | DEVELOPMENTAL DISABILITIES BASIC SUPPORT AND ADVOCACY GRANTS
"State Councils on Developmental Disabilities and Protection and Advocacy Systems"

Award: Formula Grants

Purpose: The Developmental Disabilities Basic Support and Advocacy Grants to enable individuals with developmental disabilities to become independent, productive, integrated and included into their communities. Funding under these programs is to assist States in the development of a plan for a comprehensive and coordinated system of services and other activities to enhance the lives of individuals with developmental disabilities and their families to their maximum potential.

Applicant Eligibility: State grant agencies are the designated State agencies of the respective States, the District of Columbia, Puerto Rico, Virgin Islands, Guam, Northern Mariana Islands, American Samoa. Under the basic developmental disabilities Program, the designated State agency must not provide or pay for services to individuals with developmental disabilities, unless it has held such designation on the date of the enactment of the Developmental Disabilities Assistance and Bill of Rights Act Amendments of 1994, and the Governor of the State (or the legislature, where appropriate and in accordance with State law) determines prior to June 30, 1994, not to change the designation of such agency. The State can only receive funding under the basic developmental disabilities Program if it is also participating in the protection and advocacy Program. The agency designated to implement the State system under the protection and advocacy Program cannot provide or pay for services to individuals with developmental disabilities, and that agency must have authority to obtain access to records of individuals with developmental disabilities.

Beneficiary Eligibility: To be eligible for a grant, an agency must be designated to administer the program on behalf of the State. The Basic Program benefits individuals with developmental disabilities through systems change. The Protection and Advocacy system benefits individuals with developmental disabilities. Developmental disability is defined here as a severe chronic disability of an individual that is attributable to mental, physical, or a combination of impairments, is manifested before age 22, that is likely to continue indefinitely, that results in substantial functional limitations in three or more of the following major life activities (self-care, receptive and expressive language, learning, mobility, self-direction, capacity for independent living, and economic self-sufficiency), and that reflects an individual's lifelong need for services. Infants and children from birth to age 9, inclusive, are included if they have a developmental delay or condition with a high probability of resulting in developmental disabilities if services are not provided.

Award Range/Average: Basic Support: $450,000; Protection and Advocacy: $200,000.

Funding: (Formula Grants) FY 17 $110,939,608.00; FY 18 est $116,734,000.00; FY 19 est Estimate Not Available

HQ: 330 C Street SW, Suite 1122, Washington, DC 20201

Phone: 202-795-7401 | Email: ophelia.mclain@acl.hhs.gov

HHS93.631 | DEVELOPMENTAL DISABILITIES PROJECTS OF NATIONAL SIGNIFICANCE

Award: Project Grants

Purpose: Provides for grants, contracts and cooperative agreements for projects of national significance that create opportunities for individuals with intellectual and developmental disabilities to directly and fully contribute to, and participate in, all facets of community life; and support the development of national and State policies that reinforce, promote the self-determination, independence, productivity, and integration and inclusion of individuals with intellectual and developmental disabilities in all facets of community life.

Applicant Eligibility: In general, any State, local, public or private nonprofit Organization or agency may apply.

Beneficiary Eligibility: Same as Applicant Eligibility.

Award Range/Average: The range is $50,000 to $500,000.

Funding: (Cooperative Agreements (Discretionary Grants)) FY 17 $10,000,000.00; FY 18 est $12,000,000.00; FY 19 est Estimate Not Available

HQ: 330 C Street SW, Washington, DC 20201

Phone: 202-795-7334 | Email: allison.cruz@acl.hhs.gov

http://www.acl.gov/Programs/AIDD/Index.aspx

ONDCP95.003 | DFC NATIONAL COMMUNITY ANTIDRUG COALITION INSTITUTE

"National Coalition Institute (NCI)"

Award: Project Grants

Purpose: To provide education, training, and technical assistance for anti-drug coalition leaders and community teams. It mainly focuses on developing anti-drug coalition teams serving economically disadvantaged areas.

Applicant Eligibility: Per the statute, an Organization eligible for the grant under subsection (a) is any national nonprofit Organization that represents, provides technical assistance and training to, and has special expertise and broad, national-level experience in community antidrug coalitions under section 1032 of the National Narcotics Leadership Act of 1988 (21 U.S.C. 1532).

Beneficiary Eligibility: N/A

Award Range/Average: Per the authorizing legislation, for the DFC Program, of which $2,000,000 shall be made available as directed by section 4 of Public Law 107-82, as amended by Public Law 109-469 and Public Law 115-271 (21 U.S.C. 1521 note).

Funding: (Project Grants) FY 18 $0; FY 19 est $2,000,000.00; FY 20 est $0

HQ: 1800 G Street NW, Washington, DC 20503

Phone: 202-395-6739 | Email: phuong_desear@ondcp.eop.gov

https://www.whitehouse.gov

HHS93.847 | DIABETES, DIGESTIVE, AND KIDNEY DISEASES EXTRAMURAL RESEARCH

Award: Project Grants

Purpose: To promote extramural basic and clinical biomedical research that improves the understanding of the mechanisms underlying disease and leads to improved preventions, diagnosis, and treatment of diabetes, digestive, and kidney diseases.

Applicant Eligibility: Project Grants: universities, colleges, medical, dental and nursing schools, schools of public health, laboratories, hospitals, State and local health departments, other public or private Institutions, both non-profit and for-profit, and individuals who propose to establish, expand, and improve research activities in health sciences and related fields. NRSAs: Support is provided for academic and research training only, in health and health-related areas that are periodically specified by the National Institutes of Health. To be eligible, predoctoral awardees must have completed the baccalaureate degree and postdoctoral awardees must have a professional or scientific degree (M.D., Ph.D., D.D.S., D.O., D.V.M., Sc.D., D.Eng., or equivalent domestic or foreign degree). Individuals must be nominated and sponsored by a public or nonprofit private institution having staff and facilities appropriate to the proposed research training Program. All awardees must be citizens or have been admitted to the United States for permanent residence. Nonprofit domestic Organizations may apply for the Institutional NRSA. SBIR and STTR grants can be awarded only to domestic small businesses that meet the following criteria: 1) Is independently owned and operated, is not dominant in the field of operation in which it is proposing, has a place of business in the United States and operates primarily within the United States or makes a significant contribution to the US economy, and is organized for profit; 2) Is (a) at least 51% owned and controlled by one or more individuals who are citizens of, or permanent resident aliens in, the United States, or (b) for SBIR only, it must be a for-profit business concern that is at least 51% owned and controlled by another for-profit business concern that is at least 51% owned and controlled by one or more individuals who are citizens of, or permanent resident aliens in, the United States. 3) Has, including its affiliates, an average number of employees for the preceding 12 months not exceeding 500, and meets the other regulatory requirements found in 13 C. F. R. Part 121. Business concerns are generally considered to be affiliates of one another when either directly or indirectly, (a) one concern controls or has the power to control the other; or (b) a third-party/parties controls or has the power to control both. STTR grants which "partner" with a research institution in cooperative research and development. At least 40 percent of the project is to be performed by the small business concern and at least 30 percent by the research institution. In both Phase I and Phase II, the research must be performed in the U.S. and its possessions. To be eligible for funding, a grant application must be approved for scientific merit and Program relevance by a scientific review group and a national advisory council.

Beneficiary Eligibility: Health professionals, graduate students, health professional students, scientists, and researchers, any nonprofit or for-profit organization, company, or institution engaged in biomedical research. Project Grants: Although no degree of education is either specified or required, nearly all successful applicants have doctoral degrees in one of the sciences or professions. NRSAs: Predoctoral awardees must have completed the baccalaureate degree and postdoctoral awardees must have a professional or scientific degree.

Award Range/Average: Project Grants: Range of $1,200 to $30,000,000; $442,000 averageNRSAs: Range of $358 to $735,000; $125,000 averageSBIR: Range of $30,000 to $1,803,000; $522,000 average

Funding: (Project Grants) FY 17 $1,649,244,000.00; FY 18 est $1,734,068,000.00; FY 19 est $1,613,162,000.00

HQ: 31 Center Drive Room 9A34, Bethesda, MD 20892

   Phone: 301-594-8842 | Email: Shorterm@mail.nih.gov

   http://www2.niddk.nih.gov

HHS93.321 | DIETARY SUPPLEMENT RESEARCH PROGRAM

Award: Cooperative Agreements; Project Grants

Purpose: To identify projects that should be conducted or supported by national research institutes; identify multi-disciplinary research related to dietary supplements that should be conducted or supported; and promote coordination and collaboration among entities conduction research.

Applicant Eligibility: Awards can be made to domestic, public or private, non-profit or profit Organization, institution of higher learning, University, hospital, laboratory, or other institution including state and local units of government and tribal entities. Some initiatives will accept applications from foreign Organizations. Additional details on eligibility will be specified in the funding opportunity announcement.

Beneficiary Eligibility: Institutions as described above.

Award Range/Average: The maximum funding under future program announcements is $100,000 for any single award per year.

Funding: (Project Grants) FY 17 $10,944,349.00; FY 18 est $10,312,690.00; FY 19 est $10,312,690.00

HQ: 6100 Executive Boulevard, Suite 3B01, Rockville, MD 20852

   Phone: 301-496-0168 | Email: davisci@mail.nih.gov

   http://ods.od.nih.gov

Programs Administered by Federal Headquarters

HHS93.184 | DISABILITIES PREVENTION
"Disability and Health"

Award: Cooperative Agreements

Purpose: To support National Centers on Disability to develop, implement, evaluate, and disseminate non-research activities aimed at reducing health disparities and improving the health of people with mobility limitations and/or intellectual disabilities (ID) across their lifespans.

Applicant Eligibility: Based on available funding for fiscal year 2016, CDC issued competitive awards to two National Centers on Disability and 19 State-based Disability and Health Programs. Eligibility for the National Centers on Disability included: Public and State controlled Institutions of higher education; Native American tribal Organizations (other than Federally recognized tribal Governments); Nonprofits having a 501(c)(3) status with the IRS, other than Institutions of higher education; Nonprofits without 501(c)(3) status with the IRS, other than Institutions of higher education; and Private colleges and universities. Eligibility for the State-based Disability and Health Programs included: State Governments; Native American tribal Governments (Federally recognized); and Government Organizations (States, including the District of Columbia, Territorial Governments or their bona fide agents in the Commonwealth of Puerto Rico, the Virgin Islands, the Commonwealth of the Northern Marianna Islands, American Samoa, Guam, the Federated States of Micronesia, the Republic of the Marshall Islands, and the Republic of Palau.

Beneficiary Eligibility: In addition to the eligible applicants, other groups who will receive benefits from the program include persons with disabilities and their family members of persons with disabilities, persons with limb loss, minority populations, refugees, infants, children, youth, adults, senior citizens, women, all educational levels, all income levels, urban, suburban, and rural populations, health/ rehabilitation professionals, scientists, educators, and researchers.

Award Range/Average: National Centers on Disability: FY19 and 20 funding range is $3,142,429 to $9,882,425. State-based Disability and Health Programs: FY19 and 20 funding range is $165,000 to $440,000

Funding: (Cooperative Agreements) FY 18 $16,477,926.00; FY 19 est $19,249,380.00; FY 20 est $19,249,380.00

HQ: 1600 Clifton Road NE, PO Box 88, Atlanta, GA 30333

Phone: 404-498-6730 | Email: jxt4@cdc.gov

http://www.cdc.gov/ncbddd/disabilityandhealth/index.html

DOL17.720 | DISABILITY EMPLOYMENT POLICY DEVELOPMENT
"Office of Disability Employment Policy (ODEP)"

Award: Cooperative Agreements

Purpose: Provides national leadership on disability employment policy to the Department of Labor and other Federal agencies.

Applicant Eligibility: Nonprofit and for-profit Organizations, State and local government agencies, academic Institutions, and other entities are typically eligible. Eligibility requirements are detailed in each solicitation for cooperative agreements or grant applications.

Beneficiary Eligibility: Beneficiary eligibility is detailed in each solicitation for cooperative agreements or grant applications.

Award Range/Average: Recent awards for cooperative agreements and grants have ranged from approximately $300,000 to $1,800,000 per year, depending on the project needs as detailed in the solicitation for cooperative agreement or grant applications and availability of funds. Awards have been to non-profit and for-profit organizations, State and local government agencies, academic institutions, and other entities.

Funding: (Salaries and Expenses) FY 17 Actual Not Available; FY 18 est $11,000,000.00; FY 19 Estimate Not Available

HQ: 200 Constitution Avenue NW, Room S-1303, Washington, DC 20210

Phone: 202-693-7880

http://www.dol.gov/odep

HHS93.923 | DISADVANTAGED HEALTH PROFESSIONS FACULTY LOAN REPAYMENT PROGRAM (FLRP)
"FLRP"

Award: Direct Payments for Specified Use

Purpose: The Faculty Loan Repayment Program provides loan repayment assistance to faculty members from economically and environmentally disadvantaged backgrounds with eligible health professions degree or certificates to serve at eligible academic institutions.

Applicant Eligibility: Eligible applicants must: (1) be U.S. citizens (either U.S. born or naturalized), U.S. nationals or lawful permanent residents; (2) be from an economically or environmentally disadvantaged background; (3) have a degree or certificate in one of the following health profession disciplines: allopathic, osteopathic, podiatric or veterinary medicine; dentistry, pharmacy, optometry, nursing (RN or APRN), physician assistants, allied health, or graduate Programs in public health or behavioral and mental health; or are enrolled in an approved graduate training Program in one of the health professions listed above, or are enrolled as full-time students (in the disciplines listed above) at an accredited health professions institution and are in the final course of study or Program leading to a degree from that institution; (4) have an employment commitment from an eligible health professions school for a full-time or part-time (as defined by the school) faculty position for a minimum of 2 years; and (5) have a written agreement with an eligible health professions school that has agreed to pay full or partial match toward the principal and interest for the applicant's education loans in equivalent loan repayment amounts made by HHS under FLRP. For Institutions that are unable to provide matching loan repayments, applicants must provide an official letter from the employer requesting a full or partial waiver with supporting documentation justifying the undue financial hardship necessary for a waiver to be granted.

Beneficiary Eligibility: N/A

Award Range/Average: FY 17 Range - $45,911 to $59,853; FY 17 Average: $49,709 FY 18 est Range - $10,000 to $59,853 FY 18 est Average: $56,667

Funding: (Project Grants) FY 18 $1,093,597.00; FY 19 est $1,190,000.00; FY 20 est $0.00

HQ: 5600 Fishers Lane, Rockville, MD 20857

Phone: 301-594-4130 | Email: sturnbull@hrsa.gov

http://bhw.hrsa.gov/loansscholarships/flrp

SBA59.008 | DISASTER ASSISTANCE LOANS
"7(b) Loans (DL)"

Award: Direct Loans

Purpose: Provides loans to the survivors of declared disasters for uninsured or otherwise uncompensated physical damage and economic injury.

Applicant Eligibility: Eligible applicants must have suffered physical property loss or economic injury as a result of a disaster which occurred in an area declared by the President or SBA. They must also demonstrate an ability and willingness to repay the loan. Business concerns, charitable and nonprofit Organizations and individuals are eligible to apply for assistance.

Beneficiary Eligibility: Business concerns, charitable and nonprofit organizations, and individuals. Agricultural enterprises are ineligible.

Award Range/Average: Additional information provided on SBA's website at www.sba.gov/Disaster.

Funding: (Direct Loans) FY 17 $12,970,000,000.00; FY 18 est $1,600,000,000.00; FY 19 est $1,100,000,000.00

HQ: Office of Disaster Assistance 409 3rd Street, 6th Floor, Washington, DC 20416

Phone: 202-205-6734 | Email: alan.escobar@sba.gov

http://www.sba.gov/disaster

DHS97.088 | DISASTER ASSISTANCE PROJECTS
"Earmarked Projects or Limited Scope Disaster Projects. Restricted to entities designated by DHS or congressional statute"

Award: Cooperative Agreements

Purpose: The program provides funding for disaster assistance projects that help in disaster response and recovery.

Applicant Eligibility: State (includes District of Columbia, public Institutions of higher education, and hospitals), local (includes State-designated Indian Tribes, excludes Institutions of higher education and hospitals), public nonprofit institution/ Organization (includes Institutions of higher education and hospitals), other public institution/Organization, Federally Recognized Indian Tribal Governments, individual/family, profit Organization, private nonprofit institution/Organization (includes Institutions of higher education and hospitals). Funds are restricted to nonfederal entities, e.g. State, local government, private, public, profit or nonprofit Organization, Indian Tribal government or individual specified by DHS or U.S. Appropriation Statute.

Beneficiary Eligibility: Individual/family, profit organization, private nonprofit institution/organization, State, local, public nonprofit institution/organization, other public institution/organization, Federally Recognized Indian Tribal Governments or individual specified by U.S. Appropriation Statute.

Award Range/Average: Each "earmark" or project funding is designated by the appropriation statute or identified by the

Programs Administered by Federal Headquarters

program office.

Funding: (Project Grants) FY 18 $221,791,574.00; FY 19 est $53,146,496.00; FY 20 est $55,000,000.00

HQ: Community Services Branch/Individual Assistance Division/Recovery Directorate 500 C Street SW, Washington, DC 20472

Phone: 202-646-2500

http://www.fema.gov

DHS97.036 | DISASTER GRANTS-PUBLIC ASSISTANCE (PRESIDENTIALLY DECLARED DISASTERS)

Award: Project Grants

Purpose: The program offers assistance to State and local governments and other non-profits in repairing and restoring or replacing public properties damaged during disasters and calamities.

Applicant Eligibility: State and local Governments, other political subdivisions such as a special districts, federally recognized Indian tribal Governments, Alaska Native villages or Organizations, but not Alaska Native Corporations, and certain Private Non-Profit Organizations in designated emergency or major disaster areas.

Beneficiary Eligibility: Eligible work must be required as a result of the disasters; be located in a designated emergency or major disaster area; and be the legal responsibility of the applicant.

Award Range/Average: Not Available.

Funding: (Project Grants) FY 18 $9,824,200,085.00; FY 19 est $11,370,000,000.00; FY 20 est $13,170,000,000.00

HQ: 500 C Street SW, Washington, DC 20472

Phone: 202-646-4136

http://www.fema.gov

DHS97.033 | DISASTER LEGAL SERVICES
"DLS"

Award: Direct Payments for Specified Use

Purpose: The Disaster Legal Services Program provides legal assistance to low-income individuals who are unable to secure legal services adequate to meet their disaster-related needs.

Applicant Eligibility: FEMA enters into a contract with the American Bar Association Young Lawyers Division to cover the administrative costs of implementing and managing the Disaster Legal Services Program.

Beneficiary Eligibility: The Disaster Legal Services program provides free legal advice for individuals impacted by a Presidentially-declared major disaster that includes Individual Assistance. Legal advice is limited to cases that do not produce a fee. This free legal advice extends to disaster-related issues including: assistance with insurance claims; counselling on landlord/tenant problems; assistance with home repair contracts; assistance in consumer protection matters; counselling on mortgage foreclosure problems; replacement of wills and other important legal documents; drafting powers of attorney; estate administration; preparation of guardianships and conservatorships; and referrals to local and State agencies for additional assistance.

Award Range/Average: Not Available.

Funding: (Provision of Specialized Services) FY 18 $65,000,000.00; FY 19 est $50,000,000.00; FY 20 est $50,000,000.00

HQ: Disaster Assistance Directorate Department of Homeland Security 500 C Street SW, 6th Floor, Washington, DC 20472-3100

Phone: 202-646-2500

http://www.fema.gov

USDA10.105 | DISASTER RELIEF APPROPRIATIONS ACT, EMERGENCY CONSERVATION PROGRAM
"Disaster Relief Appropriations Act, ECP"

Award: Direct Payments for Specified Use

Purpose: To help out farmers to incorporate the habit of water conservation to face natural calamities.

Applicant Eligibility: Any agricultural producer who as owner, landlord, tenant, or sharecropper on a farm or ranch, including associated groups, and bears as part of the cost of an approved conservation practice affected by Hurricane Sandy is eligible to apply for cost-share conservation assistance.

Beneficiary Eligibility: Same as Applicant Eligibility.

Funding: (Direct Payments for Specified Use) FY 17 $10,000,000.00; FY 18 est $13,381,000.00; FY 19 est Estimate Not Available

HQ: 1400 Independence Avenue SW, Washington, DC 20250

Phone: 202-205-4537 | Email: martin.bomar@wdc.usda.gov

http://www.fsa.usda.gov/programs-and-services/conservation-programs/emergency-conservation/index

DHS97.034 | DISASTER UNEMPLOYMENT ASSISTANCE "DUA"

Award: Project Grants

Purpose: The program provides benefits for individuals who lose their employment status due to a disaster and are not eligible for regular unemployment insurance.

Applicant Eligibility: The State Workforce Agency (SWA) applies for Disaster Unemployment Assistance funds to provide to eligible beneficiaries.

Beneficiary Eligibility: The (DUA) program provides weekly benefits and re-employment assistance services to individuals unemployed as a direct result of a Presidentially-declared major disaster that includes Individual Assistance. Funds are used for benefit payments to individuals and project administrative costs to States. DUA weekly benefits and re-employment assistance require proof of employment eligibility, proof of employment or self-employment to assist in determining a Weekly Benefit Amount (WBA). Aliens must prove they are "qualified aliens" (as determined by the Immigration and Naturalization Service) in order to be eligible to receive a federal public benefit.

Funding: (Direct Payments for Specified Use) FY 18 Actual Not Available; FY 19 est $45,914,780.00; FY 20 est $50,040,000.00

HQ: 500 C Street SW, 6th Floor, Washington, DC 20472-3100

Phone: 202-646-2500

http://www.fema.gov

HHS93.286 | DISCOVERY AND APPLIED RESEARCH FOR TECHNOLOGICAL INNOVATIONS TO IMPROVE HUMAN HEALTH

Award: Project Grants

Purpose: To support hypothesis, design, technology, or device-driven research related to the discovery, design, development, validation, and application of technologies for biomedical imaging and bioengineering.

Applicant Eligibility: Any corporation, public or private institution or agency, or other legal entity, either nonprofit or for-profit, may apply for a research grant. An applicant for an individual NRSA must be a citizen of the United States or lawfully admitted for permanent residence. Those on temporary or student visas are not eligible. An eligible institution for an institutional NRSA must be capable of providing predoctoral and/or postdoctoral research training opportunities for engineers, bioengineers or other. SBIR grants can be awarded only to domestic small businesses (entities that are independently owned and operated for profit; are not dominant in the field in which research is being proposed; and have no more than 500 employees). Primary employment (more than one-half time) of the principal investigator must be with the small business at the time of award and during the conduct of the proposed project. In both Phase I and Phase II, the research must be performed in the United States or its possessions. To be eligible for funding, a grant application must be reviewed for scientific merit and Program relevance by a scientific review group and a national advisory council. STTR grants can be awarded only to domestic small business concerns (entities that are independently owned and operated for profit, are not dominant in the field in which research is proposed and have no more than 500 employees) which "partner" with a research institution in cooperative research and development. At least 40 percent of the project is to be performed by the small business concern and at least 30 percent by the research institution. In both Phase I and Phase II, the research must be performed in the U.S. or its possessions. To be eligible for funding, a grant application must be approved for scientific merit and Program relevance by a scientific review group and a national advisory council.

Beneficiary Eligibility: Any nonprofit or for-profit organization, company, or institution engaged in biomedical research.

Award Range/Average: FY18 Actual Range: $2,928- $2,082,080; Avg.: $394,954 FY19 estimate Range: $3,000 - $1,899,165; Avg.: $366,008 FY20 estimate Range: $3,000 - $1,900,000; Avg.: $342,468

Funding: (Project Grants (Discretionary)) FY 18 $308,459,000.00; FY 19 est $319,891,000.00; FY 20 est $275,344,000.00

HQ: 6707 Democracy Boulevard, Bethesda, MD 20892

Phone: 301-496-9474 | Email: georged@nih.gov

https://www.nibib.nih.gov

Programs Administered by Federal Headquarters

GSA39.002 | DISPOSAL OF FEDERAL SURPLUS REAL PROPERTY

Award: Sale, Exchange, Or Donation of Property and Goods

Purpose: To assist State and local governments, and certain eligible (501(c)(3) tax-exempt status) non-profit organizations with acquiring surplus Federal real property.

Applicant Eligibility: State and local government agencies are eligible to apply for surplus real property for park and recreation, correctional facility, law enforcement, historic monument, public airport, public health, educational, homeless assistance, self help housing, emergency management, public road widening and port facilities. Eligibility for property for wildlife conservation use, other than for migratory birds and highway use, is limited to the States. Tax-supported and nonprofit medical and educational Institutions, housing assistance and homeless assistance providers which have been held exempt from taxation under 501(c)(3) of the Internal Revenue Code are also eligible to apply for property for health, educational, self help housing and homeless assistance use, respectively.

Beneficiary Eligibility: State and local governments and for certain programs, nonprofit organizations (501(c)(3) may also apply.

Funding: (Salaries and Expenses) FY 16 $4,000,000.00; FY 17 est $4,200,000.00; FY 18 est $4,300,000.00

HQ: 1800 F Street NW, Washington, DC 20405

Phone: 202-208-0324 | Email: david.stinson@gsa.gov

http://rc.gsa.gov

DOD12.440 | DISSERTATION YEAR FELLOWSHIP
"CMH Dissertation Fellowship"

Award: Project Grants

Purpose: The program is designed to support scholarly research and writing among qualified civilian graduate students preparing dissertations in the history of land warfare.

Applicant Eligibility: Applicants must be civilian U.S. citizens pursuing a doctoral degree in history. They must be unaffiliated with the federal government. Military personnel, civilian federal service employees, and contractors with the U.S. government are ineligible. Awards will be issued to individual (natural person) recipients vice to Institutions that an individual is attending for their doctoral degree.

Beneficiary Eligibility: N/A

Funding: (Project Grants (Fellowships)) FY 16 $20,000.00; FY 17 est $20,000.00; FY 18 est $20,000.00

HQ: Fort Lesley J McNair 102 4th Avenue SW, Washington, DC 20319

Phone: 202-685-2305 | Email: jeffrey.j.seiken.civ@mail.mil

http://www.history.army.mil/html/about/fellowship.html

USDA10.322 | DISTANCE EDUCATION GRANTS FOR INSTITUTIONS OF HIGHER EDUCATION IN INSULAR AREAS
"Grants for Insular Areas - Distance Education Grants for Insular Areas (DEG) [Formerly: Distance Education Grant (DEG)]"

Award: Project Grants

Purpose: To promote distance education technology, higher education in insular areas, and other teaching programs.

Applicant Eligibility: Individual land-grant colleges and universities, and other Institutions that have secured land-grant status through Federal legislation, and which are located in Insular Areas are automatically eligible for awards under the DEG grants Program, either as direct applicants or as parties to a consortium agreement.

Beneficiary Eligibility: Same as Applicant Eligibility.

Award Range/Average: If minimum or maximum amounts of funding per competitive and/or capacity project grant, or cooperative agreement are established, these amounts will be announced in the annual Competitive Request for Application (RFA).The most current RFA is available via: https://nifa.usda.gov/funding-opportunity/distance-education-grants-institutions-higher-education-insular-areas-deg

Funding: (Project Grants) FY 17 $768,000.00; FY 18 est $800,000.00; FY 19 est $1,916,160.00

HQ: Institute of Youth Family and Community Division of Community and Education 1400 Independence Avenue SW, PO Box 2250, Washington, DC 20250-2250

Phone: 202-720-2324 | Email: edwin.lewis@nifa.usda.gov

http://nifa.usda.gov/program/resident-instruction-grants-riia-and-distance-education-grants-deg-institutions-highe

USDA10.855 | DISTANCE LEARNING AND TELEMEDICINE LOANS AND GRANTS
"DLT - Distance Learning and Telemedicine"

Award: Project Grants; Direct Loans

Purpose: To promote telemedicine, telecommunications, computer networks, related advanced technologies, educational and medical benefits for those living in rural areas.

Applicant Eligibility: To be eligible to receive a grant, loan and grant combination, or loan, the applicant must be legally organized as an incorporated Organization or partnership, an Indian tribe or tribal Organization, a state or local unit of government, a consortium, or other legal entity. The applicant must have legal capacity to contract with RUS. The applicant also must propose to utilize the financing to: (i) operate a rural community facility; or (ii) deliver distance learning or telemedicine services to entities that operate a rural community facility or to residents of rural areas at rates calculated to ensure that the benefit of the financial assistance is passed through to such entities or to residents of rural areas. The applicant must not be delinquent on any Federal debt. RUS electric and telecommunications borrowers are not eligible for grants. Generally, applicants are Organizations such as schools, libraries, hospitals, medical centers, or other eligible Organizations that will be users of a telecommunications, computer network, or related advanced technology system to provide educational and/or medical benefits to rural residents.

Beneficiary Eligibility: The people living in rural areas are beneficiaries, particularly in the areas of medical and health-related services, education, training and medical services.

Award Range/Average: $50,000 to $500,000 with an average of $310,632.00

Funding: (Project Grants) FY 18 $37,000,000.00; FY 19 est $20,000,000.00; FY 20 est $20,000,000.00

HQ: 1400 Independence Avenue SW, PO Box 1590, Washington, DC 20250

Phone: 202-720-9564 | Email: chad.parker@wdc.usda.gov

http://www.rd.usda.gov/programs-services/distance-learning-telemedicine-grants

DOJ16.741 | DNA BACKLOG REDUCTION PROGRAM

Award: Cooperative Agreements

Purpose: To assist in analyzing forensic DNA and providing laboratories to process more DNA samples and other forensic technologies to track sexual assault.

Applicant Eligibility: See the current fiscal year's solicitation available at www.nij.gov.

Beneficiary Eligibility: Same as Applicant Eligibility.

Award Range/Average: See the current fiscal year's solicitation guidelines posted on the Office of Justice Programs web site at https://ojp.gov/funding/Explore/CurrentFundingOpportunities.htm.

Funding: (Formula Grants) FY 17 $97,122,118.00; FY 18 est $130,000,000.00; FY 19 est $105,000,000.00

HQ: U.S. Department of Justice National Institute of Justice 810 7th Street NW, Washington, DC 20531

Phone: 202-616-9264 | Email: charles.heurich@usdoj.gov

http://nij.gov

DOD12.560 | DOD, NDEP, DOTC-STEM EDUCATION OUTREACH IMPLEMENTATION

Award: Project Grants

Purpose: To obtain support for the management, development, and furthering of new and existing partnerships between the Department of Defense, National Defense Education Program, and Defense Ordnance Technology Consortium, for Science, Technology, Engineering, and Mathematics education and other outreach organizations, professional societies, and local education activities.

Applicant Eligibility: N/A

Beneficiary Eligibility: N/A

Funding: (Project Grants) FY 13 $4,102,404.00; FY 14 est $8,866,018.00; FY 15 est $5,000,000.00

HQ: Building 322, Picatinny Arsenal, NJ 07806

Phone: 973-724-8115 | Email: william.coolbaugh@us.army.mil

DOI15.158 | DOI NATIONAL FIRE PLAN

Award: Cooperative Agreements

Purpose: The objective of this program is to provide Cooperative Agreements to aid the Office of the Secretary, Office of Wildland Fire (OWF) in facilitating communication, cooperation and coordination between Federal, State, and local partners in support of the National Fire Plan. Funds shall be used by the recipient to assist the Office of Wildland Fire in preparation of training curriculum related to a variety of issues, such as safety and leadership.

Applicant Eligibility: Public or private nonprofit institution/Organizations.

Beneficiary Eligibility: Anyone within the Fire Use/Protection community.

Funding: (Cooperative Agreements (Discretionary Grants)) FY 17 $10,000.00; FY 18 est $10,000.00; FY 19 Estimate Not Available

HQ: Office of Wildland Fire 300 E Mallard Drive, Suite 170, Boise, ID 83706

Phone: 208-334-6195 | Email: amy_kishpaugh@ios.doi.gov

HUD14.313 | DOLLAR HOME SALES

Award: Sale, Exchange, Or Donation of Property and Goods

Purpose: Fostering housing opportunities for low-to-moderate income families and address specific community needs.

Applicant Eligibility: Local government legally authorized by local law to make the purchase.

Beneficiary Eligibility: Low- to moderate-income families and communities.

HQ: 451 7th Street SW, Washington, DC 20410

Phone: 800-225-5342

http://www.hud.gov/offices/hsg/sfh/reo/goodn/dhmabout.cfm

HHS93.815 | DOMESTIC EBOLA SUPPLEMENT TO THE EPIDEMIOLOGY AND LABORATORY CAPACITY FOR INFECTIOUS DISEASES (ELC).
"ELC"

Award: Cooperative Agreements

Purpose: The ELC Competing Supplement addresses priority domestic capacity building around Ebola and other emerging and highly-infectious diseases. The Competing Supplement provides additional resources to accelerate ELC activities around infection control assessment and response, laboratory safety, and global migration, border interventions, and migrant health.

Applicant Eligibility: Eligible applicants consist of state, local, and U.S. territory/possession Governments currently funded under CK14-1401. Specifically, these include: all 50 states, Washington, D. C., 5 largest local health departments (Chicago, Illinois; Houston, Texas; Los Angeles, California; New York City, New York; Philadelphia, Pennsylvania;), the Commonwealth of Puerto Rico, the Virgin Islands, the Commonwealth of the Northern Mariana Islands, American Samoa, Guam, the Federated States of Micronesia, the Republic of the Marshall Islands, and the Republic of Palau or their bona fide agents.

Beneficiary Eligibility: Direct beneficiaries include all 50 states, Washington, D.C., 5 largest local health departments (Chicago, Illinois; Houston, Texas; Los Angeles, California; New York City, New York; Philadelphia, Pennsylvania;), the Commonwealth of Puerto Rico, the Virgin Islands, the Commonwealth of the Northern Mariana Islands, American Samoa, Guam, the Federated States of Micronesia, the Republic of the Marshall Islands, and the Republic of Palau or their bona fide agents.

HQ: 1600 Clifton Road NE, PO Box C18, Atlanta, GA 30333

Phone: 404-639-7379 | Email: amoconnor@cdc.gov

http://www.cdc.gov

DOJ16.834 | DOMESTIC TRAFFICKING VICTIM PROGRAM

Award: Project Grants

Purpose: The Domestic Trafficking Victim Program improves the outcomes for children and youth who are victims of human trafficking. It enhances multidisciplinary and jurisdiction approach to human trafficking and responds to victims of child pornography.

Applicant Eligibility: Please contact Program office for additional information.

Beneficiary Eligibility: Same as Applicant Eligibility.

Award Range/Average: See the current fiscal year's solicitation guidelines posted on the Office of Justice Programs web site at https://ojp.gov/funding/Explore/CurrentFundingOpportunities.htm

Funding: (Project Grants) FY 18 $3,612,870.00; FY 19 est $6,000,000.00; FY 20 est $6,000,000.00

HQ: 810 7th Street NW, Washington, DC 20531

Phone: 202-353-7223 | Email: sara.gilmer@usdoj.gov

http://www.ovc.gov

GSA39.003 | DONATION OF FEDERAL SURPLUS PERSONAL PROPERTY
"Donation Program"

Award: Sale, Exchange, Or Donation of Property and Goods

Purpose: To donate Federal personal property no longer required for Federal use to eligible nonfederal entities.

Applicant Eligibility: (a) Applicants other than public airports need to have eligibility determined by their local State Agency for Surplus Property (SASP), established in each state, territory, and the District of Columbia. Public airports need to contact their local Federal Aviation Administration regional office. (b)State participation via the SASP is based upon the acceptance by the General Services Administration (GSA) of a State plan of operation as being in conformance with 40 U.S.C. 549. This State plan must establish a State agency which is responsible for the distribution of Federal surplus personal property to eligible recipients within the State on a fair and equitable basis. Eligible done categories for the distribution of property through the State Agencies for Surplus Property are defined as: (1) Public agencies which include any (i) State or department, agency, or instrumentality thereof; (ii) political subdivision of the State, including any unit of local government or economic development district, or any department, agency or instrumentality thereof; (iii) instrumentality created by compact or other agreement between State or political subdivisions; (iv) multijurisdictional sub-State district established by or pursuant to State law; and (v) Indian tribe, band, group, pueblo, or community located on a State reservation. Eligibility for public agencies is determined by the State Agency for Surplus Property. (2) Nonprofit, tax-exempt activities such as schools, colleges, universities, libraries, historic light stations, schools for the mentally challenged or physically challenged, educational radio or TV stations, childcare centers, museums, medical Institutions, hospitals, clinics, health centers, drug abuse treatment centers, providers of assistance to the homeless, providers of assistance to the impoverished and Programs for older individuals. (3) Service educational activities as determined by the Deputy Under Secretary of Defense (L/SCI). (4) Public airports. Eligibility is determined by the Federal Aviation Administration. (5) Veterans Organizations recognized by the Secretary of Veterans Affairs under section 5902 of title38.

Beneficiary Eligibility: Eligibility is determined by the SASP.

Funding: (Sale, Exchange, or Donation of Property and Goods) FY 16 $7,217,701.00; FY 17 est $6,967,143.00; FY 18 Estimate Not Available

HQ: 1800 F Street NW, Washington, DC 20405

Phone: 202-501-1700 | Email: sunny.kwa@gsa.gov

http://www.gsa.gov/property

DOD12.700 | DONATIONS/LOANS OF OBSOLETE DOD PROPERTY

Award: Use of Property, Facilities, and Equipment

Purpose: Donates or lends obsolete combat material to veterans' organizations, soldiers' monument associations, State museums, incorporated museums, and incorporated municipalities.

Applicant Eligibility: Veterans' Organizations recognized by the Office of the Deputy Under Secretary of Defense (LIMDM); museums operated and maintained for education purposes only and which are tax- exempt; and incorporated municipalities. The Department of the Navy donates or loans additional types of condemned or obsolete material and obsolete, condemned or captured vessels to States, Territories, Commonwealths, or possessions of the United States, political subdivisions or municipal incorporations thereof, the District of Columbia, the Canal Zone, libraries, historical societies, educational Institutions whose graduates or students fought in World War I or World War II, recognized veterans Organizations and to nonprofit Organizations operated and maintained for educational purposes only.

Beneficiary Eligibility: Veterans' organizations recognized by the Office of the Deputy Under Secretary of Defense (LIMDM); museums operated and maintained for education purposes only and are tax-exempt; and incorporated municipalities.

HQ: Appropriate Military Department Pentagon, Washington, DC 20301

DHS97.089 | DRIVER'S LICENSE SECURITY GRANT PROGRAM

Award: Project Grants

Purpose: The program funds to help reduce and prevent terrorism and fraud by improving the accuracy and reliability of personal identification documents like the driver's license and identification cards.

Applicant Eligibility: The issuing authority for motor vehicle licenses in each State or territory, as identified by the DHS, is the only agency eligible to apply for the Driver's License Security Grant Program.

Beneficiary Eligibility: State, U.S. Territory and local governments, intrastate, interstate, small business, general public, other public institution/organizations.

Award Range/Average: Will be identified in the solicitation/program guidance.

Programs Administered by Federal Headquarters

HQ: FEMA 400 C Street SW, Washington, DC 20472-3615
   Phone: 800-368-6498
   http://www.fema.gov/government/grant/index.shtm

ONDCP95.009 | DRUG-FREE COMMUNITIES (DFC) SUPPORT PROGRAM "DFC"

Award: Project Grants
Purpose: To establish and strengthen the collaboration among communities and agencies to support the community coalition's work to prevent and reduce substance abuse among youth.
Applicant Eligibility: The coalition must consist of one or more representatives from each of the following required 12 sectors: Parents, Youth, Business, Media, Schools, Youth-Serving Organizations, Law Enforcement, Civic/Volunteer Organizations, Religious/Fraternal Organizations, Healthcare Professionals, State/Local/Tribal Government, and Other Substance Abuse Organizations (21 USC 1532)An individual who is a member of the coalition may serve on the coalition as a representative of not more than one sector category. The coalition must demonstrate that members have worked together on substance abuse reduction initiatives for a period of not less than 6 months at the time of submission of the application, acting through entities such as task forces, subcommittees, or community boards The coalition must also demonstrate substantial participation from volunteer leaders in the community. The coalition must have as its principal mission the reduction of youth substance use, which, at a minimum, includes the use and abuse of drugs in a comprehensive and long-term manner, with a primary focus on youth in the community The coalition must have developed a 12-Month Action Plan to reduce substance use among youth which targets multiple drugs of abuse. Substances may include, but are not limited to, narcotics, depressants, stimulants, hallucinogens, inhalants, marijuana, alcohol, and tobacco, where youth use is prohibited by federal, state, or local law. The coalition must establish a system to measure and report outcomes, established and approved by the DFC Administrator, to the federal government. The applicant must demonstrate that the coalition is an ongoing concern by demonstrating that the coalition is a non-profit Organization or has made arrangements with a legal entity that is eligible to receive federal grants. The coalition must have a strategy to solicit substantial financial support from non-federal sources to ensure that the coalition is self- sustaining. The applicant must not request more than $125,000 in federal funds per year. Two DFC-funded coalitions may not serve the same zip code(s) unless both coalitions have clearly described their plan for collaboration in their application and each coalition has independently met the eligibility requirements. Grant recipients may be awarded only one grant at a time through the DFC Support Program. In order to receive a DFC grant, coalitions may not have received 10 years of DFC funding.
Beneficiary Eligibility: N/A
Award Range/Average: Estimated Award Amount per DFC grant: Up to $125,000 per the authorizing legislations, length of Project Period per DFC grant is up to 5 years with option to re-compete for a maximum of 10 Years
HQ: 1800 G Street NW, Washington, DC 20503
   Phone: 202-395-6739 | Email: phuong_desear@ondcp.eop.gov
   https://www.whitehouse.gov/ondcp

EOP95.008 | DRUG-FREE COMMUNITIES SUPPORT PROGRAM-NATIONAL YOUTH LEADERSHIP INITIATIVE

Award: Cooperative Agreements
Purpose: The program helps to implement the National Youth Leadership Initiative which helps to diversify youth population and provides technical assistance to prevent substance use and make their community a drug-free one.
Applicant Eligibility: Applicants must be a non-profit entity (501(c)3) with expert knowledge and extensive experience in community mobilizing using the Seven Strategies for Community Change. Applicants must have served as an essential partner in assisting DFC Support Program with technical assistance to community coalitions in their substance use prevention efforts.
Beneficiary Eligibility: Supports NYLI training program, where there is strong participation by DFC-funded communities.
Funding: (Cooperative Agreements) FY 18 $250,000.00; FY 19 est $0.00; FY 20 est $250,000.00
HQ: 1800 G Street NW, Washington, DC 20503
   Phone: 202-395-6739 | Email: phuong_desear@ondcp.eop.gov
   https://www.whitehouse.gov/ONDCP

HHS93.276 | DRUG-FREE COMMUNITIES SUPPORT PROGRAM GRANTS
"Drug Free Community Grants (DFC). Drug-Free Communities Mentoring Program (DFC-M)"

Award: Project Grants

Purpose: To increase the capacity of community coalitions to reduce substance abuse, and over time, to reduce substance abuse among adults through strengthening collaboration among communities, public, and private entities.

Applicant Eligibility: Community coalitions must demonstrate that the community coalition has worked together for a period of not less than 6 months on substance abuse reduction initiatives. The coalition must: meet the composition requirements; ensure that there is substantial community volunteer effort; ensure that the coalition is a nonprofit, charitable, educational Organization, or unit of local government, or is affiliated with an eligible Organization or entity; possess a strategy to be self-sustaining; provide a 100-150 percent cash or in-kind match; and agree to participate in an evaluation of the coalition's Program.

Beneficiary Eligibility: Community coalitions, children, youth, and adults, those at-risk of substance abuse, and private nonprofit, and public community agencies.

Award Range/Average: $75,000 to $125,000; Avg. $124.510

Funding: (Project Grants (Discretionary)) FY 18 $161,669,363.00; FY 19 est $94,651,962.00; FY 20 est $13,323,854.00

HQ: 5600 Fishers Lane, Rockville, MD 20857

   Phone: 240-276-1078 | Email: odessa.crocker@samhsa.hhs.gov
   http://www.samhsa.gov

HHS93.279 | DRUG ABUSE AND ADDICTION RESEARCH PROGRAMS

Award: Project Grants; Training

Purpose: To support basic and clinical neuroscience, biomedical, behavioral and social science, epidemiologic, health services and health disparity research.

Applicant Eligibility: For research grants the following Organizations /Institutions are eligible to apply: Public/State Controlled Institutions of Higher education; Private Institutions of Higher education: Hispanic-serving Institutions, Historically Black Colleges and universities (HBCUs), Tribally Controlled Colleges and universities (TCCUs), and Alaska Native and Native Hawaiian Serving Institutions; Nonprofits with 501(c)(3) IRS Status (Other than Institutions of Higher education); Nonprofits without 501(c)(3) IRS Status (Other than Institutions of Higher education); Small businesses; For-Profit Organizations (Other than Small businesses); State Governments; Indian/Native American Tribal Governments (Federally Recognized); Indian/Native American Tribally Designated Organizations; County Governments; City or Township Governments; Special District Governments; Independent School Districts; Public Housing Authorities/Indian Housing Authorities; and Other(s): Eligible Agencies of the Federal Government, Faith-based or Community-based Organizations, U.S. Territory or Possession, Indian/Native American Tribal Governments (Other than Federally Recognized), Regional Organizations, and Non-domestic (non-U.S.) Entities (Foreign Organizations). Eligible Individuals: Any individual, or individuals (multiple PDs/PIs), with the skills, knowledge, and resources necessary to carry out the proposed research as the PD/PI is invited to work with his/her Organization to develop an application for support. Individuals from underrepresented racial and ethnic groups as well as individuals with disabilities are always encouraged to apply for NIH support. SBIR grants can be awarded only to domestic small businesses (entities that are independently owned and operated for profit, are not dominant in the field in which research is proposed, and have no more than 500 employees). Primary employment (more than one-half time) of the principal investigator must be with the small business at the time of award and during the conduct of the proposed project. In both Phase I and Phase II, the research and/or development must be performed in the U.S. and its possessions. To be eligible, an SBIR grant application must be approved for scientific merit and Program relevance by a scientific review group and by a national advisory council. STTR grants can be awarded only to domestic small business concerns (entities that are independently owned and operated for profit, are not dominant in the field in which research is proposed and have no more than 500 employees) which "partner" with a research institution in cooperative research and development. At least 40 percent of the project is to be performed by the small business concern and at least 30 percent by the research institution. In both Phase I and Phase II, the research must be performed in the U.S. and its possessions. To be eligible for funding, a grant application must be approved for scientific and technical merit and Program relevance by a scientific review group and a national advisory council.

Beneficiary Eligibility: Public or private profit and nonprofit sponsored organizations and individuals, minority groups, small businesses, health professionals, students, trainees, scientists and general public.

Award Range/Average: Range- $3,000 to $5,146,000; Average- $527,100

Funding: (Project Grants) FY 18 $1,133,931,000.00; FY 19 est $1,163,419,000.00; FY 20 est $1,032,224,000

Programs Administered by Federal Headquarters

HQ: NIDA 6001 Executive Boulevard, Room 4241, Bethesda, MD 20892
  Phone: 301-827-5705 | Email: chollan1@nida.nih.gov
  http://www.drugabuse.gov

DOJ16.585 | DRUG COURT DISCRETIONARY GRANT PROGRAM
"Drug Court Program (DCP)"

Award: Project Grants

Purpose: To equip courts and community supervision systems with the necessary tools and resources, utilizing the most current evidence-based practices and principles, to intervene with participants who abuse substances while preparing them for success in the community.

Applicant Eligibility: Grants can be awarded to states, state courts, local courts, units of local government and Indian tribal Governments, acting directly or through agreements with other public or private entities. Applicants may choose to submit joint applications with other eligible jurisdictions for statewide, regional, and multijurisdictional drug court Programs. With joint applications, one Organization must be designated as the applicant and any co-applicants designated accordingly. The applicant Organization must be eligible and the other agencies/Organizations must provide supporting documentation. All applicants must demonstrate that they have the management and financial capabilities to effectively plan and implement projects of the size and scope described in the application kit. Nonprofit and for-profit agencies are not eligible applicants. For an application from a subunit of government (e.g., county probation department, district attorney's office, pretrial services agency) to be considered, it must be designated by letter as representing an eligible applicant (described above). For example, the county court or county executive may designate the county probation or county district attorney's office as its representative for the purpose of application. In this instance, the applicant continues to be the designating state, court system, or unit of local government. The county probation, district attorney's office, or other designated subunit, is the Organization authorized to submit an application on behalf of the eligible applicant.

Beneficiary Eligibility: States, local governments, Indian tribal governments, public or private entities.

Award Range/Average: Varies based upon appropriation. Consult the solicitation available at http://www.ojp.gov/funding/solicitations.htm and/or www.bja.gov.

Funding: (Project Grants) FY 18 $86,475,359.00; FY 19 est $77,000,000.00; FY 20 est $75,000,000.00

HQ: Department of Justice 810 7th Street NW, Washington, DC 20531
  Phone: 202-616-6500
  http://www.bja.gov

EOP95.005 | DRUG COURT TRAINING AND TECHNICAL ASSISTANCE

Award: Project Grants

Purpose: The grant that is awarded by the Office of National Drug Control Policy helps to establish training and technical assistance to advance criminal justice reforms that include drug courts handling justice-involved cases of individuals with substance use disorders.

Applicant Eligibility: Organizations with expert knowledge of drug courts and extensive experience in brokering and developing training and technical assistance for drug court professionals are eligible. The trainings and technical assistance will require Organizations with relevant subject matter expertise and extensive experience in developing and providing training and technical assistance for a variety of disciplines (e.g. judges, prosecutors, public defenders, defense counsel, probation and parole officers, law enforcement officers, law enforcement executives, court administrators, and treatment providers). Applicants can partner with other entities to achieve required expertise.

Beneficiary Eligibility: N/A

Award Range/Average: varies by appropriated amount

Funding: (Project Grants) FY 18 $4,000,000.00; FY 19 est $0.00; FY 20 est $2,000,000.00

HQ: 1800 G Street NW, Washington, DC 20503
  Phone: 202-395-6739 | Email: phuong_desear@ondcp.eop.gov
  https://www.whitehouse.gov/ONDCP

HHS93.685 | DRUG VIAL SIZE REPORT

Award: Formula Grants (cooperative Agreements)

Purpose: To conduct a study on healthcare costs and safety and quality concerns due to discarded drugs from disproportionate vial sizes.

Applicant Eligibility: State, Local, Unemployed, Welfare Recipient, Sponsored Organization, Low Income, Public nonprofit institution/Organization, Other public institution/Organization, Federally Recognized Indian Tribal Governments State, Intrastate, Local, Sponsored Organization, Public Nonprofit Institution/Organization, Other Public Institution/Organization, Federally Recognized Indian Tribal Government, U.S. territory/possession, individual/family.

Beneficiary Eligibility: N/A

Award Range/Average: N/A

Funding: (Formula Grants (Cooperative Agreements)) FY 18 Actual Not Available; FY 19 est $1,200,000.00; FY 20 est Estimate Not Available

HQ: 7500 Security Boulevard, Baltimore, MD 21244

Phone: 410-786-7507 | Email: alisha.williams@cms.hhs.gov

http://www.cms.gov

HHS93.314 | EARLY HEARING DETECTION AND INTERVENTION INFORMATION SYSTEM (EHDI-IS) SURVEILLANCE PROGRAM
"EHDI Information System"

Award: Cooperative Agreements

Purpose: To assist EHDI programs in developing and maintaining a sustainable, centralized newborn hearing screening tracking and surveillance system capable of accurately identifying, matching, collecting, and reporting data on all occurrent births that is unduplicated and individually identifiable.

Applicant Eligibility: N/A

Beneficiary Eligibility: State and local governments or their Bona Fide Agents (this includes the District of Columbia, the Commonwealth of Puerto Rico, the Virgin Islands, the Commonwealth of the Northern Marianna Islands, American Samoa, Guam, the Federated States of Micronesia, the Republic of the Marshall Islands, and the Republic of Palau.

Award Range/Average: FY 19/20 range is dependent upon funding availability. Award amounts range is $150,000

Funding: (Cooperative Agreements) FY 18 $7,008,952.00; FY 19 est $6,200,000.00; FY 20 est $6,000,000.00

HQ: 1600 Clifton Road NE, PO Box E87, Atlanta, GA 30333

Phone: 404-498-3034 | Email: deg4@cdc.gov

http://www.cdc.gov/ncbddd

HHS93.251 | EARLY HEARING DETECTION AND INTERVENTION

Award: Project Grants

Purpose: To support state and territory programs in developing a comprehensive and coordinated system of care targeted toward ensuring that newborns and infants receive appropriate timely services including continuous screening, evaluation, diagnosis and early intervention services.

Applicant Eligibility: Grants to states/territories and cooperative agreements to two Organizations that will provide technical assistance.

Beneficiary Eligibility: Infants and new-borns who are deaf or hard of hearing and their families/caretakers.

Award Range/Average: FY 18 $26,538- $250,000. Average award of $226,139 FY 19 $2,001- $250,000. Average award of $226,374 FY 20 est. $2,001- $250,000. Average award $235,000 Grants to LEND Audiology Programs: FY 18 $63,377- $80,000. Average award of $78,584 FY 19 $63,377- $80,000. Average award of $78,570 FY 20 est. $63,377- $80,000. Average award of $78,718 Cooperative Agreements: FY 18 $500,000- $1,200,000. Average Award of $850,000. FY 19 $500,000- $1,200,000. Average Award of $850,000. FY 20 est. $500,000- $1,200,000. Average Award of $850,000.

Funding: (Cooperative Agreements) FY 18 $2,004,000.00; FY 19 est $2,004,000.00; FY 20 est $1,604,000.00

HQ: 5600 Fishers Lane, Room 18W09A, Rockville, MD 20857

Phone: 301-443-6314 | Email: bapplebaum@hrsa.gov

http://www.hrsa.gov

HHS93.546 | EARLY RETIREE REINSURANCE PROGRAM

Award: Direct Payments for Specified Use

Purpose: To provide reimbursement to sponsors of participating employment-based plans for a portion of the cost of health benefits for early retirees and their spouses, surviving spouses, and dependents.

Applicant Eligibility: In order to have been eligible for the ERRP, a plan sponsor must have completed and submitted an ERRP application to the ERRP Center on or before May 5, 2011. In summary, the plan sponsor must be an Organization that provides health benefits to Early Retirees, have Programs and procedures in place that generate cost savings with respect to participants with chronic and high-cost conditions, use reimbursements appropriately, ensure that policies and procedures are in place to protect against fraud, waste and abuse under ERRP, and agree to the Plan Sponsor Agreement included in the ERRP application. Applications were reviewed and either approved or not approved for acceptance into the Program.

Beneficiary Eligibility: In order to be eligible to receive reimbursements under the ERRP, a plan sponsor must have completed and submitted an ERRP application to the ERRP Center on or before May 5, 2011. If approved, both the sponsor, and early retirees and their spouses, surviving spouses and their dependents are direct or indirect beneficiaries of the program. In summary, the sponsor must be an organization that provides health benefits to Early Retirees, have programs and procedures in place that generate (or have the potential to generate) cost savings with respect to participants with chronic and high-cost conditions, use reimbursements appropriately, ensure that policies and procedures are in place to protect against fraud, waste and abuse under ERRP, and agree to the Plan Sponsor Agreement included in the ERRP application.

Award Range/Average: Smallest: $50.96; Largest: $387,187,079.81; Average: $1,745,808.92 (All data as of June 2014).

Funding: (Direct Payments for Specified Use) FY 18 $31,171.00; FY 19 est $100,000.00; FY 20 est $100,000.00

HQ: 200 Independence Avenue SW, Washington, DC 20201

  Phone: 301-492-4312 | Email: michelle.feagins@hhs.gov

  http://www.cms.gov

DHS97.082 | EARTHQUAKE CONSORTIUM
"Earthquake Consortium and State Support (ECSS)"

Award: Cooperative Agreements

Purpose: The program acts as an approach to reduce the loss of lives and property to earthquakes by implementing earthquake risk-reduction activities at a local level.

Applicant Eligibility: Earthquake Direct State Assistance (EDSA)This funding opportunity is provided to those States and Territories that have been determined to be at a Moderate to Very High seismic risk as determined by the DHS, FEMA Program Office. Earthquake Consortia and Partner Support (ECPS)This funding opportunity is designed to facilitate the development and management of multi-State FEMA funded NEHRP projects and activities. Funding is provided to Earthquake Consortia and Partners through a Cooperative Agreement and applied to projects and activities submitted to FEMA by Federal earthquake partners including CUSEC, NESEC, WSSPC, CREW, EERI, FLASH, SCEC, and ATC. These earthquake mitigation efforts include 1) delivering and increasing awareness and education; 2) developing policies, tools, and products; and 3) implementing Programs or projects to support risk reduction and resilience activities from earthquakes.

Beneficiary Eligibility: Eligible States and Territories with Moderate to Very High seismic risks as determined by the Program Office, and earthquake Consortia and Partners including CUSEC, NESEC, WSSPC, CREW, EERI, FLASH, SCEC, and ATC.

Award Range/Average: Refer to the official Notice of Funding Opportunity on Grants.gov by year for actual target allocations by program by eligible applicant.

Funding: (Cooperative Agreements) FY 18 $3,430,900.00; FY 19 est $3,590,575.00; FY 20 est $3,500,000.00

HQ: Federal Insurance and Mitigation Administration (FIMA) 400 C Street SW, Washington, DC 20009

  Phone: 202-646-4037 | Email: gabriele.javier@fema.dhs.gov

  http://www.fema.gov/building-science

DOD12.219 | EASE 2.0
"Effective Absentee Systems for Elections 2.0"

Award: Project Grants

Purpose: To establish and ensure successful, sustainable, and effective methods to improve voting systems for voters protected by the Uniformed and Overseas Citizens Absentee Voting Act (UOCAVA) and to increase the percentage of ballots successfully returned by UOCAVA voters to be either equal to, or greater to that of the general population.

Applicant Eligibility: Applicants are encouraged to develop ballot delivery systems or streamlined procedures for the processing of absentee voting materials for voters covered by UOCAVA.

Beneficiary Eligibility: The amount and period of performance of each selected proposal may vary depending on the research area and technical approach pursued by the selected recipient.

Funding: (Salaries and Expenses) FY 18 $275,000.00; FY 19 est $275,000.00; FY 20 est $275,000.0

HQ: 4800 Mark Center Drive, Suite 03E25, Alexandria, VA 22350-1300

  Phone: 571-372-2614 | Email: heather.j.hay.civ@mail.mil

DOS19.124 | EAST ASIA AND PACIFIC GRANTS PROGRAM
"U.S. Department of State, Bureau of East Asian and Pacific Affairs, Grant Awards"

Award: Cooperative Agreements; Project Grants

Purpose: To support the foreign assistance goals and objectives of the Department of State, Bureau of East Asian Affairs, as delineated in the FY Bureau Strategic and Resource Plan.

Applicant Eligibility: Department of State, EAP Bureau does not issue domestic grants. Any and all grants will go to entities that operate overseas in support of our international foreign assistance goals and objectives. See www.grants.gov for specific announcement.

Beneficiary Eligibility: U.S. Department of State, EAP Bureau does not issue domestic grants. Any and all grants will go to entities that operate overseas in support of our international foreign assistance goals and objectives.

Award Range/Average: Depends on specific grant award.See www.grants.gov for specific announcement.

Funding: (Project Grants (Discretionary)); (Cooperative Agreements); (Cooperative Agreements (Discretionary Grants)); (Project Grants); (Project Grants (for specified projects))

HQ: 2201 C Street NW, Room 5313, Washington, DC 20520

Phone: 202-647-9446 | Email: wyckoffar@state.gov

HHS93.801 | EBOLA HEALTHCARE PREPAREDNESS AND RESPONSE FOR SELECT CITIES WITH ENHANCED AIRPORT ENTRANCE SCREENINGS FROM AFFECTED COUNTRIES IN WEST AFRICA

Award: Project Grants

Purpose: To enable public health departments serving regions where enhanced airport screenings are occurring to procure personal protective equipment and supplies, train staff, retrofit facilities, and carry out other necessary Ebola-specific preparedness, response, and recovery activities.

Applicant Eligibility: Eligible applicants are state or city departments of public health serving the five major airports wherein the Department of Homeland Security (DHS) is conducting enhanced airport entrance screenings for Ebola.

Beneficiary Eligibility: State or city departments of public health listed above, hospitals and supporting health care systems.

Award Range/Average: Est. Average Amount: $142,857

HQ: 200 C Street SW, Room C4K12, Washington, DC 20020

Phone: 202-245-0740 | Email: stephen.tise@hhs.gov

http://www.phe.gov

HHS93.823 | EBOLA SUPPORT: TRANSMISSION AND PREVENTION CONTROL, PUBLIC HEALTH PREPAREDNESS, VACCINE DEVELOPMENT

Award: Cooperative Agreements

Purpose: Support infection control programs throughout hospitals and other healthcare facilities to control transmission of Ebola, pathogens similar to Ebola, and those transmitted similarly to Ebola. Identify and implement healthcare worker requirements, policies and programs for training and competency of infection control practices.

Applicant Eligibility: Eligibility requirements will be delineated in the funding opportunity announcement.

Beneficiary Eligibility: All eligibility requirements will be delineated in the NOFO.

Funding: (Cooperative Agreements) FY 18 $0.00; FY 19 est $637,000.00; FY 20 est $400,000.00

HQ: 1600 Clifton Road NE, Atlanta, GA 30052

Phone: 404-718-8832 | Email: bsg2@cdc.gov

DOS19.450 | ECA INDIVIDUAL GRANTS
"Individual Grants, U.S. academics and professionals, Bureau of Educational and Cultural Affairs (ECA)"

Award: Project Grants

Purpose: Provides individual assistance awards by the Bureau of Educational and Cultural Affairs to experts and other influential or distinguished persons in the United States, including academics and professionals, athletes and coaches and creative and performing artists, with funds appropriated to and authorized by the Bureau of Educational and Cultural Affairs.

Programs Administered by Federal Headquarters

Applicant Eligibility: Individuals in fields of specialized knowledge or skill, and other influential or distinguished persons.
Beneficiary Eligibility: Beneficiaries include selected participants and the people of participating countries.
Award Range/Average: $769.93 to $820.18.
Funding: (Project Grants (including individual awards)) FY 17 $3,986.00; FY 18 est $3,986.00; FY 19 est $3,986.00
HQ: U.S. Department of State Executive Office Grants Division SA-05, Room 04 BB08, Washington, DC 20037
   Phone: 202-632-6365 | Email: thompsondl1@state.gov
   http://eca.state.gov

DOD12.617 | ECONOMIC ADJUSTMENT ASSISTANCE FOR STATE GOVERNMENTS

Award: Project Grants
Purpose: Provides technical and financial assistance to a State, or an entity of State government, to enhance its capacities to assist communities, businesses, and workers affected by Defense program activity to plan and carry out community adjustment and economic diversification activities; support local adjustment and diversification efforts; and stimulate cooperation between statewide and local adjustment and diversification efforts.
Applicant Eligibility: States, entities of States, Indian Tribal Governments, the District of Columbia, U.S. Territories and possessions. Applicants are to contact the Office of Economic Adjustment and a Project Manager will be assigned to work with the applicant to determine eligibility.
Beneficiary Eligibility: States, Indian Tribal Governments, and communities, including workers, businesses, and other community interests affected by Defense budget reductions, base closures/realignments, and/or civilian encroachment that is likely to impair the continued operational utility of a military installation.
Award Range/Average: $1,000,000 - $7,200,000, $1,900,000
Funding: (Project Grants) FY 18 $20,406,865.00; FY 19 est $15,127,205.00; FY 20 est 17,500,000.00
HQ: 2231 Crystal Drive, Suite 520, Arlington, VA 22202-3711
   Phone: 703-697-2161 | Email: karen.e.bass-mcfadden.civ@mail.mil
   http://www.oea.gov/grants

DOS19.322 | ECONOMIC STATECRAFT

Award: Project Grants
Purpose: Places economics and market forces at the center of U.S. foreign policy by both harnessing global economic forces to advance America's foreign policy and employing the tools of foreign policy to shore up our economic strength.
Applicant Eligibility: For specific information, please see announcement on www.Grants.gov.
Beneficiary Eligibility: Same as Applicant Eligibility.
Award Range/Average: For specific information, please see announcements on www.Grants.gov.
HQ: 2201 C Street NW, Room 3741, Washington, DC 20520
   Phone: 202-647-4032 | Email: hetrickc@state.gov
   http://www.state.gov/e/eb/econstatecraft/index.htm

DOJ16.752 | ECONOMIC, HIGH-TECH, AND CYBER CRIME PREVENTION

Award: Project Grants
Purpose: The Economic, High-Technology, White Collar, and Internet Crime Prevention National TTA Program prevents and investigates economic, high-tech, white collar, and internet crimes. It increases the knowledge of criminal justice practitioners and updates criminal justice agencies.
Applicant Eligibility: Eligible applicants include national, regional, State, or local public and private entities, including for-profit (commercial) and nonprofit Organizations, faith-based and community Organizations, Institutions of higher education, tribal jurisdictions, and units of local government.
Beneficiary Eligibility: State, local, tribal, and local territorial law enforcement agencies, prosecutor, and other criminal justice agencies.
Award Range/Average: Varies. See the current fiscal year's solicitation guidelines posted on the Office of Justice Programs web site at https://ojp.gov/funding/Explore/CurrentFundingOpportunities.htm.
Funding: (Cooperative Agreements) FY 18 $12,737,019.00; FY 19 est $14,000,000.00; FY 20 est $11,000,000.00
HQ: U.S. Department of Justice Bureau of Justice Assistance 810 7th Street NW, Washington, DC 20531
   Phone: 202-616-6500 | Email: david.p.lewis@usdoj.gov
   http://www.NW3C.org

DOI15.875 | ECONOMIC, SOCIAL, AND POLITICAL DEVELOPMENT OF THE TERRITORIES

Award: Formula Grants; Project Grants; Direct Payments With Unrestricted Use

Purpose: To pursue the Department's mission of Fulfilling Our Trust and Insular Responsibilities by executing activities that reinforce healthcare capacity, strengthen island economies, and fulfill U.S. Compact obligations.

Applicant Eligibility: Eligible applicants are the U.S. territories of Guam, American Samoa, the U.S. Virgin Islands, and the Commonwealth of the Northern Mariana Islands, the state of Hawaii; the Freely Associated States of the Federated States of Micronesia, the Republic of the Marshall Islands, and the Republic of Palau; and any non-profit Institutions /Organizations whose missions directly benefit the seven insular areas.

Beneficiary Eligibility: Beneficiaries are the U.S. territories of Guam, American Samoa, the U.S. Virgin Islands, and the Commonwealth of the Northern Mariana Islands; the state of Hawaii; and the Freely Associated States of the Federated States of Micronesia, the Republic of the Marshall Islands, and the Republic of Palau.

Award Range/Average: There is no minimum or maximum award. OIA financial assistance awards range from a few thousand dollars to tens of millions annually. The average award amount varies annually.

Funding: (Project Grants) FY 18 $436,417,000.00; FY 19 est Estimate Not Available; FY 20 est $299,289,000.00; - (FY 19 Exp: 312,308,000) FY 18 $436,417,000.00; FY 19 est Estimate Not Available; FY 20 est $299,289,000.00; (Direct Payments for Specified Use) FY 18 $331,073,000.00; FY 19 est $302,000,000.00; FY 20 est $302,000,000.00

HQ: Department of Interior 1849 C Street NW, PO Box 2429, Washington, DC 20240

Phone: 202-208-3913 | Email: aimee_munzi@ios.doi.gov

http://www.doi.gov/oia

HHS93.827 | EDUCATING STATE-LEVEL STAKEHOLDERS ON STRATEGIES TO ADDRESS WINNABLE BATTLES IN PUBLIC HEALTH

Award: Cooperative Agreements

Purpose: The purpose of the project is to reduce the burden of leading causes of death and disability by providing capacity building assistance to states to address priority health issues.

Applicant Eligibility: Applicants should be sufficiently connected to state executive branch and/or legislative branch members across the United States in order to accomplish the goal of working with a geographically diverse set of states from all regions of the U.S. Further, the applicant must be well versed both in public health issues such as CDC Winnable Battles and in how states approach and implement policies and practices that impact public health.

Beneficiary Eligibility: N/A

Award Range/Average: Fiscal Year:2015 Estimated Total Funding: $1,000,000 Approximate Total Fiscal Year Funding: $200,000 Approximate Project Period Funding: $1,000,000 Total Project Period Length:5 year(s) Expected Number of Awards:1 Approximate Average Award: $200,000 Per Budget Period

Funding: (Cooperative Agreements) FY 17 $15,000.00; FY 18 est $200,000.00; FY 19 est $58,750.00

NSF47.076 | EDUCATION AND HUMAN RESOURCES
"EHR"

Award: Project Grants

Purpose: To provide leadership and ensure the vitality of the Nation's science, technology, engineering and mathematics (STEM) education enterprise.

Applicant Eligibility: Except where a Program solicitation establishes more restrictive eligibility criteria, individuals and Organizations in the following categories may submit proposals: universities and colleges; Non-profit, non-academic Organizations; For-profit Organizations; State and local Governments; and unaffiliated individuals. See the NSF Grant Proposal Guide Chapter i.e. for a full description of eligibility requirements: http:// www.nsf.gov/publications/pub summ.jsp?: ods key=gpg.

Beneficiary Eligibility: N/A

Award Range/Average: Range Low $1,056 Range High $14,598,000 Average $318,070

Funding: (Project Grants) FY 18 $903,870,000.00; FY 19 est $922,000,000.00; FY 20 est $823,470,000.00

HQ: 2415 Eisenhower Avenue, Arlington, VA 22314

Phone: 703-292-8600 | Email: ssaltzma@nsf.gov

http://www.nsf.gov/dir/index.jsp?org=ehr

Programs Administered by Federal Headquarters

HUD14.416 | EDUCATION AND OUTREACH INITIATIVES
"FHIP EOI"

Award: Cooperative Agreements

Purpose: To develop, implement, carry out, or coordinate programs and/or activities to educate the public about their rights under, the Fair Housing Act (42 U.S.C. 3601-3619) or about State or local laws that provide substantially equivalent rights and remedies for alleged discriminatory housing practices.

Applicant Eligibility: Qualified Fair Housing Enforcement Organizations, other Fair Housing Enforcement Organizations, other non-profit Organizations representing groups of persons protected under Title VIII of the Civil Rights Act of 1968, State and local agencies certified by the Secretary under Section 810(f) of the Fair Housing Act, or other public or private entities that are formulating or carrying out Programs to prevent or eliminate discriminatory housing practices.

Beneficiary Eligibility: N/A

Award Range/Average: $125,000 to 1,000,000

Funding: (Cooperative Agreements) FY 17 $7,049,935.00; FY 18 est $7,450,000.00; FY 19 est $4,450,000.00

HQ: 451 7th Street SW, Room 5222, Washington, DC 20410

    Phone: 202-402-7054 | Email: paula.stone@hud.gov

    http://www.hud.gov/offices/fheo/partners.fhip/fhip.cfm

HHS93.557 | EDUCATION AND PREVENTION GRANTS TO REDUCE SEXUAL ABUSE OF RUNAWAY, HOMELESS AND STREET YOUTH
"Street Outreach Program (SOP)"

Award: Project Grants

Purpose: Provides grants available to nonprofit agencies for the purpose of providing street-based services to runaway, homeless and street youth who have been subjected to, or are at risk of being subjected to sexual abuse, prostitution, human trafficking, sexual exploitation, or other forms of victimization.

Applicant Eligibility: Private, nonprofit agencies are eligible to apply for Street Outreach Program grants. Federally recognized Indian Organizations are also eligible to apply for grants as private, non-profit agencies.

Beneficiary Eligibility: Runaway and homeless street youth are the beneficiaries of SOPs.

Award Range/Average: $100,000 to $150,000 per budget period; average award is $134,458

Funding: (Project Grants (Discretionary)) FY 18 $15,415,578.00; FY 19 est $15,373,832.00; FY 20 est $15,426,900.00

HQ: 330 C Street SW, Washington, DC 20024

    Phone: 202-205-9560 | Email: christopher.holloway@acf.hhs.gov

    http://www.acf.HHS.gov/programs/fysb

ED84.196 | EDUCATION FOR HOMELESS CHILDREN AND YOUTH

Award: Formula Grants

Purpose: To establish an Office of Coordinator for Education of Homeless Children and Youths; to develop a State plan for the education of homeless children; and to make subgrants to local educational agencies (LEAs) to support the education of those children.

Applicant Eligibility: State educational agencies in the 50 States, the District of Columbia, and Puerto Rico may apply. Funds are also reserved for the Outlying Areas and the Department of Interior/Bureau of Indian education. LEAs are eligible for State subgrants.

Beneficiary Eligibility: Homeless children and youth in elementary and secondary schools (and homeless preschool children and their parents benefit.

Award Range/Average: FY18 range of awards: $212,500- $10,563,703 FY 2018 average State award: $1,587,885. FY 19 range of awards: $233,750-11,620,515 FY 2019 average State award: $1,749,529.

Funding: (Formula Grants) FY 18 FY $85,000,000.00; 19 est $93,500,000.00; FY 20 est $93,500,000.00

HQ: Department of Education 400 Maryland Avenue SW, Washington, DC 20202

    Phone: 202-401-0962 | Email: john.mclaughlin@ed.gov

    http://www.ed.gov/programs/homeless/index.html

Programs Administered by Federal Headquarters

DOI15.959 | EDUCATION PROGRAM MANAGEMENT

Award: Direct Payments for Specified Use
Purpose: To improve the governance of education programs funded by the Bureau of Indian Education.
Applicant Eligibility: Federally Recognized Indian Tribal Governments or tribal Organizations currently served by a Bureau of Indian education funded school.
Beneficiary Eligibility: Federally Recognized Indian Tribal Governments and members of American Indian Tribes.
Award Range/Average: Range is $50,000 to $200,000;
Funding: (Direct Payments for Specified Use) FY 14 $70,000.00; FY 15 est $220,000.00; FY 16 est $70,000.00
HQ: 1849 C Street NW, Washington, DC 20240
Phone: 202-208-7658 | Email: joe.herrin@bie.edu
http://www.bie.edu

DOC11.013 | EDUCATION QUALITY AWARD AMBASSADORSHIP

Award: Cooperative Agreements
Purpose: To support Malcolm Baldrige National Quality Award Program encourages other organizations to strive for performance.
Applicant Eligibility: Applicants must have recently received the Malcolm Baldrige National Quality Award.
Beneficiary Eligibility: Public from 18 sponsored organizations.
Award Range/Average: Not to exceed $100,000 over the life of the grant.
HQ: 100 Bureau Drive, PO Box A600, Gaithersburg, MD 20899-1020
Phone: 301-975-8942 | Email: barbara.fischer@nist.gov
http://www.nist.gov/baldrige

ED84.305 | EDUCATION RESEARCH, DEVELOPMENT AND DISSEMINATION

Award: Project Grants
Purpose: To support research activities that improve the quality of education, reduce the achievement gap between high-performing and low-performing students, and increase the completion of postsecondary education.
Applicant Eligibility: Applicants that have the ability and capacity to conduct scientifically valid research are eligible to apply. Eligible applicants include, but are not limited to, non-profit and for-profit Organizations and public and private agencies and Institutions, such as colleges and universities. SBIR contract awards are limited to eligible small businesses.
Beneficiary Eligibility: Institutions and individuals involved with education will benefit.
Award Range/Average: The new 2019 grant awards ranged in size from $200,000 to $1.8 million for the first year of the awards. The 2019 SBIR awards ranged from $195,506 to $200,000 for Phase I awards and $897,103 to $900,000 for Phase II awards. Applicants for 2020 grant awards could request funding of $100,000 to $2,000,000 for projects lasting between 1 to 5 years, depending on the competition. Applicants for 2020 SBIR Phase I contract awards may request up to $200,000 for awards up to 6-months in length; the SBIR Phase II contract awards will be in amounts up to $900,000 for up to 2 years.
Funding: (Project Grants (Contracts)) FY 18 $26,410,109.00; FY 19 est $30,158,792.00; FY 20 est $37,705,157.00; (Project Grants) FY 18 $166,284,891.00; FY 19 est $162,536,208.00; FY 20 est $154,989,843.00
HQ: Department of Education 550 12th Street SW, Room 4118, Washington, DC 20202
Phone: 202-245-7833 | Email: emily.doolittle@ed.gov
http://ies.ed.gov/ncer

DOJ16.529 | EDUCATION, TRAINING, AND ENHANCED SERVICES TO END VIOLENCE AGAINST AND ABUSE OF WOMEN WITH DISABILITIES
"Disability Grant Program"

Award: Project Grants
Purpose: To provide training, consultation, and information on domestic violence, dating violence, stalking, and sexual assault against individuals with disabilities.
Applicant Eligibility: States, units of local government, Indian tribal Governments or tribal Organizations, and victim service providers, such as state or tribal domestic violence or sexual assault coalitions or nonprofit, nongovernmental Organizations serving disabled individuals. For profit Organizations and individuals are not eligible.
Beneficiary Eligibility: Beneficiaries include victim service agencies who respond to crime victims who are individuals with disabilities.
Award Range/Average: Range: $450,000 - $580,000

Programs Administered by Federal Headquarters

Funding: (Project Grants) FY 16 $3,775,000.00; FY 17 est $4,275,000.00; FY 18 est $4,100,000.00
HQ: 145 N Street NE, Suite 10W121, Washington, DC 20530
   Phone: 202-305-1177 | Email: tia.farmer@usdoj.gov
   http://www.justice.gov/ovw

NASA43.008 | EDUCATION
Award: Cooperative Agreements; Project Grants
Purpose: Provides basic research, educational outreach, or training opportunities in the area of Education.
Applicant Eligibility: Review funding opportunity announcement for additional information.
Beneficiary Eligibility: Same as Applicant Eligibility.
Funding: (Cooperative Agreements (Discretionary Grants)) FY 18 $104,038,080.45; FY 19 est $82,354,489.4.00; FY 20 est Estimate Not Available
HQ: Kennedy Space Center Central Campus, Headquarters Building M7-0301, Titusville, FL 32899
   Phone: 321-867-6988 | Email: jeppie.r.compton@nasa.gov
   http://www.nasa.gov

DOS19.022 | EDUCATIONAL AND CULTURAL EXCHANGE PROGRAMS APPROPRIATION OVERSEAS GRANTS
Award: Cooperative Agreements; Project Grants
Purpose: Provides assistance awards by U.S. diplomatic missions abroad made directly to eligible organizations in the United States using funds appropriated to and authorized by the Bureau of Educational and Cultural Affairs for the purpose of supporting international exchanges that addresses the issues of mutual interest to the United States and other countries, consistent with the program criteria established in the Department's annual appropriation.
Applicant Eligibility: Projects must support the development of mutual understanding between the United States and other countries in any area of importance to U.S. interests in those countries.
Beneficiary Eligibility: Beneficiaries include individuals selected for participation in the project, educational institutions, and Americans and people of other countries who interact with international participants.
Award Range/Average: Award amounts may vary widely depending on the nature of the project, from $3,500 up to approximately $84,328. A typical institutional award may total $50,000 or less.
Funding: (Project Grants) FY 17 $3,444,574.00; FY 18 est $3,444,574.00; FY 19 est $3,444,574.00
HQ: U.S. Department of State Executive Office Budget and Financial Management Division 2200 C Street SA-05, Room 04-P04, Washington, DC 20522-0504
   Phone: 202-632-3358 | Email: robinsonyj@state.gov
   http://exchanges.state.gov

DOJ16.751 | EDWARD BYRNE MEMORIAL COMPETITIVE GRANT PROGRAM
"Byrne Competitive Program"
Award: Project Grants
Purpose: To improve the criminal justice system by preventing crimes and enforcement of criminal law and assist in the rehabilitation, supervision, and care of criminal offenders.
Applicant Eligibility: Eligible applicants include national, regional, State, or local public and private entities, including for-profit (commercial) and nonprofit Organizations, faith-based and community Organizations, Institutions of higher education, tribal jurisdictions, and units of local government.
Beneficiary Eligibility: State and local governments, public and private organizations, individuals and tribal governments.
Award Range/Average: Varies.
Funding: (Project Grants) FY 17 $4,577,858.00; FY 18 est $1,000,000.00; FY 19 est Not Separately Identifiable
HQ: U.S. Department of Justice Bureau of Justice Assistance 810 7th Street NW, Washington, DC 20531
   Phone: 202-616-6500
   http://www.bja.gov

DOJ16.738 | EDWARD BYRNE MEMORIAL JUSTICE ASSISTANCE GRANT PROGRAM
"Byrne JAG Program"

Award: Formula Grants; Project Grants

Purpose: Providing states, tribes, and local governments with critical funding necessary to support a range of program areas including law enforcement, prosecution and court, prevention and education, corrections and community corrections, drug treatment and enforcement, planning, evaluation, and technology improvement, crime victim and witness initiatives and mental health programs, and related law enforcement and corrections programs.

Applicant Eligibility: JAG: All States, the District of Columbia, Guam, America Samoa, the Commonwealths of Puerto Rico, the Virgin Islands, and the Northern Mariana Islands. Units of local government are eligible consistent with established guidelines.

Beneficiary Eligibility: JAG grants are awarded to States, including the District of Columbia, the Commonwealth of Puerto Rico, the Northern Mariana Islands, the Virgin Islands, Guam, and American Samoa, as well as eligible units of local government (including tribes).

Award Range/Average: $10,000 to $37,000,000.

Funding: (Formula Grants) FY 18 $310,428,140.00; FY 19 est $423,500,000.00; FY 20 est $405,000,000.00

HQ: U.S. Department of Justice Bureau of Justice Assistance 810 7th Street NW, Washington, DC 20531
Phone: 202-616-6500 | Email: tracey.trautman@usdoj.gov
http://www.bja.gov/ProgramDetails.aspx?Program_ID=59

HHS93.747 | ELDER ABUSE PREVENTION INTERVENTIONS PROGRAM
"Elder Abuse Prevention Intervention Projects"

Award: Cooperative Agreements

Purpose: To develop, implement, and evaluate successful or promising interventions, practices, and programs to prevent elder abuse, neglect, and exploitation, including adult protective services programs.

Applicant Eligibility: Eligible entities for grants authorized under Section 411 of the Older Americans Act are: domestic public or private non-profit entities including state and local Governments, Indian tribal Governments and Organizations (American Indian/Alaskan Native/Native American), faith-based Organizations, community-based Organizations, hospitals, and Institutions of higher education, are eligible. For grants authorized under Section 2042 of the Patient Protection and Affordable Care Act, state government entities are eligible to apply.

Beneficiary Eligibility: N/A

Award Range/Average: FY2017: 5 New Awards (Range $176,850 - $492,500); 20 Continuation Awards (Range $100,000 - $488,550)FY2018: 22 New Awards (Range $75,000 - $500,000); 5 Continuation Awards (Range $186,021 - $581,780) FY2019: 5 New Awards (Range $150,000 - $500,000); 22 Continuation Awards (Range $75,000 - $500,000)

Funding: (Cooperative Agreements (Discretionary Grants)) FY 17 $7,748,535.00; FY 18 est $8,317,646.00; FY 19 est $6,500,000.00

HQ: Administration on Aging 330 C Street SW, Washington, DC 20201
Phone: 202-795-7467 | Email: stephanie.whittiereliason@acl.hhs.gov
http://www.acl.gov

DOD12.111 | EMERGENCY ADVANCE MEASURES FOR FLOOD PREVENTION
"Public Law 84-99 Code 500 Program"

Award: Provision of Specialized Services

Purpose: To make precautions for protecting life and property in case of a flood.

Applicant Eligibility: The Governor of the affected State must request assistance.

Beneficiary Eligibility: All persons living in areas subject to floods.

USDA10.763 | EMERGENCY COMMUNITY WATER ASSISTANCE GRANTS

Award: Project Grants

Purpose: To assist rural residents to have an adequate quantity of water that meets the standards of the Safe Drinking Water Act.

Programs Administered by Federal Headquarters

Applicant Eligibility: Eligible beneficiaries include (1) Public bodies or governmental entities such as municipalities, counties, districts, authorities, and other political subdivisions of a State, (2) nonprofit Organizations such as associations, cooperatives, and private nonprofit corporations, (3) Native American Indian Tribes on Federal and State reservations and other federally recognized Indian Tribes. projects must serve rural areas, excluding any city or town having a population greater than 10,000.
Beneficiary Eligibility: Users of the applicant systems, which are previously described as public bodies, private nonprofit corporations, and federally-recognized Indian tribes.
Award Range/Average: $15,000 to $1,000,000. Average: $335,325
Funding: (Project Grants) FY 18 $15,760,297.00; FY 19 est $19,000,000; FY est $17,650,000.00
HQ: 1400 Independence Avenue SW, Washington, DC 20250
    Phone: 202-720-0986 | Email: edna.primrose@wdc.usda.gov
    http://www.rd.usda.gov/programs-services/all-programs/water-environmental-programs

DHS97.024 | EMERGENCY FOOD AND SHELTER NATIONAL BOARD PROGRAM "EFSP"

Award: Project Grants
Purpose: The EFSP program provides economic assistance to the poor during a disaster situation to help them recover from potential burdens.
Applicant Eligibility: Public nonprofit institution/Organization (includes Institutions of higher education and hospitals), Private nonprofit institution/Organization (includes Institutions of higher education and hospitals), Quasi-public nonprofit institution/Organization since funds are initially distributed to jurisdictions based on either a National Board formula or recommendations from State Set-Aside Committees, there is no application process for jurisdictions. All jurisdictions are considered within the National Board formula and all jurisdictions in an individual State may be considered by the State Set-Aside Committee for either initial or additional (if the jurisdiction had previously been selected by the National Board) funding. At the local level, following award notification by the National Board to the jurisdiction, a Local Board is formed. The Local Board then advertises the availability of the funds to local nonprofit agencies and Governments. The Local Board must conduct a local application process for agencies to apply for funding. The Local Board selects which local nonprofit and governmental Organizations are to receive funding and submits their selections via a Local Board Plan to the National Board.
Beneficiary Eligibility: Public nonprofit institution/organization, Other public institution/organization The law directs that the Local Boards, which manage the program at the local level, shall "determine which private nonprofit organizations or public organizations of the local government in the individual locality shall receive grants to act as service providers." The range of participant groups on the Local Boards include the affiliates of the National Board membership which consists of American Red Cross, Catholic Charities USA, The Jewish Federations of North America, National Council of Churches of Christ in the USA, The Salvation Army, and United Way Worldwide, with a local government representative replacing FEMA. Also participating are thousands of independent nonprofits (such as Community Action Agencies and Food Banks and food pantries) which provide food and/or shelter services. Due to the broad category of people in need of such emergency services, the providers can include specialized groups such as domestic violence shelters and organizations providing food or shelter to: AIDS patients, handicapped individuals, the elderly, homeless veterans, non-wards of the State teenage runaways, and many other groups with emergency food and shelter needs. As noted earlier, the decisions on selections are made through the consensus of the Local Board as they have assessed their community's most urgent needs. It is important that such agencies use these funds to supplement, not replace, their current efforts. This program is intended to supplement ongoing programs and allow them to extend and expand upon their existing services.
Award Range/Average: Refer to program guidance.
Funding: (Project Grants) FY 18 $120,000,000.00; FY 19 est $120,000,000.00; FY 20 est $130,000,000.00
HQ: Community Services Branch/Individual Assistance Division/Recovery Directorate DHS 500 C Street SW, Room 614, Washington, DC 20472
    Phone: 202-646-2500
    http://www.fema.gov

DOJ16.824 | EMERGENCY LAW ENFORCEMENT ASSISTANCE GRANT "EFLEA"

Award: Project Grants
Purpose: To provide necessary law enforcement assistance to State government in response to threats to lives and property of citizens.

Applicant Eligibility: See the current fiscal year's solicitation available at the Office of Justice Programs web site at https://ojp. gov/funding/Explore/CurrentFundingOpportunities. htm.

Beneficiary Eligibility: Same as Applicant Eligibility.

Award Range/Average: Awards may be made up to the amount available under this program. For specifics, please see the current fiscal year's solicitation available at the Office of Justice Programs web site http://ojp.gov/funding/Explore/ CurrentFundingOpportunities.htm.

Funding: (Project Grants) FY 17 $13,849,826.00; FY 18 est $16,000,000.00; FY 19 est $0.00

HQ: U.S. Department of Justice Bureau of Justice Assistance 810 7th Street NW, Washington, DC 20531

    Phone: 202-616-6500 | Email: tracey.trautman@usdoj.gov

    http://www.bja.gov

DHS97.131 | EMERGENCY MANAGEMENT BASELINE ASSESSMENTS GRANT (EMBAG)
"EMBAG"

Award: Direct Payments for Specified Use

Purpose: The EMBAG Program supervises the ANSI-certified standards for emergency preparedness and response. It assesses and evaluates the State and local level emergency management organizations and also ensures that the 32 core capabilities identified in the National Preparedness Goal are delivered.

Applicant Eligibility: Private nonprofit institution/Organization (includes Institutions of higher education and hospitals) Any (two) independent, non-profit Organization (s) that can meet the objectives of this Program and sufficiently demonstrate through their application(s) that they have significant experience in developing, updating, revising, and enhancing national-level industry standards for emergency management and implementing assessments of state, local, tribal, and territorial emergency management Programs and/or professionals against these standards using peer review is eligible to apply. Each applicant should be uniquely qualified to develop, update, revise, and enhance industry standards for emergency management and implement assessments against them. At least one applicant should be capable of the above for emergency management Programs. At least one applicant should be capable of the above for emergency management professionals. The assessment and accreditation or assessment and certification process supported by the recipient(s) must include a review of the following areas (16) within an emergency management Program or for emergency management professionals, respectively: 1. Emergency Management Program Administration, including Authorities, Oversight, and Strategic Planning; 2. Development and use of a THIRA; 3. Continuity of Government and Continuity of Operations; 4. Incident Management, to include NIMS and NQS Implementation; 5. Emergency Management Finance, including Disaster Cost Recovery; 6. Operations and Procedures; 7. Consequence Analysis; 8. Emergency Planning, including Mutual Aid, Communications, and Warning; 9. Evacuation and Shelter in Place; 10. Mass Care and Sheltering; 11. Resource Management and Logistics; 12. Recovery; 13. Disaster Housing; 14. Hazard Mitigation; 15. Training and Exercises, including Alignment with the Homeland Security Exercise and Evaluation Program (HSEEP); and16. Public Affairs. For additional information, please refer to the Program notice of funding opportunity. For additional information about applicant eligibility, please refer to the Program notice of funding opportunity.

Beneficiary Eligibility: U.S. Territories, State, Local, Federally Recognized Indian Tribal GovernmentsFunding under this program is ultimately intended to benefit U.S. State, Local, Tribal, and Territorial emergency management programs.

Funding: (Direct Payments for Specified Use) FY 18 $569,379.00; FY 19 est $569,379.00; FY 20 est $569,379.00

HQ: FEMA 400 C Street NW, Washington, DC 20472-3630

    Phone: 202-786-9451 | Email: sharon.kushnir@fema.dhs.gov

    http://www.fema.gov

DHS97.027 | EMERGENCY MANAGEMENT INSTITUTE (EMI) INDEPENDENT STUDY PROGRAM
"ISP"

Award: Training

Purpose: The program provides over 195 courses on emergency management to government officials to help them prepare for threats against the national security that includes natural disasters, pandemics and acts of terrorism.

Applicant Eligibility: Unlimited Application. Anyone/general public - Any person(s), without regard to specified eligibility criteria.

Programs Administered by Federal Headquarters

Beneficiary Eligibility: Anyone/General public.
Award Range/Average: Not Applicable.
Funding: (Training) FY 18 $585,926.00; FY 19 est $693,138.00; FY 20 est $685,795.00
HQ: 16825 S Seton Avenue, Emmitsburg, MD 21727
    Phone: 301-447-1057
    http://www.training.fema.gov/is

DHS97.028 | EMERGENCY MANAGEMENT INSTITUTE (EMI) RESIDENT EDUCATIONAL PROGRAM

Award: Training
Purpose: The program helps to improve the emergency management practices in local and State level through systematic preparation against threats such as natural disasters and other acts of terrorism.
Applicant Eligibility: Individuals assigned to an emergency management position in State, local, tribal, or Territorial government are eligible. Restrictions apply, however; refer to Program guidance document or contact administering Program office for additional information.
Beneficiary Eligibility: General Public.
Funding: (Training) FY 18 $873,040.00; FY 19 est $1,028,224.00; FY 20 est $1,061,598.00
HQ: Protection and National Preparedness National Preparedness Directorate National Training and Education Division 16825 S Seton Avenue, Emmitsburg, MD 21727
    Phone: 301-447-1507
    http://www.training.fema.gov

DHS97.026 | EMERGENCY MANAGEMENT INSTITUTE TRAINING ASSISTANCE
"Student Stipend Reimbursement Program (SEP)"

Award: Direct Payments for Specified Use
Purpose: To pay for the travel expenses of state, local and tribal officials who attend training courses on emergency management for systematic preparation on terrorism, cyber attacks and other natural disasters.
Applicant Eligibility: Individuals who are assigned to an emergency management position in State, local or tribal government are eligible. Some restrictions apply, refer to Program guidance document or contact administering Program office for additional information.
Beneficiary Eligibility: State, Local Specialized Group.
Award Range/Average: Average stipend cost of $514 per student day
Funding: (Direct Payments for Specified Use) FY 18 $1,225,443.00; FY 19 est $1,263,317.00; FY 20 est $1,379,200.00
HQ: Protection and National Preparedness National Preparedness Directorate National Training and Education Division 16825 S Seton Avenue, Emmitsburg, MD 21727
    Phone: 301-447-1286
    http://www.training.fema.gov

DHS97.042 | EMERGENCY MANAGEMENT PERFORMANCE GRANTS
"EMPG"

Award: Formula Grants
Purpose: The Emergency Management Performance Grant Program assists local and State governments in emergency preparedness for natural disasters and other hazards.
Applicant Eligibility: State (includes District of Columbia, public Institutions of higher education and hospitals), U.S. Territories and possessions (includes Institutions of higher education and hospitals) All 56 States and territories, as well as the Republic of the Marshall Islands and the Federated States of Micronesia, (collectively "state or territory"), are eligible to apply for FY 2019 EMPG funds. Either the SAA or the State's EMA is eligible to apply for EMPG funds. Either the SAA or the EMA is eligible to apply directly to FEMA for EMPG funds on behalf of each state or territory. However, only one application will be accepted from each state or territory.
Beneficiary Eligibility: Funding under this program is ultimately used by emergency management organizations and programs of States, the District of Columbia, territories and possessions of the Unites States, local, and Indian Tribal governments.
Funding: (Formula Grants) FY 18 $350,099,998.00; FY 19 est $350,100,000.00; FY 20 $350,100,000.00

HQ: Department of Homeland Security 400 C Street SW, Washington, DC 20523
Phone: 800-368-6498
http://www.fema.gov/government/grant/index.shtm

HHS93.127 | EMERGENCY MEDICAL SERVICES FOR CHILDREN
"EMS for Children"

Award: Cooperative Agreements; Project Grants
Purpose: To support demonstration projects for the expansion and improvement of emergency medical services for children.
Applicant Eligibility: State Governments and Accredited Schools of Medicine.
Beneficiary Eligibility: All children will benefit from the project grants administered by this program, including children from minority groups.
Award Range/Average: (Cooperative Agreements) FY 18 average $ $1,168,739, range $599,911- $3,700,000 FY 19 $ average $1,050,000, range $699,281- $3,000,000 FY 20 average $1,161,111, range $699,281, - $3,000,000 (Project Grants) FY 18 average $148,680, range $130,000- $342,766 FY 19 average $133,627, range $130,000- $325,000 FY 20 average $142,267, range $130,000- $325,000
Funding: (Project Grants) FY 18 $9,812,899.00; FY 19 est $8,685,726.00; FY 20 est $8,820,554.00; (Cooperative Agreements) FY 18 $9,349,909; FY 19 est $9,450,000; FY 20 est $10,450,000
HQ: Maternal and Child Health Bureau 5600 Fishers Lane, Room 18N-54, Rockville, MD 20857
Phone: 301-443-1527 | Email: tmorrison-quinata@hrsa.gov
http://www.hrsa.gov

DHS97.052 | EMERGENCY OPERATIONS CENTER
"EOC"

Award: Project Grants
Purpose: The grant program provides funds for construction or renovation of a State or local emergency operations center.
Applicant Eligibility: Specific information on applicant eligibility is identified in the funding opportunity announcement and in the EOC Grant Program Guidance and Application Kit.
Beneficiary Eligibility: Funding under this program is ultimately to benefit State and local governments.
Award Range/Average: Refer to in the EOC Grant Program Guidance and Application Kit.
HQ: Grant Programs Directorate Department of Homeland Security FEMA 400 C Street SW, Washington, DC 20472-3615
Phone: 800-368-6498
http://www.fema.gov

DOD12.103 | EMERGENCY OPERATIONS FLOOD RESPONSE AND POST FLOOD RESPONSE
"Public Law 84-99 Code 200 Program"

Award: Provision of Specialized Services
Purpose: To provide emergency flood response in the time of flood or coastal storm.
Applicant Eligibility: State or local public agencies for flood response and the State for post flood response.
Beneficiary Eligibility: All persons living in areas subject to floods, and in eligible areas, are potential beneficiaries.

DOJ16.823 | EMERGENCY PLANNING FOR JUVENILE JUSTICE FACILITIES

Award: Project Grants
Purpose: To provide funds to States to address the needs of children, youth and families involved in the justice system during an emergency.
Applicant Eligibility: 1) 24-US Territories; 13-state; The only eligible applicant for these funds is the designated state agency that receives Title II Formula Grant funds from OJJDP2)50-law, justice, and legal services; 72-youth development; 58-planning3)Contact the Program office for additional information.
Beneficiary Eligibility: 1)15-local; 14-state; 79-child; 80-youth2)Contact program office for additional information.
Award Range/Average: $70,000- $91,000
Funding: (Project Grants (Discretionary)) FY 18 $449,343; FY 19 est $500,000.00; FY 20 est $500,000.00

Programs Administered by Federal Headquarters

HQ: U.S. Department of Justice Office of Juvenile Justice and Delinquency Prevention 810 7th Street NW, Washington, DC 20531
Phone: 202-514-4817 | Email: kellie.dressler@usdoj.gov
http://www.ojjdp.gov

DOD12.102 | EMERGENCY REHABILITATION OF FLOOD CONTROL WORKS OR FEDERALLY AUTHORIZED COASTAL PROTECTION WORKS
"Public Law 84-99, Code 300 Program"

Award: Provision of Specialized Services
Purpose: To restore flood control works damaged by flood and other damages caused by natural disasters.
Applicant Eligibility: Owners of damaged flood protective works, or State and local officials of public entities responsible for their maintenance, repair, and operation must meet current guidelines to become eligible for Public Law 84-99 assistance: 1. Engineering and maintenance criteria (inspection required); 2. cost-sharing (80 percent Federal and 20 percent nonfederal); and 3. public sponsorship nonfederal (items a through c pertain to nonfederal flood control projects).
Beneficiary Eligibility: All persons living in areas protected by eligible flood control or coastal protection works are potential beneficiaries of the program.

HUD14.231 | EMERGENCY SOLUTIONS GRANT PROGRAM

Award: Formula Grants
Purpose: To engage homeless individuals and families living on the street, improve their number and quality of emergency shelters, help operate these shelters, provide essential services to them, rapidly re-house them, and prevent families and individuals from becoming homeless.
Applicant Eligibility: Eligible recipients generally consist of metropolitan cities, urban counties, territories, and states, as defined in 24 CFR 576. 2. Metropolitan cities, urban counties and territories may subgrant ESG funds to private nonprofit Organizations. Local Governments may also subgrant ESG funds to public housing agencies or local redevelopment authorities. States must subgrant all of their ESG funds (except for funds for administrative costs and, under certain conditions, HMIS costs) to units of general purpose local government and/or private nonprofit Organizations. Each recipient must consult with the Continuum(s) of Care operating within the jurisdiction in determining how to allocate ESG funds.
Beneficiary Eligibility: The minimum eligibility criteria for ESG beneficiaries are as follows: For essential services related to street outreach, beneficiaries must meet the criteria under paragraph (1)(i) of the "homeless" definition under 576.2. For emergency shelter, beneficiaries must meet the "homeless" definition in 24 CFR 576.2. For essential services related to emergency shelter, beneficiaries must be "homeless" and staying in an emergency shelter (which could include a day shelter). For homelessness prevention assistance, beneficiaries must meet the requirements described in 24 CFR 576.103. For rapid re-housing assistance, beneficiaries must meet requirements described in 24 CFR 576.104. Further eligibility criteria may be established at the local level in accordance with 24 CFR 576.400(e).
Award Range/Average: The.05 percent minimum entitlement allocation resulted in $135,000 minimum grant in FY2017. The maximum entitlement allocation was $13,542,650.
Funding: (Formula Grants) FY 18 est $270,000,000.00; FY 19 est $270,000,000.00; FY 20 est $270,000,000.00
HQ: Community Planning and Development Office of Special Needs Assistance Programs 451 7th Street SW, Room 7260, Washington, DC 20410
Phone: 202-402-4773 | Email: karen.m.deblasio@hud.gov
http://www.hudexchange.info/esg

HHS93.089 | EMERGENCY SYSTEM FOR ADVANCE REGISTRATION OF VOLUNTEER HEALTH PROFESSIONALS
"ESAR-VHP"

Award: Project Grants
Purpose: To establish and maintain a national interoperable network of state systems.
Applicant Eligibility: State health departments of all 50 States, the District of Columbia, the nation's three largest municipalities (New York City, Chicago and Los Angeles County), the Commonwealths of Puerto Rico and the Northern Mariana Islands, the territories of American Samoa, Guam and the United States Virgin Islands, the Federated States of Micronesia, and the Republics of Palau and the Marshall Islands.
Beneficiary Eligibility: All State health departments listed above, hospitals and supporting health care systems.

Award Range/Average: $58,478 to $200,000 per award.
Funding: (Project Grants (Discretionary)) FY 18 $0.00; FY 19 est $0.00; FY 20 est $200,000.00
HQ: Office of Emergency Management Office of the Assistant Secretary for Preparedness and Response Department of Health and Human Services 200 C Street SW, Washington, DC 20024
> Phone: 202-245-0722 | Email: jennifer.hannah@hhs.gov
> http://www.phe.gov/esarvhp

HHS93.381 | EMERGENCY TRIAGE, TREAT, AND TRANSPORT (ET3) MODEL "ET3 Model"

Award: Formula Grants (cooperative Agreements)
Purpose: To establish a medical triage line within a region's 911 line to divert non-emergency transports and hospital admissions to appropriate healthcare within the community to improve the utilization of the regional ambulance services.
Applicant Eligibility: Applicants eligible to apply to this NOFO must have authority over the 911 system in the same geographic area as an ET3 model participant (i.e., an ambulance provider or supplier in the ET3 model).
Beneficiary Eligibility: Applicants eligible to apply to this NOFO must have authority over the 911 system in the same geographic area as an ET3 model participant (i.e., an ambulance provider or supplier in the ET3 model). Therefore, as long as an applicant meets this requirement, there is no restriction on who can apply.
Award Range/Average: The ET3 Model will award up to $34 Million in cooperative agreement funds across up to 40 awardees during the two-year performance period.
Funding: (Formula Grants (Cooperative Agreements)) FY 18 Actual Not Available; FY 19 est Estimate Not Available; FY 20 est $17,000,000.00
HQ: 7500 Security Boulevard, Baltimore, MD 21244
> Phone: 410-786-3501 | Email: alexis.lilly@cms.hhs.gov
> https://innovation.cms.gov/initiatives/et3

HHS93.317 | EMERGING INFECTIONS PROGRAMS

Award: Cooperative Agreements
Purpose: To assist in local, state, and national efforts to prevent, control, and monitor the public health impact of infectious diseases.
Applicant Eligibility: Eligibility is limited to State Governments (specifically, state health departments) or their Bona Fide Agents (this includes the District of Columbia, the Commonwealth of Puerto Rico, the Virgin Islands, the Commonwealth of the Northern Marianna Islands, American Samoa, Guam, the Federated States of Micronesia, the Republic of the Marshall Islands, and the Republic of Palau). The EIP infrastructure depends on a direct relationship with public health agencies that have sufficient legal authority and responsibility to perform public health surveillance and response activities. The network must also consist of definitive populations large enough to adequately determine disease burden, evaluate large scale interventions, and impact public health policy decisions.
Beneficiary Eligibility: Beneficiaries of this program include State and local health departments, the District of Columbia, U.S. Territories, and the general public.
Award Range/Average: Under this CFDA: awards typically range between $1.5M to 4M annually, with an average award of $2.6M.
Funding: (Cooperative Agreements) FY 18 $26,055,351.00; FY 19 est $44,837,943.00; FY 20 $45,000,000.00; For 2018: $26,055,351 awarded under this CFDA program. An additional $18,845,332 was awarded under (PPHF) CFDA 93.521.
HQ: 1600 Clifton Road NE, PO Box C18, Atlanta, GA 30329
> Phone: 404-639-6146
> http://www.cdc.gov

HHS93.860 | EMERGING INFECTIONS SENTINEL NETWORKS

Award: Cooperative Agreements
Purpose: The Emerging Infections Sentinel Networks monitors and evaluates conditions that are not covered by health department surveillance and are likely to be seen by specific kinds of health providers. They contribute to surveillance for emerging infectious diseases, including drug resistant, foodborne and waterborne, and vaccine-preventable or potentially vaccine-preventable diseases, and enhance information exchange leading to early identification of and response to trends and outbreaks.

Programs Administered by Federal Headquarters

Applicant Eligibility: Eligibility for this Program is open, however, only Institutions /Organizations that meet and can demonstrate the necessary qualifications described in the published NOFOs for this Program should apply. Additional eligibility information is also described below: There are both research and non-research funding opportunities under this Program. For the research opportunity, only Organizations currently operating a nationwide provider-based sentinel network that link academically affiliated hospital emergency departments in monitoring a variety of infectious disease problems are eligible. For the non-research opportunity, only Organizations currently operating provider-based sentinel networks that link groups of participating individuals or Organizations organized around either infectious disease clinicians or travel medicine in monitoring a variety of infectious disease problems are eligible. Applicants should refer to the published NOFOs for more information regarding applicant eligibility.
Beneficiary Eligibility: Health Professionals - Anyone/General public.
Award Range/Average: Award Range: $250k- $930kAverage Award: $530k
Funding: (Cooperative Agreements) FY 18 $1,839,926.00; FY 19 est $1,705,928.00; FY 20 est $0.00
HQ: 1600 Clifton Road NE, PO Box C18, Atlanta, GA 30329
    Phone: 404-639-7722 | Email: aslaughter@cdc.gov
    http://www.cdc.gov

USDA10.603 | EMERGING MARKETS PROGRAM
"EMP"

Award: Direct Payments for Specified Use
Purpose: The Emerging Markets Program maximizes exporting of U.S. agricultural commodities to markets of eligible organizations. It promotes food and rural businesses for emerging markets.
Applicant Eligibility: Applicants must be a: (1) U.S. agricultural or agribusiness Organization - nonprofit, trade association, University, consultant group (under certain conditions), (2) State Department of Agriculture, or (3) USDA agency (or other Federal agency involved in agricultural issues) or commercial entities.
Beneficiary Eligibility: There are 4 types of eligible activities:(1) Assistance to U.S. individual experts in assessing the food and rural business systems of other countries. This type of EMP project must include all three of the following: Conduct an assessment of the food and rural business system needs of an emerging market; Make recommendations on measures necessary to enhance the effectiveness of these systems; and; Identify opportunities and projects to enhance the effectiveness of the emerging market's food and rural business systems.(2) Travel assistance to enable individuals from emerging markets to travel to the United States so that these individuals can, for the purpose of enhancing the food and rural business systems in their countries, become familiar with U.S. technology and agribusiness and rural enterprise operations by consulting with food and rural business system experts in the United States.(3) Travel assistance to enable U.S. agricultural producers and other individuals knowledgeable in agricultural and agribusiness matters to travel to emerging markets to assist in transferring their knowledge and expertise to entities in emerging markets. Such travel must be to emerging markets. Travel to developed markets is not eligible under the program even if the travelers targeted market is an emerging market.(4) Technical assistance to implement the recommendations, projects, and/or opportunities identified by assistance under (1) above. Technical assistance that does not implement the recommendations, projects, and/or opportunities identified by assistance under (1) above is not eligible under the EMP. (Proposals that do not fall into one or more of the four categories above, regardless of previous guidance provided regarding the EMP, are not eligible for consideration under the program.).
Award Range/Average: Generally grants are for small, focused projects ranging from $7,000 up to $500,000.
Funding: (Project Grants) FY 18 $10,000,000.00; FY 19 est $8,000,000.00; FY 20 est $8,000,000.00
HQ: 1400 Independence Avenue SW, Washington, DC 20250
    Phone: 202-720-8557 | Email: robert.miller@fas.usda.gov
    http://www.fas.usda.gov/programs/emerging-markets-program-emp

DOL17.150 | EMPLOYEE BENEFITS SECURITY ADMINISTRATION
"EBSA"

Award: Dissemination of Technical Information
Purpose: The Employee Benefits Security Administration assures the security of the retirement, health and other workplace benefits. It educates workers enforces the law.
Applicant Eligibility: Plan administrators, trustees, participants, beneficiaries of employee benefit plans, or others involved in plan administration may obtain assistance in complying with the Act. Interested persons may obtain certain plan documents which are required to be filed by plan administrators.

Beneficiary Eligibility: Plan officials, trustees, participants, beneficiaries of employee benefit plans, or others involved in plan administration.
Award Range/Average: Not Available.
Funding: (Salaries and Expenses) FY 16 $181,000.00; FY 17 est $183,000.00; FY 18 est $183,296.00
HQ: Department of Labor 200 Constitution Avenue NW, Room N5623, Washington, DC 20210
    Phone: 866-444-3272
    http://www.dol.gov/agencies/ebsa

HHS93.734 | EMPOWERING OLDER ADULTS AND ADULTS WITH DISABILITIES THROUGH CHRONIC DISEASE SELF-MANAGEMENT EDUCATION PROGRAMS-FINANCED BY PREVENTION AND PUBLIC HEALTH FUNDS (PPHF)
"Chronic Disease Self-Management Education Programs"

Award: Cooperative Agreements; Project Grants
Purpose: The agreements are intended to increase the number of chronic disease self-management education program participants, while concurrently increasing the sustainability of these proven programs in the aging and disability networks.
Applicant Eligibility: Eligible applicants are domestic public or private non-profit entities including state and local Governments, Indian tribal Governments and Organizations (American Indian/Alaskan Native/Native American), faith-based Organizations, community-based Organizations, hospitals, and Institutions of higher education.
Beneficiary Eligibility: The ultimate beneficiaries of this funding opportunity are older and disabled adults with chronic conditions residing in States, Tribes and Territories.
Award Range/Average: FY 2018 Range: $145,255 - $850,000
Funding: (Salaries and Expenses) FY 17 $8,000,000.00; FY 18 est $8,000,000.00; FY 19 Estimate Not Available
HQ: U.S. Department of Health and Human Services 330 C Street SW, Washington, DC 20201
    Phone: 202-795-7379 | Email: kristie.kulinski@acl.hhs.gov
    http://www.acl.gov

HRSA93.686 | ENDING THE HIV EPIDEMIC: A PLAN FOR AMERICA-RYAN WHITE HIV/AIDS PROGRAM PARTS A AND B

Award: Cooperative Agreements
Purpose: To reduce the number of people in the United States affected by HIV infections to less than 3,000 per year by 2030.
Applicant Eligibility: Eligible applicants are: RWHAP Part A funded Eligible Metropolitan Areas (EMAs) or Transitional Grant Areas (TGAs) whose service area includes one or more of the identified 48 HIV high burden counties; and the EMAs of Washington, D. C. and San Juan, PR. RWHAP Part B funded States/Territories identified.
Beneficiary Eligibility: N/A
Award Range/Average: HRSA expects approximately $55,125,000 to be available in FY2020 It is anticipated that the total annual amount available could increase to $655,400,000 over the course of the 5 year period of performance
Funding: (Cooperative Agreements) FY 18 $0; FY 19 est $0; FY 20 est $55,125,000.00
HQ: 5600 Fishers Lane, Rockville, MD 20857
    Phone: 301-443-1993 | Email: hhauck@hrsa.gov

DOL17.310 | ENERGY EMPLOYEES OCCUPATIONAL ILLNESS COMPENSATION

Award: Direct Payments With Unrestricted Use
Purpose: Provides lump-sum monetary payments and medical benefits to covered employees and, where applicable, to survivors of such employees, of the Department of Energy (DOE), its predecessor agencies and certain of its vendors, contractors and subcontractors.
Applicant Eligibility: Employees and, where applicable, to survivors of such employees, of the Department of Energy (DOE), its predecessor agencies, certain of its vendors, contractors and subcontractors, and uranium miners, millers and ore transporters covered by section 5 of RECA, who are or were engaged in covered employment related to the testing or production of nuclear weapons.
Beneficiary Eligibility: Same as Applicant Eligibility.
Award Range/Average: Maximum monetary lump-sum payment under Part B is $150,000 per covered employee; maximum monetary lump-sum payment under Part E is $250,000 per covered employee. No limitation on payment of medical expenses.

Programs Administered by Federal Headquarters

Funding: (Direct Payments with Unrestricted Use) FY 18 $1,366,409,000.00; FY 19 est $1,418,801,000.00; FY 20 est $1,459,938,000.00

HQ: Division of Energy Employees Occupational Illness Compensation 200 Constitution Avenue NW, Washington, DC 20210
Phone: 202-693-0081
http://www.dol.gov/owcp/energy

DOS19.027 | ENERGY GOVERNANCE AND REFORM PROGRAMS

Award: Cooperative Agreements; Project Grants

Purpose: Programs support improved energy sector governance and transparency, technical engagement to build awareness of the challenges involved in developing unconventional resources, and power sector reform and development to support the expansion of access to electricity.

Applicant Eligibility: See full announcement at www.grants.gov.

Beneficiary Eligibility: Same as Applicant Eligibility.

Award Range/Average: $500,000- $600,000 to date; will vary.

Funding: (Cooperative Agreements) FY 13 $1,800,000.00; FY 14 est $1,800,000.00; FY 15 est $1,800,000.00

HQ: 2201 C Street NW, Washington, DC 20037
Phone: 202-647-9158 | Email: murphyct@state.gov

HHS93.684 | ENGAGING STATE AND LOCAL EMERGENCY MANAGEMENT AGENCIES TO IMPROVE ABILITY TO PREPARE FOR AND RESPOND TO ALL-HAZARDS EVENTS

Award: Cooperative Agreements

Purpose: The program prepares the nation's public health systems to minimize the consequences associated with all-hazards events.

Applicant Eligibility: Applicant must have experience as a professional association of and for emergency management directors from all 50 states, eight U.S. territories, and the District of Columbia, the applicant's unique ability in representing state emergency management directors will greatly assist with emergency preparedness planning and coordination efforts between public health and emergency management sectors nationally.

Beneficiary Eligibility: Applicant must have experience as a professional association of and for emergency management directors from all 50 states, eight U.S. territories, and the District of Columbia, the applicant's unique ability in representing state emergency management directors will greatly assist with emergency preparedness planning and coordination efforts between public health and emergency management sectors nationally. The nation's public is the ultimate recipient of benefits from this program.

Award Range/Average: Subject to availability of funds. Approximate Average Award: $150 KAnticipated Award Date: September 1,2019 Budget Period Length: 12 monthsProject Period Length: 5 years

Funding: (Cooperative Agreements) FY 18 $100,000.00; FY 19 est $65,000.00; FY 20 est $65,000.00

HQ: 1600 Clifton Road NE, PO Box D29, Atlanta, GA 30029-4018
Phone: 404-639-5276 | Email: vbk5@cdc.gov
http://www.cdc.gov

NSF47.041 | ENGINEERING
"ENG"

Award: Project Grants

Purpose: To improve the quality of life and the economic strength of the Nation by fostering innovation, creativity, and excellence in engineering education and research.

Applicant Eligibility: Except where a Program solicitation establishes more restrictive eligibility criteria, individuals and Organizations in the following categories may submit proposals: universities and colleges; Non-profit, non-academic Organizations; for-profit Organizations; State and local Governments; and unaffiliated individuals. See the NSF Grant Proposal Guide, Chapter i.e. for a full description of eligibility requirements: www.nsf.gov/publications/pubsumm.jsp?odskey=gpg.

Beneficiary Eligibility: N/A

Award Range/Average: Range Low $1,823 Range High $16,300,000 Average $153,866

Funding: (Project Grants) FY 18 $977,900,000.00; FY 19 est $995,770,000.00; FY 20 est $881,420,000.00
HQ: 2415 Eisenhower Avenue, Alexandria, VA 22314
    Phone: 703-292-4494 | Email: dduttere@nsf.gov
    http://nsf.gov/dir/index.jsp?org=eng

DOD12.554 | ENGLISH FOR HERITAGE LANGUAGE SPEAKERS GRANTS TO U.S. INSTITUTIONS OF HIGHER EDUCATION
"National Security Education Program (NSEP)"

Award: Project Grants
Purpose: To enable the program participants to reach a professional working proficiency in English by meeting with ILR's level 3 and/or ACTFL's superior level thereby enabling them to serve in the federal government service.
Applicant Eligibility: Any accredited U.S. institution of higher education (defined in Section 1201(a) of the Higher education Act of 1965, 20 U.S.C. 1141(a) is eligible to apply for a grant. This includes 2 and 4 year colleges and universities, both public and private. Other Organizations, associations, agencies, and foreign Institutions may be included in proposals but may not be direct recipients of a grant. Federal government schools are not eligible.
Beneficiary Eligibility: Accredited U.S. institutions of higher education, their students, and U.S. citizens with superior-level proficiency in their native language.
Funding: (Salary or Expense) FY 07 $2,000,000.00; FY 08 est Estimate Not Available; FY 09 est Estimate Not Available
HQ: 1101 Wilson Boulevard, Suite 1210, Arlington, VA 22209-2248
    Phone: 703-696-1991
    http://www.cal.org/what-we-do/projects/ehls

DOD12.555 | ENGLISH FOR HERITAGE LANGUAGE SPEAKERS SCHOLARSHIPS
"EHLS Program"

Award: Project Grants
Purpose: The English for Heritage Language Speakers (EHLS) program is designed to provide intensive English language instruction for U. S. citizens who are native speakers of critical languages.
Applicant Eligibility: Currently, the Program is administered at Georgetown University in Washington, DC through a contract.
Beneficiary Eligibility: (1) Must be a U.S. citizen at the time of application; (2) Must have a minimum proficiency in English of advanced low (as defined by ACTFL) or level 2 (as defined by ILR); (3) must also possess excellent skills in your heritage/native language (ILR level 3/ACTFL superior language proficiency or higher in all modalities of English; (4) Must have received at least an undergraduate degree by the time of application; and (5) may not be a current U.S. government employee. Eligible native languages of interest are updated annually, a list of which is available on the program web site.
Award Range/Average: Awards are for $30,000 in 2010. There is no range or average.
Funding: (Project Grants (including individual awards)) FY 17 $790,000.00; FY 18 est $790,000.00; FY 19 Estimate Not Available
HQ: 4800 Mark Center Drive, Suite 08 G 08, Alexandria, VA 22350
    Phone: 571-256-0753 | Email: kevin.j.gormley.civ@mail.mil
    http://www.cal.org/ehls

ED84.365 | ENGLISH LANGUAGE ACQUISITION STATE GRANTS

Award: Formula Grants
Purpose: To ensure that English learners (ELs), including immigrant children and youth, attain English proficiency and meet the same challenging State academic standards that all children are expected to meet.
Applicant Eligibility: States with approved State plans and outlying areas are eligible to receive funds.
Beneficiary Eligibility: English learners and immigrant children and youth benefit.
Award Range/Average: FY 19 $87,913 - $143,884,023; $12,161,101 average.
Funding: (Formula Grants) FY 18 $681,021,655.00; FY 19 est $681,021,655.00; FY 20 est $681,021,655.00
HQ: 400 Maryland Avenue SW, Washington, DC 20202
    Phone: 202-453-6827 | Email: faatimah.muhammad@ed.gov
    http://www2.ed.gov/programs/sfgp/index.html

Programs Administered by Federal Headquarters

HHS93.087 | ENHANCE SAFETY OF CHILDREN AFFECTED BY SUBSTANCE ABUSE

Award: Project Grants

Purpose: To provide, an integration of program activities and services that are designed to increase well-being, improve permanency outcomes, and enhance the safety of children who are in an out-of-home placement or are at risk of being placed in out-of-home care as a result of a parent's or caretaker's substance abuse.

Applicant Eligibility: State Governments, county Governments, local Governments, city or township Governments, regional Organizations, U.S. territory or possession, independent school districts, public and state-controlled Institutions of higher education, Indian/Native American tribal Governments (federally recognized), Indian/Native American tribal Organizations (other than federally recognized), Indian/Native American tribally designated Organizations, public/Indian housing authorities, non-profits with 501(c)(3) IRS status (other than Institutions of higher education), non-profits without 501(c)(3) IRS status (other than Institutions of higher education), private Institutions of higher education, for-profit Organizations (other than small businesses), small businesses, Hispanic-serving Institutions, historically Black colleges and universities (HBCUs), tribally controlled colleges and universities (TCCUs), Alaska Native and Native Hawaiian serving Institutions, and special district Governments. Foreign entities are not eligible under this announcement. Applications must represent regional partnerships formed by a collaborative agreement and must identify a primary applicant responsible for administering the grant. The primary applicant must be one of the regional partnership Organizations listed as an eligible applicant above. The primary applicant cannot be an individual. The regional partnership must include either the state child welfare agency that is responsible for the administration of the state plan under title IV-B or title IV-E of the Social Security Act or an Indian tribe or tribal consortium but the regional partnership may not consist of only state entities.

Beneficiary Eligibility: Agencies or organizations serving children and families who have experienced or are at risk of experiencing an out of home placement as a result of a parent's or caregiver's substance abuse.

Award Range/Average: For FY 2018, the range of grants were from $10,669 to $1,900,000 with an average grant of $782,001.

Funding: (Project Grants (Discretionary)) FY 18 $31,389,969.00; FY 19 est $28,931,506.00; FY 20 est $10,188,326.00

HQ: Office on Child Abuse and Neglect Children's Bureau 330 C Street SW, Room 3419C, Washington, DC 20201

Phone: 202-401-2887 | Email: jean.blankenship@acf.hhs.gov

http://www.acf.hhs.gov/programs/cb

HHS93.878 | ENHANCE THE ABILITY OF EMERGENCY MEDICAL SERVICES (EMS) TO TRANSPORT PATIENTS WITH HIGHLY INFECTIOUS DISEASES (HID)

Award: Cooperative Agreements

Purpose: Enhance state and local level emergency medical services operational plans for the management of confirmed or suspected high consequence infection diseases.

Applicant Eligibility: The applicant must be a nonprofit Organization representing all of the 50 state emergency medical services officials.

Beneficiary Eligibility: EMS officials and operators at the state and local levels.

Award Range/Average: $250,000- $350,000

HQ: Division of Health System Policy 200 C Street SW, Washington, DC 20201

Phone: 202-690-3830 | Email: gregg.margolis@hhs.gov

http://www.phe.gov

DOJ16.528 | ENHANCED TRAINING AND SERVICES TO END VIOLENCE AND ABUSE OF WOMEN LATER IN LIFE

"Abuse in Later Life"

Award: Project Grants

Purpose: To provide training, services, and collaboration to address the needs of victims of elder abuse, neglect, and exploitation.

Applicant Eligibility: Eligible applicants include States, tribal Governments and tribal Organizations, units of local government, population specific Organizations, victim service providers, and state, tribal, or territorial domestic violence or sexual assault coalitions.

Beneficiary Eligibility: Applicants must be part of a multidisciplinary partnership that includes law enforcement, prosecutors, a victim service provider, and a nonprofit program or government agency with demonstrated experience in assisting individuals in later life.

Award Range/Average: Range: $300,000 - $400,00

Funding: (Project Grants) FY 16 $3,438,295.00; FY 17 est $1,499,561.00; FY 18 est $4,000,000.00

HQ: 145 N Street NE, Suite 10W121, Washington, DC 20530
   Phone: 202-305-1177 | Email: tia.farmer@usdoj.gov
   http://www.justice.gov/ovw

USDA10.334 | ENHANCING AGRICULTURAL OPPORTUNITIES FOR MILITARY VETERANS COMPETITIVE GRANTS PROGRAM

Award: Project Grants
Purpose: Enhancing Agricultural Opportunities for Military Veterans provides grants for military veterans and crates farming and ranching opportunities.
Applicant Eligibility: Funds may be used to provide grants to nonprofit Organizations for Programs and services to establish and enhance farming and ranching opportunities for military veterans.
Beneficiary Eligibility: Same as Applicant Eligibility.
Award Range/Average: If minimum or maximum amounts of funding per competitive and/or capacity project grant, or cooperative agreement are established, these amounts will be announced in the annual Competitive Request for Application (RFA).The most current RFA is available via: https://nifa.usda.gov/funding-opportunity/enhancing-agricultural-opportunities-military-veterans-competitive-grants
Funding: (Project Grants (Discretionary)) FY 17 $4,979,500.00; FY 18 est $4,757,600.00; FY 19 est $0.00
HQ: 1400 Independence Avenue SW, Room 4434, Washington, DC 20250
   Phone: 202-690-3468 | Email: belrod@nifa.usda.gov
   https://nifa.usda.gov/funding-opportunity/enhancing-agricultural-opportunities-military-veterans-competitive-grants

HHS93.346 | ENHANCING THE LOGICAL OBSERVATION IDENTIFIERS NAMES AND CODES (LOINC®) STANDARD TO MEET U.S. INTEROPERABILITY NEEDS "LOINC"

Award: Cooperative Agreements
Purpose: To expedite improvements and bridge gaps between Health Level 7 International's (HL7) Fast Healthcare Interoperability Resources (FHIR).
Applicant Eligibility: The Regenstrief Institute is the only entity to apply for this award.
Beneficiary Eligibility: N/A
Award Range/Average: There has been $625,000 allocated for FY 18 for this award. One award will be made to the Regenstrief Institute.
Funding: (Cooperative Agreements) FY 17 Actual Not Available; FY 18 est $625,000.00; FY 19 est Estimate Not Available
HQ: 330 C Street SW, Washington, DC 20201
   Phone: 202-720-2919 | Email: carmel.halloun@hhs.gov
   https://www.healthit.gov

SBA59.064 | ENTREPRENEURIAL DEVELOPMENT DISASTER ASSISTANCE (DISASTER RELIEF APPROPRIATIONS ACT)

Award: Cooperative Agreements; Project Grants; Provision of Specialized Services; Advisory Services and Counseling; Dissemination of Technical Information
Purpose: Provides grants to or cooperative agreements with organizations to provide technical assistance related to disaster recovery, response, and long term resiliency to small businesses that are recovering from a natural disaster.
Applicant Eligibility: SBA is authorized to make grants (including contracts and cooperative agreements) to public or private institution of higher education, including but not limited to any land- grant college or University, any college or school of business, engineering, commerce, or agriculture, community college or junior college, to any private, nonprofit Organizations having experience in effectively training and counseling business women, or all existing and potential business owners.
Beneficiary Eligibility: Current and potential Small business persons recovering from Hurricane Sandy.

Programs Administered by Federal Headquarters

DOS19.017 | ENVIRONMENTAL AND SCIENTIFIC PARTNERSHIPS AND PROGRAMS

Award: Cooperative Agreements; Project Grants

Purpose: Supports sustainable growth across the globe, the Bureau of Oceans, Environment, and Science (OES) builds international partnerships to address environmental, scientific, and health concerns. The objective of funding includes but are not limited to, programs that address climate change and its impact, and reduce global greenhouse gas emissions; conserve natural resources and reduce international threats to biodiversity; improve access to safe drinking water; promote a level playing field with free trade partners; protect fisheries and oceans; reduce the threat from mercury and other pollutants; and foster international scientific collaboration.

Applicant Eligibility: The use of assistance is to support a wide range of partnerships responding to diverse international environmental initiatives.

Beneficiary Eligibility: N/A

Award Range/Average: Grants vary depending on program objectives and availability of funds.

Funding: (Project Grants) FY 16 $560,206,000.00; FY 17 est $7,100,000.00; FY 18 Estimate Not Available

HQ: Bureau of Oceans International Environmental and Scientific Affairs 2025 E Street NW, Room 10076 SA-09, Washington, DC 22520

   Phone: 202-472-8171 | Email: urbinama1@state.gov

   http://www.state.gov/g/oes

HHS93.113 | ENVIRONMENTAL HEALTH
"National Institute of Environmental Health Sciences"

Award: Project Grants

Purpose: To identify of agents that pose a hazard and threat of disease, disorders and defects in humans; the development of effective public health or disease prevention strategies.

Applicant Eligibility: Research Grants, Cooperative Agreements, Science education Grants, SBIR Grants, Independent Scientist Awards, Mentored Research Scientist Development Award, Mentored Clinical Scientist Development Award, and the Academic Career Awards: A University, college, hospital, State, local or tribal Governments, nonprofit research institution, or for-profit Organization may submit an application and receive a grant for support of research by a named principal investigator. Candidates for Academic Career Awards and Midcareer Investigator Awards in Patient Oriented Research must have a doctoral degree and peer-reviewed, independent, research support at the time the award is made. Candidates for Mentored Clinical Scientist Development Awards and Mentored Patient Oriented Research Career Development Awards must have a clinical degree or its equivalent and must have initiated post graduate clinical training. Candidates holding a Ph. D. degree are ineligible. Candidates who have served as principal investigators on PHS-supported research projects are ineligible. A candidate for Academic Career Awards must have a clinical or research doctorate degree. Those eligible for the Development Award must be able to devote at least 75 percent effort. SBIR grants can be awarded only to domestic small businesses (entities that are independently owned and operated for profit, are not dominant in the field in which research is proposed, and have no more than 500 employees). Primary employment (more than one-half time) of the principal investigator must be with the small business at the time of award and during the conduct of the proposed project. In both Phase I and Phase II, the research must be performed in the U.S. and its possessions. STTR grants can be awarded only to domestic small business concerns (entities that are independently owned and operated for profit, are not dominant in the field in which research is proposed and have no more than 500 employees) which "partner" with a research institution in cooperative research and development. At least 40 percent of the project is to be performed by the small business concern and at least 30 percent by the research institution. In both Phase I and Phase II, the research must be performed in the U.S. and its possessions. To be eligible for funding, a grant application must be approved for scientific merit and Program relevance by a scientific review group and a national advisory council. Centers: A University -based, nonprofit research institution, or for-profit Organization proposing an integrated research Program established to accomplish a stated mission, covering activities ranging from very basic research to the actual application of research results in the prevention and control of environmental health problems, may submit an application under the direction of a named Center Director. National Research Service Awards: (1) Nonprofit domestic Organizations may apply for the Institutional NRSA; (2) Individual NRSA awardees must be nominated and sponsored by a public for-profit or nonprofit private institution having staff and facilities appropriate to the proposed research training Program; (3) all awardees must be citizens or have been admitted to the United States for permanent residence; (4) to be eligible, predoctoral awardees must have completed the baccalaureate degree and postdoctoral awardees must have a professional or scientific degree (M.D., Ph.D., D.D.S., D.O., D.V.M., Sc.D., D.Eng., or equivalent domestic or foreign degree).

Beneficiary Eligibility: For Research Grants: Any nonprofit or for-profit organization, company, or institution engaged in biomedical research. For Centers and Training Grants: University-based nonprofit institutions; for-profit organizations conducting research; and individuals nominated by a private institution conducting research.
Award Range/Average: Range: $2,000 to $1,749,000 Average: $343,940
Funding: (Project Grants) FY 18 $354,076,000.00; FY 19 est $366,076,000.00; FY 20 est $314,583,000.00
HQ: 111 TW Alexander Drive, Research Triangle Park, NC 27709
Phone: 984-287-3784 | Email: encarna1@niehs.nih.gov
http://www.niehs.nih.gov

DOE81.214 | ENVIRONMENTAL MONITORING/CLEANUP, CULTURAL AND RESOURCE MGMT., EMERGENCY RESPONSE RESEARCH, OUTREACH, TECHNICAL ANALYSIS

Award: Cooperative Agreements
Purpose: To provide technical and financial assistance to State and local government entities to support DOE missions.
Applicant Eligibility: Research and Development Environmental Restoration.
Beneficiary Eligibility: State, Local US Territory/Possession, Minority Group, Low Income.
Award Range/Average: $0.00 to $8,792,019.00. Subject to the availibility of funds.
Funding: (Cooperative Agreements (Discretionary Grants)) FY 18 $18,355,911; FY 19 est $4,866,376.00; FY 20 est Estimate Not Available
HQ: Savannah River Site, Aiken, SC 29802
Phone: 803-952-9355 | Email: cynthia.hughes@srs.gov
http://www.srs.gov

HHS93.070 | ENVIRONMENTAL PUBLIC HEALTH AND EMERGENCY RESPONSE

Award: Cooperative Agreements
Purpose: To bring public health and epidemiologic principles together to identify, clarify, and reduce the impact of complex environmental threats, including terrorist threats and natural disasters, on populations, domestic and foreign.
Applicant Eligibility: N/A
Beneficiary Eligibility: N/A
Award Range/Average: $10,000 to $1,500,000
Funding: (Cooperative Agreements) FY 18 $45,960,170.00; FY 19 est $50,695,987.00; FY 20 est $50,695,987.00
HQ: 4770 Buford Highway NE, PO Box F45, Atlanta, GA 30341
Phone: 770-488-0563
http://www.cdc.gov

DOC11.440 | ENVIRONMENTAL SCIENCES, APPLICATIONS, DATA, AND EDUCATION

Award: Project Grants
Purpose: To promote technology development and education in environmental science.
Applicant Eligibility: Any State University, college, institute or laboratory; any public or private nonprofit institution or consortium.
Beneficiary Eligibility: Organizations and individuals with interests in support of managing effectively the Nation's oceanic and atmospheric resources.
Funding: (Cooperative Agreements) FY 16 $1,527,225.00; FY 17 est $500,000.00; FY 18 est $5,000,000.00
HQ: DOC/NOAA/NESDIS/STAR 5830 University Research Court, College Park, MD 20740
Phone: 301-683-3510 | Email: satya.kalluri@noaa.gov
http://www.nesdis.noaa.gov

Programs Administered by Federal Headquarters

HHS93.943 | EPIDEMIOLOGIC RESEARCH STUDIES OF ACQUIRED IMMUNODEFICIENCY SYNDROME (AIDS) AND HUMAN IMMUNODEFICIENCY VIRUS (HIV) INFECTION IN SELECTED POPULATION GROUPS
"Epidemiologic Research Studies of AIDS and HIV"

Award: Cooperative Agreements

Purpose: To support research of HIV-related epidemiologic issues concerning risks of transmission, the natural history and transmission of the disease in certain populations.

Applicant Eligibility: Eligible applicants include States, political subdivisions of States or their agents or instrumentalities, private research Organizations, including American Indian/Alaska Native tribal Governments or tribal Organizations located wholly or in part within their boundaries, other public and private nonprofit Organizations, and for-profit Organizations.

Beneficiary Eligibility: State and local health agencies; private research organizations, public and private nonprofit organizations, for profit organizations; minority groups, including American Indian/Alaska Native tribal governments or tribal organizations located wholly or in part within their boundaries, and persons physically afflicted with AIDS/HIV infection.

Funding: (Cooperative Agreements) FY 18 $600,000.00; FY 19 est $0.00; FY 20 est $0.00

HQ: 1600 Clifton Road NE, PO Box E07, Atlanta, GA 30333

Phone: 404-639-1877 | Email: lrw3@cdc.gov

http://www.cdc.gov

HHS93.323 | EPIDEMIOLOGY AND LABORATORY CAPACITY FOR INFECTIOUS DISEASES (ELC)
"ELC"

Award: Cooperative Agreements

Purpose: To protect the public health and safety of the American people by enhancing the capacity of public health agencies to effectively detect, respond, prevent and control known and emerging (or re-emerging) infectious diseases.

Applicant Eligibility: Eligible applicants consist of state, local, and U.S. territory/possession Governments currently funded under CDC-RFA-CI10-1012 or CDC-RFA-CK12-1201. Specifically, these include: all 50 states, Washington, D. C., 5 largest local health departments (Chicago, Illinois; Houston, Texas; Los Angeles, California; New York City, New York; Philadelphia, Pennsylvania;), the Commonwealth of Puerto Rico, the Virgin Islands, the Commonwealth of the Northern Mariana Islands, American Samoa, Guam, the Federated States of Micronesia, the Republic of the Marshall Islands, and the Republic of Palau or their bona fide agents.

Beneficiary Eligibility: Direct beneficiaries include all 50 states, Washington, D.C., 5 largest local health departments (Chicago, Illinois; Houston, Texas; Los Angeles, California; New York City, New York; Philadelphia, Pennsylvania;), the Commonwealth of Puerto Rico, the Virgin Islands, the Commonwealth of the Northern Mariana Islands, American Samoa, Guam, the Federated States of Micronesia, the Republic of the Marshall Islands, and the Republic of Palau or their bona fide agents.

Award Range/Average: Subject to availability of Funds

Funding: (Cooperative Agreements) FY 18 $217,226,427.00; FY 19 est $208,849,735.00; FY 20 est $208,849,735.00

HQ: 1600 Clifton Road NE, PO Box C18, Atlanta, GA 30333

Phone: 404-639-7379 | Email: amoconnor@cdc.gov

http://www.cdc.gov/ncezid/dpei/epidemiology-laboratory-capacity.html

HHS93.231 | EPIDEMIOLOGY COOPERATIVE AGREEMENTS

Award: Cooperative Agreements

Purpose: To fund Tribes, Tribal and urban Indian organizations, and intertribal consortia to provide epidemiological support for the AI/AN population served by IHS.

Applicant Eligibility: AI/AN Tribes, Tribal Organizations, and eligible intertribal consortia or urban Indian Organizations as defined by 25 U.S.C. 1603(e) may be eligible for a TEC cooperative agreement. Such entities must represent or serve a population of at least 60,000 AI/AN to be eligible as demonstrated by Tribal resolutions or the equivalent documentation from urban Indian clinic directors/Chief Executive Officers (CEOs). Applicants must describe the population of AI/ANs and Tribes that will be represented. The number of AI/ANs served must be substantiated by documentation describing IHS user populations, United States Census Bureau data, clinical catchment data, or any method that is scientifically and epidemiologically valid. An intertribal consortium or urban Indian Organization is eligible to receive a cooperative agreement if it is incorporated for the primary purpose of improving AI/AN health, and represents the Tribes, AN villages, or urban Indian communities in which it is located. Resolutions from each Tribe, AN village and equivalent documentation from each urban Indian community represented must be included in the application package. Collaborations with IHS Areas, Federal agencies such as the Centers for Disease Control and Prevention (CDC), State, academic Institutions or other Organizations are encouraged (letters of support and collaboration should be included in the application).

Beneficiary Eligibility: Federally-recognized Indian Tribe will benefit from the Tribal Epidemiology Centers. Federally-recognized Indian Tribe means any Indian Tribe, band, nation, or other organized group or community, including any Alaska Native village or group or regional or village corporation as defined in or established pursuant to the Alaska Native Claims Settlement Act (85 Stat. 688) [43 U.S.C. 1601, et seq.], which is recognized as eligible for the special programs and services provided by the United States to Indians because of their status as Indians. 25 U.S.C. 1603 (d).Tribal organization means the elected governing body of any Indian Tribe or any legally established organization of Indians which is controlled by one or more such bodies or by a board of directors elected or selected by one or more such bodies or elected by the Indian population to be served by such organization and which includes the maximum participation of Indians in all phases of its activities. 25 U.S.C. 1603(e).Urban Indian organization means a non-profit corporate body situated in an urban center governed by an urban Indian controlled board of directors, and providing for the maximum participation of all interested Indian groups and individuals, which body is capable of legally cooperating with other public and private entities for the purpose of performing the activities. 25 U.S.C. 1603(h).

Award Range/Average: $565,475 to $1,322,125; average award $795,535.

Funding: (Cooperative Agreements) FY 17 $7,603,660.00; FY 18 est $4,466,000.00; FY 19 $4,466,000.00

HQ: 5600 Fishers Lane, PO Box 09E70, Rockville, MD 20857
   Phone: 301-443-5204
   http://www.ihs.gov

HUD14.400 | EQUAL OPPORTUNITY IN HOUSING
"Fair Housing"

Award: Investigation of Complaints

Purpose: To provide fair housing throughout the country and an administrative enforcement system that is subject to judicial review.

Applicant Eligibility: Any aggrieved person, or the Assistant Secretary, may file a complaint based on an alleged discriminatory housing practice because of race, color, religion, sex, national origin, familial status or disability status. The complaint may be filed with the Department of Housing and Urban Development or a State or local fair housing agency whose law has been determined to be substantially equivalent to the Federal Fair Housing Act.

Beneficiary Eligibility: Anyone alleging to have been discriminated against in violation of the Fair Housing Act.

Award Range/Average: $2,800,000

HQ: 451 7th Street SW, Room 5208, Washington, DC 20410
   Phone: 202-402-3264 | Email: gordon.f.patterson@hud.gov
   http://www.hud.gov/complaints/housediscrim.cfm

DOJ16.922 | EQUITABLE SHARING PROGRAM

Award: Direct Payments for Specified Use

Purpose: The Department of Justice Asset Forfeiture Program is a law enforcement initiative that minimizes criminal organizations and assists victims.

Applicant Eligibility: A state or local law enforcement agency meeting eligibility requirements set forth in the Guide and that directly participates in an investigation or prosecution resulting in a federal forfeiture may request an equitable share of the net proceeds of the forfeiture. For purposes of equitable sharing, the Department of Justice defines a law enforcement agency as a state or local government Organization authorized to engage in, as its primary function, the investigation and apprehension, or the prosecution of individuals suspected or convicted of offenses against the criminal laws of the United States or of any state, county, municipality, or territory of the United States. A state National Guard generally does not meet the law enforcement agency criteria for participation in the Program because its primary mission is a military or other non-law enforcement purpose. However, a National Guard Counterdrug unit may qualify for sharing if: (1) It is a distinct unit of a state National Guard that has counterdrug activities as its primary mission and receives funding solely for this purpose; or (2) It is a military police or similar state National Guard unit that provides support to federal law enforcement agencies in counterdrug activities.

Programs Administered by Federal Headquarters

Beneficiary Eligibility: A state or local law enforcement agency meeting eligibility requirements set forth in the Guide and that directly participates in an investigation or prosecution that results in a federal forfeiture may request an equitable share of the net proceeds of the forfeiture.

Funding: (Direct Payments for Specified Use) FY 15 $361,589,000.00; FY 16 Estimate Not Available; FY 17 Estimate Not Available

HQ: Asset Forfeiture and Money Laundering Section 1400 New York Avenue NW, Washington, DC 20005
   Phone: 202-514-1263
   http://www.justice.gov/criminal/afmls/equitable-sharing

TREAS21.016 | EQUITABLE SHARING

Award: Direct Payments for Specified Use

Purpose: To remove the tools of crime from criminal organizations, deters crime and deprives wrongdoers of the proceeds of their criminal proceeds, and recovers property that may be used to compensate victims.

Applicant Eligibility: A state or local law enforcement agency meeting eligibility requirements set forth in the Guide and that directly participates in an investigation or prosecution that results in a federal forfeiture may request an equitable share of the net proceeds of the forfeiture. For purposes of equitable sharing, the Department of Treasury defines law enforcement agency as a state or local government Organization authorized to engage in as its primary function the investigation and apprehension, or the prosecution of individuals suspected or convicted of offenses against the criminal laws of the United States or of any state, county, municipality, or territory of the United States. A State National Guard generally does not meet the law enforcement agency criteria for participation in the Program because its primary mission is a military or other non-law enforcement purpose. However, a National Guard Counterdrug Unit may qualify for sharing if: (1) It is a distinct unit of a state National Guard that has counterdrug activities as its primary mission and receives funding solely for this purpose; or (2) It is a military police or similar state National Guard unit that provides support to federal law enforcement agencies in counterdrug activities.

Beneficiary Eligibility: A state or local law enforcement agency meeting eligibility requirements set forth in the Guide and that directly participates in an investigation or prosecution that results in a federal forfeiture may request an equitable share of the net proceeds of the forfeiture.

Award Range/Average: Not Applicable.

Funding: (Direct Payments for Specified Use) FY 18 $144.00; FY 19 est $37.00; FY 20 est $50.00

HQ: 1341 G Street NW, Suite 900, Washington, DC 20005
   Phone: 202-622-2755 | Email: jackie.jackson@treasury.gov
   http://www.treasury.gov/resource-center/terrorist-illicit-finance/pages/equitable-sharing.aspx

DOD12.130 | ESTUARY HABITAT RESTORATION PROGRAM

Award: Cooperative Agreements

Purpose: To provide Federal assistance for estuary habitat restoration projects while encouraging partnerships among public agencies and non-governmental organizations, supporting innovation, and monitoring the success of funded projects.

Applicant Eligibility: N/A

Beneficiary Eligibility: N/A

Funding: (Project Grants (Cooperative Agreements)) FY 15 Not Separately Identifiable; FY 16 est $70,000.00; FY 17 est Not Separately Identifiable

HQ: 441 G Street NW, Washington, DC 20314
   Phone: 202-761-4750 | Email: ellen.m.cummings@usace.army.mil
   http://www.usace.army.mil/missions/environmental/estuaryrestoration.aspx

DOS19.878 | EUR-OTHER

Award: Project Grants

Purpose: To promote democratic and free market transitions in the former communist countries of Central and Eastern Europe and Eurasia, enabling them to overcome their past and become reliable, productive members of the Euro-Atlantic community of Western democracies.

Applicant Eligibility: This Program is awarded on a non-competitive basis.

Beneficiary Eligibility: N/A

Funding: (Project Grants)

HQ: 2201 C Street NW, Washington, DC 20052
   Phone: 202-647-8002 | Email: gupmanam@state.gov

DOS19.123 | EUR/ACE HUMANITARIAN ASSISTANCE PROGRAM

Award: Project Grants

Purpose: Provides vital humanitarian assistance to vulnerable populations in countries of the former Soviet Union.

Applicant Eligibility: Since 1992, the EUR/ACE HA Program has been assisting those in need with food, clothing and medicine. Small Reconstruction projects fund structural repairs such as bathrooms and kitchens of recipient Institutions in a cost-effective way. Materials and engineering costs are covered by the project, unskilled labor is often provided by local residents, and contributions (such as utility costs) are sometimes made by NGOs and local Governments. The long-term result of HA is threefold: the suffering of the vulnerable is relieved, partnerships are formed between the USG and the people of the recipient country, and, from this example, their Governments are better able to recognize and react to the needs of their citizens. Since its inception in 1992, the EUR/ACE Program has provided over $4 billion worth of donated assistance to the people of the former Soviet Union. In 2012, the EUR/ACE Program provided $137. 57 million in assistance using only $10. 77 million in Program funds; that is, $12. 77 of assistance delivered for each dollar of Program funding. Similar results are expected in FY13, with diminished returns in FY14, the final year of the Program. The EUR/ACE Humanitarian Program is scheduled to phase out effective 30 September 2014.

Beneficiary Eligibility: All grantees under this program are U.S. based non-profit organizations.

Award Range/Average: between $ 100,000 and $,600,00

HQ: 2201 C Street NW, Washington, DC 20003

　　Phone: 202-647-7272 | Email: shankn@state.gov

DOS19.666 | EUR/ACE NATIONAL ENDOWMENT FOR DEMOCRACY SMALL GRANTS

"National Endowment for Democracy (NED) Small Grants Program in Europe, Eurasia and Central Asia"

Award: Project Grants

Purpose: Advances democracy in Europe, Eurasia and Central Asia by providing support to indigenous civil society organizations.

Applicant Eligibility: This Program is awarded on a non-competitive basis.

Beneficiary Eligibility: N/A

Funding: (Project Grants (Discretionary)) FY 12 Estimate Not Available

HQ: 2201 C Street NW, Washington, DC 20520

　　Phone: 202-647-7703 | Email: krystelnb@state.gov

HHS93.434 | EVERY STUDENT SUCCEEDS ACT/PRESCHOOL DEVELOPMENT GRANTS

"ESSA/Preschool Development Grants Birth - 5"

Award: Project Grants

Purpose: Seeks to assist States in helping low-income and disadvantaged children enter Kindergarten prepared and ready to succeed in school and to help improve the transitions from the early care and education setting to elementary school.

Applicant Eligibility: In addition to the 50 States eligible to apply for these grants in FY2018, the District of Columbia and Puerto Rico are also eligible. In the first year of ESSA PDG implementation (Initial Planning Grants), priority will be given to States not previously awarded under the previous PDG of 2014.

Beneficiary Eligibility: In addition to the 50 States, DC, Puerto Rico, and local communities, beneficiaries include children birth through 5 and their families.

Award Range/Average: The range of funding is anticipated to be between $5-10M per Grant Award, based on application request and supporting evidence.

Funding: (Project Grants) FY 18 $242,742,262.00; FY 19 est $242,500,000.00; FY 20 est $0.00; (Training Total) FY 18 $6,777,738.00; FY 19 est $6,940,000.00; FY 20 est $0.00; (Salaries and Expenses Total) FY 18 $480,000.00; FY 19 est $560,000.00; FY 20 est $0.00

HQ: 330 C Street SW, Room 4012E Switzer Building, Washington, DC 20201

　　Phone: 202-401-5138 | Email: richard.gonzales@acf.hhs.gov

　　https://www.acf.hhs.gov/occ/resource/pdg-b-5-initiative

Programs Administered by Federal Headquarters

HHS93.761 | EVIDENCE-BASED FALLS PREVENTION PROGRAMS FINANCED SOLELY BY PREVENTION AND PUBLIC HEALTH FUNDS (PPHF)
"Falls Prevention"

Award: Cooperative Agreements

Purpose: The cooperative agreements are intended to increase the number of evidence-based falls prevention programs available to older adults, while concurrently increasing the sustainability of these proven programs in the aging and disability networks.

Applicant Eligibility: Eligible applicants for grants are domestic public or private non-profit entities including state and local Governments, Indian tribal Governments and Organizations (American Indian/Alaskan Native/Native American), faith-based Organizations, community-based Organizations, hospitals, and Institutions of higher education. Any additional restrictions/ guidance will be provided in the funding opportunity announcement(s).

Beneficiary Eligibility: The ultimate beneficiaries of this funding opportunity are older and disabled adults at risk for falls residing in states, tribes, and territories.

Award Range/Average: FY 2018 grantee award range: $107,477 - $515,590

Funding: (Cooperative Agreements (Discretionary Grants)) FY 17 $5,000,000.00; FY 18 est $5,000,000.00; FY 19 est $5,000,000.00

HQ: U.S. Department of Health and Human Services 1 Massachusetts Avenue NW, Washington, DC 20201
Phone: 202-357-3508 | Email: casey.dicocco@acl.hhs.gov
http://www.acl.gov

TREAS21.004 | EXCHANGE OF FEDERAL TAX INFORMATION WITH STATE TAX AGENCIES

Award: Provision of Specialized Services

Purpose: To increase state tax revenues and taxpayer compliance.

Applicant Eligibility: Any agency responsible for tax administration within any of the 50 States, the District of Columbia, certain U.S. Territories, Regional Income Tax Agencies and municipalities with populations in excess of 250,000 that impose taxes on income or wages and with which the Commissioner of Internal Revenue has entered into a disclosure agreement with safeguard and confidentiality protections.

Beneficiary Eligibility: State Governments, U.S. Territories, Regional Income Tax Agencies and Municipal Governments.

Award Range/Average: Not Available.

HQ: 15 New Sudbury Street, JFK Room 825, Boston, MA 02138
Phone: 617-316-2254 | Email: william.t.crowley@irs.gov
http://www.irs.gov

USDA10.514 | EXPANDED FOOD AND NUTRITION EDUCATION PROGRAM
"EFNEP"

Award: Formula Grants; Project Grants

Purpose: The purpose of this funding is to assist socially disadvantaged families. The EFNEP assists by providing awareness of diet quality and physical activity, food resource management, food safety, and food security.

Applicant Eligibility: Only Auburn University; Alabama A & M University; Tuskegee University; University of Alaska; American Samoa Community College; University of Arizona; University of Arkansas; University of Arkansas - Pine Bluff; University of California; Central State University, Colorado State University; University of Connecticut; University of Delaware; Delaware State University; University of the District of Columbia; University of Florida; Florida A & M University; University of Georgia; Fort Valley State University; University of Guam; University of Hawaii; University of Idaho; University of Illinois; Purdue University; Iowa State University; Kansas State University; University of Kentucky; Kentucky State University; Louisiana State University; Southern University; University of Maine; University of Maryland (College Park); University of Maryland (Eastern Shore); University of Massachusetts; Michigan State University; College of Micronesia; University of Minnesota; Mississippi State University; Alcorn State University; University of Missouri; Lincoln University; Montana State University; University of Nebraska; University of Nevada; University of New Hampshire; Rutgers University; New Mexico State University; Cornell University; North Carolina State University; North Carolina A & T University; North Dakota State University; Northern Marianas College; Ohio State University; Central State University; Oklahoma State University; Langston University; Oregon State University; Pennsylvania State University; University of Puerto Rico; University of Rhode Island; Clemson University; South Carolina State University; South Dakota State

University; University of Tennessee; Tennessee State University; Texas A&M University; Prairie View A & M University; Utah State University; University of Vermont; University of the Virgin Islands; Virginia Polytechnic Institute and State University; Virginia State University; Washington State 7 University; West Virginia University; West Virginia State University; University of Wisconsin; and University of Wyoming may submit applications.

Beneficiary Eligibility: Same as Applicant Eligibility.

Award Range/Average: If minimum or maximum amounts of funding per competitive and/or capacity project grant, or cooperative agreement are established, these amounts will be announced in the annual Request for Application (RFA).The most current RFA is available via: https://nifa.usda.gov/program/expanded-food-and-nutrition-education-program-efnep. As an administrator of U.S. government support, NIFA works in partnership with grantees to ensure responsible stewardship of federal funds. Our grantees and partners are required to comply with all relevant rules and regulations. The following resources are provided to NIFA's partners and award recipients to support their adherence to federal regulations governing program performance:NIFA's primary (main) website:https://nifa.usda.gov/regulations-and-guidelinesThe following represent specific documents and direct links:POLICY GUIDENIFA's Federal Assistance Policy Guide describes agency policies and procedures.https://nifa.usda.gov/policy-guideCERTIFICATIONS AND REPRESENTATIONSCertifications and representations provided through the NIFA application process.https://nifa.usda.gov/certifications-and-representations

Funding: (Formula Grants) FY 17 $0.00; FY 18 est $0.00; FY 19 est $67,293,480.00

HQ: 1400 Independence Avenue SW, PO Box 2225, Washington, DC 20250-2225

Phone: 202-720-5004 | Email: hchipman@nifa.usda.gov

DOI15.682 | EXPERIENCED SERVICES

Award: Cooperative Agreements

Purpose: Helps to implement legislation that authorizes cooperative agreements with the eligible non-profit organizations that recruit and offer the services of professionals aged 55 and above who have the experience to support the USFWS mission.

Applicant Eligibility: Private, nonprofit Organizations designated by the Secretary of Labor under title V of the Older Americans Act of 1965, which may then recruit and provide enrollees age 55 or older who qualify for positions based on approved position descriptions provided by the contracting, Federal agency.

Beneficiary Eligibility: Individuals (Americans, age 55 and older) who qualify for temporary positions, as described in approved position descriptions provided by the contracting, Federal agency. These individuals may include Federal pension recipients.

Award Range/Average: This is a new program. The first year will be a pilot and will have a maximum of $300,000 total awarded for the year.

Funding: (Cooperative Agreements) FY 18 $0; FY 19 est $50,000.00; FY 20 est $250,000.00

HQ: 5275 Leesburg Pike, Falls Church, VA 22041

Phone: 703-358-2267 | Email: edith_thompson@fws.gov

DOI15.011 | EXPERIENCED WORKERS SUPPORT SERVICES ACTIVITIES
"Experienced Workers Program"

Award: Cooperative Agreements (discretionary Grants)

Purpose: To provide technical assistance and support to the NPS in the development and execution of natural and cultural resource conservation projects through experienced workers aged 55 and above.

Applicant Eligibility: This Program is limited to qualified non-profit Organizations subject to 26 USC 501 c (3) of the tax code, and must be designated by the Secretary of Labor under Title V of the Older Americans Act of 1965. Proof of establishment must be submitted with the application.

Beneficiary Eligibility: Private non-profit organizations that support career advancement and placement for individuals 55 years of age and older. Individuals 55 years of age and older.

Award Range/Average: Estimate that the range for FY 2020 will be: $20,000- $75,000 per funded award.

Funding: (Cooperative Agreements (Discretionary Grants)) FY 18 Actual Not Available; FY 19 est Estimate Not Available; FY 20 est $3,000,000.00

HQ: 1849 C Street NW, Room 2357, Washington, DC 20240

Phone: 202-513-7146 | Email: george_mcdonald@nps.gov

Programs Administered by Federal Headquarters

NASA43.003 | EXPLORATION
Award: Cooperative Agreements; Project Grants; Direct Payments for Specified Use; Use of Property, Facilities, and Equipment; Provision of Specialized Services; Dissemination of Technical Information; Training
Purpose: Provides basic research, educational outreach, or training opportunities in the area of space exploration.
Applicant Eligibility: Basic Research, educational Outreach, or Training Opportunities in the area of space exploration. Review funding opportunity announcement for additional information.
Beneficiary Eligibility: Review funding opportunity announcement for additional information.
Funding: (Salaries and Expenses) FY 18 $56,064,179.61; FY 19 est $38,583,420.86; FY 20 est Estimate Not Available
HQ: 300 E Street SW, Washington, DC 20546
 Phone: 202-358-2211 | Email: dtomko@nasa.gov
 http://www.nasa.gov

EXIM31.007 | EXPORT-LOAN GUARANTEE/INSURED LOANS
Award: Direct Loans; Guaranteed/insured Loans
Purpose: To support U.S. exports by providing export financing through its loan, guarantee and insurance programs in cases where the private sector is unable or unwilling to provide financing or when such support is necessary to level the playing field due to financing provided by foreign governments to their exporters that compete with U.S. exporters.
Applicant Eligibility: N/A
Beneficiary Eligibility: N/A
Award Range/Average: There is no minimum or maximum transaction size. Representative range is $25,000 to $500,000,000.
Funding: (Guaranteed/Insured Loans) FY 08 $14,398,900,000.00; FY 09 est $17,500,000,000.00; FY 10 est $16,100,000,000.00
HQ: 811 Vermont Avenue NW, Washington, DC 20571
 Phone: 800-565-3946
 http://www.exim.gov

DOS19.901 | EXPORT CONTROL AND RELATED BORDER SECURITY "EXBS"
Award: Cooperative Agreements; Project Grants
Purpose: Assists existing and potential proliferation source, transit, and transshipment countries with strengthening their strategic trade controls and border security.
Applicant Eligibility: Please see specific announcement in www.grants.gov.
Beneficiary Eligibility: Same as Applicant Eligibility.
Award Range/Average: Historically, ISN/ECC has awarded approximately $2 million in EXBS assistance awards per fiscal year. Typical award approx $85,000 See specific announcement at www.grants.gov
HQ: 2100 C Street NW, Washington, DC 20520
 Phone: 202-647-1228 | Email: mcclellanmc@state.gov
 http://www.state.gov/t/isn/ecc/index.htm

USDA10.610 | EXPORT GUARANTEE PROGRAM "The GSM-102 Program"
Award: Guaranteed/insured Loans
Purpose: The U.S. Department of Agriculture's Export Credit Guarantee Program encourages financing for commercial exports of U.S. agricultural products. It reduces financial risk. USDA's Foreign Agricultural Service administers the credit guarantees.
Applicant Eligibility: Export Credit guarantee Program (GSM-102) provides credit guarantees to encourage financing of commercial exports of U.S. agricultural products, while providing competitive credit terms to buyers. By reducing financial risk to lenders, credit guarantees encourage exports to buyers in countries, mainly developing countries, that have sufficient financial strength to have foreign exchange available for scheduled payments. This Program provides guarantees to lenders.
Beneficiary Eligibility: Exporters or the exporters assignee are the direct beneficiaries and must meet the applicant eligibility requirements. Interested parties, including U.S. exporters, foreign buyers, banks, may request that the CCC establish a GSM-102 program for a country or region. Prior to announcing the availability of guarantees, the CCC evaluates the ability of each country and foreign bank to service CCC guaranteed debt.
Funding: (Guaranteed/Insured Loans) FY 17 $1,578,800,312.00; FY 18 est $1,900,000,000.00; FY 19 est $5,500,000,000.00

HQ: 1400 independence Avenue SW, PO Box 1025, Washington, DC 20050
Phone: 202-720-9389 | Email: brad.hoppe@fas.usda.gov
http://www.fas.usda.gov/programs/export-credit-guarantee-program-gsm-102

DOC11.150 | EXPORT LICENSING SERVICE AND INFORMATION
"Export Control Exporter Assistance Program"

Award: Advisory Services and Counseling
Purpose: To respond to the needs of the exporting community and help exporters to understand the Export Administration Regulations with export license and data for shipments to foreign countries.
Applicant Eligibility: Any person, firm, Organization, or branch of government needing information or assistance on export control matters.
Beneficiary Eligibility: Same as Applicant Eligibility.
Funding: (Salary or Expense) FY 07 $1,753,000.00; FY 08 Estimate Not Available FY 09 Estimate Not Available
HQ: Department of Commerce Office of Exporter Services Outreach and Educational Services Division, Room 1099, Washington, DC 20230
Phone: 202-482-4811
http://www.bis.doc.gov

HHS93.662 | EXTRAMURAL RESEARCH FACILITIES RESTORATION PROGRAM: HURRICANES HARVEY, MARIA, AND IRMA-CONSTRUCTION

Award: Project Grants
Purpose: The program will fund disaster response and recovery, and other expenses directly related to Hurricane Harvey, Hurricane Irma, or Hurricane Maria, which are in the FEMA-declared major disaster states, relevant to supporting the recovery of losses at non-Federal biomedical or behavioral research facilities.
Applicant Eligibility: Applicants will be required to attest (at time of application) that funds requested will not be used for costs that are reimbursed by the Federal Emergency Management Agency, under a contract for insurance, or by self-insurance. Terms and Conditions of the award will stipulate that the grantee must reimburse HHS for any costs that are subsequently covered by the Federal Emergency Management Agency, under a contract for insurance, or by self-insurance. Definition: Self-Insurance is a formal plan, pursuant to law or regulation, in which amounts are set aside in a fund to cover losses of specified types and amounts, typically by a commercial insurance company. Appropriated funds are precluded from expenses that are or can be reimbursed by the formal self-insurance plan.
Beneficiary Eligibility: See individual Funding Opportunity Announcements (FOAs) for specific information.
Award Range/Average: See individual Funding Opportunity Announcements (FOAs) for specific information.
Funding: (Project Grants) FY 17 Actual Not Available; FY 18 est $25,000,000.00; FY 19 est $0.00
HQ: Bethesda, MD 20892
http://www.nih.gov

HHS93.853 | EXTRAMURAL RESEARCH PROGRAMS IN THE NEUROSCIENCES AND NEUROLOGICAL DISORDERS

Award: Project Grants
Purpose: To support extramural research funded by the National Institute of Neurological Disorders and Stroke (NINDS) including basic research that explores the fundamental structure and function of the brain and the nervous system; research to understand the causes and origins of pathological conditions of the nervous system with the goal of preventing these disorders.
Applicant Eligibility: Research Grants: Any public, private, nonprofit, or for-profit institution is eligible to apply. For-profit Institutions are not eligible for Institutional National Research Service Awards but are eligible for Individual NRSAs. All proposals are reviewed for scientific merit, for evaluation of the qualifications of the investigators, for adequacy of the research environment, and for significance of the problem. Approved proposals compete for available funds. All Career Development Program awardees, with the exception of awardees of the Pathway to Independence Award (K99/R00), must be citizens or have been admitted to the United States for permanent residence. Candidates must be nominated for the Program by a nonfederal public or private nonprofit institution located in the United States, its possessions or territories. To be eligible, postdoctoral NRSA trainees or fellows must have a professional or scientific degree (M.D., Ph.D., D.D.S., D.O., D.V.M., Sc.D., D.Eng., or equivalent domestic or foreign degree). SBIR grants can be awarded only to domestic small businesses

Programs Administered by Federal Headquarters

(entities that are independently owned and operated for profit, are not dominant in the field in which research is proposed, and have no more than 500 employees). Primary employment (more than one-half time) of the principal investigator must be with the small business at the time of award and during the conduct of the proposed project. In both Phase I and Phase II, the entire research must be performed in the United States. To be eligible for funding, a grant application must be approved for scientific merit and Program relevance by a scientific review group and a national advisory council. STTR grants can be awarded only to domestic small business concerns (entities that are independently owned and operated for profit, are not dominant in the field in which research is proposed and have no more than 500 employees) which "partner" with a research institution in cooperative research and development. At least 40 percent of the project is to be performed by the small business concern and at least 30 percent by the research institution. In both Phase I and Phase II, the research must be performed in the U.S. and its possessions. To be eligible for funding, a grant application must be approved for scientific merit and Program relevance by a scientific review group and a national advisory council.

Beneficiary Eligibility: Health professionals, graduate students, health professional students, scientists, and researchers.

Award Range/Average: Research grants: $9,219 to $6,297,501; $401,755. National Research Service Awards: Institutional $46,245 to $470,547; $209,407. Individual: $5,467 to $66,354; $42,241. SBIR/STTR: Phase 1 not to exceed $150,000; Phase II not to exceed $1,000,000; however with appropriate justification, budget caps for Phase I and Phase II are $225,000 and $1,500,00 respectively

Funding: (Project Grants (Contracts)) FY 18 $95,906,371.00; FY 19 est $109,557,690.00; FY 20 est $110,051,426.00; (Project Grants) FY 18 $1,392,406,713.00; FY 19 est $1,589,962,001.00; FY 20 est $1,387,118,098.00

HQ: 6001 Executive Boulevard, Suite 3309, Rockville, MD 20892

Phone: 301-496-9248 | Email: finkelsr@nih.gov

http://www.ninds.nih.gov

HHS93.663 | EXTRAMURAL RESEARCH RESTORATION PROGRAM: HURRICANES HARVEY, MARIA, AND IRMA-NON-CONSTRUCTION

Award: Project Grants

Purpose: The program will fund disaster response and recovery, and other expenses directly related to Hurricane Harvey, Hurricane Irma, or Hurricane Maria, which are in the FEMA-declared major disaster states, relevant to supporting the recovery of losses at non-Federal biomedical or behavioral research facilities.

Applicant Eligibility: Applicants will be required to attest (at time of application) that funds requested will not be used for costs that are reimbursed by the Federal Emergency Management Agency, under a contract for insurance, or by self-insurance. Terms and Conditions of the award will stipulate that the grantee must reimburse HHS for any costs that are subsequently covered by the Federal Emergency Management Agency, under a contract for insurance, or by self-insurance. Definition: Self-Insurance is a formal plan, pursuant to law or regulation, in which amounts are set aside in a fund to cover losses of specified types and amounts, typically by a commercial insurance company. Appropriated funds are precluded from expenses that are or can be reimbursed by the formal self-insurance plan.

Beneficiary Eligibility: Same as Applicant Eligibility.

Award Range/Average: See individual Funding Opportunity Announcements (FOAs) for specific information.

Funding: (Project Grants) FY 17 Actual Not Available; FY 18 est $25,000,000.00; FY 19 est $0.00

HQ: Bethesda, MD 20892

USDA10.613 | FACULTY EXCHANGE PROGRAM

Award: Project Grants; Direct Payments for Specified Use

Purpose: The Faculty Exchange Program promotes agricultural education and research in developing countries by providing training programs.

Applicant Eligibility: The Faculty Exchange Program solicits proposals from public universities and state cooperative Institutions in the United States.

Beneficiary Eligibility: Technical assistance and training provided through these agreements benefit foreign universities and related agricultural institutions in their countries.

Award Range/Average: Approximately $30000 - $45000 per participant.

Funding: (Direct Payments for Specified Use) FY 18 $686,129.00; FY 19 est $494,684.00; FY 20 est $500,000.00

HQ: 1400 Independence Avenue SW, Washington, DC 20250-1031

Phone: 202-720-4228 | Email: nicola.sakhleh@usda.gov

https://www.fas.usda.gov/programs/faculty-exchange-program

HUD14.401 | FAIR HOUSING ASSISTANCE PROGRAM STATE AND LOCAL
"FHAP"

Award: Project Grants

Purpose: To assist State and local fair housing enforcement agencies for complaint processing, training, technical assistance, education and outreach, data and information systems, and other activities.

Applicant Eligibility: Eligible applicants include State and local government fair housing enforcement agencies administering fair housing laws that have been certified by HUD as providing substantially equivalent rights and remedies as those provided by the Fair Housing Act and which have executed formal written Agreements with HUD to process housing discrimination complaints. In determining eligibility, HUD may also take into consideration whether a jurisdiction is already served by a FHAP agency.

Beneficiary Eligibility: Any person or group of persons aggrieved by a discriminatory housing practice because of race, color, religion, sex, disability, familial status or national origin. Also includes organizations (e.g. fair housing groups) that have suffered an injury as a result of a discriminatory housing practice.

Award Range/Average: Funding is provided for capacity building, complaint processing, training, and administrative costs. Funding may also be available for partnership efforts and special enforcement efforts.

Funding: (Formula Grants) FY 16 $19,735,652.00; FY 17 est $24,300,000.00; FY 18 est $24,300,000.00

HQ: 451 7th Street SW, Washington, DC 20410

Phone: 202-402-2126 | Email: joseph.a.pelletier@hud.gov

http://www.hud.gov/offices/fheo/partners/fhap/index.cfm

HUD14.408 | FAIR HOUSING INITIATIVES PROGRAM
"FHIP"

Award: Cooperative Agreements

Purpose: To educate the public about fair housing rights under the Fair Housing Act; 42 U.S.C. 3601-3619 or State or local laws.

Applicant Eligibility: State and local government agencies, public or private nonprofit Organizations or Institutions - and other public or private entities that are formulating or carrying out Programs to prevent or eliminate discriminatory housing practices. Applicants for funding of testing activities must have at least one year of experience in complaint intake, complaint investigation, testing for fair housing violations, and enforcement of meritorious claims. Applicants for funding of testing activities must certify that they will not solicit funds from or seek to provide services or products for compensation to any person or Organization which has been the subject of testing by the applicant for a 12-month period following a test. Fair housing enforcement Organizations and nonprofit groups organizing to build their capacity to provide fair housing enforcement are also eligible applicants. Additionally eligibility requirements are outlined in the NOFA.

Beneficiary Eligibility: Individual/Family, Minority group, Specialized group (e.g. health professionals, students, veterans). Any person or group of persons aggrieved by discriminatory housing practices because of race, color, religion, sex, disability, familial status or national origin. Also, any person or group of persons, including landlords and real estate agents, to prevent discriminatory housing practices because of race, color, religion, sex, disability, familial status or national origin.

Award Range/Average: $125,000- $1,000,000

Funding: (Project Grants) FY 17 $16,013,813.00; FY 18 est $62,480,816.00; FY 19 est $35,300,000.00

HQ: 451 7th Street SW, Room 5222, Washington, DC 20410

Phone: 202-402-7054 | Email: paula.stone@hud.gov

http://www.hud.gov/offices/fheo/partners/fhip/fhip.cfm

HUD14.417 | FAIR HOUSING ORGANIZATION INITIATIVES
"FHIP FHOI"

Award: Project Grants

Purpose: To develop, implement, carry out, or coordinate programs and/or activities that provide enforcement of fair housing rights under the Fair Housing Act; (42 U.S.C. 3601-3619) or State or local laws that provide substantially equivalent rights and remedies for alleged discriminatory housing practices.

Applicant Eligibility: Qualified Fair Housing Enforcement Organizations or Fair Housing Enforcement Organizations and nonprofit groups organizing to build their capacity to provide fair housing enforcement.

Beneficiary Eligibility: Any person or group of persons aggrieved by discriminatory housing practices because of race, color, religion, sex disability familial status or national origin. Also, any person or group of persons, including landlords or real estate agents, to prevent discriminatory housing practices because of race, color, religion, sex, disability, familial status or national origin.

Award Range/Average: $125,000- $1,000,000

Funding: (Project Grants) FY 17 $900,000.00; FY 18 est $500,000.00; FY 19 est $500,000.00

HQ: 451 7th Street SW, Room 5222, Washington, DC 20410

    Phone: 202-402-7054 | Email: paula.stone@hud.gov

    http://www.hud.gov/office/fheo/partners.FHIP/fhip.cfm

HHS93.910 | FAMILY AND COMMUNITY VIOLENCE PREVENTION PROGRAM

Award: Cooperative Agreements

Purpose: Provides support interventions to employ violence prevention and crime reduction models and a public health approach to provide critical life skills development, academic skills, career advisement, and mentoring.

Applicant Eligibility: State and local Governments or their Bona Fide Agents (this includes the District of Columbia, the Commonwealth of Puerto Rico, the Virgin Islands, the Commonwealth of the Northern Mariana Islands, American Samoa, Guam, the Federated States of Micronesia, the Republic of the Marshall Islands, and the Republic of Palau); Nonprofit with 501(c)(3) IRS status (other than institution of higher education); Nonprofit without 501(c)(3) IRS status (other than institution of higher education); For-profit Organizations (other than small business); for profit Organizations must agree to forgo any profit or management fee; Small, minority, and women-owned business; universities; Colleges; Research Institutions; Hospitals; Community-based Organizations; Faith-based Organizations; Federally recognized or state-recognized American Indian/Alaska Native Tribal Governments; American Indian/Alaska Native tribally designated Organizations; Alaska Native health Organizations; Urban Indian health Organizations; Tribal epidemiology centers; Political subdivisions of states (in consultation with states).

Beneficiary Eligibility: Target populations: Alaskan Natives; American Indians; Asians; Blacks/African Americans; Hispanics/ Latinos; Native Hawaiians and other Pacific Islanders; or subgroups of these populations; economically or environmentally disadvantaged populations; limited English populations. However, services may not be denied to otherwise eligible individuals based on race or ethnicity.

Award Range/Average: FY 2017 Awards range from $370,000 to $425,000. FY2018 Awards range from $370,000 to $425,000 FY2019 Proposed Awards range from $370,000 to $425,000

Funding: (Cooperative Agreements) FY 16 $4,746,036.00; FY 17 est $4,103,509.00; FY 18 est $4,103,509.00

HQ: 1101 Wootton Parkway, Suite 550 Tower Building, Rockville, MD 20852

    Phone: 240-453-8822 | Email: eric.west@hhs.gov

    http://www.minorityhealth.hhs.gov

HHS93.605 | FAMILY CONNECTION GRANTS

Award: Project Grants

Purpose: Provides matching grants to state, local or tribal child welfare agencies, institutions of higher education, and private nonprofit organizations that have experience in working with foster children or children in kinship care arrangements for the purpose of helping children who are in, or at risk of entering, foster care to reconnect with family members.

Applicant Eligibility: State, local or tribal child welfare agencies, Institutions of higher education, and private nonprofit Organizations that have experience in working with foster children or children in kinship care arrangements.

Beneficiary Eligibility: Public or private nonprofit agencies or organizations or tribal child welfare agencies, or institutions of higher education working with foster children, children in kinship care arrangements or children at risk of entering foster care, that help the children reconnect with family members.

Award Range/Average: For FY 2017, the range of grants were from $446,667 to $608,329 with an average of $525,028.

HQ: 330 C Street SW, Room 3503, Washington, DC 20201

    Phone: 202-205-8172 | Email: jan.shafer@acf.hhs.gov

    http://www.acf.hhs.gov/programs/cb

HHS93.260 | FAMILY PLANNING PERSONNEL TRAINING
"Family Planning Training"

Award: Project Grants

Purpose: Provides job specific training for personnel to improve the delivery of family planning services.

Applicant Eligibility: Any public entity (including city, county, local, regional, or State government) or nonprofit private entity located in a State (including the District of Columbia, Puerto Rico, the Commonwealth of the Northern Mariana Islands,

Guam, American Samoa, the Virgin Islands, the Federated States of Micronesia, the Republic of the Marshall Islands and the Republic of Palau) is eligible to apply for a grant under this Program. Faith based Organizations are eligible to apply.

Beneficiary Eligibility: Personnel delivering family planning services in Title X projects.

Award Range/Average: FY17 $800,000- $4,000,000 FY18 $895,000- $3,500,000 FY19 $900,000- $4,000,000

Funding: (Project Grants) FY 17 $10,682,950.00; FY 18 est $4,392,000.00; FY 19 est Estimate Not Available; Past Fiscal Year (2017) 2 awards, totaling $4,800,000 Current Fiscal Year (2018) 2 awards, totaling $4,395,000 Budget Fiscal Year (2019) 2 awards, totaling $4,900,000

HQ: Office of Grants Management 1101 Wootton Parkway, Suite 550 Tower Building, Rockville, MD 20852

   Phone: 240-453-8822 | Email: eric.west@hhs.gov

   http://www.hhs.gov/opa

HHS93.974 | FAMILY PLANNING SERVICE DELIVERY IMPROVEMENT RESEARCH GRANTS
"Family Planning Service Delivery Improvement"

Award: Project Grants

Purpose: The grants help develop research studies of projects under family planning service delivery improvement that falls under Title X of Section 1001 of the Public Health Service Act.

Applicant Eligibility: Any public entity (city, county, local, regional, or State government) or private nonprofit entity located in a State (including the District of Columbia, Puerto Rico, the Commonwealth of the Northern Marianas Islands, Guam, American Samoa, the Virgin Islands, the Federated States of Micronesia, the Republic of Marshall Islands and the Republic of Palau) is eligible to apply for a grant under this Program. Faith based Organizations are eligible to apply.

Beneficiary Eligibility: All levels of government and nonprofit entities responsible for the efficient and effective delivery of family planning services; providers and recipients of family planning services; and the general public.

Award Range/Average: FY17 $0 FY18 $0 FY19 $250,000 - $750,000

Funding: (Project Grants) FY 16 $1,461,000.00; FY 17 est $1,300,000.00; FY 18 Estimate Not Available

HQ: 1101 Wootton Parkway, Suite 550 Tower Building, Rockville, MD 20852

   Phone: 240-453-8822 | Email: eric.west@hhs.gov

   http://www.hhs.gov/opa

HHS93.217 | FAMILY PLANNING SERVICES

Award: Project Grants

Purpose: To establish and operate voluntary family planning services projects, which shall provide family planning services to all persons desiring such services, with priority for services to persons from low-income families.

Applicant Eligibility: Any public (including city, county, local, regional, or State government) entity or nonprofit private entity located in a State (including the District of Columbia, Puerto Rico, Guam, the Commonwealth of the Northern Mariana Islands, American Samoa, the Virgin Islands, the Federated States of Micronesia, the Republic of Marshall Islands and the Republic of Palau) is eligible to apply for a grant. Faith based Organizations are eligible to apply.

Beneficiary Eligibility: Persons who desire family planning services and who would not otherwise have access to them. Priority to be given to persons from low-income families. Individuals from other than low-income families will be charged a fee in accordance with an established fee schedule although inability to pay must not be a deterrent to services.

Award Range/Average: FY17 $150,000- $20,000,000 FY18 $150,000- $20,000,000 FY19 $150,000- $20,000,000

Funding: (Project Grants) FY 17 $255,627,000.00; FY 18 est $257,002,000.00; FY 19 Estimate Not Available

HQ: 1101 Wootton Parkway, Suite 550 Tower Building, Rockville, MD 20852

   Phone: 240-453-8822 | Email: eric.west@hhs.gov

   http://www.hhs.gov/opa

HUD14.896 | FAMILY SELF-SUFFICIENCY PROGRAM
"FSS"

Award: Project Grants

Purpose: To promote the development of local strategies to enable participating families to increase earned income and financial literacy, reduce or eliminate the need for welfare assistance, and make progress toward economic independence and self-sufficiency.

Programs Administered by Federal Headquarters

Applicant Eligibility: Eligible applicants are public housing agencies (PHAs) and Tribes /Tribally Designated Housing Entities (TDHEs).

Beneficiary Eligibility: Individuals and families who are participants in the Housing Choice Voucher program or Public Housing program are eligible to receive benefits from the FSS program.

Award Range/Average: $13,000 - $1,300,000; Average $40,000- $69,000

Funding: (Project Grants) FY 17 $149,921,000.00; FY 18 est $75,000,000.00; FY 19 est $75,000,000.00

HQ: 451 7th Street SW, Washington, DC 20410

    Phone: 202-402-2341 | Email: anice.s.chenault@hud.gov

    http://portal.hud.gov/hudportal/hud?src=/program_offices/public_indian_housing/programs/hcv/fss

HHS93.077 | FAMILY SMOKING PREVENTION AND TOBACCO CONTROL ACT REGULATORY RESEARCH
"NIH-FDA Tobacco Control Regulatory Research"

Award: Cooperative Agreements; Project Grants; Training

Purpose: To provide the authority to regulate tobacco product manufacturing, distribution and marketing.

Applicant Eligibility: Applicants should review the eligibility information in the individual funding opportunity announcements issued under this CFDA.

Beneficiary Eligibility: This Tobacco Control Regulatory Research Program will support research aimed at providing guidance and evidence to develop regulation for tobacco product manufacturing, distribution and marketing. The general public will ultimately benefit.

Funding: (Project Grants) FY 18 $79,945,805.00; FY 19 est $80,000,000.00; FY 20 est $85,590,000.00

HQ: 6100 Executive Boulevard Room 3B01, PO Box 7530, Bethesda, MD 20892-7530

    Phone: 301-451-8681

    http://prevention.nih.gov/tobacco-regulatory-science-program

HHS93.560 | FAMILY SUPPORT PAYMENTS TO STATES ASSISTANCE PAYMENTS
"Adult Programs in the Territories"

Award: Formula Grants

Purpose: Provides aid to the aged, blind, and the permanently and totally disabled in Guam, Puerto Rico, and the Virgin Islands.

Applicant Eligibility: Agencies must operate under Department of Health and Human Services (HHS) approved plans and agreements, which must comply with all Federal statutory and regulatory requirements governing these Programs.

Beneficiary Eligibility: The beneficiary must be needy - i.e., meet specific income and resource requirements. In addition, the individual must be at least age 65 to receive assistance for the aged; must be determined blind to receive aid to the blind; or must be at least 18 years of age and totally disabled to receive aid to the permanently and totally disabled. These programs also have specific unearned and earned income disregards that are applied in determining the amount of assistance payable.

Award Range/Average: This funding range is $716,830 to $31,046,869 with an average of $10,998,552.

Funding: (Formula Grants) FY 18 $32,995,657.00; FY 19 est $33,000,000.00; FY 20 est $33,000,000.00

HQ: Office of Family Assistance Department of Health and Human Services 330 C Street SW, Washington, DC 20201

    Phone: 202-401-9275 | Email: susan.golonka@acf.hhs.gov

    http://www.acf.hhs.gov/programs/ofa

HHS93.504 | FAMILY TO FAMILY HEALTH INFORMATION CENTERS
"F2F HICs"

Award: Project Grants

Purpose: To develop and support Family to Family Health Information Centers.

Applicant Eligibility: Eligible applicants include public and private entities, including an Indian tribe or tribal Organization (as those terms are defined at 25 U.S.C. 450b), faith-based Organizations, and community-based Organizations. The law limits the site of eligible Organizations to the 50 States and the District of Columbia. Although Tribes and tribal Organizations may apply, they must meet all applicable requirements, including targeting of all children and youth with special healthcare needs (CYSHCN) across the State for services. Applicants must have experience related to the purpose of the Program, the effort must be family-staffed/run, and the effort must have a focus on health for CYSHCN (as defined by the MCH Bureau). For example, if an applicant is a family Organization with a history of funding that is condition-specific or related to education, mental health or developmental disabilities, as with any applicant, evidence of health for the broad CYSHCN population must be evident in their application. Applicants MUST demonstrate that they have EXISTING and effective fiduciary, administrative and management systems. If a different fiduciary agency is needed, such as a University, activities must still be family-staffed/run for the entire grant period.

Beneficiary Eligibility: Projects will benefit (1) public or private agencies, organizations and institutions engaged in activities for CYSHCN; (2) family members and children who receive services through the program; and (3) professionals and trainees who provide services to CYSHCN.

Award Range/Average: FY18 $24,187- $96,750. Average award $95,520 FY 19 $96,750. Average award $96,750 FY 20 $96,750. Average award $96,750

Funding: (Project Grants) FY 18 $5,635,687.00; FY 19 est $5,708,250.00; FY 20 est $5,708,250.00

HQ: Maternal and Child Health Bureau Health Resources and Services Administration U.S. Department of Health and Human Services 5600 Fishers Lane, Room 18W09-A, Rockville, MD 20857

 Phone: 301-443-3740 | Email: ymazloomdoost@hrsa.gov

 http://www.mchb.hrsa.gov

HUD14.880 | FAMILY UNIFICATION PROGRAM (FUP)

Award: Direct Payments for Specified Use

Purpose: To aid families without adequate housing and youths ages 18-21 years old who left foster care at age 16 or older and lack adequate housing.

Applicant Eligibility: Applicants are limited to public housing agencies. A public housing agency (PHA) is defined as any State, county, municipality or other governmental entity or public body (or agency or instrumentality thereof) which is authorized to engage in or assist in the development or operation of housing for very low income families; and, a consortium of PHAs; any other nonprofit entity that was administering a Section 8 tenant-based Program on October 21, 1998; or, for an area outside the jurisdiction of a PHA administering a voucher Program, a private nonprofit entity or a governmental entity or public body that would otherwise lack jurisdiction to administer the Program in such area.

Beneficiary Eligibility: Families and youths that are income eligible under the HCV program regulations at 24 CFR 982.201 may receive a voucher awarded under the FUP. Families and youths must be referred to the PHA from the local Child Welfare Agency (CWA).

Award Range/Average: Serving 39 PHA's

Funding: (Direct Payments for Specified Use) FY 17 $3,450,499,867.00; FY 18 est $10,000,000.00; FY 19 est $3,910,174,977.00

HQ: 451 7th Street SW, Room 4210, Washington, DC 20410

 Phone: 202-708-0477 | Email: laure.rawson@hud.gov

 https://www.hud.gov/program_offices/public_indian_housing

HHS93.592 | FAMILY VIOLENCE PREVENTION AND SERVICES/DISCRETIONARY
"Family Violence Prevention and Services Act Discretionary Grants"

Award: Cooperative Agreements

Purpose: Funds a wide range of discretionary activities for the purpose of providing resource information, training and technical assistance to improve the capacity of individuals, organizations, government entities, and communities to prevent family violence, domestic violence, and dating violence and to provide effective intervention services.

Applicant Eligibility: Depending on the purpose of the project and the statutory requirements, an applicant may be a nonprofit private Organization, tribal Organization, federally-recognized Indian tribe, Native Hawaiian Organization, local public agency, institution of higher education, private Organization, Alaska Native Village, or nonprofit Alaska Native Regional Corporation.

Beneficiary Eligibility: These discretionary grants and contracts will benefit victims of family violence, domestic violence, dating violence, and their dependents, families, other interested persons, the general public, and communities and government entities.

Award Range/Average: FY 2019 National Hotline: $10,250,000 Discretionary National Resource Centers and Training and Technical Assistance Centers: $450,000 - $1,400,000 Specialized Services for Abused Parents and Their Children: $538,645

Funding: (Cooperative Agreements (Discretionary Grants)) FY 18 $26,860,000.00; FY 19 est $29,373,689.00; FY 20 est $29,373,689.00

HQ: 330 C Street SW, Suite 3622C, Washington, DC 20024

Programs Administered by Federal Headquarters

Phone: 202-690-6898 | Email: kenya.fairley@acf.hhs.gov
http://www.acf.hhs.gov/programs/fysb/programs/family-violence-prevention-services

HHS93.671 | FAMILY VIOLENCE PREVENTION AND SERVICES/DOMESTIC VIOLENCE SHELTER AND SUPPORTIVE SERVICES
"Family Violence Prevention and Services Act Formula Grants for States and Native American Tribes (including Alaska Native Villages) and Tribal Organizations"

Award: Formula Grants

Purpose: Assists States and Native American Tribes and Tribal Organizations in efforts to increase public awareness about, and primary and secondary prevention of family violence, domestic violence, and dating violence; and assist States and Tribes in efforts to provide immediate shelter and supportive services for victims of family violence, domestic violence, or dating violence, and their dependents.

Applicant Eligibility: Eligible applicants for the State Grants are the 50 States, the District of Columbia, the Commonwealth of Puerto Rico, and the U.S. territories of Guam, American Samoa, the United States Virgin Islands, and the Commonwealth of the Northern Mariana Islands. Eligible applicants for the Tribal Grants are the federally recognized Indian Tribes (including Alaska Native Villages), or a tribal Organization or nonprofit private Organization authorized by an Indian Tribe.

Beneficiary Eligibility: This program will benefit victims of family violence, domestic violence, and dating violence, and their dependents.

Award Range/Average: FY 2016 States: $727,182 - $8,967,078 Territories: $126,875 Indian Tribes: $17,691 - $1,592,236 FY2017 States: $727,674 - $8,999,499 Territories: $127,215 Indian Tribes: $17,600 - $1,590,000

Funding: (Formula Grants) FY 18 $124,000,000.00; FY 19 est $126,360,472.00; FY 20 est $126,360,472.00

HQ: 330 C Street SW, Suite 3620C, Washington, DC 20201

Phone: 202-205-7746 | Email: rebecca.odor@acf.hhs.gov
http://www.acf.hhs.gov/programs/fysb/programs/family-violence-prevention-services

HHS93.591 | FAMILY VIOLENCE PREVENTION AND SERVICES/STATE DOMESTIC VIOLENCE COALITIONS
"Family Violence Prevention and Services Act Grants to State Domestic Violence Coalitions"

Award: Formula Grants

Purpose: Provides funding for State Domestic Violence Coalitions to confirm the federal commitment to reducing domestic violence.

Applicant Eligibility: To be eligible for a grant under Section 10411, an entity shall be a statewide nongovernmental nonprofit private domestic violence Organization that has a membership that includes a majority of the primary-purpose domestic violence service providers in the State; has board membership that is representative of primary-purpose domestic violence service providers, and which may include representatives of the communities in which the services are being provided in the State; has as its purpose to provide education, support, and technical assistance to such service providers to enable the providers to establish and maintain shelter and supportive services for victims of domestic violence and their dependents; and serves as an information clearinghouse, primary point of contact, and resource center on domestic violence for the State and supports the development of policies, protocols, and procedures to enhance domestic violence intervention and prevention in the State.

Beneficiary Eligibility: This program will benefit youth and adult victims of family violence, domestic violence, dating violence, their children and other dependents, their families, other persons affected by such violence including friends, relatives, and the general public. The program will also benefit communities, including the State and business and nonprofit sectors.

Award Range/Average: The estimated award amount for each State and Territorial Domestic Violence Coalition for FY 2018 is $265,625.

Funding: (Formula Grants) FY 18 $14,875,000.00; FY 19 est $151,700,590.00; FY 20 est $15,170,059.00

HQ: 330 C Street SW, Suite 3620C, Washington, DC 20201

Phone: 202-205-7746 | Email: rebecca.odor@acf.hhs.gov
http://www.acf.hhs.gov/programs/fysb/programs/family-violence-prevention-services

USDA10.124 | FARM-TO-FLEET FEEDSTOCK PROGRAM BIOFUEL PRODUCTION INCENTIVE
"BFP"

Award: Direct Loans
Purpose: To produce advanced biofuels that meet military requirements at a competitive cost with petroleum and provide ready-to-market access to geographically diverse places. It helps the federal government to collaborate with the sector to make targeted investments to attain the necessary manufacturing capability needed for a robust national advanced biofuel sector.
Applicant Eligibility: The loans are awarded by the government to the Fuel Industry.
Beneficiary Eligibility: N/A
Award Range/Average: The loans awarded are based on invoices received.
Funding: (Direct Loans) FY 17 $47,927,461.00; FY 18 est $17,786,639.00; FY 19 est Estimate Not Available
HQ: 1400 Independence Avenue SW, Room 4975, Washington, DC 20250
    Phone: 202-720-4053 | Email: kelly.novak@wdc.usda.gov
    https://www.fsa.gov

USDA10.525 | FARM AND RANCH STRESS ASSISTANCE NETWORK COMPETITIVE GRANTS PROGRAM
"FRSAN"

Award: Project Grants
Purpose: Creates a network to connect farmers involved in farming or ranching to stress on assistance programs.
Applicant Eligibility: Applications may only be submitted by a collaborative state; tribal; local or regionally-based network, or partnership of qualified public and/or private entities, as determined by the Secretary. These collaborations may include the following entities: Indian Tribes (as defined in section 4 of the Indian Self-Determination and education Assistance Act (25 U.S.C. 5304)); State departments of agriculture, State cooperative extension services; and nongovernmental Organizations (NGOs).
Beneficiary Eligibility: Same as Applicant Eligibility.
Award Range/Average: If minimum or maximum amounts of funding per competitive and/or capacity project grant, or cooperative agreement are established, these amounts will be announced in the annual Request for Applications (RFA). The most current RFA is available via: https://www.nifa.usda.gov/funding-opportunity/farm-and-ranch-stress-assistance-network
Funding: (Project Grants) FY 18 $0; FY 19 est $1,920,000.00; FY 20 est $0
HQ: 1400 Independence Avenue SW, Room 4434, Washington, DC 20250
    Phone: 202-690-3468 | Email: belrod@nifa.usda.gov
    https://www.nifa.usda.gov/funding-opportunity/farm-and-ranch-stress-assistance-network

USDA10.319 | FARM BUSINESS MANAGEMENT AND BENCHMARKING COMPETITIVE GRANTS PROGRAM
"FBMB"

Award: Project Grants
Purpose: To initiate a research program and compensate for improving farm management and farm financial management.
Applicant Eligibility: Applications may be submitted by qualified public and private entities. Pursuant to 7 U.S.C. 450i(7), this includes: (A) State agricultural experiment stations; (B) colleges and universities; (C) University research foundations; (D) other research Institutions and Organizations; (E) Federal agencies; (F) national laboratories; (G) private Organizations or corporations; (H) individuals; or (I) any group consisting of 2 or more of the entities described in subparagraphs (A) through (H). Award recipients may subcontract to Organizations not eligible to apply provided such Organizations are necessary for the conduct of the project. An applicant's failure to meet an eligibility criterion by the time of an application deadline may result in the application being excluded from consideration or, even though an application may be reviewed, will preclude NIFA from making an award.
Beneficiary Eligibility: Same as Applicant Eligibility.
Award Range/Average: If minimum or maximum amounts of funding per competitive and/or capacity project grant, or cooperative agreement are established, these amounts will be announced in the annual Competitive Request for Application (RFA).The most current RFA is available via: https://nifa.usda.gov/funding-opportunity/farm-business-management-and-

Programs Administered by Federal Headquarters

benchmarking-fbmb-competitive-grants-program
Funding: (Project Grants (Cooperative Agreements)) FY 17 $1,346,556.00; FY 18 est $1,918,875.00; FY 19 est $0.00
HQ: Institute of Youth Family and Community Division of Family and Consumer Sciences 1400 Independence Avenue SW, PO Box 2250, Washington, DC 20250-2250
    Phone: 202-720-4795
    http://nifa.usda.gov/funding-opportunity/farm-business-management-and-benchmarking-fbmb-competitive-grants-program

USDA10.405 | FARM LABOR HOUSING LOANS AND GRANTS
"Labor Housing"

Award: Project Grants; Guaranteed/insured Loans
Purpose: To provide low-rent housing facilities and essential requirements for farm laborers.
Applicant Eligibility: Loans are available to farmers, family farm partnership, family farm corporations, or an association of farmers. Loans and grants are available to States, Puerto Rico, the U.S. Virgin Islands, political subdivisions of States, broad-based public or private nonprofit Organizations, federally recognized Indian Tribes and non- profit corporations of farm workers. Grants are available to eligible applicants only when there is a pressing need and when it is doubtful that such facilities could be provided unless grant assistance is available.
Beneficiary Eligibility: A domestic farm labourer is any person who receives a substantial portion of his/her income as a labourer on a farm in the United States and is either (1) a citizen of the United States, or (2) has been legally admitted for permanent residency.
Funding: (Direct Loans) FY 17 $34,900,000.00; FY 18 est $8,000,000.00; FY 19 est $8,000,000.00
HQ: 1400 Independence Avenue SW, Washington, DC 20250
    Phone: 202-720-1604 | Email: cb.alonso@wdc.usda.gov
    https://www.rd.usda.gov/programs-services/farm-labor-housing-direct-loans-grants

USDA10.175 | FARMERS MARKET AND LOCAL FOOD PROMOTION PROGRAM
"Farmers Market Promotion Program or Local Food Promotion Program"

Award: Project Grants
Purpose: Aims to support the development, coordination, and expansion of local and regional food systems through the funds granted by the Farmers Market Promotion Program (FMPP) and Local Food Promotion Program (LFPP) for processing, distributing, aggregating, and storing the food products.
Applicant Eligibility: Agricultural businesses and cooperatives, local Governments, nonprofit corporations, producer networks and associations, community supported agriculture networks and associations, public benefit corporations, economic development corporations, food councils, regional farmers market authorities, and Tribal Governments. projects and applicants must be owned, operated, and located within the 50 States, the District of Columbia, and the U.S. territories (American Samoa, Commonwealth of the Northern Mariana Islands, Guam, Puerto Rico, and U.S. Virgin Islands).
Beneficiary Eligibility: Projects that benefit producers, local and regional food business enterprises, and consumers.
Award Range/Average: FMPP - Capacity Building (CB) $50,000- $250,000 and Community Development, Training, and Technical Assistance (CTA) $250,000-500,000 LFPP - Planning projects $25,000- $100,000 and Implementation projects $100,000- $500,000.
Funding: (Project Grants) FY 18 Not Separately Identifiable; FY 19 est $23,000,000.00; FY 20 est Not Separately Identifiable
HQ: 1400 Independence Avenue SW Room 4543, PO Box 0234, Washington, DC 20250
    Phone: 202-720-0933
    http://www.ams.usda.gov/lfpp

USDA10.545 | FARMERS' MARKET SUPPLEMENTAL NUTRITION ASSISTANCE PROGRAM SUPPORT GRANTS
"Farmers Market SNAP Support Grants (FMSSG)"

Award: Salaries and Expenses; Project Grants
Purpose: Helps the farmers' markets to participate in the Supplemental Nutrition Assistance Program. It also helps to establish and expand the Electronic Benefits Transfer at farmers' markets.

Applicant Eligibility: The funds must be used to further the goals of FMSSG, which specifically relate to the operation of SNAP at farmers markets. Accordingly, uses that do not relate to that purpose are impermissible. To the extent that the entities use the funds for such purposes, they are eligible.

Beneficiary Eligibility: The funds must be used to further the goals of FMSSG, which specifically relate to the operation of SNAP at farmers' markets. Accordingly, uses that do not relate to that purpose are impermissible. To the extent that the entities use the funds for such purposes, they are eligible beneficiaries.

Award Range/Average: The range of awards are FM $15,000 to $250,000, spread over a three year period.

Funding: (Salaries and Expenses) FY 16 $532,014.00; FY 17 est $0; FY 18 est $0

HQ: 3101 Park Center Drive, Alexandria, VA 22303

  Phone: 703-756-0230 | Email: patrick.kelley@fns.usda.gov

  https://www.fns.usda.gov

SBA59.058 | FEDERAL AND STATE TECHNOLOGY PARTNERSHIP PROGRAM "FAST"

Award: Cooperative Agreements

Purpose: To strengthen the technological competitiveness of small business concerns in the U.S.

Applicant Eligibility: N/A

Beneficiary Eligibility: N/A

Award Range/Average: No more than 20 awards.

Funding: (Cooperative Agreements) FY 18 $3,000,000.00; FY 19 $3,000,000.00; FY 20 est $3,000,000.00

HQ: 409 3rd Street SW, 6th Floor, Washington, DC 20416

  Phone: 202-710-5163

  http://www.sbir.gov

ED84.268 | FEDERAL DIRECT STUDENT LOANS

Award: Direct Loans

Purpose: To provide loan support directly from the Federal government to vocational, undergraduate, and graduate postsecondary school students and their parents.

Applicant Eligibility: The applicant must be a U.S. citizen, national, or person in the United States for other than a temporary purpose. A student borrower must be enrolled or accepted for enrollment in a degree or certificate Program on at least a half-time basis as an undergraduate, graduate, or professional student at a participating postsecondary institution. An otherwise eligible student is eligible for loans during a single twelve-month period in which the student is enrolled in a non-degree/non-certificate course of study that the institution has determined is necessary in order for the student to enroll in a Program leading to a degree or certificate. Under the Direct PLUS Program, parents may borrow for dependent undergraduate students. Also, graduate and professional students are eligible to borrow PLUS Loans. Direct Unsubsidized and PLUS loans are available to eligible borrowers regardless of need. However, a financial needs test based on family income is required for an undergraduate student to receive a Direct Subsidized loan. A student that is presently enrolled at a participating institution must be maintaining satisfactory academic progress in the course of study that they are pursuing. The borrower may not owe a refund on any Title IV grant or be in default on any Title IV loan received for attendance at any institution. The borrower must also file a Statement of Registration compliance (Selective Service).

Beneficiary Eligibility: Vocational, undergraduate, and graduate postsecondary school students and their parents.

Award Range/Average: N/A

Funding: (Direct Loans) FY 18 $137,496,596,000.00; FY 19 est $143,478,719,000.00; FY 20 est $146,568,767,000.00; Figures represent Net Commitment Loan volume, without Consolidation.(Direct Loans) FY 18 $95,864,248,000.00; FY 19 est $98,181,801,000.00; FY 20 est $100,214,544,000.00; (Figures represent Net Commitment Consolidation volume) FY 18 $41,632,348,000; FY 19 est $45,296,918,000; FY 20 est $46,354,223,000

HQ: Federal Student Aid Information Center Department of Education, PO Box 84, Washington, DC 20044-0084

  Phone: 800-433-3243

  http://studentaid.ed.gov/sa/types/loans

Programs Administered by Federal Headquarters

DHS97.048 | FEDERAL DISASTER ASSISTANCE TO INDIVIDUALS AND HOUSEHOLDS IN PRESIDENTIAL DECLARED DISASTER AREAS
"IHP"

Award: Project Grants; Direct Payments for Specified Use

Purpose: The program primarily focuses on the financial assistance for housing construction or renovation for people whose shelters are affected due to natural disasters or terrorist acts.

Applicant Eligibility: Individuals and households, in areas declared an emergency or major disaster by the President, who have necessary expenses and serious needs they are unable to meet through insurance or other means, are eligible to apply for this Program. All needs must be caused by the disaster. Basic conditions of eligibility include: the individual or a member of the household must be a citizen of the United States, a non-citizen national, or a qualified alien. Housing Assistance: 1) Temporary Housing Assistance - proof of primary residence, proof of occupancy, disaster-caused displacement, and/or paid receipts for Rent or Lodging Expenses; 2) Repair - primary residence, proof of occupancy and ownership, disaster caused home damage; 3) Replacement - primary residence, proof of occupancy and ownership, home destroyed by the disaster; 4) Permanent or Semi-permanent Housing Construction - primary residence, proof of occupancy and ownership, disaster-caused home damage, home is located in an insular area outside the continental United States and in other locations in which no alternative housing resources are available, and types of temporary housing assistance are unavailable, infeasible, or not cost-effective. Other Needs Assistance: 1) Medical: disaster-caused expenses, and/or paid receipts (bills) for medical treatment; 2) Dental: disaster-caused expenses, and/or paid receipts (bills) for treatment; 3) childcare: disaster caused expenses; 4) Funeral: disaster-caused expenses, and/or paid receipts (bills) for services; 5) Personal Property: proof of ownership; disaster-caused personal property damage; 6)Transportation: proof of ownership, vehicle complies with State laws, disaster-caused vehicle damage; 7) Other Necessary Expenses and Serious Needs: the expense or need must be caused by the disaster and approved by FEMA. States and Indian Tribal Governments States and Indian Tribal Governments, in areas declared an emergency or major disaster by the president where FEMA has determined eligible individuals and households are unable to make use of financial Temporary Housing Assistance, and have a Housing Strategy approved by FEMA, are eligible to apply for financial assistance to provide direct services for Temporary Housing to eligible individuals and households. States and Indian Tribal Governments, in areas declared an emergency or major disaster by the president in insular areas outside of the continental United States and in other locations where FEMA has determined no alternative housing resources are available, and temporary housing is unavailable, infeasible, or not cost effective, and have a Housing Strategy approved by FEMA, are eligible to apply for financial assistance to provide direct services for Permanent or Semi-Permanent Housing Construction.

Beneficiary Eligibility: Individual/Family; Homeowner (located within an area which has been designated as a disaster area by Presidential declaration).

Award Range/Average: FY 18: Range - $50 - $34,000; Average - $3,279.15 - 8,905.16 - as of 0706/1125/2018 2019 FY 19: Range - $50 - $34,900; Average - $4,659.83 - as of 06/25/2019

Funding: (Project Grants) FY 18 $2,437,746,395.00; FY 19 est $1,418,400.00; FY 20 est $1,418,400,000.00

HQ: Department of Homeland Security 500 C Street SW, 6th Floor, Washington, DC 20472-3100

Phone: 202-212-1000

http://www.fema.gov/individual-disaster-assistance

DOI15.427 | FEDERAL OIL AND GAS ROYALTY MANAGEMENT STATE AND TRIBAL COORDINATION
"FOGRMA"

Award: Project Grants

Purpose: To assure that all oil, gas, and solid minerals originated on the public lands and on the Outer Continental Shelf are properly accounted for under the direction of the Secretary of the Interior, and for other purposes.

Applicant Eligibility: State and Tribal Governments as specified in Title II of the Federal Oil and Gas Royalty Management Act of 1982, as amended.

Beneficiary Eligibility: States and Federally recognized Tribal Governments that receive funds collected as a result of the compliance activities on Federal and Indian mineral leases.

Award Range/Average: Awards range from $230,000 to $3.0 million. Average is $892,000.

Funding: (Project Grants) FY 17 $13,548,000.00; FY 18 est $13,548,000.00; FY 19 est $13,548,000.00

HQ: Office of Natural Resources Revenue 1849 C Street NW, PO Box 4211, Washington, DC 20240

Phone: 202-513-0600

http://www.onrr.gov

ED84.063 | FEDERAL PELL GRANT PROGRAM

Award: Direct Payments for Specified Use

Purpose: To demonstrate financial need for undergraduate postsecondary students with grant assistance to help meet educational expenses.

Applicant Eligibility: Undergraduate students and students pursuing a teaching certificate enrolled as regular students in an eligible Program at an eligible institution of higher education and making satisfactory academic progress. The applicants must be U.S. citizens or eligible noncitizens and have a high school diploma (or its equivalent); or, for students enrolled prior to July 1, 2012, a demonstrated ability to benefit from the Program offered; or, have successfully completed six credits.

Beneficiary Eligibility: Undergraduate students and students pursuing a teaching certificate that are U.S. citizens or eligible noncitizens and meet financial need criteria. Students must be regular students in an eligible program and enrolled in institutions of higher education, making satisfactory academic progress. Incarcerated students, except those incarcerated in local penal facilities, are ineligible. Students must sign a statement of educational purpose, not owe a refund on a Title IV grant, and not be in default on a Title IV loan. Eligible males that are at least 18 years old and born after December 31, 1959, can receive aid only if they have registered with the Selective Service.

Award Range/Average: For FY 2017, grants ranged from $592- $5,920; the average grant was estimated at $4,050.For FY 2018, grants will range from $609- $6,095; the average grant is estimated at $4,137.For FY 2019, grants will range from $609- $6,095; the average grant is estimated at $4,115.

Funding: (Direct Payments for Specified Use) FY 18 $28,026,215,000.00; FY 19 est $29,747,015,000.00; FY 20 est $30,069,170,000.00

HQ: Federal Student Aid Information Center Department of Education, PO Box 84, Washington, DC 20044-0084
  Phone: 800-433-3243
  http://studentaid.ed.gov/sa/types/grants-scholarships/pell

ED84.145 | FEDERAL REAL PROPERTY ASSISTANCE PROGRAM

Award: Sale, Exchange, Or Donation of Property and Goods

Purpose: To convey surplus Federal Real Property for educational purposes at fair market value.

Applicant Eligibility: Those groups, Organizations, entities, or Institutions providing educational Programs including: States; their political subdivisions and instrumentalities; and tax supported Organizations or private nonprofit Institutions held exempt from taxation under Section 501(C)(3) of the Internal Revenue Code of 1954 may apply.

Beneficiary Eligibility: Program participants receiving educational opportunities will benefit.

Award Range/Average: Not Available.

HQ: Office of the Administrator for Management Services Department of Education 400 Maryland Avenue SW, Washington, DC 20202
  Phone: 202-260-4558
  http://www.ed.gov

ED84.007 | FEDERAL SUPPLEMENTAL EDUCATIONAL OPPORTUNITY GRANTS "FSEOG"

Award: Direct Payments for Specified Use

Purpose: To provide need-based grant aid to eligible undergraduate postsecondary students to meet their educational expenses.

Applicant Eligibility: Higher education Institutions (public, private nonprofit, postsecondary vocational, and proprietary) meeting eligibility requirements may apply.

Beneficiary Eligibility: Undergraduate students enrolled or accepted for enrollment as regular students; are maintaining satisfactory academic progress in accordance with the standards and practices of the institution, have financial need, do not owe a refund on a Title IV grant, are not in default on a Title IV loan, file a statement of educational purpose, file a statement of registration compliance (Selective Service) and meet citizen/resident requirements may benefit.

Award Range/Average: The average award in FY 2018 was $665. The average award for FY 2019 and FY 2020 is estimated to be $665.

Funding: (Direct Payments for Specified Use) FY 18 $1,130,929,000.00; FY 19 est $130,929,000.00; FY 20 est $1,130,929,000.00

HQ: Federal Student Aid Information Center Department of Education, PO Box 84, Washington, DC 20044-0084
  Phone: 800-433-3243
  http://studentaid.ed.gov/sa/types/grants-scholarships/fseog

Programs Administered by Federal Headquarters

DOJ16.578 | FEDERAL SURPLUS PROPERTY TRANSFER PROGRAM

Award: Sale, Exchange, Or Donation of Property and Goods

Purpose: To facilitate the possible no cost conveyance, by the Federal Government, to State and local governments, of surplus real and related personal property for correctional facility use, under programs or projects for the care or rehabilitation of criminal offenders, and for law enforcement purposes.

Applicant Eligibility: Eligible applicants include states, or political subdivisions or instrumentalities of states, proposing to use the subject property for law enforcement purposes or correctional facility purposes. The 50 States, the District of Columbia, the Commonwealth of Puerto Rico, Guam, American Samoa, the Virgin Islands, the Federated States of Micronesia, the Marshall Islands, Palau, and the Northern Mariana Islands.

Beneficiary Eligibility: State, local and territorial governments, that are engaged in activities to control or reduce crime and juvenile delinquency or the enforcement of criminal law including investigative activities as well as training or for the care or rehabilitation of criminal offenders.

Award Range/Average: Not Applicable.

HQ: U.S. Department of Justice Bureau of Justice Assistance 810 7th Street NW, Washington, DC 20351
Phone: 202-616-6500 | Email: laura.mizhir@usdoj.gov
https://www.bja.gov/ProgramDetails.aspx?Program_ID=61

ED84.033 | FEDERAL WORK-STUDY PROGRAM

Award: Direct Payments for Specified Use

Purpose: To provide part-time employment for the eligible postsecondary students to meet educational expenses and to encourage students for participating in community service activities.

Applicant Eligibility: Higher education Institutions (public, private nonprofit, postsecondary vocational, and proprietary) meeting eligibility requirements may apply.

Beneficiary Eligibility: Undergraduate, graduate, or professional students enrolled or accepted for enrollment as regular students; are maintaining satisfactory academic progress in accordance with the standards and practices of the institution; have financial need; do not owe a refund on a Title IV grant; are not in default on a Title IV loan; file a statement of educational purpose; file a statement of registration compliance (Selective Service); and meet citizen/resident requirements may benefit.

Award Range/Average: The average award in FY 2018 was $1,760. The average award in FY 2019 and FY 2020 is estimated at $1,760.

Funding: (Direct Payments for Specified Use) FY 17 $1,096,080,000.00; FY 18 est $1,251,425,000.00; FY 19 est $1,251,425,000.00

HQ: Department of Education PO Box 84, Washington, DC 20044-0084
Phone: 800-433-3243
https://studentaid.ed.gov/sa

VEF85.802 | FELLOWSHIP PROGRAM
"VEF Fellowship Program"

Award: Project Grants

Purpose: To promote international exchange and cooperation between the United States and Vietnam, though educational exchange.

Applicant Eligibility: Grants are solely intended for Vietnamese students who enroll in Master's and doctoral degree Programs in STEMM fields at an accredited U.S. University.

Beneficiary Eligibility: Grants are solely intended for Vietnamese Masters and doctoral students for use in their STEMM- based study at a U.S. university.

Award Range/Average: In FY14, approximately 40 grants of up to $28,000 may be awarded.

Funding: (Project Grants (Fellowships)) FY 12 $28,000.00; FY 13 est $28,000.00; FY 14 est $28,000.00

HQ: 2111 Wilson Boulevard, Suite 700, Arlington, VA 22201
Phone: 703-351-5053 | Email: margaretpetrochenkov@vef.gov
http://www.vef.gov

USDA10.934 | FERAL SWINE ERADICATION AND CONTROL PILOT PROGRAM
Award: Direct Payments for Specified Use (cooperative Agreements); Salaries and Expenses
Purpose: Allows NRCS and APHIS access to select areas to respond to feral swine threat to agriculture and human and animal health.
Applicant Eligibility: N/A
Beneficiary Eligibility: N/A
Funding: (Direct Payments for Specified Use (Cooperative Agreements)) FY 18 $0; FY 19 est $6,300,000.00; FY 20 est $10,000,000.00; (Salaries and Expenses) FY 18 $0; FY 19 est $700,000.00; FY 20 est $3,000,000.00
HQ: 1400 Independence Avenue SW Room 5204-S, PO Box 2890, Washington, DC 20250
Phone: 202-619-8569 | Email: lacey.williamson@usda.gov
https://www.nrcs.usda.gov

DHS97.132 | FINANCIAL ASSISTANCE FOR COUNTERING VIOLENT EXTREMISM "CVE"
Award: Project Grants
Purpose: Offers community-based support to curb extremism recruitment and radicalization to violence.
Applicant Eligibility: State (includes District of Columbia, public Institutions of higher education and hospitals), Local (includes State-designated Indian Tribes, excludes Institutions of higher education and hospitals, Public nonprofit institution/Organization (includes Institutions of higher education and hospitals), Federally Recognized Indian Tribal Governments, Private nonprofit institution/Organization (includes Institutions of higher education and hospitals), State Please refer to Program guidance.
Beneficiary Eligibility: The CVE Grant Program restricts Eligible Applicants to specific CVE focus areas. Applicants representing States, Local governments, Tribal government, and non-profit organizations are invited to apply for funding to implement the following program priorities: Developing resilience; Training and engagement with community members; Managing intervention activities and Applicants representing non-profit organizations and institutions of higher education are invited to apply for funding to implement the following program priorities: Challenging the narrative; and; Building capacity of community-level non-profit organizations active in CVE. Other Eligibility Criteria Civil Rights and Civil Liberties: Proposed programs, projects or activities shall not infringe on individual privacy, civil rights, and civil liberties. Applications shall describe any potential impacts to privacy, civil rights, and civil liberties and ways in which they will protect against or mitigate those impacts and administer their program(s) in a non-discriminatory manner. Applications which describe programs projects or activities which do not appropriately protect privacy, civil rights or civil liberties will be deemed ineligible for funding. Expertise: Applicants must have either an existing CVE program or demonstrable expertise to create and administer a program, project or activity which falls within one of the five advertised focus areas. Applications which do not describe an organization with appropriate expertise will be deemed ineligible for funding.
HQ: U.S. Department of Homeland Security Office of Terrorism Prevention Partnerships 880 2nd Street SW, Washington, DC 20528
Phone: 202-786-0816
http://www.fema.gov

DOC11.426 | FINANCIAL ASSISTANCE FOR NATIONAL CENTERS FOR COASTAL OCEAN SCIENCE
Award: Cooperative Agreements; Project Grants
Purpose: NCCOS provides scientific information and tools to help balance the Nation's ecological, social and economic goals. It helps coastal communities to protect themselves from harmful algae and contamination and to develop effective resources. It creates awareness of climate impacts, coastal ecosystem management, coastal pollution, and harmful algal blooms.
Applicant Eligibility: Universities, colleges, junior colleges, technical schools, institutes, laboratories, State and local government agencies, public or private profit or nonprofit entities or individuals.
Beneficiary Eligibility: Organizations and individuals utilizing science in effectively managing the Nation's coastal resources.
Award Range/Average: $20,000 to $550,000. Average $250,000.
Funding: (Cooperative Agreements) FY 16 $0.00; FY 17 est $0.00; FY 18 est $10,000.00
HQ: National Center for Coastal Ocean Science (N/SCI) 1305 E W Highway SSMC4 Station 8211, Silver Spring, MD 20910
Phone: 301-713-3020
http://coastalscience.noaa.gov

Programs Administered by Federal Headquarters

DHS97.046 | FIRE MANAGEMENT ASSISTANCE GRANT
"FMAG"

Award: Project Grants; Provision of Specialized Services

Purpose: Grants from this process are provided to the local and State governments for the management and control of any fire in a public place. The grant money is also used for other purposes such as fire suppression services and for getting emergency protective measure equipment and supplies.

Applicant Eligibility: State Governments and Indian tribal Governments are eligible for fire management assistance grants. The State or Indian tribal government may be the Recipient. The Recipient is the government entity that receives the award and is accountable for the use of funds provided.

Beneficiary Eligibility: The State Government and/or Indian tribal government, acting as the Recipient is the government to which the grant is awarded and which is accountable for the use of the funds provided. Other State entities, Indian tribal governments and local governments are eligible to apply as subrecipients.

Funding: (Project Grants) FY 18 $264,403,198.00; FY 19 est $95,941,354.00; FY 20 est $100,000,000.00

HQ: Department of Homeland Security Public Assistance Division Control Desk 500 C Street SW, 6th Floor, Washington, DC 20523

  Phone: 800-368-6498

  http://www.fema.gov

DOD12.460 | FISHER HOUSE FOUNDATION

Award: Project Grants

Purpose: To implement congressionally directed assistance to the Fisher House Foundation, Inc.

Applicant Eligibility: The only eligible applicant is the Fisher House Foundation, Inc., as directed by Congress.

Beneficiary Eligibility: The eligible applicant is the beneficiary.

Award Range/Average: Dependent on Congressional direction.

Funding: (Project Grants) FY 18 $10,000,000.00; FY 19 est $10,000,000.00; FY 20 $ Estimate Not Available.

HQ: Attention: MCMR-AAP, Fort Detrick, MD 21702-5014

  Phone: 301-619-2183

  http://www.usamraa.army.mil

DOC11.427 | FISHERIES DEVELOPMENT AND UTILIZATION RESEARCH AND DEVELOPMENT GRANTS AND COOPERATIVE AGREEMENTS PROGRAM
"The Saltonstall-Kennedy Research Grant Program"

Award: Project Grants

Purpose: To maximize the Nation's wealth and quality of life through fisheries that support fishing industry jobs and creates recreational opportunities.

Applicant Eligibility: Any U.S. citizen or national, or any citizen of the Northern Mariana Islands, the Republic of the Marshall Islands, Republic of Palau, or the Federated States of Micronesia; or group including State and local Governments, except that employees of Federal agencies, and Regional Fishery Management Councils and their employees, are not eligible.

Beneficiary Eligibility: Any U.S. citizen or national, or any citizen of the Northern Mariana Islands, the Republic of the Marshall Islands, Republic of Palau, or the Federated States of Micronesia; or group including State and local governments.

Funding: (Project Grants) FY 16 Actual Not Available; FY 17 est $10,500,000.00; FY 18 est Estimate Not Available

HQ: NOAA National Marine Fisheries Service Office of Management and Budget 1315 E W Highway, Room 14358, Silver Spring, MD 20910

  Phone: 301-427-8730 | Email: dan.namur@noaa.gov

  http://www.fisheries.noaa.gov/mb/financial_services/skhome.htm

NOAA11.477 | FISHERIES DISASTER RELIEF

Award: Project Grants

Purpose: Deals with commercial fishery failure due to the fishery resource disasters that are either natural, man-made, or undetermined.

Applicant Eligibility: Eligible applicants are agencies of State Governments or fishing communities for Programs to provide assistance to fishing communities (including fishing vessel owners, operators, and crew and United States fish processors that are based in such community).

Beneficiary Eligibility: This program directly benefits fishing communities (including fishing vessel owners, operators, crew, and U.S. fish processors based in such communities) that are adversely affected by commercial fishery failures due to a fishery resource disaster.

HQ: 1315 E W Highway, Room 13134, Silver Spring, MD 20910

    Phone: 301-713-2358 | Email: stephen.aguzin@noaa.gov

    http://www.fakr.noaa.gov/omi/grants/default.htm

DOC11.415 | FISHERIES FINANCE PROGRAM

Award: Direct Loans

Purpose: To compensate for the fisheries costs, assist first time purchasers and small vessel operators, provide buyback financing to purchase and retire fishing permits in overcapitalized fisheries.

Applicant Eligibility: Applicant must possess the ability, experience, financial resources, and other qualifications necessary to operate successfully and repay the debt.

Beneficiary Eligibility: Commercial fishermen, processors or distributors of fishery products.

Funding: (Direct Loans) FY 16 $0.00; FY 17 est $100,000,000.00; FY 18 est $0.00

HQ: Financial Services Division National Marine Fisheries Service Department of Commerce 1315 E W Highway, Silver Spring, MD 20910

    Phone: 301-713-2390

    https://www.greateratlantic.fisheries.noaa.gov/mediacenter/2016/march/29_noaa_now_accepting_applications_for_fisheries_finance_program.html

DOC11.408 | FISHERMEN'S CONTINGENCY FUND
"Fisheries Contingency Fund"

Award: Direct Payments With Unrestricted Use

Purpose: To compensate U.S. commercial fishermen for economic loss.

Applicant Eligibility: Applicant must be a U.S. commercial fisherman.

Beneficiary Eligibility: U.S. Commercial fishermen.

HQ: National Marine Fisheries Service 1315 E W Highway, Silver Spring, MD 20910

    Phone: 301-713-1306

    http://www.nmfs.noaa.gov/mb/financial_services/fcf.htm

DOS19.204 | FISHERMEN'S GUARANTY FUND
"Section 7"

Award: Insurance

Purpose: To provide for reimbursement of losses incurred as a result of the seizure of a U.S. commercial fishing vessel by a foreign country on the basis of rights or claims in territorial waters or on the high seas, which are not recognized by the United States.

Applicant Eligibility: Must be a U.S. citizen and the owner or charterer of a fishing vessel documented as such by the United States. Reimbursement of losses and costs (other than fines, license fees, registration fees and other direct costs which are reimbursable through the Secretary of State) incurred as a result of seizure. The vessel must be documented or certified under the laws of the United States.

Beneficiary Eligibility: Must be a U.S. citizen and the owner or charterer of a fishing vessel documented as such by the United States, and must have paid a premium fee, if one is required, for the year in which the seizure occurs.

Funding: (Salary or Expense) FY 07 $500,000.00; FY 08 est Estimate Not Available; FY 09 est Estimate Not Available; (Reimbursement of Losses) FY 07 $500,000; FY 08 est not available; and FY 09 est not reported.

HQ: Office of Marine Conservation Bureau of Oceans and International Environmental and Scientific Affairs, Room 5806, Washington, DC 20520-7818

    Phone: 202-647-3941

    http://www.state.gov

Programs Administered by Federal Headquarters

DOC11.413 | FISHERY PRODUCTS INSPECTION AND CERTIFICATION
"Inspection and Grading of Fishery Products"

Award: Provision of Specialized Services

Purpose: To ensure that the hygienic aspects of seafood harvesting, and processing are qualified.

Applicant Eligibility: Any individual, Federal, State, county, or municipal agencies, or carrier having a financial interest in the commodity.

Beneficiary Eligibility: General public.

HQ: Inspection Services Division National Marine Fisheries Services 1315 E W Highway, Silver Spring, MD 20910

Phone: 301-713-2355

http://www.seafood.nmfs.noaa.gov/export/export_certification/euexport.html

HHS93.367 | FLEXIBLE FUNDING MODEL-INFRASTRUCTURE DEVELOPMENT AND MAINTENANCE FOR STATE MANUFACTURED FOOD REGULATORY PROGRAMS

Award: Cooperative Agreements

Purpose: Strives for a nationally integrated food safety system (IFSS) by supporting Manufactured Food Regulatory Program Standards (MFRPS), Rapid Response Teams (RRT) and Food Protection Task Force (FPTF) programs, as well as special projects.

Applicant Eligibility: N/A

Beneficiary Eligibility: N/A

Award Range/Average: Average award $810,000

Funding: (Salaries and Expenses) FY 18 $14,539,080.00; FY 19 est $15,114,696.00; FY 20 est $14,303,490.00

HQ: 4041 Powder Mill Road, Beltsville, MD 20705

Phone: 240-402-7596 | Email: daniel.lukash@fda.hhs.gov

http://www.fda.gov/forfederalstateandlocalofficials/fundingopportunities/grantscoopagrmts/ucm539096.htm

DOI15.433 | FLOOD CONTROL ACT LANDS

Award: Direct Payments for Specified Use

Purpose: Shares 75 percent of mineral leasing revenue with the State, paid monthly and is subject to late disbursement interest.

Applicant Eligibility: Revenue from acquired Flood Control land leasing will trigger automatic payment distribution computed in accordance with the law.

Beneficiary Eligibility: ONRR distributes these funds to state governments for leased lands within a state, and the State governments has sole discretion in their use in accordance with the enabling legislation.

Award Range/Average: Not Applicable.

Funding: (Direct Payments with Unrestricted Use) FY 17 $12,512,000.00; FY 19 est $51,342,000.00; FY 18 est $47,625,000.00

HQ: Office of Natural Resources Revenue 1849 C Street NW, PO Box 4211, Washington, DC 20240

Phone: 202-513-0600

http://www.ONRR.gov

DOD12.106 | FLOOD CONTROL PROJECTS
"Small Flood Control Projects"

Award: Provision of Specialized Services

Purpose: To reduce flood damages through projects.

Applicant Eligibility: States, political subdivisions of States, or other responsible local agencies established under State law with full authority and ability to undertake necessary legal and financial responsibility.

Beneficiary Eligibility: Same as Applicant Eligibility.

Funding: (Provision of Specialized Services) FY 14 $0.00; FY 15 est $16,433.00; FY 16 est $16,000.00

DHS97.022 | FLOOD INSURANCE

Award: Insurance

Purpose: Offers flood insurance coverage to property owners in low and high-risk flood zones to reduce federal disaster assistance and to promote smarter floodplain management practices.

Applicant Eligibility: Federal flood insurance can be made available in any community (a State or political subdivision thereof with authority to adopt and enforce floodplain management measures for the areas within its jurisdiction) that adopts and enforces floodplain management measures consistent with the National Flood Insurance Program regulations.

Beneficiary Eligibility: Residential and business property owners, renters and state owned property.

Award Range/Average: Claims paid: $1 to $1,900,000; $31,802.

HQ: 400 C Street SW, Washington, DC 20024

Phone: 800-621-3363 | Email: paul.huang@fema.dhs.gov

http://www.fema.gov/national-flood-insurance-program

DHS97.029 | FLOOD MITIGATION ASSISTANCE
"FMA"

Award: Project Grants

Purpose: The program supports tribal and State governments to help reduce the loss of lives and destruction to property during natural hazards thereby reducing claims under the National Flood Insurance Program.

Applicant Eligibility: The 50 States, the District of Columbia, American Samoa, Guam, the U.S. Virgin Islands, Puerto Rico, the Northern Mariana Islands, and Federally-recognized Indian Tribal Governments may apply for FMA assistance as the Applicant to FEMA. Either the state Emergency Management Agency (EMA) or the office that has primary floodplain management responsibility is eligible to apply directly to FEMA for FMA funds as an applicant; however, only one application will be accepted from each state, tribe or territory. Applicants must have a FEMA approved mitigation plan as of the application deadline in order to apply for mitigation projects in accordance with 44 CFR Part 201.

Beneficiary Eligibility: State agencies (other than the EMA), tribal governments (non-federally recognized), and local governments and communities may apply as sub applicants for FMA grants through their applicant state/tribe/territory. Subapplicants must have a FEMA approved mitigation plan as of the application deadline in order to apply for mitigation projects in accordance with Title 44 CFR Part 201.

Award Range/Average: Not Available.

Funding: (Project Grants) FY 18 $88,000,000.00; FY 19 est $75,000,000.00; FY 20 est $75,000,000.00

HQ: 400 C Street SW, Washington, DC 20472

Phone: 202-646-3458 | Email: kayed.lakhia@fema.dhs.gov

http://www.fema.gov/flood/mitigation/assistance/grant/program

DOD12.104 | FLOOD PLAIN MANAGEMENT SERVICES
"FPMS"

Award: Advisory Services and Counseling; Dissemination of Technical Information

Purpose: To promote awareness of flood hazards in land and water and other technical assistance and provisions.

Applicant Eligibility: States, political subdivisions of States, other nonfederal public Organizations and the public.

Beneficiary Eligibility: Same as Applicant Eligibility.

HQ: U.S. Army Corps of Engineers Attention: CECW-OE, Washington, DC 20314-1000

Phone: 202-761-0169

http://www.usace.army.mil/business.html

USDA10.522 | FOOD AND AGRICULTURE SERVICE LEARNING PROGRAM
"FASLP"

Award: Project Grants

Purpose: This program promotes education on food and nutrition in the premises of educational institutions and organizations. It introduces the efforts of the farm to school programs. It implements through the food authorities the school lunch program. It introduces nutrition education in elementary and secondary schools and supports the efforts of national service.

Applicant Eligibility: The Secretary may make grants to carry out research, extension, and education under this subsection to-(A) State agricultural experiment stations; (B) colleges and universities; (C) University research foundations; (D) other research Institutions and Organizations; (E) Federal agencies; (F) national laboratories; (G) private Organizations,

Programs Administered by Federal Headquarters

foundations, or corporations; (H) individuals; or(I) any group consisting of 2 or more of the entities described in subparagraphs (A) through (H).

Beneficiary Eligibility: Same as Applicant Eligibility.

Award Range/Average: If minimum or maximum amounts of funding per competitive and/or capacity project grant, or cooperative agreement are established, these amounts will be announced in the annual Competitive Request for Application (RFA).The most current RFA is available via: https://nifa.usda.gov/funding-opportunity/food-and-agriculture-service-learning-program

Funding: (Project Grants (Discretionary)) FY 17 $0.00; FY 18 est $881,900.00; FY 19 est $0.00

HQ: 1400 Independence Avenue SW, PO Box 2225, Washington, DC 20250-2225

Phone: 202-720-5004

https://nifa.usda.gov/funding-opportunity/food-and-agriculture-service-learning-program

HHS93.103 | FOOD AND DRUG ADMINISTRATION RESEARCH
"General Grant Funding"

Award: Cooperative Agreements; Project Grants

Purpose: To assist institutions and organizations, to establish, expand, and improve research, demonstration, education and information dissemination activities.

Applicant Eligibility: Applicants should review the individual funding opportunity announcement issued under this CFDA Program to see which applicant Organizations are eligible to apply.

Beneficiary Eligibility: Same as Applicant Eligibility.

Award Range/Average: Varies by grant mechanism and program specific requirements.

Funding: (Cooperative Agreements (Discretionary Grants)) FY 18 $173,077,408.00; FY 19 est $200,887,179.00; FY 20 est $172,435,669.00

HQ: 4041 Powder Mill Road, Beltsville, MD 20705

Phone: 240-402-7610 | Email: kimberly.pendleton@fda.hhs.gov

http://www.fda.gov

USDA10.518 | FOOD ANIMAL RESIDUE AVOIDANCE DATABANK
"FARAD"

Award: Project Grants

Purpose: The FARAD provides information for the veterinarians and livestock producers on food animal products that are contaminant with drugs and pesticides.

Applicant Eligibility: Title VI Section 604 of the Agricultural Research, Extension, and education Reform Act of 1998 (7 U.S.C. 7642) states that -The Secretary of Agriculture shall continue operation of the Food Animal Residue Avoidance Database Program (referred to in this section as the FARAD Program) through contracts, grants, or cooperative agreements with appropriate colleges or universities. This 30-year-old high performing integrated consortium of collaborating Institutions currently includes at each Land Grant campus a lead PD, and his/her respective scientific staff. The Institutions involved are University of California, Davis (UCD), North Carolina State University (NCSU), University of Florida (UFL), and Kansas State University (KSU).

Beneficiary Eligibility: Same as Applicant Eligibility.

Award Range/Average: If minimum or maximum amounts of funding per competitive and/or capacity project grant, or cooperative agreement are established, these amounts will be announced in the annual Request for Application (RFA).Please refer to the Request for Applications (RFAs) for further specific and pertinent details. Contact the headquarters or regional office, for most current RFA.

Funding: (Project Grants) FY 17 $0.00; FY 18 est $0.00; FY 19 est $1,242,000.00

HQ: 1400 Independence Avenue SW, PO Box 2240, Washington, DC 20250-2220

Phone: 202-401-4892 | Email: rsmith@nifa.usda.gov

https://nifa.usda.gov/food-animal-residue-avoidance-databank

USDA10.608 | FOOD FOR EDUCATION
"McGovern-Dole International Food for Education and Children Nutrition Program"

Award: Direct Payments for Specified Use; Sale, Exchange, Or Donation of Property and Goods

Purpose: The purpose of the McGovern-Dole Program is to promote health and dietary practices. It also provides school meals and other essential assistance.

Applicant Eligibility: FAS will set forth specific eligibility information, including any factors or priorities that will affect the eligibility of an applicant or application for selection, in the full text of the applicable notice of funding opportunity posted on the U.S. government web site for grant opportunities.

Beneficiary Eligibility: The McGovern-Dole Program focuses on developing countries in which the national government of the recipient country is fully committed to achieving the goals of the World Declaration on Education for All and is taking steps to improve the quality and availability of education.

Award Range/Average: FAS encourages proposals for 5-year implementation periods, which are expected to range from $18-30 million.

Funding: (Sale, Exchange, or Donation of Property and Goods) FY 18 est $209,968,302; FY 19 est $210,000,000.00; FY 20 est Estimate Not Available

HQ: 1400 Independence Avenue SW, PO Box 1030, Washington, DC 20050

Phone: 202-720-4221

https://www.fas.usda.gov/programs/mcgovern-dole-food-education-program

USAID98.007 | FOOD FOR PEACE DEVELOPMENT ASSISTANCE PROGRAM (DAP)

Award: Project Grants; Sale, Exchange, Or Donation of Property and Goods

Purpose: The program focusses on bringing food relief to improve the health status of people living in food deprived regions.

Applicant Eligibility: Private non-profit Institutions /Organizations are eligible for this Program. Specifically, an Organization must be a Private Voluntary Organization (PVO) or cooperative. PVOs must be registered with USAID as of the date of its application. In order to be awarded a Program the Organization must also be registered with the Office of Food for Peace.

Beneficiary Eligibility: Private, non-profit institutions/organizations will benefit from this program along with vulnerable and food insecure populations in low income food deficit countries (LIFDCs) and least developed countries (LDCs).

HQ: 301 4th Street SW, Washington, DC 20547

Phone: 202-567-4688 | Email: rwillis@usaid.gov

http://www.usaid.gov

USAID98.008 | FOOD FOR PEACE EMERGENCY PROGRAM (EP)

Award: Project Grants; Sale, Exchange, Or Donation of Property and Goods

Purpose: Title II emergency program's main role is to prevent malnutrition by improving food accessibility in food insecure countries.

Applicant Eligibility: Private non-profit Institutions /Organizations are eligible for this Program. Specifically, an Organization must be a Private Voluntary Organization (PVO) or cooperative. If a U.S. based PVO, the Organization must be registered with USAID as of the date of its application. In order to be awarded a Program the Organization must also be registered with the Office of Food for Peace.

Beneficiary Eligibility: Private, non-profit institutions/organizations will benefit from this program along with vulnerable and food insecure populations.

HQ: 301 4th Street SW, Washington, DC 20547

Phone: 202-567-4688 | Email: rwillis@usaid.gov

http://www.usaid.gov

USDA10.606 | FOOD FOR PROGRESS
"FFPr"

Award: Direct Payments for Specified Use; Sale, Exchange, Or Donation of Property and Goods

Purpose: The Food for Progress program compensates for the U.S. agricultural commodities and also funds for the proceeds of the monetization. It maximizes productivity and expands trade of agricultural products.

Applicant Eligibility: A private voluntary Organization, a nonprofit agricultural Organization or cooperative, a nongovernmental Organization, or any other private entity is eligible to submit an application under this part to become a recipient under the Food for Progress Program. CCC will set forth specific eligibility information, including any factors or priorities that will affect the eligibility of an applicant or application for selection, in the full text of the applicable notice of funding opportunity posted on the U.S. government web site for grant opportunities.

Programs Administered by Federal Headquarters

Beneficiary Eligibility: The Food for Progress programs focuses on developing countries and emerging democracies that are committed to introducing or expanding free enterprise in their agricultural economies.

Award Range/Average: Food for Progress cooperative agreements generally have 3-5-year implementation periods and awards ranging from $20-30 million.

Funding: (Sale, Exchange, or Donation of Property and Goods) FY 18 $162,226,150.00; FY 19 est $161,700,000.00; FY19 est Estimate Not Available

HQ: 1400 Independence Avenue SW, PO Box 1030, Washington, DC 20050
  Phone: 202-720-4221
  http://www.fas.usda.gov/programs/food-progress

USDA10.331 | FOOD INSECURITY NUTRITION INCENTIVE GRANTS PROGRAM "FINI"

Award: Project Grants

Purpose: The Food Insecurity Nutrition Incentive program compensates for low-income consumers and the supplemental nutrition assistance program support State agencies that serve in the rural areas.

Applicant Eligibility: Eligible entities include governmental agencies and nonprofit Organizations.

Beneficiary Eligibility: Same as Applicant Eligibility.

Award Range/Average: If minimum or maximum amounts of funding per competitive and/or capacity project grant, or cooperative agreement are established, these amounts will be announced in the annual Competitive Request for Application (RFA).The most current RFA is available via: https://nifa.usda.gov/funding-opportunity/food-insecurity-nutrition-incentive-fini-grant-program

Funding: (Project Grants) FY 18 $21,015,000.00; FY 19 est $41,400,000.00; FY 20 $43,200,000.00

HQ: 1400 Independence Avenue SW, PO Box 2255, Washington, DC 20024
  Phone: 202-720-0740
  http://nifa.usda.gov/program/food-insecurity-nutrition-incentive-fini-grant-program

HHS93.448 | FOOD SAFETY AND SECURITY MONITORING PROJECT "FERN Grant Program"

Award: Cooperative Agreements

Purpose: To complement, develop and improve State, Indian Tribal, and local food safety and security testing programs.

Applicant Eligibility: These cooperative agreement and grants Programs are only available to State, Local and Tribal government Food Emergency Response (FERN) laboratories.

Beneficiary Eligibility: Successful programs will benefit the general population as more rapid and reliable food testing to enhance food safety efforts is developed. The FERN laboratory network will also benefit from better testing methods, equipment and training.

Award Range/Average: $240,000 - $618,000 total cost per award per year (for direct and indirect costs and supplemental funds as necessary, reasonable and allocable) for up to five years as referenced in the Funding Opportunity Announcement or available.

Funding: (Cooperative Agreements) FY 18 $8,894,206.00; FY 19 est $9,702,886.00; FY 20 est $0.00

HQ: 12420 Parklawn Drive, Room 3042, Rockville, MD 20857
  Phone: 301-796-5830 | Email: matthew.avis@fda.hhs.gov
  http://www.fda.gov/forfederalstateandlocalofficials/cooperativeagreementscradasgrants/default.htm

USAID98.006 | FOREIGN ASSISTANCE TO AMERICAN SCHOOLS AND HOSPITALS ABROAD (ASHA)

Award: Project Grants

Purpose: The Foreign Assistance Program provides assistance to schools and hospitals located abroad that share American vision and practices.

Applicant Eligibility: Pursuant to Section 214 of the Foreign Assistance Act of 1961, as amended, grant assistance is made available to schools and libraries outside the United States founded or sponsored by United States citizens and serving as study and demonstration centers for ideas and practices of the United States, and to hospital centers for medical education and research outside the United States, founded or sponsored by United States citizens. Grants made under this Program help such

Institutions demonstrate to people overseas the achievements of the United States in education and medicine. The applicant must be a non-profit U.S. Organization, which either founded or sponsors the institution for which assistance is sought. The applicant, for example, can be a nonprofit University or a tax exempt Organization under Section 501(c) (3) of the Internal Revenue Code of 1954 as amended. The applicant must demonstrate a continuing supportive relationship with the overseas institution. Evidence of this would be the provision of financial and management support for the institution. Other more detailed eligibility requirements are addressed in the published Request for Applications which appear on the USAID/ASHA web site and www.grants.gov.

Beneficiary Eligibility: Beneficiaries must be institutions located outside the U.S. and must not be under the control or management of a government or any other of its agencies. The majority of the users of these overseas institutions, e.g., students or patients, must be citizens of countries other than the U.S.

HQ: USAID/DCHA/ASHA Bureau for D 1300 Pennsylvania Avenue NW, Washington, DC 20523

Phone: 202-712-0510

http://www.usaid.gov/our_work/cross-cutting_programs/asha

OPIC70.002 | FOREIGN INVESTMENT FINANCING

Award: Direct Loans; Guaranteed/insured Loans

Purpose: To provide financing for projects sponsored by private U.S. businesses in developing countries and emerging economies throughout the world; and to assist in improving U.S. competitiveness, creating American jobs and increasing Unites States exports.

Applicant Eligibility: Guaranteed investor must be citizen of the United States, a corporation, partnership, or other association created under the laws of the United States or any State or territory, and more than 50 percent beneficially owned by U.S. Citizens; a foreign corporation at least 95 percent owned by such entities; or a 100 percent United States-owned foreign entity. Direct loans are reserved for projects sponsored by or significantly involving United States small businesses or cooperatives. Applicants also must meet OPIC's credit underwriting criteria.

Beneficiary Eligibility: Project must have significant participation by a United States sponsor, generally in the form of at least 25 percent equity ownership. OPIC does not support projects that will result in the loss of U.S. jobs, that would contribute to the violation of internationally recognized worker rights or involve illicit payments. OPIC only supports projects that contribute to the economic and social development of the host country.

Award Range/Average: $200,000 to $400,000,000; small business loans $200,000 to $100,000,000, $23,353,000; non-small business loans $1,166,550 to $400,000,000, $27,067,770

Funding: (Guaranteed/Insured Loans) FY 08 $1,374,000,000.00; FY 09 est $2,000,000,000.00; FY 10 est $2,350,000,000.00

HQ: 1100 New York Avenue NW, Washington, DC 20527

Phone: 202-336-8651 | Email: alison.germak@opic.gov

http://www.opic.gov

OPIC70.003 | FOREIGN INVESTMENT INSURANCE
"Political Risk Insurance"

Award: Insurance

Purpose: To insure investments of eligible U.S. investors in developing countries and emerging markets, against the political risks of inconvertibility, expropriation, and political violence.

Applicant Eligibility: Citizen of the United States; a corporation, partnership, or other association created under the laws of the United States or any State or territory, of which more than 50 percent is beneficially owned by U.S. citizens; a foreign corporation at least 95 percent owned by such entities; or any other 100 percent U.S. -owned foreign entity.

Beneficiary Eligibility: OPIC does not support projects that will result in the loss of U.S. jobs, that have a negative impact on the host country's economy or environment, or contribute to violations of internationally recognized worker rights. OPIC only supports projects that contribute to the economic and social development of the host country.

Funding: (Salary or Expense) FY 07 $1,200,000,000.00; FY 08 Estimate Not Available; FY 09 Estimate Not Available

HQ: 1100 New York Avenue NW, Suite 510C, Washington, DC 20527

Phone: 202-336-8799

http://www.opic.gov

Programs Administered by Federal Headquarters

USDA10.600 | FOREIGN MARKET DEVELOPMENT COOPERATOR PROGRAM "FMD"

Award: Direct Payments for Specified Use
Purpose: To maximize exporting markets for U.S. agricultural products to work closely with FAS and its overseas offices.
Applicant Eligibility: The Commodity Credit Corporation (CCC) enters into agreements with those nonprofit U.S. trade Organizations that have the broadest possible producer representation of the commodity being promoted. To be approved, an applicant's proposal must indicate how it can effectively contribute to the creation, expansion, or maintenance of markets abroad. FAS considers a number of factors when reviewing proposed projects. These factors include: (1) The applicant's willingness to contribute resources including cash and goods and services of the U.S. industry and foreign third party; (2) the ability of the Organization to provide an experienced U.S. -based staff and with technical and international trade expertise to ensure adequate development, supervision, and execution of the proposed project; (3) the degree to which the proposed project is likely to contribute to the development, expansion, or maintenance of foreign markets; and (4) the degree to which the strategic plan is coordinated with other private or U.S. government-funded market development projects.
Beneficiary Eligibility: Preference is given to nonprofit U.S. trade organizations which are nationwide in membership and scope.
Funding: (Formula Grants (Apportionments)) FY 18 $34,500,000.00; FY 19 est $34,500,000.00; FY 20 est $34,500,000.00
HQ: 1400 Independence Avenue SW, Washington, DC 20250
    Phone: 202-720-4327 | Email: curt.alt@fas.usda.gov
    http://www.fas.usda.gov/programs/foreign-market-development-program-fmd

HHS93.338 | FOREIGN PUBLIC HEALTH CONSTRUCTION

Award: Project Grants
Purpose: Authorizes the award of grants or cooperative agreements to public or nonprofit private institutions or agencies in foreign countries to acquire, lease, construct, alter, or renovate facilities in their country in furtherance of activities authorized under Public Health Service Act Section 307(a).
Applicant Eligibility: An eligible applicant must: (1) Be a public or nonprofit private institution or agency in a foreign country; and (2) Be located in the same foreign country as the Project. An eligible project must: (1) Be located in the same foreign country as the Recipient; (2) Be limited to approved Construction, Modernization, and Minor Alteration and Renovation activities; and (3) Result upon completion is a facility that is for use by recipient personnel only, and not for use by any U.S. government personnel; and (4) Fulfill a purpose of Public Health Service Act Section 307(a). Sub-recipients are not authorized.
Beneficiary Eligibility: Same as Applicant Eligibility.
Award Range/Average: New program with no awards to date.
HQ: 1600 Clifton Road NE, PO Box E29, Atlanta, GA 30329
    Phone: 404-639-4276 | Email: ctg8@cdc.gov
    http://www.cdc.gov

DOD12.450 | FORT HUACHUCA ENVIRONMENTAL TRAINING
"Environmental Intern Training"

Award: Cooperative Agreements
Purpose: The objective of the Fort Huachuca Environmental Intern Program is to support environmental programs through the use of student interns.
Applicant Eligibility: Unless otherwise specified in related Program announcements, all qualified entities, Institutions, and Organizations are eligible under the Program. Individuals and families are not eligible for awards under this Program.
Beneficiary Eligibility: The program provides real world training and experience for students and new graduates in the fields of cultural resources, natural resources, and compliance.
Award Range/Average: Average assistance is anticipated at $150,000. It is dependent on funding availability.
Funding: (Salaries and Expenses) FY 15 $150,000.00; FY 16 est $150,000.00; FY 17 est $150,000.00
HQ: Fort Huachuca DOC Operations, PO Box 12748, Fort Huachuca, AZ 85670-2748
    Phone: 520-533-1464 | Email: nancy.e.johnson.civ@mail.mil

DOD12.004 | FORT HUACHUCA SENTINEL LANDSCAPES FOR MILITARY TRAINING
"Sentinel Landscapes"

Award: Project Grants (cooperative Agreements)
Purpose: Mitigates future external encroachment through conservation of open space and working lands and create expanded ground operation capabilities in the Sentinel Landscapes that serves the Fort Huachuca, Arizona military training installation.
Applicant Eligibility: Sole Source Award to the US Endowment. Organizations website is below: www.usendowment. org.
Beneficiary Eligibility: Federal, State and Private Land owners may benefit from recognition and monetary incentives.
Award Range/Average: Funding in the amount of $13,000 will be provided annually.
Funding: (Project Grants (Cooperative Agreements)) FY 17 Actual Not Available; FY 18 est $13,000.00; FY 19 est $13,000.00
HQ: Auger Street Building, Suite 22208, Fort Huachuca, AZ 85613
   Phone: 520-533-1464 | Email: nancy.e.johnson.civ@mail.mil

HHS93.658 | FOSTER CARE TITLE IV-E
"Title IV-E Foster Care"

Award: Formula Grants; Project Grants
Purpose: The Title IV-E Foster Care program helps states, Indian tribes, tribal organizations and tribal consortia to provide safe and stable out-of-home care for children under the jurisdiction of the state or tribal child welfare agency until the children are returned home safely, placed with adoptive families, or placed in other planned arrangements for permanency.
Applicant Eligibility: Funds are available to states (including the District of Columbia, Puerto Rico, the U.S. Virgin Islands, Guam, and American Samoa) and to Tribes with approved title IV-E plans.
Beneficiary Eligibility: Children meeting eligibility criteria for the former Aid to Families with Dependent Children program (except for up to a 12-month period for those children placed with a parent residing in a licensed residential family-based treatment facility for substance abuse treatment) whose removal and placement in foster care are in accordance with a voluntary placement agreement or judicial determinations to the effect that continuation in the home would be contrary to the child's welfare and that reasonable efforts were made to prevent the removal (or that such efforts were not necessary), and whose placement and care are the responsibility of the state or tribal agency administering the title IV-E program. See section 472 of the Social Security Act and the Code of Federal Regulations at 45 CFR Part 1356.71 for additional details on program eligibility requirements.
Award Range/Average: FY 2016 Formula Grants: $58,993 to $2,496,685 with an average of $77,434,135. FY 2016 Plan Development/Implementation Grants: $67,891 to $1,470,700 with an average of $487,676.
Funding: (Formula Grants) FY 18 $5,022,757,197.00; FY 19 est $5,083,096.00; FY 20 est $5,231,904,151.00; (Project Grants (Discretionary)) FY 18 est $2,631,700.00; FY 19 est $2,666,398.00; FY 20 est $2,370,699.00
HQ: 330 C Street SW, Room 3512, Washington, DC 20201
   Phone: 225-654-2527 | Email: jennifer.butler-hembree@acf.hhs.gov
   http://www.acf.hhs.gov/programs/cb

ED84.116 | FUND FOR THE IMPROVEMENT OF POSTSECONDARY EDUCATION
"FIPSE"

Award: Project Grants
Purpose: To assist and support institutional reforms and innovative strategies designed to improve postsecondary instruction, quality, and to expand postsecondary opportunities.
Applicant Eligibility: Eligible applicants include Institutions of higher education, other public and private non-profit Institutions and agencies and combinations of these Institutions and agencies.
Beneficiary Eligibility: Postsecondary educational institutions and their students will benefit.
Award Range/Average: In 2018, the estimated range of awards was $1,500,000 to $4,950,000, and the estimated average size of awards was $2,475,000.
Funding: (Project Grants) FY 18 $6,000,000.00; FY 19 est $6,000,000.00; FY 20 est $0.00
HQ: 400 Maryland Avenue SW, Washington, DC 20202
   Phone: 202-453-6150 | Email: stacey.slijepcevic@ed.gov
   https://www2.ed.gov/about/offices/list/ope/fipse/index.html

Programs Administered by Federal Headquarters

HHS93.968 | FUNDING IN SUPPORT OF THE PENNSYLVANIA RURAL HEALTH MODEL

Award: Cooperative Agreements

Purpose: The purpose of this funding opportunity for the Funding in Support of Pennsylvania's Rural Health Model cooperative agreement is to provide Pennsylvania with the start-up and initial implementation funding component of the Model to assist Pennsylvania in accomplishing the health outcomes, financial, and rural hospital scale targets required of Pennsylvania under the Model.

Applicant Eligibility: This single source funding opportunity provides Pennsylvania with the necessary start-up funding for the Model and is open to Pennsylvania's Department of Health and later the Rural Health Redesign Center. First, the Pennsylvania Department of Health is uniquely positioned as the initial applicant under this funding opportunity to meet the objectives of this funding opportunity based on its existing knowledge of the Model, its regulatory authority over healthcare in Pennsylvania, and its capacity to administer the Pennsylvania Rural Health Model including operationalizing the Rural Health Redesign Center, and its existing partnerships and collaborations with Pennsylvania providers. Knowledge of the Model: The Pennsylvania Department of Health is intimately familiar with the objectives of the Model. Pennsylvania's Department of Health was a key member of the discussions between Pennsylvania and CMS during the development of the Model; the Pennsylvania's Secretary of Health and staff dedicated significant time, energy, and resources over the past year in partnering with CMS to establish the Model's financial, health outcomes, and rural hospital scale targets. This existing familiarity and knowledge of the Model will help the Pennsylvania Department of Health to expediently deploy the start-up funding offered under this funding opportunity announcement and successfully operationalize the Rural Health Redesign Center. Authority and role in administering the Model: The Pennsylvania Department of Health is responsible for ensuring that changes in Pennsylvania's health system improve the conditions and well-being of Pennsylvanians. The Pennsylvania Department of Health has broad healthcare authority to administer the payments under the model and to improve the health of Pennsylvanians and control the rate of growth in healthcare costs. Additionally, the Pennsylvania Department of Health is a signatory to the Pennsylvania Rural Health Model's State Agreement and will be supporting the State in achieving its obligations under the State Agreement. Existing partnership and collaboration: The Pennsylvania Department of Health is located in Pennsylvania and has existing relationships and a history of collaboration with Pennsylvania providers, payers, and community-based resources that would benefit from this funding opportunity. Pennsylvania's Department of Health has also been working with these stakeholders for their input and participation throughout the development of the Model. Second, the Rural Health Redesign Center as the second applicant, will also be uniquely positioned to meet the objectives of this funding opportunity. Pennsylvania's Department of Health will legislatively create the Rural Health Redesign Center as an independent entity with authority over the implementation of the Pennsylvania Rural Health Model. The RHRC will approve hospital transformation plans, global budgets, exception adjustments and changes to operational and payment mechanisms associated with the Model as defined under the State Agreement. The RHRC will also establish and build strong relationships with Pennsylvania rural hospitals as the rural hospitals implement the Model. The RHRC will continue to strengthen these relationships as it implements the activities required under the Model. Similar to Pennsylvania's Department of Health, the RHRC will be uniquely positioned to support this Model as it will be legislatively created solely to provide implementation support for the Model.

Beneficiary Eligibility: CMS is committed to achieving better care for individuals, better health for populations, and reduced expenditures for Medicare, Medicaid, and CHIP. Through the Innovation Center, CMS strives towards these goals by testing innovative payment and service delivery models. CMS believes that states can be critical partners of the federal government and other health care payers to facilitate the design, implementation, and evaluation of community-centered health systems that can deliver significantly improved cost, quality, and population health performance results for all state residents, including Medicare, Medicaid, and CHIP beneficiaries. States have policy and regulatory authorities, as well as ongoing relationships with commercial healthcare payers, health plans, and providers that can accelerate delivery system reform. CMS has previously partnered with states to accelerate delivery system reform through initiatives such as the State Innovations Model (SIM) program. SIM provides state-based healthcare transformation efforts with funding to test the ability of states to utilize policy and regulatory levers to accelerate multi-payer health care transformation. Selected states have been working with state-based payers, including Medicaid and commercial payers, and providers to design and implement care delivery and payment reform. States participating in SIM were selected through two rounds of public Funding Opportunity Announcements released on August 23, 2012 (Round 1) and May 22, 2014 (Round 2).Additionally, CMS has released guidance to SIM state participants in which CMS indicated that in certain instances it will consider state proposals for Medicare's alignment with state multi-payer payment and care delivery models. According to that guidance, CMS would assess such proposals with consideration of the following principles: 1) patient-centered, 2) accountable for total cost of care, 3) transformative, 4) broad-based, 5) feasible to implement, and 6) feasible to evaluate. Pennsylvania was one state that approached CMS with a desire for Medicare's alignment with the state's payment and care delivery model, and Pennsylvania submitted its proposal to CMS on May 23, 2016. CMS reviewed Pennsylvania's proposal and determined that it met the requirements necessary to explore in detail a potential Pennsylvania-specific model. CMS, the Governor of Pennsylvania and Pennsylvania's Department of Health, will enter into a State Agreement on the Pennsylvania Rural Health Model. Under the Model, CMS will test the effect of deliberate care delivery transformation of rural acute care hospitals and critical access hospitals (CAHs) on quality and costs of care. The Model places these hospitals on all-payer, prospective global budgets for inpatient and outpatient services. As part of the State Agreement, Pennsylvania committed to legislatively creating the Rural Health Redesign Center (the "RHRC") to operate the Model. This funding opportunity offers $5M in start-up funding to the Pennsylvania Department of Health to operationalize the RHRC. The RHRC will be the central independent entity operating the Model and supporting hospitals through technical assistance, data analytics, monitoring, and evaluation. This funding opportunity also offers the RHRC (once operationalized by the Pennsylvania Department of Health) to apply for an additional $10 million to begin implementing activities under the Model. In return, Pennsylvania commits to achieving health outcomes, financial, and Rural Hospital scale (number of Rural Hospitals participating in the Model) targets - both for Medicare and across all significant healthcare payers as defined in the State Agreement. CMS believes that model oversight, global budget administration, data analytics, technical assistance, and quality assurance will be necessary in order to implement the Model and achieve the financial, health outcomes, and rural hospital scale targets required under the Model. First, CMS will provide start-up funding to the Pennsylvania Department of Health for 12 months from the date of award. Then, CMS will provide the Rural Health Redesign Center, through a separate cooperative agreement award, with initial implementation funding for 36 months from the date of award. These cooperative agreement awards will support operationalizing the Rural Health Redesign Center and initial Model implementation efforts, and will better enable Pennsylvania to achieve the Model's financial, health outcomes, and rural hospital scale targets as defined under the State Agreement.

Award Range/Average: In 2017, up to $10M will be awarded to Pennsylvania Department of Health. In 2018, up to $7M will be awarded to the Rural Health Redesign Center. In 2019, up to $5M will be awarded to the Rural Health Redesign Center. Finally, in 2020 up to $3M will be awarded to the Rural Health Redesign Center.

Funding: (Cooperative Agreements) FY 18 est $0.00; FY 19 est $7,000,000.00; FY 20 $5,000,000.00

HQ: 7500 Security Boulevard, Baltimore, MD 21244

   Phone: 410-786-5910 | Email: cameron.williams1@cms.hhs.gov

   http://www.innovations.cms.gov

ED84.334 | GAINING EARLY AWARENESS AND READINESS FOR UNDERGRADUATE PROGRAMS
"GEAR-UP"

Award: Project Grants

Purpose: To provide 6-or 7-year grants to States and Partnerships to provide support, and maintain a commitment, to eligible low-income students, including students with disabilities.

Applicant Eligibility: A State, or a partnership consisting of one or more local educational agencies one or more degree granting Institutions of higher education.

Beneficiary Eligibility: Low-income students and students in high-poverty schools.

Award Range/Average: State grants: Average award in FY 17, $3,328,109. Partnership grants: Average award in FY 17, $1,701,679.

Funding: (Project Grants) FY 18 $350,000,000.00; FY 19 est $360,000,000.00; FY 20 est $360,000,000.00

HQ: 400 Maryland Avenue SW, Washington, DC 20202

   Phone: 202-453-7197 | Email: karmon.simms-coates@ed.gov

   http://www.ed.gov/programs/gearup/index.html

DOD12.903 | GENCYBER GRANTS PROGRAM

Award: Project Grants

Purpose: To increase diversity and interest in cybersecurity and career in the cybersecurity workforce of the Nation; to help all students understand correct and safe on-line behavior; and to improve teaching methods for delivering cybersecurity content for K-12 curricula.

Applicant Eligibility: Must be a U.S. college or University, a public or private school or school system, or a not-for-profit educational institution. The principal investigator and Program staff must be U.S. citizens or permanent residents of the United States. Program eligibility will be determined under the GenCyber Program.

Beneficiary Eligibility: Same as Applicant Eligibility.

Funding: (Project Grants) FY 15 Actual Not Available; FY 16 est $1,400,000.00; FY 17 est Estimate Not Available

Programs Administered by Federal Headquarters

HQ: 9800 Savage Road, Fort George G. Meade, MD 20755
  Phone: 443-479-1775 | Email: cmroone@radium.ncsc.mil

DOS19.700 | GENERAL DEPARTMENT OF STATE ASSISTANCE
"General Assistance Programs"

Award: Cooperative Agreements; Project Grants
Purpose: Fulfills the mission of The United States Department of State.
Applicant Eligibility: The General Assistance Programs provide information of Department of State Programs that are not elsewhere classified. See www.grants.gov for individual project information.
Beneficiary Eligibility: Same as Applicant Eligibility.
Award Range/Average: Varies
HQ: Federal Assistance Policy Federal Assistance 2201 C Street NW, Washington, DC 20522
  Phone: 703-516-1684

HUD14.506 | GENERAL RESEARCH AND TECHNOLOGY ACTIVITY

Award: Provision of Specialized Services
Purpose: To improve the operations of the Department's programs.
Applicant Eligibility: Researchers, research Organizations, State and local Governments, academic Institutions, public and/or private profit and nonprofit Organizations which have authority and capacity to carry out projects.
Beneficiary Eligibility: Same as Applicant Eligibility.
Award Range/Average: $15,000 - $20,000,000
Funding: (Provision of Specialized Services) FY 18 $60,251,538.00; FY 19 est $77,434,000.00; FY 20 est $57,000,000.00
HQ: 451 7th Street SW, Room 8230, Washington, DC 20410
  Phone: 202-402-3852 | Email: susan.s.brunson@hud.gov

DOC11.400 | GEODETIC SURVEYS AND SERVICES (GEODESY AND APPLICATIONS OF THE NATIONAL GEODETIC REFERENCE SYSTEM)
"Geodetic and Hydrographic Surveys"

Award: Project Grants
Purpose: To provide a coordinated spatial reference system at various specified intervals in the development and implementation of Multipurpose Land Information Systems, Geographic Information Systems, pilot projects and spatial reference system, etc. The Hydrographic Center improves the techniques and technology of hydrographic surveying and ocean mapping.
Applicant Eligibility: State, local, municipal, universities and/or regional agencies. For the JHC, limited to the universities.
Beneficiary Eligibility: Same as Applicant Eligibility.
Award Range/Average: For Geospatial Modeling: FY16 = $2,979,455 FY17 = $2,919,319 FY18 = $3,000,000 - Estimate For JHC, FY 14 $7,083,370; FY 15 est. $6,200,000; FY 16 est. $6,200,000
Funding: (Project Grants) FY 16 $1,839,836.00; FY 17 est $2,979,455.00; FY 18 est $2,919,319.00
HQ: Director National Geodetic Survey 1315 E W Highway SSMC3, Silver Spring, MD 20910
  Phone: 301-713-3228
  http://www.nauticalcharts.gov

NSF47.050 | GEOSCIENCES
"GEO"

Award: Project Grants
Purpose: To strengthen and enhance the national scientific enterprise through the expansion of fundamental knowledge and increased understanding of the integrated Earth system through the support of basic research in the atmospheric, earth, and ocean sciences.
Applicant Eligibility: Except where a Program solicitation establishes more restrictive eligibility criteria, individuals and Organizations in the following categories may submit proposals: universities and colleges; Non-profit, non-academic Organizations; For-profit Organizations; State and local Governments; and unaffiliated individuals. See the NSF Grant

Proposal Guide, Chapter i.e., for a full description of eligibility requirements: http://www.nsf.gov/publications/pub_summ. jsp?ods_key=gpg.

Beneficiary Eligibility: N/A

Award Range/Average: Range Low $5,000 Range High $51,941,742 Average $479,076

Funding: (Project Grants) FY 18 $907,800,000.00; FY 19 est $931,930,000.00; FY 20 est $787,050,000.00

HQ: 2415 Eisenhower Avenue, Alexandria, VA 22314

Phone: 703-292-5079 | Email: mlane@nsf.gov

http://nsf.gov/dir/index.jsp?org=geo

DOI15.434 | GEOTHERMAL RESOURCES

Award: Direct Payments for Specified Use

Purpose: Shares 50 percent of mineral leasing revenue with the State, and 25 percent with the county.

Applicant Eligibility: Revenue from government owned land leasing will trigger automatic payment distribution computed in accordance with the law.

Beneficiary Eligibility: ONRR distributes these funds to state and county governments for leased lands within the state or county and the state or county government has sole discretion in their use in accordance with the enabling legislation.

Award Range/Average: Not Applicable.

Funding: (Direct Payments for Specified Use) FY 17 $10,445,000.00; FY 18 est $11,810,000.00; FY 19 est $9,117,000.00

HQ: Office of Natural Resources Revenue 1849 C Street NW, PO Box 4211, Washington, DC 20240

Phone: 202-513-0600

http://www.ONRR.gov

HRSA93.250 | GERIATRIC ACADEMIC CAREER AWARDS DEPARTMENT OF HEALTH AND HUMAN SERVICES
"Geriatric Academic Career Award (GACA)"

Award: Project Grants

Purpose: To support the career growth of individual junior faculty in geriatrics at accredited schools to academic geriatrics specialists and provide clinical training for them.

Applicant Eligibility: Eligible applicant Organizations include accredited schools of allopathic medicine, osteopathic medicine, nursing, social work, psychology, dentistry, pharmacy, or allied health. Eligible applicant Organizations must submit applications on behalf of eligible individuals applying for a Geriatric Academic Career Award. Eligible individuals (GACA candidates) must meet the following: A. Be board certified or board eligible in internal medicine, family practice, psychiatry, or licensed dentistry, or have completed any required training in a discipline and be employed in an accredited health professions school that is approved by the Secretary; B. Have completed an approved fellowship Program in geriatrics or have completed specialty training in geriatrics as required by the discipline and any additional geriatrics training as required by the Secretary; C. Have a junior (non-tenured) faculty appointment at an accredited school of allopathic medicine, osteopathic medicine, nursing, social work, psychology, dentistry, pharmacy, or other allied health discipline in an accredited health professions school that is approved by the Secretary. Adjunct and associate professor positions are not considered eligible faculty appointments for this grant award. D. Have a full-time junior faculty appointment in an accredited school of allopathic medicine, osteopathic medicine, nursing, social work, psychology, dentistry, pharmacy, or allied health, and commitment from the institution to spend 75 percent of the total time of the individual on teaching and developing skills in interprofessional education in geriatrics. The GACA candidate receiving support from award funds must be a citizen of the United States or a foreign national having in his/her possession a visa permitting permanent residence in the United States. In addition, per the HHS GPS, a non-citizen national is eligible for a career award. The eligible applicants and eligible individuals must submit required documentation.

Beneficiary Eligibility: Junior faculty who are academic geriatric specialists at an accredited health professions school of allopathic medicine, osteopathic medicine, nursing, social work, psychology, dentistry, pharmacy, or allied health.

Award Range/Average: FY 2018: $0 FY 2019: Range $75,000- $75,000. Average: $75,000 FY 20: $0

Funding: (Project Grants) FY 18 $0; FY 19 est $1,950,000.00; FY 20 est $0

HQ: 5600 Fishers Lane, Room 15N-194A, Rockville, MD 20857

Phone: 301-443-3353 | Email: ysong@hrsa.gov

Programs Administered by Federal Headquarters

DOJ16.830 | GIRLS IN THE JUVENILE JUSTICE SYSTEM
"Delinquent Girls Program, Girls in the Juvenile Justice System"
Award: Project Grants
Purpose: To provide support for girls from entering the juvenile justice system and improve services and treatment for girls at risk, to protect victims of child sexual exploitation or domestic sex trafficking, and other efforts for the welfare of women.
Applicant Eligibility: Eligible applicants are limited to states (including territories), units of local government, federally recognized tribal Governments as determined by the Secretary of the Interior, nonprofit Organizations, and for-profit Organizations (including tribal nonprofit and for-profit Organizations), as well as Institutions of higher education (including tribal Institutions of higher education). For-profit Organizations (as well as other recipients) must agree to forgo any profit or management fee.
Beneficiary Eligibility: See applicable program announcement.
Award Range/Average: $400,000- $2,000,000
Funding: (Project Grants (Discretionary)) FY 18 $1,823,067.00; FY 19 est $2,000,000.00; FY 20 est $2,000,000.00
HQ: Office of Juvenile Justice and Delinquency Prevention 810 7th Street NW, Washington, DC 20531
Phone: 202-353-9093 | Email: kerri.shurg@usdoj.gov
http://www.ojjdp.gov

HHS93.067 | GLOBAL AIDS
Award: Project Grants
Purpose: To help save the lives of those suffering from HIV/AIDS around the world.
Applicant Eligibility: Competition is open, limited, or single eligibility by authorizing legislation.
Beneficiary Eligibility: This is only for non-research and research activities supported by CDC/ATSDR. For the definition of research, please see the CDC website at the following Internet address: http://www.cdc.gov/od/science/quality/resources.
Award Range/Average: $25,000 to $48,000,000. Average $2,700,000
Funding: (Cooperative Agreements) FY 18 $1,083,607,334.00; FY 19 est $1,752,885,349.00; FY 20 est $1,600,000,000.00
HQ: 1600 Clifton Road NE, PO Box H21-9, Atlanta, GA 30333
Phone: 404-718-6503
http://www.cdc.gov

DOS19.701 | GLOBAL COUNTERTERRORISM PROGRAMS
"Global War on Terrorism"
Award: Cooperative Agreements; Project Grants
Purpose: The Bureau for Counterterrorism develops and leads a worldwide effort to counter terrorism using all the tools of statecraft such as diplomacy, development and defense by working bilaterally, regionally, and multilaterally.
Applicant Eligibility: See Grants.gov for individual Program announcements.
Beneficiary Eligibility: Same as Applicant Eligibility.
Award Range/Average: Depending on the project, the range is $100,000 to $2,000,000. see www.grants.gov for individual announcements
Funding: (Cooperative Agreements) FY 18 est Estimate Not Available FY 17 est Estimate Not Available FY 16 Estimate Not Available - see www.grants.gov for individual announcements
HQ: 2401 E Street NW, Washington, DC 20520
Phone: 202-663-1430 | Email: coates@state.gov

USAID98.011 | GLOBAL DEVELOPMENT ALLIANCE
Award: Project Grants
Purpose: The GDA business model promotes international development objectives through the public-private alliance.
Applicant Eligibility: The eligibility criteria for potential alliance partners is broad, and the following list of potential partners is for illustrative purposes: U.S. and non-U.S. Non-Governmental Organizations, U.S. and non-U.S. private businesses, foundations, business and trade associations, international Organizations, U.S. and non-U.S. colleges and universities, U.S. cities and states, other U.S. government agencies, civic groups, other donor Governments, host country Governments, regional Organizations, host country parastals, individual and group philanthropies and funds etc. Non-Governmental Organizations (NGO) do not need to be registered as Private Voluntary Organizations to submit a proposal.

Beneficiary Eligibility: Beneficiaries are foreign governments, foreign public or private institutions or organizations, and/or the people of the developing world.
HQ: 301 4th Street SW, Washington, DC 20547
Phone: 202-567-4688 | Email: rwillis@usaid.gov
http://www.usaid.gov/our_work/global_partnerships/gda

DOS19.032 | GLOBAL ENGAGEMENT
"Special Representative to Muslim Communities"

Award: Project Grants
Purpose: Supports projects that fulfills U.S. government global engagement goals to strengthen civil society and counter extremism, including social media training, media empowerment, leadership and social entrepreneurship development that establishes civil society capacity in Muslim communities around the world.
Applicant Eligibility: See www.grants.gov for specific requests for proposals.
Beneficiary Eligibility: Same as Applicant Eligibility.
Award Range/Average: $10,000 - $100,000 dollars, average $20,000
HQ: 2201 C Street NW, HST Building, Washington, DC 20520
Phone: 202-736-7884 | Email: kifayata@state.gov

DOS19.026 | GLOBAL PEACE OPERATIONS INITIATIVE
"GPOI"

Award: Project Grants
Purpose: Global Peace Operations Initiative (GPOI) was initially envisioned as a five-year program (FY 2005-2009) to help address major gaps in international capacity to conduct peace support operations (PSOs), with a focus on Africa. Through GPOI, the United States further provides deployment support, obligating $ 76.6 million to date to facilitate the equipping, transportation, and sustainment of troops deploying to various UN and regional missions.
Applicant Eligibility: No additional information to include.
Beneficiary Eligibility: N/A
Funding: (Salaries and Expenses)
HQ: 2201 C Street NW, Suite 2811, Washington, DC 20520
Phone: 202-647-0904 | Email: hoytlv@state.gov

DOS19.033 | GLOBAL THREAT REDUCTION
"GTR"

Award: Cooperative Agreements; Project Grants
Purpose: The U.S. Department of State's Office of Cooperative Threat Reduction (ISN/CTR) supports programs aimed at reducing the threat posed by terrorist organizations or states of concern seeking to acquire weapons of mass destruction (WMD) expertise, material, and equipment. ISN/CTR programs, also known as Global Threat Reduction (GTR) programs, accomplish this task by funding a variety of projects that aim to enhance biological, chemical, and nuclear security practices and productively engage scientists with WMD-applicable expertise in civilian pursuits. In addition to continued efforts in the former Soviet Union to engage WMD experts, GTR programs are working to reduce the rapidly growing worldwide WMD threat posed by terrorists, non-state actors, and proliferant states.
Applicant Eligibility: Please see specific announcement on www.grants.gov.
Beneficiary Eligibility: Same as Applicant Eligibility.
Award Range/Average: Typical award ammount is approximately $500,000.
Funding: (Salaries and Expenses) FY 14 $41,769,557.00; FY 15 est $35,000,000.00; FY 16 est $35,000,000.00
HQ: HST 3327 - ISN/CTR 2201 C Street NW, Washington, DC 20520
Phone: 202-736-4961 | Email: walzjd@state.gov
http://www.state.gov/t/isn/58381.htm

Programs Administered by Federal Headquarters

DOI15.435 | GOMESA
Award: Direct Payments for Specified Use
Purpose: Shares 37.5 percent of selected revenue with Gulf producing states and political subdivisions; payable annually during the year after receipt in accordance with 30 CFR Section 519.418.
Applicant Eligibility: Revenue from selected leases will automatically trigger distribution to states and political subdivisions.
Beneficiary Eligibility: Eligible states and political subdivisions with Louisiana, Texas, Alabama, and Mississippi.
Award Range/Average: Not Applicable.
Funding: (Direct Payments for Specified Use) FY 17 $957,000.00; FY 18 est $187,989,000.00; FY 19 est $268,014,000.00
HQ: Office of Natural Resources Revenue 1849 C Street NW, PO Box 4211, Washington, DC 20240
    Phone: 202-513-0600
    http://www.ONRR.gov

CDC93.479 | GOOD HEALTH AND WELLNESS IN INDIAN COUNTRY
Award: Formula Grants (cooperative Agreements); Cooperative Agreements
Purpose: To reduce rates of death and disability from commercial tobacco use, heart disease and stroke, diabetes, obesity, and other chronic disease risk factors and conditions. It combines evidence-informed policy, systems, and clinical-community linkage strategies that can be culturally adapted to meet the needs of Alaska Native Village communities and Native American Tribes.
Applicant Eligibility: Component 1: Federally-recognized Tribes and Urban Indian Organizations Component 2: Tribal Organizations, up to 1 in each of the 12 IHS Administrative Areas, including the Urban Area Component 3: Tribal Organization.
Beneficiary Eligibility: N/A
Award Range/Average: Up to 29 awards will be made to address the strategies identified in 3 separate components of this NOFO. Component 1: Component 1 recipients may apply for up to $375,000 Component 2: Up to 12 tribal organizations, up to 1 in each of the 12 IHS Administrative Areas, including the Urban Area, will be funded under Component 2 of this NOFO. Recipient tribal organizations must provide subawards to at least 4 American Indian Tribes, Alaska Native Villages and Urban Indian Organizations in their Area. Component 2 recipients may apply as follows: Areas with fewer than 25 federally recognized American Indian Tribes/Alaskan Native Villages: recipients may receive up to $950,000. Areas with 25-49 federally recognized American Indian Tribes/Alaskan Native Villages: recipients may receive up to $1,250,000. Areas with 50+ federally recognized American Indian Tribes/Alaskan Native Villages: recipients may receive up to $1,450,000. Component 2 recipients must provide at least 50% of their award to Area Tribes/IUOs as subawards. These should not be Tribes/ UIOs receiving a Component 1 award from this program. Component 3: Up to 1 tribal organization will be funded under Component 3 of this NOFO. Component 3 recipient may apply for up to $800,000.
Funding: (Formula Grants (Cooperative Agreements)) FY 18 $0; FY 19 est $22,000,000.00; FY 20 est $0; (Cooperative Agreements) FY 18 $0; FY 19 est $2,000,000.00; FY 20 est $0
HQ: 4770 Buford Highway NE, PO Box F-78, Atlanta, GA 30341
    Phone: 770-488-6572 | Email: klbishop@cdc.gov

HUD14.198 | GOOD NEIGHBOR NEXT DOOR SALES PROGRAM "GNND"
Award: Sale, Exchange, Or Donation of Property and Goods
Purpose: To improve the quality of life in distressed urban communities by encouraging law enforcement officers, teachers, and firefighters/emergency medical technicians.
Applicant Eligibility: Eligible law enforcement officer must be (a) Employed full-time by a law enforcement agency of the federal government, a state, a unit of general local government, or an Indian tribal government; and (b) In carrying out such full-time employment, the person is sworn to uphold, and make arrests for violations of, Federal, state, county, or municipal law in the jurisdiction where the property is located in. A firefighter/EMT must be employed full-time as a firefighter or emergency medical technician by a fire department or emergency medical services responder unit of the federal government, a state, unit of general local government, or an Indian tribal government serving the revitalization area where the home is located. A teacher qualifies for the purposes of the GNND Sales Program if the person is: (a) Employed as a full-time teacher by a state-accredited public school or private school that provides direct services to students in grades pre-kindergarten through 12; and (b) The public or private school where the person is employed as a teacher serves students from the area where the home is located in the normal course of business. The school is located in the same revitalization area as the property. Fifty percent or more of the students that attend the school live in the revitalization area.

Beneficiary Eligibility: Law enforcement officers, firefighters, teachers, and EMTs purchasing a HUD-owned home in a designated revitalization area for use as their sole residence.

HQ: 451 7th Street SW, Washington, DC 20410

    Phone: 800-225-5342

    http://portal.hud.gov/hudportal/hud?src=/program_offices/housing/sfh/reo/goodn/gnndabot

ED84.200 | GRADUATE ASSISTANCE IN AREAS OF NATIONAL NEED

Award: Project Grants

Purpose: To provide fellowships through graduate academic departments, programs, and units of institutions of higher education to graduate students of superior ability who demonstrate financial need for the purpose of teaching and research in academic areas designated by the Secretary.

Applicant Eligibility: Academic departments and Programs of IHEs that provide courses of study leading to a graduate degree may apply. Nondegree granting Institutions may submit joint proposals with degree-granting IHEs.

Beneficiary Eligibility: Graduate students receiving fellowships must demonstrate financial need, have excellent academic records, plan to pursue the highest degree in the field, and be a U.S. citizen or a National, or a permanent resident of the U.S., or intend to become a U.S. citizen, be a permanent resident of the Trust Territory of the Pacific Islands, or a citizen of any one of the Freely Associated States.

Funding: (Project Grants) FY 18 $28,047,000.00; FY 19 est $23,047,000.00; FY 20 est $0.00

HQ: Teacher and Student Development Programs Service Graduate Assistance in Areas of National Need Program Department of Education 400 Maryland Avenue SW, Washington, DC 20202

    Phone: 202-453-6348 | Email: rebecca.ell@ed.gov

    http://www.ed.gov/programs/gaann

HHS93.191 | GRADUATE PSYCHOLOGY EDUCATION
"GPE"

Award: Project Grants

Purpose: To provide behavioral health care, including substance abuse prevention and treatment services, in a setting that provides integrated primary and behavioral health services to underserved and/or rural populations.

Applicant Eligibility: Public or private nonprofit schools, universities, or other educational entities which provide for graduate psychology education and training or other public or private nonprofit entities capable, as determined by the Secretary, of carrying out the objectives of the project. Eligible entities are American Psychological Association (APA)-accredited doctoral-level schools and Programs of health service psychology, APA-accredited doctoral internships in professional psychology, and APA-accredited post-doctoral residency Programs in practice psychology. Federally Recognized Indian Tribal Government and Native American Organizations may apply if otherwise eligible. The eligible entity must demonstrate that the training within an APA accredited psychology training school or Program, internship, and post-doctoral residency Program will occur in collaboration with two or more health disciplines other than psychology.

Beneficiary Eligibility: Doctoral students, doctoral interns, and post-doctoral residents receiving a stipend in the GPE Program must be in an APA-accredited program, a citizen of the United States, a non-citizen national of the United States, or a foreign national who possesses a visa permitting permanent residence in the United States. Individuals on temporary or student visas are not eligible participants.

Award Range/Average: FY 16: Range: $47,213 - $350,000; Average award: $249,057 FY17: Range: $93,478 - $350,000; Average award: $263,240 FY18: est Range: $94,506 - $350,000; Average award: $269,458

Funding: (Project Grants) FY 18 $8,353,211.00; FY 19 est $18,000,000.00; FY 20 $18,000,000.00

HQ: 5600 Fishers Lane, Room 11N124A Parklawn Building, Rockville, MD 20857

    Phone: 301-443-1928

    http://www.hrsa.gov

ED84.414 | GRADUATE RESEARCH OPPORTUNITIES FOR MINORITY STUDENTS (MINORITIES AND RETIREMENT SECURITY PROGRAM)

Award: Project Grants

Purpose: To support competitive post-graduate grants to apprentice scholars at selected minority-serving graduate institutions in the area of retirement security for low- to moderate-income individuals.

Programs Administered by Federal Headquarters

Applicant Eligibility: Eligible Institutions include Institutions of higher education (IHE) grantees receiving grants from the Historically Black Graduate Institutions (HBGIs) Program (84. 031B); the Master's Degrees Programs at Historically Black Colleges and universities (HBCUs) (84. 382G); the Promoting Postbaccalaureate Opportunities for Hispanic Americans Program (84. 031M); and the Master's Degree Programs at Predominantly Black Institutions (84. 382D).

Beneficiary Eligibility: Researchers and graduate students researching retirement security will benefit.

Award Range/Average: Estimated Range of Awards - $60,000- $120,000. Estimated Average Size of Awards - $90,000.

Funding: (Project Grants) FY 17 $480,000.00; FY 18 est $0.00; FY 19 est $0.00

USDA10.864 | GRANT PROGRAM TO ESTABLISH A FUND FOR FINANCING WATER AND WASTEWATER PROJECTS
"RFP Program"

Award: Project Grants

Purpose: To compensate nonprofit organizations to establish short-term loans for pre-development and water or waste disposal projects.

Applicant Eligibility: An applicant must be a private Organization, organized as a non-profit corporation. The applicant must have the legal capacity and authority to perform the obligations of the grant. The applicant must have sufficient expertise and experience in making and servicing loans.

Beneficiary Eligibility: Municipalities, counties, and other political subdivisions of a State, such as districts and authorities, associations, cooperatives, corporations operated on a not-for-profit basis, Indian tribes on Federal and State reservations and other Federally recognized Indian tribes. Facilities shall primarily serve rural residents and rural businesses. The service area shall not include any area in any city or town having a population in excess of 10,000 inhabitants according to the latest decennial census of the United States. The loan recipient must be unable to finance the proposed project from their own resources or through commercial credit at reasonable rates and terms. The loan recipient must have or will obtain the legal authority necessary for owning, constructing, operating and maintaining the proposed service or facility, and for obtaining, giving security for, and repaying the proposed loan.

Award Range/Average: $250,000 to $500,00. Average grant: $333,333

Funding: (Project Grants) FY 18 $1,000,000.00; FY 19 est $1,000,000.00; FY 20 est $1,000,000.00

HQ: 1400 Independence Avenue SW, PO Box 1548, Washington, DC 20250

Phone: 202-690-2670 | Email: edna.primrose@wdc.usda.gov

http://www.rd.usda.gov/programs-services/all-programs/water-environmental-programs

USDA10.206 | GRANTS FOR AGRICULTURAL RESEARCH-COMPETITIVE RESEARCH GRANTS
"NRI"

Award: Project Grants

Purpose: To support all components of agriculture and implement modern ideas to sustain agriculture for various purposes.

Applicant Eligibility: For research projects, the eligibility requirements for the NRI were as follows: except where otherwise prohibited by law, State agricultural experiment stations, all colleges and universities, other research Institutions and Organizations, Federal agencies, national laboratories, private Organizations or corporations, and individuals were eligible to apply for and to receive a competitive grant. The Agricultural Research Enhancement Awards (AREA) have some notable differences from these requirements. See Part II C, 2. of Fiscal Year (FY) 08 Requests for Applications (RFAs). For integrated projects, the eligibility requirements for the NRI were as follows: except where otherwise prohibited by law, State agricultural experiment stations, all colleges and universities, research foundations maintained by colleges or universities, private research Organizations with established and demonstrated capacities to perform research or technology transfer, Federal research agencies, and national laboratories were eligible to apply for and receive a competitive grant. The bridge grants have some notable differences from these requirements. See Part II, C, 3(b) of Fiscal Year (FY) 08 RFAs for details. Unsolicited applications were not considered and applications from scientists at non-United States Organizations were not accepted. Award recipients may subcontract to Organizations not eligible to apply provided such Organizations were necessary for the conduct of the project.

Beneficiary Eligibility: For research grants eligibility includes State Agricultural Experiment Stations, U.S. colleges/ universities, other U.S. research institutions and organizations, Federal agencies, national laboratories, private organizations or corporations, and individuals. For integrated research, education and extension grants eligibility includes State Agricultural

Experiment Stations, U.S. colleges/universities, research foundations maintained by colleges or universities, private research organizations with established and demonstrated capacities to perform research or technology transfer, Federal research agencies and national laboratories. Proposals from scientists at non-U.S. organizations will not be considered for support.

Award Range/Average: Minimum and maximum amounts of funding per grant were established by the annual program announcement or RFA.

HQ: 1400 Independence Avenue SW, Washington, DC 20024

Phone: 202-401-1782

http://nifa.usda.gov

USDA10.200 | GRANTS FOR AGRICULTURAL RESEARCH, SPECIAL RESEARCH GRANTS
"SRGP"

Award: Project Grants

Purpose: To enhance and expand food and agricultural research programs.

Applicant Eligibility: Special Research Grants: State agricultural experiment stations, all colleges and universities, other research Institutions and Organizations, Federal agencies, private Organizations or corporations and individuals having a demonstrable capacity to conduct research activities to facilitate or expand promising breakthroughs in areas of the food and agricultural sciences of importance to the United States.

Beneficiary Eligibility: For Special Research Grants: State agricultural experiment stations, all colleges and universities, other research institutions and organizations, Federal agencies, private organizations or corporations and individuals having a demonstrable capacity to conduct research activities to facilitate or expand promising breakthroughs in areas of the food and agricultural sciences of importance to the United States.

Award Range/Average: If minimum or maximum amounts of funding per competitive and/or capacity project grant, or cooperative agreement are established, these amounts will be announced in the annual Competitive Request for Application (RFA).The most current RFAs are available as follows: Global Change Ultraviolet Radiation Monitoring and Research Program (GC/UV-B):https://nifa.usda.gov/funding-opportunity/global-change-ultraviolet-radiation-monitoring-and-research-programMinor Crop Pest Management Program Interregional Research Project (IR-4):https://nifa.usda.gov/funding-opportunity/minor-crop-pest-management-program-interregional-research-project-4-ir-4Special Research Grants Program Potato Breeding Research:https://nifa.usda.gov/funding-opportunity/potato-breeding-researchSpecial Research Grants Program Aquaculture Research (aka Aquaculture Centers):https://nifa.usda.gov/funding-opportunity/special-research-grants-program-aquaculture-researchSupplemental and Alternative Crops Competitive Grants Program (SACC):https://nifa.usda.gov/funding-opportunity/supplemental-and-alternative-crops-sacc

Funding: (Project Grants) FY 17 $20,162,542.00; FY 18 est $21,349,723.00; FY 19 est $0.00

HQ: 1400 Independence Avenue SW, PO Box 2240, Washington, DC 20250-2210

Phone: 202-401-4939

http://nifa.usda.gov/grants

HHS93.526 | GRANTS FOR CAPITAL DEVELOPMENT IN HEALTH CENTERS
"Capital Development Grants"

Award: Project Grants

Purpose: To award Health Center Capital Development Grants for immediate facility improvements or building capacity.

Applicant Eligibility: Eligibility is limited to currently-funded health centers (see applicable Notice of Funding Opportunity available through Grants.gov for additional eligibility information).

Beneficiary Eligibility: Populations in medically underserved areas.

Award Range/Average: Varies. See applicable notice of funding opportunity.

HQ: Bureau of Primary Health Care 5600 Fishers Lane, Room 16N20, Rockville, MD 20857

Phone: 301-594-4300

http://www.hrsa.gov

Programs Administered by Federal Headquarters

HHS93.257 | GRANTS FOR EDUCATION, PREVENTION, AND EARLY DETECTION OF RADIOGENIC CANCERS AND DISEASES
"Radiation Exposure Screening and Education Program"

Award: Project Grants

Purpose: To screen individuals described under section 4 (a) (1)(A)(i) or 5(a)(1)(A) of the Radiation Exposure Compensation Act (42 U.S.C. 2210 note) for cancer as a preventative health measure.

Applicant Eligibility: The following entities, (located within the approved states of Arizona, Colorado, Idaho, Nevada, New Mexico, North Dakota, Oregon, South Dakota, Texas, Utah, Washington or Wyoming) are eligible to apply for the funds: (1) National Cancer Institute-designated cancer centers; (2) Department of Veterans Affairs hospitals or medical centers; (3) Federally Qualified Health Centers (FQHC), community health centers or hospitals; (4) agencies of any state or local government, includes any state department of health that currently provide direct healthcare services; (5) IHS healthcare facilities, including Programs provided through tribal contracts, compacts, grants, or cooperative agreements with the IHS and which are determined appropriate to raising the health status of Indians; including federally-recognized Tribal Government and Native American Organizations, and (6) nonprofit Organizations.

Beneficiary Eligibility: For purposes of the Radiation Exposure Screening and Education Program (RESEP), individuals eligible for health screening, education, medical referral, and appropriate follow-up services include an individual who either: (1) was employed in a uranium mine or uranium mill (including any individual who was employed in the transport of uranium ore or vanadium-uranium ore from such mine or mill) located in Colorado, New Mexico, Arizona, Wyoming, South Dakota, Washington, Utah, Idaho, North Dakota, Oregon, and Texas at any time during the period beginning on January 1, 1942, and ending on December 31, 1971; (2) was a miner exposed to 40 or more working level months of radiation or worked for at least 1 year during the period beginning on January 1, 1942 and ending on December 31, 1971; (3) was a miller or ore transporter who worked for at least 1 year during the period beginning on January 1, 1942, and ending on December 31, 1971; (4) was physically present in the nuclear arms affected area (which includes, in the state of Utah, the counties of Beaver, Garfield, Iron, Kane, Millard, Piute, San Juan, Sevier, Washington, and Wayne; in the state of Nevada, the counties of Eureka, Lander, Lincoln, Nye, White Pine, and that portion of Clark County that consists of townships 13 through 16 at ranges 63 through 71; and in the state of Arizona, the counties of Apache, Coconino, Gila, Navajo, and Yavapai) for a period of at least 2 years during the period beginning on January 21, 1951, and ending on October 31, 1958;(5) was physically present in the nuclear arms testing area, cited in 4. above, for the period beginning on June 30, 1962, and ending on July 31, 1962, or (6) participated onsite in a nuclear arms test involving the atmospheric detonation of a nuclear device.

Award Range/Average: Range = $100,995 to $242,525. $200,590 (average).

Funding: (Project Grants) FY 18 $1,834,000.00; FY 19 est $1,834,000.00; FY 20 est $1,834,000.00

HQ: 5600 Fishers Lane, Rockville, MD 20857

    Phone: 301-443-2702 | Email: mlincoln@hrsa.gov

    http://www.hrsa.gov/ruralhealth/about/community/resepgrant.html

HHS93.527 | GRANTS FOR NEW AND EXPANDED SERVICES UNDER THE HEALTH CENTER PROGRAM

Award: Project Grants

Purpose: To provide for expanded and sustained national investment in health centers funded under section 330 of the Public Health Service Act.

Applicant Eligibility: Eligible applicants for funding for new access points are public and private non-profit entities, including federally recognized Indian Tribal Governments and Native American, faith-based, and community-based Organizations that have the capacity to effectively administer the grant in alignment with the requirements outlined in Section 330 of the Public Health Services Act, as amended. Refer to the applicable notice of funding opportunity under this CFDA Program for additional information. Eligible applicants for funding for expanded services, integrated behavioral health services, oral health infrastructure, HIV prevention, and substance use disorder and mental health service expansion are current Health Center Program award recipients (funded under section 330 of the Public Health Service Act, as amended). Refer to the applicable notice of funding opportunity under this CFDA Program for additional information. Eligible applicants for funding for Health Center Controlled Networks are networks that are at least majority controlled and, as applicable, at least majority owned by Health Center Program award recipients; or current Health Center Program award recipients, funded for at least the 2 consecutive preceding years, applying on behalf of a Health Center Controlled Network. Refer to the applicable notice of funding opportunity under this CFDA Program for additional information.

Beneficiary Eligibility: Population groups in medically underserved areas, medically underserved populations, and special populations such migratory and seasonal agricultural workers and their families, people experiencing homelessness, and public housing residents.

Award Range/Average: Varies. See applicable notice of funding opportunity.

Funding: (Project Grants) FY 18 $388,700,000.00; FY 19 est $368,000,000.00; FY 20 est $92,000,000.00

HQ: 5600 Fishers Lane, Room 16N16, Rockville, MD 20857

Phone: 301-594-4300

http://www.hrsa.gov

DOJ16.889 | GRANTS FOR OUTREACH AND SERVICES TO UNDERSERVED POPULATIONS
"Underserved Program"

Award: Project Grants

Purpose: To develop strategies to prevent domestic violence, dating violence, sexual assault, and provide victim services.

Applicant Eligibility: Eligible applicants are: (1) population specific Organizations that have demonstrated experience and expertise in providing population specific services in the relevant underserved communities, or population specific Organizations working in partnership with a victim service provider or domestic violence or sexual assault coalition; (2) victim service providers offering population specific services for a specific underserved population; or(3) victim service providers working in partnership with a national, State, tribal, or local Organization that has demonstrated experience and expertise in providing population specific services in the relevant underserved population.

Beneficiary Eligibility: Adult and youth victims of domestic violence, dating violence, sexual assault, and stalking in underserved populations.

Award Range/Average: Funding will be available for up to $325,000.

Funding: (Project Grants) FY 16 $4,099,859.00; FY 17 est $4,550,000.00; FY 18 est $3,400,000.00

HQ: 145 N Street NE, Suite 10W121, Washington, DC 20530

Phone: 202-305-1177 | Email: tia.farmer@usdoj.gov

http://www.justice.gov/ovw

HHS93.884 | GRANTS FOR PRIMARY CARE TRAINING AND ENHANCEMENT
"Primary Care Training and Enhancement; PCTE"

Award: Project Grants

Purpose: The purpose of the PCTE program is to strengthen the primary care workforce by supporting enhanced training for future primary care. The focus of this grant is to produce primary care providers who will be well prepared to practice in and lead transforming healthcare systems aimed at improving access, quality of care, and cost effectiveness.

Applicant Eligibility: Eligible entities include accredited public or nonprofit private hospitals, schools of allopathic or osteopathic medicine, academically affiliated physician assistant training Programs, or a public or nonprofit private entity that the Secretary has determined is capable of carrying out such grants. Federally Recognized Indian Tribal Government and Native American Organizations may apply if they are otherwise eligible.

Beneficiary Eligibility: Beneficiaries include physician and physician assistant training programs that train medical students, physician assistant students, medical residents, practicing physician and physician assistants, and physician and physician assistant faculty.

Award Range/Average: Primary Care Training and Enhancement Program (PCTE):FY 2017 Range Actual: $169,995 to $580,000; Average award $366,669 for PCTE Program;Range: $1,487 to $80,000, Average MAT supplement: $69,210 FY 2018 est Range $169,826 to $500,000. Average award est. $367,394.79 Academic Units for Primary Care Training and Enhancement Program:FY 2017 Range actual: $703,396 to $749,897; Average award : $737,043 FY 2018 Range actual $727,702 to $749,802 Average award $744,446 FY 2019 Range est $727,702 to $749,802 Average award $744,446 Physician Assistant Training in Primary Care:FY 2018 est range: $194,827.00- $274,037.00; Average Award - $238,859.00 Interdisciplinary and Interprofessional Joint Degree Program:FY 2017 $0 FY 2018 $0 FY 2019 est $0

Funding: (Cooperative Agreements) FY 18 $4,765,335.00; FY 19 est $4,466,667.00; FY 20 est $0.00; (Project Grants) FY 18 $36,310,779.00; FY 19 est $37,748,265.00; FY 20 est $0.00

HQ: Bureau of Health Workforce For the Academic Units for PCTE Awards 5600 Fishers Lane, Room 15N152, Rockville, MD 20857

Phone: 301-443-2295 | Email: isandvold@hrsa.gov

http://bhpr.hrsa.gov

Programs Administered by Federal Headquarters

HHS93.501 | GRANTS FOR SCHOOL-BASED HEALTH CENTER CAPITAL EXPENDITURES
"SBHCC"

Award: Project Grants
Purpose: To award funds made available to expand school-based health center capacity to provide primary healthcareservices for school-aged children. This competitive funding opportunity is available for school-based health centers to address significant and pressing capital improvement needs, including alteration, renovation, and the purchase of equipment.
Applicant Eligibility: To be eligible for a grant under this subsection, an entity shall be a school-based health center or a sponsoring facility of a school-based health center as defined in section 2110(c)(9) of the Social Security Act (42 USC 1397jj(c)(9)). A school-based health center is defined as a health clinic that: 1. Is located in or near a school facility of a school district or board of an Indian tribe or tribal Organization; 2. Is organized through school, community, and health provider relationships; 3. Is administered by a sponsoring facility; 4. Provides through health professionals primary health services to children in accordance with State and local law, including laws relating to licensure and certification; and5. Satisfies such other requirements as a State may establish for the operation of such a clinic. A sponsoring facility includes any of the following: 1. A hospital2. A public health department3. A community health center4. A non-profit healthcare agency5. A school or school system6. A Program administered by the Indian Health Service or the Bureau of Indian Affairs or operated by an Indian tribe or a tribal Organization.
Beneficiary Eligibility: School-based health centers or a sponsoring facility of a school-based health center.
Award Range/Average: Not Applicable.
Funding: (Project Grants) FY 18 est $0.00; FY 19 est $10,000,000.00; FY 20 est $0.00
HQ: Branch Chief Capital Development Branch Health Resources and Services Administration 5600 Fishers Lane, Room 16N20, Rockville, MD 20857
Phone: 301-594-4300
http://www.hrsa.gov

ED84.369 | GRANTS FOR STATE ASSESSMENTS AND RELATED ACTIVITIES

Award: Formula Grants
Purpose: To pay the costs of developing the standards and high-quality assessments required by Title I of the ESEA.
Applicant Eligibility: State educational agencies.
Beneficiary Eligibility: States and local educational agencies.
Award Range/Average: FY 2018 range of awards to States: $3,306,849- $28,444,134 average $7,027,096. FY 2019 range of awards to States: $3,317,183- $28,368,797 average $7,027,096. FY 2020 range of awards to States: $3,317,183- $28,368,797 average $7,027,096.
Funding: (Formula Grants) FY 18 $369,100,000.00; FY 19 est $369,100,000.00; FY 20 est $369,100,000.00
HQ: Department of Education 400 Maryland Avenue SW, Washington, DC 20202
Phone: 202-453-5514 | Email: patrick.rooney@ed.gov
http://www2.ed.gov/admins/lead/account/saa.html

VA64.038 | GRANTS FOR THE RURAL VETERANS COORDINATION PILOT
"RVCP"

Award: Project Grants
Purpose: Offers grants for a two-year pilot program to aid Veterans and their families with the transition to civilian life.
Applicant Eligibility: The eligible entities that applied for the grant were (1) Private non-profit Organizations with tax exempt status (501 (C) 3) and (2) local, state and tribal government entities.
Beneficiary Eligibility: Eligible Veterans for the program are limited to Veterans and their accompanying families who are transitioning from military service to civilian life in rural areas. According to Federal Register (78 FR 12617) on February 25, 2013, which is codified at 38 CFR part 64, an eligible Veteran means a person who served in active military, naval, or air service, who was discharged or released under conditions other than dishonorable. A Veteran who is transitioning from military service to civilian life means a veteran who is separating from active military, naval, or air service in the Armed Forces to return to life as a civilian, and such veteran's date of discharge or release from active military, naval, or air service was not more than 2 years prior to the date on which the RVCP grant was awarded. A Veteran's family means those individuals who reside with the veteran in the veteran's primary residence. These individuals include a parent, a spouse, a

child, a step-family member, an extended family member, and individuals who reside in the home with the veteran but are not a member of the family of the veteran.

Award Range/Average: VA is to carry out the program in five locations to be selected by the Secretary of Veterans Affairs. Two million dollars will be allocated for the five grantees, a total of 10 million dollars for a time period of two years.

HQ: 810 Vermont Avenue NW, Washington, DC 20420

Phone: 202-461-4178 | Email: michelle.staton@va.gov

http://www.ruralhealth.va.gov/coordination-pilot/index.asp

DOJ16.590 | GRANTS TO ENCOURAGE ARREST POLICIES AND ENFORCEMENT OF PROTECTION ORDERS PROGRAM
"Arrest Program"

Award: Project Grants

Purpose: To encourage States, Indian tribal governments, State and local courts, tribal courts, and units of local government to treat domestic violence, dating violence, sexual assault, and stalking as serious violations of criminal law.

Applicant Eligibility: Grants are available to States, Indian tribal Governments, units of local government, and State, tribal, territorial, and local courts. State, tribal, and territorial domestic violence and sexual assault coalitions and victim service providers are also eligible if they partner with a state, tribal government, or unit of local government.

Beneficiary Eligibility: Beneficiaries include criminal and tribal justice practitioners, domestic violence, dating violence, sexual assault and stalking victim advocates, and other service providers who respond to victims of domestic violence, dating violence, sexual assault, and stalking.

Award Range/Average: Range: $200,00- $900,000

Funding: (Project Grants) FY 16 $29,622,711.00; FY 17 est $30,027,793.00; FY 18 est $29,500,000.00

HQ: 145 N Street NE, Suite 10W121, Washington, DC 20530

Phone: 202-305-1177 | Email: tia.farmer@usdoj.gov

http://www.justice.gov/ovw

HHS93.134 | GRANTS TO INCREASE ORGAN DONATIONS

Award: Cooperative Agreements

Purpose: To support grants for the purpose of increasing public commitment to organ donation and ultimately the number of organs recovered and transplanted.

Applicant Eligibility: Reimbursement of Travel and Subsistence Expenses Incurred toward Living Organ Donation: As specified in Section 377 of the Public Health Service Act, as amended, eligible applicants include States, transplant centers, qualified organ procurement Organizations under section 371, or other public or private entities. If the applicant is an OPTN member, and if the applicant is working with a consortium that includes OPTN members, the applicant and all other OPTN members are expected to comply with the final rule governing the operation of the OPTN Section 121. 11(b2). Faith-based, community Organizations and Federally Recognized Indian Tribal Government and Native American Organizations are eligible to apply. Increasing Organ Donation Awareness Grant Program: As specified in Section 377A(b) of the Public Health Service Act, as amended, the Secretary may make peer-reviewed grants to public and nonprofit private entities for the purpose of carrying out studies and demonstration projects to increase: organ donation and recovery rates; knowledge about opportunities for, and the risks and benefits associated with living donation; and knowledge about vascularized composite allografts (VCA) and willingness to become a VCA deceased donor or provide authorization for a deceased relative to become a VCA donor. If the applicant is an OPTN member, and if the applicant is working with a consortium that includes OPTN members, the applicant and all other OPTN members are expected to comply with the final rule governing the operation of the OPTN Section 121. 11(b2). Faith-based, community Organizations and Federally Recognized Indian Tribal Government and Native American Organizations are eligible to apply. Lost Wages Support for Living Organ Donors (Demonstration Project): As specified in Section 377A(b) of the Public Health Service Act, as amended, the Secretary may make peer-reviewed grants to public and nonprofit private entities for the purpose of carrying out studies and demonstration projects to increase organ donation and recovery rates, including living donation. If the applicant is an OPTN member, and if the applicant is working with a consortium that includes OPTN members, the applicant and all other OPTN members are expected to comply with the final rule governing the operation of the OPTN Section 121. 11(b2). Faith-based, community Organizations and Federally Recognized Indian Tribal Government and Native American Organizations are eligible to apply.

Beneficiary Eligibility: Reimbursement of Travel and Subsistence Expenses Incurred toward Living Organ Donation: Primary beneficiaries are low/moderate income living organ donors and recipients. Increasing Organ Donation Awareness Grant

Programs Administered by Federal Headquarters

Program: Beneficiaries of the grant efforts are patients on the national transplant waiting list. Lost Wages Support for Living Organ Donors (Demonstration Project): Beneficiaries include living organ donors and recipients of live organ donation.

Award Range/Average: Reimbursement of Travel and Subsistence Expenses Incurred toward Living Organ Donation: one award up to $3,250,000 Increasing Organ Donation Awareness Grant Program: $301,992 to $548,075; $398,324. Lost Wages Support for Living Organ Donors (Demonstration Project): one award up to $2,000,000.

Funding: (Project Grants) FY 18 $4,381,564.00; FY 19 est $2,265,545.00; FY 20 est $2,688,688.00; (Cooperative Agreements) FY 18 $2,744,196.00; FY 19 est $5,242,684.00; FY 20 est $5,241,574.00

HQ: Division of Transplantation 5600 Fishers Lane 08W49, Rockville, MD 20857

Phone: 301-443-7578

http://www.hrsa.gov

HHS93.918 | GRANTS TO PROVIDE OUTPATIENT EARLY INTERVENTION SERVICES WITH RESPECT TO HIV DISEASE
"Ryan White HIV/AIDS Program (RWHAP) Part C Early Intervention Services (EIS)"

Award: Project Grants

Purpose: The RWHAP Part C Early Intervention Services Program provides comprehensive HIV primary care and support services in an outpatient setting for low income, uninsured, and underserved people living with HIV (PLWH). The RWHAP Part C Capacity Development Program strengthens organizational infrastructure to respond to the changing healthcare landscape and to increase capacity to develop, enhance, or expand access to high quality HIV primary healthcare services.

Applicant Eligibility: Public and private nonprofit entities that are: federally qualified health centers under Section 1905(1)(2) (B) of the Social Security Act; recipients under Section 1001 of the PHS Act (regarding family planning) other than States; comprehensive hemophilia diagnostic and treatment centers; rural health clinics; health facilities operated by or pursuant to a contract with the Indian Health Service; community-based Organizations, clinics, hospitals and other health facilities that provide early intervention services to those persons infected with HIV/AIDS through intravenous drug use; or nonprofit private entities that provide comprehensive primary care services to populations at-risk of HIV/AIDS, including faith-based and community-based Organizations. Eligible applicants for the Capacity Development Program include public and nonprofit private entities, including faith-based and community-based Organizations, and Tribes and tribal Organizations.

Beneficiary Eligibility: Low income, uninsured, and underserved PWH.

Award Range/Average: $54,500 to $150,000;-Capacity Development Average $133,392. Capacity Development grants are limited to $150,000. $92,999 to $1,507,775-Early Intervention Services Average $520,782

Funding: (Project Grants) FY 18 $188,813,186.00; FY 19 est $185,550,928.00; FY 20 est $185,752,822.00

HQ: 5600 Fishers Lane, Room 09N16, Rockville, MD 20857

Phone: 301-443-1326 | Email: hendale@hrsa.gov

http://www.hrsa.gov

DOJ16.525 | GRANTS TO REDUCE DOMESTIC VIOLENCE, DATING VIOLENCE, SEXUAL ASSAULT, AND STALKING ON CAMPUS
"Campus Program"

Award: Project Grants

Purpose: To develop and strengthen effective security and investigation strategies to combat sexual assault, domestic violence, dating violence, and stalking on campuses; to develop and strengthen victim services in cases involving such crimes against women on campuses; and to develop and strengthen prevention education and awareness programs.

Applicant Eligibility: Institutions of higher education as defined under the Higher education Amendments of 1998 that are in compliance with the campus crime reporting requirements set forth in 20 U.S.C. 1092 (f) as amended by Public Law 105-244, 112 Stat. 1581, Sec. 486 (e) (1998). A consortia of Institutions of higher education may also apply for these grants provided that each individual consortium member is also eligible to apply.

Beneficiary Eligibility: Eligible applicants are institutions of higher education.

Award Range/Average: Range: $250,000- $550,000

Funding: (Project Grants) FY 16 $15,229,902.00; FY 17 est $16,594,162.00; FY 18 est $16,500,000.00

HQ: 145 N Street NE, Suite 10W121, Washington, DC 20530

Phone: 202-305-1177 | Email: tia.farmer@usdoj.gov

http://www.justice.gov/ovw

HHS93.597 | GRANTS TO STATES FOR ACCESS AND VISITATION PROGRAMS

Award: Formula Grants

Purpose: Enables States to create programs which support and facilitate access and visitation by non-custodial parents with their children.

Applicant Eligibility: All States, the District of Columbia, Puerto Rico, Virgin Islands and Guam.

Beneficiary Eligibility: Custodial and non-custodial parents.

Award Range/Average: The amount of funding provided to each grantee is based on an allocation formula with a designated minimum amount provided in statute.

Funding: (Formula Grants) FY 18 $10,000,000.00; FY 98 est $10,000,000.00; F20 est $10,000,000.00

HQ: 330 C Street SW, Washington, DC 20201

Phone: 202-401-5651 | Email: michael.hayes@acf.hhs.gov

http://www.acf.dhhs.gov/programs/cse

VA64.005 | GRANTS TO STATES FOR CONSTRUCTION OF STATE HOME FACILITIES

"State Home Construction"

Award: Project Grants

Purpose: To assist States to acquire or construct State home facilities for furnishing domiciliary or nursing home care to veterans.

Applicant Eligibility: Any State may apply after assuring that the assisted facility will be owned by the State; and will be used primarily for veterans.

Beneficiary Eligibility: Veterans meeting VA and State admission criteria.

HQ: 810 Vermont Avenue NW, Washington, DC 20420

Phone: 202-461-6751

http://www.va.gov

HHS93.165 | GRANTS TO STATES FOR LOAN REPAYMENT

"State Loan Repayment Program (SLRP)"

Award: Project Grants; Direct Payments for Specified Use

Purpose: To increase the availability of primary healthcare in health professional shortage areas (HPSAs) by assisting States in operating programs for the repayment of educational loans of health professionals.

Applicant Eligibility: Eligible entities include the 50 States, the District of Columbia, Guam, the Commonwealth of Puerto Rico, the Northern Mariana Islands, the U.S. Virgin Islands, American Samoa, the Federated States of Micronesia, the Republic of the Marshall Islands, and the Republic of Palau.

Beneficiary Eligibility: Applicants for State programs must have completed a course of study required to practice independently without supervision as one of the following health care professionals: Doctor of Allopathic Medicine or Osteopathic Medicine, General Practice Dentist (D.D.S. or D.M.D.), Pediatric Dentist, Primary Care Certified Nurse Practitioner, Certified Nurse-Midwife, Primary Care Registered Nurse, Pharmacist, Primary Care Physician Assistant, Registered Clinical Dental Hygienist, Health Service Psychologist (formerly Clinical or Counselling Psychologist (Ph.D. or equivalent), Licensed Clinical Social Worker (master's or doctoral degree in social work), Psychiatric Nurse Specialist, Mental Health Counselor, Licensed Professional Counselor (master's or doctoral degree with a major study in counselling), Marriage and Family Therapist (master's or doctoral degree with a major study in marriage and family therapy), Registered Nurse and Pharmacist. The primary care specialties approvable for physicians are: family medicine (and osteopathic general practice), internal medicine, including geriatricians, pediatrics, obstetrics/gynecology, and geriatrics and general psychiatry. General practitioners (physicians who have not completed residency training programs) are not eligible for funding under the SLRP. The primary care specialties approval for registered nurses, nurse practitioners and physician assistants are: adult, family, pediatrics, psychiatry/mental health, geriatrics, or women's health. Participants must provide full-time clinical service for a minimum of two years in a public or non-profit entity located in a federally designated Health Professional Shortage Area (HPSA). Refer to the NHSC State Loan Repayment Program Guidance for specific requirements.

Award Range/Average: FY 18 awards ranged from $80,000 to $1,000,000, with an average award of $337,457.73. FY 19 awards ranged from $68,000 to $1,000,000, with an average award of $ 441,392.19. FY 20 awards (est) ranged from $68,000 to $1,000,000, with an average award of $ 441,392.19.

Funding: (Project Grants) FY 18 $12,485,936.00; FY 19 est $18,979,864.00; FY 20 est $20,000,000.00

Programs Administered by Federal Headquarters

HQ: Division of National Health Service Corps Bureau of Health Workforce Department of Health and Human Services 5600 Fishers Lane, Room 14N58, Rockville, MD 20857
> Phone: 301-594-4400
> https://nhsc.hrsa.gov

HHS93.913 | GRANTS TO STATES FOR OPERATION OF STATE OFFICES OF RURAL HEALTH

"The State Offices of Rural Health (SORH) Program"

Award: Project Grants
Purpose: The Rural Outreach Benefits Counseling Program seeks to expand outreach, education and enrollment efforts to eligible uninsured individuals and families, and newly insured individuals and families in rural communities.
Applicant Eligibility: Grants: All fifty states may apply. Each state may only submit one application. Only current SORH awardees, as designated by the Governor, may apply.
Beneficiary Eligibility: Underserved populations in rural areas; facilities and services in rural areas.
Award Range/Average: $165,521 - $179,871.
Funding: (Project Grants) FY 18 $8,587,983.00; FY 19 est $8,774,156.00; FY 20 Estimate Not Available
HQ: The Federal Office of Rural Health Policy 5600 Fishers Lane, Room 17W45C, Rockville, MD 20857
> Phone: 301-443-0835 | Email: sstack@hrsa.gov
> http://www.hrsa.gov/ruralhealth

HHS93.236 | GRANTS TO STATES TO SUPPORT ORAL HEALTH WORKFORCE ACTIVITIES

Award: Project Grants
Purpose: To Support Oral Health Workforce Activities assists states to develop and implement innovative programs to address the dental workforce needs of designated Dental Health Professional Shortage Areas.
Applicant Eligibility: Eligible applicants include Governor appointed, state government entities. In addition to U.S. states, eligible applicants include: District of Columbia, Guam, the Commonwealth of Puerto Rico, the Northern Mariana Islands, the U.S. Virgin Islands, American Samoa, the Federated States of Micronesia, the Republic of the Marshall Islands, and the Republic of Palau. Each state is limited to only one application. Applicants must have significant experience with addressing oral health workforce issues in underserved populations. Federally Recognized Indian Tribal Government and Native American Organizations may apply if they are otherwise eligible.
Beneficiary Eligibility: Beneficiaries include Governor appointed, State government entities.
Award Range/Average: FY 18 Range: $121,698 to $400,000 Average award: $358,582 FY 19 Range (estimate): $181,698 to $400,000 Average award: $398,000 FY 20 (estimate) Range: $0 Average award: $0
Funding: (Project Grants) FY 18 $11,157,473.00; FY 19 est $12,001,914.00; FY 20 $0.00
HQ: Division of Medicine and Dentistry Bureau of Health Workforce 5600 Fishers Lane, Room 15N-120, Rockville, MD 20857
> Phone: 301-443-5260 | Email: srogers@hrsa.gov
> http://www.hrsa.gov

IMLS45.310 | GRANTS TO STATES

Award: Formula Grants
Purpose: Provides funds to State Library Administrative Agencies (SLAAs) using a population-based formula.
Applicant Eligibility: State library administrative agencies located in one of the 50 states of the United States, the District of Columbia, the Commonwealth of Puerto Rico, Guam, American Samoa, the U.S. Virgin Islands, the Commonwealth of the Northern Mariana Islands, the Republic of the Marshall Islands, the Federated States of Micronesia, and the Republic of Palau are eligible to submit five-year plans. For information about funding opportunities at the state level, contact the specific state library administrative agency. Section 9131 (b)(3)(C) of the Museum and Library Services Act directs that funds allotted based on the populations of the Republic of the Marshall Islands, the Federated States of Micronesia, and the Republic of Palau be used to award grants on a competitive basis taking into consideration recommendations from the Pacific Region educational Laboratory in Hawaii. These three republics, along with the U.S. Virgin Islands, Guam, American Samoa, and the Commonwealth of the Northern Marianas, are eligible to compete for the grants.

Beneficiary Eligibility: State library agencies. Through activities and services provided, beneficiaries include users of libraries and information services.

Award Range/Average: The formula determining the assistance is based on population.

Funding: (Formula Grants) FY 15 $154,848,000.00; FY 16 est $154,500,000.00; FY 17 est $154,848,000.00

HQ: 955 L'Enfant Plaza North SW, Suite 4000, Washington, DC 20024

   Phone: 202-653-4650 | Email: rdale@imls.gov

   http://www.imls.gov

SBA59.065 | GROWTH ACCELERATOR FUND COMPETITION

Award: Direct Payments for Specified Use

Purpose: To help entrepreneurs start and scale their businesses.

Applicant Eligibility: For-profit and nonprofit Organizations and the general public. Funds are intended for accelerators and other entrepreneurial ecosystem models to fund operating budgets. Organizations which provide networking opportunities, mentorship, space (can be physical or virtual) and sometimes equity to start-ups. All models are expected to have a prescribed timeline after which start ups "exit" or "graduate" their Organization to function independently in the small business economy. Consult www.sba.gov/accelerators for further information.

Beneficiary Eligibility: For-profit and nonprofit organizations, Small Businesses and the general public. Organizations which provide networking opportunities, mentorship, space (can be physical or virtual) and sometimes equity to start-ups. All models are expected to have a prescribed timeline after which start ups "exit" or "graduate" their organization to function independently in the small business economy. Consult www.sba.gov/accelerators for further information.

Award Range/Average: $2,500,000 to $4,000,000 cumulative. $50,000 to $80,000 for individual awards.

Funding: (Direct Payments for Specified Use) FY 18 $1,000,000.00; FY 19 est $3,000,000.00; FY 20 est Estimate Not Available

HQ: 409 3rd Street SW, 6th Floor, Washington, DC 20416

   Phone: 202-205-7576 | Email: nareg.sagherian@sba.gov

   http://www.sba.gov/accelerators

HHS93.090 | GUARDIANSHIP ASSISTANCE

Award: Formula Grants

Purpose: To provide Federal financial participation (FFP) to states, Indian tribes, tribal organizations and tribal consortia (tribes) who opt to provide guardianship assistance payments to relatives who have assumed legal guardianship of eligible children that they previously cared for as foster parents.

Applicant Eligibility: Funds are available to states (including the District of Columbia, Puerto Rico, the U.S. Virgin Islands, Guam and American Samoa) and to Tribes with approved Title IV-E plans.

Beneficiary Eligibility: Beneficiaries are children who meet the following requirements: (1) the child has been eligible for Title IV-E foster care maintenance payments while residing for at least six consecutive months in the home of the prospective relative guardian; (2) the state or tribe has determined that the permanency options of being returned home or adoption are not appropriate for the child; (3) the child demonstrates a strong attachment to the prospective relative guardian and the prospective guardian is committed to caring permanently for the child; and (4) for children who have attained the age of 14, the child has been consulted regarding the kinship guardianship arrangement. Beneficiaries may also be siblings of eligible children placed in the same kinship guardianship arrangement. FFP is available to states and tribes for payments made to a relative guardian in accordance with a kinship guardianship agreement that is in writing, negotiated, and binding. The program was amended (through Public Law 13-183) effective September 29, 2014 to allow continuation of Title IV-E kinship guardianship assistance payments if the relative guardian dies or is incapacitated and a successor legal guardian is named in the agreement (or in any amendments to the agreement.).

Award Range/Average: Fiscal Year 2018: Grants to states and tribes ranged from $4,290 to $62,617,561 with an average of $4,895,529.

Funding: (Formula Grants) FY 18 $154,689,581.00; FY 19 est $203,000,000.00; FY 20 est $218,000,000.00

HQ: 330 C Street SW, Room 3507A, Washington, DC 20201

   Phone: 202-205-8086 | Email: liliana.hernandez@acf.hhs.gov

   http://www.acf.hhs.gov/programs/cb

Programs Administered by Federal Headquarters

GCER87.051 | GULF COAST ECOSYSTEM RESTORATION COUNCIL COMPREHENSIVE PLAN COMPONENT PROGRAM
"RESTORE Council-Selected Restoration Component"

Award: Project Grants

Purpose: To disburse funds to eligible entities for the purpose of restoring and protecting the natural resources, ecosystems, fisheries, marine and wildlife habitats, beaches, coastal wetlands, and economy of the Gulf Coast region using the best available science.

Applicant Eligibility: The Council will periodically request proposals from its eleven state and federal members. The Council members are the only entities eligible to submit proposals. The RESTORE Council does not award Council-Selected Restoration Component grants directly to other entities or individuals. Under the RESTORE Act, Council members are the Governors of Alabama, Florida, Louisiana, Mississippi, and Texas, the Administrator of the U.S. Environmental Protection Agency, and the Secretaries of the U.S. Departments of the Interior, Commerce, Agriculture, Homeland Security, and Army. When selecting projects and Programs to be prioritized for funding under the Comprehensive Plan, the Council assigns primary authority and responsibility for overseeing and implementing projects and Programs to a Gulf Coast state or federal agency represented on the Council. Council members may select subrecipients to carryout approved projects or Programs. Interested third parties may contact the Council members listed above to learn more about how the eligible entities select proposed activities.

Beneficiary Eligibility: Beneficiaries are the people, wildlife, and natural resources of the Gulf Coast region.

Funding: (Project Grants) FY 18 $52,939,432.00; FY 19 est $37,830,000.00; FY 20 est $18,500,000.00

HQ: 500 Poydras Street, Suite 1117, New Orleans, LA 70130

Phone: 504-444-3558 | Email: kristin.smith@restorethegulf.gov

http://www.restorethegulf.gov

EPA66.130 | GULF COAST ECOSYSTEM RESTORATION COUNCIL COMPREHENSIVE PLAN COMPONENT
"EPA's RESTORE Council Component"

Award: Project Grants

Purpose: To disburse funds to eligible entities according to the funded priorities list approved by the Gulf Coast Ecosystem Restoration Council.

Applicant Eligibility: Funds are available to State and local Governments, Tribes, colleges and universities, and other public or nonprofit Organizations. Awards will be made noncompetitively or competitively based on the authority for the award and EPA procedures. Competitive awards will be made in accordance with EPA policies and procedures for competitive awards. For certain competitive funding opportunities under this CFDA assistance listing, the Agency may limit eligibility to compete to a number or subset of eligible applicants consistent with the Funded Priorities List and Agency policy.

Beneficiary Eligibility: State and local governments, interstate agencies, Tribes, colleges and universities, and other public or nonprofit organizations.

Award Range/Average: Assistance Type: Project Grants (Discretionary, Cooperative Agreements) FY 2017 - Actual ($350,000); FY 2018 - Estimate ($4,000,000); FY 2019 - Estimate ($2,250,000) Projects funded are consistent with the amounts listed in the RESTORE Council Funded Priorities List.

Funding: (Project Grants) FY 16 $0.00; FY 17 est $2,200,000.00; FY 18 est $6,400,000.00

HQ: 2510 14th Street, Suite 1212, Gulfport, MS 39501

Phone: 228-304-7441 | Email: houge.rachel@epa.gov

http://www.epa.gov/gulfofmexico

GCER87.052 | GULF COAST ECOSYSTEM RESTORATION COUNCIL OIL SPILL IMPACT PROGRAM
"RESTORE Council Oil Spill Impact Program"

Award: Project Grants

Purpose: To disburse funds to eligible entities for the purpose of restoring and protecting the natural resources, ecosystems, fisheries, marine and wildlife habitats, beaches, coastal wetlands, and economy of the Gulf Coast region.

Applicant Eligibility: Eligible applicants are specified by the RESTORE Act and regulations at 31 C. F. R. Part 34 as the five Gulf Coast States or their administrative agents, as defined in 33 U.S.C. 1321(t)(3), Alabama, Florida, Louisiana, Mississippi, and Texas. For the development of the State Expenditure Plan, the eligible entities for each Gulf Coast State are as follows: in Alabama, the Alabama Gulf Coast Recovery Council; in Florida, a consortia of local political subdivisions that includes at a minimum 1 representative of each affected county; in Louisiana, the Coastal Protection and Restoration Authority of Louisiana; in Mississippi, the Office of the Governor or an appointee of the Office of the Governor; and in Texas, the Office of the Governor or an appointee of the Office of the Governor [33 U.S.C. 1321(t)(3)(B)(iii)]. Only the above-named entities are eligible applicants who may apply for funding. The RESTORE Council does not make Spill Impact Program grants directly to other entities or individuals. States may select subrecipients to carryout approved projects in the State Expenditure Plan. Interested third parties may contact their jurisdiction listed above to learn more about how the eligible entities select proposed activities.

Beneficiary Eligibility: The principal beneficiaries are the people, wildlife, economy/businesses, and natural resources of the Gulf Coast region.

Funding: (Project Grants (for specified projects)) FY 18 $35,597,956.00; FY 19 est $28,542,000.00; FY 20 est $158,000,000.00

HQ: 500 Poydras Street, Suite 1117, New Orleans, LA 70130

    Phone: 504-444-3558 | Email: kristin.smith@restorethegulf.gov

    http://www.restorethegulf.gov

DOC11.451 | GULF COAST ECOSYSTEM RESTORATION SCIENCE, OBSERVATION, MONITORING, AND TECHNOLOGY

"National Centers for Coastal Ocean Science - NOAA RESTORE Act Science Program"

Award: Project Grants

Purpose: The RESTORE Act Science program supports the Gulf of Mexico ecosystem in its sustainability of fish stocks, wildlife, and fishing industries.

Applicant Eligibility: Institutions of higher education, not-for- profit Institutions, State, local and Indian tribal Governments, commercial Organizations and Federal agencies. All applicants will be treated equally in the competitive process.

Beneficiary Eligibility: The five Gulf Coast states: Texas, Mississippi, Louisiana, Florida, and Alabama.

Funding: (Salaries and Expenses) FY 16 $0.00; FY 17 est $4,904,381.00; FY 18 est $4,900,000.00

    HQ: 1305 E W Highway, Silver Spring, MD 20901 | Email: laurie.golden@noaa.gov

    http://restoreactscienceprogram.noaa.gov

DOJ16.843 | GULF STATES REGIONAL LAW ENFORCEMENT TECHNOLOGY TRAINING AND TECHNICAL ASSISTANCE INITIATIVE

"Regional Law Enforcement Technology Initiative"

Award: Project Grants

Purpose: Helps to identify a training and technical assistance (TTA) provider to develop a program that assists the local law agency to gather, analyse, and share information about crime and suspicious activity within the Gulf Shore states of Florida, Alabama, Louisiana, Mississippi, and Texas.

Applicant Eligibility: This solicitation will be a training and technical assistance (TTA) initiative and the eligible applicants are limited to nonprofit or for-profit Organizations (including tribal nonprofit and for-profit Organizations) and Institutions of higher education (including tribal Institutions of higher education). Applicants must possess experience in providing TTA on a national level to state, regional, county, local, and tribal law enforcement agencies and other criminal justice entities. This TTA should include information and intelligence sharing, law enforcement technology, interaction with fusion centers, responding to crimes and suspicious activities in local communities, and providing requested training both in-person and online. The applicant must have the capacity to deliver these TTA services remote locations in the Gulf States of Florida, Alabama, Louisiana, Mississippi, and Texas.

Beneficiary Eligibility: State, regional, county, local, and tribal law enforcement agencies and other criminal justice entities. The TTA will be delivered to remote locations in the Gulf States of Florida, Alabama, Louisiana, Mississippi, and Texas.

Award Range/Average: This is a new program for FY19 in the amount of $3,000,000.

Funding: (Project Grants) FY 18$0; FY 19 est $3,000,000.00; FY 20 est

HQ: 810 7th Street NW, Washington, DC 20531

    Phone: 202-616-7829 | Email: david.p.lewis@usdoj.gov

    https://www.bja.gov

Programs Administered by Federal Headquarters

DOC11.463 | HABITAT CONSERVATION
Award: Project Grants
Purpose: To conduct research on habitat modifications and contaminants on populations of living marine resources and provide grants and cooperative agreements for habitat conservation activities, which includes coastal and marine habitat restoration and protection.
Applicant Eligibility: Eligible applicants for assistance include State and local Governments, including their universities and colleges; U.S. territorial agencies; federally and State-recognized Indian Tribal Governments; private universities and colleges; private profit and nonprofit research and conservation Organizations, and/or individuals.
Beneficiary Eligibility: This program benefits Federal, State, and interstate marine resource conservation and management agencies; U.S. Territories and Freely Associated States; U.S. and foreign commercial and recreational fishing industries; conservation organizations, academic institutions; international and Indian Tribal treaties; private and public research groups; consumers; and the general public.
Award Range/Average: $15,000 to $36,000,000. Typical award: $35,000 to $200,000; CWPPRA and ARRA awards are among the largest, typically in the millions.
Funding: (Cooperative Agreements) FY 16 $75,194,939.00; FY 17 est $75,194,939.00; FY 18 Estimate Not Available
HQ: Community-based Restoration Program (CRP) 1315 E W Highway, Silver Spring, MD 20910
Phone: 301-713-0174 | Email: robin.bruckner@noaa.gov
http://www.nmfs.noaa.gov/habitat/ecosystem/index.htm

DOJ16.754 | HAROLD ROGERS PRESCRIPTION DRUG MONITORING PROGRAM "PDMP"
Award: Project Grants
Purpose: To support law enforcement agencies in enhancing prescription drug monitoring programs to safeguard public health and enhance public safety data sets and develop interventions.
Applicant Eligibility: N/A
Beneficiary Eligibility: Category 1: Implementation and Enhancement: Applicants are limited to state governments that have a pending or enacted enabling statute or regulation requiring the submission of controlled substance prescription data to an authorized state agency. Category 2: Tribal PDMP Data Sharing Grants: Applicants are limited to federally recognized tribal governments as defined under the Indian Self Determination Act, 25 U.S.C. 450b(e). Category 3: Data-Driven Multidisciplinary Approaches to Reducing Rx Abuse Grants: Applicants are limited to state agencies (health departments, law enforcement authorities, etc.) and units of county government located in states with existing and operational prescription drug monitoring programs.
Award Range/Average: See the current fiscal year's solicitation available at the Office of Justice Programs web site (https://ojp.gov/funding/Explore/CurrentFundingOpportunities.htm).
Funding: (Project Grants) FY 18 $27,278,008.00; FY 19 est $30,000,000.00; FY 20 est $30,000,000
HQ: Office of Justice Programs Bureau of Justice Assistance 810 7th Street NW, Washington, DC 20531
Phone: 202-616-6500
https://www.bja.gov/ProgramDetails.aspx?Program_ID=72

DHS97.039 | HAZARD MITIGATION GRANT "HMGP"
Award: Project Grants
Purpose: The program's objective is to provide a fund for Indian tribal, local and State governments against the loss of life or property affected by natural hazards and also, to be prepared and prevent any such further losses.
Applicant Eligibility: State and local Governments, other political subdivisions such as a special districts, Federally-recognized Indian tribal Governments, Alaska Native villages or Organizations, but not Alaska Native Corporations, and certain Private Non-Profit Organizations in designated emergency or major disaster areas shall serve as the Applicant to FEMA for HMGP assistance. A State is defined as any State of the United States, the District of Columbia, Puerto Rico, the Virgin Islands, Guam, American Samoa, the Northern Marianna Islands, the Marshall Islands and Micronesia. Applicants that have a current, approved Standard State/Tribal Mitigation Plan at the time of the declaration of a major disaster are eligible to receive up to 15% of the value of all other disaster assistance grants for HMGP. Applicants that have an approved Enhanced State/Tribal Mitigation Plan in effect may receive 20 percent of the value of all other disaster assistance grants for HMGP.

Beneficiary Eligibility: State and local governments; other political subdivisions such as a special districts, Private, non-profit organizations that own or operate a private, non-profit public facility; certain qualified conservation organizations may apply for acquisition or relocation for open space projects; Indian tribes or authorized tribal organizations and Alaska Native villages or organizations, but not Alaska native corporations with ownership vested in private individuals in designated emergency or major disaster areas are eligible to apply as sub applicants for assistance. All interested sub applicants must apply to the Applicant, who then applies to FEMA. Homeowners are not eligible to apply as sub applicants but may request their local jurisdiction to apply on their behalf.

Award Range/Average: Refer to HMA program guidance.

Funding: (Project Grants) FY 18 $971,973,247.00; FY 19 est $601,809,636.00; FY 20 est $601,809,636.00

HQ: 400 C Street SW, Washington, DC 20472

Phone: 202-646-3458 | Email: kayed.lakhia@fema.dhs.gov

http://www.fema.gov/government/mitigation.shtm

USDA10.125 | HAZARDOUS WASTE MANAGEMENT

Award: Project Grants (cooperative Agreements Or Contracts)

Purpose: Provides technical support for site investigation by soil and water sampling and remedial actions at the Commodity Credit Corporation (CCC) waste sites that may have contaminant levels that exceed natural resource degradation standards.

Applicant Eligibility: The private sector may enter into a Hazardous Waste Remediation Contract to provide technical support for site investigation and remedial actions at CCC hazardous waste sites. The objective of the Program has been and continues to be removing the financial liability associated with these sites.

Beneficiary Eligibility: The public will receive the ultimate benefit to protect the public heath.

Award Range/Average: Each fiscal year in the annual appropriation legislation, Congress authorizes CCC to not expend more than $5,000,000 for site investigation and cleanup expenses.

Funding: (Project Grants (Cooperative Agreements or Contracts)) FY 17 $8,858,152.00; FY 18 est $8,355,501.00; FY 19 est $10,842,709.00

HQ: 1400 Independence Avenue SW, Washington, DC 20024

Phone: 202-720-5104 | Email: steve.gilmore@wdc.usda.gov

HHS93.356 | HEAD START DISASTER RECOVERY

Award: Project Grants

Purpose: Funds Head Start programs for necessary expenses directly related to the consequences of Hurricanes Harvey, Irma, and Maria, including making payments under the Head Start Act.

Applicant Eligibility: Funding for Head Start Programs, for necessary expenses directly related to the consequences of Hurricanes Harvey, Irma, and Maria, including making payments under the Head Start Act.

Beneficiary Eligibility: Head Start/Early Head Start programs are for children from birth up to the age when the child enters the school system. Head Start programs serve preschool age children while Early Head Start programs serve children from birth to age three as well as pregnant women. The Early Head Start-Child Care Partnership programs are expanding access to high-quality early learning and development opportunities for infants and toddlers from birth to age three, and up to age four in family child care. No less than 10 percent of each Head Start program's enrollment shall be for children with disabilities.

Award Range/Average: The range of award amounts could vary as there is not a set maximum threshold of financial assistance a grantee may request. The Office of Head Start will review applications to determine if they are reasonable, allowable, cost effective, necessary, and directly related to the consequences of Hurricane Harvey, Irma, and/or Maria.

Funding: (Project Grants) FY 18 $862,802.00; FY 19 est $150,000,000.00; FY 20 est $200,000,000.00

HQ: 330 C Street SW, Washington, DC 20201

Phone: 202-205-7378 | Email: colleen.rathgeb@acf.hhs.gov

http://acf.hhs.gov/programs/ohs

HHS93.600 | HEAD START

Award: Project Grants; Direct Payments for Specified Use

Purpose: Promotes school readiness by enhancing the social and cognitive development of low-income children, including children on federally recognized reservations and children of migratory farm workers, through the provision of comprehensive health, educational, nutritional, social and other services; and to involve parents in their children's learning and to help parents make progress toward their educational, literacy and employment goals.

Programs Administered by Federal Headquarters

Applicant Eligibility: Any government, federally-recognized Indian tribe, or public or private nonprofit or for profit agency which meets the requirements may apply for a grant. However, applications will be considered only when submitted in response to a specific announcement, published via the Internet at the following website address: http://www.grants.gov, which solicits proposals to expand Head Start/Early Head Start Programs or establish new ones. Grantee agencies may subcontract with other child-serving agencies to provide services to Head Start children.

Beneficiary Eligibility: Head Start/Early Head Start programs are for children from birth up to the age when the child enters the school system; however, Head Start programs only serve pre-school age children while Early Head Start programs serve children from birth through age three as well as pregnant women. The Early Head Start-Child Care Partnership programs are expanding access to high quality early learning and development opportunities for infants and toddlers from birth through age four. No less than 10 percent of each Head Start program's enrollment shall be for children with disabilities.

Award Range/Average: The range of assistance is $214,489 - $144,283,203; the average is $4,490,093

Funding: (Project Grants) FY 17 $9,357,741,817.00; FY 18 est $9,414,718,228.00; FY 19 est $9,437,248,659.00

HQ: 330 C Street SW, Washington, DC 20024

Phone: 202-205-7378 | Email: colleen.rathgeb@acf.hhs.gov

https://www.acf.hhs.gov/programs/ohs

HHS93.893 | HEALTH CARE AND PUBLIC HEALTH (HPH) SECTOR INFORMATION SHARING AND ANALYSIS ORGANIZATION (ISAO)

Award: Cooperative Agreements

Purpose: The purpose of this cooperative agreement is to build the capacity of an information sharing and analysis organization to share information bi-directionally with the Health and Public Health sector and HHS about cyber threats and provide outreach and education surrounding cybersecurity awareness.

Applicant Eligibility: In order to be eligible for funding, the entity needs to be performing some of the functions of an Information Sharing and Analysis Organizations (i.e., currently sharing information bi-directionally with the Health and Public Health (HPH) sector or sectors about cyber threats and providing outreach and education surrounding cybersecurity awareness) and possess the capacity to expand.

Beneficiary Eligibility: As health care delivery impacts everyone, the beneficiary eligibility includes all of the listed groups as provided in the reference manual.

Funding: (Cooperative Agreements) FY 17 $0.00; FY 18 est $500,000.00; FY 19 est $500,000.00

HQ: 330 C Street SW, Washington, DC 20201

Phone: 202-720-2919 | Email: carmel.halloun@hhs.gov

http://www.healthit.gov

HHS93.610 | HEALTH CARE INNOVATION AWARDS (HCIA)

Award: Cooperative Agreements

Purpose: In HCIA, Round One, CMS funded 107 Awardees who proposed compelling new models of service delivery/ payment improvements that showed substantial promise of delivering the Three-Part Aim of better health, better healthcare, and lower costs through improved quality for Medicare, Medicaid, and Children's Health Insurance Program beneficiaries.

Applicant Eligibility: Round One of HCIA sought to attract a wide variety of healthcare innovators and Organizations, including: provider groups, health systems, payers and other private sector Organizations, faith-based Organizations, local Governments, and public-private partnerships. In addition, certain Organizations (such as professional associations) were eligible to apply as conveners assembling and coordinating the efforts of a group of participants. Conveners could serve as facilitators or could be direct award recipients. States were not eligible to apply to HCIA Round One. HCIA Round Two seeks to engage with a wide variety of innovators. Welcome to apply are interested parties that meet the eligibility requirements specified in the Funding Opportunity Announcement, have developed innovations that will drive significant improvement in population health, quality of care, and total cost of care, and can create a clear pathway to an alternate payment model based on their innovation. Examples of the types of Organizations expected to apply are: provider groups, health systems, payers and other private sector Organizations, faith-based Organizations, state and/or local Governments, territories or possessions, academic Institutions, research Organizations, public-private partnerships, and for-profit Organizations. By state, we refer to the definition provided under 45 CFR 74. 2 as "any of the several States of the U.S., the District of Columbia, the Commonwealth of Puerto Rico, (or) any territory or possession of the U.S. " By territory or possession, we mean Guam, the U.S. Virgin Islands, American Samoa, and the Commonwealth of the Northern Mariana Islands. In addition, certain Organizations may apply as conveners that assemble and coordinate the efforts of a group of participants. Unsuccessful applicants from prior CMS funding competitions are eligible to apply. Technology-based models need to reflect the actual use, not the development, of a product in a broader service delivery or payment model. For specific details on eligibility, see the Funding Opportunity Announcement at https://www.grantsolutions.gov/gs/preaward/previewPublicAnnouncement. do?id=17996.

Beneficiary Eligibility: The Health Care Innovation Awards initiative will fund applicants who propose the most compelling new service delivery and payment models that will drive system transformation and deliver better outcomes for Medicare, Medicaid, and CHIP beneficiaries. Proposals should be focused on innovative approaches to improving health and lowering costs for high risk/high opportunity populations, including Medicare, Medicaid, and CHIP beneficiaries. In Round Two, proposals should focus, in particular, on beneficiary care and payment in the four Innovation Categories described under the heading, "Objectives (050)," above. Round Two of the Innovation Awards encourages a strong focus on Medicaid and CHIP populations. However, CMS recognizes that in order for providers to have meaningful incentives to change their service delivery models they must engage multiple payers. Therefore, applications must include a feasible approach for securing participation of multiple payers for their proposed models. This could include demonstrable commitments from current payer partners, current contracts, letters of support or commitment from private insurers, state governments, or local governments. Preference will be given to applications that include participation by non-CMS payers at the outset of the model's implementation. Funding from CMS can only be used to provide care for beneficiaries of Medicare, Medicaid, and CHIP. For specific details, see the Funding Opportunity Announcement at https://www.grantsolutions.gov/gs/preaward/previewPublicAnnouncement.do?id=17996.

Award Range/Average: In Round Two of the healthcareInnovation Awards, the Innovation Center expects to make up to $900 million in funding available to support a diverse portfolio of new and innovative payment and service delivery models that will reduce the cost of healthcareand improve its quality in Medicare, Medicaid, and/or CHIP. CMS intends to fund the best qualified applications within the scope of available funds. CMS estimates that there will be approximately 100 awards, with a range of approximately $1 million to $30 million per award; however CMS is not obligated to fund a minimum number of applicants, or to distribute a minimum amount of funds available for the second round of healthcareInnovation Awards. Cooperative agreements will be awarded with consideration to the criteria listed above under Award Procedure (093). Awardees might not receive the award amount requested and might be asked to adjust the service delivery model, payment model, work plan, budget, or other application deliverable. For specific details, see the Funding Opportunity Announcement at https://www.grantsolutions.gov/gs/preaward/previewPublicAnnouncement.do?id=17996. In Round One, the Innovation Center made 107 awards ranging from approximately $1 million to $26.5 million for a three-year period. Cooperative agreements were awarded with consideration to: (1) available funding; (2) geographic diversity; and (3) the quality of each application and the ability to meet the goals of the project. In the first round, less than 5% percent of applications were funded. Profiles of Awardees are available on the CMS website at http://innovation.cms.gov/

HQ: 7500 Security Boulevard, Baltimore, MD 21207
Phone: 410-786-7724
http://innovation.cms.gov

HHS93.822 | HEALTH CAREERS OPPORTUNITY PROGRAM
"HCOP: National HCOP Academies"

Award: Project Grants
Purpose: The Health Careers Opportunity Program strives to develop a more competitive applicant pool to build diversity in the health professions. The program's goal is to provide students from economically and educationally disadvantaged backgrounds who are interested in pursuing a health profession to develop the needed skills to compete for, enter, and graduate from a health or allied health professions program, graduate program in behavioral and mental health, and/or programs for the training of physician assistants.
Applicant Eligibility: Eligible applicants include accredited schools of medicine, osteopathic medicine, public health, dentistry, veterinary medicine, optometry, pharmacy, allied health, chiropractic, podiatric medicine, public and nonprofit private schools that offer graduate Programs in behavioral and mental health, Programs for the training of physician assistants, and other public or private nonprofit health or educational entities including community, technical and tribal colleges. HCOP grant Programs may only operate in the fifty (50) states, the District of Columbia, Commonwealth of Puerto Rico, Commonwealth of Northern Mariana Islands, the U.S. Virgin Islands, Guam, American Samoa, the Republic of Palau, Republic of the Marshall Islands, and the Federated States of Micronesia. Federally Recognized Indian Tribal Government and Native American Organizations may apply if they are otherwise eligible.
Beneficiary Eligibility: Eligible participants of the HCOP grant program must a) meet the definition of economically disadvantaged; b) be from an "educationally disadvantaged" background; and c) express an interest in pursuing a health degree program. Individuals must be U.S. citizens, non-citizen nationals, or foreign nationals who possess a visa permitting permanent residence in the United States. An individual will be determined to be disadvantaged if he or she comes from

Programs Administered by Federal Headquarters

a background that has inhibited the individual from obtaining the knowledge, skills, and abilities required to enroll in and graduate from a health professions school or program providing education or training in an allied health profession; or comes from a family with an annual income below a level based on low income thresholds according to family size published by the Bureau of the Census, adjusted annually for changes in the Consumer Price Index, and adjusted by the Secretary for use in health professions programs.

Award Range/Average: FY 2018 range: $442,220 to $640,000 Average award: $620,077 FY 2019 est. range: $550,420 to $640,000 Average award est.: $62,261 FY 2020 est. range: $0 Average award est.: $0.

Funding: (Project Grants) FY 18 $13,021,591.00; FY 19 est $13,109,475.00; FY 20 est $0.00

HQ: Bureau of Health Workforce Health Resources and Services Administration Department of Health and Human Services 5600 Fishers Lane, Room 15N38D, Rockville, MD 20857

    Phone: 301-443-0827 | Email: tmayo-blake@hrsa.gov

    https://bhw.hrsa.gov/grants/healthcareers

HHS93.224 | HEALTH CENTER PROGRAM (COMMUNITY HEALTH CENTERS, MIGRANT HEALTH CENTERS, HEALTH CARE FOR THE HOMELESS, AND PUBLIC HOUSING PRIMARY CARE)
"Health Center Program"

Award: Project Grants

Purpose: To improve the health of the Nation's underserved communities and vulnerable populations by assuring continued access to affordable, quality primary healthcareservices.

Applicant Eligibility: Eligible applicants are domestic public and non-profit private entities, including domestic faith-based and community-based Organizations, Tribes, and tribal Organizations that have the capacity to effectively administer the grant.

Beneficiary Eligibility: Population groups in medically underserved areas, medically underserved populations, and special populations such as migratory and seasonal agricultural workers, people experiencing homelessness, and public housing residents.

Award Range/Average: $84,000 to $22,600,000; average $3,200,000.

Funding: (Project Grants) FY 18 $4,493,000,000.00; FY 19 est $4,300,000,000.00; FY 20 est $4,300,000,000.00

HQ: Bureau of Primary Health Care 5600 Fishers Lane, Room 16N09, Rockville, MD 20857

    Phone: 301-594-4300

    http://bphc.hrsa.gov/programopportunities/fundingopportunities/sac/index.html

HHS93.452 | HEALTH IMPROVEMENT FOR RE-ENTERING EX-OFFENDERS INITIATIVE (HIRE) HIV/AIDS
"HIRE Program"

Award: Cooperative Agreements

Purpose: To improve the HIV/AIDS health outcomes of ex-offenders re-entering the mainstream population (Re-entry Population) by supporting community-based efforts to ensure their successful transition from state or federal incarceration back to their communities.

Applicant Eligibility: To qualify for funding, an applicant Organization must: be located within one of the five targeted states with the highest incidence of inmates known to be infected with HIV or of inmates to have confirmed AIDS in state and federal prisons at year end 2008: Florida, New York, Texas, California, or Georgia. Furthermore, the Organization must have a minimum of five years experience in: a) providing services to the re-entry population; and b) implementing HIV/AIDS-related health and support services. Additionally, the eligible Organization must be a: Private nonprofit community-based, minority-serving Organization which addresses health, human or correctional services; or Public entity (local government) which addresses health, human or correctional services; or Tribal governmental entity which addresses health, human or correctional services; or Faith-based Organization which provides comprehensive pre-release, transitional or reentry services.

Beneficiary Eligibility: The HIRE Program places primary focus on the re-entry populations in five targeted states, with special emphasis on the following re-entry subpopulations: substance abusers, men who have sex with men, and individuals impacted by mental health disorders.

Award Range/Average: $200,000 to $250,000

HQ: 1101 Wootton Parkway, Suite 550 Tower Building, Rockville, MD 20852

    Phone: 240-453-8822 | Email: brenda.donaldson@hhs.gov

    http://www.minorityhealth.hhs.gov

HHS93.718 | HEALTH INFORMATION TECHNOLOGY REGIONAL EXTENSION CENTERS PROGRAM

Award: Cooperative Agreements

Purpose: Establish Health Information Technology Regional Extension Centers to identify and disseminate best practices and provide technical assistance supporting the adoption and meaningful use of health IT to improve care quality while protecting patient privacy.

Applicant Eligibility: N/A

Beneficiary Eligibility: N/A

Award Range/Average: Awards for regional centers are expected to average $8.5M.

HQ: Office of the National Coordinator for Health Information Technology 330 C Street SW, Suite 1100, Washington, DC 20201
Phone: 202-690-7151
http://healthit.gov

HHS93.123 | HEALTH PROFESSIONS PRE-GRADUATE SCHOLARSHIP PROGRAM FOR INDIANS

Award: Training

Purpose: To provide scholarships to American Indians and Alaska Natives for the purpose of completing pre-graduate education leading to a baccalaureate degree.

Applicant Eligibility: Individuals of American Indian or Alaska Native descent, who have successfully completed high school education or high school equivalency, and have been accepted for enrollment or are enrolled in an accredited pre-graduate Program in a pre-medicine, pre-dentistry, pre-optometry or pre-podiatry curriculum.

Beneficiary Eligibility: Individuals of American Indian or Alaska Native descent.

Award Range/Average: $23,835 - $81,091; average $34,497

Funding: (Training) FY 18 $1,332,296.00; FY 19 est $2,524,684.00; FY 20 est $2,000,000.00

HQ: 5600 Fishers Lane, PO Box 09E70, Rockville, MD 20857
Phone: 301-443-5204
http://www.ihs.gov

HHS93.971 | HEALTH PROFESSIONS PREPARATORY SCHOLARSHIP PROGRAM FOR INDIANS

Award: Training

Purpose: Provides scholarships to American Indians and Alaska Natives to complete compensatory pre-professional education to enable the recipient to qualify for enrollment or re- enrollment in a health professions school or curriculum.

Applicant Eligibility: Individuals of American Indian or Alaska Native descent, who have successfully completed high school education or high school equivalency, and have been accepted for enrollment or are enrolled in a compensatory, pre-professional general education course or curriculum.

Beneficiary Eligibility: Individuals of American Indian or Alaska Native descent.

Award Range/Average: $16,617 - $43,670; average $27,596

Funding: (Training) FY 18 $927,603.00; FY 19 est $1,065,820.00; FY 20 est $1,000,000.00

HQ: 5600 Fishers Lane, PO Box 09E70, Rockville, MD 20857
Phone: 301-443-5204
http://www.ihs.gov

HHS93.970 | HEALTH PROFESSIONS RECRUITMENT PROGRAM FOR INDIANS "Recruitment Program"

Award: Cooperative Agreements; Project Grants

Purpose: Identifies American Indians and Alaska Natives with a potential for education or training in the health professions and to encourage them to enroll in health or allied health professional schools; places health professional residents for short-term assignments at Indian Health Service facilities as a recruitment aid.

Applicant Eligibility: Public or private nonprofit health or educational entities or Indian Tribes or tribal Organizations as specifically provided in legislative authority. For Indians into Psychology, public or private nonprofit colleges and universities that offer a Ph.D. in clinical Programs accredited by the American Psychological Association will be eligible to apply for a grant under this Program. However, only one grant will be awarded and funded to a college or University per funding cycle. For Indians into Nursing, schools of nursing providing nursing education and conferring degrees are eligible for this award: A. Accredited Public or Private schools of nursing, B. Accredited Tribally controlled community colleges and Tribally controlled postsecondary vocational Institutions (as defined in section 390(2) of the Tribally Controlled Vocational Institutions Support Act of 1990 (20 U.S.C. 2397h(2)), or C. Nurse midwife Programs and nurse practitioner Programs that are provided by any public or private institution.

Beneficiary Eligibility: Preference is given to applicants in the following order of priority: (1) Indian tribes; (2) tribal organizations; (3) urban Indian organizations and other Indian health organizations; or (4) other public or nonprofit health or educational entities.

Funding: (Project Grants) FY 18 $1,819,737.00; FY 19 est $2,019,929.00; FY 20 est $2,019,929.00; (Cooperative Agreements (Discretionary Grants)) FY 18 $25,000.00; FY 19 est $0.00; FY 20 est $0.00; (Cooperative Agreements) FY 18 $1,686,705.00; FY 19 est $1,686,706.00; FY 20 est $1,686,706.00

HQ: 5600 Fishers Lane, PO Box 09E70, Rockville, MD 20857
    Phone: 301-443-5204
    http://www.ihs.gov

HHS93.972 | HEALTH PROFESSIONS SCHOLARSHIP PROGRAM

Award: Training

Purpose: Provides scholarships to American Indians and Alaska Natives at health professions schools to obtain health professionals to serve Indians. They are obligated to serve in the Indian Health Service or an Indian health organization for each year of support with a minimum of 2 years.

Applicant Eligibility: Individuals of American Indian or Alaska Native who are enrolled members of a Federally-recognized tribe are eligible. Applicants for new awards: (1) must be accepted by an accredited U.S. educational institution for a full-time or part-time course of study leading to a degree in medicine, osteopathy, dentistry, or other participating health profession which is deemed necessary by the Indian Health Service; (2) be eligible for or hold an appointment as a Commissioned Officer in the Regular or Reserve Corps of the Public Health Service; or (3) be eligible for civil service in the Indian Health Service.

Beneficiary Eligibility: Individuals of American Indian or Alaska Native who are enrolled members of Federally-recognized tribe; full-time students of medicine or other health professions; prospective or currently Commissioned Officers in the Regular or Reserve Corps of the Public Health Service; or eligible civilians of the Indian Health Service.

Award Range/Average: $11,237 - $126,920; average $48,004

Funding: (Training) FY 18 $27,062,422.00; FY 19 est $15,928,785.00; FY 20 est $14,500,000.00

HQ: 5600 Fishers Lane, PO Box 09E70, Rockville, MD 20857
    Phone: 301-443-5204
    http://www.ihs.gov

HHS93.342 | HEALTH PROFESSIONS STUDENT LOANS, INCLUDING PRIMARY CARE LOANS/LOANS FOR DISADVANTAGED STUDENTS
"HPSL, PCL, LDS"

Award: Project Grants

Purpose: To increase educational opportunities by providing long-term, low-interest loans to students in need of financial assistance.

Applicant Eligibility: Any accredited public or other nonprofit private school of medicine, dentistry, osteopathic medicine, optometry, podiatry, pharmacy, or veterinary medicine which provides a course of study leading to a degree of Doctor of Medicine or Doctor of Osteopathic Medicine for PCL and LDS borrowers, Doctor of Dentistry (or an equivalent degree), Doctor of Optometry (or an equivalent degree), Doctor of Podiatric Medicine (or an equivalent degree), Bachelor of Science in Pharmacy (or an equivalent degree), Doctor of Pharmacy (or an equivalent degree), or Doctor of Veterinary Medicine (or an equivalent degree) for HPSL and LDS borrowers. Additionally, the school must be located in the United States, the District of Columbia, the Commonwealth of Puerto Rico, the Northern Mariana Islands, the U.S. Virgin Islands, Guam, American Samoa, the Republic of Palau, the Republic of the Marshall Islands, or the Federated States of Micronesia. Federally Recognized Indian Tribal Government and Native American Organizations may apply if they are otherwise eligible.

Beneficiary Eligibility: Student applicants must display financial need and be enrolled or accepted for enrollment in a health professions school to pursue a full-time course of study leading to a degree as specified above. Students must also be citizens, nationals or lawful permanent residents of the United States, the District of Columbia, the Commonwealths of Puerto Rico, the Northern Mariana Islands, the U.S. Virgin Islands, Guam, American Samoa, the Republic of Palau, the Republic of the Marshall Islands, or the Federated States of Micronesia.

Award Range/Average: $1,780 to $5,545,683 for FY 17: Average: $369,796 per institution for FY 17.

Funding: (Project Grants (to capitalize loan funds)) FY 18 $24,406,548.00; FY 19 est $21,956,739.00; FY 20 est $18,200,000.00

HQ: Department of Health and Human Services 5600 Fishers Lane, Room 15N58, Rockville, MD 20857
   Phone: 301-443-1173 | Email: jim.essel@hrsa.hhs.gov
   http://bhw.hrsa.gov/scholarshipsloans/index.html

HHS93.161 | HEALTH PROGRAM FOR TOXIC SUBSTANCES AND DISEASE REGISTRY

Award: Project Grants

Purpose: Works closely with State, local, and other Federal agencies to reduce or eliminate illness, disability, and death resulting from exposure of the public and workers to toxic substances at spill and waste disposal sites.

Applicant Eligibility: States or political subdivisions thereof, to include the District of Columbia, American Samoa, Guam, the Commonwealth of Puerto Rico, the Commonwealth of the Northern Mariana Islands, the Federated States of Micronesia, the Virgin Islands, the Federated States of Marshall Island, the Republic of Palau, National Organizations, Federally-recognized Indian tribal Governments, public and private non-profit universities and colleges.

Beneficiary Eligibility: The general public and particularly individuals and families who reside around or near hazardous waste sites.

Award Range/Average: Average range: $130,000 to $300,000

Funding: (Cooperative Agreements) FY 16 $7,013,994.00; FY 17 est $2,497,458.00; FY 18 est $2,497,458.00

HQ: 4770 Buford Highway NE, Atlanta, GA 30341
   Phone: 770-488-0711
   http://www.cdc.gov

HHS93.542 | HEALTH PROMOTION AND DISEASE PREVENTION RESEARCH CENTERS: PPHF-AFFORDABLE CARE ACT PROJECTS
"Prevention Research Centers"

Award: Cooperative Agreements

Purpose: To maintain and operate academic-based centers for high-quality research and demonstration with respect to health promotion and disease prevention.

Applicant Eligibility: Only applicants who have applied for and have been selected as Prevention Research Centers under CDC Program Announcement DP-14-001 are eligible to apply for the annual continuation funding for the core award and Special Interest Project (SIPS) awards. Funding is limited to Prevention Research Centers under CDC Program Announcement PA DP-14-001 because they are uniquely positioned to perform, oversee, and coordinate community-based participatory research that promotes the field of prevention research due to their established relationships with community partners.

Beneficiary Eligibility: Academic health centers, scientist/researchers, operational public health programs, targeted high risk groups, selected demonstration areas, and the general public.

Funding: (Cooperative Agreements) FY 18 $38,168,000.00; FY 19 est $0.00; FY 20 est $0.00

HQ: 4770 Buford Highway NE, Atlanta, GA 30341
   Phone: 770-488-6384
   http://www.cdc.gov

HHS93.266 | HEALTH SYSTEMS STRENGTHENING AND HIV/AIDS PREVENTION, CARE AND TREATMENT UNDER THE PRESIDENT'S EMERGENCY PLAN FOR AIDS RELIEF
"Global HIV/AIDS Program"

Award: Cooperative Agreements

Purpose: To offer training and technical assistance to build and strengthen care programs and health systems.

Programs Administered by Federal Headquarters

Applicant Eligibility: Eligibility varies depending on the specific Program. Applicants should review the individual HRSA notice of funding opportunity issued under this CFDA for specific eligibility requirements.

Beneficiary Eligibility: Beneficiaries are foreign governments, foreign public or private institutions or organizations, or foreign individuals.

Award Range/Average: International Twinning Center - $500,000 to $10,000,000; Average $10,000,000 Quality Improvement Capacity for Impact Project - $6,000,000 to $20,000,000; Average $10,000,000 International AIDS Education & Training Center $1,000,000 to $60,000,000; Average $55,000,000 Resilient and Responsive Health Systems Initiative - $1,500,000 to $2,000,000; Average $1,500,000 Resilient and Responsive Health Organizations Initiative: Sustainability Communities of Practice Initiative - $750,000 Health Workforce for HIV and Chronic Disease Service Delivery Global Initiative - $30,000,000 Optimizing Momentum Toward Sustainable Epidemic Control - $10,000,000.

Funding: (Cooperative Agreements) FY 18 $39,961,000.00; FY 19 est $36,000,000.00; FY 20 est $34,000,000.00

HQ: Office of Training and Capacity Development 5600 Fishers Lane, Rockville, MD 20857
   Phone: 301-443-8109 | Email: hphillips@hrsa.gov
   http://www.hrsa.gov

HUD14.913 | HEALTHY HOMES PRODUCTION PROGRAM
"Healthy Homes Production Grant Program"

Award: Project Grants

Purpose: To address multiple residential health and safety hazards, including mold, carbon monoxide, home safety hazards, pesticides, and allergens.

Applicant Eligibility: Eligible applicants include not-for-profit Institutions and for-profit firms, state and local Governments, federally-recognized Indian Tribes, and colleges and universities located in the United States. For-profit firms are not allowed to make a profit from the project. Individuals are not eligible to apply.

Beneficiary Eligibility: Healthy Homes Production Grants provide funding to not-for-profit institutions and for-profit firms, state and local governments, federally-recognized Indian Tribes, and colleges and universities located in the United States for projects that include the assessment and mitigation of residential environmental health and safety hazards, development of local capacity and the delivery of education/outreach services to the community.

Award Range/Average: With Fiscal Year 2019, approximately 12 awards, of approximately $1,000,000 each for the entire period of performance are anticipated.

Funding: (Project Grants) FY 18 $12,000,000.00; FY 19 est $12,000,000.00; FY 20 est $12,000,000.00

HQ: 451 7th Street SW, Room 8236, Washington, DC 20410
   Phone: 202-402-7596 | Email: yolanda.a.brown@hud.gov

HUD14.906 | HEALTHY HOMES TECHNICAL STUDIES GRANTS

Award: Cooperative Agreements

Purpose: To fund technical studies and improve our knowledge of housing-related health hazards and to improve/develop new hazard assessment and control methods.

Applicant Eligibility: Academic, not-for-profit and for-profit Institutions located in the U.S. (for-profit firms are not allowed to profit from the project), state and local Governments, and federally recognized Native American Tribes are eligible under all existing authorizations. Applications for supplementation of existing projects are eligible to compete with applications for new awards. Federal agencies and federal employees are not eligible to submit applications. The General Section of the Super NOFA provides additional eligibility requirements.

Beneficiary Eligibility: Homeowners, rental property owners, and residents of rental housing and public housing.

Award Range/Average: The total amount to be awarded is approximately $6 million for Healthy Homes Technical Studies. For Healthy Homes Technical Studies, the anticipated amounts and/or numbers of individual awards will be approximately 5 - 10 cooperative agreements, ranging from approximately $300,000 to a maximum of $1,000,000.

Funding: (Cooperative Agreements) FY 18 $3,000,000.00; FY 19 est $3,000,000.00; FY 20 est $3,000,000.00

HQ: 451 7th Street SW, Room 8236, Washington, DC 20410-3000
   Phone: 202-402-7685 | Email: eugene_a_pinzer@hud.gov
   http://www.hud.gov/offices/lead

HHS93.086 | HEALTHY MARRIAGE PROMOTION AND RESPONSIBLE FATHERHOOD GRANTS
"HMRF"

Award: Project Grants; Dissemination of Technical Information
Purpose: To fund Healthy Marriage Promotion activities that will help couples, who have chosen marriage for themselves, gain greater access to marriage education services on a voluntary basis.
Applicant Eligibility: The Healthy Marriage and Relationship education Grant Program (HMRE) is part of the U.S. Department of Health and Human Services (HHS), Administration for Children and Families (ACF) efforts to promote HMRE at the community level. The Healthy Marriage Program funds Organizations that combine marriage and relationship education efforts with a robust effort to address participation barriers and the economic stability needs of their participants. The Programs directly, or through the affiliates or partners with which they are collaborating, have a physical presence in a community, city, or county where services are provided. The New Pathways for Fathers and Families Grant Program (New Pathways) is part of the U.S. Department of Health and Human Services (HHS), Administration for Children and Families (ACF) efforts to support responsible fatherhood. The New Pathways Program funds projects that integrate robust economic stability services, healthy marriage activities, and activities designed to foster responsible parenting. The Responsible Fatherhood Opportunities for Reentry and Mobility Project (Reform) is a part of the U.S. HHS' and ACF's efforts to support responsible fatherhood and ex-prisoner initiatives.
Beneficiary Eligibility: Persons who may benefit from the assistance includes, families, couples, and individuals in need of assistance with Healthy Marriage services. Services include marriage enhancement and relationship education. For the Responsible Fatherhood programs, beneficiaries are fathers (with children who are up to age 24) interested in Responsible Fatherhood activities, including parenting education, economic stability services, and marriage and relationship education. Tribal TANF Child Welfare funds assist in the efforts to enhance and expand the ability of States, Native American governments, local governments, for-profit organizations, non-profit community organizations and other public entities to provide family formation and responsible fatherhood services to those in need.
Award Range/Average: Healthy Marriage and Responsible Fatherhood Grants range from $350,000 to $2,000,000.
Funding: (Project Grants (Discretionary)) FY 18 $106,885,142.00; FY 19 est $103,387,984.00; FY 20 est $116,800,000.00
HQ: 330 C Street SW, Washington, DC 20447
　　Phone: 202-205-8184 | Email: millicent.crawford@acf.hhs.gov
　　http://hmrf.acf.hhs.gov

HHS93.926 | HEALTHY START INITIATIVE
"Healthy Start"

Award: Project Grants
Purpose: The program's purpose is to improve perinatal health outcomes by using community-based approaches to service delivery, and to facilitate access to comprehensive health and social services for women, infants, and their families.
Applicant Eligibility: Eligible Project Area All applicants applying for funding under this grant notice must identify themselves as serving an urban, rural, or border community project area. A project area is defined as a geographic community in which the proposed services are to be implemented. A project area must represent a reasonable and logical catchment area, but the defined areas do not have to be contiguous. A map of the proposed project area must be included in the application. Urban - Territory, population, and housing units located within an urbanized area (UA) or an urban cluster (UC), which has: o a population density of at least 1,000 people per square mile; and o surrounding census blocks with an overall density of at least 500 people per square mile. Rural - To determine whether the Census tract or County for your proposed project area is defined as a rural area (RA), visit the webpage Rural Health Grants Eligibility Analyzer(http://datawarehouse.hrsa. gov/RuralAdvisor/ruralhealthadvisor.aspx?ruralByAddr=1) and enter the project area address. US/Mexico Border - Border communities are those communities located within 62 miles/100 kilometers of the U.S. /Mexico border. In order to be considered for Border Community funding, the project area and the target population to be served both have to reside within 62 miles/100 kilometers of the U.S. /Mexico border. Eligible Target Population The target population is the population that the applicant will serve within their geographic project area and will determine their eligibility. The target population may range from a single racial/ethnic group to the entire project area population. The project area for which the applicant is applying and the proposed target population within that project area must be clearly identified to confirm eligibility. Eligibility Factors Demonstrating Need HRSA/MCHB must be able to verify submitted data with the appropriate state/local government agency responsible for vital statistics. Border community applicants that cannot provide this verifiable data may use the other indicators specified in the second section below. Project data for the eligibility factors for all applicants must be included in

Programs Administered by Federal Headquarters

the application's transmittal letter and in the needs assessment section of the submitted application. The existing racial/ethnic disparities in these or other perinatal indicators should also be described in the needs assessment section of the application. Applications that do not provide this information, in the manner described within this notice of funding opportunity (NOFO), will be considered ineligible and the application will be returned without review. An applicant's target population within their proposed project area must meet the following verifiable criteria using the smallest statistical level of verifiable data available - not to be any larger than a combination of counties (e.g. a city project should not report county-level data).hrsa-14-020, Urban and Rural Communities Using verifiable three-year average data for calendar years 2007 through 2009, the proposed project area for communities which meet the urban or rural community definition must meet the following indicators from the list below. The 2007-2009 combined three-year infant mortality rate (IMR, infant deaths per 1,000 live births over three years) must be equal to or more than 9. 9 deaths per 1,000 live births (1. 5 times the national average) AND there must be 20 or more infant deaths over the three years for the targeted population. If the combined 2007-2009 number of infant deaths are less than (.

Beneficiary Eligibility: Service area residents, particularly women and infants in areas with significant perinatal health disparities.

Award Range/Average: (Cooperative Agreements) FY 18 $299,979- $2,000,000. Average award $716,382 FY 19 $299,994- $2,000,000. Average award $716,384 FY 20 est. $299,994- $2,000,000. Average award $716,384 (Grants) FY 18 $304,144- $1,898,600. Average award $986,761 FY 19 $8,901- $1,070,000. Average award $1,092,120 FY 20 est. $8,901- $1,070,000. Average award $1,093,140

Funding: (Project Grants); FY 18 $98,676,104.00; FY 19 est $109,211,989.00; FY 20 $109,313,964.00; (Cooperative Agreements) FY 18 $4,298,291.00; FY 19 est $4,298,306.00; FY 20 est $4,298,306.00

HQ: 5600 Fishers Lane, Room 18N29, Rockville, MD 20857
    Phone: 301-443-0543 | Email: dcruz@hrsa.gov
    http://www.hrsa.gov

HHS93.813 | HEART DISEASE & STROKE PREVENTION PROGRAM AND DIABETES PREVENTION-STATE AND LOCAL PUBLIC HEALTH ACTIONS TO PREVENT OBESITY, DIABETES, AND HEART DISEASE AND STROKE
"State and Local Public Health Actions to Prevent Obesity, Diabetes, Heart Disease and Stroke"

Award: Cooperative Agreements

Purpose: The program's purpose is to support implementation of population-wide and priority population approaches to prevent obesity, diabetes, and heart disease and stroke and reduce health disparities in these areas among adults.

Applicant Eligibility: Eligible Applicants: State Departments of Health or their Bona Fide Agents (includes the District of Columbia) 2. Large city health departments or their bona fide agents, with populations of at least 900,000 (using July 2012 U.S. census Estimates xviii) 3. Special Eligibility Requirements: Large city applicants must work in partnership with and provide a letter of support from the state department of health or its bona fide agent documenting activities proposed.

Beneficiary Eligibility: States and communities will benefit from this assistance in many ways including through improved clinical and other preventive services for self-management of hypertension, diabetes, overweight and obesity.

Award Range/Average: Actual amounts: FY2014: $69,530,534; Anticipated amounts - FY2015: $69,500,000, FY 2016 $69,500,000. The awards may range from $1,300,000 to $1,760,000 for component 1 and $1,300.000 to $1,760,000 for component 2, and $2,600,000 to $3,520,000 per applicant

Funding: (Cooperative Agreements) FY 18 $69,500,000.00; FY 19 est $0.00; FY 20 est $0.00

HQ: 4770 Buford Highway NE, PO Box F75, Atlanta, GA 30341
    Phone: 770-488-1431 | Email: rnh2@cdc.gov
    http://www.cdc.gov

EAC90.401 | HELP AMERICA VOTE ACT REQUIREMENTS PAYMENTS
"Requirements Payment"

Award: Direct Payments for Specified Use

Purpose: To assist States in meeting the Uniform and Nondiscriminatory Election Technology and Administration Requirements in Title III of the Act and, under certain circumstances, for other activities to improve the administration of Federal elections.

Applicant Eligibility: Section 253(d) provides that States may not file a statement of certification to receive a requirements payments until the expiration of a 45-day period (or, in the case of a fiscal year other than the first fiscal year for which a requirements payment is made to the State, a 30-day period) that begins on the date the EAC publishes the State plan in the Federal Register. State, or designee, in consultation with the chief State election official, to file with EAC a statement certifying that the State is in compliance with the conditions set forth in Section 253(b). The State may meet this certification requirement by filing the following statement: hereby certifies that it is in compliance with the requirements referred to in To receive funds for a fiscal year, HAVA Section 253 requires the chief executive officer of the State, or designee, in consultation with the chief State election official, to file with EAC a statement certifying that the State is in compliance with the conditions set forth in Section 253(b). For the purpose of this requirement, the chief State election official is the individual designated by the State under section 10 of the National Voter Registration Act of 1993 (42 U.S.C. 1973gg-8) to be responsible for coordination of the States responsibilities under such Act. Section 253(b) requires the State to: have filed with EAC a State plan covering the fiscal year that the State certifies: contained each of the elements required to be in the State plan, according to HAVA Section 254, including how the State will establish a State Election Fund in accordance with Section 254(b); was developed in accordance with Section 255, which describes the process of using a committee of appropriate individuals, including the chief election officials of the two most populous jurisdictions, other local election officials, stake holders (including representatives of groups of individuals with disabilities), and other citizens to develop the plan; and met the 30-day public notice and comment requirements of Section 256. have filed with the EAC a plan for the implementation of the uniform, non-discriminatory administrative complaint procedures required under Section 402 (or has included such a plan in the State plan), and have such procedures in place. If the State did not include such an implementation plan in the State plan, the Federal Register publication and the committee development requirements of Sections 255(b) and 256 apply to the implementation plan in the same manner as they apply to the State plan. be in compliance with each of the following federal laws: The Voting Rights Act of 1965; The Voting Accessibility for the Elderly and Handicapped Act; The Uniformed and Overseas Citizens Absentee Voting Act; The National Voter Registration Act of 1993; The Americans with Disabilities Act of 1990; and The Rehabilitation Act of 1973. to the extent that any portion of the requirements payment is used for activities other than meeting the requirements of title III, have provided that: the State's proposed uses of the requirements payment are not inconsistent with the requirements of title III; and the use of the funds under this paragraph is consistent with the requirements of Section 251(b); have appropriated funds for carrying out the activities for which the requirements payment is made in an amount equal to 5 percent of the total amount to be spent for such activities (taking into account the requirements payment and the amount spent by the State) and, in the case of a State that uses a requirements payment as a reimbursement for voting equipment under Section 251(c)(2), an additional amount equal to the amount of such reimbursement.

Beneficiary Eligibility: Fifty States, the District of Columbia, American Samoa, Guam, Puerto Rico, and the U.S. Virgin Islands.

Award Range/Average: 500000-27000000

HQ: 1315 E W Highway, Suite 4300, Silver Spring, MD 20910
Phone: 202-566-2166 | Email: mabbott@eac.gov
http://eac.gov

HHS93.882 | HIGH IMPACT PILOT AWARDS
"HIP Awards"

Award: Cooperative Agreements

Purpose: The purpose of these pilots is to advance a scalable process of interoperable exchange of electronic health data using standards that will improve the delivery of how and where healthcareis delivered, improve patient outcomes, and reduce cost. All awardees will be expected to measure the progress of their pilots and the level of impact towards the advancement of interoperability and produce a final evaluation report that includes lessons learned.

Applicant Eligibility: The objective of this award is to advance a scalable process of interoperable exchange of electronic health data using standards that will improve the delivery of how and where healthcare is delivered, improve patient outcomes, and reduce cost. Collaborative groups of multiple stakeholders across different Organizations will be considered, as well as encouraged, to support widespread interoperability.

Beneficiary Eligibility: As health care delivery impacts everyone, the beneficiary eligibility includes all of the listed groups.

Award Range/Average: There has been $1,250,000 for FFY16-17 for this award. We estimate that we would award no more than four (4) awards total; the award amounts would be no less than $250,000 and may not exceed $500,000 per awardee. The award amount will be determined upon the scope and strength the awardee's proposal.

HQ: 330 C Street SW, Washington, DC 20201
Phone: 202-720-2919 | Email: carmel.halloun@hhs.gov
http://www.healthit.gov

Programs Administered by Federal Headquarters

EOP95.001 | HIGH INTENSITY DRUG TRAFFICKING AREAS PROGRAM "HIDTA"

Award: Project Grants

Purpose: The program works on reducing drug trafficking and drug production in the country by sharing information and implementing enforcement activities among tribal, local and State law enforcement agencies; support law enforcement agencies to help reduce the supply of illegal drugs in the country.

Applicant Eligibility: In order to apply for and receive funds, the law enforcement initiatives must be located and operate in an area designated as a HIDTA by the Director of ONDCP. The request for funding must be supported by the Executive Board of the regional HIDTA under which they will operate. Petitions may be submitted for consideration to become a new HIDTA or to become a part of an already existing HIDTA. In both cases the petition must be submitted by a coalition of law enforcement leaders. In the case of submitting to become a new HIDTA region, a funding request will be provided by the coalition of law enforcement officers. In the case where the petition is to become a part of an already established HIDTA, the funding request will be submitted to the Executive Board for their consideration/action. Applicants must agree to operate in accordance with HIDTA Program Policy and Budget Guidance and the Uniform Administrative Requirements, Cost Principles, and Audit Requirements for Federal Awards.

Beneficiary Eligibility: Law enforcement drug task forces; drug-related law enforcement initiatives; drug-related intelligence or information centers located in designated HIDTAs.

Award Range/Average: Award amounts vary by HIDTA.

Funding: (Project Grants) FY 18 $252,300,000.00; FY 19 est $252,300,000.00; FY 20 est $0.00

HQ: 1800 G Street NW, Washington, DC 20503

  Phone: 202-395-6739 | Email: phuong_desear@ondcp.eop.gov

  http://www.whitehouse.gov/ondcp

USDA10.210 | HIGHER EDUCATION-GRADUATE FELLOWSHIPS GRANT PROGRAM
"Institution Challenge, Multicultural Scholars & Graduate Fellowships Grant Program (Graduate Fellowships) (Formerly: National Needs Fellowship (NFF))"

Award: Project Grants

Purpose: To support students pursuing doctorates in food and agriculture sciences and studies suggested by USDA.

Applicant Eligibility: Proposals may be submitted by all U.S. colleges and universities that confer a master's or doctoral degree in at least one area of the food and agricultural sciences targeted for national needs fellowships. As defined in Section 1404 of the National Agricultural Research, Extension, and Teaching Policy Act of 1977, as amended (7 U.S.C. 3103), the terms "college" and "University " mean "an educational institution in any State which: (a) Admits as regular students only persons having a certificate of graduation from a school providing secondary education, or the recognized equivalent of such a certificate; (b) is legally authorized within such State to provide a Program of education beyond secondary education; (c) provides an educational Program for which a bachelor's degree or any other higher degree is awarded; (d) is a public or other nonprofit institution; and (e) is accredited by a nationally recognized accrediting agency or association. " Eligibility also applies to research foundations maintained by eligible colleges or universities.

Beneficiary Eligibility: Funds awarded in this program are used to support the training of graduate students to obtain either a master's or doctoral degree in one of the targeted specializations of the food and agricultural sciences.

Award Range/Average: If minimum or maximum amounts of funding per competitive and/or capacity project grant, or cooperative agreement are established, these amounts will be announced in the annual Competitive Request for Application (RFA). The most current RFA is available via: https://nifa.usda.gov/funding-opportunity/food-and-agricultural-sciences-national-needs-graduate-and-postgraduate

Funding: (Project Grants) FY 18 $3,046,422.00; FY 19 est $3,043,550.00; FY 20 est $0.00

HQ: Institute of Youth Family and Community Division of Community and Education 1400 Independence Avenue SW, PO Box 2250, Washington, DC 20250-2240

  Phone: 202-720-2324

  http://nifa.usda.gov/program/national-needs-graduate-and-postgraduate-fellowship-grants-program-funding-opportunity-nnf

USDA10.217 | HIGHER EDUCATION-INSTITUTION CHALLENGE GRANTS PROGRAM

"Institution Challenge, Multicultural Scholars & Graduate Fellowships Grant Program (Institution Higher Education Challenge) [Formerly: Challenge or HEC Grants]"

Award: Project Grants

Purpose: Responding to State, regional, national, or international educational needs by strengthening college and university teaching programs in the food and agricultural sciences, and thereby increasing institutional capacities.

Applicant Eligibility: All U.S. public and private nonprofit colleges and universities offering a baccalaureate or first professional degree in at least one discipline or area of the food and agricultural sciences.

Beneficiary Eligibility: All U.S. colleges and universities having a demonstrable capacity to teach the food and agricultural sciences.

Award Range/Average: If minimum or maximum amounts of funding per competitive and/or capacity project grant, or cooperative agreement are established, these amounts will be announced in the annual Competitive Request for Application (RFA). The most current RFA is available via: https://nifa.usda.gov/funding-opportunity/higher-education-challenge-hec-grants-program

Funding: (Project Grants) FY 18 $4,499,761.00; FY 19 est $4,522,025.00; FY 20 est $0.00

HQ: Institute of Youth Family and Community Division of Community and Education 1400 Independence Avenue SW, PO Box 2250, Washington, DC 20250-2250

Phone: 202-720-2324 | Email: edwin.lewis@nifa.usda.gov

http://nifa.usda.gov/program/higher-education-challenge-grants-program

USDA10.220 | HIGHER EDUCATION-MULTICULTURAL SCHOLARS GRANT PROGRAM

"Institution Challenge, Multicultural Scholars & Graduate Fellowships Grant Program (Multicultural Scholars)[Formerly: Minority Scholars Program]"

Award: Project Grants

Purpose: Providing grants to colleges and universities to increase the ethnic and cultural diversity of the food and agricultural scientific and professional work force, and to advance the educational achievement of minority Americans.

Applicant Eligibility: Proposals may be submitted by all U.S. colleges and universities with baccalaureate or higher degree Programs in agriculture, natural resources, forestry, veterinary medicine, home economics, and disciplines closely allied to the food and agricultural system, including land-grant colleges and universities, colleges and universities having significant minority enrollments and a demonstrable capacity to carry out the teaching of food and agricultural sciences, and other colleges and universities having a demonstrable capacity to carry out the teaching of food and agricultural sciences.

Beneficiary Eligibility: Funds awarded under this program are used to support full-time undergraduate students pursing a baccalaureate degree in an area of the food and agricultural sciences or a closely allied field. Persons eligible to receive scholarships under this program are students who either are enrolled or have been accepted as full-time baccalaureate or DVM degree candidates, and who are members of groups traditionally under-represented in food and agricultural scientific and professional fields.

Award Range/Average: If minimum or maximum amounts of funding per competitive and/or capacity project grant, or cooperative agreement are established, these amounts will be announced in the annual Competitive Request for Application (RFA). The most current RFA is available via: https://nifa.usda.gov/funding-opportunity/higher-education-multicultural-scholars-program-msp

Funding: (Project Grants) FY 17 $944,775.00; FY 18 est $944,775.00; FY 19 est $0.00

HQ: Institute of Youth Family and Community Division of Community and Education 1400 Independence Avenue SW, PO Box 2250, Washington, DC 20250-2250

Phone: 202-720-2324

http://nifa.usda.gov/program/higher-education-multicultural-scholars-program-msp

Programs Administered by Federal Headquarters

ED84.031 | HIGHER EDUCATION INSTITUTIONAL AID

Award: Project Grants

Purpose: To help eligible colleges and universities to strengthen their management and fiscal operations and to assist them to plan, develop, or implement activities for strengthening the academic quality of their institutions.

Applicant Eligibility: An institution of higher education (IHE) that qualifies as eligible using criteria as specified in the regulations. Under Part A, specific and basic requirements as stated in the Program regulations must be met. Eligible applicants include Institutions that have: (1) A low average per full-time equivalent (FTE) educational and general expenditures; (2) a substantial percentage of students having Pell Grants or other Federal need-based financial aid. However, a waiver of the low educational and general expenditure requirement and the needy student enrollment requirement may be granted to Institutions meeting the criteria specified in the existing regulations. Under Part B HBCUs, historically Black Institutions that were established prior to 1964, whose principal mission was, and is, the education of African Americans are eligible. A listing of those Institutions is published in Program regulations; these HBCUs are also eligible under the Endowment Challenge Grant Program. Institutions eligible for PBI Program grants are defined in Title III Section 318(b) of the HEA. Institutions eligible for HBGI Program grants are specified in Title III Section 326(e)(1) of the HEA. Under the Title V Programs, an HSI is defined as an institution that has an enrollment of undergraduate full-time equivalent students that is at least 25 percent Hispanic as specified in Section 502 of the HEA.

Beneficiary Eligibility: Applicant institutions of higher education, including those in the territories and possessions that meet statutory eligibility requirements will benefit.

Award Range/Average: Varies by competition

Funding: (Project Grants) FY 18 $866,203,000.00; FY 19 est $873,637,000.00; FY 20 est $542,102,000.00

HQ: 400 Maryland Avenue SW, Washington, DC 20202

Phone: 202-453-7348 | Email: james.laws@ed.gov

http://www.ed.gov/about/offices/list/ope/idues

USDA10.223 | HISPANIC SERVING INSTITUTIONS EDUCATION GRANTS
"HSI Grants"

Award: Project Grants

Purpose: To promote and strengthen the ability of Hispanic-Serving Institutions to carry out higher education programs in the food and agricultural sciences that aim to attract outstanding students. Grants under this program will be awarded to enhance educational equity for underrepresented students; strengthen institutional educational capacities; to prepare students for careers related to the food, agricultural, and natural resource systems of the United States; and to maximize the development and use of resources to improve food and agricultural sciences teaching programs.

Applicant Eligibility: Hispanic serving Institutions are eligible to receive funds under this Program. "Hispanic serving Institutions " means an institution of higher education which, at the time of application, has an enrollment of undergraduate full-time equivalent students that is at least 25 percent Hispanic students, and which (1) admits as regular students only persons having a certificate of graduation from a school providing secondary education, or the recognized equivalent of such certificate; (2) is a public or other nonprofit Institutions accredited by a nationally recognized accrediting body; and (3) is legally authorized to provide a Program of education beyond the secondary level for which a 2-year associate, baccalaureate, or higher degree is awarded. Applications may be submitted by, and awards may only be made to, public or other non-profit Hispanic-Serving Institutions as defined in the definitions section of this solicitation. For the purposes of this Program, the individual branches of a State University system or public system of higher education that are separately accredited as degree granting Institutions are treated as separate Institutions eligible for awards. Accreditation much be by an agency or association recognized by the Secretary, U.S. Department of education. Institutions also must be legally authorized to offer at least a two-year Program of study creditable toward an associate's or bachelor's degree. Separate branches or campuses of a college or University that are not individually accredited as degree granting Institutions are not treated as separate Institutions. To be eligible for competitive consideration for an award under this Program, a Hispanic-Serving Institution must at the time of application: (1) certify that it has an enrollment of undergraduate full-time equivalent students that is at least 25 percent Hispanic students; and (2) provide assurances that not less than 50 percent of the institution's Hispanic students are low-income individuals as defined in the definitions section of this solicitation.

Beneficiary Eligibility: Hispanic serving institutions, as identified above, are eligible to receive funds under this program.

Award Range/Average: If minimum or maximum amounts of funding per competitive and/or capacity project grant, or cooperative agreement are established, these amounts will be announced in the annual Competitive Request for Application (RFA).The most current RFA is available via: https://nifa.usda.gov/funding-opportunity/hispanic-serving-institutions-education-grants-program-hsi

Funding: (Project Grants) FY 17 $8,806,013.00; FY 18 est $8,808,579.00; FY 19 est $8,801,920.00

HQ: Institute of Youth Family and Community Division of Community and Education 1400 Independence Avenue SW, PO Box 2250, Washington, DC 20250-2250

    Phone: 202-720-2324

    http://nifa.usda.gov/program/hispanic-serving-institutions-education-grants-program

HUD14.520 | HISTORICALLY BLACK COLLEGES AND UNIVERSITIES PROGRAM

Award: Project Grants

Purpose: To help Historically Black Colleges and Universities (HBCUs) expand their role and strength in addressing community development needs in their localities.

Applicant Eligibility: Historically Black Colleges and universities as determined by the Department of education in 34 CFR 608. 2 pursuant to that Department's responsibilities under Executive Order 13256, dated February 12, 2002.

Beneficiary Eligibility: The principal beneficiaries of the Historically Black Colleges and Universities program will include any city, county, town, township, parish, village, or other general political subdivision of a State within which the HBCU is located. A HBCU located in a metropolitan statistical area, as established by the Office of Management and Budget, may consider its locality to be one or more of these entities within the entire area.

Award Range/Average: The maximum amount a Previously Funded HBCU applicant can request for award is $800,000 for a maximum three-year (36 months) grant performance period.The maximum amount a Previously Unfunded HBCU applicant can request for award is $500,000 for a maximum three-year (36 months) grant performance period.

Funding: (Project Grants (Discretionary)) FY 09 $9,000,000.00; FY 10 est $9,682,200.00; FY 11 est $9,780,000.00

HQ: 451 7th Street SW, Room 8226, Washington, DC 20410

    Phone: 202-402-3852 | Email: susan.s.brunson@hud.gov

    www.hud.gov/grants

HHS93.145 | HIV-RELATED TRAINING AND TECHNICAL ASSISTANCE

Award: Cooperative Agreements; Project Grants

Purpose: To assess Ryan White HIV/AIDS Program recipients' technical assistance needs and/or provide technical assistance related to building capacity and increasing their ability to provide high quality HIV care and treatment services along the HIV care continuum.

Applicant Eligibility: Entities eligible to apply include public and nonprofit entities (including faith-based and community based Organizations) and school and academic health science centers involved in addressing HIV related issues at a national level. Federally Recognized Indian Tribal Government and Native American Organizations are eligible to apply.

Beneficiary Eligibility: Persons with HIV.

Award Range/Average: FY18: $300,000 to $3,858,166; Average = $2,154,385 FY19: $300,000 to $4,049,008; Average = $2,083,555 FY20: $300,000 to $4,049,008; Average = $2,083,555 FY 18: $1,500,000 to $4,145,278; Average = $2,997,693 FY19: $375,000 to $4,693,888; Average = $2,728,640 FY20: $375,000 to $4,693,888; Average = $2,728,640

Funding: (Cooperative Agreements) FY 18 $62,761,476.00; FY 19 est $62,066,253.00; FY 20 est $64,412,546.00; (Project Grants) FY 18 $0.00; FY 19 est $0.00; FY 19 est $0.00

HQ: 5600 Fishers Lane, Room 9N-160, Rockville, MD 20857

    Phone: 301-443-8109

    http://www.hrsa.gov

HHS93.917 | HIV CARE FORMULA GRANTS

Award: Formula Grants

Purpose: To enable States to improve the quality, availability, and organization HIV/AIDS healthcare and support services for eligible individuals living with Human Immunodeficiency Virus disease.

Applicant Eligibility: All 50 States of the United States, and the District of Columbia and U.S. Territories including, the Commonwealth of Puerto Rico, Commonwealth of the Northern Mariana Islands, the Virgin Islands, Guam, American Samoa, the Republic of the Marshall Islands, Federated States of Micronesia, and the Republic of Palau.

Beneficiary Eligibility: Individuals with HIV.

Award Range/Average: $24,596 to $174,964,095 Average $23,539,326

Funding: (Project Grants) FY 18 $1,388,820,258.00; FY 19 est $1,305,660,682.00; FY 20 est $1,500,000,000.00

HQ: 5600 Fishers Lane, PO Box 09WH03, Rockville, MD 20857

    Phone: 301-443-6554 | Email: srobilotto@hrsa.gov

    http://www.hrsa.gov

Programs Administered by Federal Headquarters

HHS93.941 | HIV DEMONSTRATION, RESEARCH, PUBLIC AND PROFESSIONAL EDUCATION PROJECTS

Award: Cooperative Agreements
Purpose: To develop and test improved HIV prevention strategies.
Applicant Eligibility: States, political subdivisions of States, other public including American Indian/Alaska Native tribal Governments or tribal Organizations located wholly or in part within their boundaries, and nonprofit private entities.
Beneficiary Eligibility: Same as Applicant Eligibility.
Funding: (Cooperative Agreements) FY 18 $17,618,851.00; FY 19 est $11,086,249.00; FY 20 est $4,319,135.00
HQ: 1600 Clifton Road NE, PO Box E07, Atlanta, GA 30333
    Phone: 404-639-1877 | Email: lrw3@cdc.gov
    http://www.cdc.gov/hiv

HHS93.914 | HIV EMERGENCY RELIEF PROJECT GRANTS

Award: Project Grants
Purpose: Provides financial assistance to Eligible Metropolitan Areas (EMAs) and Transitional Grant Areas (TGAs) that are severely affected by the Human Immunodeficiency Virus (HIV) epidemic to enhance access to high quality, community-based care for low-income individuals and families with HIV and to strengthen strategies to reach minority populations.
Applicant Eligibility: RWHAP Part A recipients that were classified as an EMA or as a TGA in fiscal year (FY) 2007 and continue to meet the statutory requirements are eligible to apply for these funds. For an EMA, this is more than 2,000 cases of AIDS reported and confirmed during the most recent five calendar years, and for a TGA, this is at least 1,000, but fewer than 2,000 cases of AIDS reported and confirmed during the most recent period of five calendar years for which such data are available. Additionally, they must not have fallen below, for three consecutive years, the required incidence levels already specified AND required prevalence levels (cumulative total of living cases of AIDS reported to and confirmed by the Director of the Centers for Disease Control and Prevention (CDC) as of December 31 of the most recent calendar year for which such data are available). For an EMA, this is 3,000 living cases of AIDS, and for a TGA, this is 1, 500 living cases of AIDS, except certain areas which have a cumulative total of at least 1, 400 living cases of AIDS and which have no more than 5 percent of the total from formula grants awarded unobligated as of the end of the most recent fiscal year. Eligible metropolitan areas (EMA) with a population of 50,000 or more individuals for which the CDC has reported a cumulative total of more than 2,000 AIDS cases for the most recent period of 5 calendar years include: Atlanta, Georgia; Baltimore, Maryland; Boston, Massachusetts; Chicago, Illinois; Dallas, Texas; Detroit, Michigan, Ft. Lauderdale, Florida; Houston, Texas; Los Angeles, California; Miami, Florida; Nassau/Suffolk Counties, New York; New Haven, Connecticut; New Orleans, Louisiana; New York, New York; Newark, New Jersey; Orlando, Florida; Philadelphia, Pennsylvania; Phoenix, Arizona; San Diego, California; San Francisco, California; San Juan, Puerto Rico; Tampa-St. Petersburg, Florida; Washington, DC; and West Palm Beach, Florida. Transitional Grant areas (TGA) with a population of 50,000 or more individuals for which the CDC has reported a cumulative total of at least 1,000, but not more than 1, 999 AIDS cases for the more most recent five year period include: Austin, Texas; Baton Rouge, Louisiana; Bergen-Passaic, NJ; Charlotte, North Carolina; Cleveland, Ohio; Columbus, Ohio; Denver, Colorado; Fort Worth, Texas; Hartford, Connecticut; Indianapolis, Indiana; Jacksonville, Florida; Jersey City, New Jersey; Kansas City, Missouri; Las Vegas, Nevada; Memphis, Tennessee; Middlesex, New Jersey; Minneapolis, Minnesota; Nashville, Tennessee; Norfolk, Virginia; Oakland, California; Orange County, California; Portland, Oregon; Riverside-San Bernardino, California; Sacramento, California; St. Louis, Missouri; San Antonio, Texas; San Jose, California; and Seattle, Washington.
Beneficiary Eligibility: Individuals and families living with HIV disease.
Award Range/Average: $2,844,248 to $94,232,524; Average = $12,083,108.
Funding: (Project Grants) FY 18 $624,346,301.00; FY 19 est $628,321,646.00; FY 20 est $628,321,646.00
HQ: 5600 Fishers Lane, Room 9W12, Rockville, MD 20857
    Phone: 301-443-7136 | Email: syoung@hrsa.gov
    http://www.hrsa.gov

HHS93.940 | HIV PREVENTION ACTIVITIES HEALTH DEPARTMENT BASED "HIV Prevention Program: PS12-1201; PS15-1506; PS15-1509; PS17-1711; PS18-1802"

Award: Cooperative Agreements
Purpose: To assist States in meeting the cost of establishing and maintaining HIV prevention programs.

Applicant Eligibility: States, and in consultation with State health authorities, political subdivisions of States including American Indian/Alaska Native tribal Governments or tribal Organizations located wholly or in part within their boundaries and U.S. territories and possessions.

Beneficiary Eligibility: States, State health authorities, political subdivisions of States including American Indian/Alaska Native tribal governments or tribal organizations located wholly or in part within their boundaries and U.S. territories and possessions.

Funding: (Cooperative Agreements) FY 18 $399,583,909.00; FY 19 est $383,083,909.00; FY 20 est $0.00; (Cooperative Agreements (Discretionary Grants)) FY 18 $412,126,148.00; FY 19 est $396,160,596.00; FY 20 est $413,569,913.00

HQ: 1600 Clifton Road NE, PO Box E07, Atlanta, GA 30333

Phone: 404-639-1877 | Email: lrw3@cdc.gov

http://www.cdc.gov/hiv

HHS93.939 | HIV PREVENTION ACTIVITIES NON-GOVERNMENTAL ORGANIZATION BASED

Award: Cooperative Agreements

Purpose: To provide assistance to nonprofit organizations to develop and implement effective community-based HIV prevention programs related to achieving national goals.

Applicant Eligibility: Nongovernmental public and nonprofit private entities are eligible, including American Indian/Alaska Native tribal Governments or tribal Organizations located wholly or in part within their boundaries.

Beneficiary Eligibility: Public and nonprofit private entities.

Funding: (Cooperative Agreements) FY 18 $145,014,593.00; FY 19 est $53,265,574.00; FY 20 $53,353,122.00

HQ: 1600 Clifton Road NE, PO Box E07, Atlanta, GA 30333

Phone: 404-639-1877 | Email: lrw3@cdc.gov

http://www.cdc.gov/hiv

HHS93.015 | HIV PREVENTION PROGRAMS FOR WOMEN

Award: Cooperative Agreements

Purpose: To increase knowledge of accurate HIV prevention information among women living in rural communities in the south.

Applicant Eligibility: The applicant must be a Public College or University; a Historically Black College or University; a Hispanic Serving Institution; a Tribal College or University; a Private Non-Profit Community-Based Organization; a Native American Tribal Organization; and/or a Faith-Based Community Organization serving underserved women. Small businesses or Organizations not in an official partnership with a qualified institution are not eligible for funding under this announcement.

Beneficiary Eligibility: Underserved women living in the Rural South; Young Women Attending Minority Institutions; Native/American Indian and Alaskan Native Women Living in Rural and Frontier Indian Country; Women Incarcerated and Newly Released Living with or at Risk for HIV/AIDS/STDs; and Women Living in Puerto Rico and the U.S. Virgin Islands, will benefit from this program.

Award Range/Average: Grant program ended 8/2015

HQ: 1101 Wootton Parkway, Suite 550 Tower Building, Rockville, MD 20852

Phone: 240-453-8822 | Email: brenda.donaldson@hhs.gov

http://www.womenshealth.gov

HUD14.183 | HOME EQUITY CONVERSION MORTGAGES
"Section 255"

Award: Guaranteed/insured Loans

Purpose: To facilitate the elderly homeowners to convert equity in their homes to monthly income or lines of credit.

Applicant Eligibility: Eligible borrowers are persons 62 years of age or older and eligible non-borrowing spouses who are identified at the time of closing. Eligible borrowers and eligible non-borrowing spouses must complete HECM counseling from a HUD-approved agency prior to obtaining the loan. Eligible properties include single family one-to-four unit owner-occupied dwelling units, units within FHA-approved condominium projects and Planned Unit Developments, and manufactured homes, if they meet FHA standards.

Beneficiary Eligibility: Individuals.

Programs Administered by Federal Headquarters

Funding: (Sale, Exchange, or Donation of Property and Goods) FY 15 $15,988,470,296.00; FY 16 est $15,137,995,710.00; FY 17 est $18,468,953,952.00
HQ: 451 7th Street SW, Washington, DC 20410
   Phone: 800-225-5342
   http://portal.hud.gov/hudportal/hud?src=/program_offices/housing/sfh/hecm/hecmhome

HUD14.239 | HOME INVESTMENT PARTNERSHIPS PROGRAM
"HOME Program"

Award: Formula Grants
Purpose: To enlarge the supply of affordable housing for low and very low income Americans; to strengthen the abilities of State and local governments for designing and implementing strategies to achieve adequate supplies of affordable housing; and to increase and strengthen partnerships among all levels of government and the private sector.
Applicant Eligibility: States, cities, urban counties, and consortia (of contiguous units of general local Governments with a binding agreement) are eligible to receive formula allocations; funds are also set aside for grants to Insular Areas.
Beneficiary Eligibility: For rental housing, at least 90 percent of HOME funds must benefit low and very low income families at 60 percent of the area median income; the remaining ten percent must benefit families below 80 percent of the area median. Assistance to homeowners and homebuyers must be to families below 80 percent of the area median.
Award Range/Average: $186,048 to $69,126,329; $1,955,523 average.
Funding: (Formula Grants) FY 18 $1,362,000,000; FY 19 est $1,253,490,011; FY 20 est $0
HQ: 451 7th Street SW, Room 7164, Washington, DC 20410
   Phone: 202-708-2684 | Email: peter.h.huber@hud.gov
   http://www.hud.gov/homeprogram

DHS97.104 | HOMELAND SECURITY-RELATED SCIENCE, TECHNOLOGY, ENGINEERING AND MATHEMATICS (HS STEM) CAREER DEVELOPMENT PROGRAM
"HS-STEM Career Development Program"

Award: Project Grants
Purpose: The program funds researchers and professionals in the Homeland Security who work under the Science, Technology, Engineering and Mathematics (STEM) branch.
Applicant Eligibility: Specific information on applicant eligibility is identified in the funding opportunity announcement and Program guidance.
Beneficiary Eligibility: Other Public Institution/Organizations; Other Private Institution/Organizations; (Colleges and Universities).

USDA10.304 | HOMELAND SECURITY AGRICULTURAL
"Food And Agriculture Defense Initiative (FADI) (aka Homeland Security Program)"

Award: Cooperative Agreements
Purpose: To compensate for the agricultural products through cooperative agreements such as national animal health, plant diagnostic network, pest information platform, etc.
Applicant Eligibility: In accordance with section 1472(c) of the National Agricultural Research, Extension, and Teaching Policy Act of 1977, (NARETPA) applicant may be: State agricultural experiment stations, State cooperative extension services, all colleges and universities, other research or education Institutions and Organizations, Federal and private agencies and Organizations, individuals, and any other contractor or recipient, either foreign or domestic, to further research, extension, or teaching Programs in the food and agricultural sciences of the Department of Agriculture.
Beneficiary Eligibility: Same as Applicant Eligibility.
Award Range/Average: If minimum or maximum amounts of funding per Capacity, Competitive, and/or Non-Competitive project grant, or cooperative agreement are established, these amounts will be announced in the annual Capacity, Competitive, and/or Non-Competitive Request for Application (RFA).SPECIAL NOTE: Please refer to the following websites for further specific and pertinent details: National Plant Diagnostic Network for the Food and Agricultural Defense Initiative (NPDN):https://nifa.usda.gov/national-plant-diagnostic-networkNational Animal Health Laboratory Network (NAHLN)

for the Food and Agricultural Defense Initiativehttps://nifa.usda.gov/national-animal-health-laboratory-networkExtension Disaster Education Network (EDEN):https://nifa.usda.gov/extension-disaster-education-network
Funding: (Cooperative Agreements) FY 17 $7,680,000.00; FY 18 est $7,680,000.00; FY 19 est $0.00
HQ: 1400 Independence Avenue SW, PO Box 2201, Washington, DC 20250-2201
  Phone: 202-401-1112
  http://nifa.usda.gov/grants

DHS97.091 | HOMELAND SECURITY BIOWATCH PROGRAM

Award: Project Grants; Use of Property, Facilities, and Equipment
Purpose: The BioWatch program is an aerosolized biological agent detection and warning system that helps to prevent bioterrorist events in the country.
Applicant Eligibility: Generally, State and local Governments or as specified by U.S. Appropriation Statute. Specific applicant eligibility will be identified in the funding opportunity announcement and Program guidance.
Beneficiary Eligibility: State and local governments.
Award Range/Average: Specified in the announcement.
Funding: (Salaries and Expenses) FY 18 $27,842,000.00; FY 19 est $25,553,000.00; FY 20 est $25,553,000.00
HQ: DHS 245 Murray Lane SW, PO Box 0115, Washington, DC 20528
  Phone: 703-647-8052 | Email: daniel.yereb@hq.dhs.gov
  http://www.dhs.gov

DHS97.067 | HOMELAND SECURITY GRANT PROGRAM
"HSGP"

Award: Formula Grants
Purpose: The program's objective is to fund for the local and state's preparedness against natural calamities and terrorist and cyber terrorist activities.
Applicant Eligibility: The State Administrative Agency (SAA) is the only entity eligible to submit HSGP applications to DHS/FEMA, including those applications submitted on behalf of UASI and OPSG applicants. All 56 states and territories, including any state of the United States, the District of Columbia, the Commonwealth of Puerto Rico, the U.S. Virgin Islands, Guam, American Samoa, and the Commonwealth of the Northern Mariana Islands, are eligible to apply for SHSP funds. Tribal Governments may not apply directly for HSGP funding; however, funding may be available to Tribes under the SHSP and OPSG through the SAA. Eligible high-risk urban areas for the FY 2019 UASI Program have been determined through an analysis of relative risk of terrorism faced by the 100 most populous Metropolitan Statistical Areas (MSAs) in the United States. Subawards will be made by the SAAs to the designated high-risk urban areas. Eligible subrecipients under FY 2019 OPSG are local units of government at the county level or equivalent level of government and federally-recognized tribal Governments in states bordering Canada or Mexico and states and territories with international water borders. All applicants must have active ongoing USBP operations coordinated through a CBP sector office to be eligible for OPSG funding. Under FY 2019 OPSG, subrecipients eligible to apply for and receive a subaward directly from the SAAs are divided into three Tiers. Tier 1 entities are local units of government at the county level or equivalent and federally recognized tribal Governments that are on a physical border in states bordering Canada, states bordering Mexico, and states and territories with international water borders. Tier 2 eligible subrecipients are those not located on the physical border or international water but are contiguous to a Tier 1 county. Tier 3 eligible subrecipients are those not located on the physical border or international water but are contiguous to a Tier 2 eligible subrecipient. Tier 2 and Tier 3 eligible subrecipients may be eligible to receive funding based on border security risk as determined by the USBP.
Beneficiary Eligibility: U.S. Territories, State, Local U.S. Territories, State, Local THSGP: To be eligible to receive THSGP funding, recipients must be directly eligible Tribes. Directly eligible Tribes are Federally recognized Tribes that meet the criteria set forth in Section 2001 of the Homeland Security Act of 2002, as amended (6 U.S.C. 601). Federally recognized Tribes are those Tribes appearing on the list published by the Secretary of the Interior pursuant to the Federally Recognized Indian Tribe List Act of 1994 (Pub. L. No. 103-454) (25 U.S.C. 5131).Per 6 U.S.C. 601(4), a "directly eligible Tribe" is any Federally recognized Indian Tribe that meets the following criteria: (A)Any Indian Tribe;(i)that is located in the continental United States;(ii)that operates a law enforcement or emergency response agency with the capacity to respond to calls for law enforcement or emergency services; (iii) (I) that is located on or near (50 miles) an international border or a coastline bordering an ocean (including the Gulf of Mexico) or international waters;(II) that is located within 10 miles of a system or asset included on the prioritized critical infrastructure list established under section [2214(a)(2) of the Homeland Security Act of 2002, as amended (6 U.S.C. 124l(a)(2)] or has such a system or asset within its territory;(III) that is located within

or contiguous to one of the 50 most populous metropolitan statistical areas in the United States; or(iv) the jurisdiction of which includes not less than 1,000 square miles of Indian country, as that term is defined in section 1151 of title 18, United States Code; and(iv)that certifies to the Secretary [of Homeland Security] that a State has not provided funds under [section 2003 (UASI) or 2004 (SHSP) of the Homeland Security Act of 2002, as amended (6 U.S.C. 604 or 605, respectively)] to the Indian Tribe or consortium of Indian Tribes for the purpose for which direct funding is sought; and(B)A consortium of Indian Tribes, if each Tribe satisfies the requirements of subparagraph (A). In summary, directly eligible Tribes must meet each of the requirements set forth in (A)(i), (A)(ii), and (A)(iv). Tribes must also meet at least one of the requirements set forth in (A)(iii), that is either (A)(iii)(I), (A)(iii)(II), (A)(iii)(III), or (A)(iii)(IV). Finally, under subparagraph (B), a consortium may also be eligible to be a recipient if each Indian Tribe in the consortium meets the criteria for a directly eligible Tribe under subparagraph (A). In FY 2019, applicants must self-certify as to whether they meet the eligibility requirements. Self-certification will be provided on the THSGP Eligibility Certification Form as part of the application Investment Justification (IJ). Additionally, DHS/FEMA will verify grant recipient eligibility against these criteria. Any questions regarding an applicant's proximity to a Critical Infrastructure (CI) site, as described in the eligibility criteria, may be directed to the State Administrative Agency (SAA) for the State with which the Tribe shares a border. The State Administrative Agency Contacts List can be found at http://www.fema.gov/media-library/assets/documents/28689?id=6363.

Award Range/Average: For more information, refer to the FY 2018 HSGP and THSGP Notice of Funding Opportunity.
Funding: (Formula Grants) FY 18 $1,067,000,000.00; FY 19 est $1,095,000,000.00; FY 20 est $1,095,000,000.00
HQ: Department of Homeland Security 400 C Street SW, Washington, DC 20523
 Phone: 800-368-6498
 http://www.FEMA.gov/government/grant/index.shtm

DHS97.007 | HOMELAND SECURITY PREPAREDNESS TECHNICAL ASSISTANCE PROGRAM
"HSPTAP"

Award: Cooperative Agreements
Purpose: The Homeland Security Technical Assistance Program builds State and local capabilities to detect, prevent, protect, respond and recover from threats and acts of terrorism.
Applicant Eligibility: Eligible Applicants: DHS Preparedness Homeland Security Grant Program grantees and sub-grantees.
Beneficiary Eligibility: Refer to FY2019 HSPTAP Notice of Funding Opportunity.
Award Range/Average: Refer to program guidance document.
Funding: (Cooperative Agreements) FY 18 $525,000.00; FY 19 est $525,000.00; FY 20 est $525,000.00
HQ: FEMA DHS/FEMA 500 C Street SW, 7th Floor, Washington, DC 20472-3100
 Phone: 202-786-0849 | Email: john.allen5@fema.dhs.gov
 http://www.fema.gov

DHS97.077 | HOMELAND SECURITY RESEARCH, DEVELOPMENT, TESTING, EVALUATION, AND DEMONSTRATION OF TECHNOLOGIES RELATED TO NUCLEAR THREAT DETECTION
"Countering Weapons of Mass Destruction (CWMD)"

Award: Cooperative Agreements
Purpose: The program's objective is to prevent nuclear or radiological terrorist attacks in the country.
Applicant Eligibility: State (includes District of Columbia, public Institutions of higher education and hospitals), Local (includes State-designated Indian Tribes, excludes Institutions of higher education and hospitals, Public nonprofit institution/ Organization (includes Institutions of higher education and hospitals), Other public institution/Organization Eligible Applicants: The ARI is limited to State, public or private accredited Institutions of higher education. The ER Program supports State, Public nonprofit institution/Organizations; Private nonprofit institution/Organizations; Small businesses; Profit Organizations and Other private institution/Organizations.
Beneficiary Eligibility: ARI: State, public or private accredited institutions of higher education; Scientists/Researcher; Graduate Student; Education (13+). Exploratory Research: Public Nonprofit Institution/Organization; Small Business; Profit Organization; Private Organization; Other Private Institution/organization; Scientists/Researcher; State, public or private accredited institutions of higher education. SETCP: 10: Federal; 14 - State; 15 - Local; 20 - public non-profit; 21 - other;

22 - Federally recognized Indian Tribal Governments; 31 - Individual/Family; 35 - profit organization; 36 - private non-profit organizations.
Funding: (Cooperative Agreements) FY 18 $5,211,247.00; FY 19 est $5,399,864.00; FY 20 est $2,691,707.00
HQ: 245 Murray Lane SW DNDO, PO Box 0315, Washington, DC 20528
    Phone: 202-254-7109 | Email: richard.vojtech@hq.dhs.gov
    http://www.dhs.gov/about-domestic-nuclear-detection-office

DHS97.108 | HOMELAND SECURITY, RESEARCH, TESTING, EVALUATION, AND DEMONSTRATION OF TECHNOLOGIES

Award: Cooperative Agreements
Purpose: Provides funding and/or property to conduct research and check the readiness of homeland security agencies to respond to the terrorist threats.
Applicant Eligibility: States, local Governments, private, public, profit or nonprofit Organizations, Indian Tribal Governments, or individuals specified by U.S. Appropriation Statute, including U.S. and international Institutions of higher education and educational laboratories.
Beneficiary Eligibility: Federal, State, and local governments, private, public, profit or nonprofit organizations, Indian tribal governments, and individuals.
Award Range/Average: Refer to program guidance.
Funding: (Salaries and Expenses) FY 18 $883,395.00; FY 19 est $1,544,611.00; FY 20 est $1,544,611.00
HQ: S and T Directorate 245 Murray Lane SW, Washington, DC 20548
    Phone: 202-254-8968 | Email: kimberli.jones-holt@hq.dhs.gov
    http://www.dhs.gov

HUD14.261 | HOMELESS MANAGEMENT INFORMATION SYSTEMS TECHNICAL ASSISTANCE
"HMIS TA"

Award: Cooperative Agreements
Purpose: See HUD Community Compass CFDA14.259
Applicant Eligibility: This funding opportunity is now included in HUD Community Compass - see CFDA 14. 259.
Beneficiary Eligibility: See CFDA #14.259 - Community Compass.
Award Range/Average: See Community Compass Listing (CFDA 14.259)
HQ: Office of Special Needs Assistance Programs Office of Community Planning and Development Department of Housing and Urban Development, Room 7262, Washington, DC 20410
    Phone: 202-708-1226
    http://www.onecpd.info

HHS93.074 | HOSPITAL PREPAREDNESS PROGRAM (HPP) AND PUBLIC HEALTH EMERGENCY PREPAREDNESS (PHEP) ALIGNED COOPERATIVE AGREEMENTS
"HPP/PHEP"

Award: Formula Grants
Purpose: The purpose of the 2017-2018 HPP-PHEP aligned programs cooperative agreement is to provide resources that support state, local, territorial, and tribal public health departments and healthcare systems/organizations.
Applicant Eligibility: NA.
Beneficiary Eligibility: N/A
Award Range/Average: FY 2018: Range: $579,108 to $65,814,534 Average: $13,552,419
Funding: (Formula Grants (Cooperative Agreements)) FY 18 $851,750,000.00; FY 19 est $0.00; FY 20 est $0.00
HQ: 1600 Clifton Road NE, Atlanta, GA 30333
    Phone: 404-639-0817 | Email: lss1@cdc.gov
    http://www.cdc.gov

Programs Administered by Federal Headquarters

HHS93.817 | HOSPITAL PREPAREDNESS PROGRAM (HPP) EBOLA PREPAREDNESS AND RESPONSE ACTIVITIES

Award: Formula Grants

Purpose: The program covers two separate, but related projects which are Part A - healthcareSystem Preparedness for Ebola and Part B - Development of a Regional Network for Ebola Patient Care.

Applicant Eligibility: Eligible applicants are the 62 Hospital Preparedness Program (HPP) awardees, which include health departments in all 50 States, the District of Columbia, the Nation's three largest municipalities (Chicago, Los Angeles County, and New York City, the Commonwealths of Puerto Rico and the Northern Mariana Islands, the territories of American Samoa, Guam, and the United States Virgin Islands, the Federated States of Micronesia, and the Republics of Palau and the Marshall Islands.

Beneficiary Eligibility: Health departments listed above, hospitals and supporting health care systems.

Award Range/Average: Part A - healthcareSystem Preparedness for Ebola:Range: $202,989 - $15,229,780 Est. Average Amount: $2,612,903 Part B - Development of a Regional Network for Ebola Patient Care:Range: $3,250,000 - $4,600,000 Est. Average Amount: $3,250,000

Funding: (Formula Grants (Cooperative Agreements)) FY 18 $3,016,585.00; FY 19 est $2,414,022.00; FY 20 est $0.00

HQ: Division of National Healthcare Preparedness Programs Office of the Assistant Secretary for Preparedness and Response U.S. Department of Health and Human 200 C Street SW, Room C4K12, Washington, DC 20024

Phone: 202-245-0732 | Email: robert.dugas@hhs.gov

http://www.phe.gov

USDA10.862 | HOUSEHOLD WATER WELL SYSTEM GRANT PROGRAM "HWWS"

Award: Project Grants

Purpose: To assist nonprofit organizations in construction, refurbishing, and household water well systems in rural areas for those with low-income.

Applicant Eligibility: An applicant must be a private Organization, organized as a non-profit corporation. The applicant must have the legal capacity and authority to perform the obligations of the grant. The applicant must have sufficient expertise and experience in lending activities and promoting the safe and productive use of individually-owned household water well systems and ground water.

Beneficiary Eligibility: An individual in a household in which the combined income of all household members (for the most recent 12 months) does not exceed 100 percent of the median non-metropolitan household income for the State or territory in which the individual resides.

Award Range/Average: $89,900 to $308,000. Avg. $159,700

Funding: (Project Grants) FY 18 $1,117,900.00; FY 19 est $1,500,000.00; FY 20 est $993,000.00

HQ: Department of Agriculture 1400 Independence Avenue SW, PO Box 1548, Washington, DC 20250

Phone: 202-690-2670 | Email: christopher.mclean@wdc.usda.gov

http://www.rd.usda.gov/programs-services/all-programs/water-environmental-programs

HUD14.169 | HOUSING COUNSELING ASSISTANCE PROGRAM

Award: Project Grants

Purpose: To advocate homeowners, homebuyers, potential renters and tenants under HUD and other government programs in improving their housing conditions and meeting the responsibilities of tenancy and homeownership.

Applicant Eligibility: Qualified public or private nonprofit Organizations. There are four categories of eligible applicants: (1) HUD-approved local housing counseling agency; (2) HUD-approved national or regional intermediary; (3) State housing finance agency; and (4) multi-state Organizations.

Beneficiary Eligibility: Individuals, groups of individuals, and families who are renters, tenants, homeowners, and home buyers under HUD, conventional and other government programs.

Award Range/Average: Range and average of financial assistance: For Fiscal Year 2012, the minimum request from a local agency was $15,000 and the maximum request from an intermediary was $3,000,000. The average local agency counseling grant was approximately $20,500. The average intermediary award was approximately $990,000.

Funding: (Project Grants (Cooperative Agreements)) FY 15 $42,000,000.00; FY 16 est $45,000,000.00; FY 17 est $43,000,000.00

HQ: 451 7th Street SW, Washington, DC 20410

Phone: 800-225-5342

http://portal.hud.gov/hudportal/hud?src=/program_offices/housing/sfh/hcc/hcc_home

HUD14.316 | HOUSING COUNSELING TRAINING PROGRAM

Award: Project Grants

Purpose: To support the delivery of training activities for counselors from agencies participating in HUD's Housing Counseling program, and thereby improving the quality of counseling provided by housing counselors.

Applicant Eligibility: Applicants must be public or private nonprofit Organizations with a least two years of experience providing housing counseling training services nationwide.

Beneficiary Eligibility: Housing Counselors from HUD-approved housing counselling agencies.

Award Range/Average: Average award size is $666,666.

Funding: (Project Grants) FY 15 $3,000,000.00; FY 16 est $4,000,000.00; FY 17 est $4,000,000.00

HQ: 451 7th Street SW, Washington, DC 20410

Phone: 800-225-5342

http://portal.hud.gov/hudportal/hud?src=/program_offices/housing/sfh/hcc/hcc_home

HUD14.188 | HOUSING FINANCE AGENCIES (HFA) RISK SHARING
"542(c) Risk Sharing Program"

Award: Guaranteed/insured Loans

Purpose: To provide credit enhancement for mortgages for multifamily housing projects whose loans are underwritten, processed, serviced, and disposed of.

Applicant Eligibility: Eligible mortgagors, who include investors, builders, developers, public entities, and private nonprofit corporations or associations, may apply to a qualified HFA. To be eligible for HUD's approval, the HFA must: (1) carry the designation of "top tier" or its equivalent as evaluated by Standard and Poors or another nationally recognized rating agency; (2) receive an overall rating of "A" for the HFA for its general obligation bonds from a nationally recognized rating agency; and (3) otherwise demonstrate its capacity as a sound, well-managed agency that is experienced in financing multifamily housing.

Beneficiary Eligibility: Individuals, families, and property owners may be eligible for affordable housing.

Funding: (Guaranteed/Insured Loans) FY 15 $409,997,152.00; FY 16 est $430,586,683.00; FY 17 est $458,350,159.00

HQ: 451 7th Street SW, Washington, DC 20410

Phone: 202-402-2579 | Email: carmelita_a._james@hud.gov

http://www.hud.gov/offices/hsg/mfh/progdesc/progdesc.cfm

HUD14.241 | HOUSING OPPORTUNITIES FOR PERSONS WITH AIDS
"HOPWA"

Award: Formula Grants; Project Grants

Purpose: To provide resources and incentives to the States and localities to devise strategies for meeting the supportive housing needs of low-income persons and their families living with HIV/AIDS. To prevent homelessness and sustain housing stability for HOPWA program beneficiaries.

Applicant Eligibility: HOPWA offers two types of awards: (1) Formula entitlement grants: Eligible states and qualifying cities, as defined in 24 CFR 574. 3, qualifying for formula allocation under HOPWA. (2) Competitive grants: (a) States, units of local Governments and nonprofit Organizations for special projects of national significance; (b) States and units of local government that do not qualify for HOPWA formula allocations under the category of long-term grants; and (c) Nonprofit Organizations are eligible to apply for projects of national significance as a grantee, but may also serve as a project sponsor under any competitive or formula grantees. Additional applicant eligibility may apply depending on the competitive grant opportunity. As required by the Appropriations Acts, HUD gives funding priority to the renewal of expiring permanent supportive housing projects. When funding is available for new competitive grants, there may be additional requirements for applicant eligibility established under the Notice of Funding Availability (NOFA).

Beneficiary Eligibility: Eligible beneficiaries are low income (at or below 80% the area median income) persons living with HIV/AIDS and their families.

Award Range/Average: HOPWA formula grant awards: In FY2018, the 127 HOPWA formula eligible metropolitan statistical areas received an estimated average award amount of $2,657,480. HOPWA competitive grant awards: In FY2018, the 28 eligible permanent supportive housing renewal grants received award amounts between $269,278 and $1,501,500 with an average award amount of $1,012,333.

Funding: (Formula Grants) FY 18 $375,000,000.00; FY 19 est $393,000,000.00; FY 20 est $330,000,000.00

Programs Administered by Federal Headquarters

HQ: 451 7th Street SW, Washington, DC 20410
   Phone: 202-402-5374 | Email: rita.u.harcrow@hud.gov
   https://www.hudexchange.info/programs/hopwa

HUD14.275 | HOUSING TRUST FUND
Award: Formula Grants
Purpose: To expand and preserve the supply of affordable housing, particularly rental housing, for extremely low-income and very low income households.
Applicant Eligibility: States as defined in 24 CFR 93. 2 are eligible to receive formula allocations. Insular areas also may receive formula funds.
Beneficiary Eligibility: At least 75 percent of funds must be used for extremely low-income families, or families with incomes at or below the poverty line (whichever is greater), unless the allocation is below $1 billion, at which point 100 percent of the funds must be used for extremely low-income families.
Award Range/Average: $90,138 to $32,376,690; average is $4,670,371.
Funding: (Formula Grants) FY 18 $266,775,403.00; FY 19 est $247,526,787.00; FY 20 est $0.00
HQ: 451 7th Street SW, Room 7164, Washington, DC 20410
   Phone: 202-708-2684 | Email: peter.h.huber@hud.gov
   http://www.hudexchange.info/program/htf

SBA59.055 | HUBZONE PROGRAM
Award: Provision of Specialized Services
Purpose: To provide federal contracting assistance for qualified small business concerns (SBCs) located in Historically Underutilized Business Zones in an effort to increase employment opportunities, investment, and economic development in such areas.
Applicant Eligibility: To be eligible to participate in the Program, a firm must (1) be a small business (as defined by SBA Size Standards), (2) be at least 51% owned and controlled by one or more U.S. citizens, a Community Development Corporation, an agricultural cooperative, a Native Hawaiian Organization, or an Indian tribe, (3) be located (principal office) in a HUBZone, and (4) certify that least 35 percent of its employees are residents of a HUBZone.
Beneficiary Eligibility: The HUBZone Program is precisely targeted to provide contract opportunities - revenue sources - to firms located in approximately 19,467 qualified census tracts, 767 qualified non-metropolitan counties, 593 qualified Indian Lands, 108 qualified base closure areas, and 37 Qualified Disaster Areas.
Award Range/Average: Additional information available on SBA's website at https://www.sba.gov/contracting/government-contracting-programs/hubzone-program.
Funding: (Salaries and Expenses) FY 17 $2,792,000.00; FY 18 est $3,000,000.00; FY 19 est $2,500,000.00

HUD14.329 | HUD MULTIFAMILY PFS PILOT
"Multifamily Assisted Housing Pay For Success Energy and Water Conservation Pilot"
Award: Direct Payments for Specified Use
Purpose: To save taxpayer money; develop a Pay For Success model for funding and delivering energy and water conservation improvements; evaluate the effectiveness of energy and water conservation retrofits; and identify lessons learned and best practices in order to assess the feasibility of scaling up and replicating this approach to achieving energy and water conservation.
Applicant Eligibility: HUD will make performance-based payments to entities serving as Intermediaries under a cooperative agreement executed with the agency. Payments will be contingent on utility consumption and cost savings associated with energy and water conservation measures installed by the Intermediary at HUD-assisted multifamily properties.
Beneficiary Eligibility: HUD is the primary beneficiary of this program; energy and water conservation retrofits undertaken by program Intermediaries will result in lower utility costs for the agency once the cooperative agreements have terminated. Secondary beneficiaries are residents of the HUD-assisted multifamily properties receiving retrofits.
Funding: (Direct Payments for Specified Use (Cooperative Agreements)) FY 15 Not Separately Identifiable; FY 16 Not Separately Identifiable; FY 17 Estimate Not Available
HQ: U.S. Department of Housing and Urban Development Office of the Deputy Assistant Secretary for Multifamily Housing Programs 451 7th Street SW, Room 6106, Washington, DC 20410
   Phone: 202-402-3372 | Email: mark.a.kudlowitz@hud.gov
   http://portal.hud.gov/hudportal/hud?src=/program_offices/housing/mfh

HHS93.172 | HUMAN GENOME RESEARCH
"Human Genome Project"

Award: Project Grants

Purpose: To support the development of resources and technologies that will accelerate genome research and its application to human health and genomic medicine.

Applicant Eligibility: Research projects: Awards can be made to any public or private, for-profit or nonprofit University, college, hospital, laboratory, or other institution, including State and local units of government, qualifying small businesses (through the Small Business Innovation Research/STTR Programs, and to individuals. SBIR grants can be awarded only to domestic small businesses (entities that are independently owned and operated for profit, are not dominant in the field in which research is proposed, and have no more than 500 employees). Primary employment (more than one- half time) of the principal investigator must be with the small business at the time of award and during the conduct of the proposed project. In both Phase I and Phase II, the research must be performed in the U.S. or its territories. To be eligible for funding, an SBIR grant application must be approved for scientific merit and Program relevance by a scientific review group and a national advisory council. STTR grants can be awarded only to domestic small business concerns (entities that are independently owned and operated for profit, are not dominant in the field in which research is proposed and have no more than 500 employees) which "partner" with a research institution in cooperative research and development. At least 40 percent of the project is to be performed by the small business concern and at least 30 percent by the research institution. In both Phase I and Phase II, the research must be performed in the U.S. and its possessions. Applicants to the Small Business Innovation Research/STTR Programs must meet special requirements for small businesses, as defined by the Small Business Administration. Non-federal public and private domestic Organizations may apply for an Institutional National Research Service Award. Individual National Research Service awardees must be nominated and sponsored by a public or nonprofit private institution having staff and facilities appropriate to the proposed research training Program. All awardees must be citizens or have been admitted to the United States for permanent residence. Predoctoral awardees must have completed the baccalaureate degree, and postdoctoral awardees must have a professional or scientific degree (M.D., Ph.D., D.O., D.V.M., Sc.D., E.Eng., or equivalent domestic or foreign degree). To be eligible for funding for any award, an application must be reviewed for scientific merit by a scientific review group and for Program relevance by a national advisory council.

Beneficiary Eligibility: Any nonprofit or for-profit organization, company, or institution engaged in biomedical research can apply for research support.

Award Range/Average: For RPGS the range is from $1,192 - $19,996,553. However, the smallest RPG (5R21 HG008495-02) seems to only include funding for 2 months of support. If we exclude this grant, then the range would be $26,000 - $19,996,553.

Funding: (Project Grants) FY 18 $267,065,177.00; FY 19 est $275,654,000.00; FY 20 est $231,164,999.00; (Project Grants (for specified projects)) FY 18 $59,635,045.00; FY 19 est $58,436,999.00; FY 20 est $52,963,000.00; (Project Grants (Fellowships)) FY 18 $9,306,470.00; FY 19 est $10,314,999.00; FY 20 est $8,632,000.00

HQ: 6700B Rockledge Drive, Room 3186, Bethesda, MD 20892

Phone: 301-496-7531 | Email: grahambj@exchange.nih.gov

http://www.genome.gov

HHS93.944 | HUMAN IMMUNODEFICIENCY VIRUS (HIV)/ACQUIRED IMMUNODEFICIENCY VIRUS SYNDROME (AIDS) SURVEILLANCE
"HIV/AIDS Surveillance"

Award: Cooperative Agreements

Purpose: To continue and strengthen effective human immunodeficiency virus (HIV) and acquired immunodeficiency syndrome (AIDS) surveillance programs and to affect, maintain, measure and evaluate the extent of HIV/AIDS incidence and prevalence throughout the United States and its territories.

Applicant Eligibility: The Governments, or their agents or instrumentalities, of any of the States of the United States, the District of Columbia, the Commonwealth of Puerto Rico, territories or possessions of United States, including American Indian/Alaska Native tribal Governments or tribal Organizations located wholly or in part within their boundaries, and local Governments who are current recipients of HIV/AIDS surveillance cooperative agreements.

Beneficiary Eligibility: Official health agencies will benefit.

Funding: (Cooperative Agreements) FY 18 $51,640,351.00; FY 19 est $45,496,825.00; FY 20 est $45,759,570.00

HQ: 1600 Clifton Road NE, PO Box E07, Atlanta, GA 30333

Phone: 404-639-1877 | Email: lrw3@cdc.gov

http://www.cdc.gov

Programs Administered by Federal Headquarters

DOI15.153 | HURRICANE SANDY DISASTER RELIEF-COASTAL RESILIENCY GRANTS.

Award: Project Grants

Purpose: The main objective of this program is to provide grants for disaster assistance for Hurricane Sandy. Funds shall be used by recipients to assist Interior and its bureaus/offices to restore and rebuild national parks, national wildlife refuges, and enhance the resiliency and capacity of coastal habitat and infrastructure to withstand storms and bring down the amount of damage caused by such storms.

Applicant Eligibility: Anyone/general public.

Beneficiary Eligibility: Same as Applicant Eligibility.

Award Range/Average: New program, have not allocated yet

HQ: Department of the Interior 1849 C Street NW, Room 4257, Washington, DC 20240

Phone: 202-513-0692 | Email: megan_olsen@ios.doi.gov

DOC11.462 | HYDROLOGIC RESEARCH

Award: Project Grants

Purpose: To address hydrology issues and to establish a partnership for joint research and development on pressing surface water hydrology issues.

Applicant Eligibility: Eligible applicants are Federally recognized Institutions of higher learning, agencies of State or local Governments, quasi-public Institutions such as water supply or power companies, hydrologic consultants and companies involved in using and developing hydrologic forecasts (either for reducing flood damages or for water management decisions).

Beneficiary Eligibility: Since the benefits of the overall program are for a reduction in loss of life and damage resulting from flooding and drought, and improved utilization of water supply and water dependent industries, benefits accrue from these projects to: (1) Federal agencies responsible to forecast, assess, manage, disperse, project economic conditions based on projections of water supply for agriculture and industry, and control water resources; (2) interstate commissions to control and allocate surface waters; (3) State agencies responsible for allocating and controlling water resources and for making projections for the use of water for industry and agriculture and for planning and developing infrastructure within the State that is impacted by rivers and lakes; (4) local agencies dependent on water for economic planning, emergency preparedness, and public water supply; (5) all businesses and industries depending all or in part upon surface water supplies or adequate water in lakes for recreation, in rivers to generate power, or in production or dispersion of products or who must take action in order to ameliorate damage during flood situations, (6) wildlife interests at all levels that are dependent upon water management for managing the environment; (7) homeowners or farmers who must plan for proper responses to flooding or inadequate water supply; and (8) academic institutions which are funded for programs dealing with the studies of hydrologic science.

Award Range/Average: $80,162 to $124,999. Average: $105,789.

Funding: (Cooperative Agreements) FY 15 $10,638,580.00; FY 16 est $12,677,677.00; FY 17 est $12,500,131.00

HQ: IWRSS National Water Center 205 Hackberry Lane, Tuscaloosa, AL 35401

Phone: 205-347-1313 | Email: samcontorno@noaa.gov

http://www.noaa.gov

IAF85.750 | IAF ASSISTANCE FOR OVERSEAS PROGRAMS

Award: Project Grants

Purpose: To strengthen the bonds of friendship and understanding among the peoples in the Western Hemisphere.

Applicant Eligibility: See "Uses and Use Restrictions" above.

Beneficiary Eligibility: Same as Applicant Eligibility.

Award Range/Average: The range of financial assistance is up to $400,000 per grant award.

Funding: (Project Grants) FY 18 $17,351,991.00; FY 19 est $20,300,000.00; FY 20 est $20,300,000.00

HQ: 1331 Pennsylvania Avenue NW, Suite 1200N, Washington, DC 20004

Phone: 202-803-6098 | Email: cwood@iaf.gov

http://www.iaf.gov

DOS19.441 | IIP-AMERICAN SPACES

"U.S. Department of State, Bureau of International Information Programs, Office of American Spaces"

Award: Project Grants

Purpose: American spaces are publicly accessible facilities designed to build and strengthen relationships with foreign audiences, showcase the American culture and values, and provide information about the United States in an environment that inspires dialogue. Users get to enjoy access to physical collections and also explore the many electronic resources available.

Applicant Eligibility: The State Department's Public Diplomacy Strategic Framework calls for the revitalization of existing American Spaces and the establishment of new ones. American Spaces support one of the Secretary of State's five strategic imperatives for 21st century public diplomacy - that of building mutual trust and respect through expanded public diplomacy platforms. The new strategic approach also brings the planning and management of American Spaces into line with the goals of the Quadrennial Diplomacy and Development Review (QDDR) and the Public Diplomacy Framework. The IIP Deputy Coordinator for Regional Coordination and American Spaces leads the new American Spaces strategy. IIP coordinates with other Department bureaus (R/PPR, regional PD offices, ECA, OBO, DS, among others) as appropriate to ensure that their interests are met.

Beneficiary Eligibility: Foreign audiences. See www.grants.gov for individual award announcements.

Award Range/Average: See www.grants.gov for individual award announcements.

Funding: (Project Grants) FY 16 est $15,000,000.00

HQ: 2200 C Street NW, Washington, DC 20037

Phone: 202-632-9204 | Email: bairdem@state.gov

DOS19.440 | IIP INDIVIDUAL GRANTS

"U.S. Speaker Program Grants, Bureau of International Information Programs (IIP)"

Award: Project Grants

Purpose: The Office of the U.S. Speaker Program of the Department of State's Bureau of International Information Programs awards grants to cooperating organizations with experience in international exchanges for the administration of projects that enable U.S. experts to present lectures, serve as consultants, or conduct workshops and seminars for professional audiences worldwide.

Applicant Eligibility: N/A

Beneficiary Eligibility: N/A

Award Range/Average: see individual solicitation in www.grants.gov

Funding: (Project Grants (including individual awards)) FY 17 $3,900,000.00; FY 18 est $4,201,000.00; FY 19 Estimate Not Available

HQ: 2200 C Street NW, Washington, DC 20037

Phone: 202-632-9204 | Email: bairdem@state.gov

HHS93.268 | IMMUNIZATION COOPERATIVE AGREEMENTS

"Immunizations CoAg and Vaccines for Children Program previously published as Immunization Grants and Vaccines for Children Program"

Award: Project Grants

Purpose: To assist states and communities in establishing and maintaining preventive health service programs to immunize individuals against vaccine-preventable diseases.

Applicant Eligibility: Any U.S. state, and in consultation with state health authorities, political subdivisions of states and other public entities and U.S. territories may apply; private individuals and private nonprofit agencies are not eligible for immunization grants.

Beneficiary Eligibility: Any U.S. state, political subdivision (as described above), and other public entities will benefit.

Award Range/Average: 317 Grants: From $252,725 to $48,568,982; $6,870,723 VFC Grants: From $1,649,229 to $368,026,903; $52,334,322.

Funding: (Cooperative Agreements) FY 18 $330,791,211.00; FY 19 est $4,422,030,680.00; FY 20 est $389,151,364.00

HQ: 1600 Clifton Road NE, PO Box 19, Atlanta, GA 30333

Phone: 404-639-7824 | Email: ibr0@cdc.gov

http://www.cdc.gov/vaccines

Programs Administered by Federal Headquarters

HHS93.185 | IMMUNIZATION RESEARCH, DEMONSTRATION, PUBLIC INFORMATION AND EDUCATION TRAINING AND CLINICAL SKILLS IMPROVEMENT PROJECTS

Award: Cooperative Agreements

Purpose: Assists states, political subdivisions of states, and other public and private nonprofit entities to conduct research, demonstration projects, and provide public information on vaccine-preventable diseases and conditions.

Applicant Eligibility: Under Section 317(k) of the Public Health Service Act: States, political subdivision of states, and other public and private nonprofit entities.

Beneficiary Eligibility: Same as Applicant Eligibility.

Award Range/Average: Varies

Funding: (Cooperative Agreements) FY 18 $80,696,281.00; FY 19 est $57,881,284.00; FY 20 est $57,881,284.00

HQ: NCIRD 1600 Clifton Road NE, PO Box A27, Atlanta, GA 30333

    Phone: 404-639-2110

    http://www.cdc.gov

ED84.040 | IMPACT AID FACILITIES MAINTENANCE

Award: Project Grants

Purpose: To maintain school facilities used to serve federally connected military dependent students that are owned by the Department of Education and operated by local educational agencies (LEAs), and to transfer those facilities to the LEAs, where appropriate.

Applicant Eligibility: LEAs that operate school facilities owned by the Department of education.

Beneficiary Eligibility: Public elementary and secondary school children benefit.

Award Range/Average: Not Available.

Funding: (Project Grants) FY 18 $4,835,000.00; FY 19 est $4,835,000.00; FY 20 est $483,500.00

HQ: Department of Education 400 Maryland Avenue SW, Room 3C105, Washington, DC 20202

    Phone: 202-205-8724 | Email: marilyn.hall@ed.gov

    http://www.ed.gov/about/offices/list/oese/impactaid/index.html

ED84.041 | IMPACT AID

Award: Formula Grants; Project Grants

Purpose: To provide financial assistance to local educational agencies (LEAs) affected by Federal activities through 7002, 7003, and 7007 ESEA sections.

Applicant Eligibility: Local educational agencies that provide free public elementary or secondary education may apply. Under Section 7002, generally, assistance is provided to districts where an aggregate of 10 percent or more of the assessed valuation of all real property in the school district as of the time(s) of acquisition has been acquired by the Federal Government since 1938 and the district is not being substantially compensated by revenue from activities on the eligible Federal property. Under Section 7003, assistance is provided to districts where at least three percent or 400 of the total number of eligible federally connected children in average daily attendance (ADA) live on Federal property including Indian lands and/or have a parent who works on Federal property or is on active duty in the uniformed services. Under Section 7007(b), "heavily impacted" LEAs that enroll a high proportion (at least 40 percent) of federally connected children, or have little or no funding capacity, may be eligible for a competitive construction award.

Beneficiary Eligibility: Public elementary and secondary school children benefit.

Award Range/Average: For FY 2019, the estimated range of awards for Basic Support payments is expected to be between $560- $59,000,000 with an average award of $1,200,000; for Payments for Children With Disabilities, the estimated range of awards is expected to be between $500- $1,100,000 with an average award of $58,000.

Funding: (Project Grants (Discretionary)) FY 18 $0.00; FY 19 est $17,406,000.00; FY 20 est $17,406,000

HQ: Department of Education 400 Maryland Avenue SW, Room 3E105, Washington, DC 20202

    Phone: 202-205-8724 | Email: marilyn.hall@ed.gov

    http://www.ed.gov/about/offices/list/oese/impactaid/index.html

HHS93.850 | IMPROVING EPILEPSY PROGRAMS, SERVICES, AND OUTCOMES THROUGH NATIONAL PARTNERSHIPS
"Epilepsy Programs"

Award: Cooperative Agreements
Purpose: The purpose of this program is to reduce the treatment gap by improving professional education about epilepsy diagnosis, treatment, and management.
Applicant Eligibility: Open and full competition. However, to fulfill the requirements of the cooperative agreement, applicants must be able to demonstrate that their Organization has specialized knowledge and experience addressing the complex and challenging health and social needs of individuals with epilepsy and their families. Applicants must also be able to demonstrate that they have the ability to work at both the national level and locally in all geographical regions of the United States (Northeast, Southeast, Middle West, Southwest, and West.).
Beneficiary Eligibility: Individual/Family Racial/ethnic minority groups People with disabilities Specialty group Children Adults Older adults Schools Health Professional Educational Professional Student/trainee Low income Moderate income Rural Urban Suburban Education (0-13+)Nonprofit groups.
Award Range/Average: 1 award expected for $3,200,000;
Funding: (Cooperative Agreements) FY 18 $3,567,141.00; FY 19 est $3,917,141.00; FY 20 est $3,917,141.00
HQ: 4770 Buford Highway NE, PO Box F78, Atlanta, GA 30341
Phone: 770-488-5598 | Email: mmoore6@cdc.gov
http://www.cdc.gov

HHS93.981 | IMPROVING STUDENT HEALTH AND ACADEMIC ACHIEVEMENT THROUGH NUTRITION, PHYSICAL ACTIVITY AND THE MANAGEMENT OF CHRONIC CONDITIONS IN SCHOOLS

Award: Cooperative Agreements
Purpose: This program helps children and adolescents reduce their risk of developing any chronic or long-term disease. The program strives to achieve this by increasing the number of students who consume nutritious food and beverages, increasing the number of students who take part in a daily physical activity and prevent the outbreak of chronic illnesses at educational areas.
Applicant Eligibility: The intent of this funding opportunity announcement (FOA) is to improve the health and educational outcomes of youth/adolescents through the implementation of evidence-based strategies and activities within school settings. Funding eligibility is limited to state education agencies or equivalents since these agencies have the greatest likelihood of reaching Local education Areas, schools and the youth/adolescents they serve.
Beneficiary Eligibility: The intent of this FOA is to improve the health and educational outcomes of youth/adolescents through the implementation of evidence-based strategies and activities within school settings. Funding eligibility is limited to state education agencies or equivalents since these agencies have the greatest likelihood of reaching Local Education Areas, schools and the youth/adolescents they serve.
Award Range/Average: Estimated floor of award: $300,000 Estimated average award: $355,000 Estimated ceiling of award: $375,000
Funding: (Cooperative Agreements) FY 18 $6,693,000.00; FY 19 est $6,319,225.00; FY 20 est $6,319,225.00
HQ: 4770 Buford Highway NE, Atlanta, GA 30341
Phone: 770-488-6103
http://www.cdc.gov

HHS93.581 | IMPROVING THE CAPABILITY OF INDIAN TRIBAL GOVERNMENTS TO REGULATE ENVIRONMENTAL QUALITY
"Environmental Regulatory Enhancement (ERE)"

Award: Project Grants
Purpose: To provide funding for the costs of planning, developing, and implementing programs designed to improve the capability of tribal governing bodies to regulate environmental quality pursuant to federal and tribal environmental laws.
Applicant Eligibility: Eligible applicants include, federally recognized Indian Tribes; consortia of Indian Tribes; incorporated non-federally recognized Tribes; incorporated state-recognized Tribes; Alaska Native villages, as defined in the Alaska Native Claims Settlement Act (ANCSA) and/or non-profit village consortia; non-profit Alaska Native regional corporation/

associations in Alaska with village specific projects; other tribal or village Organizations or consortia of Indian Tribes; and Tribal governing bodies (IRA or traditional councils) as recognized by the Bureau of Indian Affairs.

Beneficiary Eligibility: Federally recognized Indian tribes; Consortia of Indian tribes; Incorporated non-federally recognized tribes; Incorporated state-recognized tribes; Alaska Native villages, as defined in the ANCSA and/or non-profit village consortia; Non-profit Alaska Native Regional Corporation/Associations in Alaska with village specific projects; Other tribal or village organizations or consortia of Indian tribes; and Tribal governing bodies (IRA or traditional councils) as recognized by the Bureau of Indian Affairs.

Award Range/Average: $100,000 - $300,000;average = $182,000 per budget period

Funding: (Project Grants) FY 18 est $1,981,267.00; FY 17 $1,694,325.00; FY 19 est $1,981,267.00

HQ: Department of Health and Human Services 330 C Street SW, Mary E Switzer Building, Washington, DC 20201
Phone: 877-922-9262 | Email: carmelia.strickland@acf.hhs.gov
https://www.acf.hhs.gov/ana

HHS93.426 | IMPROVING THE HEALTH OF AMERICANS THROUGH PREVENTION AND MANAGEMENT OF DIABETES AND HEART DISEASE AND STROKE

Award: Cooperative Agreements

Purpose: To implement and evaluate evidence-based strategies to address the challenges and systemic barriers that contribute to prevention and management of cardiovascular disease and diabetes in high-burden populations.

Applicant Eligibility: State Governments or their Bona Fide Agents (includes the District of Columbia) are eligible.

Beneficiary Eligibility: Beneficiaries of this program include: State, Local, Individual/Family, Minority Group, Anyone/General Public, Black American, American Indian, Spanish Origin, Oriental, Other Non-white, Women, Handicapped, Physically Afflicted, Senior Citizen, Rural.

Award Range/Average: Awards ranged from $980,000 to $3,800,000. Awards we based on per-capita population and the burden of disease of diabetes and heart disease and stroke in each individual state.

Funding: (Project Grants) FY 18 $90,000,002.00; FY 19 est $110,000,000.00; FY 20 est $110,000,000.00

HQ: 4770 Buford Highway NE, PO Box F75, Atlanta, GA 30341
Phone: 770-488-7431 | Email: rnh2@cdc.gov

DOJ16.758 | IMPROVING THE INVESTIGATION AND PROSECUTION OF CHILD ABUSE AND THE REGIONAL AND LOCAL CHILDREN'S ADVOCACY CENTERS "VOA"

Award: Cooperative Agreements

Purpose: To Improve the investigation and prosecution of child abuse cases, to train criminal justice system professionals, to limit the number of child victims, and to enhance medical support.

Applicant Eligibility: Please see Program announcement for specific eligibility. May be limited to national Organizations with broad membership among attorneys who prosecute criminal cases in state courts and have demonstrated experience in providing training and technical assistance to prosecutors. Or may be limited to nonprofit and for-profit Organizations (including tribal nonprofit and for-profit Organizations) and Institutions of higher education (including tribal Institutions of higher education). For-profit Organizations must agree to forgo any profit or management fee.

Beneficiary Eligibility: Contact program office for additional information.

Award Range/Average: Range and average of financial assistance varies by project and are posted at http://www.ojjdp.gov/funding/FundingList.asp as solicitations are released.

Funding: (Cooperative Agreements) FY 18 $18,392,206.00; FY 19 est $22,500,000.00; FY 20 est $20,000,000.00

HQ: U.S. Department of Justice Office of Juvenile Justice and Delinquency Prevention 810 7th Street NW, Washington, DC 20531
Phone: 202-616-3649 | Email: kristen.kracke@ojp.usdoj.gov
http://www.ojjdp.gov

HHS93.980 | INCREASING PUBLIC AWARENESS AND PROVIDER EDUCATION ABOUT PRIMARY IMMUNODEFICIENCY DISEASE

Award: Project Grants

Purpose: The program helps healthcare providers and educators to carry out public health activities in areas affected by primary immunodeficiency diseases through public awareness activities.

Applicant Eligibility: This FOA will be full and open competition. The ideal applicant will have ten years of experience in: conducting effective physician education and public awareness campaigns for primary immunodeficiency diseases, collaborating effectively with healthcare and public health partners, and maximizing resources dedicated to campaign materials development and distribution to meet outcome goals.

Beneficiary Eligibility: The general public will benefit from outcome of this FOA. The ideal applicant will have ten years of experience in: conducting effective physician education and public awareness campaigns for primary immunodeficiency diseases, collaborating effectively with health care and public health partners, and maximizing resources dedicated to campaign materials development and distribution to meet outcome goals.

Award Range/Average: FY 2017 Estimated at 921,500 FY2018 Estimated at 921,500 FY2019 Estimated at 921,500 FY2020 Estimated at 921,500 FY2021 Estimated at 921,500 Total anticipated funding is $4,607,500. Future funding is subject to availability of funds.

Funding: (Salaries and Expenses) FY 18 $921,500.00; FY 19 est $1,848,000.00; FY 20 est $921,500.00; FY 2017 Estimated at 921,500 FY2018 Estimated at 921,500 FY2019 Estimated at 921,500 FY2020 Estimated at 921,500 FY2021 Estimated at 921,500Total anticipated funding is $4,607,500. Future funding is subject to availability of funds

HQ: 1600 Clifton Road NE, Atlanta, GA 30329
Phone: 404-498-0068 | Email: sbowen1@cdc.gov
http://www.cdc.gov

HHS93.808 | INCREASING THE IMPLEMENTATION OF EVIDENCE-BASED CANCER SURVIVORSHIP INTERVENTIONS TO INCREASE QUALITY AND DURATION OF LIFE AMONG CANCER PATIENTS
"DP15-1501"

Award: Cooperative Agreements

Purpose: Funds up to six National Comprehensive Cancer Control Programs grantees to implement core surveillance activities to improve cancer survivor health in their populations.

Applicant Eligibility: No additional eligibility requirements - All eligible applicants should be current recipients of funds under DP12-1205 - Component 2 - The National Comprehensive Cancer Control Program.

Beneficiary Eligibility: Same as Applicant Eligibility.

Award Range/Average: $341,509 for each award

HQ: 4770 Buford Highway NE, PO Box F76, Atlanta, GA 30341
Phone: 770-488-4879 | Email: nnh1@cdc.gov

DOJ16.308 | INDIAN COUNTRY INVESTIGATIONS

Award: Training

Purpose: To provide training to the Bureau of Indian Affairs (BIA) and Tribal Law Enforcement Officers in conjunction with the Bureau of Indian Affairs Office of Justice Services to better conduct investigations in Indian Country.

Applicant Eligibility: BIA Investigators, Tribal Law Enforcement Officers and other law enforcement officers assigned to work in Indian Country.

Beneficiary Eligibility: Same as Applicant Eligibility.

Funding: (Training) FY 16 est $2,003,238.00; FY 17 est $2,200,000.00

HQ: 935 Pennsylvania Avenue Finance Division, Room 6712, Washington, DC 20535
Phone: 202-324-0495 | Email: michael.tyler@ic.fbi.gov
http://www.fbi.gov

ED84.299 | INDIAN EDUCATION-SPECIAL PROGRAMS FOR INDIAN CHILDREN

Award: Project Grants

Purpose: To develop, test, and demonstrate the effectiveness of services and programs to improve educational opportunities and achievement of Indian children.

Applicant Eligibility: For Demonstration grants (84. 299A), eligible applicants include State educational agencies (SEAs); local educational agencies (LEAs), including charter schools that are considered LEAs under State law; Indian Tribes; Indian Organizations; federally supported elementary or secondary schools for Indian students (including Department of the Interior/ Bureau of Indian education -funded schools); Indian Institutions (including Indian Institutions of higher education); or a consortium of any of these entities. For Professional Development grants (84. 299B), eligible applicants include Institutions of higher education, including Indian Institutions of higher education; SEAs or LEAs in consortium with an institution of higher education; Indian Tribes or Organizations in consortium with an institution of higher education; and Department of the Interior/Bureau of Indian education -funded schools in consortium with an institution of higher education. LEAs include charter schools that are considered LEAs under State law.

Beneficiary Eligibility: SEAs, LEAs, Indian students, and teachers and administrators will benefit.

Funding: (Project Grants) FY 18 $57,993,000.00; FY 19 est $57,993,000.00; FY 20 est $63,993,000.00

HQ: 400 Maryland Avenue SW, Washington, DC 20202

    Phone: 202-205-1909 | Email: angela.hernandez-marshall@ed.gov

    http://www.ed.gov/programs/indiandemo/index.html

ED84.060 | INDIAN EDUCATION GRANTS TO LOCAL EDUCATIONAL AGENCIES

Award: Formula Grants

Purpose: To address the unique educational and culturally related academic needs of Indian students; to ensure that Indian students gain knowledge and understanding of Native communities, languages, tribal histories, traditions, and cultures; and to ensure that teachers, principals, other school leaders and other staff who serve Indian students have that ability to provide culturally appropriate and effective instruction.

Applicant Eligibility: Local educational agencies (LEAs) that enroll at least 10 Indian children or in which Indians constitute at least 25 percent of the total enrollment. These requirements do not apply to LEAs serving Indian children in Alaska, California, and Oklahoma or located on, or in proximity to, an Indian reservation. Schools that receive funding from the Department of the Interior (DOI) Bureau of Indian education (BIE) under Section 1130 of the education Amendments of 1978, 25 U.S.C. 2001, are eligible to participate in this Program. If an eligible LEA does not apply, an Indian tribe or an Indian Organization that makes up at least half of the LEAs' Indian students may apply in lieu of the LEA. If no eligible LEA or Indian tribe or Indian Organization applies for a grant, an Indian community-based Organization may apply.

Beneficiary Eligibility: Eligible Indian children enrolled in eligible local educational agencies, BIE-funded schools, Indian organizations, and Indian Community Based Organizations.

Award Range/Average: Range of New Awards: $4,000- $2,854,289; Average New Award: $81,125.

Funding: (Formula Grants) FY 18 est $105,381,000.00; FY 19 est $105,381,000.00; FY 20 est $100,381,000.00

HQ: Office of Indian Education Department of Education 400 Maryland Avenue SW, Washington, DC 20202

    Phone: 202-453-6459 | Email: kimberly.smith@ed.gov

    http://www.ed.gov/about/offices/list/oese/oie/programs.html

HHS93.164 | INDIAN HEALTH SERVICE EDUCATIONAL LOAN REPAYMENT
"IHS Loan Repayment Program"

Award: Direct Payments for Specified Use

Purpose: To ensure that the Indian Health Service (IHS) has an adequate supply of trained health professionals for Indian health program facilities.

Applicant Eligibility: Eligible individuals must be enrolled: (1) In a course of study or Program in an accredited institution, as determined by the Secretary, within any State and be scheduled to complete such course of study in the same year such as individual applies to participate in such Program; (2) in an approved graduate training Program in a health profession; (3) have a degree in health profession and a license to practice a health profession; (4) be eligible for, or hold, an appointment as a commissioned officer in the Regular or Reserve Corps of the Public Health Service (PHS); (5) be eligible for selection for civilian service in the Regular or Reserve Corps of the PHS; (6) meet the professional standards for civil service employment in the IHS; (7) be employed with an Indian health Program funded under Public Law 93-638, Indian Self-Determination, Title V of Public Law 94-437 and its amendments or the Buy Indian Act (25 U.S.C. 47); (8) submit an application to participate in the IHS Loan Repayment Program. The term "State" is defined in Section 331 (i)(4) of the PHS Act.

Beneficiary Eligibility: Health professionals who have Government (Federal, State, local) and commercial unpaid educational loans will benefit from this program.

Award Range/Average: $3,000 to $51,672 for a 2-year obligation; For fiscal year 2015 the average award was $45,105.

Funding: (Direct Payments for Specified Use) FY 18 $32,345,049.00; FY 19 est $39,588,000.00; FY 20 est 35,949,091.00

HQ: 5600 Fishers Lane, PO Box 09E70, Rockville, MD 20857

    Phone: 301-443-5204

    http://www.ihs.gov

HHS93.228 | INDIAN HEALTH SERVICE, HEALTH MANAGEMENT DEVELOPMENT PROGRAM
"Indian Health"

Award: Project Grants
Purpose: To develop and enhance management infrastructure of federally recognized Tribes and Tribal organizations.
Applicant Eligibility: Federally-recognized Tribes and Tribally-sanctioned Tribal Organizations.
Beneficiary Eligibility: Individuals who are members of an eligible applicant Tribe, band, or group or village and who may be regarded as within the scope of the Indian health and medical service program and who are regarded as an Indian by the community in which he lives as evidenced by such factors as Tribal membership, enrollment, residence on tax exempt land, ownership of restricted property, active participation in Tribal affairs or other relevant factors.
Award Range/Average: $50,000 - $100,000 Range; $100,000 Average.
Funding: (Project Grants) FY 18 $2,404,664.00; FY 19 est $2,060,000.00; FY 20 est $2,456,000.00
HQ: 5600 Fishers Lane, PO Box 09E70, Rockville, MD 20857
    Phone: 301-443-5204
    http://www.ihs.gov

HHS93.441 | INDIAN SELF-DETERMINATION
"Indian Self-Determination 638 Contracts"

Award: Direct Payments for Specified Use
Purpose: To enable Indian tribes to assume the management and operation of programs, functions, services, and activities (PFSA) for the delivery of healthcareto Indian people.
Applicant Eligibility: Any federally-recognized tribe that formally requests, through a governing body action, a resolution, to enter into a self-determination contract or contracts for the purpose of planning, conducting, and administering Programs, or portions thereof, including construction Programs, provided that the T/TO submits a contract proposal that conforms to the requirements contained in 25 CFR 900. 8 may apply.
Beneficiary Eligibility: Indian tribes will benefit.
Award Range/Average: $31,963 to $25,950,652; $1,722,872.
Funding: (Direct Payments for Specified Use) FY 18 $458,327,678.00; FY 19 est $458,327,678.00; FY 20 est $458,327,678.00
HQ: 5600 Fishers Lane, PO Box 09E70, Rockville, MD 20857
    Phone: 301-443-5204
    http://www.ihs.gov

DOJ16.836 | INDIGENT DEFENSE

Award: Cooperative Agreements; Project Grants
Purpose: To enhance the capacity to deliver high-quality, fair, and comprehensive legal services to youth, to improve juvenile courts' data collection, to analyze juvenile defense system and other defense services.
Applicant Eligibility: Applicants are limited to states (including territories and the District of Columbia), federally recognized tribal Governments (as determined by the Secretary of the Interior), nonprofit and for-profit Organizations (including tribal nonprofit and for-profit Organizations) and Institutions of higher education (including tribal Institutions of higher education).
Beneficiary Eligibility: The beneficiary of these funds would be juvenile delinquents and youth.
Award Range/Average: varies by project
Funding: (Project Grants (Discretionary)) FY 18 $1,814,626.00; FY 19 est $2,000,000.00; FY 20 est $2,500,000
HQ: 810 7th Street NW, Washington, DC 20531
    Phone: 202-598-6892 | Email: julia.alanen@usdoj.gov
    http://www.ojjdp.gov

DOD12.902 | INFORMATION SECURITY GRANTS
"Information Assurance Scholarship Program"

Award: Project Grants
Purpose: To increase the number of qualified students entering the cybersecurity field to meet the DoD's increasing dependence on information technology for war fighting and the security of its information infrastructure.

Programs Administered by Federal Headquarters

Applicant Eligibility: Investigators must be an employee of a U.S. college or University. The principal investigator and supported graduate students must be a U.S. citizen or a permanent resident of the United States. Students eligibility for scholarships will determined under the DoD Information Assurance Scholarship Program.

Beneficiary Eligibility: This will benefit researchers in the information security field of computer science that are permanent residents of the United States (U.S.) as well as their students that are permanent residents of the U.S. or U.S. citizens. Scholarships will benefit those pursuing a Bachelor's, Master's or Doctoral Degree in one of the academic areas cited under the DoD Information Assurance Scholarship Program.

Award Range/Average: IASP Grants: $40,000.00 to $312,000.00 Average Award: $67,000.00

Funding: (Salaries and Expenses) FY 17 Actual Not Available; FY 18 est Estimate Not Available; FY 19 est $3,000,000.00

HQ: 9800 Savage Road, Suite 6623, Fort George G. Meade, MD 20755

Phone: 443-479-7660 | Email: diboyer@nsa.gov

HHS93.136 | INJURY PREVENTION AND CONTROL RESEARCH AND STATE AND COMMUNITY BASED PROGRAMS
"National Center for Injury Prevention and Control"

Award: Cooperative Agreements

Purpose: To support injury control research on priority issues.

Applicant Eligibility: For INJURY PREVENTION AND CONTROL RESEARCH Programs, AND INJURY CONTROL RESEARCH CENTERS: Eligible applicants may include any nonprofit or for-profit Organization; for STATE AND COMMUNITY Program GRANTS/COOPERATIVE AGREEMENTS: State and local Governments or their Bona Fide Agents (this includes the District of Columbia, the Commonwealth of Puerto Rico, the Virgin Islands, the Commonwealth of the Northern Marianna Islands, American Samoa, Guam, the Federated States of Micronesia, the Republic of the Marshall Islands, and the Republic of Palau) and political subdivisions of States (in consultation with States), Federally recognized or state-recognized American Indian/Alaska Native tribal Governments, American Indian/Alaska native tribally designated Organizations, Alaska Native health corporations, Urban Indian health Organizations, Tribal epidemiology centers; for COMMUNITY-BASED Programs: public, private, nonprofit and for-profit Organizations may be eligible.

Beneficiary Eligibility: FOR RESEARCH GRANTS: Academic health centers, scientist/researchers, operational public health programs, State and local governments, and public and private organizations involved in injury research. FOR STATE AND COMMUNITY-BASED GRANTS AND COOPERATIVE AGREEMENTS: State and local health departments, and community-based organizations.

Award Range/Average: Injury Control Research Centers: $802,300. Injury Control Research Projects: $200,000 to $300,000; $250,000. State and Community Based Injury Control Programs: $40,000 to $300,000; $170,000. Violence Prevention Programs: $80,609 to $1,946,399; $1,013,504. Motor Vehicle Prevention Programs: $247,500 to $803,000; $525,250. Prescription Drug Overdose Programs: $200,000 to $350,716; $288,586. National Violent Death Reporting System: $148,000 to $352,500; $244,985

Funding: (Cooperative Agreements) FY 18 $425,016,527.00; FY 19 est $481,698,618.00; FY 20 est $481,698,618.00

HQ: NCIPC 4770 Buford Highway NE, PO Box F63, Atlanta, GA 30341

Phone: 770-488-0143 | Email: dcameron@cdc.gov

http://www.cdc.gov

HHS93.284 | INJURY PREVENTION PROGRAM FOR AMERICAN INDIANS AND ALASKAN NATIVES COOPERATIVE AGREEMENTS

Award: Cooperative Agreements

Purpose: To improve the quality of the health of American Indians and Alaskan Natives.

Applicant Eligibility: Federally-recognized Tribes, tribal Organizations, non-profit Organizations serving primarily American Indians and Alaska Natives, and urban Indian Organizations may apply.

Beneficiary Eligibility: Individuals who are members of an eligible applicant tribe, band, or group or village and who may be regarded as within the scope of the Indian health and medical service program and who are regarded as an Indian by the community in which he lives as evidenced by such factors as tribal membership, enrollment, residence on tax exempt land, ownership or restricted property, active participation in tribal affairs or other relevant factors in keeping with general Bureau of Indian Affairs practices in the jurisdiction.

Award Range/Average: Injury Prevention: Part I - Five-Year Injury Prevention Programs, up to $100,000; Part II Effective Strategies up to $20,000.

Funding: (Cooperative Agreements) FY 17 $1,605,729.00; FY 18 est $1,325,000.00; FY 19 est $1,325,000.00
HQ: 5600 Fishers Lane, PO Box 09E70, Rockville, MD 20857
   Phone: 301-443-5204
   http://www.ihs.gov

HHS93.061 | INNOVATIONS IN APPLIED PUBLIC HEALTH RESEARCH
"Applied Public Health Research"

Award: Cooperative Agreements; Project Grants
Purpose: To foster the new knowledge necessary to develop, enhance, and disseminate effective public health services, programs, and policies.
Applicant Eligibility: Applications may be submitted by public and private nonprofit and for profit Organizations and by Governments and their agencies, such as: Public nonprofit Organizations Private nonprofit Organizations, For profit Organizations, Small, minority, women-owned businesses, universities, Colleges, Research Institutions, Hospitals, Community-based Organizations, Faith-based Organizations, Federally Recognized Indian Tribal Governments, Indian Tribes, Indian tribal Organizations, State and local Governments or their Bona Fide Agents (this includes the District of Columbia, the Commonwealth of Puerto Rico, the Virgin Islands, the Commonwealth of the Northern Marianna Islands, American Samoa, Guam, the Federated States of Micronesia, the Republic of the Marshall Islands, and the Republic of Palau), Political subdivisions of States (in consultation with States).
Beneficiary Eligibility: Beneficiary will be to public and private nonprofit and for profit organizations and by governments and their agencies, such as: Public nonprofit organizations Private nonprofit organizations, For profit organizations, Small, minority, women-owned businesses, Universities, Colleges, Research institutions, Hospitals, Community-based organizations, Faith-based organizations, Federally Recognized Indian Tribal Governments, Indian tribes, Indian tribal organizations, State and local governments or their Bona Fide Agents (this includes the District of Columbia, the Commonwealth of Puerto Rico, the Virgin Islands, the Commonwealth of the Northern Marianna Islands, American Samoa, Guam, the Federated States of Micronesia, the Republic of the Marshall Islands, and the Republic of Palau), Political subdivisions of States (in consultation with States).
Funding: (Cooperative Agreements) FY 18 $32,936,316.00; FY 19 est $32,976,315.00; FY 20 est $0.00
HQ: Deputy Director Office of Science Quality 1600 Clifton Rd, Atlanta, GA 30333
   Phone: 404-639-4639 | Email: jcyril@cdc.gov
   http://www.cdc.gov

DOJ16.817 | INNOVATIONS IN COMMUNITY-BASED CRIME REDUCTION
"CBCR"

Award: Project Grants
Purpose: The CBCR reduces crime and improves community safety and provides technical assistance by increasing law enforcement and supports agencies that are promoting public safety through all the disciplines possible.
Applicant Eligibility: See the current solicitation available at the Office of Justice Programs website https://ojp.gov/funding/Explore/CurrentFundingOpportunities. htm.
Beneficiary Eligibility: Eligible entities to serve as fiscal agent include states, unit of local governments, non-profit organizations, and federally recognized Indian tribal governments as determined by the Secretary of the Interior.
Award Range/Average: Category 1 (Implementation) Award: up to $850,000 Category 2 (Planning and Implementation) Award: up to $1 million
Funding: (Project Grants (Discretionary)) FY 18 $14,860,838.00; FY 19 est $17,000,000; FY 20 est $0.00
HQ: 810 7th Street NW, Washington, DC 20531
   Phone: 202-616-6500
   http://www.bja.gov

ED84.263 | INNOVATIVE REHABILITATION TRAINING

Award: Project Grants
Purpose: To develop new types and methods of training programs for rehabilitation personnel to individuals with disabilities by designated State rehabilitation units or other public or non-profit rehabilitation service agencies or organizations.
Applicant Eligibility: States and public or private nonprofit agencies and Organizations, including Indian Tribes and Institutions of higher education may apply.

Programs Administered by Federal Headquarters

Beneficiary Eligibility: Individuals preparing for or employed in positions relating to the rehabilitation of individuals with disabilities will benefit.
Award Range/Average: To Be Determined.
Funding: (Project Grants) FY 18 $0.00; FY 19 est $500,000.00; FY 20 est $500,000.00
HQ: OSERS Rehabilitation Services Administration 400 Maryland Avenue SW, Washington, DC 20202-2649
   Phone: 202-245-7423 | Email: mary.lovley@ed.gov
   https://www2.ed.gov/programs/rsatrain/index.html

DOJ16.828 | INNOVATIVE RESPONSES TO BEHAVIOR IN THE COMMUNITY: SWIFT, CERTAIN, AND FAIR SUPERVISION PROGRAM "SCF"

Award: Cooperative Agreements; Project Grants
Purpose: The SCF Program reduces crimes. It implements strategies to respond to offender behavior and reduces recidivism. It develops supervision strategies and reduces violence.
Applicant Eligibility: Eligible applicants for project grants under the SCF Program include states, units of local government, and federally recognized Indian tribal Governments (as determined by the Secretary of the Interior). Eligible applicants for a cooperative agreement to operate the SCF Resource Center are limited to national-scope private and nonprofit Organizations (including tribal nonprofit or for-profit Organizations), and colleges and universities, both public and private (including tribal Institutions of higher education).
Beneficiary Eligibility: See goals and objectives for additional information. Also, view the current fiscal year's solicitation available at the Office of Justice Programs web site at (https://ojp.gov/funding/Explore/CurrentFundingOpportunities.htm.
Award Range/Average: Award amounts may be up to $600,000.
Funding: (Project Grants) FY 17 $3,378,658.00; FY 18 est $3,614,134.00; FY 19 est $3,614,134.00
HQ: 810 7th Street NW, Washington, DC 20531
   Phone: 202-305-9317 | Email: emily.n.chonde@usdoj.gov
   http://www.bja.gov

HHS93.435 | INNOVATIVE STATE AND LOCAL PUBLIC HEALTH STRATEGIES TO PREVENT AND MANAGE DIABETES AND HEART DISEASE AND STROKE

Award: Cooperative Agreements
Purpose: To design, test, and evaluate novel approaches to addressing a set of evidence based strategies aimed at reducing risks, complications, and/or barriers to prevention and control of diabetes and cardiovascular disease among high-burden populations.
Applicant Eligibility: State or local health departments or their Bona Fide Agents (includes the District of Columbia)Eligibility will be limited to state and local/city/county Governments with a population of 900,000 or more with the greatest potential to reach and impact large numbers of high risk/high burden populations, or their bona fide agents. Consortia of smaller local/city/county health departments may collaborate to submit one application that, collectively, represents a population of 900,000 or more.
Beneficiary Eligibility: Beneficiaries of this program include: State, Local, Individual/Family, Minority Group, Anyone/General Public, Black American, American Indian, Spanish Origin, Oriental, Other Non-white, Women, Handicapped, Physically Afflicted, Senior Citizen, Rural.
Award Range/Average: Awards for this new program are expected to range from $1,000,000 to $3,500,000. Awards will be based on activities proposed by the applicant, the burden of disease of diabetes and heart disease and stroke, and the recipient's potential reach and effect outcomes for large numbers of adults.
Funding: (Cooperative Agreements) FY 18 $39,928,477.00; FY 19 est $41,528,477.00; FY 20 $41,528,477.00
HQ: 4770 Buford Highway NE, PO Box F75, Atlanta, GA 30341
   Phone: 770-488-7431 | Email: rnh2@cdc.gov
   http://www.cdc.gov

USAID98.005 | INSTITUTIONAL CAPACITY BUILDING (ICB) "Institutional Capacity Building"

Award: Project Grants
Purpose: Ensures food availability in food insecure regions, especially during emergency situations.

Applicant Eligibility: Private non-profit Institutions /Organizations are eligible for this Program. Specifically, an Organization must be a US Private Voluntary Organization (PVO) or cooperative headquartered in the US, that is registered with USAID as of the date of its application.

Beneficiary Eligibility: Private, non-profit institutions/organizations will benefit from this program along with vulnerable and food insecure populations in low income food deficit countries (LIFDCs) and least developed countries. (LDCs).

HQ: 301 4th Street SW, Washington, DC 20547

Phone: 202-567-4688 | Email: rwillis@usaid.gov

http://www.usaid.gov

HHS93.378 | INTEGRATED CARE FOR KIDS MODEL

Award: Formula Grants

Purpose: Helps in implementing the Integrated Care for Kids (INCK) model, which helps in improving the medical care and reducing the expenditures for children up to 21 years through early identification and treatment.

Applicant Eligibility: The InCK model will be open state Medicaid agencies and to HIPAA covered entities (including but not limited to State Medicaid Agencies, Managed Care Plans, provider groups or other HIPAA covered entities) serving Medicaid (and if applicable in the state CHIP) covered children eligible for EPSDT services.

Beneficiary Eligibility: N/A

Award Range/Average: CMS will award up to eight (8) cooperative agreements of up to $16 million per award. Funding will be awarded over a total model funding period of 7 years with an anticipated start date of FY 2020. The funding period is divided into two parts: - Pre-Implementation Period: a two year period spanning years 1-2 of the model during which the awardee will use develop capacity to operate the model - Performance Period: five year performance period spanning years 3-7 of the model during which the awardee will operate the model During the Pre-Implementation period awardees may receive up to $3 million per awardee per year for a total amount of up to $6 million. The amount available during the Performance Period is up to $2 million per awardee per year for a potential total amount of $10 million during the performance period.

Funding: (Formula Grants (Cooperative Agreements)) FY 18 $0; FY 19 est $0; FY 20 est $24,000,000.00

HQ: 7500 Security Boulevard, PO Box WB-05-53, Baltimore, MD 21244

Phone: 410-786-8917 | Email: taiwanna.lucienne@cms.hhs.gov

https://innovation.cms.gov

DOC11.012 | INTEGRATED OCEAN OBSERVING SYSTEM (IOOS) "IOOS"

Award: Project Grants

Purpose: To support projects of a national and international integrated ocean for collecting, monitoring and disseminating marine environment data.

Applicant Eligibility: Organizations and individuals with professional expertise in the sciences, engineering and economics that demonstrate how participation in the IOOS effort builds on and furthers the progress of observing system development funded by this agency.

Beneficiary Eligibility: Same as Applicant Eligibility.

Award Range/Average: Not Available.

Funding: (Project Grants) FY 16 $29,177,929.00; FY 17 est $30,394,973.00; FY 18 est $30,394,973.00

HQ: 1315 E W Highway, Silver Spring, MD 20910

Phone: 301-427-2420

http://www.ioos.noaa.gov

USDA10.303 | INTEGRATED PROGRAMS

Award: Project Grants

Purpose: To compensate for research to address agricultural requirements such as conservation of water, food safety, pest management, and critical organic farming issues.

Applicant Eligibility: State agricultural experiment stations, State cooperative extension services, all colleges and universities, other research and extension Institutions and Organizations, Federal agencies, private Organizations or corporations, and individuals to facilitate or expand promising breakthroughs in areas of the food and agricultural sciences of importance to the United States.

Beneficiary Eligibility: Same as Applicant Eligibility.

Programs Administered by Federal Headquarters

Award Range/Average: If minimum or maximum amounts of funding per competitive and/or capacity project grant, or cooperative agreement are established, these amounts will be announced in the annual Competitive Request for Application (RFA).The most current RFA is available via: Methyl Bromide Transition Program (MBT):https://nifa.usda.gov/funding-opportunity/methyl-bromide-transitionOrganic Transition-Risk Assessment (ORG):https://nifa.usda.gov/funding-opportunity/organic-transitions-orgRegional Rural Development Centers:https://nifa.usda.gov/regional-rural-development-centers
Funding: (Project Grants) FY 17 $7,571,059.00; FY 18 est $8,482,607.00; FY 19 est $0.00
HQ: 1400 Independence Avenue SW, PO Box 2210, Washington, DC 20250-2210
   Phone: 202-720-5229
   http://nifa.usda.gov/grants

HHS93.691 | INTEGRATING THE HEALTHCARE ENTERPRISE FHIR COOPERATIVE AGREEMENT PROGRAM
"IHE FHIR"

Award: Cooperative Agreements
Purpose: To advance the implementation consistency and readiness of the existing and new versions of technical implementation guides of Integrating Healthcare Enterprise (IHE). These guides include Fast Healthcare Interoperability Resource (FHIR) technical standards adopted by the healthcare industry.
Applicant Eligibility: This is a non-competitive funding opportunity and is restricted to Integrating the Healthcare Enterprise. Organizations not designated as such are not eligible to apply for this opportunity, and therefore should not submit an application. Applications submitted by Organizations not referenced in this section will not be considered.
Beneficiary Eligibility: The purpose of this cooperative agreement is to advance the market's ability to electronically exchange health information through the use of certified health IT and to ensure that the products function in the production environment in the form and manner they are certified to. While the beneficiaries are ultimately the broader public at-large, the direct beneficiaries include those who work directly with certified health IT products.
Award Range/Average: $500,000
Funding: (Cooperative Agreements) FY 18 Not Separately Identifiable; FY 19 est $500,000.00; FY 20 est Not Separately Identifiable
HQ: 330 C Street SW, Washington, DC 20201
   Phone: 202-720-2919 | Email: carmel.halloun@hhs.gov

NSF47.083 | INTEGRATIVE ACTIVITIES
"OIA"

Award: Project Grants
Purpose: To enhance the competitiveness of the Nation's research through activities that build capacity for science and engineering and broaden participation in research and education.
Applicant Eligibility: For non-EPSCoR grants, except where a Program solicitation establishes more restrictive eligibility criteria, individuals and Organizations in the following categories may submit proposals: universities and colleges; Non-profit, non-academic Organizations; For-profit Organizations; State and local Governments; and unaffiliated individuals. See the NSF Grant Proposal Guide, Chapter i.e., for a full description of eligibility requirements: http://www.nsf.gov/publications/pub_summ.jsp?ods_key=gpg.EPSCoR eligibility is based on two primary considerations: (1) a jurisdiction's demonstrated commitment to develop its research bases and to improve the quality of science, technology, engineering, and mathematics (STEM) research conducted at its universities and colleges, and (2) a jurisdiction's most recent three-year history of research funds awarded by NSF relative to the Foundation's total research budget for that same period. Regarding the second consideration, a jurisdiction is eligible to participate in EPSCoR Programs if its level of research support is equal to or less than 0. 75 percent of the total NSF research budget for that same period. Adjustments are made in the rare instances where a single large NSF-funded national or international facility skews the data.
Beneficiary Eligibility: Except where a program solicitation establishes more restrictive eligibility criteria, individuals and organizations in the following categories may submit proposals: Universities and colleges; Non-profit, non-academic organizations; for-profit organizations; State and local governments; and unaffiliated individuals. See the NSF Grant Proposal Guide, Chapter I.E. for a full description of eligibility requirements:www.nsf.gov/publications/pub summ.jsp?ods key=gpg.
Award Range/Average: Range Low $64,695 Range High $20,000,000 Average $676,480
Funding: (Project Grants) FY 18 $471,050,000; FY 19 est $546,990,000; FY 20 est $491,040,000
HQ: 2415 Eisenhower Avenue, Suite W17100, Alexandria, VA 22314
   Phone: 703-292-8040 | Email: ppage@nsf.gov

System: Programs Administered by Federal Headquarters

DOT20.703 | INTERAGENCY HAZARDOUS MATERIALS PUBLIC SECTOR TRAINING AND PLANNING GRANTS

Award: Project Grants

Purpose: To increase State, local, territorial and Native American tribal effectiveness to safely and efficiently handle hazardous materials accidents and incidents; enhance implementation of the Emergency Planning and Community Right-to-Know Act of 1986 (EPCRA); and encourage a comprehensive approach to emergency planning and training by incorporating response to transportation standards.

Applicant Eligibility: States, U.S. Territories and Federally recognized Native American Tribes may apply for either or both planning and training grants. The Governor or Tribal official of each eligible applicant has been asked to designate an agency responsible for managing the Program. DOT will work with the designated Organization.

Beneficiary Eligibility: HMEP: State, Local, Federally Recognized Indian Tribal Governments, U.S. Territories, Student/Trainee HMIT: Public nonprofit institution/organization, Private nonprofit institution/organization SPST: Public nonprofit institution/organization, Private nonprofit institution/organization ALERT: Public nonprofit institution/organization, Private nonprofit institution/organization HMCS: Public nonprofit institution/organization, Private nonprofit institution/organization All segments of the U.S. including Territories and Native American tribal populations that are involved with management of or possible exposure to hazardous materials benefit. Specifically Federal, State, and local authorities are assisted through the HMEP grant program with their responsibilities. Students and trainees in emergency response and local emergency planning activities are program beneficiaries since grant funds will be used to benefit local programs.

Award Range/Average: HMEP grant award ranges are $24,000 - $1,500,000. State and Territory HMEP awards are allocated based on a formula that accounts for risk and population. HMIT grant award ranges are $250,000- $1,000,000.SPST grant award ranges are $100,000- $3,500,000. ALERT grant award ranges are estimated to be between $500,000- $2,500,00. CS grant award ranges are estimated to between $200,000- $1,000,000

Funding: (Project Grants (Discretionary)) FY 18 $20,536,792.00; FY 19 est $20,624,744.00; FY 20 est Estimate Not Available

HQ: 1200 New Jersey Avenue SE, Washington, DC 20590

Phone: 202-366-0579 | Email: aaron.mitchell@dot.gov

http://www.phmsa.dot.gov

DHS97.057 | INTERCITY BUS SECURITY GRANTS
"Intercity Bus Security"

Award: Cooperative Agreements

Purpose: The program's objective is to strengthen the nation's preparedness and resilience against natural calamities and terrorist and cyber terrorist activities.

Applicant Eligibility: This Program is limited to applicants meeting one or both of the following criteria: (1) own/operate a fixed-route intercity bus service using over-the-road buses and providing services to a defined Urban Area Security Initiative (UASI) jurisdiction; or (2) own/operate a charter bus service using over-the-road buses providing a minimum of 50 trips annually to a defined UASI jurisdiction.

Beneficiary Eligibility: General public.

Award Range/Average: Refer to program guidance.

Funding: (Project Grants) FY 18 $2,000,000.00; FY 19 est $2,000,000.00; FY 20 est $2,000,000.00

HQ: 400 C Street SW, 3rd Floor N Control Desk, Washington, DC 20472-3635

Phone: 800-368-6498

http://www.fema.gov

HUD14.103 | INTEREST REDUCTION PAYMENTS RENTAL AND COOPERATIVE HOUSING FOR LOWER INCOME FAMILIES

Award: Direct Payments for Specified Use; Guaranteed/insured Loans

Purpose: To provide quality rental and cooperative housing for persons of low- and moderate-income.

Applicant Eligibility: Eligible mortgagors included nonprofit, cooperative, builder-seller, investor-sponsor, and limited-distribution sponsors. Public bodies did not qualify as mortgagors under this Program.

Beneficiary Eligibility: Families and individuals, including the elderly and handicapped or those displaced by government action or natural disaster, eligible to receive the benefits of the subsidies must at the time of admission fall within certain locally determined income limits. Families with higher incomes may occupy apartments, but may not benefit from subsidy payments.

Programs Administered by Federal Headquarters

HQ: 451 7th Street SW, Washington, DC 20410
    Phone: 202-402-2492 | Email: stephen.a.martin@hud.gov
    http://www.hud.gov/offices/hsg/mfh/progdesc/progdesc.cfm

DOC11.407 | INTERJURISDICTIONAL FISHERIES ACT OF 1986

Award: Formula Grants
Purpose: Assists States to manage interjurisdictional fisheries resources.
Applicant Eligibility: The agency of a State government authorized under its laws to regulate commercial fisheries, and the Pacific, Atlantic, and Gulf Interstate Marine Fisheries Commissions.
Beneficiary Eligibility: The agency of a State government authorized under its laws to regulate commercial fisheries.
Funding: (Formula Grants) FY 16 $3,386,604.00; FY 17 est $3,386,604.00; FY 18 est Estimate Not Available
HQ: 1315 E W Highway, Silver Spring, MD 20910
    Phone: 301-713-2334 | Email: steve.meyers@noaa.gov
    http://sero.nmfs.noaa.gov

SBA59.062 | INTERMEDIARY LOAN PROGRAM
"ILP"

Award: Direct Loans
Purpose: Three year pilot program in which SBA made direct loans of up to $1 million at an interest rate of 1 percent to up to 20 nonprofit lending intermediaries each year, subject to the availability of funds.
Applicant Eligibility: Applicants to the pilot Program were required to be a private nonprofit entity with not less than one year of experience of making loans to startups, newly established or growing small businesses. The applicant must have directly funded the loans and not simply provided referrals to loans made by another entity. If an applicant is made up of a consortium of Organizations, each member of the consortium must be individually eligible. Intermediaries that participate in SBA's microloan Program were not eligible to become ILP intermediaries. However, affiliates of microloan intermediaries may have applied. Refer to Federal Register Notice Vol. 76, No. 63, dated Friday, April 1, 2011 starting on page 18007 for additional information.
Beneficiary Eligibility: N/A
Award Range/Average: $1 million each for 20 ILP's with average of $1 million
HQ: 409 3rd Street SW, 8th Floor, Washington, DC 20416
    Phone: 202-619-0628 | Email: james.webb@sba.gov
    http://sero.nmfs.noaa.gov

USDA10.767 | INTERMEDIARY RELENDING PROGRAM
"IRP"

Award: Direct Loans
Purpose: To facilitate for community and business development.
Applicant Eligibility: Eligible intermediaries may include: Private nonprofit Organizations, State or local Governments, and Federally recognized Indian Tribes and cooperatives.
Beneficiary Eligibility: Ultimate recipients may include: For profit organizations, individuals, public and private nonprofit organizations.
Award Range/Average: This program has no statutory formula.Matching requirements are not applicable to this program. However, Intermediaries may not use IRP funds to finance more than 75 percent of the cost of an ultimate recipient's projectMOE requirements are not applicable to this program
Funding: (Direct Loans) FY 18 $18,889,000.00; FY 19 est $18,886,870.00; FY 20 est Estimate Not Available
HQ: 1400 Independence Avenue SW Room 4204, PO Box 3226, Washington, DC 20250
    Phone: 202-720-1400 | Email: lori.hood@wdc.usda.gov
    http://www.rd.usda.gov/programs-services/intermediary-relending-program

BBG90.500 | INTERNATIONAL BROADCASTING INDEPENDENT GRANTEE ORGANIZATIONS

Award: Project Grants

Purpose: To promote freedom and democracy and enhance understanding through multimedia communication.

Applicant Eligibility: Grants are currently only available to three existing nonprofit Organizations, Radio Free Europe/Radio Liberty, Radio Free Asia, and Middle East Broadcasting Networks as identified in authorizing or appropriations language. Grants are not available to State or local Governments or the general public.

Beneficiary Eligibility: Direct beneficiaries of these grants are three nonprofit entities based and incorporated in the United States. The grants allow these three United States-based entities to provide an objective and balanced alternative source of news, opinion, and information related to the U.S. and U.S. policy to overseas populations. Secondary beneficiaries of these grants are overseas listeners who benefit from an alternative news source that provides objective information.

Award Range/Average: FY 2009 Range: $35,919 to $110,419; Average $79,558 FY 2010 Range: $37,228 to $112,601; Average $81,914 FY 2011 Range: $38,404 to $117,462; Average $83,808(in thousands)

Funding: (Salaries and Expenses) FY 09 $238,674,000.00; FY 10 est $245,741,000.00; FY 11 est $251,423,000.00; Breakout of Funding is as follows: RFE/RL: FY 2009-$92,336; FY 2010-$95,912; FY 2011-$95,557 RFA: FY 2009-$35,919; FY 2010-$37,228; FY 2011-$38,404 MBN: FY 2009-$110,419; FY 2010-$112,601; FY 2011-$117,462 (in thousands)

HQ: 330 Independence Avenue SW, Washington, DC 20237

Phone: 202-321-4194 | Email: klarson@bbg.gov

http://www.bbg.gov

EPA66.313 | INTERNATIONAL COMPLIANCE AND ENFORCEMENT PROJECTS

Award: Project Grants

Purpose: The purpose of the proposed capacity building Projects are to protect human health and the environment while advancing U.S. national interests through international environmental collaboration on environmental compliance and enforcement by supporting by these strategic objectives: 1) Reduce Exposure to Toxic Chemicals; 2) Improve Urban Air Quality; 3) Reduce Hazardous Waste and Improve Waste Management; 4) Limit Global GHG Emissions and Other Climate-Forcing Pollutants; 5) Improve access to Clean Water; and 6) Build Strong Environmental Institutions and Legal Structures.

Applicant Eligibility: Assistance under this Program is generally available to States and local Governments, territories and possessions, foreign Governments, international Organizations, Indian Tribes, and possessions of the U.S., including the District of Columbia, public and private universities and colleges, hospitals, laboratories, other public or private nonprofit Institutions, which submit applications proposing projects with significant technical merit and relevance to EPA's Office of Enforcement and Compliance Assurance's mission. For certain competitive funding opportunities under this CFDA description, the Agency may limit eligibility to compete to a number or subset of eligible applicants consistent with the Agency's Assistance Agreement Competition Policy.

Beneficiary Eligibility: States and local governments, territories and possessions, foreign governments, international organizations, Indian Tribes, and possessions of the U.S., including the District of Columbia, public and private universities and colleges, hospitals, laboratories, other public or private nonprofit institutions.

Award Range/Average: Range: $30,000 - $1,000,000; Average: FY 2010 est. $400,000, FY 2011 est. $300,000, FY 2012 est. $620,000, FY 2013 est. $150,000, FY 2014 est. $0, FY 2015 est. $275,000, FY 2016 est. $170,000, FY 2017 est. $59,000. Annual amounts fluctuate greatly because OECA usually issues a single large grants for multiple years with interim awards for other projects at much lower levels. We do not have an estimated budget amount for FY 2018 at this time. This information will be updated when we receive further information."

Funding: (Project Grants) FY 16 $170,000.00; FY 17 est $59,000.00; FY 18 est Estimate Not Available

HQ: Ariel Rios Building 1200 Pennsylvania Avenue NW, PO Box 2201A, Washington, DC 20460

Phone: 202-564-9963 | Email: swack.david@epa.gov

http://www.epa.gov/enforcement

DOS19.452 | INTERNATIONAL EXCHANGE ALUMNI PROGRAMS

"International Exchange Alumni Programs include International Exchange Alumni Enrichment Seminars"

Award: Cooperative Agreements; Project Grants

Purpose: The Bureau of Educational and Cultural Affairs seeks to increase mutual understanding between the people of the United States and the people of other countries by means of educational and cultural exchange programs, including the exchange of scholars, researchers, professionals, students, and educators.

Programs Administered by Federal Headquarters

Applicant Eligibility: Pursuant to the Mutual educational and Cultural Exchange Act of 1961, as amended (Fulbright-Hays Act) the Bureau of educational and Cultural Affairs of the U.S. Department of State awards grants and cooperative agreements to educational and cultural public or private nonprofit foundations or Institutions. Applications may be submitted by public and private non-profit Organizations meeting the provisions described in Internal Revenue Code section 26 USC 501(c)(3). Organizations must have nonprofit status with the IRS at the time of application. Please refer to the Grants.gov or the U.S. Department of State's SAMS Domestic announcement for further eligibility criteria.

Beneficiary Eligibility: Beneficiaries include recipient organizations, educational institutions, other non-government organizations (NGOs) that meet the provisions described in Internal Revenue Code section 26 USC 501(c)(3), as well as sponsored participants, and the American people and the people of participating countries who interact with the international participants.

Award Range/Average: 2600000

Funding: (Project Grants (Cooperative Agreements)) FY 17 $2,600,000.00; FY 18 est $2,600,000.00; FY 19 est $2,600,000.00

HQ: 2200 C Street NW SA-05 01 Z03, Washington, DC 20037

Phone: 202-632-6183 | Email: bistranskysj@state.gov

http://alumni.state.gov

DOS19.087 | INTERNATIONAL FISHERIES COMMISSIONS

Award: Formula Grants

Purpose: The commissions and organizations funded by this appropriation enable the United State to promote critical U.S. economic and conservation interests.

Applicant Eligibility: The use of fund is to support a wide range of international partnerships responding to diverse climate environmental initiatives.

Beneficiary Eligibility: International Organizations.

Award Range/Average: Varies.

Funding: (Formula Grants (Apportionments)) FY 10 $53,658,536.00; FY 11 est $43,440,000.00; FY 12 est $32,200,000.00

HQ: HST Department of State 2201 C Street NW, Room 2880, Washington, DC 20520

Phone: 202-647-2198 | Email: daokt@state.gov

http://www.state.gov/g/oes

DOL17.007 | INTERNATIONAL LABOR PROGRAMS

Award: Project Grants (cooperative Agreements Or Contracts)

Purpose: The Bureau of International Labor Affairs promotes trade commitments, strengthens labor standards, and combats child labor and human trafficking.

Applicant Eligibility: N/A

Beneficiary Eligibility: N/A

Funding: (Project Grants (Cooperative Agreements or Contracts)) FY 17 Not Separately Identifiable; FY 18 Not Separately Identifiable; FY 19 Not Separately Identifiable

HQ: 200 Constitution Avenue NW, Washington, DC 20210

Phone: 202-693-4770 | Email: yoon.bruce@dol.gov

https://www.dol.gov/agencies/ilab

DOL17.401 | INTERNATIONAL LABOR PROGRAMS

Award: Project Grants

Purpose: The Bureau of International Labor Affairs (ILAB) promotes a fair global playing field for workers and businesses in the United States by enforcing trade commitments; strengthening labor standards; and combating international child labor, forced labor, and human trafficking.

Applicant Eligibility: See www.grants.gov.

Beneficiary Eligibility: Same as Applicant Eligibility.

HQ: 200 Constitution Avenue NW, Washington, DC 20210

Phone: 202-693-4876 | Email: yoon.bruce@dol.gov

DOS19.019 | INTERNATIONAL PROGRAMS TO COMBAT HUMAN TRAFFICKING

Award: Cooperative Agreements; Project Grants

Purpose: Prevents trafficking in persons, protecting and assisting trafficking victims, and prosecuting traffickers and others who profit from trafficking in persons.

Applicant Eligibility: Foreign NGOs are eligible for awards under this Program.

Beneficiary Eligibility: Same as Applicant Eligibility.

Award Range/Average: $50,000 to $750,000

HQ: 1800 G Street NW, Suite 2201 (SA 22), Washington, DC 20006

Phone: 202-312-9893 | Email: forstromma@state.gov

http://www.state.gov/g/tip

DOS19.345 | INTERNATIONAL PROGRAMS TO SUPPORT DEMOCRACY, HUMAN RIGHTS AND LABOR

Award: Project Grants

Purpose: Funds targeted democracy and human rights programs to address human rights abuses globally, where fundamental rights are threatened; open political space in struggling or nascent democracies and countries ruled by authoritarian regimes; support civil society activists worldwide; and protect at-risk populations.

Applicant Eligibility: Please see solicitation on www.grants.gov for additional eligibility criteria.

Beneficiary Eligibility: Same as Applicant Eligibility.

Award Range/Average: Please see solicitation on www.grants.gov.

HQ: 2201 C Street NW, Washington, DC 20520

Phone: 202-663-3672 | Email: mulladydk@state.gov

http://www.state.gov/g/drl/p

HHS93.989 | INTERNATIONAL RESEARCH AND RESEARCH TRAINING
"Global Health Research and Research Training"

Award: Project Grants; Training

Purpose: The John E. Fogarty International Center provides research and research training on global health and to foster a knowledge-sharing relationship between the U.S. and other scientists living abroad. It helps in conducting biological, behavioral, social science and career development researches.

Applicant Eligibility: In general, universities, colleges, hospitals, laboratories, Federal Institutions and other public or private non-profit and for-profit domestic and foreign Institutions, and State and local units of government are eligible to submit applications for research grants, research training grants, cooperative agreements, and career development awards. The grantee institution must agree to administer the grant in accordance with prevailing regulations and policies. The eligibility requirements may differ amongst FIC Programs, based on the eligibility section found in our Requests For Applications (RFAs) and Program Announcements (PAs) at: http://www.fic. nih.gov/Funding/Pages/default.aspx.

Beneficiary Eligibility: Usually any non-profit or for-profit organization, company or institution engaged in health and biomedical research.

Funding: (Project Grants (including individual awards)) FY 17 $51,379,157.00; FY 18 est $53,485,107.00; FY 19 est $54,019,955.00

HQ: 31 Center Drive Building 31 Room B2C39, PO Box 2220, Bethesda, MD 20892

Phone: 301-496-1653 | Email: flora.katz@nih.gov

http://www.fic.nih.gov

ED84.017 | INTERNATIONAL RESEARCH AND STUDIES

Award: Project Grants

Purpose: To improve foreign language, area, and other international studies training through research, studies, development and publication of specialized instructional materials developed from the result of research conducted under this program.

Applicant Eligibility: Public and private agencies, Organizations, Institutions, and individuals may apply.

Beneficiary Eligibility: Public and private agencies, organizations, institutions, and individuals will benefit.

Award Range/Average: Varies by competition.

Funding: (Project Grants) FY 18 $712,329.00; FY 19 est $712,329.00; FY 20 est $0.00

Programs Administered by Federal Headquarters

HQ: 400 Maryland Avenue SW, Washington, DC 20202
    Phone: 202-453-5690 | Email: cheryl.gibbs@ed.gov
    http://www.ed.gov/programs/iegpsirs

HHS93.830 | INTEROPERABILITY ROADMAP: PUBLIC/PRIVATE PARTNERSHIP

Award: Cooperative Agreements
Purpose: To help identify best practices in privacy law to improve interoperable exchange of health information consistent with ONC's Interoperability Roadmap.
Applicant Eligibility: This is a non-competitive funding opportunity and is restricted to the National Governors Association (NGA), a private non-profit Organization that is uniquely qualified because of its unique relationship with senior health policy leaders in executive branches of state government; its long prior collaborations with parallel Organizations that support state legislator; expanded support of gubernatorial initiatives to improve health outcomes and reduce health costs in states; and first-hand experience with the complex health privacy rules environment that exists today for patients, providers and state health policy makers. Eligible applicant is uniquely situated to lead a collaboration among high-level state health policy-making officials and ONC for the purpose of harmonizing state health privacy law to support nationwide interoperable exchange of health information for patient care.
Beneficiary Eligibility: Beneficiaries will belong to the following stakeholder groups: Federal; State; Local; Health care covered entities that conduct interstate health transactions; Health Care Consumers; Health Professionals; Scientists/Researchers; and EHR Developers.
Award Range/Average: Total funding $406,250.00 ($325,000 plus $81,250 supplemental funding).
HQ: 330 C Street SW, Washington, DC 20201
    Phone: 202-720-2919 | Email: carmel.halloun@hhs.gov

DHS97.055 | INTEROPERABLE EMERGENCY COMMUNICATIONS

Award: Project Grants
Purpose: It provides planning and training and flexibility to local and State governments to carry out interoperable emergency communications during natural disasters and acts of terrorism.
Applicant Eligibility: All 56 states and territories.
Beneficiary Eligibility: States, territories, and local and tribal governments.
Award Range/Average: Refer to program guidance document.
HQ: 400 C Street SW, Washington, DC 20523
    Phone: 800-368-6498
    http://www.fema.gov/government/grant/index.shtm

HHS93.140 | INTRAMURAL RESEARCH TRAINING AWARD
"IRTA"

Award: Direct Payments for Specified Use
Purpose: To provide opportunities for developmental training and practical research experience in a variety of disciplines related to biomedical research, medical library research, and related fields.
Applicant Eligibility: Candidates for the IRTA Program must be U.S. Citizens or Permanent Resident Aliens: 1) Postdoctoral IRTA participants must possess a Ph.D., M.D., D.D. S., D.M.D., D.V.M. or equivalent degree in biomedical, behavioral, or related sciences; or certification by a University as meeting all the requirements leading to such a doctorate; 5 or fewer years of relevant postdoctoral experience and up to 2 additional years of experience not oriented toward research (i.e., clinical training for physicians); 2) predoctoral IRTA participants must be: a) students enrolled in Ph.D., M.D., D.D.S., D.M.D., D.V.M., or equivalent degree Programs at any accredited U.S. or foreign University, which frequently involves dissertation research. The research experience is undertaken as an integral part of the student's ongoing academic preparation and is credited toward completion of degree requirements; or b) students who have been accepted into graduate or medical degree Programs and who have written permission from their school to interrupt their current schooling and to return within 1 year to their degree granting Programs; 3) postbaccalaureate IRTA participants are individuals who have received a bachelor's degree no more than 3 years prior to the activation date of the traineeship or a master's degree no more than 6 months prior to the activation date of the traineeship, and who intend to apply to graduate, other doctoral, or medical degree Programs during the Program or students who have been accepted into graduate, other doctoral, or medical degree Programs and who have written permission of their school to delay entrance for up to 1 year; and 4) student IRTA participants are at least 17 years of age and

are enrolled at least half-time in high school or have been accepted for or are enrolled as an undergraduate or graduate in an accredited college or University and are in good academic standing. U.S. citizens may be enrolled anywhere in the world; permanent residents must be enrolled in the U.S.

Beneficiary Eligibility: The IRTA Program benefits the participants by combining an opportunity for study with practical work experience and valuable research training experience at the NIH.

Award Range/Average: Fiscal Year 2018: Fogarty International Center issued two Funding Opportunities in partnership with the Office of the U.S. Global AIDS Coordinator and Health Diplomacy: Health-professional Education Partnership Initiative (HEPI: https://www.fic.nih.gov/Programs/Pages/health-professional-education-partnership-initiative-hepi.aspx) and African Association for Health Professions Education and Research (https://www.fic.nih.gov/Programs/Pages/african-association-health-professions.aspx). Both build on the Medical Education Partnership Initiative, which supported Medical Schools in Africa to increase the quality, quantity, and retention of physicians to address the HIV/AIDS crisis in Africa. The new programs extend that goal to include nurses and other allied health professionals, interprofessional training, and integrated biomedical and clinical research. Eight HEPI awards and 1 Association award were issued at the end of the fiscal year. FIC also gave first awards in a new program to reduce Stigma to improve HIV/AIDS prevention, treatment, and care in low and middle income countries (https://www.fic.nih.gov/Programs/Pages/stigma-hiv-aids.aspx). To further support our ongoing HIV programs worldwide, FIC offered supplements to develop courses and support Fellows in Mentorship and Leadership, which have large impacts on the success of scientific careers. We also participated in trans-NIH opportunities to make supplement awards to our existing programs in the areas of Alzheimer's Disease and Opioid alternative therapies. We issued a new Funding Opportunity Announcement for research training in Non-communicable Diseases Across the Lifespan (https://www.fic.nih.gov/Programs/Pages/chronic-lifespan.aspx). Finally, we made numerous new awards to our standing Funding Opportunities, including Career Development Awards for U.S. Scientists, Career Development Awards for Scientists from Low and Middle-income countries, Global Infectious Diseases Research Training, HIV Research Training, Global Fellows and Scholars Program, Bioethics, Ecology and Evolution of Infectious Diseases, Mobile Technologies and Health exploratory research grants, Non-communicable Diseases Exploratory research grants, and Brain Disorders across the Lifespan. Information on all our programs is available on our website: www.fic.nih.gov. Fiscal Year 2019: FIC made first awards in the Research Training in Non-communicable Diseases Across the Lifespan in Low and Middle Income Countries (LMICs) program. We also re-issued Funding Opportunity Announcements for the continuation of our Stigma and HIV research program and our HIV Research Training programs. Two additional awards were issued in the HEPI program (see above). We offered several opportunities for grantees to apply for targeted supplements to their grants and issued supplements for Alzheimer's Disease and Related Dementias, Bioethics Research, and Implementation Science associated with Brain and Neurological Disorders. With support from 15 NIH partners, under our Global Fellows and Scholars program we supported 116 young investigators from the U.S. and LMICs representing a large diversity of biomedical and clinical fields for one-year research training at NIH sites in LMICs. In addition, through an MOU with the Fulbright Foundation, we jointly sponsored 8 additional Fogarty-Fulbright Fellows to receive training at Global Fellows and Scholars sites. We continue to support a Bioinformatics training program through H3 Africa and a research training program for junior faculty at African medical schools. Finally, we made numerous new awards to our standing Funding Opportunities that compete on an annual basis, including Career Development Awards for U.S. Scientists, Career Development Awards for Scientists from LMICs, Global Infectious Diseases Research Training, HIV Research Training, Bioethics, Ecology and Evolution of Infectious Diseases, Mobile Technologies and Health exploratory research grants, Non-communicable Diseases and Injury Exploratory research grants, and Brain Disorders across the Lifespan research grants. Information on all our programs is available on our website: www.fic.nih.gov. Fiscal Year 2020: We anticipate continuing to fund our standing programs, as described above. We will present concepts for several new programs and issue associated Funding Opportunity announcements.

Funding: (Direct Payments for Specified Use) FY 18 $176,917,832.00; FY 19 est $179,084,641.00; FY 20 est $181,429,220.00

HQ: NIH Office of Intramural Training & Education 2 Center Drive, Bethesda, MD 20892

Phone: 301-594-2053 | Email: milgrams@od.nih.gov

http://www.training.nih.gov

DOS19.021 | INVESTING IN PEOPLE IN THE MIDDLE EAST AND NORTH AFRICA
"Investing in People/ Cultural/Educational/Alumni/Information and Media Efforts in the Middle East and North Africa"

Award: Cooperative Agreements

Purpose: Support programs, projects and activities to include (but not limited to) cultural, educational, alumni, information and media efforts in the Middle East and North Africa.

Applicant Eligibility: Not-For-Profit Organizations subject to 501(c)(3) of the U.S. tax code or registered as a non-profit Organization in the entity's home country. Organizations that have and have not previously received international Program

Programs Administered by Federal Headquarters

funding from the U.S. government. Applicants with demonstrated experience in work with vendors, suppliers, contractors, etc. and appropriately staffed offices in country will be preferred.

Beneficiary Eligibility: Local organizations, citizens of countries in the Middle East and North Africa, and the U.S.

Award Range/Average: Range: 10,000 to over 5 MillionAvg: 500,000

Funding: (Project Grants (Cooperative Agreements)) FY 17 Estimate Not Available; FY 18 est Estimate Not Available

HQ: 2201 C Street NW, HST Building, Washington, DC 20520

Phone: 202-647-6397 | Email: hollandly@state.gov

DOD12.557 | INVITATIONAL GRANTS FOR MILITARY-CONNECTED SCHOOLS
"DoDEA Grant"

Award: Project Grants

Purpose: To enhance student learning opportunities, student achievement, educator professional development, and to ease the challenges students who are military dependents face due to their parents' military station transfers or deployments.

Applicant Eligibility: These DoDEA grants are awarded to military-connected local educational agencies (LEAs) by invitation only.

Beneficiary Eligibility: K-12 students are the primary beneficiaries, although grants may also fund teacher professional development.

Award Range/Average: FY09: $300,000 to $2,500,000 FY10: $100,000 to $2,500,000 (min. and max. amounts pending)

Funding: (Project Grants (Discretionary))FY 17 Actual Not Available; FY 18 est $20,000,000; FY 19 est Estimate Not Available

HQ: 4040 N Fairfax Drive, 9th Floor, Arlington, VA 22203

Phone: 703-588-3345 | Email: brian.pritchard@hq.dodea.edu

DOS19.016 | IRAQ ASSISTANCE PROGRAM
"Iraq Assistance Programs"

Award: Cooperative Agreements

Purpose: Promotes democracy, political development and reconciliation, economic development and rule of law in Iraq.

Applicant Eligibility: U.S. or foreign non-profit Organizations; for-profit Organizations; private Institutions of higher education, public or state Institutions of higher education; public international Organizations; and small businesses with functional and regional experience. Each solicitation outlines who is eligible and what types of experience are needed to apply for funding.

Beneficiary Eligibility: U.S. or foreign non-profit organizations; for-profit organizations; private institutions of higher education, public or state institutions of higher education; public international organizations; and small businesses with functional and regional experience. Each solicitation outlines who is eligible and what types of experience are needed to apply for funding. See www.grants.gov for specific announcement.

HQ: 2430 E Street NW, Washington, DC 20037

Phone: 202-776-8691 | Email: curleysl@state.gov

http://www.state.gov

JUSFC90.300 | JAPAN-U.S. FRIENDSHIP COMMISSION GRANTS

Award: Project Grants

Purpose: Promotes educational, intellectual, artistic and cultural exchange and research between Japan and the United States.

Applicant Eligibility: Public and state-controlled Institutions of higher education; non-profits having a 501(c)(3) status with the IRS, other than Institutions of higher education; private Institutions of higher education.

Beneficiary Eligibility: Same as Applicant Eligibility.

Funding: (Project Grants) FY 10 $1,700,000.00; FY 11 est $1,600,000.00; FY 12 est $1,200,000.00

HQ: 1201 15th Street NW, Suite 330, Washington, DC 20005

Phone: 202-653-9800 | Email: mmihori@jusfc.gov

http://www.jusfc.gov

ED84.206 | JAVITS GIFTED AND TALENTED STUDENTS EDUCATION

Award: Project Grants

Purpose: To identify talented students through a coordinated program of evidence-based research, demonstration projects, innovative strategies, and similar activities designed to build and enhance the ability of elementary and secondary schools nationwide.

Government Support Index Handbook 2020

Applicant Eligibility: State and local educational agencies, the Bureaus of Indian education, Institutions of higher education, and other public and private agencies and Organizations may apply for project grants.
Beneficiary Eligibility: Students (including gifted and talented students) and their teachers benefit.
Funding: (Project Grants) FY 18 $11,998,900.00; FY 19 est $11,880,000.00; FY 20 est $0.00
HQ: 400 Maryland Avenue SW, Washington, DC 20202
　　Phone: 202-453-6661 | Email: mildred.horner-smith@ed.gov
　　http://www.ed.gov/programs/javits/index.html

DOL17.287 | JOB CORPS EXPERIMENTAL PROJECTS AND TECHNICAL ASSISTANCE

Award: Project Grants (discretionary)
Purpose: To discover whether community colleges, historically black colleges and universities and tribally controlled colleges and universities (TCUs) can provide quality job training and placement to Job Corps eligible students thereby creating better employment outcomes at a low cost than the traditional Job Corps model.
Applicant Eligibility: Eligible grant applicants are accredited, two-year, public community colleges; accredited, public, two- and four-year historically black colleges and universities or HBCUs, and accredited, two- and four-year tribally controlled colleges and universities or TCUs with at least one certification training Program that can be completed in 12 months or less. Applicants must offer a job training certificate Program that does not exceed 12 months in duration.
Beneficiary Eligibility: The beneficiaries of the Job Corps Scholars Program are: Young adults between the ages of 16 and 24, Low income, A U.S. citizen, a legal U.S. resident, or are a resident of a U.S. territory and/or are authorized to work in the United States, and; Has at least one of the characteristics that are barriers to education and employment: higher than average deficiencies in basic skills as defined in WIOA section 3, School dropout rates, Homelessness, Foster care rates, Parenthood, or Need for additional education, career and technical education or training, or workforce preparation skills to be able to obtain and retain employment that leads to self-sufficiency.
Funding: (Project Grants (Discretionary)) FY 18 Actual Not Available; FY 19 est $50,000,000.00; FY 20 est Estimate Not Available
HQ: 200 Constitution Avenue NW, Washington, DC 20210
　　Phone: 202-693-3000 | Email: carr.debra@dol.gov

HUD14.895 | JOBS-PLUS PILOT INITIATIVE
"Jobs-Plus"

Award: Project Grants
Purpose: Jobs Plus Pilot is a locally designed program implemented aiming at significantly increasing employment and income of public housing residents.
Applicant Eligibility: Public Housing Authorities (PHA).
Beneficiary Eligibility: Individuals and families who are residents of conventional public housing are eligible to receive benefits under the Job Plus program.
Award Range/Average: The range for financial assistance is $2,666,667 to $3,000,000 per grantee award.
Funding: (Project Grants) FY 17 $15,000,000.00; FY 18 est $15,000,000.00; FY 19 est $10,000,000.00
HQ: 451 7th Street SW, Room 4116, Washington, DC 20410
　　Phone: 202-402-6230 | Email: tobey.j.zimber@hud.gov

HHS93.674 | JOHN H. CHAFEE FOSTER CARE PROGRAM FOR SUCCESSFUL TRANSITION TO ADULTHOOD
"The Chafee Program"

Award: Formula Grants
Purpose: Assists states and eligible Indian tribes in establishing and carrying out programs designed to assist youth who experienced foster care at age 14 or older, youth who leave foster care for adoption or kinship guardianship after attaining age 16, and former foster care recipients between 18 and 21 years, to make a successful transition to adulthood and self-sufficiency.
Applicant Eligibility: State Governments, including the 50 states, the District of Columbia, Puerto Rico, and the U.S. Virgin Islands (hereafter "states"), and eligible Indian Tribes, Indian tribal Organizations or Indian tribal consortia (hereafter "Tribes ").

Programs Administered by Federal Headquarters

Beneficiary Eligibility: Youth who experienced foster care at 14 or older, youth who left foster care for adoption or kinship guardianship after attaining age 16, and former foster care recipients between 18 and 21 years may receive services under the Chafee program. States or tribes that operate an extended foster care program for youth up to age 21 have the option to extend services under the Chafee program to youth up to their 23rd birthday.

Award Range/Average: FY 2018 Grants for states range from $500,000 to $16,051,126 with an average of $2,600,276. FY 2018 Grants for tribes range from $10,502 to $46,552 with an average of $21,338.

Funding: (Formula Grants) FY 18 $137,900,000.00; FY 19 est $137,900,000.00; FY 20 est $140,900,000.00

HQ: 330 C Street SW, Room 3509A, Washington, DC 20201

Phone: 202-690-7888 | Email: catherine.heath@acf.hhs.gov

http://www.acf.dhhs.gov/programs/cb

USAID98.009 | JOHN OGONOWSKI FARMER-TO-FARMER PROGRAM
"Development Assistance Program"

Award: Project Grants

Purpose: Helps farmers to improve their agricultural yield by conducting technical seminars.

Applicant Eligibility: The following types of Organizations are eligible to apply for grants: agricultural producers, agriculturalists, colleges and universities (including historically black colleges and universities, land grant colleges or universities, and foundations maintained by colleges or universities), private agribusinesses, private Organizations (including grassroots Organizations with an established and demonstrated capacity to carry out such a bilateral exchange Program), private corporations, and nonprofit farm Organizations. Applicants must also be registered with USAID (if a U.S. PVO); and waive profits and/or fees under the USAID grant (if a for-profit business).

Beneficiary Eligibility: Farms, cooperatives, farmers associations, agricultural and food processing and marketing enterprises, rural finance institutions and in some cases public entities seeking assistance in improving agricultural policy and public services to the agricultural sector in developing countries, middle-income countries, emerging markets, sub-Saharan African countries, and Caribbean Basin countries.

Funding: (Project Grants) FY 16 est Not Separately Identifiable; FY 17 est Not Separately Identifiable

HQ: 301 4th Street SW, Washington, DC 20547

Phone: 202-567-4688 | Email: rwillis@usaid.gov

http://www.usaid.gov/our_work/agriculture/farmer_to_farmer.htm

DOJ16.816 | JOHN R. JUSTICE PROSECUTORS AND DEFENDERS INCENTIVE ACT
"JRJ Grant Program"

Award: Project Grants

Purpose: To encourage qualified attorneys to choose careers as prosecutors and defenders for a minimum of thirty-six (36) months.

Applicant Eligibility: Applicants are limited to state and U.S. territory government agencies, designated by their Governor, and the District of Columbia, designated by the Mayor, to manage this Program. The States, Territories, and the District of Columbia will make loan payments directly to the Institutions holding eligible beneficiary loans on behalf of eligible beneficiaries. See below for eligibility information.

Beneficiary Eligibility: For purposes of this program the following persons shall be considered eligible: Prosecutor - full-time employee of a State or unit of local government (including tribal government) who is continually licensed to practice law and prosecutes criminal or juvenile delinquency cases at the state or unit of local government level (including supervision, education, or training of other persons prosecuting such cases). 42 U.S.C. 3797cc-21(b)(1). Prosecutors who are employees of the federal government are not eligible. Public Defender - an attorney who is continually licensed to practice law and is a full time employee of a State or unit of local government (including tribal government) who provides legal representation to indigent persons in criminal or juvenile delinquency cases including supervision, education, or training of other persons providing such representation; is a full time employee of a nonprofit organization operating under a contract with a State or unit of local government who devotes substantially all of the employee's full-time employment to providing legal representation to indigent persons in criminal or juvenile delinquency cases including supervision, education, or training of other persons providing such representation; or employed as a full-time Federal defender attorney in a defender organization pursuant to subsection (g) of section 3006A of Title 18, United States Code, that provides legal representation to indigent persons in criminal or juvenile delinquency cases.

Award Range/Average: See solicitation guidelines on the Office of Justice Programs web site at https://ojp.gov/funding/Explore/CurrentFundingOpportunities.htm.

Funding: (Project Grants (Discretionary)) FY 18 $1,831,039.00; FY 19 est $2,000,000.00; FY 20 est $0.00
HQ: 810 7th Street NW, Washington, DC 20531
    Phone: 202-616-6500
    http://www.bja.gov

DOJ16.757 | JUDICIAL TRAINING ON CHILD MALTREATMENT FOR COURT PERSONNEL JUVENILE JUSTICE PROGRAMS

Award: Cooperative Agreements
Purpose: To assist the judicial system's handling of child abuse and victims of commercial sexual exploitation including sex trafficking.
Applicant Eligibility: Certain national Organizations as specified in the individual Program announcement.
Beneficiary Eligibility: N/A
Award Range/Average: Range and average of financial assistance vary by project and are posted at http://www.ojjdp.gov/funding/FundingList.asp as solicitations are released.
Funding: (Cooperative Agreements) FY 17 $1,666,643.00; FY 18 est $2,000,000.00; FY 19 est $2,000,000.00
HQ: 810 7th Street NW, Washington, DC 20531
    Phone: 202-616-3646 | Email: darian.hanrahan@usdoj.gov
    http://ojjdp.gov

DOJ16.827 | JUSTICE REINVESTMENT INITIATIVE
"JRI"

Award: Project Grants
Purpose: The Justice Reinvestment Initiative helps to respond to crime and other public safety problems. It responds to crime and cost drivers.
Applicant Eligibility: Justice Reinvestment Initiative: TTA - national scope private and nonprofit Organizations (including tribal nonprofit or for-profit Organizations) and colleges and universities, both public and private (including tribal Institutions of higher education). All recipients and sub-recipients (including any for-profit Organization) must forgo any profit or management fee. Justice Reinvestment: Reducing Violent Crime by Improving Justice System Performance - Eligible applicants are units of state government and federally recognized Indian tribal Governments (as determined by the Secretary of the Interior).
Beneficiary Eligibility: See the current fiscal year's solicitation available at the Office of Justice Programs web site at https://ojp.gov/funding/Explore/CurrentFundingOpportunities.htm.
Award Range/Average: See the current fiscal year's solicitation available at the Office of Justice Programs web site https://ojp.gov/funding/Explore/CurrentFundingOpportunities.htm.
Funding: (Project Grants (Discretionary)) FY 17 $17,151,490.00; FY 18 est $22,000,000.00; FY 19 est $20,000,000.00
HQ: 810 7th Street NW, Washington, DC 20531
    Phone: 202-514-1158 | Email: heather.tubman-carbone@usdoj.gov
    http://www.bja.gov/jri

DOJ16.596 | JUSTICE SYSTEM INFRASTRUCTURE PROGRAM FOR INDIAN TRIBES

Award: Project Grants
Purpose: Providing grant funding to support the physical tribal justice infrastructure capacity needs of Indian Country.
Applicant Eligibility: Federally recognized Indian Tribes may apply.
Beneficiary Eligibility: Same as Applicant Eligibility.
Award Range/Average: Approximately $9,000,000 is available under this program each FY. Suggested award amounts range between $1,000,000 (single jurisdiction projects) and $4,000,000 (multiple jurisdictional projects).
Funding: (Project Grants) FY 18 $9,706,336.00; FY 19 est Not Separately Identifiable; FY 20 est $ $5,000,000
HQ: 810 7th Street NW, Washington, DC 20531
    Phone: 202-616-6500
    http://www.bja.gov

Programs Administered by Federal Headquarters

DOJ16.021 | JUSTICE SYSTEMS RESPONSE TO FAMILIES
"Justice for Families Program"

Award: Cooperative Agreements

Purpose: To improve the response of all aspects of the civil and criminal justice system to families with a history of domestic violence, dating violence, sexual assault, and stalking, or in cases involving allegations of child sexual abuse.

Applicant Eligibility: Eligible applicants are states, local Governments, courts (including juvenile courts), Indian tribal Governments, nonprofit Organizations, legal services providers, and victim service providers.

Beneficiary Eligibility: Courts, supervised visitation providers, and other nonprofit organizations.

Award Range/Average: $325,000-700,000

Funding: (Cooperative Agreements (Discretionary Grants)) FY 16 $10,488,436.00; FY 17 est $10,710,302.00; FY 18 est $10,500,000.00

HQ: 145 N Street NE, Suite 10W121, Washington, DC 20530
Phone: 202-305-1177 | Email: tia.farmer@usdoj.gov
http://www.justice.gov/ovw

DOJ16.540 | JUVENILE JUSTICE AND DELINQUENCY PREVENTION
"Title II, Part B Formula Grants"

Award: Formula Grants; Project Grants; Training

Purpose: To provide grants to states to assist them in planning, establishing, operating, coordinating, and evaluating projects for the development of more effective juvenile delinquency prevention; to support technical assistance grants to facilitate state compliance; to support training and technical assistance to benefit the formula grant program; and to support research, evaluation, and statistics activities designed to benefit the formula grant program.

Applicant Eligibility: For formula grants, the eligible applicants can be found at https://www.ojjdp.gov/statecontacts/resourcelist. asp. For the training and technical assistance and research projects, please refer to the Program narrative.

Beneficiary Eligibility: Units of a State and its local government, public and private organizations, Indian tribes performing law enforcement functions, and agencies involved in juvenile delinquency prevention, treatment, and rehabilitation.

Award Range/Average: Allocation of formula grants to States and territories are based on relative populations under the age of 18. Amounts awarded for discretionary technical assistance, training, and research grants vary depending on the particular program or project being funded.

Funding: (Formula Grants) FY 18 $1,190,000.00; FY 19 est $60,000,000.00; FY 20 est $60,000,000.00

HQ: 810 7th Street NW, Washington, DC 20531
Phone: 202-532-0020 | Email: teneane.bradford@usdoj.gov
http://www.ojjdp.gov

DOJ16.726 | JUVENILE MENTORING PROGRAM
"Mentoring"

Award: Project Grants

Purpose: To improve outcomes for at-risk and high-risk youth and reduce negative outcomes through the provision of mentoring services.

Applicant Eligibility: Eligible applicants are limited to states (including territories), units of local government, federally recognized tribal Governments as determined by the Secretary of the Interior, nonprofit Organizations, and for-profit Organizations (including tribal nonprofit and for-profit Organizations), as well as Institutions of higher education (including tribal Institutions of higher education). For-profit Organizations (as well as other recipients) must agree to forgo any profit or management fee.

Beneficiary Eligibility: N/A

Award Range/Average: Award amounts vary according to solicitation.

Funding: (Project Grants) FY 18 $85,731,653; FY 19 est $9,400,000; FY 20 est $58,000,000

HQ: Office of Juvenile Justice and Delinquency Prevention 810 7th Street NW, Washington, DC 20531
Phone: 202-616-9135 | Email: jennifer.yeh@usdoj.gov
http://www.ojjdp.ncjrs.gov

HUD14.897 | JUVENILE REENTRY ASSISTANCE PROGRAM JUVENILE REENTRY ASSISTANCE PROGRAM (JRAP)

Award: Project Grants; Advisory Services and Counseling

Purpose: To provide legal services to youth had previous records with the juvenile justice system to successfully transition into the community through the expungement and sealing of their juvenile records.

Applicant Eligibility: Eligible applicants are Public Housing Authorities (PHAs) that have established a partnership with a legal aid Organizations, University legal centers, and legal service Organizations that have experience providing legal services to juveniles.

Beneficiary Eligibility: This grant program is to benefit youth (24 years or younger) who have had contact with the juvenile justice system.

Funding: (Project Grants) FY 15 est $0.00; FY 16 est $1,753,464.00; FY 17 $0.00

HQ: 451 7th Street SW, Washington, DC 20410

Phone: 202-402-7154 | Email: naana.a.boampong@hud.gov

DOJ16.840 | KEEP YOUNG ATHLETES SAFE

Award: Cooperative Agreements; Project Grants

Purpose: To safeguard young athletes in organized sports from sexual and emotional abuse and ensures prosecution for all forms of abuse to support victims of abuse.

Applicant Eligibility: Eligible applicants are nonprofit, nongovernmental entities with nationally recognized expertise in preventing and investigating sexual, physical and emotional abuse in the athletic Programs of the United States Olympic Committee, each national governing body, and each Paralympic sports Organization. Applicants must have a recognized background investigating allegations of abuse and reporting to law enforcement in order to inform training and prevention activities. Applicants must also have the capacity to develop and implement trainings on the national, statewide and local levels, as well as oversee regular and random audits to ensure the policies and procedures used to identify and prevent the abuse of amateur athletes are followed correctly. Please see Program announcement for specific eligibility.

Beneficiary Eligibility: The program will safeguard amateur athletes through the prevention of sexual, physical and emotional abuse in the athletic programs of the United States Olympic Committee, each national governing body, and each Paralympic sports organization.

Award Range/Average: Range and average of financial assistance varies by project and are posted at http://www.smart.gov/ funding as solicitations are released.

Funding: (Cooperative Agreements) FY 17 $0.00; FY 18 est $2,500,000.00; FY 19 Estimate Not Available

HQ: SMART Office, Washington, DC 20531

Phone: 202-307-5762

http://www.SMART.gov

FMCS34.002 | LABOR MANAGEMENT COOPERATION
"FMCS Labor-Management Cooperation Grant Program"

Award: Project Grants

Purpose: To support the establishment and operation of plant-level, area-wide, industry or sectoral joint labor-management committees confronting specific, definable problems for which they have developed clear, innovative, and measurable long-term solutions.

Applicant Eligibility: N/A

Beneficiary Eligibility: N/A

Award Range/Average: The grants solicitation for fiscal year 2017 will not specify range of awards based on type of committee. Grants will be awarded in amounts of up to $400,000. The amount of the grant request should be based on the reasonable needs of the committee.

Funding: (Project Grants (Discretionary)) FY 16 $514,486.00; FY 17 est $400,000.00; FY 18 est $400,000.00

HQ: 250 E Street SW, Washington, DC 20427

Phone: 202-606-8181 | Email: lgbroughton@fmcs.gov

http://www.fmcs.gov

Programs Administered by Federal Headquarters

HHS93.065 | LABORATORY LEADERSHIP, WORKFORCE TRAINING AND MANAGEMENT DEVELOPMENT, IMPROVING PUBLIC HEALTH LABORATORY INFRASTRUCTURE
"APHL-CDC Partnership for Quality Lab Practice"

Award: Cooperative Agreements
Purpose: To improve public health laboratory infrastructure, maintain a competent and trained laboratory workforce.
Applicant Eligibility: Assistance will be provided only to APHL. CDC approved single eligibility of this award. This group is the appropriate and only qualified Organization to address the activities described under this Program announcement. Application may be submitted by the APHL consistent with the single eligibility justification that follows. State Governments, specifically State public health laboratories, particularly any Organization representing state public health laboratories and having an established training network. In regards to Eligibility for Affordable Care Act (ACA) funding will be limited solely to the Association of Public Health Laboratories (APHL), the current partner in the cooperative agreement with CDC.
Beneficiary Eligibility: This project represents the front line defense against health threats to the nation's public. The nation's public is the ultimate recipient of benefits from this program.
Funding: (Cooperative Agreements) FY 18 $1,810,677.00; FY 19 est $1,810,677.00; FY 20 est $1,810,677.00
HQ: 4770 Buford Highway NE, PO Box F45, Atlanta, GA 30341
    Phone: 770-488-0563
    http://www.cdc.gov

HHS93.064 | LABORATORY TRAINING, EVALUATION, AND QUALITY ASSURANCE PROGRAMS
"Quality Assurance in Pathology and Laboratory Medicine"

Award: Cooperative Agreements
Purpose: To improve the quality of laboratory testing practices relevant to clinical and public health settings and to determine standardized approaches to quality assurance in pathology and laboratory medicine.
Applicant Eligibility: Applications may be submitted by public and private nonprofit Organizations and by Governments and their agencies, such as: Public nonprofit Organizations, private nonprofit Organizations, universities, colleges, research Institutions, hospitals, community and faith based Organizations, State and local Governments or their Bona Fide Agents (this includes the District of Columbia, the Commonwealth of Puerto Rico, the Virgin Islands, the Commonwealth of the Northern Marianna Islands, American Samoa, Guam, the Federated States of Micronesia, the Republic of the Marshall Islands, and the Republic of Palau).
Beneficiary Eligibility: Applicants must have experience in the administration and evaluation of standardized quality assurance programs in multiple, diverse laboratory sites (including community hospitals and academic medical centers). This experience is required for an applicant to be able to assess the effectiveness of these quality assurance programs and to determine best practices.
Award Range/Average: $100,000 to $500,000; $250,000
Funding: (Cooperative Agreements) FY 18 est $1,816,175.00; FY 19 est $0.00; FY 20 est $0.00
HQ: 2400 Century Parkway NE, Atlanta, GA 30345
    Phone: 404-498-0899
    http://www.cdc.gov

DOI15.152 | LAND BUY-BACK FOR TRIBAL NATIONS
"Buy-Back Program"

Award: Cooperative Agreements
Purpose: To work in partnership with the tribes to minimize the number of fractional interests in trust or restricted lands by purchasing fractional interests from willing sellers and transferring them to the tribe of jurisdiction for purposes benefitthe community.
Applicant Eligibility: Eligibility is restricted to federally recognized Indian tribal Governments with jurisdiction over fractionated lands as identified in the Land Buy-Back Program for Tribal Nation's November 2016 Status Report.
Beneficiary Eligibility: Federally recognized Indian tribal governments as identified in the Land Buy-Back Program for Tribal Nation's November 2016 Status Report.

Award Range/Average: There is no minimum or maximum award amount. Awards have averaged less than $400,000.
Funding: (Cooperative Agreements) FY 17 $1,160,122.00; FY 18 est $2,800,000.00; FY 19 est $3,400,000.00
HQ: Department of the Interior 1849 C Street NW, Room 3543, Washington, DC 20240
Phone: 703-235-3811 | Email: katherine_feiring@ios.doi.gov
http://www.doi.gov/buybackprogram

DOD12.900 | LANGUAGE GRANT PROGRAM
Award: Project Grants
Purpose: Fosters foreign language training to Americans.
Applicant Eligibility: Investigations must be an employee of a U.S. college, University or nonprofit institution as related to language.
Beneficiary Eligibility: Private, public educational institutions and other private, public nonprofit organizations which are operated primarily for language and are not organized primarily for profit.
HQ: E41, Fort George Meade, MD 20755-6000
Phone: 410-859-6087
http://www.darpa.mil/cmo

ED84.229 | LANGUAGE RESOURCE CENTERS
Award: Project Grants
Purpose: To provide grants for establishing, strengthening, and operating centers for teaching and learning foreign languages through teacher training, research, materials development, and dissemination projects.
Applicant Eligibility: An institution of higher education or a consortia of Institutions of higher education is eligible to receive an award.
Beneficiary Eligibility: Institutions of higher education or combinations of such institutions and individuals will benefit.
Award Range/Average: FY 2018: Average award was $171,000 per year; Awards ranged from $130,000- $197,000 per year.
Funding: (Project Grants) FY 18 $2,746,768.00; FY 19 est $2,746,768.00; FY 20 est $0.00
HQ: 400 Maryland Avenue SW, Washington, DC 20202
Phone: 202-453-6425 | Email: stephanie.mckissic@ed.gov
http://www.ed.gov/programs/iegpslrc

DOD12.579 | LANGUAGE TRAINING CENTER
Award: Project Grants
Purpose: A DoD-funded initiative that seeks to accelerate the development of foundational or higher-level expertise in critical and strategic languages and regional studies for DOD personnel.
Applicant Eligibility: Any accredited U.S. Institutions of higher education (defined in 20 U.S.C. 1001 of the Higher education Act of 1965) is eligible for a grant. This includes 2- and 4-year colleges and universities, both public and private. Other Organizations, associations, agencies, and foreign Institutions may be included in proposals but may not be direct recipients of a grant. Federal government schools are not eligible. Applicants must demonstrate an institutional commitment to increasing the critical language and cross-cultural proficiency of DOD personnel as well as proven institutional capability to provide quality instruction in these subject areas.
Beneficiary Eligibility: Accredited U.S. institutions of higher education.
Award Range/Average: Grant range from $150,000 to $2,000,000 annually for a single year project
Funding: (Project Grants) FY 17 $8,755,000.00; FY 18 est $5,800,000.00; FY 19 est $5,800,000.00
HQ: 4800 Mark Center Drive, Arlington, VA 22350
Phone: 571-256-0716 | Email: shirley.t.rapues.civ@mail.mil
http://www.dodltc.org

DOI15.436 | LATE DISBURSEMENT INTEREST
Award: Direct Payments With Unrestricted Use
Purpose: Pays late disbursement interest on subject payments made to States after the due date.
Applicant Eligibility: Late disbursements will trigger automatic payment distribution computed in accordance with the Law.
Beneficiary Eligibility: ONRR pays late disbursement interest on subject payments made to States after the due date.
Award Range/Average: Not Applicable.

Programs Administered by Federal Headquarters

Funding: (Direct Payments with Unrestricted Use) FY 17 $85,000.00; FY 18 est $100,000.00; FY 19 est $111,000.00
HQ: Office of Natural Resources Revenue 1849 C Street NW, PO Box 4211, Washington, DC 20240
  Phone: 202-513-0600
  http://www.ONRR.gov

IMLS45.313 | LAURA BUSH 21ST CENTURY LIBRARIAN PROGRAM
Award: Project Grants; Direct Payments for Specified Use
Purpose: To support professional development, graduate education and continuing education to help libraries and archives develop the human capital capacity they need to meet the changing learning and information needs of the American public.
Applicant Eligibility: Applicants that fulfill the general criteria for libraries may apply for Laura Bush 21st Century Librarian Grant Program. For more information about eligibility requirements, visit http://www.imls.gov/applicants/eligibility_criteria.aspx. See Program guidelines for special conditions of eligibility for this Program.
Beneficiary Eligibility: Libraries and institutions of higher education. Through activities and projects funded, beneficiaries include the general public.
Award Range/Average: Between $50,000 and $1,000,000.
Funding: (Project Grants) FY 15 $10,000,000.00; FY 16 est $10,500,000.00; FY 17 est $10,000,000.00
HQ: 955 L'Enfant Plaza North SW, Suite 4000, Washington, DC 20024
  Phone: 202-653-4730 | Email: mball@imls.gov
  http://www.imls.gov

DOJ16.300 | LAW ENFORCEMENT ASSISTANCE FBI ADVANCED POLICE TRAINING
"FBI Academy, Advanced Specialized Courses"
Award: Training
Purpose: To provide advanced training to experienced personnel of local, county, State, and selected Federal law enforcement agencies and to afford specialized advanced training to the above personnel.
Applicant Eligibility: Regular, full-time personnel of a criminal justice agency serving a municipality, county, local, or State, as well as some selected, qualified representative of Federal agencies having criminal justice responsibilities. Candidates must meet certain age, experience, education, physical, and character requirements.
Beneficiary Eligibility: Same as Applicant Eligibility.
Funding: (Training) FY 16 est $9,318,121.00; FY 17 est $8,804,322.00
HQ: 935 Pennsylvania Avenue Finance Division, Room 6712, Washington, DC 20535
  Phone: 202-324-0495 | Email: michael.tyler@ic.fbi.gov
  http://www.fbi.gov

DOJ16.301 | LAW ENFORCEMENT ASSISTANCE FBI CRIME LABORATORY SUPPORT
"FBI Laboratory"
Award: Provision of Specialized Services; Training
Purpose: To provide forensic services to the FBI and any other duly constituted law enforcement agency; and provide technical and forensic assistance through research, training, technology transfer, and access to information and forensic databases.
Applicant Eligibility: Any duly constituted State and local law enforcement agency in the United States or any of its possessions.
Beneficiary Eligibility: Same as Applicant Eligibility.
Funding: (Advisory Services and Counseling) FY 16 $23,671,109.00; FY 17 est $25,866,151.00; FY 18 est $25,598,728.00
HQ: 935 Pennsylvania Avenue Finance Division, Room 6712, Washington, DC 20535
  Phone: 202-324-0495 | Email: michael.tyler@ic.fbi.gov
  http://www.fbi.gov

DOJ16.302 | LAW ENFORCEMENT ASSISTANCE FBI FIELD POLICE TRAINING
"FBI Field Police Training"

Award: Training
Purpose: To develop the professional skills of criminal justice personnel.
Applicant Eligibility: All authorized municipal, county, local, and State criminal justice personnel.
Beneficiary Eligibility: Same as Applicant Eligibility.
Funding: (Training) FY 16 est $22,538,036.00; FY 17 est $21,290,667.00
HQ: 935 Pennsylvania Avenue Finance Division, Room 6712, Washington, DC 20535
   Phone: 202-324-0495 | Email: michael.tyler@ic.fbi.gov
   http://www.fbi.gov

DOJ16.303 | LAW ENFORCEMENT ASSISTANCE FBI FINGERPRINT IDENTIFICATION
"FBI Criminal Justice Information Services Division"

Award: Provision of Specialized Services
Purpose: To provide fingerprint and arrest-record services to U.S. Government and criminal justice agencies; and to provide arrest- record services to State and local governmental authorities.
Applicant Eligibility: All criminal justice agencies, Federal Government, and other authorized governmental and nongovernmental agencies and entities.
Beneficiary Eligibility: Same as Applicant Eligibility.
Funding: (Information) FY 16 est $76,570,578.00; FY 17 est $117,029,459.00
HQ: 935 Pennsylvania Avenue Finance Division, Room 6712, Washington, DC 20535
   Phone: 202-324-0495 | Email: michael.tyler@ic.fbi.gov
   http://www.fbi.gov

DOJ16.001 | LAW ENFORCEMENT ASSISTANCE NARCOTICS AND DANGEROUS DRUGS LABORATORY ANALYSIS

Award: Provision of Specialized Services
Purpose: To provide technical assistance to state, county, and municipal law enforcement agencies regarding specialized forensic examinations involving drug evidence.
Applicant Eligibility: Any duly constituted State and local law enforcement agency in the United States or any of its possessions.
Beneficiary Eligibility: Same as Applicant Eligibility.
Funding: (Salaries and Expenses) FY 16 $254,788.00; FY 17 est $250,000.00; FY 18 est $250,000.00
HQ: 8701 Morrissette Drive, Springfield, VA 22152
   Phone: 202-307-8866
   http://www.dea.gov

DOJ16.003 | LAW ENFORCEMENT ASSISTANCE NARCOTICS AND DANGEROUS DRUGS TECHNICAL LABORATORY PUBLICATIONS
"Microgram"

Award: Dissemination of Technical Information
Purpose: To distribute scientific information on the detection and analysis of narcotics and dangerous drugs.
Applicant Eligibility: Forensic laboratories or scientists doing work for law enforcement agencies.
Beneficiary Eligibility: Same as Applicant Eligibility.
Funding: (Salaries and Expenses) FY 16 Not Separately Identifiable; FY 17 est Not Separately Identifiable; FY 18 est $0.00
HQ: 8701 Morrissette Drive, Springfield, VA 22152
   Phone: 202-307-8866
   http://www.dea.gov

Programs Administered by Federal Headquarters

DOJ16.004 | LAW ENFORCEMENT ASSISTANCE NARCOTICS AND DANGEROUS DRUGS TRAINING

Award: Training

Purpose: To familiarize appropriate professional and enforcement personnel techniques in the conduct of drug investigations; aspects of physical security in legitimate drug distribution; techniques in analysis of drugs for evidential purpose; pharmacology; and management and supervisory training.

Applicant Eligibility: State, local, military, and other Federal law enforcement and regulatory officials; crime laboratory technicians and forensic chemists.

Beneficiary Eligibility: Same as Applicant Eligibility.

HQ: PO Box 1475, Quantico, VA 22134-1475
   Phone: 703-632-5141
   http://www.usdoj.gov

DOJ16.304 | LAW ENFORCEMENT ASSISTANCE NATIONAL CRIME INFORMATION CENTER
"NCIC"

Award: Provision of Specialized Services

Purpose: To complement the development of similar metropolitan and statewide criminal justice information systems and provide a computerized central index to documented files of local and State criminal justice agencies.

Applicant Eligibility: Local, State, and Federal criminal justice agencies may participate through their individual control terminal agency.

Beneficiary Eligibility: Same as Applicant Eligibility.

Funding: (Information) FY 16 est $17,914,864.00; FY 17 est $18,105,221.00

HQ: 935 Pennsylvania Avenue Finance Division, Room 6712, Washington, DC 20535
   Phone: 202-324-0495 | Email: michael.tyler@ic.fbi.gov
   http://www.fbi.gov

DOJ16.309 | LAW ENFORCEMENT ASSISTANCE NATIONAL INSTANT CRIMINAL BACKGROUND CHECK SYSTEM
"NICS"

Award: Provision of Specialized Services

Purpose: To provide a system so that any Federal Firearm Licensee (FFL) could receive an immediate discovery by telephone, or by other electronic means, on whether receipt of a firearm and/or explosive by a prospective buyer would violate Federal or State laws.

Applicant Eligibility: All persons purchasing firearms.

Beneficiary Eligibility: The Federal Firearm Licensees and American public.

Funding: (Information) FY 16 est $49,276,624.00; FY 17 est $52,122,496.00

HQ: 935 Pennsylvania Avenue Finance Division, Room 6712, Washington, DC 20535
   Phone: 202-324-0495 | Email: michael.tyler@ic.fbi.gov
   http://www.fbi.gov

DOJ16.305 | LAW ENFORCEMENT ASSISTANCE UNIFORM CRIME REPORTS

Award: Dissemination of Technical Information

Purpose: To furnish data for the heads of law enforcement agencies in administration and operation of their departments, and to make information/data available to judges, penologists, sociologists, legislators, media, students, and others interested in crime and its social aspects.

Applicant Eligibility: All participating law enforcement agencies including State and local Governments are furnished copies of the annual publication and preliminary annual and semiannual reports. Limited annual copies of statistics on Hate Crime and Law Enforcement Officers Killed and Assaulted, along with preliminary annual and semiannual reports are available to any interested individual who sends a request to the: Communications Unit, Criminal Justice Information Services Division, Federal Bureau of Investigation, Module D-3, 1000 Custer Hollow Road, Clarksburg, WV 26306-0154. The annual

Programs Administered by Federal Headquarters

publication is available to the general public for purchase from the Superintendent of Documents, U.S. government Printing Office, 710 North Capitol Street NW., Washington, DC 20401.

Beneficiary Eligibility: All participating State and local law enforcement agencies are furnished copies of the annual publication and preliminary annual and semiannual reports. Limited copies of preliminary annual and semi-annual reports are available to any interested individual who sends a request to the: Communications Unit, Criminal Justice Information Services Division, Federal Bureau of Investigation, Module D-3, 1000 Custer Hollow Road, Clarksburg, WV 26306-0154. The annual publication is available for sale from the Superintendent of Documents, U.S. Government Printing Office, 710 North Capitol Street, NW., Washington DC 20401.

Funding: (Advisory Services and Counseling) FY 16 est $55,592,457.00; FY 17 est $56,327,717.00

HQ: 935 Pennsylvania Avenue Finance Division, Room 6712, Washington, DC 20535

Phone: 202-324-0495 | Email: michael.tyler@ic.fbi.gov

http://www.fbi.gov

HUD14.888 | LEAD-BASED PAINT CAPITAL FUND PROGRAM

Award: Project Grants

Purpose: To assist Public Housing Authorities identify and eliminate lead-based paint hazards in public housing.

Applicant Eligibility: Only Public Housing Authorities (PHA) with the legal authority to develop, own, modernize and operate a public housing development in accordance with the 1937 Housing Act.

Beneficiary Eligibility: Public housing residents.

Award Range/Average: $0- $1,000,000; average award $500,000

Funding: (Project Grants) FY 16 Actual Not Available; FY 17 est $25,000,000.00; FY 18 est Estimate Not Available

HQ: 451 7th Street SW, Washington, DC 20410

Phone: 202-380-7369 | Email: tara.j.radosevich@hud.gov

http://www.hud.gov/offices/pih/programs/ph/capfund

HUD14.900 | LEAD-BASED PAINT HAZARD CONTROL IN PRIVATELY-OWNED HOUSING
"Lead-Based Paint Hazard Control"

Award: Project Grants

Purpose: Providing grants to aid State, Tribal, and local governments in identifying and controlling lead-based paint hazards in privately-owned housing that is owned by or rented to low- or very-low income families.

Applicant Eligibility: States, Tribes, cities or units of general local government that have a current, approved Consolidated Plan. Federal agencies and Federal employees are not eligible to submit applications. Applicants with outstanding civil rights violations are not eligible for funding.

Beneficiary Eligibility: Hazard Control Grants shall be for lead-based paint hazard control in eligible target housing, as defined under Section 217 of Public Law 104-134 (the Omnibus Consolidated Rescissions and Appropriations Act of 1996, 110 Stat. 1321, approved April 26, 1996) as amended by Section 1011(a) of the Residential Lead-Based Paint Hazard Reduction Act of 1992 (Title X). Funds shall be available only for projects conducted using contractors and inspectors certified, through an EPA authorized program, or trained in lead-safe work practices using a HUD-approved curriculum.

Award Range/Average: With Fiscal Year 2010funds an estimated 21 Lead Hazard Control grants of approximately $3 million each will be awarded totaling $62 million.

Funding: (Project Grants) FY 18 $85,000,000; FY 19 est $85,000,000; FY 20 est $85,000,000

HQ: 451 7th Street SW, Room 8236, Washington, DC 20410

Phone: 202-402-7596 | Email: yolanda.a.brown@hud.gov

http://www.hud.gov/healthyhomes

HUD14.920 | LEAD HAZARD CONTROL FOR HIGH RISK AREAS
"Lead Hazard Control for Communities with High Impact Areas"

Award: Project Grants (discretionary)

Purpose: To fund the urban areas where children have high lead levels in their blood.

Applicant Eligibility: State Governments, County Governments, City or township Governments, Special district Governments and Native American tribal Governments (Federally recognized) are eligible to apply. Applicant must demonstrate that certain designated census tracts document the highest rates of lead poisoned children in the country.

Programs Administered by Federal Headquarters

Beneficiary Eligibility: Families owning homes who earn less than 80% AMI with children under 6 in residence, and families renting who earn less than 50% AMI.

Award Range/Average: $1,000,000 - $9,000,000

Funding: (Project Grants (Discretionary)) FY 18 Actual Not Available; FY 19 est $64,000,000.00; FY 20 est Not Separately Identifiable

HQ: 451 7th Street SW, Room 8236, Washington, DC 20410

Phone: 202-402-7596 | Email: yolanda.a.brown@hud.gov

HUD14.905 | LEAD HAZARD REDUCTION DEMONSTRATION GRANT PROGRAM

Award: Project Grants

Purpose: To identify and control lead-based paint hazards in privately-owned housing that is owned by or rented to low- or very-low-income families.

Applicant Eligibility: To be eligible to apply for the Lead Hazard Reduction Demonstration Program, the applicant must be a city, county, or other unit of local government. States and Indian Tribes may apply on behalf of units of local government within their jurisdiction, if the local government designates the state or the Indian Tribe as their applicant. Multiple units of a local government (or multiple local Governments) may apply as part of a consortium; however, you must identify a prime applicant that will be responsible for ensuring compliance with all requirements specified in this NOFA. State government and Native American tribal applicants must have an EPA approved State Program for certification of lead-based paint contractors, inspectors, and risk assessors in accordance with 40 CFR 745 in effect on the application deadline date to be eligible to apply for Lead Hazard Reduction Demonstration Grant funds.

Beneficiary Eligibility: Occupants and owners of eligible target housing, Section 1011(a) of the Residential Lead-Based Paint Hazard Reduction Act of 1992 (Title X). Lead Hazard Reduction Demonstration Grants shall be for lead-based paint hazard control in this housing. Funds shall be available only for projects conducted using contractors and inspectors certified, and workers trained through an EPA authorized program. Selected beneficiaries must comply with all eligibility criteria and all applicable restrictions presented in the Appropriation language and with all requirements presented in the NOFA.

Award Range/Average: $95 million in fiscal year 2019 funds is available. The minimum award amount shall be approximately $1 million per grant up to $4.5 million per grant. Approximately 25 grants will be awarded to applicants for the Lead Hazard Reduction Demonstration Program.

Funding: (Project Grants) FY 18 $95,000,000.00; FY 19 est $95,000,000; FY 20 est $95,000,000

HQ: 451 7th Street SW, Room 8236, Washington, DC 20410

Phone: 202-402-7596 | Email: yolanda.a.brown@hud.gov

http://www.hud.gov/healthyhomes

HUD14.902 | LEAD TECHNICAL STUDIES GRANTS

Award: Cooperative Agreements

Purpose: To finance technical studies to improve methods for detecting and controlling lead-based paint hazards in housing.

Applicant Eligibility: Academic, not-for-profit and for-profit Institutions located in the U.S. (for-profit firms are not allowed to profit from the project), state and local Governments, and federally recognized Native American Tribes are eligible under all existing authorizations. Applications for supplementation of existing projects are eligible to compete with applications for new awards. Federal agencies and federal employees are not eligible to submit applications. The General Section of the Super NOFA provides additional eligibility requirements.

Beneficiary Eligibility: Homeowners, rental property owners, rental and public housing residents.

Award Range/Average: The total amount to be awarded is approximately $1 million for Lead Technical Studies. The anticipated amounts and/or numbers of individual awards will be approximately 2 - 4 cooperative agreements, ranging from approximately $250,000 to a maximum of $500,000.

Funding: (Cooperative Agreements) FY 18 est $3,000,000.00; FY 19 est $3,000,000.00; FY20 est $ 3,000,000.00

HQ: 451 7th Street SW, Room 8236, Washington, DC 20410-3000

Phone: 202-402-7685 | Email: eugene_a_pinzer@hud.gov

http://www.hud.gov

HHS93.330 | LEADERSHIP IN PUBLIC HEALTH SOCIAL WORK EDUCATION GRANT PROGRAM
"Public Health Social Work Education Grant Program, LPHSWE"

Award: Project Grants

Purpose: Provides training and education, faculty development, and curriculum enhancement to prepare students for leadership roles in public health social work through enrollment in a dual master's degree program in social work and public health.

Applicant Eligibility: Eligible applicants include accredited schools of social work/Programs that 1) offer a dual master's degree in an accredited graduate Program in social work with a macro-level concentration in management and administration and in an accredited graduate Program in public health; and 2) previously received HRSA support for dual degree enrollment, education, and graduation in the Leadership in Public Health Social Work education Program. Eligible applicants include accredited schools of social work/Programs that 1) offer a dual master's degree in an accredited graduate Program in social work with a macro-level concentration in management and administration and in an accredited graduate Program in public health; and 2) previously received HRSA support for dual degree enrollment, education, and graduation in the Leadership in Public Health Social Work education Program. Federally Recognized Indian Tribal Government and Native American Organizations may apply if they are otherwise eligible.

Beneficiary Eligibility: A student receiving a stipend in the LPHSWE Program must be a citizen of the United States, a non-citizen national of the United States, or a foreign national who possesses a visa permitting permanent residence in the United States. Individuals on temporary or student visa are not eligible participants.

Award Range/Average: FY 18 $0 FY 19 $0 FY 20 $0

HQ: 5600 Fishers Lane, Room 11N90D, Rockville, MD 20857

Phone: 301-443-6760 | Email: mgerdine@hrsa.gov

http://www.hrsa.gov

HHS93.345 | LEADING EDGE ACCELERATION PROJECTS (LEAP) IN HEALTH INFORMATION TECHNOLOGY
"LEAP"

Award: Cooperative Agreements (discretionary Grants)

Purpose: Seeks to partner with innovative organizations that can look to the future and develop leading solutions and innovations to some of these vexing problems.

Applicant Eligibility: Public or non-profit private Institutions, such as a University, college, or a faith-based or community-based Organization; units of local or state government, eligible agencies of the federal government, Indian/Native American Tribal Governments (federally recognized, other than federally recognized, and tribally designated Organizations).

Beneficiary Eligibility: N/A

Award Range/Average: There has been $2,00,000 allocated for FY 18 for this program. We estimate that we will award two (2) total; the award amounts will be $1,000,000 for each. The award amount will be determined upon the documentation, scope, and strength the awardee's proposal.

Funding: (Cooperative Agreements (Discretionary Grants)) FY 17 Actual Not Available; FY 18 est $2,000,000.00; FY 19 est Estimate Not Available

HQ: 330 C Street SW, Washington, DC 20201

Phone: 202-969-3369 | Email: kevin.chaney@hhs.gov

https://www.healthit.gov

DOD12.632 | LEGACY RESOURCE MANAGEMENT PROGRAM
"DoD Legacy Program"

Award: Cooperative Agreements; Project Grants

Purpose: A DoD Legacy Program is to provide funding to help manage and sustain DoD land in the United States.

Applicant Eligibility: Cultural Resources/Historic Preservation.

Beneficiary Eligibility: Successful applicants must have the ability to accept funds from DOD via cooperative agreement, contract, or MIPR.

Award Range/Average: Most funded projects range between $40,000 and $150,000.

Funding: (Cooperative Agreements) FY 14 $4,478,500.00; FY 15 est $2,624,000.00; FY 16 est $4,668,000.00

Programs Administered by Federal Headquarters

HQ: 4800 Mark Center Drive, Suite 16G14, Alexandria, VA 22352
   Phone: 571-372-6905 | Email: l.p.boice.civ@mail.mil
   http://www.dodlegacy.org

DOJ16.524 | LEGAL ASSISTANCE FOR VICTIMS
"LAV Program"

Award: Project Grants
Purpose: To increase the availability of comprehensive civil and criminal legal services to victims of domestic violence, dating violence, sexual assault, and stalking in matters relating to or arising from the abuse or violence.
Applicant Eligibility: Eligible grantees for this Program are private, nonprofit entities, Indian tribal Governments and tribal Organizations, territorial Organizations, and publicly funded Organizations not acting in their governmental capacity, such as law schools.
Beneficiary Eligibility: Beneficiaries include public or private nonprofit entities providing legal assistance primarily to victims of domestic violence, sexual assault, and or stalking and victims of these crimes who receive legal assistance.
Award Range/Average: Range: $350,000- $800,000
Funding: (Project Grants) FY 16 $35,733,196.00; FY 17 est $34,615,593.00; FY 18 est $35,000,000.00
HQ: 145 N Street NE, Suite 10W121, Washington, DC 20530
   Phone: 202-305-1177 | Email: tia.farmer@usdoj.gov
   http://www.justice.gov/ovw

VA64.031 | LIFE INSURANCE FOR VETERANS-DIRECT PAYMENTS FOR INSURANCE

Award: Insurance
Purpose: To provide direct insurance payments, including advance payments disbursed as loans, to Veterans and their beneficiaries for claims based on death or other qualifying circumstances.
Applicant Eligibility: Veterans currently insured under USGLI, NSLI, or VMLI. Payment cannot be made if it would cause the insurance proceeds to revert back to a State (as in cases where there are no permissible heirs to pay). 38 U.S.C. 1950; 38 U.S.C. 1917(d).
Beneficiary Eligibility: Payment may be made on a claim to a designated beneficiary, a representative of the estate, a minor or incompetent, or another designee filing for benefits. 38 U.S.C. 1917. A beneficiary may assign all or a portion of his or her share of the insurance to a restricted class of the insured's relatives. 38 U.S.C. 1918(b). Payments may also be made to the policyholder for loan or dividend amounts. 38 CFR 8.11(b); 38 CFR 6.14; 38 CFR 8.10; 38 CFR 6.11.
Award Range/Average: Not Available.
Funding: (Insurance) FY 16 $1,220,000,000.00; FY 17 est $1,220,000,000.00; FY 18 est $1,160,000,000.00
HQ: 5000 Wissahickon Avenue, Philadelphia, PA 19144
   Phone: 800-669-8477 | Email: michelle.staton@va.gov
   http://www.benefits.va.gov/insurance/index.asp

VA64.030 | LIFE INSURANCE FOR VETERANS-FACE AMOUNT OF NEW LIFE INSURANCE POLICIES ISSUED

Award: Insurance
Purpose: To provide Service Disabled Life Insurance (S-DVI) protection for other than dishonorably discharged Veterans who are service disabled and who separated from active duty on or after April 25, 1951, and to provide Veterans Mortgage Life Insurance (VMLI) for Veterans and Servicemembers who have been granted Department of Veterans Affairs (VA) specially adapted housing benefits.
Applicant Eligibility: VA may issue S-DVI to a Veteran discharged under other than dishonorable conditions from active military duty, on or after April 25, 1951, who has been granted service connection for a disability, and who, if not for the service-connected disability(ies), would be otherwise insurable in accordance with established standards of good health. The Veteran must apply for coverage within two years from the date of notification of the decision granting service connection. 38 U.S.C. 1922(a). A Veteran insured under S-DVI who qualifies for waiver of premiums, is under age 65, and applies within one year from date of notice from VA that he/she qualifies for waiver of premiums, may be issued Supplemental S-DVI coverage. 38 U.S.C. 1912(a); 38 U.S.C. 1922A(a). A Veteran or Servicemember granted VA specially adapted housing benefits will be

sent notice that he/she is automatically eligible to be insured for VMLI unless he/she elects in writing not to be so insured, or fails to respond within 60 days after VA sends a final request for information on which premiums can be based. 38 CFR 8a. 3(a).

Beneficiary Eligibility: S-DVI proceeds are payable to designated beneficiaries. 38 U.S.C. 1917(a). S-DVI may also be granted under certain conditions to mentally incompetent Veterans who were otherwise eligible for such insurance, but due to their incompetency, died without filing an application. 38 U.S.C. 1922(b). VMLI proceeds are payable to the holder of the mortgage loan. 38 U.S.C. 2106(e).

Award Range/Average: Not Available.

HQ: 5000 Wissahickon Avenue, Philadelphia, PA 19144

Phone: 800-669-8477 | Email: michelle.staton@va.gov

http://www.benefits.va.gov/INSURANCE/index.asp

VA64.103 | LIFE INSURANCE FOR VETERANS
"GI Insurance"

Award: Insurance

Purpose: To provide life insurance protection for veterans of World War I, World War II, Korean conflict, Vietnam conflict, Gulf era conflicts and service-disabled veterans separated from active duty on or after April 25, 1951.

Applicant Eligibility: All of the Programs are closed for new issues except Service-Disabled Veterans Insurance, Veterans Mortgage Life Insurance, Service members' Group Life Insurance and Veterans Group Life Insurance. A veteran discharged from active military duty, on or after April 25, 1951, who has been granted a service connection for a new disability, and who, if not for the disability would be otherwise insurable in accordance with the established standards of good health, applies for such coverage within 2 years from the date of notice of the VA service-connected rating, may be issued Service-Disabled Veterans Insurance. (The time period in which to apply is limited to one year from the date of notice of the VA service-connected rating if the notice was provided before September 1, 1991.) A veteran insured under Service-Disabled Veterans Insurance who qualifies for waiver of premiums, who is under age 65 and who applies within one year from date of notice from VA that he/she qualifies for waiver of premiums, may be issued Supplemental Service-Disabled Veterans Insurance coverage. A veteran who has been given a VA grant for specially adapted housing will be sent notice that he/she is automatically insured for mortgage protection unless he/she elects in writing not to be so insured, or fails to respond within 60 days after a final request for information on which premium can be based is mailed to him/her. Service members are automatically covered for the maximum coverage amount of life insurance on themselves and a spouse, unless the member declines or reduces the coverage in writing. Service members are also automatically covered by Servicemembers' Traumatic Injury Protection (TSGLI), which provides automatic traumatic injury coverage to all service members under SGLI. TSGLI provides for payment between $25,000 and $100,000 (depending on the type of injury) to SGLI members who sustain a traumatic injury that results in certain severe losses. Coverage of children is on "dependent" children and no premium is paid. Veterans are eligible to convert their Service members' Group Life Insurance in an amount up to the coverage held on their date of discharge. If a veteran is totally disabled at time of discharge, the veteran is eligible for a one-year disability extension of their Service members' Group Life Insurance and the conversion to Veterans' Group Life Insurance.

Beneficiary Eligibility: The veteran may apply for either type of insurance. However, if the veteran is mentally incompetent, a VA recognized fiduciary may apply on his/her behalf for Service-Disabled Veterans Insurance. Service-Disabled Veterans Insurance may also be granted under certain conditions to mentally incompetent veterans who were otherwise eligible for such insurance, but due to their incompetency, died without filing an application.

HQ: PO Box 42954, Philadelphia, PA 42954

Phone: 800-669-8477 | Email: michelle.staton@va.gov

http://www.insurance.va.gov

HHS93.072 | LIFESPAN RESPITE CARE PROGRAM
"Lifespan Respite"

Award: Cooperative Agreements

Purpose: To expand and enhance respite care services to family caregivers; improve the statewide dissemination and coordination of respite care; and to provide, supplement, or improve access and quality of respite care services to family caregivers, thereby reducing family caregiver strain.

Applicant Eligibility: N/A

Beneficiary Eligibility: N/A

Programs Administered by Federal Headquarters

Award Range/Average: FY2017 - 2 New State Grants ($200,000 per grant); 1 Continuation Award for Lifespan Respite Technical Assistance Resource Center ($239,010); 12 Advancing State Lifespan Respite Care System Awards (Range: $86,867 - $261,953)FY2018 - 12 Advancing State Lifespan Respite Care System and 1 Technical Assistance Resource Center Continuation Awards (Range: $84,275 - $254,135),13 Supplemental Awards to all 12 Advancing State Care System and Technical Assistance Resource Center (Range: $8,597 - $25,792); 4 Additional Advancing State Lifespan Respite Care System Awards that were approved but not funded in the 2017 Funding Opportunity (Range: $88,333 - $265,000)
Funding: (Cooperative Agreements) FY 17 $3,360,000.00; FY 18 est $4,110,000.00; FY 19 est Estimate Not Available.
HQ: 330 C Street SW, Washington, DC 20201
　　Phone: 202-795-7473 | Email: victoria.wright@acl.hhs.gov
　　http://www.acl.gov

HUD14.874 | LOAN GUARANTEES FOR NATIVE HAWAIIAN HOUSING "Section 184A"

Award: Guaranteed/insured Loans
Purpose: To provide greater access to private mortgage resources to eligible Native Hawaiian families by guaranteeing loans for one-to-four family housing located on Hawaiian Home Lands.
Applicant Eligibility: A Native Hawaiian family; the Department of Hawaiian Home Lands; the Office of Hawaiian Affairs; a private nonprofit Organization experienced in the planning and development of affordable housing for Native Hawaiians.
Beneficiary Eligibility: Native Hawaiian homeowners are the beneficiaries of the program.
Award Range/Average: The average loan amount in FY 2017 was $227,882.
Funding: (Guaranteed/Insured Loans) FY 17 $360,432.00; FY 18 est $556,262.00; FY 19 est $650,000.00
HQ: ONAP 451 7th Street SW, Room 5156, Washington, DC 20410
　　Phone: 202-402-4978 | Email: thomas.c.wright@hud.gov
　　http://www.hud.gov/offices/pih/ih/codetalk/onap/program184a.cfm

HHS93.232 | LOAN REPAYMENT PROGRAM FOR GENERAL RESEARCH "NIH General Research Loan Repayment Program; GR-LRP"

Award: Direct Payments for Specified Use
Purpose: To recruit and retain health professionals performing research in fields required by the NIH to carry out its mission.
Applicant Eligibility: Eligible applicants must: (1) Be a citizen, national, or permanent resident of the United States; (2) possess a M.D., Ph.D., D.O., D.D. S., D.M.D., D.V.M., D.P.M., A.D.N., B.S.N., or equivalent degree, or hold the position of Physician Assistant; (3) have qualified educational debt, which results from governmental or commercial loans obtained to support their undergraduate and/or graduate education, in excess of 20 percent of their annual NIH salary on the Program eligibility date; (4) be appointed to the NIH Intramural Research Program under any temporary or permanent employment mechanism, so long as the employment has the potential to last a minimum of three years; (5) not be under any existing service obligation to Federal, State, or other entities, until such obligation is discharged or unless it is deferred during the period of Program service; (6) submit an application to participate in the Loan Repayment Program for General Research; and (7) sign and submit to the Secretary of Health and Human Services, at the time of application submission, a contract agreeing to engage in research as an employee of the NIH for a minimum of 3 years.
Beneficiary Eligibility: NIH researchers who possess substantial unpaid educational debt relative to income will benefit from this program.
Award Range/Average: (Loan Repayment) For initial 3-year contracts, loan repayment awards may range from $7,800 to $105,000; Tax reimbursements range from $3,679 to $48,825. The average contract cost which includes loan and tax reimbursement is $102,000.
Funding: (Direct Payments for Specified Use) FY 18 $3,917,457.00; FY 19 est $4,193,697.00; FY 20 est $4,200,000
HQ: 2 Center Drive, Room 2E18 Building 2, Bethesda, MD 20892-0230
　　Phone: 301-402-1283 | Email: colep@mail.nih.gov
　　http://www.lrp.nih.gov

DOL17.302 | LONGSHORE AND HARBOR WORKERS' COMPENSATION

Award: Direct Payments With Unrestricted Use
Purpose: Provides compensation for disability or death resulting from injury, including occupational disease, to eligible private employees.

Applicant Eligibility: Longshore workers, harbor workers, and certain other employees engaged in maritime employment on the navigable waters of the United States and adjoining pier and dock areas, employees engaged in activities on the Outer Continental Shelf, employees of Non appropriated Fund Instrumentalities, employees of private employers engaged in work outside the United States under contracts with the United States Government, and others as specified, including survivors of the above. Employees of private concerns in the District of Columbia and their survivors are eligible for benefits under an extension of the Act, applicable to injuries or deaths based upon employment events that occurred prior to July 26, 1982. Puerto Rico is not covered by the Longshore and Harbor Workers' Compensation Act.

Beneficiary Eligibility: Same as Applicant Eligibility.64

Award Range/Average: Disability - 66-2/3 percent of average weekly wage; death benefits 50 percent average wages of deceased to such widow or widower, plus 16-2/3 percentfor one or more surviving children with 66-2/3 percent limit. Average benefit unknown. Weekly compensation payments limited to between 50-200 percent of national average weekly wage.

Funding: (Direct Payments with Unrestricted Use) FY 18 $110,774,000.00; FY 19 est $114,959,000.00; FY 20 est $113,118,000.00

HQ: Division of Longshore and Harbor Workers Compensation 200 Constitution Avenue NW, Washington, DC 20210
Phone: 202-693-0038
http://www.dol.gov/owcp/dlhwc

DOI15.422 | LOUISIANA STATE UNIVERSITY (LSU) COASTAL MARINE INSTITUTE (CMI)
"LSU CMI"

Award: Cooperative Agreements

Purpose: The Bureau of Ocean Energy Management (BOEM) provides major economic and energy benefits on a national and local level to the taxpayers, States and the American Indian community. The purpose of the Louisiana State University Coastal Marine Institute (CMI) is to use highly qualified scientific expertise at local levels to collect and disseminate environmental information needed for OCS oil and gas and marine minerals decisions; address local and regional OCS-related environmental and resource issues of mutual interest; and strengthen the BOEM-State partnership in addressing OCS oil and gas and marine minerals information needs.

Applicant Eligibility: To apply for a research award, the recipient is asked to provide the name of the Principal Investigator. If an applicant other than LSU wants to apply, they must do so in collaboration with an LSU research scientist.

Beneficiary Eligibility: Research scientists, Federal, State and local decision-makers, Native American Organizations, and the general public will ultimately benefit from the program.

Award Range/Average: Range is $100,000 to $450,000; Average $250,000.

Funding: (Cooperative Agreements) FY 17 $570,000.00; FY 18 Estimate Not Available; FY 19 Estimate Not Available

HQ: 45600 Woodland Road, Sterling, VA 20166
Phone: 703-787-1087 | Email: rodney.cluck@boem.gov
http://www.boem.gov

HHS93.568 | LOW-INCOME HOME ENERGY ASSISTANCE

Award: Formula Grants

Purpose: To make Low Income Home Energy Assistance Program (LIHEAP) grants available to States District of Columbia, U.S. Territories and Native American Tribes and to assist eligible households to meet the costs of home energy.

Applicant Eligibility: Energy Assistance Block Grants: All States, the District of Columbia, federally-and State-recognized Indian Tribal Governments which request direct funding, and specified Territories may receive direct grants. The prospective grantee must submit an annual application. Grantees desiring Leveraging Incentive Funds and REACH funds must submit special applications each year, if funding is available. Instructions will be issued if emergency contingency funds are released. Training and Technical Assistance: States, Indian Tribes or tribal Organizations, Territories, public agencies, and private nonprofit Organizations may apply. Nothing in the statute precludes a business concern that applies jointly with a private nonprofit Organization from receiving a training and technical assistance grant.

Beneficiary Eligibility: Energy Assistance Block Grants: All States, the District of Columbia, federally-and State-recognized Indian Tribal governments that request direct funding, and specified Territories may provide assistance to households with incomes up to the greater of 150 percent of the poverty level or 60 percent of the State median income. Grantees may establish lower income eligibility levels, but they may not set the limit below 110 percent of the poverty level. Training and Technical Assistance: States, Indian tribes or tribal organizations, Territories, public agencies, and private nonprofit organizations may apply. Nothing in the Statute precludes a business concern that applies separately or jointly with a private nonprofit organization from receiving a training and technical assistance grant.

Award Range/Average: Average is $16,053,630.

Funding: (Training) FY 18 $2,391,345.00; FY 19 est $2,195,416.00; FY 20 est $0.00; (Formula Grants) FY 18 $3,390,598,085.00; FY 19 est $3,650,412,960.00; FY 20 est $0.00

HQ: 330 C Street SW 5th Floor W, PO Box 5425, Washington, DC 20201

Phone: 202-401-4870 | Email: lauren.christopher@acf.hhs.gov

http://www.acf.hhs.gov/programs/ocs/programs/liheap

TREAS21.008 | LOW INCOME TAXPAYER CLINICS
"Low Income Taxpayer Clinic"

Award: Project Grants

Purpose: To provide matching grants to organizations providing representation of low income taxpayers in controversies with the Internal Revenue Service (IRS).

Applicant Eligibility: A qualified Organization may receive a matching grant of up to $100,000 per year for up to a three-year project period. A qualified Organization is one that represents low income taxpayers in controversies with the IRS and informs individuals for whom English is a second language (ESL taxpayers) of their taxpayer rights and responsibilities, and does not charge more than a nominal fee for its services (except for reimbursement of actual costs incurred). Examples of qualified Organizations include (1) a clinical Program at an accredited law, business, or accounting school whose students represent low income taxpayers in tax controversies with the IRS and (2) an Organization exempt from tax under IRC section 501(a) whose employees and volunteers represent low income taxpayers in controversies with the IRS and may also make referrals to qualified volunteers to provide representation.

Beneficiary Eligibility: Low-income taxpayers are those with incomes which do not exceed 250 percent of the Federal Poverty Guidelines published annually by the Department of Health and Human Services, or taxpayers for whom English is a second language.

Award Range/Average: Range of grant: $10,000 to $100,000.

Funding: (Project Grants) FY 18 $12,000,000.00; FY 19 est $12,000,000.00; FY 20 est $12,000,000.00

HQ: 24000 Avila Road, Laguna Niguel, CA 92677

Phone: 949-575-6200 | Email: beard.william@irs.gov

http://www.irs.gov/advocate

HUD14.856 | LOWER INCOME HOUSING ASSISTANCE PROGRAM SECTION 8 MODERATE REHABILITATION
"Section 8 Housing Assistance Payments Program for Very LowIncome Families-Moderate Rehabilitation"

Award: Direct Payments for Specified Use

Purpose: To assist very low income families in obtaining decent rental housing.

Applicant Eligibility: An authorized Public Housing Agency (any State, county, municipality or other governmental entity or public body (or agency or instrumentality thereof).

Beneficiary Eligibility: Very low income families (whose income does not exceed 50 percent of the median income for the area as determined by the Secretary with adjustments for smaller and larger families) and, on an exception basis, lower income families (whose income does not exceed 80 percent of the median income for the area adjusted for small and large families). A very low income or, on an exception basis, lower income single person who is elderly, disabled or handicapped, displaced, or the remaining member of an eligible tenant family is also eligible.

Award Range/Average: $4,426 to $19,549,245: Average of $1,135,021

Funding: (Direct Payments for Specified Use) FY 17 $148,539,213.00; FY 18 est $161,800,000.00; FY 19 est $154,417,000.00

HQ: 451 7th Street SW, Room 4210, Washington, DC 20410

Phone: 202-708-6050 | Email: becky.l.primeaux@hud.gov

http://www.hud.gov/progdesc/pihindx.html

HHS93.838 | LUNG DISEASES RESEARCH

Award: Project Grants

Purpose: The Division of Lung Diseases supports research and research training on the causes, diagnosis, prevention, and treatment of lung diseases and sleep disorders. Research is funded through investigator-initiated and Institute-initiated grant programs and through contract programs in areas including asthma, bronchopulmonary dysplasia, chronic obstructive pulmonary disease, cystic fibrosis, respiratory neurobiology, sleep-disordered breathing, critical care and acute lung injury, developmental biology and pediatric pulmonary diseases, immunologic and fibrotic pulmonary disease, rare lung disorders, pulmonary vascular disease, and pulmonary complications of AIDS and tuberculosis.

Applicant Eligibility: Any nonprofit Organization engaged in biomedical research and Institutions or companies organized for profit may apply for almost any kind of grant. Only domestic, non-profit, private or public Institutions may apply for NRSA Institutional Research Training Grants. An individual may apply for an NRSA or, in some cases, for a research grant if adequate facilities to perform the research are available. SBIR grants can be awarded only to United States small business concerns (entities that are independently owned and operated for profit, or owned by another small business that itself is independently owned and operated for profit and have no more than 500 employees including affiliates). Primary employment (more than one-half time) of the principal investigator must be with the small business at the time of award and during the conduct of the proposed project. In both Phase I and Phase II, the research must be performed in the U.S. or its possessions. To be eligible for funding, a grant application must be approved for scientific merit and Program relevance by a scientific review group and a national advisory council. SBIR projects are generally performed at least 67% by the applicant small business in Phase I and at least 50% of the Project in Phase II. STTR grants can be awarded only to United States small business concerns (entities that are independently owned and operated for profit and have no more than 500 employees) that formally collaborate with a University or other non-profit research institution in cooperative research and development. The principal investigator of an STTR award may be employed with either the small business concern or collaborating non-profit research institution as long as s/he has a formal appointment with or commitment to the applicant small business concern. At least 40% of the project is to be performed by the small business concern and at least 30% by the non-profit research institution. In both Phase I and Phase II, the research must be performed in the U.S. and its possessions.

Beneficiary Eligibility: Any nonprofit or for-profit organization, company or institution engaged in biomedical research. Only domestic for-profit small business firms may apply for SBIR and STTR programs.

Award Range/Average: Grants: $5,000 to $9,234,634; $459,620. SBIR Phase I - $150,000; Phase II - up to $1,000,000; STTR Phase I - $150,000; Phase II $1,000,000.

Funding: (Project Grants) FY 18 $609,357,873.00; FY 19 est $617,857,417.00; FY 20 est $617,857,417.00

HQ: National Heart Lung and Blood Institute (NHLBI) 6701 Rockledge Drive, Room 7176, Bethesda, MD 20892

Phone: 301-827-7968 | Email: pharesda@nhlbi.nih.gov

https://www.nhlbi.nih.gov/about/scientific-divisions/division-lung-diseases

HUD14.879 | MAINSTREAM VOUCHERS

Award: Direct Payments for Specified Use

Purpose: To aid persons with disabilities in getting decent, safe, and hygienic rental housing.

Applicant Eligibility: Public housing agencies (PHA)that is defined as any State, county, municipality or other governmental entity or public body (or agency or instrumentality thereof) which is authorized to engage in or assist in the development or operation of housing for very low income families; and a consortium of PHAs; any other nonprofit entity that was administering a Section 8 tenant-based Program on October 21, 1998; or, for an area outside the jurisdiction of a PHA administering a voucher Program, a private nonprofit entity or a governmental entity or public body that would otherwise lack jurisdiction to administer the Program in such area and non-profit Organization that provide services to the disabled as defined in 42 U.S.C.

Beneficiary Eligibility: Disabled family that is income-eligible under the Housing Choice Voucher program regulations at 24 CFR 982.201(b)(1)as well as other wise eligible under the regulations at 24CFR 982.201, may receive a voucher awarded on the Mainstream Program Applicants with disabilities must be selected from the PHA's or nonprofit organization's housing choice voucher waiting list.

Award Range/Average: $26,758 to $2,499,026; Average $530,237

Funding: (Direct Payments for Specified Use) FY 16 $108,041,000.00; FY 17 est $120,000,000.00; FY 18 est $107,074,000.00

HQ: 451 7th Street SW, Room 4210, Washington, DC 20410

Phone: 202-708-6050 | Email: becky.l.primeaux@hud.gov

http://www.hud.gov/offices/pih/programs/hcv/about/fact_sheet.cfm

Programs Administered by Federal Headquarters

HUD14.171 | MANUFACTURED HOME DISPUTE RESOLUTION

Award: Provision of Specialized Services

Purpose: To provide for a dispute resolution program for the timely resolution of disputes between manufacturers, retailers, and installers of manufactured homes.

Applicant Eligibility: Refer to HUD's website at www.hud.gov for additional information. Select A-Z Index at the top right of the page and scroll the alphabetical list for Manufactured Housing. There is a link on the Manufactured Housing page for Dispute Resolution. Detailed information and procedures are provided by regulation at 24CFR3288.

Beneficiary Eligibility: The program may only address disputes between manufacturers, retailers, and installers of manufactured homes regarding responsibility for the correction or repair of defects in manufactured homes that are reported during the 1-year period beginning on the date of installation. Manufactured home owners may initiate action under, and be observers to, the HUD Manufactured Home Dispute Resolution Program, as provided regulation (24CFR3288.15). There must be an alleged defect in the manufactured home that was reported within one year of installation of the home. Refer to HUD's website at www.hud.gov for additional information. Select A-Z Index at the top right of the page and scroll the alphabetical list for Manufactured Housing. There is a link on the Manufactured Housing page for Dispute Resolution. Detailed information and procedures are provided by regulation at 24CFR3288.

Award Range/Average: This program does not provide direct financial assistance.

HQ: 451 7th Street SW, Washington, DC 20410

Phone: 202-402-7112 | Email: pamela.b.danner@hud.gov

http://portal.hud.gov/hudportal/HUD?src=/program_offices/housing/rmra/mhs/mhdrp

HUD14.110 | MANUFACTURED HOME LOAN INSURANCE FINANCING PURCHASE OF MANUFACTURED HOMES AS PRINCIPAL RESIDENCES OF BORROWERS

Award: Guaranteed/insured Loans

Purpose: To provide reasonable funding of manufactured home purchases.

Applicant Eligibility: All persons are eligible to apply.

Beneficiary Eligibility: Individuals/families.

Award Range/Average: The maximum loan amount is $69,678. The average loan amount is $47,146.

Funding: (Sale, Exchange, or Donation of Property and Goods) FY 15 $32,000,000.00; FY 16 est $30,000,000.00; FY 17 est $30,000,000.00

HQ: 451 7th Street SW, Washington, DC 20410

Phone: 800-225-5342

http://portal.hud.gov/hudportal/hud?src=/program_offices/housing/sfh/title/manuf1414.117

DOC11.611 | MANUFACTURING EXTENSION PARTNERSHIP

Award: Cooperative Agreements; Dissemination of Technical Information

Purpose: To assist in productivity and technological performance in United States manufacturing and to help Manufacturing Extension Centers and services.

Applicant Eligibility: For MEP Center projects under 15 U.S.C. 278k, eligible applicants shall be U.S. based nonprofit Institutions or Organizations or a consortium thereof; Institutions of higher education; or a State, U.S. territory, local or tribal government, or groups thereof. Applicants must contribute at least 50 percent of the proposed service's capital, annual operating and maintenance costs. For competitive awards under 15 U.S.C. 278k-1, eligible applicants are existing MEP Centers. For extension service planning and pilot services agreements under 15 U.S.C. 278l, eligible applicants shall be State Governments or State- affiliated nonprofit Organizations. For multi state regional planning and pilot services agreements, eligible applicants shall be State and local Governments, representing either themselves or a consortium of States, or appropriate private or public nonprofit Organizations, operating on behalf of a consortium of States or as a representative of States.

Beneficiary Eligibility: Beneficiary shall be U.S.-based manufacturing firms, especially smaller companies.

Award Range/Average: Individual awards for extension service planning and pilot testing and special project agreements generally range between $25,000 and $100,000. Awards for Manufacturing Extension Centers generally range between of $500,000 to $15,000,000 annually. Competitive awards generally range between $500,000 and $1,000,000 annually.

Funding: (Cooperative Agreements) FY 18 $122,570,000; FY 19 est $125,275,000; FY 20 est $0;-Dissemination of Technical Information

HQ: 100 Bureau Drive, PO Box 4800, Gaithersburg, MD 20899
   Phone: 301-975-4676 | Email: carroll.thomas@nist.gov
   http://www.mep.nist.gov

DHS97.070 | MAP MODERNIZATION MANAGEMENT SUPPORT "MMMS"

Award: Project Grants
Purpose: Helps prepare and maintain flood hazard maps for the National Flood Insurance Program.
Applicant Eligibility: All States and Commonwealths (including the District of Columbia and territories and possessions of the United States), regional agencies, and communities may apply. All applicants must be communities participating and in good standing in the NFIP or agencies which service participating NFIP communities.
Beneficiary Eligibility: State; local; U.S. Territory & Possession; other public institution/organization; small business; engineer/architect; builder, contractor, developer; land/property owner; general public.
Award Range/Average: Refer to program guidance
HQ: 400 C Street SW, Washington, DC 20523
   Phone: 800-621-3363 | Email: patrick.sacbibit@fema.dhs.gov
   http://www.dhs.gov

DOD12.369 | MARINE CORPS SYSTEMS COMMAND FEDERAL ASSISTANCE PROGRAM

Award: Project Grants
Purpose: To reduce the demand for illegal drugs among America's youth by providing standardized Drug Demand Reduction (DDR) training.
Applicant Eligibility: Other private/public nonprofit Organizations which are operated primarily for educational or similar purposes in the public interest, and commercial concerns.
Beneficiary Eligibility: The beneficiaries for this program are American youth ranging from age eight through the completion of high school, not to exceed twenty years old.
Funding: (Salaries and Expenses) FY 16 Actual Not Available; FY 17 est $4,000,000.00; FY 18 est Estimate Not Available
HQ: 2200 Lester Street, Quantico, VA 22134
   Phone: 703-432-3147 | Email: angela.gorman@usmc.mil

DOC11.999 | MARINE DEBRIS PROGRAM

Award: Cooperative Agreements
Purpose: To provide grants and cooperative agreements to help identify, determine sources of, assess, reduce, and prevent marine debris and its adverse impacts on the marine environment and navigation safety within the coastal United States and territories. Awards made under this program will remove marine debris from coastal habitats; explore non-regulatory incentives to reduce the quantity and impacts of derelict fishing gear.
Applicant Eligibility: Eligible applicants for assistance include 1) state and local Governments including public universities and colleges; 2) U.S. territorial agencies and Organizations; 3) federally and State-recognized Indian Tribal Governments; 4) private universities and colleges; 5) private / commercial for-profit Organizations; and 6) nonprofit research and conservation Organizations.
Beneficiary Eligibility: This program benefits Federal, State, and interstate marine resource conservation and management agencies; U.S. Territories and Freely Associated States; U.S. and foreign commercial and recreational fishing industries; conservation organizations, academic institutions; international and Indian Tribal treaties; private and public research groups; consumers; and the general public.
Award Range/Average: Range: $15,000 - $250,000 Average: $90,000
Funding: (Salaries and Expenses) FY 16 $1,944,901.00; FY 17 est $2,213,514.00; FY 18 est $2,000,000.00
HQ: 1305 E W Highway SSMC 4, Room 13267, Silver Spring, MD 20910
   Phone: 301-713-3050 | Email: kadija.baffoeharding@noaa.gov
   http://www.marinedebris.noaa.gov

Programs Administered by Federal Headquarters

DOC11.433 | MARINE FISHERIES INITIATIVE "MARFIN"

Award: Project Grants
Purpose: To compensate for research and development projects that will deliver knowledge on fishery resources in the Southeast U. S. and in other surrounding countries.
Applicant Eligibility: States or local Governments, universities, private enterprise, individuals or any other entity, nonprofit or otherwise, if such entity is a citizen of the United States within the meaning of Section 2 of the Shipping Act, 1916, as amended, 46 U.S.C. 802.
Beneficiary Eligibility: Federal, State and local governments, universities, private enterprise, nonprofit or profit organizations, and the general public.
Funding: (Cooperative Agreements) FY 16 $11,340,211.00; FY 17 est $11,340,211.00; FY 18 est Estimate Not Available
HQ: 1305 E W Highway, Silver Spring, MD 20910
  Phone: 301-427-8771 | Email: jeffrey.kulnis@noaa.gov
  http://www.nmfs.noaa.gov

DOI15.428 | MARINE GAS HYDRATE RESEARCH ACTIVITIES

Award: Cooperative Agreements
Purpose: To characterize and oversee gas hydrate deposits and environmental conditions on OCS Block Mississippi Canyon 118 (MC-118) in the Gulf of Mexico.
Applicant Eligibility: Proposals are received from the CMRET (and qualified subcontractors through CMRET) for research and scientific sensory equipment for the monitoring station. Applicants must have expertise in marine gas hydrates.
Beneficiary Eligibility: Organizations participating in the project, as well as the general public.
Award Range/Average: $0 to $100,000
Funding: (Cooperative Agreements) FY 17 $95,000.00; FY 18 est $0.00; FY 19 est Estimate Not Available
HQ: 381 Elden Street, PO Box 4070, Herndon, VA 20170-4817
  Phone: 703-787-1514 | Email: matthew.frye@boem.gov
  http://www.boem.gov

DOC11.439 | MARINE MAMMAL DATA PROGRAM

Award: Project Grants
Purpose: To help State agencies for the information on marine mammals and to compensate for the conservation of marine mammals by improving the health and population of marine mammals.
Applicant Eligibility: State Governments and quasi-public nonprofit Institutions or Organizations. U.S. Marine Mammal Stranding Network participants, including state and local Governments, academia, aquaria, non profits, private individuals and Organizations. Eligibility may vary under Programs announced in the Federal Register.
Beneficiary Eligibility: This program benefits the States that have marine mammals in waters under State jurisdiction and supports Federal requirements for conservation of marine mammals, and other public resources. The program also benefits the active volunteer U.S. marine mammal stranding network members throughout coastal states.
Funding: (Project Grants) FY 16 $8,167,272.00; FY 17 est $8,167,272.00; FY 18 est Estimate Not Available
HQ: 1315 E W Highway, Silver Spring, MD 20910
  Phone: 301-713-2322
  http://www.nmfs.noaa.gov

DOI15.424 | MARINE MINERALS ACTIVITIES

Award: Cooperative Agreements
Purpose: To assess OCS sand deposits for coastal restoration and beach nourishment needs, and to cultivate good working relationships regarding OCS mineral issues with coastal States due to effects from hurricanes and coastal erosion.
Applicant Eligibility: Proposals are received from coastal States in need of coastal restoration.
Beneficiary Eligibility: State agencies and organizations participating in the project, as well as the general public.
Award Range/Average: Range is $500,000 to $600,000.
Funding: (Cooperative Agreements) FY 17 $500,000.00; FY 18 Estimate Not Available; FY 19 Estimate Not Available.
HQ: 381 Elden Street, PO Box E3313, Herndon, VA 20170
  Phone: 703-787-1851 | Email: keith.good@bsee.gov

http://www.boem.gov/MarineMineralsProgram

DOC11.429 | MARINE SANCTUARY PROGRAM
"Office of National Marine Sanctuaries"

Award: Project Grants
Purpose: To compensate for educational institutions and universities for providing education to the citizens of the United States.
Applicant Eligibility: Agreements to solicit private donations may only be made with nonprofit Organizations.
Beneficiary Eligibility: Financial assistance is made for a public purpose. The ultimate beneficiary is the public. The scholarship program benefits individuals who do not have the financial means of pursuing graduate level studies and, in turn, ensures that women and minorities are representative in the areas supported by the scholarship program.
Funding: (Cooperative Agreements) FY 16 $9,501,000.00; FY 17 est $7,608,471.00; FY 18 est $5,999,521.00
HQ: 1305 E W Highway SSMC4 Station 11653, Silver Spring, MD 20910
  Phone: 301-713-7241 | Email: joe.t.faulkner@noaa.gov
  http://sanctuaries.noaa.gov

USDA10.601 | MARKET ACCESS PROGRAM
"MAP"

Award: Formula Grants; Direct Payments for Specified Use
Purpose: To maximize the expansion of commercial exporting markets for U.S. agricultural commodities to organizations that develop foreign marketing.
Applicant Eligibility: To be approved, applicants must be: (1) A nonprofit U.S. agricultural trade Organization; (2) a nonprofit State regional trade group; (3) a U.S. agricultural cooperative; or (4) a State agency.
Beneficiary Eligibility: CCC will enter into MAP agreements only where the eligible agricultural commodity is comprised of at least 50 percent U.S. origin content by weight, exclusive of added water.
Funding: (Formula Grants (Cooperative Agreements)) FY 18 $200,000,000.00; FY 19 est $200,000,000.00; FY 20 est $200,000,000.00
HQ: 1400 Independence Avenue SW, Washington, DC 20250
  Phone: 202-720-4327 | Email: curt.alt@fas.usda.gov
  http://www.fas.usda.gov/programs/market-access-program-map

USDA10.123 | MARKET FACILITATION PROGRAM
"MFP"

Award: Direct Payments With Unrestricted Use
Purpose: Provides help to manufacturers of commodities considerably affected by foreign government actions resulting in the loss of traditional exports.
Applicant Eligibility: A producer must be in compliance with highly erodible land conservation and wetland conservation provisions, commonly referred to as the conservation compliance provisions. Other eligibility requirements also apply a producer's average adjusted gross income may not exceed $900,000.
Beneficiary Eligibility: N/A
Funding: (Direct Payments with Unrestricted Use) FY 17 $0; FY 18 est $500,000.00; FY 19 est Estimate Not Available
HQ: 1400 Independence Avenue SW, PO Box 0512, Washington, DC 20250-0512
  Phone: 202-720-0448 | Email: kelly.hereth@wdc.usda.gov

HHS93.983 | MARKET TRANSPARENCY PROJECT FOR HEALTH IT INTEROPERABILITY SERVICES COOPERATIVE AGREEMENT PROGRAM
"Market Transparency Project"

Award: Cooperative Agreements; Cooperative Agreements (Discretionary Grants)
Purpose: The program helps to create an awareness of the costs associated with health and IT interoperability services.
Applicant Eligibility: Must have proven knowledge of and familiarity working with either Health IT interoperability services, developing online tools for crowd sourced reporting, or a combination of the two.

Programs Administered by Federal Headquarters

Beneficiary Eligibility: Beneficiaries include healthcare CIOs, CFOs, contracting personnel, sales teams, EHR vendors, application developers, among many others that seek to determine fair market value and costs of various health IT interoperability services.

Funding: (Cooperative Agreements) FY 16 $0.00; FY 17 est $250,000.00; FY 18 est $0.00

HQ: 330 C Street SW, Washington, DC 20201

    Phone: 202-720-2919 | Email: carmel.halloun@hhs.gov

    http://www.healthit.gov

CNCS94.014 | MARTIN LUTHER KING JR DAY OF SERVICE GRANTS
"MLK Grants"

Award: Project Grants

Purpose: Martin Luther King Jr. Day of Service grant is a funding program that focuses on mobilizing more Americans to observe the Federal holiday as a day of service to their community and to create awareness on service to fellow humans.

Applicant Eligibility: See Program's Notice of Funding Opportunity.

Beneficiary Eligibility: Same as Applicant Eligibility.

Award Range/Average: See program's Notice of Funding Opportunity for matching information.

Funding: (Project Grants) FY 16 Actual Not Available; FY 17 est $506,649.00; FY 18 Estimate Not Available

HQ: 250 E Street SW, Washington, DC 20525

    Phone: 202-606-6745 | Email: pstengel@cns.gov

    http://www.nationalservice.gov/mlkday

HHS93.110 | MATERNAL AND CHILD HEALTH FEDERAL CONSOLIDATED PROGRAMS
"Special Projects of Regional and National Significance (SPRANS), including the Community Integrated Service Systems (CISS); and the Heritable Disorders Program"

Award: Project Grants

Purpose: To carry out special maternal and child health (MCH) projects of regional and national significance.

Applicant Eligibility: Training grants may be made to public or private nonprofit Institutions of higher learning. Research grants may be made to public or private nonprofit Institutions of higher learning and public or private nonprofit private agencies and Organizations engaged in research or in MCH or Children with Special healthcare Needs (CSHCN) Programs. Any public or private entity is eligible for hemophilia, genetics, and environmental health grants and other special project grants, including CISS. Eligible entities for the Heritable Disorders Program include a State or a political subdivision of a State; a consortium of two or more States of political subdivisions of States; a territory; a health facility or Program operated by or pursuant to a contract with or grant from the Indian Health Service; or any other entity with appropriate expertise in newborn screening, as determined by the Secretary. Eligible entities for the Pediatric Mental healthcare Access Program include States, political subdivisions of states, and Indian Tribes and tribal Organizations. Eligible entities for the Screening and Treatment for Maternal Depression and Related Behavior Disorders Program are states.

Beneficiary Eligibility: For training grants: (1) Trainees in the health professions related to MCH; and (2) mothers and children who receive services through training programs. For research grants: public or private nonprofit agencies and organizations engaged in research in MCH or CSHCN programs. For hemophilia, sickle cell, thalassemia, genetics, new-born screening, environmental health, and other special projects: (1) Public or private agencies, organizations and institutions; and (2) mothers and children, and individuals with genetic conditions (any age) who receive services through the programs. For Pediatric Mental Health Care Access Program: pediatric mental health care teams; pediatric primary care providers; children, youth and families who receive services from pediatric primary care providers.

Award Range/Average: $3,419 to $3,996,711; $387,145

Funding: (Project Grants) FY 18 $77,324,714.00; FY 19 est $94,877,783.00; FY 20 est $94,613,909.00; (Cooperative Agreements) FY 18 $72,482,155.00; FY 19 est $81,641,401.00; FY 20 est $94,613,909.00

HQ: 5600 Fishers Lane, Room 18W37, Rockville, MD 20857

    Phone: 301-443-2170 | Email: lkavanagh@hrsa.gov

    http://www.hrsa.gov

HHS93.687 | MATERNAL OPIOID MISUSE MODEL
"MOM Model"

Award: Formula Grants (cooperative Agreements)
Purpose: To combat the nation's opioid crisis, the MOM model aims at addressing fragmentation that cares for pregnant and postpartum Medicaid beneficiaries with opioid use disorder utilizing a state-driven transformation of the delivery system. It aims at improving the quality of care and reduces costs for mother and infants taking the support of clinical care coordination and integration of other services crucial for patient's health, wellbeing, and recovery.
Applicant Eligibility: State Medicaid agencies are eligible to apply for MOM model funding.
Beneficiary Eligibility: State Medicaid Agencies may apply for MOM model assistance.
Award Range/Average: The MOM model will award up to $64.56 million in cooperative agreement funds across up to 12 awardees during the five-year performance period.
Funding: Formula Grants (Cooperative Agreements) FY 18 Actual Not Available; FY 19 est Estimate Not Available; FY 20 est $9,000,000.00
HQ: 7500 Security Boulevard, PO Box WB-06-05, Baltimore, MD 21244
   Phone: 410-786-4338
   https://innovation.cms.gov/initiatives/maternal-opioid-misuse-model

HHS93.870 | MATERNAL, INFANT AND EARLY CHILDHOOD HOME VISITING GRANT
"MIECHV Program"

Award: Formula Grants
Purpose: The goals of the Maternal, Infant, and Early Childhood Home Visiting Program (MIECHV Program) are to improve coordination of services for at-risk communities; and identify and provide comprehensive services to improve outcomes for eligible families who reside in at-risk communities.
Applicant Eligibility: Eligible entities include those currently funded under the MIECHV Program: 47 states, 3 nonprofit Organizations serving Florida, North Dakota, and Wyoming, and 6 territories and jurisdictions serving District of Columbia, Puerto Rico, Guam, the U.S. Virgin Islands, the Commonwealth of the Northern Mariana Islands, and American Samoa. For those states that have elected not to participate in MIECHV, nonprofit Organizations with an established record of providing early childhood home visiting Programs or initiatives in a state or several states are eligible to apply to carry out Programs in those states.
Beneficiary Eligibility: As directed in statute, awardees must give priority in providing services under the MIECHV program to the following: Eligible families who reside in communities in need of such services, as identified in the statewide needs assessment required under subsection 511(b)(1)(A); Low-income eligible families; Eligible families with pregnant women who have not attained age 21; Eligible families that have a history of child abuse or neglect or have had interactions with child welfare services; Eligible families that have a history of substance abuse or need substance abuse treatment; Eligible families that have users of tobacco products in the home; Eligible families that are or have children with low student achievement; Eligible families with children with developmental delays or disabilities; and; Eligible families that include individuals who are serving or formerly served in the Armed Forces, including such families that have members of the Armed Forces who have had multiple deployments outside of the United States.
Award Range/Average: FY18 average is $6,457,041 and range is $1,200,000- $21,384,282 FY 19 average is $6,267,857 and range is $1,000,000- $20,816,822 FY 20 average is $6,267,857 and range is $1,000,000- $20,816,822
Funding: (Formula Grants) FY 18 $361,594,315.00; FY 19 est $351,000,000.00; FY 20 est $351,000,000.00; (Project Grants) FY 18 $1,200,000.00; FY 19 est $2,575,000.00; FY 20 est $2,500,000.00
HQ: 5600 Fishers Lane, Room 18N-188A, Rockville, MD 20857
   Phone: 301-443-2231 | Email: xle@hrsa.gov
   http://mchb.hrsa.gov/programs/homevisiting

HHS93.615 | MATERNAL, INFANT, AND EARLY CHILDHOOD HOME VISITING RESEARCH PROGRAMS
"Home Visiting Research Programs; MIECHV TA"

Award: Cooperative Agreements; Project Grants
Purpose: The Maternal, Infant, and Early Childhood Home Visiting Research Programs are designed to increase knowledge about the implementation and effectiveness of voluntary home visiting programs, using random assignment designs to the maximum extent feasible.

Programs Administered by Federal Headquarters

Applicant Eligibility: As cited in 42 CFR Part 51a. 3(b), only public or nonprofit Institutions of higher learning and public or private nonprofit agencies engaged in research or in Programs relating to maternal and child health and/or services for children with special healthcare needs may apply for grants, contracts or cooperative agreements for research in maternal and child health services or in services for children with special healthcare needs. Entities directly involved in the operation of home visiting Programs are not eligible to apply.

Beneficiary Eligibility: Funded research should benefit MIECHV awardees by increasing knowledge about the implementation and effectiveness of home visiting programs.

Award Range/Average: Average award $1,300,000.00 Range is $1,300,000.00

Funding: (Cooperative Agreements) FY 18 $1,300,000.00; FY 19 est $1,300,000.00; FY 20 est $1,300,000.00

HQ: 5600 Fishers Lane, Room 18N160, Rockville, MD 20857
  Phone: 301-443-7758 | Email: kpeplinski@hrsa.gov
  http://mchb.hrsa.gov/programs/homevisiting

NSF47.049 | MATHEMATICAL AND PHYSICAL SCIENCES "MPS"

Award: Project Grants

Purpose: To promote the progress of the mathematical and physical sciences and thereby strengthen the Nation's scientific enterprise; to increase the store of scientific knowledge and enhance understanding of major problems confronting the Nation.

Applicant Eligibility: Except where a Program solicitation establishes more restrictive eligibility criteria, individuals and Organizations in the following categories may submit proposals: universities and colleges; Non-profit, non-academic Organizations; for-profit Organizations; State and local Governments; and unaffiliated individuals. See the NSF Grant Proposal Guide, Chapter i.e. for a full description of eligibility requirements: http//www.nsf.gov/publications/pubsumm. jsp?odskey=gpg.

Beneficiary Eligibility: N/A

Award Range/Average: Range Low $2,460 Range High $44,194,356 Average $167,877

Funding: (Project Grants) FY 18 $1,503,412,000.00; FY 19 est $1,475,340,000.00; FY 20 est $1,255,820,000.00

HQ: 2415 Eisenhower Avenue, Alexandria, VA 22314
  Phone: 703-292-8800 | Email: ccooper@nsf.gov
  http://nsf.gov/dir/index.jsp?org=mps

DOD12.901 | MATHEMATICAL SCIENCES GRANTS

Award: Project Grants

Purpose: Program seeks to stimulate new and important developments in the field areas of algebra, discrete mathematics, number theory, probability and statistics.

Applicant Eligibility: All those receiving support from our grants must be U.S. citizens or permanent residents of the United States. Investigators must be an employee of a U.S. college or University. The principal investigator and all graduate students must be a U.S. citizen or a permanent resident of the U.S.

Beneficiary Eligibility: This will benefit researchers in the mathematical sciences who are U.S. citizens or permanent residents as well as their students who are U. S. citizens or permanent residents of the U.S.

Award Range/Average: Research Grants:Range: $5,000 - $40,000 Average Award: $26,000 Conferences:Range: $5,000 - $50,000 Average Award: $15,000 Research Experiences for Undergraduates:Range: $33,000 - $125,000 Average Award: $125,000

Funding: (Salaries and Expenses) FY 17 $2,263,987.00; FY 18 est $533,957.00; FY 19 est Estimate Not Available

HQ: 9800 Savage Road, Fort George G. Meade, MD 20755
  Phone: 443-479-7660 | Email: diboyer@nsa.gov
  https://www.nsa.gov

MCC85.002 | MCC FOREIGN ASSISTANCE FOR OVERSEAS PROGRAMS

Award: Project Grants; Direct Payments for Specified Use

Purpose: To provide United States assistance for global development through the Millennium Challenge Corporation.

Applicant Eligibility: Compacts are large, 5-year grants for countries that pass MCC's eligibility criteria. Threshold Programs are smaller grants awarded to countries that come close to passing these criteria and are firmly committed to improving their policy performance.

Beneficiary Eligibility: Beneficiaries are foreign governments, foreign public or private institutions or organizations, or foreign individuals who are eligible for MCC Compact or Threshold programs.

Funding: (Project Grants) FY 09 $7,400,000.00; FY 10 est Estimate Not Available; FY 11 est Estimate Not Available

HQ: 15th Street NW, Washington, DC 20005

    Phone: 202-521-3600 | Email: bladesjr@mcc.gov

    http://www.mcc.gov

DOC11.609 | MEASUREMENT AND ENGINEERING RESEARCH AND STANDARDS

Award: Cooperative Agreements; Project Grants

Purpose: To support scientific and engineering research for technology transfer.

Applicant Eligibility: Institutions of higher education (e.g. universities and colleges), professional institutes and associations, nonprofit Organizations, State and local Governments, laboratories, and commercial Organizations.

Beneficiary Eligibility: Universities, colleges, professional institutes and associations, nonprofit organizations, State and local governments, and commercial organizations.

Funding: (Project Grants) FY 18 est $62,521,390.00; FY 19 est $77,894,753.00; FY 20 est $33,689,000.00

HQ: 100 Bureau Drive, PO Box 1650, Gaithersburg, MD 20899

    Phone: 301-975-3086 | Email: leon.sampson@nist.gov

HHS93.857 | MEASURING INTEROPERABILITY PROGRESS THROUGH INDIVIDUALS' ACCESS AND USE OF THE ELECTRONIC HEALTH DATA

Award: Cooperative Agreements

Purpose: To establish a mechanism of collaboration with the National Partnership for Women & Families to support the development of consumer survey questions for the Health Information National Trends Survey and associated reports.

Applicant Eligibility: This is a non competitive agreement being awarded to the National Partnership for Women and Families (NPWF).

Beneficiary Eligibility: The beneficiaries will include all health care organizations and patients using electronic health records.

HQ: 330 C Street SW, Washington, DC 20201

    Phone: 202-720-2919 | Email: carmel.halloun@hhs.gov

HHS93.778 | MEDICAL ASSISTANCE PROGRAM
"Medicaid; Title XIX"

Award: Formula Grants

Purpose: Provides financial assistance to States for payments of medical assistance on behalf of cash assistance recipients, children, pregnant women and the aged who meet income and resource requirements, and other categorically-eligible groups.

Applicant Eligibility: State and local welfare agencies must operate under an HHS-approved Medicaid State Plan and comply with all Federal regulations governing aid and medical assistance to the needy.

Beneficiary Eligibility: Low-income persons who are over age 65, blind or disabled, members of families with dependent children, low- income children and pregnant women, certain Medicare beneficiaries and, in many States, medically-needy individuals may apply to a State or local welfare agency for medical assistance. At the State's option, eligibility to non-elderly individuals with family incomes up to 133 percent of the federal poverty level will start in calendar year 2014. Eligibility is determined by the State in accordance with Federal regulations.

Award Range/Average: $18,426,000 TO $59,200,006,000. Average assistance is $7,638,304,000

Funding: (Formula Grants (Apportionments)) FY 18 $441,392,376,000.00; FY 19 est $443,909,757,000.00; FY 20 est $461,306,208,000.00

HQ: 7500 Security Boulevard, Baltimore, MD 21244

    Phone: 410-786-3870 | Email: sean.danus@cms.hhs.gov

    http://www.cms.hhs.gov/contracts

HHS93.879 | MEDICAL LIBRARY ASSISTANCE

Award: Project Grants

Purpose: To meet a growing need for investigators trained in biomedical informatics research and data science by training qualified pre- and post-doctoral candidates; to conduct research in biomedical informatics, bioinformatics and related computer, information and data sciences; to facilitate management of electronic health records and clinical research data; and to advance biocomputing and bioinformatics.

Applicant Eligibility: Any individual(s) with the skills, knowledge, and resources necessary to carry out the proposed research as the project director/principal investigator (PD/PI) is invited to work with his/her Organization to develop an application for support. Individuals from underrepresented racial and ethnic groups as well as individuals with disabilities are always encouraged to apply for NIH support.

Beneficiary Eligibility: Research Grants are available to public or private, domestic or foreign, for profit or not-for-profit institutions or organizations with research capabilities in biomedical informatics, bioinformatics, computer sciences, information sciences, data sciences and related disciplines. Training Grants may be made to nonfederal public and nonprofit private institutions. With the exception of NIH Pathway to Independence awards, trainees must be citizens or non-citizen nationals of the United States or have been lawfully admitted to the United States for permanent residence. Resource grants (Information Resource, Scholarly Works) are open to any U.S. public or private nonprofit institution or organization. SBIR and STTR grants can be awarded only to domestic small businesses (entities that are independently owned and operated for profit, are not dominant in the field in which research is proposed, and have no more than 500 employees). To be eligible for funding, a grant application must be approved for scientific merit and program relevance by a scientific review group and a national advisory council.

Award Range/Average: $20,000 to $750,000 (range); $401,522 - average cost for Research Grant (R01); $99,247 - average cost for Information Resource Grant (G08); $49,021 - average total cost for Scholarly Works Grant (G13)

Funding: (Project Grants) FY 18 $61,842,104.00; FY 19 est $65,050,175.00; FY 20 est $55,258,731.00

HQ: 6705 Rockledge Drive, Suite 301, Bethesda, MD 20892

   Phone: 301-496-4621 | Email: alicia.ross@nih.gov
   http://www.nlm.nih.gov/ep/index.html

HHS93.008 | MEDICAL RESERVE CORPS SMALL GRANT PROGRAM "MRC"

Award: Cooperative Agreements

Purpose: To support the development of Medical Reserve Corps (MRC) units in communities throughout the United States.

Applicant Eligibility: Eligible applicants for this funding opportunity are national-level nonprofit Organizations with significant local, state and national networking connections.

Beneficiary Eligibility: General public.

Award Range/Average: Only one Cooperative Agreement awarded at the amount of $3,000,000

Funding: (Cooperative Agreements) FY 18 $620,000.00; FY 19 est $2,000,200.00; FY 20 est $2,000,200.00

HQ: 200 C Street SW, O'Neill Building, Washington, DC 20024

   Phone: 202-260-0400 | Email: virginia.simmons@hhs.gov
   https://www.medicalreservecorps.gov/HomePage

HRSA93.680 | MEDICAL STUDENT EDUCATION "MSE"

Award: Project Grants

Purpose: Provides grants to public institutions to support the education of medical students from underserved states.

Applicant Eligibility: The MSE Program is limited to public Institutions of higher education located in the top quintile of states with a projected primary care provider shortage in 2025, as determined by the Secretary. Public non-profit colleges of medicine in the states in the top quintile of states with projected shortage of primary care physicians in 2025.

Beneficiary Eligibility: Beneficiaries include physician training programs that train medical students. Public non-profit colleges of medicine in the states in the top quintile of states with projected shortage of primary care physicians in 2025.

Award Range/Average: FY 18 N/A FY 19 Range $1,000,000 - $1,180,000; Average $1,000,000. FY 20 Range $0; Average $0.

Funding: (Project Grants) FY 18 Actual Not Available; FY 19 est $$23,750,000.00; FY 20 est $0

HQ: 5600 Fishers Lane, Room 15N-186B, Rockville, MD 20857

   Phone: 301-443-8437 | Email: aanyanwu@hrsa.gov
   https://bhw.hrsa.gov/grants/medicine

HHS93.986 | MEDICARE ACCESS AND CHIP REAUTHORIZATION ACT (MACRA) FUNDING OPPORTUNITY: MEASURE DEVELOPMENT FOR THE QUALITY PAYMENT PROGRAM

Award: Formula Grants

Purpose: The Medicare Access and CHIP Reauthorization Act (MACRA) Funding Opportunity: Measure Development for the Quality Payment Program develops, improves or updates the quality measures to help structure a pay based on a merit-based incentive system.

Applicant Eligibility: Clinical specialty societies, clinical professional Organizations, patient advocacy Organizations, educational Institutions, independent research Organizations, health systems, and other entities engaged in quality measure development. For this funding opportunity, the above categories are referenced collectively as entity or entities. The language, engaged in quality measure development, pertains to each of the above referenced entities. Entities must: 1) demonstrate, or partner with an Organization with demonstrated, quality measure development expertise 2) be engaged in quality measure conceptualization, development, or evaluation3) be involved in developing evidence-based clinical practice guidelines Otherwise eligible entities must not be actively receiving federal funding for quality measure development, implementation, maintenance, or public reporting activities for quality measures. However, such an entity may be a sub-recipient on one or multiple applications.

Beneficiary Eligibility: Quality Payment Program provides new opportunities to improve care delivery by supporting and rewarding clinicians as they find new ways to engage patients, families, and caregivers and to improve care coordination and population health management. The quality measures in MIPS and APMs serve as the mechanism of measuring the improved care delivery. With this funding opportunity, CMS is engaging eligible entities to develop the quality measures as a way of enhancing the measure portfolio with additional measures for specialties. An enhanced measure portfolio helps to ensure that a higher percentage of providers can use quality measurement to improve their practice. This results in consumers making more informed decisions regarding their healthcare and overall health care quality improvements. The ultimate beneficiaries from this work are providers, consumers, healthcare stakeholders, and anyone interested in quality as the quality measures developed better reflect the complexity and diversity of our healthcare system and improve the quality of healthcare for everyone.

Award Range/Average: The Medicare Access and CHIP Reauthorization Act (MACRA) Funding Opportunity: Measure Development for the Quality Payment Program Cooperative Agreements expect to award 5-10 agreements with a range of $0-$2,000,000 a year for up to 3 years. The expected total funding is $10,000,000 a years for 3 years totaling $30,000,000. This is a new program with no financial assistance awards (dollars) that were made in the past and current fiscal years.

Funding: (Salaries and Expenses) FY 18 $9,228,475.00; FY 19 est $8,529,320.00; FY 20 est $8,832,783.00

HQ: 7500 Security Boulevard, Woodlawn, MD 21244

Phone: 410-786-4399 | Email: wilfred.agbenyikey@cms.hhs.gov

http://www.cms.gov

HHS93.071 | MEDICARE ENROLLMENT ASSISTANCE PROGRAM "MIPPA"

Award: Formula Grants; Project Grants

Purpose: To provide outreach to eligible Medicare beneficiaries regarding the benefits available under title XVIII of the Social Security Act.

Applicant Eligibility: Formula grants: State Governments and U.S. Territories, with distribution to designated area agencies on aging and Indian Tribal Organizations through an approved State plan. Project grants: Grants may be made to any public or nonprofit private agency, Organization, or institution.

Beneficiary Eligibility: Individuals eligible for Medicare benefits, including Part D drug benefits, and older persons eligible for benefits and services provided under Federal and state programs.

Award Range/Average: Formula Grants - Based on Statutory formulaDiscretionary Grant - one award not more than 12M

Funding: (Project Grants) FY 17 $34,912,500.00; FY 18 est $37,500,000.00; FY 19 est $37,500,000.00

HQ: 330 C Street SW, Washington, DC 20201

Phone: 202-795-7350 | Email: katherine.glendening@acl.hhs.gov

http://www.acl.gov

Programs Administered by Federal Headquarters

HHS93.773 | MEDICARE HOSPITAL INSURANCE
"Medicare Part A"

Award: Direct Payments for Specified Use

Purpose: Provides hospital insurance protection for covered services to persons age 65 or above, to certain disabled persons and to individuals with chronic renal disease.

Applicant Eligibility: Persons age 65 or over and certain disabled persons are eligible to receive hospital insurance benefits. Nearly all individuals who had reached the age of 65 before 1968 are eligible for Part A, including people not eligible for cash Social Security benefits. A person reaching the age of 65 from 1968 to the present, and who is not eligible for social security benefits, needs to have accumulated work credits (amount dependent on age) to qualify for hospital insurance benefits. Hospital insurance (Medicare Part A) is also available to persons aged 65 and over through payment of a monthly premium, which is currently $413 per month, effective January 1, 2017. A reduced Part A premium of $227 per month is applied to persons with 30 to 39 quarters in which they have paid into the social security system. This reduced Part A premium applies to their spouse, surviving spouse or divorced spouse as well. Federal employees began contributing toward Medicare hospital insurance coverage in 1983. Employees who have worked in the federal government prior to this year are still eligible to receive credit for prior non-contributory quarters of Federal employment. State and local government employees not already in Social Security-covered positions and who were hired on or after April 1, 1986 also contribute toward Medicare hospital insurance coverage. Although states may request agreements to cover individuals employed prior to April 1, 1986, no credit is given toward establishing Medicare entitlement for prior employment. Persons under the age of 65 who have been entitled to Social Security or Railroad Retirement disability benefits for at least 29 months are also eligible to receive hospital insurance benefits, as are any individuals who have been diagnosed with End Stage Renal Disease (ESRD).

Beneficiary Eligibility: Persons age 65 or over and qualified disabled persons.

Award Range/Average: Benefits may be paid based on the prospective payment amount or the reasonable costs of covered inpatient hospital services and based on the reasonable costs of covered post-hospital extended care services, which are incurred during a benefit period. For benefit periods beginning in calendar year 2019 the beneficiary is responsible for $1,364 inpatient hospital deductible, a $341 per day coinsurance amount for 61 through 90 days of inpatient hospital care, a $682 per day coinsurance amount for inpatient hospital care during the 60 lifetime reserve days, and a $170.50 per day coinsurance amount for days 21 through 100 of care in a skilled nursing facility. Home health services are paid in full.

Funding: (Insurance) FY 18 $298,824,000,000.00; FY 19 est $325,232,000,000.00; FY 20 est $346,847,000,000.00

HQ: 7500 Security Boulevard, Baltimore, MD 21244

   Phone: 410-786-5407 | Email: robert.ludwig@cms.hhs.gov

   http://www.cms.hhs.gov

HHS93.770 | MEDICARE PRESCRIPTION DRUG COVERAGE
"Medicare Part D"

Award: Direct Payments for Specified Use

Purpose: Provides prescription drugs to Medicare beneficiaries through their voluntary participation in prescription drug plans, with an additional subsidy provided to lower-income beneficiaries.

Applicant Eligibility: An entity organized and licensed under State law as a risk-bearing entity eligible to offer health insurance in each State in which it is to offer a plan, meeting the requirements in 42 CFR 423. 504 and 42 CFR 423. 505. The entity may offer prescription drug coverage in conjunction with a Medicare Advantage plan or as a separate standalone benefit.

Beneficiary Eligibility: Eligible beneficiaries include individuals who are entitled to Medicare benefits under Part A or enrolled in Part B and who reside in the plan's service area. Individuals in a Medicare Advantage Plan with Part D coverage may not be separately enrolled in a stand alone prescription drug plan.

Award Range/Average: Determined by plan offerings, number of enrollees, and utilization.

Funding: (Insurance) FY 18 $81,103,000,000.00; FY 19 est $84,656,000,000.00; FY 20 est $105,544,000,000.00

HQ: 7500 Security Boulevard, Baltimore, MD 21244

   Phone: 410-786-7625 | Email: lori.levine@cms.hhs.gov

   http://www.cms.hhs.gov

HHS93.774 | MEDICARE SUPPLEMENTARY MEDICAL INSURANCE
"Medicare Part B"

Award: Direct Payments for Specified Use

Purpose: Provides medical insurance protection for covered services to persons age 65 or over, to certain disabled persons and to individuals with end-stage renal disease.

Applicant Eligibility: All persons who are eligible for premium-free hospital insurance benefits (see 93. 773), and persons age 65 and older who reside in the United States and are either citizens or aliens lawfully admitted for permanent residence who have resided in the United States continuously during the five years immediately preceding the month in which the application for enrollment is filed, may voluntarily enroll for Part B supplementary medical insurance (SMI). The beneficiary pays a monthly premium and an annual deductible. Beginning in calendar year 2008, the Part B premiums have been set based upon beneficiary income. The calendar year 2018 premiums range from $134. 00 to $428. 60 per month. The annual deductible is $183. 00. Some States and other third parties may pay the SMI PART B premium on behalf of qualifying individuals.

Beneficiary Eligibility: All persons who qualify for hospital insurance, and those who do not qualify for hospital insurance but meet eligibility requirements and choose to purchase Part "B".

Award Range/Average: Generally, with exceptions of certain services, the beneficiary is responsible for meeting the annual $183 deductible before you may begin. Thereafter, Medicare pays a percent of the approved amount of the covered service. This percentage is 80 percent for most services.

Funding: (Insurance) FY 18 $323,097,000,000; FY 19 est $360,873,000,000; FY 20 est $391,252,000,000

HQ: 7500 Security Boulevard, Baltimore, MD 21244

    Phone: 410-786-7625 | Email: lori.levine@cms.hhs.gov

    http://www.cms.hhs.gov

HHS93.732 | MENTAL AND BEHAVIORAL HEALTH EDUCATION AND TRAINING GRANTS
"Behavioral Health Workforce Education and Training (BHWET)"

Award: Project Grants

Purpose: The BHWET Program develops and expands the behavioral health workforce serving populations across the lifespan, especially in rural and medically underserved areas.

Applicant Eligibility: Professional Track Accredited Institutions of higher education or accredited behavioral health professional training Programs in behavioral pediatrics, social work, school social work, substance use disorder prevention and treatment, marriage and family therapy, occupational therapy, school counseling, or professional counseling. Programs must require a pre-degree clinical field placement in behavioral health as part of the training and a prerequisite for graduation. Accredited schools of masters or doctoral-level training in psychiatry, psychiatric- nursing Programs. APA-accredited doctoral level schools and Programs in health service psychology or school psychology Programs with a practicum of ten or more hours per week for two semesters, and APA-accredited doctoral internship Programs in professional psychology. Paraprofessional Certificate Track Behavioral paraprofessional certificate training Programs and peer paraprofessional certificate training Programs offered by states, political subdivisions of states, Indian Tribes and tribal Organizations, public or nonprofit private health professions schools, academic health centers, state or local Governments, or other appropriate public or private nonprofit entities as determined appropriate by the Secretary. Entities must offer a certificate to the trainees upon completion of a Program in a paraprofessional behavioral health related field (i.e., peer support counselor, community health worker, outreach worker, social services aide, mental health worker, substance abuse/addictions worker, youth worker, promotor), and must include an experiential field placement component. The certificate should prepare students to apply for state licensure or certification. Students may be new to the field or may be paraprofessionals who are already practicing and want additional credentials to advance their employability. Eligible applicant Institutions /Organizations must be located in the United States, the District of Columbia, the Commonwealth of Puerto Rico, the Commonwealth of the Northern Mariana Islands, the U.S. Virgin Islands, Guam, American Samoa, the Republic of Palau, the Republic of Marshall Islands or the Federated States of Micronesia. Faith-based and community-based Organizations, Federally Recognized Indian Tribal Government and Native American Organizations may apply if they are otherwise eligible.

Beneficiary Eligibility: For all programs, students must be enrolled in the school or program receiving the grant award in order to receive stipend and tuition support. For the OWEP Paraprofessionals program, state-licensed mental health nonprofit and for-profit organizations are also eligible applicants. In addition, students/interns must be U.S. citizens, U.S. nationals, or foreign nationals who possess a visa permitting permanent residence in the United States. Individuals on temporary or student visas are not eligible to participate.

Award Range/Average: FY 17 Range: $57,142- $480,000; Average $307,637 FY 18 Range: $83,320- $480,000; Average $343,126 FY 19 est Range: $83,324- $480,000; Average $364,033

Funding: (Project Grants) FY 18 est $44,000,000.00; FY 19 est $50,000,000.00; FY 20 est $82,000,000.00

HQ: 5600 Fishers Lane, Room 11N94A, Rockville, MD 20857

    Phone: 301-443-7759

    http://www.hrsa.gov

Programs Administered by Federal Headquarters

HHS93.982 | MENTAL HEALTH DISASTER ASSISTANCE AND EMERGENCY MENTAL HEALTH
"Mental Health Disaster Assistance"
Award: Project Grants
Purpose: The program provides mental health counseling to individuals who are affected due to severe disasters.
Applicant Eligibility: Applicants may be State or local nonprofit agencies as recommended by the State Governor and accepted by the Secretary.
Beneficiary Eligibility: Individuals who were victims of major disasters.
Funding: (Project Grants (Discretionary)) FY 18 $52,299,892.00; FY 19 est $38,352,998.00; FY 20 est Estimate Not Available
HQ: 5600 Fishers Lane, Rockville, MD 20857
   Phone: 240-276-1418 | Email: roger.george@samhsa.hhs.gov
   http://www.samhsa.gov

HHS93.242 | MENTAL HEALTH RESEARCH GRANTS
Award: Cooperative Agreements; Project Grants; Training
Purpose: To transform the understanding and treatment of mental illnesses through basic and clinical research, paving the way for prevention, recovery, and cure.
Applicant Eligibility: Public, private, -profit, or nonprofit agencies (including State and local government agencies), eligible Federal agencies, universities, colleges, hospitals, and academic or research Institutions may apply for research grants. SBIR grants can be awarded only to domestic small businesses, and STTR grants can be awarded only to domestic small businesses which "partner" with a research institution in cooperative research and development. An applicant for individual predoctoral fellowship support must be enrolled in a research doctoral degree Program by the proposed activation date of the fellowship. A postdoctoral applicant must have received a Ph.D., Psy.D., M.D., D.D.S., Sc.D., D.N. S., D.O., D.S.W., or equivalent degree from an accredited institution to be eligible for an individual postdoctoral fellowship. All research training awards are made to appropriate domestic research centers, medical schools, departments of psychiatry, non-medical academic departments, psychiatric hospitals or hospitals with psychiatric services, community mental health centers, and biomedical research institutes on behalf of individuals who need the opportunity to realize research potential. Except for the NIH Pathway to Independence (PI) Award (K99/R00), the individuals must be citizens or nationals of the United States or have been lawfully admitted for permanent residence. The NIH Pathway to Independence (PI) Award (K99/R00) is open to both U.S. citizens and non-U.S. citizens. Individuals must qualify by scholastic degree and previous training and/or experience.
Beneficiary Eligibility: Individuals and public, private, profit, or nonprofit organizations.
Award Range/Average: FY 2018 range: $26 to $13,028,681 Average Cost: $480,187
Funding: (Project Grants) FY 18 $1,405,506,857.00; FY 19 est $1,503,382,736.00; FY 20 est Estimate Not Available
HQ: 6001 Executive Boulevard, Rockville, MD 20857
   Phone: 301-443-3367
   http://www.nimh.nih.gov

HHS93.856 | MICROBIOLOGY AND INFECTIOUS DISEASES RESEARCH
Award: Project Grants
Purpose: Please see program 93.855; Allergy and infectious diseases research no funding will be reported under 93.856.
Applicant Eligibility: Universities, colleges, hospitals, laboratories and other public or private nonprofit domestic Institutions, including State and local units of government. Individuals are eligible to make application for grant support of research by a named principal investigator or a research career development candidate. For-profit Organizations are also eligible, with the exception of NRSA. Individual NRSA awardees must be nominated and sponsored by a public or nonprofit private institution having staff and facilities appropriate to the proposed research training Program. All NRSA awardees must be citizens or have been admitted to the United States for permanent residence. To be eligible, predoctoral candidates must have completed the baccalaureate degree and postdoctoral candidates must have a professional or scientific degree (M.D., Ph.D., D.D.S., D.O., D.V.M., Sc.D., D.Eng.), or must have an equivalent domestic or foreign degree. SBIR grants can be awarded only to domestic small businesses (entities that are independently owned and operated for profit, are not dominant in the field in which research is being proposed and have no more than 500 employees). Primary employment (more than one-half time) of the principal investigator must be with the small business at the time of award and during the conduct of the proposed project. In both Phase I and Phase II, the research must be performed in the U.S. or its possessions. To be eligible for funding, a grant application must be approved for scientific merit and Program relevance by a scientific review group and a national advisory

council. STTR grants can be awarded only to domestic small business concerns (entities that are independently owned and operated for profit, are not dominant in the field in which researches proposed and have no more than 500 employees) which "partner" with a research institution in cooperative research and development. At least 40 percent of the project is to be performed by the small business concern and at least 30 percent by the research institution. In both Phase I and Phase II, the research must be performed in the U.S. and its possessions. To be eligible for funding, a grant application must be approved for scientific merit and Program relevance by a scientific review group and a national advisory council.

Beneficiary Eligibility: Any nonprofit or for-profit organization, company, or institution engaged in biomedical research.

SBA59.046 | MICROLOAN PROGRAM

Award: Formula Grants; Direct Loans

Purpose: To assist women, low-income, and minority entrepreneurs, business owners, and other individuals possessing the capability to operate successful business concerns and to assist small business concerns in those areas suffering from a lack of credit due to economic downturns.

Applicant Eligibility: An applicant is considered eligible to apply if it meets the definition of an intermediary lender as published in Program materials, 13 CFR, and PL 102-140, and meets published minimum experience and capability requirements.

Beneficiary Eligibility: Small businesses, minority entrepreneurs, nonprofit entities, business owners, women and low-income, and other individuals possessing the capability to operate successful business concerns.

Funding: (Direct Loans) FY 17 $44,000,000.00; FY 18 est $44,000,000.00; FY 19 est $42,000,000.00; (Advisory Services and Counseling) FY 17 $23,535,000.00; FY 18 est $31,000,000.00; FY 19 est $25,000,000.00

HQ: 409 3rd Street SW, 8th Floor, Washington, DC 20416

Phone: 202-205-7001 | Email: daniel.upham@sba.gov

http://www.sba.gov

DOS19.500 | MIDDLE EAST PARTNERSHIP INITIATIVE
"MEPI"

Award: Cooperative Agreements; Project Grants

Purpose: Supports organizations and individuals in their efforts to promote political, economic, and social engagement in the Middle East and North Africa.

Applicant Eligibility: U.S. or foreign non-profit Organizations; for-profit Organizations; private Institutions of higher education, public or state Institutions of higher education; public international Organizations; and small businesses with functional and regional experience. Each solicitation outlines who is eligible and what types of experience are needed to apply for funding.

Beneficiary Eligibility: MEPI supports projects in Algeria, Bahrain, Israel, Iraq, Jordan, Kuwait, Lebanon, Libya, Morocco, Qatar, Saudi Arabia, Syria, Tunisia, West Bank and Gaza, and Yemen. Regional and multi-country projects may include Iraqi participants, but we currently do not fund Iraq-specific projects. Any award made using State/NEA funds requires the full complement of standard federal forms and budget documents, CVs of main program staff, as dictated by the U.S. Department of State, Bureau of Administration, and the relevant OMB circulars. See www.grants.gov for specific announcement. 2 CFR 200 applies to this program.

Award Range/Average: From $10,000 to $9,600,000; average approximately $3,100,000.

HQ: 2430 E Street NW, Washington, DC 20037

Phone: 202-776-8691 | Email: curleysl@state.gov

http://mepi.state.gov

ED84.149 | MIGRANT EDUCATION COLLEGE ASSISTANCE MIGRANT PROGRAM
"CAMP"

Award: Project Grants

Purpose: To assist students whose background in migrant and other seasonal farm work, are enrolled or are admitted for enrollment on a full-time basis, at institutions of higher education and are in the first academic year at such an institution.

Applicant Eligibility: Institutions of higher education or private nonprofit agencies in cooperation with Institutions of higher education may apply.

Beneficiary Eligibility: First-year college students who are engaged, or whose immediate family member is engaged, in migrant and other seasonal farm work or who have participated or been eligible to participate in the Title I, Migrant Education Program, or the Department of Labor's National Farmworker Jobs Program.

Programs Administered by Federal Headquarters

Award Range/Average: Range: $180,000- $425,000. Average: $410,615.
Funding: (Project Grants) FY 18 $22,286,942.00; FY 19 est $22,068,084.00; FY 20 est $22,199,942.00
HQ: 400 Maryland Avenue SW, Room 3E311, Washington, DC 20202
    Phone: 202-260-1426 | Email: lisa.gillette@ed.gov
    http://www.ed.gov/programs/camp/index.html

ED84.144 | MIGRANT EDUCATION COORDINATION PROGRAM
Award: Project Grants
Purpose: To provide financial incentives to State Educational Agencies (SEAs) to participate in consortia that provide high-quality project designs and services to improve the interstate or intrastate coordination of migrant education programs for migratory children who have their education interrupted.
Applicant Eligibility: SEAs receiving MEP State Formula grants, in a consortium with another State or other appropriate entities.
Beneficiary Eligibility: Migratory children of migratory agricultural workers or migratory fishers, or individuals under 21 years old who are migratory agricultural workers or migratory fishers, or spouses of such workers or fishers whose education is interrupted benefit.
Award Range/Average: Range: $60,000- $120,000
Funding: (Project Grants) FY 18 $3,000,000.00; FY 19 est $3,000,000.00; FY 20 est $3,000,000.00
HQ: 400 Maryland Avenue SW, Washington, DC 20202-6135
    Phone: 202-260-1426 | Email: lisa.gillette@ed.gov
    http://www.ed.gov/about/offices/list/oese/ome/index.html

ED84.141 | MIGRANT EDUCATION HIGH SCHOOL EQUIVALENCY PROGRAM "HEP"
Award: Project Grants
Purpose: To assist students whose background from migrant and other seasonal farm-work to obtain the equivalent of a secondary school diploma and to gain employment or be placed in an institution of higher education or other postsecondary education or training.
Applicant Eligibility: Institutions of higher education or private nonprofit agencies in cooperation with Institutions of higher education may apply.
Beneficiary Eligibility: Persons who are engaged or whose immediate family is engaged in migrant and other seasonal farm work or who have participated or have been eligible to participate in the Title I, Migrant Education Program or the Department of Labor's National Farmworker Jobs Program. Eligible beneficiaries also must be age 16 and older or beyond the age of compulsory school attendance, and lacking a high school diploma or its equivalent.
Award Range/Average: Range: $180,000- $475,000 Average: $446,438.
Funding: (Project Grants) FY 18 $22,167,471.00; FY 19 est $22,332,475.00; FY 20 est $22,199,943.00
HQ: 400 Maryland Avenue SW, Room 3E311, Washington, DC 20202
    Phone: 202-260-1426 | Email: lisa.gillette@ed.gov
    http://www.ed.gov/program/hep/index.html

ED84.011 | MIGRANT EDUCATION STATE GRANT PROGRAM
Award: Formula Grants
Purpose: To assist States with the migratory children to meet the same challenging State content and performance standards.
Applicant Eligibility: State educational agencies or consortia of State educational agencies.
Beneficiary Eligibility: Children, ages 0 through 21, of migratory agricultural workers or migratory fishers, including children (i.e. persons age 21 or under) who are migratory-agricultural workers or migratory fishers or who are the spouses of migratory agricultural workers or migratory fishers, who have moved across school district lines within the past 36 months to obtain temporary or seasonal employment in agriculture or fishing work.
Award Range/Average: The range of awards in FY 2017 was $0 - $114,386,281.
Funding: (Formula Grants) FY 18 $364,751,000.00; FY 19 est $364,751,000.00; FY 20 est $364,751,000.00
HQ: 400 Maryland Avenue SW, Washington, DC 20202-6135
    Phone: 202-260-1426 | Email: lisa.gillette@ed.gov
    http://www.ed.gov/programs/mep/index.html

DOD12.420 | MILITARY MEDICAL RESEARCH AND DEVELOPMENT

Award: Cooperative Agreements; Project Grants

Purpose: To transform healthcare for Service Members and the American public and to investigate medical solutions for the battlefield with a focus on various areas of biomedical research.

Applicant Eligibility: Federal, State, and local Governments; public, State, and private Institutions of higher education, Federally Recognized Indian Tribal government, U.S. territory or possession, small business, profit Organization, private nonprofit institution/Organization, quasi-public nonprofit institution/Organization, other private institution/Organizations, and Native American Organizations. Awards are not made to individuals.

Beneficiary Eligibility: Federal, State, and local governments; public, State, and private institutions of higher education, Federally Recognized Indian Tribal government, U.S. territory or possession, small business, profit organization, private nonprofit institution/organization, quasi-public nonprofit institution/organization, other private institution/organizations, and Native American organizations.

Funding: (Project Grants (Discretionary)) FY 18 $993,269,424.00; FY 19 est $1,010,509,072.00; FY 20 est Estimate Not Available

HQ: Attention: MCMR-AAP, Fort Detrick, MD 21702-5014

Phone: 301-619-2183

http://mrmc.amedd.army.mil

DOI15.437 | MINERALS LEASING ACT

Award: Direct Payments for Specified Use

Purpose: Office of Natural Resources Revenue (ONRR) shares 50 percent (90 percent for Alaska) of mineral leasing revenue with States.

Applicant Eligibility: Revenue from public land leasing will trigger automatic payment distribution computed in accordance with the Law.

Beneficiary Eligibility: State governments in which Federal leased lands and minerals are located.

Award Range/Average: Not Applicable.

Funding: (Direct Payments for Specified Use) FY 17 $1,395,081,000.00; FY 18 est $1,647,867,000.00; FY 19 est $1,824,498,000.00

HQ: 1849 C Street NW, PO Box 4211, Washington, DC 20240

Phone: 202-513-0600

http://www.ONRR.gov

HHS93.307 | MINORITY HEALTH AND HEALTH DISPARITIES RESEARCH

Award: Project Grants

Purpose: To support basic, clinical, social, and behavioral research; promote research infrastructure and training; foster emerging programs; disseminate information; and reach out to minority and other health disparity communities.

Applicant Eligibility: Individuals and public and private Institutions, both non-profit and for-profit, who propose to establish, expand, and conduct research, promote or engage in research training, and outreach activities that contribute to improving minority health and/or eliminating health disparities. Endowment grants: Only NIMHD Centers of Excellence or Section 736 health professional schools (see 42 U.S.C. 293) with net endowment assets less than or equal to 50 percent of the national median of endowment funds at Institutions that conduct similar biomedical research or training of health professionals are eligible for the research endowment awards. All applicants must have an NIMHD Center of Excellence Award or HRSA Centers of Excellence Award at the time of award of an NIMHD Research Endowment Grant. SBIR grants: Domestic small businesses (entities that are independently owned and operated for profit, are not dominant in the field in which the research is proposed, and have no more than 500 employees). Primary employment (more than one-half time) of the principal investigator must be with the small business at the time of award and during the conduct of the proposed project. Small business concerns must be at least 51 percent US owned by individuals and independently operated and/or at least 51 percent owned and controlled by another (one) for-profit business concern that is at least 51 percent owned and controlled by one or more individuals. The research must be performed in the U.S. or its possessions. STTR grants: Domestic small businesses (entities that are independently owned and operated for profit, are not dominant in the field in which the research is proposed, and have no more than 500 employees) that "partner" with a research institution in cooperative research and development. At least 40 percent of the project is to be performed by the small business concern and at least 30 percent by the research institution.

Beneficiary Eligibility: Any non-profit or for-profit organization, company, or institution engaged in biomedical and behavioural research. Endowment grants: NIMHD Centers of Excellence or Section 736 institutions.

Programs Administered by Federal Headquarters

Award Range/Average: (1) Centers of Excellence (COE) grants: 14 total awards made by the NIMHD ranged from $1,091,427 to $1,563,465;average $1,412,022. (2) Endowment grants: 5 total awards made by the NIMHD ranged from $1,900,000 to $2,000,000; average $1,980,000. (3) Centers of Excellence on Environmental Health Disparities Research (P50): 2 total awards made by the NIMHD ranged from $700,000 to $799,178; average $749,589. (4) Minority Health and Health Disparities Research International Research Training (MHIRT) grants: 22 total awards made by the NIMHD ranged from $106,508 to $269,872; average $251,063. (5) Small Business Innovation Research (SBIR) grants: 21 total awards made by the NIMHD ranged from $187,157 to $755,980; average $406,131. (6) Small Business Technology Transfer (STTR) Grants: 3 total awards made by the NIMHD ranged from $220,560 to $689,032; average $394,288. (7) Health Disparities Research Project grants and cooperative agreements (RPG): 205 total awards made by the NIMHD ranged from $74,761 to $2,005,661; average $510,887. (8) Research Centers in Minority Institutions (RCMI): 18 total awards made ranged from $455,263 to $4,849,098; average $2,379,637. (9) RCMI Infrastructure for Clinical and Translational Research (RCTR): 5 total awards made ranged from $2,206,313 to $3,152,326; average $2,776,705. (10) RCMI Translational Research Network (RTRN): single award made was $2,170,006. (11) Clinical Research Education and Career Development (CRECD) Awards: 4 total awards ranged from $534,513 to $540,000; average $537,625. (12) Resource-Related and Research Capacity Building grants: 2 total awards made by the NIMHD ranged from $345,595 to $534,789; average $440,192. (13) Pathway to Independence Awards: 3 total awards made by the NIMHD ranged from $90,386 to $132,943; average $117,355. (14) NIH Research Conference Grants: 10 total awards made ranged from $49,718 to $110,000; average $58,857. (15) Transdisciplinary Collaborative Centers: 11 total awards made ranged from $1,594,338 to $3,000,000; average $2,382,557. (16) Disparities Research and Education Advancing Mission (DREAM) Career Transition Awards: single award made was $235,337. (17) Ruth L. Kirschstein NRSA Individual Fellowships: 9 total awards ranged from $28,044 to $44,044; average $40,958. (18) NIH BD2K Enhancing Diversity in Biomedical Data Science: 7 total awards ranged from $210,072 to $323,443; average $246,235. (19) NIH Director's New Innovator Award Program (DP2): single award made was $2,542,500.
Funding: (Project Grants) FY 17 $245,071,212.00; FY 18 est Estimate Not Available; FY 19 est Estimate Not Available
HQ: 7201 Wisconsin Avenue, Suite 533, Bethesda, MD 20892
    Phone: 301-594-1788 | Email: joan.wasserman@nih.gov
    http://www.nimhd.nih.gov

ED84.120 | MINORITY SCIENCE AND ENGINEERING IMPROVEMENT "MSEIP"

Award: Project Grants
Purpose: To effect long-range improvement in science and engineering education at predominantly minority institutions; and to increase the participation of underrepresented ethnic minorities, particularly minority women, in scientific and technological careers.
Applicant Eligibility: Private and public nonprofit accredited (or successfully working toward accreditation) Institutions of higher education that award baccalaureate degrees; and are minority Institutions; public or private accredited (or successfully working toward accreditation) nonprofit Institutions of higher education that award associate degrees, and are minority Institutions that have a curriculum that includes science and engineering subjects; and enters into a partnership with public or private nonprofit Institutions of higher education that award baccalaureate degrees in science or engineering. Applications may also be submitted by nonprofit science-oriented Organizations, professional scientific societies, and Institutions of higher education that award baccalaureate degrees, that provide a needed service to a group of minority Institutions; or provide in-service training for project directors, scientists, and engineers from minority Institutions; or consortia of Organizations, that provide needed services to one or more minority Institutions, the membership of which may include: Institutions of higher education which have a curriculum in science or engineering; Institutions of higher education that have graduate or professional Programs in science or engineering; research laboratories of, or under contract with the Department of Energy; private Organizations that have science or engineering facilities; or quasi-governmental entities that have a significant scientific or engineering mission.
Beneficiary Eligibility: Private or public accredited (or successfully working toward accreditation) 2- and 4-year institutions of higher education whose enrollments of a single minority or a combination of minorities exceed 50 percent of the total enrollment. The term minorities refers to American Indian; Alaskan Native; Native Hawaiian, Black (not of Hispanic origin); Hispanic (including persons of Mexican, Puerto Rican, Cuban, and Central or South American origin); Pacific Islander; or other ethnic group who are underrepresented in science and engineering.
Award Range/Average: FY 2018: Average new award was $226,683; Average continuation award was $208,528. Awards ranged from approximately $164,000 to $250,000.
Funding: (Project Grants) FY 18 $11,025,000.00; FY 19 est $11,135,000.00; FY 20 $11,135,000.00

HQ: 400 Maryland Avenue SW, Washington, DC 20202
    Phone: 202-453-7913 | Email: bernadette.hence@ed.gov
    http://www.ed.gov/programs/iduesmsi

DOJ16.015 | MISSING ALZHEIMER'S DISEASE PATIENT ASSISTANCE PROGRAM
"Alzheimer's Initiatives"

Award: Cooperative Agreements
Purpose: To assist law enforcement agencies search for missing persons with Alzheimer disease.
Applicant Eligibility: N/A
Beneficiary Eligibility: All funds must be focused solely on initiatives to benefit those with Alzheimer's disease or other forms of dementia.
Award Range/Average: BJA may make one or more awards under this category.
HQ: 810 7th Street NW, Washington, DC 20531
    Phone: 202-616-6500 | Email: david.p.lewis@usdoj.gov
    http://www.bja.gov

DOJ16.543 | MISSING CHILDREN'S ASSISTANCE
"Missing and Exploited Children (MEC) Program"

Award: Project Grants
Purpose: To coordinate missing and exploited children activities and to support research, training, technical assistance, and demonstration programs to enhance the overall response to missing and exploited children and as well as their families.
Applicant Eligibility: Eligible applicants are limited to states (including territories), units of local government, federally recognized tribal Governments as determined by the Secretary of the Interior, nonprofit and for-profit Organizations (including tribal nonprofit and for-profit Organizations), and Institutions of higher education (including tribal Institutions of higher education). For-profit Organizations (as well as other recipients) must forgo any profit or management fee.
Beneficiary Eligibility: State and local units of government, private nonprofit agencies, organizations, institutions or individuals.
Funding: (Project Grants) FY 17 $65,690,610.00; FY 18 est $76,000,000.00; FY 19 est $72,000,000.00
HQ: 810 7th Street NW, Washington, DC 20531
    Phone: 202-514-5533 | Email: james.antal@usdoj.gov
    http://www.ojjdp.gov

HHS93.311 | MOBILIZATION FOR HEALTH: NATIONAL PREVENTION PARTNERSHIP AWARDS
"NPPA"

Award: Project Grants
Purpose: To provide strategic direction for the coordination of the vaccine and immunization enterprise for the National Vaccine Plan (NVP) implementation.
Applicant Eligibility: Public (including city, county, regional, and State government) Organizations and private nonprofit entities.
Beneficiary Eligibility: All children, women (including pregnant women), and adults, including those underserved and minority populations in the US.
Award Range/Average: Program ended June,2018
HQ: 1101 Wootton Parkway, Suite 550 Tower Building, Rockville, MD 20852
    Phone: 240-453-8442 | Email: alice.bettencourt@hhs.gov
    http://www.hhs.gov/ash/public_health/indexph.html

EOP95.006 | MODEL STATE DRUG LAWS INITIATIVE

Award: Project Grants
Purpose: ONDCP's Model State Drug Laws Initiative helps to create comprehensive laws, policies and programs on current and emerging drug and alcohol issues in different States and localities.

Programs Administered by Federal Headquarters

Applicant Eligibility: Applicants must have expert knowledge and extensive experience in conducting research and analysis, providing technical assistance, and drafting model state drug and alcohol laws, policies and Programs.

Beneficiary Eligibility: N/A

Award Range/Average: range varies based upon appropriated amount

Funding: (Cooperative Agreements) FY 18 $0.00; FY 19 est $2,500,000.00; FY 20 est $0.00

HQ: 1800 G Street NW, Washington, DC 20503

Phone: 202-395-6739 | Email: phuong_desear@ondcp.eop.gov

http://www.whitehouse.gov/ondcp

HHS93.791 | MONEY FOLLOWS THE PERSON REBALANCING DEMONSTRATION
"Money Follows the Person Demonstration"

Award: Project Grants

Purpose: The Money Follows the Person Rebalancing Demonstration program was designed to assist States to balance their long-term care systems and help Medicaid enrollees transition from institutions to the community.

Applicant Eligibility: Applicants for this Demonstration Grant must be any single State Medicaid Agency, State Mental Health Agency, or instrumentality of the State. Only one application can be submitted for a given State. By "State" we refer to the definition provided under 45 CFR 74. 2 as "any of the several States of the United States, the District of Columbia, the Commonwealth of Puerto Rico, any territory or possession of the United States, or any agency or instrumentality of a State exclusive of local Governments. " By "territory or possession", we mean Guam, the U.S. Virgin Islands, American Samoa, and the Commonwealth of the Northern Mariana Islands.

Beneficiary Eligibility: As defined in Section 6071(b)(2) of the DRA and amended by Section 2403 of the Affordable Care Act, the term "eligible individual" means an individual in the State who, immediately before beginning participation in the MFP demonstration project: (i) resides (and has resided, for a period of not less than 90 consecutive days in an inpatient facility; (ii) is receiving Medicaid benefits for inpatient services furnished by such inpatient facility; and (iii) with respect to whom a determination has been made that, but for the provision of home and community-based long- term care services, the individual would continue to require the level of care provided in an inpatient facility and, in any case in which the State applies a more stringent level of care standard as a result of implementing the State plan option permitted under section 1915 (i) of the Social Security Act, the individual must continue to require at least the level of care which had resulted in admission to the institution.

Award Range/Average: There is not a prescribed or predetermined maximum floor or ceiling grant award. Each State is unique in the number of individuals that will be projected for transition under the demonstration grant. In addition, the costs of individuals transitioning to community settings may vary, by targeted population. Applicants are advised to request a grant award that is sufficient in the amount needed to transition the projected individuals into community settings. CMS reserves the right to reduce the requested grant award, based on the number and size of additional grant awards given under this demonstration, as well as because of concerns contained within a State's application (i.e., concerns with the number of costs of individuals projected for transition by the individual State.

Funding: (Formula Grants (Apportionments)) FY 18 $0.00; FY 19 est $42,000,000.00; FY 20 est $215,100,000.00

HQ: 7500 Security Boulevard, Baltimore, MD 21244

Phone: 410-786-8551 | Email: jennifer.bowdoin@cms.hhs.gov

https://www.medicaid.gov/medicaid/ltss/money-follows-the-person/index.html

VA64.032 | MONTGOMERY GI BILL SELECTED RESERVE; RESERVE EDUCATIONAL ASSISTANCE PROGRAM
"Montogomery GI Bill - Selected Reserve (MGIB-SR) Reserve Educational Assistance Program (REAP)"

Award: Direct Payments With Unrestricted Use

Purpose: To encourage membership in units of the Selected Reserve of the Ready Reserve.

Applicant Eligibility: What follows is not a complete list of eligibility requirements. For more information on MGIB-SR and REAP visit http://www.gibill. va.gov. Generally, to qualify for benefits under MGIB-SR you must (1) Have a six-year obligation to serve in the Selected Reserve signed after June 30, 1985. If you are an officer, you must have agreed to serve six years in addition to your original obligation. For some types of training, it is necessary to have a six-year commitment that begins after September 30, 1990; (2) Complete your initial active duty for training (IADT); (3) Meet the requirement to receive a high school diploma or equivalency certificate before completing IADT. You may not use 12 hours toward a college degree to meet this requirement; and (4) Remain in good standing while serving in an active Selected Reserve unit. Generally, to qualify for benefits under REAP you must have served at least 90 consecutive days on active duty as a result of a call or order to active duty from a reserve component in response to a war or national emergency declared by the President or Congress.

Beneficiary Eligibility: As stated above under Applicant Eligibility.

Award Range/Average: The amount of educational assistance an individual is entitled to under chapter 1606 is $369, based on full time training for FY 2017. Assistance under chapter 1607 for FY 2017 is $1,485.60 for consecutive service of 2 or more years, $1114.20 for one year, but less than two, and $742.80 for 90 days but less than a year of service. Chapter 1607 rates are based on MGIB chapter 30 three year rate.

HQ: Department of Veterans Affairs Central Office 810 Vermont Avenue, Washington, DC 20420
    Phone: 202-461-9800
    http://www.benefits.va.gov/gibil

UDALL85.402 | MORRIS K. UDALL NATIVE AMERICAN CONGRESSIONAL INTERNSHIP PROGRAM
"Udall Internship Program"

Award: Direct Payments for Specified Use

Purpose: To honor former Arizona Congressman Morris K. Udall through the operation of internship, scholarship and fellowship programs.

Applicant Eligibility: Applicants must be American Indian or Alaska Native; be a junior or senior in college, a recent graduate from a tribal or four-year college, or a graduate or law student; have a college grade-point average of at least a "B" or the equivalent; and be a U.S. citizen or U.S. permanent resident. Applicants should also demonstrate commitment to tribal public policy or tribal communities.

Beneficiary Eligibility: A successful applicant will demonstrate: Interest in learning how the federal government "really works" Commitment to his or her tribal community; Knowledge of Morris Udall and Stewart Udall's legacy with regard to American Indians; Awareness of issues and challenges currently facing Indian Country; Strong research and writing skills; Organizational abilities and time management skills; Maturity, responsibility, and flexibility.

Award Range/Average: Each intern receives approximately $9500 in housing, airfare, per diem and the educational stipend.

Funding: (Direct Payments for Specified Use) FY 13 $128,606.00; FY 14 est $116,000.00; FY 15 est $120,000.00

HQ: 130 S Scott Avenue, Tucson, AZ 85701
    Phone: 520-901-8500 | Email: khalil@udall.gov
    http://www.udall.gov

UDALL85.400 | MORRIS K. UDALL SCHOLARSHIP PROGRAM
"Udall Undergraduate Scholarship"

Award: Direct Payments for Specified Use

Purpose: To honor former Arizona Congressman Morris K. Udall and Secretary of Interior Stewart L. Udall through the operation of internship, scholarship, and fellowship programs.

Applicant Eligibility: Applicants must be: (1) College sophomores or juniors in the current academic year having outstanding potential and intending to pursue careers in the environment; or (2) American Indian and Alaska Native students who are college sophomores or juniors in the current academic year and have outstanding potential and intend to pursue careers in healthcare or tribal public policy. Students must be nominated by accredited colleges or universities recognized by the Department of education.

Beneficiary Eligibility: To be eligible, students must meet all of the following criteria: Be committed to a career related to the environment, OR committed to a career in tribal public policy OR Native American health care. Be a sophomore or junior-level student, enrolled full-time at a two-year or four-year accredited institution of higher education in the United States, pursuing a bachelor's or associate's degree. "Sophomore" is defined as a student who has completed at least one year of full-time undergraduate study and intends at least two more years of full-time undergraduate study at the time of application. "Junior" is defined as a student who intends at least one more year of full-time undergraduate study at the time of application. Meet the following requirements: Have a college grade-point average of at least a "B" or the equivalent; Be pursuing full-time study during academic year following the award; Be a U.S. citizen, U.S. national, or U.S. permanent resident.

Award Range/Average: $2,000 to $5,000; average $4800.

Programs Administered by Federal Headquarters

Funding: (Direct Payments for Specified Use) FY 13 $253,691.00; FY 14 est $250,000.00; FY 15 est $250,000.00
HQ: 130 S Scott Avenue, Tucson, AZ 85701
  Phone: 520-901-8564 | Email: randler@udall.gov
  http://www.udall.gov

HUD14.162 | MORTGAGE INSURANCE COMBINATION AND MANUFACTURED HOME LOT LOANS
Award: Guaranteed/insured Loans
Purpose: To make reasonable financing for the purchase of a manufactured home and a lot.
Applicant Eligibility: All persons are eligible to apply.
Beneficiary Eligibility: Individuals/families.
Award Range/Average: The maximum mortgage amount is $92,904 for a manufactured home on a suitably developed lot and $23,226 for a developed lot only.
HQ: 451 7th Street SW, Washington, DC 20410
  Phone: 800-225-5342
  http://portal.hud.gov/hudportal/hud?src=/program_offices/housing/sfh/title/manuf146

HUD14.126 | MORTGAGE INSURANCE COOPERATIVE PROJECTS
"213 Cooperatives"
Award: Guaranteed/insured Loans
Purpose: Enabling nonprofit cooperative ownership housing corporations or trusts to develop or sponsor the development of housing projects to be operated as cooperatives.
Applicant Eligibility: Eligible mortgagors are nonprofit cooperatives, ownership housing corporations or trusts which may either sponsor projects directly, sell individual units to cooperative members, or purchase projects from investor-sponsors (builders, developers, or others who meet HUD requirements).
Beneficiary Eligibility: Members of the cooperative are eligible to occupy a dwelling in the structure whose mortgage is insured under the program.
HQ: 451 7th Street SW, Washington, DC 20410
  Phone: 202-402-2579 | Email: carmelita_a._james@hud.gov
  http://www.hud.gov/offices/hsg/hsgmulti.cfm

HUD14.155 | MORTGAGE INSURANCE FOR THE PURCHASE OR REFINANCING OF EXISTING MULTIFAMILY HOUSING PROJECTS
"Section 223(f)/207"
Award: Guaranteed/insured Loans
Purpose: To provide mortgage insurance to HUD-approved lenders for the purchase or refinancing of existing multifamily housing projects.
Applicant Eligibility: Mortgagors may be either profit and non-profit.
Beneficiary Eligibility: All persons are eligible to occupy such projects subject to normal occupancy restrictions.
HQ: 451 7th Street SW, Washington, DC 20410
  Phone: 202-402-2579 | Email: carmelita_a._james@hud.gov
  http://www.hud.gov/offices/hsg/hsgmu

HUD14.119 | MORTGAGE INSURANCE HOMES FOR DISASTER VICTIMS
"203(h)"
Award: Guaranteed/insured Loans
Purpose: To help victims of a disaster declared by the President undertake homeownership on a solid basis.
Applicant Eligibility: Anyone that is a victim of a major disaster as designated by the President is eligible to apply.
Beneficiary Eligibility: Families or individuals that are victims of a major disaster as designated by the President.

HQ: 451 7th Street SW, Washington, DC 20410
    Phone: 800-225-5342
    http://portal.hud.gov/hudportal/hud?src=/program_offices/housing/sfh/ins/203h-dft

HUD14.122 | MORTGAGE INSURANCE HOMES IN URBAN RENEWAL AREAS
"220 Homes"

Award: Guaranteed/insured Loans
Purpose: To assist qualified entities to purchase and/or rehabilitate homes in urban renewal areas.
Applicant Eligibility: Eligible mortgagors include private profit motivated entities, public bodies and others who meet HUD
    requirements for mortgagors.
Beneficiary Eligibility: Families and Individuals.
HQ: 451 7th Street SW, Washington, DC 20410
    Phone: 202-402-2579 | Email: carmelita_a._james@hud.gov
    http://www.hud.gov

HUD14.117 | MORTGAGE INSURANCE HOMES
"203(b)"

Award: Guaranteed/insured Loans
Purpose: To assist people, undertake home ownership.
Applicant Eligibility: All persons with a valid Social Security Number are eligible to apply. State and local government
    agencies, HUD approved non-profit Organizations and individuals employed by the Work Bank or a foreign embassy are not
    required to provide a Social Security number.
Beneficiary Eligibility: Individuals/families.
Award Range/Average: Maximum insurable loans are as follows: In areas where 125 percent of the median house price is
    less than 65 percent of the National Conforming Loan Limit ($417,000), FHA "floor" limits are set at the 65 percent limit
    as follows: one-family $271,050; two-family $347,000; three-family $419,425; and four-family $521,250. Any area where
    the limits exceed the floor is known as a "high cost" area. In areas where 115 percent of the median house price exceeds 150
    percent of the National Conforming Loan Limit for a one unit property, the mortgage limits are set at the 150 percent amount
    (ceiling)as follows: one-unit $625,500; two-unit $800,775; three-unit $967,950; and four-unit $1,202,925.
Funding: (Sale, Exchange, or Donation of Property and Goods) FY 15 $212,961,411,747.00; FY 16 est $209,000,000,000.00;
    FY 17 est $204,000,000,000.00
HQ: 451 7th Street SW, Washington, DC 20410
    Phone: 800-225-5342
    http://portal.hud.gov/hudportal/hud?src=/program_offices/housing/sfh/ins/203h-dft

HUD14.128 | MORTGAGE INSURANCE HOSPITALS
"Section 242 - Mortgage Insurance for Hospitals"

Award: Guaranteed/insured Loans
Purpose: To facilitate the affordable financing of hospitals for the care and treatment of persons who are acutely ill or who
    otherwise require medical care.
Applicant Eligibility: Qualified applicants can be either profit or not-for-profit hospitals licensed or regulated by the State,
    municipality, or other political subdivision. At least 50 percent of the care must be for general acute patients as of June 2012.
Beneficiary Eligibility: Persons needing the services of these hospitals benefit by using the modernized facilities supported by
    the insured mortgages.
Funding: (Guaranteed/Insured Loans) FY 15 $160,000,000.00; FY 16 est $665,000,000.00; FY 17 est $300,000,000.00
HQ: 451 7th Street SW, Room 6264, Washington, DC 20410
    Phone: 202-402-2333 | Email: ivy.m.jackson@hud.gov
    http://www.fha.gov/healthcare

Programs Administered by Federal Headquarters

HUD14.123 | MORTGAGE INSURANCE HOUSING IN OLDER, DECLINING AREAS "223(e)"

Award: Guaranteed/insured Loans
Purpose: To aid in the acquisition or rehabilitation of housing in older, declining urban areas.
Applicant Eligibility: HUD-approved mortgagees.
Beneficiary Eligibility: For single family purposes, an individual or family is eligible to apply through HUD approved mortgagees. Multifamily sponsorship is determined by applicable program requirements.
HQ: 451 7th Street SW, Washington, DC 20410
    Phone: 800-225-5342
    http://portal.hud.gov/hudportal/hud?src=/program_offices/housing/sfh/ins/sfh203b

HUD14.129 | MORTGAGE INSURANCE NURSING HOMES, INTERMEDIATE CARE FACILITIES, BOARD AND CARE HOMES AND ASSISTED LIVING FACILITIES

Award: Guaranteed/insured Loans
Purpose: To assist the construction or rehabilitation of nursing homes, intermediate care facilities, board and care homes and assisted-living facilities, to allow purchase or refinancing with/without repairs of projects not requiring significant rehabilitation, and to provide loan insurance to install fire safety equipment.
Applicant Eligibility: Eligible mortgagors include investors, builders, developers, public entities, nursing homes and private nonprofit corporations or associations.
Beneficiary Eligibility: Residents requiring skilled nursing, custodial care, and assistance with activities of daily living are eligible to live in a structure whose mortgage is insured under the program.
Funding: (Guaranteed/Insured Loans) FY 15 $2,770,000,000.00; FY 16 est $2,765,000,000.00; FY 17 est $2,765,000,000.00
HQ: 451 7th Street SW, Room 6264, Washington, DC 20410
    Phone: 202-402-2333 | Email: ivy.m.jackson@hud.gov
    http://www.hud.gov/healthcare

HUD14.133 | MORTGAGE INSURANCE PURCHASE OF UNITS IN CONDOMINIUMS "203(b)"

Award: Guaranteed/insured Loans
Purpose: To enable individuals and families to buy or refinance qualified units in FHA-approved home projects.
Applicant Eligibility: All individuals and families are eligible to apply.
Beneficiary Eligibility: Individuals/families.
HQ: 451 7th Street SW, Washington, DC 20410
    Phone: 800-225-5342

HUD14.135 | MORTGAGE INSURANCE RENTAL AND COOPERATIVE HOUSING FOR MODERATE INCOME FAMILIES AND ELDERLY, MARKET INTEREST RATE "221(d)(4) Multifamily - Market Rate Housing"

Award: Guaranteed/insured Loans
Purpose: To provide quality rental or cooperative housing for moderate-income families, elderly, and disabled.
Applicant Eligibility: Public, profit-motivated sponsors, limited distribution, nonprofit cooperative, builder-seller, investor-sponsor, and general mortgagors.
Beneficiary Eligibility: All families are eligible to occupy dwellings in a structure whose mortgage is insured under the program, subject to normal tenant selection. There are no income limits. Projects may be designed specifically for the elderly and handicapped.
Funding: (Guaranteed/Insured Loans) FY 15 $3,362,376,350.00; FY 16 est $3,541,142,939.00; FY 17 est $3,786,731,323
HQ: 451 7th Street SW, Washington, DC 20410
    Phone: 202-402-2579 | Email: carmelita_a._james@hud.gov
    http://www.hud.gov

HUD14.138 | MORTGAGE INSURANCE RENTAL HOUSING FOR THE ELDERLY

Award: Guaranteed/insured Loans
Purpose: To provide quality rental housing for the elder people.
Applicant Eligibility: Eligible mortgagors include private profit-motivated developers, and nonprofit sponsors.
Beneficiary Eligibility: All elderly or handicapped persons are eligible to occupy apartments in a project whose mortgage is insured under the program.
Funding: (Guaranteed/Insured Loans) FY 15 $53,212,283.00; FY 16 est $55,170,497.00; FY 17 est $59,494,779.00
HQ: 451 7th Street SW, Washington, DC 20410
    Phone: 202-402-2579 | Email: carmelita_a._james@hud.gov
    http://www.hud.gov/offices/hsg/hsgmulti.cfm

HUD14.139 | MORTGAGE INSURANCE RENTAL HOUSING IN URBAN RENEWAL AREAS
"220 Multifamily"

Award: Guaranteed/insured Loans
Purpose: To provide quality rental housing in urban renewal areas, code enforcement areas, and areas designated for overall revitalization.
Applicant Eligibility: Eligible mortgagors include private profit motivated entities, public bodies, and others who meet HUD requirements for mortgagors.
Beneficiary Eligibility: All families eligible to occupy a dwelling in a structure whose mortgage is insured under the program, subject to normal tenant selection.
Funding: (Guaranteed/Insured Loans) FY 15 $19,694,500.00; FY 16 est $20,387,968.00; FY 17 est $22,006,608.00
HQ: 451 7th Street SW, Washington, DC 20410
    Phone: 202-402-2579 | Email: carmelita_a._james@hud.gov
    http://www.hud.gov

HUD14.134 | MORTGAGE INSURANCE RENTAL HOUSING
"Section 207"

Award: Guaranteed/insured Loans
Purpose: To increase supply of quality rental housing for middle-income families.
Applicant Eligibility: Eligible mortgagors include investors, builders, developers, and others who meet HUD requirements for mortgagors.
Beneficiary Eligibility: All families eligible to occupy dwellings in a structure whose mortgage is insured under the program, subject to normal tenant selection.
Funding: (Guaranteed/Insured Loans) FY 15 $6,422,666,988.00; FY 16 est $5,916,508,274.00; FY 17 est $5,831,984,488.00
HQ: 451 7th Street SW, Washington, DC 20410
    Phone: 202-402-2579 | Email: carmelita_a._james@hud.gov
    http://www.hud.gov/offices/hsg/hsgmulti.cfm

HUD14.184 | MORTGAGES INSURANCE FOR SINGLE ROOM OCCUPANCY (SRO) PROJECTS
"221(d) Single Room Occupancy"

Award: Guaranteed/insured Loans
Purpose: To provide mortgage insurance for multifamily properties consisting of single-room units, which is aimed at those tenants who have a source of income but are priced out of the rental apartment market.
Applicant Eligibility: Eligible applicants may be nonprofit entities; builder/sellers teamed with a nonprofit purchaser, a limited distribution entity, profit-motivated entities or public entities. Cooperative lenders or investors are not eligible.
Beneficiary Eligibility: Residents are subject to normal tenant selection procedures. There are no income limits for admission.
HQ: 451 7th Street SW, Washington, DC 20410
    Phone: 202-402-2579 | Email: carmelita_a._james@hud.gov
    http://www.hud.gov

Programs Administered by Federal Headquarters

HUD14.881 | MOVING TO WORK DEMONSTRATION PROGRAM
Award: Formula Grants
Purpose: To provide public housing agencies and the Secretary of Housing and Urban Development the flexibility to design and test different approaches for providing and administering housing assistance.
Applicant Eligibility: Public housing agencies administering the public housing Program and/or the section 8 housing assistance payments Program may be selected by the Secretary to participate.
Beneficiary Eligibility: Low-income public housing residents.
Award Range/Average: N/A
Funding: (Formula Grants) FY 16 $3,703,906,074.00; FY 17 est $3,912,687,996.00; FY 18 est $3,912,687,996
HQ: 451 7th Street SW, Washington, DC 20410
　　Phone: 202-402-4306 | Email: marianne.nazzaro@hud.gov
　　http://www.hud.gov/offices/pih/programs/ph/mtw

DHS97.123 | MULTI-STATE INFORMATION SHARING AND ANALYSIS CENTER "MS-ISAC"
Award: Cooperative Agreements
Purpose: Serves as a cyber threat monitoring center to help local and State governments to address cybersecurity issues. It also acts as a cyber security center for the nation's elections community.
Applicant Eligibility: This funding opportunity is restricted to the Multi-State Information Sharing and Analysis Center (MS-ISAC). Specific information on applicant eligibility is identified in the funding opportunity announcement.
Beneficiary Eligibility: State Governments, local government, territorial governments, tribal governments and territories.
Award Range/Average: Refer to Funding Opportunity Announcement.
Funding: (Salaries and Expenses) FY 18 $10,447,510.00; FY 19 est $10,468,300.00; FY 20 est $10,468,300.00
HQ: 245 Murray Lane SW, PO Box 0115 Attention: 720-A, Washington, DC 20528
　　Phone: 703-705-6213 | Email: donnalee.beach@hq.dhs.gov
　　http://www.dhs.gov

HUD14.319 | MULTIFAMILY ENERGY INNOVATION FUND
Award: Cooperative Agreements
Purpose: Increasing the energy efficiency of existing multifamily residential properties that can be copied by others.
Applicant Eligibility: This Program is directed at the multifamily housing market, to catalyze innovations in the residential energy efficiency sector that have promise of replicability and to help create a standardized home energy efficient retrofit market.
Beneficiary Eligibility: Must be related to eligible multifamily housing.
Award Range/Average: We expect to make awards ranging from $2.5 to $7 million. For the total amount we expect to make between five and 10 awards.
Funding: (Cooperative Agreements) FY 10$0.00; FY 11 est $0.00; FY 12 est $24,750,000.00
HQ: 451 7th Street SW, Room 6230, Washington, DC 20410
　　Phone: 202-402-8395 | Email: beverly.n.rudman@hud.gov
　　http://www.hud.gov

HUD14.191 | MULTIFAMILY HOUSING SERVICE COORDINATORS
Award: Project Grants
Purpose: To link elderly or disabled non-elderly assisted housing and neighborhood residents, prevent premature and unnecessary institutionalization, and assess individual service needs, determine eligibility for public services, and make resource allocation decisions that enable residents to stay in the community longer.
Applicant Eligibility: Eligible applicants are owners of Section 8 developments with project-based subsidy (including Rural Housing Service Section 515/8 developments); Section 202 developments as defined under 24 CFR Sections 277 and 885, and 221(d)(3) below-market interest rate and 236 developments which are insured or assisted (funded under Sections 24 CFR 221 Subpart C, 236, 277, 880, 881, 883, 885 and 886). To be eligible, developments must also be current in mortgage payments. Service coordinators for Congregate Housing Service Programs (CHSP), Section 202 developments with a Project Rental Assistance Contract (PRAC), and Section 811 developments are not eligible for funding. Owners of Section 202 PRAC developments may request an increase in their PRAC to hire a Service Coordinator by following procedures in the Office of Housing's Management Agent Hand book 4381. 5, Revision-2, Change-2, Chapter 8.

Beneficiary Eligibility: Eligible beneficiaries are residents of eligible housing or community residents who live in the vicinity of such housing. Service Coordination may be provided to elderly or disabled families. In particular, priority is given to residents who are frail (unable to perform at least three activities of daily living (ADLs)) or "at risk" elderly persons who are unable to perform 1- 2 ADLs, or non-elderly disabled or temporarily disabled residents. At least twenty-five percent of the residents of a development must be frail, at risk, or non-elderly people with disabilities for that development to be eligible for funding.

Award Range/Average: $88,825 to $402,196; $171,064.

Funding: (Project Grants) FY 15 $86,000,000.00; FY 16 est $77,000,000.00; FY 17 est $75,000,000.00

HQ: 451 7th Street SW, Room 6146, Washington, DC 20410

Phone: 202-708-3000 | Email: carissa.l.janis@hud.gov

http://portal.hud.gov/hudportal/hud?src=/program_offices/housing/mfh/scp/scphome

HHS93.373 | MULTIPLE APPROACHES TO SUPPORT YOUNG BREAST CANCER SURVIVORS AND METASTATIC BREAST CANCER PATIENTS "CDC-RFA-DP19-1906"

Award: Formula Grants (cooperative Agreements)

Purpose: To offer support for caregivers and families for these individuals, increased awareness of clinical trials by both young women diagnosed with cancer and individuals diagnosed with metastatic breast cancer, increased financial support, and improved quality of life among young breast cancer survivors.

Applicant Eligibility: Government Organizations, non-governmental Organizations, private colleges and universities, community-based Organizations, faith-based Organizations, for-profit Organizations (other than small business), and small businesses can apply.

Beneficiary Eligibility: Formula Grants

Award Range/Average: DP11-1111: $180,000 (Average award)DP14-1408: Component 1 ($200,000 - $450,000); Component 2 ($150,000 to $350,000)DP19-1906: TBD

Funding: (Formula Grants (Cooperative Agreements)) FY 18 $800,000.00; FY 19 est $0.00; FY 20 est $0.00; -(Cooperative Agreements) FY 18 $800,000.00; FY 19 est $0.00; FY 20 est $0.00

HQ: 4770 Buford Highway NE Chamblee Campus, Building 107/4th Floor, Atlanta, GA 30341

Phone: 770-488-3094 | Email: armoore@cdc.gov

HHS93.374 | MULTIPLE APPROACHES TO SUPPORT YOUNG BREAST CANCER SURVIVORS AND METASTATIC BREAST CANCER PATIENTS "CDC-RFA-DP19-1906"

Award: Cooperative Agreements (discretionary Grants)

Purpose: To offer support for caregivers and families for these individuals, increased awareness of clinical trials by both young women diagnosed with cancer and individuals diagnosed with metastic breast cancer, increased financial support, and improved quality of life among young breast cancer survivors.

Applicant Eligibility: Government Organizations, non-governmental Organizations, private colleges and universities, community-based Organizations, faith-based Organizations, for-profit Organizations (other than small business), and small businesses can apply.

Beneficiary Eligibility: N/A

Award Range/Average: DP11-1111: $180,000 (Average award)DP14-1408: Component 1 ($200,000 - $450,000); Component 2 ($150,000 to $350,000)DP19-1906: TBD

Funding: (Cooperative Agreements (Discretionary Grants)) FY 18 $2,537,154.00; FY 19 est $0.00; FY 20 est Estimate Not Available

HQ: 4770 Buford Highway NE Chamblee Campus, Building 107/4th Floor, Atlanta, GA 30341

Phone: 770-488-3094 | Email: armoore@cdc.gov

http://cdc.gov

Programs Administered by Federal Headquarters

IMLS45.309 | MUSEUM GRANTS FOR AFRICAN AMERICAN HISTORY AND CULTURE

Award: Project Grants; Direct Payments for Specified Use

Purpose: To enhance institutional capacity and sustainability through professional training, technical assistance, internships, outside expertise, and other tools.

Applicant Eligibility: Eligible applicants include museums whose primary purpose is African American life, art, history, and/ or culture, encompassing: the period of slavery; the era of Reconstruction; the Harlem renaissance; the civil rights movement; and other periods of the African American diaspora. Nonprofit Organizations whose primary purpose is to support museums identified above may also apply. Historically Black Colleges or universities (HBCUs) are also eligible. For more information about eligibility requirements, visit http://www.imls.gov/applicants/museums.aspx.

Beneficiary Eligibility: Public and private non-profit museums. Through activities and projects funded, beneficiaries include the general public.

Award Range/Average: Between $5,000 and $150,000.

Funding: (Project Grants) FY 15 $1,407,000.00; FY 16 est $1,481,000.00; FY 17 est $1,407,000.00

HQ: 955 L'Enfant Plaza North SW, Suite 4000, Washington, DC 20024

Phone: 202-653-4667 | Email: misaksen@imls.gov

http://www.imls.gov

IMLS45.301 | MUSEUMS FOR AMERICA

Award: Project Grants; Direct Payments for Specified Use

Purpose: To strengthen the ability of an individual museum to serve the public more effectively by supporting high-priority activities that advance its mission, plans, and strategic goals and objectives.

Applicant Eligibility: Museums that fulfill the eligibility criteria for museums may apply. For more information about eligibility requirements, visit http://www.imls.gov/applicants/museums.aspx.

Beneficiary Eligibility: Public and private non-profit museums. Through activities and projects funded, beneficiaries include the general public.

Award Range/Average: Between $5,000 and $150,000.

Funding: (Project Grants) FY 15 $20,200,000.00; FY 16 est $21,457,000.00; FY 17 est $20,200,000.00

HQ: 955 L'Enfant Plaza North SW, Suite 4000, Washington, DC 20024

Phone: 202-653-4636 | Email: cbodner@imls.gov

http://www.imls.gov

CDC93.387 | NATIONAL AND STATE TOBACCO CONTROL PROGRAM
"Quit lines: Tobacco Control"

Award: Cooperative Agreements

Purpose: To promote tobacco quitting among youth and adults; to eliminate exposure to second-hand smoke and tobacco-related disparities thereby reducing chronic disease morbidity, mortality, and disability related to the usage of tobacco in the United States.

Applicant Eligibility: Eligible applicants that can apply for this funding are listed below: State Governments County Governments City or township Governments Special district Governments Independent school districts Public and State controlled Institutions of higher education Native American tribal Governments (Federally recognized tribal Governments) Nonprofit with 501C3 IRS status (other than institution of higher education)Nonprofit without 501C3 IRS status (other than institution of higher education)Private Institutions of higher education For profit Organizations other than small businesses Small businesses Government Organizations: State (includes the District of Columbia)Local Governments or their bona fide agents Territorial Governments or their bona fide agents in the Commonwealth of Puerto Rico, the Virgin Islands, the Commonwealth of the Northern Marianna Islands, American Samoa, Guam, the Federated States of Micronesia, the Republic of the Marshall Islands, and the Republic of Palau State controlled Institutions of higher education American Indian or Alaska Native tribal Governments (federally recognized or state-recognized)Public Housing Authorities/Indian Housing Authorities] Non-government Organizations: American Indian or Alaska native tribally designated Organizations Other: Private colleges and universities Community-based Organizations Faith-Based Organizations.

Beneficiary Eligibility: Any State and Territorial Health Department, and other public entities will benefit.

Award Range/Average: N/A

Funding: (Cooperative Agreements) FY 18 Actual Not Available; FY 19 est $0; FY 20 est $900,000.00

HQ: 4770 Buford Highway NE, PO Box S107-7, Atlanta, GA 30341
   Phone: 770-488-5941

NARA89.001 | NATIONAL ARCHIVES REFERENCE SERVICES HISTORICAL RESEARCH

Award: Use of Property, Facilities, and Equipment; Advisory Services and Counseling; Dissemination of Technical Information
Purpose: To provide professional reference service to members of the general public and employees of the Federal government who are conducting research in Federal records or in historical materials in Presidential Libraries.
Applicant Eligibility: Anyone (general public).
Beneficiary Eligibility: Same as Applicant Eligibility.
Award Range/Average: Not Applicable.
Funding: (Salaries and Expenses) FY 16 $62,196,222.00; FY 17 est $66,084,080.00; FY 18 est $67,405,762.00
HQ: 8601 Adelphi Road, College Park, MD 20740
   Phone: 301-837-1910 | Email: benjamin.davis@nara.gov
   http://www.archives.gov

HHS93.889 | NATIONAL BIOTERRORISM HOSPITAL PREPAREDNESS PROGRAM "HPP"

Award: Formula Grants
Purpose: To ready hospitals and other healthcare systems to deliver coordinated and effective care to victims of terrorism and other public health emergencies.
Applicant Eligibility: State health departments of all 50 States, the District of Columbia, the nation's three largest municipalities (New York City, Chicago and Los Angeles County), the Commonwealths of Puerto Rico and the Northern Mariana Islands, the territories of American Samoa, Guam and the United States Virgin Islands, the Federated States of Micronesia, and the Republics of Palau and the Marshall Islands.
Beneficiary Eligibility: All State health departments listed above, hospitals and supporting health care systems.
Award Range/Average: Range in FY 13: $270,000 - to $27,000,000. FY 13 Average: $5,351,000
Funding: (Formula Grants (Cooperative Agreements)) FY 17 $150,000.00; FY 18 est $150,000.00; FY 19 est $150,000.00
HQ: 200 C E Street Concourse C4K17, Washington, DC 20024
   Phone: 202-245-0732 | Email: robert.dugas@hhs.gov
   http://www.phe.gov

HHS93.350 | NATIONAL CENTER FOR ADVANCING TRANSLATIONAL SCIENCES "NCATS"

Award: Cooperative Agreements
Purpose: To catalyze the generation of innovative methods and technologies that will enhance the development, testing, and implementation of diagnostics and therapeutics across a wide range of human diseases and conditions.
Applicant Eligibility: See above.
Beneficiary Eligibility: Biomedical investigators at any nonprofit or for-profit organization, company, or institution engaged in biomedical research.
Award Range/Average: Clinical and Translational Science Award program: $1 - $24,600,001, Therapeutics for Rare and Neglected Diseases: $49,209 - $92,677
Funding: (Project Grants) FY 18 $617,275,075.00; FY 19 est $676,537,503.00; FY 20 est $555,870,873
HQ: 6701 Democracy Boulevard, Room 970, Bethesda, MD 20892-4874
   Phone: 301-435-0860 | Email: parsonss@mail.nih.gov
   http://www.ncats.nih.gov

Programs Administered by Federal Headquarters

DOJ16.822 | NATIONAL CENTER FOR CAMPUS PUBLIC SAFETY
"National Center"

Award: Cooperative Agreements
Purpose: The National Center identifies and examines safety and security and develops resources to expand services to those who are charged with providing a safe environment on the campuses of the nation's colleges and universities.
Applicant Eligibility: A demonstrated knowledge of campus public safety needs and demonstrated experience and infrastructure for successfully carrying out a multi-faceted initiative with multiple campus stakeholder groups is required.
Beneficiary Eligibility: State, local, and tribal criminal justice agencies are the primary beneficiaries of this program.
Award Range/Average: See the current fiscal year's solicitation available at the Office of Justice Programs

HHS93.300 | NATIONAL CENTER FOR HEALTH WORKFORCE ANALYSIS
"Health Workforce Research Centers; NCHWA HWRC"

Award: Cooperative Agreements
Purpose: To provide for the development of information describing and analyzing the healthcareworkforce and workforce related issues in order to provide necessary information for decision-making regarding future directions in health professions in response to societal and professional needs.
Applicant Eligibility: Those eligible to apply are: state or local Governments, a state workforce investment board, public health or health professions schools, schools of medicine, schools of nursing, universities, academic health centers, community-based health facilities, and other appropriate public or private nonprofit entities, including faith based and community based Organizations. Federally Recognized Indian Tribal Government and Native American Organizations may apply if they are otherwise eligible.
Beneficiary Eligibility: Those who will ultimately benefit from these grants are the local, state, and federal legislators, planners, and policy makers, as well as the public, who will receive the information needed to better understand health workforce issues and trends and to make evidenced-based health workforce decisions.
Award Range/Average: FY 18. - $450,000 to $548,415; average award of $515,128 (excludes the Behavioral Health Workforce Research Center, which received funding from SAMHSA in FY 2018). FY 19 est. - $525,466 to $1,052,734; average award of $594,929 (includes the Behavioral Health Workforce Research Center, which is anticipated to be fully funded by HRSA in FY 2019). FY 20 est. - $525,466 to $1,052,734; average award of $594,929 (includes the Behavioral Health Workforce Research Center, which is anticipated to be fully funded by HRSA in FY 2019).
Funding: (Cooperative Agreements) FY 18 $4,399,029.00; FY 19 est $5,354,363.00; FY 20 $4,497,088.00
HQ: 5600 Fishers Lane, Room 11N21, Rockville, MD 20857
  Phone: 301-443-1304 | Email: rstreeter@hrsa.gov
  http://bhw.hrsa.gov/health-workforce-analysis/research/research-centers

HHS93.702 | NATIONAL CENTER FOR RESEARCH RESOURCES, RECOVERY ACT CONSTRUCTION SUPPORT

Award: Project Grants
Purpose: To renovate existing research facilities and build new research facilities to meet basic and clinical space requirements, laboratory safety, biohazard containment, and animal care standards to support the facility demands of NIH research programs.
Applicant Eligibility: Construction/Renewal/Rehabilitation.
Beneficiary Eligibility: Public nonprofit institution/organization.
Award Range/Average: Awards will range from $2M to $20M total costs. The average award is expected to be $10M.
HQ: 6701 Democracy Boulevard, Room 960, Bethesda, MD 20892
  Phone: 301-435-0877 | Email: farberg@mail.nih.gov
  http://www.ncrr.nih.gov

HHS93.233 | NATIONAL CENTER ON SLEEP DISORDERS RESEARCH

Award: Project Grants
Purpose: To support research and research training related to sleep disordered breathing, and the fundamental functions of sleep and circadian rhythms.
Applicant Eligibility: Any nonprofit Organization engaged in biomedical research and Institutions or companies organized for profit may apply for almost any kind of grant. Only domestic, non-profit, private or public Institutions may apply for

NRSA Institutional Research Training Grants. An individual may apply for an NRSA or, in some cases, for a research grant if adequate facilities to perform the research are available. SBIR grants can be awarded only to United States small business concerns (entities that are independently owned and operated for profit, or owned by another small business that itself is independently owned and operated for profit and have no more than 500 employees including affiliates). Primary employment (more than one-half time) of the principal investigator must be with the small business at the time of award and during the conduct of the proposed project. In both Phase I and Phase II, the research must be performed in the U.S. or its possessions. To be eligible for funding, a grant application must be approved for scientific merit and Program relevance by a scientific review group and a national advisory council. SBIR projects are generally performed at least 67% by the applicant small business in Phase I and at least 50% of the Project in Phase II. STTR grants can be awarded only to United States small business concerns (entities that are independently owned and operated for profit and have no more than 500 employees) that formally collaborate with a University or other non-profit research institution in cooperative research and development. The principal investigator of an STTR award may be employed with either the small business concern or collaborating non-profit research institution as long as s/he has a formal appointment with or commitment to the applicant small business concern. At least 40% of the project is to be performed by the small business concern and at least 30% by the non-profit research institution. In both Phase I and Phase II, the research must be performed in the U.S. and its possessions.

Beneficiary Eligibility: Any nonprofit or for-profit organization, company or institution engaged in biomedical research. Only domestic for-profit small business firms may apply for SBIR and STTR programs.

Award Range/Average: Grants: $25,416 to $2,620,576: $502,736. SBIR Phase I - $150,000; Phase II - up to $1,000,000; STTR Phase I - $150,000; Phase II - $1,000,000.

Funding: (Project Grants) FY 18 $67,564,617.00; FY 19 est $68,507,033.00; FY 20 est $68,507,033.00

HQ: 6701 Rockledge Drive, Room 7176, Bethesda, MD 20892

Phone: 301-827-7968 | Email: pharesda@nhlbi.nih.gov

http://www.nhlbi.nih.gov/about/scientific-divisions/national-center-sleep-disorders-research

DOJ16.027 | NATIONAL CLEARINGHOUSE ON SEXUAL ASSAULT OF AMERICAN INDIAN AND ALASKA NATIVE WOMEN

Award: Cooperative Agreements

Purpose: To provide training and technical assistance on issues relating to sexual assault of American Indian and Alaska Native women.

Applicant Eligibility: The recipient will provide training and technical assistance on sexual assault of American Indian and Alaska Native women.

Beneficiary Eligibility: Training and technical assistance under the program is available to tribes, tribal organizations, and others.

Award Range/Average: The program is awarded as a single cooperative agreement for up to the full available amount.

Funding: (Cooperative Agreements) FY 16 $500,000.00; FY 17 est $500,000.00; FY 18 est $500,000.00

HQ: 145 N Street NE, Washington, DC 20530

Phone: 202-305-1177 | Email: tia.farmer@usdoj.gov

http://www.justice.gov/ovw

HHS93.858 | NATIONAL COLLABORATION TO SUPPORT HEALTH, WELLNESS AND ACADEMIC SUCCESS OF SCHOOL-AGE CHILDREN

Award: Cooperative Agreements

Purpose: The purpose of this announcement is to fund applicants to improve the health of youth by funding NGOs to assist CDC funded grantees and the organizations' constituents to implement environmental and systems changes that support and reinforce healthful behaviors and reduce disparities. The program places a strong emphasis on training and professional development, technical assistance, dissemination and communication, and program implementation and evaluation, and all activities are to be developed and delivered within the whole school, whole community, and whole child framework.

Applicant Eligibility: Eligibility is limited to Community-Based Organizations, Faith Based Organizations, American Indian or Alaska Native Tribally-Designated organizations, Nonprofit without or with 501C3 IRS Status (other than Institution of Higher education) are eligible.

Beneficiary Eligibility: Nonprofit, Community-based, Faith based, American Indian/Alaska Native.

Award Range/Average: Funding range $300,000 - $450,000 for FY16

Funding: (Cooperative Agreements) FY 18 $2,099,750.00; FY 19 est $2,099,745.00; FY 20 est $2,099,745.00

Programs Administered by Federal Headquarters

HQ: 4770 Buford Highway NE, Atlanta, GA 30341
 Phone: 770-488-6167
 http://www.cdc.gov

HHS93.290 | NATIONAL COMMUNITY CENTERS OF EXCELLENCE IN WOMEN'S HEALTH
"Coalition for a Healthier Community (CHC)"
Award: Cooperative Agreements
Purpose: To provide 1 year of financial and technical support to an existing wellness coalition to develop a strategic action plan and implementation plan to reduce gender based health disparities in targeted communities.
Applicant Eligibility: Eligible applicants include public and private non profit Organizations (public and private academic Institutions and hospitals); community-based and faith-based Organizations, medical groups/practices and State, city, county, and local health departments, Tribes and tribal Organizations with expertise/experience in the proposed objectives. The applicant must be part of an existing coalition. At least a third of the partners should have demonstrated experience addressing gender differences through appropriate interventions, Programs, or research related to the selected objectives. Phase II: Eligible applicants are limited to Phase I grantees.
Beneficiary Eligibility: Women and girls across the life span.
Award Range/Average: Grant program last funded FY '15; program ended 8/31/16.
HQ: 1101 Wootton Parkway, Suite 550, Rockville, MD 20852
 Phone: 240-453-8822 | Email: brenda.donaldson@hhs.gov
 http://www.womenhealth.gov

NCD92.002 | NATIONAL COUNCIL ON DISABILITY
"NCD"
Award: Cooperative Agreements
Purpose: Independent federal agency charged with advising the President, Congress, and other federal agencies regarding policies, programs, practices, and procedures that affect people with disabilities.
Applicant Eligibility: NCD enters into cooperative agreements to research and produce reports on disability policy to advise the White House, Congress, Federal agencies, and to inform the general public.
Beneficiary Eligibility: The White House, Congress, Federal agencies, and the general public will benefit.
Award Range/Average: Usually for one-year cooperative agreements.
Funding: (Direct Payments for Specified Use (Cooperative Agreements)) FY 16 $605,000.00; FY 17 est $200,000.00; FY 18 est Estimate Not Available
HQ: 1331 F Street NW, Suite 850, Washington, DC 20004
 Phone: 202-272-2019 | Email: atorresdavis@ncd.gov
 http://www.ncd.gov

DOJ16.554 | NATIONAL CRIMINAL HISTORY IMPROVEMENT PROGRAM (NCHIP)
"NCHIP"
Award: Cooperative Agreements
Purpose: To enhance the quality and completeness of the nation's criminal history record systems.
Applicant Eligibility: Applicants are limited to the agency designated by the governor in each state to administer the NCHIP Program, and federally recognized tribal entities. States and Tribes may choose to submit applications as part of a multi-state consortium, multi-tribe consortium, or other entity. In such cases, please contact your BJS Program manager for further information.
Beneficiary Eligibility: Funds awarded to the state or tribe may be allocated for use in state or local/tribal agencies or the courts, but should have an impact on national record systems. Private organizations may receive funds under contract arrangements with a state/tribal agency or its subgrantees to which NCHIP funds are allocated by the state/tribe.
Award Range/Average: See the current fiscal year's solicitation guidelines posted on the Office of Justice Programs
Funding: (Project Grants) FY 17 $31,941,079.00; FY 18 est $50,000,000.00; FY 19 est $51,000,000.00

HQ: 810 7th Street NW, Washington, DC 20531
Phone: 202-307-0765 | Email: devon.adams@usdoj.gov
http://www.bjs.gov

DHS97.128 | NATIONAL CYBER SECURITY AWARENESS

Award: Cooperative Agreements
Purpose: The program helps to create a public awareness on cybersecurity and on safe ways on Internet browsing.
Applicant Eligibility: See above.
Beneficiary Eligibility: N/A
Award Range/Average: Refer to the funding opportunity announcement.
Funding: (Salaries and Expenses) FY 18 $549,996.00; FY 19 est $549,995.00; FY 20 est $550,000.00
HQ: 245 Murray Lane SW, Washington, DC 20528
Phone: 703-705-6672 | Email: latasha.mccord@hq.dhs.gov

DHS97.041 | NATIONAL DAM SAFETY PROGRAM

Award: Project Grants
Purpose: The National Dam Safety Program allows the State and local governments to conduct dam safety checks through supervision of a dam's construction, operation and maintenance and by preparing for hazard mitigation of lives and property during the failure of dams.
Applicant Eligibility: All States and U.S. territories with a legislated and approved dam safety Program are eligible for the National Dam Safety Program Assistance.
Beneficiary Eligibility: The State Dam Safety Program Office of eligible States.
Award Range/Average: Refer to program guidance.
Funding: (Project Grants) FY 18 $6,800,000.00; FY 19 est $17,000,000.00; FY 20 est $17,000,000.00
HQ: 400 C Street SW, Washington, DC 20472
Phone: 202-646-3435 | Email: james.demby@fema.dhs.gov
http://www.fema.gov

HUD14.272 | NATIONAL DISASTER RESILIENCE COMPETITION
"Community Development Block Grant P. L. 113-2"

Award: Project Grants
Purpose: To provide decent housing and a suitable living environment and expand economic opportunities mainly for persons of low and moderate income.
Applicant Eligibility: CDBG DR competitive funds are made available to States and units of general local Governments designated by the President of the United States as disaster areas. These communities must have significant unmet recovery needs and the capacity to carry out a disaster recovery Program (usually these are Governments that already receive HOME or Community Development Block Grant allocations). Grantees may use CDBG Disaster Recovery funds for recovery efforts involving housing, economic development, infrastructure and prevention of further damage to affected areas. However, CDBG DR funds may not be used for activities reimbursable by or for which funds are made available by the Federal Emergency Management Agency or the Army Corps of Engineers.
Beneficiary Eligibility: The principal beneficiaries of CDBG DR funds are low- and moderate-income persons (generally defined as a member of a family having an income equal to or less than the Section 8 low income limit established by HUD) in communities that have experienced a disaster event. Generally, grantees must use at least half of Disaster Recovery funds for activities that principally benefit low-and moderate-income persons. These can be either activities in which all or the majority of people who benefit have low or moderate incomes or activities that benefit an area or service group in which at least 51 percent of the populous are of low- and moderate-income. HUD can only waive this requirement on a showing of "compelling need.".
Award Range/Average: Thirteen (13) grants were awarded. The smallest award amount was $15 million (New Jersey) and the largest was $176 million (New York City). The average award amount was $76.8 million.
HQ: 801 Cherry Street, Suite 2800, Fort Worth, TX 76102
Phone: 817-978-5948 | Email: phyllis.j.foulds@hud.gov
http://www.hudexchange.info/programs/cdbg-dr/resilient-recove

Programs Administered by Federal Headquarters

HHS93.825 | NATIONAL EBOLA TRAINING AND EDUCATION CENTER (NETEC) "NETEC"

Award: Project Grants

Purpose: The program helps to increase the competency of healthcare and public health workers and the capability of healthcare facilities to deliver efficient and effective Ebola patient care through the nationwide, regional network for Ebola and other infectious diseases.

Applicant Eligibility: Eligible applicants are limited to healthcare facilities that have safely and successfully evaluated and treated patients with Ebola in the U.S. The lead applicant will collaborate, coordinate, plan, and work directly with the other facilities on appropriate activities described in the individual funding opportunity announcement, as well as distribute the funds from the funding opportunity announcement to support those activities.

Beneficiary Eligibility: Public health departments, hospitals and supporting health care systems.

Award Range/Average: 12000000

Funding: (Project Grants (Cooperative Agreements)) FY 18 $5,422,148.00; FY 19 est $5,397,501.00; FY 20 est $5,422,148.00

HQ: 200 C Street SW, Room C4K12, Washington, DC 20024

    Phone: 202-692-4673 | Email: melissa.harvey@hhs.gov

    http://www.phe.gov

HHS93.052 | NATIONAL FAMILY CAREGIVER SUPPORT, TITLE III, PART E

Award: Formula Grants

Purpose: To assist States, Territories in providing multifaceted systems of support services for family caregivers; and older relative caregivers.

Applicant Eligibility: Formula grants: State Governments and U.S. Territories, with distribution to designated area agencies on aging through an approved State plan and intrastate funding formula.

Beneficiary Eligibility: Family caregivers, grandparents and older individuals who are relative caregivers will benefit.

Funding: (Formula Grants) FY 17 $150,299,736.00; FY 18 est $180,586,000.00; FY 19 est $150,586,000.00

HQ: 330 C Street SW, Washington, DC 20201

    Phone: 202-795-7386 | Email: greg.link@acl.hhs.gov

    http://www.acl.gov

HHS93.054 | NATIONAL FAMILY CAREGIVER SUPPORT, TITLE VI, PART C, GRANTS TO INDIAN TRIBES AND NATIVE HAWAIIANS
"Native American Caregiver Support Program, Title VI, Part C"

Award: Project Grants

Purpose: To assist Indian Tribal and Native Hawaiian Organizations in providing multifaceted systems of support services for family caregivers; and grandparents or older individuals who are relative caregivers.

Applicant Eligibility: Indian Tribal and Native Hawaiian Organizations with approved applications under Title VI, Parts A and B.

Beneficiary Eligibility: Family caregivers, grandparents, and older individuals who are relative caregivers will benefit.

Award Range/Average: FY 16 Ranges for Part C - $14,270- $58,547 FY 17 Ranges for Part C - $13,820- $56,560

Funding: (Formula Grants) FY 16 $7,468,657.00; FY 17 est $7,478,530.00; FY 18 est Estimate Not Available.

HQ: 330 C Street SW, Washington, DC 20201

    Phone: 202-795-7380 | Email: cynthia.lacounte@acl.hhs.gov

    http://www.acl.gov

DHS97.018 | NATIONAL FIRE ACADEMY TRAINING ASSISTANCE
"Student Stipend Reimbursement Program"

Award: Direct Payments for Specified Use

Purpose: The program offers stipends to first responders and emergency managers attending the National Fire Academy courses to prepare and respond to man-made and natural disasters at a local or regional level.

Applicant Eligibility: Any student who is a member of a fire department or has significant responsibility for fire prevention and control and has been accepted into an eligible course at NFA may apply for stipend reimbursement. Federal or private industry employees or foreign students may be accepted into NFA courses but are not eligible for stipend reimbursement.

Beneficiary Eligibility: Student or sponsoring organization.

Award Range/Average: Refer to Program Guidance. Guidance can be found in the NETC Welcome Package (https://www.usfa. fema.gov/downloads/pdf/netc_welcome_package.pdf).

Funding: (Salaries and Expenses) FY 18 $1,775,000.00; FY 19 est $1,775,000.00; FY 20 est $1,737,000.00

HQ: 500 C Street SW, Washington, DC 20472

Phone: 800-238-3828

http://www.usfa.fema.gov

USDA10.328 | NATIONAL FOOD SAFETY TRAINING, EDUCATION, EXTENSION, OUTREACH, AND TECHNICAL ASSISTANCE COMPETITIVE GRANTS PROGRAM "FSMA"

Award: Project Grants

Purpose: The National Food Safety training promotes education, technical assistance, food safety methods, organic agriculture production, and other environmental practices for conservation. These programs to be promoted to all agencies that serve those eligible people.

Applicant Eligibility: The Cooperative Extension Service for a U.S. state or territory; A non-profit community-based or non-governmental Organization representing owners and operators of farms, small food processors, or small fruit and vegetable merchant wholesalers that has a commitment to public health and expertise in administering Programs that contribute to food safety; An institution of higher education (as defined in Section 101(a) of the Higher education Act of 1965 (20 U.S.C. 1001(a)) or a foundation maintained by an institution of higher education; Federal, State, Local, or Tribal Agencies, A collaboration of two or more eligible entities; or Such other appropriate entity, as determined by the Secretary of Agriculture.

Beneficiary Eligibility: Same as Applicant Eligibility.

Award Range/Average: If minimum or maximum amounts of funding per competitive and/or capacity project grant, or cooperative agreement are established, these amounts will be announced in the annual Competitive Request for Application (RFA).The most current RFA is available via: https://nifa.usda.gov/funding-opportunity/food-safety-outreach-program

Funding: (Project Grants (Discretionary)) FY 17 $4,760,653.00; FY 18 est $6,646,621.00; FY 19 est $0.00

HQ: 1400 Independence Avenue SW, PO Box 2225, Washington, DC 20024

Phone: 202-205-0250

http://nifa.usda.gov/program/food-safety

DOI15.438 | NATIONAL FOREST ACQUIRED LANDS

Award: Direct Payments for Specified Use

Purpose: Shares 25 percent of minerals leasing revenue with the State in which such National Forest is situated.

Applicant Eligibility: Revenue from acquired National Forest land leasing will trigger automatic payment distribution computed in accordance with the Law.

Beneficiary Eligibility: ONRR distributes these funds to State governments for leased lands within the state and the State government had sole discretion in their use in accordance with the enabling legislation.

Award Range/Average: Not Applicable.

Funding: (Direct Payments for Specified Use) FY 17 $6,165,000.00; FY 18 est $8,471,000.00; FY 19 est $9,144,000.00

HQ: Office of Natural Resources Revenue 1849 C Street NW, PO Box 4211, Washington, DC 20240

Phone: 202-513-0600

http://www.ONRR.gov

HHS93.528 | NATIONAL FORUM FOR STATE AND TERRITORIAL CHIEF EXECUTIVES
"National Forum"

Award: Cooperative Agreements

Purpose: To collaborate on the development and implementation of innovative strategies and best practices related to health workforce issues, health systems, and access to healthcare.

Applicant Eligibility: Eligible applicants include public and nonprofit entities. Faith-based and community-based Organizations, and Tribes and tribal Organizations as those terms are defined in 25 U.S.C. 450b, are eligible to apply. National bi-partisan Organizations representing governors and their staff of a broad cross-section of states, the Commonwealths of the Northern

Programs Administered by Federal Headquarters

Mariana Islands and Puerto Rico, the U.S. flag territories of American Samoa, Guam, and the U.S. Virgin Islands are eligible to apply.

Beneficiary Eligibility: See eligible beneficiaries listed above.

Award Range/Average: FY 17 Range: $649,800 - $649,800; Average award: $649,800.00 FY 18 Range: $600,000 - $600,000; Average award: $600,000.00 FY 19 Range: $600,000 - $600,000; Average award: $600,000.00

Funding: (Cooperative Agreements) FY 18 $600,000.00; FY 19 est $600,000.00; FY 20 est $600,000.00

HQ: 5600 Fishers Lane, Room 14W-02, Rockville, MD 20857

Phone: 301-443-0188 | Email: kfarrell@hrsa.gov

http://www.hrsa.gov

DOJ16.819 | NATIONAL FORUM ON YOUTH VIOLENCE PREVENTION
"The Forum"

Award: Project Grants

Purpose: To assist localities by participating in the Forum to address youth violence.

Applicant Eligibility: 1) 24-US Territories; 13-state; 15-local; 20-public nonprofits; 21-other public Institutions; 36 private nonprofits2)50-law, justice, legal services; 72-youth development3)Contact Program office for additional information.

Beneficiary Eligibility: 1)31-family/individual; 80-youth; 79-child, 15-local2)Contact program office for additional information.

Award Range/Average: capacity building awards: varied training and technical assistance award: varied

HQ: 810 7th Street NW, Washington, DC 20531

Phone: 202-514-3913 | Email: robin.delany-shabazz@ojp.usdoj.gov

http://ojjdp.gov

DOD12.401 | NATIONAL GUARD MILITARY OPERATIONS AND MAINTENANCE (O&M) PROJECTS

Award: Project Grants

Purpose: To provide funding for the States through cooperative agreements to support the operations and maintenance of Army National Guard (ARNG) and Air National Guard (ANG) facilities and provide authorized service support activities to National Guard units and personnel through assistance awards.

Applicant Eligibility: The 50 States, District of Columbia, Commonwealth of Puerto Rico, Virgin Islands, and Guam. The State National Guard unit must be federally recognized.

Beneficiary Eligibility: The 50 States, District of Columbia, Commonwealth of Puerto Rico, Virgin Islands, and Guam. The State National Guard must be federally recognized.

Award Range/Average: $100,000 and up.

Funding: (Salaries and Expenses) FY 13 $1,690,742,890.00; FY 14 est $1,979,661,782.00; FY 15 est $1,900,000,000.00

HQ: 1411 Jefferson Davis Highway, Suite 820, Arlington, VA 22202

Phone: 703-607-1002 | Email: maryellen.lewis@us.army.mil

http://www.ngb.army.mil

CDC93.488 | NATIONAL HARM REDUCTION TECHNICAL ASSISTANCE AND SYRINGE SERVICES PROGRAM (SSP) MONITORING AND EVALUATION FUNDING OPPORTUNITY

Award: Cooperative Agreements (discretionary Grants); Cooperative Agreements

Purpose: To strengthen harm reduction programs to prevent infectious disease occurring due to injection drug use, improve the health outcomes for drug injecting people and strengthen linkage to medication-assisted treatment by providing technical assistance, communications, monitoring, and evaluation.

Applicant Eligibility: N/A

Beneficiary Eligibility: N/A

Award Range/Average: Not Applicable.

HQ: 1600 Clifton Road, PO Box E-07, Atlanta, GA 30333

Phone: 404-639-1877 | Email: lrw3@cdc.gov

HHS93.990 | NATIONAL HEALTH PROMOTION
"APTR"

Award: Cooperative Agreements
Purpose: This program is no longer funded. The previous grant award ended on August 13, 2017.
Applicant Eligibility: This Program is no longer funded. The grant award ended on August 31, 2017.
Beneficiary Eligibility: Same as Applicant Eligibility.
Award Range/Average: Up to $200,000
Funding: (Cooperative Agreements) FY 16 $100,000.00; FY 17 est $100,000.00; FY 18 Estimate Not Available
HQ: 1101 Wootton Parkway, Suite 550, Rockville, MD 20852
   Phone: 240-453-8822 | Email: eric.west@hhs.gov
   http://www.healthypeople.gov

HHS93.162 | NATIONAL HEALTH SERVICE CORPS LOAN REPAYMENT
"NHSC Loan Repayment Program (LRP)"

Award: Direct Payments for Specified Use
Purpose: To increase the supply of primary care physicians, dentists, dental hygienists, behavioral and mental health professionals, certified nurse midwives, primary care nurse practitioners, physician assistants and, if needed by the NHSC, other health professionals in Health Professional Shortage Areas.
Applicant Eligibility: For specific Program and eligibility requirements, please see: http://nhsc.hrsa.gov/.
Beneficiary Eligibility: Primary care, oral health, mental and behavioural health and SUD professionals are eligible for the Loan Repayment Program(s). Specific specialties within these professions are selected for LRP awards based on community demand for health services.
Award Range/Average: Not Applicable.
Funding: (Direct Payments for Specified Use) FY 18 $149,888,000.00; FY 19 est $164,349,000.00; FY 20 est $167,000,000.00
HQ: 5600 Fishers Lane, Room 14N48, Rockville, MD 20857
   Phone: 301-594-4400
   http://nhsc.hrsa.gov

HHS93.288 | NATIONAL HEALTH SERVICE CORPS SCHOLARSHIP PROGRAM
"NHSC Scholarship Program (SP)"

Award: Direct Payments for Specified Use
Purpose: To increase the supply of primary care physicians, dentists, certified nurse midwives, primary care nurse practitioners, and physician assistants and, if needed by the National Health Service Corps, other health professionals in Health Professional Shortage Areas (HPSAs) within the United States by providing service-obligated scholarships to health professions students.
Applicant Eligibility: At the time of application, the applicant must be a U.S. citizen or national. The applicant must be enrolled and/or accepted for enrollment and in good academic standing in an accredited school in a State, the District of Columbia, or a U.S. Territory as a full-time student in a course of study leading to a health professional degree. The applicant must be eligible for Federal employment, be free of any Federal judgment liens, not be excluded, debarred, suspended or disqualified by a Federal agency, and have no conflicting service obligation. The applicant must submit an application and a signed contract to the National Health Service Corps agreeing to accept payment of scholarship and provide full-time primary health services in a Health Professional Shortage Area.
Beneficiary Eligibility: The participant must maintain full-time enrollment, with good academic standing in an accredited school in a State, the District of Columbia, or a U.S. Territory as a full-time student in a course of study leading to a health professional degree. The participant must maintain eligibility for Federal employment, be free of any Federal judgment liens, not be excluded, debarred, suspended or disqualified by a Federal agency, and have no conflicting service obligation.
Award Range/Average: No Current Data Available
Funding: (Direct Payments for Specified Use) FY 18 $47,126,164.00; FY 19 est $38,000,000.00; FY 20 est $38,000,000.00
HQ: 5600 Fishers Lane, Room 14N56, Rockville, MD 20857
   Phone: 301-594-4400
   http://nhsc.hrsa.gov

Programs Administered by Federal Headquarters

HHS93.547 | NATIONAL HEALTH SERVICE CORPS
"ACA National Health Service Corps - NHSC Loan Repayment Program (LRP), NHSC Scholarship Program (SP), The Students to Service (S2S) Loan Repayment Program, and State Loan Repayment Program (SLRP)"

Award: Project Grants; Direct Payments for Specified Use

Purpose: To assists Health Professional Shortage Areas (HPSAs) in every State, Territory, and Possession of the United States to meet their primary care medical, oral, and mental and behavioral health service needs by increasing the supply of clinicians.

Applicant Eligibility: For specific Program and eligibility requirements, please see: http://nhsc.hrsa.gov/.

Beneficiary Eligibility: Health professional U.S. citizen Education (13+).

Award Range/Average: Fiscal Year 2018: Since its inception in 1972, the National Health Service Corps (NHSC) has worked to support qualified healthcareproviders dedicated to working in underserved communities in urban, rural, and tribal areas. Across the nation, NHSC clinicians serve patients in Health Professional Shortage Areas (HPSAs) - communities with limited access to health care. As of September 30,2018, there were 6,815 primary care HPSAs,5,632 dental HPSAs, and 4,929 mental health HPSAs. The NHSC seeks clinicians who demonstrate a commitment to serve the Nation's medically underserved populations at NHSC-approved sites located in HPSAs. NHSC-approved sites provide care to individuals regardless of ability to pay; currently, there are over 16,400 NHSC-approved sites. Eligible sites include Federally Qualified Health Centers (FQHC) and FQHC Look-Alikes, American Indian and Native Alaska health clinics, rural health clinics, critical access hospitals and hospitals managed or owned by the Indian Health Service (IHS), school-based clinics, mobile units, free clinics, community mental health centers, state or local health departments, community outpatient facilities, federal facilities such as the Bureau of Prisons, U.S. Immigration and Customs Enforcement, IHS, and private practices. In particular, the NHSC has partnered closely with HRSA-supported FQHCs to help meet their staffing needs. Over 60 percent of NHSC clinicians serve in Health Centers around the nation, and 15 percent of clinical staff at FQHCs are NHSC clinicians. The NHSC also places clinicians in other community-based systems of care that serve underserved populations, targeting HPSAs of greatest need. As of September 30,2018, there are 10,939 primary care medical, dental, and mental and behavioral health practitioners providing service nationwide in the following programs.Account Identification

Funding: (Direct Payments for Specified Use) FY 18 $169,888,000.00; FY 19 est $184,349,000.00; FY 20 est $187,000,000.00

HQ: 5600 Fishers Lane, Room 14N56, Rockville, MD 20857

Phone: 301-594-4400

http://nhsc.hrsa.gov

NARA89.003 | NATIONAL HISTORICAL PUBLICATIONS AND RECORDS GRANTS

Award: Project Grants

Purpose: Undertakes a wide-range of activities related to the preservation, publication, and use of documentary sources relating to the history of the United States.

Applicant Eligibility: State and local Governments, U.S. territorial agencies, federally and State recognized Indian Tribes (see 44 U.S.C. 2504), and educational and other nonprofit Institutions (e.g., universities, colleges, libraries, historical societies, museums, University presses, archives, etc.).

Beneficiary Eligibility: State and local governments, U.S. territorial agencies, federally and State recognized Indian tribes, and educational and other nonprofit institutions.

Funding: (Project Grants) FY 16 $4,582,000.00; FY 17 est $5,456,000.00; FY 18 est $5,400,000.00

HQ: 8601 Adelphi Road, College Park, MD 20740

Phone: 301-837-1910 | Email: benjamin.davis@nara.gov

http://www.archives.gov/nhprc

HHS93.328 | NATIONAL IMPLEMENTATION AND DISSEMINATION FOR CHRONIC DISEASE PREVENTION
"National Organizations"

Award: Cooperative Agreements

Purpose: To support national organizations and their chapters/affiliates (sub-recipients) coalitions in implementing Socio-Ecological Model informed multi-level approaches to improve communities' health.

Applicant Eligibility: 1. Eligible Applicants: This cooperative agreement is limited to national Organizations (to include public and private nonprofit Organizations) that serve communities across the nation. Category A and B Organizations must demonstrate evidence of having members, affiliates and/or chapters within twenty-five (25) or more U.S. states and territories). Category A applicants must also demonstrate a minimum of five (5) years of experience and evidence with implementing community level improvements. For Category B, eligible Organizations must demonstrate a minimum of five (5) years of experience in providing training and technical assistance that built communities capacity to implement local-level efforts. Category B applicants must also demonstrate experience in collaborating across multiple partners to deliver training and technical assistance. Category A and B applicants must also provide supporting evidence (e.g., media reports, news/magazine articles, op-eds, community newsletters) as evidence of possessing the following desired characteristics: Have historical credibility and influence in their targeted communities (i.e., has developed and participated in community coalitions, events, and other activities Possess the demonstrated ability to influence a national dialogue. (i.e., the Organization has the ability to garner the attention and participation of other national Organizations and audiences). Have a demonstrated variety of existing communication platforms (e.g., Websites, magazines, newsletters, etc.) Have the demonstrated ability to leverage additional resources and partnerships (e.g., used non-FOA relationships and resources to maximize the impact of Organizational activities) Have the demonstrated ability to convene a national meeting In accordance with U.S. law, no Federal funds provided by CDC are permitted to be used by community grantees for lobbying or to influence, directly or indirectly, specific pieces of pending or proposed legislation at the federal, state, or local levels. The awardee should work with project officer to ensure activities adhere to federal guidelines, and federal dollars are not used to engage in unauthorized activities. Throughout all objectives and activities, the awardee should clarify that the work plan language clearly describes the role, nature, and purpose of the funded activities. This includes providing clear language focusing on the message (e.g., addressing the health risks/effects, using evidence based strategies for increasing protections) when conducting public educational initiatives. In addition, language should be included for proper engagement of elected officials as documented in the federal guidelines. Additionally, awardees should consult appropriate legal counsel to ensure compliance with all rules, regulations, and restriction of any funding sources. Title 2 of the United States Code Section 1611 states that an Organization described in Section 501(C)(4) of the Internal Revenue Code that engages in lobbying activities is no eligible to receive Federal funds constituting a grant, loan, or award. The awardee should refer to the AR-12 and CDC Guidance documents on Anti-Lobbying restrictions for more information on allowable and restricted activities. http://www.cdc.gov/od/pgo/funding/grants/additional_req.shtm#ar12 http://www.cdc.gov/obesity/downloads/Anti-Lobbying-Restrictions-for-CDC-Grantees-July2012-508.pdf.

Beneficiary Eligibility: Any U.S. state, political subdivision and U.S. territories (as described above), and other public entities will benefit.

Award Range/Average: Category A = $2,000,000 - $3,000,000 and Category B = $200,000 - $500,000

Funding: (Cooperative Agreements) FY 18 $2,653,000.00; FY 19 est $2,653,000.00; FY 20 est $0.00

HQ: 4770 Buford Highway NE, PO Box F81, Atlanta, GA 30341

Phone: 770-488-8438

http://www.cdc.gov

DHS97.107 | NATIONAL INCIDENT MANAGEMENT SYSTEM (NIMS)

Award: Project Grants

Purpose: It helps NIMS to develop a consistent system on national preparedness against terrorist threats.

Applicant Eligibility: Specific information on applicant eligibility is identified in the funding opportunity announcement and Program guidance.

Beneficiary Eligibility: State, local, Public Nonprofit Institution/Organization, Federal Recognized Indian Tribal Government, U.S. Territory/Possession, Private Organization, Other Public Institution/Organization.

Award Range/Average: Refer to program guidance

Funding: (Cooperative Agreements) FY 18 $2,000,000.00; FY 19 est $2,000,000.00; FY 20 est $2,000,000.00

HQ: 400 C Street SW, 7NW-1405, Washington, DC 20742-3620

Phone: 202-384-5008

http://www.fema.gov/national-incident-management-system

DOT20.933 | NATIONAL INFRASTRUCTURE INVESTMENTS
"TIGER Discretionary Grants"

Award: Project Grants

Purpose: Offers grants for capital investments in surface transportation infrastructure grants to be awarded to a State, local, or Tribal governments.

Programs Administered by Federal Headquarters

Applicant Eligibility: State, local, and tribal Governments, including U.S. territories, transit agencies, port authorities, metropolitan planning Organizations (MPOs), other political subdivisions of State or local Governments, and multi-State or multi-jurisdictional groups applying through a single lead applicant (for multi-jurisdictional groups, each member of the group, including the lead applicant, must be an otherwise eligible applicant as defined in this paragraph.

Beneficiary Eligibility: The ultimate benefits of this program may be received by, among others, States or local governments, transit agencies, major metropolises, and other urban, suburban, or rural areas.

Award Range/Average: FY 2020 (President's Budget Request): $1 billion FY 2018 (enacted): $1.5 billion FY 2017 (enacted): $500 million FY 2016 (enacted): $500 million In FY2019, individual BUILD Transportation grants are between $5,000,000 and $25,000,000 for projects located in an urbanized area and between $1,000,000 and $25,000,000 for projects located in a rural area

Funding: (Project Grants (Discretionary)) FY 18 $1,500,000,000.00; FY 19 est $900,000,000.00; FY 20 est Estimate Not Available

HQ: 1200 New Jersey Avenue SE, Washington, DC 20590
Phone: 202-366-0301 | Email: howard.hill@dot.gov
http://www.dot.gov/tiger

DOJ16.560 | NATIONAL INSTITUTE OF JUSTICE RESEARCH, EVALUATION, AND DEVELOPMENT PROJECT GRANTS

Award: Project Grants; Dissemination of Technical Information

Purpose: To encourage and support research, development, and evaluation to further understanding of the causes and correlates of crime and violence; methods of crime prevention and control; and criminal justice system responses to crime and violence and contribute to the improvement of the criminal justice system.

Applicant Eligibility: The National Institute of Justice (NIJ) is authorized to make grants to, or enter into contracts or cooperative agreements with States, units of local government, for-profit Organizations, nonprofit Organizations, Institutions of higher education, and qualified individuals. Applicants from the Territories of the United States, and federally recognized Indian tribal Governments that perform law enforcement functions, are also eligible to participate in this Program. Certain qualified individuals may be eligible to apply in response to some solicitations under this Program, as described in the solicitation document. Federal agencies may be eligible to apply for funding in response to a solicitation under this Program, if the solicitation specifies that Federal agencies are eligible. If an award is made to a Federal agency, it will be through an Interagency Agreement (IAA) with the National Institute of Justice, Office of Justice Programs, Department of Justice.

Beneficiary Eligibility: State and local governments; private nonprofit organizations, public nonprofit organizations, profit organizations, nonprofit organizations, institutions of higher education, and qualified individuals.

Award Range/Average: See the current fiscal year's solicitation guidelines posted on the Office of Justice Programs web site at https://ojp.gov/funding/Explore/CurrentFundingOpportunities.htm.

Funding: (Project Grants) FY 17 $33,162,241.00; FY 18 est $42,000,000.00; FY 19 est $36,000,000.00

HQ: 810 7th Street NW, Washington, DC 20531
Phone: 202-307-2942 | Email: george.tillery@ojp.usdoj.gov
http://nij.gov

DOJ16.566 | NATIONAL INSTITUTE OF JUSTICE W.E.B. DUBOIS FELLOWSHIP PROGRAM
"W.E.B. Du Bois Program of Research on Race and Crime"

Award: Project Grants

Purpose: To advance the field of knowledge regarding the confluence of crime, justice, and culture in various societal contexts. The secondary objective is to provide early career researchers an opportunity to elevate independently generated research and ideas to the level of national discussion.

Applicant Eligibility: Fellowship grants are awarded to individuals or to their parent agencies or Organizations. IPA appointments also may be negotiated with Fellows' parent agencies. Generally, researchers and academicians working in the criminal justice field, including University or college-based academic researchers and upper-level managers in criminal justice agencies are eligible.

Beneficiary Eligibility: Generally, researchers and academicians with research experience in criminal-justice or criminal-justice relevant fields are eligible for grants; those working for law enforcement related branches of State or local government units are eligible for grants or IPA appointments. Each prospective candidate must possess a terminal degree in their respective field.

Government Support Index Handbook 2020

HQ: 810 7th Street NW, Washington, DC 20531
    Phone: 202-307-2942 | Email: christine.crossland@ojp.usdoj.gov
    http://nij.gov/funding/fellowships/dubois-fellowship/Pages/welcome.aspx

HHS93.308 | NATIONAL INSTITUTE ON MINORITY HEALTH AND HEALTH DISPARITIES (NIMHD) EXTRAMURAL LOAN REPAYMENT PROGRAMS
"NIMHD Loan Repayment Programs"

Award: Direct Payments for Specified Use
Purpose: To lead scientific research to improve minority health and eliminate health disparities.
Applicant Eligibility: The following eligibility requirements apply to both: (1) Extramural Loan Repayment Program for Health Disparities Research (LRP-HDR): and (2) Extramural Clinical Research Loan Repayment Program for Individuals from Disadvantaged Backgrounds (LRP-IDB)An applicant must: (1) be a United States citizen, national, or permanent resident; (2) have an M.D., Ph.D., Pharm.D., D.D. S., D.M.D., D.C., N.D., or equivalent doctoral degree from an accredited institution; (3) conduct research that is supported by a non-profit institution, foundation, professional society or U.S. government entity; (4) commit 50 percent or more of his/her time to clinical research; (5) have total qualifying educational debt greater than or equal to 20 percent of his/her institutional base salary at the time of award; (6) conduct research in accordance with applicable Federal, state and local law; (7) not be under any existing service obligations to Federal, State, or other entities, unless and until the existing service obligation is discharged or deferred during the period of Program service; (8) not have Federal judgment liens against their property arising from a Federal debt from receiving Federal funds until all judgments have been paid in full or otherwise satisfied; (9) not be a full time employee of a Federal government agency. Part-time Federal employees who engage in qualifying research as part of their non-Federal duties are eligible to apply for loan repayment if they meet all other eligibility requirements; and (10) have the institution provide an assurance that the applicant will be provided research support for two years, that the applicant will engage in qualified clinical research for 50 percent of his/her time, that the funding foundation, professional society, or institution is considered to be non-profit pursuant to Section 501 of the Internal Revenue Code or is a U.S. government entity, and certify the applicant's annual institutional base salary. There are additional requirements for the Extramural Clinical Research Loan Repayment Program for Individuals from Disadvantaged Backgrounds (LRP-IDB). Eligible applicants must come from a disadvantaged background and adhere to the following guidelines relating to the definition of a disadvantaged background: An Individual from disadvantaged background means an individual who: (1) Comes from an environment that inhibited the individual from obtaining the knowledge, skill and ability required to enroll in and graduate from a health professions school; or(2) Comes from a family with an annual income below a level based on low-income thresholds according to family size published by the U.S. Bureau of the Census adjusted annually for changes in the Consumer Price Index, and adjusted by the Secretary for use in all health professions Programs. The Secretary periodically publishes these income levels in the Federal Register.
Beneficiary Eligibility: (1) Extramural Loan Repayment Program for Health Disparities Research (LRP-HDR), and (2) Extramural Clinical Research Loan Repayment Program for Individuals from Disadvantaged Backgrounds (LRP-IDB) contracts: Qualified health professionals who conduct minority health or other health disparities research or highly qualified health professionals from disadvantaged backgrounds who will conduct clinical research and who possess substantial unpaid educational debt relative to income.
Funding: (Direct Payments for Specified Use) FY 17 $6,579,794.00; FY 18 est Estimate Not Available; FY 19 est Estimate Not Available
HQ: 7301 Wisconsin Avenue, Suite 533, Bethesda, MD 20892
    Phone: 301-594-1788 | Email: joan.wasserman@nih.gov
    http://www.nimhd.nih.gov

HHS93.936 | NATIONAL INSTITUTES OF HEALTH ACQUIRED IMMUNODEFICIENCY SYNDROME RESEARCH LOAN REPAYMENT PROGRAM
"NIH AIDS Research Loan Repayment Program; AIDS LRP"

Award: Direct Payments for Specified Use
Purpose: To recruit trained researcher volunteers (physicians, registered nurses and scientists) with respect to AIDS at the National Institutes of Health (NIH) and helping them with repayment of their educational loans.
Applicant Eligibility: Eligible applicants must: (1) Be a citizen, national, or permanent resident of the United States; (2) possess a M.D., Ph.D., D.O., D.D.S., D.M.D., D.V.M., D.P.M., A.D.N., B.S.N., or equivalent degree, or hold the position of

Programs Administered by Federal Headquarters

Physician Assistant; 3) have educational debt, which results from governmental or commercial loans obtained to support their undergraduate and/or graduate education in excess of 20 percent of their annual NIH salary (exclusive of special allowances of any kind) on the Program eligibility date; 4) be appointed under any temporary or permanent employment mechanism in the Intramural Research Program of the NIH, so long as their employment has the potential to last a minimum of 2 years; 5) not have an existing service obligation to Federal, State, or other entities, unless deferred during period of Program service; 6) submit an application to participate in the Loan Repayment Program; and 7) submit to the Secretary for Health and Human Services, at the time of application, a signed contract agreeing to engage in AIDS research at the NIH for a minimum of 2 years.

Beneficiary Eligibility: AIDS researchers who have unpaid educational loans will benefit from this program.

Funding: (Project Grants) FY 18 $148,020.00; FY 19 est $130,974.00; FY 20 est $233,524.00

HQ: U.S. Department of Health and Human Services 2 Center Drive, Room 2E18 Building 2, Bethesda, MD 20892
  Phone: 301-402-1283 | Email: colep@mail.nih.gov
  http://www.lrp.nih.gov

HHS93.280 | NATIONAL INSTITUTES OF HEALTH LOAN REPAYMENT PROGRAM FOR CLINICAL RESEARCHERS
"NIH Clinical Research Loan Repayment Program; LRP-CR"

Award: Direct Payments for Specified Use

Purpose: To attract and retain health professionals to clinical research careers by offering educational loan repayment.

Applicant Eligibility: (1) A U.S. citizen, U.S. national, or permanent resident of the United States; (2) Have a Ph.D., M.D., D.O., D.D.S., D. M.D., D.P.M., Pharm.D., D.C., N.D., O.D. or equivalent doctoral degree from an accredited institution; (3) Have total qualifying educational loan debt equal to or in excess of 20 percent of their institutional base salary on the date of Program eligibility (the effective date that a loan repayment contract has been executed by the Secretary of Health and Human Services or designee); (4) Conduct qualifying research supported by a domestic nonprofit foundation, nonprofit professional association, or other nonprofit institution, or a U.S. or other government agency (State or local); (5) Engage in qualified clinical research. Clinical research is patient-oriented clinical research conducted with human subjects, or research on the causes and consequences of disease in human populations involving material of human origin (such as tissue specimens and cognitive phenomena) for which an investigator or colleague directly interacts with human subjects in an outpatient or inpatient setting to clarify a problem in human physiology, pathophysiology or disease, or epidemiologic or behavioral studies, outcomes research or health services research, or developing new technologies, therapeutic interventions, or clinical trials; (6) Engage in qualified clinical research for at least 50 percent of their time, i.e., not less than 20 hours per week based on a 40 hour week; (7) Agree to conduct research for which funding is not prohibited by Federal law, regulation, or HHS/NIH policy, and in accordance with applicable Federal, State and local law (e.g., applicable human subject protection regulations); and (8) Sign and submit to the Secretary of Health and Human Services, at the time of application submission, a contract agreeing to engage in clinical research in a qualifying institution for a minimum of 2 years. Full-time employees of Federal Government agencies are ineligible to apply for LRP benefits. Part-time Federal employees who engage in qualifying research as part of their nonfederal duties for at least 20 hours per week based on a 40 hour week, and who are not compensated as a Federal employee for their research, are eligible to apply for loan repayment if they meet all other eligibility requirements.

Beneficiary Eligibility: Health professionals who are interested in pursuing clinical research careers and who have unpaid educational loans will benefit from this program.

Award Range/Average: For initial two-year contract periods, loan repayment of 50 percent of education debt up to $70,000. For renewal contracts, loan repayment of 50 percent of education debt per year up to $35,000 per year.

Funding: (Direct Payments for Specified Use) FY 18 $48,533,088.00; FY 19 est $48,000,000.00; FY 20 est $48,000,000.00

HQ: 6700B Rockledge Drive, Suite 2300, Bethesda, MD 20817
  Phone: 240-380-3062 | Email: matthew.lockhart@nih.gov
  http://www.lrp.nih.gov

HHS93.285 | NATIONAL INSTITUTES OF HEALTH PEDIATRIC RESEARCH LOAN REPAYMENT PROGRAM
"NIH Pediatric Research Loan Repayment Program; LRP-PR"

Award: Direct Payments for Specified Use

Purpose: To attract and retain health professionals to pediatric research careers by offering educational loan repayment for participants.

Applicant Eligibility: Eligible applicants must: (1) be a U.S. citizen, U.S. national, or permanent resident of the United States; (2) have a Ph.D., M.D., D.O., D.D.S., D.M.D., D.P.M., Pharm.D., D.C., N.D., O.D. or equivalent doctoral degree from an accredited institution; (3) have total qualifying educational loan debt equal to or in excess of 20 percent of their institutional base salary on the date of Program eligibility (the effective date that a loan repayment contract has been executed by the Secretary of Health and Human Services or designee); (4) conduct qualifying research supported by a domestic nonprofit foundation, nonprofit professional association, or other nonprofit institution, or a U.S. or other government agency (Federal, State, or local); (5) engage in qualified pediatric research (pediatric research is research that is directly related to diseases, disorders, and other conditions in children); (6) engage in qualified pediatric research for at least 50 percent of their time, i.e., not less than 20 hours per week based on a 40 hour week; (7) agree to conduct research for which funding is not prohibited by Federal law, regulation, or HHS/NIH policy, and in accordance with applicable Federal, State and local law (e.g., applicable human subject protection regulations); and (8) sign and submit to the Secretary of Health and Human Services, at the time of application submission, a contract agreeing to engage in pediatric research in a qualifying institution for a minimum of 2 years. Full-time employees of Federal Government agencies are ineligible to apply for LRP benefits. Part-time Federal employees who engage in qualifying research as part of their non-Federal duties for at least 20 hours per week based on a 40 hour week, and who are not compensated as Federal employees for their research, are eligible to apply for loan repayment if they meet all other eligibility requirements.

Beneficiary Eligibility: Health professionals who are interested in pursuing pediatric research careers who have unpaid educational loans will benefit from this program.

Award Range/Average: For initial 2-year contract periods, loan repayment of 50 percent of education debt up to $100,000 plus tax payments. For renewal contracts, loan repayment of 50 percent of education debt per year up to $50,000 per year.

Funding: (Direct Payments for Specified Use) FY 18 $16,948,661.00; FY 19 est $17,000,000.00; FY 20 est $17,000,000.00

HQ: 6700B Rockledge Drive, Suite 2300, Bethesda, MD 20817

Phone: 240-380-3062 | Email: matthew.lockhart@nih.gov

http://www.lrp.nih.gov

IMLS45.312 | NATIONAL LEADERSHIP GRANTS

Award: Project Grants; Direct Payments for Specified Use

Purpose: To support projects that address current and future needs of the museum and library fields and that have the potential to advance practice in the profession so that museums and libraries can improve services for the American public.

Applicant Eligibility: Applicants that fulfill the general criteria for libraries may apply for National Leadership Grants for Libraries. Applicants that fulfill the general criteria for museums may apply for National Leadership Grants for Museums. For more information about eligibility requirements, visit http://www.imls.gov/applicants/eligibility_criteria.aspx. See Program guidelines for special conditions of eligibility for this Program.

Beneficiary Eligibility: Libraries, archives, and museums. Through activities and projects funded, beneficiaries include the general public.

Award Range/Average: NLG for Libraries: Between $10,000 and $2,000,000; NLG for Museums: Between $50,000 and $500,000; Sparks! Ignition Grants for Libraries and Museums: Between $10,000 and $25,000.

Funding: (Project Grants) FY 15 $19,800,000.00; FY 16 est $28,668,000.00; FY 17 est $22,840,000.00

HQ: 955 L'Enfant Plaza North SW, Suite 4000, Washington, DC 20024

Phone: 202-653-4779 | Email: hwechsler@imls.gov

http://www.imls.gov

Programs Administered by Federal Headquarters

DHS97.130 | NATIONAL NUCLEAR FORENSICS EXPERTISE DEVELOPMENT PROGRAM
"NNFEDP"

Award: Cooperative Agreements; Project Grants
Purpose: The program provides a strong foundation to develop the nuclear forensics workforce and a strong resilience against nuclear terrorism by anticipating threats and protecting the country's Chemical, Biological, Radiological and Nuclear materials from enemy access.
Applicant Eligibility: Refer to the Program guidance.
Beneficiary Eligibility: Same as Applicant Eligibility.
Award Range/Average: Refer to the funding opportunity announcements.
Funding: (Project Grants) FY 18 $500,000.00; FY 19 est $630,000.00; FY 20 est $700,000.00
HQ: 245 Murray Lane SW, Washington, DC 20528-0550
Phone: 202-254-7437 | Email: sandra.gogol@hq.dhs.gov
http://www.dhs.gov

DOC11.480 | NATIONAL OCEAN SERVICE INTERN PROGRAM
"NOS Intern Program"

Award: Project Grants
Purpose: To support unique opportunities for research and development by increasing skilled engineers, scientists, and managers who are familiar with the techniques and technologies used by the National Ocean Service.
Applicant Eligibility: Primary awards will be available to nonprofit Organizations. Internships are restricted to recent college graduates and have a maximum cumulative duration of 24 months for any individual.
Beneficiary Eligibility: Benefits to the Nation are increased opportunities for recent college graduates to increase public awareness and gain exposure to government programs that affect the Nation's coastal areas and resources. This program will also promote interest in civil service as a career. Benefits also include a transfer of the techniques, technologies, and methods used by NOS to the next generation of engineers, scientists, and managers in the environmental arena. Interns who are selected by the program will receive increased training and skill enhancement as identified by the particular Internship opportunity in which they participate.
Award Range/Average: 0 to 75000
Funding: (Salaries and Expenses) FY 16 $0.00; FY 18 est $75,000.00; FY 17 est $75,000.00
HQ: 1305 E W Highway, SSMC 4 Room 13267, Silver Spring, MD 20910
Phone: 240-533-0955 | Email: kadija.baffoeharding@noaa.gov
http://www.grants.gov

DOC11.432 | NATIONAL OCEANIC AND ATMOSPHERIC ADMINISTRATION (NOAA) COOPERATIVE INSTITUTES

Award: Cooperative Agreements
Purpose: To maximize the effectiveness of research and develop innovative approaches to education in the environmental sciences.
Applicant Eligibility: Single or multiple non-federal public and private non-profit universities, colleges and research Institutions that collectively offer accredited graduate level degree-granting Programs in NOAA related sciences.
Beneficiary Eligibility: Organizations with interests in support of the NOAA mission to understand and predict changes in Earth's environment and conserve and manage coastal and marine resources to meet the nations' economic, social, and environmental needs.
Award Range/Average: Total annual funding at current Cooperative Institutes ranges from $1,300,000 to $30,000,000. Average funding is $10,000,000
Funding: (Project Grants) FY 16 est $223,530,030.00; FY 17 est $234,706,532.00; FY 18 est $246,441,858.00
HQ: 1842 Wasp Boulevard, Building 176, Honolulu, HI 96818
Phone: 808-725-5355 | Email: candice.jongsma@noaa.gov
http://www.ci.noaa.gov

HHS93.809 | NATIONAL ORGANIZATIONS FOR CHRONIC DISEASE PREVENTION AND HEALTH PROMOTION

Award: Cooperative Agreements

Purpose: Develops effective state chronic disease prevention and health promotion programs through cross-cutting activities supportive of all chronic disease programs, focusing on Training and Technical Assistance, Performance Monitoring and Evaluation, Innovation and Leadership and Development.

Applicant Eligibility: Eligible applicants that can apply for this funding opportunity are national Organizations whose primary focus is on health education, chronic disease prevention and health promotion, and related public health training and who are of the type listed below: National Organizations that work specifically with state and territorial health departments and that have Organizational units focusing on state-based public health issues and reducing chronic diseases and their associated risk factors, are uniquely qualified to successfully implement the activities of this FOA because they have the knowledge, experience, and skills in working on reducing the burden of chronic diseases and on implementing policy, systems, and environmental changes that address chronic disease risk factors in states and community settings that no other national Organization entities have. Focusing on these types of national Organizations provides CDC the greatest potential to successfully implement the activities of this FOA. National Organizations with health departments as their members are uniquely qualified to respond to the burden of chronic diseases in their communities through their vast experience of continuous implementation of evidence - and practice-based interventions, implementation of self-management educational activities, and having the local, state, and territorial public health infrastructure in place to provide the proper foundation and support for Programs that focus on reducing the chronic disease burden across the nation.

Beneficiary Eligibility: This cooperative agreement will support the development of effective state chronic disease prevention and health promotion programs through cross-cutting activities supportive of all chronic disease programs. This FOA will serve to improve the effectiveness of chronic disease prevention and health promotion programs by focusing on cross-cutting activities that are supportive of all Chronic Disease Programs; better identify major components/priority areas based on the needs of the NCCDPHP that will serve as the core functions; increase the effectiveness of CDC's work with state chronic disease programs, so that work with state programs is more effective; and to experience the collective benefit of having strong state chronic disease programs by allowing for better coordination of efforts and greater utilization of resources, increase efficiency and minimize duplication of efforts.

Funding: (Cooperative Agreements) FY 18 $3,000,000.00; FY 19 est $3,000,000.00; FY 20 est $3,000,000.00

HQ: 4770 Buford Highway NE, PO Box F78, Atlanta, GA 30341

Phone: 770-488-5659 | Email: tnb9@cdc.gov

http://www.cdc.gov

HHS93.011 | NATIONAL ORGANIZATIONS OF STATE AND LOCAL OFFICIALS "NOSLO"

Award: Cooperative Agreements

Purpose: To support technical assistance, promotion of best practices and innovative solutions to emerging and ongoing national health priorities such as communicable disease prevention and suppression, childhood obesity, substance use disorders and/or mental health.

Applicant Eligibility: Eligible applicants include nonprofit service and/or membership Organizations that can provide training and technical assistance on a national level to strengthen the infrastructure capacities of states and local government entities. Applicants must be national in scope with a broad reach, and have established long-term relationships with at least one of the following groups: state and local health departments; state government entities such as state PCOs, SRHAs, and SORHs; state Medicaid Offices; state policymakers; state legislatures; and local county and city government entities.

Beneficiary Eligibility: Eligible beneficiaries include the following entities: Federal; Interstate; Intrastate; State; Local; Public nonprofit institution/organization; Other public institution/organization; Non-Governmental -General; Minority group; Specialized group (e.g., health professionals, students, veterans); Small business (less than 500 employees); Private nonprofit institution/organization; Quasi-public nonprofit institution/organization; Anyone/general public; Native American Organizations; Health professional; Black; American Indian; Spanish origin; Asian; Other non-white; Migrant; U.S. citizen; Refugee/Alien; Veteran/Service; Person/Reservist (including dependents); Women; Disabled (i.e., Deaf, Blind, Physically Disabled).

Award Range/Average: FY 17 Range: $765,976 - $874,902; Average award: $826,419.00 FY 18 Range: $723,750 - $817,066; Average award: $762,391.50 FY 19 Range: $874,449 - $875,000; Average award: $874,862.25

Funding: (Cooperative Agreements) FY 18 $3,049,566.00; FY 19 est $3,500,000.00; FY 20 est $$3,500,000.00

Programs Administered by Federal Headquarters

HQ: 5600 Fishers Lane Parklawn, Room 14W06, Rockville, MD 20857
Phone: 301-443-0188 | Email: kfarrell@hrsa.gov

HHS93.422 | NATIONAL PARTNERSHIPS TO PROMOTE CANCER SURVEILLANCE STANDARDS AND SUPPORT DATA QUALITY AND OPERATIONS OF NATIONAL PROGRAM OF CANCER REGISTRIES
"NPCR National Partnerships"

Award: Cooperative Agreements
Purpose: To enhance the data quality and operational efficiency of CDC's National Program of Cancer Registries (NCPR).
Applicant Eligibility: State Governments County Governments City or township Governments Special district Governments Independent school Districts Public and State controlled Institutions of higher education Native American tribal Governments (Federally recognized)Public housing authorities/Indian housing Authorities Native American tribal Organizations (other than Federally recognized tribal Governments)Nonprofits having a 501(c)(3) status with the IRS, other than Institutions of higher education Nonprofits without 501(c)(3) status with the IRS, other than Institutions of higher education Private Institutions of higher education For profit Organizations other than small businesses Small businesses Unrestricted (i.e., open to any type of entity above), subject to any clarification in text field entitled "Additional Information on Eligibility".
Beneficiary Eligibility: Benefits the general public.
Funding: (Cooperative Agreements) FY 18 $1,045,000.00; FY 19 est $1,045,000.00; FY 20 est $1,045,000.00
HQ: 4770 Buford Highway NE, PO Box F76, Atlanta, GA 30341
Phone: 770-488-8430
http://www.cdc.gov

DOI15.439 | NATIONAL PETROLEUM RESERVE-ALASKA

Award: Direct Payments for Specified Use
Purpose: Shares 50 percent of NPR-A oil and gas mineral leasing revenue with the State of Alaska.
Applicant Eligibility: Revenue from public land leasing will trigger automatic payment distribution computed in accordance with the Law.
Beneficiary Eligibility: Lease lands must be located in the National Petroleum Reserve-Alaska.
Award Range/Average: Not Applicable.
Funding: (Direct Payments for Specified Use) FY 17 $1,667,000.00; FY 18 est $21,191,000.00; FY 19 est $23,548,000.00
HQ: 1849 C Street NW, PO Box 4211, Washington, DC 20240
Phone: 202-513-0600
http://www.ONRR.gov

DOJ16.739 | NATIONAL PRISON RAPE STATISTICS PROGRAM
"PREA"

Award: Cooperative Agreements
Purpose: To collect and examine data on the incidence of sexual assault among individuals held in Federal and State prisons, local jails, and juvenile facilities as well as former inmates.
Applicant Eligibility: The Bureau of Justice Statistics is authorized to award grants and cooperative agreements to State and local Governments, private nonprofit Organizations, public nonprofit Organizations, profit Organizations, Institutions of higher education, and qualified individuals.
Beneficiary Eligibility: Eligible beneficiaries are State and local governments, private nonprofit organizations, public nonprofit organizations, profit organizations, institutions of higher education, and qualified individuals.
Award Range/Average: $1,000,000 to $10,000,000
HQ: 810 7th Street NW, Washington, DC 20531
Phone: 202-598-7610 | Email: jessica.stroop@usdoj.gov
http://bjs.gov

HHS93.292 | NATIONAL PUBLIC HEALTH IMPROVEMENT INITIATIVE
"National Public Health Improvement Initiative (NPHII) - Capacity Building Assistance to Strengthen Public Health Infrastructure and Performance; CDC-RFA-CD10-1011"

Award: Formula Grants

Purpose: To provide support for accelerating public health accreditation readiness activities; to provide additional support for performance management and improvement practices; and, for the development, identification and dissemination of evidence-based policies and practices.

Applicant Eligibility: This award will be a continuation of funds intended only for grantees previously awarded under CDC-RFA-CD10-101101PPHF12.

Beneficiary Eligibility: State health departments, large local health departments supporting cities with populations of 1 million or more inhabitants, the District of Columbia, U.S. Territories, tribal health organizations and the general public.

Award Range/Average: Component I: This amount is based on population and will continue for each year of the cooperative agreement:Below 1.5 million = $100,0001.5 million - 5 million = $200,0005 million - 8 million = $300,000 Above 8 million = $400,000 Component II: $1 million - $2.95 million

HQ: 4770 Buford Highway NE, PO Box E70, Atlanta, GA 30341
Phone: 404-498-6792 | Email: ayw3@cdc.gov

HHS93.186 | NATIONAL RESEARCH SERVICE AWARD IN PRIMARY CARE MEDICINE
"Ruth L. Kirschstein National Research Service Award Institutional Research Training Grant NRSA"

Award: Project Grants

Purpose: To prepare qualified individuals for careers that will have significant impact on the nation's primary care research agenda and ensure that a diverse and highly trained workforce is available to assume leadership roles in the area of primary healthcareresearch.

Applicant Eligibility: Eligible applicants are those entities that have received a grant under Title VII, sections 736, 739, or 747 of the Public Health Service (PHS) Act designed to prepare the primary healthcare workforce. Federally Recognized Indian Tribal Government and Native American Organizations may apply if they are otherwise eligible.

Beneficiary Eligibility: Individuals and public or private nonprofit organizations or institutions, including state or local governments and U.S. Territories. Participants must be U.S. Citizens, non-citizen nationals, or foreign nationals who possess visas permitting permanent residence in the United States. Individuals on temporary or student visas are not eligible. Postdoctoral trainees must have received, as of the beginning date of the NRSA appointment, a Ph.D., M.D., D.O., D.D.S., D.M.D., or comparable doctoral degree from an accredited domestic or foreign institution.

Award Range/Average: The range of awards in FY 2018 is $159,362 to $400,000. The average award is $365,889. The range of awards in FY 2019 is $170,319 to $403,678. The average award is $403,678. The estimated range of awards in FY 2020 is $175,000 to $405,000. The estimated average award is $400,000

Funding: (Project Grants) FY 18 $7,485,782.00; FY 19 est $8,073,567.00; FY 20 est $7,900,000.00

HQ: 5600 Fishers Lane, Room 15N130D, Rockville, MD 20857
Phone: 301-443-7271 | Email: scicale@hrsa.gov
http://www.hrsa.gov

HHS93.225 | NATIONAL RESEARCH SERVICE AWARDS HEALTH SERVICES RESEARCH TRAINING
Award: Training

Purpose: To provide predoctoral and postdoctoral training opportunities in health services research. Individual fellowships will be awarded directly to applicants for postdoctoral research training.

Applicant Eligibility: Domestic public or private nonprofit Organizations or Institutions may apply for training grants. The applicant Institutions must have or expand training Programs designed to develop competent investigators in the methods and techniques of conducting health services research. Profit-making Organizations are not eligible. Individual applicants

Programs Administered by Federal Headquarters

for postdoctoral fellowships must have received a clinical or research doctoral degree. All persons supported as fellows or trainees must be citizens or noncitizen nationals of the United States, or have been lawfully admitted for permanent residence.
Beneficiary Eligibility: Individuals and public or private nonprofit organizations or institutions are the beneficiaries of this program.
Award Range/Average: (Individual Fellowships) $60,147 to $77,762; $68,179 average. (Institutional) $361,302 to $538,374; $386,528 average. These figures are total costs.
Funding: (Training) FY 18 $8,516,246.00; FY 19 est $8,719,452.00; FY 20 est $8,719,452.00
HQ: 5600 Fishers Lane, Rockville, MD 20857
   Phone: 301-427-1528 | Email: shelley.benjamin@ahrq.hhs.gov
   http://www.ahrq.gov

HHS93.057 | NATIONAL RESOURCE CENTER FOR HIV PREVENTION AMONG ADOLESCENTS

Award: Cooperative Agreements
Purpose: To facilitate online access to practical tools and resources for service providers, community-based organizations, professionals and peer educators who serve adolescents who reside in communities with high HIV prevalence and are at-risk based on a variety of issues.
Applicant Eligibility: Public Organizations (including city, county, regional and State government) and private nonprofit entities.
Beneficiary Eligibility: Service providers, community-based organizations, and professionals who serve adolescents who reside in communities with high HIV prevalence and are at-risk. Public organizations and private nonprofit entities and institutes of higher education.
Award Range/Average: OAH awarded one (1) cooperative agreement up to $350,000 per year in FY15 for up to three (3) years contingent upon the availability of funds. No new grant awarded in FY18.
Funding: (Cooperative Agreements) FY 16 $350,000.00; FY 17 est $350,000.00; FY 18 est Estimate Not Available
HQ: 1101 Wootton Parkway, Suite 550 Tower Building, Rockville, MD 20852
   Phone: 240-453-8822 | Email: roscoe.brunson@hhs.gov
   http://www.hhs.gov/ash/oah

ED84.015 | NATIONAL RESOURCE CENTERS PROGRAM FOR FOREIGN LANGUAGE AND AREA STUDIES OR FOREIGN LANGUAGE AND INTERNATIONAL STUDIES PROGRAM AND FOREIGN LANGUAGE AND AREA STUDIES FELLOWSHIP PROGRAM

Award: Project Grants
Purpose: To promote instruction in modern foreign languages and international studies that are critical to national needs to support such programs at colleges and universities.
Applicant Eligibility: Centers: U.S. Institutions of higher education or consortia of Institutions of higher education are eligible to apply. Applying Institutions provide evidence of existing resources and institutional commitment to language and area and international studies through a curriculum that provides instruction dealing with a particular country or world area and its languages, or with international studies and modern foreign languages, including the international aspects of professional or other fields of study. Fellowships: Accredited U.S. Institutions of higher education or consortia of Institutions of higher education offering area or international studies Programs combined with language study are eligible to apply for allocations of fellowships.
Beneficiary Eligibility: Centers: U.S. institutions of higher education or consortia of institutions of higher education will benefit. Fellowships: Undergraduate and graduate students enrolled in funded centers and programs will benefit. Student candidates must be U.S. citizens or nationals or permanent residents training in area or international studies and in modern foreign languages programs that have or are developing performance-based language instruction. Undergraduate students must be engaged in intermediate level study or advanced study of a less commonly taught language. Training must be undertaken through an institution that has an allocation of Foreign Language and Area Studies (FLAS) Fellowships.
Award Range/Average: Varies by competition.
Funding: (Project Grants) FY 18 $53,595,223.00; FY 19 est $53,086,107.00; FY 20 est $0.00
HQ: 400 Maryland Avenue SW, Washington, DC 20202
   Phone: 202-453-5690 | Email: cheryl.gibbs@ed.gov
   http://www.ed.gov/programs/iegpsnrc

DOD12.552 | NATIONAL SECURITY EDUCATION PROGRAM DAVID L. BOREN FELLOWSHIPS
"Boren Fellowships Program"

Award: Cooperative Agreements

Purpose: To provide the necessary resources, accountability and flexibility to meet the national security education needs of the United States.

Applicant Eligibility: The award for this Program is made to a nonprofit Organization that administers this assistance Program on behalf of DoD. The award is typically a cooperative agreement to administer this CFDA Program as well as CFDA # 12. 550 (The Language Flagship Grants to Institutions of Higher education) and CFDA # 12. 551 (National Security education Program David L. Boren Scholarships). The award is reported to USASpending.gov under CFDA 12. 550, which has the most funding between the three Programs.

Beneficiary Eligibility: Any U.S. citizen enrolled in an accredited public or private U.S. institution of higher education (defined in 20 U.S.C. 1001 of the Higher Education Act of 1965) is eligible to apply for a graduate fellowship. Students enrolled in Federal government schools are not eligible.

Award Range/Average: Assistance to beneficiaries range: $0 - $30,000. Average for 2015: $23,000.

Funding: (Project Grants (Fellowships)) FY 18 $2,330,000.00; FY 19 est $1,500,000.00; FY 20 est $2,000,000.00

HQ: 4800 Mark Center Drive, Suite 08 G 08, Alexandria, VA 22350

   Phone: 571-256-0771 | Email: alison.m.patz.civ@mail.mil

   http://www.borenawards.org

DOD12.551 | NATIONAL SECURITY EDUCATION PROGRAM DAVID L. BOREN SCHOLARSHIPS
"Boren Scholarships Program"

Award: Cooperative Agreements

Purpose: To provide the necessary resources, accountability and flexibility to meet the national security education needs of the United States, especially as such needs change over time.

Applicant Eligibility: The award for this Program is made to a nonprofit Organization that administers this assistance Program on behalf of DoD. The award is typically a cooperative agreement made to administer this CFDA Program as well as CFDA # 12. 550 (The Language Flagship Grants to Institutions of Higher education) and CFDA # 12. 552 (National Security education Program David L. Boren Fellowships). The award is reported to USASpending.gov under CFDA 12. 550, which has the most funding between the three Programs.

Beneficiary Eligibility: Any U.S. citizen enrolled in a degree seeking program at an accredited two- or four- year public or private U.S. institution of higher education (defined in 20 U.S.C. 1001 of the Higher Education Act of 1965) is eligible to apply for an undergraduate scholarship. Students enrolled in Federal government schools are not eligible.

Award Range/Average: Assistance to beneficiaries range: $0 - $20,000. Average for 2015 - $18,000

Funding: (Cooperative Agreements) FY 18 $2,330,000.00; FY 19 est $15,000,000.00; FY 20 est $20,000,000.00

HQ: 4800 Mark Center Drive, Suite 08 G 08, Alexandria, VA 22350

   Phone: 571-256-0771 | Email: alison.m.patz.civ@mail.mil

   http://www.borenawards.org

DOJ16.833 | NATIONAL SEXUAL ASSAULT KIT INITIATIVE
"SAKI"

Award: Cooperative Agreements

Purpose: To promote government initiatives to support children of incarcerated parents and their caregivers.

Applicant Eligibility: Eligible applicants for Purpose Areas 1, 3 and 4 are law enforcement agencies of states, units of local government, and federally recognized Indian tribal Governments (as determined by the Secretary of the Interior), prosecutor's offices, or a governmental non-law enforcement agency acting as fiscal agent for one of the previously listed types of eligible applicants. Eligible applicants for Purpose Area 2 are limited to Small Law Enforcement Agencies with less than 250 sworn officers OR consortia of small law enforcement agencies. See the current solicitation available at the Office of Justice Programs website https://ojp.gov/funding/Explore/CurrentFundingOpportunities. htm.

Beneficiary Eligibility: U.S. Citizen.

Programs Administered by Federal Headquarters

Award Range/Average: See the current fiscal year's solicitation guidelines posted on the Office of Justice Programs web site at https://ojp.gov/funding/Explore/CurrentFundingOpportunities.htm.
Funding: (Project Grants) FY 17 $37,450,080.00; FY 18 est $47,500,000.00; FY 19 est $45,000,000.00
HQ: 810 7th Street NW, Washington, DC 20531

Phone: 202-307-5831 | Email: angela.williamson@usdoj.gov
http://www.bja.gov

DOC11.603 | NATIONAL STANDARD REFERENCE DATA SYSTEM
"SRD"

Award: Sale, Exchange, Or Donation of Property and Goods
Purpose: To assure scientific and technical data to scientists, engineers, and the public.
Applicant Eligibility: Federal agencies, universities, industrial laboratories, Institutions, firms, corporations, other research establishments, and individuals may purchase databases. Data compilations published and databases established by the Program are owned by the Federal government and are subject to copyright restrictions set forth in 15 US Code 290e.
Beneficiary Eligibility: Same as Applicant Eligibility.
Funding: (Sale, Exchange, or Donation of Property and Goods) FY 18 $8,305,784.00 FY 19 est $7,932,500.00; FY 20 est $8,378,900.00
HQ: 100 Bureau Drive, PO Box 6410, Gaithersburg, MD 20899

Phone: 844-374-0183 | Email: robert.hanisch@nist.gov
http://www.nist.gov/srd

HHS93.852 | NATIONAL SYNDROMIC SURVEILLANCE PROGRAM COMMUNITY OF PRACTICE (NSSP COP)

Award: Cooperative Agreements
Purpose: Funds an organization with extensive experience developing and supporting syndromic surveillance practice to develop, implement and maintain a community of practice for CDC's National Syndromic Surveillance Program.
Applicant Eligibility: Organizations with more than a decade of experience in advancing the science and practice of syndromic surveillance and managing a distributed community of practice.
Beneficiary Eligibility: States, political subdivisions of States, local health authorities, and individuals or organizations with specialized health interests will benefit. Colleges, universities, private non-profit and public nonprofit domestic organizations, research institutions, faith-based organizations, and managed care organizations for some specific programs such as Diabetes.
Award Range/Average: Average award depends on funding opportunity announcement.
Funding: (Cooperative Agreements) FY 18 $400,000.00; FY 19 est $0.00; FY 20 est $0.00
HQ: 2960 Brandywine Road, Atlanta, GA 30341

Phone: 404-498-2441
http://www.cdc.gov

DHS97.025 | NATIONAL URBAN SEARCH AND RESCUE (US&R) RESPONSE SYSTEM
"US&R"

Award: Project Grants
Purpose: The program offers development and maintenance of the national urban search and rescue capability among the 28 task forces that conducts search and rescue operations to locate people in distress.
Applicant Eligibility: Only the 28 sponsoring agencies currently designated by FEMA as members of the National Urban Search and Rescue Response System are eligible for readiness and response cooperative agreements.
Beneficiary Eligibility: Only the 28 sponsoring jurisdictions currently designated by FEMA as members of the National Urban Search and Rescue Response System are eligible for readiness and response cooperative agreements.
Award Range/Average: FY2019: $1,145,104 - $1,386,604
Funding: (Project Grants) FY 18 $34,234,232.00; FY 19 est $34,199,412.00; FY 20 est $35,000,000.00
HQ: 500 C Street SW, Washington, DC 20472

Phone: 202-212-3799 | Email: elwood.ey-iii@fema.dhs.gov
http://www.fema.gov

DOT20.934 | NATIONALLY SIGNIFICANT FREIGHT AND HIGHWAY PROJECTS
"Infrastructure For Rebuilding America"

Award: Project Grants

Purpose: To provide Federal financial assistance to projects of national or regional significance.

Applicant Eligibility: Eligible applicants for NSFHP grants are 1) a State or group of States; 2) a metropolitan planning Organization that serves an urbanized area (as defined by the Bureau of the Census) with a population of more than 200,000 individuals; 3) a unit of local government or group of local Governments; 4) a political subdivision of a State or local government; 5) a special purpose district or public authority with a transportation function, including a port authority; 6) a Federal land management agency that applies jointly with a State or group of States; 7) a tribal government or a consortium of tribal Governments; or 8) a multi-State or multijurisdictional group of public entities. Multiple States or jurisdictions that submit a joint application must identify a lead applicant as the primary point of contact. Each applicant in a joint application must be an Eligible Applicant. Joint applications must include a description of the roles and responsibilities of each applicant and must be signed by each applicant.

Beneficiary Eligibility: Same as Applicant Eligibility.

Award Range/Average: For large projects, the FAST Act specifies that an INFRA grant must be at least $25 million. The average proposed award for Small Projects in FY 2019 was $77 million. The largest proposed award was $125 million. For small projects, the minimum award is $5 million. The average proposed award was $8.5 million. The FAST Act directs that at least 25 percent of the funds provided for INFRA grants must be used for projects located in rural areas. The USDOT must consider geographic diversity among grant recipients, including the need for a balance in addressing the needs of urban and rural areas.

Funding: (Project Grants) FY 18 $825,300,000.00; FY 19 est $856,950,000.00; FY 20 est $900,000,000.00

HQ: 1200 New Jersey Avenue SE, Washington, DC 20590

    Phone: 202-366-1092

    http://www.transportation.gov/nsfhp

IMLS45.311 | NATIVE AMERICAN AND NATIVE HAWAIIAN LIBRARY SERVICES

Award: Project Grants; Direct Payments for Specified Use

Purpose: To support Native American tribes and organizations that primarily serve and represent Native Hawaiians.

Applicant Eligibility: Eligible applicants are federally recognized Indian Tribes, Alaskan Native Villages and corporations, and Organizations that primarily serve and represent Native Hawaiians. For more information about eligibility requirements, visit http://www.imls.gov/applicants/eligibility_criteria.aspx.

Beneficiary Eligibility: Indian tribes, non-profit organizations. Through activities and projects funded, beneficiaries include the general public.

Award Range/Average: Award amounts vary.

Funding: (Project Grants) FY 15 $3,861,000.00; FY 16 est $4,063,000.00; FY 17 est $3,861,000.00

HQ: 955 L'Enfant Plaza North SW, Suite 4000, Washington, DC 20024

    Phone: 202-653-4730 | Email: mball@imls.gov

    http://www.imls.gov

HHS93.340 | NATIVE AMERICAN COMMUNITY RESEARCH, DEMONSTRATION, AND PILOT PROJECTS
"Native Language Community Coordination Program (NLCC)"

Award: Cooperative Agreements

Purpose: To promote economic and social self-sufficiency for American Indians, Alaska Natives, Native Hawaiians, and other Native American Pacific Islanders from American Samoa, Guam, and the Commonwealth of the Northern Mariana Islands.

Applicant Eligibility: Federally-recognized Indian Tribes, as recognized by the Bureau of Indian Affairs; Incorporated non-federally recognized Tribes; Incorporated state-recognized Indian Tribes; Consortia of Indian Tribes; Incorporated nonprofit multi-purpose community-based Indian Organizations; Urban Indian Centers; Alaska Native villages as defined in the Alaska Native Claims Settlement Act (ANSCA) and/or non-profit village consortia; Non-profit Alaska Native Regional Corporations/Associations in Alaska with village-specific projects; Non-profit Alaska Native community entities or tribal governing bodies (Indian Re Organization Act or Traditional Councils) as recognized by the Bureau of Indian Affairs; National or regional incorporated non-profit Native American Organizations with Native American community-specific objectives; Public and nonprofit private agencies serving native peoples from Guam, American Samoa, or the Commonwealth of the Northern

Programs Administered by Federal Headquarters

Mariana Islands, Tribal Colleges and universities, and colleges and universities located in Hawaii, Guam, American Samoa, or the Tribal Colleges and universities, and colleges and universities located in Hawaii, Guam, American Samoa, or the Commonwealth of the Northern Mariana Islands which serve Native American Pacific Islanders.

Beneficiary Eligibility: American Indians, Alaska Natives, Native Hawaiians, and Native American Pacific Islanders will benefit.

Award Range/Average: Range $100,000 - $400,000;average award: $387,027.

Funding: (Cooperative Agreements) FY 18 $1,917,265.00; FY 19 est $1,927,674.00; FY 20 est $1,917,264.00

HQ: Mary E Switzer Building 330 C Street SW, PO Box 4126, Washington, DC 20024

Phone: 877-922-9262 | Email: carmelia.strickland@acf.hhs.gov

http://www.acf.hhs.gov/programs/ana

SBA59.052 | NATIVE AMERICAN OUTREACH

Award: Advisory Services and Counseling

Purpose: Funds economic development projects that will provide small business opportunities and empower American Indians, Alaska Natives and Native Hawaiian entrepreneurs located in disadvantaged and under-served Native American communities nationwide.

Applicant Eligibility: Organizations must have experience in effectively training, counseling, developing and measuring small business development in Indian Country, Alaska and Hawaii.

Beneficiary Eligibility: Native American entrepreneurs who are starting their own business or expanding their existing business.

Funding: (Advisory Services and Counseling) FY 17 $1,541,000.00; FY 18 est $2,000,000.00; FY 19 est $1,500,000.00

HQ: 409 3rd Street SW, 8th Floor, Washington, DC 20416

Phone: 202-205-7094 | Email: carol.walker@sba.gov

http://www.sba.gov/naa

HHS93.612 | NATIVE AMERICAN PROGRAMS
"Social and Economic Development Strategies (SEDS)"

Award: Project Grants

Purpose: The Social and Economic Development Strategies program promotes economic and social self-sufficiency for American Indians, Alaska Natives, Native Hawaiians, and Native American Pacific Islanders from American Samoa, Guam, and the Commonwealth of the Northern Mariana Islands.

Applicant Eligibility: Federally-recognized Indian Tribes, as recognized by the Bureau of Indian Affairs; Incorporated non-federally recognized Tribes; Incorporated state-recognized Indian Tribes; Consortia of Indian Tribes; Incorporated nonprofit multi-purpose community-based Indian Organizations; Urban Indian Centers; Alaska Native villages as defined in the Alaska Native Claims Settlement Act (ANSCA) and/or nonprofit village consortia; Nonprofit native Organizations in Alaska with village specific projects; Incorporated non-profit Alaska Native multi-purpose, community-based Organizations; Non-profit Alaska Native Regional Corporations/Associations in Alaska with village-specific projects; Non-profit Alaska Native community entities or tribal governing bodies (Indian Re Organization Act or Traditional Councils) as recognized by the Bureau of Indian Affairs; Public and nonprofit private agencies serving Native Hawaiians; National or regional incorporated nonprofit Native American Organizations with Native American community-specific objectives; Public and nonprofit private agencies serving native peoples from Guam, American Samoa, or the Commonwealth of the Northern Mariana Islands; Tribal Colleges and universities, and colleges and universities located in Hawaii, Guam, American Samoa, or the Commonwealth of the Northern Mariana Islands which serve Native American Pacific Islanders.

Beneficiary Eligibility: American Indians, Alaska Natives, Native Hawaiians, and Native American Pacific Islanders will benefit.

Award Range/Average: $100,000 to $400,000; average = $259,215 per budget period.

Funding: (Project Grants (Discretionary)) FY 18 $31,375,727.00; FY 19 est $28,369,414.00; FY 20 est $28,369,415.00

HQ: 330 C Street SW Switzer Building, PO Box 4126, Washington, DC 20447

Phone: 877-922-9262 | Email: carmelia.strickland@acf.hhs.gov

http://www.acf.hhs.gov/ana

VA64.126 | NATIVE AMERICAN VETERAN DIRECT LOAN PROGRAM
"VA Native American Veterans Housing Loan Program"

Award: Direct Loans

Purpose: To provide direct loans to certain veterans who are, or whose spouses are, Native Americans for the purchase or construction of homes.

Applicant Eligibility: Veterans who are, or whose spouses are, recognized by a Federally Recognized Tribal Government as a Native American and who: (a) Served on active duty on or after September 16, 1940, and were discharged or released under conditions other than dishonorable. If service was any time during World War II, the Korean Conflict, the Vietnam-era, or the Persian Gulf War, then the Native American Veteran must have served on active duty for 90 days or more; peacetime service only must have served a minimum of 181 days continuous active duty. If separated from enlisted service which began after September 7, 1980, or service as an officer which began after October 16, 1981, a veteran must also have served at least 24 months of continuous active duty or the full period for which called or ordered to active duty. Veterans of such recent service may qualify with less service time if they have a compensable service-connected disability or were discharged after at least 181 days, under the authority of 10 U.S. C 1171 or 1173. (b) Any veteran in the above classes with less service but discharged with a service-connected disability. (c) If acknowledged as a Native American by a Federally Recognized Tribal Government, unmarried surviving spouses of otherwise eligible veterans who died in service or whose deaths were attributable to service-connected disabilities and spouses of members of the Armed Forces serving on active duty, who are listed as missing in action, or as prisoners of war and who have been so listed 90 days or more. (d) Members of the Selected Reservists who ae, or whose spouses ae, recognized by a Federally Recognized Tribal Government as Native Americans and who are not otherwise eligible for home loan benefits and who have completed a total of 6 years in the Selected Reserves followed by an honorable discharge, placement on the retired list, or continued service.

Beneficiary Eligibility: Native Americans who are veterans, veterans who are married to a Native American, service personnel, and certain unmarried surviving spouses of veterans.

Funding: (Salary or Expense) FY 07 $7,701,000.00; FY 08 est $12,428,000.00; FY 09 est $12,676,000.00; (Loans) FY 07 $7,701,000; FY 08 est $12,428,000; FY 09 est $12,676,000

HQ: Department of Veterans Affairs 810 Vermont Avenue NW, Washington, DC 20420
Phone: 202-461-9529
http://www.va.gov

IMLS45.308 | NATIVE AMERICAN/NATIVE HAWAIIAN MUSEUM SERVICES PROGRAM

Award: Project Grants; Direct Payments for Specified Use

Purpose: To support Native American tribes and organizations that primarily serve and represent Native Hawaiians.

Applicant Eligibility: Eligible applicants are federally recognized Indian Tribes, Alaskan Native Villages and corporations, and Organizations that primarily serve and represent Native Hawaiians. For more information about eligibility requirements, visit http://www.imls.gov/applicants/tribal_Organizations.aspx.

Beneficiary Eligibility: Indian tribes, non-profit organizations. Through activities and projects funded, beneficiaries include the general public.

Award Range/Average: Between $5,000 and $50,000.

Funding: (Project Grants) FY 15 $924,000.00; FY 16 est $972,000.00; FY 17 est $924,000.00

HQ: 955 L'Enfant Plaza North SW, Suite 4000, Washington, DC 20024
Phone: 202-653-4634 | Email: snarva@imls.gov
http://www.imls.gov

ED84.259 | NATIVE HAWAIIAN CAREER AND TECHNICAL EDUCATION

Award: Project Grants

Purpose: To make grants to organizations primarily serving and representing Native Hawaiians programs authorized by, and consistent with, the Carl D. Perkins Career and Technical Education Act of 2006.

Applicant Eligibility: Community-based Organizations primarily serving and representing Native Hawaiians may apply.

Beneficiary Eligibility: Native Hawaiians individuals will benefit.

Award Range/Average: Estimated range: $250,000- $500,000; Estimated average: $289,827; Actual range: $258,219-$513,638; Actual average: $362,220

Funding: (Project Grants) FY 18 $2,981,495.00; FY 19 est $3,156,495.00; FY 20 est $3,156,495.00

Programs Administered by Federal Headquarters

HQ: 400 Maryland Avenue SW, Washington, DC 20202-7241
 Phone: 202-245-7792 | Email: linda.mayo@ed.gov
 http://cte.ed.gov/grants/discretionary-grants

ED84.362 | NATIVE HAWAIIAN EDUCATION

Award: Project Grants
Purpose: To develop innovative educational programs to assist Native Hawaiians, and to supplement and expand programs and authorities in the area of education.
Applicant Eligibility: Eligible applicants include: (1) Native Hawaiian educational Organizations and community-based Organizations; (2) public and private nonprofit Organizations, agencies, and Institutions with experience in developing or operating Native Hawaiian Programs or Programs of instruction in the Native Hawaiian language; (3) charter schools; or (4) consortia of the Organizations, agencies, and Institutions described above.
Beneficiary Eligibility: Native Hawaiian children and adults.
Award Range/Average: Range of New Awards: $250,000- $950,000; Average New Award: $425,000.
Funding: (Project Grants) FY 18 $36,397,000.00; FY 19 est $36,397,000.00; FY 20 est $0.00
HQ: 400 Maryland Avenue SW, Room 3W215, Washington, DC 20202
 Phone: 202-260-1265 | Email: joanne.osborne@ed.gov
 http://www.ed.gov/programs/nathawaiian/index.html

HHS93.932 | NATIVE HAWAIIAN HEALTH CARE SYSTEMS

Award: Project Grants
Purpose: To raise the health status of Native Hawaiians to the highest possible level through comprehensive health promotion and disease prevention services, as well as primary health services.
Applicant Eligibility: Eligible entities include Papa Ola Lokahi and the Native Hawaiian healthcare Systems (Systems). The Systems: (1) organized under the laws of the State of Hawaii; (2) provide or arrange for healthcare services through practitioners licensed by the State of Hawaii, where licensure requirements are applicable; (3) are public or nonprofit private entities; (4) involve Native Hawaiian health practitioners significantly in the planning, management, monitoring, and evaluation of healthcare services; (5) are recognized by Papa Ola Lokahi (a consortium of Hawaiian and Native Hawaiian Organizations) for the purpose of planning, conducting, or administering Programs or portions of Programs, authorized by this act for the benefit of Native Hawaiians; and (6) are certified by Papa Ola Lokahi as having the qualifications and the capacity to provide the services and meet the requirements of this Act for the benefit of Native Hawaiians.
Beneficiary Eligibility: Hawaiian natives will benefit.
Award Range/Average: $1,600,000 to $3,100,000; Average $2,600,000.
Funding: (Project Grants) FY 18 $15,624,696.00; FY 19 est $15,600,000.00; FY 20 est $15,600,000.00
HQ: 5600 Fishers Lane, Room 16N09, Rockville, MD 20857
 Phone: 301-594-4300
 http://bphc.hrsa.gov/programopportunities/fundingopportunities/nhhcs/index.html

TREAS21.012 | NATIVE INITIATIVES
"NACA Program"

Award: Project Grants
Purpose: Promotes economic revitalization and community development through financial and technical assistance to Native Community Development Financial Institutions (CDFIs).
Applicant Eligibility: Only certified CDFIs that demonstrate the majority of its activities are targeted to a Native Community are eligible to apply for Financial Assistance awards. Organizations that are Native CDFIs, Emerging CDFIs, or Sponsoring Entities and demonstrate the majority of its activities are target to a Native Community may apply for Technical Assistance awards. However, non-certified Organizations must be able to become certified within three years after receiving a TA award. Sponsoring Entities must create an Organization that must become certified within four years after receiving the TA award.
Beneficiary Eligibility: Investment Areas and Targeted Populations as defined in 12 C.F.R. 1805.
Award Range/Average: FY 2018 Range of Technical Assistance Awards was $112,293 to $150,000; FY 2018 Average Technical Assistance Awards was $143,675 and capped at $150,000. FY 2018 Range of Financial Assistance Awards was $150,000 to $1,220,000; FY 2018 Average Financial Assistance Awards was $515,808 which included Base-FA, Persistent Poverty Counties-FA and Disability Funds-FA awards.

Funding: (Project Grants) FY 18 $14,967,081.00; FY 19 est $16,000,000.00; FY 20 est $16,000,000.00
HQ: 1500 Pennsylvania Avenue NW, Washington, DC 20220
   Phone: 202-653-0300
   http://www.cdfifund.gov

DOD12.340 | NAVAL MEDICAL RESEARCH AND DEVELOPMENT

Award: Cooperative Agreements; Project Grants
Purpose: To enhance the health, safety, readiness, and performance of Navy and Marine Corps personnel through basic and applied medical research.
Applicant Eligibility: Applicants must be an institution/Organization. Applications will not be accepted from individuals.
Beneficiary Eligibility: Beneficiaries are relatively independent investigators associated with an applicant institution/organization.
Award Range/Average: $100,000 to $20,000,000. Average: $1,000,000.
Funding: (Project Grants) FY 18 Actual Not Available; FY 19 est $4,194,306.00; FY 20 est Estimate Not Available; -(Project Grants (Cooperative Agreements or Contracts)) FY 18 $14,869,700.00; FY 19 est $130,100,000.00; FY 20 est $41,800,000.00
HQ: 693 Neiman Street, Fort Detrick, MD 21702-9203
   Phone: 301-619-8433 | Email: jaclyn.p.svincek.civ@mail.mil
   http://www.nmlc.med.navy.mil

DOD12.107 | NAVIGATION PROJECTS
"Small Navigation Projects"

Award: Provision of Specialized Services
Purpose: To provide economic means through projects.
Applicant Eligibility: States, political subdivisions of States or other responsible local agencies established under State law with full authority and ability to undertake necessary legal and financial responsibilities.
Beneficiary Eligibility: Same as Applicant Eligibility.

DOD12.335 | NAVY COMMAND, CONTROL, COMMUNICATIONS, COMPUTERS, INTELLIGENCE, SURVEILLANCE, AND RECONNAISSANCE
"C4ISR"

Award: Cooperative Agreements; Project Grants
Purpose: To support basic and applied research at educational, nonprofit, or commercial research institutions.
Applicant Eligibility: Grants cannot be awarded to individuals.
Beneficiary Eligibility: Same as Applicant Eligibility.
Award Range/Average: $1,000 to $15,000,000. Average: $297,138
Funding: (Salaries and Expenses) FY 14 $60,000.00; FY 15 est $60,000.00; FY 16 est $60,000.00
HQ: 53560 Hull Street, San Diego, CA 92152-5001
   Phone: 619-524-6202
   http://www.spawar.navy.mil/sandiego

HHS93.431 | NETWORKING2SAVE: CDC'S NATIONAL NETWORK APPROACH TO PREVENTING AND CONTROLLING TOBACCO-RELATED CANCERS IN SPECIAL POPULATIONS
"Networking2Save"

Award: Cooperative Agreements
Purpose: Seek to build on the progress of the previously funded networks and expand work to address tobacco-and cancer-related health disparities among populations particularly vulnerable to tobacco industry marketing tactics and with higher cancer incidence and death rates.
Applicant Eligibility: Open competition no eligibility.
Beneficiary Eligibility: Federal, State and Local.

Programs Administered by Federal Headquarters

Funding: (Cooperative Agreements) FY 18 $3,999,345.00; FY 19 est $3,999,345.00; FY 20 est $3,999,345.00
HQ: 4770 Buford Highway NE, PO Box F50, Atlanta, GA 30341
   Phone: 770-488-8119 | Email: crecasner@cdc.gov
   http://www.cdc.gov

DOJ16.813 | NICS ACT RECORD IMPROVEMENT PROGRAM "NARIP"

Award: Cooperative Agreements
Purpose: To assist the FBI's National Instant Criminal Background Check System to improve the automation of criminal history records, records of felony convictions, records of protective orders, records of mental health adjudications, and others to reduce delays for law-abiding gun purchasers.
Applicant Eligibility: Applications must be submitted by (a) the agency designated by the Governor to administer the National Criminal History Improvement Program (NCHIP); (b) the state or territory central administrative office or similar entity designated by statute or regulation to administer federal grant funds on behalf of the jurisdiction's court system; or (c) a federally recognized Indian tribal government.
Beneficiary Eligibility: In accordance with the NICS Improvement Amendments Act (see 18 U.S.C. 922 note), there are two specific conditions that each state must satisfy before being eligible to receive grants: 1. First, "each State shall provide the Attorney General with a reasonable estimate, as calculated by a method determined by the Attorney General of the number of the records" subject to the NIAA completeness requirements. (Id.) 2. Second, "to be eligible for a grant under this [program], a State shall certify, to the satisfaction of the Attorney General, that the State has implemented a relief from disabilities program." (Id.) For the purpose of this solicitation, a "relief from disabilities program" is a program that permits persons who have been adjudicated a mental defective or committed to a mental institution to obtain relief from the firearms disabilities imposed by law as a result of such adjudication or commitment. This relief must be based on a finding, in accordance with principles of due process, by a state court, board, commission, or other lawful authority, that the circumstances of the disability and the person's record and reputation are such that the person will not be likely to act in a manner dangerous to the public safety and that the granting of relief would not be contrary to the public interest. The certification form is available on the ATF website at www.atf.gov/forms/download/atf-f-3210-12.pdf. For further information, please visit NICS Improvement Act Questions and Answers on the BJS website. Further, applications submitted on behalf of state court systems must specifically assure that: (1) the court system has the capability to contribute and will transmit pertinent information to the NICS established under section 103(b) of the Brady Handgun Violence Prevention Act (18 U.S.C. 922 note), and (2) that it will coordinate the programs proposed for NARIP funding with other federally funded information technology programs, including directly funded local programs.
Award Range/Average: See the current fiscal year's solicitation guidelines posted on the Office of Justice Programs web site at https://ojp.gov/funding/Explore/CurrentFundingOpportunities.htm.
Funding: (Cooperative Agreements) FY 17 $11,209,680.00; FY 18 est $25,000,000.00; FY 19 est $10,000,000.00
HQ: 810 7th Street NW, Washington, DC 20531
   Phone: 202-307-0765 | Email: devon.adams@usdoj.gov
   http://bjs.gov/index.cfm?ty=tp&tid=49

HHS93.142 | NIEHS HAZARDOUS WASTE WORKER HEALTH AND SAFETY TRAINING
"Superfund Worker Training Program (WTP)"

Award: Project Grants
Purpose: To provide cooperative agreements and project grant support for the development and administration of model worker health and safety training programs.
Applicant Eligibility: A public or private nonprofit entity, including tribal Governments, that provide worker health and safety education and training, may submit an application and receive a cooperative agreement or project grant for support of waste worker education and training by a named principal investigator. Recipients/grantees may use services, as appropriate, of other public or private Organizations necessary to develop, administer, or evaluate proposed worker training Programs, as long as the requirement for awards to nonprofit Organizations is not violated. Nonprofit Organizations which are incorporated under 501(c)(4) are prohibited from receiving grants.
Beneficiary Eligibility: Any public or private entity providing worker safety and health education and training will benefit from this program.

Award Range/Average: Range: $2,409 to $2,692,381 Average: $920,155
Funding: (Cooperative Agreements) FY 18 $35,886,048.00; FY 19 est $35,887,582.00; FY 20 est $32,255,399.00
HQ: 111 TW Alexander Drive, Research Triangle Park, NC 27709
    Phone: 984-287-3784 | Email: encarna1@niehs.nih.gov
    http://www.niehs.nih.gov/careers/hazmat/about_wetp/index.cfm

HHS93.143 | NIEHS SUPERFUND HAZARDOUS SUBSTANCES-BASIC RESEARCH AND EDUCATION
"NIEHS Superfund Research Program"

Award: Project Grants
Purpose: To establish a unique program linking biomedical research with engineering, geoscience and ecological research.
Applicant Eligibility: An accredited institution of higher education, as defined in the Higher education Act, 20 U.S.C. (annotated) 3381, may submit an application and receive a grant for support of research by a named principal investigator. Subcontracts may be made with public and private Organizations, including: generators of hazardous wastes; persons involved in the detection, assessment, evaluation, and treatment of hazardous substances; owners and operators of facilities at which hazardous substances are located; and State, local and Tribal Governments. Nonprofit Organizations which are incorporated under 501(c)(4) are prohibited from receiving grants. Organizations applying for a grant under the SBIR/STTR Programs must qualify as a U.S. -owned Small Business Concern (SBC).
Beneficiary Eligibility: Any accredited institution of higher education engaged in biomedical research and/or engineering and ecological research. SBIR awards are restricted to small business that meet NIH's criteria for SBC. Tribal entities that meet these requirements are eligible to apply.
Award Range/Average: Range: $7,860 to $3,067,853 Average: $697,373.
Funding: (Project Grants) FY 18 $46,724,000.00; FY 19 est $47,979,000.00; FY 20 est $39,636,000.00
HQ: 111 TW Alexander Drive, Research Triangle Park, NC 27709
    Phone: 984-287-3258 | Email: encarna1@niehs.nih.gov
    http://www.niehs.nih.gov/research/supported/centers/srp/index.cfm

HHS93.313 | NIH OFFICE OF RESEARCH ON WOMEN'S HEALTH
"NIH/ORWH"

Award: Project Grants
Purpose: To identify projects on women's health that should be conducted or supported by national research institutes.
Applicant Eligibility: Awards can be made to domestic, public or private, non-profit or profit Organization, University, hospital, laboratory, or other institution including state and local units of government and individuals. Some initiatives will accept applications from foreign Organizations. Additional details on eligibility will be specified in the funding opportunity announcement.
Beneficiary Eligibility: See information above.
Funding: (Project Grants) FY 18 $31,500,000.00; FY 19 est $32,000,000.00; FY 20 est $32,000,000.00
HQ: 6707 Democracy Boulevard, Suite 400, Bethesda, MD 20892
    Phone: 301-496-3975 | Email: beggl@od.nih.gov

DOC11.008 | NOAA MISSION-RELATED EDUCATION AWARDS
Award: Cooperative Agreements; Project Grants
Purpose: To facilitate educational activities related to NOAA's mission.
Applicant Eligibility: Eligible applicants include federal, state, and local Governments, tribal entities, universities and colleges, nonprofit and for-profit Organizations and/or individuals. Individual Federal Funding Opportunities may have more restrictive eligibility requirements.
Beneficiary Eligibility: This program benefits other Federal, state, and local governments, tribal entities, public and private universities and colleges, for-profit and nonprofit organizations, and the general public. Individual Federal Funding Opportunities may have more restrictive eligibility requirements.
Award Range/Average: Environmental Literacy Program Awards typically range from $100,000 to $1,500,000 under the competitive process, with an average award amount of approximately $500,000. Bay-Watershed Education and Training Awards typically range from of $25,000 to $80,000 per year for up to $240,000.

Programs Administered by Federal Headquarters

Funding: (Cooperative Agreements) FY 17 est $3,929,779.00; FY 18 est $5,440,758; FY 19 est $0.00
HQ: 1401 Constitution Avenue NW, Washington, DC 20230
  Phone: 202-482-3384
  http://www.noaa.gov/office-education/grants

DOC11.483 | NOAA PROGRAMS FOR DISASTER RELIEF APPROPRIATIONS ACT-NON-CONSTRUCTION AND CONSTRUCTION

Award: Cooperative Agreements; Project Grants
Purpose: To protect, restore, and manage the Use of Coastal and Ocean Resources, knowledge to Enhance Society's Ability to plan, and to respond to the society's needs for weather and water information.
Applicant Eligibility: Eligible applicants include public or private profit or not-for-profit Organizations, Institutions of higher education, state, local and Indian tribal Governments. Uses of assistance include: Mapping, charting, geodesy services marine debris surveys for coastal States impacted by Hurricane Sandy; Repair and replace ocean observing and coastal monitoring assets damaged by Hurricane Sandy; Provide technical assistance to support State assessments of coastal impacts of Hurricane Sandy; Improve weather forecasting and hurricane intensity forecasting capabilities, to include data assimilation from ocean observing platforms and satellites; Laboratories and cooperative institutes research activities associated with sustained observations weather research Programs, and ocean and coastal research; Necessary expenses related to fishery disasters during calendar year 2012 that were declared by the Secretary of Commerce as a direct result of impacts from Hurricane Sandy.
Beneficiary Eligibility: Entities impacted by Hurricane Sandy in 2012; entities benefitting from other activities funded through the Act.
Funding: (Project Grants (Cooperative Agreements)) FY 16 $0.00; FY 17 est $0.00; FY 18 est Estimate Not Available
HQ: 1315 E W Highway, Silver Spring, MD 20910
  Phone: 301-713-1364 | Email: dan.namur@noaa.gov
  http://www.noaa.gov

HHS93.424 | NON-ACA/PPHF-BUILDING CAPACITY OF THE PUBLIC HEALTH SYSTEM TO IMPROVE POPULATION HEALTH THROUGH NATIONAL NONPROFIT ORGANIZATIONS

"CBA to Strengthen the Public Health Infrastructure and Performance"

Award: Cooperative Agreements
Purpose: To cover NON-ACA/PPHF-funded capacity building assistance projects under CDC-RFA-OT13-1302.
Applicant Eligibility: 1. Eligible Applicants: Organizations with nonprofit 501(c)(3) or nonprofit 501(c)(6) IRS status (other than Institutions of higher education). 2. Special Eligibility Requirements: The applicant Organization must provide evidence of national scope of work and of public health charge or mission. 3. Justification for Less than Maximum Competition: The Program leadership in the Office of State, Tribal, Local and Territorial Support (OSTLTS) determined that in order to achieve its strategic priorities for strengthening the public health infrastructure and advancing the quality of public health decision making, OSTLTS will need to expand its capacity building assistance (CBA) efforts through national, non-profit Organizations with experience and expertise providing capacity building assistance to governmental and non-governmental components of the public health system. Eligible applicants are limited to national, non-profit professional public health mission Organizations with experience and expertise providing capacity building assistance (CBA) to governmental and non-governmental components of the public health system. The CDC is requesting the provision of capacity building assistance (CBA) to public health agencies and other public health entities across the United States and its territories in order to strengthen public health practice to improve health for all populations. These national public health mission Organizations are the only entities positioned to effectively and efficiently execute on the expected capacity building outcomes, outputs, and activities outlined in the FOA. The characteristics that position these Organizations are: 1) designated mission and experience working nationally, 2) demonstrated infrastructure, experience and expertise providing CBA, and 3) relationship to the public health system workforce across the United States and Territories. Therefore, eligibility is limited to the above specified types of applicants/Organizations that are expected to demonstrate significant experience and expertise providing capacity building assistance (CBA) to the target populations described in the attached OT13-1302 FOA. This expertise is necessary for the grantee to effectively and efficiently complete the related activities and achieve the Program outcomes described in the funding opportunity announcement. Additionally the following capacities will facilitate the completion of projects in the specified timeframe: infrastructure to organize, conduct work and disseminate key outcomes; communicate key information

to Organization members, stakeholders and the public health community on a regular basis; leverage a wide array of resources among Organization members and the public health community to expeditiously achieve results in a cost-effective manner; interact with other public health Organizations; and act as a networking hub to build the capacity of governmental and non-governmental components of the public health system.

Beneficiary Eligibility: Beneficiaries include state health departments; tribal health organizations; local health departments; the District of Columbia; U.S. Territories; and other components of the public health system. The general public will also serve as beneficiaries.

Award Range/Average: The range is $4 million to up to $20 million for Category A, $1 million to up to $15 million for Category B and $100,000 to up to $5 million for Category C. The approximate average award ranges for the 12-month budget period are up to $15 million for Category A, up to $5 million for Category B and up to $2 million for Category C.

HQ: 1825 Century Boulevard NE, PO Box V18-1, Atlanta, GA 30333

Phone: 404-498-0430

http://www.cdc.gov/stltpublichealth/funding/rfaot13.html

USAID98.004 | NON-GOVERNMENTAL ORGANIZATION STRENGTHENING (NGO)

Award: Project Grants

Purpose: The NGO Strengthening program helps local NGOs to become more efficient in their development and support services.

Applicant Eligibility: 1. Applicants must meet the following eligibility requirements. Be registered as a PVO with USAID; Receive at least 20 percent of total annual financial support for its international Programs from non-U.S. government sources; and 2. Current Matching Grants recipients are eligible.

Beneficiary Eligibility: Direct beneficiaries are foreign private institutions or organizations; indirect beneficiaries are the recipients of improved service delivery in developing countries.

HQ: 301 4th Street SW, Washington, DC 20547

Phone: 202-567-4688 | Email: rwillis@usaid.gov

http://www.usaid.gov

DHS97.008 | NON-PROFIT SECURITY PROGRAM
"NSGP"

Award: Project Grants

Purpose: The Nonprofit Security Grant Program provides preparedness activities for nonprofit organizations against terrorist attacks.

Applicant Eligibility: The SAA is the only entity eligible to apply for FY 2019 NSGP funds on behalf of eligible nonprofit Organizations. Nonprofit Organizations must apply for FY 2019 NSGP through their SAA. A list of SAA points of contact is available at: http://www.fema.gov/media-library/assets/documents/28689?id=6363. Nonprofit Organizations may not apply directly to DHS/FEMA for NSGP funds. SAAs, in coordination with the Urban Area Working Groups (UAWG) or other relevant state partners, are encouraged to notify and actively inform eligible nonprofit Organizations of the availability of FY 2019 NSGP funding. Eligible nonprofit Organizations are those Organizations that are: 1. Described under section 501(c)(3) of the Internal Revenue Code of 1986 (IRC) and exempt from tax under section 501(a) of such code. Note: The Internal Revenue Service (IRS) does not require certain Organizations such as churches, mosques, and synagogues to apply for and receive a recognition of exemption under section 501(c)(3) of the IRC. Such Organizations are automatically exempt if they meet the requirements of section 501(c)(3). These Organizations are not required to provide recognition of exemption. For Organizations that the IRS requires to apply for and receive a recognition of exemption under section 501(c)(3), the state may or may not require recognition of exemption, as long as the method chosen is applied consistently. Refer to links below for additional information: https://www.irs.gov/charities-non-profits/charitable-Organizations /exemption-requirements-section-501-c-3-Organizations https://www.irs.gov/publications/p557/ch03. htmlhttps://www.irs.gov/charities-non-profits2. Able to demonstrate, through the application, that the Organization is at high risk of a terrorist attack; and 3. For NSGP-UA, located within a UASI-designated urban area; or for NSGP-S, located outside of a UASI-designated urban area. Eligible nonprofits located within UASI-designated urban areas may apply to the SAA to receive funding only under NSGP-UA. Eligible nonprofit Organizations located outside of FY 2019 UASI-designated urban areas may apply to the SAA to receive funding only under NSGP-S. DHS/FEMA will verify that nonprofits have applied to the correct Program and may disqualify the applications of nonprofits that apply to the wrong Program.

Beneficiary Eligibility: The FY 2019 NSGP provides funding support for physical security enhancements and other security activities to nonprofit organizations that are at high risk of a terrorist attack.

Award Range/Average: Fiscal Year 2019: It is expected that the $60,000,000 funding that was appropriated, will be allocated

Programs Administered by Federal Headquarters

to support nonprofit organizations that are at high risk of a terrorist attack and located within one of the urban areas under the Fiscal year 20187 Urban Area Security Initiative (UASI).

Funding: (Formula Grants) FY 18 $60,000,000.00; FY 19 est $60,000,000.00; FY 20 est $60,000,000.00
HQ: 500 C Street SW, Washington, DC 20523
  Phone: 800-368-6498
  http://www.fema.gov/government/grant/index

USDA10.451 | NONINSURED ASSISTANCE
"NAP"

Award: Direct Payments With Unrestricted Use
Purpose: To compensate for the crops and other agricultural commodities with catastrophic risk protection.
Applicant Eligibility: Eligible crops include each commercial crop or other agricultural commodities (except livestock and their by-products; tobacco; and trees grown for wood, paper, or pulp products) that is produced for food or fiber and specifically includes: Floricultural, ornamental nursery, and Christmas tree crops, turfgrass sod, seed crops, aquaculture (including ornamental fish), and industrial crops. An eligible producer is an owner, landlord, tenant, or sharecropper: (1) Who shares in the risk of producing the crop; (2) who is entitled to share in the crop available for marketing or would have shared had the crop been produced; and (3) whose average adjusted gross income (AGI) is in accord with 7 CFR Part 1400. NAP provides catastrophic level coverage based on the amount of loss that exceeds 50 percent of expected production at 55 percent of the average market price for the crop. Additional coverage levels are available ranging from 50 to 65 percent of production, in 5 percent increments, at 100 percent of the average market price. Additional coverage must be elected by a producer by the application closing date. Producers who elect additional coverage must pay a premium in addition to the service fee. Crops intended for grazing are not eligible for additional coverage.
Beneficiary Eligibility: Eligible crops include each commercial crop or other agricultural commodities (except livestock and their by-products; tobacco; and trees grown for lumber or paper products) that is produced for food, fibre, or bioenergy conversion and specifically includes: floricultural, ornamental nursery, and Christmas tree crops, turfgrass sod, seed crops, aquaculture (including ornamental fish), and industrial crops. An eligible producer is an owner, landlord, tenant, or sharecropper: (1) who shares in the risk of producing the crop; (2) who is entitled to share in the crop available for marketing or would have shared had the crop been produced; and (3) whose average AGI is in accord with 7 CFR Part 1400.NAP provides catastrophic level coverage based on the amount of loss that exceeds 50 percent of expected production at 55 percent of the average market price for the crop. Additional coverage levels are available ranging from 50 to 65 percent of production, in 5 percent increments, at 100 percent of the average market price. Additional coverage must be elected by a producer by the application closing date. Producers who elect additional coverage must pay a premium in addition to the service fee. Crops intended for grazing are not eligible for additional coverage.
Funding: (Direct Payments with Unrestricted Use) FY 18 $183,464,000.00; FY 19 est $161,195,000.00; FY 20 est $161,195,000.00
HQ: 14th and Independence Avenue SW, PO Box 0517, Washington, DC 20250
  Phone: 202-720-5172 | Email: steve.peterson@wdc.usda.gov
  http://www.fsa.usda.gov/programs-and-services/disaster-assistance-program/noninsured-crop-disaster-assistance/index

DOS19.224 | NONPROLIFERATION AND DISARMAMENT FUND
"NDF"

Award: Cooperative Agreements; Project Grants
Purpose: Provides a pathway for the U.S. Government to respond rapidly to nonproliferation and disarmament opportunities, circumstances or conditions that are unanticipated or unusually difficult, but of high priority. Activities include assistance worldwide for various nonproliferation and disarmament projects that involves efforts to halt the spread of weapons of mass destruction, their delivery systems, and conventional weapons systems, and the destruction of existing weapons, delivery systems, and production facilities.
Applicant Eligibility: All Program grants must be related to and support nonproliferation and disarmament efforts to be eligible.
Beneficiary Eligibility: See grants.gov or Grantsolutions.gov.
Award Range/Average: $100,000 - $5,000,000
Funding: (Project Grants (for specified projects)) FY 12 $0.00; FY 13 est $5,000,000.00; FY 14 est Estimate Not Available

HQ: Main State HST, Room 3208, Washington, DC 20520
　　Phone: 202-647-3476 | Email: bluntkr@state.gov
　　http://www.state.gov/t/isn/offices/c55414.htm

USDA10.777 | NORMAN E. BORLAUG INTERNATIONAL AGRICULTURAL SCIENCE AND TECHNOLOGY FELLOWSHIP
"Borlaug Fellowship Program"
Award: Cooperative Agreements; Direct Payments for Specified Use
Purpose: The Borlaug International Agricultural Science and Technology Fellowship Program promotes food security and economic growth, educates a new generation of agricultural scientists, increases scientific knowledge, improves agricultural productivity, provides collaborative research opportunities, and reduces the barriers to technology adoption.
Applicant Eligibility: The Borlaug Fellowship Program solicits proposals from U.S. universities and state cooperative Institutions.
Beneficiary Eligibility: Technical assistance and research collaboration provided through these agreements benefit foreign governments and related agricultural institutions in their countries.
Award Range/Average: $38,000 - $50,000 per fellow.
Funding: (Project Grants (Fellowships)) FY 18 $2,079,340.00; FY 19 est $2,500,000.00; FY 20 est $2,500,000.00
HQ: 1400 Independence Avenue SW, Washington, DC 20250
　　Phone: 202-720-4228 | Email: nicola.sakhleh@usda.gov
　　http://www.fas.usda.gov/programs/borlaug-fellowship-program

NBRC90.601 | NORTHERN BORDER REGIONAL DEVELOPMENT
"Direct Grants"
Award: Project Grants
Purpose: A federal-State governmental agency concerned with the economic well-being of the citizens, businesses, and communities.
Applicant Eligibility: No additional information.
Beneficiary Eligibility: N/A
Award Range/Average: Range up to 250,000 Average $182,000
Funding: (Project Grants) FY 15 $5,000,000.00; FY 16 est $7,500,000.00; FY 17 est Estimate Not Available
HQ: 53 Pleasant Street, Suite 3602, Concord, NH 03301
　　Phone: 603-369-3001
　　http://www.nbrc.gov

DOI15.443 | NOT FOR PROFIT
Award: Cooperative Agreements
Purpose: The Bureau of Ocean Energy Management provides major economic and energy benefits on a national and local level to the taxpayers, states and the American Indian community. The purpose of the Environmental Studies Program is to obtain the information needed for the assessment and the management of environmental impacts; to predict impacts on marine biota; and to monitor the human, marine, and coastal environments to provide time series and data trend information.
Applicant Eligibility: State or political subdivision (including any agency thereof), or any not-for-profit Organization if: (1)the agreement will serve a mutual interest of the parties to the agreement in carrying out the Programs administered by BOEM; and (2) all parties will contribute resources to the accomplishment of these objectives.
Beneficiary Eligibility: Research scientists, Federal, State and local decision-makers, Native American Organizations, and the general public will ultimately benefit from the program.
Award Range/Average: Range is $25,000 to $100,000; Average $250,000.
Funding: (Cooperative Agreements) FY 17 $5,742,696.00; FY 18 est $6,400,000.00; FY 19 Estimate Not Available
HQ: 45600 Woodland Road, Sterling, VA 20166
　　Phone: 703-787-1087 | Email: rodney.cluck@boem.gov
　　http://www.boem.gov

Programs Administered by Federal Headquarters

HHS93.124 | NURSE ANESTHETIST TRAINEESHIP
"NAT"

Award: Formula Grants

Purpose: Awarded to accredited institutions that educate registered nurses to become nurse anesthetists; recipient institutions in turn disburse funds to students in the form of traineeship support.

Applicant Eligibility: Eligible applicants are accredited schools of nursing, nursing centers, academic health centers, state or local Governments, and other public or private nonprofit entities determined appropriate by the Secretary. Any school(s) of nursing affiliated with this application must be accredited to provide graduate nurse anesthesia education at the time of application - and for the duration of the award - by the Council on Accreditation of Nurse Anesthesia educational Programs. In addition to the 50 states, eligible applicants from the District of Columbia, Guam, the Commonwealth of Puerto Rico, the Northern Mariana Islands, American Samoa, the U.S. Virgin Islands, the Federated States of Micronesia, the Republic of the Marshall Islands, and the Republic of Palau may apply. Tribes and Tribal Organizations may apply for these funds, if otherwise eligible.

Beneficiary Eligibility: NAT funds are awarded to institutions, not individuals. Traineeship recipients are selected by the participating eligible institutions. A candidate must be a citizen of the United States, non-citizen national, or foreign national who possesses a visa permitting permanent residence in the United States, must be enrolled full-time in an accredited graduate-level nurse anesthesia program, must be eligible to sit for the certification examination administered by the American Association of Nurse Anesthetists Council on Certification of Nurse Anesthetists to become a Certified Registered Nurse Anesthetist upon program completion and provide the institution with the necessary information to complete the required Statement of Appointment Form. Individuals on temporary student visas are not eligible to receive NAT support.

Award Range/Average: FY 16 Range: $8,353- $97,159; Average award: $55,555 FY17 Range: $9,925- $90,512; Average award: $27,439 FY18 est Range: $11,487- $274,539; Average award: $69,406

Funding: (Formula Grants) FY 18 est $4,850,000.00; FY 19 est $2,250,000.00; FY 20 est $0.00

HQ: 5600 Fishers Lane, Room 11N74B, Rockville, MD 20857

Phone: 301-443-5787 | Email: kbreeden@hrsa.gov

http://www.hrsa.gov

HHS93.908 | NURSE CORPS LOAN REPAYMENT PROGRAM
"Nurse Corps LRP"

Award: Direct Payments for Specified Use

Purpose: The NURSE Corps Loan Repayment Program provides loan repayment assistance to professional registered nurses, including advanced practice registered nurses, in return for a commitment to work full-time in eligible healthcare facilities with a critical shortage of nurses or serve as a nurse faculty in an eligible school of nursing.

Applicant Eligibility: Individuals who satisfy the following criteria are eligible to apply: (1) have received a bachelor's degree, a master's degree, an associate degree, a diploma, or a doctoral degree in nursing; (2) have outstanding qualifying educational loans leading to a degree or diploma in nursing; (3) a U.S. citizen (either U.S. born or naturalized), U.S., national or a lawful permanent resident of the United States; (4) employed full-time (32 hours or more per week) at a critical shortage facility (CSF) or employed as a full-time nurse faculty member at an accredited, public or private nonprofit school of nursing; (5) have completed the nursing education Program for which the loan balance applies; (6) have a current, full, permanent, unencumbered, unrestricted license in the State in which they intend to practice or be authorized to practice in the State under the Nurse Licensure Compact; and (7) submit a complete application, including a signed contract to work full-time as a registered or advanced practice nurse for 2 years at an eligible healthcare facility with a critical shortage of nurses or an accredited, eligible school of nursing. Federally Recognized Indian Tribal Government and Native American Organizations may apply if they are otherwise eligible.

Beneficiary Eligibility: Beneficiaries include registered nurses who have received a diploma, an associate degree, a baccalaureate degree or a graduate degree in nursing from an accredited school of nursing.

Award Range/Average: FY18 Range for new awards - $20,766.33 to $263,992.93; Average new award - $81,617.33. FY19 est Range for new awards - $20,766.33 to $263,992.93; Average new award - $81,617.33. FY20 est Range for new awards - $20,766.33 to $263,992.93; Average new award - $81,617.33.

Funding: (Direct Payments for Specified Use) FY 18 $47,533,618.00; FY 19 est $47,533,618.00; FY 20 est $45,351,550.00

HQ: Division of Health Careers and Financial Support 5600 Fishers Lane, Rockville, MD 20857

Phone: 301-594-4130

https://bhw.hrsa.gov/loansscholarships/nursecorps/lrp

HHS93.303 | NURSE CORPS SCHOLARSHIP

Award: Direct Payments for Specified Use

Purpose: To increase the supply and maldistribution of registered nurses (RN) and nurse practitioners (NPs) in eligible healthcarefacilities across the nation, with a critical shortage of nurses by providing service-obligated scholarships to nursing students.

Applicant Eligibility: The applicant must be a U.S. citizen or national, enrolled or accepted for enrollment in a fully accredited academic institution with a graduate, baccalaureate, associate degree or diploma nursing Program located in a State, the District of Columbia, or a U.S. Territory. The applicant must be free of any Federal judgment liens, not have breached a prior service obligation, is not excluded, debarred, suspended, or disqualified by a Federal agency, and have no conflicting service obligations. Financial need is also reviewed as part of the eligibility determination. The applicant must submit an application and a signed contract, agreeing to accept payment of scholarship funds and provide healthcare services in a healthcare facility with a critical shortage of nurses for a minimum of two years.

Beneficiary Eligibility: United States citizens or nationals enrolled or accepted for enrollment in a fully accredited graduate, baccalaureate, associate degree or diploma nursing program.

Award Range/Average: FY16: average new award was $105,566. (FY 16 Range $21,106 - $262,592)FY17: average new award was $110,065; (FY 17 Range $7,000 - $280,000).

Funding: (Direct Payments for Specified Use) FY 18 $25,013,070.00; FY 19 est $25,013,070.00; FY 20 est $23,864,826.00

HQ: Division of Health Careers and Financial Support 5600 Fishers Lane, Rockville, MD 20857

   Phone: 301-594-4400

   https://bhw.hrsa.gov/loansscholarships/nursecorps/scholarship

HHS93.359 | NURSE EDUCATION, PRACTICE QUALITY AND RETENTION GRANTS "NEPQR"

Award: Cooperative Agreements; Project Grants

Purpose: Provides grant support for academic, service, and continuing education projects designed to enhance nursing education, improve the quality of patient care, increase nurse retention, and strengthen the nursing workforce.

Applicant Eligibility: Schools of nursing affiliated with the proposed project must be an accredited public or private school. Applicants must provide documentation of current accreditation by a national nurse education accrediting agency or state approval agency recognized by the U.S. Department of education for the purposes of nursing education. Eligible applicants are accredited schools of nursing, healthcare facilities, or a partnership of such a school and facilities. Individuals are not eligible to apply.

Beneficiary Eligibility: NEPQR Project participants (NEPQR-VBSN, NEPQR-IPCP BHI, NEPQR-RNPC, NEPQR-VNPC), or students in the eligible accredited nursing program, must be U.S. Citizens, non-citizen nationals, or foreign nationals who possess visas permitting permanent residence in the United States. Individuals on temporary student visas are not eligible. The program requires RNs and APRNs to hold a valid license and be an employee of the accredited school of nursing as defined by section 801(2), health care facility, or partner of such a school and/or facility. In addition, NEPQR-VBSN required and VPNC now requires student participants to be honorably or generally discharged service members or reservists, with prior medical training, who have not yet earned Bachelor of Science in Nursing (BSN) degrees. Active duty service members will also be considered eligible contingent upon their ability to meet university admission requirements, military obligations (as applicable), and commanding officer permissions.

Award Range/Average: NEPQR-VBSN: FY18 Range: $131,830- $350,000, Average: $304,184 FY 19 Range: $0 FY 20 Range: $0, Average $0 NEPQR-IPCP:BHI: FY18 Range: $350,000- $500,000, Average: $487,935; FY 19 Range: $431,718- $500,000, Average $492,441; FY 20 Range: $0, Average: $0 NEPQR-RNPC: FY18 Range: $279,104- $700,000, Average: $613,034; FY19 Range: $291,004 - $700,000, Average: 637,090 FY 20 Range: $0 Average $0 NEPQR-VNPC FY18 Range: $0 Average $0 FY19 Range: $392,846- $500,000, Average: $457,716 FY20 Range: $0 Average $0

Funding: (Project Grants) FY 18 $29,093,459.00; FY 19 est $27,043,539.00; FY 20 est $0.00; (Cooperative Agreements) FY 18 $9,642,645.00; FY 19 est $12,826,956.00; FY 20 est $0.00

HQ: Division of Nursing and Public Health Bureau of Health Workforce 5600 Fishers Lane, Room 11N-104A, Rockville, MD 20857

   Phone: 301-443-4926 | Email: kkoyama@hrsa.gov

   http://www.hrsa.gov

Programs Administered by Federal Headquarters

HHS93.264 | NURSE FACULTY LOAN PROGRAM (NFLP)
"NFLP"

Award: Formula Grants

Purpose: To increase the number of qualified nursing faculty.

Applicant Eligibility: Eligible applicants are accredited public or private collegiate schools of nursing or departments within an academic institution, that offer graduate degree nursing education Programs (master's or doctoral) that will prepare the graduate student to serve as nurse faculty. The school must be located in the 50 States, the Commonwealth of Puerto Rico, the District of Columbia, the Commonwealth of the Northern Mariana Islands, Guam, American Samoa, the U.S. Virgin Islands, the Republic of the Marshall Islands, the Federated States of Micronesia, or the Republic of Palau. Funding priority is given to applicants with doctoral-level advanced degree nursing Programs.

Beneficiary Eligibility: Eligible nursing students must: (1) be a citizen or national of the United States, or a lawful permanent resident of the United States, the Commonwealth of Puerto Rico, the District of Columbia, the Commonwealth of the Northern Mariana Islands, Guam, American Samoa, the U.S. Virgin Islands, the Republic of the Marshall Islands, the Federated States of Micronesia, or the Republic of Palau; (2) be enrolled in an advanced degree program in nursing to become qualified nursing faculty; (3) not be in default on a Federal debt; and (4) maintain good academic standing.

Award Range/Average: FY 16: 89 total awards: Range is $5,000 to $2,017,901; Average is $274,217. FY 17: 84 total awards: Range is $14,842 to $2,351,957; Average is $294.,230. FY 18: est 80 total awards:

Funding: (Formula Grants) FY 18 $26,825,131.00; FY 19 est $11,922,689.00; FY 20 est $0.00

HQ: Division of Nursing and Public Health 5600 Fishers Lane, Room 11N-104A, Rockville, MD 20857

    Phone: 301-443-4301 | Email: ewroblewski@hrsa.gov

    http://www.hrsa.gov

HHS93.361 | NURSING RESEARCH

Award: Project Grants

Purpose: To promote and improve the health of individuals, families, and communities.

Applicant Eligibility: Research Grants: Any corporation, public or private institution or agency, or other legal entity, either nonprofit or for-profit, may apply. NRSAs (Individual): An applicant must be a registered professional nurse with either a baccalaureate and/or a master's degree in nursing and must be a citizen of the United States or lawfully admitted for permanent residence. Those on temporary or student visas are not eligible. NRSAs (Institutional): An eligible institution must be capable of providing predoctoral and/or postdoctoral research training opportunities for nurses. SBIR grants: can be awarded only to domestic small businesses (entities that are independently owned and operated for profit; are not dominant in the field in which research is being proposed; and have no more than 500 employees). Primary employment (more than one-half time) of the principal investigator must be with the small business at the time of award and during the conduct of the proposed project. In both Phase I and Phase II, the research must be performed in the United States or its possessions. To be eligible for funding, a grant application must be reviewed for scientific merit and Program relevance by a scientific review group and a national advisory council. STTR grants can be awarded only to domestic small business concerns (entities that are independently owned and operated for profit, are not dominant in the field in which research is proposed and have no more than 500 employees) which "partner" with a research institution in cooperative research and development. At least 40 percent of the project is to be performed by the small business concern and at least 30 percent by the research institution. In both Phase I and Phase II, the research must be performed in the U.S. and its possessions. To be eligible for funding, a grant application must be approved for scientific merit and Program relevance by a scientific review group and a national advisory council.

Beneficiary Eligibility: Individuals and public or private institutions.

Award Range/Average: FY18 Research Grants: $10,698 to $1,649,033; Average cost $426,548; FY18 NRSA Individual Awards: $11,007 to $63,154; Average cost of FTTP/Award $38,844; FY18 NRSA Institutional Awards: $49,265 to $507,675; Average cost of FTTP $52,642/Average cost of Award $302,689

Funding: (Training) FY 18 $7,294,262.00; FY 19 est $7,452,000.00; FY 20 est $7,085,000.00; (Project Grants) FY 18 $115,247,480.00; FY 19 est $120,666,000.00; FY 20 est $102,128,000.00

HQ: 6701 Democracy Boulevard, Bethesda, MD 20892

    Phone: 301-594-1580 | Email: bryany@mail.nih.gov

    http://www.ninr.nih.gov

HHS93.364 | NURSING STUDENT LOANS
"NSL"

Award: Direct Loans

Purpose: To increase educational opportunities by providing long-term, low-interest loans to students in need of financial assistance and in pursuit of a course of nursing program.

Applicant Eligibility: All accredited public and nonprofit private schools of nursing that prepare students for practice as registered or graduate nurses, and that do not discriminate against students because of race, color, origin, sex, or handicapping conditions, are eligible to apply for funds to be disbursed to qualified nursing students. Federally Recognized Indian Tribal Government and Native American Organizations may apply if they are otherwise eligible.

Beneficiary Eligibility: The Nursing Student Loan Program provides financial assistance to nursing students who are citizens, nationals or lawful permanent residents of the United States or the District of Columbia, the Commonwealth of Puerto Rico, the Northern Mariana Islands, the U.S. Virgin Islands, Guam, American Samoa, the Republic of Palau, the Republic of the Marshall Islands, and the Federated States of Micronesia.

Award Range/Average: Range: $2,149 to $401,893 (FY16); Average: $88,690 per institution for FY 16. Range: $6,501 to $401,893,196 (FY17); Average: $203,093.07 per institution for FY 17 Est FY18 range: TBD based on returned funds and # of applicants

Funding: (Direct Loans) FY 18 $9,342,281.00; FY 19 est $7,773,916.00; FY 20 est Estimate Not Available

HQ: 5600 Fishers Lane, Room 15N58B, Rockville, MD 20857

Phone: 301-443-1173 | Email: cgrosso@hrsa.gov

http://bhw.hrsa.gov/scholarshipsloans/index.html

HHS93.178 | NURSING WORKFORCE DIVERSITY
"NWD"

Award: Project Grants

Purpose: To support projects that assist underrepresented students throughout the educational pipeline to become registered nurses, facilitate diploma or associate degree registered nurses becoming baccalaureate-prepared registered nurses, and prepare practicing registered nurses for advanced nursing education.

Applicant Eligibility: Eligible applicants are collegiate schools of nursing, nursing centers, academic health centers, State or local Governments, and other private or public entities accredited by a recognized body or bodies or state agency, approved for the purpose of nursing education by the Secretary of education. In addition to schools in the 50 states, only those in the District of Columbia, the Commonwealth of Puerto Rico, the Northern Mariana Islands, American Samoa, Guam, the U.S. Virgin Islands, the Federated States of Micronesia, the Republic of the Marshall Islands, and the Republic of Palau are eligible to apply. Federally Recognized Indian Tribal Government and Native American Organizations may apply if they are otherwise eligible.

Beneficiary Eligibility: Accredited public and nonprofit private schools of nursing and other public or nonprofit private entities. Project participants must be in an accredited program, a citizen of the United States, a non-citizen national of the United States or a foreign national who possesses a visa permitting permanent residence in the United States. Individuals on temporary or student visas are not eligible participants and may not receive NWD grant support.

Award Range/Average: FY18 Range: $245,100- $500,000; Average award: $471,500 FY19 Range: $245,100- $500,000; Average award: $471,500 FY20 est Range: $0

Funding: (Project Grants) FY 18 $13,857,483.00; FY 19 est $16,065,986.00; FY 20 est $0.00

HQ: Division of Nursing and Public Health 5600 Fishers Lane, Room 15N58B, Rockville, MD 20857

Phone: 301-443-3192 | Email: tspencer@hrsa.gov

http://www.hrsa.gov

HHS93.756 | NUTRITION AND PHYSICAL ACTIVITY PROGRAM FUNDED SOLELY BY PREVENTION AND PUBLIC HEALTH FUNDS (PPHF)
"Nutrition and Physical Activity"

Award: Cooperative Agreements

Purpose: Purpose of this program is to provide leadership of strategic public health efforts to prevent and control obesity, chronic disease, and other health conditions through regular physical activity and good nutrition.

Programs Administered by Federal Headquarters

Applicant Eligibility: Food and Nutrition, Health/Medical, Environment, Higher education, Training, Transportation, Regional Development, Youth Development.

Beneficiary Eligibility: Eligible applicants may include: States, Interstate, Intrastate, Local, Sponsored organizations, Public/ Non Profit organizations, Federally-recognized Indian Tribal Governments, U.S Territories or possessions, or Specialized groups that will be identified in individual funding opportunities. Additional eligibility requirements may apply for funding opportunities that address high needs/risks and disparate populations.

Award Range/Average: Expected $150,000 - $1,000,000. Average award depends on funding opportunity announcement. Currently in FY2016 and FY2017 this is not planned for funding.

HQ: 4770 Buford Highway NE, Atlanta, GA 30341

Phone: 404-867-9697 | Email: lbarnes@cdc.gov

http://www.cdc.gov

HHS93.649 | NUTRITION AND PHYSICAL ACTIVITY PROGRAMS
"Micronutrient"

Award: Cooperative Agreements

Purpose: The purpose of the program is to achieve two goals related to risk factors for illness, disability, and premature death as follows: Improve dietary quality to support healthy child development and reduce chronic disease and Decrease prevalence of obesity through prevention of weight gain and maintenance of healthy weight.

Applicant Eligibility: Additional eligibility requirements may apply for funding opportunities that address high needs/risks and disparate populations.

Beneficiary Eligibility: Same as Applicant Eligibility.

Award Range/Average: Average award depends on funding opportunity announcement.

Funding: (Cooperative Agreements) FY 18 $675,000.00; FY 19 est $750,000.00; FY 20 est $750,000.00

HQ: 4770 Buford Highway NE, Atlanta, GA 30341

Phone: 404-867-9697 | Email: lbarnes@cdc.gov

HHS93.053 | NUTRITION SERVICES INCENTIVE PROGRAM
"NSIP"

Award: Formula Grants

Purpose: To reward effective performance by States and Tribes in the efficient delivery of nutritious meals to older adults.

Applicant Eligibility: State Units on Aging (SUA) and Indian Tribal Organizations (ITO) that receive funding through Titles III and VI of the OAA may receive grants of cash from the Administration for Community Living, and/or USDA Foods.

Beneficiary Eligibility: For Title III congregate meals, persons who are older adults (age 60 years and above) or a spouse of an older adult, regardless of age; disabled adults who live in housing facilities primarily occupied by older adults where a congregate site is located; disabled adults under age 60, who reside at home with older adults; and volunteers, regardless of age, who assist in meal service during meal hours. For Title III home-delivered meals, an older individual (age 60 years and above) must be assessed to be homebound. The spouse of a homebound individual regardless of age or condition may receive a meal if receipt of the meal is assessed to be in the best interest of the homebound older adult. For Title VI, all of these criteria apply. In addition, an ITO may select the age that defines who is an older adult.

Award Range/Average: FY17 Range: $ 155 to $16,520,198; Average: $478,741 FY 18 Range: $72 to $16,439,201; Average $475,000

Funding: (Formula Grants) FY 17 $160,069,000.00; FY 18 est $159,795,000.00; FY 19 est $160,069,000.00

HQ: 330 C Street SW, Washington, DC 20201

Phone: 202-795-7355 | Email: holly.greuling@acl.hhs.gov

https://www.acl.gov

HHS93.262 | OCCUPATIONAL SAFETY AND HEALTH PROGRAM

Award: Project Grants; Training

Purpose: To develop specialized professional and paraprofessional personnel in the occupational safety and health field with training in occupational medicine, occupational health nursing, industrial hygiene, occupational safety, and other priority training areas.

Applicant Eligibility: Eligible applicants include for-profit or non-profit Organizations, public or private Institutions, such as universities, colleges, hospitals, and laboratories, units of State and local Governments, eligible agencies of the Federal government, domestic or foreign Institutions /Organizations, faith-based Organizations, Indian Tribes, Tribal Government, College and/or Organizations. Racial/ethnic minority individuals, women, and persons with disabilities are encouraged to apply as Principal Investigators. Training Grants: Any public or private educational institution or agency that has demonstrated competency in occupational safety and health training at the technical, professional, or graduate level may apply. Trainees must be admissible to the grantee institution and must be enrolled in occupational safety and health training Programs. SBIR grants can be awarded only to domestic small businesses (entities that are independently owned and operated for profit, are not dominant in the field in which research is proposed and have no more than 500 employees). For SBIR grants primary employment (more than one-half time) of the principal investigator must be with the small business at the time of award and during the conduct of the proposed project. In both Phase I and Phase II, the research must be performed in the U.S. and its possessions.

Beneficiary Eligibility: Research institutions and agencies as well as workers affected by occupational hazards.

Award Range/Average: General Grants and Cooperative Agreements: $15,000 to $4,924,000. Training Grants: $29,000 to $1,770,000. SBIR Grants: Phase I -up to $150,000; Phase II - up to $1,000,000.

Funding: (Project Grants) FY 18 $215,174,187.00; FY 19 est $215,000,000.00; FY 20 est $230,000,000.00

HQ: 1600 Clifton Road NE Cubicle 4201 23, PO Box E74, Atlanta, GA 30329

Phone: 404-498-2530 | Email: sshack@cdc.gov

http://www.cdc.gov/niosh/oep

DOC11.017 | OCEAN ACIDIFICATION PROGRAM (OAP)
"OAP"

Award: Cooperative Agreements; Project Grants

Purpose: The OAP assists in conducting research to enhance the conservation of marine ecosystems. It promotes ocean educational opportunities and international ocean science bodies.

Applicant Eligibility: N/A

Beneficiary Eligibility: N/A

Award Range/Average: $100,000 to $400,000

Funding: (Salaries and Expenses) FY 16 $0.00; FY 17 est $2,000,000.00; FY 18 est $2,000,000.00

HQ: SSMC3 10356, Silver Spring, MD 20910

Phone: 301-734-1288

http://oceanacidification.noaa.gov

DOC11.011 | OCEAN EXPLORATION

Award: Project Grants

Purpose: To discover the earth's unknown oceans for the advancement of knowledge and using the art technologies within Oceanic and Atmospheric Research.

Applicant Eligibility: As stated in NOAA special announcements or applicable reports in support of NOAA's mission.

Beneficiary Eligibility: Organizations and individuals with interests in support of managing effectively the Nation's ocean exploration resources.

Award Range/Average: Grants and cooperative agreements are awarded as applicable. For example, the Ocean Exploration Science Program sponsors competitive, peer-reviewed exploration projects to collaborate with and augment NOAA intramural research programs.

Funding: (Project Grants) FY 16 $1,775,174.00; FY 17 est $3,828,322.00; FY 18 est $3,500,000.00

HQ: 1315 E W Highway, Room 10210, Silver Spring, MD 20910

Phone: 301-734-1010

http://www.explorer.noaa.gov

USAID98.003 | OCEAN FREIGHT REIMBURSEMENT PROGRAM (OFR)

Award: Project Grants

Purpose: The program provides reimbursement to private voluntary organizations that ships commodities to other privately funded humanitarian programs overseas.

Applicant Eligibility: Applicants must be a U.S. PVO registered with USAID's Office of Private and Voluntary Cooperation; receive at least 20 percent of its total annual financial support for its international Programs from non-U.S. government sources; ship only those commodities and only to those countries approved by USAID; have staff or consignees in-country to ensure proper pick-up and distribution of commodities; and provide Duty-Free Certification with the application for each country to which commodities will be shipped.

Beneficiary Eligibility: Registered PVOs in the United States, as well as people located in USAID eligible countries who are in need of humanitarian assistance or relief, benefit from these grants.

HQ: 301 4th Street SW, Washington, DC 20547

Phone: 202-567-4688 | Email: rwillis@usaid.gov

http://www.usaid.gov

DOC11.473 | OFFICE FOR COASTAL MANAGEMENT

Award: Project Grants

Purpose: To assist at developing a science-based approach for the maintenance of environmental quality and economic growth.

Applicant Eligibility: Institutions of higher education s, hospitals, other nonprofits, for-profit Organizations, foreign public entities, foreign Organizations, and state, local and Indian tribal Governments.

Beneficiary Eligibility: Unrestricted.

Award Range/Average: Widely varies accounting to federal funding opportunity announcement. Contact the relevant federal program for details.

Funding: (Cooperative Agreements) FY 16 $5,520,525.00; FY 17 est $6,089,275.00; FY 18 est $6,089,275.00

HQ: 1305 E W Highway, Silver Spring, MD 20910

Phone: 301-713-3074

http://coast.noaa.gov

DOD12.582 | OFFICE FOR REINTEGRATION PROGRAMS
"Yellow Ribbon Reintegration Program"

Award: Cooperative Agreements; Project Grants

Purpose: Conducts data collection, trend analysis, and curriculum development and to prepare reports in support of activities under Section 582 of Public Law 110-181, Sec. 582 (2008), as amended by Public Law 114-92 (2016).

Applicant Eligibility: The Yellow Ribbon Reintegration Program is a DoD-wide effort to promote the well-being of National Guard and Reserve members, their families and communities, by connecting them with resources throughout the deployment cycle. Through Yellow Ribbon events, Service members and loved ones connect with local resources before, during, and after deployments. Reintegration during post-deployment is a critical time for members of the National Guard and Reserve, as they often live far from military installations and other members of their units. Commanders and leaders play a critical role in assuring that Reserve Service members and their families attend Yellow Ribbon events where they can access information on healthcare, education and training opportunities, financial, and legal benefits. We work in government and non-government partners, including the Small Business Administration and Departments of Labor and Veterans Affairs, to provide up-to-date and relevant information to the members of the All-Volunteer force and their families. Eligible applicants must be able to satisfy the needs of the Office for Reintegration Programs as outline in Public Law 110-181, Sec. 582 (2008), as amended by Public Law 114-92 (2016) stating that the Office for Reintegration Programs may make grants to conduct data collection, trend analysis, and curriculum development and to prepare reports in support of activities under this section.

Beneficiary Eligibility: Beneficiaries must be able to conduct data collection, trend analysis, and curriculum development and to prepare reports in support of activities of the Yellow Ribbon Reintegration Program as established by Public Law 110-181, Sec. 582 (2008), as amended by Public Law 114-92 (2016).

DOS19.801 | OFFICE OF GLOBAL WOMEN'S ISSUES
"Global Women's Empowerment Programs"

Award: Project Grants

Purpose: To promote sustained peace and development by empowering women around the world.

Applicant Eligibility: See individual announcements in grants.gov for further information.

Beneficiary Eligibility: Same as Applicant Eligibility.

Award Range/Average: See individual announcements in grants.gov for further information

Funding: (Cooperative Agreements) FY 16 $8,250,000.00; FY 17 est $10,000,000.00; FY 18 est $10,000,000.00

HQ: 2201 C Street NW, Room 7532, Washington, DC 20520

Phone: 202-647-5896 | Email: fotovatki@state.gov

NASA43.011 | OFFICE OF INSPECTOR GENERAL

Award: Cooperative Agreements; Project Grants; Direct Payments for Specified Use; Use of Property, Facilities, and Equipment; Provision of Specialized Services; Advisory Services and Counseling; Dissemination of Technical Information; Investigation of Complaints
Purpose: Provides basic research, educational outreach, or training opportunities in the area of Office of Inspector General.
Applicant Eligibility: Review funding opportunity announcement for additional information.
Beneficiary Eligibility: Same as Applicant Eligibility.

NSF47.079 | OFFICE OF INTERNATIONAL SCIENCE AND ENGINEERING "OISE"

Award: Project Grants
Purpose: To enable the U.S. to maintain its leadership within the global scientific community by strengthening international partnerships to advance scientific discovery and contribute to the scientific strength and welfare of the Nation.
Applicant Eligibility: Individuals and Organizations in the following categories may submit proposals: universities and colleges; Non-profit, non-academic Organizations; For-profit Organizations; State and local Governments; and unaffiliated individuals. See the NSF Grant Proposal Guide, Chapter i.e., for a full description of eligibility requirements: http://www.nsf.gov/publications/pub_summ.jsp?ods_key=gpg.
Beneficiary Eligibility: N/A
Award Range/Average: Range Low $49,999 Range High $1,000,000 Average $127,952
Funding: (Project Grants) FY 18 $48,980,000.00; FY 19 est $48,990,000.00; FY 20 est $46,240,000.00
HQ: 2415 Eisenhower Avenue, Alexandria, VA 22314

Phone: 703-292-7241 | Email: aemig@nsf.gov
http://nsf.gov/dir/index.jsp?org=oise

HUD14.893 | OFFICE OF NATIVE AMERICAN PROGRAMS TRAINING AND TECHNICAL ASSISTANCE FOR INDIAN HOUSING BLOCK GRANT PROGRAM

Award: Training
Purpose: To provide technical assistance for Indian tribes, Alaska Native villages, and tribally-designated housing entities (TDHEs) to develop viable communities.
Applicant Eligibility: Depending on the component, any national or regional T&TA provider, or any Organization with the capacity to provide services.
Beneficiary Eligibility: N/A
Award Range/Average: $9,000- $50,000; $18,000 Average
Funding: (Training) FY 17 $5,842,285.00; FY 18 est $3,500,000.00; FY 19 est $3,500,000.00
HQ: 451 7th Street SW, Washington, DC 20410

Phone: 202-402-4507 | Email: nicholas.c.zolkowski@hud.gov
http://portal.hud.gov/hudportal/hud?src=/program_offices/administration/grants/fundsavail

HUD14.894 | OFFICE OF NATIVE AMERICAN PROGRAMS TRAINING AND TECHNICAL ASSISTANCE FOR NATIVE HAWAIIAN HOUSING BLOCK GRANT PROGRAM

Award: Training
Purpose: To provide technical assistance for Native Hawaiians to develop viable communities.
Applicant Eligibility: Depending on the component, any national or regional T&TA provider, or any Organization with the capacity to provide services.
Beneficiary Eligibility: N/A
Award Range/Average: $30,000- $100,000; $20,000 Average
HQ: 451 7th Street SW, Washington, DC 20410

Phone: 202-402-4507 | Email: nicholas.c.zolkowski@hud.gov

Programs Administered by Federal Headquarters

DOS19.979 | OFFICE OF SECURITY AFFAIRS
"African Regional Security Affairs"

Award: Cooperative Agreements; Project Grants
Purpose: To support U.S. foreign policy goals in sub-Saharan Africa through a variety of programs and policies designed to bolster peace and security.
Applicant Eligibility: If you are interested in implementing AF/SA security-related assistance Programs that promote peace and stability on the continent, please see www.Grants.gov for individual solicitation opportunities.
Beneficiary Eligibility: AF/SA security-related assistance grants bolster our African partners' capacity to provide peace and security.
Award Range/Average: See www.grants.gov for individual award announcements.
HQ: 2201 C Street NW, Washington, DC 20520
   Phone: 202-647-7158 | Email: pommerercj@state.gov

DOI15.155 | OFFICE OF THE SPECIAL TRUSTEE FOR AMERICAN INDIANS, FIELD OPERATIONS
"OST- Field Ops"

Award: Project Grants
Purpose: The goal of these OST grants will be to assist and initiate a wide range of projects that facilitate Trust Improvement and Reform, including but not limited to the areas of Probate/Estates, Individual and Tribal Financial Empowerment, Trust Asset Management, Investments, and Trust administration processes generally.
Applicant Eligibility: Eligible applicants are: Indian Tribes; Alaska Native Corporations; Indian or Alaska Native Foundations; Indian or Alaska Native non-profits; qualifying corporations; qualifying contractors; qualifying individual consultants, Law Schools accredited by a recognized body or bodies or state agency, Legal Aid Organizations and ULCs. Schools must be located in the 50 states or the District of Columbia.
Beneficiary Eligibility: Beneficiaries will include organizations that will provide direct and defined service to Tribal and Individual beneficiaries. Eligible beneficiaries are: Alaska Native Corporations; Indian or Alaska Native Foundations; Indian or Alaska Native non-profits; qualifying corporations; qualifying contractors; Law Schools accredited by a recognized body or bodies or state agency, Legal Aid organizations and ULCs. Schools must be located in the 50 states or the District of Columbia. Project participants must be in an accredited program, a citizen of the United States, a non-citizen national of the United States or a foreign national who possesses a visa permitting permanent residence in the United States. Tribal Government Beneficiaries: Federally Recognized Tribal Governments' Legal Aid and Assistance programs that are qualified to perform the work specified in the Grant Notice.
Award Range/Average: FY 16: 6000.00- 149,000.00 (projected) Average award: unknown
HQ: Department of the Interior 1849 C Street NW, Room 4257, Washington, DC 20240
   Phone: 202-513-0692 | Email: megan_olsen@ios.doi.gov
   http://www.doi.gov/ost

DOJ16.029 | OFFICE ON VIOLENCE AGAINST WOMEN SPECIAL PROJECTS
"OVW Special Projects"

Award: Project Grants
Purpose: To promote promising and innovative practices to respond to violence against women, including domestic violence, dating violence, sexual assault, and stalking.
Applicant Eligibility: Further information will be available in occasional solicitations under the Program.
Beneficiary Eligibility: Beneficiaries will be specified in any solicitations issued under this program.
Award Range/Average: Range and average depend on the specific project.
HQ: 145 N Street NE, Washington, DC 20530
   Phone: 202-305-1177 | Email: tia.farmer@usdoj.gov
   http://www.justice.gov/ovw

SBA59.053 | OMBUDSMAN AND REGULATORY FAIRNESS BOARDS
Award: Investigation of Complaints

Purpose: To assure equity and fairness in federal regulation of small business by receiving comments from small businesses, small non-profit organizations or small government entities regarding regulatory compliance and enforcement involving Federal Agencies or Agency employees.

Applicant Eligibility: Small businesses, small nonprofit Organizations or small government entities (representing less than 50,000 people).

Beneficiary Eligibility: The Ombudsman's actions assist those who individually seek assistance as well as other similarly-situated small entities.

HQ: 409 3rd Street SW, 3rd Floor, Washington, DC 20416

  Phone: 202-205-6499 | Email: elahe.zahirieh@sba.gov

  http://www.sba.gov/ombudsman

DOD12.888 | OPA RESEARCH FELLOWSHIP PROGRAM

Award: Cooperative Agreements

Purpose: To solicit offers from interested applicants to establish partnership/relationship which includes a program for university students, post-doctoral researchers and faculty members to conduct mutually-benefitresearch which supports OPA's research programs.

Applicant Eligibility: To facilitate the Fellow selection, the Applicant should propose a competitive application process that incorporates OPA evaluation of the research and capability provided. It is important that a research application be consistent and complimentary with OPA facilities and interests, supporting or stimulating OPA basic and applied research Programs. The term Fellows refers to faculty, students, or post-doctoral researchers who will perform scholarly research under the OPA Research Fellowship Program cooperative agreement. NOTE: No Fellow under this Program will be considered an employee of OPA or the Department of Defense under any circumstance.

Beneficiary Eligibility: a)Provide appropriately trained and experienced undergraduate and graduate students, Post-doctoral researchers, and faculty for conducting mutually-benefitting research that is compatible with, and contributes to, OPA research, analysis, and studies; b)Match faculty expertise to mutually-benefitting research and study needs within OPAC) Facilitate a mentoring relationship between OPA researchers and undergraduate and graduate students and post-doctoral researchers; d)Provide a structured approach for OPA researchers to collaborate with university* faculty and graduate students on mutually-benefiting research projects; and e)Provide research space (to include laboratory space when applicable) for conducting research to support the OPA program if proposed by faculty.*The term "University" is used throughout this Program Announcement to refer to a post-secondary regionally accredited college or university.

Funding: (Salaries and Expenses) FY 16 $0.00; FY 17 est $500,000.00; FY 18 est $100,000.00

HQ: 4800 Mark Center Drive, Suite 06E22, Alexandria, VA 22350

  Phone: 571-372-2271 | Email: lindsey.r.schaefer.civ@mail.mil

DOJ16.842 | OPIOID AFFECTED YOUTH INITIATIVE

Award: Project Grants

Purpose: To support states and tribal government to respond to the opioid epidemic to promote public safety, to develop multi-disciplinary working groups, to prevent opioid addiction, etc.

Applicant Eligibility: The Opioid Affected Youth Initiative supports states, local units of government, and Tribal Governments in 1) the development multi-disciplinary working groups; 2) the collection and interpretation of data to assist the working group in developing strategies and Programming that will be used to better coordinate efforts; and 3) the implementation of services that will address public safety concerns, intervention, prevention and diversion services for children, youth and their families that are directly impacted by opioid addiction.

Beneficiary Eligibility: A training and technical assistance provider will: 1) assist sites with developing data sharing agreements; 2) interpreting data; 3) developing tools that can assist the sites with identifying trends, gaps in services and coordination, targeted demographics and public safety needs; 4) assist sites with developing performance and outcome measurements to improve service delivery and coordination, results and sustainability strategies; and 5) compare performance and outcome measurements across the sites to highlight changed outcomes, program impacts and lessons learned throughout the initiative to the Office of Juvenile Justice and Delinquency Prevention (OJJDP).

Award Range/Average: The Opioid Affected Youth Initiative is new this Fiscal Year (2018) and has appropriated $8,000,000 to the Office of Juvenile Justice and Delinquency Prevention.

Funding: (Project Grants (Cooperative Agreements or Contracts)) FY 18 $7,292,268.00; FY 19 est $9,000,000.00; FY 20 est $8,000,000.00

HQ: 810 7th Street NW, Washington, DC 20531

  Phone: 202-307-5911

  http://www.ojp.gov

Programs Administered by Federal Headquarters

HHS93.788 | OPIOID STR
"State Targeted Response to the Opioid Crisis Grants"

Award: Formula Grants

Purpose: Used for carrying out activities that supplement activities pertaining to opioids undertaken by the State agency responsible for administering the substance abuse prevention and treatment block grant.

Applicant Eligibility: N/A

Beneficiary Eligibility: N/A

Funding: (Formula Grants) FY 18 $1,492,704,579.00; FY 19 est $516,302,139.00; FY 20 est $963,724,307.00

HQ: 5600 Fishers Lane, Rockville, MD 20857

Phone: 240-276-1078 | Email: odessa.crocker@samhsa.hhs.gov

http://www.samhsa.gov

HHS93.121 | ORAL DISEASES AND DISORDERS RESEARCH
"Dental, Oral and Craniofacial Research"

Award: Cooperative Agreements; Project Grants

Purpose: Supports basic research examining the role of the oral microbiota in dental health and disease as well as preclinical studies aimed at developing new prevention and treatment options for dental infections.

Applicant Eligibility: Research Project Grants: Scientists at universities, medical and dental schools, hospitals, laboratories, and other public or private nonprofit and for-profit Institutions. NRSA and career development awards: (1) Nonprofit domestic Organizations may apply for institutional awards. (2) Individual candidates or applicants must arrange sponsorship by a public or nonprofit private institution having staff and facilities appropriate to the proposed research training Program. (3) All awardees must be citizens, or non-citizen nationals, of the United States or have been admitted to the United States for permanent residence, except for K99/R00 and T90/R90 grants. (4) To be eligible, postdoctoral NRSA and career development awardees must have a professional or scientific degree (M.D., Ph.D., D.D.S., D.V.M., Sc.D., D.Eng., or equivalent domestic or foreign degree). Institutional applicants must be able to provide the staff and facilities suitable for the proposed research training. SBIR and STTR grants: Can be awarded only to domestic small business concerns that meet the following criteria: 1) Is organized for profit, with a place of business located in the United States, which operates primarily within the United States or which makes a significant contribution to the United States economy through payment of taxes or use of American products, materials or labor; 2) Is in the legal form of an individual proprietorship, partnership, limited liability company, corporation, joint venture, association, trust or cooperative, except where the form is a joint venture, there must be less than 50 percent participation by foreign business entities in the joint venture; 3) Be a concern which is more than 50% directly owned and controlled by one or more individuals (who are citizens or permanent resident aliens of the United States), other business concerns (each of which is more than 50% directly owned and controlled by individuals who are citizens or permanent resident aliens of the United States), or any combination of these; no single venture capital operating company, hedge fund, or private equity firm may own more than 50% of the concern, 4) Has, including its affiliates, not more than 500 employees, and 5) meets the other regulatory requirements found in 13 C. F. R. Part 121. For STTR awards, the small business must "partner" with a research institution in a cooperative research and development project. In both Phase I and Phase II for both SBIR and STTR, the research must be performed in the U.S. and its possessions. To be eligible for funding, all grant applications must be evaluated for scientific merit and Program relevance by a peer scientific review group and the National Advisory Dental and Craniofacial Research Council.

Beneficiary Eligibility: Health professionals, graduate students, undergraduate students, health professional students, scientists, researchers, and any nonprofit or for-profit organization, company or institution engaged in biomedical research.

Award Range/Average: FY2017: research project grants: range $8042- $9,224,715, average $445,599; NRSA: range $363- $568,952, average $77,309; SBIR/STTR: range $27,916- $1,046,856, average $540,253; Career development: range $9,369- $346,329, average $134,492. FY2018: research project grants: range $7725- $9,105,814 average $454,884; NRSA: range $2027- $578,754, average $89,661; SBIR/STTR: range $145,566- $955,597, average $470,524; Career development: range $77,660- $232,667, average $139,132.

Funding: (Project Grants) FY 18 $332,520,941.00; FY 19 est $319,557,000.00; FY 20 est $297,188,000.00

HQ: 6701 Democracy Boulevard, PO Box 4878, Bethesda, MD 20892

Phone: 301-594-4890 | Email: adombroski@nidcr.nih.gov

http://www.nidcr.nih.gov

USDA10.307 | ORGANIC AGRICULTURE RESEARCH AND EXTENSION INITIATIVE "OREI"

Award: Project Grants
Purpose: To promote organic agriculture, a systematic approach to saving crops, analyzing channels for marketing products, developing international trade, understanding relationship between organic and conventional crops, and analyzing other barriers to organic farming.
Applicant Eligibility: Applications may be submitted by State agricultural experiment stations, all colleges and universities, other research Institutions and Organizations, Federal agencies, national laboratories, private Organizations or corporations, and individuals. For both ORG and OREI, all award recipients may subcontract to Organizations not eligible to apply provided such Organizations are necessary for the conduct of the project.
Beneficiary Eligibility: State agricultural experiment stations, all colleges and universities, other research institutions and organizations, Federal agencies, national laboratories, private organizations or corporations, and individuals.
Award Range/Average: If minimum or maximum amounts of funding per competitive and/or capacity project grant, or cooperative agreement are established, these amounts will be announced in the annual Competitive Request for Application (RFA).The most current RFA is available via: https://nifa.usda.gov/funding-opportunity/organic-agriculture-research-and-extension-initiative
Funding: (Project Grants) FY 17 $17,580,428.00; FY 18 est $17,601,735.00; FY 19 est $18,900,519.00
HQ: 1400 Independence Avenue SW, PO Box 2240, Washington, DC 20250-2240
   Phone: 202-401-6134
   http://nifa.usda.gov/program/organic-agriculture-program

USDA10.171 | ORGANIC CERTIFICATION COST SHARE PROGRAMS "OCCSP"

Award: Direct Payments for Specified Use
Purpose: To provide financial assistance to certified organic producers and handlers.
Applicant Eligibility: To be eligible for cost share payments, a producer or handler must possess USDA organic certification and/or transitional certification at the time of application and have paid fees/expenses related to its initial certification or renewal of its certification from a certifying agent. State Agencies are eligible to establish an agreement to administer the Program within their State.
Beneficiary Eligibility: The eligible certified producer/handler receives the OCCSP benefit.
Award Range/Average: Awards range from $2,500 - $3,000,000 annually.
Funding: (Direct Payments for Specified Use) FY 18 est $9,663,279.00; FY 19 est $13,000,000.00; FY 20 est $13,000,000.00
HQ: 1400 Independence Avenue SW, Washington, DC 20250
   Phone: 202-260-8636 | Email: rita.meade@ams.usda.gov
   http://www.fsa.usda.gov/programs-and-services/occsp

DOS19.948 | ORGANIZATION OF AMERICAN STATES PROGRAMS

Award: Cooperative Agreements; Project Grants
Purpose: Funds shall be for Organization of American States development assistance programs; building of Democracy and restoration of Peace; and Congress reaffirms its support for the work of the Inter-American Commission on Human Rights.
Applicant Eligibility: All funds may only be provided to the Organization of American States, a public international Organization.
Beneficiary Eligibility: Public International Organization.
Award Range/Average: 500,000 to $4,500,000
Funding: (Salaries and Expenses) FY 17 $9,500,000.00; FY 18 est $9,500,000.00; FY 19 est $9,000,000.00
HQ: 2201 C Street NW, Washington, DC 20520
   Phone: 202-647-9908 | Email: kodiakt@state.gov
   http://usoas.usmission.gov

Programs Administered by Federal Headquarters

HHS93.800 | ORGANIZED APPROACHES TO INCREASE COLORECTAL CANCER SCREENING
"Organized Approaches to Increase Colorectal Cancer Screening Program - DP15-1502"

Award: Cooperative Agreements

Purpose: The program's purpose is to increase CRC screening rates among an applicant-defined target population of persons 50-75 years of age within partner health system(s), defined geographical areas, or disparate populations.

Applicant Eligibility: Eligible applicants are the official State/Territorial health agencies of the United States or their bona fide agents; Tribes /Tribal Organizations and Private/Public Colleges and universities.

Beneficiary Eligibility: Same as Applicant Eligibility.

Award Range/Average: Funding for Component 1 annual awards will range from $350,000 to $800,000. Funding for Component 2 annual awards will range from $500,000 to $1,000,000.

Funding: (Cooperative Agreements) FY 18 est $22,659,654.00; FY 19 est $19,557,462.00; FY 20 est $19,557,462.00

HQ: 4770 Buford Highway NE, PO Box F76, Atlanta, GA 30341
   Phone: 770-488-1074

USDA10.443 | OUTREACH AND ASSISTANCE FOR SOCIALLY DISADVANTAGED AND VETERAN FARMERS AND RANCHERS
"USDA 2501 Grant Program"

Award: Project Grants

Purpose: The U.S. Department of Agriculture assists socially disadvantaged veteran farmers by providing education, training, and technical assistance.

Applicant Eligibility: Organizations that may apply: Any community-based Organization, network, or coalition of community-based Organizations with documented evidence of working with and on behalf of socially disadvantaged and veteran farmers and ranchers during the 3-year period preceding this application cycle and does not or has not engaged in activities prohibited under Section 501(c)(3) of the Internal Revenue Code of 1986; an 1890 or 1994 institution of higher education (as defined in 7 U.S.C. 7601); a Hispanic-Serving Institution of higher education (as defined in 7 U.S.C. 3103); American Indian tribal community colleges or Alaska Native cooperatives colleges; other Institutions of higher education with documented experience in providing agricultural education or services to socially disadvantaged or veteran farmers; Indian Tribes or national tribal Organizations with documented experience in providing agricultural education or services to socially disadvantaged or veteran farmers; Organizations or Institutions that received funding under 7 U.S.C. 2279(a) with respect to projects that the Secretary considers similar to projects previously carried out by the Organization or institution under this subsection.

Beneficiary Eligibility: A farmer or rancher who is a member of one or more of the following groups whose members have been subjected to racial or ethnic prejudice because of their identity as members of a group without regard to their individual qualities: African-Americans, American Indians, Alaskan Natives, Hispanics, Asians, and Pacific Islanders. The Secretary of Agriculture will determine on a case-by-case basis whether additional groups qualify under this definition.

Award Range/Average: $50,000 to $200,000 Average is $200,000 per award

Funding: (Project Grants) FY 18 $200,000.00; FY 19 est $750,000.00; FY 20 est $750,000.00

HQ: 1400 Independence Avenue SW, PO Box 0601, Washington, DC 20250-9600
   Phone: 202-720-6350
   http://www.outreach.usda.gov/grants/index.htm

HHS93.319 | OUTREACH PROGRAMS TO REDUCE THE PREVALENCE OF OBESITY IN HIGH RISK RURAL AREAS
"High Risk Obesity"

Award: Project Grants

Purpose: To assist Land-Grant institutions to conduct pilot programs through existing extension and outreach services to enhance and expand efforts to combat the prevalence of obesity in areas where the problem is worst, particularly rural areas.

Applicant Eligibility: (1) Must conduct activities in eligible counties (defined as having an obesity prevalence of 40%+ (based on 2006-2008 data from BRFSS, CDC County-Level Map at http://www.cdc.gov/diabetes/statistics/), and (2) Must use existing local extensions and outreach services to accomplish project.

Beneficiary Eligibility: Individual/Family (residents) in local counties/rural areas will benefit from this assistance through increased access and opportunities to healthy, affordable foods and beverages, safe and convenient places for physical activity and breastfeeding duration and support.

Funding: (Project Grants) FY 18 $10,873,643.00; FY 19 est $11,964,049.00; FY 20 est $11,962,049.00

HQ: 4770 Buford Highway NE, Atlanta, GA 30341

Phone: 404-867-9697 | Email: lbarnes@cdc.gov

ED84.022 | OVERSEAS PROGRAMS-DOCTORAL DISSERTATION RESEARCH ABROAD

Award: Project Grants

Purpose: To provide opportunities for graduate students to engage in full-time dissertation research abroad in modern foreign language and area studies with the exception of Western Europe.

Applicant Eligibility: Institutions of higher education may apply.

Beneficiary Eligibility: A candidate for Doctoral Dissertation Research Abroad Fellowship must: (1) be a (a) citizen or national of the United States; or (b) permanent resident of the United States; (2) be a graduate student in good standing at an institution of higher education who, when the fellowship period begins, has been admitted to candidacy in a doctoral degree program in modern foreign languages and area studies at that institution; (3) plan a teaching career in the United States upon graduation; (4) possess adequate skills in the foreign language(s) necessary to carry out the dissertation research project.

Award Range/Average: Not Available.

Funding: (Project Grants) FY 18 $3,744,983.00; FY 19 est $3,529,000.00; FY 20 est $0.00

HQ: 400 Maryland Avenue SW, Washington, DC 20202

Phone: 202-453-6891

http://www.ed.gov/programs/iegpsddrap

ED84.021 | OVERSEAS PROGRAMS-GROUP PROJECTS ABROAD

Award: Project Grants

Purpose: To support the development and improvement of the study of modern foreign languages and area studies in the United States by providing grants to support overseas projects in training, research, and curriculum development in modern foreign languages and area studies for teachers, students, and faculty engaged in a common endeavor.

Applicant Eligibility: Institutions of higher education, State departments of education, private nonprofit educational Organizations, and a consortium of Institutions, departments, and Organizations.

Beneficiary Eligibility: A participant must be: a citizen, or permanent resident of the United States, currently employed full-time in a United States school system, institution of higher education, local education agency or state education agency (not applicable to students), and at least one of the following: A teacher in an elementary or secondary school (please see note below); A faculty member who teaches modern foreign languages or area studies; An experienced education administrator responsible for planning, conducting, or supervising programs in modern foreign languages or area studies at the elementary, secondary, or postsecondary levels; A graduate student or junior or senior in an institution of higher education, who is a prospective teacher in the areas of social sciences, humanities and foreign languages. The student should meet the provisions set by his or her local and state education agencies; or; For the Advanced Overseas Intensive Language Training project, the participating student, other than those planning a teaching career, should be planning to apply their language skills and knowledge of countries vital to the United States national security in fields outside teaching, including government, the professions, or international development.

Award Range/Average: Varies by competition.

Funding: (Project Grants) FY 18 $2,507,307.00; FY 19 est $2,671,000.00; FY 20 est $0.00

HQ: 400 Maryland Avenue SW, Washington, DC 20202

Phone: 202-453-6391 | Email: tanyelle.richardson@ed.gov

http://www.ed.gov/programs/iegpsgpa

Programs Administered by Federal Headquarters

ED84.018 | OVERSEAS PROGRAMS SPECIAL BILATERAL PROJECTS

Award: Project Grants

Purpose: To increase mutual understanding and knowledge between the people of the United States and other countries, to participate in short-term study seminars abroad on topics in the social sciences and the humanities through qualified U.S. educators.

Applicant Eligibility: Applicants must (1) be U.S. citizens or have permanent resident status; (2) hold at least a bachelor's degree from an accredited college or University; (3) have at least 3 years full-time in teaching, administering or supervising in the humanities, the social sciences or social studies subjects; (4) be currently employed full-time in teaching, administering or supervising in the aforementioned areas; (5) meet any language requirements if applicable (see the application booklet for details). If selected, awardees must furnish evidence of good health and emotional maturity.

Beneficiary Eligibility: (1) Undergraduate faculty members of 4 year colleges/universities and 2-year community colleges in the fields of the humanities and social sciences; (2) supervisors and secondary (grades 9 through 12) and elementary and junior high school (grades K through 8) teachers of social studies and humanities; and (3) curriculum development specialists, administrators of local and State education agencies who have direct responsibility for developing curriculum in the subject areas encompassed by the social sciences and the humanities.

Award Range/Average: Varies by competition.

Funding: (Project Grants) FY 18 $680,600.00; FY 19 $552,300.00; FY 20 est $0.00

HQ: 400 Maryland Avenue SW, Washington, DC 20202

Phone: 202-453-6080 | Email: maria.chang@ed.gov

http://www.ed.gov/programs/iegpssap

DOS19.519 | OVERSEAS REFUGEE ASSISTANCE PROGRAM FOR NEAR EAST

Award: Cooperative Agreements

Purpose: Providing protection and assistance to Syrian and Iraqi refugees, conflict victims, internally displaced persons and returnees remains a high priority. Programs will assist refugee populations in neighboring countries.

Applicant Eligibility: United Nations, international and non- governmental Organizations. MRA designates primary UN or IO recipient Organizations. NGO activities must be complementary to, and coordinated with, UN Programs.

Beneficiary Eligibility: Refugees and victims of conflict requiring assistance. See www.grants.gov for individual announcement.

Funding: (Salaries and Expenses) FY 17 $23,099,109.00; FY 18 est $23,100,000.00; FY 19 est $23,100,000.00

HQ: 2025 E Street NW, 8th Floor SA 9, Washington, DC 20520

Phone: 202-453-9292 | Email: terharvs@state.gov

http://www.state.gov/j/prm/index.htm

DOS19.523 | OVERSEAS REFUGEE ASSISTANCE PROGRAM FOR SOUTH ASIA

Award: Cooperative Agreements

Purpose: The Bureau continues to support for the return and reintegration programs for Afghan refugees and Internally Displaced Persons. The Bureau will also continue supporting protection and assistance activities for refugees who remain in Pakistan and Iran and who may not repatriate.

Applicant Eligibility: United Nations (UN), international Organization (IO), and non-governmental Organizations (NGO). MRA designates primary UN or IO recipient Organizations. NGO activities must be complementary to and coordinate with, UN Programs. See www.grants.gov for individual announcement.

Beneficiary Eligibility: Refugees and victims of conflict requiring assistance. See www.grants.gov for individual announcement.

Funding: (Salaries and Expenses) FY 17 $23,099,109.00; FY 18 est $23,100,000.00; FY 19 est $23,100,000.00

HQ: 2025 E Street NW, 8th Floor SA 9, Washington, DC 20520

Phone: 202-453-9282 | Email: mestetskyea@state.gov

http://www.state.gov/j/prm/index.htm

DOS19.517 | OVERSEAS REFUGEE ASSISTANCE PROGRAMS FOR AFRICA

Award: Project Grants

Purpose: Provides assistance to the basic needs of refugees and conflict victims spread across the African continent. NGOs are key partners of international organizations in Africa, often in specialized areas such as healthcare, water, sanitation, food distribution, and education.

Applicant Eligibility: International and non- governmental Organizations. MRA designates primary UN or IO recipient Organizations. NGO activities must be complementary to, and coordinated with, UN Programs.

Beneficiary Eligibility: Refugees and victims of conflict requiring assistance.
Funding: (Cooperative Agreements) FY 16 $93,759,300.00; FY 17 est $93,000,000.00; FY 18 est $93,000,000.00
HQ: 2025 E Street NW, Washington, DC 20522-0908
    Phone: 202-453-9239 | Email: hembreeel@state.gov
    http://www.state.gov/j/prm/index.htm

DOS19.511 | OVERSEAS REFUGEE ASSISTANCE PROGRAMS FOR EAST ASIA
Award: Cooperative Agreements
Purpose: The Bureau of Population, Refugees, and Migration supports humanitarian assistance and protection programs for vulnerable populations in Australia, Bangladesh, Burma, Cambodia, Indonesia, Laos, Malaysia, Mongolia, the Philippines, Thailand, and Vietnam.
Applicant Eligibility: Non-governmental Organizations. The Migration and Refugee Assistance Account (MRA) designates primary UN or IO recipient Organizations. NGO activities must be complementary to, and coordinated with, UN Programs.
Beneficiary Eligibility: Refugees and victims of conflict requiring assistance.
Funding: (Cooperative Agreements) FY 16 $18,264,778.00; FY 17 est $18,300,000.00; FY 18 est $18,300,000.00
HQ: 2025 E Street NW, Washington, DC 20522-0908
    Phone: 202-453-9289 | Email: tranht3@state.gov
    http://www.state.gov/j/prm/index.htm

DOS19.520 | OVERSEAS REFUGEE ASSISTANCE PROGRAMS FOR EUROPE
Award: Cooperative Agreements
Purpose: Provides funding for organizations that assist refugees and internally displaced persons in Europe and Central Asia.
Applicant Eligibility: United Nations, international and non- governmental Organizations. MRA designates primary UN or IO recipient Organizations. NGO activities must be complementary to, and coordinated with, UN Programs.
Beneficiary Eligibility: Refugees and victims of conflict requiring assistance.
Award Range/Average: Not Available.
Funding: (Cooperative Agreements) FY 16 $3,098,439.00; FY 17 est $3,100,000.00; FY 18 est $3,100,000.00
HQ: 2025 E Street NW, 8th Floor SA 9, Washington, DC 20520
    Phone: 202-453-9297 | Email: irisnr@state.gov
    http://www.state.gov/j/prm/index.htm

DOS19.522 | OVERSEAS REFUGEE ASSISTANCE PROGRAMS FOR STRATEGIC GLOBAL PRIORITIES
Award: Cooperative Agreements
Purpose: Bureau support under this program includes mostly contributions to the headquarters and global program costs of the United Nations High Commissioner for Refugees, the headquarters budget of the International Committee of the Red Cross and to a smaller extent, the multiregional activities of other international and non-governmental organizations assisting refugees and other conflict victims.
Applicant Eligibility: United Nations, international and non-governmental Organizations. MRA designates primary UN or IO recipient Organizations. NGO activities must be complementary to, and coordinated with, UN Programs.
Beneficiary Eligibility: Refugees and victims of conflict requiring assistance.
Award Range/Average: Not Available.
Funding: (Cooperative Agreements) FY 16 $6,717,762.00; FY 17 est $6,700,000.00; FY 18 est $6,700,000.00
HQ: 2025 E Street NW, Washington, DC 20522-0908
    Phone: 202-453-9239 | Email: hembreeel@state.gov
    http://www.state.gov/j/prm/index.htm

DOS19.518 | OVERSEAS REFUGEE ASSISTANCE PROGRAMS FOR WESTERN HEMISPHERE
Award: Cooperative Agreements
Purpose: PRM provides assistance to internally displaced persons and refugees in Colombia and neighboring countries. PRM's assistance strategy includes ensuring adequate protection for vulnerable IDPs, filling gaps in the provision of emergency humanitarian assistance, and building local government and community capacity to meet the needs of IDPs.

Programs Administered by Federal Headquarters

Applicant Eligibility: United Nations, international and non-governmental Organizations. MRA designates primary UN or IO recipient Organizations. NGO activities must be complementary to, and coordinated with, UN Programs.
Beneficiary Eligibility: Refugees and victims of conflict requiring assistance.
Funding: (Cooperative Agreements) FY 16 $22,864,159; FY 17 est $22,800,000; FY 18 est $22,800,000
HQ: 2025 E Street NW, 8th Floor SA 9, Washington, DC 20520
　　Phone: 202-453-9297 | Email: irisnr@state.gov
　　http://www.state.gov/j/prm/index.htm

DOS19.023 | OVERSEAS SCHOOLS PROGRAM
Award: Project Grants
Purpose: Promotes quality educational opportunities at the elementary and secondary school levels for dependents of American citizens carrying out programs and interests of the U.S. Government abroad. It also works to increase mutual understanding between the people of the United States and the people of other countries through educational institutions which demonstrates American educational practices, principles and methods employed in the United States.
Applicant Eligibility: Grants are generally restricted to selected overseas schools.
Beneficiary Eligibility: Dependents of American citizens carrying out programs and interests of the U.S. Government abroad are the primary beneficiaries.
Award Range/Average: Grants range from $5000 to $400,000. Majority of grants are less than $40,000.
Funding: (Project Grants) FY 16 Actual Not Available; FY 17 est $1,200,000.00; FY 18 est $12,000,000.00
HQ: 2401 C Street NW, Room H328 SA-1, Washington, DC 20522-0103
　　Phone: 202-261-8203 | Email: lyleswm2@state.gov
　　http://www.state.gov/m/a/os

DOJ16.026 | OVW RESEARCH AND EVALUATION PROGRAM
"R&E"
Award: Project Grants
Purpose: To further develop and make maximum use of the evidence base for approaches to combating domestic violence, sexual assault, dating violence, and stalking.
Applicant Eligibility: Eligible applicants are limited to: States (including territories), units of local government, federally recognized Indian tribal Governments as determined by the Secretary of the Interior, nonprofit Organizations (including tribal nonprofit Organizations), Institutions of higher education (including tribal Institutions of higher education).
Beneficiary Eligibility: This program prioritizes research on topics for which a stronger evidence base would help OVW grantees use federal funds most effectively.
Award Range/Average: $270,000- $450,000
Funding: (Project Grants) FY 16 $3,356,608.00; FY17 est Estimate Not Available; FY 18 est Estimate Not Available
HQ: 145 N Street NE, Washington, DC 20530
　　Phone: 202-305-1177 | Email: tia.farmer@usdoj.gov
　　http://www.justice.gov/ovw

DOJ16.526 | OVW TECHNICAL ASSISTANCE INITIATIVE
"TA Program"
Award: Project Grants
Purpose: To provide communities with critical resources that assist them forge partnerships across agencies and disciplines to respond effectively to violent crimes against women.
Applicant Eligibility: Eligible applicants are nonprofit national, tribal and statewide Organizations and Institutions of higher education. In rare circumstances, state/local government agencies or local nonprofits may be eligible.
Beneficiary Eligibility: Beneficiaries are organizations or individuals partnered with organizations.
Funding: (Project Grants) FY 16 $36,638,163.00; FY 17 est Estimate Not Available; FY 18 est Estimate Not Available
HQ: 145 N Street NE, Suite 10W121, Washington, DC 20530
　　Phone: 202-305-1177 | Email: tia.farmer@usdoj.gov
　　http://www.justice.gov/ovw

DOC11.438 | PACIFIC COAST SALMON RECOVERY PACIFIC SALMON TREATY PROGRAM
"Pacific Coast Salmon Recovery - Pacific Salmon Treaty Program"

Award: Project Grants
Purpose: To assist the States in salmon restoration and support Indian tribes for salmon recovery and to meet the needs of the Pacific Salmon Commission.
Applicant Eligibility: State government agencies and treaty Indian Tribes.
Beneficiary Eligibility: This program benefits the State governments, treaty Indian tribes, Federal government, international relationships, and conservation of a public resource by ensuring that State agencies and tribal governments participate in the recovery and international management of salmon on the west coast.
Award Range/Average: Pacific Coast Salmon Recovery: Range: $30,000 to $30,000,000 Average: To Be AdvisedPacific Salmon Treaty: $25,000 - $985,000 FY 2009 Average: $661,031.00
Funding: (Project Grants) FY 16 $73,399,139.00; FY 17 est $73,399,139.00; FY 18 est Estimate Not Available
HQ: 1305 E W Highway, Silver Spring, MD 20910
   Phone: 301-427-8771 | Email: jeffrey.kulnis@noaa.gov
   http://www.nmfs.noaa.gov

DOC11.437 | PACIFIC FISHERIES DATA PROGRAM
Award: Project Grants
Purpose: To support and analyze fisheries management needs and biological data on federally managed species to the Fishery Management Councils.
Applicant Eligibility: State Governments (including territories of Guam and American Samoa and the Commonwealth of the Northern Mariana Islands) and quasi-public nonprofit institution/Organizations.
Beneficiary Eligibility: The agency of a State government authorized under its laws to regulate commercial and recreational fisheries.
Funding: (Cooperative Agreements) FY 16 $30,441,769.00; FY 17 est $30,441,769.00; FY 18 Estimate Not Available
HQ: 1305 E W Highway, Silver Spring, MD 20910
   Phone: 301-427-8771 | Email: jeffrey.kulnis@noaa.gov
   http://www.nmfs.noaa.gov

HHS93.349 | PACKAGING AND SPREADING PROVEN PEDIATRIC WEIGHT MANAGEMENT INTERVENTIONS FOR USE BY LOW-INCOME FAMILIES
"Childhood Obesity Research Demonstration"

Award: Formula Grants (cooperative Agreements)
Purpose: To increase the availability and number of packaged effective pediatric weight management interventions (PWMI) that can be used by healthcare, community or public health organizations to serve low-income children and their caregivers.
Applicant Eligibility: Eligibility will not be limited.
Beneficiary Eligibility: N/A
Award Range/Average: 3750000
Funding: (Formula Grants (Cooperative Agreements)) 17 FY 18 Estimate Not Available; FY 19 Estimate Not Available; FY 20 est $0.00
HQ: NCCDPHP 4770 Buford Highway NE, Atlanta, GA 30341
   Phone: 404-867-9697 | Email: lbarnes@cdc.gov

HHS93.325 | PARALYSIS RESOURCE CENTER
"Paralysis Resource Center & National Limb Loss Resource Center (PRC)"

Award: Cooperative Agreements
Purpose: Grant is awarded to the Christopher & Dana Reeve Foundation.
Applicant Eligibility: Eligible applicants will include public and private nonprofit entities, including universities, University-affiliated systems, not-for-profit medical centers, research Institutions and rehabilitation hospitals, disability service groups

Programs Administered by Federal Headquarters

such as advocacy and voluntary Organizations, and independent living centers, and federally recognized Indian Tribal Governments.

Beneficiary Eligibility: In addition to the eligible applicants, other groups who will receive benefits from the programs include persons individuals living with disabilities paralysis and family members of persons with disabilities, persons individuals living with limb loss, minority populations, refugees, infants, children, youth, adults, senior citizens, women, all educational levels, all income levels, urban, suburban, and rural populations, health/ rehabilitation professionals, scientists, educators, and researchers.

Funding: (Project Grants) FY 17 $7,700,000.00; FY 18 est $7,700,000.00; FY 19 est Estimate Not Available

HQ: 330 C Street SW, Washington, DC 20201

   Phone: 202-795-7401 | Email: ophelia.mclain@acl.hhs.gov

   http://www.acl.gov

USDA10.759 | PART 1774 SPECIAL EVALUATION ASSISTANCE FOR RURAL COMMUNITIES AND HOUSEHOLDS (SEARCH)
"Search Grant Program"

Award: Project Grants

Purpose: To make development grants for financially distressed communities in rural areas with water disposal projects.

Applicant Eligibility: Applicants must be (1) public bodies or governmental entities such as states, municipalities, counties, districts, authorities, and other political subdivisions of a State; (2) nonprofit Organizations such as associations, cooperatives, private nonprofit corporations, and Institutions of higher education and hospitals; (3) Native American Indian Tribes on Federal and State reservations, other federally recognized Indian Tribes, and Native American Organizations (includes Indian groups, cooperatives, corporations, partnerships, and associations).

Beneficiary Eligibility: Beneficiaries are the entities or organizations eligible to develop projects under the Water and Waste Disposal Loan and Grant Program. Eligible entities include (1) public bodies or governmental entities such as municipalities, counties, districts, authorities, and other political subdivisions of a State, (2) nonprofit organizations such as associations, cooperatives, and private nonprofit corporations, (3) Native American Indian tribes on Federal and State reservations and other federally recognized Indian tribes.

Award Range/Average: $5,000 to $30,000. Average is $26,472

Funding: (Project Grants) FY 18 $2,356,045.00; FY 19 est $3,000,000.00; FY 20 est $3,000,000.00

HQ: 1400 Independence Avenue SW, PO Box 1570, Washington, DC 20005

   Phone: 202-690-2525 | Email: stephen.saulnier@wdc.usda.gov

   http://www.rd.usda.gov/programs-services/all-programs/water-environmental-programs

HHS93.446 | PARTNER ACTIONS TO IMPROVE ORAL HEALTH OUTCOMES

Award: Cooperative Agreements; Project Grants

Purpose: To establish oral health leadership and program guidance, oral health data collection and interpretation, multi-dimensional delivery system for oral and physical health, and to implement science-based programs (including dental sealants and community water fluoridation) to improve oral and physical health.

Applicant Eligibility: Eligible applicants are the official State and territorial health agencies of the United States, the District of Columbia, tribal Organizations, the Commonwealth of Puerto, the Virgin Islands, Guam, the Northern Mariana Islands, the Federated States of Micronesia, the Republic of the Marshall Islands, the Republic of Palau, and American Samoa, or their Bona Fide Agents. For specific funding announcements, eligible applicants may be more limited; for example, State Governments, including the District of Columbia, or their Bona Fide Agents.

Beneficiary Eligibility: States, political subdivisions of States, local health authorities, and individuals or organizations with specialized health interests will benefit.

Award Range/Average: 350000

Funding: (Cooperative Agreements) FY 18 $700,000.00; FY 19 est $550,000.00; FY 20 est $550,000.00

HQ: 4770 Buford Highway NE, PO Box F80, Atlanta, GA 30341

   Phone: 770-488-6075

HHS93.814 | PARTNER SUPPORT FOR HEART DISEASE AND STROKE PREVENTION
"Partner Support"

Award: Cooperative Agreements

Purpose: The program provides partner support around cardiovascular disease prevention activities.

Applicant Eligibility: Government and non-governmental Organizations, including state, local, tribal and territorial Governments or their bona fide agents.

Beneficiary Eligibility: Non-governmental organizations, including state, local, tribal and territorial governments or their bona fide agents.

Award Range/Average: The award range is $250,000- $500,000, with an average of $400,000 per budget year.

Funding: (Cooperative Agreements) FY 18 $500,00.00; FY 19 est $500,000.00; FY 20 est $0.00

HQ: 4770 Buford Highway NE, PO Box F72, Atlanta, GA 30341
   Phone: 770-488-5108
   http://www.cdc.gov

DOD12.740 | PAST CONFLICT ACCOUNTING
"Defense POW/MIA Accounting Agency (DPAA) Past Conflict Accounting Grants and Cooperative Agreements Program (DPAA GCAP) NOTE This is a new program"

Award: Cooperative Agreements; Project Grants

Purpose: Is responsible for determining the fate of our missing and, where possible, recovering and identifying those who have made the ultimate sacrifice on behalf of a grateful nation.

Applicant Eligibility: Applicants can be any private entity. A private entity is defined as any self-sustaining, non-Federal person or Organization, established, operated, and controlled by any individual(s) acting outside the scope of any official capacity as officers, employees, or agents of the Federal Government.

Beneficiary Eligibility: Beneficiaries of an assistance award can be any private entity which is defined as any self-sustaining, non-Federal person or organization, established, operated, and controlled by any individual(s) acting outside the scope of any official capacity as officers, employees, or agents of the Federal Government.

Award Range/Average: Not yet defined as this is a new program.

Funding: (Cooperative Agreements (Discretionary Grants)) FY 17 Actual Not Available; FY 18 est $250,000.00; FY 19 est $500,000.00

HQ: 2300 Defense Pentagon, Washington, DC 20301
   Phone: 703-699-1191 | Email: george.r.gillette.civ@mail.mil

DOJ16.742 | PAUL COVERDELL FORENSIC SCIENCES IMPROVEMENT GRANT PROGRAM
"Coverdell Program"

Award: Formula Grants; Project Grants

Purpose: To fund for analysis of forensic evidence and forensic laboratory, to improve the quality and timeliness of forensic science, to address emerging forensic science issues, to educate and train forensic pathologists, and to assist medicolegal death investigators.

Applicant Eligibility: Under the Coverdell Program, SAAs may apply for both base (formula) and competitive funds. Units of local government may apply for competitive funds. Coverdell SAAs and units of local government may apply directly to NIJ for funding. The Coverdell law (at 34 USC 10562) requires that, to request a grant, an applicant for Coverdell funds must submit: 1. A certification and description regarding a plan for forensic science laboratories. Each applicant must submit a certification that the State or unit of local government has developed a plan for forensic science laboratories under a Program intended to improve the quality and timeliness of forensic science or medical examiner services in the State, including such services provided by the laboratories operated by the State and those operated by units of local government within the State. Applicants must also specifically describe the manner in which the grant will be used to carry out that plan. 2. A certification regarding use of generally accepted laboratory practices. Each applicant must submit a certification that any forensic laboratory system, medical examiner's office, or coroner's office in the State, including any laboratory operated by a unit of local government within the State, that will receive any portion of the grant amount (whether directly or through a subgrant)

Programs Administered by Federal Headquarters

uses generally accepted laboratory practices and procedures established by accrediting Organizations or appropriate certifying bodies. 3. A certification regarding forensic science laboratory accreditation. Each applicant must submit a certification that any forensic science laboratory system in the State (except with regard to any medical examiner's office, or coroner's office in the State), including any laboratory operated by a unit of local government within the State, that will receive any portion of the grant amount (whether directly or through a subgrant) either is accredited, or, is not so accredited, but will (or will be required in a legally binding and enforceable writing to) use a portion of the grant amount to prepare and apply for such accreditation not more than two (2) years after the date on which a grant is awarded under a fiscal year's grant solicitation for the Paul Coverdell Forensic Science Improvement Grants Program. 4. A certification and description regarding costs of new facilities. Each applicant must submit a certification that the amount of the grant used for the costs of any new facility constructed as part of a Program to improve the quality and timeliness of forensic science or medical examiner services will not exceed certain limitations set forth in the Coverdell law at 34 USC 10562. (See information on permissible expenses in the solicitation.) Applicants must also specifically describe any new facility to be constructed as well as the estimated costs of the facility. 5. A certification regarding external investigations into allegations of serious negligence or misconduct. Each applicant must submit a certification that a government entity exists and an appropriate process is in place to conduct independent external investigations into allegations of serious negligence or misconduct substantially affecting the integrity of the forensic results committed by employees or contractors of any forensic laboratory system, medical examiner office, coroner's office, law enforcement storage facility, or medical facility in the State that will receive a portion of the grant amount. .

Beneficiary Eligibility: Eligible applicants must be State or local (i.e., county and municipal) governments. The purpose of this solicitation is to request applications for grants from State and units of local government to improve the quality and timeliness of forensic science and medical examiner services and/or to eliminate backlogs in the analysis of forensic evidence, including firearms examination, latent prints, impression evidence, toxicology, digital evidence, fire evidence, controlled substances, forensic pathology, questioned documents, and trace evidence for criminal justice purposes in State and local forensic laboratories.

Award Range/Average: In amounts consistent with the applicant's proposed project and NIJ's plans, priorities and levels of financing.

Funding: (Formula Grants) FY 18 $27,363,404.00; FY 19 est $30,000,000.00; FY 20 $10,000,000.00

HQ: 810 7th Street NW, Washington, DC 20531

  Phone: 202-514-1287 | Email: luther.schaeffer@usdoj.gov
  http://nij.gov

HHS93.810 | PAUL COVERDELL NATIONAL ACUTE STROKE PROGRAM NATIONAL CENTER FOR CHRONIC DISEASE PREVENTION AND HEALTH PROMOTION
"Coverdell"

Award: Cooperative Agreements

Purpose: The program works to improve the quality of acute stroke care and health outcomes for acute stroke patients.

Applicant Eligibility: State Governments (this includes the District of Columbia) are eligible to apply.

Beneficiary Eligibility: Eligibility is limited to state health departments (to include the District of Columbia) with heart disease and stroke prevention programs for this cooperative agreement. State health departments are the only agencies who are uniquely positioned to develop strong state level task forces to develop these stroke systems of care that can be used to focus on an comprehensive approach to improving quality of care at all points along the continuum of care that will have the largest reach and impact on decreasing morbidity and mortality from stroke, reducing disparities in the delivery of care, and improving outcomes.

Award Range/Average: 700,000 -800,000

Funding: (Cooperative Agreements) FY 18 $6,740,000.00; FY 19 est $6,740,000.00; FY 20 est $0.00

HQ: 4770 Buford Highway NE, PO Box F72, Atlanta, GA 30341

  Phone: 770-488-6093 | Email: sweagle@cdc.gov
  http://www.cdc.gov

HUD14.273 | PAY FOR SUCCESS PERMANENT SUPPORTIVE HOUSING DEMONSTRATION
"Pay for Success Demonstration"

Award: Project Grants

Purpose: To prevent and end homelessness and reduce avoidable incarceration by increasing the provision of Permanent Supportive Housing (PSH). The PFS Demonstration is an opportunity to equip communities for funding PSH projects that will prevent returns to homelessness and reduce recidivism among the reentry population.

Applicant Eligibility: The grantee will use grant funds for assessing the feasibility of a PFS project and/or structuring PFS operations, including: partnership building, capital-raising activities, Program design for the target population at the Demonstration Site, managing contracts with service providers, making Success Payments on behalf of the government entity, and managing third-party evaluators. Intermediaries may carry out all activities directly and/or subaward funds to subrecipients or procure the services of contractors to carry out PFS activities.

Beneficiary Eligibility: See program's Notice of Funding Availability.

Award Range/Average: Range of awards is: $881,376 to $1.3 million.The average award is: $1.24 million.

HQ: 451 7th Street SW, Room 7260, Washington, DC 20410

Phone: 202-402-4773 | Email: karen.m.deblasio@hud.gov

http://hudexchange.info

DOT20.901 | PAYMENTS FOR ESSENTIAL AIR SERVICES
"EAS"

Award: Project Grants; Direct Payments for Specified Use

Purpose: To assure that air transportation is provided to eligible communities by subsidizing air carriers.

Applicant Eligibility: Air carrier must be found fit and be selected by the Department to perform the subsidized service.

Beneficiary Eligibility: Air carriers and eligible local communities.

Award Range/Average: For continental United States: range from $491,205 to $4,710,683 annually; an average of $2,189,355 annually per community per year.

Funding: (Direct Payments for Specified Use) FY 18 $325,000,000.00; FY 19 est $330,000,000.00; FY 20 est $334,000,000.00

HQ: 1200 New Jersey Avenue SE, Washington, DC 20590

Phone: 202-366-3176 | Email: kevin.schlemmer@dot.gov

http://www.dot.gov/policy/aviation-policy/small-community-rural-air-service/essential-air-service

DOT20.930 | PAYMENTS FOR SMALL COMMUNITY AIR SERVICE DEVELOPMENT
"Small Community Program or SCASDP Payments for Small Community Air Service Development"

Award: Project Grants

Purpose: To assist small communities, enhance their air service and increase access to the national transportation system.

Applicant Eligibility: In order to qualify for a SCASDP grant: 1. The airport serving the community is not larger than a small hub airport, according to FAA hub classifications effective on the date of service of the Department's Solicitation (RFP) Order or as of calendar year 1997, the airport serving the community was not larger than a small hub airport; 2. The community has insufficient air carrier service or unreasonably high air fares, 3. The airport serving the community presents characteristics, such as geographic diversity or unique circumstances that demonstrate the need for, and feasibility of, grant assistance from the Small Community Program; 4. An applicant may not receive an additional grant to support the same project from a previous grant; 5. An applicant may not receive an additional grant, prior to the completion of its previous grant; Program Limits1. No more than 4 communities or consortia of communities, or a combination thereof, from the same State may be selected to participate in the Program in any fiscal year; and2. No more than 40 communities or consortia of communities, or a combination thereof, may be selected to participate in the Program in each year for which the funds are appropriated. In addition to the statute, the Department applies the following conditions: Communities without existing air service. Communities that do not currently have commercial air service are eligible. Small communities that currently receive subsidized air service under the Essential Air Service (EAS) or Alternate Essential Air Service (AEAS) Program will not be considered for SCASDP funds. Consortium applications. The statute permits individual communities and consortia of communities to apply for grant awards under this Program. An application from a consortium of communities must be

Programs Administered by Federal Headquarters

one that seeks to facilitate the efforts of the communities working together toward a joint grant project. In other words, the application must set forth one grant project, with one joint objective, and establish one entity to ensure that the joint objective is accomplished according to the terms of a grant agreement. For example, several communities surrounding an airport may apply together to improve air services at that airport, with a joint objective of securing new or additional service to that airport. Or, surrounding airports may apply together in support of a regional plan to lower fares or reverse a decline in traffic. Multiple Applications: A community may file only one application for a grant, either individually or as part of a consortium. Prior grant recipients: Communities or members of a consortia, that were awarded grants in previous years and want to apply for a grant this year should be aware that they are precluded from seeking new funds for projects for which they have already received an award under the Small Community Program.

Beneficiary Eligibility: The legal sponsor of the proposed project must be a government entity. If the applicant is a public-private partnership, a public government member of the organization must be identified as the community's sponsor to receive project cost reimbursements. A community may designate only one government entity as the legal sponsor, even if it is applying as a consortium that consists of two or more local government entities. Private organizations may not be designated as the legal sponsor of a grant under the Small Community Program. The community has the responsibility to ensure that the recipient of any funding has the legal authority under state and local laws to carry out all aspects of the grant.

Award Range/Average: Range: $20,000 to $1.6 million

Funding: (Project Grants) FY 18 $10,000,000.00; FY 19 est $12,500,000.00; FY 20 est Estimate Not Available

HQ: 1200 New Jersey Avenue SE W86 307, Washington, DC 20590

    Phone: 202-366-0577 | Email: brooke.chapman@dot.gov

    http://www.dot.gov/policy/aviation-policy/small-community-rural-air-service/scasdp

DOI15.226 | PAYMENTS IN LIEU OF TAXES
"PILT"

Award: Direct Payments for Specified Use; Direct Payments With Unrestricted Use

Purpose: Payments in Lieu of Taxes (PILT) are Federal payments to local governments that help offset losses in property taxes due to non-taxable Federal lands.

Applicant Eligibility: Local units of government containing eligible acres of PILT entitlement land as defined in Section 6901 will receive automatic payment distribution as computed in accordance with Section 6903 of the Law.

Beneficiary Eligibility: Local units of government in which Federal lands are located or have been acquired for purposes defined under Objectives.

Award Range/Average: RangeFY 2016: $104.00- $3,498,325.00 FY 2017: TBDFY 2018: TBDAverageFY 2016: $1,749,214.50 FY 2017: TBDFY 2017: TBD

Funding: (Direct Payments with Unrestricted Use) FY 16 $451,066,792.00; FY 17 Estimate Not Available; FY 18 est Estimate Not Available; - (FY 17 Exp: TBD, FY 18 Exp: TBD); (Direct Payments for Specified Use) FY 16 $533,208.00; FY 17 Estimate Not Available; FY 18 est Estimate Not Available; - (FY 17 Exp: TBD, FY 18 Exp: TBD)

HQ: Office of Budget Department of the Interior 1849 C Street NW, PO Box 4106 MIB, Washington, DC 20240

    Phone: 202-513-7783

    http://www.doi.gov/pilt

USDA10.205 | PAYMENTS TO 1890 LAND-GRANT COLLEGES AND TUSKEGEE UNIVERSITY
"Evans-Allen Research and/or Agricultural Research at 1890 Land-Grant Institutions, Including Tuskegee University, West Virginia State University and Central State University"

Award: Formula Grants

Purpose: To support agricultural research, agriculture, and rural life.

Applicant Eligibility: Applications may be submitted by 1890 Land-Grant universities, including Tuskegee University, West Virginia State University and Central State University.

Beneficiary Eligibility: Same as Applicant Eligibility.

Award Range/Average: If minimum or maximum amounts of funding per competitive and/or capacity project grant, or cooperative agreement are established, these amounts will be announced in the annual Capacity, Competitive, and/or Non-Competitive Request for Application (RFA).The most current RFA is available via: https://nifa.usda.gov/sites/default/files/

resources/FY18 AgriculturalResearchat1890 InstitutionsModification882017.pdf
Funding: (Formula Grants (Apportionments)) FY 17 $50,780,008.00; FY 18 est $50,877,548.00; FY 19 est $50,683,295.00
HQ: 1400 Independence Avenue SW, PO Box 2250, Washington, DC 20250-2250
   Phone: 202-720-9278
   http://nifa.usda.gov/program/agricultural-research-1890-land-grant-institutions

USDA10.203 | PAYMENTS TO AGRICULTURAL EXPERIMENT STATIONS UNDER THE HATCH ACT

Award: Formula Grants
Purpose: To promote agriculture and rural life, provide support for agricultural research and compensations for agriculture research.
Applicant Eligibility: (A) The Hatch Act of 1887 (Regular Research) Hatch Act funds are provided for agricultural research on an annual basis to the State Agricultural Experiment Stations (SAES's) which were established under the direction of the college or University or agricultural departments of the college or University in each State in accordance with the act approved July 2, 1862 (7 U.S.C. 301 et seq.); or such other substantially equivalent arrangements as any State shall determine. Award recipients may subcontract to Organizations not eligible to apply for funding provided that such arrangements are necessary to complete the project. (B) The Hatch Act of 1887 (Multistate Research) Hatch Act funds are provided for agricultural research on an annual basis to the State Agricultural Experiment Stations (SAES's) which were established under the direction of the college or University or agricultural departments of the college or University in each State in accordance with the act approved July 2, 1862 (7 U.S.C. 301 et seq.); or such other substantially equivalent arrangements as any State shall determine. Award recipients may subcontract to Organizations not eligible to apply for funding provided that such arrangements are necessary to complete the project.
Beneficiary Eligibility: Funds under the Hatch Act are allocated in accordance with the statutory formula stated in the Act to the State agricultural experiment stations of the 50 States, the District of Columbia, Guam, Puerto Rico, the Virgin Islands, American Samoa, Micronesia, and Northern Mariana Islands. These institutions have been identified and declared eligible by their respective State legislatures.
Award Range/Average: If minimum or maximum amounts of funding per competitive and/or capacity project grant, or cooperative agreement are established, these amounts will be announced in the annual Competitive Request for Application (RFA). The most current RFA is available via: https://nifa.usda.gov/funding-opportunity/community-food-projects-cfp-competitive-grants-program
Funding: (Formula Grants (Apportionments)) FY 17 $228,105,022.00; FY 18 est $229,053,592.00; FY 19 est $227,669,828.00
HQ: 1400 Independence Avenue SW, PO Box 2240, Washington, DC 20250-2240
   Phone: 202-401-4939
   http://nifa.usda.gov/grants

VA64.053 | PAYMENTS TO STATES FOR PROGRAMS TO PROMOTE THE HIRING AND RETENTION OF NURSES AT STATE VETERANS HOMES

Award: Project Grants
Purpose: To obtain payments to assist a State Veterans Home (SVH) in the hiring and retention of nurses for the purpose of reducing nursing shortages at that SVH.
Applicant Eligibility: (a) To apply for payments during a Federal fiscal year, a State representative must submit to VA, in accordance with 53. 40, a completed VA Form 10-0430 and documentation specified by the form (VA Form 10-0430 is available at VA medical centers and on the Internet at http://www1.va.gov/geriatricsshg/ or may be obtained by contacting the Geriatrics and Extended Care Office at 202-461-6750, VHA Headquarters, 810 Vermont Avenue, NW., Washington, DC 20420). The submission for payments for a fiscal year must be received by VA during the last quarter (July 1-September 30) of the preceding fiscal year. The State must submit a new application for each fiscal year that the State seeks payments for an incentive Program. (b) As part of the application, the State representative must submit to VA evidence that the State has sufficient funding, when combined with the VA payments, to fully operate its employee incentive Program through the end of the fiscal year. To meet this requirement, the State representative must provide to VA a letter from an authorized State official certifying that, if VA were to approve payments under this part, the non-VA share of the funds for the Program would be by a date or dates specified in the certification, available for the employee incentive Program without further State action to make such funds available. If the certification is based on a State law authorizing funds for the employee incentive Program, a copy of the State law must be submitted with the certification. (c) If an application does not contain sufficient information for a determination under this part, the State representative will be notified in writing (electronically and by mail) of any additional

Programs Administered by Federal Headquarters

submission required and that the State has 30 calendar days from the date of the notice to submit such additional information or no further action will be taken. If the State representative does not submit all of the required information or demonstrate that he or she has good cause for failing to provide the information within 30 calendar days of the notice (which may extend beyond the last quarter of the preceding Federal fiscal year), then the State applicant will be notified in writing that the application for VA assistance will be deemed withdrawn and no further action will be taken.

Beneficiary Eligibility: There are no beneficiary benefits; this applies to a State Veterans Home and not a Veteran.

Award Range/Average: The amount of payments awarded under this part during a Federal fiscal year will be the amount requested by the State and approved by VA in accordance with this part. Payments may not exceed 50 percent of the cost of the employee incentive program for that fiscal year and may not exceed 2 percent of the amount of the total per diem payments estimated by VA to be made under 38 U.S.C. 1741 to the State for that SVH during that fiscal year for adult day health care, domiciliary care, hospital care, and nursing home care.

Funding: (Project Grants) FY 15 $113,721.00; FY 16 est $113,721.00; FY 17 Estimate Not Available

HQ: 810 Vermont Avenue NW, Washington, DC 20420

　　Phone: 814-860-2201 | Email: valarie.delanko@va.gov

　　http://www.ecfr.gov/cgi-bin/text-idx?c=ecfr&rgn=div5&view=text&node=38:2.0.1.1.24&idno=38#38:2.0.1.1.24.0.373.6

DOD12.112 | PAYMENTS TO STATES IN LIEU OF REAL ESTATE TAXES

Award: Formula Grants

Purpose: To compensate local taxing units for the loss of taxes from federally acquired lands, 75 percent of all monies received or deposited in the Treasury during any fiscal year for the account of leasing of lands acquired by the United States for flood control, navigation and allied purposes.

Applicant Eligibility: State government in which lands have been Federally acquired for purposes defined under Objectives.

Beneficiary Eligibility: State and county government being compensated and their residents.

PC45.400 | PEACE CORPS' GLOBAL HEALTH AND PEPFAR INITIATIVE PROGRAM

Award: Cooperative Agreements; Project Grants

Purpose: To support the U.S. President's Emergency Plan for AIDS Relief (PEPFAR)'s goals and programmatic strategy.

Applicant Eligibility: N/A

Beneficiary Eligibility: N/A

HQ: 1111 20th Street NW, Room 4432, Washington, DC 20526

　　Phone: 202-692-1235 | Email: jalustizaderocco@peacecorps.gov

　　http://www.peacecorps.gov

VA64.104 | PENSION FOR NON-SERVICE-CONNECTED DISABILITY FOR VETERANS
"Pension"

Award: Direct Payments With Unrestricted Use

Purpose: Assists wartime veterans in need whose non-service connected disabilities are permanent and total preventing them from following a substantially gainful occupation.

Applicant Eligibility: A Veteran who meets the wartime service requirements is potential eligible if he/she is: permanently and totally disabled for reasons not necessarily due to service, age 65 or older, or is presumed to be totally and permanently disabled for pension purposes because: o he/she is a patient in a nursing home for long-term care due to a disability, or being disabled, as determined by the Commissioner of Social Security (SS) for purposes of any benefits administered by the Commissioner, such as SS disability benefits or Supplemental Security Income. Income restrictions are prescribed in 38 U.S.C. 1521. Pension is not payable to those whose estates are so large that it is reasonable they use the estate for maintenance. A Veteran meets wartime service requirements if he/she served: a total of 90 days or more during one or more periods of war; 90 or more consecutive days that began or ended during a period of war; or for any length of time during a period of war if he/she was discharged or released for a service-connected disability. Veterans entering service after September 7, 1980, must also meet the minimum active duty requirement of 24 months of continuous service or the full period to which the Veteran was called to active duty. (38 U.S.C. 5303(A)).

Beneficiary Eligibility: Disabled veterans.

Award Range/Average: Payments are $ $12,868 annually, reduced by countable income for a Veteran without dependents ($21,466if in need of aid and attendance and $ $15,725 if housebound) and $16,851for a Veteran with one dependent ($25,488 if in need of aid and attendance and $19,710if housebound) plus $2,198for each additional dependent. Also, an additional $2,923is added if a Veteran is of the WWI or Mexican Border Period. These rates were effective December 1,2014 for Improved Law Pensions.

Funding: (Direct Payments for Specified Use) FY 16 $3,745,970,000.00; FY 17 est $3,900,824,000.00; FY 18 Estimate Not Available

HQ: 810 Vermont Avenue NW, Washington, DC 20420
   Phone: 202-461-9700
   http://www.va.gov

PBGC86.001 | PENSION PLAN TERMINATION INSURANCE "ERISA"

Award: Insurance
Purpose: To encourage the continuation and maintenance of voluntary private pension plans for the benefit of their participants.
Applicant Eligibility: Private businesses and Organizations that maintain defined benefit plans and participants (and beneficiaries) in such plans.
Beneficiary Eligibility: All participants (and their beneficiaries) in covered single-employer pension plans may be potentially eligible for plan termination insurance payments. All covered multi-employer plans may be eligible for financial assistance needed to ensure payment of guaranteed benefits.
Funding: (Salary or Expense) FY 07 Actual Not Available; FY 08 est $4,500,000,000.00; FY 09 est Estimate Not Available
HQ: 1200 K Street NW, Washington, DC 20005-4026
   Phone: 202-326-4000
   http://www.pbgc.gov

VA64.105 | PENSION TO VETERANS SURVIVING SPOUSES, AND CHILDREN "Death Pension"

Award: Direct Payments With Unrestricted Use
Purpose: Assists needy surviving spouses, and children of deceased war-time veterans whose deaths were not due to service.
Applicant Eligibility: Unmarried surviving spouses and children of deceased Veterans who met the wartime service requirements or was a wartime Veteran who was receiving (or was entitled to receive) disability compensation at the time of death. Veterans who entered service after September 7, 1980, must also have met the minimum active duty requirement of 24 months of continuous service or the full period to which the Veteran was called to active duty. Veterans discharged on or after October 16, 1981, must have served for two years or the length to which called to active duty, if less than two years, or have a service-connected disability (38 U.S.C. 5303(A)). Income restrictions are prescribed in 38 U.S.C. 1541 and 1542. A child must be unmarried and under 18, between 18 and 23 if in school, or disabled before 18 and continuously incapable of self-support. Pension is not payable to those whose estates are so large that it is reasonable they use the estate for maintenance. A Veteran meets wartime service requirements if he/she served: a total of 90 days or more during one or more periods of war; 90 or more consecutive days that began or ended during a period of war; or for any length of time during a period of war if he/she was discharged or released for a service-connected disability.
Beneficiary Eligibility: Low income surviving spouses and children of deceased war-time Veterans.
Award Range/Average: $8,630 annually, reduced by countable income for a spouse without children ($13,794 if in need of aid and attendance and $10,548 if housebound) and $11,296 for a surviving spouse with one child ($16,456 if in need of aid and attendance and $13,209 if housebound) plus $2,198 for each additional child. These rates were effective December 1,2014 for Improved Law Pensions.
Funding: (Direct Payments with Unrestricted Use) FY 16 $1,792,871,000.00; FY 17 est $1,859,608,000.00; FY 18 est $2,014,943,000.00
HQ: Washington, DC 20420
   Phone: 202-461-9700 | Email: michelle.staton@va.gov
   http://www.va.gov

Programs Administered by Federal Headquarters

HUD14.327 | PERFORMANCE BASED CONTRACT ADMINISTRATOR PROGRAM "PBCA Program"

Award: Direct Payments for Specified Use

Purpose: To implement the policy of the United States, as established in section 2 of the 1937 Act, of assisting States and their political subdivisions for aiding lower income families.

Applicant Eligibility: HUD will accept applications to provide contract administration services for the 42 States, which are listed in Appendix A of the Program Notice of Funding Availability (NOFA). State is defined in the ACC as one of the fifty United States, the District of Columbia, the United States Virgin Islands, or the Commonwealth of Puerto Rico. Please note that there have been 11 PHAs selected for PBCAs in a previous competition. HUD has already entered into an ACC with those PHAs. Entities applying to serve as PBCA in more than one State must submit a separate application for each State for which it applies. See Program NOFA for more information. HUD may enter into an ACC for the administration of a project-based Section 8 HAP contract with a legal entity that qualifies as a public housing authority as defined under section 3(b)(6) (a) of the Housing Act of 1937.

Beneficiary Eligibility: Families currently receiving assistance as long as their income does not exceed 80 percent of area median income adjusted for family size.

Award Range/Average: estimated $20 million per month for entire program.

Funding: (Salaries and Expenses) FY 15 $273,000,000; FY 16 est $338,000,000; FY 17 est $295,000,000

HQ: 451 7th Street SW, Office of Housing Assistance and Contract Administration, Washington, DC 20410

Phone: 202-402-2768 | Email: deborah.k.lear@hud.gov

http://portal.hud.gov/hudportal/hud?src=/program_offices/housing/mfh/rfp/sec8rfp

DOD12.355 | PEST MANAGEMENT AND VECTOR CONTROL RESEARCH

Award: Cooperative Agreements; Project Grants

Purpose: To develop new interventions for protection of deployed military personnel from diseases caused by arthropod-borne pathogens and to improve control of filth flies.

Applicant Eligibility: Applicants must be a public or private educational institution, nonprofit Organizations operated for purposes in the public interest and commercial firms.

Beneficiary Eligibility: Beneficiaries are relatively independent investigators associated with an applicant organization.

Award Range/Average: $100- $250K per year/per award.

Funding: (Cooperative Agreements) FY 17 $145,000.00; FY 18 est $500,000.00; FY 19 est $1,479,376.00

HQ: 110 Thomas Johnson Drive, Frederick, MD 21702

Phone: 301-619-2446 | Email: richard.w.totten2.civ@mail.mil

http://www.3.natick.army.mil

DOT20.721 | PHMSA PIPELINE SAFETY PROGRAM ONE CALL GRANT

Award: Project Grants

Purpose: Provides funding to State agencies in promoting damage prevention, including changes with their State underground damage prevention laws, related compliance activities, training and public education.

Applicant Eligibility: A state is eligible if it qualifies under section 49 USC 6104 (b).

Beneficiary Eligibility: State (Includes District of Columbia and Puerto Rico) Also, State agency with a Certification or Agreement under 60105 or 60106 of Title 49 USC.

Award Range/Average: The range for grants awarded $10,000 to $45,000

Funding: (Project Grants (Discretionary)) FY 18 $1,110,539.00; FY 19 est $1,218,889.00; FY 20 est Estimate Not Available

HQ: 1200 New Jersey Avenue SE, Washington, DC 20590

Phone: 405-834-8344 | Email: zach.barrett@dot.gov

http://www.phmsa.dot.gov

DOT20.723 | PHMSA PIPELINE SAFETY RESEARCH AND DEVELOPMENT "OTHER TRANSACTION AGREEMENTS"

Award: Project Grants

Purpose: Sponsors research and development projects focused on providing near-term solutions that will improve the safety, reduce environmental impact, and enhance the reliability of the Nation's pipeline transportation system.

Applicant Eligibility: Universities and other academic Institutions, individual, profit Organization, nonprofit Organization, State (includes D. C.), U.S. Territories and possessions, Indian Tribes, local government, other entities are eligible to apply.

Beneficiary Eligibility: Anyone/general public can receive benefits from the eligible applicant.

Award Range/Average: The range of awards is $40,000 to $856,000. The average is $189,000.

Funding: (Project Grants) FY 18 $10,029,765.00; FY 19 est $10,600,000.00; FY 20 est Estimate Not Available

HQ: 1200 New Jersey Avenue SE, Washington, DC 20590

Phone: 919-238-4759 | Email: robert.w.smith@dot.gov

http://www.phmsa.dot.gov

DOT20.725 | PHMSA PIPELINE SAFETY UNDERGROUND NATURAL GAS STORAGE GRANT

Award: Formula Grants

Purpose: Through annual Certification/Agreements with PHMSA, inspects and enforces the federal underground storage regulations for intrastate underground natural gas storage facilities located within the state.

Applicant Eligibility: State must have a 60105 Certification or 60106 Agreement with PHMSA. The Department provides Federal funds, up to 80 percent of the State's total Program costs to any State agency with a certificate under Section 60105 of Title 49, United States Code, an agreement under Section 60106 of Title 49, United States Code, or to any State acting as a DOT agent on interstate pipelines.

Beneficiary Eligibility: State (Includes District of Columbia and Puerto Rico) Also, State agency with a Certification or Agreement under 60105 or 60106 of Title 49 USC.

Funding: (Formula Grants) FY 18 $3,707,058.00; FY 19 est $7,146,926.00; FY 20 est Estimate Not Available

HQ: 1200 New Jersey Avenue SE, Washington, DC 20590

Phone: 405-834-8344 | Email: zach.barrett@dot.gov

http://www.phmsa.dot.gov

USDA10.615 | PIMA AGRICULTURE COTTON TRUST FUND

Award: Direct Payments With Unrestricted Use

Purpose: The Pima Agriculture Cotton Trust compensates for accidents to the domestic textile manufacturers resulting from U.S. import tariffs on cotton fabric.

Applicant Eligibility: Payments to reduce the injury to domestic textile manufacturers resulting from U.S. import tariffs on cotton fabric that are higher than tariffs on certain apparel articles made of cotton fabric.

Beneficiary Eligibility: Beneficiaries limited to: one or more nationally recognized associations established for the promotion of pima cotton in apparel; yarn spinners of pima cotton that produce ring spun cotton yarns in the United States, and manufacturers who cut and sew cotton shirts in the United States who certify that they used imported cotton fabric in 2013.

Award Range/Average: Range: $273,000 to $4,285,000.Average: $1,800,000.

Funding: (Direct Payments with Unrestricted Use) FY 17 $16,000,000.00; FY 18 est $16,000,000.00; FY 19 Estimate Not Available

HQ: 1400 Independence Avenue SW, Washington, DC 20250

Phone: 202-720-3538 | Email: amy.harding@fas.usda.gov

http://www.fas.usda.gov

DOT20.700 | PIPELINE SAFETY PROGRAM STATE BASE GRANT

Award: Formula Grants

Purpose: Develops, supports, and maintains inspection and enforcement activities for State gas and hazardous liquid pipeline safety programs.

Programs Administered by Federal Headquarters

Applicant Eligibility: State must have a 60105 Certification or 60106 Agreement with PHMSA. The Department provides Federal funds (limited to congressional appropriations), up to 80 percent of the State's total Program costs to any State agency with a certificate under Section 60105 of Title 49, United States Code, an agreement under Section 60106 of Title 49, United States Code, or to any State acting as a DOT agent on interstate pipelines.

Beneficiary Eligibility: State, District of Columbia, and Puerto Rico.

Award Range/Average: The range of grants awarded $11,826 - $ 4,507,570.

Funding: (Formula Grants) FY 18 $56,030,237.00; FY 19 est $53,169,623.00; FY 20 est Estimate Not Available.

HQ: 1200 New Jersey Avenue SE, Washington, DC 20590

Phone: 405-834-8344 | Email: zach.barrett@dot.gov

http://www.phmsa.dot.gov

DOT20.724 | PIPELINE SAFETY RESEARCH COMPETITIVE ACADEMIC AGREEMENT PROGRAM (CAAP)

Award: Project Grants

Purpose: To spur innovation by enabling an academic research focus on high-risk and high pay-off solutions for the many pipeline safety challenges.

Applicant Eligibility: Applicants must be non-profit Institutions of higher education located in the United States or a U.S. territory or possession.

Beneficiary Eligibility: Solutions from academic research agreements to non-profit institutions of higher education will benefit the American public who has a stake in safe, reliable and environmentally friendly pipeline transportation of hydrocarbons.

Award Range/Average: The current program level of $2,000,000 (six individual awards at up to $300,000 each) is anticipated.

Funding: (Cooperative Agreements) FY 18 $3,855,575; FY 19 est $1,956,810; FY 20 est Estimate Not Available;-This program is designed to be administered as an annual announcement with up to six awards of $300,000 each, or up to $2,000,000 for the overall annual program. If a large number of high-quality applications are received, and there are remaining funds available, PHMSA may award more than six agreements.

HQ: Pipeline & Hazardous Materials Safety Administration Acquisition Services Division 1200 New Jersey Avenue SE, Washington, DC 20590

Phone: 202-366-6085 | Email: joshua.arnold@dot.gov

http://www.phmsa.dot.gov/pipeline

USDA10.617 | PL-480 MARKET DEVELOPMENT AND TECHNICAL ASSISTANCE "Section 108"

Award: Project Grants

Purpose: The Foreign Agricultural Service promotes a grant program to assist in the implementation of market development and agricultural technical assistance activities.

Applicant Eligibility: Priority applicants will be U.S. agricultural non profit trade Organizations who will conduct market development and technical assistance activities designed to increase or maintain U.S. agricultural exports.

Beneficiary Eligibility: U.S. agricultural entities are expected to benefit from the growth of U.S. export markets.

Funding: (Project Grants (Discretionary)) FY 18 $5,000,000.00; FY 19 est $3,000,000.00; FY 20 est 1,500,000.00

HQ: 1400 Independence Avenue SW, Washington, DC 20250

Phone: 202-720-4327 | Email: curt.alt@fas.usda.gov

DOD12.110 | PLANNING ASSISTANCE TO STATES "Section 22"

Award: Provision of Specialized Services

Purpose: To assist State in the plans for the conservation of water and land resources within the State.

Applicant Eligibility: The 50 States, the District of Columbia, Guam, American Samoa, the Commonwealth of the Northern Marinas, Palau Island, the Commonwealth of Puerto Rico, the Virgin Islands, and Federally recognized Indian Tribes.

Beneficiary Eligibility: Same as Applicant Eligibility.

HQ: 441 G Street NW, Washington, DC 20314

Phone: 202-761-1504 | Email: donnie.l.tew@usace.army.mil

http://www.usace.army.mil/business.html

HHS93.835 | PLANNING GRANT FOR HEALTHCARE AND PUBLIC HEALTH SECTOR CYBERSECURITY INFORMATION SHARING

Award: Cooperative Agreements
Purpose: The objectives of this award are to gain an understanding of the cybersecurity threat information needs and to increase organizational capacity and develop a strategy to expand cybersecurity threat information sharing.
Applicant Eligibility: N/A
Beneficiary Eligibility: Select as many that apply (see pages 11 through 14 of the Reference Manual); Nonprofit with 501(c)3 IRS status (other than institution of higher education); Nonprofit without 501(c)3 IRS status (other than institution of higher education); Universities; Colleges; Research institutions; Hospitals; Community-based organizations; Faith-based organizations.
Award Range/Average: 150000
Funding: (Cooperative Agreements (Discretionary Grants)) FY 18 $500,000.00; FY 19 est $500,000.00; FY 20 est $500,000.00
HQ: 200 C Street SW, Washington, DC 20024

Phone: 202-260-0400 | Email: virginia.simmons@hhs.gov
http://phe.gov

HHS93.253 | POISON CENTER SUPPORT AND ENHANCEMENT GRANT
"Poison Control Centers (PCCs)"

Award: Project Grants
Purpose: To support PCCs' efforts to prevent, and provide treatment recommendations, for poisonings.
Applicant Eligibility: U.S. accredited Poison Control Centers. Unaccredited centers are eligible for a grant waiver if such centers can reasonably demonstrate that they will obtain such accreditation within a reasonable period of time.
Beneficiary Eligibility: Residents of the 50 United States, Puerto Rico, the District of Columbia, the U.S. Virgin Islands, Guam, American Samoa, and the Federated States of Micronesia.
Award Range/Average: Range: $12,466 to $2,185,501. Average: $356,711.
Funding: (Project Grants) FY 18 est $18,549,001.00; FY 19 $20,400,000.00; FY 20 estEstimate Not Available
HQ: 5600 Fishers Lane, Room 08W 26, Rockville, MD 20857

Phone: 301-443-8177 | Email: sstevenson1@hrsa.gov
http://www.hrsa.gov

NSF47.078 | POLAR PROGRAMS
"OPP"

Award: Project Grants
Purpose: To strengthen and enhance the national scientific enterprise through the expansion of fundamental knowledge and increased understanding of the polar regions.
Applicant Eligibility: Except where a Program solicitation establishes more restrictive eligibility criteria, individuals and Organizations in the following categories may submit proposals: universities and colleges; Non-profit, non-academic Organizations; For-profit Organizations; State and local Governments; and unaffiliated individuals. See the NSF Grant Proposal Guide Chapter i.e. for a full description of eligibility requirements: http://www.nsf.gov/publications/pubsumm. jsp?odskey=gpg.
Beneficiary Eligibility: N/A
Award Range/Average: Range Low $9,766 Range High $2,403,846 Average $276,709
Funding: (Project Grants) FY 18 $501,720,000.00; FY 19 est $469,160,000.00; FY 20 est $403,390,000.00
HQ: 2415 Eisenhower Avenue, Alexandria, VA 22314

Phone: 703-292-5079 | Email: mlane@nsf.gov
http://nsf.gov/dir/index.jsp?org=opp

HHS93.239 | POLICY RESEARCH AND EVALUATION GRANTS

Award: Project Grants
Purpose: To support research that is relevant to policy development and evaluation of current and proposed programs of interest to the Secretary, the Administration, and the Congress.

Programs Administered by Federal Headquarters

Applicant Eligibility: Assistance may be provided to State and local Governments, Institutions of higher education, nonprofit Organizations and individuals. Occasionally, awards are made to for-profit Organizations when deemed by the Assistant Secretary to be consistent with the legislative intent and purpose of the Program.

Beneficiary Eligibility: Federal, State and local governments will benefit. (Note: Projects do not provide any direct assistance to individuals.

Award Range/Average: for FY2016 one cooperative agreement award at estimated $1,900,000, In FY2017 the single award was increased to $2,050,000. For FY2018 it is estimated that the award will return to $1,900,000

Funding: (Project Grants) FY 16 Actual Not Available; FY 17 est $2,050,000.00; FY 18 est $1,900,000.00

HQ: 200 Independence Avenue SW, Room 405F, Washington, DC 20201

Phone: 202-690-8410 | Email: don.oellerich@hhs.gov

http://aspe.hhs.gov

DOT20.823 | PORT INFRASTRUCTURE DEVELOPMENT PROGRAM

Award: Project Grants (discretionary)

Purpose: To improve the port facilities available at coastal seaports.

Applicant Eligibility: An eligible applicant for a Port Infrastructure Development Program discretionary grants is a port authority, a commission or its subdivision or agent under existing authority, as well as a State or political subdivision of a State or local government, a Tribal government, a public agency or publicly chartered authority established by one or more States, a special purpose district with a transportation function, a multistate or multijurisdictional group of entities, or a lead entity described above jointly with a private entity or group of private entities.

Beneficiary Eligibility: Same as Applicant Eligibility.

Funding: (Project Grants (Discretionary)) FY 18 Actual Not Available; FY 19 est $292,730,000.00; FY 20 est Estimate Not Available

HQ: 1200 New Jersey Avenue SE, Washington, DC 20590

Phone: 202-366-5076 | Email: robert.bouchard@dot.gov

DHS97.056 | PORT SECURITY GRANT PROGRAM
"PSGP"

Award: Project Grants

Purpose: The Port Security Grant Program's function is to enhance the nation's preparedness and resilience against natural calamities and terrorist and cyber terrorist activities.

Applicant Eligibility: Pursuant to the Maritime Transportation Security Act of 2002, as amended (MTSA), DHS established a risk-based grant Program to support maritime security risk management. Funding is directed towards the implementation of AMSPs, Facility Security Plans (FSP), and Vessel Security Plans (VSPs) among port authorities, facility operators, and state and local government agencies that are required to provide port security services. In administering the grant Program, national, economic, energy, and strategic defense concerns based upon the most current risk assessments available will be considered.

Beneficiary Eligibility: Critical national seaports and terminals.

Funding: (Project Grants) FY 18 $100,000,000.00; FY 19 est $100,000,000.00; FY 20 est $100,000,000.00

HQ: 400 C Street SW, Washington, DC 20523

Phone: 800-368-6498

http://www.fema.gov/government/grant/index.shtm

VA64.027 | POST-9/11 VETERANS EDUCATIONAL ASSISTANCE
"Post 9/11 GI Bill - Chapter 33 - Veterans Benefits Administration"

Award: Direct Payments for Specified Use

Purpose: To help servicepersons adjust to civilian life after separation from military service, assist in the recruitment and retention of highly qualified personnel in the active and reserve components in the Armed Forces.

Applicant Eligibility: What follows is not a complete list of eligibility requirements. For more information on the latest changes to the Post-9/11 GI Bill go to the VA web-site address listed below. Individuals who entered active duty after September 10, 2001 may be eligible for the Post-9/11 GI Bill. Individuals can use the Post-9/11 GI Bill after serving 90 days on active duty (excluding entry level and skill training). Only periods of active duty under title 10 will be used to establish eligibility for the Post 9/11 GI Bill. A high school diploma or equivalency certificate is always required for eligibility. Individuals who are eligible for the Montgomery GI Bill - Active Duty (chapter 30), the Montgomery GI Bill - Selected Reserve (chapter 1606), or the Reserve educational Assistance Program (REAP) will have to make an irrevocable election to relinquish eligibility under one of those benefit Programs to establish eligibility under the Post-9/11 GI Bill. The dependent children of a person who died in the line of duty while serving as a member of the Armed Forces may be eligible to use benefits under the Fry Scholarship provision of the Post-9/11 GI Bill. The spouse and/or child(ren) of a veteran or service member may be eligible for the Post 9/11 GI Bill if the veteran or service member transfers entitlement to those dependents. Eligibility to transfer entitlement to dependents is determined by the Department of Defense.

Beneficiary Eligibility: As stated above under Applicant Eligibility.

Award Range/Average: The amount of educational assistance an individual is entitled to varies based on the amount of time served on active duty, the amount of tuition and fees charged, and the Basic Allowance for Housing payable for an E-5 with dependents in the zip code where the student attends school. In most cases, the benefits last for 36 (48 months when combined with other VA education benefits) calendar months of full-time training. The work-study allowance is limited to the higher of the Federal minimum wage or the State minimum wage where the work is performed. Tutorial assistance may not exceed $1200 and reimbursement for a licensing or certification test may not exceed $2000. The rural benefit is a one-time payment of $500.

HQ: Department of Veterans Affairs Central Office 810 Vermont Avenue, Washington, DC 20420

Phone: 202-461-9800 | Email: michelle.staton@va.gov

http://www.gibill.va.gov

VA64.120 | POST-VIETNAM ERA VETERANS' EDUCATIONAL ASSISTANCE
"Voluntary-Contributory Matching Program"

Award: Direct Payments With Unrestricted Use

Purpose: To provide educational assistance to persons entering the Armed Forces after December 31, 1976, and before July 1, 1985.

Applicant Eligibility: The participant must have entered on active duty on or after January 1, 1977, and before July 1, 1985, and either served on active duty for more than 180 continuous days receiving an other than dishonorable discharge, or have been discharged after January, 1, 1977 because of a service-connected disability. Also eligible are participants who serve for more than 180 days and who continue on active duty and have completed their first period of obligated service (or 6 years of active duty, whichever comes first). Participants must also have satisfactorily contributed to the Program. (Satisfactory contribution consists of monthly deduction of $25 to $100 from military pay, up to a maximum of $2,700 for deposit in a special training fund.) Participants may make lump-sum contributions. No individuals on active duty in the Armed Forces may initially begin contributing to this Program after March 31, 1987.

Beneficiary Eligibility: Post-Vietnam era veterans.

HQ: 810 Vermont Avenue NW, Washington, DC 20420

Phone: 202-461-9700

http://www.gibill.va.gov

DOJ16.820 | POSTCONVICTION TESTING OF DNA EVIDENCE
"Kirk Bloodsworth Program"

Award: Project Grants

Purpose: To fund projects that assist States with postconviction DNA testing in cases of violent offenses to ensure fair and impartial administration of justice for all citizens.

Applicant Eligibility: Eligible applicants are States, units of local government, and public Institutions of higher education (including tribal Institutions of higher education). For the purposes of agency Program announcements, the term State includes the District of Columbia, the Commonwealth of Puerto Rico, the U.S. Virgin Islands, American Samoa, Guam, and the Northern Mariana Islands.

Beneficiary Eligibility: Ensures the availability of fair and impartial administration of justice to Americans who may have been unjustly convicted.

Award Range/Average: See the current fiscal year's solicitation guidelines posted on the Office of Justice Programs web site at https://ojp.gov/funding/Explore/CurrentFundingOpportunities.htm.

Funding: (Project Grants (Discretionary)) FY 17 $3,333,287.00; FY 18 Not Separately Identifiable; FY 19 Not Separately Identifiable

Programs Administered by Federal Headquarters

HQ: 810 7th Street NW, Washington, DC 20531
    Phone: 202-307-2942
    http://www.nij.gov

ED84.408 | POSTSECONDARY EDUCATION SCHOLARSHIPS FOR VETERAN'S DEPENDENTS
"Iraq and Afghanistan Service Grant (IASG)"

Award: Direct Payments for Specified Use

Purpose: Provides eligible veteran's dependent undergraduate postsecondary students with non-need based grant assistance to help meet educational expenses.

Applicant Eligibility: The student must be an eligible Veteran's dependent whose parent or guardian was a member of the Armed Forces of the United States and died as a result of performing military service in Iraq or Afghanistan after September 11, 2001. At the time of the parent or guardian's death, the student was less than 24 years of age or enrolled at an institution of higher education. The applicants must be U.S. citizens or eligible noncitizens and have a high school diploma, or a GED. Applicants must apply annually using the Free Application for Federal Student Aid (FAFSA). To be eligible, the applicant must meet all IAS Grant eligibility requirements, and must not have a Federal Pell Grant eligible Expected Family Contribution (EFC).

Beneficiary Eligibility: Eligible veteran's dependent undergraduate students, and students pursuing a teaching certificate that are U.S. citizens or eligible noncitizens. Students must be regular students in an eligible program and enrolled in institutions of higher education, making satisfactory academic progress. Incarcerated students, except those incarcerated in local penal facilities, are ineligible. Students must sign a statement of educational purpose, not owe a refund on a Title IV grant, and not be in default on a Title IV loan. Eligible males that are at least 18 years old and born after December 31, 1959, can receive aid only if they have registered with the Selective Service. The eligible veteran's dependent student cannot receive both an Iraq and Afghanistan Service Grant and Federal Pell Grant during the same award year.

Award Range/Average: For FY 2018, grants ranged from $569- $5,693; the average grant was estimated at $5,160. For FY 2019, grants are expected to range from $581- $5,811; the average grant is estimated at $5,293. For FY 2020, grants are expected to range from $620- $6,195, the average grant is estimated at $5,619.

Funding: (Formula Grants) FY 18 $329,000.00; FY 19 est $317,000.00; FY 20 est $307,000.00

HQ: PO Box 84, Washington, DC 20044-0084
    Phone: 800-433-3243
    https://studentaid.ed.gov/sa

HHS93.765 | PPHF-CDC PARTNERSHIP: STRENGTHENING PUBLIC HEALTH LABORATORIES

Award: Formula Grants

Purpose: The major objective is to enhance and strengthen the work and functionality of public health laboratories both domestically and abroad. The overall goal of the program is to improve several aspects of public health laboratories.

Applicant Eligibility: Eligible applicants that can apply for this funding opportunity are listed below: Nonprofit Organizations Small, minority, and women-owned businesses universities Colleges Research Institutions Hospitals Community-based Organizations Faith-based Organizations Federally recognized or state-recognized American Indian/Alaska Native tribal Governments American Indian/Alaska native tribally designated Organizations Alaska Native health corporations Urban Indian health Organizations Tribal epidemiology centers State and local Governments or their Bona Fide Agents (this includes the District of Columbia, the Commonwealth of Puerto Rico, the Virgin Islands, the Commonwealth of the Northern Marianna Islands, American Samoa, Guam, the Federated States of Micronesia, the Republic of the Marshall Islands, and the Republic of Palau)Political subdivisions of States (in consultation with States)A Bona Fide Agent is an agency/Organization identified by the state as eligible to submit an application under the state eligibility in lieu of a state application. If applying as a bona fide agent of a state or local government, a legal, binding agreement from the state or local government as documentation of the status is required. Attach with Other Attachment Forms when submitting via www.grants.gov.

Beneficiary Eligibility: Applicants must have experience with enhancing and strengthening the work and functionality of public health laboratories both domestically and abroad. The overarching goal is to improve several aspects of public health laboratories. The nation's public is the ultimate recipient of benefits from this program.

Award Range/Average: FY 2015 PPHF actual awarded amount $3,046,800. FY2016 anticipated PPHF awarded amount: $4,000,000; FY 2017 estimated PPHF award: $4,000,000 FY 2018 estimated PPHF award $4,000,000; FY 2019 estimated

PPHF award $4,000,000; FY2020 estimated PPHF award amount $4,000,000. Total anticipated PPHF award from FY2015 -FY2020 : 19,046,800.
Funding: (Formula Grants (Cooperative Agreements)) FY 18 $27,552,526.00; FY 19 est $1,284,500.00; FY 20 est $0.00
HQ: 2400 Century Parkway NE, PO Box V24-3, Atlanta, GA 30345
    Phone: 404-639-3008 | Email: sfs5@cdc.gov
    http://www.cdc.gov

HHS93.531 | PPHF-COMMUNITY TRANSFORMATION GRANTS AND NATIONAL DISSEMINATION AND SUPPORT FOR COMMUNITY TRANSFORMATION GRANTS-FINANCED SOLELY BY PREVENTION AND PUBLIC HEALTH FUNDS
"Community Transformation Grants and National Dissemination and Support for Community Transformation Grants"

Award: Cooperative Agreements
Purpose: To reduce death and disability from the five leading causes of death through the prevention and control these conditions and their risk factors.
Applicant Eligibility: Applications may be submitted by State or local Governments or their Bona Fide Agents (this includes the District of Columbia, the Commonwealth of Puerto Rico, the Virgin Islands, the Commonwealth of the Northern Marianna Islands, American Samoa, Guam, the Federated States of Micronesia, the Republic of the Marshall Islands, and the Republic of Palau). Eligible applicants also include public and private nonprofit Organizations, for profit Organizations, small, minority, women-owned businesses, universities, colleges, research Institutions, hospitals, community-based Organizations, faith-based Organizations, Federally recognized Indian tribal Governments, Indian Tribes, and Indian tribal Organizations. Additional guidance may be provided in individual Program announcements.
Beneficiary Eligibility: The general public will benefit from the objectives of this program.
Award Range/Average: Community Transformation Grants Expected: $50,000 - $500,000 National Dissemination and Support for Community Transformation Grants Expected - $350,000 - 3,500,000
HQ: 4770 Buford Highway NE, PO Box K40, Atlanta, GA 30333
    Phone: 770-488-2524 | Email: rrb7@cdc.gov
    http://www.cdc.gov

HHS93.764 | PPHF-COOPERATIVE AGREEMENTS TO IMPLEMENT THE NATIONAL STRATEGY FOR SUICIDE PREVENTION (SHORT TITLE: NATIONAL STRATEGY GRANTS)
Award: Cooperative Agreements
Purpose: Supports states in implementing the 2012 National Strategy for Suicide Prevention (NSSP) goals and objectives focused on preventing suicide and suicide attempts among adults aged 25-64 years old in order to reduce the overall suicide rate and number of suicides in the U.S. nationally.
Applicant Eligibility: Eligibility is limited to the Mental Health Authority in states, territories, and the District of Columbia. The purpose of this Program is to support states in implementing the 2012 National Strategy for Suicide Prevention (NSSP) goals and objectives focused on preventing suicide and suicide attempts among working-age adults 25-64 years old in order to reduce the overall suicide rate and number of suicides in the U.S. nationally. The Mental Health Authority within states and territories are uniquely positioned and have the necessary statewide infrastructure in place to promote suicide prevention as a core component of healthcare services and to coordinate the required activities, including convening all other relevant state agencies to advise and/or participate in the initiative.
Beneficiary Eligibility: Consumers that are working-age adults between 25-64 years old.
Award Range/Average: up to $587,524 per year
Funding: (Cooperative Agreements) FY 17 est $0.00; FY 19 $2,350,097.00; FY 20 est $0.00
HQ: 5600 Fishers Lane, Rockville, MD 20857
    Phone: 240-276-1418 | Email: roger.george@samhsa.hhs.gov
    http://www.samhsa.gov

Programs Administered by Federal Headquarters

HHS93.749 | PPHF-PUBLIC HEALTH LABORATORY INFRASTRUCTURE-FINANCED SOLELY BY PREVENTION AND PUBLIC HEALTH FUND

Award: Cooperative Agreements

Purpose: The Association of Public Health Laboratories (APHL) will engage in activities to strengthen public health infectious disease laboratory infrastructure by addressing gaps in public health laboratory practice, and assist with development, implementation and ongoing support of laboratory technologies for use in public health.

Applicant Eligibility: Eligibility is limited to the Association of Public Health Laboratories (APHL), a private nonprofit Organization and the current grantee. CDC approved single eligibility of this award. This group is the appropriate and only qualified Organization to address the activities described under the Program announcement.

Beneficiary Eligibility: Students/trainees and any U.S. state, political subdivision and U.S. territories (as described above), and other public entities will benefit.

Award Range/Average: Awards will range from approximately $1 million to $3 million with an average of approximately $2 million.

HQ: 1600 Clifton Road NE, PO Box E94, Atlanta, GA 30333

    Phone: 404-498-6451

    http://www.cdc.gov

HHS93.305 | PPHF 2018: OFFICE OF SMOKING AND HEALTH-NATIONAL STATE-BASED TOBACCO CONTROL PROGRAMS-FINANCED IN PART BY 2018 PREVENTION AND PUBLIC HEALTH FUNDS (PPHF)

"National Tobacco Control Program"

Award: Cooperative Agreements

Purpose: Addresses tobacco uses and secondhand smoke exposure in the United States and supports four National Tobacco Control Program goals.

Applicant Eligibility: State departments of health are essential for coordinating the public health response to prevent tobacco use and protect the population from second hand smoke exposure. They have experience with implementing evidence-based interventions and strategies that use environment, policy, and system approaches that have the potential to reach large numbers of people in the state. State departments of health have experience working with an array of state and local governmental and non-governmental Organizations to leverage resources that can support tobacco control efforts across a number of categorical Programs and sectors. State departments of health are uniquely positioned to carry out the activities outlined in this funding opportunity announcement. State departments of health serve as the lead for tobacco control in every state. State departments of health have existing personnel who are able to provide technical assistance based on their area of expertise (e.g., environment, policy, and systems approaches, Program planning, implementation, and evaluation, health communication, surveillance and epidemiology, partnership development) which conserves valuable resources. All this infrastructure and capacity can be integrated and employed by state departments of health to: Leverage partnerships to support the implementation of evidence-based interventions and strategies to prevent and control tobacco at the state and local levels; implement policy and Programmatic strategies that cut across multiple chronic conditions and that leverage individual categorical efforts and create synergies and efficiencies across multiple state Programmatic efforts also funded by CDC, given the high level of co-morbidities among people with chronic diseases and conditions (e.g., obesity, diabetes, hypertension, heart disease and stroke); utilize the public health resources and capacity unique to state departments of health to achieve a comprehensive state-based tobacco control Program; develop models that integrate with other state departments of health chronic disease Programs affecting similar populations; collect state-wide surveillance data on tobacco use, secondhand smoke exposure, and the populations most affected through data sources that are uniquely available to state departments of health.

Beneficiary Eligibility: General Public would benefit.

Funding: (Cooperative Agreements) FY 18 $54,442,137.00; FY 19 est $55,224,826.00; FY 20 est $0.00

HQ: 4770 Buford Highway NE, PO Box F79, Atlanta, GA 30341

    Phone: 770-488-5218 | Email: ksneegas@cdc.gov

    http://www.cdc.gov

HHS93.430 | PPHF 2018: PREVENTION HEALTH AND HEALTH SERVICES-STRENGTHENING PUBLIC HEALTH SYSTEMS AND SERVICES THROUGH NATIONAL PARTNERSHIPS TO IMPROVE AND PROTECT THE NATION'S HEALTH-FINANCED IN PART BY PREVENTION AND PUBLIC HEALTH FUNDS (PPHF) "CDC-RFA-OT18-1802"

Award: Cooperative Agreements
Purpose: To announce a program to strengthen the nation's public health infrastructure, ensure a competent, current and connected public health system, and improve delivery of essential services through capacity building assistance (CBA).
Applicant Eligibility: Organizations deemed eligible to apply must also meet responsiveness criteria as outlined in the "Additional Information on Eligibility" in CDC-RFA-OT18-1802.
Beneficiary Eligibility: Beneficiaries include state health departments; tribal health organizations; local health departments; the District of Columbia; U.S. Territories; and other components of the public health system. The general public will also serve as beneficiaries.
Award Range/Average: The approximate average award ranges for the 12-month budget period are $2 million for Category A, up to $1 million for Category B and up to $500,000 for Category C. This average is based on funding provided during funding strategy 1, as outlined in CDC-RFA-OT18-1802.
Funding: (Salaries and Expenses) FY 18 $37,525,640.00; FY 19 est $50,000,000.00; FY 20 est $50,000,000.00
HQ: 1825 Century Boulevard NE MS V18-1, Room 1014, Atlanta, GA 30345
　Phone: 770-488-1522
　https://www.cdc.gov/publichealthgateway/partnerships/capacity-building-assistance-OT18-1802.html

HHS93.539 | PPHF CAPACITY BUILDING ASSISTANCE TO STRENGTHEN PUBLIC HEALTH IMMUNIZATION INFRASTRUCTURE AND PERFORMANCE FINANCED IN PART BY PREVENTION AND PUBLIC HEALTH FUNDS
"Prevention and Public Health Fund (Affordable Care Act) - Immunization Program"

Award: Cooperative Agreements
Purpose: To support efforts to transition immunization programs supported by Section 317 funding to the healthcare environment being transformed by the Affordable Care Act (ACA).
Applicant Eligibility: Eligibility is limited to existing grantees under the Immunization Program (CFDA 93. 268) which includes all 50 U.S. states, the District of Columbia, local health departments (Chicago, Houston, New York City, Philadelphia, San Antonio) and U.S. territories (Commonwealth of Puerto Rico, Virgin Islands, Commonwealth of the Northern Mariana Islands, American Samoa, Guam, Federated States of Micronesia, Republic of the Marshall Islands, Republic of Palau). Private individuals, private nonprofit agencies, and Indian Tribes are not eligible.
Beneficiary Eligibility: Any U.S. state, political subdivision and U.S. territories (as described above), and other public entities will benefit.
Award Range/Average: Award ranges and averages vary based on program areas and supplemental projects funded through these cooperative agreements.
HQ: 1600 Clifton Road NE, PO Box A19, Atlanta, GA 30333
　Phone: 404-639-7824 | Email: ibr0@cdc.gov
　http://www.cdc.gov

HHS93.748 | PPHF COOPERATIVE AGREEMENTS FOR PRESCRIPTION DRUG MONITORING PROGRAM ELECTRONIC HEALTH RECORD (EHR) INTEGRATION AND INTEROPERABILITY EXPANSION
"PPHF-2012: PDMP EHR Integration and Interoperability (TI-12-011)"

Award: Cooperative Agreements
Purpose: Purpose of this program is to improve real-time access to PDMP data by integrating PDMPs into existing technologies like EHRs, in order to improve the ability of State PDMPs to reduce the nature, scope, and extent of prescription drug abuse.

Programs Administered by Federal Headquarters

Applicant Eligibility: Grant funds will enable States to integrate their PDMPs into EHR and other health information technology systems to expand utilization by increasing the production and distribution of unsolicited reports and alerts to prescribers and dispensers of prescription data. Grant funds will also be used by States to allow for modification of their systems to expand interoperability.

Beneficiary Eligibility: Eligible applicants are the immediate office of the Chief Executive (e.g., Governor) in the 49 States and 1 U.S. territory (i.e., Guam) that have enacted legislation or regulations that permit the following: implementation of a State PDMP; imposition of appropriate penalties for the unauthorized use and disclosure of information maintained in the program; and ability to share PDMP data (de-identified or anonymized) with CDC for research purposes. Eligibility is limited to States/Territory with enacted PDMP legislation because only these States/Territory have the capability to collect the required information and make that information available to prescribers, dispensers, and under controls, other States. PDMPs that are not actively collecting information cannot link their systems to EHRs or share information with other State PDMPs. Due to State laws establishing PDMPs, privacy, confidentiality, security, and other limitations on PDMPs, PDMP EHR Integration and Interoperability grants are limited to State and applicable territorial government entities.

HQ: 5600 Fishers Lane, Rockville, MD 20857
Phone: 240-276-1418 | Email: roger.george@samhsa.hhs.gov
http://www.samhsa.gov

HHS93.969 | PPHF GERIATRIC EDUCATION CENTERS
"Geriatric Workforce Enhancement Program (GWEP)"

Award: Cooperative Agreements

Purpose: The cooperative agreement program's purpose is to establish and operate geriatric education centers that will implement the Geriatric Workforce Enhancement Program to develop a healthcare workforce that maximizes patient and family engagement and improves health outcomes for older adults by integrating geriatrics with primary care. These centers improve the training of health professionals and individuals in geriatrics, including geriatric residencies, traineeships or fellowships and develops and disseminates curricula relating to the treatment of the health problems of elderly individuals.

Applicant Eligibility: Eligible applicants are accredited health professions schools and Programs. The following entities are eligible applicants: Schools of Allopathic Medicine; Schools of Veterinary Medicine; Schools of Dentistry; Schools of Public Health; Schools of Osteopathic Medicine; Schools of Chiropractic; Schools of Pharmacy; Physician Assistant Programs; Schools of Optometry; Schools of Allied Health; Schools of Podiatric Medicine; and Schools of Nursing The following accredited graduate Programs are also eligible applicants: Health Administration; and Behavioral Health and Mental Health Practice, including: Clinical Psychology, Clinical Social Work, Professional Counseling, and Marriage and Family Therapy. In addition these are also eligible entities under GWEP: a healthcare facility, a Program leading to certification as a certified nurse assistant, a partnership of a school of nursing such and facility, or a partnership of such a Program and facility Faith-based and community-based Organizations, Federally Recognized Indian Tribal Governments and Native American Organizations may apply if otherwise eligible. Applicants must be located in the United States, the District of Columbia, the Commonwealth of Puerto Rico, the Commonwealth of the Northern Mariana Islands, the U. S Virgin Islands, Guam, American Samoa, the Republic of Palau, the Republic of the Marshall Islands, or the Federated States of Micronesia.

Beneficiary Eligibility: Accredited health professions schools.

Award Range/Average: FY 18 Range: $589,616 - $881,825 Average Award: $857,500 FY 19 Range: $590,000 - $750,000 Est Average Award: $740,384 FY 20 est Range: $0 Average Award: $0

Funding: (Project Grants) FY 18 $35,839,723.00; FY 19 est $37,729,921.00; FY 20 est $0.00

HQ: Division of Medicine and Dentistry 5600 Fishers Lane, Room 15N194B, Rockville, MD 20857
Phone: 301-443-5626 | Email: ntumosa@hrsa.gov
http://www.hrsa.gov

HHS93.507 | PPHF NATIONAL PUBLIC HEALTH IMPROVEMENT INITIATIVE

Award: Cooperative Agreements

Purpose: To increase the performance management capacity of public health departments in order to ensure that public health goals are effectively and efficiently met.

Applicant Eligibility: Eligible applicants include all 50 states, Washington, D. C., 9 large local health departments supporting cities with populations of 1 million or more inhabitants (Chicago, Illinois; Dallas, Texas; Houston Texas; Los Angeles, California; New York City, New York; Philadelphia, Pennsylvania; Phoenix, Arizona; San Antonio, Texas; San Diego, California), 5 U.S. Territories 3 U.S. Affiliated Pacific Islands, and up to 7 federally-recognized Tribes with an established public health departments structure (or their equivalent) that provide public health services to their tribal members or their bona fide agents.

Beneficiary Eligibility: State health departments, large local health departments supporting cities with populations of 1 million or more inhabitants, the District of Columbia, U.S. Territories, tribal health organizations and the general public.

Award Range/Average: Component I: This amount is based on population and will continue for each year of the cooperative agreement: Below 1.5 million = $100,000 1.5 million - 5 million = $200,000 5 million - 8 million = $300,000 Above 8 million = $400,000. Component II: $1M - $2.95M.

HQ: 2500 Century Parkway, Atlanta, GA 30329
   Phone: 404-498-6792 | Email: ayw3@cdc.gov
   http://www.cdc.gov

HHS93.744 | PPHF: BREAST AND CERVICAL CANCER SCREENING OPPORTUNITIES FOR STATES, TRIBES AND TERRITORIES SOLELY FINANCED BY PREVENTION AND PUBLIC HEALTH FUNDS
"Breast and Cervical Cancer Screening Opportunities through the National Breast and Cervical Cancer Early Detection Program (NBCCEDP) - PPHF Funds (DP12-1218)"

Award: Cooperative Agreements

Purpose: Purpose of the FOA is to enhance and leverage existing organized systems for breast and cervical cancer screening to provide high quality screening with tracking and follow-up including patient navigation to low income, uninsured and under-insured women.

Applicant Eligibility: Eligibility is limited to the currently funded states or their bona fide agents, tribal and territorial recipients under CDC-RFA-DP12-1205. Cancer Prevention and Control Programs for State, Territorial and Tribal Organizations.

Beneficiary Eligibility: The general public will benefit from the objectives of this program. Additionally states, tribes and territories funded under DP12-1205 will benefit from this program.

Award Range/Average: Expected Approximately: $15,000 - $700,000 (estimated based on availability of funds).

HQ: 4770 Buford Highway NE, PO Box F76, Atlanta, GA 30341
   Phone: 770-488-4880 | Email: fwong@cdc.gov
   http://www.cdc.gov

HHS93.739 | PPHF: CHRONIC DISEASE INNOVATION GRANTS-FINANCED SOLELY BY PUBLIC PREVENTION HEALTH FUNDS
"National Diabetes Prevention Program Evidence-Based Lifestyle Intervention to Prevent Type 2 Diabetes in Underserved Communities"

Award: Cooperative Agreements

Purpose: The purpose of the program is to expand the National Diabetes Prevention Program, an evidence-based lifestyle change program in populations at high-risk for developing type 2 diabetes that includes African American; American Indian/Alaska Native; Hispanic/Latino, Low Social Economic Status; and women with a history of Gestational Diabetes.

Applicant Eligibility: Eligible Applicants: Nonprofits with 501(c)(3) IRS Status (Other than Institutions of Higher education); For-Profit Organizations; Small, minority, and women-owned businesses; Indian/Native American Tribal Governments (Federally Recognized); Hospitals; Regional Organizations; Faith-based or Community-based Organizations.

Beneficiary Eligibility: The general public will benefit from the objectives of this program. More specifically, populations at high-risk for developing type 2 diabetes (African American; American Indian/Alaska Native; Hispanic/Latino, Low Social Economic Status; Women with a history of Gestational Diabetes) will benefit from the objectives of this program.

Award Range/Average: N/A

HQ: 4770 Buford Highway NE, PO Box K10 NCCDPHP, Atlanta, GA 30333
   Phone: 770-488-1097 | Email: djt4@cdc.gov
   http://www.cdc.gov

Programs Administered by Federal Headquarters

HHS93.751 | PPHF: CONSORTIUM FOR TOBACCO USE CESSATION TECHNICAL ASSISTANCE FINANCED BY SOLELY BY PREVENTION AND PUBLIC HEALTH FUNDS
"PPHF2013: Consortium for Tobacco Use Cessation Technical Assistance"

Award: Cooperative Agreements

Purpose: Develops a consortium for tobacco use cessation technical assistance. The aim of the consortium is to provide technical assistance to state tobacco control programs and other partners by translating the science of tobacco control cessation into public health action to further increase the rate of cessation among tobacco users in the United States.

Applicant Eligibility: A Bona Fide Agent is an agency/Organization identified by the state as eligible to submit an application under the state eligibility in lieu of a state application. If applying as a bona fide agent of a state or local government, a legal, binding agreement from the state or local government as documentation of the status is required.

Beneficiary Eligibility: The general public will benefit from the objectives of this program.

Award Range/Average: Awards will range from approximately $75,000 to $450,000 with an average of approximately $112,500.

Funding: (Cooperative Agreements) FY 18 $450,000.00; FY 19 est $0.00; FY 20 est $0.00

HQ: 4770 Buford Highway NE, PO Box K50, Atlanta, GA 30341
   Phone: 770-488-1172 | Email: sbabb@cdc.gov
   http://www.cdc.gov

HHS93.742 | PPHF: EARLY CHILDCARE AND EDUCATION OBESITY PREVENTION PROGRAM-OBESITY PREVENTION IN YOUNG CHILDREN-FINANCED SOLELY BY PUBLIC PREVENTION AND HEALTH FUNDS
"Early Care and Education Statewide Collaboratives to Improve Nutrition, Breastfeeding Support, Physical Activity and Screen Time Practices for Obesity Prevention in Young Children"

Award: Cooperative Agreements

Purpose: The program is an obesity prevention effort targeting the early care and education setting (ECE) to reach most children in the U.S. to reverse obesity trends through helping ECE providers across the nation to adopt healthier policies and practices around physical activity and nutrition, including limiting screen time and supporting breastfeeding.

Applicant Eligibility: Selected applicant under initial solicitations are eligible applicants for future years.

Beneficiary Eligibility: N/A

Award Range/Average: est $4,000,000

HQ: 4770 Buford Highway NE, PO Box F77, Atlanta, GA 30341
   Phone: 770-488-6042 | Email: lbarnes@cdc.gov
   http://www.cdc.gov

HHS93.745 | PPHF: HEALTH CARE SURVEILLANCE/HEALTH STATISTICS-SURVEILLANCE PROGRAM ANNOUNCEMENT: BEHAVIORAL RISK FACTOR SURVEILLANCE SYSTEM FINANCED IN PART BY PREVENTION AND PUBLIC HEALTH FUND
"Behavioral Risk Factor Surveillance System (BRFSS)"

Award: Cooperative Agreements

Purpose: Provides assistance to State and Territorial Health Departments to maintain and expand: Specific health surveillance using telephone and multi-mode survey methodology for the behaviors of the general population that contribute to the occurrences and prevention of chronic diseases, injuries, and other public health threats.

Applicant Eligibility: Eligibility includes all 50 states, Washington D. C., Puerto Rico, the U.S. Virgin Islands, Guam, American Samoa, Palau, and the Federated States of Micronesia, who are currently funded through the Behavioral Risk Factor Surveillance System (BRFSS) Funding Opportunity Announcements (CDC-RFA-SO11-1101 and CDC-RFA-SO11-1102).

Beneficiary Eligibility: Any U.S. State, political subdivision, and U.S. Territories as described above.
Award Range/Average: Awards will range from approximately $50,000 through $125,000 with an average award of approximately $80,000 for FY12. Awards will range from approximately $50,000 through $100,000 with an average award of approximately $68,000 for FY13.
HQ: 4602 Buford Highway, PO Box F78, Atlanta, GA 30341
  Phone: 770-488-4588
  http://www.grants.gov

HHS93.738 | PPHF: RACIAL AND ETHNIC APPROACHES TO COMMUNITY HEALTH PROGRAM FINANCED SOLELY BY PUBLIC PREVENTION AND HEALTH FUNDS
"Racial and Ethnic Approaches to Community Health (REACH)"
Award: Cooperative Agreements
Purpose: The proposed FY2012 REACH program supports the implementation of projects to reduce racial and ethnic health disparities.
Applicant Eligibility: Applications may be submitted by State or local Governments or their Bona Fide Agents (this includes the District of Columbia, the Commonwealth of Puerto Rico, the Virgin Islands, the Commonwealth of the Northern Marianna Islands, American Samoa, Guam, the Federated States of Micronesia, the Republic of the Marshall Islands, and the Republic of Palau). Eligible applicants also include public and private nonprofit Organizations, for profit Organizations, small, minority, women-owned businesses, universities, colleges, research Institutions, hospitals, community-based Organizations, faith-based Organizations, Federally recognized Indian tribal Governments, Indian Tribes, and Indian tribal Organizations. Additional guidance may be provided in individual Program announcements.
Beneficiary Eligibility: The general public will benefit from the objectives of this program. Additionally, colleges, universities, private non-profit and public nonprofit domestic organizations, research institutions, and faith-based organization, states, political subdivisions of states, local health authorities, and individuals or organizations with specialized health interests will benefit.
Funding: (Cooperative Agreements) FY 18 $23,197,325.00; FY 19 est $23,197,156.00; FY 20 est $23,197,156.00
HQ: 4770 Buford Highway NE, PO Box K30, Atlanta, GA 30333
  Phone: 404-498-3058 | Email: scoulberson@cdc.gov
  http://www.cdc.gov

HHS93.548 | PPHF: STATE NUTRITION, PHYSICAL ACTIVITY, AND OBESITY PROGRAMS-FINANCED IN PART BY PPHF
"Nutrition, Physical Activity, and Obesity Programs - financed solely by PPHF funds"
Award: Cooperative Agreements
Purpose: To provide leadership of strategic public health efforts to prevent and control obesity, chronic disease, and other health conditions through regular physical activity and good nutrition.
Applicant Eligibility: N/A
Beneficiary Eligibility: N/A
Award Range/Average: $50,000 to $16M
HQ: NCCDPHP 4770 Buford Highway NE, Atlanta, GA 30341
  Phone: 404-867-9697 | Email: lbarnes@cdc.gov
  http://www.grants.gov

HHS93.437 | PPHF2018-NATIONAL ORGANIZATION FOR CHRONIC DISEASE PREVENTION AND HEALTH PROMOTION-FINANCED IN PART BY 2018 PREVENTION AND PUBLIC HEALTH FUNDS
Award: Cooperative Agreements
Purpose: Supports the development of effective state chronic disease programs to strengthen public health science and practice by addressing crosscutting functions, domains, settings, risk factors and diseases.

Programs Administered by Federal Headquarters

Applicant Eligibility: The intent of this funding is to support the development of effective state chronic disease Programs by disseminating effective chronic disease prevention and health promotion approaches to strengthen public health science and practice. Funding eligibility is limited to national, public non-profit Organizations, that work with state and territorial health departments and whose primary focus is chronic disease prevention and health promotion.
Beneficiary Eligibility: Same as Applicant Eligibility.
Funding: (Cooperative Agreements) FY 18 $0.00; FY 19 est 0.00; FY 20 est $0.00
HQ: 477 Buford Highway NE, Atlanta, GA 30341
    Phone: 770-488-0877
    http://www.cdc.gov

DHS97.047 | PRE-DISASTER MITIGATION
"PDM"

Award: Project Grants
Purpose: The program provides funds for Indian tribal governments, communities and territories to prepare for pre-disaster mitigation by addressing the natural hazards at an early stage.
Applicant Eligibility: Applications are reviewed by DHS/FEMA Program and administrative staff. Any issues or concerns noted in the application will be negotiated with the successful applicant prior to the award being issued. Applicants/recipients are responsible for distributing funds to sub-applicants/sub-recipients.
Beneficiary Eligibility: State agencies, Indian Tribal governments, and local governments and communities are eligible to apply as sub applicants for assistance under the PDM program. All interested sub applicants must apply to the Applicant. Homeowners are not eligible to apply as sub applicants but may request their local jurisdiction to apply on their behalf.
Funding: (Project Grants) FY 18 $50,000,000.00; FY 19 est $62,500,000.00; FY 20 est $75,000,000.00
HQ: 400 C Street, Washington, DC 20472
    Phone: 202-646-3458 | Email: kayed.lakhia@fema.dhs.gov
    http://www.fema.gov/pre-disaster/mitigation/grant/program

DOJ16.735 | PREA PROGRAM: STRATEGIC SUPPORT FOR PREA
IMPLEMENTATION
"PREA"

Award: Cooperative Agreements; Project Grants
Purpose: To support efforts in the confinement facilities that are covered by the PREA Standards to achieve compliance with the standards.
Applicant Eligibility: Eligible applicants include states, units of local government, and federally-recognized Indian Tribes, as well as any national nonprofit Organization, for-profit (commercial) Organization (including tribal nonprofit or for-profit Organizations), or institution of higher education (including tribal Institutions of higher education) that have expertise and experience managing and delivering training and technical assistance on complex corrections or criminal justice issues at the national and local levels. For-profit Organizations (as well as other recipients) (including tribal Institutions of higher education) must forgo any profit or management fee.
Beneficiary Eligibility: Local agencies that oversee small- and medium-sized jails (i.e., with 500 beds or less), lockups, and juvenile facilities.
Funding: (Project Grants) FY 18 $10,207,126.00; FY 19 est Estimate Not Available; FY 20 est $15,500,000.00
HQ: 810 7th Street NW, Washington, DC 20531
    Phone: 202-616-6500
    http://www.bja.gov

HHS93.500 | PREGNANCY ASSISTANCE FUND PROGRAM
"PAF"

Award: Project Grants
Purpose: Provides support for States and Tribes to develop and implement programs to improve the educational, health, and social outcomes for expectant and parenting teens, women, fathers, and their families.
Applicant Eligibility: Eligible applicants are from States, which include the District of Columbia, any commonwealth, possession, or other territory of the of the United States and any Federally-recognized Indian tribe, reservation or consortium

or council (referred to as States or Tribes), for the development and implementation of Programs for expectant and parenting teens, women, fathers and their families. The authorized representative from the State or tribe must apply for grant funds available through this announcement to assist expectant and parenting teens, women, fathers and their families.

Beneficiary Eligibility: 1. States, which include the District of Columbia, any commonwealth, possession, or other territory of the United States, and any Federally-recognized Indian Tribe, reservation, consortium or council2. Education, Health, Non-profits, Community-based organizations, and entities within tribal communities.

Award Range/Average: $250,000 - $1,000,000 per year.

Funding: (Project Grants) FY 17 $23,300,000.00; FY 18 est Estimate Not Available; FY 19 est Estimate Not Available

HQ: 1101 Wootton Parkway, Suite 550 Tower Building, Rockville, MD 20852

  Phone: 240-453-8822 | Email: alice.bettencourt@hhs.gov

  http://www.hhs.gov/ash/oah

DHS97.133 | PREPARING FOR EMERGING THREATS AND HAZARDS

Award: Project Grants

Purpose: Provides federal assistance to communities to help prepare for new and emerging threats and hazards.

Applicant Eligibility: Please refer to the FY2016 Funding Opportunity Announcement.

Beneficiary Eligibility: Preparedness is the shared responsibility of our entire nation. Each community contributes to achieving the National Preparedness Goal by assessing and preparing for the risks that are most relevant and urgent for them individually, which in turn strengthens our collective security and resilience as a Nation. As new threats and hazards emerge, communities need to assess the risk to their community and take the necessary steps to prepare. Emerging threats and hazards include technological advancements, new environmental challenges, emerging diseases, and evolving terrorist tactics.

Award Range/Average: To Be Determined.

HQ: FEMA 500 C Street SW, Washington, DC 20472

  Phone: 800-368-6498

  http://www.fema.gov

DOI15.683 | PRESCOTT MARINE MAMMAL RESCUE ASSISTANCE

Award: Project Grants (discretionary)

Purpose: To rescue, treat, and release marine species such as polar bears, sea otters, West Indian manatees, and Pacific walruses, and collect data related to these species.

Applicant Eligibility: To be eligible, an applicant must be a current participant or researcher associated with marine mammal stranding efforts and must demonstrate they have authorization under the Marine Mammal Protection Act (MMPA; 16 U.S.C. 1361, et seq.) and the Endangered Species Act (ESA; 16 U.S.C. 1531, et seq.), if the marine mammal species is listed under the ESA. Authorization may include a permit issued under section 104(c) or an agreement under section 112(c) to take marine mammals as described in section 109(h)(1) in response to stranded marine mammals. Eligibility also includes Federal (except DOI and DOC), State, or local government employees operating in the course of their official duties as indicated under 109(h).

Beneficiary Eligibility: The recipients are the primary beneficiaries. The projects may have secondary benefits to States that have the identified marine mammal species in waters under State jurisdiction and supports Federal requirements for conservation of marine mammals, and other public resources.

Funding: (Project Grants (Discretionary)) FY 18 $0; FY 19 est $0; FY 20 est $920,000.00

HQ: 1849 C Street NW, Washington, DC 20240

  Phone: 703-358-2171

DHS97.050 | PRESIDENTIAL DECLARED DISASTER ASSISTANCE TO INDIVIDUALS AND HOUSEHOLDS-OTHER NEEDS
"ONA"

Award: Direct Payments for Specified Use

Purpose: The program offers financial support for disaster survivors whose financial needs aren't met by the insurance.

Applicant Eligibility: Individuals and households, in areas declared an emergency or major disaster by the President, who have necessary expenses and serious needs they are unable to meet through insurance or other means, are eligible for Other Needs Assistance. Basic conditions of eligibility include: the individual or a member of the household must be a citizen of the United States, a non-citizen national, or a qualified alien. 1) Medical: disaster-caused expenses, and/or paid receipts (bills)

Programs Administered by Federal Headquarters

for medical treatment; 2) Dental: disaster-caused expenses, and/or paid receipts (bills) for treatment; 3) childcare: disaster-caused expenses; 4) Funeral: disaster-caused expenses, and/or paid receipts (bills) for services; 5) Personal Property: proof of ownership, disaster- caused personal property damage; 6) Transportation: proof of ownership, vehicle complies with State laws, disaster-caused vehicle damage; and 7) Other Necessary Expenses and Serious Needs: the expense or need must be caused by the disaster and approved by FEMA.

Beneficiary Eligibility: Individual/Family; expenses/losses must have occurred within an area which has been designated as a disaster area by Presidential declaration.

Award Range/Average: FY 18: Range - $50 - $34,000; Average - $2,742.55 - as of 06/25/2019 FY 19: Range - $50 - $34,900; Average - $4,489.18- as of 06/25/2019

Funding: (Direct Payments for Specified Use) FY 18 Actual Not Available; FY 19 est Not Separately Identifiable; FY 20 est $31,200,000.00

HQ: FEMA 500 C Street SW, Washington, DC 20472
Phone: 800-368-6498
http://www.dhs.gov

DHS97.134 | PRESIDENTIAL RESIDENCE PROTECTION SECURITY GRANT "PRPA Grant"

Award: Project Grants

Purpose: The Fiscal Year 2018 Presidential Residence Protection Assistance Grant provides reimbursement to law enforcement agencies from Federal funds for any law enforcement personnel costs that incurs while protecting the President during any non-governmental residential tenure.

Applicant Eligibility: Eligible applicants are limited to state and local law enforcement agencies, directly or through the State Administrative Agency, that conducted protection activities associated with any non-governmental residence of the President of the United States designated or identified to be secured by the United States Secret Service.

Beneficiary Eligibility: N/A

Award Range/Average: This was a new program in FY 2017, so there were no previous program budgets.

Funding: (Project Grants) FY 18 $41,000,000.00; FY 19 est $41,000,000.00; FY 20 est $0.00

HQ: 400 C Street SW, Washington, DC 20472
Phone: 202-510-0986 | Email: margaret.wilson@fema.dhs.gov
http://fema.gov/grants

HHS93.613 | PRESIDENT'S COMMITTEE FOR PEOPLE WITH INTELLECTUAL DISABILITIES (PCPID) "PCPID"

Award: Dissemination of Technical Information

Purpose: The President's Committee for People with Intellectual Disabilities provides advice to the President and to the Secretary of Health and Human Services, concerning a broad range of topics relating to people with intellectual disabilities.

Applicant Eligibility: General public.

Beneficiary Eligibility: Same as Applicant Eligibility.

Award Range/Average: Education of Legislators PIE states facilitated Take Your Legislator to Work Day, where state legislators attended the workplace of a youth employee with I/DD to learn about the youths' employment experiences firsthand. This helped policymakers understand that youth are motivated to, interested in, and excel at working. PIE states also brought self-advocates to meet with state and national legislators to share their employment experiences and make the case for increasing employment opportunities for people with disabilities. Improved Support to Families To dispel misunderstandings about youths' desires for employment, support families to help youth reach their employment goals, and expose families to new opportunities and expectations around youth employment, PIE states engaged parents and families of youth with I/DD through various methods, including through surveys, trainings, and Parent and Family Coalitions. Family Coalitions provided information about employment to families, and also provided forums for families to engage with state agency representatives to provide comments on state plans. Change Employers Attitudes PIE consortia recognized that engaging businesses, changing businesses' expectations and attitudes about hiring youth with I/DD, and forming relationships with businesses are important to finding and creating job opportunities for youth with I/DD. As a result, grantees employed a variety of methods to engage businesses. Ex. Alaska's consortium, the Alaska Integrated Employment Initiative, created the Business Employment Services Team (BEST), an interdepartmental business engagement that includes support from various Alaska

State agencies. Alaska's consortium, the Alaska Integrated Employment Initiative, created the Business Employment Services Team (BEST), an interdepartmental business engagement Support for Employers PIE states created resources and trainings to help employers better support and provide reasonable accommodations for employees with I/DD. Benefits Education States created tools and resources to help youth and families understand the impact employment will have on benefits. Shift in Thinking Focused on building opportunities, policies, and practices within formal and informal systems aimed at supporting all to have a "good life". Local Learning States exchanged information related to their efforts to improve supports to families consistent with the Life Course framework Leverage Current Opportunities States reported that efforts to support families could not be a separate initiative. Lasting and sustainable change meant embedding the values of supporting families across all departments, initiatives, policies, practices, and the community. Create Space for Innovation States reevaluated their efforts to support individuals and families with regard to how the needs of the entire family are considered and addressed going forward. Understanding the benefits of working collaboratively across all entities available to support families helped participants identify and form new partnerships and alliances that they may not have considered. It gave participants permission to be open to possibilities and test new approaches, and this freedom helped them be creative and arrive at new solutions to the common issues they faced. Education for Teachers: Gave the keynote address at a Tennessee conference with 25,000 education professionals and a breakout sessions for about 200. Teachers are often the ones who recommend guardianship for their students Education for Judges and Attorneys: A partner (American Bar Association) created the P.R.A.C.T.I.C.A.L tool aims to help lawyers identify and implement decision-making options for persons with disabilities that are less restrictive than guardianship. State Grants: Awarded two cohorts of state grantees to review guardianship policy and procedure in their states and develop innovative methods to increase knowledge, access to, and implementation of Supported Decision Making. Grant recipients included: Delaware Developmental Disabilities Council, the Arc of Indiana, Disability Rights Maine, First In Families of North Carolina, Wisconsin Board for People with Developmental Disabilities, the Northern Florida Office of Public Guardian, the University of Georgia, Disability Rights Maine, the Second Judicial District Court in Nevada, the Brookdale Center for Healthy Aging of Hunter College and the Arc Tennessee. Transportation Research & Demonstration Program: Tools The Transportation4all website contains resources, tools and stories to assist organizations to empower people with I/DD and older adults to be actively involved in designing and implementing coordinated transportation systems. Pathway to Inclusion is a tool that organizations can use with participants to discuss and evaluate where the organization is in terms of inclusion. At the lower end of the pathway (least inclusive) there is "programs are developed for participants" and at the highest end of pathway (most inclusive) there is "participants play lead roles" in the organization The National knowledge sharing network of local/regional/state model projects and national experts to serve as a resource for communities interested in replicating best practices and testing new approaches to achieve the goals of this project State Grants - Awarded 17 small grants to test the replication of proven best practices as well as new models and approaches to successfully empower people with disabilities and older adults to be actively involved in the planning and implementation of coordinated transportation systems. Grantees included United Way of Northwest Vermont, District of Columbia DOT; City of Evanston, Il; Central Pennsylvania Transportation Authority; Economic Assistance League, Inc., Alice, TX; Northern Arizona Intergovernmental Public Transportation Authority; King County Metro, Seattle, WA; PEAC, Inc., Ypsilanti, MI.; Inclusive Coordinated Transportation Planning Grantees; Ride Connection, Portland OR; Jewish Council for the Aging, The Arc Connecticut Alaska Mobility Coalition Area Agency on Aging 1-B, Lewis and Clark County and Knoxville-Knox County Community Action Committee Self-Advocacy Resource Center-Building leaders Tools and Reach Presented to People First of South Korea on the history of self- advocacy in the U.S. 14 people registered for the National Conference from Northern Mariana Islands. Estimated reach is a minimum of 30,593 discreet individuals from website Leadership 2 cohorts of fellows,12 people with self-advocates, received a year-long experience at non-profit organizations Self Advocates are in leadership roles as Co-Chairs of Conference Planning Committee and Program Planning Sub-Committee. Employment The project continues to employ 8 self-advocates. A self-advocate who spent many hours at the NEAT regional meetings receiving hands on training is now working with the Sexual Assault Response Unit with the MA Disabled Persons Protection Council Alaska will no longer allow workers with disabilities to be paid less than minimum wage. Longitudinal Data Collection - The data collection projects have made an impact in several areas: AIDD grantees use the information for future planning and setting goals People with I/DD and family members use the information to compare their states with others regarding DD services The information is used to prepare testimony before the U.S. Congress and state legislatures Policymakers use the information as background to change law Journalists use the information to write in-depth stories

Funding: (Formula Grants) FY 17 $248,294.00; FY 18 est $242,916.00; FY 19 est Estimate Not Available

HQ: 330 C Street SW, Washington, DC 20201

    Phone: 202-795-7309 | Email: melissa.oritiz@acl.hhs.gov

    http://www.acl.gov

Programs Administered by Federal Headquarters

HHS93.289 | PRESIDENT'S COUNCIL ON FITNESS, SPORTS, AND NUTRITION "PCFSN"

Award: Advisory Services and Counseling

Purpose: To expand interest in and awareness of the importance of regular physical activity, fitness, sports participation and good nutrition for Americans of all ages by encouraging the development, improvement, or enhanced coordination of programs that promote healthy lifestyles.

Applicant Eligibility: General public.

Beneficiary Eligibility: General public. The PCFSN provides programs and public information on physical activity, fitness, sports, and nutrition programs. The PCFSN has no grant-making authority.

Award Range/Average: The PCFSN has no grant-making authority.

Funding: (Salaries and Expenses) FY 16 $707,000.00; FY 17 est $668,000.00; FY 18 est $827,480.00

HQ: 1101 Wootton Parkway, Suite 560 PCFSN Tower Building, Rockville, MD 20852

Phone: 240-276-9567 | Email: shannon.feaster@hhs.gov

http://www.fitness.gov

HHS93.816 | PREVENTING HEART ATTACKS AND STROKES IN HIGH NEED AREAS

Award: Cooperative Agreements

Purpose: The purpose of the program is to support implementation of population-wide and priority population approaches to prevent and control high blood pressure, and reduce health disparities associated with high blood pressure, among adults in Mississippi's 18-county Delta Region, which is an underserved and rural area.

Applicant Eligibility: The Mississippi Department of Health / Mississippi Delta Health Collaborative is uniquely qualified positioned to carry out the activities outlined in this FOA because: - To meet Congressional intent detailed in the FY 2015 Appropriations language, CDC needs to continue supporting the Mississippi Department of Health / Mississippi Delta Health Collaborative's work related to policy, systems, and environmental approaches, as well as community-clinical linkages for the prevention and control of chronic diseases, such as heart disease and stroke. - The Mississippi Department of Health's mission is to promote and protect the health of the citizens of Mississippi. In addition, The Mississippi Department of Health is designated as the sole and official agency to administer and supervise all health planning responsibilities for the state, as established by Section 41-7-171 et seq., of the Mississippi Code 1972. Therefore they are uniquely qualified to identify those areas of greatest need in the state; develop strategies to reduce barriers and deficiencies in the state's public healthcare system; and establish policies to encourage the provision of appropriate and quality care in the public and private healthcare system. Through its Program, the Mississippi Delta Health Collaborative, reach of the Mississippi Department of Health is further extended to address health issues of rural areas of the state (i.e., the 18-county MS Delta Region). The MS Delta Region bears a disproportionate burden of heart disease and stroke, and related conditions as compared to the rest of Mississippi and to the nation. - Mississippi Delta Health Collaborative has provided leadership and coordination of heart disease and stroke prevention and control efforts in communities across the MS Delta Region. Also, by directly engaging, and providing funding and technical assistance to community Organizations to promote coordination of public health efforts, the Mississippi Delta Health Collaborative is poised to expeditiously and successfully implement strategies related to policy, systems, and environmental approaches; health systems; and community-clinical linkages to prevent and control heart disease and stroke in the MS Delta Region.

Beneficiary Eligibility: The ultimate benefits of this program will be received by the general and priority adult populations in a local, rural area of Mississippi (i.e., the MS Delta Region) who have high blood pressure, and experience health disparities associated with high blood pressure. Priority adult populations are those adult population subgroups in the MS Delta Region who experience racial/ethnic and socioeconomic disparities, including inadequate access to care and poor quality of care. Strategies related to the prevention and control of heart disease and stroke will be implemented and tailored to meet the unique local needs of the MS Delta Region and to achieve the greatest impact.

Award Range/Average: Funding for the Mississippi Department of Health / Mississippi Delta Health Collaborative has ranged from $1,058,464 to $ 4,000,000. FY16 and 17 supports new FOA DP16-1612

Funding: (Cooperative Agreements) FY 18 $3,150,000.00; FY 19 est $3,150,000.00; FY 20 est $3,150,000.00

HQ: 4770 Buford Highway NE, Atlanta, GA 30341

Phone: 770-488-5519 | Email: rmoeti@cdc.gov

http://www.cdc.gov

CDC93.478 | PREVENTING MATERNAL DEATHS: SUPPORTING MATERNAL MORTALITY REVIEW COMMITTEES

Award: Cooperative Agreements

Purpose: It aims at identifying pregnancy-related deaths, abstract clinical and non-clinical data into MMRIA, a standard data system. By identifying and describing the maternal deaths, it makes the policy and prevention strategies to reduce it.

Applicant Eligibility: N/A

Beneficiary Eligibility: N/A

Award Range/Average: Awards are expected to range from $150,000 to $600,000 per year.

HQ: 4770 Buford Highway NE, Atlanta, GA 30341

    Phone: 770-488-6553

CDC93.377 | PREVENTION AND CONTROL OF CHRONIC DISEASE AND ASSOCIATED RISK FACTORS IN THE U.S. AFFILIATED PACIFIC ISLANDS, U.S. VIRGIN ISLANDS, AND P. R.

Award: Cooperative Agreements (discretionary Grants)

Purpose: To help reduce the disability and rates of death due to chronic illnesses in the U.S. Affiliated Pacific Islands by preventing and controlling such chronic diseases.

Applicant Eligibility: Applicants much provide proof of ability to serve populations in one of the following jurisdictions: Commonwealth of the Northern Mariana Islands (CNMI), American Samoa, Guam, Federated States of Micronesia (FSM), Republic of the Marshall Islands (RMI), Republic of Palau, U.S. Virgin Islands, Puerto Rico.

Beneficiary Eligibility: Northern Mariana Islands, American Samoa, Guam, Federated States of Micronesia, Republic of the Marshall Islands, Republic of Palau, U.S. Virgin Islands, Puerto Rico.

Award Range/Average: Awards are expected to range from $250,000 to $1,500,000 (total award for both Core and Competitive Components, where applicable). All activities supported through this NOFO must contribute to health improvements across the target population and across population subgroups. Funding strategy will also include the awardees' proposed activities and goals, estimated population reach, and program capacity as described in the application.

Funding: (Cooperative Agreements (Discretionary Grants)) FY 18 Actual Not Available; FY 19 est $3,286,054.00; FY 20 est $3,286,054.00

HQ: 4770 Buford Highway NE, PO Box F-80, Atlanta, GA 30341

    Phone: 770-488-6393 | Email: sdejesus@cdc.gov

HHS93.792 | PREVENTION AND CONTROL OF CHRONIC DISEASE AND ASSOCIATED RISK FACTORS IN THE U.S. AFFILIATED PACIFIC ISLANDS, U.S. VIRGIN ISLANDS, AND P. R.

Award: Cooperative Agreements (discretionary Grants)

Purpose: The five-year program reduces the rates of disability and death associated with chronic disease in the U.S. Affiliated Pacific Islands, U.S. Virgin Islands, and Puerto Rico.

Applicant Eligibility: Applicants much provide proof of ability to serve populations in one of the following jurisdictions: Commonwealth of the Northern Mariana Islands (CNMI), American Samoa, Guam, Federated States of Micronesia (FSM), Republic of the Marshall Islands (RMI), Republic of Palau, U.S. Virgin Islands, Puerto Rico.

Beneficiary Eligibility: N/A

Award Range/Average: Awards are expected to range from $250,000 to $1,500,000 (total award for both Core and Competitive Components, where applicable). All activities supported through this NOFO must contribute to health improvements across the target population and across population subgroups. Funding strategy will also include the awardees' proposed activities and goals, estimated population reach, and program capacity as described in the application.

HQ: 4770 Buford Highway NE, PO Box F80, Atlanta, GA 30341

    Phone: 770-488-6393 | Email: sdejesus@cdc.gov

Programs Administered by Federal Headquarters

HHS93.357 | PREVENTION AND CONTROL OF CHRONIC DISEASE AND ASSOCIATED RISK FACTORS IN THE U.S. AFFILIATED PACIFIC ISLANDS, U.S. VIRGIN ISLANDS, AND PUERTO RI

Award: Cooperative Agreements

Purpose: To reduce the rates of disability and death associated with chronic disease in the U.S. Affiliated Pacific Islands, U.S. Virgin Islands, and Puerto Rico.

Applicant Eligibility: State Governments, county Governments, city or township Governments, special district Governments, independent school districts, public and state controlled Institutions of higher education, Native American tribal Governments (Federally recognized), Public housing authorities/Indian housing authorities, Native American tribal Organizations (other than Federally recognized tribal Governments), Nonprofits having 501(c)(3) status with the IRS, other Institutions of higher education; Nonprofits without 501 (c)(3) status with the IRS, other than Institutions of higher education, private Institutions of higher education, For profit Organizations other than small businesses, small businesses, Territorial Governments or their bona fide agents in the Commonwealth of Puerto Rico, the Virgin Islands, the Commonwealth of the Northern Mariana Islands, American Samoa, Guam, Federated States of Micronesia, Republic of the Marshall Islands, and the Republic of Palau, State Controlled Institutions of higher education, American Indian or Alaska Native tribal Governments, American Indian or Alaska Native tribally designated Organizations, Ministries of Health Applicants must provide proof of ability to serve populations in one of the following jurisdictions: Commonwealth of the Northern Mariana Islands (CNMI), American Samoa, Guam, Federated States of Micronesia (FSM), Republic of the Marshall Islands (RMI), Republic of Palau, U.S. Virgin Islands, Puerto Rico.

Beneficiary Eligibility: Beneficiaries of this NOFO are anyone/general public currently living in the Commonwealth of the Northern Mariana Islands, American Samoa, Guam, Federated States of Micronesia, Republic of the Marshall Islands, Republic of Palau, U.S. Virgin Islands, Puerto Rico.

Award Range/Average: Awards are expected to range from $250,000 to $1,500,000 (total award for both Core and Competitive Components, where applicable). All activities supported through this NOFO must contribute to health improvements across the target population and across population subgroups. Funding strategy will also include the awardees' proposed activities and goals, estimated population reach, and program capacity as described in the application.

Funding: (Cooperative Agreements) FY 18 Actual Not Available; FY 19 est $8,000,000.00; FY 20 est $0.00

HQ: 4770 Buford Highway NE, PO Box F80, Atlanta, GA 30341

Phone: 770-488-6393 | Email: sdejesus@cdc.gov

HHS93.533 | PREVENTION AND PUBLIC HEALTH FUND (AFFORDABLE CARE ACT): ENHANCED SURVEILLANCE FOR NEW VACCINE PREVENTABLE DISEASE "NVSN"

Award: Cooperative Agreements

Purpose: To support a network of sites that provide surveillance and data collection on new vaccine use, the impact of new and upcoming vaccines and other immunoprophylaxis, new vaccine policies/policies under consideration, through enhanced inpatient and Emergency Department (ED) surveillance, applied epidemiologic research, and investigator-initiated investigations.

Applicant Eligibility: Higher education Institutions: Public/State Controlled Institutions of Higher education Private Institutions of Higher education The following types of Higher education Institutions are always encouraged to apply for CDC support as Public or Private Institutions of Higher education: Hispanic-serving Institutions Historically Black Colleges and universities (HBCUs)Tribally Controlled Colleges and universities (TCCUs) Alaska Native and Native Hawaiian Serving Institutions Nonprofits Other Than Institutions of Higher education Nonprofits (Other than Institutions of Higher education) Governments State Governments County Governments City or Township Governments Special District Governments Indian/Native American Tribal Governments (Federally Recognized) Indian/Native American Tribal Governments (Other than Federally Recognized)Eligible Agencies of the Federal Government U.S. Territory or Possession Other Independent School Districts Public Housing Authorities/Indian Housing Authorities Native American tribal Organizations (other than Federally recognized tribal Governments)Faith-based or Community-based Organizations Regional Organizations Bona Fide Agents Entities must be States (or bona fide agents of States), political subdivision of States, or other public or non-profit private entities.

Beneficiary Eligibility: Any U.S. state, political subdivision and U.S. territories (as described above), and other public entities will benefit.

Award Range/Average: Awards will range from approximately $450,000 to $550,000 with an average of approximately $500,000. Supplemental award possible subject to all necessary procedures and approvals.

Funding: (Cooperative Agreements) FY 18 $19,577,284.00; FY 19 est $19,577,284.00; FY 20 est $0.00

HQ: 1600 Clifton Road NE, Atlanta, GA 30329
  Phone: 404-639-1305 | Email: tlockhart@cdc.gov

HHS93.084 | PREVENTION OF DISEASE, DISABILITY, AND DEATH BY INFECTIOUS DISEASES

Award: Cooperative Agreements
Purpose: To prevent disease, disability and death by infectious diseases.
Applicant Eligibility: Dependent upon the individual NOFO, eligibility may range from open competition, limited competition, single-source, domestic and/or international in accordance with the authorizing legislation.
Beneficiary Eligibility: N/A
Award Range/Average: $100,000 - $10,000,000; Average $3,000,000
Funding: (Cooperative Agreements (Discretionary Grants)) FY 18 $19,761,909.00; FY 19 est $20,000,000.00; FY 20 est $20,000,000.00
HQ: 1600 Clifton Road NE, PO Box E60, Atlanta, GA 30333
  Phone: 404-718-8832 | Email: bsg2@cdc.gov

HHS93.083 | PREVENTION OF DISEASE, DISABILITY, AND DEATH THROUGH IMMUNIZATION AND CONTROL OF RESPIRATORY AND RELATED DISEASES

Award: Project Grants
Purpose: To strengthen capacity to prevent disease, disability, and death through immunization and control of respiratory and related diseases.
Applicant Eligibility: Dependent on the NOFO, eligibility may range from open competition, limited competition, single-source, domestic and/or international in accordance with the authorizing language.
Beneficiary Eligibility: N/A
Award Range/Average: $500,000 - $2,000,000, Average $1,000,000
Funding: (Cooperative Agreements) FY 18 $13,075,054.00; FY 19 est $14,000,000.00; FY 20 est $14,000,000.00
HQ: 1600 Clifton Road NE, PO Box E60, Atlanta, GA 30333
  Phone: 404-718-8832 | Email: bsg2@cdc.gov

HHS93.117 | PREVENTIVE MEDICINE RESIDENCY

Award: Project Grants
Purpose: To promote postgraduate medical education in the specialty of preventive medicine and to enhance preventive medicine education through incorporation of evidence-based integrative medicine curricula into such programs.
Applicant Eligibility: Eligible Preventive Medicine Residency Program grants are: (1) an accredited school of public health or school of medicine or osteopathic medicine; (2) an accredited public or private nonprofit hospital; (3) a State, local, or tribal health department; or (4) a consortium of 2 or more entities described in (1) through (3). Refer to the relevant Notice of Funding Opportunity for more specific information regarding eligibility. Federally Recognized Indian Tribal Government and Native American Organizations may apply if they are otherwise eligible.
Beneficiary Eligibility: For Preventive Medicine Residency program grants, each trainee receiving stipend support must: (a) be a citizen of the United States, a non-citizen U.S. national, or a foreign national having in his or her possession a visa permitting permanent residence in the United States; (b) be a physician who has graduated from an accredited school of medicine or osteopathic medicine in the United States; or if a graduate from a foreign school, meet the criteria of the Educational Commission for Foreign Medical Graduates, for entry into the program supported by this grant; and (c) plan to complete the grant-supported program and engage in the practice and/or teaching of preventive medicine, especially in positions which meet the needs of medically underserved populations.
Award Range/Average: Preventive Medicine Residency FY 2018 Range: $340,000 to $500,847; Average award $446,905 FY 2019 est Range $234,439 to $400,000; Average award $382,352 FY 2020 est Range: $0; Average award: $0
Funding: (Project Grants) FY 18 $4,469,058; FY 19 est $6,499,989; FY 20 est $0.00
HQ: 5600 Fishers Lane, Room 15N 144A, Rockville, MD 20857
  Phone: 301-945-3336 | Email: scoulter@hrsa.gov
  http://www.hrsa.gov

Programs Administered by Federal Headquarters

USDA10.112 | PRICE LOSS COVERAGE
"PLC"

Award: Direct Payments for Specified Use

Purpose: The Price Loss Coverage program compensates producers for price loss payments.

Applicant Eligibility: An eligible producer is eligible to enter into a contract if 1) the owner of the farm has an ownership of a crop and assumes all or a part of the risk producing a crop that is commensurate with that claimed ownership of the crop; 2) a producer, other than the owner, on a farm with a share-rent lease for such farm, regardless of the length of the lease, if the owner of the farm enters into the same contract; 3) a producer, other than an owner, on a farm who rents such farm under a lease expiring on or after September 30 of the year of the contract in which case the owner is not required to enter into the contract; 4) a producer, other than an owner, on a farm who cash rents such farm under a leasing expiring before September 30 of the year of the contract; 5)An owner of an eligible farm who cash rents such farm and the lease expires before September 30 of the year of the contract, if the tenant declines to enter into a contract for the applicable year.

Beneficiary Eligibility: PLC provides payments to eligible producers on farms enrolled for the 2014 through 2018 crop years.

Funding: (Direct Payments for Specified Use) FY 18 $1,231,000,000.00; FY 19 est $3,965,000,000.00; FY 20 est $4,691,000,000.00

HQ: 1400 Independence Avenue SW, Room 4759 S, Washington, DC 20024
Phone: 202-720-7641 | Email: brent.orr@wdc.usda.gov
http://www.fsa.usda.gov

HHS93.976 | PRIMARY CARE MEDICINE AND DENTISTRY CLINICIAN EDUCATOR CAREER DEVELOPMENT AWARDS
"Career Development Awards (CDA)"

Award: Project Grants

Purpose: The career development awards are targeted towards physicians, dentists and dental hygienists who act as role models by improving the standards of primary care medicine and dentistry faculty and also plan to teach in primary care fields.

Applicant Eligibility: Eligible applicant Organizations include schools of allopathic or osteopathic medicine, academically affiliated physician assistant training Programs, dental and dental hygiene schools, accredited public or nonprofit private hospitals, or a public or nonprofit private entity that the Secretary has determined is capable of carrying out such grants. If the applicant Organization is not a medical school, physician assistant training Program, dental or dental hygiene school, they must be affiliated with one of the listed schools or training Programs and provide a letter of agreement from the relevant Organization. Faith-based and community-based Organizations, Federally Recognized Indian Tribal Government and Native American Organizations may apply for these funds, if otherwise eligible.

Beneficiary Eligibility: Eligible junior faculty candidates (Project Directors/Principal Investigators) are identified individuals who are applying to HRSA for a clinician educator faculty award through the applicant organization. Candidates must hold a non-tenured faculty appointment (i.e., be a junior faculty such as instructor or assistant professor) before the award is made. The faculty appointment must not be contingent on receipt of the award.

Award Range/Average: FY 2018: Range $89,549 to $200,000; Average: $186,074 FY 2019: est Range $91,643 to $200,000; Average: $184,689 FY 2020: est $0 Oral Health FY 2018: Range $147,992 to $199,364; Average $180,797 FY 2019: est Range: $148,020 to $199,946; Average $180,959 FY 2020: est. $0

Funding: (Project Grants) FY 18 $3,161,510.00; FY 19 est $4,063,148.00; FY 20 est $0.00

HQ: 5600 Fishers Lane, Room 15N186A, Rockville, MD 20857
Phone: 301-945-3368
http://www.hrsa.gov

SBA59.050 | PRIME TECHNICAL ASSISTANCE
"Prime"

Award: Project Grants

Purpose: To increase the number of microenterprises and to enhance the management capability of microentrepreneurs in starting, expanding and/or growing their business.

Applicant Eligibility: Grant recipients shall be non-profit microenterprise development or Program (or a collaborative thereof) that has a demonstrated record of delivering microenterprise services to disadvantaged entrepreneurs, an intermediary, a microenterprise development Organization or Program that is accountable to a local community, working in conjunction with a State or local government or Indian tribe, or an Indian tribe acting on its' own, if the tribe can certify that no private Organization or Program referred to in this paragraph exists within its' jurisdiction.

Beneficiary Eligibility: Disadvantaged entrepreneurs, microenterprises, and microenterprise development organizations as defined in the Act.

Funding: (Project Grants) FY 17 $4,700,000.00; FY 18 est $5,000,000.00; FY 19 est $0.00

HQ: 409 3rd Street SW, 5th Floor, Washington, DC 20416

Phone: 202-401-6365 | Email: manuel.hidalgo@sba.gov

http://www.sba.gov

USIP91.005 | PRIORITY GRANT COMPETITION

Award: Project Grants

Purpose: To seek and develop the international conflict resolution and peacebuilding field.

Applicant Eligibility: Nonprofit or public Institutions are eligible to apply. USIP does not accept applications from individuals who are not affiliated with an eligible institution. Funding is not available for degree work (payment of tuition fees or support for M.A. or Ph.D. -related work). Inquiries for dissertation research support should be directed to USIP's Jennings Randolph Peace Scholar Dissertation Program. Applications that list as participants, consultants, or project personnel members of USIP's Board of Directors, staff or fellows will not be accepted. USIP does not fund grant proposals of a partisan political nature or proposals that would inject the grantee or USIP into the policy processes of the United States government or any foreign government or international Organization. In addition, in accord with the United States of Peace Act, Section 1709 (b), USIP will not use political tests or political qualifications in selecting or monitoring any grantees. projects that lead to policy recommendations for Governments, international Organizations, or nongovernmental Organizations are welcome and encouraged, although such recommendations will be those of the grantee and not USIP. USIP does not provide support for the creation of a new Organization, construction or maintenance purposes, direct social services, or microenterprise projects, nor does it provide funding to government agencies or to individuals working for government agencies. All application materials must be in English unless specified otherwise in the specific call for proposals.

Beneficiary Eligibility: N/A

Award Range/Average: Range $30,000 - $190,000. Average $60,000.

Funding: (Project Grants) FY 18 $1,238,599.00; FY 19 est Estimate Not Available; FY 20 est Estimate Not Available

HQ: 2301 Constitution Avenue NW, Washington, DC 20037

Phone: 202-429-3841 | Email: seisenberg@usip.gov

http://www.usip.org

HUD14.418 | PRIVATE ENFORCEMENT INITIATIVES
"FHIP PEI"

Award: Cooperative Agreements

Purpose: To develop, implement, and carry out, related activities and enforcement under the or State or local laws that provide substantially equivalent rights and remedies for alleged discriminatory housing practices. Objectives include carrying out testing and other investigative activities.

Applicant Eligibility: Eligible applicants are other private Institutions /Organizations with at least one year of enforcement related experience.

Beneficiary Eligibility: Any person or group of persons aggrieved by discriminatory housing practices because of race, color, religion, sex disability familial status or national origin. Also, any person or group of persons, including landlords or real estate agents, to prevent discriminatory housing practices because of race, color, religion, sex, disability, familial status or national origin.

Award Range/Average: $300,000 per project period. $900,000 total funding for multi-year (3 years)

Funding: (Cooperative Agreements) FY 17 $16,013,813.00; FY 18 est $30,750,000.00; FY 19 est $30,350,000.00

HQ: 451 7th Street SW, Room 5222, Washington, DC 20410

Phone: 202-402-7054 | Email: paula.stone@hud.gov

http://www.hud.gov/offices/fheo/partners/fhip/fhip.cfm

Programs Administered by Federal Headquarters

DOD12.002 | PROCUREMENT TECHNICAL ASSISTANCE FOR BUSINESS FIRMS "PTAP"

Award: Cooperative Agreements

Purpose: To maximize the contracts of businesses with government.

Applicant Eligibility: Eligible applicants. Only those entities listed in this section are eligible to apply. a. States. State means a State of the United States, the District of Columbia, a territory or possession of the United States, an agency or instrumentality of a State, and a multi-State, regional, or interstate entity having governmental duties and powers (refer to 10 U.S.C. 2411(1)(A)). b. Local Governments. Local government, means a unit of government in a State, a local public authority, a special district, an intrastate district, a council of Governments, a sponsor group representative Organization, an interstate entity, or another instrumentality of a local government (refer to 10 U.S.C. 2411(1)(B)). c. Private nonprofit Organizations. Private nonprofit Organization means an entity which is exempt from federal income taxation under Section 501 of the Internal Revenue Code, and no part of its earnings inure to the benefit of any private shareholder or individual, and no substantial part of its activities is carrying on propaganda or otherwise attempting to influence legislation or participating in any political campaign on behalf of any candidate for public office (refer to 10 U.S.C. 2411(1)(C)). d. Economic enterprises. Economic enterprise means any Indian-owned (as defined by the Secretary of the Interior) commercial, industrial, or business activity established or organized for profit purposes or for nonprofit purposes. Provided, that such Indian ownership constitutes not less than 51 percent of the enterprise (refer to 10 U.S.C. 2411(1)(D)). e. Tribal Organizations. Tribal Organization means the recognized governing body of any Indian tribe; any legally established Organization of Indians which is controlled, sanctioned, or chartered by such governing body, or which is democratically elected by the adult members of the Indian community to be served by such Organization and which includes the maximum participation of Indians in all phases of its activities. Provided, that in any case where a cooperative agreement is made to an Organization to perform services benefiting more than one Indian tribe, the approval of each such Indian tribe shall be a prerequisite to the making of such cooperative agreement (refer to 10 U.S.C. 2411(1)(D)).

Beneficiary Eligibility: Any established US business who wants to sell goods or services to any US government agency.

Award Range/Average: The smallest award is about $64,000 and serves businesses in one or a few counties and the largest is $750,000 and serves businesses throughout an entire state.

Funding: (Cooperative Agreements) FY 18 $37,300,000.00; FY 19 est $41,000,000.00; FY 20 est $42,000,000.00

HQ: 8725 John J Kingman Road, Suite 1127, Fort Belvoir, VA 22060

Phone: 703-767-0192

https://www.dla.mil/SmallBusiness/PTAP

DOS19.415 | PROFESSIONAL AND CULTURAL EXCHANGE PROGRAMS-CITIZEN EXCHANGES

Award: Cooperative Agreements; Project Grants

Purpose: Seeks to increase mutual understanding between the people of the United States and the people of other countries by means of educational and cultural exchange programs, including the exchange of scholars, researchers, professionals, students, and educators.

Applicant Eligibility: Pursuant to the Mutual educational and Cultural Exchange Act of 1961, as amended (Fulbright-Hays Act) the Bureau of educational and Cultural Affairs of the U.S. Department of State awards grants and cooperative agreements to educational and cultural public or private nonprofit foundations or Institutions. Applications may be submitted by public and private non-profit Organizations meeting the provisions described in Internal Revenue Code section 26 USC 501(c)(3). Organizations must have nonprofit status with the IRS at the time of application. Please refer to the Grants.gov or the U.S. Department of State's SAMS Domestic announcement for further eligibility criteria.

Beneficiary Eligibility: Beneficiaries include recipient organizations, educational institutions, other non-government organizations (NGOs) that meet the provisions described in Internal Revenue Code section 26 USC 501(c)(3), as well as sponsored participants, and the American people and the people of participating countries who interact with the international participants.

Award Range/Average: $119,875 to $16,673,716.

Funding: (Project Grants) FY 17 $120,595,927.00; FY 18 est $120,595,927.00; FY 19 est $120,595,927.00

HQ: 2200 C Street NW SA-05, Room 3B13, Washington, DC 20037

Phone: 202-632-6070 | Email: hadjigeorgalisea@state.gov

http://eca.state.gov/about-bureau-0/organizational-structure/office-citizen-exchanges

DOS19.402 | PROFESSIONAL AND CULTURAL EXCHANGE PROGRAMS-INTERNATIONAL VISITOR LEADERSHIP PROGRAM
"International Visitor Leadership Program"

Award: Project Grants

Purpose: Seeks to increase mutual understanding between the people of the United States and the people of other countries by means of educational and cultural exchange programs, including the exchange of scholars, researchers, professionals, students, and educators.

Applicant Eligibility: Pursuant to the Mutual educational and Cultural Exchange Act of 1961, as amended (Fulbright-Hays Act) the Bureau of educational and Cultural Affairs of the U.S. Department of State awards grants and cooperative agreements to educational and cultural public or private nonprofit foundations or Institutions. Applications may be submitted by public and private non-profit Organizations meeting the provisions described in Internal Revenue Code section 26 USC 501(c)(3). Organizations must have nonprofit status with the IRS at the time of application. Please refer to the Grants.gov or the U.S. Department of State's SAMS Domestic announcement for further eligibility criteria.

Beneficiary Eligibility: Beneficiaries include recipient organizations, educational institutions, other non-government organizations (NGOs) that meet the provisions described in Internal Revenue Code section 26 USC 501(c)(3), as well as sponsored participants, the American people and the people of participating countries who interact with the international participants.

Award Range/Average: $300,000 to $18,106,089.

Funding: (Cooperative Agreements) FY 17 $65,947,690.00; FY 18 est $65,947,690.00; FY 19 est $65,947,690.00

HQ: 2200 C Street NW SA-05, Room 03BB06, Washington, DC 20037

  Phone: 202-632-9384 | Email: rathburntg@state.gov

  http://eca.state.gov/ivlp

DOS19.012 | PROFESSIONAL AND CULTURAL EXCHANGE PROGRAMS-SPECIAL PROFESSIONAL AND CULTURAL PROGRAMS
"Special Professional and Cultural Programs include the Ngwang Choephel Fellows Program"

Award: Project Grants

Purpose: Seeks to increase mutual understanding between the people of the United States and the people of other countries by means of educational and cultural exchange programs. The purpose of the Special Professional and Cultural Programs is to carry out congressionally directed initiatives that support professional exchanges between the United States and select countries through grants to American non-profit, non-governmental institutions and organizations, including community organizations, professional associations, and universities.

Applicant Eligibility: Pursuant to the Mutual educational and Cultural Exchange Act of 1961, as amended (Fulbright-Hays Act) the Bureau of educational and Cultural Affairs of the U.S. Department of State awards grants and cooperative agreements to educational and cultural public or private nonprofit foundations or Institutions. Applications may be submitted by public and private non-profit Organizations meeting the provisions described in Internal Revenue Code section 26 USC 501(c)(3). Organizations must have nonprofit status with the IRS at the time of application. Please refer to the Grants.gov or the U.S. Department of State's SAMS Domestic announcement for further eligibility criteria.

Beneficiary Eligibility: Beneficiaries include recipient organizations, educational institutions, other non-government organizations (NGOs) that meet the provisions described in Internal Revenue Code section 26 USC 501(c)(3), as well as sponsored participants, and the American people and the people of participating countries who interact with the international participants.

Award Range/Average: 287500

Funding: (Project Grants) FY 17 $575,000.00; FY 18 est $575,000.00; FY 19 est $575,000.00

HQ: 2200 C Street NW SA-05, Room 3B13, Washington, DC 20037

  Phone: 202-632-6070 | Email: hadjigeorgalisea@state.gov

  http://eca.state.gov/about-bureau-0/organizational-structure/office-citizen-exchanges

Programs Administered by Federal Headquarters

DOS19.300 | PROGRAM FOR STUDY OF EASTERN EUROPE AND THE INDEPENDENT STATES OF THE FORMER SOVIET UNION

Award: Project Grants

Purpose: Sustains and strengthens American expertise on the independent states of the former Soviet Union and countries of Eastern Europe, by supporting graduate training; advanced research; public dissemination of research data, methods, and findings; contact and collaboration among Government and private specialists; and firsthand experience of these countries by American specialists, including on site conduct of advanced training and research.

Applicant Eligibility: Applicants must be nonprofit Organizations or Institutions of higher education with an established track record in conducting research and training Programs on the independent states of the former Soviet Union and countries of Eastern Europe. These Organizations must run national Programs of: advanced research; graduate training; language training; public dissemination of research data, methods, and findings; contact and collaboration among Government and private specialists; and/or firsthand experience of the area by U.S. specialists.

Beneficiary Eligibility: Graduate students, individual scholars, nonprofit organizations and institutions of higher education active in the study of the Independent States of the former Soviet Union and countries of Eastern Europe.

Award Range/Average: Avg. Approx $500000

Funding: (Project Grants) FY 16 $2,000,000.00; FY 17 est $200,000.00; FY 18 Estimate Not Available

HQ: 2201 C Street NW, Washington, DC 20520

Phone: 202-736-4562 | Email: dechaines@state.gov

http://www.state.gov/s/inr/grants

ED84.240 | PROGRAM OF PROTECTION AND ADVOCACY OF INDIVIDUAL RIGHTS

Award: Formula Grants

Purpose: To provide grants for States to support systems for protection and advocacy for the rights of individuals with disabilities who are ineligible for advocacy services from the other protection and advocacy programs or whose problems fall outside the scope of services available from the Client Assistance Program (CAP).

Applicant Eligibility: Only designated protection and advocacy agencies in each State and Territory, and the protection and advocacy system serving the American Indian Consortium, may apply. With the exception of the protection and advocacy system serving the American Indian Consortium, the Governor designates the protection and advocacy agency.

Beneficiary Eligibility: Individuals with disabilities will benefit.

Award Range/Average: For FY 2019, the estimated range of State awards (including the District of Columbia and Puerto Rico) under the distribution formula is $147,598 to $1,775,273, with a median award of $200,001. The estimated award for each of the four outlying areas is $85,799.

Funding: (Formula Grants) FY 18 $17,650,000.00; FY 19 est $17,650,000.00; FY 20 est $17,650,000.00

HQ: 400 Maryland Avenue SW, Washington, DC 20202

Phone: 202-245-6493 | Email: samuel.pierre@ed.gov

http://www.rsa.ed.gov/programs.cfm

HHS93.116 | PROJECT GRANTS AND COOPERATIVE AGREEMENTS FOR TUBERCULOSIS CONTROL PROGRAMS

Award: Cooperative Agreements

Purpose: To assist State, local health agencies, political subdivisions, and other government entities to conduct TB preventive health service programs to assist in carrying out tuberculosis (TB) control activities designed to prevent transmission of infection and disease.

Applicant Eligibility: Under Section 317 of the Public Health Service Act, official public health agencies or their bona fide agents of State and local Governments, including the District of Columbia, the Commonwealth of Puerto Rico, the Virgin Islands, Guam, the Northern Mariana Islands, the Federated States of Micronesia, the Republic of the Marshall Islands, the Republic of Palau, and American Samoa.

Beneficiary Eligibility: Official public health agencies of State and local governments, including the District of Columbia, the Commonwealth of Puerto Rico, the Virgin Islands, Guam, the Northern Mariana Islands, the Federated States of Micronesia, the Republic of the Marshall Islands, the Republic of Palau, and American Samoa.

Award Range/Average: $86,938 to $9,9,317,764 with an average of $1,454,714

Funding: (Cooperative Agreements) FY 18 $85,104,273.00; FY 19 est $86,481,851.00; FY 20 est $80,498,900.00

HQ: Division of Tuberculosis Elimination 1600 Clifton Road NE, PO Box E10, Atlanta, GA 30333
Phone: 404-639-5259 | Email: kak4@cdc.gov
http://www.cdc.gov/tb

HUD14.326 | PROJECT RENTAL ASSISTANCE DEMONSTRATION (PRA DEMO) PROGRAM OF SECTION 811 SUPPORTIVE HOUSING FOR PERSONS WITH DISABILITIES

Award: Project Grants
Purpose: Implementing the new requirements for the new project rental assistance authority rendered by the Melville Act.
Applicant Eligibility: Any housing agency currently allocating Low Income Housing Tax Credits (LIHTC) under IRS Section 42 or any housing or Community Development Agency currently allocating and overseeing in good standing HOME Funds or the Section 8 Program or a similar Program are eligible applicants, and only one housing agency per state is eligible. Only states that are developing partnerships or that have existing partnerships with State healthcare and Human Service Agency or agencies and the state Medicaid Agency for supportive services are eligible.
Beneficiary Eligibility: Extremely low-income non-elderly (18-62 years of age) persons with disabilities that are eligible for community-based, long-term care as provided through Medicaid waivers, Medicaid state plan options or other appropriate services. Eligible applicants will provide these PRA Demo project-based rental assistance funds to not more than 25% of the units in multifamily developments for extremely low-income persons with disabilities which are the beneficiaries.
Award Range/Average: To Be Determined.
Funding: (Project Grants) FY 15 $82,000,000.00; FY 16 est $67,000,000.00; FY 17 est $3,000,000.00
HQ: 451 7th Street SW, Washington, DC 20410
Phone: 202-708-3000 | Email: lessie.p.evans@hud.gov

DOJ16.609 | PROJECT SAFE NEIGHBORHOODS
"PSN"

Award: Project Grants
Purpose: To create and foster safer neighborhoods through a sustained diminution in violent crime, including, but not limited to, addressing criminal gangs and the felonious possession and use of firearms.
Applicant Eligibility: Eligible applicants are PSN Task Force fiscal agents for the U.S. Attorney districts and federally recognized Indian tribal Governments (as determined by the Secretary of the Interior). All fiscal agents must be certified by the relevant U.S. Attorney's Office (USAO). Eligible USAO-certified fiscal agents include states, units of local government, educational Institutions, faith-based and other community Organizations, private nonprofit Organizations, and federally recognized Indian tribal Governments (as determined by the Secretary of the Interior).
Beneficiary Eligibility: State and local governments, public and private organizations, Indian Tribal government, prosecutor offices.
Award Range/Average: Prior awards have ranged from approximately $200,000 to $500,000.
Funding: (Project Grants) FY 18 $33,230,672.00; FY 19 est $20,000,000.00; FY 20 est $0.00
HQ: 810 7th Street NW, Washington, DC 20735
Phone: 202-598-5248
http://www.bja.gov

HHS93.150 | PROJECTS FOR ASSISTANCE IN TRANSITION FROM HOMELESSNESS (PATH)
"PATH"

Award: Formula Grants
Purpose: To provide financial assistance to States to support services for individuals who are suffering from serious mental illness or serious mental illness and substance abuse; and are homeless or at imminent risk of becoming homeless.
Applicant Eligibility: States, District of Columbia, Guam, American Samoa, the Commonwealths of Puerto Rico and the Northern Mariana Islands, and the Virgin Islands.
Beneficiary Eligibility: Individuals who have a serious mental illness or serious mental illness and substance abuse; and are homeless or are at imminent risk of becoming homeless.

Programs Administered by Federal Headquarters

Award Range/Average: Range - $50,000 to $8,812,865; Avg. - $1,099,933.96
Funding: (Formula Grants) FY 18 est $61,596,302.00; FY 19 est $61,581,202.00; FY 20 est $2,705,569.00
HQ: 5600 Fishers Lane, Rockville, MD 20857
   Phone: 240-276-1078 | Email: odessa.crocker@samhsa.hhs.gov
   http://www.samhsa.gov

HHS93.587 | PROMOTE THE SURVIVAL AND CONTINUING VITALITY OF NATIVE AMERICAN LANGUAGES

"Native American Language Preservation and Maintenance (P&M) and the Esther Martinez Immersion (EMI)"

Award: Project Grants
Purpose: Provides financial assistance to eligible applicants for the purpose of promoting the survival and continued vitality of native languages.
Applicant Eligibility: Federally-recognized Indian Tribes, as recognized by the Bureau of Indian Affairs, Incorporated non-federally recognized Tribes Incorporated state-recognized Indian Tribes Consortia of Indian Tribes Incorporated nonprofit multi-purpose community-based Indian Organizations Urban Indian Centers Alaska Native villages as defined in the Alaska Native Claims Settlement Act (ANSCA) and/or nonprofit village consortia Nonprofit native Organizations in Alaska with village specific projects Incorporated non-profit Alaska Native multi-purpose, community-based Organizations Non-profit Alaska Native Regional Corporations/Associations in Alaska with village-specific projects Non-profit Alaska Native community entities or tribal governing bodies (Indian Re Organization Act or Traditional Councils) as recognized by the Bureau of Indian Affairs, Public and nonprofit private agencies serving Native Hawaiians, National or regional incorporated nonprofit Native American Organizations with Native American community-specific objectives, Public and nonprofit private agencies serving native peoples from Guam, American Samoa, or the Commonwealth of the Northern Mariana Islands, Tribal Colleges and universities, and colleges and universities located in Hawaii, Guam, American Samoa, or the Tribal Colleges and universities, and colleges and universities located in Hawaii, Guam, American Samoa, or the Commonwealth of the Northern Mariana Islands which serve Native American Pacific Islanders.
Beneficiary Eligibility: American Indians, Alaska Natives, Native Hawaiians, and Native American Pacific Islanders will benefit.
Award Range/Average: $100,000- $300,000. Average per Budget Period: $278,000
Funding: (Project Grants) FY 18 $10,158,410.00; FY 19 est $11,768,118.00; FY 20 est $11,768,118.00
HQ: Division of Program Operations 330 C Street SW Switzer Building, PO Box 4126, Washington, DC 20201
   Phone: 877-922-9262 | Email: carmelia.strickland@acf.hhs.gov
   http://www.acf.hhs.gov/programs/ana

DOJ16.203 | PROMOTING EVIDENCE INTEGRATION IN SEX OFFENDER MANAGEMENT DISCRETIONARY GRANT PROGRAM

Award: Project Grants; Training
Purpose: To support the Adam Walsh Act (AWA) by administering grant programs related to sex offender registration and notification as authorized under AWA or directed by the Attorney General and provide technical assistance to states, the District of Columbia, principal U.S. territories, units of local government, tribal governments, and other public and private entities involved in activities related to sex offender registration or notification or to other measures for the protection of children or other members of the public from sexual abuse or exploitation. To assist states, the District of Columbia, the principal U.S. territories, local, and tribal jurisdictions in improving their adult and/or juvenile sex offender management policies and practices by supporting training, technical assistance, demonstration projects, and fellowships in the Office of Sex Offender Sentencing, Monitoring, Apprehending, Registering and Tracking (SMART).
Applicant Eligibility: Non-profit Organizations (including tribal Organizations), Institutions of higher education (including tribal Institutions of higher education), for-profit Organizations, states, the District of Columbia, the Commonwealth of Puerto Rico, the Virgin Islands, America Samoa, Guam, the Commonwealth of the Northern Mariana Islands, local, and tribal communities who are interested in addressing the management of juvenile, adult, or a mixed population of sex offenders are eligible to apply for this grant Program. Applicants must coordinate their proposal with others in their jurisdiction to ensure a collaborative response to this solicitation as well as to ensure that agencies within a single jurisdiction are not competing against one another in the grant process. For sex offender management fellowships, eligible applicants include individuals.

Beneficiary Eligibility: State, local, and tribal agencies (e.g. parole, probation, pretrial services, etc.) responsible for sex offender management, accountability, registration, and supervision. Non-profit or for-profit organizations, institutions of higher education, and tribal entities. For sex offender management fellowships: individuals with knowledge and experience in the field of sex offender management.

Award Range/Average: Up to $500,000 for sex offender management enhancement programs, up to $1,000,000 for training and technical assistance, and up to $250,000 per fellowship opportunity.See the current fiscal year's solicitations on Grants.gov and at the SMART Office's Funding Opportunities page.

Funding: (Project Grants) FY 17 $853,266.00; FY 18 est Not Separately Identifiable; FY 19 est Not Separately Identifiable

HQ: 810 7th Street NW, Washington, DC 20531

    Phone: 202-307-5762

    http://www.smart.gov

HHS93.845 | PROMOTING POPULATION HEALTH THROUGH INCREASED CAPACITY IN ALCOHOL EPIDEMIOLOGY
"Alcohol Epidemiology"

Award: Cooperative Agreements

Purpose: The purpose of this FOA is to support the building of capacity in alcohol epidemiology in state and large city Health Departments and help provide the tools needed to perform core public health functions. This increased epidemiologic capacity will help build the public health infrastructure that is needed to address excessive alcohol use in the U.S.

Applicant Eligibility: Eligibility will be limited to State and District of Columbia Health Departments, large city health departments (900,00 residents or more), or their Bona Fide Agents.

Beneficiary Eligibility: State and local health departments' work may benefit work may benefit others outside the institution including health professionals, non-profit organizations, and the general public.

Funding: (Cooperative Agreements) FY 18 $750,000.00; FY 19 est $750,000.00; FY 20 est $750,000.00

HQ: 4770 Buford Highway NE, PO Box F78, Atlanta, GA 30341

    Phone: 770-488-8063

    http://www.cdc.gov

HHS93.556 | PROMOTING SAFE AND STABLE FAMILIES

Award: Formula Grants; Project Grants

Purpose: To prevent child maltreatment among families at risk through the provision of supportive family services.

Applicant Eligibility: (1) Formula Grants: States, the District of Columbia, Puerto Rico, the U.S. Virgin Islands, the Northern Marianas, Guam, American Samoa, and Federally-recognized Indian Tribes are eligible applicants. For caseworker visit funds, only states and territories are eligible applicants. (2) Discretionary Grants: States, local Governments, Tribes, public agencies or private agencies or Organizations (or combinations of such agencies or Organizations) with expertise in providing, evaluating and/or providing technical assistance related to family preservation, family support, family reunification and adoption promotion and support.

Beneficiary Eligibility: Families and children who need services to assist them to stabilize their lives, strengthen family functioning, prevent out-of-home placement of children, enhance child development and increase competence in parenting abilities, facilitate timely reunification of the child, and promote appropriate adoptions.

Award Range/Average: In FY 2017, formula grants for main grant program: states, territories, and tribes ranged from $1,935 to $26,939,151 with an average of $1,333,355.

Funding: (Formula Grants) FY 18 $325,364,129.00; FY 19 est $321,902,509.00; FY 20 est $344,820,510.00; (Cooperative Agreements (Discretionary Grants)) FY 18 $1,972,245.00; FY 19 est $14,792,875.00; FY 20 est $1,972,244.00

HQ: 330 C Street SW, Room 3509A, Washington, DC 20201

    Phone: 202-690-8888 | Email: catherine.heath@acf.hhs.gov

    http://www.acf.hhs.gov/programs/cb

Programs Administered by Federal Headquarters

HHS93.832 | PROMOTING THE CANCER SURVEILLANCE WORKFORCE, EDUCATION AND DATA USE

Award: Cooperative Agreements

Purpose: The purpose of this program is to expand the capacity of CDC-funded National Program of Cancer Registries through external partners, to pursue activities that impact the national cancer surveillance workforce.

Applicant Eligibility: Nonprofit with 501C3 IRS status (other than institution of higher education)Nonprofit without 501C3 IRS status (other than institution of higher education)Private colleges and universities.

Beneficiary Eligibility: Same as Applicant Eligibility.

Award Range/Average: The award range is $200,000 per budget year for five years.

Funding: (Cooperative Agreements) FY 18 $200,000.00; FY 19 est $200,000.00; FY 20 est $199,999.00

HQ: 4770 Buford Highway NE, PO Box F76, Atlanta, GA 30341

    Phone: 770-488-8430

    http://www.cdc.gov

NEA45.024 | PROMOTION OF THE ARTS GRANTS TO ORGANIZATIONS AND INDIVIDUALS

Award: Project Grants

Purpose: To support public engagement with, and access to, various forms of excellent art across the nation, the creation of art that meets the highest standards of excellence.

Applicant Eligibility: Tax-exempt Organizations meeting the following conditions may apply: (1) No part of any earnings may benefit a private stockholder or individual, and (2) donations to the Organization are allowable as charitable deductions under Section 170(c) of the Internal Revenue Code. Examples of eligible Organizations are arts Institutions, arts service Organizations, local arts agencies, official units of state and local Governments, federally recognized tribal communities, and Indian Tribes. Generally, an Organization may submit only one application for a single project under one of the category deadlines; must have a three-year history of arts Programming prior to the application deadline; and must have submitted acceptable final reports by the due date for all National Endowment for the Arts grants previously received. Individuals must be U.S. citizens or permanent residents and, according to 20 U.S.C. 954 (c), must demonstrate exceptional talent. Currently, the only individuals eligible to apply directly are published creative writers and translators. Certain master artists who have made extraordinary contributions to the arts in the United States are eligible for honorary fellowships awarded on the basis of nominations. See respective funding opportunities, guidelines, or Program announcements for further information.

Beneficiary Eligibility: Through activities and services supported, beneficiaries include the general public and artists as well as nonprofit organizations, state and local governments, local arts agencies, local education agencies (school districts), federally recognized tribal communities and Indian tribes, literary artists, and master artists.

Award Range/Average: Most of the National Endowment for the Arts' regular grants range from $10,000 to $100,000. Grants of $100,000 or more are made only in rare instances, and only for projects that the National Endowment for the Arts determines demonstrate exceptional national or regional significance and impact. In the past few years, well over half of our grants have been for amounts less than $25,000.

Funding: (Project Grants (Discretionary)) FY 18 $70,313,432.00; FY 19 est $69,942,424.00; FY 20 Estimate Not Available

HQ: 400 7th Street SW, Washington, DC 20506

    Phone: 202-682-5441 | Email: chauveauxt@arts.gov

    http://www.arts.gov

NEA45.025 | PROMOTION OF THE ARTS PARTNERSHIP AGREEMENTS

Award: Project Grants; Advisory Services and Counseling

Purpose: To develop and maintain partnerships with the state and jurisdictional arts agencies (SAAs) and their regional arts organizations (RAOs) to advance the mission of the National Endowment for the Arts.

Applicant Eligibility: Agencies that are officially designated as the state arts agency by the state government in each of the 50 States and six special U.S. jurisdictions, and that meet the National Endowment for the Arts' eligibility requirements for SAAs as outlined in the Partnership Agreements guidelines on our website; regional arts Organizations that represent state arts agencies and that meet the National Endowment for the Arts' eligibility requirements for RAOs as outlined in the Partnership Agreements guidelines on our website; and Organizations providing support services to state and regional arts agencies at a national level.

Beneficiary Eligibility: The official arts agencies of the 50 states and six U.S. jurisdictions, regional arts organizations, and organizations providing support services to SAAs and RAOs at the national level. Through activities and services supported, beneficiaries include the general public, local arts agencies, nonprofit organizations, and artists.

Award Range/Average: FY 2019 Partnership Agreements for SAAs range from $289,300 to $1,167,300, averaging approximately $750,000. The range of FY 2019 RAO awards is $1,106,200 to $1,713,600, averaging approximately $1,450,000.

Funding: (Project Grants (with Formula Distribution)) FY 18 $50,706,790.00; FY 19 est $51,956,500.00; FY 20 Estimate Not Available

HQ: 400 7th Street SW, Washington, DC 20506
Phone: 202-682-5469 | Email: orlovem@arts.gov
http://www.arts.gov

NEH45.130 | PROMOTION OF THE HUMANITIES CHALLENGE GRANTS

Award: Project Grants

Purpose: To strengthen the institutional base of the humanities by supporting infrastructure development and capacity building.

Applicant Eligibility: U.S. public and nonprofit 501(c)(3) Organizations (including Institutions of higher education), state and local governmental agencies, and federally recognized Native American tribal Governments. The following eligible entities are subject to the one-to-one matching requirement: public and 501(c)(3) nonprofit community colleges and post-secondary two-year Institutions of higher education; public and nonprofit 501(c)(3) U.S. historically black colleges or universities, as defined by Executive Order 13532; public and nonprofit 501(c)(3) Hispanic-serving Institutions of higher education; and U.S. tribal college or University, as defined by Executive Order 13270.

Beneficiary Eligibility: All applicant organizations and institutions and all users of their humanities resources, programs, or activities; humanities scholars, and the general public.

Award Range/Average: Applicants may request up to $750,000. In fiscal year 2017, the largest award offered was $338,000, the smallest was $1,500; and the average award was approximately $72,240.

Funding: (Project Grants) FY 18 $4,776,710; FY 19 est $9,194,550; FY 20 est Estimate Not Available;-FY19 obligations include awards made but not fully processed.

HQ: 400 7th Street SW, Washington, DC 20506
Phone: 202-606-8309
http://www.neh.gov

NEH45.149 | PROMOTION OF THE HUMANITIES DIVISION OF PRESERVATION AND ACCESS

Award: Project Grants

Purpose: To ensure the long-term and wide availability of primary resources in the humanities by funding projects that promote preserving, creating, and providing intellectual access to resources held in libraries, museums, archives, historical organizations, and other collections.

Applicant Eligibility: U.S. public and nonprofit 501(c)(3) Organizations (including Institutions of higher education), state and local governmental agencies, and federally recognized Native American tribal Governments.

Beneficiary Eligibility: U.S. public and nonprofit 501(c)(3) organizations (including institutions of higher education), state and local governmental agencies, federally recognized Native American tribal governments, humanities scholars, and the general public.

Award Range/Average: FY 18 from $6,000 to $350,000; average $98,850

Funding: (Project Grants) FY 18 $19,372,200.00; FY 19 est $19,631,350.00; FY 20 Estimate Not Available

HQ: 400 7th Street SW, Washington, DC 20506
Phone: 202-606-8570
http://www.neh.gov/divisions/preservation

NEH45.129 | PROMOTION OF THE HUMANITIES FEDERAL/STATE PARTNERSHIP

Award: Formula Grants

Purpose: To promote local, statewide, and regional humanities programming through annual grants to humanities councils in each of the 50 States, the District of Columbia, Puerto Rico, the U.S. Virgin Islands, Northern Mariana Islands, Guam, and American Samoa.

Programs Administered by Federal Headquarters

Applicant Eligibility: Nonprofit 501(c)(3) state and jurisdictional humanities councils which conform to the requirements of 20 U.S.C. 956(f). See https://www.neh.gov/about/state-humanities-councils.

Beneficiary Eligibility: State and local governments; sponsored organizations; public and private nonprofit institutions/ organizations; other public institutions/organizations; Federally recognized Indian tribal governments; Native American organizations; U.S. Territories; non-government general; minority organizations; other specialized groups; and quasi-public nonprofit institutions which apply directly to the State Humanities Council.

Award Range/Average: In FY 2018 the range of assistance was $384,160 to $2,446,300. Average was $823,747.

Funding: (Project Grants) FY 18 $47,503,308; FY 19 est $48,385,840.00; FY 20 est Estimate Not Available

HQ: 400 7th Street SW, Washington, DC 20506

   Phone: 202-606-8254

   http://www.neh.gov/divisions/fedstate

NEH45.160 | PROMOTION OF THE HUMANITIES FELLOWSHIPS AND STIPENDS

Award: Project Grants

Purpose: To provide support for scholars to undertake full-time independent research and writing in the humanities. Grants are available for six to-12-month fellowships and two months of summer study.

Applicant Eligibility: All applicants must be U.S. citizens, native residents of U.S. jurisdictions, foreign nationals who have been legal residents in the U.S. or its jurisdictions for at least the three years immediately preceding the application deadline. Fellowships: Faculty members at colleges and universities, individuals affiliated with other Institutions, independent scholars, and others who work in the humanities are eligible. Applicants need not have advanced degrees, but they must have completed their formal academic training. Active candidates for degrees and persons seeking support for work leading to degrees are not eligible. Summer Stipends: University and college faculty members must be nominated by their academic Institutions. Faculty members with terminating appointments, independent scholars, and nonfaculty college and University staff members are exempt from nomination and may apply directly. Awards for Faculty are offered to full-time faculty members at Historically Black Colleges and universities, Hispanic-Serving Institutions, and Tribal Colleges and universities as designated by the White House offices charged with the implementation of Executive Orders 12876, 13230, 13021.

Beneficiary Eligibility: Fellowships and Stipends: College and university faculty and staff, individuals affiliated with institutions other than colleges and universities, and scholars and writers working independently. Awards for Faculty: faculty members at Historically Black Colleges and Universities, Hispanic-Serving Institutions, and Tribal Colleges and Universities.

Award Range/Average: Fellowships and Awards for Faculty: An award of $5,000 per month for a grant period of from 3 to 12 months. Summer Stipends: All awards are $6,000 for a grant periodof 8 weeks.

Funding: (Project Grants (Fellowships)) FY 18 $5,061,600.00; FY 19 est $5,450,000.00; FY 20 est Estimate Not Available

HQ: Division of Research Programs 400 7th Street SW, Washington, DC 20506

   Phone: 202-606-8200

   https://www.neh.gov/divisions/research

NEH45.169 | PROMOTION OF THE HUMANITIES OFFICE OF DIGITAL HUMANITIES

Award: Project Grants

Purpose: Supports innovative humanities projects that utilize or study the impact of digital technology for research, preservation, access, education, and public programming.

Applicant Eligibility: U.S. public and 501(c)(3) nonprofit Organizations (including Institutions of higher education); state and local governmental agencies and Native American tribal Organizations.

Beneficiary Eligibility: U.S. public and nonprofit organizations (including institutions of higher education); state and local governmental agencies and Native American tribal organizations; U.S. citizens; and humanities scholars.

Award Range/Average: FY 18 from $25200 to $325000.

Funding: (Project Grants) FY 18 $4,822,974.00; FY 19 est $5,323,000.00; FY 20 est Estimate Not Available

HQ: 400 7th Street SW, Washington, DC 20506

   Phone: 202-606-8400

   http://www.neh.gov

NEH45.163 | PROMOTION OF THE HUMANITIES PROFESSIONAL DEVELOPMENT

Award: Project Grants

Purpose: Seminars and Institutes promote better teaching and research in the humanities through faculty development.

Applicant Eligibility: Distinguished scholar/teachers in the humanities may apply through a sponsoring institution to direct a seminar or institute for college teachers or schoolteachers. For Landmarks in American History and Culture, the following may apply: U.S. public and nonprofit 501(c)(3) Organizations (including Institutions of higher education), state and local governmental agencies, and federally recognized Native American tribal Governments.

Beneficiary Eligibility: U.S. public and nonprofit 501(c)(3) organizations (including institutions of higher education), state and local governmental agencies, federally recognized Native American tribal governments, humanities scholars, and the general public. For Seminars and Institutes and Landmarks of American History and Culture -primarily K-12 or college teachers, depending on the particular project -as well as their colleagues and students.

Award Range/Average: Not Available.

Funding: (Project Grants) FY 18 $8,845,400; FY 19 est $8,965,000.00; FY 20 est Estimate Not Available

HQ: Division of Education Programs 400 7th Street SW, Washington, DC 20506

Phone: 202-606-8463

https://www.neh.gov/divisions/education

NEH45.164 | PROMOTION OF THE HUMANITIES PUBLIC PROGRAMS

Award: Project Grants

Purpose: To provide opportunities for the American public to explore human history and culture through humanities programs in museums, historical organizations, libraries, community centers, and other gathering places.

Applicant Eligibility: U.S. public and private 501(c)(3) nonprofit Institutions /Organizations (including Institutions of higher education); state and local governmental agencies; and Federally recognized Indian tribal Governments.

Beneficiary Eligibility: U.S. public and private nonprofit institutions/organizations (including institutions of higher education); state and local governmental agencies; and Federally recognized Indian tribal governments, humanities scholars, and the general public.

Award Range/Average: FY 18 from $1,000 to $460,000.

Funding: (Project Grants) FY 18 $13,840,100.00; FY 19 est $14,500,000; FY 20 est Estimate Not Available

HQ: Division of Public Programs 400 7th Street SW, Washington, DC 20506

Phone: 202-606-8269

http://www.neh.gov/divisions/public

NEH45.161 | PROMOTION OF THE HUMANITIES RESEARCH

Award: Project Grants

Purpose: To advance knowledge and understanding of the humanities and strengthen the intellectual foundations of the humanities.

Applicant Eligibility: For Collaborative Research and Scholarly Editions and Translations, U.S. public and 501(c)(3) nonprofit Organizations (including Institutions of higher education), state and local Governments, federally recognized Native American tribal Governments, and individuals (U.S. citizens and foreign nationals who have been living in the United States or its jurisdictions for at least the three years immediately prior to the time of application). For Fellowship Programs at Independent Research Institutions (FPIRI), U.S. nonprofit 501(c)(3) Organizations, a state or local governmental agency, or a federally recognized Indian tribal government with existing fellowship Programs may apply. FPIRI applicant Institutions must be financed, governed and administered independently of Institutions of higher education.

Beneficiary Eligibility: U.S. citizens and residents, State and local governments, sponsored organizations, public and private nonprofit institutions/organizations, other public institutions/organizations, Federally recognized Indian tribal governments, Native American organizations, U.S. territories; non-governmental-general; minority organizations, other specialized groups; and quasi-public nonprofit institutions benefit.

Award Range/Average: FY 17 from $50,400 to $330,000; $177,300 average.

Funding: (Project Grants) FY 18 $8,526,700.00; FY 19 est 8,850,000; FY 20 est Estimate Not Available

HQ: Division of Research Programs 400 7th Street SW, Washington, DC 20506

Phone: 202-606-8200

Programs Administered by Federal Headquarters

NEH45.162 | PROMOTION OF THE HUMANITIES TEACHING AND LEARNING RESOURCES AND CURRICULUM DEVELOPMENT

Award: Project Grants

Purpose: Humanities Initiatives at Historically Black, Hispanic-Serving Institutions, and Tribal Colleges and Universities are designed to strengthen humanities teaching and learning at these institutions.

Applicant Eligibility: Public and nonprofit U.S. Historically Black Colleges or universities (HBCU) as defined by Executive Order 13532, Hispanic-serving Institutions of higher education (HSI) recognized by the U.S. Department of education, tribal colleges or universities as defined by Executive Order 13270, and public and nonprofit 501(c)(3) community colleges.

Beneficiary Eligibility: U.S. public and nonprofit 501(c)(3) organizations (including institutions of higher education), state and local governmental agencies, federally recognized Native American tribal governments, humanities scholars, and the general public.

Award Range/Average: Humanities Connections Planning Grants do not exceed $35,000. Humanities Connections Implementation Grants and Humanities Initiatives at Historically Black, Hispanic-Serving Institutions, and Tribal Colleges and Universities do not exceed $100,000.

Funding: (Project Grants) FY 18 $1,479,000.00; FY 19 est $4,225,000.00; FY 20 Estimate Not Available

HQ: Division of Education Programs 400 7th Street SW, Washington, DC 20506

  Phone: 202-606-8500

  http://www.neh.gov

HUD14.142 | PROPERTY IMPROVEMENT LOAN INSURANCE FOR IMPROVING ALL EXISTING STRUCTURES AND BUILDING OF NEW NONRESIDENTIAL STRUCTURES

Award: Guaranteed/insured Loans

Purpose: To assist the financing of improvements to homes and other property types.

Applicant Eligibility: Eligible borrowers include the owner of the property to be improved, a lessee having a lease extending at least 6 months beyond maturity of the loan, or a purchaser of the property under a land installment contract.

Beneficiary Eligibility: Individuals/families.

Funding: (Sale, Exchange, or Donation of Property and Goods) FY 15 $90,000,000.00; FY 16 est $90,000,000.00; FY 17 est $90,000,000.00

HQ: 451 7th Street SW, Washington, DC 20410

  Phone: 800-225-5342

  http://portal.hud.gov/hudportal/hud?src=/program_offices/housing/sfh/title/ti_home

HHS93.318 | PROTECTING AND IMPROVING HEALTH GLOBALLY: BUILDING AND STRENGTHENING PUBLIC HEALTH IMPACT, SYSTEMS, CAPACITY AND SECURITY "Global Health"

Award: Cooperative Agreements

Purpose: To assist Ministries of Health and other international partners to plan, manage effectively, and evaluate public health programs.

Applicant Eligibility: Dependent on the FOA, eligibility may range from open, competitive, limited, or single eligibility in accordance with authorizing legislation.

Beneficiary Eligibility: This will benefit individuals worldwide, including in the U.S., through collaborations with national Ministries of Health and other organizations/institutions. This is only for non-research activities supported by CDC/ATSDR. For the definition of research, please see http://www.cdc.gov/od/science/quality/resources.

Funding: (Cooperative Agreements) FY 18 $90,695,262.00; FY 19 est $28,454,661.00; FY 20 est $28,454,661.00

HQ: 1600 Clifton Road NE, PO Box H21-9, Atlanta, GA 30333

  Phone: 404-718-6503

  http://www.cdc.gov

HHS93.138 | PROTECTION AND ADVOCACY FOR INDIVIDUALS WITH MENTAL ILLNESS
"PAIMI"

Award: Formula Grants

Purpose: To enable the expansion of the Protection and Advocacy system established in each State.

Applicant Eligibility: State, local, and territory government agencies, public or private Organizations designated by the Governor under Part C of the Developmental Disabilities Assistance and Bill of Rights Acts as systems to protect and advocate the rights of persons with developmental disabilities in that State.

Beneficiary Eligibility: Individuals with significant mental illness or severe emotional impairment (children) who are at risk for abuse, neglect, or civil rights violations while residing in care or treatment facilities have service priority. Persons with significant mental illness and severe emotional impairment living in the community, including their own home, may be served as determined by their state protection and advocacy systems PAIMI program funded priorities and objectives and available resources includes persons who are in the process of being admitted to a facility rendering care or treatment, persons being transported to such a facility, or persons who are involuntarily confined in a municipal detention facility, jails, or prisons.

Award Range/Average: $229,300 to $3,140,635; Avg. $619,645

Funding: (Formula Grants) FY 18 $35,329,908.00; FY 19 est $35,335,256.00; FY 20 est $35,335,256.00

HQ: 5600 Fishers Lane, Rockville, MD 20857

Phone: 240-276-1078 | Email: odessa.crocker@samhsa.hhs.gov

http://www.samhsa.gov

DOD12.105 | PROTECTION OF ESSENTIAL HIGHWAYS, HIGHWAY BRIDGE APPROACHES, AND PUBLIC WORKS
"Emergency Bank Protection"

Award: Provision of Specialized Services

Purpose: To fund for bridges, churches, hospitals, schools and other nonprofit public services endangered by flood-caused erosion.

Applicant Eligibility: States, political subdivisions of States or other responsible local agencies established under State law with full authority and ability to undertake necessary legal and financial responsibilities.

Beneficiary Eligibility: Same as Applicant Eligibility.

DOD12.109 | PROTECTION, CLEARING AND STRAIGHTENING CHANNELS
"Section 3, Emergency Dredging Projects"

Award: Provision of Specialized Services

Purpose: To restore navigations for flood control.

Applicant Eligibility: States, political subdivisions of States or other responsible local agencies established under State law with full authority and ability to undertake necessary legal and financial responsibilities.

Beneficiary Eligibility: Same as Applicant Eligibility.

HHS93.427 | PROVISION OF TECHNICAL ASSISTANCE AND TRAINING ACTIVITIES TO ASSURE COMPREHENSIVE CANCER CONTROL OUTCOMES.

Award: Cooperative Agreements

Purpose: To fund up to two national organizations with proven capacities and expertise in chronic disease prevention and health promotion to provide technical assistance and training to National Comprehensive Cancer Control Program awardees and their coalitions to implement evidence-based and promising comprehensive cancer control interventions in the areas of primary prevention, screening and survivorship.

Applicant Eligibility: Eligible applicants: National 501(c) 3 Organizations; Public Non-for profits National 501(c)3 Organizations comprised of affiliates or chapters at state and/or local levels or universities with national reach who have the capacity to provide technical assistance and training to all funded grantees of the National Comprehensive Cancer Control Program.

Beneficiary Eligibility: Federal, State, Local.

Funding: (Cooperative Agreements) FY 18 $1,400,000.00; FY 19 est $1,900,000.00; FY 20 est $1,900,000.00

Programs Administered by Federal Headquarters

HQ: Public Health Advisor 4770 Buford Highway NE, PO Box 76, Atlanta, GA 30341
  Phone: 770-488-4296 | Email: jfonseka@cdc.gov
  http://www.cdc.gov

HUD14.865 | PUBLIC AND INDIAN HOUSING INDIAN LOAN GUARANTEE PROGRAM
"Loan Guarantees for Indian Housing"

Award: Guaranteed/insured Loans
Purpose: With the help of a guaranteed mortgage loan program available through private financial institutions, homeownership opportunities are provided to the Native Americans, Tribes, Indian Housing Authorities including Tribally Designated Housing Entities (TDHEs), and Indian Housing Authorities on Indian land.
Applicant Eligibility: The loan applicant must be members of a federally recognized Indian tribe, band or community, which includes Native Americans, Alaska Natives, or an Indian Housing Authority including a Tribally Designated Housing Authority (TDHE) or a Tribe which meets certain requirements. Applicant eligibility is validated by current enrollment in a federally recognized tribe.
Beneficiary Eligibility: The homeowner is the ultimate beneficiary of the program. When the Indian Housing Authority, TDHE or Tribe is the homebuyer, they may then rent the property. In these cases, the person renting the home would be an indirect beneficiary.
Award Range/Average: The average loan amount in FY 2014 was $176,000.
Funding: (Guaranteed/Insured Loans) FY 16 $4,492,000.00; FY 17 est $4,999,000.00; FY 18 est $4,006,000.00
HQ: 451 7th Street SW, Room 5156, Washington, DC 20410
  Phone: 202-402-4978 | Email: thomas.c.wright@hud.gov
  http://www.hud.gov/offices/pih/ih/homeownership/184

HUD14.891 | PUBLIC AND INDIAN HOUSING TRANSFORMATION INITIATIVE (TI) TECHNICAL ASSISTANCE (TA)

Award: Provision of Specialized Services
Purpose: To increase the operational efficiency of PIH processes, which is a key step toward capacity building and technical awareness of HUD's mission.
Applicant Eligibility: Increasing the operation efficiency of PIH processes is a key step toward capacity building and technical awareness that are at the heart of HUD's mission.
Beneficiary Eligibility: Public and Indian Housing Transformation Initiatives Technical Assistance ultimate beneficiaries are those who receive assistance. These initiatives will improve the way the Department operates.
Award Range/Average: Range $34,000 - $5,320,000 Average $2,130,000
HQ: 451 7th Street SW, Room 4246, Washington, DC 20410
  Phone: 202-402-4307 | Email: gary.f.vanbuskirk@hud.gov

HUD14.850 | PUBLIC AND INDIAN HOUSING

Award: Direct Payments for Specified Use
Purpose: To supply and function cost-effective, respectable, safe and affordable dwellings for lower income families through a licensed local Public Housing Agency (PHA).
Applicant Eligibility: Public Housing Agencies established in accordance with State law are eligible. The proposed Program must be approved by the local governing body. Pursuant to the Native American Housing Assistance and Self Determination Act of 1996, Indian Housing Authorities (IHAs) are no longer eligible for funding under the U.S. Housing Act (of 1937) or the Indian Housing Act.
Beneficiary Eligibility: Lower income families which include citizens or eligible immigrants. The term "Families" includes but is not limited to: (1) a family with or without children; (2) an elderly family (head, spouse, or sole member 62 years or older), (3) near elderly family (head, spouse, or sole member 50 years old but less than 62 years old); (4) a disabled family; (5) a displaced family; (6) the remaining member of a tenant family; or (7) a single person who is neither elderly, near-elderly, displaced, or a person with disabilities.
Award Range/Average: From $2,510 to $900,775,513; Average $1,423,394
Funding: (Formula Grants) FY 18 est $3,900,000,000.00; FY 16 $4,037,051,000.00; FY 17 est $4,400,000,000.00

HQ: 451 7th Street SW, Washington, DC 20410
Phone: 202-402-4192 | Email: kevin.j.gallagher@hud.gov
http://www.hud.gov/offices/pih/programs/ph/am

HHS93.007 | PUBLIC AWARENESS CAMPAIGNS ON EMBRYO ADOPTION
"Embryo Donation/Adoption"

Award: Project Grants
Purpose: To increase public awareness of embryo adoption as a method of family building and to provide services to infertile individuals.
Applicant Eligibility: Eligible applicants include public agencies, nonprofit Organizations, and for-profit Organizations. Eligibility to compete for this announcement is limited to particular applicant Organizations. Only agencies and Organizations, not individuals, are eligible to apply. One agency must be identified as the applicant Organization and will have legal responsibility for the project. Additional agencies and Organizations can be included as co-participants, subgrantees, subcontractors, or collaborators if they will assist in providing expertise and in helping to meet the needs of the recipients. Faith-based and community-based Organizations meeting the eligibility requirements may apply, or they may be included as co-participants, subgrantees, subcontractors, or collaborators if they will assist in providing expertise and in helping to meet the needs of recipients. Eligibility is limited to Organizations that can demonstration previous experience with embryo adoption and are knowledgeable in all elements of the process of embryo adoption.
Beneficiary Eligibility: The beneficiaries for this program are potential donors and/or recipients of frozen embryos.
Award Range/Average: Fiscal Year 2017 $150,000 - $299,000 Fiscal Year 2018 $150,000 - $299,000 Fiscal Year 2019 $100,000 - $300,000
Funding: (Project Grants) FY 16 $680,000.00; FY 17 est $688,000.00; FY 18 est Estimate Not Available
HQ: 1101 Wootton Parkway, Suite 550 Tower Building, Rockville, MD 20852
Phone: 240-453-8822 | Email: eric.west@hhs.gov
http://www.opa.gov

DOS19.501 | PUBLIC DIPLOMACY PROGRAMS FOR AFGHANISTAN AND
PAKISTAN

Award: Cooperative Agreements
Purpose: To promote diplomatic solutions, through language training, critical skills development and other public diplomacy programs.
Applicant Eligibility: Not-for-profit Organizations subject to 501(c)(3) of the U.S. tax code or registered as a non-profit Organization in the entity's home country. Organizations that have and have not previously received international Program funding from the U.S. government. Applicants with demonstrated experience in working with vendors, suppliers, contractors, etc. and appropriately staffed offices in country will be preferred.
Beneficiary Eligibility: Citizens of Afghanistan, Pakistan, and the United States.
Award Range/Average: grants are estimated to range between 300000 - 2000000.
Funding: (Project Grants) FY 12 $107,000,000.00; FY 14 est $88,900,000.00; FY 13 est $110,000,000.00
HQ: 2201 C Street NW, Washington, DC 20520
Phone: 202-647-8667 | Email: humphriesgj@state.gov

DOS19.040 | PUBLIC DIPLOMACY PROGRAMS

Award: Project Grants
Purpose: To support the achievement of U.S. foreign policy goals and objectives, advance national interests, and enhance national security by informing and influencing foreign publics.
Applicant Eligibility: See specific announcement in www.grants.gov.
Beneficiary Eligibility: Local organizations, See specific announcement in www.grants.gov.Citizens throughout the world as determined by post.
Award Range/Average: Range between $10,000 and $5,000,000. Average $50,000.
HQ: 2200 C Street NW R/PPR/R, 5th Floor, Washington, DC 20522
Phone: 202-632-3341 | Email: keithcf@state.gov

Programs Administered by Federal Headquarters

HHS93.339 | PUBLIC HEALTH CONFERENCE SUPPORT
"Centers for Disease Control and Prevention (CDC) National Center for HIV, Viral Hepatitis, Sexually Transmitted Disease and Tuberculosis Prevention (NCHHSTP) Public Health Conference Support"

Award: Cooperative Agreements
Purpose: Allows state and local governments, their Bona Fide Agents, non-governmental organizations and the general public to request funds for partial support for public health conferences related to the health promotion, education and prevention of HIV, Viral Hepatitis, STD and TB Prevention.
Applicant Eligibility: N/A
Beneficiary Eligibility: N/A
Award Range/Average: Awards will range from approximately $25,000 to $125,000 with an average of approximately $30,000.
Funding: (Formula Grants (Cooperative Agreements)) FY 18 $500,000.00; FY 19 est $500,000.00; FY 20 est Estimate Not Available; (Cooperative Agreements) FY 18 $221,463.00; FY 19 est $0.00; FY 20 est $0.00
HQ: 1600 Clifton Road NE, PO Box E07, Atlanta, GA 30333
Phone: 404-639-1877 | Email: lrw3@cdc.gov
http://www.cdc.gov

HHS93.069 | PUBLIC HEALTH EMERGENCY PREPAREDNESS
"PERLC: PREPAREDNESS AND EMERGENCY RESPONSE LEARNING CENTER Supporting PHEP; awards other than PHEP Cooperative agreement not recorded under 93.074"

Award: Cooperative Agreements
Purpose: To offer critical source of funding, guidance, and technical assistance for state, territorial, and local public health departments.
Applicant Eligibility: State health departments of all 50 States, the District of Columbia, the nation's three largest municipalities (New York City, Chicago and Los Angeles County), the Commonwealths of Puerto Rico and the Northern Mariana Islands, the territories of American Samoa, Guam and the U.S. Virgin Islands, the Federated States of Micronesia, and the Republics of Palau and the Marshall Islands.
Beneficiary Eligibility: All State, County, and Local Health Departments.
Award Range/Average: Average: $10,004,032 Range: Minimum $374,216 Maximum $41,896,344
Funding: (Cooperative Agreements) FY 18 $0.00; FY 19 est $620,250,000.00; FY 20 est $620,250,000.00
HQ: 1600 Clifton Road NE, PO Box D29, Atlanta, GA 30329-4018
Phone: 404-639-5276 | Email: vbk5@cdc.gov
http://www.cdc.gov

HHS93.354 | PUBLIC HEALTH EMERGENCY RESPONSE: COOPERATIVE AGREEMENT FOR EMERGENCY RESPONSE: PUBLIC HEALTH CRISIS RESPONSE
"Public Health Crisis Response Awards"

Award: Cooperative Agreements
Purpose: To fund state, local, and territorial public health departments for HHS Secretarial declared and non-declared public health emergencies having an overwhelming impact on jurisdictional resources.
Applicant Eligibility: State government public health departments or their bona fide agents (N=50); Local health departments or their bona fide agents (N=6) (city or county) consistent with PHEP and ELC awardees, which include: Chicago Department of Public Health, District of Columbia Department of Health, Houston Department of Health and Human Services, Los Angeles County Department of Health Services - Public Health, New York City Department of Health and Mental Hygiene, and Philadelphia Department of Public Health; Territorial Governments or their bona fide agents (N=8) in the Commonwealth of Puerto Rico, the US Virgin Islands, the Commonwealth of the Northern Marianna Islands, American Samoa, Guam, the Federated States of Micronesia, the Republic of the Marshall Islands, and the Republic of Palau; Tribal Public Health Departments - (N=5) Federally recognized tribal Governments meeting the core criteria outlined for all eligible applicants and that serve, through their own PH infrastructure, at least 50,000 people and have demonstrable PH capacity.

Beneficiary Eligibility: Same as Applicant Eligibility.
Funding: (Cooperative Agreements) FY 18 Not Separately Identifiable; FY 19 est Estimate Not Available; FY 20 est $0.00
HQ: 1600 Clifton Road NE, PO Box D29, Atlanta, GA 30329
 Phone: 404-639-0817 | Email: ssharpe@cdc.gov

HHS93.316 | PUBLIC HEALTH PREPAREDNESS AND RESPONSE SCIENCE, RESEARCH, AND PRACTICE
"Public Health Preparedness Science"

Award: Cooperative Agreements; Project Grants
Purpose: To conduct research and related public health preparedness and response (PHPR) program activities to build the scientific evidence base for public health preparedness, response, and recovery (PHPRR).
Applicant Eligibility: Eligible applicants may include public and private nonprofit and for profit Organizations and Governments and their agencies, such as: public nonprofit Organizations private nonprofit Organizations, for-profit Organizations, small, minority, women-owned businesses, universities, colleges, research Institutions, hospitals, community-based Organizations, faith-based Organizations, Federally Recognized Indian Tribal Governments, Indian Tribes, Indian tribal Organizations, state and local Governments or their bona fide agents (this includes the District of Columbia, the Commonwealth of Puerto Rico, the Virgin Islands, the Commonwealth of the Northern Marianna Islands, American Samoa, Guam, the Federated States of Micronesia, the Republic of the Marshall Islands, and the Republic of Palau), political subdivisions of states (in consultation with States).
Beneficiary Eligibility: Eligible beneficiaries may include public and private nonprofit and for profit organizations and governments and their agencies, such as: public nonprofit organizations private nonprofit organizations, for-profit organizations, small, minority, women-owned businesses, universities, colleges, research institutions, hospitals, community-based organizations, faith-based organizations, Federally Recognized Indian Tribal Governments, Indian tribes, Indian tribal organizations, state and local governments or their bona fide agents (this includes the District of Columbia, the Commonwealth of Puerto Rico, the Virgin Islands, the Commonwealth of the Northern Marianna Islands, American Samoa, Guam, the Federated States of Micronesia, the Republic of the Marshall Islands, and the Republic of Palau), political subdivisions of states (in consultation with states).
HQ: Resource Management 1600 Clifton Road NE, PO Box D29, Atlanta, GA 30329
 Phone: 404-639-5276 | Email: vbk5@cdc.gov
 http://www.cdc.gov/phpr/science/research.htm

HHS93.343 | PUBLIC HEALTH SERVICE EVALUATION FUNDS
"PHS Evaluation Funds"

Award: Cooperative Agreements
Purpose: To carry out evaluations of teen pregnancy prevention approaches.
Applicant Eligibility: Nonprofit, for profit, small businesses, community based Organizations, faith based Organizations, universities, hospitals, state and local Governments, US territories and possessions, tribal entities, native American Organizations are eligible to apply.
Beneficiary Eligibility: Researchers, Policymakers, Teens, Parents.
Award Range/Average: $357,345 awarded for a fully funded 2 year project period from FY16-FY18
Funding: (Cooperative Agreements) FY 17 $1,500,000.00; FY 18 Estimate Not Available; FY 19 Estimate Not Available
HQ: 1101 Wootton Parkway, Suite 550, Rockville, MD 20852
 Phone: 240-453-8822 | Email: alice.bettencourt@hhs.gov
 http://www.hhs.gov/oah

HHS93.516 | PUBLIC HEALTH TRAINING CENTERS PROGRAM
"Regional Public Health Training Center (PHTC) and the National Coordinating Center for Public Health Training (NCCPHT) Programs"

Award: Cooperative Agreements; Project Grants
Purpose: To improve the Nation's public health system by strengthening the technical, scientific, managerial and leadership competencies of the current and future public health workforce through the provision of education, training and consultation services.

Programs Administered by Federal Headquarters

Applicant Eligibility: Accredited school of public health, or another public or nonprofit private institution accredited for the provision of graduate or specialized training in public health. This Program also includes a statutory funding preference for accredited schools of public health. Federally Recognized Indian Tribal Government and Native American Organizations may apply if they are otherwise eligible.

Beneficiary Eligibility: Each trainee receiving stipend support must be a citizen of the United States, a non-citizen U.S. national, or a foreign national having in his or her possession a visa permitting permanent residence in the United States.

Award Range/Average: FY 18 Range: Regional PHTCs: - $705,000 to $1,005,000 Average: $895,380 FY 18 Range: NCCPHT: - $845,000. FY 19 Range: Regional PHTCs: - $780,000 to $1,105,000 Average: $895,380 FY 19 Range: NCCPHT: - $0 FY 20 Range: $0

Funding: (Cooperative Agreements) FY 18 $9,095,000.00; FY 19 est $ 9,100,000.00; FY 20 est Estimate Not Available

HQ: Department of Health and Human Services 5600 Fishers Lane 11N94D, Rockville, MD 20857

Phone: 301-443-1057 | Email: mjenkins@hrsa.gov
http://www.hrsa.gov

HUD14.872 | PUBLIC HOUSING CAPITAL FUND
"CFP"

Award: Formula Grants

Purpose: To provide funds annually to Public Housing Agencies (PHAs) for capital and management activities and permit PHAs to use Capital Funds for financing activities, in standard PHA developments and in mixed-finance developments.

Applicant Eligibility: The PHA must demonstrate that it has the legal authority to develop, own, modernize and operate a public housing development in accordance with the 1937 Act.

Beneficiary Eligibility: Low-income public housing residents.

Award Range/Average: $5,527 to $300,862,746; Average: $583,427

Funding: (Formula Grants) FY 17 $1,785,565,332.00; FY 18 est $2,750,000,000.00; FY 19 est $0.00

HQ: 451 7th Street SW, Washington, DC 20410

Phone: 202-402-2488 | Email: ivan.m.pour@hud.gov
http://www.hud.gov/offices/pih/programs/ph/capfund/index.cfm

HUD14.877 | PUBLIC HOUSING FAMILY SELF-SUFFICIENCY UNDER RESIDENT OPPORTUNITY AND SUPPORTIVE SERVICES
"PH FSS"

Award: Project Grants

Purpose: To promote the development of local strategies and enable participating families to achieve economic independence and housing self-sufficiency.

Applicant Eligibility: Public Housing Authorities (PHAs) and Tribes and tribally designated housing entities (TDHEs).

Beneficiary Eligibility: Individuals and families who are residents of conventional public or Indian housing are eligible to receive benefits from the ROSS program.

Award Range/Average: The average financial assistance was $60,036.

HQ: 451 7th Street SW, Room 4238, Washington, DC 20410

Phone: 202-402-2341 | Email: anice.m.schervish@hud.gov
http://www.hud.gov/offices/pih/programs/ph/ross

DOJ16.571 | PUBLIC SAFETY OFFICERS' BENEFITS PROGRAM
"PSOB"

Award: Direct Payments With Unrestricted Use

Purpose: To provide death benefits to the eligible survivors of federal, state, or local public safety officers whose deaths are the direct and proximate result of a traumatic injury sustained in the line of duty.

Applicant Eligibility: Public safety officer means -(A) an individual serving a public agency in an official capacity, with or without compensation, as a law enforcement officer, as a firefighter, or as a chaplain; (B) an employee of the Federal Emergency Management Agency who is performing official duties of the Agency in an area, if those official duties (i) are related to a major disaster or emergency that has been, or is later, declared to exist with respect to the area under the Robert

T. Stafford Disaster Relief and Emergency Assistance Act; and(ii) are determined by the Administrator of the Federal Emergency Management Agency to be hazardous duties; (C) an employee of a State, local, or tribal emergency management or civil defense agency who is performing official duties in cooperation with the Federal Emergency Management Agency in an area, if those official duties (i) are related to a major disaster or emergency that has been, or is later, declared to exist with respect to the area under the Robert T. Stafford Disaster Relief and Emergency Assistance Act; and(ii) are determined by the head of the agency to be hazardous duties; or(D) a member of a rescue squad or ambulance crew who, as authorized or licensed by law and by the applicable agency or entity, is engaging in rescue activity or in the provision of emergency medical services. Disabled public safety officers and eligible survivors of deceased public safety officers in the District of Columbia, Puerto Rico, Guam, Virgin Islands, American Samoa, the Pacific Trust Territories and the Northern Mariana Islands are also eligible for benefits under the Act. Death benefit coverage for (1) state and local law enforcement officers and firefighters applies to deaths occurring on or after September 29, 1976; (2) federal law enforcement officers and firefighters applies to deaths occurring on or after October 12, 1984; (3) federal, state, and local rescue squad and ambulance crew members applies to death occurring on or after October 15, 1986; (4) members of certain nonprofit rescue squads and ambulance crews applies to deaths occurring on or after June 1, 2009; and (5) Federal Emergency Management Agency (FEMA) personnel and state, local, and tribal emergency management and civil defense agency employees applies to deaths occurring on or after October 30, 2000. Disability benefit coverage for federal, state, and local law enforcement officers, firefighters and members of public rescue squads and ambulance crews applies to injuries sustained on or after November 29, 1990. FEMA personnel and state, local, and tribal emergency management and civil defense agency employees are covered for such injuries sustained on or after October 30, 2000. Disability benefit coverage for federal, state, and local law enforcement officers, firefighters and members of public rescue squads and ambulance crews applies to injuries sustained on or after November 29, 1990. FEMA personnel and state, local, and tribal emergency management and civil defense agency employees are covered for such injuries sustained on or after October 30, 2000 and Chaplains as of September 11, 2001. As of January 2, 2013, disability benefit coverage for members of public agency and certain nonprofit rescue squads and ambulance crews applies to injuries sustained on or after June 1, 2009; for injuries sustained between June 29, 1990, and June 1, 2009, disability benefit coverage extends only to members of public agency rescue squads and ambulance crews.

Beneficiary Eligibility: The Public Safety Officers' Benefits (PSOB) Act, enacted in 1976, was designed to offer peace of mind to men and women seeking careers in public safety and to make a strong statement about the value American society places on the contributions of those who serve their communities in potentially dangerous circumstances. The PSOB Program provides a one-time financial benefit to the eligible survivors of public safety officers whose deaths are the direct and proximate result of a traumatic injury sustained in the line of duty. The benefit is determined by the date of the fatal or totally and permanently disabling injury and is adjusted annually for inflation. A table with the annually adjusted amounts is contained here: https://www.psob.gov/benefits_by_year.html.

Award Range/Average: Not Available.

Funding: (Direct Payments with Unrestricted Use) FY 18 $112,081,003.00; FY 19 est $104,000,000.00; FY 20 est $115,000,000.00

HQ: 810 7th Street NW, Washington, DC 20531
    Phone: 888-744-6513
    http://www.psob.gov

DOJ16.615 | PUBLIC SAFETY OFFICERS' EDUCATIONAL ASSISTANCE "PSOEA"

Award: Direct Payments With Unrestricted Use

Purpose: To provide financial assistance for higher education to the spouses and children of public safety officers killed in line of duty.

Applicant Eligibility: Spouses and children who attend a Program of education at an eligible institution and are the spouse and/ or surviving children under the age of 27 of federal, state, and local public safety officers whose deaths or permanent and totally disabling injuries are covered by the Public Safety Officers' Benefits (PSOB) Program (34 U.S.C. 10281-10288) are eligible for this Program. The maximum age of eligibility for surviving children will be extended by the amount of time a claim for death, disability, or education benefits has been pending before the Bureau of Justice Assistance in excess of one year. A public safety officer is (A) an individual serving a public agency in an official capacity, with or without compensation, as a law enforcement officer, as a firefighter, or as a chaplain; (B) an employee of the Federal Emergency Management Agency who is performing official duties of the Agency in an area, if those official duties (i) are related to a major disaster or emergency that has been, or is later, declared to exist with respect to the area under the Robert T. Stafford Disaster Relief and Emergency Assistance Act; and(ii) are determined by the Administrator of the Federal Emergency Management Agency to be hazardous duties; (C) an employee of a State, local, or tribal emergency management or civil defense agency who is

Programs Administered by Federal Headquarters

performing official duties in cooperation with the Federal Emergency Management Agency in an area, if those official duties (i) are related to a major disaster or emergency that has been, or is later, declared to exist with respect to the area under the Robert T. Stafford Disaster Relief and Emergency Assistance Act; and(ii) are determined by the head of the agency to be hazardous duties; or(D) a member of a rescue squad or ambulance crew who, as authorized or licensed by law and by the applicable agency or entity, is engaging in rescue activity or in the provision of emergency medical services.

Beneficiary Eligibility: The spouse and surviving children of federal, state, and local public safety officers receive the ultimate benefits from this program. The children may receive benefits for classes taken before their 27th birthday. (The maximum age of eligibility for surviving children will be extended by the amount of time a claim for death, disability, or education benefits has been pending before the Bureau of Justice Assistance in excess of one year.) There is no age restriction for spouses.

Award Range/Average: For classes taken since October 1,2016, the rates of assistance are $1024 per month for full-time students, $767 for three-quarter-time students, $510 for half-time students, and $256 for less-than-half-time students. The amount of assistance is subject to change consistent with the current computation of educational assistance allowance set forth in Title IV of the Higher Education Act, Section 3532 of Title 38, U.S.C.

Funding: (Direct Payments with Unrestricted Use) FY 18 $4,745,613.00; FY 19 est $24,800,000.00; FY 20 $24,800,000.00

HQ: 810 7th Street NW, Washington, DC 20531

  Phone: 202-616-6500

  https://www.bja.gov/ProgramDetails.aspx?Program_ID=78

DOJ16.710 | PUBLIC SAFETY PARTNERSHIP AND COMMUNITY POLICING GRANTS
"COPS Office"

Award: Project Grants

Purpose: To advance public safety through the implementation of community policing strategies that entail developing partnerships between law enforcement agencies and the communities they serve so they can work collaboratively to resolve problems and build community trust.

Applicant Eligibility: States, units of local government, Federally Recognized Indian tribal Governments, U.S. territories or possessions (including the Commonwealth of Puerto Rico, the Virgin Islands, Guam, American Samoa, and the Mariana Islands), other public and private entities, and multi-jurisdictional or regional consortia thereof.

Beneficiary Eligibility: Same as Applicant Eligibility.

Award Range/Average: Range: $10,390.00 - $3,513,921.00 Average award: $167,547.00

Funding: (Project Grants) FY 16 $167,422,943.00; FY 17 est Estimate Not Available; FY 18 est Estimate Not Available

HQ: 145 N Street NE, Washington, DC 20530

  Phone: 202-514-8553 | Email: david.neely2@usdoj.gov

  http://www.cops.usdoj.gov

VA64.029 | PURCHASE CARE PROGRAM
"Purchase Care Program - VA Health Administration Center"

Award: Direct Payments for Specified Use

Purpose: The Chief Business Office represents a single accountable authority for development of the administrative processes, policy, regulations, and the directives associated with the delivery of VA health benefit programs.

Applicant Eligibility: What follows is not a comprehensive listing of eligibility requirements. For detailed eligibility requirements the USC and CFR's of each Program should be consulted. For Veterans generally eligibility is established by evidence of service by DD Form 214 or through the Veterans Benefits Administration. Benefits provided are based on eligibility as established at 8 levels approved by the VHA Deputy Under Secretary for Health. For Non Veteran Beneficiaries eligibility is established by adjudication of the Sponsoring Veteran as Permanently and Totally disabled (P&T) (38 CFR 17. 52(a)(1)(iii)) and that the Non Veteran Beneficiary is a dependent of the Veteran by the VBA and is eligible for Chapter 35 Benefits.

Beneficiary Eligibility: As stated above under Applicant Eligibility.

Award Range/Average: The amount of medical benefits paid for Veterans varies according to the need of the individual. Some eligible's make no claim in a benefit year. Others have claims paid as required. The NonVA Purchase Care Program paid an average of $4051.00 for each of 920,404 unique patients in FY09.

Funding: (Direct Payments for Specified Use) FY 15 $6,647,184,786.00; FY 16 est $6,304,350,411.00; FY 17 est Estimate Not Available

HQ: 810 Vermont Avenue NW, Washington, DC 20420
  Phone: 303-370-5061 | Email: michelle.staton@va.gov
  http://vaww1.va.gov/cbo/index.asp

HUD14.189 | QUALIFIED PARTICIPATING ENTITIES (QPE) RISK SHARING
"542(b) Risk Sharing Program"

Award: Guaranteed/insured Loans
Purpose: To provide reinsurance on multifamily housing projects whose loans are originated, underwritten, serviced, and disposed of.
Applicant Eligibility: Eligible mortgagors include investors, builders, developers, public entities, and private nonprofit corporations or associations may apply to a qualified QPE and/or its lender.
Beneficiary Eligibility: Individuals, families, and property owners may be eligible for affordable housing.
Funding: (Guaranteed/Insured Loans) FY 15 $14,352,529.00; FY 16 est $40,873,150.00; FY 17 est $66,633,349.00
HQ: 451 7th Street SW, Washington, DC 20410
  Phone: 202-402-2579 | Email: carmelita_a._james@hud.gov
  http://www.hud.gov/offices/hsg/hsgmulti.cfm

USDA10.605 | QUALITY SAMPLES PROGRAM
"QSP"

Award: Direct Payments for Specified Use
Purpose: The Quality Samples Program maximizes exporting of U.S. agricultural commodities by assisting U.S. entities to promote a high quality of U.S. agricultural commodities.
Applicant Eligibility: To be approved, an applicant must be a U.S. private or government entity.
Beneficiary Eligibility: The Quality Samples Program is intended to benefit a represented U.S. industry rather than a specific company or brand.
Award Range/Average: range $15,000 to $75,000
Funding: (Project Grants) FY 18 $2,500,000.00; FY 19 est $2,500,000.00; FY 20 est $2,500,000.00
HQ: 1400 Independence Avenue SW, Washington, DC 20050
  Phone: 202-720-7927 | Email: vincent.cornetto@fas.usda.gov
  http://www.fas.usda.gov/programs/quality-samples-program-qsp

HHS93.743 | RACIAL AND ETHNIC APPROACHES TO COMMUNITY HEALTH: OBESITY AND HYPERTENSION DEMONSTRATION PROJECTS FINANCED SOLELY BY PREVENTION AND PUBLIC HEALTH FUNDS
"Racial and Ethnic Approaches to Community Health (REACH)"

Award: Cooperative Agreements
Purpose: Supports the implementation of projects to reduce racial and ethnic health disparities.
Applicant Eligibility: Applications may be submitted by State or local Governments or their Bona Fide Agents (this includes the District of Columbia, the Commonwealth of Puerto Rico, the Virgin Islands, the Commonwealth of the Northern Marianna Islands, American Samoa, Guam, the Federated States of Micronesia, the Republic of the Marshall Islands, and the Republic of Palau). Eligible applicants also include public and private nonprofit Organizations, for profit Organizations, small, minority, women-owned businesses, universities, colleges, research Institutions, hospitals, community-based Organizations, faith-based Organizations, Federally recognized Indian tribal Governments, Indian Tribes, and Indian tribal Organizations. Additional guidance may be provided in individual Program announcements.
Beneficiary Eligibility: The general public will benefit from the objectives of this program. Additionally, colleges, universities, private non-profit and public nonprofit domestic organizations, research institutions, and faith-based organization, states, political subdivisions of states, local health authorities, and individuals or organizations with specialized health interests will benefit.
Award Range/Average: Range and Average of Financial Assistance: Expected:1,500,000 - 4,000,000
HQ: 4770 Buford Highway NE, PO Box K40 NCCDPHP, Atlanta, GA 30333
  Phone: 770-488-2524 | Email: rrb7@cdc.gov

Programs Administered by Federal Headquarters

HHS93.304 | RACIAL AND ETHNIC APPROACHES TO COMMUNITY HEALTH
"REACH National Networks"

Award: Cooperative Agreements

Purpose: To fund National Networks to fund, manage, support, and monitor sub-recipients to address health disparities and implement evidence- and practice-based strategies that reduce health disparities for intervention population(s) experiencing high burden of disease or risk factors.

Applicant Eligibility: In continuation years, eligibility is limited to the six (6) existing original awardees: Asian and Pacific Islander American Health Forum; Hidalgo Medical Services; National Council of Young Men's Christian Association of the USA; National REACH Coalition; Regents of the University of California, Los Angeles; University of Colorado Denver.

Beneficiary Eligibility: The general public will benefit from the objectives of this program.

Funding: (Cooperative Agreements) FY 18 est $23,197,325.00; FY 19 est $23,197,156.00; FY 20 $23,197,156.00

HQ: 4770 Buford Highway NE, PO Box F81, Atlanta, GA 30341

    Phone: 770-488-8438

    http://www.cdc.gov

DHS97.075 | RAIL AND TRANSIT SECURITY GRANT PROGRAM
"TSGP/IPR (AMTRAK)"

Award: Project Grants

Purpose: The TSGP and IPR lay a few sets of measures for the Homeland Security to strengthen the nation's preparedness and resilience against terrorist and cyber attacks.

Applicant Eligibility: Agencies eligible for the FY 2019 TSGP are determined based upon daily unlinked passenger trips (ridership) and transit systems that serve historically eligible Urban Area Security Initiative (UASI) jurisdictions as indicated below. Certain ferry systems are eligible to participate in the FY 2019 TSGP and receive funds under this Program. However, any ferry system electing to participate in and receive funds under the FY 2019 TSGP will not be eligible to participate under the FY 2019 Port Security Grant Program (PSGP) and will not be considered for funding under the FY 2019 PSGP. Likewise, any ferry system that participates in the FY 2019 PSGP will not be eligible for funding under the TSGP. Sections 1405 (6 U.S.C. 1134) and 1406 (6 U.S.C. 1135) of the Implementing Recommendations of the 9/11 Commission Act of 2007 require that high risk public transportation agencies that receive grant funding develop a security plan based on a security assessment. Additionally, the statutes direct that grant funds be used to address items in the security assessment or the security plan. To be eligible for the FY 2019 TSGP, transit agencies must have developed or updated their security plan. The security plan must be based on a security assessment, such as the Baseline Assessment for Security Enhancement (BASE), which is performed by the Transportation Security Inspectors-Surface Division of the Transportation Security Administration (TSA). This security assessment must have been conducted within the three years prior to receiving an FY 2019 TSGP award. A copy of the security plan and security assessment must be provided to DHS/FEMA upon request. Please see the Preparedness Grants Manual for more information on security plan requirements. Entities providing transit security (e.g., city/county police departments or the public transportation agencies own police departments) for a public transportation agency must approve the security plan. The signature of a responsible official from the agency's transit security provider serves as this approval. If there is more than one provider in the core service area, all transit security providers must review and concur with the plan. Associated documentation of this approval must be provided to DHS/FEMA upon request. In addition, agencies transit security providers are encouraged to review the Investment Justifications (IJs) prior to submission. Each public transportation agency receiving funds through this Program must also participate in a Regional Transit Security Working Group (RTSWG) or develop a RTSWG if one does not already exist. The RTSWG should serve as the forum for regional partners to discuss risk, planning efforts, and mitigation strategies. These discussions should be held regardless of funding to continue enhancing the overall security of the region. Regional working groups are a best practice for enhancing security and are encouraged for all jurisdictions. The National Passenger Railroad Corporation (Amtrak) is the only entity eligible to apply for funding under FY 2019 IPR Program. For more information, refer to the FY 2019 TSGP and IPR Program Notice of Funding Opportunity (NOFO) National Incident Management System (NIMS) Implementation. In accordance with Homeland Security Presidential Directive (HSPD)-5, Management of Domestic Incidents, the adoption of NIMS is a requirement to receive Federal preparedness assistance, through grants, contracts, and other activities. Prior to allocation of any Federal preparedness awards in FY 2019, grantee must ensure compliance and/or alignment with the NIMS implementation plan. The list of objectives against which progress and achievement are assessed and reported can be found at http://www.fema.gov/emergency/nims/ImplementationGuidanceStakeholders. shtm#item2. The primary grantee/administrator of FY 2019 TSGP and IPR Program award funds is responsible for determining if sub-awardees have demonstrated sufficient progress in NIMS implementation to disburse awards.

Beneficiary Eligibility: Specialized group; general public.
Award Range/Average: For more information, refer to the FY 2019 TSGP and IPR Program Notice of Funding Opportunity (NOFO).
Funding: (Project Grants) FY 18 $98,000,000.00; FY 19 est $98,000,000.00; FY 20 est $98,000,000.00
HQ: 400 C Street SW, Washington, DC 20523
    Phone: 800-368-6498
    http://www.fema.gov/government/grant/index.shtm

HHS93.315 | RARE DISORDERS: RESEARCH, SURVEILLANCE, HEALTH PROMOTION, AND EDUCATION
"Rare Disorders and Health Outcomes"

Award: Cooperative Agreements
Purpose: To promote public health capacity by conducting research to expand the knowledge base around people with complex disabling conditions, including muscular dystrophy, fragile X syndrome and spina bifida across the lifespan.
Applicant Eligibility: N/A
Beneficiary Eligibility: State; Local; Public nonprofit institution/organization; Federally Recognized Indian Tribal Governments; Individuals/Families affected by rare disorder/conditions; Private nonprofit institution/organizations, minority populations including Spanish speaking populations.
Award Range/Average: FY19/20 range is dependent upon funding availability. Award Amounts range from $20,530 to $500,000.
Funding: (Cooperative Agreements) FY 18 $5,818,927.00; FY 19 est $5,742,899.00; FY 20 est $5,742,899.00
HQ: 1600 Clifton Road NE, PO Box E88, Atlanta, GA 30329-4027
    Phone: 404-498-3042

HHS93.576 | REFUGEE AND ENTRANT ASSISTANCE DISCRETIONARY GRANTS

Award: Project Grants
Purpose: Grant programs seeks to decrease the numbers of refugees on public assistance and the length of time refugees require such assistance.
Applicant Eligibility: Public and private nonprofit agencies may apply for these grants.
Beneficiary Eligibility: Refugees, certain Amerasians, Cuban and Haitian entrants, asylees, certified victims of a severe form of trafficking, and Special Immigrants from Iraq and Afghanistan.
Award Range/Average: Refugee Health Promotion grants range from a minimum of $75,000 to a maximum of $195,000. The remaining 6 Discretionary grant programs range from a minimum of $90,000 to a maximum of $3,144,736.
Funding: (Project Grants) FY 18 $4,600,000.00; FY 19 est $4,600,000.00; FY 20 est $402,000.00; (Project Grants (Discretionary)) FY 18 $37,569,915.00; FY 19 est $37,679,308.00; FY 20 est $31,437,000.00
HQ: Mary E Switzer Building 330 C Street SW, PO Box 5123, Washington, DC 20201
    Phone: 202-401-4559 | Email: anastasia.brown@acf.hhs.gov
    http://www.acf.hhs.gov/programs/orr/programs

HHS93.566 | REFUGEE AND ENTRANT ASSISTANCE STATE/REPLACEMENT DESIGNEE ADMINISTERED PROGRAMS
"Refugee Cash and Medical Assistance Program and Refugee Social Services Program"

Award: Formula Grants
Purpose: Reimburses States and State Replacement Designees for the cost of cash and medical assistance provided to refugees, certain Amerasians from Vietnam, Cuban and Haitian entrants, asylees, victims of a severe form of trafficking, and Iraqi and Afghan Special Immigrants during the first eight months after their arrival in this country or grant of asylum.
Applicant Eligibility: State agencies, State Replacement Designees, and Wilson/Fish Alternative projects are eligible to apply for these funds.
Beneficiary Eligibility: Refugees, certain Amerasians from Vietnam, Cuban and Haitian entrants, asylees, victims of a severe form of trafficking, and Iraqi and Afghan Special Immigrants are eligible for benefits and services.

Programs Administered by Federal Headquarters

Award Range/Average: In FY 2018, the Refugee Cash and Medical Assistance program grants ranged from $11,070 to $38,763,643: the Refugee Support Services program grants ranged from $75,000 to $35,298,954.
Funding: (Formula Grants) FY 18 $388,157,330.00; FY 19 est $ 422,474,692.00; FY 20 est $371,875,590.00
HQ: 330 C Street SW, 8th Floor W Mary E Switzer Building, Washington, DC 20201
  Phone: 202-205-5933 | Email: carl.rubenstein@acf.hhs.gov
  http://www.acf.hhs.gov/programs/orr

HHS93.567 | REFUGEE AND ENTRANT ASSISTANCE VOLUNTARY AGENCY PROGRAMS
"Matching Grant Program"

Award: Formula Grants
Purpose: Assists refugees in becoming self-supporting and independent members of American society by providing grant funds to private nonprofit organizations to support case management, transitional assistance, and social services for new arrivals.
Applicant Eligibility: Grant awards are limited to private nonprofit Organizations that have a Reception and Placement Cooperative Agreement with the Department of State or Department of Homeland Security.
Beneficiary Eligibility: Enrollment must occur within 31 days of the individual's date of eligibility. The date of eligibility for Matching Grant Services is counted from the date of arrival into the country for refugees and Amerasians; the date a Cuban/Haitian becomes an entrant; the date of the final grant of asylum for asylees; the date of the certification or eligibility letter for Victims of Severe Forms of Trafficking; and the date an SIV arrives in the U.S. or the date of adjustment of status if applying for Special Immigrant Status within the U.S. At least one member of the case unit must be deemed 'employable' for the case to be enrolled in the Matching Grant Program, and all other members must be otherwise Program eligible.
Award Range/Average: In FY 2018, the grants ranged from $1,740,000 to $10,072,200 with an average award of $5,222,222.
Funding: (Formula Grants) FY 18 $47,000,000.00; FY 19 est $47,500,000.00; FY 20 est $47,000,000.00
HQ: 330 C Street SW, Mary E Switzer Building, Washington, DC 20201
  Phone: 202-401-4559 | Email: anastasia.brown@acf.hhs.gov
  http://www.acf.hhs.gov/programs/orr/programs

HHS93.583 | REFUGEE AND ENTRANT ASSISTANCE WILSON/FISH PROGRAM
"Wilson-Fish Program"

Award: Cooperative Agreements
Purpose: To develop alternative projects which promote early employment of refugees, certain Amerasians from Vietnam, Cuban and Haitian entrants, asylees, victims of a severe form of trafficking, and Iraqi and Afghan Special Immigrants.
Applicant Eligibility: Beginning in FY2015/2016, funding under this Program is open only to those agencies that currently administer a Wilson-Fish project. ORR requires that appropriate proposals and applications are submitted and that a determination is made that the grantees are the ones that can best perform the services in accordance with 8 U.S.C. 1522(a)(4)(A). Wilson-Fish grantees include States, voluntary resettlement agencies (local and national), and a private non-profit agency. There are 12 state-wide Wilson-Fish projects in the following States: Alabama, Alaska, Colorado, Idaho, Kentucky, Louisiana, Massachusetts, Nevada, North Dakota, South Dakota, Tennessee and Vermont, plus one county-wide project in San Diego County, California. No separate funding is appropriated for Wilson-Fish projects. Funds are drawn instead from funds earmarked for refugee cash and medical assistance grants and refugee support services allocations for the State-administered Program (93. 566) according to ORR projections.
Beneficiary Eligibility: Refugees, certain Amerasian immigrants from Vietnam, Cuban/Haitian entrants, asylees, victims of a severe form of trafficking, and Iraqi and Afghan Special Immigrants are eligible for services and assistance through funded projects in a community. Cash assistance is transitional for up to 8 months; services may be provided for up to five years.
Award Range/Average: In FY 2017 awards ranged from $295,996 to $7,364,452
Funding: (Cooperative Agreements) FY 18 $14,907,877.00; FY 19 est $4,414,000.00; FY 20 est $8,891,442.00
HQ: 330 C Street SW, Mary E Switzer Building, Washington, DC 20201
  Phone: 202-205-5266 | Email: colleen.mahar-piersma@acf.hhs.gov
  http://www.acf.hhs.gov/programs/orr

FEMA97.111 | REGIONAL CATASTROPHIC PREPAREDNESS GRANT PROGRAM (RCPGP)
"RCPGP"

Award: Salaries and Expenses; Project Grants
Purpose: Aims at closing the known capability gaps and encourage innovative regional solutions to issues in connection with catastrophic incidents.
Applicant Eligibility: Refer to Program notice of funding opportunity.
Beneficiary Eligibility: Same as Applicant Eligibility.
Award Range/Average: Refer to program guidance.
Funding: (Salaries and Expenses) FY 18 $0; FY 19 est $10,000,000.00; FY 20 est $0
HQ: 400 C Street SW, Washington, DC 20472
> Phone: 202-212-3330
> http://www.fema.gov

DOS19.221 | REGIONAL DEMOCRACY PROGRAM
"Iran Assistance"

Award: Cooperative Agreements; Project Grants
Purpose: Supports democracy and human rights in the Near East region.
Applicant Eligibility: Non-profit, for-profit Organizations or state and local Governments interested in partnering with the NEA/AC to promote democratic change in the Near East.
Beneficiary Eligibility: Any award made using State/NEA funds requires the full complement of standard federal forms and budget documents, CVs of main program staff, as dictated by the U.S. Department of State, Bureau of Administration, and the relevant OMB circulars. See www.grants.gov for specific announcement. OMB Circular No. A-87 applies to this program.
Award Range/Average: The range is $500,000 to $2,500,000 with an average of $1,500,000.
Funding: (Project Grants) FY 17 est Estimate Not Available; FY 18 est Estimate Not Available
HQ: 2430 E Street NW, Washington, DC 20037
> Phone: 202-776-8691 | Email: curleysl@state.gov

DOC11.441 | REGIONAL FISHERY MANAGEMENT COUNCILS

Award: Project Grants
Purpose: The Regional Fishery Management Council monitors fishery management and collects data for domestic and foreign fishing within the 200-mile U.S. Exclusive Economic Zone.
Applicant Eligibility: Eight Regional Fishery Management Councils (New England, Mid-Atlantic, South Atlantic, Gulf of Mexico, Caribbean, Pacific, North Pacific and Western Pacific) as established by the MSFCMA. These councils can best be described as "quasi-government" because they are sponsored by the Federal government, specifically funded by Congress but the members are appointed by the Secretary of Commerce from the private sector; they are not Federal employees.
Beneficiary Eligibility: This program benefits commercial and recreational fishing enterprises in the EEZ. Foreign fishing enterprises may also benefit from this program if authorized to conduct fishing operations. U.S. consumers will benefit as a result of availability of seafood. Imports may be reduced and exports may be increased.
Award Range/Average: $890,400 to $2,451,000
Funding: (Project Grants) FY 16 $31,871,198.00; FY 17 est $31,871,198.00; FY 18 Estimate Not Available
HQ: 1305 E W Highway, Silver Spring, MD 20910
> Phone: 301-427-8771 | Email: jeffrey.kulnis@noaa.gov
> http://www.nmfs.noaa.gov/sfa/domes_fish/index.htm

USDA10.177 | REGIONAL FOOD SYSTEM PARTNERSHIPS
"RFSP, Partnerships"

Award: Project Grants
Purpose: To support the partnerships between public and private resources in the planning and development of local or regional food systems and also to encourage food economy viability and flexibility. It accelerates the local or regional food system growth through increased access to local knowledge and networks.

Programs Administered by Federal Headquarters

Applicant Eligibility: Applications can be submitted by an eligible entity or eligible partner. An application must have at least one eligible entity and eligible partner to be considered for funding. Eligible entities include producers; producer networks or associations; farmer or rancher cooperatives; majority-controlled producer-based business ventures; food councils; local or Tribal Governments; nonprofit corporations; economic development corporations; public benefit corporations; community-supported agriculture networks or associations; and regional farmers market authorities. Eligible partners include State agencies or regional authorities; philanthropic Organizations; private corporations; institution of higher education s; and commercial, Federal, or Farm Credit System lending Institutions. projects and applicants must be owned, operated, and located within the 50 States, the District of Columbia, and the U.S. territories (American Samoa, Commonwealth of the Northern Mariana Islands, Guam, Puerto Rico, and U.S. Virgin Islands.

Beneficiary Eligibility: Projects that benefit producers, local and regional food business enterprises, and consumers.

Award Range/Average: See Request for Applications for more information.

Funding: (Project Grants) FY 18 Not Separately Identifiable; FY 19 est $5,000,000.00; FY 20 est $5,000,000.00

HQ: 1400 Independence Avenue SW, Washington, DC 20250

    Phone: 202-690-1300

    https://www.ams.usda.gov/services/grants

DOJ16.610 | REGIONAL INFORMATION SHARING SYSTEMS
"RISS"

Award: Project Grants

Purpose: To assist agencies in reducing violent crime and support law enforcement through officer safety, enhance the ability to identify, target, and remove criminal conspiracies and activities spanning multi-jurisdictional, multi-state, and sometime international boundaries.

Applicant Eligibility: Six RISS Centers are authorized as eligible to receive funding to provide services to law enforcement agencies throughout the nation. The Centers are: The Middle Atlantic Great-Lakes Organized Crime Law Enforcement Center (MAGLOCLEN), the Mid-States Organized Crime Information Center (MOCIC), the New England State Police Information Network (NESPIN), the Regional Organized Crime Information Center (ROCIC), the Rocky Mountain Information Network (RMIN), and the Western States Information Network (WSIN). Additionally, a competitively selected entity will serve as the administrator of network and support system capabilities serving the aforementioned six RISS Centers. Applications are limited to these six RISS Centers and the competitive process to select an awardee for the purpose of administration and on behalf of the RISS Technology Service Center (RTSC).

Beneficiary Eligibility: State and local criminal justice agencies; Federal, State, local, tribal, and territorial law enforcement agencies and personnel benefit from this program.

Award Range/Average: See the current fiscal year's solicitation guidelines posted on the Office of Justice Programs web site at https://ojp.gov/funding/Explore/CurrentFundingOpportunities.htm.

Funding: (Project Grants) FY 18 $32,814,530.00; FY 19 est $37,000,000.00; FY 20 est $10,000,000.00

HQ: Bureau of Justice Assistance 810 7th Street NW, Washington, DC 20531

    Phone: 202-616-6500 | Email: david.p.lewis@usdoj.gov

    http://www.riss.net

SBA59.067 | REGIONAL INNOVATION CLUSTERS
"RICs"

Award: Direct Payments for Specified Use

Purpose: To connect and enhance regional cluster initiatives so that small businesses can effectively leverage them to commercialize new technologies and expand into new markets, thereby positioning themselves and their regional economies for growth.

Applicant Eligibility: Educational Institutions, public or private Organizations and businesses, individuals, State and local Governments, Indian Tribes and lending and financial Institutions and sureties that have the capability to provide the required business assistance.

Beneficiary Eligibility: Small business concerns as defined by industry size standards established by the U.S. Small Business Administration.

Award Range/Average: $5,000,000 to $6,000,000 cumulative.

Funding: (Direct Payments for Specified Use) FY 17 $3,259,000.00; FY 18 est $5,000,000.00; FY 19 est $0.00

ED84.129 | REHABILITATION LONG-TERM TRAINING

Award: Project Grants

Purpose: To support academic training project in areas of personnel shortages identified by the Secretary and to increase the number of personnel trained in vocational rehabilitation services to individuals with disabilities.

Applicant Eligibility: States and public or private nonprofit agencies and Organizations, including Indian Tribes and Institutions of higher education.

Beneficiary Eligibility: Individuals preparing for employment in the field of rehabilitation counselling of individuals with disabilities.

Award Range/Average: To Be Determined.

Funding: (Project Grants) FY 18 $18,973,666.00; FY 19 est $15,659,000.00; FY 20 est $15,620,000

HQ: OSERS Rehabilitation Services Administration 400 Maryland Avenue SW, Washington, DC 20202

Phone: 202-245-7343 | Email: mary.lovley@ed.gov

http://www.ed.gov/about/offices/list/osers/rsa/index.html

HUD14.108 | REHABILITATION MORTGAGE INSURANCE "203(k)"

Award: Guaranteed/insured Loans

Purpose: To rehabilitate and repair single family properties. The program will allow a purchase or refinance transaction along with the loan amount the cost of making repairs and/or nonluxury improvements.

Applicant Eligibility: Individual and families.

Beneficiary Eligibility: Individuals and families.

HQ: Federal Housing Administration 451 7th Street SW, Washington, DC 20410

Phone: 800-225-5342

ED84.250 | REHABILITATION SERVICES AMERICAN INDIANS WITH DISABILITIES

Award: Project Grants

Purpose: To provide vocational rehabilitation services to American Indians with disabilities that reside on or near Federal or State reservations.

Applicant Eligibility: Service projects: Governing bodies of Indian Tribes, consortia of such governing bodies, or tribal Organizations established and controlled by the governing bodies of Indian Tribes, located on or near Federal and State reservations may apply. Training and technical assistance: State, local, or tribal Governments, non-profit Organizations, or Institutions of higher education that have experience in the operation of AIVRS Programs.

Beneficiary Eligibility: American Indians with disabilities residing on or near a Federal or State reservation who meet the definition of an individual with a disability in Section 7 (8) (A) of the Rehabilitation Act.

Award Range/Average: Range of new awards in FY 2016 was $365,000 to $1,550,000; Median new award: $550,000. No new awards were made in fiscal years 2017 and 2018. New awards are planned for fiscal year 2019.

Funding: (Project Grants) FY 18 $40,188,809.00; FY 19 est $43,300,000.00; FY 20 est $43,300,000.00

HQ: OSERS Rehabilitation Services Administration 400 Maryland Avenue SW, Washington, DC 20202

Phone: 202-245-6529 | Email: corinne.weidenthal@ed.gov

https://www2.ed.gov/programs/vramerind/index.html

ED84.161 | REHABILITATION SERVICES CLIENT ASSISTANCE PROGRAM "CAP"

Award: Formula Grants

Purpose: To establish client assistance programs that provide information for clients and client-applicants of available benefits under the Rehabilitation Act; to assist clients and client-applicants in their relationships with projects and programs providing services under this Act; to inform individuals with disabilities in the State, of the services and benefits available under the Act and under Title I of the Americans with Disabilities Act.

Applicant Eligibility: States and Territories (through the Governor) and the protection and advocacy system serving the American Indian Consortium, are eligible for awards. With the exception of the protection and advocacy system serving the American Indian Consortium, the Governor designates a public or private agency to conduct the State's Program.

Programs Administered by Federal Headquarters

Beneficiary Eligibility: Clients and client-applicants receiving services or interested in seeking assistance under the Rehabilitation Act of 1973, as amended, will benefit from CAP services.

Award Range/Average: For FY 2019, the estimated range of State awards (including the District of Columbia and Puerto Rico) under the distribution formula is $131,917 to $1,322,898, with a median award of $149,038. The FY 2019 amount for each of the four outlying areas and the American Indian Consortium is $59,477.

Funding: (Formula Grants) FY 17 $13,000,000.00; FY 18 est $13,000,000.00; FY 19 est $13,000,000.00

HQ: OSERS Rehabilitation Services Administration 400 Maryland Avenue SW, Washington, DC 20202
Phone: 202-245-6074 | Email: april.trice@ed.gov

ED84.235 | REHABILITATION SERVICES DEMONSTRATION AND TRAINING PROGRAMS

Award: Project Grants

Purpose: To provide financial assistance to projects that expands and improve the provision of rehabilitation and research and evaluation activities authorized under the Act.

Applicant Eligibility: Eligible applicants are States and public or nonprofit Organizations. Grants cannot be made directly to individuals.

Beneficiary Eligibility: Individuals with disabilities.

Award Range/Average: To Be Determined.

Funding: (Project Grants) FY 18 $5,796,000.00; FY 19 est $5,796,000.00; FY 20 est $5,796,000.00

HQ: OSERS Rehabilitation Services Administration 400 Maryland Avenue SW, Washington, DC 20202
Phone: 202-245-7423 | Email: mary.lovley@ed.gov
http://www.ed.gov/offices/OSERS/RSA/Programs/Discretionary/demotrain.html

ED84.177 | REHABILITATION SERVICES INDEPENDENT LIVING SERVICES FOR OLDER INDIVIDUALS WHO ARE BLIND

Award: Project Grants

Purpose: To provide any independent living services that are described in 34 CFR Section 367.3(b) to older individuals who are blind that improve or expand services for these individuals.

Applicant Eligibility: Any State agency in the 50 States and the District of Columbia and territories (Commonwealth of Puerto Rico and Virgin Islands) and outlying areas (Guam, American Samoa, and the Commonwealth of the Northern Mariana Islands) designated by the State as the State agency and authorized to provide rehabilitation services to blind individuals may apply. In order to receive assistance under this Program, a designated state agency (DSA) must- submit in a timely manner and obtain approval from the Department of an application containing the agreements, assurances, and information that the Department determines to be necessary to carry out this Program.

Beneficiary Eligibility: Older individuals who are blind, as defined in 34 C.F.R. 367.5 of the ILOIB program regulations are the primary beneficiaries of assistance under this program. This term means "An individual aged 55 or older whose severe visual impairment makes competitive employment extremely difficult to obtain but for whom independent living goals are feasible.".

Award Range/Average: For FY 2019, the estimated range of State awards (including the District of Columbia and Puerto Rico) under the distribution formula is $225,000 to $3,332,107, with a median award of $421,728. The statutory amount for each of the four outlying areas is $40,000.

Funding: (Project Grants) FY 17 $33,317,000.00; FY 18 est $33,317,000.00; FY 19 est $33,317,000.00

HQ: 400 Maryland Avenue SW, Washington, DC 20202
Phone: 202-245-7273 | Email: james.billy@ed.gov
https://www2.ed.gov/programs/rsailob/index.html

ED84.126 | REHABILITATION SERVICES VOCATIONAL REHABILITATION GRANTS TO STATES

Award: Formula Grants

Purpose: To assist States in operating comprehensive, coordinated, effective, efficient and accountable programs of vocational rehabilitation (VR); to assess, plan, develop, and provide VR services for individuals with disabilities and engage in competitive integrated employment.

Applicant Eligibility: State agencies in all States (including territories/possessions) designated as the State agency to administer the VR Program may receive funds with the submission and approval a VR services portion of the Unified or Combined State plan in accordance with section 101(a) of the Rehabilitation Act of 1973, as amended.

Beneficiary Eligibility: In order to be eligible for VR services, an individual must have a physical and/or mental impairment, which, for such an individual, constitutes or results in a substantial impediment to employment, and requires VR services to achieve an employment outcome.

Award Range/Average: 9 In FY 2018 initial annual allotments to States, including D.C. and Puerto Rico ranged from $10.8 million to $303.7 million, with a median award of $45.2 million. Grants to territories ranged from $0.9 million to $3.1 million.

Funding: (Formula Grants) FY 18 $3,184,848,745.00; FY 19 est $3,260,626,620.00; FY 20 est $3,355,549,540.00

HQ: 400 Maryland Avenue SW, Washington, DC 20202

Phone: 202-245-7454 | Email: suzanne.mitchell@ed.gov

http://www.rsa.ed.gov/programs.cfm

ED84.246 | REHABILITATION SHORT-TERM TRAINING

Award: Project Grants

Purpose: To support special seminars, institutes, workshops, and other short-term courses in technical matters relating to the delivery of vocational, medical, social, and psychological services.

Applicant Eligibility: State vocational rehabilitation agencies (including territories), and other public or nonprofit agencies and Organizations, including Institutions of higher education may apply.

Beneficiary Eligibility: Individuals preparing for or employed in positions relating to the rehabilitation of individuals with disabilities will benefit. Projects under this program are designed to provide short-term training and technical instruction in areas of special significance to the delivery of vocational, medical, social, and psychological rehabilitation services.

Award Range/Average: To Be Determined.

Funding: (Project Grants) FY 18 $200,000.00; FY 19 est $200,000.00; FY 20 est $200,000.00

HQ: OSERS Rehabilitation Services Administration 400 Maryland Avenue SW, Washington, DC 20202

Phone: 202-245-7343 | Email: mary.lovley@ed.gov

http://www.ed.gov/offices/osers/rsa

ED84.264 | REHABILITATION TRAINING TECHNICAL ASSISTANCE CENTERS

Award: Project Grants

Purpose: To improve the capacity of State Vocational Rehabilitation agencies and their partners to equip individuals with disabilities to help them obtain high quality competitive integrated employment.

Applicant Eligibility: States and public or nonprofit agencies and Organizations, including Indian Tribes and Institutions of higher education.

Beneficiary Eligibility: Individuals employed in positions related to the rehabilitation of individuals with disabilities will benefit.

Award Range/Average: In FY 2019, the estimated range of awards is $1,500,000 to $2,500,000.

Funding: (Project Grants) FY 18 $6,169,112.00; FY 19 $7,498,388.00; est FY 20 est $6,000,000.00

HQ: OSERS Rehabilitation Services Administration 400 Maryland Avenue SW, Washington, DC 20202

Phone: 202-245-7343 | Email: mary.lovley@ed.gov

http://www.ed.gov/offices/osers/rsa

USDA10.098 | REIMBURSEMENT TRANSPORTATION COST PAYMENT PROGRAM FOR GEOGRAPHICALLY DISADVANTAGED FARMERS AND RANCHERS "RTCP"

Award: Direct Payments With Unrestricted Use

Purpose: To provide reimbursement for the geographically disadvantaged farmers.

Applicant Eligibility: To be eligible to receive Program benefits, a geographically disadvantaged farmer or rancher must: (1) Be a producer of an eligible agricultural commodity in substantial commercial quantities(2) Incur transportation costs for the transportation of the agricultural commodity or input used to produce the agriculture commodity(3) Submit an application for payment during the specified period applicable for each fiscal year. (4) Be in compliance with conservation and wetland protection requirements on all their land(5) Be a citizen of or legal resident alien of the U.S. Eligible commodities include

Programs Administered by Federal Headquarters

any agricultural commodity (including horticulture, aquaculture, and floriculture) food, feed, fiber, livestock (including elk, reindeer, bison, horses, and deer), insects or products thereof.

Beneficiary Eligibility: The U.S. farmers and ranchers outside the continental U.S.(the 48 contiguous U.S.) receive the ultimate benefit from the program because they operate at a competitive disadvantage relative to farmers and ranchers in the continental U.S. This disadvantage is due to the high cost of transporting agricultural commodities from those areas to markets in the continental U.S. and in other countries, and the high cost of transporting agricultural inputs to those areas. Geographically disadvantage farmers and ranchers located in Hawaii, Alaska, or an insular area such as the Commonwealth of Puerto Rico, Guam, American Samoa, the Commonwealth of the Northern Mariana Islands, the Federated States of Micronesia, the Republic of the Marshall Islands, the Republic of Palau, and the Virgin Islands of the U.S. are the primary beneficiaries.

Funding: (Direct Payments with Unrestricted Use) FY 18 $1,996,000.00; FY 19 est $1,996,000.00; FY 20 est $0.00

HQ: 1400 Independence Avenue SW, Washington, DC 20250-0512

  Phone: 202-720-1919 | Email: danielle.cooke@wdc.usda.gov

  http://www.fsa.usda.gov/programs-and-services/price-support/rtcp-program/index

DOE81.092 | REMEDIAL ACTION AND WASTE MANAGEMENT
"Federal Facility Agreement"

Award: Project Grants

Purpose: To perform actions that include conducting site and engineering evaluation, remedial investigations, remedial actions, and following-up with the evaluations to ensure success in various stages of the CERCLA process.

Applicant Eligibility: N/A

Beneficiary Eligibility: N/A

Award Range/Average: This Financial Assistance award ranges between $2,700,000 and $4,000,000. The average is $3,012,772.

Funding: (Project Grants) FY 18 $4,000,000.00 FY 19 est $2,416,133.00; FY 20 est $4,037,024

HQ: 1000 Independence Avenue SW, Washington, DC 20585

  Phone: 202-586-1487 | Email: andrew.wirkkala@em.doe.gov

USDA10.515 | RENEWABLE RESOURCES EXTENSION ACT AND NATIONAL FOCUS FUND PROJECTS
"RREA and RREA-NFF"

Award: Formula Grants; Project Grants

Purpose: To assist forest and range landowners in making resource management decisions and also, to support during rangeland resource issues. Rangeland management includes vegetation, water, fisheries, wildlife, etc.

Applicant Eligibility: RREA: In accordance with the Renewable Resources Extension Act of 1978, applications may only be submitted by the following State colleges and universities. Auburn University; Alabama A&M University; Tuskegee University; University of Alaska - Fairbanks; University of Arizona; University of Arkansas; University of Arkansas at Pine Bluff; University of California; Central State University; Colorado State University; University of Connecticut; University of Delaware; Delaware State University; University of the District of Columbia; University of Florida; Florida A&M University; University of Georgia; Fort Valley State University; University of Guam; University of Hawaii; University of Idaho; University of Illinois; Purdue University; Iowa State University; Kansas State University; University of Kentucky; Kentucky State University; Louisiana State University; Southern University; University of Maine; University of Maryland (College Park); University of Maryland (Eastern Shore); University of Massachusetts; Michigan State University; University of Minnesota; Mississippi State University; Alcorn State University; University of Missouri; Lincoln University; Montana State University; University of Nebraska; University of Nevada; University of New Hampshire; Rutgers University; New Mexico State University; Cornell University; North Carolina State University; North Carolina A&T State University; North Dakota State University; The Ohio State University; Oklahoma State University; Langston University; Oregon State University; Pennsylvania State University; University of Puerto Rico; University of Rhode Island; Clemson University; South Carolina State University; South Dakota State University; University of Tennessee; Tennessee State University; Texas A&M University; Prairie View A&M University; Utah State University; University of Vermont; University of the Virgin Islands; Virginia Polytechnic Institute and State University Virginia State University; Washington State University; West Virginia University; West Virginia State University; University of Wisconsin; and University of Wyoming. RREA-NFF: Applications may only be submitted by 1862 and 1890 land-grant Institutions. Project Directors must have an extension appointment.

An extension appointment is a formal appointment by an Extension Director/Administrator in the institution's cooperative extension service. Failure to meet an eligibility criterion by the application deadline may result in the application being excluded from consideration or, even though an application may be reviewed, will preclude NIFA from making an award.

Beneficiary Eligibility: Same as Applicant Eligibility.

Award Range/Average: If minimum or maximum amounts of funding per competitive and/or capacity project grant, or cooperative agreement are established, these amounts will be announced in the annual Competitive Request for Application (RFA).SPECIAL NOTE: Please refer to the Request for Applications (RFAs) for further specific and pertinent details. The most current RFAs are available as follows: RREA:https://nifa.usda.gov/sites/default/files/resources/FY%202017%20 Renewable%20Resources%20Extension%20Act%20Program%20Modifications.pdfRREA-NFF:https://nifa.usda.gov/sites/ default/files/rfa/FY%202017%20 RREA%20NATIONAL%20FEDERAL%20FOCUS.pdfRFAs are generally released annually. Hence, the RFAs provide the most current and accurate information available. Any specific instructions in the RFAs supersede the general information provided in the CFDA database. Further, the National Program Leader(s) reflected per Section # 152 - Headquarters, can be contacted for the most recent RFA(s).

HQ: Institute of Bioenergy Climate and Environment (IBCE) Division of Environmental Systems Forest Resource Management 1400 Independence Avenue SW, PO Box 2210, Washington, DC 20250-2210

Phone: 202-720-0740 | Email: enorland@nifa.usda.gov

http://nifa.usda.gov/program/renewable-resources-extension-act-capacity-grant

HUD14.149 | RENT SUPPLEMENTS RENTAL HOUSING FOR LOWER INCOME FAMILIES
"Rent Supplement Program"

Award: Direct Payments for Specified Use

Purpose: To provide quality rental housing to low income families at a cost they can afford.

Applicant Eligibility: Eligible sponsors included nonprofit, cooperative, builder-seller, investor-sponsor, and limited-distribution mortgagors.

Beneficiary Eligibility: Families incomes must be within the income limits prescribed for admission to Section 8 housing in order to qualify for benefits under this program. Families may continue in occupancy if 30 percent of monthly income exceeds the market rent.

Funding: (Direct Payments for Specified Use) FY 15 $11,000,000.00; FY 16 est $12,000,000.00; FY 17 est $4,000,000.00

HQ: 451 7th Street SW, Washington, DC 20410

Phone: 202-402-2614 | Email: brandt.t.witte@hud.gov

DHS97.092 | REPETITIVE FLOOD CLAIMS
"RFC"

Award: Project Grants

Purpose: Assists the local and State governments to reduce the long-term risk of flood damage to structures by removing them from flood hazard areas.

Applicant Eligibility: Entities eligible to apply for RFC grants include the emergency management agency (EMA) or a similar office of the 50 States, the District of Columbia, American Samoa, Guam, the U.S. Virgin Islands, Puerto Rico, the Northern Mariana Islands, and Federally recognized Indian Tribal Governments. Each State, Territory, Commonwealth, or Federally recognized Indian Tribal government shall designate one agency to serve as the Applicant for each HMA Program. Please see the HMA Program guidance for more detailed information.

Beneficiary Eligibility: State agencies (other than the EMA), Indian Tribal governments (non-federally recognized), and local governments and communities are eligible to apply as sub applicants for assistance under the RFC program. All interested sub applicants must apply to their State/Tribe/Territory Applicant. Subapplicants (and Applicants) may submit applications on behalf of homeowners and property owners. Please see the HMA program guidance for detailed information.

Award Range/Average: Refer to HMA program guidance.

HQ: 400 C Street SW, Washington, DC 20472

Phone: 202-646-3458 | Email: kayed.lakhia@fema.dhs.gov

http://www.fema.gov

Programs Administered by Federal Headquarters

USDA10.866 | REPOWERING ASSISTANCE
"Section 9004 Repowering Assistance"

Award: Direct Payments for Specified Use

Purpose: To assist biorefineries for restoring fossil fuels with renewable biomass.

Applicant Eligibility: A Biorefinery facility (including equipment and processes) that converts renewable biomass into biofuels and biobased products, and may produce electricity. An eligible biorefinery producer, whose primary production is biofuels; that meets all requirements of this Program. The biorefinery must have been in existence on or before June 18, 2008.

Beneficiary Eligibility: For biorefineries in existence on June 18, 2008 Primary production is biofuels.

Award Range/Average: Determined on a project bases.

Funding: (Direct Payments with Unrestricted Use) FY 18 $5,000,000.00; FY 19 est $0.00; FY 20 $0.00

HQ: 1400 Independence Avenue SW, PO Box 3225, Washington, DC 20250-3225

Phone: 202-690-0784

http://www.rd.usda.gov/programs-services/repowering-assistance-program

EOP95.007 | RESEARCH AND DATA ANALYSIS

Award: Cooperative Agreements

Purpose: The program involves research and analysis of data pertaining to drug policy.

Applicant Eligibility: Applicants must have expert knowledge and extensive experience in conducting research and analysis.

Beneficiary Eligibility: Same as Applicant Eligibility.

Funding: (Cooperative Agreements) FY 18 $3,500,000.00; FY 19 est $0.00; FY 20 est $0.00

HQ: 1800 G Street NW, Washington, DC 20503

Phone: 202-395-6739 | Email: phuong_desear@ondcp.eop.gov

https://www.whitehouse.gov/ONDCP

DOS19.031 | RESEARCH AND DEVELOPMENT-PHYSICAL SECURITY PROGRAMS
"Research and Development"

Award: Cooperative Agreements

Purpose: Program evaluates and recommends physical security countermeasures against terrorism threat for blast mitigation, anti-ram barriers, and forced-entry ballistic-resistant systems.

Applicant Eligibility: The Vehicle Anti-Ram Program develop passive and active anti-ram designs to lower the cost of providing anti-ram protection. The Blast Mitigation Program develops, tests, and fields systems and techniques that protect USG employees and property from the effects of attacks employing explosives. The Force-Entry Ballistic-Resistance Program develops and certifies FE/BR construction products and systems to protect USG employees and property from the effects of forced-entry attacks.

Beneficiary Eligibility: USG Personnel and Facilities are the beneficiary of all research and development programs and products.

Funding: (Salaries and Expenses) FY 16 Estimate Not Available; FY 17 est $1,222,000.00; FY 18 est $250,000.00

HQ: 1400 Wilson Boulevard, Arlington, VA 22209

Phone: 703-312-3125 | Email: norrisrj@state.gov

VA64.054 | RESEARCH AND DEVELOPMENT

Award: Project Grants

Purpose: To submit applications for VA employees to conduct research for the purpose of improving Veterans' health and well-being. Investigator-initiated research proposals is the foundation to achieving ORD's mission to discover knowledge, develop VA researchers and healthcareleaders, and create innovations that advance healthcarefor our Veterans.

Applicant Eligibility: The Principal Investigator (PI) and any Co-Principal Investigator (Co-PI) must have employment status of at least 25 hours per week (5/8ths) and activities that demonstrate a primary professional commitment to VA, including research, patient care, teaching, committee work, etc. The eligibility of each prospective PI (and Co-PI) must be established prior to the funding of a research proposal.

Beneficiary Eligibility: VA Research's fundamental mission is to advance the healthcare of Veterans.

Award Range/Average: VA-ORD awards are for terms ranging from one to seven years, as specified in each FOA/RFA. Availability of funds is dependent on Congressional appropriation and adjustments to budgets may be imposed after an award is initiated.

Funding: (Project Grants) FY 16 Not Separately Identifiable; FY 17 est $536,000,000.00; FY 18 est Estimate Not Available
HQ: 810 Vermont Avenue NW, Washington, DC 20420

Phone: 202-443-5600

http://www.research.va.gov

HUD14.536 | RESEARCH AND EVALUATIONS, DEMONSTRATIONS, AND DATA ANALYSIS AND UTILIZATION

Award: Cooperative Agreements
Purpose: Through Notice of Funding Availability (NOFA), HUD plans to solicit applications for cooperative agreements to engage in research, evaluations, demonstrations, and data analysis and utilization activities.
Applicant Eligibility: N/A
Beneficiary Eligibility: N/A
Award Range/Average: $100,000 minimum funding amount for successful applicants.
Funding: (Cooperative Agreements) FY 18 $890,661.00; FY 19 est $2,623,000.00; FY 20 est $3,000,000
HQ: 451 7th Street SW, Room 8230, Washington, DC 20410

Phone: 202-402-3852 | Email: susan.s.brunson@hud.gov

DOD12.615 | RESEARCH AND TECHNICAL ASSISTANCE

Award: Cooperative Agreements; Project Grants
Purpose: To make awards to, or conclude cooperative agreements with States or local governments, or any nongovernmental or other private entity, to conduct research, and provide technical assistance related to community economic adjustment needs and assistance under 10 U.S.C. Section 2391(c), or Executive Order 12788, as amended.
Applicant Eligibility: Eligible respondents include any governmental or private entity. A "private entity" is defined for purposes of this listing as any entity that is non-governmental.
Beneficiary Eligibility: States and communities, including workers, businesses, and other community interests that may be affected by Department of Defense activity.
Award Range/Average: $400,000-550,000; $477,247
Funding: (Project Grants (Cooperative Agreements)) FY 15 $609,556.00; FY 17 est Estimate Not Available FY 16 est $954,493.00
HQ: 2231 Crystal Drive, Suite 520, Arlington, VA 22202-3711

Phone: 703-697-2130

HHS93.213 | RESEARCH AND TRAINING IN COMPLEMENTARY AND INTEGRATIVE HEALTH

"National Center for Complementary and Integrative Health"

Award: Project Grants; Training
Purpose: To evaluate complementary and integrative health approaches.
Applicant Eligibility: Universities, colleges, hospitals, laboratories, and other public or private nonprofit domestic Institutions, including State and local units of government, and individuals are eligible to make application for grant support of research by a named principal investigator or a research career development candidate. For-profit Organizations are also eligible, with the exception of NRSA. Individual NRSA awardees must be nominated and sponsored by a public or nonprofit private institution having staff and facilities appropriate to the proposed research training Program. All NRSA awardees must be citizens or have been admitted to the United States for permanent residence. To be eligible, predoctoral candidates must have completed the baccalaureate degree, and postdoctoral awardees must have a professional or scientific degree (M.D., Ph.D., D.D.S., D.O., ND, DC, D.V.M., Sc.D., D.Eng., or equivalent domestic or foreign degree). SBIR grants can be awarded only to domestic small businesses (entities that are independently owned and operated for profit, are not dominant in the field in which research is being proposed and have no more than 500 employees). Primary employment (more than one-half time) of the principal investigator must be with the small business at the time of award and during the conduct of the proposed project. In both Phase I and Phase II, the research must be performed in the U.S. or its possessions. STTR grants can be awarded only to domestic small business concerns (entities that are independently owned and operated for profit, are not dominant in the field in which researches proposed and have no more than 500 employees) which "partner" with a research institution in cooperative research and development. At least 40 percent of the project is to be performed by the small business concern and

Programs Administered by Federal Headquarters

at least 30 percent by the research institution. In both Phase I and Phase II, the research must be performed in the U.S. and its possessions. To be eligible for funding, a grant application must be approved for scientific merit and Program relevance by a scientific review group and a national advisory council.

Beneficiary Eligibility: Any nonprofit or for-profit organization, company, or institution engaged in biomedical research.

Award Range/Average: FY2018 total costs (i.e., the sum of the direct costs plus the facilities and administration costs) for grants/awards ranged from low to high: R13 - $30,000 to DP2 - $2,336,250; average financial assistance was: $389,691.

Funding: (Project Grants) FY 18 $126,928,685.00; FY 19 est $130,344,368.00; FY 20 est $112,226,501

HQ: NCCIH 6707 Democracy Boulevard, Suite 401, Bethesda, MD 20892

Phone: 301-594-3462 | Email: partap.khalsa@nih.gov

http://nccih.nih.gov

DOT20.762 | RESEARCH GRANTS

Award: Project Grants

Purpose: Carries various research grants on improving transportation field by funding for research such as the Rural Transportation Research Initiative by North Dakota State University's Upper Great Plains Transportation Institute, Hydrogen-Powered Transportation Research Initiative by the University of Montana, Cold Region and Rural Transportation Research, Maintenance, and Operations by Montana State University's Western Transportation Institute, Advanced Vehicle Technology by the University of Kansas Transportation Research Institute, Renewable Transportation Systems Research by University of Vermont, Alternative Fuels and Life Cycle Engineering by Rochester Institute of Technology, and National Cooperative Freight Research Program by National Academy of Sciences.

Applicant Eligibility: Legislated grants in SAFETEA-LU Section 5513(d), (g) and (i) and Section 5209.

Beneficiary Eligibility: All listed beneficiaries will benefit from results produced by these research efforts.

Award Range/Average: $500K to $22M. Averaged $2.25M

HQ: 1200 New Jersey Avenue SE E33-464, Washington, DC 20590

Phone: 202-366-7253 | Email: dawn.tucker-thomas@dot.gov

http://www.rita.dot.gov

ED84.324 | RESEARCH IN SPECIAL EDUCATION

Award: Project Grants

Purpose: Supports scientifically rigorous research contributing to the solution of specific early intervention and education problems associated with children with disabilities.

Applicant Eligibility: Applicants that have the ability and capacity to conduct scientifically valid research are eligible to apply. Eligible applicants include, but are not limited to, non-profit and for-profit Organizations and public and private agencies and Institutions, such as colleges and universities.

Beneficiary Eligibility: Infants, toddlers, and children with disabilities or at risk for disabilities benefit from this research.

Award Range/Average: The FY 2018 grant awards ranged in size from $85,467 to $1,137,615 for the first year of the 1 to 5 year awards. Award maximums vary depending on the type of project. The FY 2019 grant awards ranged in size from $250,000 to $4,000,000 for 1 to 5 years projects. The FY 2020 awards are estimated to range in size between $100,000 and $800,000 for the first year of the 1 to 5 year awards. Award maximums vary depending on the type of project.

Funding: (Project Grants) FY 18 $54,536,601.00; FY 19 est $54,829,123.00; FY 20 est $52,669,977.00

HQ: National Center for Special Education Research 550 12th Street SW, Room 4144, Washington, DC 20202

Phone: 202-245-8201 | Email: joan.mclaughlin@ed.gov

http://ies.ed.gov/ncser

HHS93.351 | RESEARCH INFRASTRUCTURE PROGRAMS
"Comparative Medicine, Instrumentation, Research Infrastructure"

Award: Project Grants

Purpose: To supporting research infrastructure and related research programs. ORIP consists of the Division of Comparative Medicine (DCM); and Division of Construction and Instruments (DCI).

Applicant Eligibility: Comparative Medicine: Institutions of higher education, hospitals, and other Institutions and Organizations, both nonprofit and for-profit, seeking to establish, continue, or enlarge Programs consistent with the objectives of the Program. Applicants for NRSA must be citizens of the United States or be admitted to the United States for permanent residency. Applicants must be nominated and sponsored by a public or private nonprofit institution with staff and facilities suitable for the proposed research training. Nonprofit domestic Organizations may apply for the institutional NRSA. Research Career Development: Applications may be submitted on behalf of candidates by domestic, nonfederal Organizations, public or private Institutions of higher education.

Beneficiary Eligibility: Biomedical investigators at any nonprofit or for-profit organization, company, or institution engaged in biomedical research.

Award Range/Average: Awards vary in range depending on the particular activity codes. Research Centers grants have much larger ranges - from hundreds of thousands to several million dollars. All costs are shown on a single year basis. Awards may be for up to five years.

Funding: (Project Grants) FY 18 $267,342,483.00; FY 19 est $260,292,600.00; FY 20 est $260,292,600.00; (Project Grants (Capacity Building and Complaint Processing, Training)) FY 18 $7,366,915.00; FY 19 est $6,823,308.00; FY 20 est $6,823,308.00

HQ: 6701 Democracy Boulevard Room 956, PO Box 4874, Bethesda, MD 20892-4874

Phone: 301-435-0864 | Email: pnewman@mail.nih.gov

http://orip.nih.gov

USDA10.255 | RESEARCH INNOVATION AND DEVELOPMENT GRANTS IN ECONOMIC (RIDGE)

Award: Dissemination of Technical Information

Purpose: ERS provides help for development, administration, and evaluation of agricultural and rural policies.

Applicant Eligibility: Any individual or Organization in the U.S. and U.S. Territories is eligible to receive the popular or technical research publications that convey the research results, although there may be a fee.

Beneficiary Eligibility: Same as Applicant Eligibility.

Funding: (Formula Grants (Cooperative Agreements)) FY 17 $600,000.00; FY 18 est $600,000.00; FY 19 est $0.00

HQ: 355 E Street SW, Room 5-254, Washington, DC 20024-3231

Phone: 202-694-5008 | Email: nthomas@ers.usda.gov

http://www.ers.usda.gov

DOD12.360 | RESEARCH ON CHEMICAL AND BIOLOGICAL DEFENSE

Award: Cooperative Agreements; Project Grants

Purpose: To improve the capability to prevent, detect, diagnose and treat the effects of chemical, radiological and biological warfare agents.

Applicant Eligibility: Applicants must be a public or private educational institution, a nonprofit Organizations operated for purposes in the public interest, or a commercial firm.

Beneficiary Eligibility: Beneficiaries are relatively independent investigators associated with an applicant organization.

Funding: (Project Grants) FY 17 $0.00; FY 18 est $1,000,000.00; FY 19 est $336,754.00

HQ: 110 Thomas Johnson Drive, Frederick, MD 21702

Phone: 301-619-2446 | Email: richard.w.totten2.civ@mail.mil

HHS93.226 | RESEARCH ON HEALTHCARE COSTS, QUALITY AND OUTCOMES

Award: Project Grants

Purpose: To support research and evaluations, demonstration projects, research networks, and multidisciplinary centers and to disseminate information on healthcareand on systems for the delivery.

Applicant Eligibility: Federal, State or local government agencies, federally-recognized Indian Tribal Governments, U.S. Territories, non-government Organizations, public or private Institutions of higher education, and other public or nonprofit private agencies, Institutions, or Organizations. For-profit Organizations are eligible to apply for these grants only if "cooperative agreement" is the designated funding mechanism. Organizations described in section 501(c)4 of the Internal Revenue Code that engage in lobbying are not eligible.

Beneficiary Eligibility: Federal, State or local government agencies, federally-recognized Indian Tribal Governments, public or private nonprofit institutions, U.S. territories, Native American organizations, consumers, students, minority groups, specialized groups, health or education professionals, individuals, scientist/researchers, and the general public.

Award Range/Average: $3,956 to $1,149,308; $282,712 average. These are total cost figures (direct costs plus associated facilities and administrative costs, if appropriate).

Funding: (Project Grants) FY 18 $108,016,631.00; FY 19 est $112,170,165.00; FY 20 est $84,941,313.00

Programs Administered by Federal Headquarters

HQ: 5600 Fishers Lane, Rockville, MD 20857
   Phone: 301-427-1447 | Email: george.gardner@ahrq.hhs.gov
   http://www.ahrq.gov

HHS93.085 | RESEARCH ON RESEARCH INTEGRITY
Award: Project Grants
Purpose: To solicit applications for competing grant awards for the planning and implementation of conferences or workshops.
Applicant Eligibility: Public, private or nonprofit agencies (including State and local government agencies) eligible Federal agencies, universities, colleges, hospitals and academic or research Institutions may apply for research grants.
Beneficiary Eligibility: Individuals and public, private, profit or nonprofit organizations.
Award Range/Average: 2016: $249971 - $49,971- $50,000 2017 - $49971 - $50,000 Total $249,971 2018 - $48321 - $50,000 Total $98,321
Funding: (Project Grants (Discretionary)) FY 17 $249,971.00; FY 18 est $98,321.00; FY 19 est Estimate Not Available
HQ: 1101 Wootton Parkway, Suite 550 Tower Building, Rockville, MD 20852
   Phone: 240-453-8822 | Email: roscoe.brunsont@hhs.gov
   http://ori.hhs.gov

HHS93.173 | RESEARCH RELATED TO DEAFNESS AND COMMUNICATION DISORDERS
Award: Project Grants
Purpose: To investigate solutions to problems directly relevant to individuals with deafness or disorders of human communication in the areas of hearing, balance, smell, taste, voice, speech, and language.
Applicant Eligibility: Project Grants and Centers Grants: Any public, private, nonprofit, or for-profit institution is eligible to apply. For-profit Institutions are not eligible for institutional National Research Service Awards. All proposals are reviewed for scientific merit, for evaluation of the qualifications of the investigators, for adequacy of the research and/or research training environment and for significance of the problem. Approved proposals compete for available funds. Awardees of almost all Research Career Development Programs must be citizens or have been admitted to the United States for permanent residence. Candidates must be nominated for the Program by a nonfederal public or private nonprofit institution located in the United States, its possessions or Territories. To be eligible, postdoctoral NRSA trainees and fellows must have a professional or scientific doctoral degree (PhD, MD, DO, DC, DDS, DVM, OD, DPM, ScD, EngD, Dr PHPhD, MD, DO, DC, DDS, DVM, OD, DPM, ScD, EngD, Dr PH, DNSc, ND {Doctor of Naturopathy}, PharmD, DSW, PsyD, AUD or equivalent doctoral degree from an accredited domestic or foreign institution). SBIR grants can be awarded only to domestic small businesses (entities that are independently owned and operated for profit, and have no more than 500 employees). Primary employment (more than one-half time) of the principal investigator must be with the small business at the time of award and during the conduct of the proposed project. In both Phase I and Phase II, the research must be performed in the United States or its possessions. To be eligible for funding, an SBIR grant application must be approved for scientific merit and Program relevance by a scientific review group and a national advisory council. STTR grants can be awarded only to domestic small business concerns which "partner" with a research institution in cooperative research and development. At least 40 percent of the project is to be performed by the small business concern and at least 30 percent by the research institution. In both Phase I and Phase II, the research must be performed in the U.S. and its possessions. To be eligible for funding, a grant application must be approved for scientific merit and Program relevance by a scientific review group and a national advisory council.
Beneficiary Eligibility: Health professionals; student/trainee; scientists/researchers; consumer.
Award Range/Average: Project Grants: FY18 - Ranged from $100 to $2,474,742; Average was $346,647.
Funding: (Project Grants) FY 18 $378,191,652.00; FY 19 est $387,231,000.00; FY 20 est $331,266,000.00
HQ: 6001 Executive Boulevard Room 8328, PO Box 9670, Bethesda, MD 20892-9670
   Phone: 301-496-8693 | Email: holmesd@mail.nih.gov
   http://www.nidcd.nih.gov

HHS93.344 | RESEARCH, MONITORING AND OUTCOMES DEFINITIONS FOR VACCINE SAFETY
"Vaccine Safety Research"

Award: Cooperative Agreements

Purpose: Collaborates with federal partners to provide strategic direction for the coordination of the vaccine and immunization enterprise for the National Vaccine Plan (NVP) implementation.

Applicant Eligibility: Public (including city, county, regional, and State government) Organizations and private nonprofit entities.

Beneficiary Eligibility: Improving vaccine safety for adults.

Award Range/Average: Estimated Funds Available for Competition $750,000

Funding: (Cooperative Agreements) FY 16 $250,000.00; FY 17 est $750,000.00; FY 18 est Estimate Not Available

HQ: 1101 Wootton Parkway, Suite 550 Tower Building, Rockville, MD 20852

Phone: 240-453-8822 | Email: eric.west@hhs.gov

http://www.hhs.gov/nvpo

HHS93.942 | RESEARCH, PREVENTION, AND EDUCATION PROGRAMS ON LYME DISEASE IN THE UNITED STATES
"Lyme Disease"

Award: Cooperative Agreements

Purpose: To develop, implement and evaluate measures for the prevention of Lyme disease in the United States.

Applicant Eligibility: Public and nonprofit Organizations able to provide services to geographical areas where Lyme disease is endemic or found to be newly emerging in the continental United States. Thus, universities, colleges, research Institutions, State and local health departments, and private nonprofit Organizations are eligible.

Beneficiary Eligibility: States, political subdivisions of states, and other public and nonprofit private entities and the general public who may be exposed to the threat of Lyme disease in certain geographical areas.

Award Range/Average: $250,000 to $500,000; Average award depends on Notice of Funding Opportunity (NOFO).

Funding: (Cooperative Agreements (Discretionary Grants)) FY 18 $462,404.00; FY 19 est $339,906.00; FY 20 est $0.00

HQ: CDC1600 Clifton Road NE E60, Atlanta, GA 30329-4018

Phone: 404-718-8845 | Email: cmorrison@cdc.gov

http://www.cdc.gov

DOS19.018 | RESETTLEMENT SUPPORT CENTERS (RSCS) FOR U.S. REFUGEE RESETTLEMENT

Award: Cooperative Agreements

Purpose: Assists the Bureau in preparing the necessary casework for persons eligible for interview by United States Citizenship and Immigration Services (USCIS) of the Department of Homeland Security (DHS) under the U.S. Refugee Admissions Program and, for those approved, to provide assistance in completing the additional requirements for refugee admission under Section 207 of the Immigration and Nationality Act.

Applicant Eligibility: International and non-governmental Organizations.

Beneficiary Eligibility: Refugees approved under the U.S. Refugee Admissions Program will benefit.

Funding: (Cooperative Agreements) FY 16 $52,847,676.00; FY 17 est $53,000,000.00; FY 18 est $53,000,000.00

HQ: 2025 E Street NW, 8th Floor SA 9, Washington, DC 20520

Phone: 202-453-9253 | Email: smithjl1@state.gov

http://www.state.gov/j/prm/index.htm

Programs Administered by Federal Headquarters

USDA10.308 | RESIDENT INSTRUCTION GRANTS FOR INSULAR AREA ACTIVITIES
"Grants for Insular Areas - RIIA"

Award: Project Grants

Purpose: The secretary of agriculture shall fund for education infrastructure with required equipment, encourage UG and PG students to pursue studies in agriculture sciences, support organizations in the private sector, and provide training for agricultural scientists.

Applicant Eligibility: The Secretary of Agriculture shall ensure that each eligible institution, prior to receiving grant funds under subsection (a), shall have a significant demonstrable commitment to higher education Programs in the food and agricultural sciences and to each specific subject area for which grant funds under this section are to be used. The Secretary of Agriculture may require that any grant awarded under this section contain provisions that require funds to be targeted to meet the needs identified in section 1402.

Beneficiary Eligibility: Same as Applicant Eligibility.

Award Range/Average: If minimum or maximum amounts of funding per competitive and/or capacity project grant, or cooperative agreement are established, these amounts will be announced in the annual Competitive Request for Application (RFA).The most current RFA is available via: https://nifa.usda.gov/funding-opportunity/resident-instruction-grants-program-institutions-higher-education-insular-areas

Funding: (Project Grants) FY 17 $1,150,200.00; FY 18 est $1,200,000.00; FY 19 est $0.00

HQ: Institute of Youth Family and Community Division of Community and Education 1400 Independence Avenue SW, PO Box 2250, Washington, DC 20250-2250

    Phone: 202-720-2324 | Email: edwin.lewis@nifa.usda.gov

    http://nifa.usda.gov/program/resident-instruction-grants-riia-and-distance-education-grants-deg-institutions-higher

HUD14.870 | RESIDENT OPPORTUNITY AND SUPPORTIVE SERVICES-SERVICE COORDINATORS
"ROSS Service Coordinators"

Award: Project Grants

Purpose: To provide service coordinator positions to organize supportive services, resident empowerment activities and/or assisting residents in becoming economically self-sufficient or age-in-place.

Applicant Eligibility: Public Housing Authorities (PHAs), Tribes and tribally designated housing entities (TDHEs), resident councils and nonprofit entities supported by residents. Applicants must establish partnerships to leverage resources.

Beneficiary Eligibility: Individuals, families, children, youth, adults as well as elderly/persons with disabilities who are residents of conventional public or Indian housing are eligible to receive benefits from the ROSS program.

Award Range/Average: Average $360,000

Funding: (Project Grants) FY 17 $45,962,000.00; FY 18 est $35,000,000.00; FY 19 est $0.00

HQ: 451 7th Street SW, Room 4130, Washington, DC 20410

    Phone: 202-402-2341 | Email: anice.m.schervish@hud.gov

DOI15.012 | RESIDENTIAL ENVIRONMENTAL LEARNING CENTERS
"RELCs"

Award: Cooperative Agreements (discretionary Grants)

Purpose: To develop and promote educational opportunities through field-science and stewardship of environmental education programs by collaborating with the National Park Service.

Applicant Eligibility: Applicant may be State and local agencies, public or private nonprofit Institutions /Organizations, Federally recognized Indian tribal Governments, State colleges and universities, public and private colleges and universities.

Beneficiary Eligibility: Educators will bring real-world, place-based science to students in accordance with state education standards.

Award Range/Average: $1 - $500,000

Funding: (Cooperative Agreements (Discretionary Grants)) FY 18 Not Separately Identifiable; FY 19 est Not Separately Identifiable; FY 20 est $500,000.00

HQ: 1849 C Street NW, PO Box 3322, Washington, DC 20240

    Phone: 202-513-7247 | Email: tom_medema@nps.gov

DOJ16.593 | RESIDENTIAL SUBSTANCE ABUSE TREATMENT FOR STATE PRISONERS
"RSAT"

Award: Formula Grants

Purpose: To assist states and units of local and tribal governments to break the cycle of incarceration for drug addiction and violence by reducing the demand for, use, and trafficking of illegal drugs.

Applicant Eligibility: States, the District of Columbia, the Commonwealth of Puerto Rico, the Virgin Islands, America Samoa, Guam, and the Northern Mariana Islands are eligible to apply. By statute 42 U.S.C. 3796ff-1(e), the Bureau of Justice Assistance must award RSAT grants to the State office (www.ojp. usdoj.gov/saa/index. htm) designated to administer the Byrne Justice Assistance Grant Program. The State office may award subgrants to state agencies and units of local government (including federally recognized Indian tribal Governments that perform law enforcement functions, as determined by the Secretary of the Interior). Applicant States must agree to implement or continue to require urinalysis and/ or other proven reliable forms of drug and alcohol testing of individuals assigned to residential substance abuse treatment Programs in correctional facilities.

Beneficiary Eligibility: State and local correctional agencies will implement programs to provide treatment to incarcerated offenders.

Award Range/Average: Individual state and territory awards ranged from $35,000 to $908,000.

Funding: (Formula Grants) FY 18 $27,170,769; FY 19 est $30,000,000; FY 19 est $30,000,000

HQ: Bureau of Justice Assistance 810 7th Street NW, Washington, DC 20531

    Phone: 202-616-7385 | Email: timothy.jeffries@usdoj.gov

    http://www.bja.gov

DOJ16.028 | RESOURCE CENTER ON WORKPLACE RESPONSE TO DOMESTIC VIOLENCE, DATING VIOLENCE, SEXUAL ASSAULT, AND STALKING
"Workplace Resource Center"

Award: Cooperative Agreements

Purpose: To provide for establishment and operation of a national resource center on workplace responses to help victims of domestic and sexual violence.

Applicant Eligibility: To be eligible to receive a grant under this section, an entity or Organization shall submit an application to the Attorney General at such time, in such manner, and containing such information as the Attorney General may require, including; (1) information that demonstrates that the entity or Organization has nationally recognized expertise in the area of domestic or sexual violence; (2) a plan to maximize, to the extent practicable, outreach to employers (including private companies and public entities such as public Institutions of higher education and State and local Governments) and labor Organizations described in subsection (a) of this section concerning developing and implementing workplace responses to assist victims of domestic or sexual violence; and(3) a plan for developing materials and training for materials for employers that address the needs of employees in cases of domestic violence, dating violence, sexual assault, and stalking impacting the workplace, including the needs of underserved communities.

Beneficiary Eligibility: An entity or organization that receives a grant under this section may use the funds made available through the grant for staff salaries, travel expenses, equipment, printing, and other reasonable expenses necessary to develop, maintain, and disseminate to employers and labour organizations described in subsection (a) of this section, information and assistance concerning workplace responses to assist victims of domestic or sexual violence.(2) Responses referred to in paragraph (1) may include;(A) providing training to promote a better understanding of workplace assistance to victims of domestic or sexual violence;(B) providing conferences and other educational opportunities; and(C) developing protocols and model workplace policies.

Award Range/Average: Project is issued as a single award for up to the full available amount.

Funding: (Cooperative Agreements) FY 18 est $500,000.00; FY 17 est $500,000.00; FY 16 $500,000.00

HQ: 145 N Street NE, Washington, DC 20530

    Phone: 202-305-1177 | Email: tia.farmer@usdoj.gov

    http://www.justice.gov/ovw

Programs Administered by Federal Headquarters

TREAS21.015 | RESOURCES AND ECOSYSTEMS SUSTAINABILITY, TOURIST OPPORTUNITIES, AND REVIVED ECONOMIES OF THE GULF COAST STATES
"Gulf RESTORE - Direct Component and Centers of Excellence Research Grant Programs"

Award: Formula Grants

Purpose: To disburse funds to eligible entities for the ecological and economic restoration of the Gulf Coast Region.

Applicant Eligibility: The RESTORE Act specifies who may apply to receive funds under the Direct Component Grant Program. Treasury's regulations list the Direct Component eligible states, counties, and parishes who may apply as follows: in Alabama, the Alabama Gulf Coast Recovery Council or such administrative agent as it may designate; in Florida, the Florida counties of Bay, Charlotte, Citrus, Collier, Dixie, Escambia, Franklin, Gulf, Hernando, Hillsborough, Jefferson, Lee, Levy, Manatee, Monroe, Okaloosa, Santa Rosa, Pasco, Pinellas, Sarasota, Taylor, Wakulla, and Walton; in Louisiana, the Coastal Protection and Restoration Authority Board of Louisiana through the Coastal Protection and Restoration Authority of Louisiana; in Louisiana, the Louisiana parishes of Ascension, Assumption, Calcasieu, Cameron, Iberia, Jefferson, Lafourche, Livingston, Orleans, Plaquemines, St. Bernard, St. Charles, St. James, St. John the Baptist, St. Martin, St. Mary, St. Tammany, Tangipahoa, Terrebonne, and Vermilion; In Mississippi, the Mississippi Department of Environmental Quality; and In Texas, the Office of the Governor or an appointee of the Office of the Governor. The RESTORE Act also specifies who may apply to receive funds under the Centers of Excellence Research Grants Program. Treasury's final rule, lists the Centers of Excellence Research Grants Program eligible applicants for each state as follows: in Alabama, the Alabama Gulf Coast Recovery Council or such administrative agent as it may designate; in Florida, the Florida Institute of Oceanography; in Louisiana, the Coastal Protection and Restoration Authority Board of Louisiana through the Coastal Protection and Restoration Authority of Louisiana; in Mississippi, the Mississippi Department of Environmental Quality; and in Texas, the Office of the Governor or an appointee of the Office of the Governor.

Beneficiary Eligibility: The beneficiaries are the coastal communities of the Gulf Coast Region.

Funding: (Formula Grants) FY 18 $18,231,789.00; FY 19 est $119,000,000.00; FY 20 est Estimate Not Available.

HQ: 1500 Pennsylvania Avenue NW, Washington, DC 20220
   Phone: 202-622-0904

HUD14.898 | ROSS SUPPORTIVE SERVICES PROGRAMS

Award: Project Grants

Purpose: To address the needs of public housing residents by providing supportive services, resident empowerment activities, and/ or assisting residents of all ages in becoming economically self-sufficient through a variety of innovative programs/initiatives.

Applicant Eligibility: Public Housing Authorities (PHAs), Tribes and tribally designated housing entities (TDHEs), resident councils and nonprofit entities supported by residents. Applicants must establish partnerships to leverage resources.

Beneficiary Eligibility: Individuals, families, children, youth, adults as well as elderly/persons with disabilities who are residents of conventional public or Indian housing are eligible to receive benefits from the ROSS program.

Award Range/Average: TBD by each individual program/initiative in accordance with the NOFA.

Funding: (Project Grants) FY 16 $1,753,464.00; FY 17 est $3,000,000.00; FY 18 est $0.00

HQ: 451 7th Street SW, Washington, DC 20410
   Phone: 202-402-2430 | Email: dina.lehmann-kim@hud.gov

DOD12.357 | ROTC LANGUAGE AND CULTURE TRAINING GRANTS
"ROTC Project GO (Global Officers)"

Award: Project Grants

Purpose: A DoD-funded initiative that promotes critical language education, study abroad, and intercultural dialogue opportunities within the ROTC student population in order to develop future military officers.

Applicant Eligibility: Any accredited U.S. institution of higher education (defined in 20 U.S.C. 1001 of the Higher education Act of 1965, is eligible to apply for a grant. This includes 2 and 4 year colleges and universities, both public and private. Other Organizations, associations, agencies, and foreign Institutions may be included in proposals but may not be direct recipients of a grant. Federal government schools are not eligible. Applicants must demonstrate an institutional commitment to increasing the critical language and cross-cultural proficiency of their ROTC students as well as proven institutional capability to provide quality instruction in these subject areas. Institutions applying for institutional grants must have an ROTC unit on their campus.

Beneficiary Eligibility: Accredited U.S. institutions of higher education and their ROTC students.
Award Range/Average: Grants range from $150,000 to $350,000 annually for multi-year projects.
Funding: (Salaries and Expenses) FY 17 $8,550,000.00; FY 18 est $7,000,000.00; FY 19 est $19,109,834.00
HQ: 4800 Mark Center Drive, Suite 8G08, Alexandria, VA 22350-7000

    Phone: 571-256-0716 | Email: shirley.t.rapues.civ@mail.mil

HHS93.449 | RUMINANT FEED BAN SUPPORT PROJECT
"BSE Grant Program"

Award: Cooperative Agreements
Purpose: To assist in an increased surveillance presence throughout the commercial feed channels to prevent the introduction or amplification of Bovine Spongiform Encephalopathy (BSE).
Applicant Eligibility: This cooperative agreement grant Program is only available to State and Tribal Feed/BSE regulatory Programs.
Beneficiary Eligibility: The general public, State and Tribal Feed/BSE regulatory programs.

USDA10.886 | RURAL BROADBAND ACCESS LOANS AND LOAN GUARANTEES
"Farm Bill Broadband Loans & Loan Guarantees"

Award: Direct Loans; Guaranteed/insured Loans
Purpose: To assure that people in rural communities have access to broadband services.
Applicant Eligibility: (a) To be eligible for a broadband loan, an applicant may be either a nonprofit or for-profit Organization, and must take one of the following forms: (1) Corporation; (2) Limited liability company (LLC); (3) Cooperative or mutual Organization; (4) Indian tribe or tribal Organization as defined in 25 U.S.C. 450b; or (5) State or local government, including any agency, subdivision, or instrumentality thereof. (b) To be eligible for a broadband loan, the applicant must: (1) Submit a loan application which meets the requirements set forth the regulation; (2) Agree to complete the build-out of the broadband system described in the loan application within three years from the day the applicant is notified that loan funds are available. The loan application must demonstrate that all proposed construction be completed within this three year period with the exception of CPE. CPE can be funded throughout the forecast period; (3) Demonstrate an ability to furnish, improve, or extend broadband facilities to provide service at the broadband lending speed in rural areas; (4) Demonstrate an equity position equal to at least 10 percent of the amount of the loan requested in the application; and (5) Provide additional security if it is necessary to ensure financial feasibility as determined by the Administrator. An eligible entity that provides telecommunications or broadband service to at least 20 percent of the households in the United States may not receive a total amount of loans or guarantees for a fiscal year in excess of 15 percent of the funds authorized and appropriated for that fiscal year.
Beneficiary Eligibility: Residents and businesses of eligible rural areas.
Award Range/Average: In FY18 1 Loan was approved for $19.8 Million
Funding: (Direct Loans) FY 18 $19,884,000.00; FY 19 est $23,700,000.00; FY 20 est $23,700,000.00
HQ: Telecommunications Program 1400 Independence Avenue SW, PO Box 1590, Washington, DC 20250

    Phone: 202-720-9564 | Email: chad.parker@wdc.usda.gov

    http://www.rd.usda.gov/programs-services/farm-bill-broadband-loans-loan-guarantees

USDA10.351 | RURAL BUSINESS DEVELOPMENT GRANT
"RBDG"

Award: Project Grants
Purpose: To support economic development in various disciplines and businesses in rural communities.
Applicant Eligibility: Applicants eligible for RBDG grants are government entities, Indian Tribes or nonprofit corporations serving rural areas such as States, counties, cities, townships, and incorporated towns and villages, boroughs, authorities, districts and Indian Tribes on Federal and State reservations which will serve rural areas. Applicants eligible for TD grants are statewide, private, nonprofit, public television systems whose coverage is predominantly rural. Rural area for this Program is defined as a city, town, or unincorporated area that has a population of 50,000 inhabitants or less, other than an urbanized area immediately adjacent to a city, town, or unincorporated area that has a population in excess of 50,000 inhabitants.
Beneficiary Eligibility: Rural communities and small and emerging private business enterprises which will employ 50 or less new employees and have less than $1.0 million in projected gross revenue. Government entities, private nonprofit

Programs Administered by Federal Headquarters

corporations, and Federally recognized Indian tribes that receive the grant to assist a business type operation. Grants are not made directly to a business.

Award Range/Average: $25,000 to $500,000. Average is less than $100,000.

Funding: (Formula Grants) FY 18 $34,000,000.00; FY 19 est $43,000,000; FY 20 est Estimate Not Available

HQ: 1400 Independence Avenue SW, PO Box 3226, Washington, DC 20250

    Phone: 202-692-5303 | Email: sami.zarour@wdc.usda.gov

    http://www.rd.usda.gov/programs-services/rural-business-development-grants

USDA10.773 | RURAL BUSINESS OPPORTUNITY GRANTS
"RBOG Combined with RBEG 10.769 and RBDG 10.35"

Award: Project Grants

Purpose: To promote economic development in rural communities.

Applicant Eligibility: Grants may be made to public bodies, nonprofit corporations, Federally-Recognized Native American Tribes, and cooperatives with members that are primarily rural residents and that conduct activities for the mutual benefit of the members.

Beneficiary Eligibility: Rural communities and businesses in rural areas.

Award Range/Average: Varies from year to year

Funding: (Cooperative Agreements) FY 17 $30,000,000.00; FY 18 est $28,000,000.00; FY 19 est $0.00

HQ: 1400 Independence Avenue SW, Washington, DC 20250

    Phone: 202-720-1400 | Email: sami.zarour@wdc.usda.gov

    http://www.rd.usda.gov/programs-services/rural-business-development-grants

HUD14.265 | RURAL CAPACITY BUILDING FOR COMMUNITY DEVELOPMENT AND AFFORDABLE HOUSING GRANTS
"Rural Capacity Building Program"

Award: Project Grants

Purpose: The capacity of rural housing development organizations, Community Development Corporations (CDCs), Community Housing Development Organizations (CHDOs), local governments, and the eligible beneficiaries of the Indian tribes are built by the Rural Capacity Building program in order to serve their communities and low- and moderate-income families with community development and low-cost housing activities.

Applicant Eligibility: Only National Organizations that are 503(c)(3) nonprofits, other than Institutions of higher education, can apply for RCB funding. For the purpose of the RCB Program, a National Organization must be a single Organization that has experience conducting RCB eligible activities with RCB eligible beneficiaries within the last ten years in at least seven Federal HUD regions. Having relevant experience working in one state in a HUD region is sufficient for counting that region towards the seven-region minimum. Federal regions are described on HUD's website at: http://portal.hud.gov/hudportal/HUD?src=/localoffices/regions.

Beneficiary Eligibility: RCB program Eligible Beneficiaries are limited to a local organization serving rural areas that are one of the following types of organizations: - Rural housing development organization, - Community Development Corporation (CDC), - Community Housing Development Organization (CHDO), - Local government, and/or - Indian tribe. RCB program Eligible Beneficiaries must serve rural areas. Eligible Beneficiaries in the RCB program are not Eligible Applicants for the RCB program. By definition, RCB Eligible Beneficiaries are not eligible to apply to this RCB NOFA; National Organizations are the only organizations that can be deemed to be Eligible Applicants by successfully meeting the requirements of a National Organization established in Section I.A.4 and Section III.C of this FY 2018 RCB NOFA. Only Eligible Applicants can apply to HUD directly for RCB program funds through this NOFA. Successfully funded RCB program National Organizations are required to work with Eligible Beneficiaries with their RCB program grant award.

Award Range/Average: The minimum grant award is $1,000,000 and the maximum grant award is $2,500,000. In FY 2017 there were four awards made, with the largest grant at $2,000,000 and the smallest at $1,000,000.

Funding: (Project Grants) FY 18 $5,000,000.00; FY 19 est $5,000,000.00; FY 20 est $5,000,000.00

HQ: 451 7th Street SW, Washington, DC 20410

    Phone: 202-402-4385 | Email: diane.m.schmutzler@hud.gov

    http://www.hudexchange.info/programs/rural-capacity-building

USDA10.446 | RURAL COMMUNITY DEVELOPMENT INITIATIVE "RCDI"

Award: Project Grants
Purpose: To assist low-income rural communities to improve housing, economic development, and other essential facilities for standard living.
Applicant Eligibility: Rural Community Development Initiative grants may be made to a legally qualified private or public (including tribal) Organization that provides technical assistance to nonprofit community-based housing and community development Organizations, and low income rural communities. The grantee must provide a Program of technical assistance to the recipient entity. The grantee must have been legally organized for a minimum of three years prior experience working with nonprofit Organizations or low-income rural communities in the areas of housing, community facilities, or community and economic development. Assistance is authorized for eligible applicants in rural areas of the States, Puerto Rico, the Virgin Islands, Guam, American Samoa, the commonwealth of the Northern Mariana Islands, the Marshall Islands, the Republic of Palaw, and the Federated States of Micronesia.
Beneficiary Eligibility: Recipient entities must be legally organized private, nonprofit community-based housing and community development organizations, low income rural communities, and Federally recognized Indian Tribes.
Award Range/Average: FY 2017 grant range: $50,000 to $250,000. Average: $194,691
Funding: (Project Grants) FY 17 $4,000,000.00; FY 18 est $4,000,000.00; FY 19 est $4,000,000.00
HQ: 1400 Independence Avenue SW, Washington, DC 20250
  Phone: 202-205-9685 | Email: shirley.stevenson@wdc.usda.gov
  http://www.rd.usda.gov/had-rcdi_grants.html

USDA10.771 | RURAL COOPERATIVE DEVELOPMENT GRANTS "RCDG"

Award: Project Grants
Purpose: To assist people and businesses in rural areas for improving economic condition through Cooperative Development Centers.
Applicant Eligibility: Applicants are not eligible if they have been debarred or suspended or otherwise excluded from participation in Federal assistance Programs under Executive Order 12549, Debarment and Suspension. Applicants are not eligible if they have an outstanding judgement obtained by the U.S. in a Federal Court (other than U.S. Tax Court), are delinquent on the payment of Federal income taxes, or are delinquent on a Federal debt. Any corporation that has been convicted of a felony criminal violation under any Federal law within the past 24 months or that has any unpaid Federal tax liability that has been assessed, for which all judicial and administrative remedies have been exhausted or have lapsed, and that is not being paid in a timely manner pursuant to an agreement with the authority responsible for collecting the tax liability, is not eligible for funding.
Beneficiary Eligibility: Ultimate beneficiaries must be located in rural areas.
Award Range/Average: Average = $180,000 Range = $70,000 (minimum) to $200,000 (maximum)
Funding: (Project Grants) FY 18 $6,000,000.00; FY 19 est $5,800,000.00; FY 20 est Estimate Not Available
HQ: 1400 Independence Avenue SW Room 4208-S, PO Box 3253, Washington, DC 20250-3253
  Phone: 202-690-1374
  http://www.rd.usda.gov/programs-services/rural-cooperative-development-grant-program

USDA10.890 | RURAL DEVELOPMENT COOPERATIVE AGREEMENT PROGRAM "RCAP"

Award: Project Grants
Purpose: To maximize effectiveness of Federal programs affecting the rural areas.
Applicant Eligibility: Applicants are not eligible if they have been debarred or suspended or otherwise excluded from participation in Federal assistance Programs under Executive Order 12549, Debarment and Suspension. Applicants are not eligible if they have an outstanding judgement obtained by the U.S. in a Federal Court (other than U.S. Tax Court), are delinquent on the payment of Federal income taxes, or are delinquent on a Federal debt. Any corporation that has been convicted of a felony criminal violation under any Federal law within the past 24 months or that has any unpaid Federal tax liability that has been assessed, for which all judicial and administrative remedies have been exhausted or have lapsed,

Programs Administered by Federal Headquarters

and that is not being paid in a timely manner pursuant to an agreement with the authority responsible for collecting the tax liability, is not eligible for funding.

Beneficiary Eligibility: Ultimate beneficiaries must be located in rural areas.

Award Range/Average: Average = $130,000 Range = $30,000 (minimum) to $1,000,000 (maximum)

Funding: (Project Grants) FY 17 $785,981.00; FY 18 est $864,580.00; FY 19 Estimate Not Available

HQ: 1400 Independence Avenue SW Room 4208-S, PO Box 3253, Washington, DC 20250-3253
   Phone: 202-690-1374
   http://www.rd.usda.gov/programs-services/all-programs

USDA10.448 | RURAL DEVELOPMENT MULTI-FAMILY HOUSING RURAL HOUSING VOUCHER DEMONSTRATION PROGRAM
"Rural Development Voucher Demonstration Program"

Award: Direct Payments for Specified Use

Purpose: The Rural Housing Voucher Demonstration program assists the tenants to prepay their rural development mortgage through rental housing assistance vouchers. Prepaying opportunities are located in Puerto Rico, the U.S. Virgin Islands, and Guam.

Applicant Eligibility: Applicants must (a) be residing in the Section 515 project on the date of the prepayment of the Section 515 loan or upon foreclosure by Rural Development; (b) the date of the prepayment or foreclosure must be after September 30, 2005; (c) as required by 42 U.S.C. 1436a the tenant must be a citizen, U.S. non-citizen national or qualified alien and will so provide proof of citizenship.

Beneficiary Eligibility: Applicants must be citizens, U.S. non-citizen nationals or qualified aliens and have an adjusted household income at or below 80 percent of area median income as determined annually by the U.S. Department of Housing and Urban Development (HUD) to be eligible for a rural housing voucher.

Funding: (Direct Payments for Specified Use) FY 17 $22,000,000.00; FY 18 est $25,000,000.00; FY 19 est $19,000,000.00

HQ: USDA Rural Development 1400 Independence Avenue SW, PO Box 0782, Washington, DC 20250-0782
   Phone: 202-720-9728 | Email: janet.stouder@wdc.usda.gov
   http://www.rd.usda.gov

DOJ16.589 | RURAL DOMESTIC VIOLENCE, DATING VIOLENCE, SEXUAL ASSAULT, AND STALKING ASSISTANCE PROGRAM
"Rural Program"

Award: Project Grants

Purpose: To identify, assess, and appropriately respond to child, youth and adult victims of domestic violence, sexual assault, dating violence, and stalking in rural communities.

Applicant Eligibility: States, Indian Tribes, Territories, local Governments, and nonprofit, public or private entities, including tribal nonprofit Organizations, are eligible to carry out Programs serving rural areas or rural communities that address sexual assault, domestic violence, dating violence, and stalking.

Beneficiary Eligibility: Beneficiaries include eligible applicants who propose to serve victims of sexual assault, domestic violence, dating violence, and stalking in a rural area or rural community, as defined by 42 U.S.C., 13925(a)(21) to mean (a) any area or community, respectively, no part of which is within an area designated as a standard metropolitan statistical area by the Office of Management and Budget; or (b) any area or community, respectively, that is (i) within an area designated as a metropolitan statistical area or considered part of a metropolitan statistical area; and (ii) located in a rural census tract.

Award Range/Average: Range: $200,000-750,000

Funding: (Project Grants) FY 16 $24,231,823.00; FY 17 est $26,130,481.00; FY 18 est $24,000,000.00

HQ: 145 N Street NE, Suite 10W121, Washington, DC 20530
   Phone: 202-305-1177 | Email: tia.farmer@usdoj.gov
   http://www.justice.gov/ovw

USDA10.752 | RURAL ECONNECTIVITY PILOT PROGRAM
"ReConnect Program"

Award: Project Grants (discretionary); Direct Loans

Purpose: To improve the broadband connectivity in rural areas that do not have sufficient broadband access.

Applicant Eligibility: Applicants must submit unqualified, audited financial statements for the two previous years from the date the application is submitted. Applicants may have limited eligibility for the Program depending on the characteristics of the proposed funded service area defined in the application.

Beneficiary Eligibility: N/A

Award Range/Average: FY 2018: $600,000,000, to remain available until expended FY 2019: $550,000,000 (of which, $125,000,000 is to remain available until expended and $425,000,000 is to be treated as a reprogramming per Sec. 716 of the Consolidated Appropriations Act,2019, also to remain available until expended)

Funding: (Project Grants (Discretionary)) FY 18 $600,000,000.00; FY 19 est $550,000,000.00

HQ: 1400 Independence Avenue SW, Washington, DC 20250

Phone: 202-720-9554 | Email: chad.parker@usda.gov

https://www.usda.gov/reconnect

USDA10.854 | RURAL ECONOMIC DEVELOPMENT LOANS AND GRANTS
"REDLG"

Award: Project Grants; Direct Loans

Purpose: To promote rural economic development and job creation projects.

Applicant Eligibility: Electric and telephone utilities that have current loans with the Rural Utilities Service (RUS), Rural Telephone Bank loans, or guarantees outstanding and are not delinquent on any Federal debt or in bankruptcy proceedings.

Beneficiary Eligibility: Rural/General Public.

Award Range/Average: Loans and Grants to establish Revolving Loan Fund Programs.

Funding: (Loan Guarantees/Grants) FY 18 $0.00; FY 19 est $46,900,000.00; FY 20 est Estimate Not Available; (Project Grants) FY 18 $10,000,000.00; FY 19 est Estimate Not Available; FY 20 est Estimate Not Available; (Direct Loans) FY 18 $58,000,000.00; FY 19 est Estimate Not Available; FY 20 est Estimate Not Available

HQ: 1400 Independence Avenue SW, PO Box 3226, Washington, DC 20250

Phone: 202-720-1400 | Email: sami.zarour@wdc.usda.gov

http://www.rd.usda.gov/programs-services/rural-economic-development-loan-grant-program

ED84.358 | RURAL EDUCATION

Award: Formula Grants

Purpose: Provides financial assistance to rural districts to carry out activities to help improve the quality of teaching and learning in their schools.

Applicant Eligibility: For SRSA, eligible recipients are local educational agencies (LEAs) in which (1) the total number of students in average daily attendance at all of the schools served by the LEA is less than 600 or where each school in the LEA is located in a county with a total population density of less than 10 persons per square mile; and (2) all of the schools served by the LEA are designated as rural by the U.S. Department of education 's National Center for education Statistics (NCES) using the NCES school locale methodology in place at the time of enactment of the Every Student Succeeds Act (ESSA) or the LEA is located in an area of the State defined as rural by a State governmental agency. For RLIS, eligible recipients are State educational agencies (SEAs). SEAs then must distribute funds to local educational agencies (LEAs) on a formula or competitive basis. An LEA is eligible to receive a grant under RLIS only if (1) at least 20 percent of the school children ages 5-17 in the LEA come from families with incomes below the poverty line; and (2) all of the schools served by the LEA are designated with a school locale code of 32, 33, 41, 42, or 43 under the NCES school locale methodology in place at the time of ESSA's enactment. If an SEA chooses not to participate in the Program, the Secretary uses the State's allocation to make direct grants to eligible LEAs in the State. If an LEA is eligible for both SRSA and RLIS, the LEA may choose in which Program to participate.

Beneficiary Eligibility: Elementary and secondary schools, students, and teachers in rural schools.

Award Range/Average: For Fiscal Year 2018: Range of new awards for SRSA: $140 - $51,294; Average new award for SRSA: $22,478.Estimated range of new subgrants for RLIS: $17 - $266,500; Average new subgrants for RLIS: $34,102.

Funding: (Formula Grants) FY 18 $180,840,000.00; FY 19 est $180,840,000.00; FY 20 est $180,840,000.00

Programs Administered by Federal Headquarters

HQ: Department of Education 400 Maryland Avenue SW, Washington, DC 20202
   Phone: 202-260-7349
   http://www2.ed.gov/nclb/freedom/local/reap.html

USDA10.850 | RURAL ELECTRIFICATION LOANS AND LOAN GUARANTEES
"Electric Loans and Loan Guarantees"

Award: Direct Loans; Guaranteed/insured Loans
Purpose: To assist with electric services in rural areas and provide awareness on-grid and off-grid renewable energy systems.
Applicant Eligibility: Rural electric cooperatives, public utility districts, municipalities, corporations, and other qualified power suppliers including those located in the U.S. Territories, the Federated States of Micronesia, the Republic of the Marshall Islands, and the Republic of Palau.
Beneficiary Eligibility: Persons, businesses, public bodies, tribal entities, and other entities in rural areas (as defined in program regulations) or those currently served through RUS electric loans. Rural areas are defined in the Rural Electrification Act and program regulations as any area of the United States, or eligible insular areas, other than a city, town, or unincorporated area that has a population of greater than 20,000 inhabitants, or any area within a service area of an entity with an outstanding Rural Electrification Act loan on June 18, 2008.
Award Range/Average: Average Guaranteed FFB: $32,668,948 Average.
Funding: (Guaranteed/Insured Loans) FY 18 $2,922,444,000.00; FY 19 est $5,500,000,000.00; FY 20 est $5,500,000,000.00
HQ: Electric Programs 1400 Independence Avenue SW, PO Box 1560, Washington, DC 20250
   Phone: 202-720-9545 | Email: christopher.mclean@wdc.usda.gov
   http://www.rd.usda.gov/programs-services/all-programs/electric-programs

DHS97.120 | RURAL EMERGENCY MEDICAL COMMUNICATIONS DEMONSTRATION PROJECT
"REMCDP"

Award: Project Grants
Purpose: This grant provides training and education and also helps to improve the communication infrastructure and operational effectiveness on rural medical services.
Applicant Eligibility: Please refer to the Notice of Funding Opportunity Announcement.
Beneficiary Eligibility: Refer to program guidance for further information.
Award Range/Average: Refer to program guidance.
Funding: (Salaries and Expenses) FY 18 $2,000,000.00; FY 19 est $0.00; FY 20 est $0.00
HQ: Cyber Security and Communications (CS and C)/Office of Emergency Communications (OEC) NPPD 4200 Wilson Boulevard, Arlington, VA 22201
   Phone: 703-235-4025
   http://www.dhs.gov

USDA10.868 | RURAL ENERGY FOR AMERICA PROGRAM
"REAP"

Award: Loan Guarantees/grants
Purpose: To compensate for agricultural producers and rural small businesses to promote renewable energy systems and to compensate government entities, educational institutions, and public power entities to assist agricultural producers and rural small businesses with renewable energy systems.
Applicant Eligibility: To be eligible for renewable energy systems or energy efficiency improvement assistance, an applicant must be an agricultural producer or rural small business. Rural small businesses must be located in a rural area. The applicant or owner must not have an outstanding judgment, delinquent on any Federal debt or debarred from receiving Federal assistance. Under the Energy Audit and Renewable Energy Development Assistance Programs eligible applicants include governmental entities and their instrumentalities, educational Institutions, rural electric cooperatives, Resource Conservation and Development Councils, and public power entities.
Beneficiary Eligibility: For energy efficiency improvements and renewable energy systems the program is for agricultural producers and rural small businesses. For energy audits and renewable energy development assistance grants, units of State,

tribal, and local governments; land-grant colleges, universities, and other institutions of higher education; rural electric cooperatives and public power entities; instrumentalities of a state, tribal, and local governments; and Resource Conservation and Development Councils are eligible for the assistance.

Award Range/Average: Grant Range $2,500 to $500,000; Average $45,000 Guaranteed Loan Range $5,000 to $25,000,000; Average $85,000.

Funding: (Loan Guarantees/Grants) FY 18 $0.00; FY 19 est $25,000,000.00; FY 20 est Estimate Not Available; (Project Grants) FY 18 $25,000,000.00; FY 19 Estimate Not Available; FY 20 est Estimate Not Available; (Guaranteed/Insured Loans) FY 18 $530,000,000.00; FY 19 est $500,025,502.00; FY 20 est Estimate Not Available

HQ: Energy Division 511 W 7th Street, Atlantic, IA 50022

Phone: 712-243-2107 | Email: lisa.noty@wdc.usda.gov

USDA10.751 | RURAL ENERGY SAVINGS PROGRAM (RESP) "RESP"

Award: Direct Loans
Purpose: To assist in cost savings for the rural and small business families.
Applicant Eligibility: N/A
Beneficiary Eligibility: N/A
Award Range/Average: Range of loan size is from $200,000 to $13,000,000.00.The average is $3,034,147.00
Funding: (Direct Loans) FY 18 $21,500,000.00; FY 19 est $56,000,000.00; FY 20 est $133,000,000.00
HQ: Electric Programs 1400 Independence Avenue SW, PO Box 1560, Washington, DC 20250

Phone: 202-720-9545 | Email: christopher.mclean@wdc.usda.gov

https://www.rd.usda.gov/programs-services/rural-energy-savings-program

USDA10.516 | RURAL HEALTH AND SAFETY EDUCATION COMPETITIVE GRANTS PROGRAM

"Rural Health and Safety Education Competitive Grants Program-RHSE"

Award: Project Grants
Purpose: The Rural Health and Safety Education provide programs for individuals and families, promotes rural health leadership development, farm safety, information and training to farm workers.
Applicant Eligibility: Applications may be submitted by 1862 and 1890 Land Grant colleges and universities that are eligible to receive funds under the Act of July 2, 1862 (7 U.S.C. 301 et seq.), and the Act of August 30, 1890 (7 U.S.C. 321 et seq.), including Central State University, Tuskegee University, West Virginia State University and the University of the District of Columbia. Applications also may be submitted by any of the Tribal colleges and universities designated as 1994 Land Grant Institutions under the educational Land-Grant Status Act of 1994, as amended.
Beneficiary Eligibility: Same as Applicant Eligibility.
Award Range/Average: If minimum or maximum amounts of funding per competitive and/or capacity project grant, or cooperative agreement are established, these amounts will be announced in the annual Competitive Request for Application (RFA).The most current RFA is available via: https://nifa.usda.gov/funding-opportunity/rural-health-and-safety-education-competitive-grants-program-rhse
HQ: Institute of Youth Family and Community (IYFC) Division of Family and Consumer Sciences 1400 Independence Avenue SW, PO Box 2250, Washington, DC 20250-2250

Phone: 202-720-2324 | Email: ashipley@nifa.usda.gov

https://nifa.usda.gov/program/rural-health-and-safety

HHS93.912 | RURAL HEALTH CARE SERVICES OUTREACH, RURAL HEALTH NETWORK DEVELOPMENT AND SMALL HEALTH CARE PROVIDER QUALITY IMPROVEMENT

Award: Project Grants
Purpose: The Rural healthcareCoordination Network Partnership Program supports the development of formal and mature rural health networks that focus on care coordination activities for the following chronic conditions: diabetes, congestive heart failure and chronic obstructive pulmonary disease. Care coordination in the primary care practice involves deliberately organizing

Programs Administered by Federal Headquarters

patient care activities and sharing information among all of the participants concerned with a patient's care to achieve safer and more effective care.

Applicant Eligibility: Rural healthcare Services Outreach, Rural Health Network Development and Rural Health Network Development Planning Programs: Applicants applying to these Programs can be rural public or rural nonprofit private entities. These include faith-based Organizations, health departments, Tribal Governments whose grant-funded activities are conducted in a federally recognized Tribal area, Organizations that serve migrant and seasonal farm- workers in rural areas etc. that include three or more healthcare providers that provide or support the delivery of healthcare services. The administrative headquarters of the Organization must be located in a rural county or a rural zip code of an urban county. Small healthcare Provider Quality Improvement Program: This Program is available to rural public or rural nonprofit private healthcare provider or provider of healthcare services, such as a critical access hospital or a rural health clinic; or network of small rural providers (including faith-based Organizations and federally recognized Tribal Governments) that deliver healthcare services in rural areas. Eligible applicants must be located in a non-metropolitan county or in a rural census tract of a metropolitan county and all services must be provided in a non-metropolitan county or rural census tract. Delta States Rural Development Network Program: This Program is available to rural, nonprofit or public entities located in the eight Delta States (Alabama, Arkansas, Illinois, Kentucky, Louisiana, Mississippi, Missouri, and Tennessee) that represent a consortium of three or more diverse Organizations that deliver healthcare services in eligible rural Delta counties/parishes. Rural Health Opioid Program: This Program is available to rural public or rural nonprofit private entities (including faith-based Organizations and federally recognized Tribal Governments) that include three or more healthcare providers. The administrative headquarters/lead applicant of the Organization must be located in a rural county or a rural zip code of an urban county. Delta Region Community Health Systems Development Program: Eligible applicants include domestic public, private, and non-profit Organizations, including Tribes and tribal Organizations, and faith-based and community-based Organizations. Rural Maternity and Obstetrics Management Strategies Program: Applicants applying to these Programs can be public or nonprofit private entities. These include faith-based Organizations, health departments, Tribal Governments whose grant-funded activities are conducted in a federally recognized Tribal area, Organizations that serve migrant and seasonal farm- workers in rural areas etc. that are part of a network. A network is defined as an Organizational arrangement among three or more separately owned domestic public and/or private entities, including the applicant Organization. For the purposes of this Program, the applicant must have a network composition that includes: 1) at least two rural hospitals or CAHs; 2) at least one health center under section 330 of the Public Health Service Act (Federally Qualified Health Center (FQHC) or FQHC look-alike); 3) state Home Visiting and Healthy Start Programs if regionally available; and 4) the state Medicaid agency. Rural Communities Opioids Response Program - Planning: Eligible applicants include all domestic public or private, non-profit or for-profit, entities, including faith-based and community-based Organizations, Tribes, and tribal Organizations, who will serve rural communities at the highest risk for substance use disorder. To ascertain rural eligibility, please refer to http://datawarehouse.hrsa.gov/RuralAdvisor/. This website can be searched by eligibility by county and by address. Federally-recognized Tribal Government and Native American Organizations are eligible to apply as long as they meet the eligibility requirements.

Beneficiary Eligibility: Medically underserved populations in rural areas will receive expanded services in rural communities where they did not previously exist.

Award Range/Average: Program: Rural healthcareServices Outreach Program; Maximum award: $200,000; Minimum award: $191,755; Average Award: $199,352. Program: Rural Health Network Development Planning Program; Maximum award: $100,000; Minimum award: $ $94,698; Average Award: $99,744. Program: Rural Health Network Development Program; Maximum award: $300,000; Minimum award: $199,562; Average Award: $294,362. Program: Delta States Rural Development Network Program; Maximum award: $945,000; Minimum award: $584,999; Average Award: $839,995. Program: Small healthcareProvider Quality Improvement Program; Maximum award: $200,000; Minimum award: $167,431; Average Award: $198,265. Program: Rural Health Opioid Program; Maximum award: $250,000; Minimum award: $173,934; Average Award: $246,133. Program: Delta Region Community Health Systems Development; Maximum award $4,000,000; Minimum award $4,000,000. Average Award: $4,000,000. Program: Rural Maternity and Obstetrics Management Strategies Program; Maximum award: $600,000; minimum awards: TBD; Average Award: Yet to be Determined Program: Rural Communities Opioid Response Program- Planning: Maximum award $200,000; Minimum award $200,000. Average award: $200,000 Program: Rural Communities Opioid Response Program- Implementation: Maximum award $1,000,0000; Minimum award $1,000,000. Average award: $1,000,000 Program: Rural Communities Opioid Response Program- Medication Assisted Treatment Expansion: Maximum award: $725,000; Minimum award: $725,000. Average award: $725,000 Program: Rural Communities Opioid Response Program- Technical Assistance: Maximum Award: $6,000,000; Minimum award: $3,000,000. Average award: $6,000,000

Funding: (Project Grants) FY 18 $58,913,526.00; FY 19 est $151,179,478.00; FY 20 est $96,502,892.00

HQ: Community-Based Division 5600 Fishers Lane, Rockville, MD 20857

Phone: 301-443-7444 | Email: kumali@hrsa.gov

http://www.hrsa.gov/ruralhealth

HHS93.155 | RURAL HEALTH RESEARCH CENTERS

Award: Cooperative Agreements

Purpose: To increase the amount of publicly available, high quality, impartial, policy-relevant research to assist decision makers at the federal, state and local levels to better understand the challenges faced by rural communities and providers.

Applicant Eligibility: The Rural Health Research Center and Telehealth Focused Rural Health Research Center cooperative agreements are open to domestic public, for-profit, and non-profit entities. Institutions of higher education, faith-based and community based Organizations, Tribes, and tribal Organizations are eligible to apply. The Frontier Community Health Integration Project Technical Assistance, Tracking and Analysis Program is open to all public, private, and nonprofit Organizations, including faith-based and community Organizations, as well as federally-recognized tribal Governments and Organizations. The Rural Health Research Dissemination cooperative agreement is open to all domestic public and private entities, nonprofit and for-profit. Eligible entities may include, but are not limited to, public and private Institutions for higher education, public and private health research Organizations, foundations, Tribes and tribal Organizations, and faith based entities. Rural Policy Analysis award eligibility is open to public, private, and nonprofit Organizations including faith-based and community Organizations, state Governments and their agencies such as universities, colleges, research Institutions, hospitals, and local Governments or their bona fide agents. Federally recognized tribal Governments, Tribes, and tribal Organizations are also eligible. Please see individual grant FOA at www.grants.gov for Program -specific eligibility. Eligible applicants for the National Rural Health Best Practices and Community Development Program include public, private and nonprofit Organizations including faith-based and community Organizations, state Governments and their agencies such as universities, colleges, research Institutions, hospitals, and local Governments or their bona fide agents. Federally recognized tribal Governments, Tribes, and tribal Organizations are also eligible. The Rapid Response Rural Data Analysis and Issue Specific Rural Research Studies cooperative agreement is open to all domestic public and private entities, nonprofit and for-profit. Eligible entities may include, but are not limited to, public and private Institutions for higher education, public and private health research Organizations, foundations, Tribes and tribal Organizations, and faith based entities. National Rural Health Best Practices and Community Development Program eligibility is open to public, private and non-profit Organizations, including faith-based and community-based Organizations. Please see individual grant FOA at www.grants. gov for Program -specific eligibility. Rural Health Value Cooperative Agreement Program eligibility is open to public, private, and nonprofit Organizations, including faith-based and community Organizations, as well as federally recognized tribal Governments and Organizations. Please see individual grant FOA at www.grants.gov for Program -specific eligibility. Medicare Rural Hospital Flexibility Program Evaluation Cooperative Agreement: Eligible applicants include public and private nonprofit entities. Faith-based and community Organizations are eligible to apply for this cooperative agreement. Federally recognized tribal government and Native American Organizations are eligible to apply. Information Services to Rural Hospital Flexibility Program: Any public or private entity is eligible to apply for this Federal funding opportunity. Applicant Organizations that are federally recognized Native American Tribes or tribal Organizations are eligible to apply. Faith-based and community-based Organizations are eligible to apply for this cooperative agreement. The State Rural Health Coordination and Development Cooperative Agreement (SRHCD-CA) applicant is an Organization that is national in scope with experience providing coordination and development to enhance the rural health infrastructure in each of the 50 states. Federally recognized tribal Government and Native American Organizations are eligible to apply. Rural Quality Improvement Technical Assistance Cooperative Agreement: Eligible applicants include domestic public, private, and nonprofit Organizations, including Tribes and tribal Organizations, and faith-based and community-based Organizations. The Rural Health Clinic Technical Assistance Cooperative Agreement: Eligible applicants include domestic public, private, for-profit and nonprofit Organizations, as well as faith-based and community-based Organizations and federally recognized tribal Governments and Organizations. Rural Residency Technical Assistance and Development Cooperative Agreement: Eligible entities include any domestic public or private nonprofit entities including faith-based and community-based Organizations; state Governments and their agencies such as universities, colleges and research Institutions; hospitals; local Governments or their bona fide agents; and federally recognized tribal Governments, Tribes and tribal Organizations. Vulnerable Rural Hospitals Assistance Program Eligible applicants include domestic public or private, non-profit entities. Domestic faith-based and community-based Organizations, Tribes, and tribal Organizations are also eligible to apply. The eligible applicant (VRHAP recipient) shall provide targeted assistance to selected rural hospitals in need. Rural hospitals are eligible to receive targeted assistance from the VRHAP recipient. Rural Residency Planning and Development (RRPD) Program Hospitals, medical schools and community-based ambulatory settings with rural designation along with consortia of urban and rural partnerships are eligible to apply for the award. The applicant Organization must demonstrate it has the capacity to acquire accreditation and provide ongoing support for resident training, including financially, by the end of the period of performance. Rural Communities Opioid Response Program -Evaluation cooperative agreement: Eligible applicants include domestic public or private, non-profit or for-profit Organizations. Institutions of higher education, faith-based and community-based Organizations, Tribes, and tribal Organizations are eligible to apply. Applicants may be a single entity or a consortium. Rural Communities Opioid Response Program - Rural Centers of Excellence on Substance Use Disorder: Eligible applicants include

Programs Administered by Federal Headquarters

all domestic public or private, non-profit or for-profit entities, including state, county, or city or township Governments; independent school districts; public housing authorities or Indian housing authorities; public or private Institutions of higher education; small businesses; faith-based and community-based Organizations; and federally recognized Tribes, tribal Organizations, and tribal Governments; or consortia of these Organizations.

Beneficiary Eligibility: The entities that will benefit from this program are health care personnel, health research personnel, policy makers, and the general public. Underserved populations in rural areas; facilities and services in rural areas States with at least one hospital located in a non-metropolitan statistical area or county and provides CMS with necessary assurances.

Award Range/Average: For Rural Health Research Centers (eight awards): Range $699,363- $700,000 For Telehealth Research Center (one award): $750,0000 For Rural Health Research Dissemination (one award): $120,000- $135,000 For Frontier Community Health Integration Project Technical Assistance, Tracking and Analysis (one award): $484,097- $497,734 For Rural Policy Analysis (one award): $224,986- $225,000 For Rapid Response Rural Data Analysis and Issue Specific Rural Research Studies (one award) : $450,000 For National Rural Health Best Practice and Community Development Program (one award): $1,799,843- $1,799,997 For Rural Health Value (one award): $500,000 For the Information Services to Rural Hospital Flexibility Program Awardees: $957,510- $1,100,000 For the Medicare Rural Hospital Flexibility Program Evaluation Cooperative Agreement: $1,500,000 (one award) For the State Rural Health Coordination and Development Cooperative Agreement (SRHCD-CA): - $750,000 (one award) For Rural Quality Improvement Technical Assistance Cooperative Agreement: $ $500,000 (one award) For Rural Health Clinic Technical Assistance Cooperative Agreement (one award): $100,000 For Rural Residency Technical Assistance and Development Cooperative Agreement (one award): $666,666 For Vulnerable Rural Hospitals Assistance Program Cooperative Agreement (one award): $800,000 The Rural Residency Planning and Development Program (one award): FY'20 amount TBD For Rural Communities Opioid Response Program- Evaluation (one award): $3,000,000 For Rural Communities Opioid Response Program- Rural Centers of Excellence on Substance Use Disorder (three awards): $2,200,000 per year, per award.

Funding: (Cooperative Agreements) FY 18 $13,266,454.00; FY 19 est $23,670,706.00; FY 20 est $17,944,057.00; (Project Grants) FY 18 Actual Not Available; FY 19 est $800,000.00; FY 20 est Estimate Not Available

HQ: 5600 Fishers Lane, PO Box 17W59-D, Rockville, MD 20857

Phone: 301-945-3985 | Email: jburges@hrsa.gov

http://www.hrsa.gov/ruralhealth

HUD14.250 | RURAL HOUSING AND ECONOMIC DEVELOPMENT

Award: Project Grants

Purpose: To build capacity at the State and local level for rural housing and economic development, and to assist innovative housing and economic development activities.

Applicant Eligibility: Local rural nonprofit Organizations, community development corporations, Federally recognized Indian Tribes, State Housing Financing Agencies and State Community and/or Economic Development Agencies.

Beneficiary Eligibility: Local and rural communities.

Award Range/Average: The maximum amount awarded to a successful applicant is $300,000.

HQ: U.S. Department of Housing and Urban Development Office of Rural Housing and Economic Development, Room 7137, Washington, DC 20410

Phone: 202-708-2290 | Email: thann.young@hud.gov

http://www.hud.gov/offices/cpd/economicdevelopment/programs

USDA10.433 | RURAL HOUSING PRESERVATION GRANTS

Award: Project Grants

Purpose: To support low-income rural residents to renovate their houses and develop standard living.

Applicant Eligibility: Must be a State or political subdivision, public nonprofit corporation, Indian tribal corporations, authorized to receive and administer housing preservation grants, private nonprofit corporation, or a consortium of such eligible entities. Applicants must provide assistance under this Program to persons residing in open country and communities with a population of 10,000 that are rural in character and places with a population of up to 20,000 under certain conditions. Applicants in towns with population of 10,000 to 20,000 should check with local Rural Development office to determine if the Agency can serve them. Assistance is authorized for eligible applicants in the United States, Puerto Rico, Virgin Islands, and the territories and possessions of the United States.

Beneficiary Eligibility: Very low and low-income rural individuals and families who are homeowners and need resources to bring their housing up to code standards, rental property owners, or co-ops.

Funding: (Project Grants) FY 17 $4,890,755.00; FY 18 est $5,000,000.00; FY 19 est $0.00

HQ: Multi-Family Housing Preservation and Direct Loan Division 1400 Independence Avenue SW, Washington, DC 20250-0788
Phone: 202-720-1604 | Email: bonnie.edwards@wdc.usda.gov
https://www.rd.usda.gov/programs-services/housing-preservation-grants

USDA10.411 | RURAL HOUSING SITE LOANS AND SELF HELP HOUSING LAND DEVELOPMENT LOANS
"Section 523 and 524 Site Loans"

Award: Direct Loans

Purpose: To support public and private nonprofit organization with sites for development and provide families those who have low-income with loans.

Applicant Eligibility: A private or public nonprofit Organization that will provide the developed sites to qualified borrowers on a cost of development basis in open country and towns of 10,000 population or less and places up to 25,000 population under certain conditions. Applicants from towns of 10,000 to 25,000 population should check with local RD office to determine if agency can serve them. Assistance is available to eligible applicants in States, Puerto Rico, the Virgin Islands, Guam, and the Northern Marianas.

Beneficiary Eligibility: Sites developed with Section 524 loans must be for housing low and very low income families and may be sold to families, nonprofit organizations, public agencies and cooperatives eligible for assistance under any Section of Title V of the Housing Act of 1949, or under any other law which provides financial assistance. Sites developed with Section 523 loans must be for housing to be built by the self-help method.

Award Range/Average: Loan amounts vary based on proposed project size.

Funding: (Direct Loans) FY 17 $1,000,000.00; FY 18 est $0.00; FY 19 est $$10,000,000.00

HQ: 1400 Independence Avenue SW, Washington, DC 20250
Phone: 804-287-1559 | Email: myron.wooden@usda.gov
https://www.rd.usda.gov

HUD14.268 | RURAL HOUSING STABILITY ASSISTANCE PROGRAM

Award: Project Grants; Direct Payments for Specified Use

Purpose: To provide aid for rural counties to re-house or improve the housing situations of individuals and families who are homeless, at risk of homelessness, or in the worst housing situations, stabilize them, and improve their ability afford stable housing.

Applicant Eligibility: Counties, that meet the definition of a rural county (a county that has no part of it within an area designated as a standard metropolitan statistical area by OMB; a county that is within an area designated as a metropolitan statistical area or considered as part of a metropolitan statistical area and at least 75 percent of its population is located on U.S. Census blocks classified as non-urban; a county that is located in a State that has population density of less than 30 persons per square mile [as reported in the most recent decennial census], and of which at least 1. 25 percent of the total acreage of such State is under Federal jurisdiction, provided that no metropolitan city in such State is the sole beneficiary of the grant amounts awarded under this part. A metropolitan city means a city that was classified as a metropolitan city under section 102(a) of the Housing and Community Development Act of 1974 (42 U.S.C. 5302(a)) for the fiscal year immediately preceding the fiscal year for which Emergency Solutions Grant Program funds are made available. Recipient includes the District of Columbia.) local units of government authorized by the county and private non-profit Organizations authorized by the county.

Beneficiary Eligibility: Individuals and families who are homeless, at risk of homelessness or are in a worst housing situation. Worst housing situation is defined as housing that has serious health and safety defects and at least one major system that has failed or is failing.

HQ: 451 7th Street SW, Room 7260, Washington, DC 20410
Phone: 202-402-4773 | Email: karen.m.deblasio@hud.gov
http://www.hudexchange.info/rural

Programs Administered by Federal Headquarters

USDA10.870 | RURAL MICROENTREPRENEUR ASSISTANCE PROGRAM "RMAP"

Award: Project Grants; Direct Loans

Purpose: To provide financial assistance for operations of rural microenterprises. Microenterprise Development Organizations support rural microenterprise development. These grants are known as technical assistance and used by an MDO to provide marketing, management, and other technical assistance to microentrepreneurs.

Applicant Eligibility: To be eligible to apply for Microlender status under the Rural Microentrepreneur Assistance Program, an applicant must be a non-profit entity, an Indian tribe, or a public institution of higher education. Applicants must be at least 51 percent controlled by persons who are either (i) citizens of the United States, the Republic of Palau, the Federated States of Micronesia, the Republic of the Marshall Islands, or American Samoa; or (ii) legally admitted permanent residents residing in the U.S. The applicant or owner must not have an outstanding judgment, be delinquent on any Federal debt or debarred from receiving Federal assistance.

Beneficiary Eligibility: Microentrepreneur is defined as an owner and operator, or prospective owner and operator, of a rural microenterprise who is unable to obtain sufficient training, technical assistance, or as determined by the Secretary. All microentrepreneurs must be located in a rural area.

Award Range/Average: Range of financial assistance is outlined in the Notice of Funding Availability published in the federal register, however prior loans has ranged from $131,250 to $500,000.

Funding: (Direct Loans) FY 18 $7,000,000.00; FY 19 est $10,504,202.00; FY 20 est Estimate Not Available; (Project Grants Total) FY 18 $2,500,000.00; FY 19 est $2,000,000.00; FY 20 est Estimate Not Available

HQ: Speciality Program 1400 Independence Avenue SW, Washington, DC 20250

Phone: 202-720-1400 | Email: sami.zarour@wdc.usda.gov

http://www.rd.usda.gov/programs-services/rural-microentrepreneur-assistance-program

USDA10.427 | RURAL RENTAL ASSISTANCE PAYMENTS "Rental Assistance"

Award: Direct Payments for Specified Use

Purpose: The Rural Housing Service reduced the rent for less-income families in rural areas based on the sections 515, 514, and 516.

Applicant Eligibility: To be eligible to participate in the rental assistance Program, borrowers must have an eligible project. All projects must convert to Interest Credit Plan II before they are eligible, except direct RRH and insured RRH loans approved prior to August 1, 1968, and LH loans and grants. For a borrower to have an eligible project, the loan must be an RRH insured or direct loan made to a broad-based nonprofit Organization, or State or local agency or; an RRH insured loan made to an individual or Organization who has or will agree to operate the housing on a limited profit basis as defined in 7 CFR 3560. 254 (a) or; an RCH insured or direct loan or; an LH loan, or an LH loan and grant combination made to a broad-based nonprofit Organization or nonprofit Organization of farm workers or a State or local public agency. New construction and/or rehabilitation projects, utilizing the Section 8 Program from HUD will not be considered eligible projects, although it may be used for eligible families in existing projects utilizing Section 8 for part of the units.

Beneficiary Eligibility: Any very low and low-income family, handicapped or senior citizen that is unable to pay the approved rental rate for an eligible RHS rental assistance unit within 30 percent of their adjusted monthly income. Households eligible for rental assistance are those 1) whose net tenant contribution to rent, determined in accordance with 3560.203 (a)(2), is less than the basic rent for the unit; 2) who meet the occupancy rules established by the borrower in accordance with 3560.155 (e); and 3) who have a signed, unexpired tenant certification form on file with the borrower. Additional eligibility requirements must be met for Section 514 Farm Labour Housing Program occupancy.

Award Range/Average: From 30 to 90 days from the time Form RD 3560-25, "Request for Rental Assistance is filed.

Funding: (Direct Payments for Specified Use) FY 17 $1,365,018,600.00; FY 18 est $1,395,000,000.00; FY 19 est $1,351,000,000.00

HQ: Multi-Family Housing Portfolio Management Division Rural Housing Service Department of Agriculture 1400 Independence Avenue SW, Washington, DC 20250

Phone: 202-720-9728 | Email: janet.stouder@wdc.usda.gov

http://www.rd.usda.gov

USDA10.415 | RURAL RENTAL HOUSING LOANS

Award: Project Grants; Direct Loans

Purpose: To provide rural residents with rental and housing related facilities.

Applicant Eligibility: Applicants may be individuals, cooperatives, nonprofit Organizations, State or local public agencies, profit corporations, trusts, partnerships, limited partnerships, and be unable to finance the housing either with their own resources or with credit obtained from private sources. However, applicants must be able to assume the obligations of the loan, furnish adequate security, and have sufficient income for repayment. They must also have the ability and intention of maintaining and operating the housing for purposes for which the loan is made. Loans may be made in communities up to 10,000 people in MSA areas and some communities up to 20,000 population in non- MSA areas. Applicants in towns of 10,000 to 20,000 should check with their local Rural Development; office to determine if the agency can serve them. Assistance is available to eligible applicants in States, Puerto Rico, the Virgin Islands, Guam, American Samoa, the Northern Mariana's, and the Trust Territory of the Pacific Islands.

Beneficiary Eligibility: Occupants must be very low-, low- or moderate-income families households, elderly, handicapped, or disabled persons.

Funding: (Direct Loans) FY 17 $33,204,553.00; FY 18 est $39,000,000.00; FY 19 est $0.00

HQ: Multi-Family Housing Direct Loan Division Rural Development, Washington, DC 20250

  Phone: 202-720-1604

  https://www.rd.usda.gov/programs-services/multi-family-housing-direct-loans

USDA10.420 | RURAL SELF-HELP HOUSING TECHNICAL ASSISTANCE
"Section 523 Technical Assistance"

Award: Project Grants

Purpose: The Self-help Technical Assistance Grants financial support to those with less income to construct homes with the self-help method and assistance to nonprofit organizations. Section 523 provides up to $10,000 for qualified organizations.

Applicant Eligibility: Must be a State or political subdivision, public nonprofit corporation or a private nonprofit corporation. Assistance is authorized for eligible applicants in the United States, Puerto Rico, Virgin Islands, Guam, and the Northern Marianas.

Beneficiary Eligibility: Very low and low-income rural families, usually in groups of 6 to 10 families.

Funding: (Project Grants) FY 17 $27,626,751.00; FY 18 est $29,000,000.00; FY 19 est $0.00

HQ: 1400 Independence Avenue SW, Washington, DC 20250

  Phone: 804-287-1559 | Email: myron.wooden@wdc.usda.gov

  http://www.rurdev.usda.gov

USDA10.851 | RURAL TELEPHONE LOANS AND LOAN GUARANTEES
"Telecommunications Infrastructure Loan Program"

Award: Direct Loans; Guaranteed/insured Loans

Purpose: To assist those in rural areas to have telecommunications services.

Applicant Eligibility: Telephone companies or cooperatives, nonprofit associations, limited dividend associations, mutual associations or public bodies including those located in the U.S. Territories and countries included in the Compact of Free Association Act of 1985, providing or proposing to provide telecommunications service to meet the needs of rural areas.

Beneficiary Eligibility: Residents and businesses of eligible rural areas.

Award Range/Average: Direct Loans - $2,183,000 to $13,659,000 Avg. $7,921,000 Guaranteed Loans - $2,183,000 to $20,360,000 Avg. $11,271,500

Funding: (Direct Loans) FY 18 $99,006,000.00; FY 19 est $345,000,000.00; FY 20 est $345,000,000.00; (Guaranteed/Insured Loans) FY 18 $62,932,000.00; FY 19 est $1,000,000.00; FY 20 est $100,000,000.00

HQ: 1400 Independence Avenue SW Room 5151, PO Box 1590, Washington, DC 20250

  Phone: 202-720-9554 | Email: chad.parker@wdc.usda.gov

  http://www.rd.usda.gov/programs-services/telecommunications-infrastructure-loans-loan-guarantees

Programs Administered by Federal Headquarters

HHS93.924 | RYAN WHITE HIV/AIDS DENTAL REIMBURSEMENT AND COMMUNITY BASED DENTAL PARTNERSHIP GRANTS

Award: Formula Grants; Project Grants

Purpose: The Dental Reimbursement Program partially compensates accredited dental schools, postdoctoral dental education programs, and dental hygiene education programs for unreimbursed costs they have incurred in providing oral health services to low income, uninsured, and underserved people living with HIV (PLWH). The Community Based Dental Partnership Program aims to improve access to oral healthcare services for low income, uninsured and underserved PLWH in underserved geographic areas.

Applicant Eligibility: Applicants are limited to accredited dental schools and other accredited dental education Programs such as dental hygiene Programs or those sponsored by a school of dentistry, a hospital, or a public or private institution that offers postdoctoral training in the specialties of dentistry, advanced education in general dentistry, or a dental general practice residency.

Beneficiary Eligibility: Low income, uninsured, and underserved people with HIV.

Award Range/Average: Dental Reimbursement: $6,195 to $ 1,545,922; Average $174,345. Community-Based Dental Partnership grants: $219,230 to $364,172; Average $289,939.

Funding: (Project Grants) FY 18 $3,475,672.00; FY 19 est $3,475,672.00; FY 20 $ $3,475,672.00; (Formula Grants) FY 18 $8,891,572.00; FY 19 est $8,977,802.00; FY 20 est $8,977,802

HQ: 5600 Fishers Lane, Room 09N09, Rockville, MD 20857
  Phone: 301-443-2075 | Email: mmofidi@hrsa.gov
  http://www.hrsa.gov

DOI15.441 | SAFETY AND ENVIRONMENTAL ENFORCEMENT RESEARCH AND DATA COLLECTION FOR OFFSHORE ENERGY AND MINERAL ACTIVITIES
"Office of Offshore Regulatory Programs (OORP)"

Award: Cooperative Agreements

Purpose: The Agency oversees the exploration and development of oil, natural gas and other materials and renewable energy alternatives on the Nation's outer continental shelf. Bureau of Safety and Environmental Enforcement continues to look for better ways to serve the American people and to ensure that the nation receives the best oversight and regulation of National resource development now and into the future. The purposes of the Office of Offshore Regulatory Program (OORP) is to obtain the information needed to improve the knowledge, practices, and technologies used to promote operational safety and pollution prevention for offshore oil and gas activities and alternate energy projects.

Applicant Eligibility: State agencies and public universities may apply. More than one institution may collaborate in the preparation of an application for assistance.

Beneficiary Eligibility: Research scientists, Federal, State and local decision-makers, and the general public will ultimately benefit from the program.

Award Range/Average: Range is $100,000 to $5,000,000; Average $350,000.

Funding: (Cooperative Agreements) FY 17 $501,000.00; FY 18 est Estimate Not Available; FY 19 est Estimate Not Available

HQ: 45600 Woodland Road, Sterling, VA 20164
  Phone: 703-787-1844 | Email: andre.king@bsee.gov
  http://www.bsee.gov

GSA39.007 | SALE OF FEDERAL SURPLUS PERSONAL PROPERTY
"Sales Program"

Award: Sale, Exchange, Or Donation of Property and Goods

Purpose: To sell personal property no longer needed by the Government in an expeditious, economical and efficient manner and to obtain the maximum net return from sales.

Applicant Eligibility: Competitive bid sales are open to the general public, however bidders must be at least 18 years of age. Individuals cannot successfully register to bid on items without providing a Taxpayer Identification Number (TIN). A TIN is defined as an individual's Social Security Number (SSN) or business entity's Employer Identification Number (EIN).

Beneficiary Eligibility: General public.

Funding: (Salaries and Expenses) FY 16 $8,984,591.00; FY 17 est $9,154,565.00; FY 18 est Estimate Not Available

HQ: 1800 F Street NW, Washington, DC 20405
Phone: 202-501-1700 | Email: sunny.kwa@gsa.gov
http://www.govsales.gov

SBA59.069 | SBA EMERGING LEADERS INITIATIVE
"Emerging Leaders"

Award: Direct Payments for Specified Use
Purpose: Provides executives with the organizational framework and resources to build sustainable businesses and support economic development within underserved communities.
Applicant Eligibility: Existing small business owners that meet criteria, this training is for established business owners and is not for start-ups or people who are thinking about starting a business. The Emerging Leaders Initiative advanced training series is open to small business owners and executives that: Have annual revenues of at least $400,000Have been in business for at least 3 years Have at least one employee, other than self.
Beneficiary Eligibility: Existing small business owners.

HHS93.261 | SCALING THE NATIONAL DIABETES PREVENTION PROGRAM TO PRIORITY POPULATIONS
"National Diabetes Prevention Program"

Award: Cooperative Agreements
Purpose: To scale (expand) and sustain the National Diabetes Prevention Program (National DPP).
Applicant Eligibility: Nonprofit Organizations; For-Profit Organizations; Indian/Native American Tribal Governments; Faith-based Organizations.
Beneficiary Eligibility: Any U.S. state, political subdivision and U.S. territories (as described above), and other public entities will benefit.
Award Range/Average: $750,000 - $ 2 million
Funding: (Cooperative Agreements) FY 18 $14,165,143.00; FY 19 est $14,165,143.00; FY 20 est $14,165,143.00
HQ: 4770 Buford Highway NE, PO Box K75, Atlanta, GA 30341
Phone: 404-498-5759
http://www.cdc.gov/diabetes/prevention

HHS93.925 | SCHOLARSHIPS FOR HEALTH PROFESSIONS STUDENTS FROM DISADVANTAGED BACKGROUNDS
"Scholarships for Disadvantaged Students (SDS)"

Award: Project Grants
Purpose: The SDS program promotes service in primary care and in medically underserved communities by providing grants to eligible health professions and nursing schools for use in awarding scholarships to students from disadvantaged backgrounds who have financial need for such scholarships.
Applicant Eligibility: Accredited public or non-profit private schools of medicine, nursing, osteopathic medicine, dentistry, pharmacy, podiatric medicine, optometry, veterinary medicine, chiropractic, allied health, public health, a school offering a graduate Program in behavioral and mental health practice, or an entity providing Programs for the training of physician assistants. 1) At least 20 percent of the total enrollment (full-time enrolled) of a Program during the specified academic year must be students from disadvantaged backgrounds; and2) At least 20 percent of the total graduates (who were full-time students) of a Program during the specified academic year must have been from disadvantaged backgrounds. Faith-based and community-based Organizations, Federally Recognized Indian Tribal Government and Native American Organizations are eligible to apply if all other eligibility requirements are met.
Beneficiary Eligibility: Students who are citizens, nationals, or lawful permanent residents of the United States or the District of Columbia, the Commonwealths of Puerto Rico or the Northern Mariana Islands, the U.S. Virgin Islands, Guam, the American Samoa, the Republic of Palau, the Republic of the Marshall Islands, the Federated States of Micronesia; and enrolled full-time in health professions or nursing schools. A student who is in this country on a student or visitor's visa is not eligible.
Award Range/Average: Range: FY 2016: $28,000 to $650,000; Average $546,428.Range FY 2017: $26,615 to $617,837;Average $545,828.Range FY est 2018: $28,000 to $650,000;Average est $578,812.

Programs Administered by Federal Headquarters

Funding: (Project Grants) FY 18 $45,726,127.00; FY 19 est $45,354,203.00; FY 20 est $0.00
HQ: Bureau of Health Workforce 5600 Fishers Lane, Room 15N78, Rockville, MD 20857
  Phone: 301-443-1173 | Email: dsorrell@hrsa.gov
  http://bhw.hrsa.gov/loansscholarships/schoolbasedloans

USDA10.524 | SCHOLARSHIPS FOR STUDENTS AT 1890 INSTITUTIONS
"1890 Scholarships"

Award: Project Grants (discretionary)
Purpose: To provide scholarships for deserving students at all the 1890 Land-Grant Institutions and Tuskegee University.
Applicant Eligibility: Applications may only be submitted by 1890 Land-grant Institutions and Tuskegee University. Alabama A&M University Alcorn State University Central State University Delaware State University Florida A&M University Fort Valley State University Kentucky State University Langston University Lincoln University (MO)North Carolina A&T State University Prairie View A&M University South Carolina State University Southern University and A&M College Tennessee State University Tuskegee University of Arkansas-Pine Bluff University of Maryland-Eastern Shore Virginia State University West Virginia State University.
Beneficiary Eligibility: N/A
Award Range/Average: If minimum or maximum amounts of funding per competitive and/or capacity project grant, or cooperative agreement are established, these amounts will be announced in the annual Request for Applications (RFA). The most current RFA is available via: https://nifa.usda.gov/funding-opportunity/scholarships-students-1890-institutions
Funding: (Project Grants (Discretionary)) FY 18 $0; FY 19 est $0; FY 20 est $$9,600,000.00
HQ: 1400 Independence Avenue SW, PO Box 2201, Washington, DC 20250-2201
  Phone: 202-720-0742 | Email: antonio.a.mclaren@nifa.usda.gov

USDA10.532 | SCHOOL NUTRITION TRAINING GRANT FOR ALLIED PROFESSIONAL ORGANIZATIONS

Award: Project Grants (special)
Purpose: Guides associated professional organizations in planning, designing, supporting, and assessing a workforce development and training initiative to provide skills-based training and technical aid to school nutrition experts to enhance the skills and expertise of school meal program operators in school nutrition activities.
Applicant Eligibility: Competition for this grant is open to all national allied professional Organizations operating in the United States to which school nutrition professionals are eligible to join as a member, which provides membership representation for school nutrition professionals, and whose mission seeks to further the school nutrition field and the interests of school nutrition professionals. Applicants must clearly describe how their Organization (s) meets the definition of allied professional Organization, as stated above, and submit Organization bylaws which clearly define the scope of members. All non-profit Organizations must include their 501(c)(3) or 501(c)(4) determination letter issued by the Internal Revenue Service (IRS).
Beneficiary Eligibility: Grant funds will ultimately benefit school food service program staff, school nutrition personnel, school nutrition professionals, school nutrition employees, school nutrition directors, school nutrition managers/supervisors, front-line staff through a job-skills and workforce development training.
Award Range/Average: Under this grant opportunity, one award of up to $2 million is competitively available to eligible entities.
Funding: (Project Grants (Special)) FY 17 $0; FY 18 est $0; FY 19 est $2,000,000.00
HQ: 3101 Park Center Drive, Room 628, Alexandria, VA 22302
  Phone: 703-305-2590 | Email: cindy.long@fns.usda.gov

ED84.184 | SCHOOL SAFETY NATIONAL ACTIVITIES (FORMERLY, SAFE AND DRUG-FREE SCHOOLS AND COMMUNITIES-NATIONAL PROGRAMS)

Award: Project Grants
Purpose: To improve safety and well-being for students during and after the school day.
Applicant Eligibility: Public and private entities, and individuals.
Beneficiary Eligibility: State educational agencies, local educational agencies, institutions of higher education, public and private organizations and institutions will benefit.
Funding: (Project Grants) FY 18 $90,000,000.00; FY 19 est $95,000,000.00; FY 20 est $95,000,000.00

HQ: 400 Maryland Avenue SW, Room 3E330 LBJ Building, Washington, DC 20202
Phone: 202-453-6727 | Email: paul.kesner@ed.gov
http://www2.ed.gov/about/offices/list/oese/oshs/index.html

DOC11.620 | SCIENCE, TECHNOLOGY, BUSINESS AND/OR EDUCATION OUTREACH

Award: Cooperative Agreements

Purpose: To assist in the efforts innovative approaches and various methods of development measures of NIST research. It also supports small businesses and other research programs.

Applicant Eligibility: Public and private Institutions of higher education, public and private hospitals, and other quasi-public and private non-profit Organizations such as, but not limited to, community action agencies, research institutes, educational associations, and health centers. The term may include commercial Organizations, foreign or international Organizations (such as agencies of the United Nations) which are recipients, subrecipients, or contractors or subcontractors of recipients or subrecipients at the discretion of the DoC. The term does not include government-owned contractor-operated facilities or research centers providing continued support for mission-oriented, large-scale Programs that are government-owned or controlled, or are designated as federally-funded research and development centers.

Beneficiary Eligibility: Public and private institutions of higher education, public and private hospitals, and other quasi-public and private non-profit organizations such as, but not limited to, community action agencies, research institutes, educational associations, and health centers. The term may include commercial organizations, foreign or international organizations (such as agencies of the United Nations) which are recipients, subrecipients, or contractors or subcontractors of recipients or subrecipients at the discretion of the DoC. The term does not include government-owned contractor-operated facilities or research centers providing continued support for mission-oriented, large-scale programs that are government-owned or controlled, or are designated as federally-funded research and development centers. Institutions of research and/or education, professional institutes and associations, non-profit organizations, state and local governments, and commercial organizations.

Award Range/Average: Dependent upon nature and type of grant

Funding: (Cooperative Agreements) FY 18 $32,008,610.00; FY 19 est $33,449,247.00; FY 20 est $34,100,000.00

HQ: 100 Bureau Drive, PO Box 1090, Gaithersburg, MD 20899
Phone: 301-975-2371 | Email: brandi.toliver@nist.gov
http://www.nist.gov

DOD12.330 | SCIENCE, TECHNOLOGY, ENGINEERING & MATHEMATICS (STEM) EDUCATION, OUTREACH AND WORKFORCE PROGRAM

Award: Cooperative Agreements; Project Grants

Purpose: To offer support to educational programs in Science, Technology, Engineering and Mathematics (STEM) Education, Outreach and Workforce Program.

Applicant Eligibility: All responsible sources from public nonprofit Institutions /Organizations to include elementary, middle and high schools, private non-profit Institutions /Organizations, small businesses, profit Organizations, and other private Institutions /Organizations may submit proposals. Grants cannot be awarded to individuals.

Beneficiary Eligibility: Black Colleges and Universities (HBCUs), and Minority Institutions (MIs).

Award Range/Average: $200,000 - $1,000,000

Funding: (Project Grants) FY 18 $6,195,009.00; FY 19 est $8,000,000.00; FY 20 est $8,575,000.00

HQ: 875 N Randolph Street, Arlington, VA 22203
Phone: 703-696-4601 | Email: susan.sutherland@navy.mil
http://www.onr.navy.mil

DOD12.631 | SCIENCE, TECHNOLOGY, ENGINEERING AND MATHEMATICS (STEM) EDUCATIONAL PROGRAM: SCIENCE, MATHEMATICS AND RESEARCH FOR TRANSFORMATION (SMART)
"STEM"

Award: Cooperative Agreements; Project Grants

Purpose: To increase the intellectual capacity and proficiency of future scientists and engineers in disciplines critical to defense.

Programs Administered by Federal Headquarters

Applicant Eligibility: Subject to language in any announcement for competitive procedures.

Beneficiary Eligibility: All applicants for scholarships must be at least 18 years of age and U.S. citizens. Applicants must be an undergraduate or graduate student majoring in a DoD-relevant STEM field. Applicants participate in internships at DoD laboratories. Participants will be required to obtain and/or maintain a security clearance. Upon completion of their degree, applicants are expected to work full-time for the DoD.

Award Range/Average: See above.

Funding: (Project Grants) FY 17 $30,000,000.00; FY 18 est $35,000,000.00; FY 19 est $30,419,552.00

HQ: 800 Park Office Drive, Suite 4229, Research Triangle Park, NC 27709

  Phone: 919-549-4338 | Email: andrew.l.fiske.civ@mail.mil

NASA43.001 | SCIENCE

Award: Cooperative Agreements; Project Grants; Direct Payments for Specified Use; Use of Property, Facilities, and Equipment; Training

Purpose: To offer basic research, educational outreach, or training opportunities in the area of science.

Applicant Eligibility: Basic Research, educational Outreach, or Training Opportunities in the area of Science. Science funds (Treasury Account Symbol = 80 0120) will be used to fund NASA Federal Financial Assistance awards. Review funding opportunity for specific eligibility requirements.

Beneficiary Eligibility: Basic Research, Educational Outreach, or Training Opportunities in the area of Science. Science funds (Treasury Account Symbol = 800120) will be used to fund NASA Federal Financial Assistance awards with institutions of higher education and/or other non-profit entities.

Funding: (Cooperative Agreements (Discretionary Grants)) FY 18 $518,461,297.31.00; FY 19 est $642,085,168.68.00; FY 20 est Estimate Not Available

HQ: 300 E Street SW, Washington, DC 20546

  Phone: 202-358-0879 | Email: max.bernstein@nasa.gov

  http://www.nasa.gov

USDA10.961 | SCIENTIFIC COOPERATION AND RESEARCH
"SCRP"

Award: Cooperative Agreements; Direct Payments for Specified Use

Purpose: To leverage resources to advance cooperative research extension in agriculture.

Applicant Eligibility: Institutions of higher education in the United States, including state cooperative Institutions.

Beneficiary Eligibility: Beneficiaries will be specified in the Notice of Funding Opportunities, and are generally nationals of an eligible beneficiary country.

Award Range/Average: Research projects up to 24 months. Individual projects may not exceed $50,000 of program funding.

Funding: (Cooperative Agreements) FY 18 $0.00; FY 19 est $493,910.00; FY 20 est $500,000.00

HQ: 1400 Independence Avenue SW, Washington, DC 20250

  Phone: 202-720-4228 | Email: nicola.sakhleh@usda.gov

  https://www.fas.usda.gov/programs/scientific-cooperation-research-program

USDA10.614 | SCIENTIFIC COOPERATION EXCHANGE PROGRAM WITH CHINA
"SCEP"

Award: Project Grants; Direct Payments for Specified Use

Purpose: To encourage agricultural research between the United States and China through mutual cooperation.

Applicant Eligibility: U.S. Institutions of higher-learning, and public and private nonprofit Organizations whose primary purpose is agriculture, natural resources management and/or rural development (including those located in U.S. territories).

Beneficiary Eligibility: U.S. institutions from the public, private, and academia sectors.

Award Range/Average: Exchange visits last approximately two weeks. Average cost per participant is $8,000.

Funding: (Project Grants (Cooperative Agreements or Contracts)) FY 18 $216,896.00; FY 19 est $0.00; FY 20 est $0.00

HQ: 1400 Independence Avenue SW, Washington, DC 20250-1031

  Phone: 202-720-4228 | Email: nicola.sakhleh@usda.gov

  https://www.fas.usda.gov/programs/scientific-cooperation-exchange-program

DHS97.062 | SCIENTIFIC LEADERSHIP AWARDS

Award: Project Grants; Direct Payments for Specified Use

Purpose: The program helps attract highly talented students and other professionals such as scholars and fellows to work on emerging areas of science and technology that is of high importance to the homeland security.

Applicant Eligibility: US accredited MSIs are eligible to apply. Student recipients must be U.S. citizens studying in one of the following areas including: computer science, engineering, life sciences, math, physical sciences, psychology, social sciences, Students must have career and employment goals aligned with the mission and objectives of the U.S. Department of Homeland Security.

Beneficiary Eligibility: Undergraduate Student, Graduate Student, and Minority Serving Institution Faculty.

Award Range/Average: Refer to program guidance.

Funding: (Project Grants) FY 18 $3,396,347.00; FY 19 est $3,396,438.00; FY 20 est $3,396,438.00

HQ: Office of University Programs S and T 245 Murray Lane Building 410, PO Box 0217, Washington, DC 20523

Phone: 202-254-5631

http://www.hsuniversityprograms.org

DOD12.351 | SCIENTIFIC RESEARCH-COMBATING WEAPONS OF MASS DESTRUCTION

Award: Cooperative Agreements; Project Grants

Purpose: To support and stimulate basic, applied and advanced research at educational or research institutions, non-profit organizations, and commercial firms.

Applicant Eligibility: As stated in individual Program BAAs. Generally, competitions are open to private and public educational accredited Institutions of higher education that carry out science and engineering research and/or related science and engineering education on a non-profit basis. Some awards are made to other non-profit and for profit Organizations that conduct research. Awards are not made to individuals.

Beneficiary Eligibility: N/A

Award Range/Average: Range from $100,000 per year to $1,000,000 per year over a 5-year period.

Funding: (Project Grants) FY 18 $68,070,710.00; FY 19 est $62,467,600.00; FY 20 est $63,249,100.00

HQ: 8725 John J Kingman Road, Fort Belvoir, VA 22060

Phone: 571-616-6159 | Email: mary.k.chase2.civ@mail.mil

SBA59.026 | SCORE

Award: Project Grants

Purpose: To use the management experience of retired and active business professionals to counsel and train potential and existing small business owners.

Applicant Eligibility: All existing and potential small business owners are eligible. The business must be independently owned and operated, not dominant in its field, and must conform to SBA size standards.

Beneficiary Eligibility: Current and potential small business persons.

Award Range/Average: FY 15 $8,000,000 FY 16 $10,500,000 FY 17 $10,300,000

Funding: (Project Grants) FY 17 $10,500,000.00; FY 18 est $10,500,000.00; FY 19 est $9,900,000.00

HQ: 409 3rd Street SW, 6th Floor, Washington, DC 20416

Phone: 202-205-7007 | Email: nvbishop@sba.gov

http://www.sba.gov

DOC11.417 | SEA GRANT SUPPORT

Award: Project Grants

Purpose: To assist major university centers for marine resources research, education, and training and to support marine advisory services.

Applicant Eligibility: Universities, colleges, junior colleges, technical schools, institutes, laboratories; any public or private corporation, partnership, or other association or entity; any State, political subdivision of a State or agency or officer thereof; any individual.

Beneficiary Eligibility: Organizations and individuals with professional interest in marine affairs.

Funding: (Project Grants) FY 16 $72,492,871.00; FY 17 est $74,789,001.00; FY 18 est $0.00

Programs Administered by Federal Headquarters

HQ: 1315 E W Highway, Silver Spring, MD 20910
   Phone: 301-713-2448
   http://www.noaa.gov

DOJ16.812 | SECOND CHANCE ACT REENTRY INITIATIVE
"SCA"

Award: Cooperative Agreements; Project Grants
Purpose: To compensate for the programs that assist those individuals from prison to the community is successful.
Applicant Eligibility: See current solicitation at the Office of Justice Programs website http://ojp.gov/funding/Explore/CurrentFundingOpportunities. htm.
Beneficiary Eligibility: N/A
Award Range/Average: Varies, see solicitation guidelines posted on the Office of Justice Programs web site at http://www.ojp.gov/funding/solicitations.htm or www.bja.gov.
Funding: (Cooperative Agreements) FY 18 $69,005,755.00; FY 19 est $87,500,000.00; FY 20 est $85,000,000.00
HQ: Bureau of Justice Assistance 810 7th Street NW, Washington, DC 20531
   Phone: 202-616-6500
   http://www.bja.gov

USDA10.226 | SECONDARY AND TWO-YEAR POSTSECONDARY AGRICULTURE EDUCATION CHALLENGE GRANTS
"SPECA Grants Program"

Award: Project Grants
Purpose: To encourage agricultural education for the students to promote agribusiness and agriscience.
Applicant Eligibility: Public secondary schools or public or private nonprofit junior and community colleges.
Beneficiary Eligibility: Same as Applicant Eligibility.
Award Range/Average: If minimum or maximum amounts of funding per competitive and/or capacity project grant, or cooperative agreement are established, these amounts will be announced in the annual Competitive Request for Application (RFA).The most current RFA is available via: https://nifa.usda.gov/funding-opportunity/secondary-education-two-year-postsecondary-education-and-agriculture-k-12
Funding: (Project Grants) FY 18 $858,600.00; FY 19 est $857,250.00; FY 20 est $0.00
HQ: National Program Leader Institute of Youth Family and Community Division of Community and Education 1400 Independence Avenue SW, PO Box 2250, Washington, DC 20250-2250
   Phone: 202-720-2324
   http://nifa.usda.gov/program/secondary-education-two-year-postsecondary-education-and-agriculture-k-12-classroom

HUD14.252 | SECTION 4 CAPACITY BUILDING FOR COMMUNITY DEVELOPMENT AND AFFORDABLE HOUSING
"Section 4 Capacity Building"

Award: Project Grants
Purpose: To build the capacity of Community Development Corporations (CDCs) and Community Housing Development Organizations (CHDOs) to serve their communities and low- and moderate-income families.
Applicant Eligibility: By law, there are only three eligible applicants for the Section 4 Program. The competition is limited to the Organizations identified in Section 4 of the HUD Demonstration Act of 1993 (Pub. L. 103-120, 107 Stat. 1148, 42 U.S.C. 9816 note), as amended. These Organizations are: 1. Enterprise Community Partners, Inc. (formerly The Enterprise Foundation); 2. the Local Initiatives Support Corporation (LISC), and 3. Habitat for Humanity International. Specifically, the only applicants eligible for this competition are the three Organizations located at the following addresses: 1. Enterprise Community Partners, Inc., 11000 Broken Land Parkway, Suite 700, Columbia, MD 21044. 2. Local Initiatives Support Corporation, 501 Seventh Avenue, 7th Floor, New York, NY 10018 3. Habitat for Humanity International, 121 Habitat Street, Americus, GA 31709. Affiliates and local offices of these Organizations and their community partners are not eligible to compete either directly or independently for capacity building grants under this notice, but rather may seek funding from the above Organizations.

Beneficiary Eligibility: Community Development Corporations (CDCs) and Community Housing Development Organizations (CHDOs) are the only eligible beneficiaries.

Award Range/Average: There have been three grant awards made each fiscal year ranging from $5 million to $15 million over the past three years.

Funding: (Project Grants) FY 18 $35,000,000.00; FY 19 est $35,000,000.00; FY 20 est $35,000,000.00

HQ: 451 7th Street SW, Washington, DC 20410

Phone: 202-402-4385 | Email: diane.m.schmutzler@hud.gov

http://www.hudexchange.info/programs/section-4-capacity-building

USDA10.438 | SECTION 538 RURAL RENTAL HOUSING GUARANTEED LOANS

Award: Guaranteed/insured Loans

Purpose: To support by providing loans for multifamily housing in rural areas.

Applicant Eligibility: The applicant in this Program is the lender. The lender must be approved and currently active with Fannie Mae, Freddie Mac, HUD/FHA insurance Programs, Ginnie Mae or be a State or local Housing Finance Agency. A member of the Federal Home Loan Bank System or other lender may be able to participate if they can demonstrate satisfactory experience with multifamily lending.

Beneficiary Eligibility: Occupants must be families or persons with income not in excess of 115 percent of the Median Income at the time of initial occupancy.

Award Range/Average: Not Applicable.

Funding: (Guaranteed/Insured Loans) FY 18 $185,639,985.00; FY 19 est $230,000,000.00; FY 20 $250,000,000.00

HQ: 1400 Independence Avenue SW, Washington, DC 20250

Phone: 202-720-1604

http://www.rd.usda.gov

HUD14.195 | SECTION 8 HOUSING ASSISTANCE PAYMENTS PROGRAM
"Project-based Section 8"

Award: Direct Payments for Specified Use

Purpose: To provide rental aid to very low income individuals and families helping them live in low-cost, decent, safe, and sanitary housing.

Applicant Eligibility: No funding is available to new applicants. Funding is currently available only for the owners of record of projects with an existing expiring project-based Section 8 contract. The project must meet minimum decent, safe, and sanitary standards.

Beneficiary Eligibility: Families currently receiving assistance as long as their income does not exceed 80 percent of area median income adjusted for smaller or larger families.

Award Range/Average: Eligible tenants pay no more than 30 percent of their monthly adjusted income for rent.

Funding: (Direct Payments for Specified Use) FY 15 $9,537,000,000.00; FY 16 est $10,393,000,000.00; FY 17 est $10,707,000,000.00

HQ: 451 7th Street SW, Washington, DC 20410

Phone: 202-402-6732 | Email: catherine.m.brennan@hud.gov

http://portal.hud.gov/hudportal/HUD?src=/program_offices/housing/mfh/mfhsec8

HUD14.871 | SECTION 8 HOUSING CHOICE VOUCHERS

Award: Direct Payments for Specified Use

Purpose: Aiding very low-income families in obtaining decent, safe, and sanitary rental housing.

Applicant Eligibility: Applicants are limited to public housing agencies. A public housing agency (PHA) is defined as any State, county, municipality or other governmental entity or public body (or agency or instrumentality thereof) which is authorized to engage in or assist in the development or operation of housing for very low income families; and, a consortium of PHAs; any other nonprofit entity that was administering a Section 8 tenant-based Program on October 21, 1998; or, for an area outside the jurisdiction of a PHA administering a voucher Program, a private nonprofit entity or a governmental entity or public body that would otherwise lack jurisdiction to administer the Program in such area.

Beneficiary Eligibility: Very low income families (whose income does not exceed 50 percent of the median income for the area as determined by the Secretary with adjustments for smaller and larger families) and, on an exception basis, lower income families (whose income does not exceed 80 percent of the median income for the area, adjusted for smaller and larger families). At least 75 percent of families admitted to the voucher program during the PHA fiscal year must be extremely low income families (whose income does not exceed 30 percent of the median income for the area).

Award Range/Average: $5,618 to $1,074,563,247 average of 7,142,148

Funding: (Direct Payments for Specified Use) FY 17 $16,740,888,987.00; FY 18 est $17,211,712,441.00; FY 19 est $16,425,500,023.00

HQ: 451 7th Street SW, Washington, DC 20410
  Phone: 202-402-6050 | Email: becky.l.primeaux@hud.gov

HUD14.249 | SECTION 8 MODERATE REHABILITATION SINGLE ROOM OCCUPANCY

Award: Project Grants

Purpose: To provide rental assistance to homeless individuals.

Applicant Eligibility: An eligible applicant is a PHA or private nonprofit Organization. Private nonprofits have to contract with a PHA to administer the rental assistance.

Beneficiary Eligibility: Homeless individuals.

HQ: Office of Special Needs Assistance Programs 400 Maryland Avenue SW 451 7th Street SW, Room 7266, Washington, DC 20410
  Phone: 202-402-4080 | Email: brian.p.fitzmaurice@hud.gov
  http://www.hudexchange.info/sro

DHS97.106 | SECURING THE CITIES PROGRAM
"STC"

Award: Cooperative Agreements; Use of Property, Facilities, and Equipment; Dissemination of Technical Information

Purpose: The program seeks to prevent the smuggling of nuclear and radiological components and weaponry into the country by enhancing the nuclear detection capabilities of the local, State and Federal territorial agencies.

Applicant Eligibility: Specific information on applicant eligibility is identified in the funding opportunity announcement and Program guidance, or as specified by U.S. Appropriation Statute.

Beneficiary Eligibility: State, and local governments, Interstate or intrastate governmental organizations, and Indian tribal governments.

Award Range/Average: See Program Guidance.

Funding: (Cooperative Agreements (Discretionary Grants)) FY 18 $18,974,000.00; FY 19 est $30,000,000.00; FY 20 est $22,000,000.00

HQ: DNDO 245 Murray Lane, PO Box 0550, Washington, DC 20528
  Phone: 202-254-7223 | Email: kimberly.patten@hq.dhs.gov
  http://www.dhs.gov

HUD14.247 | SELF-HELP HOMEOWNERSHIP OPPORTUNITY PROGRAM
"SHOP"

Award: Project Grants

Purpose: To assist and support innovative home-ownership opportunities through the provision of self-help home-ownership.

Applicant Eligibility: Funds are awarded competitively to national or regional nonprofit Organizations or consortia that have capacity and experience in providing or facilitating self-help housing homeownership opportunities. Grantees must use a significant amount of SHOP grant funds in at least two states. Grantees may award grant funds to local non-profit affiliate Organizations.

Beneficiary Eligibility: Eligible homebuyers are low-income families, (including individuals) who are otherwise unable to afford to purchase a dwelling, and who provide significant amounts of sweat equity towards the development of the dwellings.

Award Range/Average: Four grants were awarded with FY 2018 funds. They ranged from $1,104,723 to 5,187,271. The average grant was $2,500,000.

Funding: (Project Grants) FY 18 $30,000,000.00; FY 19 est $20,000,000.00; FY 20 est Estimate Not Available; (Project Grants (for specified projects)) FY 18 $10,000,000.00; FY 19 est $10,000,000.00; FY 20 est $10,000,000.00

HQ: 451 7Th Street SW, Washington, DC 20410
  Phone: 202-402-4464 | Email: thann.young@hud.gov
  www.hud.gov/offices/cpd/affordablehousing/programs/shop/index.cfm

CNCS94.012 | SEPTEMBER 11TH NATIONAL DAY OF SERVICE AND REMEMBRANCE GRANTS
"September 11th Grants"

Award: Project Grants

Purpose: The September 11th National Day of Service and Remembrance Grants program engages Americans to serve actively for their community and also honor the brave hearts who sacrificed their lives on September 11, 2001.

Applicant Eligibility: See Program's Notice of Funding Opportunity.

Beneficiary Eligibility: Same as Applicant Eligibility.

Award Range/Average: See program's Notice of Funding Opportunity for matching information.

Funding: (Project Grants) FY 16 Actual Not Available; FY 17 est $463,934.00; FY 18 est Estimate Not Available

HQ: 250 E Street SW, Washington, DC 20525

    Phone: 202-606-6745 | Email: pstengel@cns.gov

    http://www.nationalservice.gov/911day

DOJ16.320 | SERVICES FOR TRAFFICKING VICTIMS

Award: Project Grants; Direct Payments for Specified Use

Purpose: To provide comprehensive and specialized services to victims of human trafficking; to develop multidisciplinary task forces with federal, state, and local law enforcement, service providers, and community- and faith-based organizations to ensure that trafficking victims are identified and referred for appropriate services; to conduct training, technical assistance and public awareness activities for professionals and community members in order to improve their knowledge of human trafficking and their ability to identify and respond to victims; and to conduct data collection and evaluation activities to determine if the program is meeting stated goals and objectives.

Applicant Eligibility: The Attorney General may make grants to States, Indian Tribes, units of local government, and nonprofit, non- governmental victim service Organizations.

Beneficiary Eligibility: Eligible victim assistance agencies. Eligibility depends on the nature of they may vary depending on specific grant types but generally includes victims and potential victims of human trafficking, as defined in TVPA, but may include a wide variety of public and private nonprofit agencies.

Award Range/Average: OJP anticipates awarding grants of up to $925,000 (depending on the program) for 3 years to support enhanced services to trafficking victims, training and technical assistance, and research and evaluation.

Funding: (Project Grants) FY 18 $62,942,886.00; FY 19 est $85,000,000.00; FY 20 est $850,000,000.00

HQ: Office of Victims of Crime Department of Justice Office of Justice Programs Office of Victims of Crime 810 7th Street NW, Washington, DC 20531

    Phone: 202-305-2601 | Email: zoe.french@usdoj.gov

    http://www.ovc.gov

HHS93.598 | SERVICES TO VICTIMS OF A SEVERE FORM OF TRAFFICKING

Award: Project Grants; Direct Payments for Specified Use

Purpose: Provides outreach to, identification of, and service referrals to individuals who may be victims of a severe form of trafficking. To provide comprehensive case management services to alien victims of a severe form of trafficking.

Applicant Eligibility: Eligible Organizations includes: state Governments, Tribes, units of local government, and non-profit, non-governmental victim service Organizations. Victim service Organizations include those who by nature of their current operations serve victims of sexual assault, sexual violence, domestic violence, human trafficking, and youth homelessness. Victim services Organizations may also include faith-based Organizations that are addressing human trafficking in their services. Individuals (including sole proprietorship's) and foreign entities are not eligible.

Beneficiary Eligibility: Under the TVPA, as amended, alien victims of a severe form of trafficking in persons are eligible for benefits and services to the same extent as refugees. Beneficiaries are adult alien victims of a severe form of trafficking who have been certified by the Department of Health and Human Services (HHS)/OTIP. Alien children under 18 years of age subjected to a severe form of trafficking who have received letters of eligibility from HHS/OTIP are considered eligible for services. Certain family members of victims of a severe form of trafficking are eligible for federally funded or administered benefits and services to the same extent as refugees if they hold "derivative T visas" (T-2, T-3, T-4, or T-5 visa). Potential victims of trafficking are also eligible for assistance through discretionary grant programs.

Award Range/Average: In FY 2018, grants ranged from $90,000 per budget period to $3,750,000 per budget period. The average grant amount was $490,605.

Programs Administered by Federal Headquarters

Funding: (Project Grants) FY 18 $11,925,000.00; FY 19 est $13,740,000.00; FY 20 est $15,490,000.00; (Salaries and Expenses) FY 18 $380,000.00; FY 19 est $400,000.00; FY 20 est $400,000.00
HQ: 330 C Street SW, 4th Floor, Washington, DC 20201
Phone: 202-401-9372 | Email: katherine.chon@acf.hhs.gov
https://www.acf.hhs.gov/otip

DHS97.110 | SEVERE REPETITIVE LOSS PROGRAM
"SRL"

Award: Project Grants
Purpose: It assists local and State governments to help reduce the long-term risk of flood damage to insured properties by removing such structures from flood hazard areas in the shortest time possible.
Applicant Eligibility: Entities eligible to apply for SRL grants include the emergency management agency (EMA) or a similar office of the 50 States, the District of Columbia, American Samoa, Guam, the U.S. Virgin Islands, Puerto Rico, the Northern Mariana Islands, and Federally recognized Indian Tribal Governments. Each State, Territory, Commonwealth, or Federally recognized Indian Tribal government shall designate one agency to serve as the Applicant for each FMA Program. Please see the HMA Program guidance for more detailed information.
Beneficiary Eligibility: State agencies, (other than EMA) Indian Tribal governments (non-federally recognized), and local governments and communities are eligible to apply as sub applicants for assistance under the SRL program. All interested sub applicants must apply to their Applicant State/tribe/territory. Subapplicants (and Applicants) may submit applications on behalf of homeowners and property owners. Please see the HMA program guidance for detailed information.
Award Range/Average: Refer to HMA program guidance document.
HQ: 400 C Street SW, Washington, DC 20472
Phone: 202-646-3458 | Email: kayed.lakhia@fema.dhs.gov

DOJ16.023 | SEXUAL ASSAULT SERVICES CULTURALLY SPECIFIC PROGRAM
"SAS Culturally Specific Program"

Award: Project Grants
Purpose: To increase culturally specific intervention, advocacy, accompaniment, support services, and related assistance for victims of sexual assault; family and household members of such victims; and those collaterally affected by the victimization, except for the perpetrator of such victimization.
Applicant Eligibility: Eligible entities for this Program are private nonprofit Organizations for which the primary purpose of the Organization as a whole is to provide culturally specific services to one or more of the following racial and ethnic communities: American Indians (including Alaska Natives, Eskimos, and Aleuts); Asian Americans; Native Hawaiians and other Pacific Islanders; Blacks; and Hispanics.
Beneficiary Eligibility: Beneficiaries are adult, youth, and child victims of sexual assault, family and household members of such victims, and those collaterally affected by the victimization, except the perpetrator.
Award Range/Average: up to $300,000
Funding: (Project Grants) FY 16 $3,463,319.00; FY 17 est $3,600,000.00; FY 18 est $3,500,000.00
HQ: 145 N Street NE, Suite 10W121, Washington, DC 20530
Phone: 202-305-1177 | Email: tia.farmer@usdoj.gov
http://www.justice.gov/ovw

DOJ16.017 | SEXUAL ASSAULT SERVICES FORMULA PROGRAM

Award: Formula Grants
Purpose: To increase intervention, advocacy, accompaniment, support services, and related assistance for adult, youth and child victims of sexual assault.
Applicant Eligibility: Eligible applicants are States and territories.
Beneficiary Eligibility: Beneficiaries are rape crisis centers and other nonprofit, nongovernmental organizations or tribal programs and activities.
Award Range/Average: Range: $12,678 - $437,011
Funding: (Formula Grants) FY 16 $22,750,000.00; FY 17 est $22,750,000.00; FY 18 est $22,750,000.00
HQ: 145 N Street NE, Suite 121, Washington, DC 20530
Phone: 202-305-1177 | Email: tia.farmer@usdoj.gov
http://www.justice.gov/ovw

HHS93.060 | SEXUAL RISK AVOIDANCE EDUCATION
"SRAE"

Award: Project Grants
Purpose: To promote sexual risk avoidance education, as defined by section 1110 of the Social Security Act, for adolescents.
Applicant Eligibility: Grants made under the authority of section 1110 of the Social Security Act, 42 U.S.C. 1310 grants shall be made only to public and private entities that agree to use medically accurate information referenced to peer-reviewed publications by educational, scientific, governmental, or health Organizations; implement an evidence-based approach integrating research findings with practical implementation that aligns with the needs and desired outcomes for the intended audience; and teach the benefits associated with self-regulation, success sequencing for poverty prevention, healthy relationships, goal setting, and resisting sexual coercion, dating violence, and other youth risk behaviors such as underage drinking or illicit drug use without normalizing teen sexual activity.
Beneficiary Eligibility: Vulnerable populations of youth with a focus on those that are most likely to bear children out-of-wedlock or who live in areas with high teen birth rates.
Award Range/Average: $350,000 to $450,000. The average estimate award amount is $450,000.
Funding: (Project Grants (Discretionary)) FY 17 $13,447,039.00; FY 18 est $24,341,891.00; FY 19 est $24,341,891.00
HQ: 330 C Street SW, Room 3614 Mary E Switzer Building, Washington, DC 20024
   Phone: 202-205-9605 | Email: lebretia.white@acf.hhs.gov
   http://www.acf.hhs.gov/programs/fysb

HHS93.977 | SEXUALLY TRANSMITTED DISEASES (STD) PREVENTION AND CONTROL GRANTS
"Sexually Transmitted Diseases (STD) Prevention and Control Grants: PS13-1306, PS14-1402, PS18-1808"

Award: Project Grants
Purpose: The program provides grants to the State and local STD prevention programs under Section 318 to implement prevention and control programs against sexually transmitted diseases.
Applicant Eligibility: Any State, and, in consultation with the appropriate State Health Authority, any political subdivision of a State, including American Indian/Alaska Native tribal Governments or tribal Organizations located wholly or in part within their boundaries; academic Institutions, and national and public health Organizations.
Beneficiary Eligibility: Any State or authorized subdivision including American Indian/Alaska Native tribal governments or tribal organizations located wholly or in part within their boundaries, academic institutions, and public health organizations.
Award Range/Average: Range: $149,560 to $2,817,271; Average: $3,571,002
Funding: (Cooperative Agreements) FY 18 $185,469,304.00; FY 19 est $193,103,652.00; FY 20 est $192,938,000.00
HQ: 1600 Clifton Road NE, PO Box E07, Atlanta, GA 30333
   Phone: 404-639-8531 | Email: eow1@cdc.gov
   http://www.cdc.gov/std

HHS93.978 | SEXUALLY TRANSMITTED DISEASES (STD) PROVIDER EDUCATION GRANTS
"STD Prevention Training Centers: PS14-1407, PS14-1408, PS15-1504, PS17-1707, PS17-1708"

Award: Project Grants
Purpose: The programs funds clinical and public health organizations to develop, deliver and evaluate the educational and clinical skill improvement activities for the healthcare professionals to prevent, control or clinically manage sexually transmitted diseases.
Applicant Eligibility: Academic Institutions and national, state and Tribal clinical and public health training Organizations.
Beneficiary Eligibility: Private and public clinical providers, such as physicians, nurse practitioners, nurses, physician assistants, pharmacists, and others. Any academic institutions and national, state and Tribal clinical and public health training organizations may apply for assistance.
Award Range/Average: Range: $83,800 to $6,188,272; Average: $2,781,692

Programs Administered by Federal Headquarters

Funding: (Cooperative Agreements) FY 18 $14,685,572.00; FY 19 est $14,540,571.00; FY 20 est $14,383,572.00
HQ: 1600 Clifton Road NE, PO Box E07, Atlanta, GA 30333
    Phone: 404-639-1877 | Email: lrw3@cdc.gov
    http://www.cdc.gov/std

DC90.199 | SHARED SERVICES
Award: Project Grants
Purpose: To deliver services of the federal government in the most cost-effective manner by reducing administrative and overhead costs.
Applicant Eligibility: Varies per federal agency requirements.
Beneficiary Eligibility: General public.
Funding: (Project Grants) FY 16 $0.00; FY 17 est $100,000.00; FY 18 est $100,000.00
HQ: 510 L Street, Suite 410, Anchorage, AK 99501
    Phone: 907-271-1414 | Email: ceilo@denali.gov

USDA10.173 | SHEEP PRODUCTION AND MARKETING GRANT PROGRAM "SPMGP"
Award: Project Grants
Purpose: To develop projects to enhance the marketing and production of sheep and sheep products in the United States through innovative approaches solving long-term needs and improving infrastructure and business and developing the resources.
Applicant Eligibility: National entities whose mission is consistent with strengthening and enhancing the production and marketing of sheep and sheep products in the United States.
Beneficiary Eligibility: U.S. sheep producers.
Award Range/Average: Not to exceed $2,000,000.
HQ: 1400 Independence Avenue SW Room 4534, PO Box 0234, Washington, DC 20250
    Phone: 202-720-1403 | Email: john.miklozek@ams.usda.gov
    https://www.ams.usda.gov/spmgp

HUD14.238 | SHELTER PLUS CARE
Award: Project Grants
Purpose: To assist through Tenant-based Rental Assistance (TRA), Sponsor-based Rental Assistance (SRA), Project-based Rental Assistance (PRA), (4) and Single Room Occupancy for Homeless Individuals (SRO).
Applicant Eligibility: An eligible applicant is a State, unit of general local government, or public housing agency (PHA).
Beneficiary Eligibility: Homeless persons with disabilities and their families. Except in single room occupancy dwellings that are only for homeless individuals with disabilities.
HQ: Office of Special Needs Assistance Programs 451 7th Street SW, Room 7262, Washington, DC 20410
    Phone: 202-402-4080 | Email: brian.p.fitzmaurice@hud.gov
    https://www.hudexchange.info/spc

HHS93.365 | SICKLE CELL TREATMENT DEMONSTRATION PROGRAM "SCDTDP"
Award: Cooperative Agreements
Purpose: To improve the prevention and treatment of sickle cell disease complications, including the coordination of service delivery for individuals with sickle cell disease; genetic counseling and testing; bundling of technical services.
Applicant Eligibility: Eligible entities include, Federally-qualified health center, as defined in section 1905(10(2)(B) of the Social Security Act (42 U.S.C. 1396d(10(2)(B), nonprofit hospital or clinic, or University health center that provides primary healthcare, that: (1) has a collaborative agreement with a community-based Sickle Cell Disease Organization or a nonprofit entity with experience in working with individuals who have Sickle Cell Disease; and (2) demonstrates that either the Federally-qualified health center, the nonprofit hospital or clinic, the University health center, the community-based Sickle Cell Disease Organization or the Sickle Cell Disease experts who serve as consultants to the project have at least 5 years of experience in working with individuals who have Sickle Cell Disease.

Beneficiary Eligibility: Projects will benefit individuals with Sickle Cell Disease and health professionals who provide care for individuals with Sickle Cell Disease.

Award Range/Average: FY 18 $347,436 - $1,042,304; $694,869 FY 19 $350,000 - $1,042,300; $712,397 FY 20 est. $350,000 - $1,042,300; $694,997

Funding: (Cooperative Agreements) FY 18 $3,474,358.00; FY 19 est $3,561,986.00; FY 20 est $3,574,986

HQ: 5600 Fishers Lane, Room 18W56, Rockville, MD 20857

Phone: 301-443-9775 | Email: eivy@hrsa.gov

http://www.hrsa.gov

HUD14.311 | SINGLE FAMILY PROPERTY DISPOSITION

Award: Sale, Exchange, Or Donation of Property and Goods

Purpose: To sell the inventory of HUD-acquired properties, and expand home ownership opportunities, strengthen neighborhoods and communities, and guarantee a maximum return to the FHA mortgage insurance fund.

Applicant Eligibility: Local Governments and Nonprofit Organizations: HUD contractors in the specific area should be contacted regarding eligibility requirements. Contact HUD at Toll free: (800) CALL FHA or (800) 225-5342 for a listing of nationwide HUD contractors. You can also visit: http://portal.hud.gov/hudportal/HUD?src=/Program _offices/housing/sfh/reo/mm/mminfo for the contact information for the M&M contractors. FHA Insured Financing: Generally, anyone who has a satisfactory credit rating; enough cash to close the loan; sufficient, steady income to make the monthly payments without difficulty; and who will live in the home can be approved for an FHA insured mortgage. Income is only one of several factors that apply in the lending process. Interested buyers should contact their lender for more information.

Beneficiary Eligibility: Individual, governmental and organizational homebuyers.

Funding: (Sale, Exchange, or Donation of Property and Goods) FY 15 $4,382,890,349.00; FY 16 est $1,571,887,224.00; FY 17 est $10,777,393,429.00

HQ: 451 7th Street SW, Washington, DC 20410

Phone: 800-225-5342

SBA59.037 | SMALL BUSINESS DEVELOPMENT CENTERS
"SBDC"

Award: Project Grants; Provision of Specialized Services; Advisory Services and Counseling; Dissemination of Technical Information

Purpose: Provides management counseling, training, and technical assistance to the small business community through Small Business Development Centers (SBDCs).

Applicant Eligibility: SBA is authorized to make grants (including contracts and cooperative agreements) to any public or private institution of higher education, including but not limited to any land- grant college or University, any college or school of business, engineering, commerce, or agriculture, community college or junior college. SBA is also authorized to renew the funding of other entities currently funded as SBDCs providing SBA affirmatively determines that such applicants have their own budget and will primarily utilize Institutions of higher education to provide the services to the small business community.

Beneficiary Eligibility: Current and potential Small business persons.

Funding: (Formula Grants) FY 17 $126,532,000.00; FY 18 est $125,000,000.00; FY 19 est $110,000,000.00

HQ: 409 3rd Street SW, 6th Floor, Washington, DC 20416

Phone: 202-205-7176 | Email: victoria.mundt@sba.gov

http://www.sba.gov/sbdc

USDA10.212 | SMALL BUSINESS INNOVATION RESEARCH
"SBIR Program - Phase I and II"

Award: Project Grants

Purpose: To implement technological creations in all businesses and in other research and development aspects.

Applicant Eligibility: (1) is organized for profit, with a place of business located in the United States, which operates primarily within the United States, or which makes a significant contribution to the United States economy through the payment of taxes or use of American products, materials or labor; (2) is in the legal form of an individual proprietorship, partnership, limited liability company, corporation, joint venture, association, trust or cooperative, except that where the form is a joint venture, there can be no more than 49 percent participation by foreign business entities in the joint venture; (3) is at least 51 percent owned and controlled by one or more individuals who are citizens of, or permanent resident aliens in, the United

Programs Administered by Federal Headquarters

States, except in the case of a joint venture, where each entity in the venture must be 51 percent owned and controlled by one or more individuals who are citizens of, or permanent resident aliens in the United States; and (4) has, including its affiliates, not more than 500 employees. The term "affiliates" is defined in greater detail in 13 CFR 121. 103. The term "number of employees" is defined in 13 CFR 121. 106.

Beneficiary Eligibility: Small businesses.

Award Range/Average: If minimum or maximum amounts of funding per competitive and/or capacity project grant, or cooperative agreement are established, these amounts will be announced in the annual Competitive Request for Application (RFA).The most current RFA is available via: SBIR Phase Ihttps://nifa.usda.gov/funding-opportunity/small-business-innovation-research-program-phase-iSBIR Phase IIhttps://nifa.usda.gov/funding-opportunity/small-business-innovation-research-program-phase-ii

Funding: (Project Grants) FY 17 $22,893,330.00; FY 18 est $24,209,624.00; FY 19 est $17,151,241.00

HQ: National Program Leader Institute of Bioenergy Climate and Environment - Division of Environmental Systems 1400 Independence Avenue SW, PO Box 2210, Washington, DC 20250-2210

    Phone: 202-720-5229

    http://nifa.usda.gov/grants

SBA59.011 | SMALL BUSINESS INVESTMENT COMPANIES
"SBIC; SSBIC"

Award: Guaranteed/insured Loans

Purpose: To establish privately owned and managed investment companies, which are licensed and regulated by the U.S. Small Business Administration.

Applicant Eligibility: Any chartered small business investment company having private capital of not less than $5 million, having qualified management, giving evidence of sound operation, and establishing the need for SBIC financing in the geographic area in which the applicant proposes to operate.

Beneficiary Eligibility: Individual businesses (single proprietorship, partnership or corporation) which satisfy the established criteria of a small business. SSBICs beneficiary must also be a business owned and operated by socially or economically disadvantaged individuals.

Award Range/Average: Additional information available at SBA's website

Funding: (Guaranteed/Insured Loans) FY 17 $196,000,000.00; FY 18 est $4,000,000,000.00; FY 19 est $4,000,000,000.00

HQ: 409 3rd Street SW, 6th Floor, Washington, DC 20416

    Phone: 202-619-0384

    http://www.sba.gov

HHS93.301 | SMALL RURAL HOSPITAL IMPROVEMENT GRANT PROGRAM
"Small Rural Hospital Improvement Program"

Award: Project Grants

Purpose: Supports small rural hospitals in their quality improvement efforts and with adapting to changing payment systems through investments in hardware, software, and related trainings.

Applicant Eligibility: The State Office of Rural Health (SORH) in each state will be the official awardee of record, as they will act as a fiscal intermediary for all hospitals within their state. Each SORH will be charged with organizing the distribution of funds to eligible hospitals. Only SORHs are eligible to apply for this grant. Federally-recognized Tribal Government and Native American Organizations are selected if they are eligible to apply.

Beneficiary Eligibility: Small rural hospitals must meet the following eligibility requirements in order to be eligible for SHIP funds: "Small" is a facility with 49 or fewer available beds, as reported on the hospital's most recent Medicare Cost Report. "Rural area" is either (a) being located outside of a Metropolitan Statistical Area (MSA); (b) being located within a rural census tract of a MSA, as determined under the Goldsmith Modification or the Rural Urban Commuting Areas; or (c) being treated as if it is located in a rural area pursuant to 42 U.S.C. 1395(d)(8)(E)."Hospital" is a non-federal, short-term, general acute care facility. Hospitals may be for-profit or not-for-profit. All Critical Access Hospitals are eligible for the program. In addition, hospitals with fewer than 50 beds located in a designated rural area, designated by any state law or regulation, are eligible. Tribally operated hospitals under Titles I and V of P.L. 93-638 are eligible to the extent that such hospitals meet the above criteria.

Award Range/Average: Range = $20,340 to $1,118,700. $351,970 (average award amount).

Funding: (Project Grants) FY 18 $15,631,528.00; FY 19 est $18,665,218; FY 20 est Estimate Not Available

HQ: 5600 Fishers Lane, Rockville, MD 20857
    Phone: 301-443-0456 | Email: sbarrie@hrsa.gov
    http://www.hrsa.gov

DOJ16.825 | SMART PROSECUTION INITIATIVE
"IPI"

Award: Project Grants
Purpose: The Innovative Prosecution Initiative helps prosecutors to develop practices to evaluate new solutions for public safety concerns.
Applicant Eligibility: Site-based - Eligible applicants are limited to state, local, and tribal prosecutor agencies or a government agency acting as fiscal agent for the applicant. TTA - Eligible applicants are limited to for-profit (commercial) Organizations, nonprofit Organizations, and Institutions of higher learning that support national initiatives to improve the functioning of the criminal justice system. For-profit Organizations must agree to waive any profit or fees for services.
Beneficiary Eligibility: N/A
Award Range/Average: See the current fiscal year's solicitation guidelines posted on the Office of Justice Programs web site at https://ojp.gov/funding/Explore/CurrentFundingOpportunities.htm.
Funding: (Project Grants (Discretionary)) FY 18 $2,256,584.00; FY 19 est $8,000,000.00; FY 20 est $0.00
HQ: Bureau of Justice Assistance 810 7th Street NW, Washington, DC 20531
    Phone: 202-514-5309
    http://www.smartprosecution.apainc.org

USDA10.511 | SMITH-LEVER FUNDING (VARIOUS PROGRAMS)
"1862 LGI's: 1862 CES (Smith-Lever) and DCPPERA, 1862 Smith-Lever Special Needs, and Smith-Lever Special Needs-Competitive"

Award: Formula Grants; Project Grants
Purpose: To increase agricultural extension activities, education, emergency preparedness for natural and human-made disasters.
Applicant Eligibility: 1862 CES Capacity & DCPPERA: Joint Cooperative Extension Programs at 1862 Land-Grant Institutions applications may only be submitted by the following 1862 Land-grant Institutions: Auburn University, University of Alaska-Fairbanks, American Samoa Community College, University of Arizona, University of Arkansas, University of California, Colorado State University, University of Connecticut, University of Delaware, University of Florida, University of Georgia, University of Guam, University of Hawaii, University of Idaho, University of Illinois, Purdue University, Iowa State University, Kansas State University, University of Kentucky, Louisiana State University, University of Maine, University of Maryland-College Park, University of Massachusetts, Michigan State University, College of Micronesia, University of Minnesota, Mississippi State University, University of Missouri, Montana State University, University of Nebraska, University of Nevada-Reno, University of New Hampshire, Rutgers University, New Mexico State University, Cornell University, North Carolina State University, North Dakota State University, Northern Marianas College, Ohio State University, Oklahoma State University, Oregon State University, Pennsylvania State University, University of Puerto Rico, University of Rhode Island, Clemson University, South Dakota State University, University of Tennessee, Texas A & M University, Utah State University, University of Vermont, Virginia Polytechnic Institute & State University, University of the Virgin Islands, Washington State University, West Virginia University, University of Wisconsin, and University of Wyoming. University of the District of Columbia Public Postsecondary education Re Organization Act Program (DCPPERA): Applications may only be submitted by the University of the District of Columbia. 1862 Special Needs Capacity (SLSN): Applications may only be submitted by the following 1862 Land-grant Institutions: University of Alaska-Fairbanks, University of Arizona, Colorado State University, University of Idaho, Kansas State University, Montana State University, University of Nebraska, University of Nevada-Reno, New Mexico State University, North Dakota State University, Oregon State University, South Dakota State University, Texas A&M University, Utah State University, University of Vermont, and University of Wyoming. Smith-Lever Special Needs Competitive (SLSNCGP): Applications may only be submitted by 1862 Land-grant Institutions in the 50 states and the U.S. territories, American Samoa, Guam, Micronesia, Northern Marianas, Puerto Rico, and the U.S. Virgin Islands.
Beneficiary Eligibility: Same as Applicant Eligibility.
Award Range/Average: If minimum or maximum amounts of funding per capacity project grant, or cooperative agreement are established, these amounts will be announced in the annual Request for Application (RFA).The most current RFAs are available as follows: 1862 Cooperative Extension Capacity & District of Columbia Postsecondary Reorganization

Programs Administered by Federal Headquarters

Act (1862 CES Capacity & DCPPERA):https://nifa.usda.gov/sites/default/files/resources/FY%202017%20SLBC%20 and%20DCPPERA%20modifications.pdfreorganization-act-program-cooperative1862 Smith Lever Special Needs Capacity (SLSN):https://nifa.usda.gov/sites/default/files/resources/FY%202017%20CES%201862%20Special%20Needs%20 Capacity%20RFA%20-%20MODIFIED%20%202008-30-16.pdfSmith Lever Special Needs Competitive (SLSNCGP):https:// nifa.usda.gov/sites/default/files/rfa/FY%20%2717%20SLSNCGP%20RFA%20-FINAL.pdf

HQ: National Program Leader Institute of Food Production and Sustainability Division of Agricultural Systems 1400 Independence Avenue SW, PO Box 2240, Washington, DC 20250-2220

Phone: 202-720-6059 | Email: wesley.dean@nifa.usda.gov

http://nifa.usda.gov/program/district-columbia-public-postsecondary-education-reorganization-act-program-cooperative

DOD12.108 | SNAGGING AND CLEARING FOR FLOOD CONTROL
"Section 208"

Award: Provision of Specialized Services
Purpose: To reduce flood damages.
Applicant Eligibility: States, political subdivisions of States or other responsible local agencies established under State law with full authority and ability to undertake necessary legal and financial responsibilities.
Beneficiary Eligibility: Same as Applicant Eligibility.

TREAS21.017 | SOCIAL IMPACT PARTNERSHIPS TO PAY FOR RESULTS ACT (SIPPRA)
"SIPPRA"

Award: Project Grants (discretionary)
Purpose: To fund the social programs thereby improving the lives of needed families and individuals in the United States and to ensure whether the Federal funds are effectively used on social services. It also focuses on facilitating the creation of public-private partnerships for effective social interventions that are already being implemented by private organizations and local governments across the country.
Applicant Eligibility: Only State and local Governments may apply.
Beneficiary Eligibility: N/A
Award Range/Average: No SIPPRA project or feasibility awards have been made. Treasury expects to award up to approximately $70,000,000 in competitive project and feasibility study grants. SIPPRA provides that not less than 50 percent of all federal payments made to carry out social impact partnership project agreements shall be used for initiatives that directly benefit children.
Funding: (Project Grants (Discretionary)) FY 18 $765,000.00; FY 19 est Estimate Not Available; FY 20 est Estimate Not Available
HQ: 1500 Pennsylvania Avenue NW, Washington, DC 20220
Phone: 202-622-0262 | Email: william.girardo@treasury.gov

RRB57.001 | SOCIAL INSURANCE FOR RAILROAD WORKERS
"Railroad retirement and railroad unemployment-sickness insurance programs"

Award: Direct Payments With Unrestricted Use
Purpose: Provide income security for retired and disabled railroad workers, their family members, and survivors, and financial benefits for railroad workers who are unemployed or unable to work due to illness or injury.
Applicant Eligibility: Under the Railroad Retirement Act, for employee, spouse and survivor benefits, the employee must have had 10 or more years of railroad service or, for annuities beginning January 2002 or later, 5 years of railroad service rendered after 1995. For survivors to be eligible for benefits, the employee must also have been insured at death. Under the Railroad Unemployment Insurance Act, an employee must have earned at least $3,637. 50 in calendar year 2016, $3,862. 50 in calendar year 2017, and $3,900 in calendar year 2018 (counting no more than $1,455 in 2016, $1,545 in 2017, and $1,560 in 2018).
Beneficiary Eligibility: Individuals, families, pension recipients.
Award Range/Average: Amounts for 2018: Employee initially awarded age annuities - monthly maximum $5,274, average $2,904; employee disability - monthly maximum $5,143, average $2,816; employee supplemental annuities - monthly

maximum $70, average $42; married spouse benefits - monthly maximum $2,521, average $1,077; widows and widowers - monthly maximum $5,033, average $1,754; widowed mothers and fathers - monthly maximum $4,438, average $1,919; children - monthly maximum $2,929, average $1,152; unemployment and sickness - weekly maximum for benefit year 2019-2020 $367, expected average $367.

Funding: (Direct Payments with Unrestricted Use) FY 18 $13,216,000,000.00; FY 19 est $13,130,000,000.00; FY 20 est $13,298,000,000.00; (Salaries and Expenses) FY 18 $141,500,000.00; FY 19 est $142,100,000.00; FY 20 est $132,375,000.00

HQ: 844 N Rush Street 4NE, Chicago, IL 60611-1275

Phone: 312-751-4932 | Email: bruce.rodman@rrb.gov

http://www.rrb.gov

SSA96.001 | SOCIAL SECURITY DISABILITY INSURANCE

Award: Direct Payments for Specified Use; Direct Payments With Unrestricted Use

Purpose: To financially support a person who has been physically or mentally impaired and cannot continue their work.

Applicant Eligibility: A disabled worker is entitled to Social Security disability benefits if he or she has worked for a sufficient period of time under Social Security to be insured, has not attained "full-benefit retirement age" (66 years old for workers age 62 in 2005), has filed an application, and is under a disability as defined in the Social Security law. The law defines disability as the inability to do any substantial gainful activity by reason of any medically determinable physical or mental impairment which can be expected to result in death or which has lasted or can be expected to last for a continuous period of not less than 12 months. The insured status requirements depend upon the age of the applicant and the date he or she became disabled. Coverage credits under the social security systems of certain foreign countries with which the U.S. has reciprocal agreements may be taken into account to meet the requirements. Certain family members of disabled workers are also entitled to benefits: (1) Unmarried children under age 18, or under age 19 for full-time students in elementary or secondary school; (2) unmarried adult offspring at any age if continuously disabled since before age 22; (3) wife or husband at any age if child in his or her care is receiving benefits on worker's Social Security record and is under age 16 or disabled; (4) spouse age 62 or over; and (5) divorced wives or husbands age 62 or over who were married to the worker for at least 10 years. (Benefits are also payable to auxiliaries, including certain disabled widow(er)s, disabled surviving divorced spouses, children under age 19 who are full-time students in an elementary or secondary school, and disabled children of the worker, after the worker dies. See 96.004 "Social Security-Survivors' Insurance".) For workers who are first entitled after 1985 for both (a) a pension based on non-covered employment; and (b) Social Security disability (or retirement) benefits, a less generous benefit formula applies. In addition, Social Security disability benefits are reduced (offset) by the amount that the sum of all disability benefits payable under Social Security and certain Federal, State, or local public disability and workers' compensation laws or plans exceeds the higher of 80 percent of the worker's average current earnings or the total Social Security benefit that would otherwise be payable on the disabled worker's record. The Social Security benefit for a spouse of a disabled worker is subject to a pension offset if the spouse receives a governmental pension based on his or her own work in non-covered employment. However, the offset does not apply if: (i) the person received or became eligible to receive the pension before December 1, 1982, and can meet requirements for Social Security auxiliaries' benefit as they existed in January 1977; or (ii) if the person received, or was eligible to receive, the pension before July 1, 1983, and the person was dependent on his or her spouse for at least one-half support at the time the spouse died, became disabled or became entitled to Social Security benefits. The amount of the public pension used for purposes of the offset against Social Security spouse's benefits is equal to two-thirds of the public pension. The Social Security benefit for the spouse of a disabled worker is also offset dollar for dollar by the amount of any Social Security benefit the spouse receives based on his or her own work. All benefits to spouses and children of disabled workers are subject to an earnings test unless those beneficiaries are full-benefit retirement age or older. Beginning with the year 2000, the retirement earnings test was eliminated beginning with the month in which the beneficiary reaches full-benefit retirement age (FRA). A person at and above FRA will not have Social Security benefits reduced because of earnings. In the calendar year in which a beneficiary reaches FRA, benefits are reduced $1 for every $3 of earnings above the limit allowed by law, $31,800 in 2005, but this reduction is applied only to months prior to attainment of FRA. For years before the year the beneficiary attains FRA, the reduction in benefits is $1 for every $2 of earnings over the annual exempt amount. Further, no benefit can be paid to an alien in the United States unless he or she is lawfully present in the United States. In addition, an alien cannot qualify for benefits if he or she never had a work-authorized Social Security Number (SSN) (effective for benefit applications based on SSNs issued after 2003).

Beneficiary Eligibility: Qualified disabled workers under full retirement age (FRA). Under the definition of disability in the Social Security Law, disability benefits are provided to a person who is unable to engage in any substantial gainful activity by reason of a medically determinable physical or mental impairment that has lasted or is expected to last at least 12 months, or to result in death. Disabled widow(er)s' benefits are covered under survivors insurance. Felony-related impairments and confinement-related impairments cannot be considered in determining whether an individual is under a disability if the individual has been convicted of a felony which was committed after October 19, 1980. Effective for claims finally

Programs Administered by Federal Headquarters

adjudicated on or after March 29, 1996, (or for claims approved before then, with benefits payable beginning January 1, 1997) eligibility can no longer be based on drug addiction or alcoholism.

Award Range/Average: Monthly cash benefits for a worker disabled in 2005 range up to a maximum of $2,099 based on the level of the worker's earnings and the age at which a worker becomes disabled. The corresponding maximum for such a worker with a family is $3,148.60 As of December 31,2004, the average benefit paid to a disabled worker alone was $880 and the average amount payable to a disabled worker with eligible dependents was $1,496. This takes into account stipulations set forth in Public Law 96-265 and Public Law 97-35. Under Public Law 97-123, the minimum amount is no longer applicable for workers who either become disabled or first met the insured status requirements after December 1981, and a lesser amount can be paid, depending on the worker's average earnings.

HQ: Baltimore, MD 21235
   Phone: 800-772-1213
   http://www.socialsecurity.gov

SSA96.002 | SOCIAL SECURITY RETIREMENT INSURANCE

Award: Direct Payments With Unrestricted Use

Purpose: To financially support the workers after their retirement.

Applicant Eligibility: Retired workers age 62 and over who have worked the required number of years under Social Security are eligible for monthly benefits. Coverage credits under the social security systems of certain foreign countries with which the U.S. has reciprocal agreements may be taken into account to meet the requirements. If an eligible worker age 62 or over receives benefits before full-benefit retirement age (FRA)(age 66 for workers age 62 in 2005), the individual's retirement benefit will be permanently reduced. Also, certain family members can receive benefits including: (1) A wife or husband age 62 or over; (2) a spouse at any age, if a child who is under age 16 or is disabled is in his or her care and is entitled to benefits based on the worker's record; (3) unmarried children under age 18 (or under age 19 for students in elementary or secondary school); (4) unmarried adult offspring at any age if disabled before age 22; and (5) divorced wives or husbands age 62 or over who were married to the worker for at least 10 years. Beginning January 1985, spouses ages 62 or over who have been divorced for at least 2 years (and married to the worker for at least 10 years) may become entitled to benefits regardless of whether the former spouse who is at least age 62 and fully insured has applied for benefits. Effective January 1991, the 2-year waiting period for payment of divorced spouse's benefits without regard to the former spouse's earnings was waived if the former spouse was entitled to benefits prior to the divorce. All benefits, other than benefits to disabled beneficiaries, and beneficiaries FRA and older, are subject to an earnings test. Beginning with the year 2000, the retirement earnings test was eliminated beginning with the month in which the beneficiary reaches FRA. A person at and above FRA will not have Social Security benefits reduced because of earnings. In the calendar year in which a beneficiary reaches FRA, benefits are reduced $1 for every $3 of earnings above the limit allowed by law, $31,800 in 2005, but this reduction is applied only to months prior to attainment of FRA. For years before the year the beneficiary attains FRA, the reduction in benefits is $1 for every $2 of earnings over the annual exempt amount, $16,920 in 2017. For workers who are first eligible after 1985 for both (a) a pension based on non-covered employment; and (b) Social Security retirement (or disability) benefits, a different benefit formula applies which provides somewhat lower benefits. The Social Security benefit for a spouse of a retired worker is subject to a pension offset if the spouse receives a governmental pension based on his or her own work in non-covered employment. However, the offset does not apply if: (i) the person has received or became eligible to receive the pension before December 1, 1982, and met eligibility requirements for Social Security auxiliaries' benefits as they existed in January 1977; or (ii) if the person receives, or is eligible to receive, the pension before July 1, 1983, and the person was dependent on his or her spouse for at least one-half support at the time the spouse died, became disabled or became entitled to Social Security benefits. The amount of the public pension used for purposes of the offset against Social Security spouse's benefits is equal to two-thirds of the public pension. The benefit for the spouse of a retired worker is also offset dollar for dollar by the amount of any Social Security benefit the spouse receives based on his or her own work. Effective for those who have reached age 62 since August 1981, a retired worker or spouse can receive benefits only for months in which he or she has attained at least age 62 for the entire month. No benefit can be paid to an alien in the United States unless he or she is lawfully present in the United States. In addition, an alien cannot qualify for benefits if he or she never had a work-authorized Social Security Number (SSN) effective for benefit applications based on SSNs issued after 2003.

Beneficiary Eligibility: Benefits are paid to retired workers age 62 and over who have worked the required number of years under Social Security, and to certain family members.

Award Range/Average: Monthly cash benefits for a worker retiring at full retirement age (FRA) in 2017 range up to $2,687 and to a maximum of $4,702.60 for a family of such a worker receiving benefits. As of December 31,2016, the average benefit paid to a retired worker alone (no family members receiving benefits) was $1,360 and the average amount payable to a retired worker with an eligible spouse was $1,574.

HQ: Office of Public Inquiries, Room 4100 Annex, Baltimore, MD 21235
    Phone: 800-772-1213
    http://www.socialsecurity.gov

SSA96.004 | SOCIAL SECURITY SURVIVORS INSURANCE

Award: Direct Payments for Specified Use; Direct Payments With Unrestricted Use
Purpose: To financially support the dependents of workers due to the worker's demise.
Applicant Eligibility: Benefits are payable only if the deceased was insured for survivors insurance protection. Coverage credits under the social security systems of certain foreign countries with which the U.S. has reciprocal agreements may be taken into account to meet the requirements. Survivors eligible for monthly cash benefits are the following: widows or widowers age 60 or over; surviving divorced spouses age 60 or over (married to the deceased worker for at least 10 years); disabled widows, widowers or surviving divorced spouses ages 50- 59; widows, widowers, or surviving divorced spouses at any age who have in their care a child under age 16 or disabled and entitled to benefits on the deceased worker's Social Security record; unmarried children under age 18, under age 19 and a full time student in elementary or secondary school; or age 18 or older and under a disability which began before age 22; and dependent parents age 62 and over. All survivors benefits, other than for beneficiaries at full retirement age (FRA) or older, are subject to an earnings test. Beginning with the year 2000, the retirement earnings test was eliminated beginning with the month in which the beneficiary reaches FRA. A person at and above FRA will not have Social Security benefits reduced because of earnings. In the calendar year in which a beneficiary reaches FRA, benefits are reduced $1 for every $3 of earnings above the limit allowed by law, $44,880 in 2017, but this reduction is applied only to months prior to attainment of FRA. For years before the year the beneficiary attains FRA, the reduction in benefits is $1 for every $2 of earnings over the annual exempt amount, $16,920 in 2017. Except for benefits to children and dependent parents, all survivors benefits are subject to a pension offset if the person is also receiving a governmental pension based on his or her own work in non-covered employment. However, the offset does not apply: (1) If the person receives, or is eligible to receive, the pension before December 1, 1982, and can meet the requirements for the Social Security auxiliary's benefit as they existed in January 1977; or (2) if the person receives, or is eligible to receive, the pension before July 1, 1983, and the person was dependent on his or her spouse for at least one-half support at the time the spouse died, became disabled or became entitled to Social Security benefits; or 3) if the last 60 months of a person's government service before retirement was covered by both Social Security and the pension plan that provides the government pension. The amount of the public pension used for purposes of the offset against Social Security survivor's benefits is equal to two-thirds of the public pension. Benefits for widows/widowers and surviving divorced spouses are also offset dollar for dollar by any Social Security benefit the surviving spouse receives based on his or her own work. Under certain conditions, a lump-sum death payment of $255 is payable to the widow or children of the deceased worker. Further, no benefit can be paid to an alien in the United States unless he is lawfully present in the United States. Also, an alien cannot qualify for benefits if he or she never had a work-authorized Social Security Number (SSN) (effective for benefit applications based on SSNs issued after 2003).
Beneficiary Eligibility: Widows, widowers, and surviving divorced spouses age 60 or over are entitled as long as the worker met the insurance requirements. Widows, widowers, and surviving divorced spouses also qualify at any age if they have entitled children of the worker under age 16 or disabled children in their care; unmarried children: under age 18, under age 19 and a full-time student in elementary or secondary school or age 18 or older and under a disability which began before age 22; and dependent parents age 62 and over. To claim benefits as disabled widows, widowers, or surviving divorced spouses, individuals ages 50-59 must show that they have a disability that started no later than 7 years after the insured died or 7 years after certain other events. "Disability" currently has the same meaning for these entitlements as it does for workers who claim disability insurance (see 96.001). As in worker disability claims, there is also a 5-month waiting period after the disability began before benefits begin and entitlement to Medicare after 24 months of entitlement to benefits. Children of the worker claiming benefits because of disability are also subject to the definition of disability used for workers and must show that they have been disabled since before they reached age 22. There is no waiting period for these benefits.
HQ: Office of Public Inquiries, Room 4100 Annex, Baltimore, MD 21235
    Phone: 800-772-1213
    http://www.socialsecurity.gov

Programs Administered by Federal Headquarters

HHS93.647 | SOCIAL SERVICES RESEARCH AND DEMONSTRATION
"SSRD"

Award: Project Grants
Purpose: Promotes research and demonstrations related to the prevention and reduction of dependency or the administration and effectiveness of programs related to that purpose.
Applicant Eligibility: Grants and cooperative agreements may be made to or with governmental entities, colleges, universities, nonprofit and for-profit Organizations (if fee is waived), and faith-based and community Organizations. Grants and cooperative agreements cannot be made directly to individuals.
Beneficiary Eligibility: Children, youth, and families, especially low-income families, will benefit.
Award Range/Average: Range from $24,918 to $100,000; Average being $70,772.75
Funding: (Project Grants) FY 18 $99,481.00; FY 19 est $149,958.00; FY 20 est $250,000.00
HQ: 330 C Street SW, Room 4625A, Washington, DC 20201
    Phone: 202-401-5803 | Email: sheila.celentano@acf.hhs.gov
    http://www.acf.hhs.gov/programs/opre

NSF47.075 | SOCIAL, BEHAVIORAL, AND ECONOMIC SCIENCES
"SBE"

Award: Project Grants
Purpose: To contribute to the scientific strength and welfare of the Nation through the promotion of basic research and education in the social, behavioral and economic sciences and through monitoring and understanding the resources invested in science and engineering in the United States.
Applicant Eligibility: Except where a Program solicitation establishes more restrictive eligibility criteria, individuals and Organizations in the following categories may submit proposals: universities and colleges; Non-profit, non-academic Organizations; For-profit Organizations; State and local Governments; and unaffiliated individuals. See the NSF Grant Proposal Guide, Chapter i.e., for a full description of eligibility requirements: http://www.nsf.gov/publications/pubsumm. jsp?odskey=gpg.
Beneficiary Eligibility: N/A
Award Range/Average: Range Low $3,543 Range High $11,999,950 Average $121,500
Funding: (Project Grants) FY 18 $250,690,000.00; FY 19 est $270,420,000.00; FY 20 est $230,080,000.00
HQ: Senior Information Technology 2415 Eisenhower Avenue, Alexandria, VA 22314
    Phone: 703-292-8700 | Email: dlivings@nsf.gov
    http://nsf.gov/dir/index.jsp?org=sbe

USDA10.871 | SOCIALLY-DISADVANTAGED GROUPS GRANT
"SSDG"

Award: Project Grants
Purpose: To assist financially distressed groups through Cooperative Development Centers.
Applicant Eligibility: Eligible applicants are cooperatives, groups of cooperatives, and cooperative development centers that serve socially-disadvantaged groups and whose governing board is comprised of a majority of individuals who are members of a socially-disadvantaged group. Applicants are not eligible if they have been debarred or suspended or otherwise excluded from participation in Federal assistance Programs under Executive Order 12549, Debarment and Suspension. Applicants are not eligible if they have an outstanding judgement obtained by the U.S. in a Federal Court (other than U.S. Tax Court), are delinquent on the payment of Federal income taxes, or are delinquent on a Federal debt. Any corporation that has been convicted of a felony criminal violation under any Federal law within the past 24 months or that has any unpaid Federal tax liability that has been assessed, for which all judicial and administrative remedies have been exhausted or have lapsed, and that is not being paid in a timely manner pursuant to an agreement with the authority responsible for collecting the tax liability, is not eligible for funding.
Beneficiary Eligibility: Ultimate beneficiaries must be located in rural areas, as defined by 7 U.S.C. 1991(a).
Award Range/Average: Average = $150,000 Range = $37,000 (minimum) to $175,000 (maximum)
Funding: (Project Grants) FY 18 $3,000,000.00; FY 19 est $1,828,008.95.00; FY 20 est Estimate Not Available;- Project usually fund with $3,000,000 annually

HQ: Cooperative Programs Grants Division 1400 Independence Avenue SW Room 4208-S, PO Box 3253, Washington, DC 20250
> Phone: 202-690-1374
> http://www.rd.usda.gov/programs-services/socially-disadvantaged-groups-grant

USDA10.464 | SOCIALLY DISADVANTAGED FARMERS AND RANCHERS POLICY RESEARCH CENTER
"Policy Research Center"

Award: Project Grants
Purpose: The Policy Research Center assists socially disadvantaged farmers and ranchers. The program also creates awareness of socially disadvantaged farmers and ranchers.
Applicant Eligibility: Only 1890 Institutions as defined in 7 U.S.C. 7601, including Tuskegee University, may apply and are eligible to receive funds under the Act of August 30, 1890 (& U.S.C. 321 et seq.).
Beneficiary Eligibility: Minority Farmers and Ranchers.
Award Range/Average: 525000
Funding: (Project Grants) FY 18 est $400,000.00; FY 19 est $525,000.00; FY 20 est $525,000.00
HQ: 1400 Independence Avenue SW Room 520-A, PO Box 0601, Washington, DC 20250
> Phone: 202-720-6350
> http://www.outreach.usda.gov/education/index.htm

HHS93.082 | SODIUM REDUCTION IN COMMUNITIES

Award: Cooperative Agreements
Purpose: To reduce Americans' sodium intake to limits recommended by the Dietary Guidelines.
Applicant Eligibility: A. An official state health department (or its bona fide agent), or its equivalent, as designated by the Governor, is to serve as the lead/fiduciary agency for Small City and Rural Community applications. For this announcement, the term State includes the 50 states and the District of Columbia. The term small city is defined as a local health department that serves a jurisdiction with a population between 50,000 - 250,000 people. The term rural area is defined as a local health department that serves a jurisdiction with a population of 50,000 people and below. b. An official local health department (or its bona fide agent), or its equivalent, as designated by the mayor, county executive, or other equivalent governmental official, will serve as the lead/fiduciary agent for a Large City application. For this announcement, the term large city is defined as a local health department that serves a jurisdiction with a population of more than 500,000 people. c. Federally recognized Tribal Governments, Regional Area Indian Health Boards, Urban Indian Organizations, and Inter-Tribal Councils will serve as the lead/fiduciary agency for Tribal Community applications.
Beneficiary Eligibility: Any U.S. state, political subdivision and U.S. territories (as described above), and other public entities will benefit.
Award Range/Average: 250,000 for Large City Applicants; $350,000 for state coordinated applicants (this amount is subject to the availability of funds
Funding: (Cooperative Agreements) FY 18 $2,999,949.00; FY 19 est $2,999,948.00; FY 20 est $299,949.00
HQ: 4770 Buford Highway NE, PO Box F72, Atlanta, GA 30341
> Phone: 770-488-2047 | Email: kmugavero@cdc.gov
> http://www.cdc.gov

DOS19.024 | SOFT TARGET PROGRAM FOR OVERSEAS SCHOOLS
"Soft Target Program"

Award: Project Grants
Purpose: Improves physical security of overseas schools to prevent or lessen the impact of terrorism and/or violent crime.
Applicant Eligibility: N/A
Beneficiary Eligibility: N/A
Award Range/Average: Range: $1K - $1.5M Avg: $800K
Funding: (Project Grants)
HQ: 1701 Fort Myer Drive, Arlington, VA 22209
> Phone: 703-516-1615 | Email: adamsmr@state.gov

Programs Administered by Federal Headquarters

USDA10.762 | SOLID WASTE MANAGEMENT GRANTS
Award: Project Grants
Purpose: To minimize pollution of water and management of solid waste disposal facilities in rural areas.
Applicant Eligibility: Entities eligible for grants are nonprofit Organizations, including: Private, nonprofit Organizations that have been granted tax exempt status by the Internal Revenue Service (IRS); and public bodies including local governmental-based multijurisdictional Organizations. Applicants must have the proven ability, background, experience, legal authority, and actual capacity to provide technical assistance and/or training on a regional basis to eligible beneficiaries.
Beneficiary Eligibility: The entities that receive assistance are: (1) municipalities, counties, districts, authorities, and other political subdivisions of a State; (2) organizations operated on a not-for-profit basis, such as associations, cooperatives, and private nonprofit corporations; (3) and, Indian tribes on Federal and State reservations and other federally recognized Indian tribes.
Award Range/Average: $74,477 to $900,000. Average: $200,137
Funding: (Project Grants) FY 18 est $4,202,873; FY 19 est $4,075,773; FY 20 est $4,000,000
HQ: Water and Environmental Programs Department of Agriculture 1400 Independence Avenue SW, PO Box 1548, Washington, DC 20250
    Phone: 202-720-0986 | Email: edna.primrose@wdc.usda.gov
    http://www.rd.usda.gov/programs-services/all-programs/water-environmental-programs

DOI15.440 | SOUTH HALF OF THE RED RIVER
Award: Direct Payments for Specified Use
Purpose: Shares 37.5 percent of mineral leasing revenue with the State of Oklahoma paid monthly and is subject to late disbursement interest.
Applicant Eligibility: Revenue from public land leasing will trigger automatic payment distribution computed in the accordance with the Law.
Beneficiary Eligibility: ONRR distributes these funds to the State of Oklahoma for leased lands located within the south half of the Red River.
Award Range/Average: Not Applicable.
Funding: (Direct Payments for Specified Use) FY 17 $9,000.00; FY 18 est $11,000.00; FY 19 est $12,000.00
HQ: Department of the Interior Office of Natural Resources Revenue 1849 C Street NW, PO Box 4211, Washington, DC 20240
    Phone: 202-513-0600
    http://www.ONRR.gov

DOC11.435 | SOUTHEAST AREA MONITORING AND ASSESSMENT PROGRAM "SEAMAP"
Award: Project Grants
Purpose: To maintain State and Federal agencies in coordination and collect information on marine fisheries to support State Territorial fisheries management programs.
Applicant Eligibility: Eligible applicants are the Marine Fishery Conservation agencies of the States of Alabama, Florida, Georgia, Louisiana, Mississippi, North Carolina, South Carolina, Texas, Puerto Rico, the U.S. Virgin Islands, the Atlantic and Gulf States Marine Fishery Commissions.
Beneficiary Eligibility: This program benefits Federal, State and interstate marine resource conservation and management agencies; U.S. and foreign commercial and recreational fishing industries; conservation organizations; academic institutions; international and Indian Tribal treaties; private and public research groups; consumers; and the general public.
Award Range/Average: $71,500 - $1,372,023. Average: $337,845.
Funding: (Project Grants) FY 16 $3,653,166.00; FY 17 est $3,653,166.00; FY 18 est Estimate Not Available
HQ: 1305 E W Highway, Silver Spring, MD 20910
    Phone: 301-427-8771 | Email: jeffrey.kulnis@noaa.gov
    http://caldera.sero.nmfs.gov/grants/programs/seamap.htm

NASA43.007 | SPACE OPERATIONS
Award: Cooperative Agreements; Project Grants
Purpose: Provides basic research, educational outreach, or training opportunities in the area of space exploration.

Applicant Eligibility: Basic Research, educational Outreach, and Training Opportunities in the area of Space Operations. Review funding opportunity announcement for additional information.

Beneficiary Eligibility: See funding opportunity announcement for additional information.

Funding: (Salaries and Expenses) FY 18 $39,322,160.42.00; FY 19 est $31,734,267.48.00; FY 20 est Estimate Not Available

HQ: 300 E Street SW, PO Box LH010, Washington, DC 20546

Phone: 202-358-4683 | Email: diane.c.malarik@nasa.gov

http://www.nasa.gov

NASA43.012 | SPACE TECHNOLOGY

Award: Cooperative Agreements; Project Grants; Direct Payments for Specified Use; Use of Property, Facilities, and Equipment; Training

Purpose: Responsible for developing the crosscutting, pioneering, new technologies and capabilities needed by the agency to achieve its current and future missions.

Applicant Eligibility: Generally, applications are solicited from Institutions of higher learning and non-profit Organizations. All applicants should review the appropriate funding announcement to determine eligibility for a specific project.

Beneficiary Eligibility: Review funding opportunity announcement for additional information.

Funding: (Cooperative Agreements (Discretionary Grants)) FY 18 $23,988,866.17; FY 19 est $36,808,845.4; FY 20 est Estimate Not Available

HQ: 300 E Street SW, Washington, DC 20546

Phone: 216-977-7511 | Email: claudia.m.meyer@nasa.gov

DOJ16.734 | SPECIAL DATA COLLECTIONS AND STATISTICAL STUDIES
"Statistics"

Award: Cooperative Agreements

Purpose: To make grants to or enter into cooperative agreements or contracts with public agencies, institutions of higher education, private organizations, or private individuals for purposes of collecting and analyzing criminal justice statistics.

Applicant Eligibility: The Bureau of Justice Statistics is authorized to award grants and cooperative agreements to State and local Governments, private nonprofit Organizations, public nonprofit Organizations, profit Organizations, Institutions of higher education, and qualified individuals. Applicants from the Territories of the United States and federally recognized Indian Tribal Governments are also eligible to participate in this Program.

Beneficiary Eligibility: Eligible beneficiaries are State and local governments, private nonprofit organizations, public nonprofit organizations, profit organizations, institutions of higher education, and qualified individuals.

Award Range/Average: $50,000 to $1,000,000

Funding: (Cooperative Agreements) FY 17 $41,755,090.00; FY 18 est $48,000,000.00; FY 19 est $41,000,000.00

HQ: Bureau of Justice Statistics 810 7th Street NW, Washington, DC 20531

Phone: 202-307-0765 | Email: allina.lee@usdoj.gov

http://www.bjs.gov

HHS93.237 | SPECIAL DIABETES PROGRAM FOR INDIANS DIABETES PREVENTION AND TREATMENT PROJECTS
"Indian Health"

Award: Project Grants

Purpose: To promote improved healthcareamong American Indians/Alaska Natives through special diabetes prevention and treatment services with objectives and priorities determined at the local level.

Applicant Eligibility: The Public Health Service Act, as amended, states that the following groups are eligible to apply for grants: Indian Health Service (IHS) entities: Indian Tribes or tribal Organizations who operate an Indian Health Program. This includes Program under a contract, grant, cooperative agreement or compact with the IHS under the Indian Self-Determination Act; and Urban Indian Organizations that operate an urban Indian Health Program. This includes Programs under a grant or contract with the IHS under Title V of the Indian healthcare Improvement Act.

Beneficiary Eligibility: American Indians/Alaskan Natives will be the ultimate beneficiaries of the funded projects through either prevention or direct treatment services.

Funding: (Project Grants) FY 18 est $138,700,000.00; FY 19 est $138,700,000.00; FY 20 est $138,700,000.00

Programs Administered by Federal Headquarters

HQ: Grants Policy Office 5600 Fishers Lane, PO Box 09E70, Rockville, MD 20857
   Phone: 301-443-5204

DOJ16.025 | SPECIAL DOMESTIC VIOLENCE CRIMINAL JURISDICTION IMPLEMENTATION
"SDVCJ Program"
Award: Project Grants
Purpose: To assist tribal governments in implementing the Special Domestic Violence Criminal Jurisdiction, which was created by section 904 of the Violence Against Women Reauthorization Act of 2013.
Applicant Eligibility: Eligible applicants are tribal Governments.
Beneficiary Eligibility: Beneficiaries include the tribal criminal justice system and victim service providers.
Award Range/Average: 495000
Funding: (Project Grants (Discretionary)) FY 16 $2,219,939.00; FY 17 est $3,465,000.00; FY 18 est $2,200,000.00
HQ: 145 N Street NE, Suite 10W121, Washington, DC 20530
   Phone: 202-305-1177 | Email: tia.farmer@usdoj.gov
   http://www.justice.gov/tribal/grants.html

ED84.380 | SPECIAL EDUCATION-OLYMPIC EDUCATION PROGRAMS
Award: Project Grants
Purpose: To promote the expansion of Special Olympics and the design and implementation of Special Olympics education programs.
Applicant Eligibility: Special Olympics is the only eligible recipient of funds.
Beneficiary Eligibility: Individuals with and without intellectual disabilities.
Award Range/Average: One award for $15,083,000 in FY 18 and one award for $17,583,000 in FY 19.
Funding: (Project Grants) FY 18 $15,083,000.00; FY 19 est $17,583,000.00; FY 20 est $17,583,000.00
HQ: OSERS Office of Special Education Programs 400 Maryland Avenue SW, Washington, DC 20202
   Phone: 202-245-6039 | Email: terry.jackson@ed.gov
   http://www2.ed.gov/programs/osepoly/index.html

ED84.181 | SPECIAL EDUCATION-GRANTS FOR INFANTS AND FAMILIES
Award: Formula Grants
Purpose: To provide grants to States to assist them to implement and maintain a Statewide, comprehensive, coordinated, multidisciplinary, interagency system to make available early intervention services to infants and toddlers with disabilities and their families.
Applicant Eligibility: Eligible applicants are the following 57 entities: the 50 States, the District of Columbia, the Commonwealth of Puerto Rico, the Bureau of Indian education within the U.S. Department of the Interior and the following four outlying area jurisdictions: Guam, American Samoa, the Virgin Islands, and the Commonwealth of the Northern Mariana Islands.
Beneficiary Eligibility: The beneficiaries are infants and toddlers with disabilities aged birth through 2 and their families and at the State's option, children with disabilities ages three through five and their families.
Award Range/Average: For 2019, regular annual allotments to States, including DC and Puerto Rico, ranged from, $2,301,492 to $54,9831652; with an average award of $8,860,943.
Funding: (Formula Grants) FY 18 $470,000,000.00; FY 19 est $470,000,000.00; FY 20 est $470,000,000.00
HQ: Office of Special Education Programs Department of Education 400 Maryland Avenue SW, Washington, DC 20202
   Phone: 202-245-7309 | Email: gregg.corr@ed.gov
   http://www2.ed.gov/about/offices/list/osers/osep/programs.html

ED84.325 | SPECIAL EDUCATION-PERSONNEL DEVELOPMENT TO IMPROVE SERVICES AND RESULTS FOR CHILDREN WITH DISABILITIES
Award: Project Grants
Purpose: To help address State identified needs for highly qualified personnel in special education, related services, early intervention, and regular education to work with infants, toddlers, and children with disabilities.

Applicant Eligibility: State educational agencies, local education agencies, public charter schools that are LEAs under State law, Institutions of higher education, other public agencies, private nonprofit Organizations, outlying areas, Indian Tribes or tribal Organizations, and, if approved by the Secretary, for-profit Organizations.

Beneficiary Eligibility: Infants, toddlers, and children with disabilities are the primary beneficiaries under this program.

Award Range/Average: The range and average vary by competition.

Funding: (Project Grants) FY 18 $83,700,000.00; FY 19 est $87,200,000.00; FY 20 est $87,200,000.00

HQ: OSERS Office of Special Education Programs Potomac Center Plaza 550 12th Street SW, Washington, DC 20202

Phone: 202-245-7875 | Email: sarah.allen@ed.gov

http://www.ed.gov/about/offices/list/osers/osep/index.html

ED84.323 | SPECIAL EDUCATION-STATE PERSONNEL DEVELOPMENT

Award: Project Grants

Purpose: To assist State educational agencies in reforming and improving their systems for personnel preparation and professional development in early intervention, educational and transition services, to improve results for children with disabilities.

Applicant Eligibility: State educational Agencies. A State educational agency of one of the 50 States, the District of Columbia, the Commonwealth of Puerto Rico, and the outlying areas (U.S. Virgin Islands, Guam, American Samoa, and the Commonwealth of the Northern Mariana Islands) may apply.

Beneficiary Eligibility: Infants and toddlers with disabilities as defined in the IDEA and their families, and children with disabilities as defined in the IDEA and their parents benefit from this program.

Award Range/Average: For 2019, the range of awards is expected to be between $500,000 and $1,750,000; the average award is expected to be about $1,000,000, excluding outlying areas.

Funding: (Project Grants) FY 18 $38,630,000.00; FY 19 est $38,630,000.00; FY 20 est $38,630,000.00

HQ: OSERS Office of Special Education Programs 400 Maryland Avenue SW, Washington, DC 20202

Phone: 202-245-6529 | Email: corinne.weidenthal@ed.gov

https://www2.ed.gov/programs/vramerind/index.html

ED84.327 | SPECIAL EDUCATION EDUCATIONAL TECHNOLOGY MEDIA, AND MATERIALS FOR INDIVIDUALS WITH DISABILITIES

Award: Project Grants

Purpose: To improve results for children with disabilities by promoting the development, demonstration, and use of technology.

Applicant Eligibility: State educational agencies (SEAs), local educational agencies (LEAs), public charter schools that are LEAs under State law, Institutions of higher education (IHEs), other public agencies, private nonprofit Organizations, outlying areas, freely associated States, Indian Tribes or tribal Organizations, and, if approved by the Secretary, for-profit Organizations.

Beneficiary Eligibility: Infants, toddlers, children, and other individuals with disabilities, their families, as well as practitioners and service providers benefit from this program.

Award Range/Average: The range and average vary by competition.

Funding: (Project Grants) FY 18 $28,047,000.00; FY 19 est $28,047,000.00; FY 20 est $28,047,000.00

HQ: Office of Special Education Programs, Room 5158 Potomac Center Plaza, Washington, DC 20202

Phone: 202-245-6039 | Email: terry.jackson@ed.gov

http://www2.ed.gov/programs/oseptms/index.html

ED84.027 | SPECIAL EDUCATION GRANTS TO STATES

Award: Formula Grants

Purpose: To provide grants to States to assist them in providing special education and related services to all children with disabilities.

Applicant Eligibility: State educational agencies in the 50 States, District of Columbia, Puerto Rico, American Samoa, Commonwealth of the Northern Mariana Islands, Guam and Virgin Islands, the Department of the Interior, and freely associated States. Local educational agencies apply to their State educational agency for subgrants.

Beneficiary Eligibility: Children with disabilities will benefit.

Award Range/Average: In FY 2017, regular annual allotments to States, including DC and Puerto Rico, ranged from $18.9 million to $1.2 billion, with an average award of $228 million. Grants to outlying areas ranged from $4.8 million to $14 million. The Department of Interior received $95 million.

Funding: (Formula Grants) FY 18 $12,002,848,000.00; FY 19 est $12,364,392,000.00; FY 20 $12,364,392,000.00

Programs Administered by Federal Headquarters

HQ: Department of Education 401 Maryland Avenue SW, Washington, DC 20202
  Phone: 202-245-7309 | Email: gregg.corr@ed.gov
  http://www.ed.gov/about/offices/list/osers/osep/index.html

ED84.328 | SPECIAL EDUCATION PARENT INFORMATION CENTERS
Award: Project Grants
Purpose: To ensure that parents of children with disabilities receive training and information to help improve results for their children.
Applicant Eligibility: Parent Organizations, as defined in Section 671(a)(2) of the Individuals with Disabilities education Act are eligible for parent center awards under IDEA sections 671 and 672. For section 672 funding, these parent centers must meet additional conditions set forth in section 672. For IDEA section 673, State educational agencies (SEAs), local educational agencies (LEAs), public charter schools that are LEAs under State law, Institutions of higher education (IHEs), other public agencies, private nonprofit Organizations, outlying areas, freely associated States, Indian Tribes or tribal Organizations, and, if the Secretary approves, for-profit Organizations, are eligible for technical assistance for parent training and information center awards.
Beneficiary Eligibility: Infants, toddlers, children and youth with disabilities, and their families, benefit from this program.
Award Range/Average: The range and average vary by competition.
Funding: (Project Grants) FY 18 $27,411,000.00; FY 19 est $27,411,000.00; FY 20 est $27,411,000.00
HQ: Department of Education OSERS Office of Special Education Programs 400 Maryland Avenue SW, Room 5162 PCP, Washington, DC 20202
  Phone: 202-245-6595 | Email: carmen.sanchez@ed.gov
  http://www2.ed.gov/programs/oseppic/index.html

ED84.173 | SPECIAL EDUCATION PRESCHOOL GRANTS
Award: Formula Grants
Purpose: To provide grants to States to assist them in providing special education and related services to children with disabilities ages 3 through 5 years, and to 2- year- old children with disabilities who will reach age three during the school year.
Applicant Eligibility: State educational agencies in the 50 States, the District of Columbia, and the Commonwealth of Puerto Rico. Local educational agencies apply to their State educational agency for sub-grants.
Beneficiary Eligibility: Children aged 3 through 5 with disabilities, and (at the State's option) 2-year- old children with disabilities that will reach age 3 during the school year, that require special education and related services.
Award Range/Average: For FY 2019, regular annual allotments to States, including DC and Puerto Rico, ranged from $250,970 to $39,237,787, with an average award of $7,521,538.
Funding: (Formula Grants) FY 18 $381,120,000.00; FY 19 est $391,120,000.00; FY 20 est $391,120,000.00
HQ: Department of Education 402 Maryland Avenue SW, Washington, DC 20202
  Phone: 202-245-7309 | Email: gregg.corr@ed.gov
  http://www.ed.gov/about/offices/list/osers/osep/programs.html

ED84.329 | SPECIAL EDUCATION STUDIES AND EVALUATIONS
Award: Project Grants
Purpose: To provide free appropriate public education to children with disabilities; and early intervention services to infants and toddlers with disabilities who would be at risk of having substantial developmental delays if early intervention services were not provided.
Applicant Eligibility: Applicants that have the ability and capacity to conduct scientifically valid evaluations are eligible to apply. Eligible applicants include, but are not limited to, non-profit and for-profit Organizations.
Beneficiary Eligibility: Infants, toddlers, and children with disabilities, and other individuals with disabilities, and their families benefit from this program.
Funding: (Project Grants (Contracts)) FY 18 $10,818,000.00; FY 19 est $10,818,000.00; FY 20 est $10,818,000.00
HQ: 550 12th Street SW, Room 4104, Washington, DC 20208
  Phone: 202-245-7474 | Email: lauren.angelo@ed.gov
  http://ies.ed.gov/ncee

ED84.326 | SPECIAL EDUCATION TECHNICAL ASSISTANCE AND DISSEMINATION TO IMPROVE SERVICES AND RESULTS FOR CHILDREN WITH DISABILITIES

Award: Project Grants

Purpose: To improve Services and Results for Children with Disabilities program is to promote academic achievement and to improve results for children with disabilities by providing technical assistance (TA).

Applicant Eligibility: State educational agencies (SEAs), local educational agencies (LEAs), public charter schools that are LEAs under State law, Institutions of higher education (IHEs), other public agencies, private nonprofit Organizations, outlying areas, freely associated States, Indian Tribes or tribal Organizations, and, if approved by the Secretary, for-profit Organizations.

Beneficiary Eligibility: Infants, toddlers, children, and other individuals with disabilities, their families as well as practitioners and service providers benefit from this program.

Award Range/Average: The range and average vary by competition.

Funding: (Project Grants) FY 18 $44,345,000.00; FY 19 est $44,345,000.00; FY 19 $44,345,000.00

HQ: Office of Special Education Programs, Room 5136 Potomac Center Plaza, Washington, DC 20202
Phone: 202-245-6674 | Email: tina.diamond@ed.gov
http://www.ed.gov/about/offices/list/osers/osep/index.html

ED84.373 | SPECIAL EDUCATION TECHNICAL ASSISTANCE ON STATE DATA COLLECTION

Award: Project Grants

Purpose: Provides technical assistance needed, to improve the capacity of States to meet the data collection requirements of the IDEA.

Applicant Eligibility: Public and private agencies and Organizations, including for profit and non-profit agencies and Organizations.

Beneficiary Eligibility: Infants, toddlers, and children with disabilities benefit from this program.

Funding: (Project Grants) FY 18 est $21,000,000.00; FY 19 est $21,000,000.00; FY 20 est $10,000,000.00

HQ: OSERS Office of Special Education Programs 400 Maryland Avenue SW, Washington, DC 20202
Phone: 202-245-7334 | Email: david.egnor@ed.gov
http://www.ed.gov/about/offices/list/osers/osep/index.html

DOS19.451 | SPECIAL INTERNATIONAL EXCHANGE GRANT PROGRAMS

Award: Cooperative Agreements; Project Grants

Purpose: Provides special grants for international exchanges and other activities that support and address current and emerging issues of mutual interest to the United States and other countries, consistent with the program criteria established in the Department's annual appropriation.

Applicant Eligibility: Pursuant to the Mutual educational and Cultural Exchange Act of 1961, as amended (Fulbright-Hays Act) the Bureau of educational and Cultural Affairs of the U.S. Department of State awards project grants and cooperative agreements to educational and cultural public or private nonprofit foundations or Institutions. Applications may be submitted by public and private non-profit Organizations meeting the provisions described in Internal Revenue Code section 26 USC 501(c)(3). Organizations must have nonprofit status with the IRS at the time of application. Please refer to the Grants.gov or the U.S. Department of State's SAMS Domestic announcement for further eligibility criteria. OMB Guidance 2 CFR Part 200 Subpart E Cost Principles applies to this Program.

Beneficiary Eligibility: Same as Applicant Eligibility.

Award Range/Average: 8401984

Funding: (Cooperative Agreements) FY 17 $8,401,984.00; FY 18 est $8,401,984.00; FY 19 est $8,401,984.00

HQ: Office of Academic Exchanges E Asia and Pacific Branch 2200 C Street NW SA-05 4-L11, Washington, DC 20037
Phone: 202-632-3216 | Email: marshallt@state.gov
http://exchanges.state.gov

Programs Administered by Federal Headquarters

DOC11.460 | SPECIAL OCEANIC AND ATMOSPHERIC PROJECTS
"Ocean Exploration"

Award: Cooperative Agreements

Purpose: To acquire information on all oceans and their dimensions for advancing knowledge and technologies within Oceanic and Atmospheric Research.

Applicant Eligibility: As stated in NOAA special announcements or applicable reports in support of NOAA's mission.

Beneficiary Eligibility: Organizations and individuals with interests in support of managing effectively the Nation's oceanic and atmospheric resources.

Funding: (Cooperative Agreements) FY 16 $13,770,306.00; FY 17 est $17,939,678.00; FY 18 est $23,265,000.00

HQ: 1315 E W Highway, Silver Spring, MD 20910

Phone: 301-713-1010

HHS93.044 | SPECIAL PROGRAMS FOR THE AGING, TITLE III, PART B, GRANTS FOR SUPPORTIVE SERVICES AND SENIOR CENTERS

Award: Formula Grants

Purpose: To encourage State Agencies on Aging and Area Agencies on Aging to concentrate resources to develop and implement comprehensive and coordinated community-based systems of service for older individuals.

Applicant Eligibility: Only State and U.S. Territories which have State Agencies on Aging designated by the Governors are eligible to receive these grants.

Beneficiary Eligibility: Individuals age 60 and over, targeting those older individuals with the greatest economic needs, the greatest social needs, and those residing in rural areas.

Award Range/Average: Average $6,511,854

Funding: (Formula Grants) FY 17 $357,063,000.00; FY 18 est $385,074,000.00; FY 19 est $350,224,000.00

HQ: 330 C Street SW, Washington, DC 20201

Phone: 202-795-7386 | Email: greg.link@acl.hhs.gov

http://acl.gov

HHS93.045 | SPECIAL PROGRAMS FOR THE AGING, TITLE III, PART C, NUTRITION SERVICES

Award: Formula Grants

Purpose: To provide grants to States and U.S. Territories to support nutrition services including nutritious meals, nutrition education and other appropriate nutrition services for older adults.

Applicant Eligibility: Only States and U.S. Territories which have State Units on Aging designated by the governors are eligible to receive these grants.

Beneficiary Eligibility: For Title III congregate meals, persons who are older adults (age 60 years and above) or a spouse of an older adult, regardless of age; disabled adults who live in housing facilities primarily occupied by older adults where a congregate site is located; disabled adults under age 60, who reside at home with older adults; and volunteers, regardless of age, who assist in meal service during meal hours. For Title III home-delivered meals, an older individual must be assessed to be homebound. The spouse of a homebound individual regardless of age or condition may receive a meal if receipt of the meal is assessed to be in the best interest of the homebound older adult.

Award Range/Average: Congregate Nutrition Services: FY16: RANGE: $278,155 to $45,269,354 AVERAGE: $5,270,768 FY 17: RANGE: $278,636 to $45,730,530 AVERAGE: $7,961,029 FY18 Range $302,513 to $50,682,482 AVERAGE: $ 8,643,237 Home-Delivered Nutrition Services:FY 16: RANGE: $140,421 to $23,435,646 AVERAGE: $4,012,033 FY17: RANGE: $140,659 to $23,603,150 AVERAGE: $4,018,820 FY 18: Range $151,968- $25,494,622, Average: $4,341,937

Funding: (Formula Grants) FY 17 $688,488,000.00; FY 18 est $688,684,000.00; FY 19 Estimate Not Available FY 16 $669,721,620.00; Congregate Nutrition Services: FY16: RANGE: $278,155 to $45,269,354 AVERAGE: $5,270,768 FY 17: RANGE: $278,636 to $45,730,530 AVERAGE: $7,961,029 FY18 Range $302,513 to $50,682,482 AVERAGE: $ 8,643,237Home-Delivered Nutrition Services:FY 16: RANGE: $140,421 to $23,435,646 AVERAGE: $4,012,033 FY17: RANGE: $140,659 to $23,603,150 AVERAGE: $4,018,820 FY 18: Range $151,968- $25,494,622, Average: $4,341,937

HQ: Office of Nutrition and Health Promotion Programs Administration on Aging DHHS 330 C Street SW, Washington, DC 20201

Phone: 202-795-7355 | Email: holly.greuling@acl.hhs.gov

HHS93.043 | SPECIAL PROGRAMS FOR THE AGING, TITLE III, PART D, DISEASE PREVENTION AND HEALTH PROMOTION SERVICES

Award: Formula Grants
Purpose: To develop or strengthen preventive health service and health promotion systems through designated State Agencies on Aging and Area Agencies on Aging.
Applicant Eligibility: Only States and U.S. Territories which have State Agencies on Aging designated by the governors are eligible to receive these grants.
Beneficiary Eligibility: Older individuals, age sixty and older, especially those living in areas of States which are medically underserved and in which there are a large number of older individuals who have the greatest economic need for the services.
Award Range/Average: FY17 est $12,281 - $1,992,449; $350,884
Funding: (Formula Grants) FY 17 $19,664,255.00; FY 18 est $24,599,520.00; FY 19 est $24,599,520.00
HQ: 330 C Street SW, Washington, DC 20201
  Phone: 617-565-1170 | Email: casey.dicocco@acl.hhs.gov
  http://www.acl.gov/programs/health-wellness/disease-prevention

HHS93.048 | SPECIAL PROGRAMS FOR THE AGING, TITLE IV, AND TITLE II, DISCRETIONARY PROJECTS

Award: Cooperative Agreements
Purpose: To support the development and testing of innovative programs, services and systems of support that respond to the needs of the nation's growing elderly population and those individuals in need of long term services and supports (LTSS).
Applicant Eligibility: Grants may be made to any public or nonprofit private agency, Organization, or institution. Contracts may be awarded to any agency, Organization or institution. Grants and contracts are not available to individuals.
Beneficiary Eligibility: Older individuals aged 60 and older, family caregivers and grandparents, and older individuals who are relative caregivers, individuals at high-risk of institutional placement, and individuals in need of assistance with or planning ahead for their long-term care needs.
Award Range/Average: Not Available.
Funding: (Cooperative Agreements (Discretionary Grants)) FY 17 $36,323,928.00; FY 18 est $36,323,928.00; FY 19 est $35,323,928.00
HQ: Department of Health and Human Services 330 C Street SW, Room 1144, Washington, DC 20201
  Phone: 202-795-7386 | Email: greg.link@acl.hhs.gov
  http://www.acl.gov

HHS93.047 | SPECIAL PROGRAMS FOR THE AGING, TITLE VI, PART A, GRANTS TO INDIAN TRIBES, PART B, GRANTS TO NATIVE HAWAIIANS

Award: Formula Grants
Purpose: To promote the delivery of supportive services, including nutrition services, to American Indians, Alaskan natives, and Native Hawaiians.
Applicant Eligibility: Tribal Organizations of Indian Tribes eligible for assistance under Section 4 of the Indian Self-Determination and education Assistance Act (25 U.S.C. 450b), and public or nonprofit private Organizations which serve Native Hawaiian Elders, which represent at least 50 Indians or Hawaiians 60 years of age or older. Applicants must demonstrate that they have the ability to deliver supportive and nutrition services.
Beneficiary Eligibility: Indians who are 60 years of age and older, and in the case of nutrition services, their spouses. Tribes also have the authority to define Indians under 60 years of age as "older Indian" making them eligible for services.
Award Range/Average: FY 16 Ranges for Part A - $75,540- $186,042; Part B - $1,505,000 FY 17 Ranges for Part A - $73,990-$181,831; Part B - $1,505,000
Funding: (Formula Grants) FY 17 $31,158,000.00; FY 18 est $31,923,872.00; FY 19 Estimate Not Available
HQ: 330 C Street SW, Washington, DC 20201
  Phone: 202-357-0148 | Email: cynthia.lacounte@acl.hhs.gov
  http://www.acl.gov

HHS93.042 | SPECIAL PROGRAMS FOR THE AGING, TITLE VII, CHAPTER 2, LONG TERM CARE OMBUDSMAN SERVICES FOR OLDER INDIVIDUALS
"State Grants for Long Term Care Ombudsman Services"

Award: Formula Grants
Purpose: To investigate and resolve complaints made by or on behalf of residents of nursing homes or other long-term care facilities.
Applicant Eligibility: All States and U.S. Territories which have State Agencies on Aging designated by the governors.
Beneficiary Eligibility: Individuals residing in long-term care facilities or requiring assistance in entering or transferring from such facilities.
Award Range/Average: FY15 Range: $9,829 - $1,618,546; Average: $280,824
Funding: (Formula Grants) FY 17 $15,885,000.00; FY 18 est $16,885,000.00; FY 19 est Estimate Not Available
HQ: Department of Health and Human Services 330 C Street SW, Washington, DC 20201
   Phone: 206-615-2514 | Email: louise.ryan@acl.hhs.gov
   http://www.acl.gov

HHS93.041 | SPECIAL PROGRAMS FOR THE AGING, TITLE VII, CHAPTER 3, PROGRAMS FOR PREVENTION OF ELDER ABUSE, NEGLECT, AND EXPLOITATION

Award: Formula Grants
Purpose: To develop, strengthen, and carry out programs for the prevention, detection, assessment, and treatment of, intervention in, investigation of, and response to elder abuse, neglect, and exploitation.
Applicant Eligibility: All States and U.S. Territories which have State Agencies on Aging designated by the governors.
Beneficiary Eligibility: Individuals 60 years of age and older, targeting those older individuals with the greatest social needs and those with the greatest economic needs.
Award Range/Average: Average: $84,500 FY16 Range $2,958- $471,073.
Funding: (Formula Grants) FY 16 $4,751,881.00; FY 17 est $4,742,357.00; FY 18 Estimate Not Available
HQ: 330 C Street SW, Washington, DC 20201
   Phone: 202-795-7467 | Email: stephanie.whittiereliason@acl.hhs.gov
   http://www.acl.gov

HHS93.928 | SPECIAL PROJECTS OF NATIONAL SIGNIFICANCE
"SPNS"

Award: Cooperative Agreements; Project Grants
Purpose: To respond to the care and treatment needs of individuals receiving assistance under the Ryan White HIV/AIDS program (RWHAP). Special Projects of National Significance (SPNS) also supports the development and implementation of innovative delivery models of HIV care, services, and capacity development initiatives.
Applicant Eligibility: Academic Institutions, non-profit Organizations including faith-based Organizations, and those eligible for funding under Parts A-D authorized by Title XXVI of the Public Health Service (PHS) Act as amended by the Ryan White HIV/AIDS Treatment Extension Act of 2009. Additionally, federally recognized Indian Tribal Governments and tribal Organizations are also eligible to apply for these funds.
Beneficiary Eligibility: Individuals with HIV.
Award Range/Average: Project Grants: $263,206 to $482,500; Average $300,000; Coop. Agreements: $ 500,000 to $3,049,198. Average $550,000.
Funding: (Project Grants) FY 18 $7,155,077.00; FY 19 est $4,179,396.00; FY 20 est $2,396,543.00; (Cooperative Agreements) FY 18 $15,785,011.00; FY 19 est $18,217,687.00; FY 20 est $20,195,873.00
HQ: 5600 Fishers Lane, Room 9N-114, Rockville, MD 20857
   Phone: 301-443-8109 | Email: hphillips@hrsa.gov
   http://www.hrsa.gov

DOC11.553 | SPECIAL PROJECTS
Award: Project Grants
Purpose: To assist organizations and new sources of advanced telecommunications.

Applicant Eligibility: Organizations specifically identified by Congress in agency appropriations legislation or other authority that provides for non-competitive grants.

Beneficiary Eligibility: Beneficiaries are those served by the organizations receiving awards.

HQ: 1401 Constitution Avenue NW, Room 4888 NTIA/OPCM, Washington, DC 20230

Phone: 202-482-5515 | Email: writchie@ntia.doc.gov

https://www.ntia.doc.gov/home

HUD14.279 | SPECIALIZED HOUSING AND SERVICES FOR VICTIMS OF HUMAN TRAFFICKING

Award: Salaries and Expenses

Purpose: To address the housing and service needs of victims affected by sex and labour trafficking.

Applicant Eligibility: Human Trafficking Program Eligible Applicants: For the purposes of housing and trauma-informed, client centered services under this NOFA, of which $13,500,000 is available, additional eligible applicants, and subrecipients, defined as other Governments, e.g., town, borough, parish, village or other general purpose political subdivision of a state, territory, or federally recognized Indian tribe government. Additionally, Institutions of higher education are eligible if they hold an IRS 501(c)(3) final determinate letter. If the applicant chooses to include subrecipients, the subrecipients must meet the same eligibility requirements as the applicant. If a non-profit Organization will submit the application, a copy of the IRS 501(c)(3) must be attached to this application. Additionally, if the application includes subrecipients, non-profit documentation for the subrecipients must also be attached to this application. Human Trafficking Technical Assistance Eligible Applicants: For the purposes of the technical assistance under this NOFA, of which $1,000,000 is available, the following lists eligible applicants in addition to the eligible applicants listed above under Program eligible applicants: Non-profits without 501(c)(3) status with IRS, other than Institutions of higher education; Private Institutions of higher education; Private Institutions other than small businesses; and Small businesses.

Beneficiary Eligibility: Program - Housing and Services: other governments, e.g., town, borough, parish, village or other general purpose political subdivision of a state, territory, or federally recognized Indian tribe government Technical Assistance: Non-profits without 501(c)(3) status with IRS, other than institutions of higher education; Private institutions of higher education; Private institutions other than small businesses and Small businesses.

Award Range/Average: $500,000 to $600,000 for program operations, housing and services $1,000,000 for technical assistance

Funding: (Salaries and Expenses Total) FY 18 $0; FY 19 est $12; FY 20 est $12

HQ: 451 7th Street SW, Room 7260, Washington, DC 20410

Phone: 202-402-4773 | Email: karen.m.deblasio@hud.gov

https://www.grants.gov

VA64.051 | SPECIALLY ADAPTED HOUSING ASSISTIVE TECHNOLOGY GRANT PROGRAM

"SAHAT"

Award: Project Grants

Purpose: To provide grants of financial assistance to develop new assistive technology.

Applicant Eligibility: As authorized by 38 U.S.C. 2108, the Secretary may award grants to a person or entity for the development of specially adapted housing assistive technologies. In order to foster competition and best serve the needs of Veterans and Servicemembers, VA is placing no restrictions on the types of eligible entities outside of threshold criteria listed in the NOFA. All technology grant recipients, including individuals and entities formed as for-profit entities, will be subject to the rules of the Uniform Administrative Requirements for Grants and Agreements With Institutions of Higher education, Hospitals, and other Non-profit Organizations, as found at 2 CFR Part 200. Where the Secretary determines that 2 CFR Part 200 is not applicable or where the Secretary determines that additional requirements are necessary due to the uniqueness of a situation, the Secretary will apply the same standard applicable to exceptions under 2 CFR 200. 102.

Beneficiary Eligibility: Projects funded under this announcement must involve new assistive technologies the Secretary determines could aid or enhance the ability of a Veteran or Servicemember to live in an adapted home. However, projects funded under this announcement must not be used for the completion of activities which were to have been completed under a prior grant.

Award Range/Average: Grantees can be awarded no more than $200,000

Funding: (Project Grants) FY 15 Actual Not Available; FY 16 est $1,000,000.00; FY 17 est Estimate Not Available

Programs Administered by Federal Headquarters

HQ: 810 Vermont Avenue NW, Washington, DC 20420
   Phone: 202-632-8801 | Email: betty.rhoades@va.gov
   http://www.benefits.va.gov/homeloans/adaptedhousing.asp

VA64.106 | SPECIALLY ADAPTED HOUSING FOR DISABLED VETERANS
"Paraplegic Housing"

Award: Direct Payments for Specified Use
Purpose: To help certain severely disabled veterans acquire a home which is suitably adapted to meet the needs of their disabilities.
Applicant Eligibility: For a SAH grant, veterans are eligible if they are entitled to disability compensation for a permanent, total, and service-connected disability due to: (1) loss or loss of use of both lower extremities, such as to preclude locomotion without the aid of braces, canes, crutches, or a wheelchair; (2) blindness in both eyes, having only light perception, plus loss or loss of use of one lower extremity; (3) loss or loss of use of one lower extremity, together with residuals of organic disease or injury, or the loss or loss of use of one upper extremity, which so affect the functions of balance or propulsion as to preclude locomotion without the aid of braces, crutches, canes, or a wheelchair; or (4) loss or loss of use, of both upper extremities such as to preclude use of the arms at or above the elbows; (5) a severe burn injury. It must be medically feasible for the veteran to reside in the particular home involved. For an SHA grant, veterans are eligible if they are entitled to disability compensation for a permanent and total service-connected disability that (1) is due to blindness in both eyes with 5/200 visual acuity or less, or (2) includes the anatomical loss or loss of use of both hands, or (3) a severe burn injury.
Beneficiary Eligibility: Permanently and totally disabled veterans.
Award Range/Average: SAH: For the housing unit, land, fixtures, and allowable expenses, up to $73,768. SHA: For adaptations to the veteran's residence, up to $14,754.
Funding: (Direct Payments for Specified Use) FY 16 $117,885,000.00; FY 17 est $124,626,000.00; FY 18 Estimate Not Available
HQ: Department of Veterans Affairs 810 Vermont Avenue NW, Washington, DC 20420
   Phone: 202-461-9500
   http://www.benefits.va.gov/homeloans/adaptedhousing.asp

USDA10.309 | SPECIALTY CROP RESEARCH INITIATIVE
"SCRI"

Award: Project Grants
Purpose: The Specialty Crop Research Initiative resolves issues of industries. It promotes projects that address innovations and technology for advancing agriculture, management of pests, food safety, etc.
Applicant Eligibility: Applications may be submitted by Federal agencies, national laboratories, colleges and universities, research Institutions and Organizations, private Organizations or corporations, State agricultural experiment stations, individuals, or groups consisting of two or more of these entities.
Beneficiary Eligibility: Same as Applicant Eligibility.
Award Range/Average: If minimum or maximum amounts of funding per competitive and/or capacity project grant, or cooperative agreement are established, these amounts will be announced in the annual Competitive Request for Application (RFA).The most current RFA is available via: https://nifa.usda.gov/funding-opportunity/specialty-crop-research-initiative-scri
Funding: (Project Grants (Cooperative Agreements)) FY 17 $69,578,033.00; FY 18 est $69,796,077.00; FY 19 est $74,795,599.00
HQ: National Program Leader Institute of Food Production and Sustainability Division of Plant Systems-Production 1400 Independence Avenue SW, PO Box 2240, Washington, DC 20250-2240
   Phone: 202-401-4202
   http://nifa.usda.gov/program/specialty-crop-research-initiative

DHS97.083 | STAFFING FOR ADEQUATE FIRE AND EMERGENCY RESPONSE (SAFER)
"SAFER ACT"

Award: Project Grants

Purpose: SAFER grant program assists the local fire departments with staffing and deployment to respond quickly to emergencies. The program also ensures that communal areas have adequate protection from fire and fire-related hazards.

Applicant Eligibility: This Program is restricted to the jurisdictions/Organizations described in Program guidance documents. For specific information, refer to the Notice of Funding Opportunity. In summary, for the purpose of this Program, "State" is defined as the fifty States, the District of Columbia, Puerto Rico, the U.S. Virgin Islands, Guam, American Samoa, and the Commonwealth of the Northern Mariana Islands. The Alaska Village Initiative, a nonprofit Organization incorporated in the State of Alaska, shall also be considered eligible for purposes of receiving assistance under this Program on behalf of Alaska Native villages. A "fire department" is defined as an agency or Organization that has a formally recognized arrangement with a State, territory, local, or tribal authority (city, county, parish, fire district, township, town, or other governing body) to provide fire suppression on a first-due basis to a population within a fixed geographical area. Fire departments may be comprised of members who are all volunteer, combination volunteer/career, or all career.

Beneficiary Eligibility: Local or tribal communities serviced by the fire department including, local businesses, homeowners and property owners.

Award Range/Average: Refer to Notice of Funding Opportunity document.

Funding: (Project Grants) FY 18 $350,000,000.00; FY 19 est $350,000,000.00; FY 20 est $350,000,000.00

HQ: Department of Homeland Security/FEMA Grant Programs Directorate Assistance to Firefighters Grant 400 C Street SW 3N, Washington, DC 20742-3635

Phone: 866-274-0960

http://www.fema.gov/firegrants

DOC11.604 | STANDARD REFERENCE MATERIALS
"SRM"

Award: Sale, Exchange, Or Donation of Property and Goods

Purpose: Standard Reference Materials are issued by NIST for analysis, strategies for quality control and to assess material performance, steps to measure materials, etc.

Applicant Eligibility: Federal agencies, State and local Governments, societies, Institutions, firms, corporations, and individuals may purchase the materials.

Beneficiary Eligibility: N/A

Funding: (Sale, Exchange, or Donation of Property and Goods) FY 18 $20,101,453.00; FY 19 est $23,144,000.00; FY 20 est $22,119,800.00

HQ: 100 Bureau Drive, PO Box 2300, Gaithersburg, MD 20899

Phone: 301-975-3096 | Email: steven.choquette@nist.gov

http://www.nist.gov/srm

HHS93.831 | STANDARDS DEVELOPMENT ORGANIZATION COLLABORATION TO ENHANCE STANDARDS ALIGNMENT, TESTING, AND MEASUREMENT

Award: Cooperative Agreements

Purpose: To establish a mechanism for ongoing collaboration among ONC and various SDOs. It aims to provide support to these organizations for standards and interoperability within these organizations portfolio's that is of mutual interest to ONC.

Applicant Eligibility: Applicants must be a United States-based non-profit institution or Organization, state or local government, agency or group.

Beneficiary Eligibility: The beneficiaries will include all health care organizations and patients using electronic health records.

Award Range/Average: Average of $100,000.

Funding: (Cooperative Agreements) FY 18 $100,000.00; FY 19 est $0.00; FY 20 est Estimate Not Available

HQ: 330 C Street SW, Washington, DC 20201

Phone: 202-720-2919 | Email: carmel.halloun@hhs.gov

http://www.healthit.gov

Programs Administered by Federal Headquarters

HHS93.883 | STANDARDS EXPLORATION AWARD

Award: Cooperative Agreements

Purpose: The Office of the National Coordinator for Health Information Technology funds up to four pilot programs that will advance a scalable process of interoperable exchange of electronic health data using standards that will improve the delivery of how and where healthcare is delivered, improve patient outcomes, and reduce cost.

Applicant Eligibility: The objective of this award is to advance a scalable process of interoperable exchange of electronic health data using standards that will improve the delivery of how and where healthcare is delivered, improve patient outcomes, and reduce cost. Collaborative groups of multiple stakeholders across different Organizations will be considered, as well as encouraged, to support widespread interoperability.

Beneficiary Eligibility: As health care delivery impacts everyone, the beneficiary eligibility includes all of the listed groups as provided in the reference manual.

Award Range/Average: There has been $250,000 for FFY16-17 for this award. We estimate that we would award no more than four (4) awards total; the award amounts would be no less than $20,000 and may not exceed $75,000 per awardee. The award amount will be determined upon the scope and strength the awardee's proposal.

HQ: 330 C Street SW, Washington, DC 20201
  Phone: 202-720-2919 | Email: carmel.halloun@hhs.gov

DOC11.610 | STANDARDS INFORMATION CENTER
"SIC"

Award: Dissemination of Technical Information

Purpose: To assist information center and referral services and guidance on standards to provide regulatory and certification information to U.S. exporters and manufacturers.

Applicant Eligibility: State and local government, private, public, profit Organizations, nonprofit Institutions and individuals.

Beneficiary Eligibility: State and local government, private, public, profit organizations, nonprofit institutions and individuals will benefit.

Funding: (Formula Grants) FY 18 $180,174.00; FY 19 est $188,834.00; FY 20 est $150,750.00

HQ: 100 Bureau Drive, PO Box 2100, Gaithersburg, MD 20899
  Phone: 301-975-5571 | Email: kerry.miles@nist.gov
  https://www.nist.gov/standardsgov/what-we-do/trade-regulatory-programs/standards-information-center

HHS93.366 | STATE ACTIONS TO IMPROVE ORAL HEALTH OUTCOMES AND PARTNER ACTIONS TO IMPROVE ORAL HEALTH OUTCOMES
"Oral Health"

Award: Cooperative Agreements; Project Grants

Purpose: To establish oral health leadership and program guidance, oral health data collection and interpretation, multi-dimensional delivery system for oral and physical health, and to implement science-based programs to improve oral and physical health.

Applicant Eligibility: States, political subdivisions of States, local health authorities, and individuals or Organizations with specialized health interests will benefit.

Beneficiary Eligibility: Same as Applicant Eligibility.

Funding: (Cooperative Agreements) FY 18 $8,319,096.00; FY 19 est $8,383,485.00; FY 20 est $8,383,485.00

HQ: 4770 Buford Highway NE, PO Box F80, Atlanta, GA 30341
  Phone: 770-488-6075
  http://www.cdc.gov

USDA10.531 | STATE AGENCY: FARM TO SCHOOL PROGRAM TRAINING AND CURRICULA

Award: Cooperative Agreements

Purpose: Conduct a needs assessment among agricultural producers and provide the necessary knowledge and skills to train the producers to overcome their challenges in selling their goods to the school food authorities.

Applicant Eligibility: The cooperative agreement is only open to accredited public or private academic institute of higher education, a research or training institution, or nonprofit or for-profit Organizations. Special consideration will be given to applicants who have an established producer and State Agency network and/or have successfully implemented training initiatives with a producer on a national level. Please see the RFP for a full explanation of eligibility requirements.

Beneficiary Eligibility: Please see the RFP for additional information.

Award Range/Average: $1,000,000 - $2,000,000

Funding: (Cooperative Agreements) FY 18 $1,829,282.00 FY 19 est Not Separately Identifiable; FY 20 est Not Separately Identifiable

HQ: 3101 Park Center Drive, Alexandria, VA 22302
  Phone: 703-457-7803

DOJ16.614 | STATE AND LOCAL ANTI-TERRORISM TRAINING "SLATT"

Award: Advisory Services and Counseling; Dissemination of Technical Information; Training

Purpose: To prevent terrorism and promote the Nation's Security Consistent with the Rule of Law by assisting state, local, and tribal law enforcement in identifying, investigating, and preventing criminal acts of terror through training, technical assistance, and resources that build law enforcement's knowledge and capacity to identify and respond to possible domestic terrorism.

Applicant Eligibility: For-profit (commercial) Organizations; nonprofit Organizations; faith-based and community Organizations; Institutions of higher education; and consortiums with significant and demonstrated experience in terror prevention strategies and in delivering training and technical assistance to law enforcement and tribal communities are eligible to apply. For-profit Organizations must agree to waive any profit or fees for services. Joint applications from a consortium must identify the primary applicant and co-applicant(s), and letters of support that outline the partners' responsibilities must be provided.

Beneficiary Eligibility: State, local, and tribal criminal justice agencies are the primary beneficiaries of this program.

Award Range/Average: One cooperative agreement for up to $2 million was competitively awarded in FY 2018 for a project period of 24 months.

Funding: (Project Grants) FY 18 $2,000,000.00; FY 19 est $0.00; FY 20 est $0.00

HQ: Bureau of Justice Assistance 810 7th Street NW, Washington, DC 20531
  Phone: 202-616-6500
  http://www.ojp.usdoj.gov/training/training.htm

DHS97.005 | STATE AND LOCAL HOMELAND SECURITY NATIONAL TRAINING PROGRAM
"FY 2014 Homeland Security National Training Program National Domestic Preparedness Consortium (NDPC) and Continuing Training Grants (CTG)"

Award: Project Grants

Purpose: The Homeland Security National Training Program together with the National Domestic Preparedness Consortium and Continuing Training Grants program helps in implementing the National Preparedness System to help build a secure and resilient nation against terrorist attacks and natural disasters.

Applicant Eligibility: The HSNTP/NDPC is a closed solicitation, available only to eligible Organizations. Non-Federal members that make up the National Domestic Preparedness Consortium (NDPC) which consist of the following Institutions: Louisiana State University, Texas A&M, New Mexico Institute of Mining and Technology, and the University of Hawaii. The Continuing Training Grants (CTG) Program is an open competition to develop and deliver training in selected focus areas. Through the CTG, FEMA identifies important focus areas for applicants to use in the development of their application. Applicants may submit only one application per focus area. Applications will undergo a review to determine whether all required guidelines are followed and selection criteria are met. The full application review process will conclude with a rigorous, competitive review process used to select Programs for recommendation for award. NDPC To receive funding under this Program, recipients must be members of the NDPC as defined by 6 U.S.C. 1102PC.

Beneficiary Eligibility: State and Local units of government, public non-profits, and Federally recognized tribal entities.

Award Range/Average: $5,000,000 (low) to $25,000,000 (high).

Funding: (Cooperative Agreements) FY 18 $188,000,000.00; FY 19 est $188,000,000.00; FY 20 est $109,000,000.00

HQ: National Preparedness Directorate (NPD) Grants Program Directorate (GPD) FEMA Department of Homeland Security National Training and Education Division 400 C Street SW, Washington, DC 20472
  Phone: 800-368-6498
  http://www.fema.gov/government/grant/index.shtm

Programs Administered by Federal Headquarters

DOC11.549 | STATE AND LOCAL IMPLEMENTATION GRANT PROGRAM "SLIGP"

Award: Project Grants
Purpose: To assist State and local jurisdictions in implementing effective ways for utilizing equipment and architecture for safety broadband network and wireless communications.
Applicant Eligibility: 1. Grants were awarded to eligible States and Territories. 2. The grants will be used to assist applicants with activities related to planning for the establishment of a nationwide public safety broadband network. 3. The State must designate a single officer or governmental body to serve as the coordinator of the grant funds.
Beneficiary Eligibility: Indirect beneficiaries of the grants are law enforcement officers, fire fighters, emergency medical professionals and other public safety officials, as well as the general public, who will receive improved communications capabilities from the creation of the single, nationwide interoperable public safety broadband network that these grants will facilitate.
Award Range/Average: SLIGP 2.0 awards for the first increment of funding ranged from $200,000 to $425,000. For the second increment of funding, awards ranged from $102,645 to $695,000.
Funding: (Project Grants) FY 18 $12,629,323.00; FY 19 est $20,680,038.00; FY 20 est $0.00
HQ: Office of Public Safety Communications U.S. Department of Commerce 1401 Constitution Avenue NW, Room 4086, Washington, DC 20230
Phone: 202-482-2236
https://www.ntia.doc.gov/category/state-and-local-implementation-grant-program-20

HHS93.757 | STATE AND LOCAL PUBLIC HEALTH ACTIONS TO PREVENT OBESITY, DIABETES, HEART DISEASE AND STROKE (PPHF)
"State and Local Public Health Actions to Prevent Obesity, Diabetes, Heart Disease and Stroke"

Award: Cooperative Agreements
Purpose: The purpose of this program is to support statewide implementation of cross-cutting, evidence-based approaches to promote health and prevent and control chronic diseases and their risk factors.
Applicant Eligibility: (1) Eligible Applicants: State Departments of Health or their Bona Fide Agents funded under CDC-RFA-DP13-1305 (2.) Special Eligibility Requirements: Letters of Support (LOS) for key collaborations involved with promoting and/or implementing activities. In addition there may be requirements for demonstrated capacity in key (or specific) areas, and/or to reach highest need areas or disparate populations.
Beneficiary Eligibility: States and communities will benefit from this assistance in many ways including through improved clinical and other preventive services for self management of hypertension, diabetes, overweight and obesity.
Award Range/Average: The awards may range from $550,000 for basic component and $1,000,000 to $1,700,000 per applicant
HQ: 4770 Buford Highway NE, PO Box K10, Atlanta, GA 30341
Phone: 770-488-5007 | Email: rif6@cdc.gov
http://www.cdc.gov

HHS93.699 | STATE AND NATIONAL TOBACCO CESSATION SUPPORT SYSTEMS "Quitlines"

Award: Cooperative Agreements
Purpose: The program supports state quitline capacity in order to respond to federal initiatives such as the National Tobacco Education Campaign. This program addresses the "Healthy People 2020" focus area of tobacco uses and the goal of reducing illness, disability, and death related to tobacco uses and secondhand smoke exposure.
Applicant Eligibility: Eligible applicants that can apply for this funding are listed below: State Governments County Governments City or township Governments Special district Governments Independent school districts Public and State controlled Institutions of higher education Native American tribal Governments (Federally recognized tribal Governments) Nonprofit with 501C3 IRS status (other than institution of higher education)Nonprofit without 501C3 IRS status (other than institution of higher education)Private Institutions of higher education For profit Organizations other than small businesses Small businesses Government Organizations: State (includes the District of Columbia)Local Governments or their bona fide agents Territorial Governments or their bona fide agents in the Commonwealth of Puerto Rico, the Virgin Islands, the

Programs Administered by Federal Headquarters

Commonwealth of the Northern Marianna Islands, American Samoa, Guam, the Federated States of Micronesia, the Republic of the Marshall Islands, and the Republic of Palau State controlled Institutions of higher education American Indian or Alaska Native tribal Governments (federally recognized or state-recognized)Public Housing Authorities/Indian Housing Authorities] Non-government Organizations: American Indian or Alaska native tribally designated Organizations Other: Private colleges and universities Community-based Organizations Faith-Based Organizations.
Beneficiary Eligibility: N/A
Award Range/Average: Not available Pending FY19 funding
HQ: 4770 Buford Highway NE, Atlanta, GA 30341
    Phone: 770-488-5941
    http://www.cdc.gov

HHS93.240 | STATE CAPACITY BUILDING
"Site Specific Activities Cooperative Agreement Program"

Award: Project Grants
Purpose: To fulfill the mandated objectives of the Comprehensive Environmental Response, Compensation, and Liability Act of 1980 (CERCLA) and the Superfund Amendments and Reauthorization Act (SARA) of 1986.
Applicant Eligibility: Eligible applicants are the official public health agencies of States or their bona fide agents or instrumentalities, to include the District of Columbia, American Samoa, the Commonwealth of Puerto Rico, the Virgin Islands, the Federated States of Micronesia, Guam, the Northern Marina Islands, the Republic of the Marshall Islands, and the Republic of Palau, and the Federally- recognized Indian tribal Governments.
Beneficiary Eligibility: Beneficiaries are individuals and/or families living in communities near or in proximity of Superfund sites.
Award Range/Average: $150,000 to $350,000
Funding: (Cooperative Agreements) FY 16 $10,442,338.00; FY 17 Estimate Not Available; FY 18 Estimate Not Available
HQ: 4770 Buford Highway NE, Atlanta, GA 30341
    Phone: 770-488-0711
    http://www.atsdr.cdc.gov

CNCS94.003 | STATE COMMISSIONS
"Commission Support Grants"

Award: Project Grants
Purpose: The State Commission program helps to develop State plan and provide an oversight of AmeriCorps programs within each State. It also helps the State to form a 15 to 25 member commission to implement service programs in their State.
Applicant Eligibility: Eligibility is limited to State or Territory Commissions for national service. State Governments may house or form non-profit Organizations as commissions to receive awards. Use of assistance must be consistent with funded approved grant application.
Beneficiary Eligibility: States will benefit. See program's Application Instructions.
Award Range/Average: Range may vary based on annual appropriations and population based formulas. Range has been from $250,000 to $755,810 over the course of the program.
Funding: (Project Grants) FY 16 $130,613,495.00; FY 17 est $128,804,807.00; FY 18 est Estimate Not Available
HQ: 250 E Street SW, Washington, DC 20525
    Phone: 202-606-6905 | Email: jgraham@cns.gov
    http://www.nationalservice.gov

HHS93.586 | STATE COURT IMPROVEMENT PROGRAM
"State and Tribal Court Improvement Programs"

Award: Formula Grants; Project Grants
Purpose: Provides three grant opportunities to state courts to improve court efficiency and the quality of legal representation; a basic grant for assessment work; a grant for data collection and analysis; and a grant to increase training of court personnel, including cross training with agency staff.
Applicant Eligibility: The highest state courts in each of the 50 states, the District of Columbia, Puerto Rico and the U.S. Virgin Islands are eligible to apply for funding. The term "highest state court" means the judicial tribunal which is the ultimate court

Programs Administered by Federal Headquarters

of appeals in the state. Tribal courts or tribal Governments of federally recognized Tribes may apply for grants. To be eligible, a tribe must be operating an approved title IV-E Program in accordance with section 479B of the Social Security Act (the Act); or plan to operate a title IV-E Program and have received a title IV-E plan development grant, as authorized by section 476 of the Act; or have a court responsible for proceedings related to foster care or adoption (section 438(c)(3)(A)(iv) of the Act).

Beneficiary Eligibility: Families and children who are served by state and tribal courts in proceedings related to foster care, guardianship and adoption.

Award Range/Average: FY 2017: State grant awards ranged from $86,408 to $571,308 with an average of $158,094. FY 2017: Tribal grant awards ranged from $31,282 to $140,000 with an average of $103,444.

Funding: (Project Grants (Discretionary)) FY 18 est $934,000.00; FY 19 est $937999.00; FY 20 est $1,000,000.00; (Formula Grants) FY 18 $29,058,245.00; FY 19 est $29,058,243.00; FY 20 est $30,972,245.00

HQ: 330 C Street SW, Room 3512, Washington, DC 20201

Phone: 202-205-8552 | Email: gail.collins@acf.hhs.gov

http://www.acf.hhs.gov/programs/cb

DOJ16.606 | STATE CRIMINAL ALIEN ASSISTANCE PROGRAM "SCAAP"

Award: Direct Payments for Specified Use

Purpose: The goal of the program is to refund state and local jurisdictions for housing criminal noncitizens in the state and local jails.

Applicant Eligibility: Eligible applicants include States, the District of Columbia, Puerto Rico, Guam, the Virgin Islands and localities or local jurisdictions exercising authority with respect to the incarceration of an undocumented criminal alien. This covers state prison facilities and local jails, whether operated by counties or cities. Applicants are generally States and units of local government. Note: Only one application is accepted from each separate political division (i.e., State, county, city).

Beneficiary Eligibility: States, the District of Columbia, Puerto Rico, Guam, the Virgin Islands and localities or local jurisdictions.

Award Range/Average: Contact Bureau of Justice Assistance for funding information or see the SCAAP Guidelines at https://www.bja.gov/ProgramDetails.aspx?Program_ID=86.

Funding: (Direct Payments with Unrestricted Use) FY 18 $540,000.00; FY 19 est $243,500,000.00; FY 20 est $0.00

HQ: Bureau of Justice Assistance 810 7th Street NW, Washington, DC 20531

Phone: 202-353-4411

http://www.bja.gov

DOT20.720 | STATE DAMAGE PREVENTION PROGRAM GRANTS

Award: Project Grants

Purpose: Improves State Damage Prevention programs, which are intended to protect underground facilities from excavation damage.

Applicant Eligibility: Any State (including U.S. Territory or possessions) authority designated by the Governor is eligible to apply for a grant as long an agency within the State (including U.S. Territory or possessions) has an annual Section 60105 (49 U.S.C.) certification or Section 60106 (49 U.S.C.) agreement in effect with PHMSA. If a State (including U.S. Territory or possessions) does not have a certification or agreement with PHMSA, then no State (including U.S. Territory or possessions) authority can receive a grant.

Beneficiary Eligibility: State Government, U.S. Territory and possessions would receive the ultimate benefit from this program.

Award Range/Average: The range is $0- $100,000.

Funding: (Project Grants (Discretionary)) FY 18 $1,497,888.00; FY 19 est $1,500,000.00; FY 20 est Estimate Not Available

HQ: 1200 New Jersey Avenue SE, Washington, DC 20590

Phone: 202-366-0568 | Email: hung.nguyen@dot.gov

http://www.phmsa.dot.gov

DOJ16.556 | STATE DOMESTIC VIOLENCE AND SEXUAL ASSAULT COALITIONS "State Coalitions Program"

Award: Project Grants

Purpose: To collaborate and coordinate with Federal, State, and local entities engaged in violence against women activities.

Applicant Eligibility: Each State domestic violence coalition as determined by the Secretary of Health and Human Services under the Family Violence Prevention and Services Act and each State sexual assault coalition as determined by the Center for Injury Prevention and Control at the Centers for Disease Control and Prevention under the Public Health Service Act.
Beneficiary Eligibility: State domestic violence, and sexual assault coalitions.
Award Range/Average: State DV Coalitions:Range: $91,443- $91,443 Average: $91,443 State SA Coalitions:Range: $147,693-$147,693 Average: $147,693
Funding: (Formula Grants) FY 16 $13,413,792.00; FY 17 est $13,391,656.00; FY 18 est $13,390,000.00
HQ: 145 N Street NE, Suite 10W121, Washington, DC 20530
    Phone: 202-305-1177 | Email: tia.farmer@usdoj.gov
    http://www.justice.gov/ovw

DHS97.043 | STATE FIRE TRAINING SYSTEMS GRANTS
"National Fire Academy State Fire Training Grants"

Award: Project Grants
Purpose: The program supports training programs to the fire and emergency response community irrespective of local or State agencies to meet individual training standards based on NFA course guidelines.
Applicant Eligibility: Representatives from the 50 State Fire Training Systems.
Beneficiary Eligibility: Specialized Group; fire and emergency response personnel.
Award Range/Average: Refer to program guidance.
Funding: (Project Grants) FY 18 $960,000.00; FY 19 est $0.00, FY 20 est $0,00
HQ: United States Fire Administration FEMA 16825 S Seton Avenue, Emmitsburg, MD 21727
    Phone: 301-447-1376 | Email: diane.close@fema.dhs.gov
    http://www.usfa.fema.gov

HHS93.873 | STATE GRANTS FOR PROTECTION AND ADVOCACY SERVICES
"Protection and Advocacy for Traumatic Brain Injury"

Award: Formula Grants
Purpose: To make grants to Protection and Advocacy systems established in each State to provide services to individuals with traumatic brain injury which may include information, referrals, and advice; and individual and family advocacy.
Applicant Eligibility: State Grant Agencies.
Beneficiary Eligibility: Individuals with disabilities and family members.
Award Range/Average: Range is $20,000 to $145,583; Average is $50,000
Funding: (Formula Grants) FY 17 $3,099,589.00; FY 18 est $4,000,000.00; FY 19 Estimate Not Available
HQ: 330 C Street SW, PO Box 1104-B, Washington, DC 20201
    Phone: 202-795-7474 | Email: yi-hsin.yan@acl.hhs.gov

HHS93.324 | STATE HEALTH INSURANCE ASSISTANCE PROGRAM
"SHIP"

Award: Cooperative Agreements
Purpose: Provides information, counseling, and assistance relating to obtaining adequate and appropriate health insurance coverage to individuals eligible to receive benefits under the Medicare program.
Applicant Eligibility: Grants or cooperative agreements may be made to States and U.S. Territories with approved State regulatory Programs under section 1882 of the Social Security Act.
Beneficiary Eligibility: Individuals eligible for Medicare benefits, including Part D drug benefits, and older persons eligible for benefits and services provided under Medicare, their families, and caregivers.
Award Range/Average: FY 17: 54 awards that range from $50,000 to $5,003,012 per budget period
Funding: (Cooperative Agreements (Discretionary Grants)) FY 17 $52,115,000.00; FY 18 est $49,115,000.00; FY 19 est $49,115,000.00
HQ: 330 C Street SW, Washington, DC 20201
    Phone: 202-795-7375 | Email: rebecca.kinney@acl.hhs.gov

Programs Administered by Federal Headquarters

DOJ16.550 | STATE JUSTICE STATISTICS PROGRAM FOR STATISTICAL ANALYSIS CENTERS
"SACs"

Award: Cooperative Agreements
Purpose: To give financial and technical help to state governments for the establishment and operation of Statistical Analysis Centers (SACs) to collect, analyze, and disseminate justice statistics.
Applicant Eligibility: Eligible applicants are state agencies whose responsibilities include statistical activities consistent with the goals of the specific Programs and are designated as the state Statistical Analysis Center through an Executive Order or legislation.
Beneficiary Eligibility: Eligible beneficiaries are state agencies whose responsibilities include statistical activities consistent with the goals of the specific programs.
Award Range/Average: See the current fiscal year's solicitation guidelines posted on the Office of Justice Programs web site at https://ojp.gov/funding/Explore/CurrentFundingOpportunities.htm.
Funding: (Cooperative Agreements) FY 17 $3,400,000.00; FY 18 est $5,500,000.00; FY 19 est $6,000,000.00
HQ: Bureau of Justice Statistics 810 7th Street NW, Washington, DC 20531
　　Phone: 202-307-0765 | Email: stephanie.burroughs@usdoj.gov
　　http://www.bjs.gov/index.cfm?ty=tp&tipd=48

HHS93.775 | STATE MEDICAID FRAUD CONTROL UNITS
"SMFCU's"

Award: Formula Grants
Purpose: Strives to eliminate fraud and patient abuse in the State Medicaid Programs.
Applicant Eligibility: An established State Medicaid Fraud Control Unit must be a single identifiable entity of the State government which the Secretary certifies (and the Office of Inspector General annually re-certifies) as complying with the requirements of 1903(q) of the Social Security Act (42 CFR 1007) regarding location, function and procedure. Applicants must also comply with section 1902 (a)(61) of the Act as amended by the Omnibus Budget Reconciliation Act of 1993. Tribes (American Indian/Alaskan Native/Native American) are not eligible to apply.
Beneficiary Eligibility: Grantees are State entities.
Award Range/Average: FY 2019: Range $335,896 to $44,036,860; Average $5,400,000
Funding: (Formula Grants) FY 18 $270,000,000.00; FY 19 est $280,800,000.00; FY 20 est $290,000,000.00
HQ: 330 Independence Avenue SW, Cohen Building, Washington, DC 20201
　　Phone: 202-619-0480 | Email: richard.stern@oig.hhs.gov
　　http://www.oig.hhs.gov

DOD12.113 | STATE MEMORANDUM OF AGREEMENT PROGRAM FOR THE REIMBURSEMENT OF TECHNICAL SERVICES
"DSMOA"

Award: Project Grants
Purpose: To reimburse each State and territory for their costs incurred by providing technical services in support of Department of Defense Environmental Restoration Program activities.
Applicant Eligibility: State and territorial Governments only.
Beneficiary Eligibility: State and territorial governments, local governments, public nonprofit organization/institution, public institution/organization, profit organization, private nonprofit institution/organization.
Funding: (Salaries and Expenses) FY 07 $1,700,000.00; FY 08 est Estimate Not Available; FY 09 est Estimate Not Available; (Salaries and Expenses) FY 07 $1,700,000 FY 08 est not reported; and FY 09 est not reported. (Cooperative Agreements) FY 07 $41,844,600; FY 08 est not reported; and FY 09 est not reported. Note: No current information provided by Agency.
HQ: CEMP-RI 20 Massachusetts Avenue NW, Washington, DC 20314
　　Phone: 202-504-4950

HHS93.296 | STATE PARTNERSHIP GRANT PROGRAM TO IMPROVE MINORITY HEALTH

"State Partnership Initiative to Improve Minority Health"

Award: Project Grants

Purpose: To facilitate the improvement of minority health and eliminate health disparities.

Applicant Eligibility: Any state, which includes the District of Columbia, any commonwealth possession, or other territory of the United States. If the applicant is a state, the application must include the state office of minority health/healthy equity (or other state entity with similar function) and the state health agency as partners. Any Federally-recognized or State-recognized American Indian/Alaska Native tribal government or consortium or council. If applicant is a tribe, the application must include a tribal government, consortium or council and an affiliated health agency/ office as partners.

Beneficiary Eligibility: Targeted populations: Alaskan Natives; American Indians; Asians; Blacks/African Americans; Hispanics/Latinos; Native Hawaiians and other Pacific Islanders; or subgroups of these populations. However, services may not be denied to any individual on the basis of race or ethnicity.

Award Range/Average: Range from $175,000 to $200,000

Funding: (Project Grants) FY 16 $4,150,105.00; FY 17 est $4,150,105.00; FY 18 est $4,150,105.00

HQ: 1101 Wootton Parkway, Suite 550 Tower Building, Rockville, MD 20852

   Phone: 240-453-8822 | Email: eric.west@hhs.gov

HHS93.439 | STATE PHYSICAL ACTIVITY AND NUTRITION (SPAN

Award: Project Grants

Purpose: To implement state and local nutrition and physical activity interventions that support healthy nutrition, safe and accessible physical activity, and breastfeeding within states and/or the District of Columbia.

Applicant Eligibility: Applicants must provide evidence of the authority to direct work on government public health systems at the state and local levels to readily implement this state based Program.

Beneficiary Eligibility: Same as Applicant Eligibility.

Award Range/Average: Base funding level is $13,000,000 with potential for up to $15,000,000 annually for each of the five year budget periods. Based on available funding. $600,000 - $1,250,000 annually.

Funding: (Project Grants) FY 18 $14,088,691.00; FY 19 est $14,088,691.00; FY 20 est $14,088,691.00

HQ: NCCDPHP 4770 Buford Highway NE, Atlanta, GA 30341

   Phone: 404-867-9697 | Email: lbarnes@cdc.gov

   http://www.cdc.gov

HHS93.735 | STATE PUBLIC HEALTH APPROACHES FOR ENSURING QUITLINE CAPACITY-FUNDED IN PART BY PREVENTION AND PUBLIC HEALTH FUNDS (PPHF)

Award: Cooperative Agreements

Purpose: The program addresses the "Healthy People 2020" focus area of tobacco uses and the goal of reducing illness, disability, and death related to tobacco uses and secondhand smoke exposure.

Applicant Eligibility: Eligible applicants that can apply for this funding opportunity are listed below: Eligibility is limited to currently funded recipients under RFA-DP09-901 and RFA-DP09-902. These include state, District of Columbia, and the U.S. territorial health departments of Guam and Puerto Rico because they are the only entities with the authority to prevent and control tobacco use and which provide quitline services within the states and territories. State and territorial health departments are also uniquely qualified to address the anticipated increase in calls to quitlines due to federal media education campaigns, while expanding capacity and eligibility to ensure all callers receive some form of assistance. These agencies are also uniquely qualified to promote the quitline, increase quit attempts, and increase public and private partnerships to ensure quitline sustainability.

Beneficiary Eligibility: Any State and territorial health department, and other public entities will benefit.

Award Range/Average: $50,000- $2,771,803.

Funding: (Cooperative Agreements (Discretionary Grants)) FY 18 $16,357,470.00; FY 19 est $12,268,103.00; FY20 est $0.00

HQ: 4770 Buford Highway NE, PO Box K50, Atlanta, GA 30341

   Phone: 770-488-1221 | Email: ksneegas@cdc.gov

   http://www.cdc.gov

Programs Administered by Federal Headquarters

HHS93.241 | STATE RURAL HOSPITAL FLEXIBILITY PROGRAM
"The Rural Hospital Flexibility Program (Flex) The Rural Veterans Health Access Program"

Award: Project Grants

Purpose: Engages state designated entities in activities relating to planning and implementing rural healthcare plans and networks; designating facilities as Critical Access Hospitals; providing support for CAHs for quality improvement, quality reporting, performance improvements, and benchmarking; and integrating rural emergency medical services.

Applicant Eligibility: Flex and Rural Veterans Recipients: Only states with certified Critical Access Hospitals are eligible for this Program. The Governor designates the eligible applicant from each state. All other states need to submit an application to the Regional Administrator of their CMS Regional Office that expresses the state's interest in developing a Medicare Rural Hospital Flexibility Program before they can apply for funds.

Beneficiary Eligibility: States with at least one hospital located in a non-metropolitan statistical area or county that provide CMS with necessary assurances.

Award Range/Average: Medicare Rural Hospital Flexibility Program $316,735 to $968,815; Average, $592,440 Rural Veterans Health Access Program: $300,000

Funding: (Cooperative Agreements) FY 18 $28,947,420.00; FY 19 est $29,559,826.00; FY 20 est Estimate Not Available

HQ: 5600 Fishers Lane, Rockville, MD 20857

Phone: 301-443-5905

http://www.hrsa.gov/ruralhealth

DOI15.429 | STATE SELECT

Award: Direct Payments With Unrestricted Use

Purpose: Shares 90 percent of oil and gas royalties with the State to be paid monthly subject to late disbursement interest.

Applicant Eligibility: Revenue from public land leasing will trigger automatic payment distribution computed in accordance with the law.

Beneficiary Eligibility: ONRR distributes these funds to state governments for leased lands within the State and the State government has sole discretion in their use in accordance with the enabling legislation.

Award Range/Average: Not Applicable.

Funding: (Direct Payments with Unrestricted Use) FY 17 $263,000.00; FY 18 est $311,000.00; FY 19 est $344,000.00

HQ: Office of Natural Resources Revenue 1849 C Street NW, PO Box 4211, Washington, DC 20240

Phone: 202-513-0600

http://www.ONRR.gov

HHS93.777 | STATE SURVEY AND CERTIFICATION OF HEALTH CARE PROVIDERS AND SUPPLIERS (TITLE XVIII) MEDICARE

Award: Formula Grants

Purpose: Provides financial assistance to any State which is able to determine through an appropriate State agency that providers and suppliers of healthcare services are in compliance with Federal regulatory health and safety standards and conditions of participation.

Applicant Eligibility: Under Title XVIII, States enter into Section 1864 agreements with the Secretary of Health and Human Services whereby the designated agency of the State will be supported or reimbursed for on-site inspection of healthcare providers and suppliers. The designated State agency is usually that unit performing licensure activities within the State health department.

Beneficiary Eligibility: N/A

Award Range/Average: FY 18 range is from $559,205 to $46,106,561 with an average of $6,603,238 (includes IMPACT Act funding).

Funding: (Direct Payments for Specified Use) FY 18 $363,178,086.00; FY 19 est $366,123,636.00; FY 20 est $397,334,000.00

HQ: 7500 Security Boulevard, Baltimore, MD 21244

Phone: 410-786-9493 | Email: david.wright@cms.hhs.gov

http://www.cms.hhs.gov/contracts

HHS93.796 | STATE SURVEY CERTIFICATION OF HEALTH CARE PROVIDERS AND SUPPLIERS (TITLE XIX) MEDICAID

Award: Formula Grants

Purpose: Provides Medicaid financial assistance to any State which is able and willing to determine through its State health agency or other appropriate State agency that providers and suppliers of healthcare services are in compliance with Federal regulatory health and safety standards and conditions of participation.

Applicant Eligibility: The Federal government reimburses States for the Federal Financial Participation share for costs of inspection. Such participation is dependent on an approved State activity plan.

Beneficiary Eligibility: N/A

Award Range/Average: FY 18 range is from $479,794 to $37,750,211 with an average of $5,154,420.

Funding: (Formula Grants) FY 18 Actual Not Available; FY 19 $282,000,000.00; FY 20 est $286,750,000.00

HQ: 7500 Security Boulevard, Baltimore, MD 21244

  Phone: 410-786-9493 | Email: david.wright@cms.hhs.gov

  http://www.cms.hhs.gov/contracts

SBA59.061 | STATE TRADE EXPANSION

Award: Cooperative Agreements; Project Grants

Purpose: To increase the number of small businesses that are exporting and increase the value of exports for those small businesses that are currently exporting.

Applicant Eligibility: States, defined as the 50 states, District of Columbia, Puerto Rico, US Virgin Islands, Guam, American Samoa, and the Commonwealth of Northern Mariana Islands.

Beneficiary Eligibility: N/A

Funding: (Cooperative Agreements) FY 18 $18,000,000.00; FY 19 est $18,000,000.00; FY 20 est $8,000,000.00

HQ: 409 3rd Street SW, 2nd Floor, Washington, DC 20416

  Phone: 202-205-3644 | Email: james.parker@sba.gov

  http://www.sba.gov

ED84.415 | STATE TRIBAL EDUCATION PARTNERSHIP (STEP)

Award: Project Grants

Purpose: To promote tribal self-determination in education.

Applicant Eligibility: Eligible entities include an Indian tribe or tribal Organization approved by an Indian tribe, or a tribal educational agency.

Beneficiary Eligibility: TEAs, SEAs, LEAs, Indian students, and teachers will benefit.

Award Range/Average: The average award is expected to be $240,000 for a single TEA or $400,000 for a consortium of TEAs.

Funding: (Project Grants) FY 18 $2,000,000.00; FY 19 est $2,000,000.00; FY 20 est $2,000,000.00

HQ: Office of Indian Education Department of Education 400 Maryland Avenue SW, Washington, DC 20202

  Phone: 202-453-5602 | Email: shahla.ortega@ed.gov

  http://www2.ed.gov/about/offices/list/oese/oie/index.html

HHS93.066 | STATE VITAL STATISTICS IMPROVEMENT PROGRAM

Award: Cooperative Agreements

Purpose: To enhance the performance of the National Vital Statistics System (NVSS) by convening states to aid in improving vital statistics data quality, timeliness and public health utility, increasing the competencies of the vital statistics workforce, and promoting accreditation of jurisdictional vital statistics programs consistent with National Center for Health Statistics goals.

Applicant Eligibility: Any application requesting an award higher than the funded amount is considered nonresponsive and will receive no further review. In addition, application will be considered non-responsive if they do not contain a letter of support written on behalf of the 57 jurisdictions' vital statistics offices. The letter of support must include the following information or the application will be considered non-responsive: confirmation that the applicant has established relationships with all 57 jurisdiction vital statistics offices, including experience in supporting vital statistics standards and best practices and convening vital statistics offices to advance vital statistics initiatives.

Beneficiary Eligibility: An organization with demonstrated support of the 57 jurisdiction vital statistics offices. (See eligibility requirements.).

Award Range/Average: $694,500 per year (5-year Cooperative Agreement)

Programs Administered by Federal Headquarters

Funding: (Cooperative Agreements) FY 18 $694,450.00; FY 19 est $819,401.00; FY 20 est $694,500.00
HQ: 4024 Stirrup Creek Drive, Durham, NC 27703
   Phone: 919-541-4414
   http://www.cdc.gov

DRA90.204 | STATES' ECONOMIC DEVELOPMENT ASSISTANCE PROGRAM "SEDAP"

Award: Project Grants
Purpose: To improve regional economic opportunity by helping to create jobs, build communities, and improve the lives of the 10 million people who reside in the 252 counties and parishes of the eight state Delta region.
Applicant Eligibility: The 252 counties and parishes served by the Delta Regional Authority make up the most distressed area of the country. According to the USDA, the most severe rates of poverty are historically found in the South, especially in the Mississippi River delta region. In fact, 4 of the 10 most impoverished counties and parishes in the country are located within the DRA footprint.
Beneficiary Eligibility: For more information, please visit the DRA website at www.dra.gov.
HQ: 236 Sharkey Avenue, Suite 400, Clarksdale, MS 38614
   Phone: 662-483-8212 | Email: shoskins@dra.gov
   http://www.dra.gov

ED84.310 | STATEWIDE FAMILY ENGAGEMENT CENTERS

Award: Project Grants
Purpose: To provide financial support to statewide organizations that conduct parent education and family engagement programs to support family-school partnerships.
Applicant Eligibility: Statewide Organizations or consortia of such Organizations may apply.
Beneficiary Eligibility: State educational agencies, local educational agencies, schools, and families will benefit.
Award Range/Average: Varies by competition.
Funding: (Project Grants) FY 18 $10,000,000.00; FY 19 est $10,000,000.00; FY 20 est $0.00
HQ: 400 Maryland Avenue SW, Washington, DC 20202
   Phone: 202-453-6723 | Email: norris.dickard@ed.gov
   http://www.ed.gov/programs/pirc/index.html

ED84.372 | STATEWIDE LONGITUDINAL DATA SYSTEMS

Award: Project Grants
Purpose: To design, develop, and implement statewide, longitudinal data systems to efficiently and accurately manage, analyze, disaggregate, and use individual student data, consistent with the Elementary and Secondary Education Act of 1965 and to facilitate analyses and research to improve student academic achievement and close achievement gaps.
Applicant Eligibility: State educational agencies.
Beneficiary Eligibility: State educational agencies, local educational agencies, non-profit and for-profit organizations, and individuals involved with education will benefit.
Award Range/Average: The 2015 grant awards ranged in size from approximately $3.5 million to $7 million for 4-year projects.
Funding: (Project Grants (Contracts)) FY 18 $6,000,000.00; FY 19 est $6,000,000.00; FY 20 est $0.00; (Project Grants) FY 18 $26,281,000.00; FY 19 est $26,281,000.00; FY 20 est $0.00
HQ: 550 12th Street SW, Room 9101, Washington, DC 20006
   Phone: 202-245-7689 | Email: nancy.sharkey@ed.gov
   http://nces.ed.gov/programs/slds

HHS93.645 | STEPHANIE TUBBS JONES CHILD WELFARE SERVICES PROGRAM

Award: Formula Grants
Purpose: Purpose of the Stephanie Tubbs Jones Child Welfare Services program is to promote state and tribal flexibility in the development and expansion of a coordinated child and family services program that utilizes community-based agencies and ensures all children are raised in safe, loving families.

Applicant Eligibility: Territories and possessions include only Puerto Rico, U.S. Virgin Islands, Northern Marianas, Guam, and American Samoa.

Beneficiary Eligibility: Families and children in need of child welfare services will benefit.

Award Range/Average: FY 2017: Awards for states and territories ranged from $107,236 to $29,787,966 with an average of $4,661,994. FY 2017: Awards for Tribes ranged from $1,162 to $927,457 with an average of $32,847.

Funding: (Formula Grants (Apportionments)) FY 18 $268,735,000.00; FY 19 est $268,000,000.00; FY 20 est $268,735,000

HQ: 330 C Street SW, Room 3509B, Washington, DC 20201

Phone: 202-690-7888 | Email: catherine.heath@acf.hhs.gov

http://www.acf.hhs.gov/programs/cb

DOJ16.839 | STOP SCHOOL VIOLENCE

Award: Project Grants

Purpose: To promote education for students on preventing violence and assists officials in responding to mental health crises.

Applicant Eligibility: The STOP School Violence Act of 2018 describes those who are eligible to apply are States, local units of government, and Indian Tribes.

Beneficiary Eligibility: The STOP School Violence Act of 2018 states that training for teachers and education of students to prevent violence against others and self. This will include specialized training for school officials responding to mental health crisis.

Award Range/Average: Award amounts will range from $100,000 up to $500,000. See solicitation for specifics at https://ojp.gov/funding/Explore/CurrentFundingOpportunities.htm

Funding: (Cooperative Agreements) FY 17 $0.00; FY 18 est $75,000,000.00; FY 19 est Estimate Not Available

HQ: 810 7th Street NW, Washington, DC 20351

Phone: 202-616-6500

http://bja.gov

HHS93.078 | STRENGTHENING EMERGENCY CARE DELIVERY IN THE UNITED STATES HEALTHCARE SYSTEM THROUGH HEALTH INFORMATION AND PROMOTION

Award: Cooperative Agreements; Project Grants

Purpose: To assist in planning or developing emergency care health information and promotion activities, documents or materials.

Applicant Eligibility: Domestic public or private non-profit entities including state and local Governments, Indian tribal Governments and Organizations (American Indian/Alaskan Native/Native American), faith-based Organizations, community-based Organizations, hospitals, and Institutions of higher education.

Beneficiary Eligibility: Same as Applicant Eligibility.

Funding: (Cooperative Agreements) FY 18 $220,000.00; FY 19 est $300,000.00; FY 20 est $300,000.00

HQ: 200 C Street SW, 1st Floor Cube C1A04 O'Neill Federal Building, Washington, DC 20024

Phone: 202-631-2013 | Email: kristen.finne@hhs.gov

http://www.phe.gov

ED84.382 | STRENGTHENING MINORITY-SERVING INSTITUTIONS

Award: Project Grants

Purpose: To strengthen Predominantly Black Institutions (PBI); Asian American and Native American Pacific Islander-Serving Institutions (AANAPISI); and Native American-Serving Nontribal Institutions (NASNTI) that propose to carry out activities to improve and expand such institution's capacity to serve low-income and minority students.

Applicant Eligibility: At the time of application, PBIs must have an enrollment of undergraduate students that is at least 40 percent African American students. AANAPISI and NASNTI applicants must have, at the time of application, an enrollment of undergraduate students not less than 10 percent Asian American and Native American Pacific Islanders and Native Americans, respectively. Institutions eligible for master's Degree Programs at HBCUs and PBIs are specified in Title VII Sections 723 and 724 of the HEA. An institution that is eligible for and receives an award under HEA's Title III Historically Black Graduate Institutions (HBGIs) or Title V Promoting Postbaccalaureate Opportunities for Hispanic Americans (Section 512) for a fiscal year is not eligible to apply for a grant or receive grant funding under Section 897 master's Degree Programs for HBCUs and PBIs for the same fiscal year.

Programs Administered by Federal Headquarters

Beneficiary Eligibility: The authorized beneficiaries are underrepresented; low-income; first-generation; minority; undergraduate students.
Award Range/Average: Varies by competition
Funding: (Project Grants) FY 18 $31,921,000.00; FY 19 est $32,107,000.00; FY 20 est $8,657,000.00
HQ: Washington, DC 20202
   Phone: 202-453-7605 | Email: winston.skerrett@ed.gov
   http://www2.ed.gov/about/offices/list/ope/idues/index.html

HHS93.018 | STRENGTHENING PUBLIC HEALTH SERVICES AT THE OUTREACH OFFICES OF THE U.S.-MEXICO BORDER HEALTH COMMISSION

Award: Cooperative Agreements
Purpose: To provide leadership to optimize health and quality of life for residents in the border region.
Applicant Eligibility: This is a limited eligibility cooperative agreement offered to the Arizona Department of Health Services/ Office of Border Health; the California Department of Public Health/California Office of Bi-national Border Health; the New Mexico Department of Health/Office of Border Health; and the Texas Department of State Health Services/Office of Border Health. The BHC's establishing legislation (22 U.S.C. 290n) calls for close coordination and integration with each of the four state offices of border health, and enabled the Commission to locate its border health operations within those existing state offices to avoid duplicative efforts. The four U.S. offices of border health have extensive experience supporting the BHC's bi-national goals, objectives, and initiatives, and maintain important working relationships and shared ongoing initiatives with Mexico through the appropriate BHC outreach office(s) on the Mexican side of the border. Continuity and consistency in this bi-national effort in the border region is essential to the productivity and success of the BHC.
Beneficiary Eligibility: This funding is intended to support projects aligned with the goals of the United States-Mexico Border Health Commission, and its mission to provide leadership to optimize health and quality of life for residents in the border region. Special target populations and organizations can include specific sub-groups of interest, such as disadvantaged or medically underserved areas, limited-English speaking groups, migrant populations, native communities, and community-based organizations. The cooperative agreement mechanism encourages the formation and development of collaborative partnerships to facilitate sustainability of efforts and to maximize impact in the border region.
Award Range/Average: Fiscal Year 2014: $1,300,000 Fiscal Year 2015: $1,350,000 Fiscal Year 2016: $1,300,000 Fiscal Year 2017: $1,100,000 Anticipated future budget period amounts are dependent on the availability of funding.
Funding: (Cooperative Agreements) FY 16 $1,300,000.00; FY 17 est $1,100,000.00; FY 18 est Estimate Not Available
HQ: DeWayne Wynn 1101 Wootton Parkway, Suite 550, Rockville, MD 20852
   Phone: 240-453-8822 | Email: eric.west@hhs.gov
   http://www.hhs.gov/about/agencies/oga/index.html

HHS93.421 | STRENGTHENING PUBLIC HEALTH SYSTEMS AND SERVICES THROUGH NATIONAL PARTNERSHIPS TO IMPROVE AND PROTECT THE NATION'S HEALTH
"CDC-RFA-OT18-1802"

Award: Cooperative Agreements
Purpose: To fund nongovernmental organizations with demonstrated capability, expertise, resources, national reach, and track record to strengthen governmental public health system's infrastructure and core services through provision of capacity building assistance.
Applicant Eligibility: Organizations deemed eligible to apply must also meet responsiveness criteria as outlined in the "Additional Information on Eligibility" in CDC-RFA-OT18-1802.
Beneficiary Eligibility: Beneficiaries include state health departments; tribal health organizations; local health departments; the District of Columbia; U.S. Territories; and other components of the public health system. The general public will also serve as beneficiaries.
Award Range/Average: The approximate average award ranges for the 12-month budget period are $2 million for Category A, up to $1 million for Category B and up to $500,000 for Category C. This average is based on funding provided during funding strategy 1, as outlined in CDC-RFA-OT18-1802.
Funding: (Cooperative Agreements) FY 18 $94,421,972.00; FY 19 est Estimate Not Available; FY 120 est $120,000,000.00
HQ: 1825 Century Boulevard NE MS V18-1, Atlanta, GA 30345
   Phone: 770-488-1522

HHS93.326 | STRENGTHENING PUBLIC HEALTH THROUGH SURVEILLANCE, EPIDEMIOLOGIC RESEARCH, DISEASE DETECTION AND PREVENTION
"Global Health Research"

Award: Cooperative Agreements
Purpose: To assist Ministries of Health and other international partners to plan, effectively manage and conduct public health research in the intent of public health protection; achieve U.S. Government program and international organization goals to improve health; including surveillance, intervention and prevention in global health programs.
Applicant Eligibility: Dependent on the FOA, eligibility may range from open, competitive, limited or single eligibility in accordance with authorizing legislation. May include non-profit Organizations who may be domestic, international or Ministries of Health. Domestic academic Institutions, community Organizations, universities.
Beneficiary Eligibility: This will benefit individuals worldwide, including in the U.S., through collaborations with the national Ministries of Health and other organizations/institutions. This is only for research activities supported by CDC/ATSDR. For the definition of research, please see http:/www.cdc.gov/od/science/quality/resources.
Funding: (Cooperative Agreements) FY 18 $12,305,285.00; FY 19 est $3,790,159.00; FY 20 est $3,790,159.00
HQ: 1600 Clifton Road, Atlanta, GA 30047
    Phone: 404-639-7618 | Email: lek7@cdc.gov

HHS93.097 | STRENGTHENING THE NATION'S PUBLIC HEALTH SYSTEM THROUGH A NATIONAL VOLUNTARY ACCREDITATION PROGRAM FOR STATE, TRIBAL, LOCAL AND TERRITORIAL HEALTH DEPARTMENTS
"A National Voluntary Accreditation Program for State, Tribal, Local and Territorial Health Departments"

Award: Cooperative Agreements
Purpose: To support the operations and continuous improvement of a national accreditation program for state, tribal, local and territorial public health departments.
Applicant Eligibility: 1. Eligible Applicants: Public Health Accreditation Board (PHAB), a nonprofit with 501(c)3 IRS status. 2. Special Eligibility Requirements: The only eligible applicant for this award is the Public Health Accreditation Board (PHAB), a 501(c)3 independent accrediting body that administers the national voluntary public health department accreditation Program. 3. Justification for Less than Maximum Competition: The nature of the activities under this award are best employed by focusing on the entity to which this cooperative agreement is limited, per memorandum for approval for single-eligibility competition, which was approved and dated December 20, 2012. PHAB was found to be uniquely qualified, as it is the Organization that has been established as the national accrediting body for state, tribal, local and territorial health departments. PHAB was determined to have the experience and Program infrastructure, which includes field-driven and tested standards, measures and accreditation assessment process. PHAB is also widely accepted as the national accrediting body for state, local tribal and territorial health departments by the constituency Organizations for these agencies and as evidenced by the visible mention of PHAB within national policy documents (e.g., Institute of Medicine reports, Healthy People 2020).
Beneficiary Eligibility: State, Tribal, Local and Territorial Public Health Departments via a National Voluntary Accreditation Program administered by the Public Health Accreditation Board (PHAB), a 501(c)3 independent accrediting entity.
Award Range/Average: 1 award at an approximate average award of: $900,000.
Funding: (Cooperative Agreements) FY 18 $935,000.00; FY 19 est $1,050,000.00; FY 20 est $900,000.00
HQ: 1600 Clifton Road NE, PO Box E70, Atlanta, GA 30333
    Phone: 770-488-1523
    http://www.cdc.gov

Programs Administered by Federal Headquarters

HHS93.874 | STRENGTHENING THE PUBLIC HEALTH SYSTEM IN U.S.-AFFILIATED PACIFIC ISLANDS (NON-PPHF)
"CBA to Strengthen Public Health Infrastructure and Performance in USAPIs (Non-PPHF)"

Award: Cooperative Agreements

Purpose: The purpose of this funding initiative is to ensure provision of capacity building assistance (CBA) to the USAPI's public health officials and public health systems by the formation of sound policies, strengthened organizational structures, effective management and revenue control, and address important cross-cutting issues such as health equity programs and services, and improved accountability measures for performance effectiveness and efficiency.

Applicant Eligibility: The only eligible applicant for this award is the Pacific Island Health Officers Association (PIHOA), a 501(c)3 independent accrediting body that administers the national voluntary public health department accreditation Program.

Beneficiary Eligibility: Governmental public health departments, workforce segments across governmental public health departments, and/or nongovernmental public health professionals in the US-Affiliated Pacific Islands (USAPI). The US-Affiliated Pacific Islands (USAPI) consist of three U.S. Flag Territories of American Samoa, Guam, and the Commonwealth of the Northern Mariana Islands, as well as three sovereign states that have a Compact of Free Association with the United States (US) - Freely Associated States of the Republic of the Marshall Islands, Republic of Palau, and Federated States of Micronesia.

Award Range/Average: 1 award at approximate average award of 2,000,000

Funding: (Cooperative Agreements) FY 18 $2,528,795.00; FY 19 est $2,000,000.00; FY 20 est $2,000,000.00

HQ: 1825 Century Boulevard NE, PO Box V18-1, Atlanta, GA 30345

   Phone: 770-488-1522

   http://www.cdc.gov/stltpublichealth

HHS93.861 | STRENGTHENING THE PUBLIC HEALTH SYSTEM IN U.S. AFFILIATED PACIFIC ISLANDS (PPHF)
"CBA to Strengthen Public Health Infrastructure and Performance in USAPIs"

Award: Cooperative Agreements

Purpose: The purpose of this funding initiative is to ensure provision of capacity building assistance to the USAPI's public health officials and public health systems through the formation of sound policies, strengthened organizational structures, effective management and revenue control, building jurisdictional partnerships, and by addressing important cross-cutting issues such as health equity programs and services, and improved accountability measures for performance effectiveness and efficiency.

Applicant Eligibility: The only eligible applicant for this award is the Pacific Island Health Officers Association (PIHOA), a 501(c)3 independent accrediting body that administers the national voluntary public health department accreditation Program.

Beneficiary Eligibility: Governmental public health departments, workforce segments across governmental public health departments, and/or nongovernmental public health professionals in the US-Affiliated Pacific Islands (USAPI). The US-Affiliated Pacific Islands (USAPI) consist of three U.S. Flag Territories of American Samoa, Guam, and the Commonwealth of the Northern Mariana Islands, as well as three sovereign states that have a Compact of Free Association with the United States (US)-Freely Associated States of the Republic of the Marshall Islands, Republic of Palau, and Federated States of Micronesia.

Award Range/Average: 1 award at approximate average award of $2,000,000

Funding: (Cooperative Agreements) FY 18 $250,000.00; FY 19 est $200,000.00; FY 20 est $200,000.00

HQ: 1825 Century Boulevard NE, PO Box V18-1, Atlanta, GA 30345

   Phone: 770-488-1522

   https://www.cdc.gov/publichealthgateway/partnerships/pihoa.html

DOE81.102 | STUDENT DRIVEN RESEARCH AND LONG TERM MONITORING OF SELECTED POPULATIONS IN THE VALLEY AND RIDGE ECO-REGION
"CRESO"

Award: Project Grants (contracts)

Purpose: Aims at providing a mechanism that engages high school and undergraduate college students in long-term environmental field studies conducted in the Oak Ridge area and maintains a cooperative relationship with the residents over there.

Applicant Eligibility: N/A

Beneficiary Eligibility: N/A

Funding: (Project Grants (Contracts)) FY 18 $ $88,600.00; FY 19 est $88,600.00; FY 20 est $0

HQ: 1000 Independence Avenue SW, Washington, DC 20585

  Phone: 202-586-1487 | Email: andrew.wirkkala@em.doe.gov

HHS93.275 | SUBSTANCE ABUSE AND MENTAL HEALTH SERVICES-ACCESS TO RECOVERY
"ATR I, ATR II, ATRIII"

Award: Project Grants

Purpose: To implement voucher programs for substance abuse clinical treatment and recovery support services pursuant to sections 501 (d)(5) and 509 of Public Health Service Act (42 U.S.C. sections 290aa(d)(5) and 290bb-2).

Applicant Eligibility: Eligibility for Access to Recovery (ATR) grants is limited to the immediate office of the Chief Executive (e.g., Governor) in the States, Territories, District of Columbia; or the head of a Tribal Organization. (A "Tribal Organization " means the recognized governing body of any Indian tribe or any legally established Organization of Indians, including urban Indian health boards, inter-tribal councils, or regional Indian health boards, which is controlled, sanctioned, or chartered by such governing body or which is democratically elected by the adult members of the Indian community to be served by such an Organization.) The Chief Executive of the State, Territory, or District of Columbia, or the head of the Tribal Organization must sign the application. Eligibility is limited to the immediate office of these Chief Executives because only they have the authority to leverage funding across the State, implement the necessary policy changes, manage the fiscal responsibilities, and coordinate the range of Programs necessary for successful implementation of the voucher Programs to be funded through these grants. No more than on application from any one Chief Executive or head of a Tribal Organization will be funded.

Beneficiary Eligibility: Eligibility for Access to Recovery (ATR) grants is limited to the immediate office of the Chief Executive (e.g., Governor) in the States, Territories, District of Columbia; or the head of a Tribal Organization" means the recognized governing body of any Indian tribe or any legally established organization of Indians, including urban health boards, inter-tribal councils, or regional Indian health boards, which is controlled, sanctioned, or chartered by such governing body or which is democratically elected by the adult members of the Indian community to be served by such an organization.

HQ: 5600 Fishers Lane, Rockville, MD 20857

  Phone: 240-276-1418 | Email: roger.george@samhsa.hhs.gov

  http://www.samhsa.gov

HHS93.243 | SUBSTANCE ABUSE AND MENTAL HEALTH SERVICES PROJECTS OF REGIONAL AND NATIONAL SIGNIFICANCE
"PRNS"

Award: Project Grants

Purpose: To address priority substance abuse treatment, prevention and mental health needs of regional and national significance through assistance (grants and cooperative agreements) to States, political subdivisions of States, Indian tribes and tribal organizations, and other public or nonprofit private entities.

Applicant Eligibility: Public Organizations, such as units of State and local Governments and to domestic private nonprofit Organizations such as community-based Organizations, universities, colleges and hospitals.

Beneficiary Eligibility: Other non-profits.

Award Range/Average: $17,692 to $7,099,783; $417,410

Funding: (Project Grants) FY 18 $986,796,092.00; FY 19 est $910,083,518.00; FY 20 est 767,503,517.00

HQ: 5600 Fishers Lane, Rockville, MD 20857

  Phone: 240-276-1418 | Email: roger.george@samhsa.hhs.gov

  http://www.samhsa.gov

Programs Administered by Federal Headquarters

HHS93.664 | SUBSTANCE USE-DISORDER PREVENTION THAT PROMOTES OPIOID RECOVERY AND TREATMENT (SUPPORT) FOR PATIENTS AND COMMUNITIES ACT
"Section 1003 Demonstration Project to Increase Substance Use Provider Capacity"

Award: Project Grants

Purpose: Enhances the treatment capacity of providers participating in Medicaid to provide substance use disorder (SUD) treatment or recovery services and supporting the development of state infrastructure to recruit prospective providers to treat substance use disorders and training for those providers.

Applicant Eligibility: The statutory authority limits eligibility to states including the District of Columbia. Eligible applicants are State Medicaid Agencies (SMAs).

Beneficiary Eligibility: Planning grants are aimed to increase the capacity of Medicaid providers to provide SUD treatment or recovery services to: Medicaid eligible individuals; low income individuals/families; individuals with disabilities; consumers; individuals with behavioural health disorders including mental health and substance use disorders.

Award Range/Average: N/A

Funding: (Project Grants) FY 18 $0; FY 19 est $50,000,000.00; FY 20 est $0

HQ: 7500 Security Boulevard, Baltimore, MD 21244

    Phone: 410-786-1095 | Email: melanie.brown@cms.hhs.gov

    https://www.medicaid.gov/medicaid/benefits/bhs/support-act-provider-capacity-demos/index.html

DOI15.563 | SUISUN MARSH PRESERVATION AGREEMENT
"SMPA"

Award: Cooperative Agreements

Purpose: To ensure adequate water is supplied to protect and preserve the Suisan Marsh fish and wildlife habitat.

Applicant Eligibility: Per P. L. 99-546 and the SMPA limits the applicant to the State of California.

Beneficiary Eligibility: State of California and individual landowners within the Suisun Marsh as represented by Suisun Resource Conservation District.

Award Range/Average: Range is $0 to $1,430,000 Average is $908,333.

Funding: (Cooperative Agreements) FY 13 $0; FY 14 est $1,351,000.00; FY 15 est $1,374,000.00

HQ: 801 I Street, Suite 140, Sacramento, CA 95814

    Phone: 916-414-2429 | Email: rvictorine@usbr.gov

    http://www.usbr.gov/mp

USDA10.320 | SUN GRANT PROGRAM

Award: Project Grants

Purpose: To promote biobased energy technology and related research and to provide funds for promoting educational programs to implement biobased technology in the rural U.S.

Applicant Eligibility: Only the Sun Grant Centers and Subcenter as specifically designated in 7 U.S.C. 8114 are eligible to apply for funding under this Program.

Beneficiary Eligibility: Same as Applicant Eligibility.

Award Range/Average: If minimum or maximum amounts of funding per competitive and/or capacity project grant, or cooperative agreement are established, these amounts will be announced in the annual Competitive Request for Application (RFA). The most current RFA is available via: https://nifa.usda.gov/funding-opportunity/sun-grant-program

Funding: (Project Grants (Cooperative Agreements)) FY 17 $2,787,840.00; FY 18 est $2,815,488.00; FY 19 est $0.00

HQ: 1400 Independence Avenue SW, PO Box 2210, Washington, DC 20250-2210

    Phone: 202-401-5244

    http://nifa.usda.gov/funding-opportunity/sun-grant-program

HUD14.151 | SUPPLEMENTAL LOAN INSURANCE MULTIFAMILY RENTAL HOUSING
"241(a)"

Award: Guaranteed/insured Loans
Purpose: To provide quality rental housing.
Applicant Eligibility: Owners of a multifamily project or facility already subject to a mortgage insured by HUD or held by HUD.
Beneficiary Eligibility: Individuals/families and owners of multifamily projects.
HQ: 451 7th Street SW, Washington, DC 20410
   Phone: 202-402-2579 | Email: carmelita_a._james@hud.gov
   http://www.hud.gov/offices/hsg/hsgmulti.cfm

USDA10.090 | SUPPLEMENTAL REVENUE ASSISTANCE PROGRAM
"SURE"

Award: Direct Payments for Specified Use
Purpose: The SURE program assists farmers by compensating them for the crops destroyed due to the natural calamities.
Applicant Eligibility: An eligible applicant or eligible "producer on a farm", is an individual or entity who assumes the production and market risks associated with the agricultural production of crops or livestock. An individual or entity is a citizen of the United States (U.S.), a resident alien, or a partnership of citizens of the U.S.
Beneficiary Eligibility: The SURE program will provide financial assistance to an eligible producer on a farm who has insurable or non insurable commodity or agricultural commodity (except livestock) for which the producer on a farm is eligible to obtain a policy or plan of insurance. Benefits are also extended to the Socially Disadvantaged Farmer or Rancher who has been subject to racial or ethnic prejudice because of his or her identity as members of a group without regard to their individual qualities; a beginning farmer or rancher who has not operated a farm or ranch for more than 10 years and materially and substantially participates in the operation; and limited resource producer with direct or indirect gross farm sales not more than $100,000 in both of the previous two years, adjusted upwards for any general inflation since fiscal year 2004, and if the total household income is at or below the national poverty level for a family of four or less than 50 percent of county median household income in bother of the previous two years.
Funding: (Direct Payments for Specified Use) FY 18 $198,098,000.00; FY 19 est $0.00; FY 20 est $0.00
HQ: 14th and Independence Avenue SW, PO Box 0517, Washington, DC 20250
   Phone: 202-720-5172 | Email: steve.peterson@wdc.usda.gov
   http://www.fsa.gov

DOJ16.750 | SUPPORT FOR ADAM WALSH ACT IMPLEMENTATION GRANT PROGRAM
"Adam Walsh Act"

Award: Project Grants
Purpose: To assist U.S. territories, tribes and local jurisdictions with developing programs to implement requirements of the Sex Offender Registration and Notification Act, where the offender lives, works and goes to school.
Applicant Eligibility: States, the District of Columbia, the Commonwealth of Puerto Rico, the Virgin Islands, America Samoa, Guam, the Northern Mariana Islands, and Federally recognized Indian Tribes who have elected to carry out the requirements of SORNA. Only applicant jurisdictions that are enhancing, maintaining, or working towards substantial implementation of SORNA are eligible to apply for AWA Implementation Grants. Nonprofit Organizations, for-profit Organizations, and Institutions of higher learning may apply for training and technical assistance and other AWA-authorized grant Programs. For sex offender management fellowships, eligible applicants include individuals.
Beneficiary Eligibility: State (including the District of Columbia), local governments (through funds granted to States), U.S. territory and tribal government agencies that have sex offender registry and tracking responsibilities. For training and technical assistance funds: nonprofit and for-profit organizations with experience in SORNA implementation and sex offender management practices. For NSOPW: nonprofit and/or for-profit organizations with experience in providing web site development, hosting and management, web services, service-oriented architecture, and distributed information sharing systems.

Programs Administered by Federal Headquarters

Award Range/Average: Up to $400,000 each for Adam Walsh Act (AWA) Implementation grants, up to $1,000,000 for the National Sex Offender Public Website (NSOPW), up to $1,000,000 for tribal training and technical assistance and $150,000 per fellowship opportunity
Funding: (Project Grants) FY 17 $16,883,370.00; FY 18 est $20,000,000.00; FY 19 est $20,000,000.00
HQ: 810 7th Street NW, Washington, DC 20531
    Phone: 202-307-5762
    http://smart.gov

HHS93.634 | SUPPORT FOR OMBUDSMAN AND BENEFICIARY COUNSELING PROGRAMS FOR STATES PARTICIPATING IN FINANCIAL ALIGNMENT MODEL DEMONSTRATIONS FOR DUALLY ELIGIBLE INDIVIDUALS
"Support for Demonstration Ombudsman Programs Serving Beneficiaries of State Demonstrations to Integrate Care for Medicare-Medicaid"

Award: Cooperative Agreements
Purpose: CMS is presenting this Funding Opportunity Announcement to ensure that the beneficiaries of the Financial Alignment Demonstration models - as well as their caregivers and authorized representatives - have access to person-centered assistance in resolving problems and selecting appropriate healthcare coverage related to the Plans and providers.
Applicant Eligibility: States which have signed an MOU with CMS to implement one of the financial alignment demonstration models.
Beneficiary Eligibility: States which have signed an MOU with CMS to implement one of the financial alignment demonstration models. Enrollees and caregivers in the Financial Alignment Demonstration.
Award Range/Average: Awards range from $149,000- $ $1,494,476 per year.
Funding: (Cooperative Agreements) FY 18 $27,614,601.00; FY 19 est $28,092,794.00; FY 20 est $25,404,250.00
HQ: 7500 Security Boulevard, Baltimore, MD 21207
    Phone: 410-786-8200 | Email: kemuel.johnson@cms.hhs.gov
    http://www.cms.gov/Medicare-Medicaid-Coordination/Medicare-and-Medicaid-Coordination/Medicare-Medicaid-Coordination-Office/FinancialModelstoSupportStatesEffortsinCareCoordination.html

HHS93.818 | SUPPORT TO THE WORLD HEALTH ORGANIZATION (WHO) FOR RESPONSE TO THE EBOLA VIRUS DISEASE OUTBREAK IN WESTERN AFRICA

Award: Cooperative Agreements
Purpose: The project's objective is to contribute to on-going efforts to reduce the morbidity, mortality and to break the chain of transmission of EVD by strengthening capacities at the district level of affected countries in western Africa to actively find, investigate and refer cases, register all potential contacts and monitor them for symptom development.
Applicant Eligibility: World Health Organization (WHO). For purposes of this document, the term WHO includes its regional offices (e.g., PAHO, EMRO, AFRO, SEARO, etc.).
Beneficiary Eligibility: Individuals worldwide, including the U.S.
Award Range/Average: Range and Average Award for FY2015: Approx $50M
HQ: 1600 Clifton Road NE, PO Box E29, Atlanta, GA 30329
    Phone: 404-639-4276 | Email: ctg8@cdc.gov
    http://www.cdc.gov

ED84.187 | SUPPORTED EMPLOYMENT SERVICES FOR INDIVIDUALS WITH THE MOST SIGNIFICANT DISABILITIES
"Supported Employment State Grants"

Award: Formula Grants
Purpose: To provide grants for time limited services leading to supported employment for individuals with the most severe disabilities.
Applicant Eligibility: The State VR agency designated in the VR services portion of the Unified or Combined State plan to administer the VR Program is eligible to receive Federal funds under this Program.

Beneficiary Eligibility: Individuals with the most significant disabilities who have been determined eligible for VR services under Title I of the Rehabilitation Act and whose individualized plan for employment identifies supported employment as the employment outcome.

Award Range/Average: In FY 2019, the estimated range of awards is $28,185 (territories) to $2,020,1858, with a median State award, excluding territories, of $300,000.

Funding: (Formula Grants) FY 18 $22,548,000.00; FY 19 est $22,548,000.00; FY 20 est $22,548,000.00

HQ: 400 Maryland Avenue SW, Washington, DC 20202

Phone: 202-245-7454 | Email: suzanne.mitchell@ed.gov

http://www2.ed.gov/about/offices/list/osers/rsa/index.html

HHS93.833 | SUPPORTING AND MAINTAINING A SURVEILLANCE SYSTEM FOR CHRONIC KIDNEY DISEASE (CKD) IN THE UNITED STATES
"Chronic Kidney Disease (CKD)"

Award: Cooperative Agreements

Purpose: The award will build upon previous work to continue developing, supporting and enhancing the CKD Surveillance System in the United States, to monitor the burden and trends of CKD and its risk factors over time, and monitor and evaluate trends in achieving Healthy People 2020 objectives.

Applicant Eligibility: Public nonprofit Organizations; Private nonprofit Organizations; For profit Organizations; Small, minority, and women-owned businesses; universities; Colleges; Research Institutions; Hospitals; Community-based Organizations; Faith-based Organizations; Indian/Native American Tribal Governments (Federally Recognized); Indian/Native American Tribal Governments (other than Federally recognized); Indian/Native American Tribally Designated Organizations State and local Governments or their Bona Fide Agents (this includes the District of Columbia, the Commonwealth of Puerto Rico, the Virgin Islands, the Commonwealth of the Northern Marianna Islands, American Samoa, Guam, the Federated States of Micronesia, the Republic of the Marshall Islands, and the Republic of Palau). Note: A Bona Fide Agent is an agency/Organization identified by the state as eligible to submit an application under the state eligibility in lieu of a state application.

Beneficiary Eligibility: The general public will benefit from the objectives of this program. Kidney diseases are the ninth leading cause of death in the United States and more than 1 of 10 US adults may have CKD. The CKD Surveillance System is intended to raise awareness about CKD and its risk factors, promote early diagnosis, and improve outcomes for those living with CKD.

Award Range/Average: Current FOA DP11-1109 funds three awardee ranging from 200000 - 400000; new FY16 will fund two range is contingent upon funding request.

Funding: (Cooperative Agreements) FY 18 $1,311,429.00; FY 19 est $1,350,455.00; FY 20 est $1,350,455

HQ: 4770 Buford Highway NE, PO Box F75, Atlanta, GA 30341

Phone: 770-488-1057 | Email: nmr0@cdc.gov

http://www.cdc.gov

ED84.367 | SUPPORTING EFFECTIVE INSTRUCTION STATE GRANTS (FORMERLY IMPROVING TEACHER QUALITY STATE GRANTS)

Award: Formula Grants

Purpose: To provide grants to State Educational Agencies (SEAs), to increase student academic achievement consistent with challenging State academic standards.

Applicant Eligibility: NOTE: State educational Agencies (SEAs) are the only eligible State agencies. The 50 States, the District of Columbia, the Bureau of Indian education, Puerto Rico, American Samoa, Guam, the Northern Marianas, and the Virgin Islands receive funding.

Beneficiary Eligibility: Elementary and secondary schools, teachers, paraprofessionals, principals and other school leaders; and students will benefit.

Award Range/Average: FY 18: Range: $9,789,945 to $230,422,543 (for State awards); Average: $38,944,141 FY 19: Range: $9,857,080 to $229,489,744 (for State awards); Average $38,944,141 FY 20: Not applicable.

Funding: (Formula Grants) FY 18 $2,055,830,000.00; FY 19 est $2,055,830,000.00; FY 20 est $0.00

HQ: 400 Maryland Avenue SW, Washington, DC 20202

Phone: 202-453-7019 | Email: patrick.rooney@ed.gov

http://www.ed.gov/programs/teacherqual/index.html

Programs Administered by Federal Headquarters

HUD14.181 | SUPPORTIVE HOUSING FOR PERSONS WITH DISABILITIES
"Section 811"

Award: Direct Payments for Specified Use

Purpose: To enlarge the supply of supportive housing for very low-income disabled persons.

Applicant Eligibility: Eligible Sponsors are nonprofit Organizations with a Section 501(c)(3) tax exemption from the Internal Revenue Service. Eligible Owner entities are nonprofit Organizations with a 501(c)(3) tax exemption from the Internal Revenue Service and, if the proposed project involves mixed financing, for-profit limited partnerships with a nonprofit entity as the sole general partner.

Beneficiary Eligibility: Beneficiaries of housing developed under this program must be very low-income (equal to or less than 50% AMI) adults (18 or older) with a physical, mental, or emotional impairment that is expected to be of long-continued and indefinite duration, that substantially impedes his or her ability to live independently, and is of a nature that such ability could be improved by more suitable housing conditions.

Award Range/Average: $422,600 to $4,092,000 (FY10/11)

Funding: (Direct Payments for Specified Use) FY 15 $125,000,000.00; FY 16 est $129,000,000.00; FY 17 est $146,000,000.00

HQ: 451 7th Street SW, Room 6142, Washington, DC 20410

   Phone: 202-708-3000 | Email: marvis.s.hayward@hud.gov

   http://portal.hud.gov/hudportal/hud?src=/program_offices/housing/mfh/progdesc/disab811

HUD14.157 | SUPPORTIVE HOUSING FOR THE ELDERLY
"Section 202"

Award: Direct Payments for Specified Use

Purpose: To enlarge the supply of multifamily housing for very low income elderly persons.

Applicant Eligibility: Eligible Sponsors include private nonprofit Organizations and nonprofit consumer cooperatives. Eligible Owner entities include private nonprofit corporations, nonprofit consumer cooperatives, and if the proposed project involves mixed-financing, for-profit limited partnerships with a nonprofit entity as the sole general partner. Public bodies and their instrumentalities are not eligible Section 202 applicants.

Beneficiary Eligibility: Beneficiaries of housing developed under this program must be elderly (62 years of age or older) and have very low-incomes.

Funding: (Direct Payments for Specified Use) FY 15 $354,000,000.00; FY 16 est $356,000,000.00; FY 17 est $430,000,000.00

HQ: 451 7th Street SW, Room 6152, Washington, DC 20410

   Phone: 202-708-3000 | Email: alicia.anderson@hud.gov

   http://portal.hud.gov/hudportal/hud?src=/program_offices/housing/mfh/progdesc/eld202

HUD14.235 | SUPPORTIVE HOUSING PROGRAM

Award: Project Grants; Direct Payments for Specified Use

Purpose: To promote the development of supportive housing and services to assist homeless individuals and families and to enable them to live as independently.

Applicant Eligibility: States, local Governments, other governmental entities, private nonprofit Organizations, and community mental health associations that are public nonprofit Organizations.

Beneficiary Eligibility: Homeless individuals and families with children.

Award Range/Average: HUD imposes the following limitations: (1) Acquisition and/or rehabilitation construction grants for the Supportive Housing Program may not exceed 200,000 (up to $400,000 in high cost areas); new construction may not exceed $400,000; (2) funding of up to 75 percent for operating costs; (3) funding of up to 80 percent for supportive services and HMIS costs; and (4) the program provides grants for leasing costs for up to 3 years.

HQ: 451 7th Street SW, Room 7256, Washington, DC 20410

   Phone: 202-402-5697 | Email: tonya.proctor@hud.gov

   http://www.hudexchange.info/shp

SBA59.016 | SURETY BOND GUARANTEES

Award: Insurance

Purpose: To guarantee surety bonds issued by commercial surety companies for small businesses unable to obtain a bond without an SBA guarantee.

Applicant Eligibility: Guarantees are limited to those surety companies holding certificates of authority from the Secretary of the Treasury as an acceptable surety for bonds on Federal contracts. Specific criteria apply to the Prior Approval and PSB Sureties.

Beneficiary Eligibility: For Federal contracts, a small business is eligible for the surety bond program if it qualifies as a small business under Code of Federal Regulations Subpart 121, Size Eligibility Provisions and Standards.

Award Range/Average: Additional information available on SBA's website at www.sba.gov.

Funding: (Insurance (Guaranteed Surety Bonds)) FY 17 $1,392,000,000.00; FY 18 est $6,000,000,000.00; FY 19 est $6,000,000,000.00

HQ: 409 3rd Street SW, 8th Floor, Washington, DC 20416
Phone: 202-205-6548 | Email: peter.gibbs@sba.gov
http://www.sba.gov/osg

DOT20.932 | SURFACE TRANSPORTATION DISCRETIONARY GRANTS FOR CAPITAL INVESTMENT
"TIGER Grants (Transportation Investment Generating Economic Recovery)"

Award: Project Grants

Purpose: To preserve and create jobs and promote economic recovery.

Applicant Eligibility: The Federal share of the costs for which an expenditure is made under this Program may have been up to 100 percent, however, the Department gave priority to projects that required a contribution of Federal funds in order to complete an overall financing package, and to projects that are expected to be completed by February 17, 2012.

Beneficiary Eligibility: The ultimate benefits of this program may have been received by, among others, State or local governments, transit agencies, builders/contractors/developers, major metropolises, and other urban, suburban, or rural areas.

Award Range/Average: Grants provided under this program generally were not less than $20,000,000 and not greater than $300,000,000, however, some cases the Department waived the minimum grant size for the purpose of funding significant projects in smaller cities, regions, or States.

HQ: 1200 New Jersey Avenue SE, Washington, DC 20590
Phone: 202-366-0301 | Email: howard.hill@dot.gov
http://www.dot.gov/tiger

HHS93.291 | SURPLUS PROPERTY UTILIZATION
"Federal Real Property Assistance Program"

Award: Sale, Exchange, Or Donation of Property and Goods

Purpose: To convey or lease all surplus Federal real properties made available by the disposal agency which are needed and usable by eligible organizations and institutions to carry out health programs.

Applicant Eligibility: States, their political subdivisions and instrumentalities; tax-supported public health Institutions, and nonprofit Institutions which (except for Institutions which lease property to assist the homeless under Title V of Public Law 100-77) have been held exempt from taxation under Section 501 (c) (3) of the 1986 Internal Revenue Code.

Beneficiary Eligibility: Anyone attending, working with or for, or served by the eligible applicants. Examples of potentially eligible use programs are hospitals, public health clinics, water and sewer systems, institutions for the rehabilitation of mentally or physically disabled, health research institutions, homeless assistance facilities, and other institutions with basic health programs.

HQ: 7700 Wisconsin Avenue, Suite 8216, Bethesda, MD 20814
Phone: 301-443-2265 | Email: theresa.ritta@psc.hhs.gov
https://www.psc.gov/services/property-assistance-program

HHS93.755 | SURVEILLANCE FOR DISEASES AMONG IMMIGRANTS AND REFUGEES FINANCED IN PART BY PREVENTION AND PUBLIC HEALTH FUNDS (PPHF)

Award: Cooperative Agreements

Purpose: Conducts surveillance to detect, prevent and control diseases and evaluate existing health programs to improve the health of refugees and/or immigrants that are newly arrived in the United States.

Programs Administered by Federal Headquarters

Applicant Eligibility: Eligibility is limited to any domestic entity providing healthcare services to immigrants and refugees newly arrived in the United States.

Beneficiary Eligibility: Any U.S. state, political subdivision and U.S. territories and other public entities providing healthcare services to newly arrived refugees and immigrants will benefit.

Award Range/Average: Awards will range from approximately $25,000 to $150,000 with an average of approximately $80,000.

HQ: 1600 Clifton Road NE, PO Box E03, Atlanta, GA 30333

    Phone: 404-639-0712

    http://www.cdc.gov/immigrantrefugeehealth

VA64.117 | SURVIVORS AND DEPENDENTS EDUCATIONAL ASSISTANCE

Award: Direct Payments for Specified Use

Purpose: Provides educational opportunities to the dependents of certain disabled and deceased veterans.

Applicant Eligibility: Spouses, surviving spouses, and children (including stepchild or adopted child) between age 18 and 26 of veterans who died from service-connected disabilities, of living veterans whose service-connected disabilities are considered permanently and totally disabling, of those who died from any cause while such service-connected disabilities were in existence, of servicepersons who have been listed for a total of more than 90 days as currently missing in action, or as currently prisoners of war, a service member who VA determines has a service connected permanent and total disability and at the time of VA's determination is a member of the Armed Forces who is hospitalized or receiving outpatient medical care, services, or treatment; and is likely to be discharged or released from service for this service-connected disability. Children under the age of 18 may be eligible under special circumstances.

Beneficiary Eligibility: See Applicant Eligibility.

Funding: (Direct Payments for Specified Use) FY 07 $423,335,000.00; FY 08 est $450,646,000.00; FY 09 est $478,067,000.00

HQ: Department of Veterans Affairs Central Office 810 Vermont Avenue, Washington, DC 20420

    Phone: 202-461-9800

    http://www.gibill.va.gov

USDA10.215 | SUSTAINABLE AGRICULTURE RESEARCH AND EDUCATION "SARE"

Award: Project Grants

Purpose: To support agriculture products, sustain domestic and wildlife habitat, conservation of land and natural resources, and provide employment opportunities.

Applicant Eligibility: Land-grant colleges or universities, other universities, State agricultural experiment stations, State cooperative extension services, nonprofit Organizations, and individuals with demonstrable expertise, or Federal or State governmental entities.

Beneficiary Eligibility: Same as Applicant Eligibility.

Award Range/Average: If minimum or maximum amounts of funding per competitive and/or capacity project grant, or cooperative agreement are established, these amounts will be announced in the annual Competitive Request for Application (RFA). The most current RFA is available via: https://nifa.usda.gov/funding-opportunity/sare-regional-host-institution

Funding: (Project Grants) FY 18 $32,770,088.00; FY 19 est $34,667,520; Fy 20 est $17,741,448

HQ: 1400 Independence Avenue SW, PO Box 2240, Washington, DC 20250-2240

    Phone: 202-401-0151

    http://nifa.usda.gov/program/sustainable-agriculture-program

DOS19.601 | SYRIA ASSISTANCE PROGRAM "NEA Syria"

Award: Cooperative Agreements; Project Grants

Purpose: Supports the foreign assistance goals and objectives of the Department of State, Bureau of Near Eastern Affairs, as delineated in the Fiscal Year Bureau Strategic and Resource Plan. This program is for all grant awards for the entire fiscal year funded through State/NEA for Syria programming.

Applicant Eligibility: U.S. or foreign non-profit Organizations; for-profit Organizations; private Institutions of higher education, public or state Institutions of higher education; public international Organizations; and small businesses with functional and regional experience. Each solicitation outlines who is eligible and what types of experience are needed to apply for funding.

Any award made using State/NEA funds requires the full complement of standard federal forms and budget documents as required in 2 CFR 200 and 2 CFR 600. See www.grants.gov for specific announcement. 2 CFR 200 applies to this Program.

Beneficiary Eligibility: U.S. or foreign non-profit organizations; for-profit organizations; private institutions of higher education, public or state institutions of higher education; public international organizations; and small businesses with functional and regional experience. Each solicitation outlines who is eligible and what types of experience are needed to apply for funding. See www.grants.gov for specific announcement.

Award Range/Average: Depends on specific grant award. See www.grants.gov for specific announcement.

HQ: 2430 E Street NW, Washington, DC 20037

Phone: 202-776-8691 | Email: curleysl@state.gov

DOI15.444 | TAKE PRIDE

Award: Cooperative Agreements

Purpose: The Bureau of Ocean Energy Management (BOEM) oversees the exploration and development of oil, natural gas and other minerals and renewable energy alternatives on the Nation's outer continental shelf. The purpose of the Environmental Studies Program is to obtain the information needed for the assessment and the management of environmental impacts; to predict impacts on marine biota; and to monitor the human, marine, and coastal environments to provide time series and data trend information.

Applicant Eligibility: Public and private Organizations.

Beneficiary Eligibility: Research scientists, Federal, State and local decision-makers, Native American Organizations, and the general public will ultimately benefit from the program.

Award Range/Average: Range is $25,000 to $100,000; Average $250,000.

Funding: (Cooperative Agreements) FY 17 $5,742,696.00; FY 18 est $6,400,000.00; FY 19 Estimate Not Available

HQ: 45600 Woodland Road, Sterling, VA 20166

Phone: 703-787-1087 | Email: rodney.cluck@boem.gov

http://www.boem.gov

HHS93.475 | TANF POLICY ACADEMY FOR INNOVATIVE EMPLOYMENT STRATEGIES (PAIES)
"PAIES"

Award: Cooperative Agreements

Purpose: Work with successful state TANF applicants to design, plan and refine components and strategies to improve employment outcomes for TANF program participants.

Applicant Eligibility: State (including the District of Columbia, Guam, Puerto Rico, and the Virgin Islands) human services agencies are eligible to receive assistance.

Beneficiary Eligibility: State (including the District of Columbia, Guam, Puerto Rico, and the Virgin Islands) human services agencies are eligible to receive assistance to participate in the PAIES to design, plan and refine components and strategies to improve employment outcomes for TANF program participants.

Award Range/Average: For Fiscal Year 2018, the grants were $125,000 each.

Funding: (Cooperative Agreements) FY 18 $500,000.00; FY 19 est $0.00; FY 20 est Estimate Not Available

HQ: 330 C Street SW, Suite 3026, Washington, DC 20002

Phone: 202-401-5141 | Email: lwashington-thomas@acf.hhs.gov

http://www.acf.hhs.gov/ofa

TREAS21.006 | TAX COUNSELING FOR THE ELDERLY

Award: Project Grants

Purpose: To authorize the Internal Revenue Service to enter into agreements with private or public nonprofit agencies or organizations.

Applicant Eligibility: Tax Counseling for the Elderly sponsors must be private or public nonprofit Organizations with experience in coordinating volunteer Programs. Federal, State, and local governmental agencies are not eligible to sponsor a Program. Applicants must be tax compliant and not debarred or suspended.

Beneficiary Eligibility: Elderly taxpayers, age 60 or older.

Funding: (Cooperative Agreements (Discretionary Grants)) FY 18 $8,890,000.00; FY 19 est $8,890,000.00; FY 20 est $8,890,000.00

Programs Administered by Federal Headquarters

HQ: 5000 Ellin Road NCFB C4 110, Lanham, MD 20706
 Phone: 404-338-7894
 http://www.irs.gov/individuals/tax-counseling-for-the-elderly

ED84.379 | TEACHER EDUCATION ASSISTANCE FOR COLLEGE AND HIGHER EDUCATION GRANTS (TEACH GRANTS)

Award: Direct Payments for Specified Use
Purpose: To provide annual grants of up to $4,000 to eligible undergraduate and graduate students who agree to teach specified high-need subjects at schools serving primarily disadvantaged populations for four years within eight years of graduation.
Applicant Eligibility: Undergraduate and graduate students completing coursework or other requirements necessary to begin a career in teaching. Students must attend an institution of higher education that provides high-quality teacher preparation and professional development services; is financially sound; provides, or assists in the provision, of pedagogical coursework; and provides, or assists in the provision, of supervision and support services to teachers.
Beneficiary Eligibility: Students must have a grade-point-average (GPA) comparable to a 3.25 on a scale of zero to 4.0, except that, if the student is in the first year of undergraduate education, the grade point average is determined based on the student's cumulative secondary school grade point average. A student applying for a grant to obtain a graduate degree must be a teacher or a retiree from another occupation with expertise in a field in which there is a shortage of teachers; grants for graduate education may also be obtained by a student who is or was a teacher who is pursuing high-quality alternative certification. In addition, students must sign an agreement to serve as a full-time teacher for not less than four years within eight years of completing the course of study for which they received a TEACH Grant. Service must be performed at a school serving a primarily disadvantaged population and must be in one of the following fields: mathematics, science, a foreign language, bilingual education, special education, as a reading specialist, or in another field documented as high-need. Students must also agree to provide evidence of qualifying employment upon completion of each year of service. Failure to complete the service requirements results in the student's TEACH Grants being treated as Federal Direct Unsubsidized Stafford Loans, with interest accrued from the date of award. Students must also sign a statement of educational purpose, not owe a refund on a Title IV grant, and not be in default on a Title IV loan. Eligible males that are at least 18 years old and born after December 31, 1959, can receive aid only if they have registered with the Selective Service.
Funding: (Direct Payments for Specified Use) FY 18 $88,979,000.00; FY 19 est $95,800,000.00; FY 20 est $97,173,000.00
HQ: PO Box 84, Washington, DC 20044-0084
 Phone: 800-433-3243
 http://www2.ed.gov/programs/tqpartnership/index.html

HHS93.530 | TEACHING HEALTH CENTER GRADUATE MEDICAL EDUCATION PAYMENT
"THCGME Payment Program"

Award: Formula Grants
Purpose: To expand primary care and dental residency training programs in community based settings.
Applicant Eligibility: Eligible entities include community-based ambulatory patient care centers that operate a primary care residency Program. Specific examples of eligible entities include, but are not limited to: Federally qualified health centers, as defined in section 1905(l)(2)(B) of the Social Security Act Community mental health centers, as defined in section 1861(ff)(3)(B) of the Social Security Act Rural health clinics, as defined in section 1861(aa) of the Social Security Act Health centers operated by the Indian Health service, an Indian tribe, or tribal Organization, or an urban Indian Organization, as defined in section 4 of the Indian healthcare Improvement Act An entity receiving funds under Title X of the Public Health Service Act. In addition, the eligible entity must be listed as the institutional sponsor by the relevant accrediting body, including the Accreditation Council for Graduate Medical education (ACGME), American Osteopathic Association (AOA), or the Council on Dental Accreditation (CODA)Federally Recognized Indian Tribal Government and Native American Organizations may apply if they are otherwise eligible.
Beneficiary Eligibility: The program supports high-quality primary care residency training in community based settings. Eligible entities include community-based ambulatory patient care centers that operate a primary care residency program. Specific examples of eligible entities include, but are not limited to: Federally qualified health centers, as defined in section 1905(l)(2)(B) of the Social Security Act; Community mental health centers, as defined in section 1861(ff)(3)(B) of the Social Security Act; Rural health clinics, as defined in section 1861(aa) of the Social Security Act; Health centers operated by the Indian Health service, an Indian tribe, or tribal organization, or an urban Indian organization, as defined in section 4 of the

Indian Health Care Improvement Act; An entity receiving funds under Title X of the Public Health Service Act. In addition, the eligible entity must be listed as the institutional sponsor by the relevant accrediting body, including the Accreditation Council for Graduate Medical Education (ACGME), American Osteopathic Association (AOA), or the Council on Dental Accreditation (CODA)Federally Recognized Indian Tribal Government and Native American Organizations may apply if they are otherwise eligible.

Award Range/Average: The current interim payment rate is set at $150,000 per resident FTE.

Funding: (Formula Grants) FY 18 $119,498,802.00; FY 19 est $121,092,500.00; FY 20 est $120,092,500.00

HQ: 5600 Fishers Lane, Room 15N146A, Rockville, MD 20857

    Phone: 301-443-6535

    http://www.hrsa.gov

USDA10.960 | TECHNICAL AGRICULTURAL ASSISTANCE
"International Capacity Building and Development Assistance Programs"

Award: Cooperative Agreements; Direct Payments for Specified Use

Purpose: To identify agricultural issues and problems and to maximize the capabilities of U.S. educational institutions and nonprofit agencies in agricultural technical assistance and research.

Applicant Eligibility: Institutions of higher education, state cooperative Institutions, non-profit Organizations, and public international Organizations.

Beneficiary Eligibility: Technical assistance provided through these agreements generally benefits agricultural institutions in specified locations, or supports programming that does so.

Award Range/Average: Most awards are between $25,000 - $1,500,000.

Funding: (Cooperative Agreements) FY 18 $24,407,456.00; FY 19 est $25,000,000.00; FY 20 est $20,000,000.00

HQ: 400 Independence Avenue SW, Washington, DC 20250

    Phone: 202-720-5337 | Email: lawrence.trouba@usda.gov

    http://www.fas.usda.gov

HHS93.129 | TECHNICAL AND NON-FINANCIAL ASSISTANCE TO HEALTH CENTERS
"State and Regional Primary Care Associations and National Cooperative Agreements"

Award: Cooperative Agreements

Purpose: To provide necessary technical and non-financial assistance to potential and existing health centers, including training and assistance.

Applicant Eligibility: Eligible applicants include domestic public or private, non-profit, and for-profit entities, including federally recognized Indian Tribal Governments and Native American and faith-based Organizations, that can provide training and technical assistance on a national or state/regional level to community-based Organizations and public entities that have or are seeking Health Center Program award recipient or look-alike designation status. Applications may be submitted by current State and Regional Primary Care Associations, National Cooperative Agreements, or new Organizations.

Beneficiary Eligibility: Population groups in medically underserved areas, medically underserved populations, and special populations such migratory and seasonal agricultural workers, people experiencing homelessness, and public housing residents.

Award Range/Average: $448,662 to $6,375,000; Average $1,909,130

Funding: (Cooperative Agreements) FY 18 $76,732,625.00; FY 19 est $78,000,000.00; FY 20 est $78,000,000.00

HQ: 5600 Fishers Lane, Room 16N16, Rockville, MD 20857

    Phone: 301-594-4300

    http://www.hrsa.gov/about/contact/bphc.aspx

HHS93.019 | TECHNICAL ASSISTANCE AND PROVISION FOR FOREIGN HOSPITALS AND HEALTH ORGANIZATIONS

Award: Project Grants

Purpose: To provide support for a quality of care improvement project based in a partner healthcare institution around the world.

Programs Administered by Federal Headquarters

Applicant Eligibility: N/A
Beneficiary Eligibility: Citizens of the world.
Award Range/Average: $650,000.00 to $7,900,000
Funding: (Salaries and Expenses) FY 18 est $1,760,969.00; FY 19 est $1,300,000.00; FY 20 est $1,300,000.00
HQ: 200 Independence Avenue SW, Washington, DC 20201

Phone: 202-205-1435 | Email: julie.schafer@hhs.gov
http://www.phe.gov

USDA10.761 | TECHNICAL ASSISTANCE AND TRAINING GRANTS
"TAT Grants"

Award: Project Grants
Purpose: To identify water and waste disposal problems in rural areas and to provide maintenance facilities.
Applicant Eligibility: Eligible entities must be private nonprofit Organizations. Applicants must have proven ability, background, experience, legal authority and actual capacity to provide technical assistance and/or training on a regional basis to associations.
Beneficiary Eligibility: Entities that may be eligible for water and waste disposal loans and grants (10.760) such as municipalities, counties, districts, authorities, and other political subdivisions of a State, organizations operated on a not-for-profit basis, such as associations, cooperatives, or private corporations, Indian tribes on Federal and State reservations and other federally recognized Indian tribes.
Award Range/Average: $100,000 to $9,939,370. Average: $1,286,404
Funding: (Project Grants) FY 18 est $41,164,931.00; FY 19 est $30,083,280.00; FY 20 est $40,000,000
HQ: 1400 Independence Avenue SW, PO Box 1548, Washington, DC 20250

Phone: 202-720-0986 | Email: edna.primrose@wdc.usda.gov
http://www.rd.usda.gov/programs-services/water-waste-disposal-technical-assistance-training-grants

USDA10.604 | TECHNICAL ASSISTANCE FOR SPECIALTY CROPS PROGRAM
"TASC"

Award: Direct Payments for Specified Use
Purpose: The Technical Assistance for Specialty Crops Program is for U.S. organizations to address sanitary, phytosanitary, and technical barriers that threaten the export of U.S. specialty crops.
Applicant Eligibility: To be approved, an applicant must be a: (1) U.S. government agency; (2) U.S. State government agency; (3) U.S. non-profit trade association; (4) U.S. University; (5) U.S. agricultural cooperative; (6) U.S. private company or (7) any other U.S. Organization.
Beneficiary Eligibility: The Technical Assistance for Specialty Crops Program is intended to benefit the represented U.S. industry rather than a specific company or brand.
Award Range/Average: Projects funded on a project by project basis for up to $500,000 per year.
Funding: (Formula Grants (Apportionments)) FY 18 $9,000,000.00; FY 19 est $9,000,000.00 FY 20 est $9,000,000.00
HQ: 1400 Independence Avenue SW, Washington, DC 20250

Phone: 202-401-0100 | Email: richard.chavez@fas.usda.gov
http://www.fas.usda.gov/programs/technical-assistance-specialty-crops-tasc

DOT20.710 | TECHNICAL ASSISTANCE GRANTS
"Information Grants to Communities - Technical Assistance Grant"

Award: Project Grants
Purpose: Promotes development of engineering or other scientific analysis of pipeline safety issues, including the promotion of public participation in official proceedings.
Applicant Eligibility: As well as private nonprofit Institutions /Organizations and public nonprofit Institutions /Organizations.
Beneficiary Eligibility: N/A
Award Range/Average: The range is $0 - $100,000
Funding: (Project Grants (Discretionary)) FY 18 $1,487,634.00; FY 19 est $1,500,000.00; FY 20 Estimate Not Available
HQ: 1200 New Jersey Avenue SE E22 105, Washington, DC 20590

Phone: 202-366-6855 | Email: karen.lynch@dot.gov
http://primis.phmsa.dot.gov/tag

USDA10.350 | TECHNICAL ASSISTANCE TO COOPERATIVES
"TAC"

Award: Provision of Specialized Services; Advisory Services and Counseling; Dissemination of Technical Information; Training
Purpose: To promote research, technical assistance, educational programs in various disciplines, especially on farmer and farming aspects in rural areas.
Applicant Eligibility: Farmer and rural cooperatives and rural residents in all U.S. States and Territories.
Beneficiary Eligibility: Ultimate beneficiaries must be located in rural areas.
Award Range/Average: Non-monetary, This program offers technical assistance and advise
HQ: 1400 Independence Avenue SW Room 5803 S, PO Box 3201, Washington, DC 20250
   Phone: 202-690-1374
   http://www.rd.usda.gov/about-rd/agencies/rural-business-cooperative-service

HHS93.348 | TECHNICAL ASSISTANCE TO INCREASE TOBACCO CESSATION

Award: Cooperative Agreements
Purpose: To provide technical assistance to state tobacco control programs and national and state partners.
Applicant Eligibility: N/A
Beneficiary Eligibility: N/A
Award Range/Average: DP13-1316 $450K
Funding: (Cooperative Agreements) FY 18 Actual Not Available; FY 19 est $450,000.00; FY 20 est $450,000.00
HQ: 4770 Buford Highway NE, PO Box S107 7, Atlanta, GA 30341
   Phone: 770-488-2499
   http://www.cdc.gov

DOC11.616 | TECHNOLOGY INNOVATION PROGRAM (TIP)
"TIP"

Award: Project Grants
Purpose: The Technology Innovation Program supports innovation in the United States especially in the areas of critical national need.
Applicant Eligibility: A U.S. -owned, single, small-sized or medium-sized company doing a majority of its business in the United States or a joint venture may apply for TIP funding. Members of joint ventures that are companies must also be doing a majority of their business in the United States. In addition, a company incorporated in the United States that has a parent company incorporated in another country may apply as either a single applicant or a joint venture member provided that certain requirements are met. Institutions of higher education, national laboratories, governmental laboratories (not including NIST), and nonprofit research Institutions may also participate as a member of a joint venture.
Beneficiary Eligibility: Same as Applicant Eligibility.
Award Range/Average: New program; therefore, no range and average available.
HQ: 100 Bureau Drive, Gaithersburg, MD 20899
   Phone: 301-975-4429 | Email: heather.mayton@nist.gov
   http://www.nist.gov

HHS93.297 | TEENAGE PREGNANCY PREVENTION PROGRAM
"TPP"

Award: Cooperative Agreements
Purpose: To support competitive grants to public and private entities to replicate evidence-based teen pregnancy prevention program models that have been shown to be effective through rigorous evaluation and research and demonstration projects to develop and test additional models and innovative strategies to prevent teen pregnancy.
Applicant Eligibility: Nonprofit with or without 501C3 IRS status; For profit Organizations; Small, minority, and women owned businesses; universities and colleges; Research Institutions; Hospitals; Community-based Organizations; Faith-based Organizations; Federally recognized or state-recognized American Indian/Alaska Native tribal Governments; American Indian/Alaska Native tribally designated Organizations; Alaska Native health corporations; Urban Indian health Organizations; Tribal epidemiology centers; State and local Governments or their Bona Fide Agents; Political subdivisions of States.

Programs Administered by Federal Headquarters

Beneficiary Eligibility: Teenagers in the US.
Award Range/Average: $250,000 - $2,000,000 per year. TPP Program grants in FY18 are funded through 6 different Funding Opportunity Announcements.
Funding: (Cooperative Agreements) FY 16 est $101,000,000.00; FY 17 $101,000,000.00; FY 18 Estimate Not Available
HQ: 1101 Wootton Parkway, Suite 550 Tower Building, Rockville, MD 20852
    Phone: 240-453-8822 | Email: alice.bettencourt@hhs.gov
    http://www.hhs.gov/ash/oah

HHS93.211 | TELEHEALTH PROGRAMS

Award: Project Grants
Purpose: To fund programs that demonstrate how telehealth networks improve healthcare services in rural communities. The current cohort is focused on telehealth services delivered through school-based health centers/clinics (SBHC), particularly those serving high-poverty populations.
Applicant Eligibility: Telehealth Network Program (TNGP) - Eligible applicants include public and private non-profit entities, including faith-based and community Organizations, as well as federally recognized tribal Governments and Organizations. National Telehealth Resource Center Program (NTRC) and Regional Telehealth Resource Center Program (RTRC) - Eligible applicants include public and private non-profit entities. Faith-based and community-based Organizations, Tribes, and tribal Organizations are eligible to apply. Licensure Portability Program (LPP) - Eligible applicants are limited by statute to state professional licensing boards. Note: American Indian and/or Alaska Native Tribal Organizations are eligible provided those Organizations meet the eligibility requirements above. Evidence-Based Tele-Emergency Network Program (EB TNGP) - Eligible applicants include public, private, and non-profit Organizations, including faith-based and community Organizations, as well as federally recognized tribal Governments and Organizations. Evidence-Based Tele-Behavioral Health Network Program (EB-THNP) - Eligible applicants include domestic public or private, non-profit entities, including faith-based and community-based Organizations, Tribes, and tribal Organizations. The Rural Child Poverty Telehealth Network Program (RCP-TNGP) - Eligible applicants include public and private non-profit entities, including faith-based and community Organizations, as well as federally recognized Indian tribal Governments and Organizations. The Substance Abuse Treatment Telehealth Network Program (SAT-TNGP) - Eligible applicants include public and private non-profit entities, including faith-based and community Organizations, as well as federally recognized Tribes and tribal Governments and Organizations. The Telehealth Center of Excellence Program - Eligible applicants must be public academic medical centers located in states with high chronic disease prevalence, high poverty rates, and a large percentage of medically underserved rural areas. The Telehealth Center of Excellence will be located in a public academic medical center that: 1. Has a successful telehealth Program with a high annual volume of telehealth visits; 2. Has an established reimbursement structure that allows telehealth services to be financially self-sustaining; and 3. Has established Programs that provide telehealth services in medically underserved areas with high chronic disease prevalence and high poverty rates.
Beneficiary Eligibility: Telehealth Network Grant Program (TNGP) - Health care providers in rural areas, in medically underserved areas, in frontier communities, and for medically underserved populations. TNGP grantees include in the network at least two (2) of the following entities (at least one (1) of which shall be a community-based health care provider: (a) community or migrant health centers or other federally qualified health centers; (b) health care providers, including pharmacists, in private practice; (c) entities operating clinics, including rural health clinics; (d) local health departments; (e) nonprofit hospitals, including community (critical) access hospitals; (f) other publicly funded health or social service agencies; (g) long-term care providers; (h) providers of health care services in the home; (i) providers of outpatient mental health services and entities operating outpatient mental health facilities; (j) local or regional emergency health care providers; (k) institutions of higher education; or (l) entities operating dental clinics; and (m) school based health centers/clinics. National Telehealth Resource Center Program (NTRC) and Regional Telehealth Resource Center Program (RTRC)- Health care providers in rural areas, in medically underserved areas, in frontier communities, and medically underserved populations. The TRCs must support the activities of existing or developing telehealth networks to meet the health care needs of rural or other populations to be served, including the improvement of access to services and the quality of the services received by those populations. American Indian and/or Alaska Native Tribal Organizations are eligible beneficiaries provided those organizations meet the beneficiary requirements above. Licensure Portability Grant Program (LPGP) - State professional licensing boards carry out programs under which licensing boards of various states cooperate to develop and implement state policies that will reduce statutory and regulatory barriers to telemedicine. State licensing boards, their members, and the general public are beneficiaries of the services conducted under this grant. Evidence-Based Tele-Emergency Network Grant Program (EB TNGP) - The Tele-Emergency Network shall include at least five members. Network members may include representation from the following categories: Hospitals, including community (critical) access hospitals; Local or regional emergency health care providers; Institutions of higher education with experience in data collection and analysis including but not limited to claims-level data; Medical research institutions; Tertiary providers with specialized experience in emergency

medicine, stroke and the use of telehealth services in those clinical areas. The Rural Child Poverty Telehealth Network Grant Program (RCP-TNGP) - Health care providers serving rural areas and frontier communities. The RCP-TNGP Network shall include at least two (2) of the following entities (at least one of which shall be a community-based health care provider): Community or migrant health centers or other federally-qualified health centers; Health care providers, including pharmacists, in private practice; Entities operating clinics, including rural health clinics; Local health departments; Nonprofit hospitals, including community access hospitals; Other publicly funded health or human/social service agencies; Long-term care providers; Providers of health care services in the home; Providers of outpatient mental health services and entities operating outpatient mental health facilities; Local or regional emergency health care providers; Institutions of higher education; and Entities operating dental clinics. If available in their area, applicants should consider partnering or collaborating with other federally-funded programs that target or have demonstrable effects on the health of impoverished children living in rural areas, including: USDA Cooperative Extension System Offices; Healthy Start; Healthy Tomorrows Partnership for Children; WIC; Maternal, Infant and Early Childhood Home Visitation programs; Head Start and Early Head Start; Temporary Assistance to Needy Families; Community Action Agencies; and other human/social service-focused providers. The Substance Abuse Treatment Telehealth Network Grant Program (SAT-TNGP) - The network must include at least two (2) of the following entities (at least one of which shall be a community-based health care provider): (a) Small hospital (defined as less than 50 available beds, as reported on the hospital's most recently filed Medicare Cost Report); (b) Community or migrant health centers or other federally-qualified health centers; (c) Health care providers, including pharmacists, in private practice; (d) entities operating clinics, including rural health clinics; (e) local health departments; (f) nonprofit hospitals, including community (critical) access hospitals; (g) other publicly funded health or social service agencies; (h) long-term care providers; (i) providers of health care services in the home; (j) providers of outpatient mental health services and entities operating outpatient mental health facilities; (k) local or regional emergency health care providers; (l) institutions of higher education; or (m) entities operating dental clinics. As noted in the Consolidated Appropriations Act 2017 (Public Law No. 115-31), preference will be given to networks that include small hospitals serving communities with high rates of poverty, unemployment, and substance abuse. The Telehealth Center of Excellence Program (COE) - Health care providers in rural areas, in medically underserved areas, in frontier communities, and medically underserved populations. The TRCs must support the activities of existing or developing telehealth networks to meet the health care needs of rural or other populations to be served, including the improvement of access to services and the quality of the services received by those populations.
Funding: (Project Grants) FY 18 $24,263,994.00; FY 19 est $21,705,486.00; FY 20 est Estimate Not Available
HQ: 5600 Fishers Lane, Rockville, MD 20857
   Phone: 301-443-0835 | Email: cmena@hrsa.gov
   http://www.hrsa.gov/ruralhealth/telehealth/index.html

HHS93.558 | TEMPORARY ASSISTANCE FOR NEEDY FAMILIES "TANF"

Award: Formula Grants; Dissemination of Technical Information
Purpose: To provide grants to States, Territories, the District of Columbia, and federally recognized Indian Tribes.
Applicant Eligibility: In general, all States, Territories, the District of Columbia, and all Federally-recognized Tribes in the lower 48 States and 13 specified entities in Alaska are eligible. State and local agencies and Tribes that operate TANF Programs must do so under plans determined to be complete (or for Tribes approved) by the Department of Health and Human Services (HHS). For Contingency Funds, all States and the District of Columbia are eligible if they are determined to be a "needy State" by satisfying criteria related to the state's unemployment rate or the average number of participants in the Supplemental Nutrition Assistance Program (or SNAP, formerly known as food stamps). Territories and Tribes are not eligible for Contingency Funds.
Beneficiary Eligibility: Needy families with children, as determined eligible by the State, Territory, or Tribe in accordance with the State or Tribal plan submitted to HHS.
Award Range/Average: State and Tribal Family Assistance grants are estimated from $77,195 to $3,637,503,251 with an average of $125,451,428.
Funding: (Formula Grants) FY 18 est $17,119,754,574.00; FY 19 est $17,119,754,574.00; FY 20 est $17,119,754,574.00
HQ: 330 C Street SW, Washington, DC 20201
   Phone: 202-401-9275 | Email: susan.golonka@acf.hhs.gov
   http://www.acf.hhs.gov/programs/ofa

Programs Administered by Federal Headquarters

HUD14.322 | TENANT RESOURCE NETWORK PROGRAM
"TRN"

Award: Cooperative Agreements
Purpose: To make grants to applicant organizations to help, communicate, educate and engage tenants of eligible project-based Section 8-assisted properties.
Applicant Eligibility: Eligible applicants are non profit Organizations with current IRS 501(c)(3) tax-exempt status. Eligible applicants shall demonstrate a minimum of five years of tenant outreach and organizing work, and may not have an identity of interest with any owner or management entity of any property where TRN activities are proposed.
Beneficiary Eligibility: Tenants in identified TRN eligible properties will ultimately benefit from the program.
Award Range/Average: 200000 to 720000
HQ: 451 7th Street SW, Room 6178, Washington, DC 20410
　　Phone: 202-402-3263 | Email: carol.schrader@hud.gov
　　http://portal.hud.gov/hudportal/hud?src=/program_offices/housing/mfh/grants/trn

HHS93.609 | THE AFFORDABLE CARE ACT-MEDICAID ADULT QUALITY GRANTS
"Measuring and Improving the Quality of Maternity Care in Medicaid"

Award: Project Grants
Purpose: Supports State Medicaid agencies in testing, collecting, and reporting the Initial Core Set of healthcareQuality Measures for Adults Enrolled in Medicaid to CMS. Additionally, the grant funding will also support States' efforts to use these data for improving the quality of care for adults covered by Medicaid.
Applicant Eligibility: Grant applicants are limited to the 51 State Medicaid Agencies and the Medicaid Agencies in the US Territories.
Beneficiary Eligibility: N/A
Award Range/Average: Grant awards up to $1 million for each 12-month budget period, with an estimated total of up to $2 million per Grantee over the two-year project period.
HQ: 200 Independence Avenue SW, Room 733H 02, Washington, DC 20201
　　Phone: 301-492-4312 | Email: michelle.feagins@cms.hhs.gov
　　http://www.medicaid.gov/medicaid-chip-program-information/by-topics/quality-of-care/adult-medicaid-quality-grants.html

HHS93.521 | THE AFFORDABLE CARE ACT: BUILDING EPIDEMIOLOGY, LABORATORY, AND HEALTH INFORMATION SYSTEMS CAPACITY IN THE EPIDEMIOLOGY AND LABORATORY CAPACITY FOR INFECTIOUS DISEASE (ELC) AND EMERGING INFECTIONS PROGRAM (EIP) COOPERATIVE AGREEMENTS; PPHF
"ELC/EIP - Prevention and Public Health Fund and other Capacity-Building Activities"

Award: Cooperative Agreements
Purpose: To provide for expanded and sustained national investment in prevention and public health programs to improve health and help restrain the rate of growth in private and public sector healthcarecosts.
Applicant Eligibility: Eligible applicants include the current ELC and EIP grantees which consists of all U.S. states, 6 large local health departments (Los Angeles County, Philadelphia, New York City, Chicago, Houston, and the District of Columbia), U.S. territories (Puerto Rico, Guam, U.S. Virgin Islands) and other U.S. affiliates in the Pacific (American Samoa, the Republic of Palau, Federated States of Micronesia, Marshall Islands, Mariana Islands and American Samoa).
Beneficiary Eligibility: State health departments, large local health departments, the District of Columbia, U.S. Territories, and the general public.
Funding: (Cooperative Agreements); FY 18 est $37,690,664.00; FY 19 est $37,690,664.00; FY 20 $0.00
HQ: 1600 Clifton Road NE, PO Box C18, Atlanta, GA 30333
　　Phone: 404-639-7379 | Email: amoconnor@cdc.gov
　　http://www.cdc.gov

CDC93.380 | THE CDC PUBLIC HEALTH CANCER GENOMICS PROGRAM: TRANSLATING RESEARCH INTO PUBLIC HEALTH PRACTICE
"Genomics Program"

Award: Cooperative Agreements
Purpose: Translates evidence-based recommendation of activities such as screening for cancer genomics in public health settings.
Applicant Eligibility: Non-profit Organizations, state health department or tribal Organization, universities.
Beneficiary Eligibility: Same as Applicant Eligibility.
Award Range/Average: 5-programs are currently funded in FY18, at about $350,000 each. They were funded at a similar amount in FY17.
Funding: (Cooperative Agreements) FY 18 $0; FY 19 est $2,100,516.00; FY 20 est $2,100,516.00
HQ: 4770 Buford Highway NE, PO Box F-76, Atlanta, GA 30341
    Phone: 770-488-3086

HHS93.881 | THE HEALTH INSURANCE ENFORCEMENT AND CONSUMER PROTECTIONS GRANT PROGRAM

Award: Project Grants
Purpose: The Health Insurance Enforcement and Consumer Protections grants will provide states with the opportunity to ensure their laws, regulations, and procedures are in line with federal requirements and that states are able to effectively oversee and enforce the PHS Act's title XXVII Part A provisions with respect to health insurance issuers.
Applicant Eligibility: The Health Insurance Enforcement and Consumer Protections grant is open to all states that are currently enforcing the ACA market Reforms and also for those states who are not currently enforcing the ACA market Reforms to assist with their respective transition to an active enforcement role for all the market Reforms and consumer protections under Part A of Title XXVII of the Public Health Service Act.
Beneficiary Eligibility: Grants to States' (including the District of Columbia) for planning and/or implementing the market reforms and consumer protections in Part A of title XXVII of the PHS Act.
Award Range/Average: Grantees will receive a minimum of $476,998 as a baseline award amount.
Funding: (Project Grants) FY 18 $8,616,955.00; FY 19 Estimate Not Available; FY 20 Estimate Not Available
HQ: 200 Independence Avenue SW, Washington, DC 20201
    Phone: 301-492-4182 | Email: james.taing@cms.hhs.gov
    https://www.cms.gov/CCIIO/Programs-and-Initiatives/Health-Insurance-Market-Reforms/Health_Insurance_Enforcement_and_Consumer_Protections-Grants-.html

HHS93.334 | THE HEALTHY BRAIN INITIATIVE: TECHNICAL ASSISTANCE TO IMPLEMENT PUBLIC HEALTH ACTIONS RELATED TO COGNITIVE HEALTH, COGNITIVE IMPAIRMENT, AND CAREGIVING AT THE STATE AND LOCAL LEVELS
"Healthy Brain Initiative"

Award: Cooperative Agreements
Purpose: To implement public health actions through engagement of national partners and public health networks at national, state and local levels to apply public health strategies to promote cognitive health; address cognitive impairment, including Alzheimer's disease; and support the needs of care partners.
Applicant Eligibility: Eligible applicants are limited to national, non-profit professional public health or cognitive health/cognitive impairment mission Organizations with experience and expertise providing technical assistance and support to governmental and non-governmental components of the public health system.
Beneficiary Eligibility: Anyone/General public.
Funding: (Cooperative Agreements) FY 18 $1,366,098.00; FY 19 est $1,443,322.00; FY 20 est $0.00
HQ: 4770 Buford Highway NE, PO Box F78, Atlanta, GA 30341
    Phone: 770-488-5998
    http://www.cdc.gov

Programs Administered by Federal Headquarters

DOD12.550 | THE LANGUAGE FLAGSHIP GRANTS TO INSTITUTIONS OF HIGHER EDUCATION
"The Language Flagship"

Award: Cooperative Agreements; Project Grants

Purpose: To establish centers for the teaching of critical languages that enable students to reach or exceed Level 3 in proficiency based on the Interagency Language Roundtable (ILR) scale in African Languages, Arabic, Chinese, Hindi/Urdu, Korean, Persian, and Russian.

Applicant Eligibility: The award for this Program is made to a nonprofit Organization that administers this assistance Program on behalf of DoD. The award is typically a cooperative agreement made to administer this CFDA Program as well as CFDA # 12. 551 (National Security education Program David L. Boren Scholarships) and CFDA # 12. 552 (National Security education Program David L. Boren Fellowships). The award is reported to USASpending.gov only under this CFDA number since it has the most funding of the three Programs.

Beneficiary Eligibility: Any accredited U.S. institution of higher education (defined in 20 U.S.C. 1001 of the Higher Education Act of 1965) is eligible to apply for assistance (subaward) under this program. This includes 2 and 4 year colleges and universities, both public and private. Other organizations, associations, agencies, and foreign institutions may be included in proposals for subawards but may not be receive assistance directly from the administering nonprofit organization. Eligible entities for subawards must be located within the fifty (50) states, the District of Columbia, Commonwealth of Puerto Rico, Commonwealth of Northern Mariana Islands, the U.S. Virgin Islands, Guam, American Samoa, the Republic of Palau, Republic of the Marshall Islands, and the Federated States of Micronesia.

Award Range/Average: Subawards range from $200,000 to $500,000 depending on type of project. The average award is estimated at $325,000 per subaward for each budget period. The core program has four-year project periods pending availability of funds.

Funding: (Salaries and Expenses) FY 17 $24,494,000.00; FY 18 est $18,330,000.00; FY 19 est $41,730,948.00

HQ: 4800 Mark Center Drive, Suite 08 G 08, Alexandria, VA 22350

Phone: 571-256-0756 | Email: g.e.mcdermott.civ@mail.mil

http://www.thelanguageflagship.org

USDA10.447 | THE RURAL DEVELOPMENT (RD) MULTI-FAMILY HOUSING REVITALIZATION DEMONSTRATION PROGRAM (MPR)
"Restructuring Program"

Award: Project Grants

Purpose: The RHS under Section 515 provides for the low-income residents with affordable housing.

Applicant Eligibility: Owners or buyers of financially viable Section 515 financed rental or Section 514/516 labor housing properties.

Beneficiary Eligibility: Low-income rural residents needing safe, decent, and sanitary rental housing are eligible.

Award Range/Average: The underwriting guidelines include, but are not limited to, the following: The maximum soft-second loan will be limited to no more than $5,000 per unit; revitalization grants limited to $5,000 per unit; total assistance provided from a revitalization grant, revitalization zero percent loan, and/or a soft-second loan is limited to $10,000 per unit; and the maximum Section 515 loan or Section 514/516 loan and grant is limited to no more than $20,000 per unit.

Funding: (Direct Loans) FY 17 $37,000,000.00; FY 18 est $40,000,000.00; FY 19 est $0.00

HQ: 1400 Independence Avenue SW, PO Box 0782, Washington, DC 20250-0781

Phone: 202-720-1604

http://www.rd.usda.gov

DOS19.301 | THE SECRETARY'S OFFICE OF THE GLOBAL PARTNERSHIP INITIATIVE (S/GPI) GRANT PROGRAMS
"Global Partnership Initiative"

Award: Project Grants

Purpose: Supports the foreign assistance goals and objectives of the Department of State, Secretary's Office of the Global Partnership Initiative (S/GPI), as delineated in the FY Bureau Strategic and Resource Plan and other strategic planning documents.

Applicant Eligibility: Uses of assistance vary according to the individual award. Please see www.grants.gov for specific announcement.

Beneficiary Eligibility: U.S. Department of State, Secretary's Office of the Global Partnership Initiative, issues grants to domestic and international entities that implement programs abroad. Primary beneficiaries are residents of any community abroad where program activities are taking place. See www.grants.gov for specific application.

Award Range/Average: Grants can range from small amounts (thousands of dollars) up to $1 million.

HQ: 2201 C Street NW, Suite 6817, Washington, DC 20520

Phone: 202-647-9097 | Email: debass@state.gov

http://www.state.gov/partnerships

HHS93.413 | THE STATE FLEXIBILITY TO STABILIZE THE MARKET GRANT PROGRAM

Award: Project Grants

Purpose: To provide a funding source to enhance the role of states in the implementation and planning for several of the Federal market reforms and consumer protections under Part A of Title XXVII of the Public Health Service Act (PHS Act).

Applicant Eligibility: This Funding Opportunity Announcement is open to all fifty States and the District of Columbia for planning and/or implementing one or more of the three pre-selected market Reforms and consumer protections in Part A of title XXVII of the PHS Act. Only one application per state is permitted, except in a state in which there is more than one regulating entity, each with a primary responsibility over the regulation of a portion of the private health insurance market.

Beneficiary Eligibility: Grants to States' (including the District of Columbia) for planning and/or implementing the market reforms and consumer protections in Part A of title XXVII of the PHS Act.

Award Range/Average: Grantees will receive a minimum of $156,000 as a baseline award amount.

Funding: (Cooperative Agreements) FY 18 $8,616,955.00; FY 19 est Estimate Not Available; FY 20 est Estimate Not Available

HQ: 200 Independence Avenue SW, Washington, DC 20201

Phone: 301-492-4182 | Email: james.taing@cms.hhs.gov

https://www.cms.gov/CCIIO/Programs-and-Initiatives/Health-Insurance-Market-Reforms/State-Flexibility.html

DOS19.029 | THE U.S. PRESIDENT'S EMERGENCY PLAN FOR AIDS RELIEF PROGRAMS
"PEPFAR"

Award: Cooperative Agreements; Project Grants

Purpose: The Office of the U.S. Global AIDS Coordinator coordinates and oversees the U.S. global response to HIV/AIDS through the U.S. President's Plan for Emergency AIDS Relief (PEPFAR). The key aspect of the program is to provide support in achieving the HIV/AIDS care, treatment, and prevention goals of PEPFAR as detailed in the PEPFAR Blueprint.

Applicant Eligibility: Please visit grants.gov for specific Program announcements.

Beneficiary Eligibility: Same as Applicant Eligibility.

Funding: (Project Grants (Discretionary)) FY 15 est Estimate Not Available

HQ: 2100 Pennsylvania Avenue NW, Room 200, Washington, DC 20037

Phone: 202-663-2109 | Email: ewingwf@state.gov

http://www.pepfar.gov

DOS19.013 | THOMAS R. PICKERING FOREIGN AFFAIRS FELLOWSHIP PROGRAM
"Pickering Fellowship Program"

Award: Cooperative Agreements; Project Grants

Purpose: The program offers only graduate fellowships. The purpose of the program is to attract outstanding students who represent all ethnic and social backgrounds and who have an interest in pursuing a Foreign Service career in the U.S. Department of State. This program encourages the application of members of minority groups historically underrepresented in the Foreign Service, women and those with financial need.

Applicant Eligibility: N/A

Beneficiary Eligibility: N/A

Programs Administered by Federal Headquarters

Award Range/Average: Please see obligations.
Funding: (Salaries and Expenses)
HQ: 2401 E Street NW, Room H 518, Washington, DC 20522
    Phone: 202-261-8892 | Email: georgecm@state.gov

ED84.010 | TITLE I GRANTS TO LOCAL EDUCATIONAL AGENCIES
"Title I Basic, Concentration, Targeted and Education Finance Incentive Grants"

Award: Formula Grants
Purpose: To improve teaching and learning in high-poverty schools in particular for children falling through local educational agencies (LEAs).
Applicant Eligibility: SEAs including for the Outlying Areas and the Secretary of the Interior. Local educational agencies (LEAs) and Indian tribal schools are subgrantees.
Beneficiary Eligibility: In a targeted assistance program, children who are failing, or most at risk of failing, to meet challenging State academic standards. In a schoolwide program, all children in the school.
Award Range/Average: The range of awards in FY 2018 is $1,000,000 - $1,988,156,056. The average award is $271,634,517. The estimated range of awards in FY 2018 is $1,000,000 - $1,963,753,367. The estimated average award is $273,358,655. The estimated range of awards in FY 2019 is $1,000,000 - $1,961,725,794. The estimated average award is $273,358,655.
Funding: (Formula Grants) FY 18 $15,754,802,000.00; FY 19 est $15,854,802,000.00; FY 20 est $15,854,802,000.00
HQ: 400 Maryland Avenue SW, Washington, DC 20202
    Phone: 202-453-5514 | Email: patrick.rooney@ed.gov
    http://www.ed.gov/programs/titleiparta/index.html

ED84.013 | TITLE I STATE AGENCY PROGRAM FOR NEGLECTED AND DELINQUENT CHILDREN AND YOUTH

Award: Formula Grants
Purpose: To provide educational continuity for neglected and delinquent children and youth in State-run institutions for juveniles and in adult correctional institutions.
Applicant Eligibility: SEAs. State agencies responsible for providing free public education for children and youth (1) in Institutions for neglected or delinquent children and youth; (2) attending community day Programs for neglected or delinquent children and youth; or (3) in adult correctional Institutions may apply to their SEA for subgrants.
Beneficiary Eligibility: Children and youth in institutions for neglected or delinquent children and youth, community day programs for neglected or delinquent children and youth, and adult correctional institutions.
Award Range/Average: FY 18 est: Range $49,389-2,305,162; Average: $828,994. FY19 est: Range: $86,204-2,604,392; Average: $892,763.
Funding: (Formula Grants) FY 18 $47,614,000.00; FY 19 est $47,614,000.00; FY 20 est $47,614,000.00
HQ: 400 Maryland Avenue SW, Room 3E244, Washington, DC 20202
    Phone: 202-401-3617 | Email: jasmine.akinsipe@ed.gov
    http://www.ed.gov/programs/titleipartd/index.html

HHS93.471 | TITLE IV-E KINSHIP NAVIGATOR PROGRAM
"Kinship Navigator"

Award: Formula Grants
Purpose: To help caregivers learn, find, and use programs and facilities to satisfy the requirements of the kids they raise and their own needs and promote efficient government and private partnerships to guarantee that the family caregivers are served.
Applicant Eligibility: State and Tribal agencies directly administering approved title IV-E Plans may participate in the kinship navigator Program.
Beneficiary Eligibility: Kinship caregivers and the children they are raising are eligible beneficiaries.
Funding: (Formula Grants) FY 18 $0; FY 19 est $0; FY 20 est $708,000.00
HQ: 330 C Street SW, Room 3512, Washington, DC 20201
    Phone: 202-205-8552 | Email: gail.collins@acf.hhs.gov
    http://www.acf.hhs.gov/programs/cb

HHS93.472 | TITLE IV-E PREVENTION AND FAMILY SERVICES AND PROGRAMS
"Title IV-E Prevention Services"

Award: Formula Grants

Purpose: To provide time-limited prevention services for mental health or substance abuse and also services for in-home parent skill-based programs targeted on candidates needing who are at imminent risk of removal from foster care.

Applicant Eligibility: State and Tribal agencies directly administering approved title IV-E Plans may participate in the prevention services Program.

Beneficiary Eligibility: Children designated as candidates for foster care and those who are pregnant/parenting in foster care along with the parents or kin caregivers of these children.

HQ: 330 C Street SW, Room 3403, Washington, DC 20447

Phone: 202-205-7941 | Email: elaine.stedt@acf.hhs.gov

http://www.acf.hhs.gov/programs/cb

DOJ16.548 | TITLE V DELINQUENCY PREVENTION PROGRAM
"Delinquency Prevention Program"

Award: Formula Grants

Purpose: To reduce risks and enhancing protective factors to prevent youth at risk of becoming delinquent from entering the juvenile justice system and to intervene with first-time and nonserious offenders to keep them out of the juvenile justice system.

Applicant Eligibility: Contact Program office for additional information.

Beneficiary Eligibility: Same as Applicant Eligibility.

Award Range/Average: Available in the OJP Program Announcement available at http://www.ojp.gov/funding/solicitations.htm.

Funding: (Formula Grants) FY 16 $9,014,278.00; FY 17 est $14,500,000.00; FY 18 est $17,000,000.00

HQ: 810 7th Street NW, Washington, DC 20531

Phone: 202-616-9135

http://www.ojjdp.ncjrs.org/titleV

HHS93.787 | TITLE V SEXUAL RISK AVOIDANCE EDUCATION PROGRAM (DISCRETIONARY GRANTS)
"Title V SRAE - Discretionary Grants"

Award: Project Grants

Purpose: The program provides messages to youth that normalizes the optimal health behavior of avoiding non-marital sexual activity.

Applicant Eligibility: Faith-based and community Organizations that meet the eligibility requirements are eligible to receive awards under the Competitive Title V SRAE Discretionary Grants and National SRA Resource Center funding opportunity announcements.

Beneficiary Eligibility: Title V SRAE Discretionary Grant Program will fund States and other entities to provide youth ages 10 to 19 with education on sexual risk avoidance (meaning voluntarily refraining from sexual activity).

Award Range/Average: The range of awards for discretionary Title V Competitive SRAE is $13,500 to $400,000.

Funding: (Project Grants (Discretionary)) FY 18 $4,762,870.00; FY 19 est $6,821,526.00; FY 20 est $4,300,000.00

HQ: 330 C Street SW, Washington, DC 20021

Phone: 202-205-9605 | Email: lebretia.white@acf.hhs.gov

http://www.acf.hhs.gov/programs/fysb

HHS93.235 | TITLE V STATE SEXUAL RISK AVOIDANCE EDUCATION (TITLE V STATE SRAE) PROGRAM

Award: Formula Grants

Purpose: To provide messages to youth that normalizes the optimal health behavior of avoiding non-marital sexual activity.

Applicant Eligibility: Eligible applicants include all 50 States, the District of Columbia, Puerto Rico, U.S. Virgin Islands, Guam, American Samoa, Commonwealth of the Northern Mariana Islands, Federate States of Micronesia, the Republic of the Marshall Islands, and Republic of Palau.

Programs Administered by Federal Headquarters

Beneficiary Eligibility: Title V State SRAE will fund states to provide youth ages 10 to 19 with education on sexual risk avoidance (meaning voluntarily refraining from sexual activity).
Award Range/Average: The range of awards for Title V SRAE was $13,500 to $7,389,100.
Funding: (Formula Grants) FY 18 $46,994,375.00; FY 19 est $52,118,958.00; FY 20 est $52,118,958.00
HQ: 330 C Street SW, Washington, DC 20021
  Phone: 202-205-9605 | Email: lebretia.white@acf.hhs.gov
  http://www.acf.hhs.gov/programs/fysb

DOD12.129 | TITLE VI-CHEYENNE RIVER SIOUX TRIBE, LOWER BRULE SIOUX TRIBE, AND TERRESTRIAL WILDLIFE HABITAT RESTORATION, SOUTH DAKOTA

Award: Cooperative Agreements
Purpose: Exclusive legislation to the transfer in fee title of Corps of Engineers lands at directed locations to the Cheyenne River Sioux Tribe (CRST), the South Dakota Department of Game, Fish and Parks (SDGFP), and the Lower Brule Sioux Tribe (LBST).
Applicant Eligibility: N/A
Beneficiary Eligibility: N/A

HUD14.869 | TITLE VI FEDERAL GUARANTEES FOR FINANCING TRIBAL HOUSING ACTIVITIES

Award: Guaranteed/insured Loans
Purpose: To obtain financing for affordable housing activities.
Applicant Eligibility: The applicant must be a Federally recognized Indian tribe or TDHE that is either a beneficiary or recipient of Indian Housing Block Grants (IHBG) funds.
Beneficiary Eligibility: Indian tribes and their members are the beneficiaries. A TDHE acts on behalf of a tribe, as authorized by Tribal and TDHE resolutions.
Award Range/Average: A borrower's guaranteed obligations may not exceed an amount equal to the borrower's IHBG, less the amount needed to operate and maintain current assisted stock (CAS), times five (IHBG - CAS X 5 = maximum guaranteed amount).
Funding: (Guaranteed/Insured Loans) FY 16 $5,760,000.00; FY 17 est $2,000,000.00; FY 18 est $2,000,000.00
HQ: 451 7th Street SW, Room 5156, Washington, DC 20410
  Phone: 202-402-4978 | Email: thomas.c.wright@hud.gov
  http://www.hud.gov/offices/pih/ih/homeownership/titlevi

CDC93.376 | MULTIPLE APPROACHES TO SUPPORT YOUNG BREAST CANCER SURVIVORS AND METASTATIC BREAST CANCER PATIENTS

Award: Cooperative Agreements (discretionary Grants)
Purpose: Provides support to breast cancer survivors and metastatic breast cancer patients, increases awareness on clinical trials, increases the financial support, improves the quality of life, and offers support to the family and caregivers of breast cancer patients.
Applicant Eligibility: Government Organizations, non-governmental Organizations, private colleges and universities, community-based Organizations, faith-based Organizations, for-profit Organizations (other than small business), and small businesses can apply.
Beneficiary Eligibility: General public.
Award Range/Average: 150000 - 350000
Funding: (Cooperative Agreements (Discretionary Grants)) FY $0; FY 19 est $1,800,000.00; FY 20 est $1,800,000.00
HQ: 4770 Buford Highway NE Chamblee Campus, Building 107 4th Floor, Atlanta, GA 30341
  Phone: 770-488-3094 | Email: armoore@cdc.gov

HHS93.465 | TOBACCO PREVENTION AND CONTROL LEGAL TECHNICAL ASSISTANCE
"Legal TA"

Award: Cooperative Agreements

Purpose: To provide legal technical assistance and consultation to OSH and NTCP grantees awardees on questions related to the identification, development, adoption, and implementation of evidence-based interventions and policies nationwide.

Applicant Eligibility: In addition to the above list, legal centers are eligible for this FOA. Due to the strategies, activities and approaches required by this cooperative agreement, it is essential that the potential awardee has a) deep institutional knowledge specific to current and historical U.S. tobacco control issues, b) is an experienced national Organization with capacity to work at the national level in tobacco control legal TA, and c) does not have any present or historical links to the tobacco industry and should provide a statement to such effect.

Beneficiary Eligibility: The immediate beneficiaries of the program include the federal government, state, local, territorial and Federally Recognized Indian Tribal Governments, as well as other CDC Office on Smoking and Health Awardees such as the National Networks, which include a range of non profit organizations. The ultimate beneficiary of the program is the general public, as the program seeks to support population-wide environmental changes that help to transform the nation's health and provide individuals with equitable opportunities to take charge of their health. Smokers are more likely to be in lower socioeconomic groups; tobacco control work is a proven strategy to reduce health inequities.

Award Range/Average: $250,000 per year for 5 years

Funding: (Cooperative Agreements (Discretionary Grants)) FY 18 $235,000.00; FY 19 est $235,000.00; FY 20 est $235,000.00

HQ: 4770 Buford Highway NE, Atlanta, GA 30341

    Phone: 770-488-6204 | Email: sedwards2@cdc.gov

    http://www.cdc.gov

HHS93.851 | TRACKING ELECTRONIC HEALTH RECORD ADOPTION AND CAPTURING RELATED INSIGHTS IN U.S. HOSPITALS

Award: Cooperative Agreements

Purpose: Significant federal investments to accelerate the adoption of electronic health records and exchange of clinical data are now in place. It is critical to continue to track the adoption and use of EHRs. The data generated under this funding opportunity will enable ONC and researchers to carry out these important activities for inpatient settings.

Applicant Eligibility: This is a non-competitive funding opportunity and is restricted to a designated Organization. Organizations not designated as such are not eligible to apply for this opportunity, and therefore should not submit an application. Applications submitted by Organizations not designated below will not be considered. The designated Organization for this opportunity is the American Hospital Association (AHA).

Beneficiary Eligibility: The beneficiaries will include the Office of the National Coordinator for Health Information Technology, the American Hospital Association, and any researchers or members of the general public interested in survey data on the adoption and use of health IT by U.S. hospitals.

Funding: (Cooperative Agreements) FY 18 $105,000.00; FY 19 est $180,000.00; FY 20 est Estimate Not Available

HQ: 330 C Street SW, Washington, DC 20201

    Phone: 202-720-2919 | Email: carmel.halloun@hhs.gov

USDA10.178 | TRADE MITIGATION PROGRAM ELIGIBLE RECIPIENT AGENCY OPERATIONAL FUNDS

Award: Formula Grants

Purpose: To make funds available to the Emergency Food Assistance Program eligible recipient agencies such as food banks, soup kitchens, and other organizations thereby supporting the costs of food storage and distribution and also to supplement the diets of low-income persons.

Applicant Eligibility: N/A

Beneficiary Eligibility: Public or private non-profit organizations, such as food banks, food pantries, and soup kitchens, which provide food assistance to low-income persons.

Funding: (Formula Grants) FY 18 Not Separately Identifiable; FY 19 est $50,000,000.00; FY 20 est Not Separately Identifiable

HQ: 3101 Park Center Drive, Alexandria, VA 22302

    Phone: 703-305-4386 | Email: polly.fairfield@usda.gov

    http://fns.usda.gov

Programs Administered by Federal Headquarters

ED84.315 | TRADITIONALLY UNDERSERVED POPULATIONS
"Capacity Building"

Award: Project Grants

Purpose: To enhance the capacity and increase the participation of historically Black colleges and universities, Hispanic serving institutions of higher education, and other institutions of higher education where minority enrollment is at least 50 percent.

Applicant Eligibility: States and public and nonprofit agencies and Organizations may apply.

Beneficiary Eligibility: Historically Black colleges and universities; (2) Hispanics serving institutions of higher education; (3) Indian tribal colleges and universities (4) other institutions of higher education whose minority student enrollment is at least 50 percent; and (5) Indian Tribes.

Funding: (Project Grants) FY 18 $910,490.00; FY 19 est $910,490.00; FY 20 est $910,490.00

HQ: Department of Education OSERS Rehabilitation Services Administration 400 Maryland Avenue SW, Washington, DC 20202

Phone: 202-245-7423 | Email: mary.lovley@ed.gov

http://www.ed.gov/about/offices/list/osers/rsa/index.html

DOD12.501 | TRAINING AND SUPPORT-COMBATING WEAPONS OF MASS DESTRUCTION

Award: Cooperative Agreements

Purpose: Offers support and stimulate training and collaborative efforts for solutions to combat or counter weapons of mass destruction (WMD).

Applicant Eligibility: Applicant eligibility is specified in individual Program announcements, funding opportunities, award documents, and codified regulations applicable to award.

Beneficiary Eligibility: Competitions are open to private and public accredited institutions of higher education, non-profit organizations, non-Federal government entities and other qualified organizations as listed in the appropriate funding opportunity. Review funding opportunity for additional information.

Funding: (Salaries and Expenses) FY 17 $0.00; FY 18 est $10,000,000.00; FY 19 est $10,000,000.00

HQ: 8725 John J Kingman Road, Fort Belvoir, VA 22060

Phone: 703-767-3527 | Email: mary.k.chase2.civ@mail.mil

CNCS94.009 | TRAINING AND TECHNICAL ASSISTANCE
"Regional Training Conferences"

Award: Dissemination of Technical Information; Training

Purpose: The program conducts training conferences to strengthen the AmeriCorps programs and Senior Corps projects across various regions of the country.

Applicant Eligibility: Restrictions on use of funds are described in Program's Notice of Federal Funding and Application Instructions. Use of funds must be consistent with the funded application, and are subject to CNCS's grants administration laws, regulations, and policies. Applications are limited to State Service Commissions (or approved alternative administrative entities) or partnerships/consortia of State Service Commissions.

Beneficiary Eligibility: AmeriCorps State and National programs and Senior Corps projects, AmeriCorps Indian Tribes programs, AmeriCorps VISTA programs (especially multi-site projects), Social Innovation Fund recipients, Operation AmeriCorps grant recipients and AmeriCorps National Civilian Community Corps (NCCC) staff will benefit.

Award Range/Average: Range will vary as determined by the scope of the projects. CNCS will make awards in the range of $75,000 to $115,000.

Funding: (Cooperative Agreements (Discretionary Grants)) FY 16 Actual Not Available; FY 17 est $578,000.00; FY 18 est $0.00

HQ: 250 E Street SW, Washington, DC 20525

Phone: 202-606-3915 | Email: rlampi@cns.gov

http://www.nationalservice.gov

HHS93.059 | TRAINING IN GENERAL, PEDIATRIC, AND PUBLIC HEALTH DENTISTRY

"General, Pediatric, and Public Health Dentistry and Dental Hygiene"

Award: Project Grants

Purpose: To improve access to and the delivery of oral healthcareservices for all individuals, particularly low income, underserved, uninsured, minority, health disparity, and rural populations.

Applicant Eligibility: Eligible applicants include accredited schools of dentistry and dental hygiene, postdoctoral training Programs in general, pediatric, or public health dentistry that have Programs in dental schools, or approved residency or advanced education Programs in the practice of general dentistry, pediatric dentistry, or dental public health. Public or non-profit hospitals, or other public or private not-for-profit entities including faith-based and community-based Organizations, community colleges, as well as Tribes and Tribal Organizations, are eligible provided they are otherwise eligible and the Secretary has determined they are capable of carrying out such grants.

Beneficiary Eligibility: Beneficiaries include a full range of trainees: dental or dental hygiene students, dental hygienists, dental residents, practicing dentists, and other approved primary care dental trainees and dental faculty.

Award Range/Average: Predoctoral Training in General, Pediatric and Public Health Dentistry and Dental Hygiene: FY 16.: Range: $315,311 to $350,000; Average award: $344,097 FY 17 Range: $315,000 to $350,000; Average award: $344,000 FY 18 est.: Range: $315,000 to $350,000; Average award: $344,000 Postdoctoral Training in General, Pediatric and Public Health Dentistry: FY 16: Range: $242,937 to $749,055; Average award: $549,392 FY 17: Range: $242,000 to $749,000; Average award: $549,000 FY 18 est: Range: $242,000 to $749,000; Average award: $549,000 Faculty Development in General, Pediatric and Public Health Dentistry and Dental Hygiene:FY 16: Range: $343,887 to $500,000; Average award: $457,418 FY 17: Program has ended. FY 18 est.: Program has ended.Dental Faculty Development and Loan Repayment Program:FY 16: Range: $138,862 to $200,000; Average award: $180,959. FY 17: Range: $208,293 to $300,000; Average award: $236,175 FY 18 est: Range: $236,765 to $300,000; Average award: $285,367 Dental Faculty Loan Repayment Program:FY 16: Range: program did not existFY 17: Range: $54,000 to $100,000; Average award $88,492 FY 18 est.: Range: $79,715 to $150,000; Average award: $115,780

Funding: (Project Grants) FY 18 $24,936,547.00; FY 19 est $26,112,543.00; FY 20 est $0.00

HQ: 5600 Fishers Lane, Room 15N 120, Rockville, MD 20857

Phone: 301-443-5260 | Email: srogers@hrsa.gov

http://www.hrsa.gov

ED84.160 | TRAINING INTERPRETERS FOR INDIVIDUALS WHO ARE DEAF AND INDIVIDUALS WHO ARE DEAF-BLIND

Award: Project Grants

Purpose: To support projects that improve the skills of manual, tactile, oral, and cued speech interpreters providing services to individuals who are deaf and individuals who are deaf-blind.

Applicant Eligibility: Public or private nonprofit agencies and Organizations, including Institutions of higher education are eligible for assistance.

Beneficiary Eligibility: Individuals preparing for employment as interpreters for individuals who are deaf and individuals who are deaf- blind individuals who are presently serving as interpreters and wish to maintain or raise the level of their skills, and the persons who will receive the services of interpreters are beneficiaries of this program.

Award Range/Average: To Be Determined.

Funding: (Project Grants) FY 18 $2,399,507.00; FY 19 est $2,399,996.00; FY 20 est $2,399,750.00

HQ: 400 Maryland Avenue SW, Washington, DC 20202

Phone: 202-245-7423 | Email: mary.lovley@ed.gov

http://rsa.ed.gov/programs.cfm?pc=traindeaf

DOS19.705 | TRANS-NATIONAL CRIME

Award: Cooperative Agreements; Project Grants

Purpose: To minimize the impact of transnational crime and criminal networks on the U.S. and its allies through enhanced international cooperation and foreign assistance.

Applicant Eligibility: Please see announcements in www.grants.gov.

Beneficiary Eligibility: Same as Applicant Eligibility.

Award Range/Average: Range varies widely. Please see announcements in www.grants.gov.

Programs Administered by Federal Headquarters

HQ: 2430 E Street NW, Washington, DC 20037
   Phone: 202-776-8774 | Email: steinlf@state.gov

HHS93.310 | TRANS-NIH RESEARCH SUPPORT
"Common Fund Research Support"

Award: Project Grants; Training
Purpose: To provide support for new initiatives designed to address major opportunities and gaps in biomedical research.
Applicant Eligibility: Awards can be made to domestic, public or private, for-profit or nonprofit Organization, University, college, hospital, laboratory, or other institution, including State and local units of government, and individuals. Some initiatives will accept applications from foreign Organizations. Additional details on eligibility are specified in the Common Fund Grants and Funding Opportunities funding announcement, listed at http://commonfund. nih.gov/.
Beneficiary Eligibility: Institutions as described above.
Award Range/Average: $10,000 to $15,462,500 with the average being $737,000
Funding: (Project Grants) FY 18 $911,714,752.00; FY 19 est $911,000,000.00; FY 20 est $911,000,000.00
HQ: 6001 Executive Boulevard Room 8180D, PO Box 9500, Rockville, MD 20852
   Phone: 301-402-7617 | Email: michael.morse@nih.gov
   http://commonfund.nih.gov

DOS19.222 | TRANS-SAHARA COUNTERTERRORISM PARTNERSHIP (TSCTP)

Award: Cooperative Agreements; Project Grants
Purpose: The main objective is to create an environment that will disrupt the ability of terrorists, violent extremist organizations (VEOs), and traffickers to operate by promoting regional government and non-government capacity building partnerships in the Sahel and Maghreb.
Applicant Eligibility: TSCTP Programs are designed to be proactive and preventive in nature, to combat terrorism and violent extremism through both civilian and military efforts. These Programs are structured in a way that empowers local law enforcement authorities to effectively address the threat of terrorist Organizations, while also respecting national sovereignty and cultural sensitivities of countries in the region.
Beneficiary Eligibility: TSCTP supports projects in Burkina Faso, Cameroon, Chad, Mali, Mauritania, Niger, Nigeria, and Senegal in sub-Saharan Africa, and Algeria, Morocco, and Tunisia in North Africa.
Award Range/Average: See www.grants.gov for individual notice of funding opportunities or www.USASpending.gov for previous award information.
Funding: (Cooperative Agreements (Discretionary Grants)) FY 16 Actual Not Available; FY 17 est $7,000,000.00; FY 18 est Estimate Not Available
HQ: 2430 E Street NW, Washington, DC 20520
   Phone: 202-776-6831 | Email: edgertonna@state.gov

HUD14.525 | TRANSFORMATION INITIATIVE RESEARCH GRANTS: DEMONSTRATION AND RELATED SMALL GRANTS

Award: Project Grants
Purpose: To enhance the demonstrations of Office of Policy Development and Research by providing a vehicle for conducting a number of small research projects.
Applicant Eligibility: Nonprofit Organizations, for profit Organizations located in the U. S (HUD will not pay fee or profit for the work conducted under this Program), foundations, think tanks, consortia, Institutions of higher education accredited by a national or regional accrediting agency recognized by the U.S. Department of education and other entities that will sponsor a researcher, expert and analyst.
Beneficiary Eligibility: The purpose of this program is to enhance these demonstrations by providing a vehicle for conducting a number of small research projects aimed at collecting additional/supplemental information and analyses. Eligibility of tribes and tribal organizations applies only to the small grant program associated with the Sustainable Construction in Indian Country demonstration.
Award Range/Average: $25,000- $500,000 per grant for a maximum three-grant performance period. Awards under this NOPI will be made in the form of a Cooperative Agreement, and minimum and maximum award amounts will be specified under each NOPI.

HQ: 451 7th Street SW, Room 8230, Washington, DC 20410
  Phone: 202-402-3852 | Email: susan.s.brunson@hud.gov

HUD14.524 | TRANSFORMATION INITIATIVE RESEARCH GRANTS: NATURAL EXPERIMENTS

Award: Project Grants
Purpose: To provide funding to support scientific research to evaluate the impact on local, state, and federal policies.
Applicant Eligibility: Nonprofit Organizations, for profit Organizations located in the U. S (HUD will not pay fee or profit for the work conducted under this Program), foundations, think tanks, consortia, Institutions of higher education accredited by a national or regional accrediting agency recognized by the U.S. Department of education and other entities that will sponsor a.
Beneficiary Eligibility: The research funded by these HUD grants should be state-of-the-art natural experiments and result in substantive contributions to the existing pool of scientific theory and evidence on the effectiveness of public policies. It should also yield methodological advances to evaluating public policy - preference will be given to proposals aimed at developing general solutions that may be applied to additional problems. Projects may focus on any local, state, or federal policy relevant to HUD's mission of increasing homeownership, supporting community development, and increasing access to affordable housing free from discrimination. HUD is particularly interested in funding evaluations that can help this Administration and subsequent Administrations determine how to spend taxpayer dollars effectively and efficiently, though other types of projects will also be considered.
Award Range/Average: An applicant can request $100,000 to $250,000 per award, depending on the scope of the research proposed. Awards under this NOFA will be made in the form of a Cooperative Agreement.
HQ: 451 7th Street SW, Room 8230, Washington, DC 20410
  Phone: 202-402-3852 | Email: susan.s.brunson@hud.gov

HUD14.523 | TRANSFORMATION INITIATIVE RESEARCH GRANTS: SUSTAINABLE COMMUNITY RESEARCH GRANT PROGRAM

Award: Cooperative Agreements
Purpose: To fill key data and information gaps and to develop and evaluate policy alternatives that communities can choose to facilitate decision making about various community investments.
Applicant Eligibility: Nationally recognized and accredited institutes of higher education; non-profit foundations, research consortia or policy institutes; for-profit Organizations located in the U.S. and contract research Institutions or academic entities that will sponsor a researcher or experts as the applicant. However, the sponsored researcher assumes the sole responsibility for the completion of the application and conducting the research. In addition, the researcher must meet the following Program requirements: a. Be a U.S. citizen or U.S. national (such as a person born in the Swains Island or American Samoa) within the meaning of 8 U.S.C. 1408, or be a lawful permanent resident (a recipient of an Alien Registration Recipient Card-Form I-551, commonly referred to as a Green Card), or other qualified alien (such as, an alien who has been granted asylum or refugee status) within the meaning of 8 U.S.C. 1651(b); and b. The proposed research project can be completed within the 24 months grant performance period.
Beneficiary Eligibility: The purpose of this NOFA is to inform the research community of the opportunity to submit grant applications to fund quality research under the broad subject area of sustainable development. HUD is primarily interested in sponsoring cutting edge research in the areas of affordable housing development and preservation; transportation-related issues; economic development and job creation; land use planning and urban design; green and sustainable energy practices; and a range of issues related to sustainability.
Award Range/Average: An applicant may request a minimum of $150,000, up to $500,000 for an award, depending on the scope and scale of the proposed research. Awards under this NOFA will be made in the form of Cooperative Agreements.
HQ: 451 7th Street SW, Room 8230, Washington, DC 20410
  Phone: 202-402-3852 | Email: susan.s.brunson@hud.gov

HUD14.008 | TRANSFORMATION INITIATIVE: CHOICE NEIGHBORHOODS DEMONSTRATION SMALL RESEARCH GRANT PROGRAM

Award: Cooperative Agreements
Purpose: To fund research related to choose neighborhoods that complements the work already being funded by HUD through the Choice baseline research project.

Programs Administered by Federal Headquarters

Applicant Eligibility: Since one purpose of this NOFA is to broaden the community of researchers working on Choice Neighborhoods, HUD will not directly fund entities or individuals already involved in HUD-funded Choice Neighborhoods research under Task Order C-CHI-01127/TO001.

Beneficiary Eligibility: The goal of this research program is to fund research related to Choice Neighbourhoods that complements the work already being funded by HUD through the Choice baseline research project (C-CHI-01127/TO001). Since the Choice baseline research project will focus on implementation grants in Boston, Chicago, and New Orleans, applicants are encouraged to identify research projects in other Choice Neighbourhood implementation or planning grant sites. Research projects in Boston, Chicago, and New Orleans will be eligible but the applicant must demonstrate how the proposed research would complement research already planned through the Choice baseline research project. 4 There are some substantial challenges in evaluating a program like Choice Neighborhoods. First, it is difficult to establish a convincing counterfactual of what would have happened to the neighborhood and its residents in the absence of the Choice Neighbourhoods intervention. Second, because Choice Neighbourhoods combines a variety of services and investments-related to housing, education, public safety, job training, etc.-it is difficult to explain why a particular approach does or doesn't work. Third, neighborhoods are dynamic-the people and businesses that participate in, or rely upon, a neighborhood are constantly changing. The Choice Neighbourhoods investment may have benefits that accrue to individuals, businesses, or other entities not captured in the Choice baseline research project, which focuses on the neighborhood and the individuals living there at baseline. Applicants are encouraged to identify research that will overcome these challenges and provide clear evidence of the impact of Choice Neighborhoods. HUD is using this NOFA rather than a contract (or task order under the existing BPA) for two reasons: 1. To solicit research ideas that are related to Choice Neighborhoods, but that are not already apparent to HUD, and 2. To broaden the community of researchers working on Choice Neighborhoods. Proposals should identify research questions that will help to demonstrate the impacts of Choice Neighbourhoods or to help improve the program.

Award Range/Average: An applicant may request up to $200,000 for an award, depending on the scope and scale of the proposed research. Awards under this NOFA will be made in the form of Cooperative Agreements. A Cooperative Agreement means that HUD will have substantial involvement during performance of the contemplated research project.

HQ: 451 7th Street SW, Room 8230, Washington, DC 20410

Phone: 202-402-3852 | Email: susan.s.brunson@hud.gov

HHS93.651 | "TRANSFORMING CLINICAL PRACTICE INITIATIVE (TCPI)-SUPPORT AND ALIGNMENT NETWORK (SAN) 2.0"

Award: Cooperative Agreements

Purpose: Works to leverage primary and specialist care transformation work and learning in the field. SAN 2.0 awardees add a valuable technical assistance asset to TCPI that will catalyze the accelerated adoption of Alternative Payment Models, prior to 2019, at very large scale, and with very low cost.

Applicant Eligibility: Applications will be screened for completeness and adherence to eligibility. Applications received late or that fail to meet the eligibility requirements or do not include the required forms will not be reviewed.

Beneficiary Eligibility: The Beneficiary eligibility includes the list as noted above with the exception of Federal, Interstate-Intrastate-Student/Trainee and Graduate Students-Artist/Humanist-Engineer/Architect, Builder/Contractor/Developer-Farmer/Rancher/Agriculture Producer-Industrialist/Business Person-Small Business Person-Homeowner-Property Owner-Anyone/General public.

Award Range/Average: Budget Fiscal Year 2017: $700,000 - $110,000

Funding: (Formula Grants (Cooperative Agreements)) FY 17 $1,712,720.00; FY 18 est $0.00; FY 19 est 0.00

SBA59.066 | TRANSITION ASSISTANCE-ENTREPRENEURSHIP TRACK (BOOTS TO BUSINESS)

"Boots to Business"

Award: Cooperative Agreements

Purpose: Funds eligible organizations to provide follow-on online entrepreneurship training, information and resources, and domestic and global delivery of the B2B.

Applicant Eligibility: Eligible applicants may be a non-profit Organization, a state, local, or tribal government agency, an institution of higher learning, a for-profit Organization, or collaboration between such entities.

Beneficiary Eligibility: First beneficiaries are eligible transitioning service members, spouses and family members, and veterans, as defined by DOD policy.

Award Range/Average: $3,500,000
Funding: (Advisory Services and Counseling) FY 17 $12,572,000.00; FY 18 est $12,300,000.00; FY 19 est $11,250,000.00
HQ: 409 3rd Street SW, 5th Floor, Washington, DC 20416
    Phone: 202-205-7034 | Email: dena.moglia@sba.gov
    http://www.sba.gov/bootstobusiness

DOL17.807 | TRANSITION ASSISTANCE PROGRAM
"TAP - Department of Labor Employment Workshops (DOL EW)"

Award: Provision of Specialized Services
Purpose: Provides employment instructions, information and assistance to separating and retiring military personnel and their spouses through domestic and overseas installations.
Applicant Eligibility: Contractor, as determined by the Department of Labor's Contracting Officer.
Beneficiary Eligibility: Service members within two years of retirement or one year of separation and their spouses.
Funding: (Provision of Specialized Services) FY 18 $19,499,432.00; FY 19 est $23,379,000.00; FY 20 est $29,379,000.00
HQ: 200 Constitution Avenue NW, Room S 1312, Washington, DC 20210
    Phone: 202-693-4705 | Email: winter.timothy@dol.gov
    http://www.dol.gov/vets

ED84.407 | TRANSITION PROGRAMS FOR STUDENTS WITH INTELLECTUAL DISABILITIES INTO HIGHER EDUCATION

Award: Project Grants
Purpose: To support competitive grants to institutions of higher education (IHEs) (as defined under section 101(a) of the Higher Education Act of 1965, as amended (HEA)), or consortia of IHEs, to create or expand high-quality, inclusive model comprehensive transition and postsecondary programs for students with intellectual disabilities.
Applicant Eligibility: Institutions of higher education (IHEs) (as defined under section 101(a) of the Higher education Act of 1965, as amended) and consortia of IHEs are eligible to receive grants under the TPSID Program. All grant recipients must partner with one or more local educational agencies to support students with intellectual disabilities who are still eligible for special education and related services under the Individuals with Disabilities education Act (IDEA). Proprietary schools (for-profit entities) are not eligible to apply for a grant under this Program.
Beneficiary Eligibility: Grant funds establish model comprehensive transition and postsecondary programs for students with intellectual disabilities at institutions of higher education. Funds also support a Coordinating Center that: provides technical assistance for all comprehensive transition and postsecondary programs for students with intellectual disabilities; conducts and disseminates research to the public on strategies to promote academic, social, employment, and independent living outcomes for students with intellectual disabilities; and builds capacity of Kindergarten through Grade 12 transition services and supports of local and State education agencies.
Award Range/Average: Not currently available
Funding: (Project Grants) FY 18 $11,800,000.00; FY 19 est $11,800,000.00; FY 20 est $11,800,000.00
HQ: 400 Maryland Avenue SW 4C144, Washington, DC 20202
    Phone: 202-453-7090 | Email: shedita.alston@ed.gov
    http://www2.ed.gov/programs/tpsid/index.html

DOJ16.736 | TRANSITIONAL HOUSING ASSISTANCE FOR VICTIMS OF DOMESTIC VIOLENCE, DATING VIOLENCE, STALKING, OR SEXUAL ASSAULT
"Transitional Housing"

Award: Project Grants
Purpose: To provide transitional housing assistance and related support services to minors, adults, and their dependents who are homeless, or in need of transitional housing or other housing assistance.
Applicant Eligibility: Eligible applicants are States, Indian tribal Governments, units of local government, and other Organizations, including domestic violence and sexual assault victim service providers, domestic violence and sexual assault coalitions, other nonprofit, nongovernmental Organizations, or community-based and culturally specific Organizations, that have a documented history of effective work concerning domestic violence, dating violence, sexual assault, or stalking.

Programs Administered by Federal Headquarters

Beneficiary Eligibility: Beneficiaries include minors, adults, and their dependants who are homeless or in need of transitional housing or other housing assistance, as a result of a situation of domestic violence; and for whom emergency shelter services or other crisis intervention services are unavailable or insufficient.

Award Range/Average: Range: $200,000 to $350,000

Funding: (Project Grants) FY 16 $25,135,181.00; FY 17 est $25,379,034.00; FY 18 est $25,379,000.00

HQ: 145 N Street NE, Suite 10W121, Washington, DC 20530

   Phone: 202-305-1177 | Email: tia.farmer@usdoj.gov

   http://www.justice.gov/ovw

HHS93.550 | TRANSITIONAL LIVING FOR HOMELESS YOUTH
"Transitional Living Program (TLP) and Maternity Group Homes (MGH)"

Award: Project Grants

Purpose: To help runaway and homeless youth between the ages of 16 to under 22 establish sustainable living and well-being for themselves and if applicable, their dependent child(ren).

Applicant Eligibility: States, localities, private entities, and coordinated networks of such entities are eligible to apply for a Transitional Living Program grant unless they are part of the law enforcement structure or the juvenile justice system. Federally recognized Indian Organizations are also eligible to apply for grants as private, nonprofit agencies. Faith-based Organizations and small community-based Organizations are eligible to apply.

Beneficiary Eligibility: Homeless youth (ages 16 to under 22) are the beneficiaries.

Award Range/Average: Range of grant is $100,000 to $200,000; the average grant is $193,910.

Funding: (Project Grants) FY 18 Not Separately Identifiable; FY 19 est $43,274,791.00; FY 20 est $43,274,791.00

HQ: 330 C Street SW, Washington, DC 20201

   Phone: 202-205-9560 | Email: christopher.holloway@acf.hhs.gov

   https://www.acf.hhs.gov/fysb

HHS93.840 | TRANSLATION AND IMPLEMENTATION SCIENCE RESEARCH FOR HEART, LUNG, BLOOD DISEASES, AND SLEEP DISORDERS

Award: Project Grants

Purpose: To foster late-stage translation phase 4 research and facilitate the understanding of multi-level processes and factors associated with successful and sustainable integration of evidence-based interventions within specific clinical and public health settings related to heart, lung, and blood diseases and sleep diseases and disorders for diverse populations across the lifespan, including those that reduce health inequities within the U.S. and globally.

Applicant Eligibility: Any nonprofit Organization engaged in biomedical research and Institutions or companies organized for profit may apply for almost any kind of grant. Only domestic, non-profit, private or public Institutions may apply for NRSA Institutional Research Training Grants. An individual may apply for an NRSA or, in some cases, for a research grant if adequate facilities to perform the research are available. SBIR grants can be awarded only to United States small business concerns (entities that are independently owned and operated for profit, or owned by another small business that itself is independently owned and operated for profit and have no more than 500 employees including affiliates). Primary employment (more than one-half time) of the principal investigator must be with the small business at the time of award and during the conduct of the proposed project. In both Phase I and Phase II, the research must be performed in the U.S. or its possessions. To be eligible for funding, a grant application must be approved for scientific merit and Program relevance by a scientific review group and a national advisory council. SBIR projects are generally performed at least 67% by the applicant small business in Phase I and at least 50% of the Project in Phase II. STTR grants can be awarded only to United States small business concerns (entities that are independently owned and operated for profit and have no more than 500 employees) that formally collaborate with a University or other non-profit research institution in cooperative research and development. The principal investigator of an STTR award may be employed by either the small business concern or collaborating non-profit research institution as long as s/he has a formal appointment with or commitment to the applicant small business concern. At least 40% of the project is to be performed by the small business concern and at least 30% by the non-profit research institution. In both Phase I and Phase II, the research must be performed in the U.S. and its possessions.

Beneficiary Eligibility: Any nonprofit or for-profit organization, company or institution engaged in biomedical research. Only domestic for-profit small business firms may apply for SBIR and STTR programs.

Award Range/Average: Range of Dollar Amount: $30,000 - $821,921. Average Dollar Amount: $194,768.

Funding: (Project Grants) FY 18 $17,035,756.00; FY 19 est $17,273,377.00; FY 20 est $17,273,377.00

HQ: 6701 Rockledge Drive, Room 7176, Bethesda, MD 20892
Phone: 301-827-7968 | Email: pharesda@nhlbi.nih.gov
http://www.nhlbi.nih.gov/about/scientific-divisions/center-translation-research-and-implementation-science

DOT20.931 | TRANSPORTATION PLANNING, RESEARCH AND EDUCATION
"Innovative and Advanced Transportation Research"

Award: Project Grants
Purpose: Provides funds to conduct research and development on innovative transportation systems and related applied technologies.
Applicant Eligibility: These grants are mandated by Congress in US DOT's Annual Appropriation Legislation. Therefore, only those Organizations specifically identified in the appropriation legislation can apply.
Beneficiary Eligibility: Public Non-Profit Institutions/Organizations; Sponsored Organizations; State; Local; Other Public Institutions; Federal Recognized Indian Tribal Government; US Territory or Possession; Private Non-Profit Institutions/ Organizations; Quasi-Public Non-Profit Institutions/Organizations; Native American Organizations.
Award Range/Average: No funding beyond FY 2014.
HQ: 1200 New Jersey Avenue SE, Washington, DC 20950
Phone: 202-366-3252 | Email: caesar.singh@dot.gov

HHS93.234 | TRAUMATIC BRAIN INJURY STATE DEMONSTRATION GRANT PROGRAM
"TBI State Implementation grants"

Award: Project Grants
Purpose: To improve access to rehabilitation and other services for individuals with Traumatic Brain Injury (TBI) and their families.
Applicant Eligibility: State, Territorial Governments, and Federally recognized Indian Tribal government and Native American Organizations are eligible to apply for funding under the TBI grant Program. The application for Implementation Partnership funds may only come from the State agency designated as the lead for TBI services. The State maternal and child health Program is expected to be involved in the Program. Only one application from each State may enter the review process and be considered for an award under this Program.
Beneficiary Eligibility: Individuals with TBI and their families, including those in high risk groups, such as children and youth, the elderly, Native Americans and Alaska Natives, military service members and veterans.
Award Range/Average: $100,000 to $250,000; average $249,252
Funding: (Project Grants) FY 17 $4,734,432.00; FY 18 est $5,090,467.00; FY 19 est Estimate Not Available
HQ: 330 C Street SW, Washington, DC 20201
Phone: 202-475-2482 | Email: elizabeth.leef@acl.hhs.gov
http://www.acl.gov

DOJ16.815 | TRIBAL CIVIL AND CRIMINAL LEGAL ASSISTANCE GRANTS, TRAINING AND TECHNICAL ASSISTANCE
"Tribal Civil and Criminal Legal Assistance (TCCLA)"

Award: Project Grants
Purpose: To enhance tribal justice systems and technical assistance for the development and enhancement of tribal justice systems.
Applicant Eligibility: Applicants for Tribal Legal Assistance Grants are limited to non-profit Organizations, as defined by (Internal Revenue Code 501(c)(3)), including tribal enterprises and educational Institutions (public, private, and tribal colleges and universities), with experience providing legal assistance services to eligible individuals pursuant to federal poverty guidelines, federally-recognized Indian Tribes, or tribal justice systems. Tribal Justice Training and Technical Assistance (TTA) Grants: Applicants are limited to national or regional membership Organizations and associations whose membership or a membership section consists of judicial system personnel within tribal justice systems. Judicial system personnel are defined as any judge, magistrate, court counselor, court clerk, court administrator, bailiff, probation officer, officer of the court, dispute resolution facilitator, or other official, employee (e.g., tribal defenders and tribal prosecutors), or volunteer within the tribal judicial system. Tribal justice systems are defined as a federally recognized Indian Tribes entire

Programs Administered by Federal Headquarters

judicial branch, including traditional methods and forums for dispute resolution, trial courts, appellate courts, inter-tribal courts, alternative dispute resolution systems, and circuit rider systems, established by inherent tribunal authority whether or not they constitute a court of record.

Beneficiary Eligibility: N/A

Award Range/Average: The awards vary by fiscal year and resources appropriated. Please see the solicitation for current fiscal year funding amounts at https://ojp.gov/funding/Explore/index.htm or www.bja.gov; Range: FY 18: $300,000 - $600,000.

Funding: (Formula Grants) FY 17 $97,122,118; FY 18 est $130,000,000; FY 19 est $105,000,000

HQ: 810 7th Street NW, Washington, DC 20531

   Phone: 202-927-5657

   http://www.bja.gov

USDA10.221 | TRIBAL COLLEGES EDUCATION EQUITY GRANTS
"Higher Education Native American Formula and/or Higher Education Native American Institutions"

Award: Project Grants

Purpose: To promote and strengthen higher education instruction in the food and agricultural sciences at the 34 Tribal Colleges. The purpose of the TCEG Program is to fund and enhance educational opportunities for Native Americans in the food and agricultural sciences. The TCEG program also strengthens institutional capacity to deliver relevant formal education opportunities.

Applicant Eligibility: Applications may be submitted by any of the Tribal colleges and universities designated as 1994 Land-Grant Institutions under the educational Land-Grant Status Act of 1994, as amended. This Act, as amended in Section 533(a), requires that each 1994 Land-Grant Institution be accredited or making progress towards accreditation and be recognized as a legal entity. If accreditation is being sought, a college must demonstrate its progress towards accreditation by a letter from a nationally recognized accreditation agency affirming receipt of application for an accreditation site visit or other such documentation. An applicant's failure to meet an eligibility criterion by the time of an application deadline will result in NIFA returning the application without review or, even though an application may be reviewed, will preclude NIFA from making an award. Award recipients may subcontract to Organizations not eligible to apply provided such Organizations are necessary for the conduct of project goals and objectives.

Beneficiary Eligibility: Current Listing of 1994 Land-Grant Institutions (aka Tribal Colleges):Aaniiih Nakoda College; Bay Mills Community College; Blackfeet Community College; Cankdeska Cikana Community College; Chief Dull Knife College; College of Menominee Nation; College of the Muscogee Nation; Dine' College; Fond du Lac Tribal and Community College; Fort Peck Community College; Haskell Indian Nations University; Ilisagvik College; Institute of American Indian Arts; Keweenaw Bay Ojibwa Community College; Lac Courte Oreilles Ojibwa Community College; Leech Lake Tribal College; Little Big Horn College; Little Priest Tribal College; Navajo Technical University; Nebraska Indian Community College; Nueta, Hidatsa and Sahnish College; Northwest Indian College; Oglala Lakota College; Saginaw Chippewa Tribal College; Salish Kootenai College; Sinte Gleska University; Sisseton Wahpeton College; Sitting Bull College; Southwestern Indian Polytechnic Institute; Stone Child College; Tohono O'odham Community College; Turtle Mountain Community College; United Tribes Technical College; and White Earth Tribal and Community College.

Award Range/Average: Appropriated funds are to be awarded to the 1994 Land-Grant Institutions (hereinafter referred to as 1994 Institutions) for Education capacity building and funds are to be distributed equally among institutions that meet eligibility requirements. Equity Funds for ineligible 1994 institutions or of those who fail to apply by the application submission date will be redistributed equally among the remaining eligible 1994 institutions. Under this RFA, only new applications for four-year continuation awards may be submitted to the TCEG Program. These are project applications not previously submitted to TCEG. All new applications will be reviewed by a review panel using the process and criteria described in Part V of the RFA - Application Review Requirements. If minimum or maximum amounts of funding per competitive and/or capacity project grant, or cooperative agreement are established, these amounts will be announced in the annual Competitive Request for Application (RFA).The most current RFA is available via: https://nifa.usda.gov/funding-opportunity/tribal-colleges-education-equity-program-tceg

Funding: (Project Grants) FY 17 $3,439,000.00; FY 18 est $3,439,000.00; FY 19 est $3,432,000.00

HQ: 1400 Independence Avenue SW, PO Box 2250, Washington, DC 20250

   Phone: 202-720-2324

   http://nifa.usda.gov/program/tribal-equity-grants-program

USDA10.222 | TRIBAL COLLEGES ENDOWMENT PROGRAM
"Tribal Colleges Endowment Interest Programaka 1994 Institutions Endowment Interest Program"

Award: Formula Grants

Purpose: Strengthening the thirty-four (34) Land Grant Institutions' teaching programs in the food and agricultural sciences in targeted need areas, and thereby, enhancing their educational opportunities.

Applicant Eligibility: Eligibility is defined by legislation. An institution must be an accredited 1994 Land Grant Institution with current accreditation from a recognized accreditation Organization. Section 7402 of the Food, Conservation, and Energy Act of 2008 (FCEA) (Pub. L. 110-246), amends Section 532 of the Equity in educational Land-Grant Status Act of 1994 (7 U.S.C. 301 note: Public Law 103-382) by adding at the end the following: (34) Ilisagvik College. The complete listing of 1994 Land-Grant Institutions (LGIs) is as follows: Bay Mills Community College, Blackfeet Community College, Cankdeska Cikana Community College, Chief Dull Knife College, College of the Menominee Nation, D-Q University, Dine College, Fond du Lac Tribal and Community College, Fort Belknap College, Fort Berthold Community College, Fort Peck Community College, Haskell Indian Nations University, Ilisagvik College, Institute of American Indian Arts, Leech Lake Tribal College, Little Big Horn College, Little Priest Tribal College, Navajo Technical College, Nebraska Indian Community College, Northwest Indian College, Oglala Lakota College, Saginaw Chippewa Tribal College, Salish Kootenai College, Si Tanka University, Sinte Gleska University, Sisseton Wahpeton College, Sitting Bull College, Southwestern Indian Polytechnic Institute, Stone Child College, Tohono odham Community College, Turtle Mountain Community College, United Tribes Technical College, Lac Courte Oreilles Ojibwa Community College, and White Earth Tribal and Community College.

Beneficiary Eligibility: Eligibility is defined by legislation. An institution must be an accredited 1994 Land Grant Institution with current accreditation from a recognized accreditation organization. Section 7402 of the Food, Conservation, and Energy Act of 2008 (FCEA) (Pub. L. 110-246), amends Section 532 of the Equity in Educational Land-Grant Status Act of 1994 (7 U.S.C. 301 note: Public Law 103-382) by adding at the end the following: "(34) Ilisagvik College." The complete listing of 1994 Land-Grant Institutions (LGIs) is as follows: Bay Mills Community College, Blackfeet Community College, Cankdeska Cikana Community College, Chief Dull Knife College, College of the Menominee Nation, D-Q University, Dine' College, Fond du Lac Tribal and Community College, Fort Belknap College, Fort Berthold Community College, Fort Peck Community College, Haskell Indian Nations University, Ilisagvik College, Institute of American Indian Arts, Leech Lake Tribal College, Little Big Horn College, Little Priest Tribal College, Navajo Technical College, Nebraska Indian Community College, Northwest Indian College, Oglala Lakota College, Saginaw Chippewa Tribal College, Salish Kootenai College, Si Tanka University, Sinte Gleska University, Sisseton Wahpeton College, Sitting Bull College, Southwestern Indian Polytechnic Institute, Stone Child College, Tohono O'odham Community College, Turtle Mountain Community College, United Tribes Technical College, Lac Courte Oreilles Ojibwa Community College, and White Earth Tribal and Community College.

Award Range/Average: The Endowment Interest distribution increases each year in proportion to the Endowment Corpus and the interest earnings for each year; as well as the number of American Indians enrolled at each institution. The highest amount awarded was in 2009 was $299,509 and the lowest amount was $57,866. Three Institutions received amounts over $200,000; 11 Institutions received amounts over $100,000 and 18 Institutions received amounts under $99,000. NOTE: For Fiscal Year (FY) 2009, two (2) LGIs did not meet eligibility criteria for interest distribution.

Funding: (Formula Grants (Apportionments)) FY 17 $4,629,955.00; FY 18 est $4,376,381.00; FY 19 est $4,473,600.00

HQ: 1400 Independence Avenue SW, PO Box 2250, Washington, DC 20250

Phone: 202-720-2324

http://nifa.usda.gov/program/tribal-college-endowment-program

USDA10.517 | TRIBAL COLLEGES EXTENSION PROGRAMS

Award: Project Grants

Purpose: The TCEP-SE promotes the development of sustainable energy, global food security, adaptation of natural resources to global change, minimizing childhood and adolescent obesity, increasing food safety, energy conservation, adapting tribal culture, etc.

Applicant Eligibility: TCEP-SE and TCEP: The educational Land-Grant Status Act of 1994, as amended in Section 533(a), requires that each 1994 Land-Grant Institution be accredited or making progress towards accreditation and be recognized as a legal entity. If accreditation is being sought, a college must demonstrate its progress towards accreditation by a letter from a nationally recognized accreditation agency affirming receipt of application for an accreditation site visit or other such documentation. FRTEP: Applications may be submitted by1862 or 1890 Land-Grant Institutions that have a Federally Recognized Tribe within their state jurisdiction. For a state-by-state listing of Indian Tribes or groups that are federally recognized, see http://www.ncsl.org/research/state-tribal-institute/list-of-federal-and-state-recognized-Tribes.aspx.

Programs Administered by Federal Headquarters

Beneficiary Eligibility: Same as Applicant Eligibility.

Award Range/Average: If minimum or maximum amounts of funding per competitive and/or capacity project grant, or cooperative agreement are established, these amounts will be announced in the annual Competitive Request for Application (RFA).The most current RFA is available via: TCEP-SE: https://nifa.usda.gov/sites/default/files/11_Tribal%20Colleges%20 Extension%20-%20Special%20Emphasis_0.pdf TCEP https://www.nifa.usda.gov/funding-opportunity/tribal-colleges-extension-services-program-capacity-tcepFRTEP https://nifa.usda.gov/sites/default/files/rfa/FY%202017%20 FRTEP_final. pdf

Funding: (Project Grants (Discretionary)) FY 17 $0.00; FY 18 est $0.00; FY 19 est $7,160,210.00

HQ: 1400 Independence Avenue SW, PO Box 2250, Washington, DC 20250

Phone: 202-690-0402 | Email: erin.riley@nifa.usda.gov

DOJ16.557 | TRIBAL DOMESTIC VIOLENCE AND SEXUAL ASSAULT COALITIONS GRANT PROGRAM
"Tribal Coalitions"

Award: Project Grants

Purpose: To increase awareness of domestic violence and sexual assault against the American Indian and Alaska Native women.

Applicant Eligibility: Tribal coalitions that meet the criteria of a tribal coalition under 24 U.S.C. 13925(a), provide services to Indian Tribes, and are recognized by the Office on Violence Against Women.

Beneficiary Eligibility: Tribal sexual assault and domestic violence coalitions.

Award Range/Average: $298,564- $318,008

Funding: (Project Grants) FY 16 $5,641,616.00; FY 17 est $5,724,144.00; FY 18 est $5,724,000.00

HQ: 145 N Street NE, Suite 10W121, Washington, DC 20530

Phone: 202-305-1177 | Email: tia.farmer@usdoj.gov

http://www.justice.gov/ovw

HUD14.899 | TRIBAL HUD-VA SUPPORTIVE HOUSING PROGRAM
"Tribal HUD-VASH Program"

Award: Project Grants

Purpose: To provide rental assistance and supportive services to Native American veterans who are homeless or at risk of homelessness living on or near a reservation or other Indian areas.

Applicant Eligibility: Housing assistance under this Program is made available by grants to Tribes and tribally designated housing entities (TDHEs) that are eligible to receive Indian Housing Block Grant funding under the Native American Housing Assistance and Self-Determination Act of 1996 (NAHASDA).

Beneficiary Eligibility: Beneficiaries of the Tribal HUD-VASH program are Native American veterans who are Homeless or At Risk of Homelessness. The tribe/TDHE must accept all VA referrals of Native American veterans and their families from its VA partner and screen for the following eligibility requirements: a. A determination that the veteran is "Indian" as)defined in section 4(10) of NAHASD (b) A determination that the Native American veteran is income-eligible. To be eligible, a veteran household's annual income must be no more than 80 percent of the greater of the median income for the Indian area, or the median income for the United States as prescribed by Section 4(15) of NAHASDA. c. A determination that the veteran is not registered as a lifetime sex offender. As part of the eligibility screening process, a tribe/TDHE must perform a background check to see if the referred veteran or any household member is subject to a lifetime sex offender registration requirement in the State where the housing is located and in other States where the household members are known to have resided.

Award Range/Average: $100,000- $400,000

Funding: (Project Grants (Discretionary)) FY 17 Actual Not Available; FY 18 est Estimate Not Available; FY 19 Estimate Not Available

HQ: 451 7th Street SW, Room 5156, Washington, DC 20410

Phone: 202-402-3057 | Email: marco.c.santos@hud.gov

https://www.hud.gov/program_offices/public_indian_housing/ih/headquarters/gm

DOJ16.608 | TRIBAL JUSTICE SYSTEMS AND ALCOHOL AND SUBSTANCE ABUSE "TCAP"

Award: Project Grants
Purpose: To develop, support, and enhance adult and juvenile tribal justice systems and the prevention of violent crime and crime related to opioid, alcohol, and other substance abuse. The main objective is to support the critical and priority needs of tribal justice systems, to prevent crime and to ensure tribal safety through the development, implementation, and enhancement of strategies.
Applicant Eligibility: Federally recognized Indian Tribal Governments are eligible to apply for and receive funds under this Program.
Beneficiary Eligibility: Indian Tribal governments.
Award Range/Average: See solicitation guidelines posted on the Office of Justice Programs web site at http://www.ojp.gov/funding/solicitations.htm and/or www.bja.gov.
Funding: (Project Grants) FY 18 $21,318,696.00; FY 19 est $16,800,000.00; FY 20 est Not Separately Identifiable
HQ: 810 7th Street NW, Washington, DC 20531
    Phone: 202-307-0581
    http://www.bja.gov

HHS93.872 | TRIBAL MATERNAL, INFANT, AND EARLY CHILDHOOD HOME VISITING

"Tribal MIECHV, Tribal Home VisitingTribal Research Center for Early Childhood (TRCEC)"

Award: Cooperative Agreements
Purpose: The Tribal Maternal, Infant, and Early Childhood Home Visiting Program offers assistance to eligible Tribes (or consortia of Tribes), Tribal Organizations, and Urban Indian Organizations, to strengthen and improve maternal and child health programs, improve service coordination for at-risk communities, and identify and provide comprehensive evidence-based home visiting services to families who reside in at-risk communities. The program's goal is to support the development of happy, healthy, and successful American Indian and Alaska Native children and families through a coordinated home visiting strategy that addresses critical maternal and child health, development, early learning, family support, and child abuse and neglect prevention needs.
Applicant Eligibility: Specifically: Only Tribes (or a consortium of Indian Tribes), Tribal Organizations, or Urban Indian Organizations, as defined by Section 4 of the Indian healthcare Improvement Act, Public Law 94-437, are eligible applicants for the Tribal MIECHV Grant Program. Only Tribes (or a consortium of Indian Tribes), Tribal Organizations, or Urban Indian Organizations, as defined by Section 4 of the Indian healthcare Improvement Act, Public Law 94-437, are eligible applicants for the Tribal MIECHV Grant Program. For the TRCEC, eligibility is open to public and private entities that include state, city, and local Governments; public, private, and state-controlled Institutions of higher education; private, non-profit Organizations with, and without, 501(c)(3) IRS tax status; Native American tribal Governments (federally recognized) and Native American tribal Organizations; and for-profit Organizations that are not sole proprietorship's.
Beneficiary Eligibility: Eligible families in at-risk AIAN communities include pregnant women, expectant fathers, parents, and primary caregivers of children aged birth through kindergarten entry, including grandparents or other relatives of the child, foster parents who are serving as the child's primary caregiver, and non-custodial parents who have an ongoing relationship with, and at times provide physical care for, the child. Specifically: Eligible families residing in at-risk American Indian/Alaskan Native communities in need of such services, as identified in a needs assessment; Low-income eligible families; Eligible families who are pregnant women under age 21; Eligible families with a history of child abuse or neglect or have had interactions with child welfare services; Eligible families with a history of substance abuse or need substance abuse treatment; Eligible families that have users of tobacco products in the home; Eligible families that are or have children with low student achievement; Eligible families with children with developmental delays or disabilities; and; Eligible families who, or that include individuals serving or formerly serving in the Armed Forces, including those with members who have had multiple deployments outside the U.S. Eligible family: A woman who is pregnant, and the father of the child if available, or; A parent or primary caregiver of the child, including grandparents or other relatives and foster parents serving as the child's primary caregiver from birth until kindergarten entry, including a noncustodial parent with an ongoing relationship with, and at times provides physical care for the child.
Award Range/Average: The range of funding is $250,000- $895,000 per budget period for Tribal MIECHV grants.For the TRCEC, the range of funding is up to $600,000 per budget period and the average is $250,000.

Programs Administered by Federal Headquarters

Funding: (Cooperative Agreements) FY 18 $12,000,000.00; FY 19 est $12,000,000.00; FY 20 est $12,000,000.00
HQ: 330 C Street SW, Suite 3014F Mary E Switzer Building, Washington, DC 20201
  Phone: 202-260-8515 | Email: anne.bergan@acf.hhs.gov
  http://www.acf.hhs.gov/ecd/home-visiting/tribal-home-visiting

HHS93.772 | TRIBAL PUBLIC HEALTH CAPACITY BUILDING AND QUALITY IMPROVEMENT UMBRELLA COOPERATIVE AGREEMENT
"Tribal Umbrella CoAg"

Award: Cooperative Agreements
Purpose: This program's ultimate outcomes are decreased morbidity and mortality among American Indians and Alaska Natives and advanced capacity of Indian Country to identify, respond to, and mitigate public health threats.
Applicant Eligibility: Executive Order 13175, Consultation and Coordination with Indian Tribal Governments, 65 FR 67, 249, issued by President Clinton on November 6, 2000, and the Presidential Memorandum for the Heads of Executive Departments and Agencies on Tribal Consultation, 74 FR 57881, signed by President Obama on November 5, 2009 [http://www.gsa.gov/ portal /content/101569] encourage strengthening intergovernmental relations between the federal government and AI/AN tribal nations. As such, eligibility for this CoAg is limited to federally recognized American Indian and Alaska Native (AI/ AN) tribal nations and regional tribally designated Organizations. AI/AN tribal nations have the right of self-determination and governance over their citizens. In addition, AI/AN tribal nations and regional tribally designated Organizations have a unique understanding of AI/AN cultures, fluency in Native languages, knowledge of indigenous history and traditional practices. These entities are the best qualified to address AI/AN public health needs in an efficient, effective, and culturally-appropriate manner. AI/AN tribal public health infrastructure and capacity initiatives and quality improvements are more likely to be sustained when they begin as tribal initiatives rather than as external initiatives. This CoAg will further efforts in Indian Country by supporting a culturally- appropriate approach advocated for and by the CDC/ATSDR Tribal Advisory Committee, tribal public health practitioners and partners. Direct funding will support tribal Governments and tribal-serving Organizations in making sound and efficient public health planning and resource allocation. The funding method for this CoAg will allow for more Programs in CDC to provide direct funding to Indian Country in order to improve tribal public health systems and reach the outcomes stated in the logic model.
Beneficiary Eligibility: Eligible applicants should be able to demonstrate tribal affiliation including (1) a record of effectively working with American Indian and Alaska Native populations (2) an ability to methodically and efficiently reach tribal members in American Indian and Alaska Native communities and (3), if recipient is a tribally owned and operated organization, it should provide a letter of approval from Tribal council for the proposed program.
Funding: (Cooperative Agreements) FY 18 $15,431,446.00; FY 19 est $12,780,459.00; FY 20 est $13,500,000
HQ: 1600 Clifton Road NE, PO Box V18-1, Atlanta, GA 30329
  Phone: 404-498-6121 | Email: kjwilson@cdc.gov
  http://www.cdc.gov/tribal

HHS93.098 | TRIBAL PUBLIC HEALTH CAPACITY BUILDING AND QUALITY IMPROVEMENT
"CBQI"

Award: Cooperative Agreements
Purpose: To provide funding to improve tribal health systems' quality, effectiveness, and efficiency in the delivery of public health services to American Indians/Alaska Natives (AI/AN).
Applicant Eligibility: This Program will provide funding to improve tribal health systems quality, effectiveness, and efficiency in the delivery of public health services to American Indians/Alaska Natives (AI/AN). The intent is to provide support to optimize the quality and performance of tribal public health systems, tribal public health practice and services, tribal public health partnerships, and tribal public health resources.
Beneficiary Eligibility: Tribal Public Health Capacity Building and Quality Improvement Infrastructure and Tribal Entities and Organizations as described/listed in Section (080) Eligibility Requirements, above.
Award Range/Average: Subject to the availability of Funds; Fiscal Year: 2013-2018, Approximate Total Fiscal Year Funding: $587274, Approximate Average Award: $97,500, Approximate Total Project Period Funding: $2,925,000.
Funding: (Cooperative Agreements) FY 18 $550,000.00; FY 19 est $0.00; FY 20 est $0.00

HQ: 1825 Century Boulevard NE, Atlanta, GA 30345
Phone: 404-498-2208
https://www.cdc.gov/tribal/cooperative-agreements/index.html#1

DOJ16.019 | TRIBAL REGISTRY

Award: Project Grants
Purpose: To develop and maintain a national tribal sex offender registry and a tribal protection order registry issued by Indian tribes and participating jurisdictions.
Applicant Eligibility: Eligible applicants are Tribes, tribal Organizations, or tribal nonprofit Organizations.
Beneficiary Eligibility: Beneficiaries include tribes and tribal law enforcement.
HQ: 145 N Street NE, Suite 10W121, Washington, DC 20530
Phone: 202-305-1177 | Email: tia.farmer@usdoj.gov
http://www.justice.gov/ovw

HHS93.210 | TRIBAL SELF-GOVERNANCE PROGRAM: IHS COMPACTS/FUNDING AGREEMENTS
"OTSG Compacts"

Award: Direct Payments for Specified Use
Purpose: To allow federally recognized Indian Tribes to enter into an agreement with the Indian Health Service (IHS) to assume full funding and control over programs, services, functions and activities (PSFA).
Applicant Eligibility: Per 42 C. F. R. 137. 18, to be eligible to participate in the IHS Tribal Self-Governance Program (Program), any Federally recognized Indian tribe must: (a) successfully complete the planning phase described in 42 C. F. R. 137. 20; (b) request participation in the Program by resolution or other official action by the governing body of each Indian tribe to be served; and (c) demonstrate financial stability and financial management capability for three fiscal years. Per 42 C. F. R. 137. 21, the Indian tribe provides evidence that, for the three years prior to participation in the Program, the Indian tribe has had no uncorrected significant and material audit exceptions in the required annual audit of the Indian tribe's self-determination contracts or self-governance funding agreements with any federal agency. Per 42 C. F. R. 137. 22, if the Indian Tribe chooses to centralize its self-determination or self-governance financial and administrative functions with non-self-determination or non-self-governance financial and administrative functions, such as personnel, payroll, property management, etc., the Secretary may consider uncorrected significant and material audit exceptions related to the integrity of a cross-cutting centralized function in determining the Indian Tribe's eligibility for participation in the self-governance Program. Per 42 C. F. R. 137. 26, an Indian tribe does not need to receive a planning or negotiation cooperative agreement to be eligible to participate in the IHS Tribal Self-Governance Program. An Indian tribe may use other resources to meet the planning requirement and to negotiate. Under 25 U.S.C. 458aaa-2(b)(1), each year, an additional 50 Indian Tribes that meet the eligibility criteria are entitled to participate in the IHS Tribal Self-Governance Program.
Beneficiary Eligibility: Federally-recognized Indian tribes and tribal organizations (as defined in 25 U.S.C. 458aaa-(b)) may benefit.
Award Range/Average: Range $79,000 to $153,000,000; Average $16,563,000
Funding: (Direct Payments for Specified Use) FY 18 $2,017,100,000.00; FY 19 est $2,042,100,000.00; FY 20 est $2,042,100,000.00
HQ: 5600 Fishers Lane, PO Box 09E70, Rockville, MD 20857
Phone: 301-443-5204
http://www.ihs.gov

HHS93.444 | TRIBAL SELF-GOVERNANCE PROGRAM: PLANNING AND NEGOTIATION COOPERATIVE AGREEMENT
"Tribal Self Governance"

Award: Cooperative Agreements
Purpose: To enable federally recognized Indian tribes to enter into agreements that would allow them to assume programs, services, functions, and activities (PSFA) that the IHS would otherwise provide for Indians because of their status as Indians.
Applicant Eligibility: For Planning Cooperative Agreements, any Federally recognized tribe that (1) formally requests, through a governing body action, a Planning Cooperative Agreement for the purpose of preparing to enter the IHS Tribal

Programs Administered by Federal Headquarters

Self-Governance Program and (2) has furnished Organization -wide single audit reports as prescribed by Pub. L. 96-502, the Single Audit Act of 1984, as amended, for the previous three years that contain no uncorrected significant and material audit exceptions. See OMB Circular No. A-133 (June 27, 2003 and June 26, 2007). For Negotiation Cooperative Agreements, in addition to the two criteria listed above, applicants must have successfully completed the planning phase as described at 42 C. F. R. 137. 20.

Beneficiary Eligibility: Federally recognized Indian tribes and tribal organizations (as defined in 25 U.S.C. 458aaa-(b)) may benefit.

Award Range/Average: Range $48,000 to $120,000

Funding: (Cooperative Agreements) FY 17 $216,000.00; FY 18 est $840,000.00; FY 19 est $840,000.00

HQ: 5600 Fishers Lane, PO Box 09E70, Rockville, MD 20857

   Phone: 301-443-5204

   http://www.ihs.gov

DOJ16.024 | TRIBAL SEXUAL ASSAULT SERVICES PROGRAM "TSASP"

Award: Project Grants

Purpose: To support programs or projects in Indian tribal lands and Alaska native villages that increase intervention, advocacy, accompaniment, support services, and related assistance for victims of sexual assault; family and household members of such victims; and those collaterally affected by the victimization, except for the perpetrator of such victimization.

Applicant Eligibility: Eligible applicants are Indian Tribes, tribal Organizations, and nonprofit tribal Organizations.

Beneficiary Eligibility: Beneficiaries are tribal organizations and nonprofit tribal organizations, as well as Indian or Alaska native victims of sexual assault.

Award Range/Average: $345,000- $526,500

Funding: (Project Grants) FY 16 $3,465,000.00; FY 17 est $3,468,000.00; FY 18 est $3,500,000.00

HQ: 145 N Street NE, Suite 10W121, Washington, DC 20530

   Phone: 202-305-1177 | Email: tia.farmer@usdoj.gov

   http://www.justice.gov/ovw

DOI15.960 | TRIBAL TECHNICAL COLLEGES

Award: Project Grants

Purpose: To provide grants for operating postsecondary career and technical education programs for Indian students at tribally-controlled postsecondary career and technical institutions.

Applicant Eligibility: Funding is limited to the United Tribes Technical College (UTTC) located in Bismarck, North Dakota; and the Navajo Technical College (NTC) located in Crown point, New Mexico. UTTC is a regionally accredited institution, having achieved accreditation through the Higher Learning Commission of the North Central Association of Colleges and Schools. In addition, UTTC is the first tribal college in the nation authorized to offer full on-line degree Programs. NTC is accredited by the Higher Learning Commission to offer associate of applied science degrees and certificates.

Beneficiary Eligibility: United Tribes Technical College is a 501(c)(3) non-profit corporation chartered by the state of North Dakota and operated by these five tribes: Three Affiliated Tribes of Fort Berthold, the Spirit Lake Tribe, the Sisseton-Wahpeton Oyate, the Standing Rock Sioux Tribe, and the Turtle Mountain Band of Chippewa Indians. The college serves students from federally recognized Indian Tribes, but welcomes and serves students of all backgrounds. Navajo Technical College primarily services Navajo students but has an open door admissions policy.

Award Range/Average: FY 2015 UTTC was awarded $4,565,000, NTC was awarded $2,249,000. The amount of the award is determined by the annual appropriations. Indian Tribes may choose to supplement the funding provided by the grant program by identifying additional amounts in the Tribal Priority Allocations portion of the Bureau of Indian Affairs budget.

Funding: (Project Grants) FY 14 $6,465,000.00; FY 15 est $6,814,000.00; FY 16 est $6,911,000.00

HQ: 1849 C Street NW Bureau of Indian Education, PO Box 4657-MIB, Washington, DC 20240

   Phone: 202-208-3559 | Email: juanita.mendoza@bie.edu

   http://www.bie.edu

HHS93.594 | TRIBAL WORK GRANTS
"Native Employment Works; NEW"

Award: Formula Grants
Purpose: Allows eligible Indian Tribes and Alaska Native organizations to operate a program to make work activities available.
Applicant Eligibility: An Indian Tribe or Alaska Native Organization that conducted a Tribal JOBS (Job Opportunities and Basic Skills Training) Program in fiscal year 1995.
Beneficiary Eligibility: Service areas and populations as designated by the eligible Indian Tribe or Alaska Native organization.
Award Range/Average: From $5,187 to $1,752,666; $96,000, on average.
Funding: (Formula Grants) FY 18 $7,535,110.00; FY 19 est $7,535,110.00; FY 20 est $7,535,110.00
HQ: 330 C Street SW, Washington, DC 20201

Phone: 202-401-5457 | Email: stanley.koutstaal@acf.hhs.gov
http://www.acf.hhs.gov/programs/ofa/programs/tribal/new

DOJ16.731 | TRIBAL YOUTH PROGRAM
"TYP"

Award: Project Grants
Purpose: To assist tribes in responding to myriad issues facing tribal nations. It includes creating, expanding, or strengthening tribally-driven approaches along the juvenile justice continuum that can range from prevention to intervention and treatment.
Applicant Eligibility: Only federally recognized Indian Tribes, as determined by the Secretary of Interior, may apply. This includes Alaska Native villages and tribal consortia consisting of two or more federally recognize Indian Tribes. Applicants will be asked to submit documentation reflective of their legal authority to apply for funds on behalf of their Tribes. Recognizing that Tribes have different forms of tribal governance and tribal laws vary, no prescribed form of documentation will be required.
Beneficiary Eligibility: N/A
Funding: (Project Grants (Discretionary)) FY 17 $9,666,150.00; FY 18 est $5,000,000.00; FY 19 est $0.00
HQ: 810 7th Street NW, Washington, DC 20531

Phone: 202-514-1289 | Email: jennifer.yeh@usdoj.gov
http://www.ojjdp.gov

ED84.245 | TRIBALLY CONTROLLED POSTSECONDARY CAREER AND TECHNICAL INSTITUTIONS

Award: Project Grants
Purpose: To provide career and technical education (CTE) services and basic support for the education and training of Indian students through tribally controlled postsecondary career and technical institutions.
Applicant Eligibility: A tribally controlled postsecondary career and technical institution that: (1) Is formally controlled, or has been formally sanctioned or chartered, by the governing body of an Indian tribe or Indian Tribes; (2) offers a technical degree- or certificate-granting Program; (3) is governed by a board of directors or trustees, a majority of whom are Indians; (4) demonstrates adherence to stated goals, a philosophy, or a plan of operation, that fosters individual Indian economic and self-sufficient opportunity, including Programs that are appropriate to stated tribal goals of developing individual entrepreneurships and self-sustaining economic infrastructures on reservations; (5) has been in operation for at least 3 years; (6) holds accreditation with or is a candidate for accreditation by a nationally recognized accrediting authority for postsecondary vocational and technical education; (7) enrolls the full-time equivalent of not less than 100 students, of whom a majority are Indians; and (8) receives no Federal funds under the Tribally Controlled College or University Act of 1978 or the Navajo Community College Act may apply.
Beneficiary Eligibility: Indian students and tribally controlled postsecondary career and technical institutions not receiving Federal funds under the Tribally Controlled College or University Act of 1978 or the Navajo Community College Act may benefit.
Award Range/Average: Estimated range: $2,500,000- $5,000,000; Estimated average: $3,000,000
Funding: (Project Grants) FY 18 $9,469,000.00; FY 19 est $9,564,000.00; FY 20 est $9,564,000.00
HQ: 400 Maryland Avenue SW, Washington, DC 20202

Phone: 202-245-7790 | Email: gwen.washington@ed.gov
http://www2.ed.gov/about/offices/list/ovae/programs.html

Programs Administered by Federal Headquarters

ED84.066 | TRIO EDUCATIONAL OPPORTUNITY CENTERS

Award: Project Grants

Purpose: To provide information on financial and academic assistance available for qualified adults to pursue postsecondary education program and to assist them in applying for admission to institutions of postsecondary education.

Applicant Eligibility: Institutions of Higher education, public and private agencies and Organizations including community-based Organizations with experience in serving disadvantaged youth, combinations of such Institutions, agencies and Organizations, and as appropriate to the purposes of the Program; secondary schools.

Beneficiary Eligibility: Persons residing in the target area who need one or more of the services provided by the project in order to pursue a program of postsecondary education and who desire to pursue or who are pursuing a program of postsecondary education. Two-thirds of the participants must be low-income individuals who are also potential first-generation college students. Project participants must be at least nineteen years old (exceptions allowed). Required low-income criteria for participants are stated in application materials.

Award Range/Average: Varies by competition. In 2017, awards ranged from $141,575 to $1,201,831; the average award was approximately $356,688.

Funding: (Project Grants) FY 18 $49,661,000.00; FY 19 est $54,101,000.00; FY 20 est $54,101,000.00

HQ: 400 Maryland Avenue SW, Washington, DC 20202

Phone: 202-502-7655 | Email: rachel.couch@ed.gov

http://www.ed.gov/programs/trioeoc

ED84.217 | TRIO MCNAIR POST-BACCALAUREATE ACHIEVEMENT

Award: Project Grants

Purpose: To provide grants for institutions of higher education to prepare participants for doctoral studies through involvement in research and other scholarly activities.

Applicant Eligibility: Institutions of higher education or combinations of Institutions of higher education may apply.

Beneficiary Eligibility: 2/3 of participants must be low-income first generation college students. The remaining participants must be students from groups underrepresented in graduate education. All participants must be enrolled in a degree program at an eligible institution of higher education.

Award Range/Average: Varies by competition. In FY 2017, awards ranged from approximately $225,064 to $388,253; the average award was approximately $245,434.

Funding: (Project Grants) FY 18 $45,886,000.00; FY 19 est $50,027,000.00; FY 20 est $50,027,000.00

HQ: 400 Maryland Avenue SW, Washington, DC 20202

Phone: 202-453-7095 | Email: katie.blanding@ed.gov

http://www.ed.gov/programs/triomcnair

ED84.103 | TRIO STAFF TRAINING PROGRAM

Award: Project Grants

Purpose: To provide training for staff and leadership personnel employed in, or preparing for employment in, projects funded under the Federal TRIO Programs (program numbers 84.042, 84.044, 84.047, 84.066, and 84.217.

Applicant Eligibility: Institutions of higher education and other public and private nonprofit Institutions and Organizations.

Beneficiary Eligibility: Leadership personnel, full-time and part- time staff members of projects under the Federal TRIO Programs, and individuals preparing for employment as staff or leadership personnel in projects under the Federal TRIO Special Programs will benefit.

Award Range/Average: FY 18, awards ranged from $97,230 to $343,119. The average award was approximately $215,769.

Funding: (Project Grants) FY 18 $3,078,000.00; FY 19 est $3,219,000.00; FY 20 $3,219,000.00

HQ: 400 Maryland Avenue SW, Washington, DC 20202

Phone: 202-453-7691 | Email: suzanne.ulmer@ed.gov

http://www.ed.gov/programs/triotrain

ED84.042 | TRIO STUDENT SUPPORT SERVICES

Award: Project Grants

Purpose: To support disadvantaged college students and to enhance their potential for successfully completing the postsecondary education programs in which they are enrolled and increase their transfer rates from 2-year to 4-year institutions.

Applicant Eligibility: Institutions of higher education and combinations of Institutions of higher education may apply.

Beneficiary Eligibility: Low-income, first generation college students or disabled students who are enrolled or accepted for enrollment at the institution that is the recipient of the grant and who are in need of academic support in order to successfully pursue a program of postsecondary education. At least two-thirds of the project participants must be disabled or must be low-income individuals who are first generation college students. The remaining participants must be disabled, low-income individuals, or first generation college students. One-third of the disabled participants must be low-income. Required low-income criteria for participants are stated in application materials.

Award Range/Average: Awards in 2017 ranged from $116,111 to $1,464,591; the average award was $290,030.

Funding: (Project Grants) FY 18 $303,361,000.00; FY 19 est $336,224,000.00; FY 20 est $336,380,000.00

HQ: 400 Maryland Avenue SW, Washington, DC 20202

Phone: 202-453-7814 | Email: james.davis@ed.gov

http://www.ed.gov

ED84.044 | TRIO TALENT SEARCH

Award: Project Grants

Purpose: To identify qualified disadvantaged youths and to encourage them in completing secondary school and in enrolling in programs of postsecondary education.

Applicant Eligibility: Institutions of higher education (IHEs), public and private agencies and Organizations including community-based Organizations with experience in serving disadvantaged youth, combinations of such Institutions, agencies and Organizations, and as appropriate to the purposes of the Program, secondary schools.

Beneficiary Eligibility: Individuals residing in the target area or attending a target school who have potential for education at the postsecondary level and who can benefit from one or more of the services provided by the project. Two-thirds must be low-income individuals who are also potential first generation college students. Project participants must be between 11 and 27 years old (exceptions allowed). Required low-income criteria for participants are stated in application materials.

Award Range/Average: Varies by competition. In FY 17, awards ranged from approximately $185,152 to $914,012; the average award was $320,873. The statutory minimum is $200,000, unless the applicant requests a smaller amount.

Funding: (Project Grants) FY 18 $151,817,000.00; FY 19 est $184,534,000.00; FY 20 est $165,391,000.00

HQ: 400 Maryland Avenue SW, Washington, DC 20202

Phone: 202-453-6195 | Email: craig.pooler@ed.gov

http://www.ed.gov/programs/triotalent

ED84.047 | TRIO UPWARD BOUND

Award: Project Grants

Purpose: To increase the academic performance and motivational levels of low-income and potential first-generation college students and veterans to complete secondary and postsecondary school.

Applicant Eligibility: Institutions of higher education, public and private agencies and Organizations including community-based Organizations with experience in serving disadvantaged youth, combinations of such Institutions, agencies and Organizations, and as appropriate to the purposes of the Program, secondary schools.

Beneficiary Eligibility: Low-income individuals and potential first generation college students who have a need for academic support in order to successfully pursue a program of postsecondary education. Two-thirds of the participants must be low-income individuals who are also potential first generation college students. The remaining one-third must be either low-income, first-generation college students, or students who have a high risk for academic failure. Required low-income criteria are stated in application materials. Except for veterans, who can be served regardless of age, project participants must be between 13 and 19 years old and have completed the eighth grade but have not entered the twelfth grade (exceptions allowed).

Award Range/Average: Varies by competition. In FY 2017, the smallest award was $226,637 and the largest award was $900,511. The average award was $326,415.

Funding: (Project Grants) FY 18 $387,364,000.00; FY 19 est $427,854,000.00; FY 20 est $426,580,000.00

HQ: 400 Maryland Avenue SW, Washington, DC 20202

Phone: 202-453-6273 | Email: ken.waters@ed.gov

http://www.ed.gov/programs/trioupbound

Programs Administered by Federal Headquarters

DOD12.620 | TROOPS TO TEACHERS GRANT PROGRAM
"Troops to Teachers Program"

Award: Project Grants

Purpose: To facilitate employment of eligible members of the armed forces in schools identified in 10 U.S.C. 1154.

Applicant Eligibility: Grant opportunity is for one or more, or a consortia of such States, to receive grant funding to develop and implement a replicable model for attracting and assisting eligible members and former members of the armed forces to obtain employment as teachers.

Beneficiary Eligibility: Beneficiaries of the program are eligible members of the armed forces, as specified in 10 U.S.C. 1154.

Award Range/Average: Grants range from $100,000 to $400,000 annually for multi-year projects. Average award is approximately $200,000 Total funding = $5,000,000.

Funding: (Salaries and Expenses) FY 17 $5,000,000.00; FY 18 est $5,000,000.00; FY 19 est $3,581,414.00

HQ: 6490 Saufley Field Road, Pensacola, FL 32508

   Phone: 850-452-1940 | Email: kim.h.day@navy.mil

   http://www.proudtoserveagain.com

HHS93.347 | TRUSTED EXCHANGE FRAMEWORK AND COMMON AGREEMENT (TEFCA) RECOGNIZED COORDINATING ENTITY (RCE) COOPERATIVE AGREEMENT
"TEFCA RCE Cooperative Agreement"

Award: Cooperative Agreements

Purpose: To advance the establishment of an interoperable health system that empowers individuals to use their electronic health information to the fullest extent.

Applicant Eligibility: Any entity applying for a cooperative agreement must satisfy the following criteria: 1. Be a United States-based not-for-profit entity; 2. Has an existing (or previous) agreement (or single collective set of existing policies) which the applicant determines, oversees, or administers that defines the business, operational, technical, or other conditions or requirements for enabling or facilitating access, exchange, or use of electronic health information between or among two or more unaffiliated individuals or entities. 3. Currently operates or has previously operated across two (2) or more state jurisdictions and can demonstrate governance over data sharing across these jurisdictions; 4. Demonstrates, through letters of support, previous or current participation and membership in a public-private collaborative across two or more state jurisdictions and from multiple types of stakeholders. Such stakeholders can include, but are not limited to, healthcare systems, payers, purchasers, care providers (i.e. long-term and post-acute care, behavioral health, community-based and safety net providers, and emergency medical services), key partners and stakeholders, health IT developers; health information networks, and/or other multi-stakeholder collaboratives that enable widespread health information exchange to occur; 5. Demonstrates the presence of a current (or previous) board or commission with broad stakeholder representation, that has governing authority over the entity, and the ability to modify as needed immediately upon award; 6. Has a mission statement or similar principal Organizational goal indicating their commitment to the advancement of healthcare interoperability; and 7. Demonstrates a commitment to transparent, fair, and nondiscriminatory data exchange by participants through existing Organizational policies and governing structure. a. The existing Organizational policies must include policies that prevent conflicts of interest. b. The applicant must not be majority controlled by any single entity. c. If awarded, the applicant may never be affiliated with a QHIN and must make an attestation specifically to this requirement.

Beneficiary Eligibility: N/A

Award Range/Average: There has been $500,000 allocated for FY 18 for this award. We estimate that we will award one (1) total.

Funding: (Cooperative Agreements) FY 17 Actual Not Available; FY 18 est $499,997.00; FY 19 Estimate Not Available

HQ: 330 C Street SW, Washington, DC 20201

   Phone: 202-774-2466 | Email: hibah.qudsi@hhs.gov

   http://www.healthit.gov

HHS93.947 | TUBERCULOSIS DEMONSTRATION, RESEARCH, PUBLIC AND PROFESSIONAL EDUCATION

Award: Cooperative Agreements

Purpose: Assists States and other public and nonprofit private entities in conducting research into prevention and control of tuberculosis nationally and internationally.

Applicant Eligibility: States, political subdivisions of States, and other public and nonprofit private entities.

Beneficiary Eligibility: States, political subdivisions of States, other public and nonprofit private entities, serving persons with TB infection and disease.

Award Range/Average: $100,000 to $1,000,000 with an average of $120,000.

Funding: (Cooperative Agreements) FY 18 $80,268,900.00; FY 19 est $80,268,900.00; FY 20 est $0.00

HQ: 1600 Clifton Road NE, PO Box E10, Atlanta, GA 30333

Phone: 404-639-5259 | Email: kak4@cdc.gov

http://www.cdc.gov/tb

ED84.287 | TWENTY-FIRST CENTURY COMMUNITY LEARNING CENTERS

Award: Formula Grants

Purpose: To provide opportunities for communities to establish community learning centers high-poverty and low-performing school students.

Applicant Eligibility: State educational agencies (SEAs) are eligible for funds under this Program. Local educational agencies, community-based Organizations, and other public or private entities are eligible to apply to the SEA in state in which they are located for subgrants.

Beneficiary Eligibility: School-aged children and their families.

Award Range/Average: For Fiscal Year 2018: Range: $708,746 - $139,212,692; Average: $21,044,847.

Funding: (Project Grants) FY 18 $1,199,556,270.00; FY 19 est $1,209,456,270.00; FY 20 est $0.00

HQ: 400 Maryland Avenue SW, Washington, DC 20202

Phone: 202-401-2871

http://www.ed.gov/programs/21stcclc/index.html

NRC77.006 | U. S. NUCLEAR REGULATORY COMMISSION NUCLEAR EDUCATION GRANT PROGRAM

"Nuclear Education Grant Program - Curricula Development"

Award: Project Grants

Purpose: To provide assistance to accredited U.S. colleges and universities in support of courses, studies, training, curricula, and disciplines relevant to nuclear safety, nuclear security, nuclear environmental protection, or any other field that the Commission determines to be critical to its regulatory mission.

Applicant Eligibility: Applicants must be a U.S. public or private institution of higher education, accredited by the U.S. Department of education.

Beneficiary Eligibility: Accredited U.S. public or private institutions of higher education will benefit.

Award Range/Average: Award amounts range from $87,000.00 to $200,000.00.

HQ: 11545 Rockville Pike, PO Box TWFN- 8E06M, Rockville, MD 20852

Phone: 301-415-6869 | Email: mlita.carr@nrc.gov

http://www.nrc.gov

DOS19.025 | U.S. AMBASSADORS FUND FOR CULTURAL PRESERVATION
"AFCP, USAFCP"

Award: Project Grants

Purpose: Supports the preservation of cultural heritage overseas, shows respect for the cultural heritage of other countries and supports U.S. diplomatic objectives and foreign policy goals.

Applicant Eligibility: The U.S. Ambassadors Fund for Cultural Preservation supports the preservation of cultural heritage in more than 130 eligible countries around the world. Eligible entities may apply through U.S. embassies for fund support for

Programs Administered by Federal Headquarters

the preservation of cultural sites, cultural objects and collections, and forms of traditional cultural expression (intangible heritage).

Beneficiary Eligibility: Eligible countries: Afghanistan, Albania, Algeria, Angola, Antigua & Barbuda, Armenia, Azerbaijan, Bangladesh, Barbados, Belarus, Belize, Benin, Bhutan, Bolivia, Bosnia & Herzegovina, Botswana, Brazil, Bulgaria, Burkina Faso, Burma, Burundi, Cambodia, Cameroon, Cape Verde, Central African Republic, Chad, China, Colombia, Comoros, Congo (Democratic Republic of the), Congo (Republic of), Costa Rica, Cote d'Ivoire, Cuba, Djibouti, Dominica, Dominican Republic, Ecuador, Egypt, El Salvador, Equatorial Guinea, Eritrea, Ethiopia, Fiji, Gabon, Gambia, Georgia, Ghana, Grenada, Guatemala, Guinea, Guinea-Bissau, Guyana, Haiti, Honduras, India, Indonesia, Iraq, Jamaica, Jordan, Kazakhstan, Kenya, Kiribati, Kosovo, Kyrgyzstan, Laos, Lebanon, Lesotho, Liberia, Libya, Macedonia, Madagascar, Malawi, Malaysia, Maldives, Mali, Marshall Islands, Mauritania, Mauritius, Mexico, Micronesia, Moldova, Mongolia, Montenegro, Morocco, Mozambique, Namibia, Nauru, Nepal, Nicaragua, Niger, Nigeria, Oman, Pakistan, Palau, Panama, Papua New Guinea, Paraguay, Peru, Philippines, Romania, Russian Federation, Rwanda, Saint Kitts & Nevis, Saint Lucia, Saint Vincent & the Grenadines, Samoa, Sao Tome & Principe, Senegal, Serbia, Seychelles, Sierra Leone, Solomon Islands, South Africa, South Sudan, Sri Lanka, Sudan, Suriname, Swaziland, Syria, Tajikistan, Tanzania, Thailand, Timor-Leste, Togo, Tonga, Trinidad & Tobago, Tunisia, Turkey, Turkmenistan, Tuvalu, Uganda, Ukraine, Uzbekistan, Vanuatu, Venezuela, Vietnam, Yemen, Zambia, and Zimbabwe.

Award Range/Average: Awards in Fiscal Year 2015 ranged from $10,000 to $695,000 with an average award amount of $154,000.

Funding: (Project Grants) FY 16 est $5,750,000.00; FY 17 est $5,750,000.00

HQ: Department of State SA-05 C2, Washington, DC 20522-0582
   Phone: 202-632-6308 | Email: perschlermj@state.gov
   http://go.usa.gov/jeUC

VEF85.801 | U.S. FACULTY SCHOLAR GRANTS

Award: Project Grants

Purpose: To promote international exchange and cooperation between the United States and Vietnam.

Applicant Eligibility: Grants are solely intended for U.S. professors for use in teaching in the STEMM fields in Vietnam.

Beneficiary Eligibility: Same as Applicant Eligibility.

Award Range/Average: In 2014,4 grants of up to $40,000 may be awarded.

Funding: (Project Grants (Fellowships)) FY 12 Not Separately Identifiable; FY 13 est Not Separately Identifiable; FY 14 est Not Separately Identifiable.

HQ: 2111 Wilson Boulevard, Suite 700, Arlington, VA 22201
   Phone: 703-351-5053 | Email: margaretpetrochenkov@vef.gov
   http://www.vef.gov

DOD12.432 | U.S. MILITARY ACADEMY ATHLETIC PROGRAMS AT WEST POINT

Award: Cooperative Agreements

Purpose: Supports athletic programs of the U.S. Military Academy at West Point, NY.

Applicant Eligibility: The intent is to issue a cooperative agreement, without using competitive procedures, to the Army West Point Athletic Association in accordance with 10 U.S.C. 4362(a)(1) and subject to the conditions in 10 U.S.C. 4362(g).

Beneficiary Eligibility: N/A

Award Range/Average: Not Available.

Funding: (Project Grants (Cooperative Agreements)) FY 16 $0.00; FY 17 est $3,181,814.00; FY 18 est $13,142,624.00

HQ: 800 Park Office Drive, Suite 4229, Research Triangle Park, NC 27709
   Phone: 919-549-4338 | Email: andrew.l.fiske.civ@mail.mil

NRC77.007 | U.S. NUCLEAR REGULATORY COMMISSION MINORITY SERVING INSTITUTIONS PROGRAM (MSIP)
"NRC Minority Serving Institutions Program"

Award: Project Grants

Purpose: To provide assistance for minority serving programs and activities to include, but not limited to mentoring, leadership development, training, instruction, developmental learning, research and development, program evaluation, and technical assistance.

Applicant Eligibility: Minority Serving Institutions and Organizations that provide services to Minority Serving Institutions and their students and faculty.

Beneficiary Eligibility: Accredited U.S. public and private Minority Serving Institutions of higher education and their students and facility will benefit.

Award Range/Average: Award amounts range from $5,000.00 to $400,000.00.

HQ: 11545 Rockville Pike, PO Box TWFN-8E06M, Rockville, MD 20852

    Phone: 301-415-6869 | Email: mlita.carr@nrc.gov

    http://www.nrc.gov

NRC77.009 | U.S. NUCLEAR REGULATORY COMMISSION OFFICE OF RESEARCH FINANCIAL ASSISTANCE PROGRAM

"NRC Office of Research Grant and Cooperative Agreement Program"

Award: Cooperative Agreements; Project Grants

Purpose: To provide technical advice, technical tools and information for identifying and resolving safety issues, making regulatory decisions, and promulgating regulations and guidance.

Applicant Eligibility: N/A

Beneficiary Eligibility: N/A

Award Range/Average: Award amounts range from $5,000.00 to $225,000.00.

Funding: (Project Grants) FY 18 $803,399.00; FY 19 est $341,621.00; FY 20 Estimate Not Available

HQ: 11545 Rockville Pike, Rockville, MD 20852

    Phone: 301-415-6869 | Email: mlita.carr@nrc.gov

    http://www.nrc.gov

NRC77.008 | U.S. NUCLEAR REGULATORY COMMISSION SCHOLARSHIP AND FELLOWSHIP PROGRAM

"NRC Scholarship/Fellowship and Faculty Development Program"

Award: Project Grants

Purpose: To provide funding for undergraduate scholarships, graduate fellowships, and trade school and community college scholarships; and to support faculty development in the nuclear-related fields of Nuclear Engineering, Health Physics, Radiochemistry and related disciplines as determined by the NRC.

Applicant Eligibility: Applicants must be a U.S. public or private Institutions of higher education, accredited by the U.S. Department of education.

Beneficiary Eligibility: Individual Recipients must be undergraduate and graduate students of accredited U.S. public or private institutions of higher education. Candidates for the Faculty Development program are targeted for probationary, tenure-track faculty in nuclear related fields during the first 6 years of their career. All recipients must be U.S. citizens or noncitizen national of the U.S. or have been lawfully admitted to the U.S. for permanent residence (i.e., in possession of a currently valid Alien Registration Receipt Card I-551, or other legal verification of such status).

Award Range/Average: Award amounts range from $150,000.00 to $450,000.00 (depending on the program).

Funding: (Project Grants) FY 16 $15,000,000.00; FY 17 est $15,000,000.00; FY 18 Estimate Not Available

HQ: 11545 Rockville Pike, Rockville, MD 20852

    Phone: 301-415-6869 | Email: mlita.carr@nrc.gov

    http://www.nrc.gov

DOS19.510 | U.S. REFUGEE ADMISSIONS PROGRAM

Award: Cooperative Agreements

Purpose: Provides initial reception and placement program for refugees approved for admission in the United States. Program objectives include: arranging for refugees' placement by ensuring that approved refugees are sponsored and offered appropriate assistance upon arrival in the United States; providing them with basic necessities and core services during their initial resettlement period in the United States; and by promoting refugee self-sufficiency through employment as soon as possible after arrival in the United States in coordination with other refugee service and assistance programs.

Applicant Eligibility: Private non-profit Organizations.

Beneficiary Eligibility: Refugees approved under the U.S. Refugee Admissions Program will benefit.

Programs Administered by Federal Headquarters

Funding: (Cooperative Agreements) FY 16 $227,636,918.00; FY 17 est $227,000,000.00; FY 18 est $227,000,000
HQ: 2025 E Street NW, Washington, DC 20522-0908
    Phone: 202-453-9261 | Email: daybj@state.gov
    http://www.state.gov/j/prm/index.htm

HHS93.579 | U.S. REPATRIATION
"Repatriation Program"

Award: Cooperative Agreements
Purpose: To provide temporary assistance to U.S. citizens and their dependents who have been identified by the Department of State (DOS) as having returned, or been brought from a foreign country to the U.S. because of destitution, illness, war, threat of war, or a similar crisis, and are without available resources immediately accessible to meet their needs.
Applicant Eligibility: Social service Organizations with expertise in mental health, child welfare, the criminal justice system, and emergency assistance.
Beneficiary Eligibility: ORR authorized staff determines eligibility for citizens and their dependents who have been identified by the Department of State (DOS) as having returned, or been brought from a foreign country to the U.S. because of destitution, illness, war, threat of war, or a similar crisis, and are without resources immediately accessible to meet their needs. In addition, U.S. nationals who are determined eligible by an authorized ORR staff in accordance to 211.3.
Award Range/Average: One Cooperative Agreement non-competing continuation is awarded each year of the project period. When funds are available, reimbursement is provided to states and applicable support agencies for emergency management activities.
Funding: (Cooperative Agreements) FY 18 $1,000,000.00; FY 19 est $938,000.00; FY 20 est $941,000.00
HQ: 330 C Street SW, Mary E Switzer Building, Washington, DC 20201
    Phone: 202-401-4845 | Email: elizabeth.russell@acf.hhs.gov
    https://www.acf.hhs.gov

HHS93.676 | UNACCOMPANIED ALIEN CHILDREN PROGRAM

Award: Project Grants
Purpose: The Unaccompanied Alien Children's program is designed to provide for the care and placement of unaccompanied alien minors who are apprehended in the U.S. by Homeland Security agents, Border patrol agents, or other federal law enforcement agencies and are taken into care pending resolution of their claims for relief under U.S. immigration law or release to parent, adult family members or another responsible adult.
Applicant Eligibility: Also, State and Local Governments, private non-profit Organizations. Faith-based and private for-profit Organizations who can provide state licensed residential capacity or other requisite services.
Beneficiary Eligibility: Beneficiaries are unaccompanied alien children who are in Federal custody by reason of their immigration status.
Award Range/Average: In FY 2018, award amounts ranged from $2,841,419 to $314,740,477. Average of Awards: $88,079,443.
Funding: (Project Grants (Cooperative Agreements)) FY 18 $1,911,084,434.00; FY 19 est $4,568,025,150.00; FY 20 est $2,041,245,000.00
HQ: 330 C Street SW, Washington, DC 20201
    Phone: 202-401-4997 | Email: jallyn.sualog@acf.hhs.gov
    http://www.acf.hhs.gov/programs/orr

DOC11.452 | UNALLIED INDUSTRY PROJECTS

Award: Project Grants
Purpose: To compensate for biological and other research and administration projects to benefit U.S. fisheries industries for qualitative products and for predicting disasters on the Gulf's fishery resources. The FISHTEC applies new technology in molecular biology for marine fisheries to evaluate the status of fish populations and fishery-related industries.
Applicant Eligibility: Eligible applicants for assistance include State and local Governments, including their universities and colleges; U.S. territorial agencies; Federal and State-recognized Indian Tribal Governments; private universities and colleges; private profit and nonprofit research and conservation Organizations and/or individuals.
Beneficiary Eligibility: This program benefits Federal, State, and interstate marine resource conservation and management agencies; U.S. and foreign commercial and recreational fishing industries; conservation organizations, academic institutions; international and Indian Tribal treaties; private and public research groups; consumers; and the general public.

Award Range/Average: Range and Average of Financial Assistance: $50,000 to $1,361,000.
Funding: (Cooperative Agreements) FY 16 $757,640.00; FY 17 est $728,151.00; FY 18 est $750,000.00
HQ: 1315 E W Highway, Silver Spring, MD 20910
   Phone: 301-713-1364 | Email: dan.namur@noaa.gov
   http://sero.nmfs.noaa.gov/grants/uip.htm

DOC11.454 | UNALLIED MANAGEMENT PROJECTS
Award: Project Grants
Purpose: To provide economic and other information needed by Federal and State natural resource administrators for conserving, managing fishery resources, sociological case studies, policy and systems analyses, etc.
Applicant Eligibility: Eligible applicants for assistance include: State and local Governments, including their universities and colleges; U.S. territorial agencies; federally and state recognized Indian Tribal Governments; private universities and colleges; private profit and nonprofit research and conservation Organizations and individuals.
Beneficiary Eligibility: This program benefits Federal, State and interstate marine resource conservation and management agencies; U.S. and foreign commercial and recreational fishing industries; conservation organizations; academic institutions; international and Indian Tribal treaties; private and public research groups; consumers; and the general public.
Award Range/Average: Range and Average of Financial Assistance: $146,500 to $1.27 million.
Funding: (Cooperative Agreements) FY 16 $13,467,493.00; FY 17 est $13,467,493.00; FY 18 Estimate Not Available
HQ: 1315 E W Highway, Silver Spring, MD 20910
   Phone: 301-713-1364 | Email: dan.namur@noaa.gov
   http://www.nmfs.noaa.gov

DOC11.472 | UNALLIED SCIENCE PROGRAM
Award: Project Grants
Purpose: To compensate for the cooperative agreements of biological and physical science research on the stocks of the fishery that will contribute to their optimal management for the benefit of the Nation.
Applicant Eligibility: Eligible applicants for assistance include: State and local Governments, including their universities and colleges; U.S. territorial agencies; federally and State-recognized Indian Tribal Governments; private universities and colleges; private profit and nonprofit research and conservation Organizations and/or individuals.
Beneficiary Eligibility: This program benefits Federal, State and interstate marine resource conservation and management agencies; U.S. and foreign commercial and recreational fishing industries; conservation organizations, academic institutions; international and Indian Tribal treaties; private and public research groups; consumers; and the general public.
Funding: (Cooperative Agreements) FY 16 $23,624,864.00; FY 17 est $23,624,864.00; FY 18 Estimate Not Available
HQ: National Marine Fisheries Services, Office of Management and Budget, 1305 E W Highway, Silver Spring, MD 20910
   Phone: 301-713-1364 | Email: dan.namur@noaa.gov
   http://www.nmfs.noaa.gov

ED84.016 | UNDERGRADUATE INTERNATIONAL STUDIES AND FOREIGN LANGUAGE PROGRAMS
Award: Project Grants
Purpose: To assist institutions of higher education to plan, develop, and carry out a program to strengthen and improve undergraduate instruction in international studies and foreign languages.
Applicant Eligibility: Accredited colleges and universities, and public and nonprofit private agencies and Organizations.
Beneficiary Eligibility: Accredited colleges and universities, and public and nonprofit private agencies and organizations will benefit.
Award Range/Average: Varies by competition.
Funding: (Project Grants) FY 18 $2,353,717.00; FY 19 est $2,863,000.00; FY 20 est $0.00
HQ: 400 Maryland Avenue SW, Washington, DC 20202
   Phone: 202-453-6391 | Email: tanyelle.richardson@ed.gov
   http://www2.ed.gov

Programs Administered by Federal Headquarters

HHS93.187 | UNDERGRADUATE SCHOLARSHIP PROGRAM FOR INDIVIDUALS FROM DISADVANTAGED BACKGROUNDS
"NIH Undergraduate Scholarship Program (UGSP)"

Award: Direct Payments for Specified Use

Purpose: To provide service-conditioned scholarships to individuals from disadvantaged backgrounds who agree to pursue undergraduate education at accredited institutions.

Applicant Eligibility: An eligible applicant must be (1) A U.S. citizen, national, or permanent resident; (2) enrolled or accepted for enrollment as a full-time student at an accredited undergraduate institution (4 year school) of higher education; (3) from a disadvantaged background as determined by the Secretary of Health and Human Services; (4) in good academic standing (minimum GPA of 3. 3 or be in the top 5 percent) with his/her educational institution; and (5) submit an application to participate in the Undergraduate Scholarship (UGS) Program; (6) agree to serve as a full-time NIH employee for not less than 10 consecutive weeks of each year during which the individual is attending the educational institution and receiving a scholarship; (7) agree to serve as a full-time NIH employee for 12 months for each academic year during which the scholarship was provided, not later than 60 days after obtaining his or her academic degree, unless a service deferment is granted.

Beneficiary Eligibility: Undergraduate students from disadvantaged backgrounds pursuing academic programs supporting professions needed by the NIH.

Award Range/Average: Scholarship awards over the past seven years have ranged from $2,000- $20,000, with the average award amount of $9,000.

Funding: (Direct Payments for Specified Use) FY 18 est $3,803,279.00; FY 19 est $4,100,500.00; FY 20 est $4,200,000.00

HQ: 2 Center Drive, Dr Building 2 Room 2E20, Bethesda, MD 20892

Phone: 301-594-2222 | Email: murrayda@mail.nih.gov

http://www.training.nih.gov/programs/ugsp

DOD12.750 | UNIFORMED SERVICES UNIVERSITY MEDICAL RESEARCH PROJECTS
"Uniformed Services University (USU)"

Award: Project Grants

Purpose: Is authorized by status (10 U.S.C. 2113) to enter into grant agreements on a sole-source basis with the Henry M. Jackson Foundation to carry out cooperative enterprises in medical research, medical consultation and medical education.

Applicant Eligibility: Used for medical research and education grants.

Beneficiary Eligibility: Available to USU Scientists/Researchers.

Award Range/Average: Range: $50K - $80 MAverage: $1.5M

Funding: (Salaries and Expenses) FY 14 $224,421,949.00; FY 15 est $45,000,000.00; FY 16 est $220,000,000.00

HQ: 4301 Jones Bridge Road, Bethesda, MD 20814

Phone: 301-295-3861 | Email: kbell@usuhs.mil

http://www.usuhs.mil

HHS93.632 | UNIVERSITY CENTERS FOR EXCELLENCE IN DEVELOPMENTAL DISABILITIES EDUCATION, RESEARCH, AND SERVICE
"University Centers (UCEDD)"

Award: Project Grants

Purpose: To pay the Federal share of the cost of administration and operation of interdisciplinary centers that (1) provide interdisciplinary training for personnel concerned with developmental disabilities; (2) provide community service activities that include training and technical assistance and may include direct services, e.g., family support, individual support, educational, vocational, clinical, health and prevention; (3) conduct research, evaluation and analysis of public policy in areas affecting individuals with developmental disabilities; and (4) disseminate information as a national and international resource.

Applicant Eligibility: Existing Centers; A public or nonprofit entity which is associated with, or is an integral part of a college or University and which provides at least: interdisciplinary training; demonstration of exemplary services, technical assistance, research and dissemination of findings.

Beneficiary Eligibility: Individuals of all ages with developmental disabilities attributable to a mental and/or physical impairment, their families, and personnel and trainees providing services to them.

Award Range/Average: All Centers receive the same award amount. FY 2017 award amount was $547,000 per Center.

Funding: (Project Grants (Discretionary)) FY 18 $38,619,000.00; FY 19 est $40,619,000; FY 20 est Estimate Not Available

HQ: 330 C Street SW, Washington, DC 20201

    Phone: 202-795-7417 | Email: pamela.o'brien@acl.hhs.gov

    http://www.acl.gov/programs/aidd/programs/ucedd/index.aspx

DOT20.701 | UNIVERSITY TRANSPORTATION CENTERS PROGRAM
"UTC Program"

Award: Project Grants

Purpose: To provide grants to nonprofit institutions of higher learning for the purpose of establishing and operating university transportation centers that conduct research, education, and technology transfer programs.

Applicant Eligibility: For the Program's competitive grants, public and private nonprofit Institutions of higher learning that have established transportation research Programs. Non-competitive grants must also be to public and private nonprofit Institutions of higher learning but may or may not have established Programs.

Beneficiary Eligibility: Same as Applicant Eligibility.

Award Range/Average: Fiscal Year 2019: Accomplishments of the UTC Program are expected to continue advancing the capabilities of the nation's universities to conduct needed transportation research on local, regional and national issues, and educate the future transportation workforce, while continuing to enhance the degree of collaboration between and among universities, develop partnerships with state and local government.

Funding: (Project Grants) FY 18 $67,745,500.00; FY 19 est $8,147,000.00; FY 20 est $77,500,000.00

HQ: 1200 New Jersey Avenue SE, Washington, DC 20590

    Phone: 202-366-4985 | Email: denise.e.dunn@dot.gov

    http://www.transportation.gov/utc

DOI15.535 | UPPER COLORADO RIVER BASIN FISH AND WILDLIFE MITIGATION
"Section 314c Projects"

Award: Cooperative Agreements

Purpose: Protects, restores and enhances wetland and upland ecosystems for the conservation of fish and wildlife resources in the upper Colorado River Basin.

Applicant Eligibility: -Under Section 314(c) projects, state and local government agencies, Federally recognized Indian Tribal Governments, private nonprofit Institutions /Organizations; public nonprofit Institutions /Organizations; for-profit Organizations, interstate and intrastate entities, and individuals. While entities within the state of Utah are eligible to receive funds under this Program, funds must be expended for project activities outside the State of Utah. -The State of Utah manages the June sucker Interim Hatchery. Therefore, funding is granted to the State. -The JSRIP is provided funding under the June Sucker Recovery Implementation Program Agreement-The Fish and Wildlife Service is provided funding under the Endangered Species Status Review Agreement.

Beneficiary Eligibility: For Section 314(c) projects, state and local government agencies, Federally recognized Indian Tribal governments, private nonprofit institutions/organizations; public nonprofit institutions/organizations; for-profit organizations, interstate and intrastate entities, and individuals. While entities within the state of Utah are eligible to receive funds under this program, funds must be expended for project activities outside the State of Utah. -The State of Utah manages the June sucker Interim Hatchery. Therefore, funding is granted to the State.-The JSRIP is provided funding under the June Sucker Recovery Implementation Program Agreement -The Fish and Wildlife Service is provided funding under the Endangered Species Status Review Agreement.

Award Range/Average: Range $ 3,000 - $ 582,881 Average $ $356,049

Funding: (Cooperative Agreements (Discretionary Grants)) FY 17 $421,000.00; FY 18 est $385,000.00; FY 19 est $391,000.00

HQ: 1849 C Street NW, PO Box MIB6640, Washington, DC 20240

    Phone: 801-379-1254 | Email: rswanson@uc.usbr.gov

    http://www.cupcao.gov

Programs Administered by Federal Headquarters

DOD12.987 | UPPER SAN PEDRO PARTNERSHIP SUPPORT
"Upper San Pedro Partnership"

Award: Cooperative Agreements

Purpose: To assist in meeting the long-term water needs of the Sierra Vista Subwatershed by achieving sustainable yield of the regional aquifer, and thereby preserving the San Pedro Riparian National Conservation Area and ensuring the long-term viability of Fort Huachuca.

Applicant Eligibility: Solicit and award cooperative agreement for implementing water conservation, reuse, or recharge projects in support of Endangered Species Act compliance in the SV subwatershed of the Upper San Pedro Basin. projects may include design/construction of rainwater harvesting systems, stormwater recharge systems, installation of water conservation devices, and other measures to reduce groundwater usage or increase aquifer recharge in the SV subwatershed. Administer the Partnership's Water Conservation Business Grant Program to include issuing grant funds to those businesses and Institutions that are selected by the Partnership's Retail Work Group to receive a water conservation business grant or to those businesses that provide labor and/or materials to implement grant projects.

Beneficiary Eligibility: This effort supports long-range water conservation for the Sierra Vista sub watershed through the use of the Upper San Pedro Partnership Agreement.

Award Range/Average: Average assistance is anticipated at $100,000. It is dependent on funding availability.

Funding: (Cooperative Agreements) FY 16 $50,000.00; FY 17 est $100,000.00; FY 18 est $100,000.00

HQ: ACC APG Huachuca Division, PO Box 12748, Fort Huachuca, AZ 85670-2748
　　Phone: 520-533-1464 | Email: nancy.e.johnson.civ@mail.mil

HHS93.193 | URBAN INDIAN HEALTH SERVICES
"The Indian Health Service (IHS)"

Award: Cooperative Agreements; Project Grants

Purpose: To provide health-related services to Urban Indians.

Applicant Eligibility: Urban Indian Organizations, as defined by 25 U.S.C. 1603(29), operating a Title V Urban Indian Health Program that currently has a grant or contract with the IHS under Title V of the Indian healthcare Improvement Act, (Pub. L. 93-437).

Beneficiary Eligibility: Urban Indians residing in the urban centers in which the organization is located.

Award Range/Average: $149,950 to $1,096,176; $280,678.

Funding: (Cooperative Agreements (Discretionary Grants)) FY 18 $1,125,517.00; FY 19 est $1,125,000.00; FY 20 est $1,125,000.00; (Project Grants (Discretionary)) FY 18 $7,708,341.00; FY 19 est $8,508,341.00; FY 20 est $ 8,508,341.00

HQ: 5600 Fishers Lane, PO Box 09E70, Rockville, MD 20857
　　Phone: 301-443-5204
　　http://www.ihs.gov

USAID98.012 | USAID DEVELOPMENT PARTNERSHIPS FOR UNIVERSITY COOPERATION AND DEVELOPMENT

Award: Project Grants

Purpose: The program provides support for USAID's strategic objectives through higher education resources and talents.

Applicant Eligibility: US Institutions of higher education, including community colleges, are eligible to apply, subject to the terms of any solicitation. Solicitations and any additional eligibility requirements unique to the solicitation are published at www.HEDProgram. org/.

Beneficiary Eligibility: Same as Applicant Eligibility.

HQ: 301 4th Street SW, Washington, DC 20547
　　Phone: 202-567-4688 | Email: rwillis@usaid.gov
　　http://www.usaid.gov

USAID98.001 | USAID FOREIGN ASSISTANCE FOR PROGRAMS OVERSEAS

Award: Project Grants

Purpose: The program supports foreign policy objectives on a long-term by supporting economic growth, trade and agriculture.

Applicant Eligibility: While an individual grant may include limitations on whom may apply, generally any type of applicant may apply.

Beneficiary Eligibility: Beneficiaries are foreign governments, foreign public or private institutions or organizations, or foreign individuals.
HQ: 301 4th Street SW, Washington, DC 20547
   Phone: 202-567-4688 | Email: rwillis@usaid.gov
   http://www.usaid.gov

USDA10.612 | USDA LOCAL AND REGIONAL FOOD AID PROCUREMENT PROGRAM

Award: Cooperative Agreements
Purpose: The FAS compensates for the purchase of commodities through the U.S. Department of Agriculture. The FAS also provides food assistance in the form of emergency response.
Applicant Eligibility: N/A
Beneficiary Eligibility: Only food-insecure populations in developing countries are eligible beneficiaries under the USDA LRP Program.
Award Range/Average: Individual applications may be valued between $3 and $5 million.
Funding: (Project Grants (Cooperative Agreements)) FY 18 $10,000,000.00; FY 19 est $15,000,000.00; FY 20 est $0.00
HQ: 1400 Independence Avenue SW, PO Box 1030, Washington, DC 20050
   Phone: 202-720-4221
   http://www.fas.usda.gov/programs/local-and-regional-food-aid-procurement

USDA10.528 | USDA WIC TELEHEALTH EVALUATION COLLABORATIVE "WIC TEC"

Award: Cooperative Agreements
Purpose: To implement telehealth innovations that supplement the WIC nutrition education through selected state agencies and to evaluate the interventions implemented by sub-grantees that include process evaluation and cost estimate.
Applicant Eligibility: Eligible entities include public and private colleges and universities and other non-profit research Organizations. This Request for Application (RFA) is open to all Accredited Colleges/universities, and Private or Public Non-profit Research Institutions or Organizations.
Beneficiary Eligibility: WIC participants may benefit from telehealth funded subgrant projects.
Award Range/Average: In a 5 year funding cycle, the USDA anticipates awarding up to $8,500,000 in grant funding to support the creation of the WIC Telehealth Evaluation Collaborative, a WIC telehealth innovations research facility. The majority of these funds, $5,000,000, shall be awarded as sub-grants through a competitive process to WIC State Agencies for the purpose of implementing telehealth innovations that supplement the nutrition education and breastfeeding support offered in the WIC clinic.
Funding: (Cooperative Agreements) FY 18 Actual Not Available; FY 19 est $8,500,000.00; FY 20 est Not Separately Identifiable
HQ: 3101 Park Center Drive, Alexandria, VA 22302
   Phone: 703-305-2732 | Email: karen.castellanos-brown@usda.gov

VA64.034 | VA GRANTS FOR ADAPTIVE SPORTS PROGRAMS FOR DISABLED VETERANS AND DISABLED MEMBERS OF THE ARMED FORCES

Award: Project Grants
Purpose: To promote the lifelong health and to motivate, encourage and sustain participation and competition in adaptive sports from the local level through elite levels among disabled Veterans and disabled members of the Armed Forces.
Applicant Eligibility: The Secretary may award the grants to eligible entities with significant experience in managing large-scale adaptive sports Programs, in order to plan, develop, manage, and implement Programs to provide adaptive sports opportunities for disabled Veterans and disabled members of the Armed Forces. Partnerships are authorized between the recipient adaptive sports and Organizations with significant experience in the training and support of disabled athletes and the promotion of disabled sports and local, regional, and national levels.
Beneficiary Eligibility: In accordance with 38 U.S.C. Section 521A, awards will be made to eligible adaptive sports entities. In addition, partnership agreements may be developed by adaptive sports entities with organizations with significant experience in the training and support of disabled athletes. The partnership agreements must be with organizations that are able to

Programs Administered by Federal Headquarters

recruit, support, equip, encourage, schedule, facilitate, supervise, and implement the participation of disabled Veterans and disabled members of the Armed Forces. Those eligible to apply include Paralympic Sport Clubs, colleges/ universities, Veterans Service Organizations (VSOs), Parks and Recreation Departments, hospitals, and community-based organizations. In addition, these organizations must also: 1. Serve disabled Veterans or disabled members of the Armed Forces or both.2. Provide regular, frequent activity over an extended period of time (weeks or months) - one-time events will not be funded unless the event serves as a launching or focal point for ongoing adaptive sport programming.3. Be designed for long-term sustainability.4. Have specific objectives and measurable outcomes for participation, community involvement, publicity, skill progress and/or other factors.

Award Range/Average: The range and average of financial assistance is to be determined.

Funding: (Project Grants) FY 15 $8,000,000.00; FY 16 est $8,000,000.00; FY 17 est $8,000,000.00

HQ: 810 Vermont Avenue NW, Suite 912D, Washington, DC 20420

   Phone: 202-632-7136

   http://www.va.gov/adaptivesports

VA64.024 | VA HOMELESS PROVIDERS GRANT AND PER DIEM PROGRAM

Award: Project Grants

Purpose: To assist public and nonprofit private entities in establishing new programs and service centers to furnish supportive services and supportive housing for homeless veterans through grants.

Applicant Eligibility: Applicants eligible for grants include public and nonprofit private entities with the capacity to effectively administer a grant; which demonstrate that adequate financial support will be available to carry out the project; and which agree to and demonstrate capacity to meet the applicable criteria and requirements of the grant Program. Applicants eligible for per diem payments include public or nonprofit private entities who are either grant recipients, or who are eligible to receive a grant.

Beneficiary Eligibility: Veterans, meaning a person who served in the active military, naval or air service, and who was discharged or released there from under conditions other than dishonorable.

Award Range/Average: Capital grants have ranged from $12,610 to $1,000,000 for with an average award of $250,000.00. Per Diem is a based on the operational costs and income of each project per the requirements of 38 CFR 61.33. To receive per diem the bed must be occupied. The maximum per diem is $43.32; the average per diem is $31.45 with the average number of beds per project at 22. With an eighty-five per cent occupancy rate the result is an average per diem of approximately $588.

Funding: (Project Grants) FY 15 $214,990,000.00; FY 16 est $171,094,000.00; FY 17 Estimate Not Available

HQ: 10770 N 46th Street, Suite C 200, Tampa, FL 33617

   Phone: 877-322-0334

   http://www.va.gov/homeless/gpd.asp

VA64.033 | VA SUPPORTIVE SERVICES FOR VETERAN FAMILIES PROGRAM

Award: Project Grants

Purpose: To provide supportive services grants to private non-profit organizations and consumer cooperatives who will coordinate or provide supportive services to very low-income Veteran families.

Applicant Eligibility: Applicants eligible for grants must be either a private non-profit Organization or a consumer cooperative. The SSVF Program defines a private non-profit Organization as: 1. An incorporated private institution or foundation that (a) has no part of the net earnings that inure to the benefit of any member, founder, contributor, or individual; (b) has a governing board that is responsible for the operation of the supportive services; and (c) is approved by VA as to financial responsibility; 2. A for-profit limited partnership, the sole general partner of which is an Organization that (a) has no part of the net earnings that inure to the benefit of any member, founder, contributor, or individual; (b) has a governing board that is responsible for the operation of the supportive services; and (c) is approved by VA as to financial responsibility; 3. A corporation wholly owned and controlled by an Organization that (a) has no part of the net earnings that inure to the benefit of any member, founder, contributor, or individual; (b) has a governing board that is responsible for the operation of the supportive services; and (c) is approved by VA as to financial responsibility; or 4. A tribally designated housing entity (as defined in section 4 of the Native American Housing Assistance and Self-Determination Act of 1996 (25 U.S.C. 4103)). The SSVF Program defines a consumer cooperative as having the meaning given such term in section 202 of the Housing Act of 1959 (12 U.S.C. 1701q).

Beneficiary Eligibility: Veteran families, meaning families in which the head of household or the spouse of the head of household served in the active military, naval, or air service, and who was discharged or released therefrom under conditions other than dishonorable. Eligible Veteran families must be very-low income, meaning their annual income, as determined in accordance with 24 CFR 5.609, does not exceed 50 percent of the median income for an area or community. Eligible Veteran families must also fall within one of the following categories: (i) residing in permanent housing; (ii) homeless and scheduled to become a resident of permanent housing within 90 days pending the location or development of housing suitable for permanent housing; or (iii) exited permanent housing within the previous 90 days to seek other housing that is responsive to the very low-income Veteran family's needs and preferences.

Award Range/Average: Annual range and average of grant awards have varied over funding rounds, ranging from $118,000 to $6,800,000 and averaging $1.1 million per award.

Funding: (Project Grants) FY 15 $297,997,000.00; FY 16 est $300,000,000.00; FY 17 Estimate Not Available

HQ: 4100 Chester Avenue, Suite 201, Philadelphia, PA 19104

Phone: 877-737-0111

http://www.va.gov/homeless/ssvf.asp

VA64.037 | VA U.S. PARALYMPICS MONTHLY ASSISTANCE ALLOWANCE PROGRAM

Award: Direct Payments With Unrestricted Use

Purpose: To promote the lifelong health and to motivate, encourage and sustain participation and competition in adaptive sports from the local level through elite levels among disabled Veterans and disabled members of the Armed Forces.

Applicant Eligibility: To receive an allowance, a disabled Veteran must submit a complete application, as well as established training and competition plans and is responsible for turning in monthly and quarterly reports in order to continue receiving the monthly assistance allowance. The disability of the Veteran may be service-connected or non-service-connected if the veteran meets the minimum military standard or higher in his or her respective Paralympic sport at a recognized competition level. The Veteran also must meet eligibility criteria established by the International Paralympic Committee for participants in Paralympic sports.

Beneficiary Eligibility: To receive an allowance, a Veteran must submit a complete application identifying any dependents upon which a higher payable rate of allowance may be based; and the appropriate National Governing Body or equivalent Paralympic entity must provide certification of the Veteran's participation in training or competition sponsored by the USOC, applicable Paralympic sport entity for U.S. Commonwealths or Territories, or the International Paralympic Committee (IPC), or residence at a USOC training center, for a period for which payment is requested. The certification must specify whether the payment is due for training, competition, or residence, and the dates of the training, competition, or residence for which payment is due.

Award Range/Average: The monthly assistance allowance is based on 38 U.S.C. Chapter 31 Vocational Rehabilitation and Employment (VR&E) rates. For FY 2016, a disabled Veteran athlete approved for monetary assistance normally ranges from $605.44 up to $1,143.00 per month, depending on the number of dependents.

Funding: (Direct Payments for Specified Use) FY 15 $2,000,000.00; FY 16 est $2,000,000.00; FY 17 est $2,000,000.00

HQ: 90 K Street NE, Room 707, Washington, DC 20002

Phone: 202-632-7136

http://www.va.gov/adaptivesports

USDA10.352 | VALUE-ADDED PRODUCER GRANTS
"VAPG"

Award: Project Grants

Purpose: To support agricultural producers in expanding marketing opportunities and to have increased income by providing new products.

Applicant Eligibility: Applicants are not eligible if they have been debarred or suspended or otherwise excluded from participation in Federal assistance Programs under Executive Order 12549, Debarment and Suspension. Applicants are not eligible if they have an outstanding judgement obtained by the U.S. in a Federal Court (other than U.S. Tax Court), are delinquent on the payment of Federal income taxes, or are delinquent on a Federal debt. Any corporation that has been convicted of a felony criminal violation under any Federal law within the past 24 months or that has any unpaid Federal tax liability that has been assessed, for which all judicial and administrative remedies have been exhausted or have lapsed, and that is not being paid in a timely manner pursuant to an agreement with the authority responsible for collecting the tax liability, is not eligible for funding.

Beneficiary Eligibility: Agricultural producers.

Award Range/Average: Average = $120,000 Range = $5,000 (minimum) to $250,000 (maximum)

Funding: (Project Grants) FY 18 $11,250,000.00; FY 19 est $13,000,000.00; FY 20 est Estimate Not Available

HQ: 1400 Independence Avenue SW Room 4208-South, PO Box 3253, Washington, DC 20250

Phone: 202-690-1374

http://www.rd.usda.gov/programs-services/value-added-producer-grants

Programs Administered by Federal Headquarters

USDA10.417 | VERY LOW-INCOME HOUSING REPAIR LOANS AND GRANTS
"Section 504 Rural Housing Loans and Grants"

Award: Project Grants; Direct Loans

Purpose: Section 504 compensates for those in rural areas to repair their properties.

Applicant Eligibility: Applicants must own and occupy a home in a rural area; and be a citizen of the United States or reside in the United States after having been legally admitted for permanent residence or on indefinite parole. Loan recipients must have sufficient income to repay the loan. Grant recipients must be 62 years of age or older and be unable to repay a loan for that part of the assistance received as a grant. Applicant's income may not exceed the very low-income limit set forth in RD Instructions.

Beneficiary Eligibility: Applicants must own and occupy a home in a rural area; and be a citizen of the United States or reside in the United States after having been legally admitted for permanent residence or on indefinite parole. Loan recipients must have sufficient income to repay the loan. Grant recipients must be 62 years of age or older and be unable to repay a loan for the part of the assistance received as a grant. Applicant's income may not exceed the very low-income limit set forth in RD Instructions.

Award Range/Average: FY 2017 average loan amount is $5,724. FY 2017 average grant amount is $6,060 FY 2018 average loan amount is $6,154. FY 2018 average grant amount is $6,172 FY 2018 averages are estimates.

Funding: (Project Grants) FY 17 $28,873,909.00; FY 18 est $26,000,000.00; FY 19 est $0.00; (Direct Loans) FY 17 $19,637,606.00; FY 18 est $19,000,000.00; FY 19 est $0.00

HQ: 1400 Independence Avenue SW, Washington, DC 20250

   Phone: 804-287-1559 | Email: myron.wooden@wdc.usda.gov

   http://www.rurdev.usda.gov

USDA10.410 | VERY LOW TO MODERATE INCOME HOUSING LOANS
"Section 502 Rural Housing Loans"

Award: Direct Loans; Guaranteed/insured Loans

Purpose: To support those who receive low-income with permanent housing and essential requirements.

Applicant Eligibility: Applicants must have very low-, low- or moderate incomes. Very low-income is defined as below 50 percent of the area median income (AMI); low-income is between 50 and 80 percent of AMI; moderate income is below 115 percent of AMI. Families must be without adequate housing, but able to afford the housing payments, including principal, interest, taxes, and insurance (PITI). Qualifying repayment ratios are 29 percent for PITI to 41 percent for total debt. In addition, applicants must be unable to obtain credit elsewhere, yet have an acceptable credit history.

Beneficiary Eligibility: Applicants must meet eligibility requirements. Guaranteed Loan Low and Moderate income eligible.

Award Range/Average: FY 17 Average: 502 Direct Loans ($139,158) Guaranteed Loans ($143,804)FY 18 Average: 502 Direct Loans ($151,469) Guaranteed Loans ($147,318)FY 18 are estimates. Loans in high cost areas may be higher.

Funding: (Guaranteed/Insured Loans) FY 17 $19,279,916,900.00; FY 18 est $17,416,823,972.00; FY 19 est $24,000,000,000.00; (Direct Loans) FY 17 $999,991,163.00; FY 18 est $1,000,000,000.00; FY 19 est $0.00

HQ: 1400 Independence Avenue SW, Washington, DC 20250

   Phone: 202-720-1532 | Email: myron.wooden@wdc.usda.gov

   http://www.rurdev.usda.gov

VA64.203 | VETERANS CEMETERY GRANTS PROGRAM

Award: Project Grants

Purpose: Assists States and federally recognized tribal governments in the establishment, expansion, and improvement of veterans' cemeteries.

Applicant Eligibility: Any State may apply. Any federal recognized tribal government.

Beneficiary Eligibility: The cemetery must be used solely for the interment of veterans, their wives, husbands, surviving spouses, minor children, and unmarried adult children who were physically or mentally disabled and incapable of self support: section 38 CFR Part 38.620.

Award Range/Average: Range of Financial Assistance from 1980 $2,897 to 14,000,000

Funding: (Project Grants) FY 15 $46,678,221.00; FY 16 Estimate Not Available; FY 17 Estimate Not Available

HQ: 810 Vermont Avenue NW, Washington, DC 20420

   Phone: 202-632-7369

   http://www.va.gov

VA64.109 | VETERANS COMPENSATION FOR SERVICE-CONNECTED DISABILITY
"Compensation"

Award: Direct Payments With Unrestricted Use

Purpose: To compensate veterans for disabilities incurred or aggravated during military service according to the average impairment in earning capacity.

Applicant Eligibility: Persons who have suffered disabilities resulting from service in the Armed Forces of the United States. The disability must have been incurred or aggravated by service in the line of duty. Separation from service must have been under other than dishonorable conditions for the period in which the disability was incurred or aggravated.

Beneficiary Eligibility: Disabled veterans.

Funding: (Direct Payments for Specified Use) FY 07 $29,091,160,000.00; FY 08 est $32,456,880,000.00; FY 09 est $34,689,066,000.00; (Direct Payments) FY 07 $29,091,160,000; FY 08 est $32,456,880,000; and FY 09 est $34,689,066,000.

HQ: Washington, DC 20420
    Phone: 202-461-9700
    http://www.va.gov

VA64.011 | VETERANS DENTAL CARE

Award: Provision of Specialized Services

Purpose: Provides dental services.

Applicant Eligibility: Must have enlisted in the armed forces before September 7, 1980. Veterans who enlisted in the armed forces after September 7, 1980 or entered on active duty after October 16, 1981, must have 24 continuous months of active duty service or completed the full period of time for which the individual was called or ordered to active duty.

Beneficiary Eligibility: Dental care may be provided for those veterans (1) who have a service-connected compensable dental disability or condition; (2) who have a service-connected, non-compensable dental condition or disability and were former prisoners of war; (3) who have a service-connected, non-compensable condition or disability resulting from combat wounds or service trauma; (4) who were held as a prisoner of war for a period of not less than 90 days; (5) who have a service-connected disability rated as total; (6) who have been found in need of training authorized under 38 U.S.C. Chapter 31; (7) who have a dental condition which is having a direct and material detrimental effect upon a service-connected condition; (8) who have service-connected, non- compensable disability and who apply for treatment of such condition within 90 days following discharge or release from active duty of not less than 180 days, or in the case of a veteran who served on active duty during the Persian Gulf War, 90 days (treatment under this latter authority is limited to one-time correction of the service-connected dental condition); and (9) those receiving outpatient or scheduled for inpatient care may receive dental care if the dental condition is clinically determined to be complicating a medical condition currently under treatment.

Funding: (Salaries and Expenses) FY 07 $418,671,000.00; FY 08 est $451,490,000.00; FY 09 est $485,454,000.00

HQ: Washington, DC 20420
    Phone: 202-273-8303
    http://www.va.gov

VA64.110 | VETERANS DEPENDENCY AND INDEMNITY COMPENSATION FOR SERVICE-CONNECTED DEATH
"DIC and Death Compensation"

Award: Direct Payments With Unrestricted Use

Purpose: To compensate surviving spouses, children and parents for the death of any servicemember who died while on active duty, active duty for training, or inactive duty training, OR any veteran.

Applicant Eligibility: Death Compensation is payable to an unmarried surviving spouse, unmarried children and dependent parent or parents of the deceased Veteran who died before January 1, 1957, because of a service-connected disability. For deaths on or after January 1, 1957, Dependency and Indemnity Compensation (DIC) is payable to an unmarried surviving spouse, unmarried children and dependent parent or parents of the deceased Veteran. DIC is a tax free monetary benefit paid to eligible survivors of a military servicemember who died in the line of duty or eligible survivors of a Veteran who: died from an injury or disease deemed to be related to military service, OR died from a non service-related injury or disease, but was receiving, or was entitled to receive, VA Compensation for a service-connected disability or disabilities that was rated as totally disabling: for at least 10 years immediately preceding death, OR since the Veteran's release from active duty and for at least five years immediately preceding death, OR for at least one year before death if the Veteran was a former prisoner of war who died after September 30, 1999. The surviving parent(s) must have an income below a limit established by law, 38

Programs Administered by Federal Headquarters

U.S. Code 5312. Effective January 2005, surviving spouses who receive DIC and have one or more children under age 18 will receive $250 a month in addition to their current rate. Only one monthly child supplement payment is made, regardless of the number of minor children on the surviving spouse's award. This increased rate applies only to months "occurring" during the two-year period beginning on the date entitlement to DIC began. It ceases on the first month beginning after the expiration of the two-year period or the month in which all of the surviving spouse's children have attained the age of 18, or are removed from the award, whichever is earlier. A surviving spouse who remarries after age 57 retains eligibility for DIC.

Beneficiary Eligibility: Surviving spouses, children and parents of deceased Veterans.

Award Range/Average: Monthly rates of DIC range from $529.55 for one child when no spouse is entitled; from $1,254.19 to $2,677.67 for a surviving spouse, with $310.71 additional if the surviving spouse is in need of aid and attendance, or $145.55 if housebound. A surviving spouse is also entitled to an additional $310.71 monthly for each child under age 18. Monthly rates for parents range from $5 to $621 depending upon income and whether single or married. An additional $336 is payable if the parent is in need of aid and attendance. Monthly Death Compensation ranges from $87 for a surviving spouse to $121 for a surviving spouse with one child; plus $29 for each additional child. An additional allowance or $79 if widow, widower or dependent parent is in need of aid and attendance. Assistance for a dependent parent is $75 for one alone and $80 for two. These rates were effective December 1,2014 for DIC and Parents DIC.

Funding: (Direct Payments with Unrestricted Use) FY 16 $6,589,909,000.00; FY 17 est $6,950,613,000.00; FY 18 est Estimate Not Available

HQ: 810 Vermont Avenue NW, Washington, DC 20420
  Phone: 202-461-9700
  http://www.va.gov

VA64.008 | VETERANS DOMICILIARY CARE
"Domiciliary Residential Rehabilitation And Treatment Program (DRRTP)"

Award: Provision of Specialized Services

Purpose: To provide residential care for ambulatory veterans disabled by age or illness who are not in need of acute hospitalization and who do not need the skilled nursing services provided in nursing homes.

Applicant Eligibility: Veterans who meet basic VA eligibility requirement for VA healthcare and who are assessed as: not meeting criteria for acute inpatient mental health or medical admission; having tried a less restrictive treatment alternative, or one was unavailable; having identified rehabilitation and treatment needs requiring the structure and support of a residential treatment environment; not a significant risk of harm to self or others; lacking a stable lifestyle or living arrangement that is conducive to the Veteran's goal of recovery; being capable of self-preservation and basic self-care.

Beneficiary Eligibility: Veterans meeting the above requirements.

Award Range/Average: Not Applicable.

Funding: (Project Grants) FY 15 $729,752,605.00; FY 16 est $728,933,266.00; FY 17 est $721,104,018.00

HQ: Washington, DC 20420
  Phone: 202-461-4154
  http://www.va.gov

VA64.052 | VETERANS EMPLOYMENT PAY FOR SUCCESS PROGRAM
"VEPFS - Veterans Employment Pay for Success Program"

Award: Project Grants

Purpose: To provide grants to eligible recipients to assist veterans in highly rural areas through innovative transportation services to travel to Department of Veterans Affairs Medical Centers.

Applicant Eligibility: Applicants must be prepared to provide documentation of eligibility criteria and other support documentation described in the notice of funds availability (NOFA). This competition is open to public or nonprofit agencies, including Institutions of higher learning as defined in 38 U.S.C. 3119. Eligible nonprofit Organizations include those defined in 2 C. F. R 200. 70. Eligible applicants must serve low-income communities or address a specific issue area (e.g., employment or mental health challenges) in geographical areas that have the highest need in that issue area.

Beneficiary Eligibility: This competition is open to public or nonprofit agencies, including institutions of higher learning as defined in 38 U.S.C. 3119. Eligible nonprofit organizations include those defined in 2 C.F.R 200.70. Eligible applicants must serve low-income communities or address a specific issue area (e.g., employment or mental health challenges) in geographical areas that have the highest need in that issue area.

Award Range/Average: The grant amount will be specified in the NOFA.

Funding: (Project Grants) FY 15 Not Separately Identifiable; FY 16 est $1,500,000.00; FY 17 est $1,500,000.00 `
HQ: 810 Vermont Avenue NW, Washington, DC 20420

Phone: 202-256-7176 | Email: michelle.staton@va.gov

VA64.118 | VETERANS HOUSING DIRECT LOANS FOR CERTAIN DISABLED VETERANS

Award: Direct Loans
Purpose: To provide veterans who are eligible for a Specially Adapted Housing grant with loan directly from the VA.
Applicant Eligibility: Veterans who served on active duty on or after September 16, 1940 and are eligible for a Specially Adapted Housing grant.
Beneficiary Eligibility: Permanently and totally disabled veterans.
HQ: Washington, DC 20420

Phone: 202-461-9511

http://www.va.gov

VA64.114 | VETERANS HOUSING GUARANTEED AND INSURED LOANS
"VA Home Loans"

Award: Guaranteed/insured Loans
Purpose: To assist veterans, certain service personnel, and certain unmarried surviving spouses of veterans, in obtaining credit for the purchase, construction or improvement of homes on more liberal terms.
Applicant Eligibility: (a) Veterans who served on active duty on or after September 16, 1940, and were discharged or released under conditions other than dishonorable. Veterans who served any time during World War II, the Korean Conflict, the Vietnam-era, or the Persian Gulf War must have served on active duty 90 days or more; veterans with peacetime service only must have served a minimum of 181 days continuous active duty. All veterans separated from enlisted service which began after September 7, 1980, or service as an officer which began after October 16, 1981, must also have served at least 24 months of continuous active duty or the full period for which the person was called or ordered to active duty. Veterans of such recent service may qualify with less service time if they have a compensable service-connected disability or were discharged after at least 181 days (90 days during Persian Gulf War), under the authority of 10 U.S.C. 1171 or 1173; or (b) any veteran in the above classes with less service but discharged with a service-connected disability; (c) individuals may also be eligible if they were released from active duty due to an involuntary reduction in force, certain medical conditions, or in some instances, for the convenience of the Government; (d) unmarried surviving spouses of otherwise eligible veterans who died in service or whose deaths were attributable to service-connected disabilities Note: A surviving spouse who remarries on or after attaining age 57, may be eligible for the home loan benefit. However, a surviving spouse who remarried before December 16, 2003, must have applied no later than December 15, 2004 to establish home loan eligibility. VA must deny applications from surviving spouses who remarried before December 16, 2003; (e) service personnel who have served at least 181 days on continuous active duty status (90 days until the ending date for the Persian Gulf War has been set); (f) spouses of members of the Armed Forces serving on active duty, who are listed as missing in action, or as prisoners of war and who have been so listed 90 days or more; (g) members of the Selected Reserve who are not otherwise eligible for home loan benefits and who have completed a total of six (6) years in the Selected Reserves, followed by an honorable discharge, placement on the retired list, or continued service. Individuals who completed less than 6 years may be eligible if discharged for a service connected disability. Applicants must have sufficient present and prospective income to meet loan repayment terms and have a satisfactory credit record.
Beneficiary Eligibility: Veterans, service personnel, and unmarried surviving spouses of veterans.
Funding: (Salary or Expense) FY 07 $24,186,118,000.00; FY 08 est $34,761,311,000.00; FY 09 est $35,816,558,000.00
HQ: Washington, DC 20420

Phone: 202-461-9500

http://www.va.gov

Programs Administered by Federal Headquarters

HUD14.278 | VETERANS HOUSING REHABILITATION AND MODIFICATION PROGRAM

Award: Project Grants

Purpose: To award grants to nonprofit veterans service organizations to rehabilitate and modify the particular residence of disabled and low-income veterans.

Applicant Eligibility: Nonprofits Organizations that provide nationwide or statewide Programs that primarily serve veterans or low-income individuals. Applicants that are nonprofits Organizations as described in section 501(c) (3) or 501 (a) (19) of the Internal Revenue Code of 1986 and exempt from tax under section 501 (a) of such Code.

Beneficiary Eligibility: Eligible recipients for use of the Veterans Housing Rehabilitation and Modification Program include disabled and low-income veterans.

Award Range/Average: Up to $1,000,000 per grant.

Funding: (Salaries and Expenses) FY 18 $3,000,000.00; FY 19 est $8,000,000.00; FY 20 est $5,000,000.00

HQ: 451 7th Street SW, Room 7240, Washington, DC 20410

Phone: 877-787-2526 | Email: jackie.williams@hud.gov

http://www.hud.gov/ruralgateway

SBA59.044 | VETERANS OUTREACH PROGRAM
"Veterans Business Outreach Center Program (VBOC)"

Award: Cooperative Agreements

Purpose: Organizations provide information on small business ownership to service members and military spouses by facilitating and instructing the U.S. Small Business Administration's "Introduction to Entrepreneurship" known as "Boots to Business" which is a course offered within the Department of Defense Transition Assistance Program in accordance with Public Law of 110-186.

Applicant Eligibility: Eligible applicants may be education Institutions, private businesses, veterans nonprofit community-based Organizations, and Federal, State, local and tribal government agencies.

Beneficiary Eligibility: First beneficiaries are eligible veterans, active duty service members, Guard & Reserve members and military spouses who seek to start and manage a small business; second beneficiaries are all others.

Funding: (Project Grants) FY 17 $12,572,000.00; FY 18 est $12,500,000.00; FY 19 est $11,250,000.00

HQ: 409 3rd Street SW, 5th Floor, Washington, DC 20416

Phone: 202-205-6777 | Email: raymond.milano@sba.gov

http://www.sba.gov

VA64.012 | VETERANS PRESCRIPTION SERVICE
"Medicine For Veterans"

Award: Sale, Exchange, Or Donation of Property and Goods

Purpose: To provide eligible veterans and certain dependents and survivors of veterans with prescription drugs and expendable medical supplies from VA pharmacies upon presentation of prescription(s) from a VA provider.

Applicant Eligibility: Veterans receiving outpatient care (see Veterans Outpatient Care 64. 011); service connected veterans and World War I veterans if they are authorized non-VA care (Fee Basis) are eligible for prescriptions. Also, veterans in receipt of aid and attendance or housebound benefits are eligible for prescriptions. Veterans whose pension payments have been discontinued because their annual income exceeds the applicable maximum limitations may continue to be eligible for prescription drugs and expendable medical supplies until their income exceeds the maximum limitation by more than $1,000.

Beneficiary Eligibility: Same as Applicant Eligibility.

Funding: (Salaries and Expenses) FY 07 $4,324,952,000.00; FY 08 est $4,688,246,000.00; FY 09 est $5,100,409,000.00

HQ: Washington, DC 20420

Phone: 202-273-8429

http://www.va.gov

VA64.013 | VETERANS PROSTHETIC APPLIANCES
"Prosthetics Services"

Award: Provision of Specialized Services

Purpose: To provide, through purchase and/or fabrication, prosthetic and related appliances, equipment and services to eligible veterans.

Applicant Eligibility: Any disabled veteran or authorized representative on his behalf meeting the criteria below may apply for prosthetic appliances or services. VA may not furnish sensory-neural aids, e.g., eye glasses, hearing aids, etc., other than in accordance with guidelines established by the Secretary.

Beneficiary Eligibility: Veterans eligible for prosthetic services are service-connected veterans seeking care for a service-connected disability; veterans with compensable service-connected disabilities generally rated 10 percent or more; former prisoners of war, veterans discharged or released from active military service for a disability that was incurred or aggravated in the line of duty, and veterans who are in receipt of Section 1151 benefits; veterans who are in receipt of increased pension based on a need of regular aid and attendance or by reason of being permanently housebound; veterans who have annual income and net worth below the "means test" threshold; all other veterans who are not required to pay a co-payment for their care, i.e., veterans of the Mexican border period and World War I, compensated zero (0) percent service-connected veterans who are receiving statutory awards, veterans exposed to a toxic substance, radiation or environmental hazard (limited to certain disabilities); and veterans who must pay a co-payment for their care. Ineligible veterans are nonservice-connected veterans residing or sojourning in foreign lands.

Funding: (Salary or Expense) FY 07 $1,236,275,000.00; FY 08 est $1,320,834,000.00; FY 09 est $1,454,528,000.00

HQ: Washington, DC 20420
Phone: 202-254-0440
http://vaww1.va.gov/prosthetics

VA64.026 | VETERANS STATE ADULT DAY HEALTH CARE

Award: Formula Grants

Purpose: To provide a community-based program designed to meet the needs of adults with impairments through individual plans of care. This type of structured, comprehensive, nonresidential program provides a variety of health, social, and related support services in a protective setting.

Applicant Eligibility: 52. 50 Eligible veterans. A veteran is an eligible veteran under this part if VA determines that the veteran meets the definition of a veteran in 38 U.S.C. 101, is not barred from receiving this VA care under 38 U.S.C. 5303, 5303A, needs adult day healthcare, and is within one of the following Categories listed below: Public Law 106-117 Section 101, Adult Day Health-Eligibility. (a) Veterans with service-connected disabilities; (b) Veterans who are former prisoners of war; (c) Veterans who were discharged or released from active military service for a disability incurred or aggravated in the line of duty; (d) Veterans who receive disability compensation under 38 U.S.C. 1151; (e) Veterans whose entitlement to disability compensation is suspended because of the receipt of retired pay; (f) Veterans whose entitlement to disability compensation is suspended pursuant to 38 U.S.C. 1151, but only to the extent that such veterans continuing eligibility for adult day healthcare is provided for in the judgment or settlement described in 38 U.S.C. 1151; (g) Veterans who VA determines are unable to defray the expenses of necessary care as specified under 38 U.S.C. 1722(a); (h) Veterans of the Mexican Border period or of World War I; (i) Veterans solely seeking care for a disorder associated with exposure to a toxic substance or radiation or for a disorder associated with service in the Southwest Asia theater of operations during the Gulf War, as provided in 38 U.S.C. 1710(e); (j) Veterans who agree to pay to the United States the applicable co-payment determined under 38 U.S.C. 1710(f) and 1710(g), if they seek VA (Department of Veterans Affairs) hospital, nursing home, or outpatient care. (Authority: 38 U.S.C. 101, 501, 1741, 1743).

Beneficiary Eligibility: A veteran eligible for care in a VA facility needing adult day health care and meeting one of the following conditions: (a) has a service-connected disability for which such care is being provided; (b) has a non-service connected disability and sates under oath his inability to defray the expenses of necessary adult day health care; (c) was discharged or related from active military, naval and air services for a disability incurred or aggravated in the line of duty; or (d) is in receipt of, or but for the receipt of retirement pay would be entitled to receive disability compensation. A veteran must also meet State admission criteria.

Award Range/Average: $22,686 to $165,077; average $93,882

HQ: Department of Veterans Affairs 810 Vermont Avenue NW, Washington, DC 20420
Phone: 202-461-6771
http://www.va.gov

Programs Administered by Federal Headquarters

VA64.014 | VETERANS STATE DOMICILIARY CARE

Award: Formula Grants

Purpose: To provide financial assistance to States furnishing domiciliary care to eligible veterans in State Veterans' Homes.

Applicant Eligibility: Applicant is any State which operates a designated facility to furnish domiciliary care primarily for veterans.

Beneficiary Eligibility: Veterans eligible for care in a VA facility needing domiciliary care and meeting one of the following conditions: (a) has a service-connected disability for which such care is being provided; (b) has a nonservice-connected disability and states under oath his inability to defray the expenses of necessary care; (c) was discharged or released from active military, naval and air service for a disability incurred or aggravated in line of duty; or (d) is in receipt of, or but for the receipt of, retirement pay would be entitled to receive disability compensation. A veteran must also meet State admission criteria.

Funding: (Formula Grants) FY 07 $45,034,000.00; FY 08 est $49,339,000.00; FY 09 est $51,190,000.00

HQ: Washington, DC 20420

    Phone: 202-461-6771

    http://www.va.gov

VA64.015 | VETERANS STATE NURSING HOME CARE

Award: Formula Grants

Purpose: To provide financial assistance to States furnishing domiciliary care to eligible veterans in State Veterans' Homes.

Applicant Eligibility: Applicant is any State which operates a designated facility to furnish nursing home care primarily for veterans.

Beneficiary Eligibility: A veteran eligible for care in a VA facility needing nursing home care and meeting one of the following conditions: (a) has a service-connected disability for which such care is being provided; (b) has a nonservice-connected disability and states under oath his inability to defray the expenses of necessary nursing home care; (c) was discharged or released from active military, naval and air services for a disability incurred or aggravated in line of duty; or (d) is in receipt of, or but for the receipt of retirement pay would be entitled to receive disability compensation. A veteran must also meet State admission criteria.

Funding: (Formula Grants) FY 07 $451,644,000.00; FY 08 est $501,046,000.00; FY 09 est $524,739,000,000.00

HQ: Washington, DC 20420

    Phone: 202-461-6771

    http://www.va.gov

VA64.035 | VETERANS TRANSPORTATION PROGRAM
"Veterans Transportation Program/Grants for Transportation in Highly Rural Areas"

Award: Project Grants

Purpose: This program furthers the Department's mission by establishing a program to provide grants to eligible recipients to assist veterans in highly rural areas through innovative transportation services to travel to Department of Veterans Affairs Medical Centers.

Applicant Eligibility: The Secretary may award the grants to an eligible entity which is defined as either a Veterans Service Organization or State Veterans Service Agency, in accordance with paragraphs (a)(2)(A)-(B) of section 307 of the 2010 Act.

Beneficiary Eligibility: A "participant" would be defined as a veteran in a highly rural area who receives transportation services from a grantee.

Award Range/Average: The grant amounts will be specified in the Notice of Fund Availability, but that no single grant will exceed $50,000, to comply with paragraph (a)(4) of section 307 of the 2010 Act.

Funding: (Project Grants) FY 11 Not Separately Identifiable; FY 12 est Not Separately Identifiable; FY 13 est $275,000.00

HQ: 2957 Clairmont Road, Suite 200, Atlanta, GA 30329

    Phone: 404-828-5380 | Email: michelle.staton@va.gov

USDA10.313 | VETERINARY MEDICINE LOAN REPAYMENT PROGRAM "VLMRP"

Award: Direct Payments for Specified Use

Purpose: To encourage veterinarians to serve in socially disadvantaged areas and the SCA shall provide them with loans and necessary assistance.

Applicant Eligibility: The Secretary may enter into agreements with veterinarians under which the veterinarians agree to provide, for a period of time as determined by the Secretary and specified in the agreement, veterinary services in veterinarian shortage situations.

Beneficiary Eligibility: Same as Applicant Eligibility.

Award Range/Average: Minimum and maximum amounts of funding per grant are established by the annual program announcement.

Funding: (Direct Payments for Specified Use) FY 17 $5,850,000.00; FY 18 est $7,200,000.00; FY 19 est $0.00

HQ: 1400 Independence Avenue SW, PO Box 2240, Washington, DC 20250-2240

    Phone: 202-401-6134

    http://nifa.usda.gov

USDA10.336 | VETERINARY SERVICES GRANT PROGRAM "VSGP"

Award: Cooperative Agreements; Project Grants

Purpose: The Veterinary Services Grant Program is to support and promote veterinary services and to encourage education, training, and expand veterinary practices.

Applicant Eligibility: A qualified entity shall be eligible to receive a grant described in paragraph (1) if the entity carries out Programs or activities that the Secretary determines will: (A) Substantially relieve veterinarian shortage situations; (B) Support or facilitate private veterinary practices engaged in public health activities; or (C) support or facilitate the practices of veterinarians who are providing or have completed providing services under an agreement entered into with the Secretary under section 1415A(a)(2). The term ˜qualified entity means: (A) A for-profit or nonprofit entity located in the United States that, or an individual who, operates a veterinary clinic providing veterinary services: (i) In a rural area, as defined in section 343(a) of the Consolidated Farm and Rural Development Act (7 U.S.C. 1991(a)); and (ii) In a veterinarian shortage situation; (B) A State, national, allied, or regional veterinary Organization or specialty board recognized by the American Veterinary Medical Association; (C) A college or school of veterinary medicine accredited by the American Veterinary Medical Association; (D) A University research foundation or veterinary medical foundation; (E) A department of veterinary science or department of comparative medicine accredited by the Department of education; (F) A State agricultural experiment station; or (G) A State, local, or tribal government agency. The term ˜veterinarian shortage situation means a veterinarian shortage situation as determined by the Secretary under section 1415A.

Beneficiary Eligibility: A qualified entity shall be eligible to receive a grant described in paragraph (1) if the entity carries out programs or activities that the Secretary determines will: (A) Substantially relieve veterinarian shortage situations; (B) Support or facilitate private veterinary practices engaged in public health activities; or (C) support or facilitate the practices of veterinarians who are providing or have completed providing services under an agreement entered into with the Secretary under section 1415A(a)(2). The term qualified entity' means: (A) A for-profit or nonprofit entity located in the United States that, or an individual who, operates a veterinary clinic providing veterinary services: (i) In a rural area, as defined in section 343(a) of the Consolidated Farm and Rural Development Act (7 U.S.C. 1991(a)); and (ii) In a veterinarian shortage situation; (B) A State, national, allied, or regional veterinary organization or specialty board recognized by the American Veterinary Medical Association; (C) A college or school of veterinary medicine accredited by the American Veterinary Medical Association; (D) A university research foundation or veterinary medical foundation; (E) A department of veterinary science or department of comparative medicine accredited by the Department of Education; (F) A State agricultural experiment station; or (G) A State, local, or tribal government agency. The term veterinarian shortage situation' means a veterinarian shortage situation as determined by the Secretary under section 1415A.

Award Range/Average: If minimum or maximum amounts of funding per competitive and/or capacity project grant, or cooperative agreement are established, these amounts will be announced in the annual Competitive Request for Application (RFA).The most current RFA is available via: https://nifa.usda.gov/program/veterinary-services-grant-program

Funding: (Cooperative Agreements (Discretionary Grants)) FY 17 $2,350,736.00; FY 18 est $2,354,305.00; FY 19 est $0.00

HQ: 1400 Independence Avenue SW, PO Box 2240, Washington, DC 20024

    Phone: 202-401-6802

    https://nifa.usda.gov/program/veterinary-services-grant-program

Programs Administered by Federal Headquarters

VA64.049 | VHA COMMUNITY LIVING CENTER
"USASpending.gov"
Award: Direct Payments for Specified Use
Purpose: To account for Veterans healthcarespending and display the spending by the beneficiary residence.
Applicant Eligibility: Nursing Home care in VHA Community Living Centers provided to Veterans.
Beneficiary Eligibility: 38 USC 1705: patient enrollment system Text contains those laws in effect on December 1, 2013From Title 38-VETERANS' BENEFITSPART II-GENERAL BENEFITSCHAPTER 17-HOSPITAL, NURSING HOME, DOMICILIARY, AND MEDICAL CARESUBCHAPTER I-GENERAL 1705. Management of health care: patient enrollment system(a) In managing the provision of hospital care and medical services under section 1710(a) of this title, the Secretary, in accordance with regulations the Secretary shall prescribe, shall establish and operate a system of annual patient enrollment. The Secretary shall manage the enrollment of veterans in accordance with the following priorities, in the order listed:(1) Veterans with service-connected disabilities rated 50 percent or greater.(2) Veterans with service-connected disabilities rated 30 percent or 40 percent.(3) Veterans who are former prisoners of war or who were awarded the Purple Heart, veterans who were awarded the medal of honour under section 3741, 6241, or 8741 of title 10 or section 491 of title 14, veterans with service-connected disabilities rated 10 percent or 20 percent, and veterans described in subparagraphs (B) and (C) of section 1710(a)(2) of this title.(4) Veterans who are in receipt of increased pension based on a need of regular aid and attendance or by reason of being permanently housebound and other veterans who are catastrophically disabled.(5) Veterans not covered by paragraphs (1) through (4) who are unable to defray the expenses of necessary care as determined under section 1722(a) of this title.(6) All other veterans eligible for hospital care, medical services, and nursing home care under section 1710(a)(2) of this title.
Award Range/Average: According to the cost of the services.
HQ: 100 Grandview Road, Suite 114, Braintree, MA 02184
Phone: 781-849-1837 | Email: michelle.staton@va.gov
http://www.va.gov

VA64.050 | VHA DIAGNOSTIC CARE
"USASpending.gov"
Award: Direct Payments for Specified Use
Purpose: To account for Veterans healthcarespending and display the spending by the beneficiary residence.
Applicant Eligibility: All services provided to eligible recipients for Outpatient Diagnostic Care. This includes the Pathology, Radiology, Nuclear Medicine and other Diagnostic Clinics.
Beneficiary Eligibility: 38 USC 1705: patient enrollment system Text contains those laws in effect on December 1, 2013From Title 38-VETERANS' BENEFITSPART II-GENERAL BENEFITSCHAPTER 17-HOSPITAL, NURSING HOME, DOMICILIARY, AND MEDICAL CARESUBCHAPTER I-GENERAL 1705. Management of health care: patient enrollment system(a) In managing the provision of hospital care and medical services under section 1710(a) of this title, the Secretary, in accordance with regulations the Secretary shall prescribe, shall establish and operate a system of annual patient enrollment. The Secretary shall manage the enrollment of veterans in accordance with the following priorities, in the order listed:(1) Veterans with service-connected disabilities rated 50 percent or greater.(2) Veterans with service-connected disabilities rated 30 percent or 40 percent.(3) Veterans who are former prisoners of war or who were awarded the Purple Heart, veterans who were awarded the medal of honour under section 3741, 6241, or 8741 of title 10 or section 491 of title 14, veterans with service-connected disabilities rated 10 percent or 20 percent, and veterans described in subparagraphs (B) and (C) of section 1710(a)(2) of this title.(4) Veterans who are in receipt of increased pension based on a need of regular aid and attendance or by reason of being permanently housebound and other veterans who are catastrophically disabled.(5) Veterans not covered by paragraphs (1) through (4) who are unable to defray the expenses of necessary care as determined under section 1722(a) of this title.(6) All other veterans eligible for hospital care, medical services, and nursing home care under section 1710(a)(2) of this title.
Award Range/Average: According to the cost of the services.
HQ: 100 Grandview Road, Suite 114, Braintree, MA 02184
Phone: 781-849-1837 | Email: michelle.staton@va.gov
http://www.va.gov

VA64.044 | VHA HOME CARE
"USASpending.gov"

Award: Direct Payments for Specified Use

Purpose: To account for Veterans healthcarespending and display the spending by the beneficiary residence.

Applicant Eligibility: Management of healthcare: patient enrollment system(a) In managing the provision of hospital care and medical services under section 1710(a) of this title, the Secretary, in accordance with regulations the Secretary shall prescribe, shall establish and operate a system of annual patient enrollment. The Secretary shall manage the enrollment of veterans in accordance with the following priorities, in the order listed: (1) Veterans with service-connected disabilities rated 50 percent or greater. (2) Veterans with service-connected disabilities rated 30 percent or 40 percent. (3) Veterans who are former prisoners of war or who were awarded the Purple Heart, veterans who were awarded the medal of honor under section 3741, 6241, or 8741 of title 10 or section 491 of title 14, veterans with service-connected disabilities rated 10 percent or 20 percent, and veterans described in subparagraphs (B) and (C) of section 1710(a)(2) of this title. (4) Veterans who are in receipt of increased pension based on a need of regular aid and attendance or by reason of being permanently housebound and other veterans who are catastrophically disabled. (5) Veterans not covered by paragraphs (1) through (4) who are unable to defray the expenses of necessary care as determined under section 1722(a) of this title. (6) All other veterans eligible for hospital care, medical services, and nursing home care under section 1710(a)(2) of this title.

Beneficiary Eligibility: Same as Applicant Eligibility.

Award Range/Average: According to the cost of the services.

HQ: 100 Grandview Road, Suite 114, Braintree, MA 02184
Phone: 781-849-1837 | Email: michelle.staton@va.gov
http://www.va.gov

VA64.040 | VHA INPATIENT MEDICINE
"USASpending.gov"

Award: Direct Payments With Unrestricted Use

Purpose: To account for Veterans healthcarespending and display the spending by the beneficiary residence.

Applicant Eligibility: Management of healthcare: patient enrollment system(a) In managing the provision of hospital care and medical services under section 1710(a) of this title, the Secretary, in accordance with regulations the Secretary shall prescribe, shall establish and operate a system of annual patient enrollment. The Secretary shall manage the enrollment of veterans in accordance with the following priorities, in the order listed: (1) Veterans with service-connected disabilities rated 50 percent or greater. (2) Veterans with service-connected disabilities rated 30 percent or 40 percent. (3) Veterans who are former prisoners of war or who were awarded the Purple Heart, veterans who were awarded the medal of honor under section 3741, 6241, or 8741 of title 10 or section 491 of title 14, veterans with service-connected disabilities rated 10 percent or 20 percent, and veterans described in subparagraphs (B) and (C) of section 1710(a)(2) of this title. (4) Veterans who are in receipt of increased pension based on a need of regular aid and attendance or by reason of being permanently housebound and other veterans who are catastrophically disabled. (5) Veterans not covered by paragraphs (1) through (4) who are unable to defray the expenses of necessary care as determined under section 1722(a) of this title. (6) All other veterans eligible for hospital care, medical services, and nursing home care under section 1710(a)(2) of this title.

Beneficiary Eligibility: Same as Applicant Eligibility.

HQ: 100 Grandview Road, Suite 114, Braintree, MA 02184
Phone: 781-849-1837 | Email: michelle.staton@va.gov
http://www.va.gov

VA64.046 | VHA INPATIENT PSYCHIATRY
"USASpending.gov"

Award: Direct Payments for Specified Use

Purpose: To account for Veterans healthcarespending and display the spending by the beneficiary residence.

Applicant Eligibility: Management of healthcare: patient enrollment system(a) In managing the provision of hospital care and medical services under section 1710(a) of this title, the Secretary, in accordance with regulations the Secretary shall prescribe, shall establish and operate a system of annual patient enrollment. The Secretary shall manage the enrollment of veterans in accordance with the following priorities, in the order listed: (1) Veterans with service-connected disabilities rated 50 percent or greater. (2) Veterans with service-connected disabilities rated 30 percent or 40 percent. (3) Veterans who are former prisoners of war or who were awarded the Purple Heart, veterans who were awarded the medal of honor under section 3741, 6241, or 8741 of title 10 or section 491 of title 14, veterans with service-connected disabilities rated 10 percent or 20 percent, and veterans described in subparagraphs (B) and (C) of section 1710(a)(2) of this title. (4) Veterans who are in receipt of increased pension based on a need of regular aid and attendance or by reason of being permanently housebound and other veterans who are catastrophically disabled. (5) Veterans not covered by paragraphs (1) through (4) who are unable to defray the expenses of necessary care as determined under section 1722(a) of this title. (6) All other veterans eligible for hospital care, medical services, and nursing home care under section 1710(a)(2) of this title.

Beneficiary Eligibility: Same as Applicant Eligibility.

Award Range/Average: According to the cost of the services.

HQ: 100 Grandview Road, Suite 114, Braintree, MA 02184
   Phone: 781-849-1837 | Email: michelle.staton@va.gov
   http://www.va.gov

VA64.042 | VHA INPATIENT SURGERY
"USASpending.gov"

Award: Direct Payments for Specified Use

Purpose: To account for Veterans healthcarespending and display the spending by the beneficiary residence.

Applicant Eligibility: Management of healthcare: patient enrollment system(a) In managing the provision of hospital care and medical services under section 1710(a) of this title, the Secretary, in accordance with regulations the Secretary shall prescribe, shall establish and operate a system of annual patient enrollment. The Secretary shall manage the enrollment of veterans in accordance with the following priorities, in the order listed: (1) Veterans with service-connected disabilities rated 50 percent or greater. (2) Veterans with service-connected disabilities rated 30 percent or 40 percent. (3) Veterans who are former prisoners of war or who were awarded the Purple Heart, veterans who were awarded the medal of honor under section 3741, 6241, or 8741 of title 10 or section 491 of title 14, veterans with service-connected disabilities rated 10 percent or 20 percent, and veterans described in subparagraphs (B) and (C) of section 1710(a)(2) of this title. (4) Veterans who are in receipt of increased pension based on a need of regular aid and attendance or by reason of being permanently housebound and other veterans who are catastrophically disabled. (5) Veterans not covered by paragraphs (1) through (4) who are unable to defray the expenses of necessary care as determined under section 1722(a) of this title. (6) All other veterans eligible for hospital care, medical services, and nursing home care under section 1710(a)(2) of this title.

Beneficiary Eligibility: Same as Applicant Eligibility.

HQ: 100 Grandview Road, Suite 114, Braintree, MA 02184
   Phone: 781-849-1837 | Email: michelle.staton@va.gov
   http://www.va.gov

VA64.048 | VHA MENTAL HEALTH CLINICS
"USASpending.gov"

Award: Direct Payments for Specified Use

Purpose: To account for Veterans healthcarespending and display the spending by the beneficiary residence.

Applicant Eligibility: 38 USC 1705: patient enrollment system Text contains those laws in effect on December 1, 2013From Title 38-VETERANS' BENEFITSPART II-GENERAL BENEFITSCHAPTER 17-HOSPITAL, NURSING HOME, DOMICILIARY, AND MEDICAL CARESUBCHAPTER I-GENERAL1705. Management of healthcare: patient enrollment system(a) In managing the provision of hospital care and medical services under section 1710(a) of this title, the Secretary, in accordance with regulations the Secretary shall prescribe, shall establish and operate a system of annual patient enrollment. The Secretary shall manage the enrollment of veterans in accordance with the following priorities, in the order listed: (1) Veterans with service-connected disabilities rated 50 percent or greater. (2) Veterans with service-connected disabilities rated 30 percent or 40 percent. (3) Veterans who are former prisoners of war or who were awarded the Purple Heart, veterans who were awarded the medal of honor under section 3741, 6241, or 8741 of title 10 or section 491 of title 14, veterans with service-connected disabilities rated 10 percent or 20 percent, and veterans described in subparagraphs (B) and (C) of section 1710(a)(2) of this title. (4) Veterans who are in receipt of increased pension based on a need of regular aid and attendance or by reason of being permanently housebound and other veterans who are catastrophically disabled. (5) Veterans not covered by paragraphs (1) through (4) who are unable to defray the expenses of necessary care as determined under section 1722(a) of this title. (6) All other veterans eligible for hospital care, medical services, and nursing home care under section 1710(a)(2) of this title.

Beneficiary Eligibility: Veterans are eligible for services under Title 38 USC 1705: Management of health care: patient enrollment system.

Award Range/Average: According to the cost of the services

HQ: 100 Grandview Road, Suite 114, Braintree, MA 02184

Phone: 781-849-1837 | Email: michelle.staton@va.gov

http://www.va.gov

VA64.043 | VHA MENTAL HEALTH RESIDENTIAL
"USASpending.gov"

Award: Direct Payments for Specified Use

Purpose: To account for Veterans healthcarespending and display the spending by the beneficiary residence.

Applicant Eligibility: Management of healthcare: patient enrollment system(a) In managing the provision of hospital care and medical services under section 1710(a) of this title, the Secretary, in accordance with regulations the Secretary shall prescribe, shall establish and operate a system of annual patient enrollment. The Secretary shall manage the enrollment of veterans in accordance with the following priorities, in the order listed: (1) Veterans with service-connected disabilities rated 50 percent or greater. (2) Veterans with service-connected disabilities rated 30 percent or 40 percent. (3) Veterans who are former prisoners of war or who were awarded the Purple Heart, veterans who were awarded the medal of honor under section 3741, 6241, or 8741 of title 10 or section 491 of title 14, veterans with service-connected disabilities rated 10 percent or 20 percent, and veterans described in subparagraphs (B) and (C) of section 1710(a)(2) of this title. (4) Veterans who are in receipt of increased pension based on a need of regular aid and attendance or by reason of being permanently housebound and other veterans who are catastrophically disabled. (5) Veterans not covered by paragraphs (1) through (4) who are unable to defray the expenses of necessary care as determined under section 1722(a) of this title. (6) All other veterans eligible for hospital care, medical services, and nursing home care under section 1710(a)(2) of this title.

Beneficiary Eligibility: Same as Applicant Eligibility.

Award Range/Average: According to the cost of the services.

HQ: 100 Grandview Road, Suite 114, Braintree, MA 02184

Phone: 781-849-1837 | Email: michelle.staton@va.gov

http://www.va.gov

VA64.045 | VHA OUTPATIENT ANCILLARY SERVICES
"USASpending.gov"

Award: Direct Payments for Specified Use

Purpose: To account for Veterans healthcarespending and display the spending by the beneficiary residence.

Applicant Eligibility: Management of healthcare: patient enrollment system(a) In managing the provision of hospital care and medical services under section 1710(a) of this title, the Secretary, in accordance with regulations the Secretary shall prescribe, shall establish and operate a system of annual patient enrollment. The Secretary shall manage the enrollment of veterans in accordance with the following priorities, in the order listed: (1) Veterans with service-connected disabilities rated 50 percent or greater. (2) Veterans with service-connected disabilities rated 30 percent or 40 percent. (3) Veterans who are former prisoners of war or who were awarded the Purple Heart, veterans who were awarded the medal of honor under section 3741, 6241, or 8741 of title 10 or section 491 of title 14, veterans with service-connected disabilities rated 10 percent or 20 percent, and veterans described in subparagraphs (B) and (C) of section 1710(a)(2) of this title. (4) Veterans who are in receipt of increased pension based on a need of regular aid and attendance or by reason of being permanently housebound and other veterans who are catastrophically disabled. (5) Veterans not covered by paragraphs (1) through (4) who are unable to defray the expenses of necessary care as determined under section 1722(a) of this title. (6) All other veterans eligible for hospital care, medical services, and nursing home care under section 1710(a)(2) of this title.

Beneficiary Eligibility: Same as Applicant Eligibility.

Award Range/Average: According to the cost of the services.

HQ: 100 Grandview Road, Suite 114, Braintree, MA 02184

Phone: 781-849-1837 | Email: michelle.staton@va.gov

http://www.va.gov

Programs Administered by Federal Headquarters

VA64.041 | VHA OUTPATIENT SPECIALTY CARE
"USASpending.gov"
Award: Direct Payments for Specified Use
Purpose: To account for Veterans healthcarespending and display the spending by the beneficiary residence.
Applicant Eligibility: Management of healthcare: patient enrollment system(a) In managing the provision of hospital care and medical services under section 1710(a) of this title, the Secretary, in accordance with regulations the Secretary shall prescribe, shall establish and operate a system of annual patient enrollment. The Secretary shall manage the enrollment of veterans in accordance with the following priorities, in the order listed: (1) Veterans with service-connected disabilities rated 50 percent or greater. (2) Veterans with service-connected disabilities rated 30 percent or 40 percent. (3) Veterans who are former prisoners of war or who were awarded the Purple Heart, veterans who were awarded the medal of honor under section 3741, 6241, or 8741 of title 10 or section 491 of title 14, veterans with service-connected disabilities rated 10 percent or 20 percent, and veterans described in subparagraphs (B) and (C) of section 1710(a)(2) of this title. (4) Veterans who are in receipt of increased pension based on a need of regular aid and attendance or by reason of being permanently housebound and other veterans who are catastrophically disabled. (5) Veterans not covered by paragraphs (1) through (4) who are unable to defray the expenses of necessary care as determined under section 1722(a) of this title. (6) All other veterans eligible for hospital care, medical services, and nursing home care under section 1710(a)(2) of this title.
Beneficiary Eligibility: Same as Applicant Eligibility.
Award Range/Average: According to the cost of services
HQ: 100 Grandview Road, Suite 114, Braintree, MA 02184
Phone: 781-849-1837 | Email: michelle.staton@va.gov
http://www.va.gov

VA64.047 | VHA PRIMARY CARE
"USASpending.gov"
Award: Direct Payments for Specified Use
Purpose: To account for Veterans healthcarespending and display the spending by the beneficiary residence.
Applicant Eligibility: Management of healthcare: patient enrollment system(a) In managing the provision of hospital care and medical services under section 1710(a) of this title, the Secretary, in accordance with regulations the Secretary shall prescribe, shall establish and operate a system of annual patient enrollment. The Secretary shall manage the enrollment of veterans in accordance with the following priorities, in the order listed: (1) Veterans with service-connected disabilities rated 50 percent or greater. (2) Veterans with service-connected disabilities rated 30 percent or 40 percent. (3) Veterans who are former prisoners of war or who were awarded the Purple Heart, veterans who were awarded the medal of honor under section 3741, 6241, or 8741 of title 10 or section 491 of title 14, veterans with service-connected disabilities rated 10 percent or 20 percent, and veterans described in subparagraphs (B) and (C) of section 1710(a)(2) of this title. (4) Veterans who are in receipt of increased pension based on a need of regular aid and attendance or by reason of being permanently housebound and other veterans who are catastrophically disabled. (5) Veterans not covered by paragraphs (1) through (4) who are unable to defray the expenses of necessary care as determined under section 1722(a) of this title. (6) All other veterans eligible for hospital care, medical services, and nursing home care under section 1710(a)(2) of this title.
Beneficiary Eligibility: Same as Applicant Eligibility.
Award Range/Average: According to the cost of the services.
HQ: 100 Grandview Road, Suite 114, Braintree, MA 02184
Phone: 781-849-1837 | Email: michelle.staton@va.gov
http://www.va.gov

DOJ16.587 | VIOLENCE AGAINST WOMEN DISCRETIONARY GRANTS FOR INDIAN TRIBAL GOVERNMENTS
Award: Project Grants
Purpose: To increase tribal capacity to respond to violent crimes against Indian women and to develop and strengthen victim services in cases involving violent crimes against the Indian women.
Applicant Eligibility: Indian tribal Governments and authorized designees of tribal Governments. The term "tribal government" means - (A) the governing body of an Indian tribe; or (B) a tribe, band, pueblo, nation, or other organized group or community of Indians, including any Alaska Native village or regional or village corporation (as defined in, or established

pursuant to, the Alaska Native Claims Settlement Act (43 U.S.C. 1601 et seq.)), that is recognized as eligible for the special Programs and services provided by the United States to Indians because of their status as Indians.

Beneficiary Eligibility: Tribal governments and authorized designees of tribal governments.

Funding: (Project Grants) FY 16 $33,647,321.00; FY 17 est $34,137,475.00; FY 18 est $33,500,000.00

HQ: 145 N Street NE, Suite 10W121, Washington, DC 20530
Phone: 202-305-1177 | Email: tia.farmer@usdoj.gov
http://www.justice.gov/tribal/grants.html

DOJ16.588 | VIOLENCE AGAINST WOMEN FORMULA GRANTS
"STOP Violence Against Women Formula Grants"

Award: Formula Grants

Purpose: To develop and strengthen effective law enforcement and prosecution strategies to combat violent crimes against women and develop and strengthen victim services in cases involving crimes against women.

Applicant Eligibility: All States, Puerto Rico, Guam, American Samoa, the Virgin Islands, the Northern Mariana Islands, and the District of Columbia, are eligible.

Beneficiary Eligibility: State and local units of government, nonprofit nongovernmental victim service programs, state, local, and tribal courts, and Indian tribal governments.

Award Range/Average: Range: $616,994 - $12,654,241

Funding: (Formula Grants) FY 16 $151,085,699.00; FY 17 est $150,050,789.00; FY 18 est $150,050,000.00

HQ: 145 N Street NE, Suite 10W121, Washington, DC 20530
Phone: 202-305-1177 | Email: tia.farmer@usdoj.gov
http://www.justice.gov/ovw

HHS93.270 | VIRAL HEPATITIS PREVENTION AND CONTROL
"Viral Hepatitis Prevention, Screening, Linkage to Care, and Education"

Award: Cooperative Agreements

Purpose: Funding will allow for CDC to partner with multiple organizations to benefit individuals by substantially reducing viral hepatitis transmission, identifying those that are acutely and chronically infected, and linking infected individuals with treatment if appropriate.

Applicant Eligibility: Applicants include State or local Governments or their Bona Fide Agents, public and private nonprofit Organizations, for profit Organizations, small, minority, women-owned businesses, universities, colleges, research Institutions, hospitals, community-based Organizations, faith based Organizations, Federally recognized Indian tribal Governments, Indian Tribes, and Indian tribal Organizations. Additional guidance may be provided in individual Program announcements. In addition, funds may be used for costs associated with establishing and maintaining a prevention and control Program directed towards prevention of viral hepatitis infections and their manifestations. Recipients may only expend funds for reasonable policies, systems and Program purposes including personnel, travel, supplies and services, such as reducing transmission of HAV, HBV and HCV, preventing and delaying the progress of chronic infection, as well as educating and training of the general public and healthcare providers. Recipients may not use funds for clinical care. Recipients may not generally use funding for the purchase of furniture or equipment. Any such proposed spending must be identified in the budget. The recipient must perform a substantial role in carrying out project objectives and not merely serve as a conduit for an award in another party or provider who is eligible.

Beneficiary Eligibility: The individual will benefit from the objectives of this program as well as the community at large, and society from the savings realized from treating those who are infected with viral hepatitis.

Award Range/Average: Awards will range from approximately $30,000 to $500,000, with an average award of $150,000.

Funding: (Cooperative Agreements) FY 18 $39,664,480.00; FY 19 est $41,774,015.00; FY 20 est $22,500,000.00

HQ: 1600 Clifton Road NE, PO Box G37, Atlanta, GA 30333
Phone: 404-718-8504 | Email: jle1@cdc.gov
http://www.cdc.gov

CPSC87.002 | VIRGINIA GRAEME BAKER POOL AND SPA SAFETY

Award: Project Grants

Purpose: To reduce the number of drowning and drain entrapment-related injuries and deaths of children associated with pools and spas.

Programs Administered by Federal Headquarters

Applicant Eligibility: Local Governments, including a county, municipality, city, town, township, local public authority, school district, special district, intrastate district, council of Governments (whether or not incorporated as a non-profit corporation under State law), any other regional or interstate government entity, or any agency or instrumentality of a local government. To be eligible for an award under this Program, an applicant shall demonstrate that it has enacted a State statute or local ordinance or code, or has amended an existing State statute or local ordinance or code, that meets the requirements specified in title XIV - Pool and Spa Safety Bill (15 U.S.C. 8001), Sections 1405 and 1406 of the Virginia Graeme Baker Pool and Spa Safety Act. Grant awards will be determined in accordance with CFR 2, Parts 255 (OMB Circular A-87), and OMB Circular No. A-102.

Beneficiary Eligibility: State, local, U.S. Territories/Possessions, Consumers.

Award Range/Average: Not Applicable.

Funding: (Project Grants) FY 15 Not Separately Identifiable; FY 16 est $781,536.00; FY 17 Estimate Not Available

HQ: 4330 E W Highway, Bethesda, MD 20814

Phone: 301-504-7261 | Email: apiesen@cpsc.gov

http://www.cpsc.gov

HHS93.867 | VISION RESEARCH

Award: Project Grants

Purpose: To support eye and vision research projects that address the leading causes of blindness and impaired vision in the U.S.

Applicant Eligibility: Public/State-controlled Institutions of higher education, private Institutions of higher education, Hispanic-serving Institutions, Historically Black Colleges and universities, tribally-controlled colleges and universities, Alaska Native- and Native Hawaiian-serving Institutions, nonprofits with or without 501(c)(3) IRS status, Small businesses, for-profit Organizations, federal Institutions, and State and local units of government are eligible to make application for research grants, cooperative agreements, and career development awards. Foreign Institutions may apply for research grants and cooperative agreements only. The grantee institution must agree to administer the grant in accordance with prevailing regulations and policies. Candidates for the Mentored Clinical Scientist Development and Mentored-Patient Oriented Research Career Awards are restricted to those holding health professional degrees in the clinical sciences (M.D., O.D., D.D.S., D.V.M., or equivalent). Individual and institutional NRSAs are provided for predoctoral and postdoctoral research training. Individual postdoctoral NRSAs may be made for applicants who hold a professional or scientific degree (M.D., Ph.D., O.D., D.D.S., D.V.M., Sc.D., D.Eng., or equivalent degree). Predoctoral awardees must have completed the baccalaureate degree. All awardees must be citizens of the United States, or have been admitted to the U.S. for permanent residence prior to award. Individual NRSA awardees must be nominated and sponsored by a Federal, public or private nonprofit institution having staff and facilities suitable to the proposed research training. Federal and for-profit Organizations, and State and local Governments may not apply for an institutional NRSA. Refer to the NIH Program Guidelines on NRSAs for further information. The Small Business Innovation grants: SBIRs can be awarded only to domestic small businesses (entities that are independently owned and operated for profit, are not dominant in the field in which research is proposed, and have not more than 500 employees). Primary employment (more than one-half time) of the Principal Investigator must be with the small business at the time of the award and during the conduct of the proposed project. The research during both Phase I and Phase II must be performed in the U.S. or its possessions. STTR grants can be awarded only to domestic small business concerns (entities that are independently owned and operated for profit, are not dominant in the field in which research is proposed and have no more than 500 employees) which "partner" with a research institution in cooperative research and development. At least 40 percent of the project is to be performed by the small business concern and at least 30 percent by the research institution. In both Phase I and Phase II, the research must be performed in the U.S. and its possessions. Individuals applying for the NIH Loan Repayment Programs must be engaged in patient oriented research and be trained in a medical subspecialty as defined under Section 206 of Public Law 106-505. These individuals must be U.S. citizens, U.S. citizen nationals, or lawfully admitted for permanent residence in the U.S.; have a student loan debt which equals or exceeds 20 percent of their University compensation; have no Federal judgment lien against their property arising from a Federal debt; and owe no obligation of health professional service to the Federal government, a State, or other entity unless deferrals are granted during the length of their Loan Repayment Program service obligation.

Beneficiary Eligibility: Any nonprofit or for-profit organization, company, or institution engaged in biomedical research.

Award Range/Average: Grants and Cooperative Agreements: $13,587 to $4,500,000; $777,643. NRSA (Institutional): $25,240 to $505,935; $162,521. NRSA (Individual): $10,576 to $63,078; $ 45,562. SBIR Phase I: $136,774 to $299,999; $216,691. SBIR Phase II: $171,203 to $1,165,695; $499,120. STTR Phase I: $147,349 to $299,999; $206,034 STTR Phase II: $136,774 to $899,580; $684,190.

Funding: (Project Grants) FY 17 $572,203,845.00; FY 18 est $602,608,017.00; FY 19 est $562,363,947.00

HQ: 6700B Rockledge Drive, Room 3438, Bethesda, MD 20892

Phone: 301-451-2020 | Email: paul.sheehy@nih.gov

http://www.nei.nih.gov

VEF85.803 | VISITING SCHOLAR GRANTS
"VEF Visiting Scholar Grants"

Award: Project Grants
Purpose: Promotes international exchange and cooperation between the United States and Vietnam, through educational exchanges.
Applicant Eligibility: Grants cover living expenses and expenses related to the professional development of the Visiting Scholar while they are pursuing their approved project/course of study at a U.S. University.
Beneficiary Eligibility: Grants cover living expenses and expenses related to the professional development of the Visiting Scholar while they are pursuing their approved project/course of study at a U.S. university. Scholars must be Vietnamese citizens and must have completed a doctoral degree.
Award Range/Average: Financial assistance is limited to $2,300 per month as a stipend and up to $300 per month for professional development for no less than 5 months and for no more than 12 months. Funds may be spent as specified in the VEF Professional Development Grant policy. Funding may be provided for a project/course of study from 5 to 12 months. In FY 2015, up to 3 Visiting Scholar grants may be funded.
Funding: (Project Grants (Fellowships)) FY 12 Not Separately Identifiable; FY 13 est Not Separately Identifiable; FY 14 est Not Separately Identifiable
HQ: 2111 Wilson Boulevard, Suite 700, Arlington, VA 22201
   Phone: 703-351-5053 | Email: margaretpetrochenkov@vef.gov
   http://www.vef.gov

DOJ16.841 | VOCA TRIBAL VICTIM SERVICES SET-ASIDE PROGRAM
"VOCA Tribal Set-Aside Program"

Award: Project Grants
Purpose: To provide support to Indian tribes through the Tribal Set-Aside Training and Technical Assistance Program to assist crime victims and provide technical assistance for Indian tribes and tribal consortia.
Applicant Eligibility: Indian Tribes and tribal consortia (NOTE: eligible applicants may also include tribal Organizations and Organizations that directly serve Indian Tribes).
Beneficiary Eligibility: The following will receive the ultimate benefits of the funding: Federally-Recognized Indian Tribal Governments Native American Organizations American Indians/Alaska Natives.
Award Range/Average: In FY19: Tribal Set-Aside: Up to $720,000 per award
Funding: (Cooperative Agreements (Discretionary Grants)) FY 18 $121,808,565.00; FY 19 est $167,650,000.00; FY 20 est $115,000,000.00
HQ: 810 7th Street NW, Washington, DC 20531
   Phone: 202-307-5983 | Email: allison.turkel@ojp.usdoj.gov
   http://www.ovc.gov

VA64.125 | VOCATIONAL AND EDUCATIONAL COUNSELING FOR SERVICEMEMBERS AND VETERANS
"Chapter 36 Counseling"

Award: Advisory Services and Counseling
Purpose: To offer vocational and educational counseling to service members within 180 days of their projected discharge or release from active duty and to veterans within one year from the date of their discharge or release from active duty.
Applicant Eligibility: Service members must be within 180 days of projected discharge or release from active duty. Veterans must be within 1 year from the date of discharge or release from active duty. For servicemembers, the projected discharge or release from active duty must be under conditions other than dishonorable. For veterans, the discharge or release from active duty must have been under conditions other than dishonorable. This counseling is also available to individuals who are eligible for VA educational assistance including: Chapter 30 - All-Volunteer Force educational Assistance Program; Chapter 31 - Vocational Rehabilitation and Employment; Chapter 32 - Post-Vietnam Era Veterans' educational Assistance; Chapter 33 - Post 9/11 educational Assistance; Chapter 35 - Survivors' and Dependents' educational Assistance; Chapter 1606 - educational Assistance for Members of the Selective Service; and Chapter 1607 - Reserve educational Assistance Program.
Beneficiary Eligibility: Service members must be within 180 days of projected discharge or release from active duty. Veterans must be within 1 year from the date of discharge or release from active duty. For service members, the projected discharge or release from active duty must be under conditions other than dishonorable. For veterans, the discharge or release from

active duty must have been under conditions other than dishonorable. This counselling is also available to individuals who are eligible for VA educational assistance including: Chapter 30 - All-Volunteer Force Educational Assistance Program; Chapter 31 - Vocational Rehabilitation and Employment; Chapter 32 - Post-Vietnam Era Veterans' Educational Assistance; Chapter 33 - Post 9/11 Educational Assistance; Chapter 35 - Survivors' and Dependents' Educational Assistance; Chapter 1606 - Educational Assistance for Members of the Selective Service; and Chapter 1607 - Reserve Educational Assistance Program.

Award Range/Average: Not Applicable.

HQ: 810 Vermont Avenue NW, Washington, DC 20420

Phone: 202-461-9600

http://www.va.gov

VA64.116 | VOCATIONAL REHABILITATION FOR DISABLED VETERANS
"Vocational Rehabilitation"

Award: Direct Payments With Unrestricted Use

Purpose: To provide all services and assistance necessary to enable service-disabled veterans and service persons hospitalized or receiving outpatient medical care services or treatment for a service- connected disability pending discharge to get and keep a suitable job.

Applicant Eligibility: Veterans of World War II and later service with a service-connected disability or disabilities rated at least 20 percent compensable and certain service-disabled servicepersons pending discharge or release from service if VA determines the servicepersons will likely receive at least a 20 percent rating and they need vocational rehabilitation because of an employment handicap. Veterans with a 10 percent service-connected disability may be eligible if they first applied for vocational rehabilitation prior to November 1, 1990, and they have an employment handicap. In addition, veterans with compensable ratings of 10 percent may also be eligible if they are found to have a serious employment handicap.

Beneficiary Eligibility: Veterans of World War II and later service with a service-connected disability or disabilities rated at least 20 percent compensable and certain service-disabled servicepersons pending discharge or release from service if VA determines the servicepersons will likely receive at least a 20 percent rating and they need vocational rehabilitation because of an employment handicap. Veterans with compensable ratings of 10 percent may also be eligible if they are found to have a serious employment handicap.

Award Range/Average: Full cost of tuition, books, fees, supplies and rehabilitation services. Monthly full-time allowances for veterans participating in training during fiscal year 2009 range from $541.05 for a single veteran to $790.87 for a veteran with two dependents, plus $57.65 for each dependent in excess of two. Non-interest bearing loans of up to $1,082.10 and a work-study allowance not to exceed the higher of 25 times the Federal or State minimum hourly wage times the number of weeks in the enrollment.

HQ: 810 Vermont Avenue NW, Washington, DC 20420

Phone: 202-461-9600

http://www.va.gov

VA64.128 | VOCATIONAL TRAINING AND REHABILITATION FOR VIETNAM VETERANS' CHILDREN WITH SPINA BIFIDA OR OTHER COVERED BIRTH DEFECTS

Award: Direct Payments With Unrestricted Use

Purpose: Provides vocational training and rehabilitation to certain children born with spina bifida or other covered birth defects who are children of Vietnam veterans and some Korean veterans.

Applicant Eligibility: A child born with spina bifida or other covered birth defects, except spina bifida occulta, who is the natural child of a Vietnam veteran and some Korean veterans, regardless of the age or marital status of the child, conceived after the date on which the veteran first served in the Republic of Vietnam during the Vietnam era and in particular areas near the DMZ in the Korean conflict. VA must also determine that it is feasible for the child to achieve a vocational goal.

Beneficiary Eligibility: Children born with spina bifida.

HQ: 810 Vermont Avenue NW, Washington, DC 20420

Phone: 202-461-9600

http://www.va.gov

CNCS94.021 | VOLUNTEER GENERATION FUND

Award: Project Grants

Purpose: The Volunteer Generation Fund helps to expand the volunteer capacity through recruitment, management, support and retention of volunteers, especially during days of high-quality assignments such as 11th National Day of Service and Remembrance.

Applicant Eligibility: Use of assistance must be consistent with the funded, approved grant application.

Beneficiary Eligibility: N/A

Award Range/Average: See program's Notice of Federal Funding for matching information.

Funding: (Project Grants) FY 16 $3,879,866.00; FY 17 est $3,800,000.00; FY 18 Estimate Not Available

HQ: Grants and Initiatives 250 E Street SW, Washington, DC 20525

    Phone: 202-606-6745 | Email: pstengel@cns.gov

    http://www.nationalservice.gov/programs/volunteer-generation-fund

TREAS21.009 | VOLUNTEER INCOME TAX ASSISTANCE (VITA) MATCHING GRANT PROGRAM

Award: Project Grants

Purpose: To provide direct funding that will enable VITA initiatives to extend services to underserved populations and hardest-to-reach areas, both urban and non-urban; specific objectives as they relate to the VITA Program.

Applicant Eligibility: Non-profit Organization or state or government entity.

Beneficiary Eligibility: Providing assistance to low to moderate income individuals and families.

Funding: (Project Grants (Discretionary)) FY 18 $15,000,000.00; FY 19 est $15,000,000.00; FY 20 est $15,000,000.00

HQ: 401 W Peachtree Street NW, PO Box 420-D, Atlanta, GA 30308

    Phone: 404-338-7894

    http://www.irs.gov

HHS93.618 | VOTING ACCESS FOR INDIVIDUALS WITH DISABILITIES-GRANTS FOR PROTECTION AND ADVOCACY SYSTEMS
"PAVA"

Award: Formula Grants; Project Grants

Purpose: Section 291 of HAVA provides that funds be made available to Protection and Advocacy Systems to: ensure full participation in the electoral process for individuals with disabilities.

Applicant Eligibility: States and Territories who have a Protection and Advocacy System in place in accordance with the Developmental Disabilities Assistance and Bill of Rights Act of 2000 with the exception of the Commonwealth of the Northern Mariana Islands and Native Americans.

Beneficiary Eligibility: Individuals with a full-range of disabilities.

Award Range/Average: The awards range from $35,000 to $348,000. The average award amount is approximately $144,000.

Funding: (Formula Grants) FY 16 $4,963,000.00; FY 17 est $4,963,000.00; FY 18 Estimate Not Available

HQ: 330 C Street SW, Washington, DC 20201

    Phone: 202-795-7472 | Email: melvenia.wright@acl.hhs.gov

    http://www.acl.gov/Programs/AIDD/Index.aspx

USDA10.770 | WATER AND WASTE DISPOSAL LOANS AND GRANTS (SECTION 306C)
"Section 306C"

Award: Project Grants; Direct Loans

Purpose: To provide for the low-income rural communities who face significant health risks with water and waste disposal facilities.

Applicant Eligibility: Local level Governments, Indian Tribes on Federal and State reservations, and other federally recognized Indian Tribes, U.S. Territories and possessions, and nonprofit associations can receive assistance under this Program. Except for rural areas known as "Colonia" along the U.S. /Mexico border, the projects funded under this Program must primarily provide water and/or waste disposal services to residents of a county where the per capita income of the residents is not more

Programs Administered by Federal Headquarters

than 70 percent of the most recent national average per capita income, as determined by the U.S. Department of Commerce, and unemployment rate of the residents is not less than 125 percent of the most recent national average unemployment rate, as determined by the Bureau of Labor Statistics. Also the residents must face significant health risks due to not having access to an affordable community water and/or waste disposal system.

Beneficiary Eligibility: Users of the applicant systems, which are previously described as public bodies, private nonprofit corporations, Indian tribes, and individuals.

Award Range/Average: Colonias Grants - $20,000 to $8,030,000 Average: $2,405,293. Native American Tribe Grants - $52,000 to $2,000,000 Average: $1,193,199

Funding: (Project Grants (Discretionary)) FY 18 $56,325,978.00; FY 19 est $50,000,000.00; FY 20 est $50,000,000.00

HQ: 1400 Independence Avenue SW, Washington, DC 20250

　　Phone: 202-720-0986 | Email: edna.primrose@wdc.usda.gov

　　http://www.rd.usda.gov

USDA10.760 | WATER AND WASTE DISPOSAL SYSTEMS FOR RURAL COMMUNITIES

Award: Project Grants; Direct Loans; Guaranteed/insured Loans

Purpose: To compensate for financially distressed communities for water and waste projects.

Applicant Eligibility: Municipalities, counties, other political subdivisions of a State such as districts and authorities, associations, cooperatives, corporations operated on a not-for-profit basis, Indian Tribes on Federal and State reservations and other Federally recognized Indian Tribes. The applicant must: (1) be unable to finance the proposed project from its own resources or through commercial credit at reasonable rates and terms; and (2) have the legal authority necessary for constructing, operating, and maintaining the proposed facility or service, and for obtaining, giving security for, and repaying the proposed loan. Assistance is authorized for eligible applicants in rural areas of the United States, Puerto Rico, the Virgin Islands, Guam, Commonwealth of Northern Mariana Islands, American Samoa, and to the extent the Secretary determines feasible and appropriate, the Trust Territory of the Pacific Islands.

Beneficiary Eligibility: Users of the applicant systems, which are previously described as public bodies, private nonprofit corporations, Indian tribes, and individuals.

Award Range/Average: (Direct Loans) $16,000 to $9,900,000; average $2,354,392 (Grants) $8,000 to $22,437,000; average $1,284,000 (Guaranteed/Insured Loans) $450,000 to $7,371,000; average $1,415,325

Funding: (Direct Loans) FY 18 $1,911,766,480; FY 19 est $1,540,000,000.00; FY 20 est $1,200,000,000.00; (Guaranteed/Insured Loans) FY 18 $25,486,642.00; FY 19 est $50,000,000.00; FY 20 est $$0.00; (Project Grants) FY 18 $857,712,118.00; FY 19 est $448,682,500.00; FY 20 est $418,357,000.00

HQ: 1400 Independence Avenue SW, PO Box 1548, Washington, DC 20250

　　Phone: 202-690-2670 | Email: edna.primrose@wdc.usda.gov

　　http://www.rd.usda.gov

DOS19.800 | WEAPONS REMOVAL AND ABATEMENT
"PM/WRA"

Award: Cooperative Agreements; Project Grants

Purpose: Reduces the threats posed to civilian security by at-risk, illicitly proliferated, and indiscriminately used conventional weapons.

Applicant Eligibility: All projects must have a clear focus on CWD Program goals and objectives.

Beneficiary Eligibility: N/A

Award Range/Average: Grants range from $25,000 to $30,000,000.

Funding: (Project Grants (Discretionary)) FY 16 $179,532,000.00; FY 17 est $189,000,000.00; FY 18 est $196,900,000.00

HQ: 2121 Virginia Avenue NW, Suite 6100, Washington, DC 20037

　　Phone: 202-663-0085 | Email: murguiace@state.gov

　　http://www.state.gov

DOC11.459 | WEATHER AND AIR QUALITY RESEARCH

Award: Project Grants

Purpose: To analyze and develop scientific information for short and long-term climate changes.

Applicant Eligibility: Universities, colleges, junior colleges, technical schools, Institutions, laboratories; any State, political subdivision of a State or agency or officer thereof; any individual.

Beneficiary Eligibility: Organizations and individuals with interests in meteorology, oceanography, climate, and air-quality research and prediction and organizations and individuals in the social sciences with interests in the linkages between human systems and the aforementioned interest areas.

Funding: (Project Grants (Contracts)) FY 16 $8,838,244.00; FY 17 est $13,094,248.00; FY 18 est $15,430,129.00

HQ: National Oceanic and Atmospheric Administration 1315 E W Highway, Silver Spring, MD 20910

    Phone: 301-713-9397

    http://owaq.noaa.gov

DOC11.606 | WEIGHTS AND MEASURES SERVICE

Award: Provision of Specialized Services; Advisory Services and Counseling; Dissemination of Technical Information; Training

Purpose: To assist with technical resources in all commercial transactions in the U.S. by harmonizing national and international metrology standards to facilitate the metric system.

Applicant Eligibility: States, political subdivisions of States, private industry, and the general public.

Beneficiary Eligibility: Same as Applicant Eligibility.

Award Range/Average: Not Applicable.

Funding: (Sale, Exchange, or Donation of Property and Goods) FY 18 $5,093,400.00; FY 19 est $5,038,400.00; FY 20 est $4,993,400.00

HQ: 100 Bureau Drive, PO Box 8400, Gaithersburg, MD 20899

    Phone: 301-975-4290 | Email: patrick.hovis@nist.gov

    http://www.nist.gov/pml/wmd/index.cfm

HHS93.595 | WELFARE REFORM RESEARCH, EVALUATIONS AND NATIONAL STUDIES
"Welfare Research"

Award: Project Grants

Purpose: Supports research on the benefits, effects, and costs of operating different State welfare programs, including studies on the effects of different programs and the operation of such programs on welfare dependency, employment rates, child well-being, family formation and healthy marriage, illegitimacy, teen pregnancy, and others.

Applicant Eligibility: Grants and cooperative agreements may be made to or with governmental entities, colleges, universities, nonprofit and for-profit Organizations (if fee is waived), and faith- and community-based Organizations. Grants or cooperative agreements cannot be made directly to individuals.

Beneficiary Eligibility: Children, youth, and families, especially low-income families, will benefit.

Award Range/Average: For FY18 there was a single grant continuation for $50,000.

Funding: (Project Grants) FY 18 $50,000.00; FY 19 est $0.00; FY 20 est $800,000.00

HQ: 330 C Street SW 4625A, Washington, DC 20201

    Phone: 202-401-5803 | Email: sheila.celentano@acf.hhs.gov

    http://www.acf.hhs.gov/programs/opre

HHS93.436 | WELL-INTEGRATED SCREENING AND EVALUATION FOR WOMEN ACROSS THE NATION (WISEWOMAN)
"WISEWOMAN"

Award: Cooperative Agreements

Purpose: To fund state health departments and tribal organizations to extend services to improve prevention, detection, and control of CVD risk factors for low-income, uninsured, or underinsured women by offering CVD screening, risk reduction counseling, referral to medical services, referral to programs, and resources to support positive cardiovascular health.

Applicant Eligibility: State and the District of Columbia government; local government or their Bona Fide Agent; U.S. Territory or Possession; Federally Recognized Indian Tribal Government; Native American Organization (American Indian/Alaska native tribally designated Organization). 1. Eligible Applicants: State and local Governments or their Bona Fide Agents (this includes the District of Columbia, the Commonwealth of Puerto Rico, the Virgin Islands, the Commonwealth of the Northern Marianna Islands, American Samoa, Guam, the Federated States of Micronesia, the Republic of the Marshall Islands, and the

Programs Administered by Federal Headquarters

Republic of Palau). American Indian/Alaska Native tribal Governments (federally recognized or state-recognized) American Indian/Alaska native tribally designated Organizations 2. Special Eligibility Requirements: Applicants must be recipients of the NBCCEDP Program funding.

Beneficiary Eligibility: Beneficiaries of this program include: Women who are ages 40-64 and eligible through the National Breast and Cervical Cancer Early Detection Program criteria.

Award Range/Average: Awards are expected to range from $500,000 to $2,500,000 (total award for both Core and innovation Components, were applicable). All activities supported through this NOFO must contribute to health improvements across the target population and across population subgroups. Award recipients must demonstrate significant disease burden to allow the strategies supported by this NOFO to reach a significant proportion of the target population. Funding strategy will also include the awardees' proposed activities and goals, estimated population reach, and program capacity as described in the application.

Funding: (Cooperative Agreements (Discretionary Grants)) FY 18 $16,700,000.00; FY 19 est $16,700,000.00; FY 20 est $16,700,000.00

HQ: 4770 Buford Highway NE, PO Box F75, Atlanta, GA 30341
   Phone: 770-488-6215
   http://www.cdc.gov

HHS93.094 | WELL-INTEGRATED SCREENING AND EVALUATION FOR WOMEN ACROSS THE NATION
"WISEWOMAN"

Award: Cooperative Agreements

Purpose: To improve the cardiovascular health of low-income, uninsured and under-insured women, ages 40-64, who are participants in the National Breast and Cervical Cancer Early Detection Program (NBCCEDP).

Applicant Eligibility: Applicants must be recipients of the National Breast and Cervical Cancer Early Detection Program (NBCCEDP).

Beneficiary Eligibility: Low Income, uninsured or under-insured women.

Award Range/Average: Awards will range from approximately $500,000 to $2,000,000 with an average of approximately $780,000.

Funding: (Cooperative Agreements) FY 18 $16,700,000.00; FY 19 est $16,700,000.00; FY 20 est $16,700,000.00

USDA10.129 | WILDFIRES AND HURRICANES INDEMNITY PROGRAM PLUS
"WHIP Plus"

Award: Direct Payments With Unrestricted Use

Purpose: Reimburses bush, crop, tree, and vine producers who suffered losses due to disaster events in 2018 or 2019.

Applicant Eligibility: Agriculture producers are eligible to apply.

Beneficiary Eligibility: N/A

Award Range/Average: Producers are subject to a $125,000 payment limitation for all eligible losses under WHIP+. A producer can receive a higher payment if three-fourths or more of their income is derived from farming or another agricultural-based business. Producers who derived 75 percent of their income in tax years 2015,2016, and 2017 will be subject to a $900,000 payment limitation for all eligible losses under WHIP+.

HQ: 1400 Independence Avenue SW, Washington, DC 20228
   Phone: 202-720-9882 | Email: jennifer.fiser@usda.gov

USDA10.318 | WOMEN AND MINORITIES IN SCIENCE, TECHNOLOGY, ENGINEERING, AND MATHEMATICS FIELDS
"WAMS; Women and Minorities in Science, Technology, Engineering, and Mathematics Fields (STEM) program"

Award: Project Grants

Purpose: The WAMS supports women by providing them the education in the fields such as Science, Technology, Engineering, and Mathematics. STEM supports women in rural areas by providing them with career and other skills necessary.

Applicant Eligibility: State agricultural experiment stations; colleges and universities; University research foundations; other research Institutions and Organizations; Federal agencies; national laboratories; private Organizations or corporations; individuals; or any group consisting of 2 or more of these entities.

Beneficiary Eligibility: Same as Applicant Eligibility.

Award Range/Average: If minimum or maximum amounts of funding per competitive and/or capacity project grant, or cooperative agreement are established, these amounts will be announced in the annual Competitive Request for Application (RFA).

Funding: (Cooperative Agreements (Discretionary Grants)) FY 17 $378,600.00; FY 18 est $363,000.00; FY 19 est $0.00

HQ: 1400 Independence Avenue SW, PO Box 2250, Washington, DC 20024-2250

Phone: 202-720-2324

http://nifa.usda.gov/program/women-and-minorities-science-technology-engineering-and-mathematics-fields-grant-program

DOL17.701 | WOMEN IN APPRENTICESHIP AND NONTRADITIONAL OCCUPATIONS ("WANTO") TECHNICAL ASSISTANCE GRANT PROGRAM
"WANTO Grants"

Award: Project Grants (for Specified Projects)

Purpose: To provide technical assistance to employers and labour unions to encourage women employment in apprenticeship and nontraditional occupations.

Applicant Eligibility: Community Based Organizations (CBOs).

Beneficiary Eligibility: N/A

Award Range/Average: Between (2) and six (6) grants of $250,000 to $500,000

Funding: (Project Grants (for specified projects)) FY 18 $1,403,190.00; FY 19 est $1,500,000.00; FY 20 est $1,500,000.00

HQ: 200 Constitution Avenue NW, Washington, DC 20210

Phone: 202-693-6710 | Email: daniel.reeba@dol.gov

https://www.dol.gov/wb/media/wantogrants.htm

DOL17.700 | WOMEN'S BUREAU

Award: Advisory Services and Counseling

Purpose: To formulate standards and policies to promote the welfare of wage-earning women, improve their working conditions, increase their efficiency, and advance their opportunities for profitable employment.

Applicant Eligibility: Any individual or group located in the United States or its territories may benefit from Women's Bureau projects and/or Programs. The Women's Bureau does not provide financial assistance to individuals.

Beneficiary Eligibility: Any individual or group (especially women or women's organizations) located in the United States or its territories may benefit from Women's Bureau projects and/or programs. The Women's Bureau does not provide financial assistance to individuals.

Award Range/Average: The Women's Bureau does not provide financial assistance to individuals.

Funding: (Salaries and Expenses) FY 16 $11,529,084.00; FY 17 est $11,330,000.00; FY 18 est $2,925,000.00

HQ: 200 Constitution Avenue NW, Room S3002, Washington, DC 20210

Phone: 202-693-6710

http://www.dol.gov/wb

SBA59.043 | WOMEN'S BUSINESS OWNERSHIP ASSISTANCE
"Women's Business Center"

Award: Project Grants

Purpose: To fund private, nonprofit organizations to assist, through training and counseling, small business concerns owned and controlled by women and to remove.

Applicant Eligibility: Private, nonprofit Organizations having experience in effectively training and counseling business women. Public educational Institutions and State and local Governments are not eligible.

Beneficiary Eligibility: Women entrepreneurs starting their own business or expanding their existing business.

Award Range/Average: Additional information available at www.sba.gov/wbc

Funding: (Project Grants) FY 17 $15,849,000.00; FY 18 est $18,000,000.00; FY 19 est $16,000,000.00

Programs Administered by Federal Headquarters

HQ: 409 3rd Street SW, 6th Floor, Washington, DC 20416
Phone: 202-205-7532 | Email: bruce.purdy@sba.gov
http://www.sba.gov/wbc

DOD12.010 | YOUTH CONSERVATION SERVICES
Award: Cooperative Agreements
Purpose: To expand educational opportunities for water resources projects through the Secretary, who provide agreements with nonprofit entities for natural resources conservation.
Applicant Eligibility: N/A
Beneficiary Eligibility: N/A
Funding: (Cooperative Agreements) FY 14 $0.00; FY 15 est $3,000.00; FY 16 est $3,000.00
HQ: Strategic Operations Division 441 G Street NW, Washington, DC 20314-1000
Phone: 202-761-8645 | Email: robin.a.baldwin@usace.army.mil
http://www.usace.army.mil

DOJ16.544 | YOUTH GANG PREVENTION
"Gangs and youth violence prevention"
Award: Project Grants
Purpose: To provide funding to states, local units of government, and federal recognized tribes to implement programs and strategies to prevent and intervene youth-gang-related violence.
Applicant Eligibility: Part D funds are available under the Juvenile Justice and Delinquency Prevention Act of 1974, as amended, to public or private nonprofit agencies, Organizations or individuals. Please contact Program office for additional information.
Beneficiary Eligibility: Contact program office for additional information.
Award Range/Average: Varies.
Funding: (Formula Grants) FY 17 $3,333,287.00; FY 18 est $0.00; FY 19 est $0.00
HQ: 810 7th Street NW, Washington, DC 20351
Phone: 202-514-4817 | Email: kellie.dressler@usdoj.gov
http://www.ojjdp.gov

HUD14.276 | YOUTH HOMELESSNESS DEMONSTRATION PROGRAM
Award: Direct Payments for Specified Use
Purpose: To promote a community-wide commitment to the goal of ending youth homelessness and promote access and effective utilization of mainstream programs and optimizes self-sufficiency among youth experiencing homelessness.
Applicant Eligibility: Homeless unaccompanied youth (age 24 and younger) and homeless youth (age 24 and younger) with children.
Beneficiary Eligibility: Same as Applicant Eligibility.
Award Range/Average: The allocation for selected communities ranges between $1 million and $15 million. The allocation is abased upon a formula that considers the number of youth in the community and the local poverty rate.
Funding: (Project Grants (Discretionary)) FY 18 est $80,000,000.00; FY 19 est Estimate Not Available; FY 20 est Estimate Not Available
HQ: 451 7th Street SW, Room 7256, Washington, DC 20410
Phone: 202-402-5183 | Email: lisa.a.hill@hud.gov
http://www.hudexchange.info/programs/yhdp

PROGRAMS ADMINISTERED BY REGIONAL - STATE - LOCAL OFFICES

Programs Administered by Regional - State - Local Offices

ADVANCED RESEARCH PROJECTS AGENCY
Regional - State - Local Offices

USA Cold Regions Research and Engineering Laboratory
Mr. Peter Smallidge | 72 Lynn Road, Hanover, NH 03755-1290 603-646-4445

USA Construction Engineering Research Laboratories
Ms. Bea Shahim | 2902 Newmark Drive, Champaign, IL 61821-1075 800-872-2375

USA Topographic Engineering Center
Mr. Charles McKenna | Cude Building No. 2592, Ft. Belvoir, VA 22060-5546 703-355-3133

USAE Hydrologic Engineering Center
Mr. Arlen Feldman | 609 Second Street, Davis, CA 95616-4887 916-756-1104

USAE Institute for Water Resources
Casey Building No. 2594, Ft. Belvoir, VA 22060-5586 703-355-3084

USAE Waterways Experiment Station
Mr. William McGleese | 3909 Falls Ferry Road, Vicksburg, MI 39180-6199 601-634-2512

DOD12.910 | RESEARCH AND TECHNOLOGY DEVELOPMENT
Award: Cooperative Agreements
Purpose: To assist and induce the basic research, applied research, and advanced research at educational institutions, nonprofit organizations, and commercial firms.
Applicant Eligibility: For grants, eligibility is limited to public and private educational Institutions and nonprofit Organizations operated for purposes in the public interest. For cooperative agreements, eligibility is limited to educational Institutions, nonprofit Organizations, and commercial firms. Eligibility for TIAs is the same as for cooperative agreements. Individuals are not eligible for these awards.
Beneficiary Eligibility: Public and private educational institutions. Nonprofit organizations operated for purposes in the public interest and commercial firms.
Funding: (Project Grants) FY 18 $195,089,926.00; FY 19 $223,864,806.00 est FY 20 est $246,000,000.00
HQ: 675 N Randolph Street, Arlington, VA 22203
Phone: 703-696-2434 | Email: scott.ulrey@darpa.mil

AGRICULTURAL MARKETING SERVICE
Regional – State – Local Offices

COTTON DIVISION

Standardization and Quality Assurance Branch
Don West, Chief | 3275 Appling Road, Memphis, TN 38133 901-384-3015

Tennessee
J. Jerome Boyd | 3275 Appling Road, Memphis, TN 38133 901-384-3000

DAIRY DIVISION

Illinois
800 Roosevelt Road Building A Suite 370, Glen Ellyn, IL 60137 708-790-6920

USDA, AMS, Dairy Division, Marketing Division
2811 Agricultural Drive, Madison, WI 53704-6777 608-224-5080

FRUIT AND VEGETABLE DIVISION

Alabama
Robert Spann, Federal Supervisor, In-Charge | 1557 Reeves Street PO Box 1368, Dothan, AL 36302 334-792-5185

Arizona
James E. Nowlin | 1688 W Adams Room 415, Phoenix, AZ 85007 602-542-0880

Jerry W. Taylor, Regional Director | Tucson Federal Building PO Box FB30 300 W Congress Street Room 7, Tucson, AZ 85701-1319 520-670-4793

Stephen Skuba, In-Charge | 522 N Central Avenue Room 106, Phoenix, AZ 85004 602-379-3066

Baltimore, Washington
Nathaniel Taylor IV, In-Charge | USDA AMS F&VD Baltimore-Washington Terminal Market Office 8610 Baltimore-Washington Boulevard Suite 212, Jessup, MD 20794 301-317-4387, 4587

Programs Administered by Regional - State - Local Offices

California
Clifton Harada, In-Charge | 1320 E Olympic Avenue Room 212, Los Angeles, CA 90021 213-894-2489, 6553

Dale I. Scarborough, Inspector | Inspection Point of Fresno CA 45-116 Commerce Street Suite 15, Indio, CA 92201-3440 619-347-1057

Frederick Teensma, In-Charge | 630 Sansome Street Room 727, San Francisco, CA 94111 415-705-1300

John Henry, In-Charge | 1320 E Olympic Boulevard Room 212, Los Angeles, CA 90021-1948 213-894-3173

Kevin Morris, In-Charge | 2202 Monterey Street Suite 104-A, Fresno, CA 93721 209-487-5178

Kurt J. Kimmel, In-Charge | USDA AMS MFO 2202 Monterey Street Suite 102-B, Fresno, CA 93721 209-487-5901

Michael Shine, In-Charge | 1320 E Olympic Boulevard Suite 212, Los Angeles, CA 90021-1907 213-894-3077

Michael V. Morrelli, Federal Supervisor, In-Charge | 1220 N Street Room A-270 PO Box 942871, Sacramento, CA 94271-0001 916-654-0810, 13, 15

Yoshiki Kagawa Jr., In-Charge | 2202 Monterey Street Suite 102-A, Fresno, CA 93721-3129 209-487-5210

Colorado
Ronald D. Nightengale, Federal Supervisor, In-Charge | 2331 W 31st Avenue, Denver, CO 80211 303-844-4570

Tom Guttierrez, In-Charge | Greeley Producers Building 711 O Street, Greeley, CO 80631 970-351-7097, 351-8256

Connecticut
Peter Bucci, Federal Supervisor, In-Charge | Connecticut Regional Market 101 Reserve Road Room 5, Hartford, CT 06114 860-240-3446

Delaware
Clifford W. Hudson, In-Charge | State of Delaware Department of Agriculture 2320 S DuPont Highway, Dover, DE 19901 302-736-4811

Eastern Region
Terry B. Bane, Director | 800 Roosevelt Road Building A Suite 380, Glen Ellyn, IL 60137-5875 630-790-6957

Florida
775 Warner Lane, Orlando, FL 32803 407-897-5950

Ann S. Pinner, In-Charge | 98 3rd Street SW, Winter Haven, FL 33880-2909 941-294-7416

Christian Nissen, In-Charge | PO Box 2276 301 3rd Street NW Suite 206, Winter Haven, FL 33881 941-299-4770, 4886

Clyde Thornhill, In-Charge | 6966 NW 36th Avenue, Miami, FL 33147-6506 305-835-7626

James Dunn, In-Charge | Techniport Building Room 556 5600 NW 36 Street, Miami, FL 33122 305-870-9542

Jim Cunningham, In-Charge | Brickell Plaza Building 909 SE 1st Avenue Suite 424, Miami, FL 33131 305-373-2955

Georgia
John Kerrens, In-Charge | 203 Administration Building 16 Forest Parkway, Forest Park, GA 30050 404-763-7297

John Pollard, In-Charge | 1555 Saint Joseph Avenue, East Point, GA 30344-2591 404-763-7495

Larry Ivaska, In-Charge | Administration Building Room 205 16 Forest Parkway, Forest Park, GA 30050 404-366-7522

Richard DeMenna, In-Charge | PO Box 1447 Georgia State Farmers Market Stall 39 502 Smith Avenue U.S. Highway 84, Thomasville, GA 31799 912-228-1208

Hawaii
Walter T. Mitsui, Federal Supervisory, Inspector | State of Hawaii Department of Agriculture 1428 S King Street PO Box 22159, Honolulu, HI 96823-2159 808-973-9566

Warren Maeda, Assistant Federal Supervisor, In-Charge | 1428 S King Street PO Box 22159, Honolulu, HI 96823-2159 808-973-9566

Idaho
Scott P. Brubaker, Federal Supervisor, In-Charge | Idaho State Department of Agriculture 2270 Old Penitentiary Road, Boise, ID 83712 208-332-8670

Thomas L. Cooper, In-Charge | 1820 E 17th Street Suite 130, Idaho Falls, ID 83404 208-526-0166

Illinois
Greg Braun, Regional Director | USDA AMS F&V PACA Branch 800 Roosevelt Road Building A Suite 360, Glen Ellyn, IL 60137-5832 630-790-6929

Steven D. Dailey, In-Charge | JC Kluczynski Building 230 S Dearborn Street Room 512, Chicago, IL 60604 312-353-0111

Indiana
Anthony Chartrand, In-Charge | 4318 Technology Drive, South Bend, IN 46628-9752 219-287-5407

Richard Barlow, Federal Supervisor, In-Charge | PO Box 427, Greenfield, IN 46140-0427 317-462-5897

Kentucky
Jesse M. Stockton, Federal Supervisor, In-Charge | No 1 Produce Terminal, Louisville, KY 40218 502-595-4266, 4278

Louisiana
John Crose, Federal Supervisor, In-Charge | U.S. Postal Service Building 701 Loyola Avenue Room 11036, New Orleans, LA 70113 504-589-6741, 6742

Thomas Clominger, USDA Inspector | (Inspection Point of E Point GA) Commerce Building Suite 3 1942 Williams Boulevard, Kenner, LA 70062-6285 504-466-0343

Maine
Ed Margeson, Federal Supervisor, In-Charge | PO Box 1058 744 Main Street Suite 4, Presque Isle, ME 04769 207-764-2100

Wallace Fengler, In-Charge | 165 Lancaster Street, Portland, ME 04101-2499 207-772-1588

Maryland
Holly R. Mozal, In-Charge | Maryland Wholesale Produce Market Building B Room 101 7460 Conowingo Avenue, Jessup, MD 20794 301-621-1261

Norman Upton, In-Charge | Hunt Valley Professional Building 9 Schilling Road, Hunt Valley, MD 21031-1106

Programs Administered by Regional - State - Local Offices

William V. Kaier, Inspector | (Inspector Point of Hunt Valley MD) 102 Maryland Avenue, Easton, MD 21601-3409 410-822-3383

Massachusetts

James Calnan, In-Charge | Boston Market Terminal 34 Market Street Room 10, Everett, MA 02149 617-387-4498, 4615, 4681

Susan Taylor, Federal Supervisor, In-Charge | Boston Market Terminal Building 34 Market Street Room 1, Everett, MA 02149 617-389-2480, 2481

Michigan

Charles W. Hackensmith II, In-Charge | PO Box 1204 Federal Building 175 Territorial Road Room 201, Benton Harbor, MI 49023 616-925-3270, 3271

Gary Reij, USDA Inspector | (Inspection Point of S Bend IN) c/o Vroom Cold Storage Russell Road, Hart, MI 49420-0113 616-873-5654

Michael Rann, In-Charge Union Produce Terminal | 7201 W Fort Street Room 53, Detroit, MI 48209 313-841-1111

Michael W. Moore, Federal Supervisor | 90 Detroit Union Produce Terminal 7201 W Fort Street, Detroit, MI 48209 313-226-6059, 6225

Minnesota

Gregory Stevens, USDA Inspector | (Inspection Point of Ripon WI) 2126 Hoffman Road, Mankato, MN 56001-5863 507-387-6101

Mark Inverson, Federal Supervisor, In-Charge | 90 W Plato Boulevard, Saint Paul, MN 55107 612-296-8557, 0593

Missouri

Arne Stokke, In-Charge | Gumbel Building Room 502 801 Walnut Street, Kansas City, MO 64106 816-374-6273

Charles M. Gore, In-Charge | Unit 1 Produce Row Room 101, Saint Louis, MO 63102-1418 314-425-4520

Larry Wenger, In-Charge | Unit 1 Produce Row 1st Floor Room 100, Saint Louis, MO 63102 314-425-4514, 4515

New Jersey

Michiko F. Shaw, Regional Director | PACA Branch USDA AMS F&V Division 622 Georges Road Suite 303, North Brunswick, NJ 08902-3303 908-846-8222

Park Plaza Professional Building Suite 304 622 Georges Road, North Brunswick, NJ 08902-3313 908-545-0939

Tom Robertson, In-Charge | Federal Building 970 Broad Street Room 1430, Newark, NJ 07102 201-645-2636

New York

Bruce Copeland | (Inspection Point of N Brunswick NJ) Genesee Valley Regional Market 900 Jefferson Road Room 110, Rochester, NY 14623-3289 716-424-2092, 2096

C. Michael Wells, In-Charge | 465B Hunts Point Market, Bronx, NY 10474 718-991-7665, 7669

Paul Beattie, Federal Supervisor, In-Charge | Division of Food Safety & Inspection Service Department of Agriculture Capital Plaza 1 Winners Circle Building No 2 Second Floor, Albany, NY 12235 518-457-1211, 457-2090, 457-1982

Philip H. Montgomery, In-Charge | 5A NYC Terminal Market Halleck Street at Edgewater Road, Bronx, NY 10474-7355 718-542-2225

Ohio

Francis Allard, Federal Supervisor, In-Charge | Fresh Fruit & Vegetable Division Ohio Department of Agriculture Division of Food Dairy & Drugs 8995 E Main Street Building 2, Reynoldsburg, OH 43068 614-728-6350

Randall T. Edwards, In-Charge | 3716 Croton Avenue, Cleveland, OH 44115 216-522-2135

Oklahoma

716 S 2nd Street Suite 106, Stilwell, OK 74960-4806 918-696-6333

James W. Goodson, In-Charge | 2800 N Lincoln Boulevard, Oklahoma City, OK 73105 405-521-3864

Oregon

Dick C. Harms, Federal Supervisor, In-Charge | 635 Capitol Street NE, Salem, OR 97310-0110 503-986-4629

Gary Olson, In-Charge | 1220 SW 3rd Avenue Room 369, Portland, OR 97204 503-326-2724, 2725

Gary Sheltor, USDA Inspector | (Inspection Point of Yakima WA) 111 S Main Street, Milton-Freewater, OR, 97862-1342 541-938-3251

Jack Whitt, In-Charge | 340 High Street NE, Salem, OR 97301-3631 503-399-5761

Pennsylvania

Armia Lawandy, In-Charge | 210 Produce Building 3301 S Galloway Street, Philadelphia, PA 19148 215-336-0845, 0846

Dennis Jemmerson, In-Charge | 2100 Smallman Street Room 207, Pittsburgh, PA 15222 412-644-5847

James Prady, In-Charge | Pittsburgh Produce Terminal Building Room 206 2100 Smallman Street, Pittsburgh, PA 15222 412-261-6435

Michael Cramer, In-Charge | Room 261 3301 S Galloway Street, Philadelphia, PA 19148 215-597-4536

Thomas Yawman, Federal Supervisor, In-Charge | 2301 N Cameron Street Room 112, Harrisburg, PA 17110 717-787-5107, 5108

Puerto Rico

Luis Aponte, Federal Supervisor, In-Charge | Federal State Inspection Service GSA Center 651 Federal Drive Suite 103-05, Guaynabo, PR 00965-1030 809-783-2230, 4116

Tennessee

Jerry L. Cook, In-Charge | 3211 Alcoa Highway, Knoxville, TN 37920 423-577-2633

Michael W. Golightly, Federal Supervisor, In-Charge | PO Box 40627 Melrose Station, Nashville, TN 37204 615-360-0169

Texas

Alfonso T. Briones, USDA Inspector | 319 Market Street, Laredo, TX 78040-8529 210-726-2258

Belinda G. Garza, In-Charge | McAllen Marketing Field Office Fruit & Vegetable Division Agricultural Marketing Services USDA 1313 E Hackberry, McAllen, TX 78501 956-682-2833

Programs Administered by Regional - State - Local Offices

Byron E. White, Regional Director | PACA Branch USDA AMS F&U 1200 E Copeland Road Suite 404, Arlington, TX 76011-4938 817-885-7805

Calvin Harvey, In-Charge | 8001 E N Mesa Suite 303, El Paso, TX 79932 505-589-3753

D.C. Benavides Jr., In-Charge | Administration Building Room 244 1500 S Zarzamora Street, San Antonio, TX 78207 210-222-2751

Daniel Frey, Inspector | 2320 La Branch Street Federal Building Room 1011, Houston, TX 77004-1036 713-659-3836

Desiree Shaw, In-Charge | 1406 Parker Street Room 201, Dallas, TX 75215 214-767-5375, 5376, 5377

Dwain Parrish, In-Charge | 117 So Westgate, Weslaco, TX 78596-2701 210-968-2772, 2126

Gary Verheek, Federal Supervisor, In-Charge | 1301 W Expressway PO Box 107, San Juan, TX 78589 210-787-4091, 6881

Ken Edwards, In-Charge | 3100 Produce Row Room 1A, Houston, TX 77023 713-923-2557, 2558

Timothy J. Peppel, In-Charge | 1406 Parker Street Suite 203, Dallas, TX 75215 214-767-5337, 5338

Utah

350 N Redwood Road Room 217, Salt Lake City, UT 84116 801-538-7187

Virginia

8700 Centerville Road Suite 206, Manassas, VA 22110 703-330-4455

Raymond Oliver, In-Charge | No 1 N 14th Street Room 332, Richmond, VA 23219-3691 804-786-0930

Washington

Dale Guyant, Federal Supervisor, In-Charge | PO Box 42560 National Resources Building 2nd Floor 1111 Washington Street, Olympia, WA 98504-2560 360-902-1831

Frank V. Warren, In-Charge | 32 N 3rd Street Room 212, Yakima, WA 98901-2791 509-575-5869

Jeffrey Main, In-Charge | Agricultural Service Center 2015 S 1st Street Room 4, Yakima, WA 98903 509-575-2492, 2493

Peter Echanove, In-Charge | Interwest Savings Bank 15111 8th Avenue SW Suite 302 PO Box 48099, Seattle, WA 98148-0099 206-764-3804, 3753

Western Region

Romeo V. Villaluz, Regional Director | 2202 Monterey Street Suite 102-C, Fresno, CA 93721-3175 209-487-5891

Wisconsin

Milborn Beaty, In-Charge | 742 E Fond du Lac Street, Ripon, WI 54971-9555 414-748-2287

LIVESTOCK DIVISION

Alabama

F. David Gonsoulin | 1445 Federal Drive Room 107 PO Box 3336, Montgomery, AL 36109-0336 334-223-7488

Arizona

Donald W. Perkins | Stockyards Building 5001 E Washington Street Room 102, Phoenix, AZ 85034-2010 602-379-4376

Arkansas

Steve R. Cheney | PO Box 391 2301 S University Room 110-B, Little Rock, AR 72203-3910 501-671-2203

Colorado

Dale Krows | 400 Livestock Exchange Building, Denver, CO 80216-2139 303-294-7676

Keith L. Padgett | 711 O Street, Greeley, CO 80631-9540 970-353-9750

Florida

Ronald Carpenter | 775 Warner Lane, Orlando, FL 32803 407-897-2708

Georgia

Terry Harris | Georgia State Farmers Market PO Box 86 502 Smith Avenue Stall 38, Thomasville, GA 31792-0086 912-226-2198

Illinois

James Epstein | Illinois Department of Agriculture Division of Marketing State Fairgrounds PO Box 19281, Springfield, IL 62794-9281 217-782-4925

Richard Johnson | 800 Roosevelt Road Building A Suite 330, Glen Ellyn, IL 60137-5832 708-790-6905

Iowa

C. Thomas Sandau | PO Box 2437 800 Cunningham Drive Room 225, Sioux City, IA 51107-2437 712-252-3286

Michael Sheats | 210 Walnut Street Room 767, Des Moines, IA 50309-2106 515-284-4460

Richard Jones | 210 Walnut Street Room 575-A, Des Moines, IA 50309-2106 515-284-7166

Kansas

R. Gary Mills | 100 Military Avenue Suite 217, Dodge City, KS 67801-4945 316-227-8881

Kentucky

Jack L. Colley | 1321 Story Avenue, Louisville, KY 40206-1884 502-582-5287

Louisiana

David H. Foster, Director | PO Box 3334 Capitol Station 5825 Florida Boulevard, Baton Rouge, LA 70821-3334 504-922-1328

Minnesota

Robert Brommer | New Livestock Exchange Building Suite 208, South Saint Paul, MN 55075-5598 612-451-1565

Missouri

Phil B. McFall | 601 Illinois Avenue Room 210, Saint Joseph, MO 64504-1396 816-238-0678

Montana

Russ Travelute | PO Box 1191 Public Auction Yards Building 112 S 18th & Minnesota Avenue Room 206, Billings, MT 59103-1191 406-657-6285

Nebraska

Evan Stachowicz | 204 Livestock Exchange Building 29th & O Streets, Omaha, NE 68107-2603 402-733-4833

Programs Administered by Regional - State - Local Offices

Gary R. Kinder | 213 Livestock Exchange Building 29th & O Street, Omaha, NE 68107-2603 402-731-4520

New Mexico
John Langenegger | 2507 N Telshor Boulevard Suite 4, Las Cruces, NM 88001 505-521-4928

Oklahoma
Robert P. Miles | Livestock Exchange Building Room 140 2501 Exchange Avenue, Oklahoma City, OK 73108-2477 405-232-5425

Oregon
Lowell C. Serfling | 1220 SW 3rd Avenue Room 1772, Portland, OR 97204-2899 503-326-2237

Pennsylvania
James L. Anderson | c/o New Holland Sales Stables 101 W Fulton Street PO Box 155, New Holland, PA 17557 717-354-2391

South Carolina
Daniel Schussler | PO Box 13405 Youngblood Building 1001 Bluff Road, Columbia, SC 29201-3405 803-737-4491

South Dakota
Charles E. McIntyre | 803 E Rice Street Room 103, Sioux Falls, SD 57103-0193 605-338-4061

Tennessee
Lewis Langell | PO Box 40627 Melrose Station Ellington Agriculture Center Hogan Road, Nashville, TN 37204-0627 615-781-5406

Texas
Cecil R. Rains | PO Box 30217 Livestock Exchange Building 101 S Manhattan Street, Amarillo, TX 79104 806-373-7111

Kenneth Gladney | Livestock Exchange Building PO Box 30217 101 S Manhattan Street 1st Floor, Amarillo, TX 79104-0217 806-372-6361

Rebecca Saunder | Producer's Livestock Auction Building PO Box 30160, San Angelo, TX 76903-0160 915-653-1778

Washington
Vern Larson | 988 Juniper Street, Moses Lake, WA 98837-2250 509-765-3611

Wyoming
Ray Leach | 1834 E A Street, Torrington, WY 82240-1813 307-532-4146

POULTRY DIVISION

Arkansas
Larry Poldrack | 1 Natural Resources Drive Room 110 PO Box 8521, Little Rock, AR 72215-8521 501-324-5955

California
Gerald Brockman | 2909 Coffee Road Suite 4, Modesto, CA 95355-3188 209-522-5251

James Derby | 5600 Rickenbacker Road Building 6 Section E, Bell, CA 90201-6418 213-269-4154

Connecticut
Patricia Bussy, Administrative Assistant | Connecticut Department of Agriculture Marketing Division 165 Capital Avenue State Office Building Room 263, Hartford, CT 06106-1688 860-566-3671

District of Columbia
Richard Parsons, USDA National Poultry Supervisor | S Building Room 3960 PO Box 96456, Washington, DC 20090-6456 202-720-6911

Georgia
Johnny Freeman | 60 Forsyth Street SW Room 6M80, Atlanta, GA 30303

Iowa
Jerry Mason | Room 777 Federal Building 210 Walnut Street, Des Moines, IA 50309-2100 515-284-4581

Mary Adkins | 210 Walnut Street Room 951, Des Moines, IA 50309-2103 515-284-4545

Louisiana
David H. Foster, Director | Louisiana Department of Agriculture PO Box 3334 HJ Wilson Building, Baton Rouge, LA 70821-3334 504-922-1328

Mississippi
Gary Brown | 352 E Woodrow Wilson PO Box 4629, Jackson, MS 39296-4629 601-965-4662

North Carolina
Douglas N. Lecher | 635 Cox Road Suite G, Gastonia, NC 28054-3441 704-867-3871

Spurgeon Hyder, Manager | N Carolina Department of Agriculture PO Box 27647 State Agriculture Building Room 402 2 W Edenton Street, Raleigh, NC 27611-7647 919-733-7252

Texas
Neal Alexander, Director, Market Information | Texas Department of Agriculture PO Box 12847 Capitol Station 1700 N Congress Avenue, Austin, TX 78711-2847 512-463-7628

Virginia
Linda M. Kelley, Reporter | Virginia Department of Agriculture & Consumer Services Market News 116 Reservoir Street, Harrisonburg, VA 22801-4232 540-434-0779

SCIENCE DIVISION

Alabama
Bobby L. Joyner, Supervisory Chemist | Aflatoxin Laboratories 3119 Wesley Way, Dothan, AL 36301-2020 334-794-5070

Melvin C. Ginn, Laboratory Supervisor | PO Box 1368 1557 Reeves Street, Dothan, AL 36302 334-792-5185

Florida
James Carson, Supervisory Chemist | Eastern Laboratories 98 3rd Street SW Suite 211, Winter Haven, FL 33880-2909 941-299-7958

Georgia
Donald Johnson, Laboratory Supervisor | 610 N Main Street, Blakely, GA 31723 912-723-4570

Lorine Lewis, Laboratory Supervisor | PO Box 488, Ashburn, GA 31714 912-567-3703

Thomas E. Parris, Laboratory Supervisor | 1211 Schley Avenue, Albany, GA 31707 912-430-8490

Walter K. Wills Jr., Laboratory Supervisor | PO Box 272, Dawson, GA 31742 912-995-7257

Illinois

Dr. Fred Pepper, Laboratory Director | Midwestern Laboratory 3570 No Avondale Avenue, Chicago, IL 60618-5391 312-353-6525

North Carolina

James G. Hess, Laboratory Director | Eastern Laboratory 2311-B Aberdeen Boulevard, Gastonia, NC 28054-0614 704-867-3873

Laboratory Address 645 Cox Road, Gastonia, NC 28054-0614 704-867-1882

Michael S. Lyons, Laboratory Supervisor | PO Box 279 301 W Pearl Street, Aulander, NC 27805 919-345-1661, Ext. 156

Oklahoma

John Mangham, Laboratory Supervisor | 107 S 4th Street, Madill, OK 73446 405-795-5615

Virginia

Bonnie Poli, Branch Chief | Pesticide Records Branch 8700 Centreville Road Suite 200, Manassas, VA 22110-0031 703-330-7826

Robert L. Epstein, Acting Branch Chief | Residue Branch 8700 Centreville Road Suite 200, Manassas, VA 22110-0031 703-330-2300

Virginia L. Meeks, Laboratory Supervisor | PO Box 1130 308 Culloden Street, Suffolk, VA 23434 757-925-2286

TOBACCO DIVISION

Kentucky

Everette B. Mace | 771 Corporate Drive Suite 500, Lexington, KY 40503 606-224-1088

North Carolina

Ralph W. Lowery | 1306 Annapolis Drive Room 205, Raleigh, NC 27608-0001 919-856-4584

USDA10.153 | MARKET NEWS

Award: Dissemination of Technical Information
Purpose: To give the exact fare list to the State department of agriculture on all U.S. agricultural products.
Applicant Eligibility: State Departments of Agriculture may subscribe to existing market news reports or bulletins pertaining to specific agricultural commodities and markets.
Beneficiary Eligibility: State Departments of Agriculture.
Award Range/Average: Not Applicable.
Funding: (Information) FY 17 $33,659,000.00; FY 18 est $33,659,000.00; FY 19 est $28,281,000.00
HQ: 1400 Independence Avenue SW, Washington, DC 20250
   Phone: 202-690-4024 | Email: erin.morris@ams.usda.gov
   http://www.ams.usda.gov

USDA10.155 | MARKETING AGREEMENTS AND ORDERS

Award: Provision of Specialized Services; Advisory Services and Counseling
Purpose: To increase infrastructure of the marketing facilities by providing quality commodities.
Applicant Eligibility: Marketing orders are issued by the Secretary of Agriculture only after a public hearing where milk, fruit and vegetable producers, marketers, and consumers testify, and after farmers vote approval through a referendum. Growers of certain fruits, vegetables, and specialty crops (like nuts, raisins, olives, and hops). Dairy farmers are the primary applicants.
Beneficiary Eligibility: The beneficiaries are producers of milk, fruit and vegetable products.
Award Range/Average: Not Applicable.
Funding: (Salaries and Expenses) FY 17 $20,705,000.00; FY 18 est $20,489,000.00; FY 19 est $20,489,000.00
HQ: 1400 Independence Avenue SW, Washington, DC 20250
   Phone: 202-690-4024 | Email: erin.morris@ams.usda.gov
   http://www.ams.usda.gov

USDA10.156 | FEDERAL-STATE MARKETING IMPROVEMENT PROGRAM "FSMP"

Award: Project Grants
Purpose: To increase the market value for the U.S. agriculture products and enhance the marketing system in the U.S.
Applicant Eligibility: State Departments of Agriculture, State Agricultural Experiment Stations and other appropriate State agencies including State universities, State colleges, and State government entities such as State departments of forestry, natural resources, or energy.
Beneficiary Eligibility: Farmer/Rancher/Agriculture Producer, Consumer, State Producers, processors, marketing agencies, and general public.

Programs Administered by Regional - State - Local Offices

Award Range/Average: $25,000 to $1,000,000. Average: $148,000.
Funding: (Project Grants (for specified projects)) FY 17 $981,682.00; FY 18 est $1,109,000.00; FY 19 est $0.00
HQ: 1400 Independence Avenue SW Room 4543, PO Box 0234, Washington, DC 20250
　　Phone: 202-260-8449 | Email: martin.rosier@ams.usda.gov
　　https://www.ams.usda.gov/fsmip

USDA10.162 | INSPECTION GRADING AND STANDARDIZATION
"Agricultural Fair Practices Act"

Award: Provision of Specialized Services
Purpose: To provide qualitative infrastructure for the agriculture commodities and egg hatcheries.
Applicant Eligibility: Any owner of or dealer in agricultural commodities who (a) has a financial interest in the commodity to be graded and (b) is located within the United States and its Territories. All hatcheries and shell egg handlers having an annual production from 3,000 or more hens who pack for the retail consumer and are located within the U.S. or its Territories.
Beneficiary Eligibility: Buyers and sellers of agricultural commodities. Shell egg handlers having an annual production from 3,000 or more hens who pack for the retail consumer and are located in the U.S. or its Territories.
Award Range/Average: Not Applicable.
Funding: (Salaries and Expenses) FY 17 $157,759,000.00; FY 18 est $160,473,000.00; FY 19 est $160,473,000.00
HQ: 1400 Independence Avenue SW, Washington, DC 20250
　　Phone: 202-690-4024 | Email: erin.morris@ams.usda.gov
　　http://www.ams.usda.gov

USDA10.163 | MARKET PROTECTION AND PROMOTION

Award: Provision of Specialized Services; Advisory Services and Counseling; Training
Purpose: To reduce misbranding of seeds and to analyze pesticide usage in the agriculture commodities.
Applicant Eligibility: Any State government, public and private Organization and institution, business and industry, or individual may apply for technical assistance or service. State, trade associations, and universities may be eligible for cooperative agreements.
Beneficiary Eligibility: Any State government, public and private organization and institution, business and industry, or individual may apply for technical assistance or service.
Award Range/Average: Not Applicable.
Funding: (Salaries and Expenses) FY 17 $63,000,000.00; FY 18 est $65,000,000.00; FY 19 est $35,000,000.00
HQ: 1400 Independence Avenue SW, Washington, DC 20250
　　Phone: 202-690-4024 | Email: erin.morris@ams.usda.gov
　　http://www.ams.usda.gov

USDA10.164 | WHOLESALE FARMERS AND ALTERNATIVE MARKET DEVELOPMENT

Award: Advisory Services and Counseling; Training
Purpose: To create apt infrastructure for the U.S. marketing.
Applicant Eligibility: Other government agencies and private industry. State, trade associations, universities, and other nonprofit Organizations are eligible to apply for cooperative agreements.
Beneficiary Eligibility: Producers, processors, marketing agencies, and general public.
Award Range/Average: Not Applicable.
Funding: (Advisory Services and Counseling) FY 17 $5,246,000.00; FY 18 est $4,254,000.00; FY 19 est $4,250,000.00
HQ: 1400 Independence Avenue SW, Washington, DC 20250
　　Phone: 202-690-1300 | Email: arthur.neal@ams.usda.gov
　　http://www.ams.usda.gov

USDA10.165 | PERISHABLE AGRICULTURAL COMMODITIES ACT

Award: Investigation of Complaints
Purpose: To detect fraud practices of supplying unreliable agricultural products and reduce wastage of the products.
Applicant Eligibility: Business and industry or individuals may apply for a PACA license.
Beneficiary Eligibility: Same as Applicant Eligibility.

Award Range/Average: Not Applicable.
Funding: (Investigation of Complaints) FY 17 $10,423,000.00; FY 18 est $10,590,000.00; FY 19 est $10,733,000.00
HQ: 1400 Independence Avenue SW, Washington, DC 20250
  Phone: 202-690-4024 | Email: erin.morris@ams.usda.gov
  http://www.ams.usda.gov

USDA10.167 | TRANSPORTATION SERVICES
Award: Advisory Services and Counseling; Training
Purpose: To increase income for rural Americans by providing agricultural transportation facilities.
Applicant Eligibility: Any State government, public and private Organization and institution, business and industry, or individual may apply for technical assistance or service. State, trade associations, universities, and nonprofit Organizations may be eligible for cooperative agreements.
Beneficiary Eligibility: Producers, processors, and general public.
Award Range/Average: Not Applicable.
Funding: (Advisory Services and Counseling) FY 17 $3,928,999.00; FY 18 est $2,929,000.00; FY 19 est $2,933,000.00
HQ: 1400 Independence Avenue SW, Washington, DC 20250
  Phone: 202-690-1300 | Email: arthur.neal@ams.usda.gov
  http://www.ams.usda.gov

USDA10.168 | FARMERS MARKET PROMOTION PROGRAM
"FMPP"
Award: Project Grants
Purpose: To promote better marketing facilities and infrastructure for increasing marketing opportunities.
Applicant Eligibility: Agricultural cooperatives, local Governments, nonprofit corporations, producer networks, producer associations, community supported agriculture networks, community supported agriculture associations, public benefit corporations, economic development corporations, regional farmers market authorities, and Tribal Governments. projects and applicants must be owned, operated, and located within the 50 States, the District of Columbia, and the U.S. territories (American Samoa, Commonwealth of the Northern Mariana Islands, Guam, Puerto Rico, and U.S. Virgin Islands.
Beneficiary Eligibility: Projects that benefit producers, direct marketing enterprises, and consumers.
Award Range/Average: Capacity Building (CB) - $50,000- $250,000 Community Development, Training, and Technical Assistance (CDTTA) - $250,000-500,000
Funding: (Project Grants) FY 17 $13,965,000.00; FY 18 est $14,010,000.00; FY 19 est $0.00
HQ: USDA FMPP 1400 Independence Avenue SW, Washington, DC 20250
  Phone: 202-720-8317
  http://www.ams.usda.gov/FMPP

USDA10.172 | LOCAL FOOD PROMOTION PROGRAM
"LFPP"
Award: Project Grants
Purpose: To enhance marketing opportunities for regionally produced agricultural products.
Applicant Eligibility: Agricultural businesses and cooperatives, local Governments, nonprofit corporations, producer networks, producer associations, community supported agriculture networks, community supported agriculture associations, public benefit corporations, economic development corporations, regional farmers market authorities, and Tribal Governments. projects and applicants must be owned, operated, and located within the 50 States, the District of Columbia, and the U.S. territories (American Samoa, Commonwealth of the Northern Mariana Islands, Guam, Puerto Rico, and U.S. Virgin Islands.
Beneficiary Eligibility: Projects that benefit producers, local and regional food business enterprises, and consumers.
Award Range/Average: As provided for in the applicable request for applications. For planning grants, the minimum grant request is $25,000; maximum grant request is $100,000. For implementation grants, the minimum grant request is $100,000; maximum grant request is $500,000.
Funding: (Project Grants) FY 17 $13,965,000.00; FY 18 est $14,010,000.00; FY 19 est $0.00
HQ: 1400 Independence Avenue SW Room 4543, PO Box 0234, Washington, DC 20250
  Phone: 202-720-8713
  http://www.ams.usda.gov

Programs Administered by Regional - State - Local Offices

USDA10.174 | ACER ACCESS DEVELOPMENT PROGRAM
Award: Project Grants
Purpose: To assist the research institutions, producers, and States to increase products based on maple.
Applicant Eligibility: State agencies, tribal Governments, and research Institutions.
Beneficiary Eligibility: Producers, processors, marketing agencies, and general public.
Award Range/Average: $100,000 to $500,000. Average $350,000.
Funding: (Project Grants) FY 18 $3,000,000.00; FY 19 est $3,000,000.00; FY 20 est $0.00
HQ: 1400 Independence Avenue SW Room 4543, PO Box 0234, Washington, DC 20250
    Phone: 202-260-8449 | Email: martin.rosier@ams.usda.gov
    http://www.ams.usda.gov/grants

AGRICULTURAL RESEARCH SERVICE
Regional – State – Local Offices

Beltsville Area
Building 003 Room 203 BARC W, Beltsville, MD 20705 301-504-7019

Maryland
Financial Management & Agreements Division 5601 Sunnyside Avenue Room 3-2175 PO Box 5110, Beltsville, MD 20705-5110 301-504-1702

Midsouth Area
Delta States Research Center PO Box 225, Stoneville, MS 38776

Midwest Area
Northern Regional Research Center 1815 N University Street, Peoria, IL 61604

North Atlantic Area
Eastern Regional Research Center 600 E Mermaid Lane, Philadelphia, PA 19118

Northern Plains Area
1201 Oakridge Drive Suite 150, Fort Collins, CO 80525-5526 303-229-5513

Pacific West Area
Western Regional Research Center 800 Buchanan Street, Albany, CA 94710

South Atlantic Area
Richard B Russell Research Center College Station Road, Athens, GA 30604-5677 706-546-3532

Southern Plains Area
7607 Eastmark Drive Suite 230, College Station, TX 77840 979-960-9444

USDA10.001 | AGRICULTURAL RESEARCH BASIC AND APPLIED RESEARCH
"Extramural Research"
Award: Project Grants
Purpose: To attain other possible ways of agricultural techniques and scientific information on agriculture.
Applicant Eligibility: Usually nonprofit Institutions of higher education or other nonprofit research Organizations, whose primary purpose is conducting scientific research.
Beneficiary Eligibility: Same as Applicant Eligibility.
Award Range/Average: $5,000 to $50,000. Average $20,000
Funding: (Project Grants) FY 18 $6,271,318.00; FY 19 est $4,704,045.00; FY 20 est $4,713,453.00
HQ: 5601 Sunnyside Avenue, PO Box 5110, Beltsville, MD 20705
    Phone: 301-504-1702 | Email: kathleen.townson@ars.usda.gov
    http://www.ars.usda.gov

USDA10.700 | NATIONAL AGRICULTURAL LIBRARY
Award: Dissemination of Technical Information
Purpose: To provide agricultural information on products to agencies of the USDA, public organizations, and individuals.
Applicant Eligibility: Individuals, State and local Governments, educational Organizations, research societies, business and industry including those located in the U.S. Territories.
Beneficiary Eligibility: Same as Applicant Eligibility.
Funding: (Cooperative Agreements) FY 17 $24,000,000.00; FY 18 est $24,000,000.00; FY 19 est $22,000,000.00

HQ: 5601 Sunnyside Avenue, PO Box 5110, Batesville, MD 20705
Phone: 301-504-1702 | Email: kathleen.townson@ars.usda.gov
http://www.nal.usda.gov

ANIMAL AND PLANT HEALTH INSPECTION SERVICE
Regional – State – Local Offices

Central Region
3505 Boca Chica Boulevard Suite 360, Brownsville, TX
78521-4065 956-504-4150
Dr. R. Harrington Jr., Regional Director | 100 W Pioneer Park-
way Suite 100, Arlington, TX 76010 817-276-2201

Eastern Region
Gary E. Larson, Regional Director | 3322 W End Avenue Suite
301, Nashville, TN 37203 615-736-2007
Jerry L. Fowler, Regional Director | Blason II 2nd Floor 505 S
Lenola Road, Moorestown, NJ 08057-1549 609-968-4970

Northern Region
Thomas Holt, Acting Regional Director | 1 Winner's Circle
Suite 100, Albany, NY 12205 518-453-0103

Southeast Region
Harold McCoy, Assistant Regional Director | 500 E Zack Street
Suite 410, Tampa, FL 33602-3945 813-228-2952

Jerry L. Fowler, Regional Director | 3505 25th Avenue Building
1, Gulfport, MS 39501 601-863-1813

Western Region
James R. Reynolds, Regional Director | 9580 Micron Avenue
Suite I, Sacramento, CA 95827 916-857-6065
Michael Worthen, Regional Director | 12345 W Alameda Park-
way Suite 204, Lakewood, CO 80228 303-969-6560
W.W. Buisch, Acting Regional Director | 384 Inverness Drive S
Suite 150, Englewood, CO 80112 303-784-6202

NATIONAL WILDLIFE RESEARCH CENTER
Colorado
Richard Curnow | 1201 Oakridge Drive, Fort Collins, CO
80525 970-223-1588

USDA10.025 | PLANT AND ANIMAL DISEASE, PEST CONTROL, AND ANIMAL CARE
Award: Project Grants
Purpose: To ensure the safety of U.S. agriculture including plants and animals.
Applicant Eligibility: Foreign, State, local, and U.S. Territorial government agencies, nonprofit Institutions of higher education, and nonprofit associations or Organizations requiring Federal support to eradicate, control, or assess the status of injurious plant and animal diseases and pests that are a threat to regional or national agriculture and conduct related demonstration projects.
Beneficiary Eligibility: Farmers, ranchers, agriculture producers, State, local, U.S. Territorial government agencies, public and private institutions and organizations benefit from Federal assistance to eradicate or control injurious plant and animal diseases and pests that are a threat to regional or national agriculture.
Funding: (Salaries and Expenses) FY 18 $246,769,118.00; FY 19 est $249,527,131.00; FY 20 est $280,732,387.00
HQ: 4700 River Road, Unit 55, Riverdale, MD 20737
Phone: 301-851-2856 | Email: eileen.m.berke@aphis.usda.gov
http://www.aphis.usda.gov

USDA10.028 | WILDLIFE SERVICES
Award: Project Grants
Purpose: To implement human methods to safeguard from zoonotic disease.
Applicant Eligibility: State and local Governments, federally recognized Indian tribal Governments, public/private nonprofit Organizations, nonprofit Institutions of higher education, and individuals.
Beneficiary Eligibility: States, local jurisdictions, U.S. Territorial government agencies, federally recognized Indian tribal governments, public and private institutions and organizations, farmers, ranchers, agricultural producers, and land/property owners benefit from Federal assistance in the control of nuisance mammals and birds and those mammal and bird species that are reservoirs for zoonotic diseases.
Funding: (Salaries and Expenses) FY 18 $7,905,018.00; FY 19 est $8,063,118.00; FY 20 est $13,466,274.00
HQ: 4700 River Road Unit 55, Suite 3B06 3, Riverdale, MD 20737
Phone: 301-851-2856 | Email: eileen.m.berke@aphis.usda.gov
http://www.aphis.usda.gov

Programs Administered by Regional - State - Local Offices

USDA10.030 | INDEMNITY PROGRAM
Award: Direct Payments With Unrestricted Use
Purpose: The animal and plant health inspection service provide compensation for the destroyed agriculture crops and cattle under the section 415 Plant Protection Act.
Applicant Eligibility: N/A
Beneficiary Eligibility: N/A
Funding: (Direct Payments with Unrestricted Use) FY 18 $6,586,698.00; FY 19 est $13,751,903.00; FY 20 est $14,400,228.00
HQ: 100 N 6th Street, Suite 510C, Minneapolis, MN 55403
    Phone: 612-336-3261 | Email: donna.r.cichy@aphis.usda.gov

BUREAU OF INDIAN AFFAIRS AND BUREAU OF INDIAN EDUCATION
Regional – State – Local Offices

Alaska
101 12th Avenue Room 16 Metlakatla Field Office PO Box 450, Metlakatla, AK 99926 907-886-3791

1675 C Street Suite 211, Anchorage, AK 99501-5198 907-271-4088

1675 C Street Suite 279, Anchorage, AK 99501-5198 907-271-4086

1675 C Street, Anchorage, AK 99501 907-271-4115

Fairbanks Agency, Fairbanks, AK 99701-6270 907-456-0222

PO Box 25520, Juneau, AK 99802-5520 907-586-7177

Arizona
10000 E McDowell Road, Scottsdale, AZ 85256 602-640-2168

400 N 5th Street PO Box 10, Phoenix, AZ 85001 602-379-3944

Building 38 Blue Canyon Highway 110 PO Box 110, Fort Defiance, AZ 86504-0110 520-729-7251

Highway 264 PO Box 568 Keams, Canyon, AZ 86034 520-738-2262

Highway 73 & Elm Street PO Box 920, White River, AZ 85941 520-338-5441

Navjo Route 7 PO Box 6003, Chinle, AZ 86503 520-674-5130, Ext. 201

PO Box 11000, Yuma, AZ 85366-1000 760-572-0248

PO Box 127, Tuba City, AZ 86045 520-283-2254, 2252

PO Box 158 Keams, Canyon, AZ 86034 520-738-2228

PO Box 209, San Carlos, AZ 85550 520-475-2321

PO Box 37, Valentine, AZ 86437 520-769-2286

PO Box 560, Whiteriver, AZ 85941 520-338-5353

PO Box 578, Sells, AZ 85634 520-383-3286

PO Box 619, Fort Defiance, AZ 86504 520-729-7217, 7218

PO Box 7 H, Chinle, AZ 86503 520-674-5100

PO Box 8, Sacaton, AZ 85247 520-562-3326

Route 1 PO Box 9-C, Parker, AZ 85344 520-669-7111

S Building 49 PO Box 38, Sells, AZ 85634 520-383-3292

Two Arizona Center 12th Floor PO Box 10 MS-100, Phoenix, AZ 85001-0010 602-379-6600

Western Navajo Agency-Education Highway 160 & Warrior Drive Building 407 PO Box 746, Tuba City, AZ 86045 520-283-2218

California
1824 Tribute Road Suite J, Sacramento, CA 95815 916-566-7121

1900 Churn Creek Road Suite 300, Redding, CA 96002 530-246-5141

2038 Iowa Avenue Suite 101, Riverside, CA 92507-0001 909-276-6624

2800 Cottage Way, Sacramento, CA 95825 916-979-2560, Ext. 234

Federal Office Building 2800 Cottage Way, Sacramento, CA 95825-1846 916-979-2600

PO Box 2245 650 E Tahquitz Canyon Way Suite A, Palm Springs, CA 92262 760-416-2133

Colorado
PO Box 315, Ignacio, CO 81137 970-563-4511

Ute Mountain Ute Field Office PO Box KK, Towaoc, CO 81334 970-565-8473

District of Columbia
1849 C Street NW PO Box 4140 MIB, Washington, DC 20240 202-208-5116

Florida
6075 Sterling Road, Hollywood, FL 33024 954-356-7288

Idaho
Plummer Subagency PO Box 408 850 A Street, Plummer, ID 83851 208-686-1887

PO Box 220, Fort Hall, ID 83203 208-238-2301

PO Box 277, Lapwai, ID 83540 208-843-2300

Kansas
Haskell Indian Nations University 155 Indian Avenue, Lawrence, KS 66046 785-749-8404

PO Box 31, Horton, KS 66439 785-486-2161

Michigan
2901 5 Interstate75 Business Spur, Sault Ste Marie, MI 49783 906-632-6809

Midwest Region
One Federal Drive Room 550, Saint Snelling, MN 55111 612-713-4400, Ext. 1020

Red Lake Field Office, Red Lake, MN 56671 218-679-3361

Minneapolis Area Education Office
331 S 2nd Avenue, Minneapolis, MN 55401-2241 612-373-1000, Ext. 1090

Programs Administered by Regional - State - Local Offices

Minnesota
Room 418 Federal Building 522 Minnesota Avenue NW, Bemidji, MN 56601-3062 218-751-2011

Mississippi
421 Powell Street, Philadelphia, MS 39350 601-656-1522, Crow Agency, MT 59022 406-638-2672

Montana
316 N 26th Street, Billings, MT 59101 406-247-7943

Northern Cheyenne Agency PO Box 40, Lame Deer, MT 59043 406-477-8242

PO Box 40, Pablo, MT 59855-5555 406-675-0242

PO Box 637, Poplar, MT 59255 406-768-5312

PO Box 69 Billings Area Education Office 316 N 26th Street, Billings, MT 59101-1397 406-247-7953

PO Box 880, Browning, MT 59417 406-338-7544

Rural Route 1 PO Box 542, Elder, MT 59521 406-395-4476

Rural Route 1 PO Box 980, Harlem, MT 59526 406-353-2901, Ext. 23

Nebraska
PO Box 18, Winnebago, NE 68071 402-878-2502

Nevada
1555 Shoshone Circle, Elko, NV 89801 775-738-0569

1677 Hot Springs Road, Carson City, NV 89706 775-887-3500

New Hampshire
PO Box 1448, Laguna, NH 87026 505-552-6001

New Mexico
1 Main Street Building 222 PO Box 328, Crownpoint, NM 87313 505-786-6150

1000 Indian School Road NW PO Box 1667, Albuquerque, NM 87103 505-346-2431

1Mile N of Espanola Highway 68 PO Box 4269 Fairview Station, Espanola, NM 87533 505-753-1465

615 1st Street NW PO Box 26567, Albuquerque, NM 87125-6567 505-346-7590

9169 Coors Road NW PO Box 10146-9196, Albuquerque, NM 87184 505-346-2343

Eastern Navajo Agency PO Box 328, Crownpoint, NM 87313 505-786-6100

Highway 666N PO Box 3239, Shiprock, NM 87420-3239 505-368-4427, Ext. 360

PO Box 1060, Gallup, NM 87305 505-863-8314

PO Box 1667, Albuquerque, NM 87103 505-346-2424

PO Box 167, Dulce, NM 87528 505-759-3951

PO Box 189, Mescalero, NM 88340 505-671-4423

PO Box 369, Zuni, NM 87327 505-782-5591

PO Box 4269 Fairview Station, Espanola, NM 87533 505-753-1400

PO Box 966, Shiprock, NM 87420 505-368-3300

Route 2 PO Box 14, Ramah, NM 87321 505-775-3235

New York
PO Box 7366, Syracuse, NY 13261-7366 315-448-0620

North Carolina
N Carolina Cherokee Agency, Cherokee, NC 28719 704-497-9131

North Dakota
Education School Street PO Box 30, Belcourt, ND 58316 701-477-6471, Ext. 211

Main Street off Highway 106 Agency Avenue PO Box E, Fort Yates, ND 58538 701-854-3497

PO Box 270, Fort Totten, ND 58335 701-766-4545

PO Box 370, New Town, ND 58763 701-627-4707

PO Box 60, Belcourt, ND 58316 701-477-3191

Standing Rock Agency PO Box E, Fort Yates, ND 58538 701-854-3433

Oklahoma
100 N 5th Street, Muskogee, OK 74401-6206 918-687-2295

1500 N Country Club Road PO Box 2240, Ada, OK 74821 580-436-0784

4149 Highline Boulevard Suite 380, Oklahoma City, OK 73108 605-945-6051, Ext. 301

624 W Independence Suite 114, Shawnee, OK 74801 405-273-0317

Concho Field Office PO Box 68, El Reno, OK 73036-0068 405-262-7481

PO Box 1060, Wewoka, OK 74884 405-257-6259

PO Box 1539, Pawhuska, OK 74056 918-287-1032

PO Box 309, Anadarko, OK 73005 405-247-6677

PO Box 368, Anadarko, OK 73005-0368 405-247-6673, Ext. 257

PO Box 370, Okmulgee, OK 74447 918-756-3950

PO Box 391, Miami, OK 74355 918-542-3396

PO Box 440, Pawnee, OK 74058-0440 918-762-2585

Talihina Office PO Box H, Talihina, OK 74571 918-567-2207

Oregon
911 N E 11 Avenue, Portland, OR 97232-4169 503-872-2743

911 NE 11th Avenue, Portland, OR 97232 503-231-6702

PO Box 1239, Warm Springs, OR 97761 541-553-2411

PO Box 520, Pendleton, OR 97801 541-278-3786

PO Box 569, Siletz, OR 97380 541-444-2679

South Dakota
100 N Main PO Box 2020, Eagle Butte, SD 51625 605-964-8722

1001 Avenue D PO Box 669, Mission, SD 57555 605-856-4478, Ext. 261

101 Main Street PO Box 333, Pine Ridge, SD 57770 605-867-1306

115 4th Avenue SE, Aberdeen, SD 57401-4382 605-226-7343

140 Education Avenue PO Box 139, Fort Thompson, SD 57339 605-245-2398

PO Box 1203, Pine Ridge, SD 57770 605-867-5125

PO Box 139, Fort Thompson, SD 57339 605-245-2311

PO Box 190, Lower Brule, SD 57548 605-473-5512

PO Box 325, Eagle Butte, SD 57625 605-964-6611

PO Box 550, Rosebud, SD 57570 605-747-2224

PO Box 577, Wagner, SD 57380 605-384-3651

PO Box 688, Agency Village, SD 57262 605-698-3001

Utah
PO Box 130, Fort Duchesne, UT 84026 435-722-4300

PO Box 720, Saint George, UT 84771 435-674-9720

Programs Administered by Regional - State - Local Offices

Virginia
3701 N Fairfax Drive Suite 260, Arlington, VA 22203
703-235-3006

Washington
2707 Colby Avenue Suite 1101, Everett, WA 98201
425-258-2651
PO Box 111, Nespelem, WA 99155-0111 509-634-2316
PO Box 115 Neah Bay, Pine Ridge, WA 98357 360-645-3232
PO Box 389, Wellpinit, WA 99040 509-258-4561

PO Box 48, Aberdeen, WA 98520 360-533-9100
Yakima Agency PO Box 151 (Tribal), Toppenish, WA 98948
509-865-5121

Wisconsin
615 Main Street W PO Box 273, Ashland, WI 54806-0273
715-682-4527

Wyoming
PO Box 158, Fort Washakie, WY 82514 307-332-7810

DOI15.020 | AID TO TRIBAL GOVERNMENTS
Award: Direct Payments for Specified Use
Purpose: To provide funds to Indian tribal governments to support general tribal government operations; to maintain up-to-date tribal registration; to conduct tribal elections; and to develop appropriate tribal policies, legislation, and regulations.
Applicant Eligibility: Federally Recognized Indian Tribal Governments.
Beneficiary Eligibility: Federally Recognized Indian Tribal Governments and members of American Indian Tribes.
HQ: Sovereignty in Indian Education Program 1849 C Street NW, PO Box MIB-3610, Washington, DC 20240
    Phone: 202-208-6123 | Email: juanita.mendoza@bie.edu
    http://www.bia.gov

DOI15.021 | CONSOLIDATED TRIBAL GOVERNMENT
Award: Direct Payments for Specified Use
Purpose: To promote Indian self-determination and improve the quality of life in Tribal communities by providing greater flexibility in planning programs and meeting the needs of communities.
Applicant Eligibility: Federally Recognized Indian Tribal Governments.
Beneficiary Eligibility: Federally Recognized Indian Tribal Governments and members of American Indian Tribes.
Award Range/Average: The range is $1,300 to $2,400,000; average $500,000.
HQ: 1849 C Street NW, PO Box 4657-MIB, Washington, DC 20240
    Phone: 202-208-3559 | Email: juanita.mendoza@bie.edu
    http://www.bia.gov

DOI15.022 | TRIBAL SELF-GOVERNANCE
Award: Direct Payments for Specified Use
Purpose: To promote Indian self-determination by providing funds to administer a wide range of programs with broad administrative and programmatic flexibility.
Applicant Eligibility: Federally Recognized Indian Tribal Governments and tribal consortia authorized by the Federally Recognized Indian Tribal Governments to be served.
Beneficiary Eligibility: Federally Recognized Indian Tribal Governments and their Members.
Award Range/Average: $9,705 to $27,537,488; Avearge $434,655.
HQ: 1849 C Street NW Bureau of Indian Education, PO Box 4657-MIB, Washington, DC 20240
    Phone: 202-208-3559 | Email: juanita.mendoza@bie.edu
    http://www.doi.gov/bureau-indian-affairs.html

DOI15.024 | INDIAN SELF-DETERMINATION CONTRACT SUPPORT
"Contract Support"
Award: Direct Payments for Specified Use
Purpose: To provide funds to federally recognized Indian Tribal Governments and to tribal organizations to fund the indirect costs incurred in administering Federal programs.
Applicant Eligibility: Federally Recognized Indian Tribal Governments and tribal Organizations authorized by Indian Tribal Governments.
Beneficiary Eligibility: Federally Recognized Indian Tribal Governments.

Award Range/Average: The range is $10,000 to $8,000,000; average $190,000.
HQ: 1849 C Street NW, PO Box 4657-MIB, Washington, DC 20240
    Phone: 202-208-3559 | Email: juanita.mendoza@bie.edu

DOI15.025 | SERVICES TO INDIAN CHILDREN, ELDERLY AND FAMILIES
"Social Services"

Award: Direct Payments for Specified Use
Purpose: To provide funds to federally recognized Indian Tribal Governments to administer welfare assistance programs for American Indians; to support caseworkers and counselors; and to support tribal programs to reduce the incidence of substance abuse and alcohol abuse in Indian country.
Applicant Eligibility: Federally Recognized Indian Tribal Governments.
Beneficiary Eligibility: Federally Recognized Indian Tribal Governments, adult American Indians in need of financial assistance or social services counselling, American Indian children who require foster care services, and American Indian youth requiring temporary, emergency shelter.
Award Range/Average: The range is $10,000 to $4,800,000; average $100,000.
HQ: 1849 C Street NW, PO Box 4657-MIB, Washington, DC 20240
    Phone: 202-208-3559 | Email: juanita.mendoza@bie.edu
    http://www.bia.gov

DOI15.026 | INDIAN ADULT EDUCATION

Award: Direct Payments for Specified Use
Purpose: To improve the educational opportunities for Indian adults who lack the level of literacy skills necessary for effective citizenship and productive employment, and to encourage the formation of adult education programs.
Applicant Eligibility: Federally Recognized Indian Tribal Governments.
Beneficiary Eligibility: Federally Recognized Indian Tribal Governments and members of American Indian Tribes.
Award Range/Average: Range is $100 to $297,000; Average $35,900.
HQ: 1849 C Street NW, Washington, DC 20240
    Phone: 202-208-5810 | Email: james.martin@bie.edu
    http://www.bie.gov

DOI15.027 | ASSISTANCE TO TRIBALLY CONTROLLED COMMUNITY COLLEGES
AND UNIVERSITIES

Award: Project Grants
Purpose: To provide funds for the operation and improvement of Tribal Colleges and Universities (TCUs) to insure continued and expanded educational opportunities for Indian students, and to allow for the improvement and expansion of their physical resources.
Applicant Eligibility: Colleges chartered by Federally Recognized Indian Tribes or tribal Organizations which are governed by a board of directors, are in operation more than one year, admit students with a certificate of graduation from a secondary institution or equivalent, provide certificates, associate, baccalaureate and graduate degrees, are nonprofit and nonsectarian, and are accredited by a nationally recognized agency or association.
Beneficiary Eligibility: Indian students who are a member of or are at least a one-fourth degree Indian blood descendant of a member of an Indian tribe which is eligible for the special programs and services provided by the United States through the Bureau of Indian Affairs to Indians because of their status as Indians.
Award Range/Average: FY 2015: Range is $273,790 to $13,598,820; Average $2,467,250. The amount of the award is determined by the number of eligible Indian students enrolled in the college. Indian Tribes may choose to supplement the funding provided by the grant program by identifying additional amounts in the Tribal Priority Allocations portion of the Bureau of Indian Affairs budget.
HQ: 1849 C Street NW Bureau of Indian Education, PO Box 4657-MIB, Washington, DC 20240
    Phone: 202-208-3559 | Email: juanita.mendoza@bie.edu
    http://www.bie.edu

Programs Administered by Regional - State - Local Offices

DOI15.028 | TRIBALLY CONTROLLED COMMUNITY COLLEGE ENDOWMENTS
Award: Project Grants
Purpose: To provide funds to establish endowments for the Tribally Controlled Community Colleges and Universities.
Applicant Eligibility: Colleges chartered by Federally Recognized Indian Tribes which are governed by an Indian board of directors, are in operation more than one year, admit students with a certificate of graduation from a secondary institution or equivalent, provide certificates, associate, baccalaureate and graduate degrees, are nonprofit and nonsectarian, and are accredited by a nationally recognized agency or association.
Beneficiary Eligibility: Indian students who are a member of or are at least a one-fourth degree Indian blood descendant of a member of an Indian tribe which is eligible for the special programs and services provided by the United States through the Bureau of Indian Affairs to Indians because of their status as Indians.
Award Range/Average: Range is $0.00 to $5,700; Average $5,700
HQ: 1849 C Street NW, Washington, DC 20240
    Phone: 202-208-3559 | Email: juanita.mendoza@bie.edu
    http://www.bie.edu

DOI15.029 | TRIBAL COURTS
Award: Direct Payments for Specified Use
Purpose: To provide grants to federally recognized Indian Tribal Governments to operate a judicial branch of government.
Applicant Eligibility: Federally Recognized Indian Tribal Governments exercising law enforcement jurisdiction on their reservation.
Beneficiary Eligibility: Federally Recognized Indian Tribal Governments.
Award Range/Average: The range is $15,000 to $800,000; average $50,000.
HQ: 1849 C Street NW Bureau of Indian Education, PO Box 4657-MIB, Washington, DC 20240
    Phone: 202-208-3559 | Email: juanita.mendoza@bie.edu
    http://www.bia.gov

DOI15.030 | INDIAN LAW ENFORCEMENT
"Law Enforcement"

Award: Direct Payments for Specified Use
Purpose: To provide grants to Indian Tribal Governments to operate police departments and detention facilities.
Applicant Eligibility: Federally Recognized Indian Tribal Governments exercising Federal criminal law enforcement authority over crimes under the Major Crimes Act (18 U.S.C. 1153) and other Federal statutes on their reservations and operating a Law Enforcement Services Program.
Beneficiary Eligibility: Federally Recognized Indian Tribal Governments.
Award Range/Average: The range is $20,000 to $20,000,000; average $200,000.
HQ: 1849 C Street NW, PO Box 4657-MIB, Washington, DC 20240
    Phone: 202-208-3559 | Email: juanita.mendoza@bie.edu

DOI15.031 | INDIAN COMMUNITY FIRE PROTECTION
"Community Fire Protection"

Award: Direct Payments for Specified Use
Purpose: To provide grants to perform fire protection services for Indian Tribal Governments that do not receive fire protection support from State or local government.
Applicant Eligibility: Federally Recognized Indian Tribal Governments performing fire protection services on their reservation.
Beneficiary Eligibility: Federally Recognized Indian Tribal Governments.
Award Range/Average: $200 to $138,000; $10,000.
HQ: 1849 C Street NW, PO Box 4657-MIB, Washington, DC 20240
    Phone: 202-208-3559 | Email: juanita.mendoza@bie.edu
    http://www.bia.gov

DOI15.032 | INDIAN ECONOMIC DEVELOPMENT

Award: Direct Payments for Specified Use

Purpose: To aid federally Recognized Indian Tribal Governments by catering the resources necessary to develop a self-sustaining economic base. The program provides opportunities for business development, the coordination and integration of programs throughout the Federal government, and the partnering of federally Recognized Indian Tribal Governments with local government and the public and private business sector.

Applicant Eligibility: Federally Recognized Indian Tribal Governments.

Beneficiary Eligibility: Federally Recognized Indian Tribal Governments and their members.

Award Range/Average: $5,000 to $300,000; $215,000.

HQ: 1849 C Street NW, PO Box 4657-MIB, Washington, DC 20240

Phone: 202-208-3559 | Email: juanita.mendoza@bie.edu

DOI15.033 | ROAD MAINTENANCE INDIAN ROADS

Award: Direct Payments for Specified Use

Purpose: To issue limited routine and preventive maintenance on BIA transportation facilities as described below: (1) BIA road systems and related road appurtenances such as signs, traffic signals, pavement striping, trail markers, guardrails, etc.; (2) Highway bridges and drainage structures; (3) Airport runways and heliport pads, including runway lighting; (4) Boardwalks; (5) Adjacent parking areas; (6) Maintenance yards; (7) Bus stations; (8) System public pedestrian walkways, paths, bike and other trails; (9) Motorized vehicle trails; (10) Public access roads to heliports and airports; (11) BIA and tribal post-secondary school roads and parking lots built with IRR Program funds; and (12) Public ferry boats and boat ramps.

Applicant Eligibility: Federally Recognized Indian Tribal Governments with BIA transportation facilities qualifying for this Program.

Beneficiary Eligibility: Federally Recognized Indian Tribal Governments; individual tribal members and the public that use the BIA transportation system on Indian Reservation and lands.

HQ: 1849 C Street NW, PO Box 4657-MIB, Washington, DC 20240

Phone: 202-208-3559 | Email: juanita.mendoza@bie.edu

DOI15.034 | AGRICULTURE ON INDIAN LANDS

Award: Direct Payments for Specified Use; Provision of Specialized Services; Advisory Services and Counseling

Purpose: To safeguard and restore the agricultural (cropland and rangeland) resources on trust lands and ease the development of renewable agricultural resources.

Applicant Eligibility: Native American individuals, tribal Governments and native Organizations authorized by tribal Governments, and individuals and entities authorized to make use of Indian agricultural lands and resources.

Beneficiary Eligibility: Native American landowners, Indian tribes and their members, native organizations authorized by tribal governments, and individuals and entities authorized to make use of Indian agricultural lands and resources. Agricultural grant programs (Rangeland Inventory and Noxious Weed Control) are not currently available to individuals or to non-tribal land-user entities.

Award Range/Average: Agriculture: $200 to $575,000; $50,000. Noxious Weed Eradication: $500 to $300,000; $6,200.

HQ: 1849 C Street NW, PO Box 4657-MIB, Washington, DC 20240

Phone: 202-208-3559 | Email: juanita.mendoza@bie.edu

DOI15.035 | FORESTRY ON INDIAN LANDS

Award: Direct Payments for Specified Use; Provision of Specialized Services; Advisory Services and Counseling

Purpose: To preserve, protect, strengthen, and develop Indian forest resources through the execution of forest management activities.

Applicant Eligibility: Federally Recognized Indian Tribal Governments and Native American Organizations authorized by Indian tribal Governments.

Beneficiary Eligibility: Federally Recognized Indian Tribal Governments and their members and Native American Organizations.

HQ: Office of Trust Services Division of Forestry and Wildland Fire Management 1849 C Street NW, PO Box 4513 MIB, Washington, DC 20240

Phone: 202-208-4620 | Email: bill_downes@bia.gov

Programs Administered by Regional - State - Local Offices

DOI15.036 | INDIAN RIGHTS PROTECTION
Award: Direct Payments for Specified Use
Purpose: To secure Indian rights guaranteed through treaty or statute by acquiring the services or information needed to litigate challenges to these rights.
Applicant Eligibility: Federally Recognized Indian Tribal Governments and Native American Organizations authorized by Indian tribal Governments.
Beneficiary Eligibility: Federally Recognized Indian Tribal Governments and their members.
Award Range/Average: Range is $1,000 to $100,000; Average $25,000.
HQ: 1849 C Street NW, PO Box 4657-MIB, Washington, DC 20240
    Phone: 202-208-3559 | Email: juanita.mendoza@bie.edu

DOI15.037 | WATER RESOURCES ON INDIAN LANDS
Award: Direct Payments for Specified Use; Provision of Specialized Services; Advisory Services and Counseling
Purpose: To assist Indian tribes in the effective and efficient management, planning, and use of their water resources.
Applicant Eligibility: Federally Recognized Indian Tribal Governments and Native American Organizations authorized by Indian tribal Governments.
Beneficiary Eligibility: Federally Recognized Indian Tribal Governments and their members and Native American Organizations.
Award Range/Average: The range is $10,000 to $200,000.
HQ: 1849 C Street NW, Washington, DC 20240
    Phone: 202-083-5590 | Email: juanita.mendoza@bie.edu

DOI15.038 | MINERALS AND MINING ON INDIAN LANDS
Award: Direct Payments for Specified Use; Provision of Specialized Services; Dissemination of Technical Information
Purpose: The key aspect of the Energy and Mineral Development Program are to provide funds to Tribes to perform technical evaluations of the energy (both renewable and conventional) and mineral resource potential of Indian reservations and provide Tribes with geological, geophysical and engineering reports, maps, and other data concerning their energy and mineral resources; and technical assistance on using and interpreting assessment information so that Tribes can understand and plan for the potential development of these resources; and with an outreach vehicle to promote their lands and resources to potential partners if they so desire. Those projects that fell into economic development categories will be considered for funding through the Office of Indian Energy and Economic Development.
Applicant Eligibility: Federally Recognized Indian Tribes and Individual American Indian mineral owners.
Beneficiary Eligibility: Federally Recognized Indian Tribal Governments and their members, Native American Organizations, and/or individual American Indian mineral property owners.
Award Range/Average: Minerals and Mining: Currently not contracted by any of the tribal governments. Mineral Assessments range is $10,000 to $250,000; average $75,000.
HQ: 1849 C Street NW Bureau of Indian Education, PO Box 4657-MIB, Washington, DC 20240
    Phone: 202-208-3559 | Email: juanita.mendoza@bie.edu
    http://www.doi.gov/whoweare/as-ia/ieed

DOI15.040 | REAL ESTATE PROGRAMS INDIAN LANDS
Award: Direct Payments for Specified Use
Purpose: To render real property management, counseling, and land use planning services to individual Indian allottees and Indian tribal and Alaska Native entities who own an interest in almost 56 million acres of trust land; to provide real estate appraisal services required in processing land transactions, and to safeguard and enhance the Indian leasehold estate by providing individual Indian landowners and Indian tribes with lease compliance activities.
Applicant Eligibility: Federally Recognized Indian Tribal Governments, Native American Organizations authorized by Tribes, and individual American Indians.
Beneficiary Eligibility: Federally Recognized Indian Tribal Governments and their members.
Award Range/Average: For Real Estate Services, tribal award amounts vary from approximately $1,000 to $500,000. For Real Estate Appraisals, the cost of most appraisals is less than $500 but can range up to approximately $2,500 or more for large or complex properties; the average is $1000. Lease Compliance awards range from $250 to $30,000 with most awards less than $5,000.

HQ: 1849 C Street NW, PO Box 4657-MIB, Washington, DC 20240

Phone: 202-208-3559 | Email: juanita.mendoza@bie.edu

DOI15.041 | ENVIRONMENTAL MANAGEMENT INDIAN

Award: Direct Payments for Specified Use

Purpose: To calculate environmental impacts of Federal projects on Indian lands; to conduct surveys of Bureau of Indian Affairs controlled Federal lands and facilities, and of Indian lands, in order to recognize hazardous waste sites, evaluate the potential threat to health and the environment, and develop the necessary remedial actions; to train area, agency and tribal staff in waste management principles; and to respond to emergencies and alleviate adverse health or environmental impacts.

Applicant Eligibility: Federally Recognized Indian Tribal Governments and Native American Organizations authorized by the Tribes.

Beneficiary Eligibility: Federally Recognized Indian tribes.

Award Range/Average: Range is $5,000 to $250,000; Average $25,000.

HQ: 1849 C Street NW Bureau of Indian Education, PO Box 4657-MIB, Washington, DC 20240

Phone: 202-208-3559 | Email: juanita.mendoza@bie.edu

http://www.doi.gov/bureau-indian-affairs.html

DOI15.042 | INDIAN SCHOOL EQUALIZATION
"ISEP"

Award: Direct Payments for Specified Use

Purpose: To allocate funding for primary and secondary education.

Applicant Eligibility: Federally Recognized Indian Tribes or tribal Organizations currently served by a Bureau of Indian education funded school.

Beneficiary Eligibility: Children between the ages of 5 and 21 who are a member of or are at least a one-fourth degree Indian blood descendant of a member of an Indian tribe which is eligible for the special programs and services provided by the United States through the Bureau of Indian Affairs to Indians because of their status as Indians.

Award Range/Average: The FY 2014 range was $161,000 to $8,930,300. The average was $2,007,600 per grant school.

HQ: 1849 C Street NW, PO Box 4657-MIB, Washington, DC 20240

Phone: 202-208-7658 | Email: joe.herrin@bie.edu

http://www.bie.edu

DOI15.043 | INDIAN CHILD AND FAMILY EDUCATION
"FACE"

Award: Project Grants; Training

Purpose: The Family and Child Education (FACE) program is aimed to serve families with children from prenatal to age five in home and center-based settings. Families may receive services in one or both settings. The program provides early childhood for all children from birth to age five and adult education for their parents through family literacy, parental involvement, increasing school readiness, high school graduation rates among Indian parents, and encouraging life-long learning.

Applicant Eligibility: Federally Recognized Indian Tribal Governments and tribal Organizations authorized by Indian tribal Governments on reservations with Bureau of Indian education funded elementary schools may apply to administer the Program.

Beneficiary Eligibility: Parents and their Indian children under 5 years of age who live on a reservation with a Bureau-funded school.

Award Range/Average: Each site receives approximately $289,910.

HQ: Division of Performance and Accountability 1011 Indian School Road NW, 3rd Floor Suite 332 BIA Building 2, Albuquerque, NM 87104

Phone: 505-563-5260 | Email: jeffrey.hamley@bie.edu

http://www.bie.edu

Programs Administered by Regional - State - Local Offices

DOI15.044 | INDIAN SCHOOLS STUDENT TRANSPORTATION
"Student Transportation"

Award: Direct Payments for Specified Use

Purpose: To assign funds to each Bureau of Indian Education (BIE) funded school for the round trip transportation of students between home and the school site.

Applicant Eligibility: Federally Recognized Indian Tribes or tribal Organizations currently served by a BIE-funded school.

Beneficiary Eligibility: Children between the ages of 5 and 21 who are members of or are at least a one-fourth degree Indian blood descendant of a member of an Indian tribe which is eligible for the special programs and services provided by the United States through the Bureau of Indian Affairs to Indians because of their status as Indians.

Award Range/Average: Range is $2,870 to $1,630,820; Average $328,061.

HQ: 1849 C Street NW Bureau of Indian Education, PO Box 4657-MIB, Washington, DC 20240

Phone: 202-208-7658 | Email: joe.herrin@bie.edu

http://www.bie.edu

DOI15.046 | ADMINISTRATIVE COST GRANTS FOR INDIAN SCHOOLS

Award: Project Grants

Purpose: To allocate grants to tribes and tribal organizations operating schools for the purpose of paying administrative and indirect costs.

Applicant Eligibility: Federally Recognized Indian Tribal Governments or Tribal Organizations operating a Bureau of Indian education funded school.

Beneficiary Eligibility: Indian Tribal Governments or tribal organizations operating a Bureau funded elementary or secondary school under a Public Law 100.297 grant or Public Law 93-638 Self-determination Contract with the Bureau of Indian Education.

Award Range/Average: Range is $127,600 to $1,166,200; Average $405,967.

HQ: 1849 C Street NW, PO Box 3609-MIB, Washington, DC 20240

Phone: 202-208-7658 | Email: joe.herrin@bie.edu

http://www.bie.edu

DOI15.047 | INDIAN EDUCATION FACILITIES, OPERATIONS, AND MAINTENANCE

Award: Direct Payments for Specified Use

Purpose: To allocate funds to BIE funded elementary schools, secondary schools and peripheral dormitories for facilities operations and maintenance.

Applicant Eligibility: Federally Recognized Indian Tribal Governments or tribal Organizations currently served by a Bureau of Indian education (BIE) funded elementary school, secondary school or peripheral dormitory.

Beneficiary Eligibility: Federally Recognized Indian Tribal Governments and occupants and visitors of BIE funded elementary or secondary schools or peripheral dormitories.

Award Range/Average: Range and Average of Financial Assistance (123): FY 2014 Range was $58,374 to $2,385,121; Average $533,888. Federally Recognized Indian Tribal Governments or tribal organizations currently served by a Bureau of Indian Education (BIE) funded elementary school, secondary school or peripheral dormitory.

HQ: 1849 C Street NW, PO Box 4657-MIB, Washington, DC 20240

Phone: 202-208-7658 | Email: joe.herrin@bie.gov

http://www.bie.edu

DOI15.048 | BUREAU OF INDIAN AFFAIRS FACILITIES OPERATIONS AND MAINTENANCE

Award: Direct Payments for Specified Use

Purpose: To assign funds for basic operating services to Bureau-owned or Bureau-operated non-education facilities and to maintain these facilities in a safe operating condition for the conduct of Bureau programs.

Applicant Eligibility: Federally Recognized Indian Tribal Governments who have Bureau-owned or Bureau-operated facilities on their reservation.

Beneficiary Eligibility: Federally Recognized Indian Tribal Governments and occupants and visitors of Bureau-owned or Bureau-operated facilities.

Award Range/Average: Not Available.

HQ: 1849 C Street NW Bureau of Indian Education, PO Box 4657-MIB, Washington, DC 20240
Phone: 202-208-3559 | Email: juanita.mendoza@bie.edu
http://www.indianaffairs.gov/as-ia/ofpsm/dfmc/om

DOI15.051 | ENDANGERED SPECIES ON INDIAN LANDS

Award: Direct Payments for Specified Use; Advisory Services and Counseling; Dissemination of Technical Information

Purpose: To adhere with the Endangered Species Act, the Northern Spotted Owl Recovery plan, and to carry out the Endangered Species Recovery on Indian lands.

Applicant Eligibility: Federally Recognized Indian Tribal Governments and Native American Organizations authorized by Indian tribal Governments whose reservations are in areas inhabited by these specific endangered species.

Beneficiary Eligibility: Federally Recognized Indian Tribal Governments and Native American Organizations authorized by Indian tribal governments.

Award Range/Average: Range is $20,000 to $140,000; Average $50,000.

HQ: 1849 C Street NW, PO Box 4657-MIB, Washington, DC 20240
Phone: 202-208-3559 | Email: juanita.mendoza@bie.edu

DOI15.052 | LITIGATION SUPPORT FOR INDIAN RIGHTS

Award: Direct Payments for Specified Use

Purpose: To implement or safeguard the Indian property or treaty rights through judicial, administrative, or settlement actions.

Applicant Eligibility: Federally Recognized Indian Tribal Governments and Native American Organizations authorized by these Tribes.

Beneficiary Eligibility: Federally Recognized Indian Tribes and their members.

Award Range/Average: Funding range and average is not available. Approximately 30 funding requests are received on an annual basis; between 20 and 25 are funded each year.

HQ: 1849 C Street NW, PO Box 4657-MIB, Washington, DC 20240
Phone: 202-208-3559 | Email: juanita.mendoza@bie.edu

DOI15.053 | ATTORNEY FEES INDIAN RIGHTS

Award: Direct Payments for Specified Use

Purpose: To help or aid federally Recognized Tribes in protecting their treaty rights and other rights established through Executive Order or court action.

Applicant Eligibility: Federally Recognized Indian Tribal Governments.

Beneficiary Eligibility: Federally Recognized Indian Tribes and their members.

HQ: 1849 C Street NW Bureau of Indian Education, PO Box 4657-MIB, Washington, DC 20240
Phone: 202-208-3559 | Email: juanita.mendoza@bie.edu

DOI15.057 | NAVAJO-HOPI INDIAN SETTLEMENT

Award: Direct Payments for Specified Use; Provision of Specialized Services

Purpose: To carry out those provisions of the Navajo-Hopi Settlement Act of 1974, as amended, which are allocated to the Department of the Interior; and to introduce conservation practices and methods to restore the grazing potential of rangelands lying within the former Navajo/Hopi Joint Use Area.

Applicant Eligibility: Federally Recognized Indian Tribal Governments of the Navajo and Hopi Tribes and Native American Organizations authorized by either Tribe.

Beneficiary Eligibility: Federally Recognized Indian Tribal Governments of the Navajo and Hopi Tribes and individual members of both Tribes.

HQ: 1849 C Street NW, PO Box 4657-MIB, Washington, DC 20240
Phone: 202-208-3559 | Email: juanita.mendoza@bie.edu
http://www.doi.gov/bureau-indian-affairs.html

Programs Administered by Regional - State - Local Offices

DOI15.058 | INDIAN POST SECONDARY SCHOOLS
"Haskell Indian Nations University (Haskell) and SouthwesternIndian Polytechnic Institute (SIPI)"

Award: Training
Purpose: To arrange or layout postsecondary educational opportunities for American Indian Students.
Applicant Eligibility: American Indians and Alaskan Natives.
Beneficiary Eligibility: Same as Applicant Eligibility.
Award Range/Average: Not identifiable.
HQ: 1849 C Street NW, PO Box 4657-MIB, Washington, DC 20240
   Phone: 202-208-3559 | Email: juanita.mendoza@bie.edu

DOI15.059 | INDIAN GRADUATE STUDENT SCHOLARSHIPS
"Special Higher Education Scholarships"

Award: Project Grants
Purpose: To assign financial aid to eligible Indian students to enable them to obtain advanced degrees.
Applicant Eligibility: Individual applicants must be Indian students who are members of Federally Recognized Indian Tribes, who have been admitted to a graduate Program and have unmet financial need.
Beneficiary Eligibility: Members of Federally Recognized Indian Tribes who are a member of or are at least one-fourth degree Indian blood descendant of a member of an Indian tribe which is eligible for the special programs and services provided by the United States through the Bureau of Indian Affairs to Indians because of their status as Indians.
Award Range/Average: Range is $250 to $4,000; Average $3,947.
HQ: 1849 C Street NW, PO Box 4657-MIB, Washington, DC 20240
   Phone: 202-208-3559 | Email: juanita.mendoza@bie.edu
   http://www.bie.edu/contact.htm

DOI15.060 | INDIAN VOCATIONAL TRAINING UNITED TRIBES TECHNICAL COLLEGE

Award: Direct Payments With Unrestricted Use; Training
Purpose: To render vocational training to individual American Indians through the United Tribes Technical College, located in Bismarck, North Dakota.
Applicant Eligibility: Application to administer the Program is limited to the United Tribes Technical College. Individual American Indian applicants must be a member of a Federally Recognized Indian Tribe, be in need of financial assistance, and reside on or near an Indian reservation under the jurisdiction of the Bureau of Indian Affairs.
Beneficiary Eligibility: Individual American Indians who are members of a Federally Recognized Indian Tribe and reside on or near an Indian reservation under the jurisdiction of the Bureau of Indian Affairs. Complete information on beneficiary eligibility is found in 25 CFR, Parts 26 and 27.
Award Range/Average: Range is between $500 to $3,000; Average $2,500.
HQ: 1849 C Street NW, PO Box 4657-MIB, Washington, DC 20240
   Phone: 202-208-3559 | Email: juanita.mendoza@bie.edu

DOI15.061 | INDIAN JOB PLACEMENT UNITED SIOUX TRIBES DEVELOPMENT CORPORATION
"United Sioux Tribes"

Award: Direct Payments With Unrestricted Use; Advisory Services and Counseling
Purpose: To render job development, counseling, social adjustment guidance, and referrals to job training programs and other assistance programs through the United Sioux Tribes Development Corporation, located in Pierre, South Dakota.
Applicant Eligibility: Application to administer the Program is limited to the United Sioux Tribes Development Corporation. Individual American Indian applicants must be a member of a Federally Recognized Indian Tribe, be in need of financial assistance, and reside on or near an Indian reservation under the jurisdiction of the Bureau of Indian Affairs.

Beneficiary Eligibility: Must be an American Indian member of a Federally Recognized Indian Tribe and reside on or near an Indian reservation under the jurisdiction of the Bureau of Indian Affairs. Complete information on beneficiary eligibility is found in 25 CFR, Parts 26 and 27.

Award Range/Average: Students receive $185 per week for the duration of the program for room and board and miscellaneous expenses. Work clothes and tools are also provided.

HQ: 1849 C Street NW, PO Box 4657-MIB, Washington, DC 20240
   Phone: 202-208-3559 | Email: juanita.mendoza@bie.edu

DOI15.062 | REPLACEMENT AND REPAIR OF INDIAN SCHOOLS

Award: Direct Payments for Specified Use

Purpose: To provide safe, functional, code-compliant, economical, and energy efficient education facilities for American Indian students attending Bureau of Indian Affairs owned or funded primary and secondary schools and/or residing in Bureau owned or funded dormitories. Additional objectives for ARRA funded projects comprise of having a demonstrated or potential ability to deliver programmatic results, optimizing economic activity and the number of jobs created or saved, obtaining long-term public benefits from improved school infrastructure, fostering energy independence or improving educational quality.

Applicant Eligibility: Federally Recognized Indian Tribal Governments and Tribal Organizations, including School Boards, who have a prioritized Replacement School Construction or Facilities Improvement and Repair, for which funds have been specifically approved through the appropriation process, or for which ARRA funds have been allocated.

Beneficiary Eligibility: American Indian children attending Bureau owned or funded primary and secondary schools and/or American Indian children residing in Bureau owned or funded dormitories.

Award Range/Average: The amount of financial assistance can range from approximately $6 million to $25 million depending on the size of the school, both grade level and student enrollment, the program requirements, and the location. For the higher amounts, funding may be incremental over 2,3, or even 5 years. Because of the limited number of schools that have received funding in the last few years and the increasing costs for construction, there is no way to determine a true representative "average" of financial assistance. Facilities Improvement and Repair: The amount of financial assistance can range significantly from a few thousand dollars to approximately $7 million. There are several categories of projects that are included under Facilities Improvement and Repair, such as, Emergency, Roofing, Replacement/Repair, and Portable Classrooms. The average amount of financial assistance can vary depending on the category. An average amount is not calculable.

HQ: 1849 C Street NW Bureau of Indian Education, PO Box 4657-MIB, Washington, DC 20240
   Phone: 202-208-3559 | Email: juanita.mendoza@bie.edu
   http://www.bia.gov

DOI15.063 | IMPROVEMENT AND REPAIR OF INDIAN DETENTION FACILITIES

Award: Direct Payments for Specified Use

Purpose: To help in providing a safe, functional, code and standards compliant, economical, and energy-efficient adult and/or juvenile detention facilities. Additional objectives for ARRA-funded projects consists of having a demonstrated or potential ability to deliver programmatic results, optimizing economic activity and the number of jobs created or saved, achieving long-term public benefits from improved detention facilities, infrastructure, fostering energy independence.

Applicant Eligibility: Federally Recognized Indian Tribal Governments or Tribal Organizations who have a prioritized Facilities Improvement and Repair and for which funds have been specifically approved through the appropriation process or for which ARRA funds have been allocated.

Beneficiary Eligibility: Federally Recognized Indian Tribal Governments in Bureau owned or funded Law Enforcement/ Detention Facilities.

Award Range/Average: Facilities Improvement and Repair: The amount of financial assistance can range significantly from a few thousand dollars to approximately $3 million. There are several categories of projects that are included under Facilities Improvement and Repair, such as, Emergency, Roofing and Environmental. The average amount of financial assistance can vary depending on the category. ARRA-funded projects range from less than $1.1 million to $1.6 Million.

HQ: 1849 C Street NW Bureau of Indian Education, PO Box 4657-MIB, Washington, DC 20240
   Phone: 202-208-3559 | Email: juanita.mendoza@bie.edu

DOI15.065 | SAFETY OF DAMS ON INDIAN LANDS

Award: Direct Payments for Specified Use

Purpose: To enhance the structural integrity of dams on Indian lands, including operations and maintenance of these dams.

Programs Administered by Regional - State - Local Offices

Applicant Eligibility: Federally Recognized Indian Tribal Governments and Native American Organizations authorized by Indian tribal Governments to be benefited by the award.

Beneficiary Eligibility: Federally Recognized Indian Tribal Governments and their members and Native American Organizations.

Award Range/Average: Range is variable depending upon the scope of work. Awards are commonly awarded for various phases of the safety program. For example, conception design $100,000 to $300,000; final design $300,000 to $1,000,000; and construction repair $1,000,000 to $17,000,000. For the non-construction portion, awards can be from $10,000 up to $250,000.

HQ: PE Office of Trust Services Division of Water and Power Branch of Safety of Dams 13922 Denver W Parkway, Lakewood, CO 80401
Phone: 303-231-5222 | Email: jack.byers@bia.gov

DOI15.066 | TRIBAL GREAT LAKES RESTORATION INITIATIVE
"Tribal GLRI"

Award: Project Grants

Purpose: The BIA Tribal GLRI Program offers financial assistance to Great Lakes tribes to protect, enhance, and restore the Great Lakes. Priority actions are to identify, protect, conserve, manage, enhance, or restore species or habitat, as well as to build tribal capacity to oversee natural resources within the Great Lakes Basin.

Applicant Eligibility: Federally-recognized Indian Tribes and Native American Organizations authorized by Indian tribal Governments.

Beneficiary Eligibility: Same as Applicant Eligibility.

Award Range/Average: Projects may range from $1,000 to $500,000, or greater. Average over two years is $162,000.

Funding: (Project Grants (Discretionary)) FY 16 Not Separately Identifiable; FY 17 est Not Separately Identifiable; FY 18 est Not Separately Identifiable

HQ: 5600 W American Boulevard, Suite 500, Bloomington, MN 55437
Phone: 612-725-4529 | Email: merben.cebrian@bia.gov

DOI15.067 | STRENGTHENING TRIBAL NATIONS

Award: Cooperative Agreements; Advisory Services and Counseling; Dissemination of Technical Information; Training

Purpose: To allocate funding to advance nation-to-nation relationships, support Indian families and protect Indian country, support sustainable stewardship of trust resources, and advance Indian education.

Applicant Eligibility: N/A

Beneficiary Eligibility: American Indians/Alaska Natives will be the ultimate beneficiaries of the funded projects either directly or indirectly depending upon the nature of the project.

HQ: 1849 C Street NW Bureau of Indian Education, PO Box 4657-MIB, Washington, DC 20240
Phone: 202-208-3559 | Email: juanita.mendoza@bie.edu
http://www.bia.gov

DOI15.108 | INDIAN EMPLOYMENT ASSISTANCE
"Employment Assistance Program"

Award: Direct Payments for Specified Use

Purpose: To render vocational training and employment opportunities to eligible American Indians and Alaska Natives to reduce Federal dependence.

Applicant Eligibility: Federally Recognized Indian Tribal Governments and Native American Organizations authorized by Indian Tribal Governments may apply to administer the Program. Individual American Indian and Alaska Native applicants must be a member of a Federally Recognized Indian Tribe, be in need of financial assistance, and reside on or near an Indian reservation or in Alaska under the jurisdiction of the Bureau of Indian Affairs.

Beneficiary Eligibility: Members of Federally Recognized Indian Tribes who are unemployed, underemployed, or in need of training to obtain reasonable and gainful employment. Complete information on beneficiary eligibility is found in 25 CFR, Part 26.

Award Range/Average: Not Available.

HQ: 1849 C Street NW Bureau of Indian Education, PO Box 4657-MIB, Washington, DC 20240
Phone: 202-208-3559 | Email: juanita.mendoza@bie.edu
http://www.bia.gov

DOI15.113 | INDIAN SOCIAL SERVICES WELFARE ASSISTANCE

Award: Direct Payments for Specified Use

Purpose: To offer financial assistance for basic needs of needy eligible American Indians who reside on or near reservations, including those American Indians living under Bureau of Indian Affairs service area jurisdictions, when such backing is not available from State or local public agencies.

Applicant Eligibility: An American Indian who is a member of a federally recognized Indian Tribe, who resides on or near a federally recognized Indian reservations, who is in need of financial assistance and who meets the eligibility criteria in 25 CFR Part 20.

Beneficiary Eligibility: American Indians who are members of federally recognized Indian Tribes.

Award Range/Average: May range from a few hundred to several hundred dollars monthly depending upon the assistance provided.

HQ: 1849 C Street NW Bureau of Indian Education, PO Box 4657-MIB, Washington, DC 20240
Phone: 202-208-3559 | Email: juanita.mendoza@bie.edu
http://www.bia.gov

DOI15.114 | INDIAN EDUCATION HIGHER EDUCATION GRANT
"Higher Education"

Award: Project Grants

Purpose: To offer financial aid to eligible Indian students to enable them to attend accredited institutions of higher education.

Applicant Eligibility: Federally Recognized Indian Tribal Governments and tribal Organizations authorized by Indian Tribal Governments may apply to administer the Program. Individuals who are members of Federally Recognized Indian Tribes may submit applications for benefits directly to the Bureau of Indian Affairs if the Bureau agency serving their reservation provides direct services for this Program. Individuals must be enrolled in an accredited college and have financial need as determined by the institution's financial aid office.

Beneficiary Eligibility: Members of a Federally Recognized Indian Tribe who are enrolled or accepted for enrollment in an accredited college and have financial need as determined by the institution's financial aid office.

Award Range/Average: Range is $300 to $5,000; Average $2,700.

HQ: Office of Indian Education Programs Bureau of Indian Affairs 1849 C Street NW, PO Box 4657-MIB, Washington, DC 20240
Phone: 202-208-7658 | Email: joe.herrin@bie.edu
http://www.bie.edu

DOI15.124 | INDIAN LOANS ECONOMIC DEVELOPMENT
"Loan Guaranty, Insurance, and Interest Subsidy Program"

Award: Guaranteed/insured Loans

Purpose: To render assistance to federally Recognized Indian Tribal Governments, Native American Organizations, and individual American Indians in acquiring financing from private sources to promote business development initiatives to improve the economies of federally Recognized Indian Reservations.

Applicant Eligibility: Federally Recognized Indian Tribal Governments, Native American Organizations authorized by Indian tribal Governments, and individual American Indians.

Beneficiary Eligibility: Federally Recognized Indian Tribal Governments, Native American Organizations, and individual American Indians or Alaska natives. Complete information on beneficiary eligibility is found in 25 CFR, Part 103.

HQ: 1849 C Street NW Bureau of Indian Education, PO Box 4657-MIB, Washington, DC 20240
Phone: 202-208-3559 | Email: juanita.mendoza@bie.edu

DOI15.130 | INDIAN EDUCATION ASSISTANCE TO SCHOOLS
"Johnson-O'Malley"

Award: Direct Payments for Specified Use

Purpose: To finance programs that meets the unique and specialized needs of eligible Indian students.

Applicant Eligibility: Tribal Organizations, Indian Corporations, school districts or States which have eligible Indian children attending public school districts and have established Indian education Committees to approve supplementary or operational support Programs beneficial to Indian students. Current funding is calculated with the 1995 JOM student count.

Beneficiary Eligibility: Children who are enrolled members of, or at least one-fourth or more degree of Indian blood descendant of a member of a federally recognized Indian tribal government eligible for service by the Bureau, and are between age 3 through grade 12 with priority given to those residing on or near Indian reservations.

Award Range/Average: Range is $100 to $3,360,980; TPA Average $77,300

Funding: (Direct Payments for Specified Use) FY 16 Not Separately Identifiable; FY 17 est Not Separately Identifiable: FY 18 est Not Separately Identifiable

HQ: 1849 C Street NW Bureau of Indian Education, PO Box 4657-MIB, Washington, DC 20240

Phone: 202-208-4397 | Email: jennifer.davis@bie.edu

http://www.bie.edu

DOI15.133 | NATIVE AMERICAN BUSINESS DEVELOPMENT INSTITUTE "NABDI"

Award: Formula Grants

Purpose: Under its Native American Business Development Institute (NABDI) conceived in FY 2006, IEED has established partnerships with U.S. graduate schools to help tribal business evaluate financial opportunities and prepare economic feasibility studies. Assistance by way of Public Law 93-638 agreements between tribes and participating business schools. During FY 2006- 2010, NABDI assisted tribes to estimate the potential of economic opportunities as diverse as a business park, a meat packing plant, a wind energy project, a security business, a medical supply business, upland bird hunting, new uses for a dormant tribal wellness/recreation center, and a greenhouse heated by way of woody biomass. Starting in FY 2011, NABDI funding will be dispersed on a competitive basis following notice in the Federal Register. Applicants will be free to choose private consultants in addition to graduate schools.

Applicant Eligibility: Federally Recognized Indian Tribal Governments.

Beneficiary Eligibility: Federally Recognized Indian Tribal governments and their members.

Award Range/Average: Determined on an annual basis, subject to appropriations.

HQ: 1849 C Street NW Bureau of Indian Education, PO Box 4657-MIB, Washington, DC 20240

Phone: 202-208-3559 | Email: juanita.mendoza@bie.edu

DOI15.141 | INDIAN HOUSING ASSISTANCE

Award: Project Grants; Dissemination of Technical Information

Purpose: To utilize the Housing Improvement Program (HIP) resources of the Bureau of Indian Affairs to remove substantially substandard Indian owned and inhabited housing for very low income eligible Indians living in approved tribal service areas. This effort is assisted by the Indian Health Service (Department of Health and Human Services) which provides water and sanitary systems for houses repaired or built with HIP funds.

Applicant Eligibility: Federally Recognized Indian Tribal Governments and tribal Organizations to administer the Program who have eligible applicants with identified housing needs. Individual members of Federally recognized Indian Tribes living in approved tribal service areas in need of housing assistance who are unable to obtain assistance from any other source, and who meet the eligibility criteria of the HIP regulations (25 CFR Part 256 "Housing Improvement Program ").

Beneficiary Eligibility: Individual members of Federally recognized Indian tribes.

Award Range/Average: For HIP, maximum of $35,000 for repairs and renovations; $2,500 for interim improvements. The average cost of repair has been approximately $17,500. New housing does not have a specified maximum amount but is intended to provide only a modest standard dwelling. Average new housing construction cost has been approximately $100,000.

HQ: 1849 C Street NW Bureau of Indian Education, PO Box 4657-MIB, Washington, DC 20240

Phone: 202-208-3559 | Email: juanita.mendoza@bie.edu

DOI15.144 | INDIAN CHILD WELFARE ACT TITLE II GRANTS

Award: Project Grants

Purpose: To foster the stability and security of American Indian tribes and families by protecting American Indian children and avert the separation of American Indian families and providing assistance to Indian tribes in the operation of child and family service programs designed to prevent the breakup families.

Applicant Eligibility: Federally Recognized Indian Tribal Governments.

Beneficiary Eligibility: American Indian children and families.

Award Range/Average: $26,449 to $750,000; $60,000.

HQ: 1849 C Street NW Bureau of Indian Education, PO Box 4657-MIB, Washington, DC 20240
Phone: 202-208-3559 | Email: juanita.mendoza@bie.edu

DOI15.146 | IRONWORKER TRAINING

Award: Project Grants

Purpose: To render ironworker vocational training, apprenticeships, and job placement to eligible American Indians through the National Ironworkers Training Program, located in Broadview, Illinois.

Applicant Eligibility: Applicants must be an American Indian who is a member of a Federally Recognized Indian Tribe, at least 18 years old, possess a high school diploma or General Equivalency Development (GED) Certificate, be in good physical health, and reside on or near an Indian reservation under the jurisdiction of the Bureau of Indian Affairs.

Beneficiary Eligibility: American Indian who is a member of a Federally Recognized Indian Tribal Government, at least 18 years old, possess a high school diploma or General Equivalency Development (GED) Certificate, be in good physical health, and reside on or near an Indian reservation under the jurisdiction of the Bureau of Indian Affairs. Complete information on beneficiary eligibility is found in 25 CFR, Part 26.

Award Range/Average: Students receive $185 per week for the duration of the program for room and board and miscellaneous expenses. Work clothes and tools are also provided.

HQ: 1849 C Street NW Bureau of Indian Education, PO Box 4657-MIB, Washington, DC 20240
Phone: 202-208-3559 | Email: juanita.mendoza@bie.edu

DOI15.147 | TRIBAL COURTS TRUST REFORM INITIATIVE

Award: Project Grants

Purpose: To allocate grant funds to federally Recognized Indian Tribal Governments that operate a judicial branch of government which has assumed the increased responsibilities required by 25 CFR Part 115-Trust Funds for Individual Indians Money accounts.

Applicant Eligibility: Federally Recognized Indian Tribal Governments that operate a judicial branch of government which has assumed the increased responsibilities required by 25 CFR Part 115.

Beneficiary Eligibility: Federally Recognized Indian Tribal Governments that operate a tribal judicial branch which has assumed the increased responsibilities required by 25 CFR Part 115 and its members.

Award Range/Average: $3,000 to $216,000; $50,000

HQ: 1849 C Street NW Bureau of Indian Education, PO Box 4657-MIB, Washington, DC 20240
Phone: 202-208-3559 | Email: juanita.mendoza@bie.edu

DOI15.148 | TRIBAL ENERGY DEVELOPMENT CAPACITY GRANTS "TEDC "

Award: Direct Payments for Specified Use

Purpose: To allocate development grants to Indian tribes for use in developing and sustaining the managerial and technical capacity needed to enhance their energy resources, and to properly account for resulting energy production and revenues. Proposals from tribes should strive to obtain the following stated goals: To evaluate the type and range of energy development activities that a tribe way want to assume under a TERA; To determine the current level of scientific, technical, administrative, for financial management capacity of the tribe to assume responsibility for the identified development activities; and to determine which scientific, technical, administrative, or financial management capacities needs enhancement and what process and/or procedures the grantee may use to eliminate these capacity gaps.

Applicant Eligibility: Federally Recognized Indian Tribal Governments.

Beneficiary Eligibility: Federally Recognized Tribal Governments and their members.

Award Range/Average: Determined on an annual basis, subject to appropriations.

HQ: 1849 C Street NW Bureau of Indian Education, PO Box 4657-MIB, Washington, DC 20240
Phone: 202-208-3559 | Email: juanita.mendoza@bie.edu

Programs Administered by Regional - State - Local Offices

DOI15.149 | FOCUS ON STUDENT ACHIEVEMENT
"Focus"

Award: Project Grants

Purpose: The FOCUS program focuses on schools where student achievement is close to achieving annual measurable objectives as set by their state's achievement test and where additional resources could facilitate achievement of Adequate Yearly Progress (AYP) as required by Public Law 107-110, the No Child Left Behind Act of 2001.

Applicant Eligibility: Federally Recognized Indian Tribal Governments and tribal Organizations authorized by Indian tribal Governments on reservations with Bureau-funded schools may apply to administer the Program.

Beneficiary Eligibility: Children between the ages of 5 and 21 who are members of or are at least a one-fourth degree Indian blood descendant of a member of an Indian tribe which is eligible for the special programs and services provided by the United States through the Bureau of Indian Affairs to Indians because of their status as Indians.

Award Range/Average: Range is $100,000 to $225,000; Average $153,333.

HQ: Division of Performance and Accountability 1011 Indian School Road NW, Suite 332 BIA Building 2 3rd Floor, Albuquerque, NM 87104

Phone: 505-563-5250 | Email: joel.longie@bie.edu
http://www.bie.edu

DOI15.150 | JUVENILE DETENTION EDUCATION

Award: Project Grants

Purpose: The Juvenile Detention Education Program offers education services to detained and incarcerated youth in the 24 Bureau of Indian Affairs funded juvenile detention centers.

Applicant Eligibility: Federally Recognized Indian Tribal Governments and tribal Organizations authorized by Indian tribal Governments on reservations with BIA-funded JDCs.

Beneficiary Eligibility: Children between the ages of 5 and 21 who are members of or are at least a one-fourth degree Indian blood descendant of a member of an Indian tribe which is eligible for the special programs and services provided by the United States through the Bureau of Indian Affairs to Indians because of their status as Indians.

Award Range/Average: In Fiscal Year 2010 the average grant/and contract was $34,444, minimum grant was $19,000, maximum grant was $56,000.

HQ: Division of Performance and Accountability 1011 Indian School Road NW, Suite 332 BIA Building 2 3rd Floor, Albuquerque, NM 87104

Phone: 505-563-5250 | Email: jeffrey.hamley@bie.edu

DOI15.151 | EDUCATION ENHANCEMENTS
"BIE Reads!and Math Counts"

Award: Cooperative Agreements

Purpose: Education Program Enhancements offers resources for special studies, projects, new activities, and other costs associated with enhancing the basic educational programs provided to students. These funds allow BIE to provide specialized assistance to schools struggling to make Adequate Yearly Progress (AYP) that is focused to address the schools' unique needs and specific gaps in achievement. Typically, assistance comprises of implementation of specialized programs in reading and math, and staff development for principals, teachers and support staff.

Applicant Eligibility: Federally Recognized Indian Tribal Governments and tribal Organizations authorized by Indian tribal Governments on reservations with Bureau-funded schools may apply to administer the Program.

Beneficiary Eligibility: Children between the ages of 5 and 21 who are members of or are at least a one-fourth degree Indian blood descendant of a member of an Indian tribe which is eligible for the special programs and services provided by the United States through the Bureau of Indian Affairs to Indians because of their status as Indians.

Award Range/Average: In Fiscal Year 2012 the average Reads grant was $23,052, and the maximum Reads grant was $176,038; the average Math Counts grant was $17,353 and the maximum Math Counts grant was 232,507.

HQ: Division of Performance and Accountability 1011 Indian School Road NW, Suite 332 BIA Building 2 3rd Floor, Albuquerque, NM 87104

Phone: 505-563-5250 | Email: joel.longie@bie.edu

DOI15.156 | TRIBAL CLIMATE RESILIENCE
"Climate Change"
Award: Direct Payments for Specified Use
Purpose: The Cooperative Landscape Conservation (CLC) program allocates funds and technical support to enable tribal governments and trust land managers to better understand potential impacts and vulnerabilities of communities, ecosystems and built systems to climate-related change, to enable them to develop information and tools to support planning and decision making, to establish strategies that elevates the preparedness and resilience of communities in the face of a changing climate and address the potential for increased peak weather events. The program also enables tribal participation in ocean and coastal planning.
Applicant Eligibility: Direct Support Awards: Federally Recognized Indian Tribal Governments, Native American Organizations authorized by Indian tribal Governments and Native American non-profit Organizations, federally/ tribally chartered tribal colleges and universities. Providers of Training and Technical Support Awards: Native American Organizations authorized by Indian tribal Governments, federally/tribally chartered tribal colleges and universities, Native American tribal and non-profit Organizations, and public universities. (Contact BIA Central Office for details).
Beneficiary Eligibility: Federally Recognized Indian Tribal Governments and consortia, tribal and public colleges and universities, and Native American organizations.
Award Range/Average: Not Available.
HQ: 1849 C Street NW, PO Box 4635 MIB, Washington, DC 20240
  Phone: 202-513-0337 | Email: sean.hart@bia.gov
  http://www.bia.gov

DOI15.159 | CULTURAL RESOURCES MANAGEMENT
Award: Project Grants; Direct Payments for Specified Use
Purpose: To verify the proper management, protection, and preservation of cultural resources over which the BIA maintains responsibility; furnish secure, short-term housing and care for cultural resources regained during investigations; provide for the curation, stewardship, and public access to BIA museum collections and other cultural resources, including the increase of public awareness, appreciation, and knowledge of these resources.
Applicant Eligibility: State and local agencies, sponsored Organizations, public nonprofit Institutions /Organizations, other public Institutions /Organizations, Federally-recognized Indian Tribal Governments, specialized groups, small businesses, profit Organizations, private nonprofit Institutions /Organizations, quasi-public nonprofit Institutions /Organizations, other private Institutions /Organizations, and Native American Organizations, educational or scientific Organization, or any institution, corporation, association, or individual that possesses the requisite professional expertise. Applicant eligibility will be specified in the Funding Opportunity Announcement, if applicable.
Beneficiary Eligibility: State and local governments, Federally recognized Indian Tribal governments, nonprofit organizations, educational or scientific institutions, universities, associations, and entities that have an education mission or mission-component, and museums and/or repositories that meet the standards of the Department of the Interior, Department Manual, Part 411.
HQ: 12220 Sunrise Valley Drive, Room 6084, Reston, VA 20191
  Phone: 703-390-6343 | Email: anna.pardo@bia.gov
  http://www.bia.gov

DOI15.160 | BIA WILDLAND URBAN INTERFACE COMMUNITY FIRE ASSISTANCE
Award: Cooperative Agreements; Use of Property, Facilities, and Equipment; Dissemination of Technical Information; Training
Purpose: To establish the National Fire Plan and help communities at risk from catastrophic wildland fires by providing assistance in the following areas: Community programs that develop local capability including; assessment and planning, mitigation activities, and community and homeowner education and action; plan and implement hazardous fuels reduction activities, including the training, monitoring or maintenance associated with such hazardous fuels reduction activities, on federal land, or on adjacent nonfederal land for activities that mitigate the threat of catastrophic fire to communities and natural resources in high risk areas; improve local and small business employment opportunities for rural communities; enhance the knowledge and fire protection capability of rural fire districts by providing aid in education and training; assist with the prevention and detection of wildfires to minimize the risk and impact to communities and their values.
Applicant Eligibility: States and local Governments at risk as published in the Federal Register, Indian Tribes, public and private education Institutions, nonprofit Organizations, and rural fire departments serving a community with a population of 10,000 or less in the wildland/urban interface.

Programs Administered by Regional - State - Local Offices

Beneficiary Eligibility: Same as Applicant Eligibility.
HQ: 12220 Sunrise Valley Drive, Room 6084, Reston, VA 20191
   Phone: 703-390-6343 | Email: anna.pardo@bia.gov

DOI15.161 | NATIVE LANGUAGE IMMERSION GRANT
Award: Direct Payments for Specified Use
Purpose: Offers capacity building grants for Bureau-funded schools to amplify existing language immersion programs or create new programs that will lead to oral Native language proficiency.
Applicant Eligibility: Specialized group: Bureau of Indian education Funded Schools.
Beneficiary Eligibility: American Indian Student.
Award Range/Average: Range: $1,000.00 - $95,000, or greater. Average: $48,500 over one year.
Funding: (Direct Payments for Specified Use) FY 17 Actual Not Available; FY 18 est $2,000,000.00; FY 19 est Estimate Not Available
HQ: 1849 C Street NW, PO Box MIB 3610, Washington, DC 20240
   Phone: 202-208-6123 | Email: juanita.mendoza@bie.edu

DOI15.162 | TIWAHE HOUSING
Award: Project Grants
Purpose: According to the FY 17 Appropriations Bill, to enhance tribal communities in Indian country by leveraging programs and resources; to maximize the number of single families and veterans assisted; and to address the dilapidated and overcrowded housing conditions in Tribes' service.
Applicant Eligibility: Tribe must hold status as an active Tiwahe Initiative Tribe with an approved Tiwahe Initiative Plan that includes a plan and budget for Tiwahe housing funds.
Beneficiary Eligibility: Federally Recognized Indian Tribal Government.
Award Range/Average: At the present time, $1,688,304 has been allotted. However, additional funds may become available.
Funding: (Project Grants) FY 17 Actual Not Available; FY 18 est $281,384.00; FY 19 Estimate Not Available
HQ: 1849 C Street NW, Washington, DC 20240
   Phone: 202-513-7712 | Email: meredes.garcia@bia.gov
   http://www.bia.gov/bia/ois

DOI15.163 | TRIBAL EDUCATION DEPARTMENTS "TED"
Award: Direct Payments for Specified Use
Purpose: Allocates grants and offers technical assistance to tribes for the development and operation of tribal departments or divisions of education for the purpose of planning and coordinating all education programs of the tribe.
Applicant Eligibility: Specialized group: Indian Tribes which are federally recognized as eligible by the U.S. government through the Secretary of the Interior for the special Programs and services provided by the Secretary because of their status as Indians.
Beneficiary Eligibility: Same as Applicant Eligibility.
Award Range/Average: $50,000.00 - $300,000.00
HQ: 1849 C Street NW, PO Box MIB-3610, Washington, DC 20240
   Phone: 505-563-5397 | Email: maureen.lesky@bie.edu
   http://www.bie.edu

BUREAU OF LABOR STATISTICS
Regional – State – Local Offices

Boston, New York

Bureau of Labor Statistics JFK Federal Building Room E- 310,

Boston, MA 02203 617-565-2331

Chicago Region

Bureau of Labor Statistics JCK Federal Office Building 9th Floor 230 S Dearborn Street, Chicago, IL 60604 312-353-7226

Programs Administered by Regional - State - Local Offices

Dallas, Kansas City
Bureau of Labor Statistics Federal Office Building 525 Griffin Street Room 221, Dallas, TX 75202 972-850-4882

Kansas
Bureau of Labor Statistics Two Pershing Square Building 2300 Main Street Room 1190, Kansas City, MO 64108 816-285-7018

New York
Bureau of Labor Statistics 201 Varick Street Room 808, New York, NY 10014 212-337-2500

Philadelphia
Bureau of Labor Statistics The Curtis Center Suite 610 E 170 S Independence Mall W, Philadelphia, PA 19106 215-861-5600

San Francisco
Bureau of Labor Statistics SF Federal Building 14th Floor 90 7th Street, San Francisco, CA 94103 415-625-2245

REGIONAL OFFICES

Atlanta
Bureau of Labor Statistics Room 7 T50 61 Forsyth Street SW, Atlanta, GA 30303 404-893-8300

DOL17.002 | LABOR FORCE STATISTICS
Award: Project Grants; Dissemination of Technical Information
Purpose: To provide payroll employment and occupational employment and provide regular wages.
Applicant Eligibility: SWAs designated under Section 4 of the Wagner-Peyser Act (as amended by the Workforce Investment Act and subsequently the Workforce Innovation and Opportunity Act) are eligible to apply for cooperative agreement funding to operate the Current Employment Statistics (CES), Local Area Unemployment Statistics (LAUS), Quarterly Census of Employment and Wages (QCEW), and Occupational Employment Statistics (OES) Programs in the states. BLS may select an alternative applicant if a SWA declines to apply for cooperative agreement funding or otherwise substantially fails to meet BLS application and performance requirements. Requests for technical information may be made by the general public.
Beneficiary Eligibility: General public may request information from the SWAs and the Bureau of Labour Statistics.
Award Range/Average: The size of each cooperative agreement reflects the staff and non-personal resources required to operate the programs in a state. The range of awards in fiscal year 2018 was from $52,000 (Guam) to $7,329,000 (California). The average was $1,303,000.
Funding: (Salaries and Expenses) FY 18 $272,759,101.00; FY 19 est $276,000,000.00; FY 20 est Estimate Not Available; (Grants) FY 18 $70,386,000; FY 19 est $70,126,000; and FY 20 est Not Available
HQ: 2 Massachusetts Avenue NE, Washington, DC 20212
Phone: 202-691-5400 | Email: robertson.kenneth@bls.gov
https://www.bls.gov

DOL17.003 | PRICES AND COST OF LIVING DATA
Award: Dissemination of Technical Information
Purpose: To provide assistance in export and import price changes and consumer expenditures.
Applicant Eligibility: Request for information may be made by the general public.
Beneficiary Eligibility: General public.
Award Range/Average: Not Applicable.
Funding: (Salaries and Expenses) FY 18 $209,657,080.00; FY 19 est $210,000,000.00; FY 20 est Estimate Not Available
HQ: 2 Massachusetts Avenue NE, Washington, DC 20212
Phone: 202-691-6960 | Email: friedman.david@bls.gov
http://www.bls.gov

DOL17.004 | PRODUCTIVITY AND TECHNOLOGY DATA
Award: Dissemination of Technical Information
Purpose: To assist in productivity trends in the U.S. economy and examines the factors for productivity change.
Applicant Eligibility: N/A
Beneficiary Eligibility: N/A
Award Range/Average: Not Applicable.
Funding: (Salaries and Expenses) FY 18 $10,749,395.00; FY 19 est $10,500,000.00; FY 20 Estimate Not Available

Programs Administered by Regional - State - Local Offices

HQ: 2 Massachusetts Avenue NE, Washington, DC 20212
Phone: 202-691-5600 | Email: eldridge.lucy@bls.gov
http://www.bls.gov

DOL17.005 | COMPENSATION AND WORKING CONDITIONS

Award: Project Grants; Dissemination of Technical Information

Purpose: To assist in the measures of employee compensation, including cost, wages and to improve the measurement process.

Applicant Eligibility: State agencies or designated local Governments are eligible to apply for cooperative agreement funding to share costs in operating statistical Programs dealing with occupational safety and health statistics. Request for copies of published studies and reports may be made by the general public.

Beneficiary Eligibility: General public.

Award Range/Average: The size of each cooperative agreement reflects the staff and nonpersonal resources required to operate the program. The range of awards in fiscal year 2018 was from $9,000 (Idaho) to $745,000 (California). The average was $123,000.

Funding: (Salaries and Expenses) FY 18 $82,790,968.00; FY 19 est $83,500,000.00; FY 20 Estimate Not Available; (Grants) FY 17 $6,743,000; FY 18 est $7,093,000; and FY 19 est Not Available.

HQ: 2 Massachusetts Avenue NE, Washington, DC 20212
Phone: 202-691-7527 | Email: monaco.kristen@bls.gov
http://www.bls.gov

BUREAU OF LAND MANAGEMENT
Regional – State – Local Offices

REGIONAL OFFICES

Alaska
227 W 7th Avenue 13, Anchorage, AK 99513 907-267-4323

Arizona
1 Central Avenue Suite 800, Phoenix, AZ 85004-4427 602-417-9296

California
2800 Cottage Way Suite W-1834, Sacramento, CA 85825-1886 916-978-4527

Colorado
2850 Youngfield Street, Lakewood, CO 80215-7076 303-239-3677

District of Columbia
20 M Street SE, Washington, DC 20003-0047 801-539-4178

Nevada
1340 Financial Boulevard, Reno, NV 89520-0006 702-861-6559

New Mexico
100 Sun Avenue NE Pan American Building Suite 300, Albuquerque, NM 87109 505-761-8917

Oregon
1515 SW 5th Avenue, Portland, OR 97208 503-952-6220

Utah
440 W 200 S Suite 500, Salt Lake City, UT 84101 801-539-4177

Wyoming
5353 Yellowstone Road PO Box 1828, Cheyenne, WY 82005 307-775-6056

RESEARCH HEADQUARTERS

Idaho
1387 S Vinnell Way, Boise, ID 83709-1657 208-373-3909

Montana
5001 Southgate Drive, Billings, MT 59101 406-896-5188

DOI15.214 | NON-SALE DISPOSALS OF MINERAL MATERIAL

Award: Sale, Exchange, Or Donation of Property and Goods

Purpose: To allow free use of certain mineral material from federally owned lands under the jurisdiction of the Bureau of Land Management by governmental units and nonprofit organizations.

Applicant Eligibility: Any Federal or State agency, unit, or subdivision, including municipalities, where material will be used for public project; or any nonprofit association or corporation. A free use permit will not be issued upon the determination that the applicant owns or control an adequate supply of suitable mineral materials that are readily available and can be mined in a manner which is economically and environmentally acceptable. Mineral material obtained under a free use permit may not be bartered or sold.

Beneficiary Eligibility: Federal or State agencies, units, or subdivisions, including municipalities, where material will be used for public project; or any nonprofit association or corporation.

Award Range/Average: Not Applicable.

Funding: (Sale, Exchange, or Donation of Property and Goods) FY 18 $14,391,000.00; FY 19 est Estimate Not Available; FY 20 est Estimate Not Available

HQ: Solid Minerals Division (WO-320) 1849 C Street NW, Room 2134 LM, Washington, DC 20240
Phone: 570-593-8659 | Email: gbrown@blm.gov
http://www.blm.gov/nhp/index.htm

DOI15.222 | COOPERATIVE INSPECTION AGREEMENTS WITH STATES AND TRIBES
"Section 202 Agreements"

Award: Cooperative Agreements

Purpose: Assists the Bureau of Land Management (BLM) to enter into cooperative agreements with Tribes so that authorized Tribal inspectors can perform inspection activities on Indian oil and gas leases within Tribal jurisdiction.

Applicant Eligibility: Indian Tribes with producing tribal oil and gas leases for which with Federal government has trust responsibility. State may enter into a cooperative agreement for inspection of tribal oil and gas leases with the permission of the Tribe.

Beneficiary Eligibility: Indian tribes with producing tribal oil and gas leases for which the Federal government has trust responsibility. States that have tribal permission to enter into cooperative agreements to conduct inspections on tribal oil and gas leases.

Award Range/Average: Past partnership projects have ranged from $200,000 to $494,708. Average amount is $273,064 or less.

Funding: (Cooperative Agreements (Discretionary Grants)) FY 18 $2,088,240; FY 19 est Estimate Not Available; FY 20 est Estimate Not Available

HQ: Division of Lands and Realty Bureau of Land Management (WO 350) 20 M Street SE, Room 2134, Washington, DC 20003
Phone: 202-912-7350 | Email: kim_berns@blm.gov
http://www.blm.gov/nhp/index.htm

DOI15.224 | CULTURAL AND PALEONTOLOGICAL RESOURCES MANAGEMENT

Award: Cooperative Agreements

Purpose: To organize and safeguard cultural resources on the public lands and to increase public awareness and appreciation of these resources. Most of these lands are located in the Western United States and Alaska.

Applicant Eligibility: Anyone/general public.

Beneficiary Eligibility: Same as Applicant Eligibility.

Award Range/Average: Past partnership projects have ranged from $3,000 to $100,000. Average amount is $45,000 or less.

Funding: (Cooperative Agreements (Discretionary Grants)) FY 17 $3,938,237.00; FY 18 est $2,500,000.00; FY 19 Estimate Not Available

HQ: Division of Lands and Realty Bureau of Land Management (WO 350) 20 M Street SE, Room 2134, Washington, DC 20003
Phone: 202-912-7350 | Email: kim_berns@blm.gov
http://www.blm.gov

DOI15.225 | RECREATION AND VISITOR SERVICES

Award: Cooperative Agreements

Purpose: Public lands administered by the BLM that offers some of the most diverse outdoor recreation opportunities on Federal lands in the western United States. The BLM's Recreation and Visitor Services Program manages a broad and complex set of recreation related and social management activities and programs. Recreation Management activities support efforts to provide resource-related recreational opportunities for a wide range of activities and furnish quality visitor services; and also, to provide diversity of recreational facilities and visitor centers. Objective of this program are to provide: recreation planning and visitor use monitoring; trails, access, and rivers management including: off-highway vehicle, public access, and comprehensive travel and transportation management; visitor services, information, interpretation and stewardship education; visitor health, safety, and accessibility for persons with disabilities; trail maintenance, including visitor centers; and recreation and community support partnerships including tourism and marketing.

Applicant Eligibility: Anyone/general public.

Programs Administered by Regional - State - Local Offices

Beneficiary Eligibility: Same as Applicant Eligibility.

Award Range/Average: Past partnership projects have ranged from $2000 to $552,400. Average amounts approximately $60,000 or less.

Funding: (Cooperative Agreements (Discretionary Grants)) FY 18 $3,817,749.00; FY 19 est $2,942,585.00; FY 20 est Estimate Not Available

HQ: 20 M Street SE, Washington, DC 20003
   Phone: 202-912-7256 | Email: jmccusker@blm.gov
   http://www.blm.gov/nhp/index.htm

DOI15.228 | BLM WILDLAND URBAN INTERFACE COMMUNITY FIRE ASSISTANCE

Award: Cooperative Agreements; Use of Property, Facilities, and Equipment; Dissemination of Technical Information; Training

Purpose: To implement the National Fire Plan and assist communities at risk from catastrophic wildland fires by providing assistance in developing local capability including; assessment and planning, mitigation activities, and community and homeowner education and action; plan and implement hazardous fuels reduction activities, including the training, monitoring or maintenance associated with such hazardous fuels reduction activities, on federal land, or on adjacent nonfederal land for activities that mitigate the threat of catastrophic fire to communities and natural resources in high risk areas.

Applicant Eligibility: States and local Governments at risk as published in the Federal Register, Indian Tribes, public and private education Institutions, nonprofit Organizations, and rural fire departments serving a community with a population of 10,000 or less in the wildland/urban interface.

Beneficiary Eligibility: Same as Applicant Eligibility.

Award Range/Average: Past partnership projects have ranged from $5,000 to $686,000. Average amount is $47,400 or less.

Funding: (Cooperative Agreements (Discretionary Grants)) FY 18 $4,864,265.00; FY 19 est $4,999,996.00; FY 20 est Estimate Not Available

HQ: Division of Fire Planning and Fuels Management National Interagency Fire Center 3833 S Development Avenue, Boise, ID 83705
   Phone: 208-387-5321 | Email: jskinner@blm.gov
   http://www.nifc.gov

DOI15.229 | WILD HORSE AND BURRO RESOURCE MANAGEMENT

Award: Cooperative Agreements

Purpose: The objective of the Wild Horses and Burro Resource Management program is to manage wild horses and burros as an integral part of the natural system of the public lands under the principle of multiple use.

Applicant Eligibility: Anyone/general public.

Beneficiary Eligibility: Same as Applicant Eligibility.

Funding: (Cooperative Agreements (Discretionary Grants)) FY 18 $3,350,246.00; FY 19 est $3,200,000.00; FY 19 est $3,500,000.00

HQ: Division of Wild Horses and Burros 20 M Street SE, Washington, DC 20003
   Phone: 202-912-7350
   http://www.wildhorseandburro.blm.gov

DOI15.230 | INVASIVE AND NOXIOUS PLANT MANAGEMENT

Award: Cooperative Agreements; Training

Purpose: Develop and implement projects that foster consultation and cooperation among stakeholders, interested parties, and the public and to organize, finalize, and develop projects to implement IPM plans for noxious weeds or invasive species within a specific geographic area.

Applicant Eligibility: N/A

Beneficiary Eligibility: Awards under the Plant Protection Act of 2000, 7 USC, Chapter 61 Noxious Weeds 2814 and Good Neighbour Authority. 16 USC 2113a (b)(1)(A) are limited to State and local governments.

Award Range/Average: Past partnership projects have run between $1,000 to $567,000. Average amounts run about $31,600 or less.

Funding: (Cooperative Agreements (Discretionary Grants)) FY 18 $4,386,504.00; FY 19 est $5,213,539.00; FY 20 est Estimate Not Available

HQ: 20 M Street SE, Washington, DC 20240
   Phone: 202-912-7226 | Email: gramos@blm.gov
   http://www.blm.gov/wo/st/en/prog/more/weeds/html

DOI15.231 | FISH, WILDLIFE AND PLANT CONSERVATION RESOURCE MANAGEMENT

Award: Cooperative Agreements; Training
Purpose: Provides national leadership to promote conservation of fish, wildlife and plant conservation, which will help restore and protect lands containing noteworthy resource values for regionally significant species of management concern or wetland and riparian areas; restore and protect crucial habitat through vegetation treatments, installation of wildlife friendly fences, and creating fish passages or barriers to protect aquatic species.
Applicant Eligibility: Anyone/general public.
Beneficiary Eligibility: Same as Applicant Eligibility.
Award Range/Average: Past partnership projects have ranged from $10,000 to $1,000,000. Average amounts approximately $68,300 or less.
Funding: (Cooperative Agreements (Discretionary Grants)) FY 18 $28,668,498.00; FY 19 est $12,423,000.00; FY 20 est Estimate Not Available.
HQ: 20 M Street SE, Washington, DC 20003
   Phone: 202-912-7230 | Email: gwalsh@blm.gov
   http://www.blm.gov/nhp/index.htm

DOI15.232 | WILDLAND FIRE RESEARCH AND STUDIES

Award: Cooperative Agreements
Purpose: To encourage interested parties to perform research and studies pertaining to wildland fire and resource management, to develop products and tools for all levels of decision making to meet the objectives of the National Fire Plan, and to seek information to improve decision making in wildland fire management.
Applicant Eligibility: Anyone/General Public.
Beneficiary Eligibility: Same as Applicant Eligibility.
Award Range/Average: Past partnership projects range from $15,000 to $90,000. Average amounts are $30,000 or less. For the Joint Fire Science Program awards range from $60,000 to $500,000. Average amounts are $350,000 or less.
Funding: (Cooperative Agreements (Discretionary Grants)) FY 17 $5,374,206.00; FY 18 est $650,000.00; FY 19 est $950,000.00
HQ: Bureau of Land Management (WO 350) 20 M Street SE, Room 2134, Washington, DC 20003
   Phone: 202-912-7350 | Email: kim_berns@blm.gov
   http://www.forestsandrangelands.gov

DOI15.233 | FORESTS AND WOODLANDS RESOURCE MANAGEMENT

Award: Cooperative Agreements
Purpose: The Forest and Woodland Management program provides financial assistance, through grants or cooperative agreements, to public or private organizations for the improvement of forests on public lands. Stewardship Authority provides financial assistance for Stewardship projects that achieve land management goals for the public lands that meet local and rural community needs. Good Neighbor Authority provides financial assistance for Good Neighbor projects that consist of Authorized Restoration Services which include treatment of insect and disease infected trees, hazardous fuels reduction, or any other activities to restore or improve forest, rangeland, and watershed health, including fish and wildlife habitat.
Applicant Eligibility: Anyone/General public. State Government only (Good Neighbor Authority).
Beneficiary Eligibility: Anyone/General public.
Award Range/Average: Past partnership projects have ranged from $1,000 to $450,900. Average amounts approximately $50,000 or less.
Funding: (Cooperative Agreements (Discretionary Grants)) FY 18 $831,800.00; FY 19 est $16,238,500.00; FY 20 est Estimate Not Available
HQ: Forest Rangeland Riparian & Plant Conservation (WO 220) 20 M Street SE, Room 2134, Washington, DC 20003
   Phone: 202-912-7220 | Email: jbowmer@blm.gov
   http://www.blm.gov/wo/st/en/prog/more/forests_and_woodland.html

Programs Administered by Regional - State - Local Offices

DOI15.234 | SECURE RURAL SCHOOLS AND COMMUNITY SELF-DETERMINATION

Award: Cooperative Agreements; Training

Purpose: To reinstate stability and predictability to the annual payments made to States and counties containing National Forest System lands and Oregon and California and Coos Bay Wagon Road lands managed by the Bureau of Land Management.

Applicant Eligibility: State and local Governments, public nonprofit Institutions /Organizations, other public institution/ Organization, private nonprofit institution/Organization, other private institution/Organization and landowners.

Beneficiary Eligibility: Anyone/General public.

Award Range/Average: Past partnership projects have run between $1,100 to $596,700. Average amounts run about $83,600 or less.

Funding: (Cooperative Agreements (Discretionary Grants)) FY 18 $133,511.00; FY 19 est $180,094.00; FY 20 est Estimate Not Available

HQ: 20 M Street SE, Washington, DC 20003
Phone: 202-912-7220 | Email: jbowmer@blm.gov
http://www.blm.gov/or/rac/ctypayhistory.php

DOI15.235 | SOUTHERN NEVADA PUBLIC LAND MANAGEMENT

Award: Cooperative Agreements

Purpose: To contribute for the acquisition of environmentally sensitive lands in the State of Nevada.

Applicant Eligibility: Local Governments and regional government entities within the State of Nevada as specifically identified in Public Law 105-263, as amended.

Beneficiary Eligibility: N/A

Award Range/Average: Past partnership projects have been between $30,000 to $30,500,000. Average project amount is $2,500,000 or less.

Funding: (Cooperative Agreements (Discretionary Grants)) FY 18 $845,991.00; FY 19 est $62,862,977; FY 20 Estimate Not Available

HQ: 1340 Financial Boulevard, Reno, NV 89520-0006
Phone: 775-861-6613
http://www.nv.blm.gov/snplma/

DOI15.236 | ENVIRONMENTAL QUALITY AND PROTECTION

Award: Cooperative Agreements

Purpose: To render financial assistance, through grants or cooperative agreements as a partnership to reduce or remove pollutants in the environment for the protection of human health, water and air resources; to restore damaged or degraded watersheds; and to respond to changing climate. Objectives are implemented through core programs such as: the Abandoned Mine Land program, Hazmat program and the Soil, Water and Air (SWA) program.

Applicant Eligibility: Anyone/General public.

Beneficiary Eligibility: Same as Applicant Eligibility.

Award Range/Average: Past partnership projects have ranged from $1,000 to 1,762,000. Average amount is $62,700 or less.

Funding: (Cooperative Agreements (Discretionary Grants)) FY 18 $5,321,592.00; FY 19 est $6,000,000.00; FY 20 est Estimate Not Available

HQ: Division of Environmental Quality and Protection Bureau of Land Management (WO 280) 1849 C Street NW, Room 5284, Washington, DC 20003
Phone: 202-208-6731 | Email: lbaker@blm.gov
http://www.blm.gov

DOI15.237 | RANGELAND RESOURCE MANAGEMENT

Award: Cooperative Agreements

Purpose: Provides financial assistance to manage, develop and protect public lands and enhance the understanding of rangeland and watershed resources, their ecological processes, and capabilities in order to meet rangeland and water quality standards for the improvement of rangelands on public lands. Projects and livestock administration for the management of rangeland ecosystems are conducted in a coordinated manner and consider the interrelationships of living organisms of plants and animals, the physical environment of soil, water, air, and landscape characteristics when developing and implementing resource objectives and management actions.

Applicant Eligibility: N/A
Beneficiary Eligibility: N/A
Award Range/Average: Past partnership projects have been awarded between $7,000 to $501,000. Average amounts run about $57,891 or less.
Funding: (Cooperative Agreements (Discretionary Grants)) FY 18 $719,000.00; FY 19 est $496,996.00; FY 20 est Estimate Not Available
HQ: 20 M Street SE, Washington, DC 20003
Phone: 202-912-7364 | Email: jbowmer@blm.gov
http://www.blm.gov/programs/natural-resources

DOI15.238 | CHALLENGE COST SHARE

Award: Cooperative Agreements
Purpose: Works through cooperative partners to help accomplish high priority work to support habitat improvement, comprehensive travel management, recreation and cultural projects.
Applicant Eligibility: N/A
Beneficiary Eligibility: N/A
Award Range/Average: Past partnership projects have been between $5,000 to $182,000 depending on the policies of that particular state and the money available. Average amounts are $25,100 or less.
HQ: Bureau of Land Management (WO 350) 20 M Street SE, Room 2134, Washington, DC 20003
Phone: 202-912-7350 | Email: kim_berns@blm.gov
http://www.blm.gov/

DOI15.239 | MANAGEMENT INITIATIVES

Award: Cooperative Agreements
Purpose: Supports mission program efforts for the management, protection, and development of public lands managed by the Bureau of Land Management. Awards are typically supported by funding one-time specific legislation and internal projects and programs.
Applicant Eligibility: Anyone/General public.
Beneficiary Eligibility: Same as Applicant Eligibility.
Award Range/Average: Past partnerships have been between $2,900 to $800,000. Average amounts are $117,400 or less.
Funding: (Cooperative Agreements (Discretionary Grants)) FY 18 est $0.00; FY 19 est $1,000,000.00; FY 20 est $4,000,000.00
HQ: 20 M Street SE, Washington, DC 20003
Phone: 801-539-4178 | Email: mgochis@blm.gov
http://www.blm.gov/

DOI15.241 | INDIAN SELF-DETERMINATION ACT CONTRACTS, GRANTS AND COOPERATIVE AGREEMENTS

Award: Cooperative Agreements; Training
Purpose: To provide the full participation of the Indian tribes in programs and services conducted by the Bureau of Land Management for Indians and to encourage the development of human resources of the Indian people; and to establish program assistance to upgrade Indian education that will support the right of Indian citizens and for other purposes.
Applicant Eligibility: Federally recognized Indian tribal Governments and any Alaska Native Village, or regional or village corporation.
Beneficiary Eligibility: Federally recognized Indian tribal governments and American Indians.
Award Range/Average: Past partnership projects range between $12,600 to $1,302,100. Average amount is $244,300 or less.
Funding: (Cooperative Agreements (Discretionary Grants)) FY 18 $3,172,128.00; FY 19 est Estimate Not Available; FY 20 est Estimate Not Available
HQ: 1849 C Street NW, Room 2134LM, Washington, DC 20240
Phone: 202-912-7245
http://www.blm.gov

Programs Administered by Regional - State - Local Offices

DOI15.243 | YOUTH CONSERVATION OPPORTUNITIES ON PUBLIC LANDS
Award: Cooperative Agreements

Purpose: Promotes and stimulate public purposes such as education, job training, development of responsible citizenship, productive community involvement, and further the understanding and appreciation of natural and cultural resources through the involvement of youth and young adults in the care and enhancement of public resources.

Applicant Eligibility: Any qualified youth or conservation corps that supports youth career training and development in the areas of appropriate natural and cultural resource conservation projects. A qualified service and conservation corps means any Program established by a State, or local government, by the governing body of any Indian tribe, or by a nonprofit Organization.

Beneficiary Eligibility: Youth and local communities that benefit from conservation improvements and involvement in youth programs activities on Bureau of Land Management public lands and facilities.

Award Range/Average: Past partnership projects have ranged from $2,500 to $250,000. Average amounts approximately $150,000 or less.

Funding: (Cooperative Agreements (Discretionary Grants)) FY 18 $9,408,497.00; FY 19 est $3,875,000; FY 20 est Estimate Not Available

HQ: Division of Education Interpretation and Partnerships 1849 C Street NW, Room 2134LM, Washington, DC 20240-9998
Phone: 202-912-7454 | Email: jady@blm.gov
http://www.blm.gov/nhp/index.htm

DOI15.244 | FISHERIES AND AQUATIC RESOURCES MANAGEMENT
Award: Cooperative Agreements

Purpose: Bureau of Land Management (BLM) provides national leadership to promote conservation of aquatic habitats, healthy aquatic ecosystems, and the fish, aquatic wildlife, and invertebrate species that are dependent upon them including native, non-native, subsistence, sportfish and aquatic invasive species. Aquatic resources on BLM-managed public lands support the nation's aquatic biodiversity, support public recreation, and help sustain Native American cultural heritages. The BLM works to ensure the resiliency of public trust aquatic species and habitats through on the ground programs and activities including conducting instream habitat and riparian vegetation treatments; removing passage barriers to aquatic organisms; preserving water quantity and quality; taking actions that prevent the introduction, spread, and establishment of aquatic invasive species; conducting family, youth and veterans education and outreach programs; and inventorying, assessing and monitoring aquatic organisms and habitats. The BLM manages these resources in cooperation with states, tribes, other federal agencies, and non-governmental organizations.

Applicant Eligibility: N/A

Beneficiary Eligibility: All Public Land users.

Award Range/Average: Past partnership projects have ranged from $10,000 to $1,000,000. Average amounts approximately $68,300 or less.

Funding: (Cooperative Agreements (Discretionary Grants)) FY 18 $29,323,127.00; FY 19 est $878,260.00; FY 20 Estimate Not Available

HQ: 20 M Street SE, Washington, DC 20003-3503
Phone: 202-912-7202 | Email: gtoevs@blm.gov
http://www.blm.gov/nhp/index.htm

DOI15.245 | PLANT CONSERVATION AND RESTORATION MANAGEMENT
Award: Cooperative Agreements; Training

Purpose: Bureau of Land Management (BLM) Plant Conservation & Restoration Program provides national leadership to support field office habitat management efforts to restore sage grouse, mule deer, desert tortoise, and wild game species habitats; and increase on-the-ground project work to restore and reduce the threats to sage-grouse, mule deer, and other sensitive species in high priority habitats; conduct seed collection through the Seeds of Success (SOS) Program within priority species habitat; continue to work with growers to develop genetically appropriate native plant material for use in habitat restoration; continue to support and increase labor and operations of the BLM National Seed Warehouse System to assist field offices with seed procurement; support studies to improve the effectiveness of seed and seeding treatments through partners, State Offices, and Eco regional Programs; continue to monitor and protect more than 1,700 rare plant species, ~400 of which are found exclusively on BLM lands; continue to work with partners to prioritize and implement priority species conservation actions; continue to assist Emergency Stabilization & Restoration in identifying imminent post-wildfire threats, managing unacceptable risks, and restoring public lands with the use of native plant materials.

Applicant Eligibility: Anyone/general public.

Beneficiary Eligibility: Same as Applicant Eligibility.

Award Range/Average: Past partnership projects have ranged from $10,000 to $1,000,000.

Funding: (Cooperative Agreements (Discretionary Grants)) FY 18 $8,964,833.00; FY 19 est $78,866,810.00; FY 20 est Estimate Not Available.

HQ: 20 M Street SE, Washington, DC 20003

    Phone: 202-912-7222 | Email: jtague@blm.gov

    http://www.blm.gov/programs/natural-resources/native-plant-communities

DOI15.246 | THREATENED AND ENDANGERED SPECIES

Award: Cooperative Agreements

Purpose: The Bureau of Land Management (BLM) implements tasks identified in T&E recovery plans developed by the U.S. Fish and Wildlife Service (USFWS) and National Marine Fisheries Service. It also implements conservation actions for sensitive and candidate species to preclude the need for federal listing. The Threatened and Endangered Species Program works to conserve and recover federally-listed animal and plant species and their habitat on public lands and shares cooperative responsibility with other BLM programs and partners for conservation of candidate and sensitive species.

Applicant Eligibility: Anyone/general public with the exception of other federal agencies. Applicants must competitively apply to postings on Grants.gov to opportunities posted by the office that has funding and the desire to accomplish conservation cooperatively with an applicant that can deliver to a level of public purpose that addresses the wildlife conservation need outlined in the opportunity listing.

Beneficiary Eligibility: All Public Land users.

Award Range/Average: Past partnership projects have ranged from $5,000 to $2,000,000. Average amounts approximately $68,300 or less.

Funding: (Cooperative Agreements (Discretionary Grants)) FY 18 $735,719.00; FY 19 est $1,059,564.00; FY 20 est Estimate Not Available

HQ: 20 M Street SE, Washington, DC 20003-3503

    Phone: 202-912-7220 | Email: jbowmer@blm.gov

DOI15.247 | WILDLIFE RESOURCE MANAGEMENT

Award: Cooperative Agreements

Purpose: The Bureau of Land Management's Wildlife Program manages wildlife habitat to help ensure self-sustaining, abundant and diverse populations of wildlife on public lands. In order to provide for the long-term conservation of wildlife resources, it supports numerous habitat maintenance and restoration activities. BLM-managed lands are vital to thousands of mammals, reptile, avian, and amphibian species. Managing more wildlife habitat than any other federal agency, the wildlife program helps ensure self-sustaining populations and a natural abundance and diversity of wildlife (a publicly owned resource) on public lands.

Applicant Eligibility: Anyone/general public with the exception of other federal agencies. Applicants must competitively apply to postings on Grants.gov to opportunities posted by the office that has funding and the desire to accomplish conservation cooperatively with an applicant that can deliver to a level of public purpose that addresses the wildlife conservation need outlined in the opportunity listing.

Beneficiary Eligibility: All Public Land users.

Award Range/Average: Past partnership projects have ranged from $10,000 to $1,000,000. Average amounts approximately $68,300 or less.

Funding: (Cooperative Agreements (Discretionary Grants)) FY 18 $30,850,320.00; FY 19 est $15,135,700.00; FY 20 est Estimate Not Available

HQ: 20 M Street SE, Washington, DC 20003

    Phone: 202-912-7271 | Email: gwalsh@blm.gov

BUREAU OF RECLAMATION
Regional – State – Local Offices

Lower Colorado Region	Mid - Pacific Region
1340 Financial Boulevard, Reno, NV 89520-0006 702-861-6559	2800 Cottage Way Suite W-1834, Sacramento, CA 85825-1886 916-978-4527

Programs Administered by Regional - State - Local Offices

Upper Colorado Region
440 W 200 S Suite 500, Salt Lake City, UT 84101 801-539-4177

REGIONAL OFFICES

Commissioner's Office, Denver, Colorado
Denver Federal Center Building 53 PO Box 45047, Denver,
CO 80225-0047 303-236-6309

Great Plains Region
5001 Southgate Drive, Billings, MT 59101 406-896-5188

Pacific Northwest Region
1387 S Vinnell Way, Boise, ID 83709-1657 208-373-3909

DOI15.504 | TITLE XVI WATER RECLAMATION AND REUSE
"Title XVI Program"

Award: Formula Grants
Purpose: Directs the Secretary of Interior to undertake a program to identify and investigate opportunities to reclaim and reuse wastewaters and naturally impaired ground and surface water in the 17 Western States and Hawaii. It also provides authority for the Secretary to provide up to the lesser of 25 percent of, or the Federal appropriations ceiling (typically $20 million), for the cost of planning, design, and construction of specific water recycling projects, as well as up to 50 percent of the cost of Title XVI feasibility studies and 25 percent of the cost of Title XVI water reclamation and reuse research studies.
Applicant Eligibility: Eligible recipients of Title XVI funding are identified under the 1902 Act and include State, regional, or local authorities; Indian Tribes or tribal Organizations; or other entities such as a water conservation or conservancy district, wastewater district, rural water district, all located within the 17 Western States or Hawaii. To be eligible to receive funding for construction activities, a water reclamation and reuse project must be specifically authorized under Title XVI or eligible under the amendments in section 4009(c) of the Water Infrastructure Improvements for the Nation (WIIN) Act.
Beneficiary Eligibility: Water users, including municipal, industrial, and agricultural, that benefit from the additional drought resistant water source created.
Award Range/Average: Range: $75,000 to $5,250,000 Average: $1,000,000
Funding: (Cooperative Agreements) FY 17 $23,619,391.00; FY 18 est $21,500,000.00; FY 19 est $3,000,000.00
HQ: Denver Federal Center, PO Box 84-51000 PO Box 25007, Denver, CO 80225
Phone: 303-445-3577
http://www.usbr.gov/watersmart/title/index.html

DOI15.506 | WATER DESALINATION RESEARCH AND DEVELOPMENT

Award: Cooperative Agreements
Purpose: Goals of the program: augment the supply of usable water in the United States; understand the environmental impacts of desalination and develop approaches to minimize these impacts relative to other water supply alternatives; develop approaches to lower the financial costs of desalination so that it is an attractive option relative to other alternatives in locations where traditional sources of water are inadequate.
Applicant Eligibility: Any responsible source, to include individuals, State and local entities, public nonprofit Institutions / Organizations, other public Institutions /Organizations, Federally recognized Indian Tribal Governments, small businesses, profit Organizations, private nonprofit Institutions /Organizations, quasi-public nonprofit Institutions /Organizations, and other private Institutions /Organizations may submit a proposal which will be considered by Reclamation. Foreign entities are not eligible for funding. Federal agencies are not eligible to apply.
Beneficiary Eligibility: Individuals, State and local entities, public nonprofit institutions/organizations, other public institutions/ organizations, Federally recognized Indian Tribal Governments, small businesses, profit organizations, private nonprofit institutions/organizations, quasi-public nonprofit institutions/organizations and other private institutions/organizations.
Award Range/Average: Range is $100,000 - $500,000, Average $150,000.
Funding: (Cooperative Agreements) FY 17 $3,610,000.00; FY 18 est $1,250,000.00; FY 19 est $1,250,000.00
HQ: Denver Federal Center, PO Box 84-51000 PO Box 25007, Denver, CO 25007
Phone: 303-445-2265 | Email: yporrasmendoza@usbr.gov
http://www.usbr.gov/pmts/water/desalination/index.html

DOI15.507 | WATER SMART (SUSTAINING AND MANAGE AMERICA'S RESOURCES FOR TOMORROW)
"Water SMART Grants"

Award: Cooperative Agreements

Purpose: Makes funding available for eligible applicants to leverage their money and resources by cost sharing with Reclamation on projects that save water; mitigate conflict risk in areas at a high risk of water conflict; and accomplish other benefits to increase the reliability of existing supplies; development of water marketing strategies that will help prevent water conflicts and will contribute to water supply reliability; and small-scale water efficiency projects to that have been identified through previous planning efforts to conserve and use water more efficiently.

Applicant Eligibility: In accordance with P.L. 111-11, Section 9502, eligible applicants include any: University, nonprofit research institution, or other Organization with water or power delivery authority. Applicants must also be located in the western U.S. or Territories as identified in the Reclamation Act of June 17, 1902, as amended and supplemented; specifically, Arizona, California, Colorado, Idaho, Kansas, Montana, Nebraska, Nevada, New Mexico, North Dakota, Oklahoma, Oregon, South Dakota, Texas, Utah, Washington, Wyoming, American Samoa, Guam, the Northern Mariana Islands, and the Virgin Islands.

Beneficiary Eligibility: The general public, agricultural, municipal and industrial water users; irrigation or water districts; and state governmental entities with water or power delivery authority, located in the states identified in the Act of June 17, 1902.

Award Range/Average: Range: $75,000- $1,000,000 Average: $300,000

Funding: (Cooperative Agreements (Discretionary Grants)) FY 19 est $10,000,000.00; FY 18 est $23,365,000.00; FY 17 $27,500,000.00

HQ: Denver Federal Center, PO Box 84-51000 PO Box 25007, Denver, CO 80225
Phone: 303-445-2839 | Email: jgerman@usbr.gov
http://www.usbr.gov/WaterSMART/grants.html

DOI15.508 | PROVIDING WATER TO AT-RISK NATURAL DESERT TERMINAL LAKES
"Desert Terminal Lakes Program"

Award: Project Grants

Purpose: Under this authority, Reclamation will fund various activities for the benefit of at-risk terminal lakes to provide water and assistance to a terminal lake to carry out research, support, and conservation activities for associated fish, wildlife, plant, and habitat resources in Nevada and California.

Applicant Eligibility: All funding allocated for grants, interagency agreements and 93-638 grants and contracts has been obligated, if additional funding is realized, the following would apply: State and local public agencies, Indian Tribes, nonprofit Organizations, educational Institutions, and individuals may submit a proposal which will be considered by Reclamation. Foreign entities and Federal agencies are not eligible to apply.

Beneficiary Eligibility: All funding allocated for grants, interagency agreements and 93-638 grants and contracts has been obligated, if additional funding is realized, the following would apply: State and local entities, public nonprofit institutions/organizations, other public institutions/organizations, Federally recognized Indian Tribal Governments, individuals, small businesses, profit organizations, private organizations, quasi-public nonprofit organizations, other private institutions/organization, general public, Native American organizations, higher education institutions, irrigation districts, municipal water authorities, farmers/ranchers/agriculture producers, and land/property owners.

Award Range/Average: Range: $168,236 to $3,000,000 in FY17 Average: $1,047,081.89 in FY17

Funding: (Cooperative Agreements (Discretionary Grants)) FY 17 $4,188,327.00; FY 18 est $1,850,000.00; FY 19 est $0.00

HQ: Lahontan Basin Area 705 N Plaza Street, Room 320, Carson City, NV 89701-4015
Phone: 775-882-3436 | Email: abrinnand@usbr.gov
http://www.usbr.gov/mp/lbao

Programs Administered by Regional - State - Local Offices

DOI15.509 | TITLE II, COLORADO RIVER BASIN SALINITY CONTROL
"Basinwide Program"

Award: Cooperative Agreements

Purpose: Provides financial and technical assistance to identify salt source areas; develop project plans to carry out conservation practices to reduce salt loads; install conversation practices to reduce salinity levels; carry out research, education, and demonstration activities; carry out monitoring and devaluation activities; and to decrease salt concentration and salt loading which causes increased salinity levels within the Colorado River and to enhance the supply and quality of water available for use in the United States and the Republic of Mexico.

Applicant Eligibility: Any legal entity that is the owner or operator of the features to be replaced and/or to be constructed and capable of contracting with Reclamation.

Beneficiary Eligibility: Any person who uses or reuses Colorado River water for irrigation, domestic, municipal or industrial water supply, or for fish and wildlife habitat will benefit.

Award Range/Average: Range $11,962,857 to $12,210,000 Average $10,914,762

Funding: (Cooperative Agreements (Discretionary Grants)) FY 17 $12,210,000.00; FY 18 est $11,962,857.00; FY 19 est $8,571,429.00

HQ: 2764 Compass Drive, Grand Junction, CO 81506
Phone: 970-248-0637 | Email: tstroh@usbr.gov
http://www.usbr.gov/uc/progact/salinity/index.html

DOI15.510 | COLORADO UTE INDIAN WATER RIGHTS SETTLEMENT ACT
"Colorado Ute Settlement Act/Animas La Plata"

Award: Cooperative Agreements; Project Grants; Direct Payments for Specified Use

Purpose: Provides municipal and industrial water supply to the Ute Mountain Ute, Southern Ute Indian Tribe, the Navajo Nation and non-Tribal participants from the Animas-La Plata Project in settlement of water rights claims for the Tribes, and also fulfill other project activities that may be required as a result of the construction, such as relocation of roads and moving powerlines.

Applicant Eligibility: Federally Recognized Indian Tribal Government - projects shall be subject to the provisions of the Indian Self-Determination and education Assistance Act (ii Stat. 2203; 25 U.S.C. 450 et seq.) to the same extent as if such functions were performed by the Bureau of Indian Affairs; and for projects not awarded subject to Public Law 93-638: State, local, Federally recognized Indian Tribal Governments, small businesses, individuals, and profit Organizations.

Beneficiary Eligibility: Federally recognized Indian Tribal Government members and the general public in southwestern Colorado and north-western New Mexico.

Award Range/Average: Range: $4,128,239.07 Average: $ 1,592,746.36

Funding: (Direct Payments for Specified Use) FY 17 $250,000.00; FY 18 est $0.00; FY 19 est $0.00

HQ: FCCO 100 Four Corners Construction Office 1235 La Plata Highway, Farmington, NM 87401
Phone: 505-324-5000 | Email: blongwell@usbr.gov
http://www.usbr.gov/library/annual_reports/FY2008/MDAPart1.pdf

DOI15.511 | CULTURAL RESOURCES MANAGEMENT

Award: Cooperative Agreements

Purpose: Manages and protects cultural resources on Reclamation land; provide for the curation of and public access to collectible heritage assets, including the increase of public awareness, appreciation, and knowledge of these resources; and provide for the protection and preservation of the tribal cultural resources impacted by operations of some Reclamation projects.

Applicant Eligibility: State and local agencies, sponsored Organizations, public nonprofit Institutions /Organizations, other public Institutions /Organizations, Federally-recognized Indian Tribal Governments, minority groups, specialized groups, small businesses, profit Organizations, private nonprofit Institutions /Organizations, quasi-public nonprofit Institutions / Organizations, other private Institutions /Organizations, and Native American Organizations, educational or scientific Organization, or any institution, corporation, association, or individual that possesses the requisite professional requirements.

Beneficiary Eligibility: State and local governments, Tribes, universities, anyone/general public, entities that have an education mission or mission-component, and repositories that meet the standards of the Department of the Interior, Department Manual, Part 411: Identifying and Managing Museum Property, for facilities managing Federal museum property. Further information regarding the general purpose and scope of the Department Manual (DM) is included in Part 001, Chapter 1, of the DM. The DM may be accessed at http://elips.doi.gov/app_DM/index.cfm?fuseaction=home.

Award Range/Average: Range $ 15,144 - $ 69,342 Average $ 42,243

Funding: (Cooperative Agreements (Discretionary Grants)) FY 18 est $168,827.00; FY 17 $247,798.00; FY 19 est $151,247.00
HQ: PO Box 25007 PO Box 84-57000 Denver Federal Center, Denver, CO 80225-0007
  Phone: 303-445-3311
  http://www.usbr.gov/cultural

DOI15.512 | CENTRAL VALLEY IMPROVEMENT ACT, TITLE XXXIV

Award: Cooperative Agreements
Purpose: Central Valley Project Improvement Act (CVPIA) protects, restores, and enhances fish, wildlife, and associated habitats in the Central Valley and Trinity River basins of California; to address impacts of the Central Valley Project on fish, wildlife, and associated habitats; to improve the operational flexibility of the Central Valley Project; to increase water-related benefits provided by the Central Valley Project to the State of California through expanded use of voluntary water transfers and improved water conservation; to contribute to the State of California's interim and long-term efforts to protect the San Francisco Bay/ Sacramento-San Joaquin Delta Estuary and to achieve a reasonable balance among competing demands for use of Central Valley Project water, including the requirements of fish and wildlife, agricultural, municipal and industrial and power contractors.
Applicant Eligibility: State of California or an agency or subdivision thereof, Indian Tribes, or nonprofit entities concerned with restoration, protection, or enhancement of fish, wildlife, habitat, or environmental values that are able to assist implementing any action authorized by the title in an efficient, timely, and cost effective manner, [Section 9404(e) of PL 102-575, Title XXXIV].
Beneficiary Eligibility: Anyone/General public.
Award Range/Average: Range is $10,000,000 to $12,000,000; Average $ 10,750,000
Funding: (Cooperative Agreements (Discretionary Grants)) FY 17 $10,024,159.00; FY 18 est $12,000,000.00; FY 19 est $12,000,000.00
HQ: http://www.usbr.gov/mp/cvpia

DOI15.514 | RECLAMATION STATES EMERGENCY DROUGHT RELIEF
"Emergency Drought Relief and Drought Contingency Planning"

Award: Cooperative Agreements; Project Grants
Purpose: Develops and updates comprehensive drought contingency plans and implements projects that will build long-term resiliency to drought.
Applicant Eligibility: 1) Drought contingency planning: Applicants eligible to apply for funding to develop or update drought contingency plans include: States, cities, or sub-divisions of a state or city; Indian Tribes or tribal water Organizations; irrigation and water districts, water conservancy districts and other Organizations with water or power delivery authority located within the following 17 Western U.S. States: Arizona, California, Colorado, Idaho, Kansas, Montana, Nebraska, Nevada, New Mexico, North Dakota, Oklahoma, Oregon, South Dakota, Texas, Wyoming, Utah, and Washington; and Hawaii. 2) Drought resiliency projects: Applicants eligible to apply for funding for drought resiliency projects include: States, cities, or sub-divisions of a state or city; Indian Tribes or tribal water Organizations; irrigation and water districts, water conservancy districts, and other Organizations with water or power delivery authority. Applicants must also be located in the western United States or Territories as identified in the Reclamation Act of June 17, 1902, as amended and supplemented; specifically: Arizona, California, Colorado, Idaho, Kansas, Montana, Nebraska, Nevada, New Mexico, North Dakota, Oklahoma, Oregon, South Dakota, Texas, Utah, Washington, Wyoming, American Samoa, Guam, the Northern Mariana Islands, and the Virgin Islands.
Beneficiary Eligibility: General public; Federal, State and local governments; and Federally Recognized Indian Tribal Governments.
Award Range/Average: Range is $ 35,000 - $ 750,000; Average $270,000.
Funding: (Cooperative Agreements (Discretionary Grants)) FY 17 $6,900,000.00; FY 18 est $3,250,000.00; FY 19 est $2,900,000.00
HQ: PO Box 25007 PO Box 84-57000 Denver Federal Center, Denver, CO 80225-0007
  Phone: 303-445-3121 | Email: dmayhorn@usbr.gov
  https://www.usbr.gov/drought

Programs Administered by Regional - State - Local Offices

DOI15.516 | FORT PECK RESERVATION RURAL WATER SYSTEM
"Fort Peck Water Supply Project"

Award: Project Grants; Direct Payments for Specified Use

Purpose: Ensures a safe and adequate municipal, rural and industrial water supply and assist the citizens in developing safe and adequate municipal, rural, and industrial water supplies.

Applicant Eligibility: The Fort Peck Tribal Executive Board, Dry Prairie Rural Water Association Incorporated (or any successor non-Federal entity).

Beneficiary Eligibility: The Fort Peck Indian Reservation, the Dry Prairie Rural Water Association, and the residents of all or portions of Valley, Daniels, Sheridan and Roosevelt counties in the State of Montana.

Funding: (Project Grants (Cooperative Agreements or Contracts)) FY 17 $15,250,000.00; FY 18 est $6,000,000.00; FY 19 est $4,731,000.00

HQ: PO Box 36900, Billings, MT 59107

Phone: 406-247-7710 | Email: douglasdavis@usbr.gov

DOI15.517 | FISH AND WILDLIFE COORDINATION ACT

Award: Cooperative Agreements

Purpose: Provides financial assistance through grants or cooperative agreements and to public or private organizations for the improvement of fish and wildlife habitat associated with water systems or water supplies affected by Bureau of Reclamation projects.

Applicant Eligibility: State and local Governments, nonprofit Organizations and Institutions, public and private Institutions and Organizations, Federally recognized Indian Tribal Governments, individuals, small businesses, for-profit Organizations, and Native American Organizations.

Beneficiary Eligibility: Anyone/general public, governmental entities, Tribal governments, Native American organizations, and/or public or private organizations in the specific project area.

Award Range/Average: Range $10,0000 to $11,000,000 Average $430,000

Funding: (Cooperative Agreements (Discretionary Grants)) FY 17 $31,227,958.00; FY 18 est $20,000,000.00; FY 19 est $20,000,000.00

HQ: 1849 C Street NW, Washington, DC 20240

Phone: 202-208-3100

http://www.usbr.gov/cultural

DOI15.518 | GARRISON DIVERSION UNIT

Award: Project Grants

Purpose: Provides funds on a non-reimbursable basis for the planning and construction of a multi-purpose water resource development project for irrigation; municipal, rural, and industrial water; fish, wildlife, and other natural resource conservation and development; recreation; flood control; augmented stream flows; ground water recharge; and other project purposes.

Applicant Eligibility: The State of North Dakota, the Garrison Conservancy District, the Standing Rock Sioux, the Three Affiliated Tribes, the Spirit Lake Nation, the Turtle Mountain Band of Chippewa and the Trenton Indian Service Area.

Beneficiary Eligibility: The citizens of the State of North Dakota and the Standing Rock Sioux, the Three Affiliated Tribes, the Spirit Lake Nation, the Turtle Mountain Band of Chippewa and the Trenton Indian Service Area.

Award Range/Average: Range $2,000 to $40,000,000 Average $567,000

Funding: (Project Grants (Cooperative Agreements or Contracts)) FY 17 $22,676,904.00; FY 18 est $9,600,000.00; FY 19 est $4,980,000.00

HQ: 2021 4th Avenue N, PO Box 36900, Billings, MT 59101

Phone: 406-247-7789 | Email: lparker@usbr.gov

http://www.usbr.gov/gp/

DOI15.519 | INDIAN TRIBAL WATER RESOURCES DEVELOPMENT, MANAGEMENT, AND PROTECTION
"Indian Tribal Water Resources"

Award: Cooperative Agreements; Direct Payments for Specified Use

Purpose: Increases the opportunities for Indian tribes to develop, manage, and protect their water resources.

Applicant Eligibility: Federally recognized Indian Tribes, Institutions of higher education, national Indian Organizations, and tribal Organizations located in the 17 western States identified in the Act of June 17, 1902, as amended; specifically, Arizona, California, Colorado, Idaho, Kansas, Montana, Nebraska, Nevada, New Mexico, North Dakota, Oklahoma, Oregon, South Dakota, Texas, Utah, Washington, and Wyoming.

Beneficiary Eligibility: Federally recognized Indian tribes in the 17 western states.

Award Range/Average: Range $2,000 to $1,300,000 Average $125,000

Funding: (Cooperative Agreements (Discretionary Grants)) FY 17 $3,600,000.00; FY 19 est $3,500,000.00; FY 18 est $3,500,000.00

HQ: Native American and International Affairs Office 1849 C Street NW, Washington, DC 20240

Phone: 202-513-0550

http://www.usbr.gov/native

DOI15.520 | LEWIS AND CLARK RURAL WATER SYSTEM
"Lewis and Clark Project"

Award: Cooperative Agreements

Purpose: Provides safe and adequate municipal, rural, and industrial water supplies, mitigation of wetland areas and water conservation for the Lewis and Clark Rural Water System.

Applicant Eligibility: The Lewis and Clark Rural Water Supply System, Inc., and its member entities (rural water systems and municipalities the meet the requirements for membership in the Lewis and Clark Rural Water Supply System, Inc.).

Beneficiary Eligibility: Fifteen communities and 5 rural water systems in Lake, McCook, Minnehaha, Turner, Lincoln, Clay, and Union Counties, in south-eastern South Dakota; Rock and Nobles Counties, in Southwestern Minnesota; and Lyon, Sioux, Osceola, O'Brien Dickinson, and Clay Counties, in north-western Iowa.

Award Range/Average: Range $2,432,000.00 to $ 8,775,000.00 Average $5,000,000

Funding: (Cooperative Agreements) FY 17 $9,522,000.00; FY 18 est $3,650,000.00; FY 19 est $100,000.00

HQ: 316 N 26th Street, PO Box 36900, Billings, MT 59101-6900

Phone: 406-247-7684 | Email: lnafts@usbr.gov

http://www.lcrws.org/

DOI15.521 | LOWER RIO GRANDE VALLEY WATER RESOURCES CONSERVATION AND IMPROVEMENT
"Lower Rio Grande Valley Irrigation Projects"

Award: Cooperative Agreements

Purpose: Program includes the review of studies and planning reports, conduct of or participation in funding engineering work, infrastructure construction, and improvements for the purpose of conserving and transporting raw water.

Applicant Eligibility: The State of Texas, water users in the Program area, specified irrigation districts, and other non-Federal entities.

Beneficiary Eligibility: The general public located in the state of Texas.

Award Range/Average: Range $ 0 - 435,000 Average $ 140,449

Funding: (Cooperative Agreements) FY 17 $321,348.00; FY 18 est $50,000.00; FY 19 est $50,000.00

HQ: 316 N 26th Street, PO Box 36900, Billings, MT 59101

Phone: 406-247-7710 | Email: kbanks@gp.usbr.gov

http://www.usbr.gov/gp

DOI15.522 | MNI WICONI RURAL WATER SUPPLY PROJECT
"Mni Wiconi Project"

Award: Project Grants

Purpose: Ensures a safe and adequate municipal, rural, and industrial water supply for the residents of the Pine Ridge Indian, Rosebud Indian, and Lower Brule Indian Reservations in South Dakota; to assist the citizens of Haakon, Jackson, Jones, Lyman, Mellette, Pennington, and Stanley Counties, South Dakota, to develop safe and adequate municipal, rural, and industrial water supplies to promote the implementation of water conservation programs at these locations.

Programs Administered by Regional - State - Local Offices

Applicant Eligibility: West River/Lyman-Jones Water Systems; the Oglala, Rosebud, and Lower Brule Sioux Tribes; and non-Federal entity or entities. Section 3(b) of Public Law 100-516 states the Secretary, with the concurrence of the Oglala Sioux Tribal Council, shall enter into agreements with the appropriate non-Federal entity or entities for planning, designing, constructing, operating, maintaining and replacing the Oglala Sioux Rural Water Supply System.

Beneficiary Eligibility: The citizens of the southwest quarter of the State of South Dakota, including the Oglala, Rosebud, and Lower Brule Indian Reservations.

Award Range/Average: Range $ 50,000 to $ 20,000,000 Average $ 12,000,000

HQ: 2021 4th Avenue N, PO Box 36900, Billings, MT 59107-6900

   Phone: 406-247-7789 | Email: lparker@usbr.gov

   http://www.usbr.gov

DOI15.524 | RECREATION RESOURCES MANAGEMENT

Award: Cooperative Agreements

Purpose: Provides cost-share opportunities with non-Federal recreation partners to assist in planning, development, operation, maintenance, and replacement of recreation and fish and wildlife resource facilities at partner managed Reclamation project recreation areas.

Applicant Eligibility: Non-Federal managing partners (e.g., state, county, local government entities, etc.), that currently manage or will be managing one or more Reclamation project recreation areas.

Beneficiary Eligibility: Non-Federal recreation management partners.

Award Range/Average: Range $485,000 to $2,500,000 Average $3,398,215

Funding: (Cooperative Agreements (Discretionary Grants)) FY 18 est $8,960,439.00; FY 17 $7,490,397.00; FY 19 est $6,288,761.00

HQ: PO Box 25007 PO Box 84-57000 Denver Federal Center, Denver, CO 80225-0007

   Phone: 303-445-2712 | Email: jljackson@usbr.gov

   http://www.usbr.gov/recreation

DOI15.525 | ROCKY BOY'S/NORTH CENTRAL MONTANA REGIONAL WATER SYSTEM
"North Central Montana Rural Water Supply Project"

Award: Project Grants

Purpose: Ensures a safe and adequate rural, municipal, and industrial water supply for the residents of the Rocky Boy's Reservation in the State of Montana.

Applicant Eligibility: The Chippewa-Cree of the Rocky Boy's Indian Reservation and the North Central Montana Regional Water Authority.

Beneficiary Eligibility: The Chippewa-Cree of the Rocky Boy's Indian Reservation and inhabitants of the areas served by the North Central Montana Regional Water Authority in Chouteau, Glacier, Hill, Liberty, Pondera, Teton, and Toole Counties, Montana.

Funding: (Project Grants (Cooperative Agreements or Contracts)) FY 17 $13,091,919.00; FY 18 est $4,850,000.00; FY 19 est $3,984,000.00

HQ: Great Plains Regional Office 316 N 26th Street, PO Box 36900, Billings, MT 59101

   Phone: 406-247-7710 | Email: douglasdavis@usbr.gov

DOI15.526 | SAN GABRIEL BASIN RESTORATION

Award: Project Grants

Purpose: Designs, constructs, operates, and maintains water quality projects within the San Gabriel Basin, Los Angeles County, California.

Applicant Eligibility: San Gabriel Basin Water Quality Authority (or its successor agency) and/or the Central Basin Municipal Water District.

Beneficiary Eligibility: General public, all users and indirect users of groundwater supplies in the San Gabriel Basin.

Award Range/Average: Range $0 to $0 Average $0.

HQ: PO Box 61470, Boulder City, NV 89006

   Phone: 702-293-8438 | Email: mthiemann@usbr.gov

   http://www.usbr.gov/lc/socal

DOI15.527 | SAN LUIS UNIT, CENTRAL VALLEY

Award: Cooperative Agreements

Purpose: Provides drainage service to lands within the San Luis Unit of the Central Valley Project of central California.

Applicant Eligibility: Any responsible source, to include irrigation and/or water districts, State and local entities, public nonprofit Institutions /Organizations, other public Institutions /Organizations, Federally recognized Indian Tribal Governments, small businesses, profit Organizations, private nonprofit Institutions /Organizations, quasi-public nonprofit Institutions /Organizations, and other private Institutions /Organizations.

Beneficiary Eligibility: Irrigation and/or water districts, State and local entities, farmers and ranchers, agricultural producers, and owners of drainage impacted land within the San Luis Unit of the Central Valley Project.

Award Range/Average: Range $32,600 - $122,700 Average $124,014.67

Funding: (Project Grants (Cooperative Agreements)) FY 17 $3,047,817.00; FY 18 est $2,000,000.00; FY 19 est $3,000,000.00

HQ: Washington, DC

http://www.usbr.gov/mp

DOI15.529 | UPPER COLORADO AND SAN JUAN RIVER BASINS ENDANGERED FISH RECOVERY

"Upper Colorado and San Juan River Recovery Implementation Program"

Award: Project Grants

Purpose: Authorizes the U.S. Bureau of Reclamation (USBR) to provide cost sharing for the endangered fish recovery implementation programs for the Upper Colorado and San Juan River Basins.

Applicant Eligibility: Federal, Interstate, Intrastate, State and Local Governments; Public Institution/Organizations, and Federally Recognized Indian Tribal Governments and private contractors.

Beneficiary Eligibility: Indian Tribes in the location of the San Juan River Basin and in the Duchesne River Basin, and the general public in the Colorado River Basin.

Award Range/Average: Range $5,000 to $1,800,000 per award Average $1,208,532

Funding: (Project Grants (Cooperative Agreements)) FY 17 $8,334,955.00; FY 18 est $8,477,356.00; FY 19 est $8,731,677.00

HQ: 125 South State Street Room 8100, Salt Lake City, UT 84138 | Email: mmckinstry@usbr.gov

http://www.usbr.gov/uc/wcao/rm/sjrip

DOI15.530 | WATER CONSERVATION FIELD SERVICES (WCFS)

Award: Cooperative Agreements

Purpose: Encourages water conservation in the operations of recipients of water from Federal water projects, to assist agricultural and urban water districts in preparing and implementing water conservation plans in accordance with the Reclamation Reform Act of 1982 (RRA).

Applicant Eligibility: Eligible applicants include any State, Indian tribe, irrigation district, water district, or other Organization with water or power delivery authority. Applicants must also be located in the western U.S. or Territories as identified in the Reclamation Act of June 17, 1902, as amended and supplemented; specifically, Arizona, California, Colorado, Idaho, Kansas, Montana, Nebraska, Nevada, New Mexico, North Dakota, Oklahoma, Oregon, South Dakota, Texas, Utah, Washington, Wyoming, American Samoa, Guam, the Northern Mariana Islands, and the Virgin Islands. Each funding announcement may include additional eligibility requirements.

Beneficiary Eligibility: The general public and irrigation or water districts located in the 17 western States identified in the Act of June 17, 1902, as amended; specifically, Arizona, California, Colorado, Idaho, Kansas, Montana, Nebraska, Nevada, New Mexico, North Dakota, Oklahoma, Oregon, South Dakota, Texas, Utah, Washington, and Wyoming.

Award Range/Average: Range $6,938 - $100,000 Average $50,000

Funding: (Cooperative Agreements (Discretionary Grants)) FY 17 $4,179,000.00; FY 18 est $4,038,000.00; FY 19 est $1,750,000.00

HQ: PO Box 25007 PO Box 84-57000 Denver Federal Center, Denver, CO 80225

Phone: 303-445-3577 | Email: dmarrone@usbr.gov

https://www.usbr.gov/waterconservation

Programs Administered by Regional - State - Local Offices

DOI15.531 | YAKIMA RIVER BASIN WATER ENHANCEMENT (YRBWE)

Award: Cooperative Agreements

Purpose: Within the Yakima River Basin to safeguard, mitigate, and enhance fish and wildlife through improved water management; improved instream flows; improved water quality; protection, creation and enhancement of wetlands; and by other appropriate means of habitat improvement; to improve the reliability of water supply for irrigation; to authorize a Yakima River basin water conservation program that will improve the efficiency of water delivery and use; enhance basin water supplies; improve water quality; protect, create and enhance wetlands, and determine the amount of basin water needs that can be met by water conservation measures.

Applicant Eligibility: State of Washington, and Federally Recognized Indian Tribal Governments, water and irrigation districts, and water rights owners located in the project area.

Beneficiary Eligibility: Anyone/General Public, Intrastate, Local, Individual/Family, and Federally Recognized Indian Tribal Governments within the project area.

Award Range/Average: Range $ 5,000 to $ 44,700,000 Average $ 6,687,907

Funding: (Cooperative Agreements) FY 17 $8,401,840.00; FY 18 est $3,490,000.00; FY 19 est $4,544,458.00

HQ: 1849 C Street NW, Washington, DC 20240

Phone: 202-208-3100

http://www.usbr.gov/pn/

DOI15.532 | CENTRAL VALLEY, TRINITY RIVER DIVISION, TRINITY RIVER FISH AND WILDLIFE MANAGEMENT
"Trinity River Restoration Program"

Award: Cooperative Agreements

Purpose: Addresses the impacts of the Central Valley Project (CVP) on fish, wildlife, and associated habitats by protecting, restoring, and enhancing such habitats and to address other identified adverse environmental impacts.

Applicant Eligibility: State and local entities, public nonprofit Institutions /Organizations, other public Institutions / Organizations, Federally recognized Indian Tribal Governments, small businesses, profit Organizations, private nonprofit Institutions /Organizations, quasi- public nonprofit Institutions /Organizations, and other private Institutions /Organizations.

Beneficiary Eligibility: General public, public institutions/organizations, Federally recognized Indian Tribal Governments, small businesses, profit organizations, private nonprofit institutions/organizations, quasi-public nonprofit institutions/organizations, and other private institutions/organizations.

Award Range/Average: Range $48,652- $3,862,051 Average $1,115,849

Funding: (Cooperative Agreements (Discretionary Grants)) FY 17 $7,707,625.00; FY 18 est $8,875,640.00; FY 19 est $9,117,640.00

HQ: Bureau of Reclamation, Trinity River Restoration Program, PO Box 1300, Washington, DC 96093

Phone: 530-623-1811 | Email: mdixon@usbr.gov

http://www.usbr.gov/mp/ncao

DOI15.533 | CALIFORNIA WATER SECURITY AND ENVIRONMENTAL ENHANCEMENT
"California Bay-Delta Authorization Act (CALFED)"

Award: Cooperative Agreements

Purpose: Primary objectives of the program are to expand water supplies to ensure efficient use through an array of projects and approaches, to improve water quality from source to tap, improve the health of the Bay-Delta system through restoring and protecting habitats and native species, and improve the Bay-Delta levees to provide flood protection, ecosystem benefits, and protect water supplies.

Applicant Eligibility: Agencies of the state of California.

Beneficiary Eligibility: State agencies within the CALFED solution area as defined in the CALFED Bay-Delta Program Record of Decision.

Award Range/Average: Range: $438,640 to $750,000 Average: $3,753,144

Funding: (Cooperative Agreements) FY 17 $521,436.00; FY 18 est $0.00; FY 19 est $589,975.00

HQ: DC

http://www.mp.usbr.gov

DOI15.537 | MIDDLE RIO GRANDE ENDANGERED SPECIES COLLABORATIVE
"Collaborative Program"

Award: Cooperative Agreements

Purpose: A collaborative effort consisting of 16 stakeholders including federal, state, and local governmental entities; Indian tribes and pueblos; and non-governmental organizations representing diverse interests working to support compliance with the Endangered Species Act (ESA). The purpose of the Program is to protect and improve the status of endangered listed species along the Middle Rio Grande (MRG) by implementing certain recovery activities to benefit those species and their associated habitats.

Applicant Eligibility: Federal, Interstate, Intrastate, State, Local, Public nonprofit institution/Organization, Other public institution/Organization, Federally Recognized Tribal Government, Specialized Group, Private Non-profit Institution/Organization.

Beneficiary Eligibility: Same as Applicant Eligibility.

Award Range/Average: Range: $25,000 to $200,000 Average: $ 125,000

Funding: (Cooperative Agreements (Discretionary Grants)) FY 17 $155,301.00; FY 18 est $405,960.00; FY 19 est $404,278.00

HQ: Albuquerque Area Office 555 Broadway Boulevard NE, Albuquerque, NM 87102

Phone: 505-462-3540

http://www.usbr.gov/uc/albuq/index.html

DOI15.538 | LOWER COLORADO RIVER MULTI-SPECIES CONSERVATION
"MSCP"

Award: Cooperative Agreements

Purpose: Protects the lower Colorado River environment while ensuring the certainty of existing river water and power operations, address the needs of threatened and endangered wildlife under the Endangered Species Act, and reduce the likelihood of listing additional species along the lower Colorado River.

Applicant Eligibility: State and local Governments, nonprofit Organizations and Institutions, public and private Institutions and Organizations, Federally recognized Indian Tribal Governments, individuals, small businesses, for-profit Organizations, and Native American Organizations.

Beneficiary Eligibility: Anyone/general public, governmental entities, Tribal governments, Native American organizations, and/or public or private organizations in the specific project area.

Award Range/Average: Range: $1,739 to $285,374 Average: $ 1,613,317

Funding: (Cooperative Agreements (Discretionary Grants)) FY 17 $1,509,950.00; FY 18 est $1,665,000.00; FY 19 est $1,665,000.00

HQ: PO Box 61470, Boulder City, NV 89006

Phone: 702-293-8555

http://www.lcrmscp.gov

DOI15.539 | EQUUS BEDS DIVISION ACQUIFER STORAGE RECHARGE
"Equus Beds Aquifer Storage Recharge Project"

Award: Cooperative Agreements

Purpose: Designs and constructs the City of Wichita's Aquifer Storage and Recovery project to divert flood flows from the Little Arkansas River into the Equus Beds Aquifer in order to recover depleted storage and protect the Aquifer.

Applicant Eligibility: The City of Wichita.

Beneficiary Eligibility: M & I and agricultural waters users of South-central Kansas.

HQ: Great Plains Regional Office 316 N 26th Street, PO Box 36900, Billings, MT 59101-6900

Phone: 406-247-7684 | Email: lnafts@usbr.gov

http://www.usbr.gov/gp

Programs Administered by Regional - State - Local Offices

DOI15.540 | LAKE MEAD/LAS VEGAS WASH
"LVW"

Award: Cooperative Agreements
Purpose: Develops and implements management strategies to improve water quality, habitat integrity, and reduce the salinity and sediment transport while providing environmental enhancement and recreational opportunities.
Applicant Eligibility: The Southern Nevada Water Authority (SNWA), a Special District Government.
Beneficiary Eligibility: The Southern Nevada Water Authority (SNWA) and the General Public.
Award Range/Average: Range $384,510.93 Average $101,106.40
Funding: (Cooperative Agreements (Discretionary Grants)) FY 17 $300,000.00; FY 18 est $300,000.00; FY 19 est $300,000.00
HQ: Boulder City, NV 89006
Phone: 702-293-8109
http://www.usbr.gov

DOI15.541 | COLORADO RIVER BASIN ACT OF 1968
"Colorado River Basin Projects Act"

Award: Cooperative Agreements
Purpose: Provides a program for the further comprehensive development of water resources of the Colorado River Basin and for the provision of additional and adequate water supplies for the use in the upper as well as in the lower Colorado Basin.
Applicant Eligibility: Must have a water allocation and water delivery from a Reclamation water resource project or State responsibility for various project purposes.
Beneficiary Eligibility: The general public in the state of Arizona and southwestern New Mexico, irrigation and water districts and local entities.
Award Range/Average: Range $0 Average $0
HQ: 6150 W Thunderbird Road, Glendale, AZ 85306-4001
Phone: 623-773-6215
http://www.usbr.gov/lc/phoenix

DOI15.542 | ARIZONA WATER SETTLEMENT ACT OF 2004
"Arizona Water Settlement Act"

Award: Project Grants; Direct Payments for Specified Use
Purpose: Provide for adjustments to the Central Arizona Project in Arizona, to authorize the Gila River Indian Community water rights settlement, to reauthorize and amend the Southern Arizona Water Rights settlement Act of 1982.
Applicant Eligibility: Must be authorized to receive funds by Congress in the statute.
Beneficiary Eligibility: Authorized beneficiaries are identified in the statute and include the state of Arizona, state of New Mexico, various irrigation and water districts, local entities and municipalities and Tribal Governments.
Award Range/Average: Range: $25,000,000 to $100,000,000 Average: $69,300,000
HQ: Phoenix Area Office 6150 W Thunderbird Road, Glendale, AZ 85306-4001
Phone: 623-773-6200
http://www.usbr.gov/lc/phoenix

DOI15.543 | LAKE TAHOE REGIONAL WETLANDS DEVELOPMENT

Award: Cooperative Agreements
Purpose: Assists in addressing the past degradation of Lake Tahoe and its watershed by undertaking projects to meet the environmental thresholds as defined in the Tahoe Regional Planning Agency's Environmental Improvement Program (EIP). The environmental thresholds of interest include water quality, soil conservation, wildlife, fisheries and vegetation.
Applicant Eligibility: State and local agencies, public nonprofit Institutions /Organizations, other public Institutions / Organizations, Federally-recognized Indian Tribal Governments, profit Organizations, private nonprofit Institutions / Organizations, other private Institutions /Organizations, and educational or scientific Organizations may apply.
Beneficiary Eligibility: Awards made under this program are intended to benefit the public by maintaining and improving the environmental quality in general, and water quality in particular, of the Lake Tahoe Basin.
Award Range/Average: Range: $0 to $ 320,029 Average: $ 106,676

Funding: (Cooperative Agreements (Discretionary Grants)) FY 17 $150,000.00; FY 18 est $0.00; FY 19 est $0.00
HQ: 2800 Cottage Way, Sacramento, CA 95825
  Phone: 916-978-5045
  http://www.usbr.gov/mp

DOI15.544 | PLATTE RIVER RECOVERY IMPLEMENTATION "PRRIP"

Award: Cooperative Agreements
Purpose: Implements certain aspects of the U.S. Fish and Wildlife Service's recovery plans for four target species (interior least tern, whooping crane, piping plover and pallid sturgeon) listed as threatened or endangered pursuant to the Endangered Species Act.
Applicant Eligibility: Legislation authorizes the agreement. The term Agreement means the Platte River Recovery Implementation Program Cooperative Agreement entered into by the Governors of the States of Wyoming, Nebraska, and Colorado and the Secretary.
Beneficiary Eligibility: General public, irrigation and/or water districts, State and local entities, farmers and ranchers, agricultural producers, property owners, municipal water users, and power users.
Award Range/Average: Range $1,000,000 to $22,000,000 Average $16,605,536.00
Funding: (Cooperative Agreements (Discretionary Grants)) FY 17 $19,674,308.00; FY 18 est $12,959,000.00; FY 19 est $11,959,000.00
HQ: Great Plains Region PO Box 36900, Billings, MT 59107-6900
  Phone: 307-261-5671
  http://www.platteriverprogram.org

DOI15.545 | BUNKER HILL GROUNDWATER BASIN, RIVERSIDE-CORONA FEEDER
"Riverside Corona Feeder"

Award: Cooperative Agreements
Purpose: Directs the Secretary of the Interior to participate in the planning, design, and construction of the Riverside-Corona Feeder Project.
Applicant Eligibility: The Secretary is authorized to cooperate with the Western Municipal Water District, Riverside County, California, in the planning, design, and construction of the Riverside-Corona Feeder Project.
Beneficiary Eligibility: Water users serviced by the Western Municipal Water District.
Award Range/Average: Range: $ 0 to $ 0 Average: $ 0
HQ: Office of Policy and Administration Denver Federal Center, PO Box 84-51000 PO Box 25007, Denver, CO 80225
  Phone: 303-445-3577
  http://www.usbr.gov/lc/socal

DOI15.546 | YOUTH CONSERVATION

Award: Cooperative Agreements
Purpose: Promotes and stimulates the public purposes such as education, job training, development of responsible citizenship, productive community involvement, and furthering the understanding and appreciation of natural and cultural resources.
Applicant Eligibility: Eligibility for conservation activities is limited to qualified youth or conservation corps that are able to involve youth ages 15-25 in the 17 states west of the Mississippi river. Eligibility for the Intern Program is limited to non-profit Organizations other than Institutions of higher education that are capable of recruiting qualified youth interns for positions located at Reclamation offices and facilities. A qualified service and conservation corps means any Program established by a State, or local government, by the governing body of any Indian tribe, or by a nonprofit Organization that 1) is capable of offering meaningful, full-time, productive work for individuals between the ages of 16 and 30, inclusive, in a natural or cultural resource setting; 2) gives participants a mix of work experience, basic and life skills, education, training and support services; and 3) provides participants with the opportunity to develop citizenship values and skills through service to their community and the United States.
Beneficiary Eligibility: Youth and local communities that benefit from conservation improvements and involvement in youth programs activities on Reclamation-owned lands and facilities.

Programs Administered by Regional - State - Local Offices

Award Range/Average: Range: $4,000 to $500,000 Average: $50,000
HQ: PO Box 25007 PO Box 84-57000 Denver Federal Center, Denver, CO 80255
    Phone: 303-445-2632 | Email: rfarrell@usbr.gov
    http://www.usbr.gov/youth

DOI15.548 | RECLAMATION RURAL WATER SUPPLY
"Rural Water Program"

Award: Cooperative Agreements
Purpose: Provides the basic requirements and framework for conducting water and related resource feasibility studies in order to formulate, evaluate, and select project plans for implementation.
Applicant Eligibility: Eligible applicants include states and political subdivisions of states, such as departments, agencies, municipalities, counties, and other regional or local authorities; Indian Tribes and tribal Organizations; and entities created under state law that have water management or water delivery authority, such as irrigation or water districts, canal companies, water users associations, rural water associations or districts, joint powers authorities, and other qualifying entities; and any combination of the entities listed above. Applicants must be located in the 17 Western States as identified in the Reclamation Act of June 17, 1902, as amended.
Beneficiary Eligibility: Eligible beneficiaries include small communities or group of small communities, including Indian tribes and tribal organizations. For the purpose of the Rural Water Supply Program, a small community is defined as having a population of no more than 50,000 people. More than one small community may be served by a rural water project if each small community has a population of 50,000 or less.
Award Range/Average: Range $0 Average $0
HQ: Water and Environmental Resources Division Building 67, PO Box 84-51000 PO Box 25007, Denver, CO 80225-0007
    Phone: 303-445-2711
    http://www.usbr.gov/ruralwater

DOI15.550 | FISHING EVENTS FOR DISADVANTAGED CHILDREN

Award: Cooperative Agreements
Purpose: Provide opportunities for disabled and disadvantaged children to use and enjoy public waters and related lands; to assist Reclamation in meeting its goal to provide accessible programs, facilities and activities to create a positive outdoor experience for all citizens; to increase awareness of all the participants to the capabilities of disabled and disadvantaged children; and to provide educational opportunities for disabled and disadvantaged children to learn more about fish and water as natural resources.
Applicant Eligibility: Eligible applicants are State Governments, County Governments, City or townships Governments, Special districts Governments, Independent school districts, Public and State controlled Institutions of higher education, Native American tribal Governments (federally recognized), Public Housing Authorities/Indian Housing Authorities, Native American tribal Organization (other than Federally recognized tribal Governments) Non-Profits having a 501(c)(3) status with the Internal Revenue Survive (IRS), other than Institutions of higher education, Private Institutions of higher education, Individuals, Small businesses.
Beneficiary Eligibility: Disabled and disadvantaged children.
Award Range/Average: Range: $50,000 - 118,000 Average: $136,000
Funding: (Cooperative Agreements (Discretionary Grants)) FY 17 $132,000.00; FY 18 est $0.00; FY 19 est $0.00
HQ: Financial Assistance Services Denver Federal Center, PO Box 84-51000 PO Box 25007, Denver, CO 80255
    Phone: 303-445-2025 | Email: ihoiby@usbr.gov

DOI15.552 | NAVAJO-GALLUP WATER SUPPLY

Award: Project Grants
Purpose: Provides financial aid to design and construct portions of the Navajo-Gallup Water Supply Project.
Applicant Eligibility: Native American Organization (Navajo Nation) Local Governments (City of Gallup New Mexico) Profit Organization (s)Private nonprofit institution(s)/Organization (s).
Beneficiary Eligibility: Federally Recognized Indian Tribal Government (Navajo Nation)Local Governments (City of Gallup New Mexico).
Award Range/Average: Range: $499,985 - $32,409,679 Average: $14,647,328 Average from FY11-FY17

Funding: (Project Grants (Cooperative Agreements)) FY 17 $1,806,336.00; FY 18 est $60,000,000.00; FY 19 est $20,300,000.00

HQ: FCCO 100 Four Corners Construction Office 103 Everett Street, Durango, CO 81303
  Phone: 505-325-1794 | Email: blongwell@usbr.gov

DOI15.553 | EASTERN NEW MEXICO RURAL WATER SYSTEM "ENMRWS"

Award: Project Grants

Purpose: Provides potable surface water to communities in Eastern New Mexico.

Applicant Eligibility: Eastern New Mexico Water Utility Authority (Authority) was formed for the sole purpose of administration of this new water supply project for the surrounding communities.

Beneficiary Eligibility: The Project would pipe 16,450 acre-feet of surface water per year from Ute Reservoir to the eastern New Mexico municipalities of Clovis, Elida, Grady, Melrose, Portales, and Texico currently relying on the declining quantity and quality of the Ogallala Aquifer. Curry County, Roosevelt County, and Cannon Air Force Base (CAFB) are also beneficiaries of the Project. The present population of the Project service area is about 60,000 people.

Award Range/Average: Range: $ 1,875,000 Average:N/A

Funding: (Project Grants (Cooperative Agreements)) FY 17 $5,000,000; FY 18 est $1,875,000.00; FY 19 est $0.00

HQ: 555 Broadway Boulevard NE, Albuquerque, NM 87102
  Phone: 505-462-3655 | Email: jirizarrynazario@usbr.gov
  http://www.enmwua.com

DOI15.554 | COOPERATIVE WATERSHED MANAGEMENT "CWMP"

Award: Project Grants

Purpose: Enhances water conservation, uses; improve water quality and ecological resiliency of a river or stream; and to reduce conflicts over water at the watershed level by supporting the formation of watershed groups to develop local solutions to address water management issues.

Applicant Eligibility: Watershed Group Development and Restoration Planning (Phase I): Applicants eligible to receive financial assistance through Phase I of the Cooperative Watershed Management Program include: States; Indian Tribes; Local and special districts; (e.g., irrigation and water districts, county soil conservation districts, etc.); Local governmental entities; and non-profit Organizations, including watershed groups. To be eligible, applicants must also significantly affect or be affected by the quality or quantity of water in a watershed; be capable of promoting the sustainable use of water resources within the given watershed area; and be located within the 17 western United States or Territories as identified in the Reclamation Act of June 17, 1902, as amended and supplemented. Implementation of Watershed Management projects (Phase II): An eligible applicant is an established watershed group as defined in the Section 6001(5) of the Cooperative Watershed Management Act (Act) that has met the requirements outlined in Section 6002(c)(2)(A)(iv) of the Act (see Section A. 3. Statutory Authority for full citation). In summary, the applicant must be a grassroots, non-regulatory entity that addresses water availability and quality issues within the relevant watershed, represents a diverse group of stakeholders, and is capable of promoting the sustainable use of water resources in the watershed. The applicant must also have approved articles of incorporation, bylaws, and a mission statement; hold regular meetings; and have developed a restoration plan and project concepts for the watershed. Applicants must also be located in the Western United States or Territories as identified in the Reclamation Act of June 17, 1902, as amended and supplemented.

Beneficiary Eligibility: The Cooperative Watershed Management Program benefits a diverse array of stakeholders, which may include but is not limited to, private property owners, Federal, State, or local agencies, and Indian tribes that are located in the 17 western States identified in the Act of June 17, 1902, as amended, and have authority with respect to the watershed.

Award Range/Average: Range: $20,000 - $100,000 Average: $80,000

Funding: (Project Grants (Cooperative Agreements)) FY 17 $560,000.00; FY 18 est $3,250,000.00; FY 19 est $250,000.00

HQ: Office of Policy and Administration Denver Federal Center, PO Box 84-51000 PO Box 25007, Denver, CO 80225
  Phone: 303-445-2906 | Email: aomorgan@usbr.gov
  http://www.usbr.gov/watersmart/cwmp/index.html

Programs Administered by Regional - State - Local Offices

DOI15.555 | SAN JOAQUIN RIVER RESTORATION

Award: Project Grants

Purpose: Implements the Stipulation of Settlement in NRDC, which is consistent with and as supplement by, the San Joaquin River Restoration Settlement Act. It restores and maintains fish populations in "good condition" in the main stem of the San Joaquin River below Friant Dam to the confluence of the Merced River, including naturally-reproducing and self-sustaining populations of salmon and other fish.

Applicant Eligibility: State, tribal, and local governmental agencies, and with private parties, including agreements related to construction, improvement, and operation and maintenance of facilities, subject to any terms and conditions that the Secretary deems necessary to achieve the purposes of the Settlement.

Beneficiary Eligibility: State, tribal, and local governmental agencies, private parties, and the general public.

Award Range/Average: Range: $ 5,000,000 Average: $ 2,294,246

Funding: (Project Grants (Cooperative Agreements)) FY 19 est $6,600,000.00; FY 17 $4,339,481.00; FY 18 est $21,101,965.00

HQ: 2800 Cottage Way MP-170, Sacramento, CA 95825

Phone: 916-978-5464 | Email: alubaswilliams@usbr.gov

http://www.restoresjr.net

DOI15.556 | CROW TRIBE WATER RIGHTS SETTLEMENT
"Crow Tribe Water Rights Settlement Act of 2010"

Award: Direct Payments for Specified Use

Purpose: Rehabilitates and improves the water diversion and delivery features of the Crow Irrigation Project (CIP) and to construct a new municipal, rural and industrial (MR&I) water system for the benefit of the Crow Tribe and its members.

Applicant Eligibility: The Crow Tribe of Montana.

Beneficiary Eligibility: Irrigable lands within the Crow Reservation. Drinking water for people on the reservation.

Award Range/Average: Range: $2,000,000 to $12,772,000 Average: $9,361,286

Funding: (Direct Payments for Specified Use) FY 17 $12,772,000.00; FY 18 est $12,772,000.00; FY 19 est $12,772,000.00

HQ: 2021 4th Avenue N, Billings, MT 59101

Phone: 406-247-7710 | Email: douglasdavis@usbr.gov

DOI15.557 | APPLIED SCIENCE GRANTS
"Landscape Conservation Cooperatives (LCC)"

Award: Project Grants

Purpose: Enhances the management of natural and cultural resources that have a nexus to water resource management. It also includes developing tools to assess and adapt to the impacts of climate change and other landscape scale stressors within the geographic boundaries.

Applicant Eligibility: Eligible applicants include any: States; Tribes; Irrigation districts; Water districts; Organizations with water or power delivery in the Western United States or Territories as identified in the Reclamation Act of June 17, as amended and supplemented; specifically, Arizona, California, Colorado, Idaho, Kansas, Montana, Nebraska, Nevada, New Mexico, North Dakota, Oklahoma, Oregon, South Dakota, Texas, Utah, Washington, Wyoming, American Samoa, Guam, the Northern Mariana Islands, and the Virgin Islands); universities located in the United States; Non-profit research Institutions located in the United States; or Non-profit Organizations (Non-profit Organizations are eligible to apply for funding under all three task areas so long as the proposal addresses fish or wildlife habitat in wetland, riparian, or aquatic areas and there is a nexus to a Reclamation project.).

Beneficiary Eligibility: The general public; agricultural, municipal and industrial water users; irrigation or water districts; state governmental entities with water or power delivery authority; tribes; non-profit research institutions; and non-profit organizations located in the states identified in the Act of June 17, 1902.

Award Range/Average: Range: $25,000 $150,000 Average: $100,000

Funding: (Project Grants (Cooperative Agreements)) FY 16 $15,649.00; FY 17 est $700,000.00; FY 18 est $700,000.00

HQ: Office of Policy and Administration Denver Federal Center, PO Box 84-51000 PO Box 25007, Denver, CO 80225

Phone: 303-445-2906 | Email: aomorgan@usbr.gov

http://www.usbr.gov/watersmart/lcc/index.html

DOI15.558 | WHITE MOUNTAIN APACHE TRIBE RURAL WATER SYSTEM
"Miner Flat Project"

Award: Direct Payments for Specified Use
Purpose: Assists in planning, engineering, design and construction of the Miner Flat Project.
Applicant Eligibility: White Mountain Apache Tribe.
Beneficiary Eligibility: Same as Applicant Eligibility.
Award Range/Average: Range: $ 0 Average: $ 0
HQ: 6150 W Thunderbird Road, Glendale, AZ 85306-4001
   Phone: 623-773-6200
   http://www.usbr.gov/lc/phoenix

DOI15.559 | NEW MEXICO RIO GRANDE BASIN PUEBLOS IRRIGATION INFRASTRUCTURE
"New Mexico Pueblos Irrigation Project"

Award: Project Grants; Direct Payments for Specified Use
Purpose: Rehabilitates and repairs the irrigation infrastructure of the Rio Grande Pueblos and helps in conserving water and addressing potential conflicts over water in the Rio Grande Basin.
Applicant Eligibility: Federally Recognized Indian Tribal Government 18 New Mexico Rio Grande Pueblos only: Taos, Picuris, Ohkay Owingeh, Santa Clara, San Ildefonso, Tesuque, Pojoaque, Nambe, Cochiti, Santo Domingo, San Felipe, Santa Ana, Sandia, Isleta, Acoma, Laguna, Jemez, Zia.
Beneficiary Eligibility: Same as Applicant Eligibility.
Award Range/Average: Range: $12,000 - $400,000 Average: $130,000
Funding: (Direct Payments for Specified Use (Cooperative Agreements)) FY 17 $300,000.00; FY 18 est $1,000,000.00; FY 19 est $1,000,000.00
HQ: 1849 C Street NW, Washington, DC 20240-0001
   Phone: 202-513-0558
   http://www.usbr.gov/uc/albuq/progact/NMPueblos/index.html

DOI15.560 | SECURE WATER ACT-RESEARCH AGREEMENTS

Award: Project Grants
Purpose: Research activities designed to conserve water resources, increases the efficiency of the use of water resources, and enhances the management of water resources, including increasing the use of renewable energy in the management and delivery of water.
Applicant Eligibility: In accordance with P. L. 111-11, Section 9504(b), eligible applicants include any: University, nonprofit research institution, or other Organization with water or power delivery authority. In accordance with P. L. 111-11, Section 9509, there are no restrictions on the type of Organization eligibility.
Beneficiary Eligibility: The general public; agricultural, municipal and industrial water users; irrigation or water districts; and state governmental entities with water or power delivery authority.
Award Range/Average: Range: $36,000 - $420,000 Average: $105,000
Funding: (Project Grants (Cooperative Agreements)) FY 17 $3,466,553.00; FY 18 est $3,000,000.00; FY 19 est $3,000,000.00
HQ: Acquisition and Assistance Management Division Denver Federal Center, PO Box 84-51000 PO Box 25007, Denver, CO 80225
   Phone: 303-445-2490 | Email: jablack@usbr.gov

DOI15.564 | CENTRAL VALLEY PROJECT CONSERVATION
"CVPCP"

Award: Project Grants
Purpose: Provides financial support for activities to benefit federally listed endangered and threatened species to compensate for impacts to species resulting from the operation and maintenance of the Central Valley Project (CVP).
Applicant Eligibility: Any person(s) without regard to specified eligibility criteria.
Beneficiary Eligibility: Anyone/General public.

Programs Administered by Regional - State - Local Offices

Award Range/Average: Range: $ 25,000 to $1,000,000 Average: $ 1,132,347
Funding: (Project Grants) FY 17 $1,142,000.00; FY 18 est $1,122,000.00; FY 19 est $1,130,000.00
HQ: 1849 C Street NW, PO Box MIB6640, Washington, DC 20240
   Phone: 202-208-3100 | Email: rswanson@uc.usbr.gov
   http://www.usbr.gov/mp/cvpcp

DOI15.565 | IMPLEMENTATION OF THE TAOS PUEBLO INDIAN WATER RIGHTS SETTLEMENT

Award: Project Grants
Purpose: The Act authorizes and directs the Bureau of Reclamation to provide financial assistance in the form of grants on a non-reimbursable basis to plan, permit, design, engineer, and construct Mutual-Benefit Projects that will minimize adverse effects on the Pueblo's water resources by moving future non-Indian ground water pumping away from the Pueblo's Buffalo Pasture, a culturally sensitive wetland.
Applicant Eligibility: Only the eligible non-Pueblo entities identified in section 503(1) of the Settlement Act are eligible to receive financial assistance.
Beneficiary Eligibility: Only the eligible non-Pueblo entities identified in section 503(1) are eligible to receive financial assistance.
Award Range/Average: Range: $8,000 to $12.5 million Average: TBD
Funding: (Project Grants (Cooperative Agreements)) FY 17 $4,000,000.00; FY 18 est $6,000,000.00; FY 19 est $12,500,000.00
HQ: Denver Federal Center, Room 1000 25007 Building 56, Denver, CO 80225
   Phone: 303-445-2490

DOI15.566 | UPPER KLAMATH BASIN HYDROLIC ANALYSES

Award: Formula Grants; Project Grants; Direct Payments for Specified Use; Dissemination of Technical Information
Purpose: Studies the hydrologic characteristics of Upper Klamath Basin to include the quantity, quality and distribution of all water, both above and below ground surface, and the geologic environment in which the water resides.
Applicant Eligibility: Federal - Department and establishment of the Federal government which are responsible for enforcement and the fulfillment of public policy. These departments and establishments directly administer and exercise jurisdiction over matters assigned to them, and are the administering agencies of Federal domestic assistance Programs. Interstate - An Organizational unit established by two or more States to coordinate certain regional Programs relating usually to boundaries for the control and improvement of rivers for irrigation or water power, conservation of natural resources, public utility regulation, development of ports, regional educational development, and regional planning. State - Any agency or instrumentality of the fifty States and the District of Columbia excluding the political subdivisions of State, but including public Institutions of higher education and hospitals. (This term does not include U.S. possessions or territories.) Local - Political subdivisions of a State created under general law or State charter that regulate and administer matters chiefly of local concern. These subdivisions include cities, parishes, counties, municipalities, towns, townships, villages, school districts, special districts, or agencies or instrumentalities of local government, exclusive of Institutions of higher education and hospitals. Included are Indian Tribes on State reservations, Indian school boards, and State-designated Indian Tribes. Sponsored Organizations - A public purpose group other than a unit of government that is a beneficiary under a plan or Program administered by a State, or political subdivision of a State or local government, and which is subject to approval by a Federal agency. Usually organized to work for a specific purpose. Examples: Community development agencies, model cities, community action agencies. Public nonprofit institution/Organizations - A publicly owned agency or Organization established to perform specialized functions or services for the benefit of all or part of the general public either without charge or at cost, making no profits and having no shareholders to receive dividends. Includes Institutions of higher education and hospitals. Federally Recognized Indian Tribal Government - The governing body or a governmental agency of an Indian tribe, Nation, pueblo, or other organized group or community (including any Native village as defined in the Alaska Native Claims Settlement Act) certified by the special Programs and services provided through the Bureau of Indian Affairs. Minority group - A group regarded as a subgroup of the majority to include African Americans, Americans of Spanish descent, Asians, and other nonwhite persons. It may include disadvantaged or under-represented groups, such as women, Vietnam-era veterans, and the physically challenged/disabled. Small business - A business of less than 500 employees, independently owned and not dominant in its field. (Detailed criteria are established by the Small Business Administration.) Profit Organization - A public or private Organization designed to produce product or deliver services to the public through a business enterprise which is structured and managed for profit. Private nonprofit institution/Organization - A privately owned Organization or institution that represents community special interests through community service networks, public information, technical assistance,

and public education. Operated exclusively for charitable, scientific, literary or educational purposes such that no part of its earnings is for the benefit of any private shareholder or individual. Includes private Institutions of higher education and hospitals. Examples: Girl Scouts, American Civil Liberties Union. Other private institution/Organization - A privately owned agency that operates for profit and disburses dividends to shareholders. Native American Organization - Groups of Indians to include urban Indian groups, cooperatives, corporations, partnerships, and associations. Also, include Indians as a minority group.

Beneficiary Eligibility: N/A
Award Range/Average: Range: $50,000 - $1,500,000 Average: 300,000
Funding: (Formula Grants) FY 17 $511,000.00; FY 18 est $576,000.00; FY 19 est $500,000.00
HQ: 6600 Washburn Way, Klamath Falls, OR 97603
   Phone: 541-880-2571 | Email: ckittner@usbr.gov
   http://www.usbr.gov/mp/cvpia

DOI15.567 | COLORADO RIVER CONSERVATION SYSTEM (PILOT))
Award: Cooperative Agreements
Purpose: Conservation projects that creates "system water" through voluntary compensated reductions in water use. All water conserved as a result of the SCPP becomes system water with the sole purpose of increasing storage levels in Lakes Powell and Mead and does not accrue to the benefit of any individual user.
Applicant Eligibility: Eligibility of the Upper Colorado River Commission established through PL 113-235.
Beneficiary Eligibility: Pursuant to PL 113-235, participation in the Pilot Program is limited to Entitlement Holders in the Lower Colorado Division States and Colorado River Water Users in the Upper Colorado River Basin.
Award Range/Average: Range: $1,065,000 Average: $1,065,000
Funding: (Cooperative Agreements) FY 17 $1,000,000.00; FY 18 est $0.00; FY 19 est $0.00
HQ: Upper Colorado Regional Office, Salt Lake City, CO 84138

CORPORATION FOR NATIONAL AND COMMUNITY SERVICE
Regional – State – Local Offices

Alabama
950 22nd Street N Suite 428, Birmingham, AL 35203 205-731-1580

Alabama, District of Columbia, Florida, Georgia, Kentucky, Mississippi, North Carolina, South Carolina, Tennessee, Virginia, West Virginia
Harold Williams, Director | 60 Forsyth Street SW Suite 3M40, Atlanta, GA 30323-2301 404-562-4055

Alaska, California, Hawaii, Idaho, Montana, Nevada, Oregon, Utah, Washington, Wyoming
Lee Spencer, Director | PO Box 29996, Presidio of San Francisco, CA 94129-0996 415-561-5960

Arizona
230 N 1st Avenue Suite 200, Phoenix, AZ 85003 602-514-7171

Arkansas
Federal Building Room 2506, Little Rock, AR 72201 501-324-5235

Arkansas, Arizona, Colorado, Kansas, Louisiana, Missouri, New Mexico, Oklahoma, Texas
James Parker, Director | 1999 Bryan Street Room 2050, Dallas, TX 75201 214-880-7050

California
11150 W Olympia Boulevard Suite 670, Los Angeles, CA 90064 310-893-2287

Colorado
Denver Federal Center Building 46, Denver, CO 80225-0505 303-390-2212

Connecticut
William R Cotter Federal Building, Hartford, CT 06103 860-240-3240

Connecticut, Delaware, Massachusetts, Maryland, Maine, New Hampshire, New Jersey, New York, Pennsylvania, Puerto Rico, Rhode Island, Vermont
Rocco Gaudio, Director | 801 Arch Street Suite 103, Philadelphia, PA 19107-2416 215-597-9972

District of Columbia
250 E Street SW Suite 300, Washington, DC 20024 202-606-6818

Florida
3165 McCrory Place Suite 115, Orlando, FL 32803 407-587-2975

Georgia
401 W Peachtree Street NW Suite 1600, Atlanta, GA 30303-2587 404-965-2102

Hawaii
300 Ala Moana Boulevard Room 6-213, Honolulu, HI 96850 801-524-2832

Programs Administered by Regional - State - Local Offices

Idaho
550 W Fort Street Suite 395, Boise, ID 83724 208-334-1645

Illinois
77 W Jackson Boulevard Suite 442, Chicago, IL 60604-3511 312-897-2121

Indiana
46 E Ohio Street Room 226, Indianapolis, IN 46204-4317 317-226-6724

Iowa
Federal Building Room 917, Des Moines, IA 50309-2195 515-776-4553

Iowa, Illinois, Indiana, Michigan, Minnesota, Nebraska, North Dakota, Ohio, South Dakota, Wisconsin
Mary Lubertozzi, Director | 77 W Jackson Boulevard Suite 442, Chicago, IL 60604-3511 312-353-7705

Kentucky
600 Martin L King Place, Louisville, KY 40202 502-582-6385

Louisiana
707 Florida Street Suite 316, Baton Rouge, LA 70801 225-389-0471

Maryland
Fallon Federal Building, Baltimore, MD 21201 410-962-4443

Massachusetts
10 Causeway Street Room 473, Boston, MA 02222-1038 857-317-5285

Michigan
477 Michigan Avenue Suite 1870, Detroit, MI 49226-2576 313-989-4571

Minnesota
431 S 7th Street Room 2405, Minneapolis, MN 55415-1854 612-607-7799

Mississippi
210 E Capitol Street Room 920, Jackson, MS 39201 601-965-4463

Missouri
2345 Grand Boulevard Suite 650, Kansas City, MO 64108 816-905-3706

Montana
208 N Montana Avenue Suite 206, Helena, MT 59601-3837 406-449-5404

Nebraska
100 Centennial Mall N Room 256, Lincoln, NE 68508-3896 402-437-5474

Nevada
400 S Virginia Street Suite 548, Reno, NV 89501 775-784-7474

New Hampshire
JC Cleveland Federal Building, Concord, NH 03301 603-225-1450

New Jersey
402 E State Street Suite 3050, Trenton, NJ 08608 609-503-2043

New Mexico
120 S Federal Place Room 315, Santa Fe, NM 87501-2026 505-988-6577

New York
Leo O'Brien Federal Building, Albany, NY 12207 518-649-8042

North Carolina
Federal Building PO Century Station 300 Fayetteville Street Room 104, Raleigh, NC 27601 984-269-4523

North Dakota
657 2nd Avenue N Room 347, Fargo, ND 58102 701-232-0320

Ohio
200 N High Street Room 616, Columbus, OH 43215 614-493-2755

Oklahoma
215 Dean A McGee Suite 324, Oklahoma City, OK 73102 405-231-5201

Oregon
620 SW Main Street Room 312, Portland, OR 97205 503-821-2161

Pennsylvania
601 Walnut Street Suite 876 E, Philadelphia, PA 19106-3323 215-964-6350

Puerto Rico
150 Carlos Chardon Avenue Suite 662, San Juan, PR 00918-1737 787-766-5247

Rhode Island
655 Broad Street Suite 103, Providence, RI 02907 401-528-5426

South Carolina
1835 Assembly Street Suite 872, Columbia, SC 29201 803-765-5774

Tennessee
233 Cumberland Bend Drive Suite 112, Nashville, TN 37228 615-736-5563

Texas
300 E 8th Street Suite G-169, Austin, TX 78701-3220 512-391-2900

Utah
125 S State Street Suite 2420, Salt Lake City, UT 84138 801-524-5411

Virginia
400 N 8th Street Suite 446 PO Box 10066, Richmond, VA 23219-2197 804-771-2197

Washington
Jackson Federal Building, Seattle, WA 98174-1103 206-607-2603

West Virginia
Robert C. Byrd | United States Courthouse, Charleston, WV
25301-2535 304-347-5246

Wyoming
308 W 21st Street Suite 206, Cheyenne, WY 82001-3663
307-772-2385

Wisconsin
517 E Wisconsin Avenue Room 462, Milwaukee, WI 53202
414-944-7747

CNCS94.002 | RETIRED AND SENIOR VOLUNTEER PROGRAM
"RSVP"

Award: Project Grants
Purpose: The Retired and Senior Volunteer Program provides grants for volunteers aged 55 and older who serve in various community programs and respond to the National Performance Measures.
Applicant Eligibility: See the Program's Notice of Funding Availability/Opportunity.
Beneficiary Eligibility: Persons age 55 and older who are willing to volunteer on a regular basis by serving in a diverse range of activities that meet specific community needs. See the program's Notice of Federal Funding for additional information.
Award Range/Average: The range of financial assistance ranges from $0 to $728,668.The average amount of financial assistance requested is $80,239.
Funding: (Project Grants (Discretionary)) FY 17 $46,508,000.00; FY 18 est $45,031,000.00; FY 19 est Estimate Not Available
HQ: RSVP 250 E Street SW, Washington, DC 20525
  Phone: 202-606-5000 | Email: tbecton@cns.gov
  http://www.nationalservice.gov/programs/senior-corps

CNCS94.007 | PROGRAM DEVELOPMENT AND INNOVATION GRANTS
"Basic Innovative Grants"

Award: Project Grants
Purpose: Innovation grants program supports other service programs such as the Day of Service grants, September 11th and Disability Outreach grants which help to build service ethics amongst all Americans.
Applicant Eligibility: See Program's Notice of Federal Funding.
Beneficiary Eligibility: Same as Applicant Eligibility.
Award Range/Average: See program's Notice of Federal Funding for matching information.
HQ: 250 E Street SW, Washington, DC 20525
  Phone: 202-606-6667 | Email: jbastresstahmasebi@cns.gov
  http://www.nationalservice.gov

CNCS94.011 | FOSTER GRANDPARENT PROGRAM
"FGP"

Award: Project Grants
Purpose: The Foster Grandparent Program provides grants to volunteers with limited income from agencies and organizations that take care of critical community needs. The program also provides supportive services to children with special needs that might otherwise limit their social or emotional development.
Applicant Eligibility: See the Program's Notice of Funding Availability/Opportunity.
Beneficiary Eligibility: Foster Grandparents must be: 55 years of age or older, with an income of up to 200 percent of poverty, based on the Department of Health and Human Services Poverty Guidelines, and interested in serving infants, children, and youth with special or exceptional needs. (However, individuals who are not income eligible may serve as non-stipendvolunteers under certain conditions.) Foster Grandparents must be physically, mentally, and emotionally capable and willing to serve selected infants, children or youth on a person-to-person basis. See the program's Notice of Funding Availability/Opportunity for additional information.
Award Range/Average: The range of financial assistance is from $0 to $1,917,775. The average of financial assistance is $310,711.
Funding: (Project Grants (Discretionary)) FY 17 $100,953,000.00; FY 18 est $99,093,000.00; FY 19 Estimate Not Available

Programs Administered by Regional - State - Local Offices

HQ: Senior Corps - FGP 250 E Street SW, Washington, DC 20525
   Phone: 202-606-5000 | Email: tbecton@cns.gov
   http://www.nationalservice.gov/programs/senior-corps/foster-grandparents

CNCS94.013 | VOLUNTEERS IN SERVICE TO AMERICA
"AmeriCorps VISTA, VISTA, or Volunteers In Service To America"

Award: Provision of Specialized Services

Purpose: AmeriCorps Volunteers in Service to America (VISTA) is a service program that takes efforts to eradicate poverty by engaging volunteers aged 18 and older to develop or expand programs that helps to bring individuals and communities out of poverty.

Applicant Eligibility: The proposed project must have a clear anti-poverty focus, include the involvement of the low-income community, and the activities must lead towards sustainability of the project. The activities of the VISTA members may not supplant staff or current volunteers. See Program's Notice of Federal Funding for more information.

Beneficiary Eligibility: VISTA activities must benefit low-income persons and communities by building the capacity of the sponsoring organization to find permanent solutions to poverty. VISTAs live and serve in some of our nation's poorest areas. They receive a modest living allowance and other benefits during their service. After successfully completing a term of service, VISTAs and Summer Associates may receive a Segal AmeriCorps Education Award, which can be used to pay for college or student loans, or an end-of-service cash stipend. Sponsors may contribute to the cost of a VISTA through "cost share," but are under no obligation to do so.

Award Range/Average: See program's Notice of Funding Opportunity for information.

Funding: (Provision of Specialized Services) FY 17 $92,364,000.00; FY 18 est $92,364,000.00; FY 19 est $92,364,000.00

HQ: 250 E Street SW, Washington, DC 20525
   Phone: 202-606-6849
   http://www.nationalservice.gov/programs/americorps/americorps-vista

CNCS94.016 | SENIOR COMPANION PROGRAM
"SCP"

Award: Project Grants

Purpose: The Senior Companion Program provides grants to volunteers with limited income and aged 55 and above from agencies and organizations that take care of adults with special needs.

Applicant Eligibility: See the Program's Notice of Funding Availability/Opportunity.

Beneficiary Eligibility: Senior Companions must be: 55 years of age or older, with an income of up to 200 percent of poverty, based on the Department of Health and Human Services Poverty Guidelines; interested in serving special-needs adults, especially the frail elderly, and must be physically, mentally and emotionally capable, and willing to serve on a person-to-person basis. However, non-income eligible individuals may serve as non-stipendvolunteers under certain conditions.

Award Range/Average: The range of financial assistance is from $0 to $779,169.The average of financial assistance is $228,258.

Funding: (Project Grants) FY 17 $42,277,000.00; FY 18 est $41,692,000.00; FY 19 Estimate Not Available

HQ: Senior Corps - SCP 250 E Street SW, Washington, DC 20525
   Phone: 202-606-5000 | Email: tbecton@cns.gov
   http://www.nationalservice.gov/programs/senior-corps/senior-companions

CNCS94.017 | SENIOR DEMONSTRATION PROGRAM
"SDP"

Award: Project Grants

Purpose: The program provides grants to agencies that involve older Americans as volunteers to carry out innovative activities in their community.

Applicant Eligibility: See Program's Notice of Federal Funding or Invitation to Apply.

Beneficiary Eligibility: Persons age 55 and older who are willing to volunteer by serving in a diverse range of activities that meet specific community needs. See the program's Notice of Federal Funding/Opportunity for additional information.

Award Range/Average: The range and average are not applicable to this program.

Funding: (Project Grants (Discretionary)) FY 17 $0.00; FY 18 est $0.00; FY 19 Estimate Not Available

CNCS94.019 | SOCIAL INNOVATION FUND
"SIF"

Award: Cooperative Agreements
Purpose: The Corporation for National and Community Service rolls out the Social Innovation Fund to non-profit community organizations that are high-performing and provides promising solutions to their community problems.
Applicant Eligibility: See Program's Notice of Funding Opportunity.
Beneficiary Eligibility: Same as Applicant Eligibility.
HQ: 250 E Street SW, Washington, DC 20525
  Phone: 202-606-6939 | Email: lzandniapour@cns.gov
  http://www.nationalservice.gov/programs/social-innovation-fund

CNCS94.020 | CNCS DISASTER RESPONSE COOPERATIVE AGREEMENT
"CNCS AmeriCorps Disaster Response Team"

Award: Cooperative Agreements
Purpose: The CNCS Disaster Response Cooperative Agreement is an initiative which helps the national service programs provide physical support to communities affected by a disaster and monetary reimbursements for any expense during such times.
Applicant Eligibility: See application instructions.
Beneficiary Eligibility: Same as Applicant Eligibility.
Award Range/Average: Variable depending on levels of disaster activity across the country.
HQ: 250 E Street SW, Suite 300, Washington, DC 20525
  Phone: 202-606-3906 | Email: jmurphy@cns.gov
  http://www.nationalservice.gov/focus-areas/disaster-services

CNCS94.023 | AMERICORPS VISTA TRAINING & LOGISTICS SUPPORT
"VISTA (Volunteers in Service to America)"

Award: Dissemination of Technical Information; Training
Purpose: The program offers training and technical assistance to members of the AmeriCorps VISTA program and the staff at community-based organizations.
Applicant Eligibility: The use of this cooperative agreement is limited to overall support of VISTA Training.
Beneficiary Eligibility: Any US Citizen or legal resident, 18 years of age or older, with no history of crime against a minor, is eligible to serve as a VISTA member and therefore be trained through the assistance of this cooperative agreement. Equally any organization whose mission is to eradicate poverty in the US may apply to "sponsor" a VISTA member or members, and as such is eligible to be trained through assistance of this cooperative agreement.
Award Range/Average: Currently not active.
HQ: 250 E Street SW, Washington, DC 20525
  Phone: 202-606-3774
  http://www.nationalservice.gov

CNCS94.024 | SOCIAL INNOVATION FUND PAY FOR SUCCESS
"Pay for Success"

Award: Project Grants
Purpose: Pay for Success program conducts grant competitions that implement Pay for Success strategies to improve the low-income community areas and people living in it.
Applicant Eligibility: See Program's Notice of Federal Funding.
Beneficiary Eligibility: Same as Applicant Eligibility.

Programs Administered by Regional - State - Local Offices

HQ: 250 E Street SW, Washington, DC 20525
   Phone: 202-606-6961 | Email: lzandniapour@cns.gov
   http://www.nationalservice.gov/programs/social-innovation-fund/our-programs/pay-success

CNCS94.025 | OPERATION AMERICORPS

Award: Project Grants
Purpose: The Corporation for National and Community Service partners with all 3 streams of AmeriCorps members to address high-priority problems put forward by the tribal and local leaders.
Applicant Eligibility: See Program's Notice of Federal Funding.
Beneficiary Eligibility: Same as Applicant Eligibility.
Award Range/Average: See program's Notice of Federal Funding for matching information.
HQ: 250 E Street SW, Washington, DC 20525
   Phone: 202-606-6745 | Email: pstengel@cns.gov
   http://www.nationalservice.gov/programs/americorps/operation-americorps

CNCS94.026 | NATIONAL SERVICE AND CIVIC ENGAGEMENT RESEARCH COMPETITION

Award: Cooperative Agreements
Purpose: The program conducts research, addresses gaps and provides new ideas and approaches on effective strategies for national and community service and volunteering.
Applicant Eligibility: See Program's Notice of Funding Opportunity.
Beneficiary Eligibility: Same as Applicant Eligibility.
Funding: (Cooperative Agreements) FY 17 $1,300,000.00; FY 18 est $1,500,000.00; FY 19 est Estimate Not Available
HQ: 250 E Street SW, Washington, DC 20525
   Phone: 202-606-6687 | Email: arobles@cns.gov
   http://www.nationalservice.gov

DEPARTMENT OF EDUCATION
Regional – State – Local Offices

California
Gilbert Williams | Federal Office Building 50 United Nations Plaza Room 215, San Francisco, CA 94102 415-437-7840

Jane Bryson, Regional Director, VIII-X | 50 United Nations Plaza Room 227 PO Box 09-8080, San Francisco, CA 94102-4987 415-556-8382

Loni Hancock | 50 United Nations Plaza Room 205, San Francisco, CA 94102-4987 415-437-7520

Colorado
Harry Shriver, Chief Institutional Review Branch | 1244 Speer Boulevard Room 322, Denver, CO 80204 303-844-3676

Lynn Simons | Federal Regional Office Building 1244 Speer Boulevard Room 310, Denver, CO 80204-3582 303-844-3544

District of Columbia
David B. Hakola, Office of Administrator for Management Services, Director for the Western Zone(VI, VII, VIII, IX, X) | 400 Maryland Avenue SW Room 2C107, Washington, DC 20202 202-401-0506

Georgia
Dr. Ralph Pacinelli | 61 Forsyth Street SW Room 18T91, Atlanta, GA 30303 404-562-6330

Judith G. Brantley, Acting Regional Director | PO Box 1692, Atlanta, GA 30301 404-331-0556

Stan Williams | 61 Forsyth Street SW Room 19T40, Atlanta, GA 30303 404-562-6225

Illinois
Douglas Parrott, Chief | 401 S State Street Room 700-D PO Box 05-4080, Chicago, IL 60605 312-353-0375

Dr. Douglas L. Burleigh | 111 N Canal Street Suite 510, Chicago, IL 60606

Stephanie Jones | 111 N Canal Street Room 1094, Chicago, IL 60606 312-553-8192

Massachusetts
David C. Bayer, Regional Director, I-III | 5 Post Office Square PO Box 01-0070 McCormack PO & Courthouse Room 502, Boston, MA 02109 617-223-9328

Jan Pashcal | McCormack PO & Courthouse Room 540, Boston, MA 02109 617-223-9317

John J. Szufnarowski | McCormack PO & Courthouse Room 232, Boston, MA 02109-4557 617-223-4085

Peter Wieczorek | McCormack PO & Courthouse Room 536, Boston, MA 02109-4557 617-223-9321

Missouri

Dr. Douglas L. Burleigh | 10220 N Executive Hills Boulevard, Kansas City, MO 64153-1367 816-880-4107

Sandra Walker | 10220 N Executive Hills Boulevard Suite 720, Kansas City, MO 64153-1367 816-880-4000

Steve Dorssom, Chief Institutional Review Branch | 10220 N Executive Hills Boulevard 9th Floor, Kansas City, MO 64153 816-880-4054

New York

John J. Szufnarowski | 75 Park Place 12th Floor, New York, NY 10007 212-264-4016

John Mahoney | 75 Park Place 12th Floor, New York, NY 10007 212-637-6283

Robert J. McKiernan, Chief Institutional Review Branch | 75 Park Place 12th Floor, New York, NY 10007 212-637-6423

Pennsylvania

Dr. Ralph Pacinelli | 100 Penn Square E Suite 512, Philadelphia, PA 19107

Nancy Klingler, Acting Regional Director | 3535 Market Street Room 16200 PO Box 03-2080, Philadelphia, PA 19104 215-596-1018

Wilson Goode | 100 Penn Square E Suite 505, Philadelphia, PA 19107 215-656-6010

Texas

Loerance Deaver | Harwood Center 1999 Bryan Street, Dallas, TX 75201-6817 214-880-4927

Sally Cain | 1999 Bryan Street Suite 2700, Dallas, TX 75201-6817 214-880-3011

W. Carl Hammack, Regional Director, IV-VII | 1200 Main Tower Building Room 2150 PO Box 06-5080, Dallas, TX 75202 214-767-3811

Washington

Carla Nuxoll | 915 2nd Avenue Room 3362, Seattle, WA 98174-1099 206-220-7800

Richard Corbridge, Assistant Regional Commissioner | 915 2nd Avenue Room 2848, Seattle, WA 98174-1099 206-220-7840

Susan Bowder, Regional Director | 1000 2nd Avenue Room 1200, Seattle, WA 98174-1099 206-287-1770

ED84.165 | MAGNET SCHOOLS ASSISTANCE

Award: Project Grants

Purpose: To provide grants to eligible local educational agencies (LEAs) to establish and operate magnet schools to eliminate, reduce, or prevent minority-group isolation in elementary and secondary schools under court-ordered, agency-ordered, or federally approved voluntary desegregation plans.

Applicant Eligibility: LEAs that are implementing court-ordered, agency-ordered or federally approved voluntary desegregation plans that include magnet schools are eligible to apply.

Beneficiary Eligibility: LEAs and participating students will benefit.

Award Range/Average: Range of awards: $350,000- $3,000,000 (estimated).

Funding: (Project Grants) FY 18 $105,000,000.00; FY 19 est $107,000,000.00; FY 20 est $107,000,000.00

HQ: 400 Maryland Avenue SW, Washington, DC 20202

Phone: 202-205-5471 | Email: vicki.robinson@ed.gov

http://www.ed.gov/programs/magnet/index.html

ED84.215 | INNOVATIVE APPROACHES TO LITERACY, FULL-SERVICE COMMUNITY SCHOOLS; AND PROMISE NEIGHBORHOODS

"Innovative Approaches to Literacy (IAL); Full-service Community Schools (FSCA); Promise Neighborhoods (PN)"

Award: Project Grants

Purpose: To conduct nationally significant programs for all elementary and secondary students to quality education and assist them to meet challenging State content standards.

Applicant Eligibility: Local educational agencies, the Bureau of Indian education, Institutions of higher education, Indian Tribes or tribal Organizations, public and private Organizations and Institutions may apply.

Beneficiary Eligibility: Local educational agencies, institutions of higher education, Indian tribes or tribal organizations, public and private organizations and institutions will benefit.

Award Range/Average: Varies by competition.

Funding: (Project Grants) FY 18 $122,754,000.00; FY 19 est $122,754,000.00; FY 20 est $0.00

HQ: Office of Elementary and Secondary Education (OESE) 400 Maryland Avenue SW, Washington, DC 20202

Phone: 202-260-2551 | Email: sylvia.lyles@ed.gov

http://www2.ed.gov

Programs Administered by Regional - State - Local Offices

ED84.282 | CHARTER SCHOOLS

Award: Project Grants

Purpose: To support startup of new charter schools and the replication and expansion of high-quality charter schools.

Applicant Eligibility: State entities, including State educational agencies, State charter school boards, Governors, and statewide charter school Organizations, in States in which State law authorizes charter schools are eligible. If no State entity in a State receives a grant, charter school developers in the State that have applied to an authorized public chartering authority to operate a charter school, and provided adequate and timely notice to that authority, may apply directly to the Secretary. Charter management Organizations with experience operating or managing high-quality quality schools are also separately eligible for grants. Lastly, States are eligible for grants for charter school per-pupil facilities aid Programs.

Beneficiary Eligibility: School administrators, teachers, and students and their parents are beneficiaries.

Award Range/Average: Range of awards: $100,000 - $45,000,000

Funding: (Project Grants) FY 18 $345,685,153.00; FY 19 est $379,561,485.00; FY 20 est $384,250,000.00

HQ: Office of Innovation and Improvement Parental Options and Information 400 Maryland Avenue SW, Washington, DC 20202

Phone: 202-453-7660 | Email: ellen.safranek@ed.gov

http://www.ed.gov/programs/charter/index.html

ED84.295 | READY-TO-LEARN TELEVISION

Award: Project Grants

Purpose: To provide educational program with accompanying educational support materials, for preschool and early elementary school children and their families.

Applicant Eligibility: To be eligible to receive a grant, contract, or cooperative agreement, an entity shall be a public telecommunications entity that can demonstrate a capacity to: (1) develop and disseminate educational and instructional television Programming nationwide; (2) contract with the producers of children's television Programming; (3) negotiate such contracts in a manner that returns an appropriate share of ancillary income from sales of Program -related products; and (4) localize Programming and materials to meet specific State and local needs.

Beneficiary Eligibility: Programming is to be made widely available, with support materials as appropriate, to young children, their parents, child care workers, and Head Start and Even Start providers.

Funding: (Project Grants) FY 18 $27,741,000.00; FY 19 est $27,741,000.00; FY 20 est $0.00

HQ: 400 Maryland Avenue SW, Washington, DC 20202

Phone: 202-205-5633 | Email: brian.lekander@ed.gov

http://www.ed.gov/programs/rtltv/index.html

ED84.336 | TEACHER QUALITY PARTNERSHIP GRANTS

Award: Project Grants

Purpose: To improve the quality of new and prospective teachers by improving the preparation of prospective teachers and enhancing professional development activities for new teachers.

Applicant Eligibility: States and partnerships that consist of at least one institution of higher education, a school, department or Program of education within the partner institution, one school of arts and sciences within the partner institution, one high-need local educational agency, and a high-need school or a consortium of high-need schools served by the high-need local educational agency. A high-need local educational agency; is an agency that serves an elementary school or secondary school located in an area containing: (1) A high percentage of individuals or families with incomes below the poverty line, (2) a high percentage of secondary teachers not teaching in the content area that they were trained to teach, or (3) a high teacher turnover rate. An accredited institution of higher education, with a teacher training Program must demonstrate the following: (A) A graduate from the teacher training Program exhibits strong performance on State-determined qualifying assessments for new teachers through demonstrating that 80 percent or more of the graduates of the Program intending to enter the field of teaching have passed all of the applicable State qualification assessments for new teachers including an assessment of each prospective teacher's subject matter knowledge in the content area or areas in which the teacher intends to teach; (B) be ranked among the highest-performing teacher preparation Programs in the State as determined by the State; (C) the teacher training Program requires all the students of the Program to participate in intensive clinical experience that meets high academic standards in the case of secondary candidates to successfully complete an academic major in the subject area in which the candidate intends to teach; (D) competence through a high level of performance in relevant content area; (F) successful completion of an academic major in the arts and sciences in the case of elementary school candidates, or (G) competence through a high level of performance in core academic subjects areas. (Note: Entities that may constitute a partnership are specifically listed in the Law.).

Beneficiary Eligibility: Students in high-need schools and school districts are the primary beneficiaries.

Award Range/Average: An average award is $1.5 million per year.
Funding: (Project Grants) FY 18 $43,092,000.00; FY 19 est $43,092,000.00; FY 20 $0.00
HQ: 400 Maryland Avenue SW, Washington, DC 20202
  Phone: 202-401-9501 | Email: ashlee.schmidt@ed.gov
  http://www2.ed.gov/programs/tqpartnership/index.html

ED84.351 | ARTS IN EDUCATION

Award: Project Grants
Purpose: Provides competitive grants that support the integration of the arts into the elementary and secondary school curriculum, with particular focus on improving the academic achievement of low-income students.
Applicant Eligibility: State educational agencies; local educational agencies in which 20 percent or more of the students served are from low-income families; Institutions of higher education; museums and other cultural Institutions; the Bureau of Indian education; a national nonprofit Organization; and any other public or private agencies, Institutions, or Organizations.
Beneficiary Eligibility: Arts educators and administrators, and their students benefit.
Award Range/Average: Range of new awards: $100,000 to $6,700,000.
Funding: (Project Grants) FY 18 $29,000,000.00.00; FY 19 est $29,000,000.00; FY 20 est $0.00
HQ: Office of Innovation and Improvement 400 Maryland Avenue SW, Washington, DC 20202
  Phone: 202-260-1816 | Email: anna.hinton@ed.gov
  http://www2.ed.gov/programs/artsnational/index.html

ED84.354 | CREDIT ENHANCEMENT FOR CHARTER SCHOOL FACILITIES

Award: Project Grants
Purpose: Provides grants to eligible entities to leverage funds through credit enhancement initiatives in order to assist charter schools in using private-sector capital to acquire, construct, renovate, or lease academic facilities.
Applicant Eligibility: A public entity, such as a State or local government entity, a private nonprofit entity, or a consortium of such entities may apply.
Beneficiary Eligibility: Public charter schools as defined in Section 5210, ESEA.
Award Range/Average: Range: $8,000,000- $12,000,000. Average: $10,000,000.
Funding: (Project Grants) FY 18 $39,922,000.00; FY 19 est $44,900,000.00; FY 20 est $95,000,000.00
HQ: 400 Maryland Avenue SW 4W244, Washington, DC 20202
  Phone: 202-453-7660 | Email: ellen.safranek@ed.gov
  http://innovation.ed.gov/what-we-do/charter-schools/credit-enhancement-for-charter-school-facilities-program

ED84.370 | DC SCHOOL CHOICE INCENTIVE PROGRAM

Award: Project Grants
Purpose: To provide low-income parents residing in the District of Columbia (District) with expanded options for the education of their children.
Applicant Eligibility: An educational entity of the District of Columbia Government; a nonprofit Organization; or a consortium of nonprofit Organizations.
Beneficiary Eligibility: To receive an award under this program, an applicant must ensure that a majority of the members of its voting board or governing organization are residents of the District of Columbia. The Secretary gives priority to applications from eligible entities that will most effectively provide students and families with the widest range of educational options; to applications from eligible entities that will most effectively target resources to students and families who lack the financial resources to take advantage of available educational options; and to applications from eligible entities that will most effectively give priority to (A) eligible students who, in the school year preceding the school year in which the student would use the scholarship, attend an elementary or secondary school identified for improvement, corrective action, or restructuring under section 1116 of the Elementary and Secondary Education Act of 1965, as amended (ESEA) (20 U.S.C. 6316); (B) students who have been awarded a scholarship in a preceding year under the current authorizing legislation or the DC School Choice Incentive Act of 2003, as such Act was in effect on the day before the date of the enactment of the current authorizing legislation, but who have not used the scholarship, including eligible students who were provided notification of selection for a scholarship for school year 2009-2010, which was later rescinded in accordance with direction from the Secretary of Education; and (C) students whose household includes a sibling or other child who is already participating in the program of the eligible entity under this division, regardless of whether such students have, in the past, been assigned as members of a control study group for the purposes of an evaluation.

Programs Administered by Regional - State - Local Offices

Award Range/Average: Average new awards: $13,000,000.
Funding: (Project Grants) FY 18 $13,939,394.00; FY 19 est $17,000,000.00; FY 20 est $29,100,000.00
    HQ: 400 Maryland Avenue SW, Washington, DC 20202 | Email: elson.nash@ed.gov
    https://innovation.ed.gov/what-we-do/parental-options/district-of-columbia-opportunity-scholarship-program/

ED84.374 | TEACHER AND SCHOOL LEADER INCENTIVE GRANTS (FORMERLY THE TEACHER INCENTIVE FUND)
"TSL"

Award: Project Grants
Purpose: To help eligible entities develop, implement, improve, or expand human capital management systems or performance-based compensation systems for teachers, principals, or other school leaders in schools (and especially those in high-need schools) served by the grantees.
Applicant Eligibility: Eligible applicants are local educational agencies (LEAs), including charter schools that are LEAs in their State; State educational agencies (SEAs) or other State agencies; the Bureau of Indian education (BIE); and partnerships of (1) one or more LEAs, State agencies, or the BIE and, (2) and at least one nonprofit or for-profit entity. An LEA may receive a grant, whether individually or as part of a partnership, only twice.
Beneficiary Eligibility: SEAs, LEAs, the BIE, non-profit and for profit organizations, and students, teachers, principals, and other school leaders in an LEA's high-need schools.
Award Range/Average: FY 18 range $599,000 to $14,853,000 (continuation awards) and $535,000 to $12,880,000 (new awards). FY 19 $781,000 to $14,871,000 (continuation awards). FY 20 $678,000 to $13,635,000 (continuation awards; $1,000,000 to $15,000,000 (new awards).
Funding: (Project Grants) FY 18 $200,000,000.00; FY 19 est $200,000,000.00; FY 20 est $200,000,000.00
HQ: 400 Maryland Avenue SW, Washington, DC 20202
    Phone: 202-401-1259 | Email: Gillian.cohen@ed.gov
    https://innovation.ed.gov/what-we-do/teacher-quality/teacher-and-school-leader-incentive-program/

ED84.411 | EDUCATION INNOVATION AND RESEARCH (FORMERLY INVESTING IN INNOVATION (I3) FUND)

Award: Project Grants
Purpose: To support the creation, development, implementation, replication, and scaling up of evidence-based, field-initiated innovations designed to improve student achievement.
Applicant Eligibility: (1) Local educational agencies (LEAs); (2) State educational agencies (SEAs); (3) the Bureau of Indian education (BIE); (4) consortia of LEAs or SEAs; (5) nonprofit Organizations; or (6) SEAs, LEAs, or the BIE in consortia with a nonprofit Organization, a business, an educational service agency, or an institution of higher education.
Beneficiary Eligibility: High-need students in LEAs will benefit.
Award Range/Average: Range: $4,000,000- $15,000,000; Average: $7,727,000.
Funding: (Project Grants) FY 18 $120,000,000.00; FY 19 est $130,000,000.00; FY 20 est $300,000,000.00
HQ: 400 Maryland Avenue SW, Washington, DC 20202
    Phone: 202-260-0819 | Email: soumya.sathya@ed.gov
    http://www.ed.gov/programs/innovation/index.html

ED84.417 | DIRECTED GRANTS AND AWARDS

Award: Direct Payments for Specified Use
Purpose: Awards are made to specified institutions for purposes specified in the appropriations or authorization bills.
Applicant Eligibility: The use of the grants varies based on the appropriation and authorization language.
Beneficiary Eligibility: The National Technical Institute for the Deaf (NTID), American Printing House for the Blind (APHB), Gallaudet University, Howard University, and other institutions and organization will benefit.
HQ: 400 Maryland Avenue SW, Room 5W327, Washington, DC 20202
    Phone: 202-401-0292 | Email: nancy.martin@ed.gov

ED84.419 | PRESCHOOL DEVELOPMENT GRANTS

Award: Project Grants
Purpose: Supports effort to build, develop, and expand voluntary, high-quality preschool programs.
Applicant Eligibility: Eligible applicants are States.
Beneficiary Eligibility: Children age 4 from families at or below 200 percent of the Federal poverty line.
Award Range/Average: Range of awards $5- $35 million; average award est. $20 million.
Funding: (Project Grants) FY 18 $250,000,000.00; FY 19 est $250,000,000.00; FY 20 est $250,000,000.00
HQ: 400 Maryland Avenue SW, Washington, DC 20202
   Phone: 202-260-7803 | Email: tammy.proctor@ed.gov
   http://www.ed.gov/earlylearing

ED84.422 | AMERICAN HISTORY AND CIVICS EDUCATION
"American History and Civics Academies: National Activities Grants"

Award: Project Grants
Purpose: The program supports American History and Civics Academies grants and National Activities grants.
Applicant Eligibility: N/A
Beneficiary Eligibility: N/A
Award Range/Average: American History and Civics Academies: Anticipated range of awards is $300,000- $700,000 per year. National Activities: Anticipated range of awards is $200,000- $700,000 per year.
Funding: (Project Grants (Discretionary)) FY 18 $3,515,000.00; FY 19 est $4,815,000.00; FY 20 est $0.00
HQ: Office of Innovation and Improvement 400 Maryland Avenue SW, Room 4W205 LBJ Building, Washington, DC 20202-5960
   Phone: 202-260-7350 | Email: christine.miller@ed.gov
   http://innovation.ed.gov/what-we-do/american-history-and-civics-academies

ED84.423 | SUPPORTING EFFECTIVE EDUCATOR DEVELOPMENT PROGRAM
"SEED"

Award: Project Grants
Purpose: To support pathways that allow teachers, principals, or other school leaders with nontraditional preparation and certification to obtain employment in traditionally underserved local educational agencies (LEAs).
Applicant Eligibility: The only eligible applicants are Institutions of higher education and nonprofit entities meeting specific statutory requirements, the Bureau of Indian education, and partnerships of one or more of those entities and a for-profit entity.
Beneficiary Eligibility: Educators and prospective educators benefit from this program.
Award Range/Average: The Department held one competition in FY 2018 and made 15 awards ranging from $971,000 to $8,444,000 for the initial funding period.
Funding: (Project Grants) FY 18 est $75,000,000.00; FY 19 est $75,000,000.00; FY 20 est $0.00
HQ: 400 Maryland Avenue SW, Washington, DC 20202
   Phone: 202-401-1259 | Email: gillian.cohen-boyer@ed.gov
   http://innovation.ed.gov/what-we-do/teacher-quality/supporting-effective-educator-development-grant-program

ED84.424 | STUDENT SUPPORT AND ACADEMIC ENRICHMENT PROGRAM
"SSAE"

Award: Formula Grants
Purpose: To provide all students with access to a well-rounded education; and improve school conditions for student learning.
Applicant Eligibility: SEAs must submit a Program or consolidated state plan to the Secretary for review and approval.
Beneficiary Eligibility: LEAs, schools, and their community stakeholders will benefit directly by improving students' academic achievement by increasing the capacity to: (1) provide all students with access to a well-rounded education; (2) improve school conditions for student learning: and (3) improve the use of technology in order to improve the academic achievement and digital literacy for all students.
Award Range/Average: FY 17 range: $1,940,000- $46,418,059; FY 17 average: $7,000,000. FY 18 est range: $5,308,325- $127,291,818; FY 18 est average: $19,153,750.

Programs Administered by Regional - State - Local Offices

Funding: (Formula Grants) FY 18 $1,072,610,000.00; FY 19 est $1,140,867,000.00; FY 20 est $0.00
HQ: 400 Maryland Avenue SW, Washington, DC 20202
  Phone: 202-453-6727 | Email: paul.kesner@ed.gov
  http://www2.ed.gov/programs/ssae/index.html

ED84.938 | HURRICANE EDUCATION RECOVERY

Award: Formula Grants; Project Grants
Purpose: Assists in meeting the educational needs of individuals affected by a 2017 Presidentially declared major disaster or emergency related to the consequences of Hurricanes Harvey, Irma, and Maria and the 2017 California wildfires.
Applicant Eligibility: State educational agencies (SEAs) and Institutions of higher education (IHEs) in affected areas or which enrolled students displaced from an affected area. Local educational agencies (LEAs) and public and non-public schools in affected areas are subgrantees.
Beneficiary Eligibility: State educational agencies, local educational agencies, postsecondary institutions and students in areas affected by Hurricanes Harvey, Irma, and Maria and the 2017 California wildfires will benefit.
Award Range/Average: Not Applicable.
Funding: (Formula Grants) FY 18 $2,700,000,000.00; FY 19 est $165,000,000.00; FY 20 est $ 0.00
HQ: 400 Maryland Avenue SW, Room 3W311, Washington, DC 20202
  Phone: 202-401-8368 | Email: meredith.miller@ed.gov
  http://www.ed.gov/disasterrelief

DOE81.005 | ENVIRONMENTAL MONITORING, INDEPENDENT RESEARCH, TECHNICAL ANALYSIS

Award: Cooperative Agreements (discretionary Grants)
Purpose: To provide technical and financial assistance to State of New Mexico Environment Department and the Regents of New Mexico State University/Carlsbad Environmental Monitoring and Research Center (NMSU/CEMRC) for the conduct of projects/activities to support DOE's and the Waste Isolation Pilot Plant (WIPP) mission and to provide the public assurances that implemented DOE programs are protective of human health and the environment.
Applicant Eligibility: Eligibility for this Program is restricted to the following: The Board of Regents New Mexico State University - Carlsbad Environmental Monitoring and Research Center and the State of New Mexico.
Beneficiary Eligibility: N/A
Award Range/Average: 500,000 to 3,300,000 per fiscal year
Funding: (Cooperative Agreements (Discretionary Grants)) FY 18 $0.00; FY 19 est $0.00; FY 20 est $6,674,130.00
HQ: 1000 Independence Avenue SW, Washington, DC 20585
  Phone: 301-903-8466 | Email: alton.harris@em.doe.gov
  http://www.energy.gov

DOE81.036 | INVENTIONS AND INNOVATIONS
"I&I"

Award: Project Grants; Advisory Services and Counseling; Dissemination of Technical Information
Purpose: To provide financial and technical assistance to projects that have a potential for significant energy savings and future commercialization markets through a competitive solicitation process.
Applicant Eligibility: N/A
Beneficiary Eligibility: N/A
Award Range/Average: $500,000 to $1,000,000
HQ: 15013 Denver W Parkway, Golden, CO 80401
  Phone: 240-562-1456 | Email: james.cash@ee.doe.gov
  http://www.eere.energy.gov

DOE81.041 | STAT

E ENERGY PROGRAM
"SEP"

Award: Formula Grants; Dissemination of Technical Information

Purpose: To increase market transformation of energy efficiency and renewable energy technologies; and to provide financial and technical assistance to State governments to create and implement a variety of energy efficiency and conservation projects.

Applicant Eligibility: All States plus the District of Columbia, the U.S. Virgin Islands, Puerto Rico, Guam, Samoa, and the Commonwealth of the Northern Mariana Islands.

Beneficiary Eligibility: The ultimate potential beneficiaries will be the people affected by the plan that each State develops. This is anticipated to be the State's population.

Award Range/Average: $1- $5,000,000

Funding: (Formula Grants) FY 18 $41,978,435.00; FY 19 est $41,433,043.00; FY 20 est Estimate Not Available

HQ: 15013 Denver W Parkway, Golden, CO 80401

Phone: 240-562-1456 | Email: james.cash@ee.doe.gov

http://www.eere.energy.gov

DOE81.042 | WEATHERIZATION ASSISTANCE FOR LOW-INCOME PERSONS
"WAP"

Award: Formula Grants

Purpose: To improve home energy efficiency by reducing fossil fuel emissions and reducing the total energy usage.

Applicant Eligibility: States and Territories, including the District of Columbia, Puerto Rico, U.S. Virgin Islands, American Samoa, Guam, Commonwealth of the Northern Marianas, and, Native American tribal Organizations (Navajo Nation, Northern Cheyenne, Intertribal Council of Arizona). In the event a State does not apply, a unit of general purpose local government, or community action agencies and/or other nonprofit agencies within that State becomes eligible to apply.

Beneficiary Eligibility: All low-income households are eligible to receive weatherization assistance. A low-income household is one whose combined income falls at or below 200 percent of the Federal poverty level determined by the Office of Management and Budget's poverty income guidelines or the basis on which Federal, State, or local cash assistance payments have been made. A State may also elect to make all homes eligible under the HHS Low-income Home Energy Assistance Program (LIHEAP) eligible for weatherization assistance and may use either 150 percent of poverty or 60 percent of State median income.

Award Range/Average: Up to $7,541 per dwelling unit.

Funding: (Formula Grants) FY 18 $214,720,034.00; FY 19 est $239,891,480.00; FY 20 est Estimate Not Available

HQ: 15013 Denver W Parkway, Golden, CO 80401

Phone: 240-562-1456 | Email: james.cash@ee.doe.gov

http://www.eere.energy.gov

DOE81.049 | OFFICE OF SCIENCE FINANCIAL ASSISTANCE PROGRAM

Award: Project Grants

Purpose: To deliver scientific discoveries and major scientific tools to transform the understanding of nature and advance the energy, economic and national security of the United States.

Applicant Eligibility: Except where a Program solicitation establishes more restrictive eligibility criteria, individuals and Organizations in the following categories may submit proposals: Institutions of higher education; National Laboratories; Nonprofit and for-profit private entities; State and local Governments; and consortia of entities described above.

Beneficiary Eligibility: N/A

Award Range/Average: $10,000 to $2,500,000; $250,000.

Funding: (Project Grants (Cooperative Agreements)) FY 18 $1,332,804,781.00; FY 19 est $1,225,000,000.00; FY 20 est $1,225,000,000.00; Total fiscal year (FY) obligations for the Office of Science financial assistance awards are as follows: FY 14: $1,134,524,873, FY 15: $1,123,478,061; and FY 16: $1,153,268,755, FY17: $1,134,577,949, FY18$1,1332,804,781

HQ: 19901 Germantown Road, Germantown, MD 20874

Phone: 301-903-4946 | Email: michael.zarkin@science.doe.gov

http://science.energy.gov/grants

Programs Administered by Regional - State - Local Offices

DOE81.057 | UNIVERSITY COAL RESEARCH

Award: Project Grants

Purpose: To fund Fossil Energy's coal-related programs and improve scientific and technical understanding of the chemistry and physics involved in the conversion and utilization of coal.

Applicant Eligibility: Only US colleges and universities can apply.

Beneficiary Eligibility: In accordance with 2 CFR 910.124, eligibility for award is restricted to U.S. colleges, universities, and university-affiliated research institutions. Grants awarded through the UCR Program are for maintaining and upgrading the educational, training and research capabilities of U.S. universities and colleges in the fields of science, environment, energy and technology related to coal. The involvement of professors and students generates fresh research ideas and enhances the education of future scientists and engineers. To assure the program continues to support the performance of high quality fundamental research by professors and students at U.S. colleges and universities, applications may be submitted by U.S. colleges, universities and university-affiliated research institutions provided the following criteria are met: (1) Principal Investigator or a Co-Principal Investigator listed in the application is a teaching professor at the submitting university. If this condition is met, other participants, Co-Principal Investigators or research staff, who do not hold teaching positions may be included as part of the research team; (2) Applications from university-affiliated research institutions must be submitted through the college or university with which they are affiliated; and (3) At least one student registered at that university is to receive compensation for performing research.

Award Range/Average: Maximum funding for 36 month project is $400,000.

Funding: (Project Grants) FY 18 $1,971,000.00; FY 19 est $2,798,244.00; FY 20 est $3,825,000.00

HQ: Washington, DC 20585

Phone: 301-903-2827 | Email: regis.conrad@hq.doe.gov

http://www.netl.doe.gov/technologies/coalpower/advresearch

DOE81.065 | NUCLEAR LEGACY CLEANUP PROGRAM
"Consultation and Cooperation Financial Assistance"

Award: Project Grants; Direct Payments for Specified Use

Purpose: To carry out the purposes of the Nuclear Waste Policy Act of 1982, Public Law 97-425, as amended (NWPA); to conduct and participate in licensing activities in accordance with the NWPA.

Applicant Eligibility: Local Governments, elected officials and affected Indian Tribes surrounding DOE facilities. Designation of a local government or tribe as an "Affected Unite of Local Government" or "Affected Tribe is done pursuant to the NWPA.

Beneficiary Eligibility: States, affected units of local government and affected American Indian tribes will benefit, as well as the clean-up work at the Department of Energy.

Funding: (Direct Payments for Specified Use (Cooperative Agreements)) FY 17 $730,000.00; FY 18 est $535,000.00; FY 19 est $750,000.00

HQ: 1000 Independence Avenue SW, Washington, DC 20585

Phone: 202-586-2904 | Email: elizabeth.lisann@em.doe.gov

DOE81.079 | REGIONAL BIOMASS ENERGY PROGRAMS

Award: Project Grants

Purpose: To help meet the goal by significantly increasing America's use of fuels, chemicals, materials, and power made from domestic biomass on a sustainable basis.

Applicant Eligibility: Profit Organizations; private nonprofit Institutions /Organizations; intrastate, interstate, State and local government agencies, and universities may apply.

Beneficiary Eligibility: Profit organizations; private nonprofit institutions/organizations; intrastate, interstate, State and local government agencies, universities will benefit.

Award Range/Average: Varies.

HQ: 15013 Denver W Parkway, Golden, CO 80401

Phone: 240-562-1456 | Email: james.cash@ee.doe.gov

http://www.eere.energy.gov

DOE81.086 | CONSERVATION RESEARCH AND DEVELOPMENT
"Energy Efficiency (EE)"

Award: Project Grants
Purpose: To conduct a balanced, long-term research effort in Buildings Technologies, Industrial Technologies, Vehicle Technologies, Solid State Lighting Technologies, and Advanced Manufacturing Technologies.
Applicant Eligibility: For-profit Organizations, private nonprofit Institutions /Organizations, State and local Governments may apply.
Beneficiary Eligibility: Same as Applicant Eligibility.
Award Range/Average: Varies.
Funding: (Cooperative Agreements) FY 18 $156,699,907.00; FY 19 est $42,285,303.00; FY 20 est Estimate Not Available
HQ: 15013 Denver W Parkway, Golden, CO 80401
    Phone: 240-562-1456 | Email: james.cash@ee.doe.gov
    http://www.eere.energy.gov

DOE81.087 | RENEWABLE ENERGY RESEARCH AND DEVELOPMENT
"Renewable Energy (RE)"

Award: Project Grants
Purpose: To conduct balanced research and development efforts in the fields like solar, biomass, hydrogen fuel cells and infrastructure, wind and hydropower, and geothermal.
Applicant Eligibility: For-profit Organizations, private nonprofit Institutions /Organizations, intrastate, interstate, and local agencies and universities may apply.
Beneficiary Eligibility: For-profit organizations, private nonprofit institutions/organizations, intrastate, interstate, State and local agencies and universities will benefit.
Award Range/Average: Varies.
Funding: (Cooperative Agreements) FY 18 $249,020,499.00; FY 19 est $88,560,662.00; FY 20 est Estimate Not Available
HQ: 15013 Denver W Parkway, Golden, CO 80401
    Phone: 240-562-1456 | Email: james.cash@ee.doe.gov
    http://www.eere.doe.gov

DOE81.089 | FOSSIL ENERGY RESEARCH AND DEVELOPMENT

Award: Cooperative Agreements
Purpose: To promote the development and use of environmentally and economically superior technologies for supply, conversion, delivery, utilization and reliability constraints of producing and using fossil fuels.
Applicant Eligibility: States, local Governments, universities, governmental entities, consortia, nonprofit Institutions, commercial corporations, joint Federal/Industry corporations, U.S. Territories, and individuals are eligible to apply.
Beneficiary Eligibility: Federal, State, local governments, universities, consortia, nonprofit institutions, commercial corporations, joint Federal/Industry corporations, and individuals will benefit.
Award Range/Average: Award size varies according to the funding opportunity announcement. A majority of the active projects are in the range from $200,000 to $10,000,000+.
Funding: (Cooperative Agreements (Discretionary Grants)) FY 18 $291,492,545.00; FY 19 est $328,621,789.00; FY 20 est $291,000,000.00
HQ: 1000 Independence Avenue SW, Washington, DC 20623
    Phone: 202-586-7661 | Email: miranda.johnson@hq.doe.gov
    https://www.energy.gov

DOE81.104 | ENVIRONMENTAL REMEDIATION AND WASTE PROCESSING AND DISPOSAL
"Environmental Management"

Award: Cooperative Agreements; Project Grants
Purpose: To support the development of technologies to safely expedite tank waste processing and tank closure, remediation of contaminated groundwater and soil, disposition of nuclear materials and spent (used) nuclear fuel, and deactivation and decommissioning of contaminated excess facilities.

Programs Administered by Regional - State - Local Offices

Applicant Eligibility: Public, quasi-public, private industry, individuals, groups, educational Institutions, Organizations, and nonprofit Organizations may apply including State or local level Governments, federally recognized Indian tribal Governments, and Institutions in U.S. Territories and possessions may apply. Determinations are made by DOE EM Headquarters or EM Field Offices, or both.

Beneficiary Eligibility: States, affected Indian tribes, regional organizations, (including U.S. Territories) local governments, and the public will benefit.

Funding: (Cooperative Agreements) FY 18 $33,956,580.00; FY 19 est $25,000,000.00; FY 20 est $25,000,000.00

HQ: EM-412 1000 Independence Avenue SW, Washington, DC 20585

   Phone: 301-903-7654 | Email: latrincy.bates@em.doe.gov

   http://www.em.doe.gov

DOE81.105 | NATIONAL INDUSTRIAL COMPETITIVENESS THROUGH ENERGY, ENVIRONMENT, AND ECONOMICS
"NICE3 or NICE Cube"

Award: Project Grants

Purpose: This program is in close-out. Financial assistance will not be provided in the future.

Applicant Eligibility: N/A

Beneficiary Eligibility: Both state and local governments benefited from these grants. Commercial firms with expertise in waste reduction and pollution prevention, large and small businesses, and others in the business of preventing pollution and energy conserving technologies also benefited.

HQ: 15013 Denver W Parkway, Golden, CO 80401

   Phone: 240-562-1456 | Email: james.cash@ee.doe.gov

   http://www.eere.energy.gov

DOE81.106 | TRANSPORT OF TRANSURANIC WASTES TO THE WASTE ISOLATION PILOT PLANT: STATES AND TRIBAL CONCERNS, PROPOSED SOLUTIONS
"Transport of Transuranic Waste to the Waste Isolation Pilot Plant (WIPP): States and Tribal Concerns, Proposed Solutions"

Award: Project Grants

Purpose: To enlist cooperation among the Tribal and the Southern, Western, and Midwest state governments along the Waste Isolation Pilot Plant (WIPP) shipping corridors for the safe and uneventful transportation of transuranic waste from storage facilities to the WIPP.

Applicant Eligibility: Eligibility is restricted by action of the Western Governors' Association, Southern States Energy Board, the State of New Mexico, Council of State Governments (midwest region), and tribal Governments along WIPP transportation routes. DOE administers agreements with 10 southern State Governments, and two Midwest state Governments. The Western Governors' Association is the negotiating body for 12 western states on the WIPP transportation route. Each tribal government on the WIPP transportation route elected to represent themselves. Participation in this Program is restricted to the above list of Organizations and to the affected tribal Governments.

Beneficiary Eligibility: Benefits from this program will go to DOE and the State and tribal governments located on the WIPP disposal phase shipping corridor.

Award Range/Average: $50,000 to $3,000,000 per year

Funding: (Project Grants (Cooperative Agreements or Contracts)) FY 18 $4,587,850.00; FY 19 est $5,339,303.00; FY 20 est $6,674,130.00

HQ: 1000 Independence Avenue SW, Washington, DC 20585

   Phone: 301-903-8466 | Email: alton.harris@em.doe.gov

   http://www.wipp.energy.gov

DOE81.108 | EPIDEMIOLOGY AND OTHER HEALTH STUDIES FINANCIAL ASSISTANCE PROGRAM
"Health Studies"

Award: Project Grants

Purpose: To provide financial support for research, education, conferences, communication, and other activities relating to the health of Department of Energy workers and others who are exposed to health hazards associated with energy production, transmission, and use.

Applicant Eligibility: Colleges and universities, businesses, and nonprofit Institutions may apply.

Beneficiary Eligibility: Colleges and universities, businesses, and nonprofit institutions will benefit.

Award Range/Average: $10,000 to $6,500,000. Average about $2.0 Million.

Funding: (Project Grants) FY 17 $14,447,254.00; FY 18 est $26,910,000.00; FY 19 est $26,910,000.00

HQ: 1000 Independence Avenue SW, Washington, DC 20585

Phone: 301-903-1244 | Email: ron.barnes@hq.doe.gov

http://energy.gov/ehss/environment-health-safety-security

DOE81.112 | STEWARDSHIP SCIENCE GRANT PROGRAM
"Stewardship Science Academic Alliances Programs (SSAP)"

Award: Cooperative Agreements; Project Grants

Purpose: To grow the U.S. scientific community through the areas of fundamental science and technology; to promote and sustain scientific interactions between the academic community and scientists at the NNSA laboratories; to train scientists in specific areas; to increase the availability of unique experimental facilities sited at NNSA's laboratories; and to develop and maintain a long-term recruiting pipeline to NNSA's laboratories.

Applicant Eligibility: Some solicitations are open to Institutions of higher education only and others include nonprofit Organizations and for profit commercial Organizations. See individual funding opportunity announcements for details on eligibility.

Beneficiary Eligibility: Depending upon the eligibility requirements of the individual solicitation, U.S. public and private institutions of higher education and/or nonprofit organizations and for profit commercial organizations will benefit. The Federal government will also benefit from the research of these grants.

Award Range/Average: grants $50,000 - $750,000 per yearCooperative agreements $1,000,000- $68,000,000 per year

Funding: (Project Grants (Cooperative Agreements)) FY 18 $237,174,283.00; FY 19 est $215,360,283.00; FY 20 est $116,625,000.00

HQ: 19901 Germantown Road, Germantown, MD 20874

Phone: 301-903-7423 | Email: terri.stone@nnsa.doe.gov

http://www.nnsa.energy.gov

DOE81.113 | DEFENSE NUCLEAR NONPROLIFERATION RESEARCH
"Defense Nuclear Nonproliferation Research and Development"

Award: Project Grants

Purpose: To conduct basic and applied research and development that enhances U.S. national security and reduces the global danger from the proliferation of weapons of mass destruction and special nuclear materials.

Applicant Eligibility: Universities (public and private), Institutions of higher education, whose activities benefit the general public through results which are available to the National Nuclear Security Administration (NNSA), other U.S. government agencies, and universities and Institutions of higher learning may apply.

Beneficiary Eligibility: The NNSA, other U.S. government agencies, universities and institutions of higher learning will benefit.

Award Range/Average: The expected range of Awards is approximately $25,000,000; $5,000,000/year for five years for the lifecycle of the project.

Funding: (Project Grants (Cooperative Agreements)) FY 18 $15,000,000.00; FY 19 est $15,000,000.00; FY 20 est $15,000,000.00

HQ: 1000 Independence Avenue SW, Washington, DC 20585

Phone: 202-586-2246 | Email: ivy.martin@nnsa.doe.gov

http://www.nnsa.doe.gov/na-20

DOE81.117 | ENERGY EFFICIENCY AND RENEWABLE ENERGY INFORMATION DISSEMINATION, OUTREACH, TRAINING AND TECHNICAL ANALYSIS/ASSISTANCE

Award: Project Grants

Purpose: To provide financial assistance for information dissemination, outreach, training and related technical analysis/assistance for the Department of Energy (DOE).

Applicant Eligibility: Profit Organizations, individuals, private nonprofit Institutions /Organizations, public nonprofit Institutions /Organizations, State and local Governments, Native American Organizations, Alaskan Native corporations and universities may apply. DOE Laboratories are not eligible.

Beneficiary Eligibility: Profit organizations, individuals, private nonprofit institutions/organizations, public nonprofit institutions/organizations, State and local governments, Native American organizations, Alaskan Native corporations and universities benefit.

Award Range/Average: Varies

Funding: (Cooperative Agreements) FY 18 $21,691,756.00; FY 19 est $9,642,517.00; FY 20 Estimate Not Available

HQ: 15013 Denver W Parkway, Golden, CO 80401

  Phone: 240-562-1456 | Email: james.cash@ee.doe.gov

  http://www.eere.energy.gov

DOE81.119 | STATE ENERGY PROGRAM SPECIAL PROJECTS
"SEP Competitive Grants"

Award: Project Grants

Purpose: To allow States to submit proposals to implement specific Department of Energy (DOE) Office of Energy Efficiency and Renewable Energy deployment activities and initiatives as Special Projects under the State Energy Program.

Applicant Eligibility: All States plus the District of Columbia, the U.S. Virgin Islands, Puerto Rico, Guam, American Samoa, and the Commonwealth of the Northern Mariana Islands may apply.

Beneficiary Eligibility: States, territories, and their project partners will benefit.

Award Range/Average: 500,000 - 1,000,000

Funding: (Cooperative Agreements) FY 18 $0.00; FY 19 est $4,888,218.00; FY 20 est Estimate Not Available

HQ: 15013 Denver W Parkway, Golden, CO 80401

  Phone: 240-562-1456 | Email: james.cash@ee.doe.gov

  http://www.eere.energy.gov

DOE81.121 | NUCLEAR ENERGY RESEARCH, DEVELOPMENT AND DEMONSTRATION
"NE RD&D"

Award: Project Grants

Purpose: To provide financial assistance to address key issues affecting the worldwide use of nuclear energy through the research, development, and demonstration of science and technology fields.

Applicant Eligibility: Federal, State, local Governments, universities, consortia, nonprofit Institutions, commercial corporations, and individuals may apply.

Beneficiary Eligibility: Any individual, partnership, corporation, association, joint venture, institution of higher education, or nonprofit organization will benefit.

Award Range/Average: The range of awards vary per funding opportunity and depends on available program funding. Information on awards is published in the Funding Opportunity Announcements and can be found on the NEUP.gov website. For example, NEUP awards typically range from $400,000 to $1,000,000; however, they can be more or less, as described in the FOA. NEUP R&D awards are capped at $800,000, whereas IRP awards can exceed $1,000,000, based upon the program's R&D focus and available funds. NEUP R&D awards with Nuclear Science User Facility (NSUF) access vary in that they can be funded both by DOE award and with NSUF resources and funding. Infrastructure awards greater than $250,000 require the university to share costs, calculated as a percentage of the amount over the $250,000 threshold. For IUP, Fellowship awards are typically $155,000 and Scholarship awards are $7,500 per student

Funding: (Project Grants (Cooperative Agreements)) FY 18 $167,853,383.00; FY 19 est $148,000,000.00; FY 20 est $145,000,000.00

HQ: 1000 Independence Avenue SW, Washington, DC 20585
    Phone: 301-903-7991 | Email: aaron.gravelle@nuclear.energy.gov
    http://www.ne.doe.gov

DOE81.122 | ELECTRICITY DELIVERY AND ENERGY RELIABILITY, RESEARCH, DEVELOPMENT AND ANALYSIS

Award: Project Grants
Purpose: To develop cost-effective technology that enhances the reliability, efficiency, and resiliency of the electric grid for the effective utilization of emerging and renewable generation sources.
Applicant Eligibility: All types of domestic entities are eligible to apply, such as profit Organizations, private nonprofit Institutions /Organizations, universities, research Organizations, and state and local Governments.
Beneficiary Eligibility: Profit organizations, private nonprofit institutions/organizations, universities, research organizations, and state and local governments benefit.
Award Range/Average: $500,000- $5,000,000; Average $2,500,000
Funding: (Cooperative Agreements) FY 18 $8,000,000.00; FY 19 est $7,000,000.00; FY 20 est $10,000,000.00
HQ: Washington, DC 20585
    Phone: 202-586-4936 | Email: rusty.perrin@hq.doe.gov
    http://www.oe.energy.gov

DOE81.123 | NATIONAL NUCLEAR SECURITY ADMINISTRATION (NNSA) MINORITY SERVING INSTITUTIONS (MSI) PROGRAM
"Minority Serving Institutions Partnership Program (MSIPP)"

Award: Project Grants
Purpose: To focus on building sustainable pipeline between DOE/NNSA's sites/labs and MSIs in STEM disciplines, and bring an awareness of NNSA plants and laboratories to MSIs.
Applicant Eligibility: Historically Black Colleges and universities (HBCUs), Hispanic Serving Institutions (HSIs), Tribal Colleges and universities (TCUs) and non-profit Institutions servicing HBCUs, HSIs and TCUs.
Beneficiary Eligibility: The general public, scientists, researchers, student/trainee, graduate students, institutions of higher learning, NNSA, and other US government agencies will benefit. Elementary, Middle and high school students will also benefit due to the institutions of higher learning's programs supported by NNSA.
Award Range/Average: Grant awards range from $750K to $5M annually over either a three or five year period.
Funding: (Project Grants) FY 17 $18,956,000.00; FY 18 est $18,832,000.00; FY 19 est $18,832,000.00
HQ: 1000 Independence Avenue SW, Washington, DC 20585
    Phone: 202-586-6019 | Email: jonathan.jackson@nnsa.doe.gov
    http://www.nnsa.doe.gov

DOE81.124 | PREDICTIVE SCIENCE ACADEMIC ALLIANCE PROGRAM
"Office of Advanced Simulation and Computing (ASC)"

Award: Project Grants
Purpose: To focus on code validation and verification in the predictive science; to promote scientific interactions between the academic community and scientists at the NNSA laboratories; and to train scientists in specific areas.
Applicant Eligibility: Only U.S. Public and Private education Institutions with Ph.D. granting Programs can apply.
Beneficiary Eligibility: Same as Applicant Eligibility.
Award Range/Average: $17M for each award for 5 project years ranging from mid-FY08 to mid-FY13 (under a one year no cost time extension, with $3.4 M as the average annual award amount. The 6 new Centers that started in FY14 will receive $4M each year for 5 years for 3 Multidisciplinary Simulation Centers (MSC) and $2M each year for 5 years for 3 Single-Discipline Centers (SDC). The latter 6 Centers will receive this money annually for 5 years. We will request an additional sixth year for the Centers to receive awards out of FY19 funds.
Funding: (Project Grants) FY 18 $17,000,000.00; FY 19 est $9,000,000.00; FY 20 est $20,000,000.00
HQ: 1000 Independence Avenue SW, Washington, DC 20585
    Phone: 202-586-8081 | Email: david.etim@nnsa.doe.gov
    https://www.sandia.gov/psaap/index.html

Programs Administered by Regional - State - Local Offices

DOE81.126 | FEDERAL LOAN GUARANTEES FOR INNOVATIVE ENERGY TECHNOLOGIES
"Loan Programs Office"

Award: Direct Loans; Guaranteed/insured Loans

Purpose: To promote the new or significantly improved technologies in energy projects and their commercial use in the United States of America.

Applicant Eligibility: For innovative clean energy projects: including advanced fossil energy, nuclear energy, renewable energy, and energy efficiency. Eligible projects must utilize a new or significantly improved technology, avoid, reduce or sequester greenhouse gases, be located in the United States, and have a reasonable prospect of repayment. Further information may be found at http://www.energy.gov/lpo/innovative-clean-energy-projects -title-xvii-loan-Program For ATVM loans, automotive or component manufacturers for reequipping, expanding, or establishing manufacturing facilities in the United States that produce fuel - efficient advanced technology vehicles or qualifying components, or for engineering integration performed in the U.S. for ATVMs or qualifying components. Further information may be found at http://www.energy.gov/lpo/advanced-technology-vehicles-manufacturing-atvm-loan-Program For Title XVII there is no legal restriction regarding eligible applicants. An applicant can be a corporation, company, partnership, association, society, trust, joint venture, joint stock company, or governmental nonfederal entity, that has the authority to enter into, and is seeking, a loan guarantee for a loan or other debt obligation of an Eligible Project. Glossary of Termshttp://www.energy.gov/lpo/about-us/glossary-terms.

Beneficiary Eligibility: Small businesses, profit organizations, quasi-public nonprofits, public institutions and interstate, intrastate, State and local governments will benefit from the loan guarantee program. For ATVM, DOE has promulgated regulations defining the eligibility requirements for automobile manufacturers.For more information, please visit: http://www.energy.gov/lpo/loan-programs-office.

Award Range/Average: The value of the loan or guarantee will be determined on a project by project basis.

Funding: (Guaranteed/Insured Loans) FY 18 $0.00; FY 19 est $3,702,619,385.00; FY 20 est Estimate Not Available

HQ: 1000 Independence Avenue SW, Washington, DC 20585

Phone: 202-586-5059 | Email: jeffrey.walker@hq.doe.gov

http://www.energy.gov/lpo/loan-programs-office

DOE81.127 | ENERGY EFFICIENT APPLIANCE REBATE PROGRAM (EEARP)
"EEARP"

Award: Formula Grants

Purpose: To provide financial and technical assistance to States for establishing residential energy star rated appliance rebate programs.

Applicant Eligibility: Assistance available to States and US Territories and possessions.

Beneficiary Eligibility: Individuals and families are the ultimate beneficiaries.

Award Range/Average: Range: 500k-6 million

HQ: 15013 Denver W Parkway, Golden, CO 80401

Phone: 240-562-1456 | Email: james.cash@ee.doe.gov

http://energy.gov/eere/office-energy-efficiency-renewable-energy

DOE81.129 | ENERGY EFFICIENCY AND RENEWABLE ENERGY TECHNOLOGY DEPLOYMENT, DEMONSTRATION AND COMMERCIALIZATION

Award: Cooperative Agreements; Project Grants

Purpose: To provide financial assistance for the technology deployment, demonstration, and commercialization of Energy Efficiency and Renewable Energy technologies.

Applicant Eligibility: Anyone who meets the requirements specified in the funding opportunity announcement at http://www.grants.gov may apply.

Beneficiary Eligibility: Beneficiaries are states and local governments and other public and private institutions.

Award Range/Average: Not Available.

HQ: 15013 Denver W Parkway, Golden, CO 80401

Phone: 240-562-1456 | Email: james.cash@ee.doe.gov

http://www.eere.energy.gov

DOE81.135 | ADVANCED RESEARCH PROJECTS AGENCY-ENERGY "ARPA-E"

Award: Cooperative Agreements
Purpose: To support the President's National Objectives for the Department of Energy.
Applicant Eligibility: As described in the Funding Opportunity Announcement.
Beneficiary Eligibility: General public.
Award Range/Average: $250,000 to $10,000,000 (average range is $2 million)
Funding: (Cooperative Agreements) FY 18 $129,705,947.00; FY 19 est $334,750,000.00; FY 20 Estimate Not Available
HQ: 1000 Independence Avenue SW, Washington, DC 20585
    Phone: 202-287-6583 | Email: hai.duong@hq.doe.gov
    http://www.arpa-e.energy.gov

DOE81.136 | LONG-TERM SURVEILLANCE AND MAINTENANCE

Award: Project Grants
Purpose: To ensure the future protection of human health and the environment through Office of Legacy Management department.
Applicant Eligibility: N/A
Beneficiary Eligibility: N/A
Award Range/Average: The range us $4,000 to $450,000. The average is $89,736
Funding: (Project Grants (Cooperative Agreements)) FY 18 est $7,182,594.00; FY 19 est $6,549,109.00; FY 20 est $7,000,000.00
HQ: 1000 Independence Avenue SW, Washington, DC 20585
    Phone: 202-586-1431 | Email: ingrid.colbert@hq.doe.gov
    http://www.lm.doe.gov

DOE81.137 | MINORITY ECONOMIC IMPACT "Minority Education Awards and Minority Business and Economic Development Programs"

Award: Cooperative Agreements
Purpose: To engage minority serving institutions (MSIs) in DOE mission activities, collaborative research projects throughout the DOE, and future workforce development.
Applicant Eligibility: Historically Black Colleges and universities (HBCUs), Hispanic Serving Institutions (HSIs), Tribal Colleges and universities (TCUs), Asian American Pacific Islander (AAPI) Serving Institutions, and non-profit Institutions servicing HBCUs, HSIs, TCUs, and AAPIs. Additionally, minority business enterprises, and Organizations the primary purpose which is to assist in the development of those communities will be able to participate in the research, development, demonstration, and contract activities of the Department.
Beneficiary Eligibility: The general public, scientists, researchers, student/trainee, graduate students, institutions of higher learning, DOE, minority business enterprises, and organizations the primary purpose which is to assist in the development of those communities and other US government agencies will benefit. Middle and high school will also benefit due to the institutions of higher learning's programs supported by DOE.
Funding: (Formula Grants (Cooperative Agreements)) FY 17 $1,370,961.68; FY 18 est $1,009,000.00; FY 19 est $1,500,000.00
HQ: 1000 Independence Avenue SW, Washington, DC 20585
    Phone: 202-586-8383
    http://energy.gov/diversity

DOE81.138 | STATE HEATING OIL AND PROPANE PROGRAM "SHOPP"

Award: Cooperative Agreements
Purpose: To enable a joint data collection effort between heating oil and propane consuming States across the United States and the U.S. Department of Energy/U.S. Energy Information Administration (EIA).

Programs Administered by Regional - State - Local Offices

Applicant Eligibility: SHOPP is a joint data collection effort between States that consume heating oil and propane for residential heating purposes across the United States and the U.S. Department of Energy/Energy Information Administration (EIA).

Beneficiary Eligibility: Beneficiaries are States and their agencies that have the resources to conduct the program, and whose residents consume heating oil and/or propane for residential purposes.

Award Range/Average: The range of individual awards is from $1,900 to $24,000. $250,000 is allocated annually for financial assistance to States for SHOPP.

Funding: (Salaries and Expenses) FY 18 $188,814.00; FY 19 est $189,605.00; FY 20 est $200,000.00

HQ: 1000 Independence Avenue SW, Washington, DC 20585

Phone: 202-586-4412 | Email: marcela.rourk@eia.gov
http://www.eia.gov

DOE81.139 | ENVIRONMENTAL MANAGEMENT R&D AND VALIDATION TESTING ON HIGH EFFICIENCY PARTICULATE AIR (HEPA) FILTERS
"Environmental Management R&D"

Award: Cooperative Agreements

Purpose: To support the safety and quality of permanent containment and confinement ventilation systems as well as modular worksite and breathing-zone ventilation systems used to support nuclear, radiological, chemical, and other high-consequence facility and environmental operations.

Applicant Eligibility: A publicly-owned agency or Organization established to perform specialized functions or services for the benefit of all or part of the general public either without charge or at cost, making no profits and having no shareholders to receive dividends. Includes Institutions of higher education and hospitals. Determinations are made by DOE EM Headquarters or EM Field Offices, or both.

Beneficiary Eligibility: The following organizations will significantly benefit from improved, more reliable, and safer advanced HEPA filters: Federal/ State radioactive treatment and/or storage facilities, commercial nuclear power industry, workers in a radioactive environment, industrial, military or medical processes that require very stringent filtering and the general public, particularly landowners or homeowners in proximity to radioactive facilities. Indirect benefits include more accurate known and understood HEPA filter failure mechanisms and limits, margins, and operational constraints, especially in emergency situations such as fire or a seismic event. Indirect benefits include deceased operating costs, and potentially improvements to the American Society of Mechanical Engineering (ASME) AG-1 code, the US national consensus standard for nuclear air handling and treatment systems.

Funding: (Salaries and Expenses) FY 18 $5,000,000.00; FY 19 est $5,000,000.00; FY 20 est $5,000,000.00

HQ: Office of Technology Development 1000 Independence Avenue SW, Washington, DC 20585

Phone: 202-287-1348 | Email: rodrigo.rimando@em.doe.gov
http://www.energy.gov

DOE81.140 | LOS ALAMOS NATIONAL LABORATORY-FIRE PROTECTION
"Los Alamos Fire Department Cooperative Agreement"

Award: Project Grants

Purpose: To provide an enhanced level of fire department services, including advanced nuclear facility capable, industrial fire suppression, advanced emergency medical, rescue, hazardous materials response, and other services for County of Los Alamos through its municipal fire department.

Applicant Eligibility: EMERGENCY PREPAREDNESS: The fire department has an authorized staffing level of 139 fire fighters and officers and 11 civilian support staff. The fire department staff, in addition to being trained as conventional fire fighters responding to fires in residence and businesses, is also trained to respond to fires and other emergencies at nuclear and high hazard facilities. PLANNING: The fire department is responsible for the development of Pre-Incident Plans at necessary LANL buildings and facilities. PUBLIC WORKS: The fire department is responsible for hydrant testing at LANL. TRAINING: Fire fighters receive special training prior to engaging in fire fighting or emergency operations at nuclear and high hazard facilities at LANL, not only to ensure their safety, but to ensure that their actions contribute to control of the incident, versus making the incident worse by possibly spreading contamination or taking actions which result in unnecessary damage to mission critical or costly equipment.

Beneficiary Eligibility: Los Alamos Fire Department is an agency within Los Alamos County. Los Alamos County is a political subdivision of the State of New Mexico.

Award Range/Average: For the 1st term of the Cooperative Agreement (FY09-FY13), Federal assistance ranged from $13,978,318 to $15,731,859 (estimated). For the 2nd term of the Cooperative Agreement (FY14-FY18), Federal assistance is estimated at $17,478,712 to $19,038,838. For the 3rd term of the Cooperative Agreement (FY19-FY23), Federal assistance is estimated at $19,216,331 to $21,266,489.

Funding: (Project Grants (Cooperative Agreements)) FY 18 $18,585,361.00: FY 19 est $19,216,331.00; FY 20 est $20,350,045.00

HQ: 3747 W Jamez Road, Los Alamos, NM 87544

Phone: 505-665-0838 | Email: james.rast@nnsa.doe.gov

http://nnsa.energy.gov

DOE81.250 | ENERGY POLICY AND SYSTEMS ANALYSIS

Award: Cooperative Agreements

Purpose: To enhance intergovernmental coordination and collaboration on key analytical and policy issues; and to provide technical assistance and guidance to states and local governments on energy planning and measures.

Applicant Eligibility: State, local, and/or tribal nonprofit Institutions /Organizations and "instrumentalities of the states" are eligible.

Beneficiary Eligibility: State, local, and tribal government officials benefit.

Award Range/Average: $100,000 to $1,000,000 per year per award (maximum of 6 awards)

Funding: (Cooperative Agreements) FY 18 $0.00; FY 19 est $ 0.00; FY 19 est $ 0.00; FY2015 $0 FY2016 NCSL: $137,500 NASEO: $137,500 NARUC: $92,500 NGA: $97,500 FY2017: NCSL: $0 NASEO: $125,000 NARUC: $75,000 NGA: $83,850

HQ: 1000 Independence Avenue SW, Washington, DC 20585

Phone: 202-287-1040 | Email: quinntella.wilson@hq.doe.gov

http://www.energy.gov/policy

ECONOMIC DEVELOPMENT ADMINISTRATION
Regional – State – Local Offices

Atlanta Region

William J. Day Jr., Regional Director | 401 W Peachtree Street NW Suite 1820, Atlanta, GA 30308-3510 404-730-3002

Austin Region

903 San Jacinto Suite 206, Austin, TX 78701-5595 512-381-8144

Chicago Region

C. Robert Sawyer, Regional Director | 111 N Canal Street Suite 855, Chicago, IL 60606-7204 312-353-8143

Denver Region

Robert Olsen, Regional Director | 1244 Speer Boulevard Room 670, Denver, CO 80204 303-844-4715

Philadelphia

Paul M. Raetsch, Regional Director | Curtis Center Independence Square W Suite 140 S, Philadelphia, PA 19106 215-597-4603

Seattle

A. Leonard Smith, Regional Director | 915 2nd Avenue Jackson Federal Building Suite 1856, Seattle, WA 98174 206-220-7660

DOC11.020 | CLUSTER GRANTS

Award: Project Grants

Purpose: The Regional Innovation Strategies program assists innovators and entrepreneurs and provides operational support for organizations.

Applicant Eligibility: N/A

Beneficiary Eligibility: N/A

Award Range/Average: For the 2019 i6 Challenge the maximum Federal share of each i6 Challenge grant is $750,000 and EDA plans to award up to 32 grants. For the 2019 SFS Grant Competition, the maximum Federal share of each SFS Grant is $300,000, and EDA plans to award up to 16 grants.

Funding: (Project Grants) FY 18 $21,000,000.00; FY 19 est $23,500,000.00; FY 20 est $ Estimate Not Available

HQ: Office of Innovation and Entrepreneurship 1401 Constitution Avenue NW, Washington, DC 20230

Phone: 202-482-8001

http://www.eda.gov

Programs Administered by Regional - State - Local Offices

DOC11.300 | INVESTMENTS FOR PUBLIC WORKS AND ECONOMIC DEVELOPMENT FACILITIES

Award: Project Grants

Purpose: The Public Works program helps distressed communities and facilities to implement regional development strategies, regional prosperity, water and sewer system improvements, industrial parks, shipping and logistics facilities, workforce training facilities, etc. Public Works program follows the standards of EDA.

Applicant Eligibility: EDA is not authorized to provide grants or cooperative agreements under its Public Works or EAA Programs to individuals or to for-profit entities. Requests from such entities will not be considered for funding. Pursuant to Section 3 of PWEDA (42 U.S.C. 3122) and 13 C. F. R. 300. 3, eligible applicants for EDA financial assistance under the Public Works and EAA Programs include a(n): (i) District Organization of an EDA-designated Economic Development District; (ii) Indian Tribe or a consortium of Indian Tribes; (iii) State, county, city, or other political subdivision of a State, including a special purpose unit of a State or local government engaged in economic or infrastructure development activities, or a consortium of political subdivisions; (iv) institution of higher education or a consortium of Institutions of higher education; or (v) public or private non-profit Organization or association acting in cooperation with officials of a political subdivision of a State.

Beneficiary Eligibility: N/A

Award Range/Average: The average size of a Public Works investment has been approximately $1.4 million, and investments generally range from $600,000 to $3,000,000. Historically, EDA has awarded funds for between 80 and 150 Public Works projects a year.

Funding: (Project Grants) FY 18 $117,500,000.00; FY 19 est $117,500,000.00; FY 20 est Estimate Not Available.

HQ: 1401 Constitution Avenue NW, Room 71030, Washington, DC 20230

Phone: 202-400-0662 | Email: psaputo@eda.gov

http://www.eda.gov

DOC11.302 | ECONOMIC DEVELOPMENT SUPPORT FOR PLANNING ORGANIZATIONS

"Planning Investments and Comprehensive Economic Development Strategies"

Award: Project Grants

Purpose: The Planning program provides assistance to create regional economic development plans in order to stimulate and guide the economic development efforts of a community or region by helping to create and retain higher-skill, higher-wage jobs, particularly for the unemployed and underemployed in the Nation's most economically distressed regions. In addition, EDA provides Partnership Planning grants to Indian Tribes to help organize and assist with the implementation of economic development activities within their areas.

Applicant Eligibility: Pursuant to PWEDA, eligible applicants for and recipients of EDA investment assistance include a(n): (a) District Organization (as defined in 13 CFR 304. 2); (b) Indian Tribe or a consortium of Indian Tribes; (c) State, city, or other political subdivision of a State, including a special purpose unit of a State or local government engaged in economic or infrastructure development activities, or a consortium of political subdivisions; (d) institution of higher education or a consortium of Institutions of higher education; or (e) public or private non-profit Organization or association acting in cooperation with officials of a political subdivision of a State. See section 3 of PWEDA (42 U.S.C. 3122) and 13 CFR 300. 3. As used in this paragraph, State includes the Commonwealth of Puerto Rico, the U.S. Virgin Islands, Guam, American Samoa, and the Commonwealth of the Northern Mariana Islands, the Republic of the Marshall Islands, the Federated States of Micronesia, and the Republic of Palau. See 13 CFR 300. 3 and 301. 2.

Beneficiary Eligibility: EDA Planning investments provide support to Planning Organizations for the development, implementation, revision, or replacement of a CEDS. They also may provide support for related short-term planning investments and State plans designed to create and retain higher-skill, higher-wage jobs, particularly for the unemployed and underemployed in the nation's most economically distressed regions.

Award Range/Average: The average size of a Planning investment has been approximately $70,000, and investments generally range from $40,000 to $200,000.

Funding: (Project Grants) FY 18 $33,000,000.00; FY 19 est $33,000,000.00; FY 20 est Estimate Not Available

HQ: 1401 Constitution Avenue NW, Room 71030, Washington, DC 20230

Phone: 202-482-0529 | Email: dives@eda.gov

http://www.eda.gov

DOC11.303 | ECONOMIC DEVELOPMENT TECHNICAL ASSISTANCE
"National Technical Assistance"

Award: Project Grants

Purpose: EDA's NTA supports projects that provide technical assistance at a national scope to solve problems related to economic development and provides training, information, and implementation of economic development practices.

Applicant Eligibility: Pursuant to PWEDA, eligible applicants for and eligible recipients of EDA investment assistance under this NOFO include a(n): a. District Organization; b. Indian Tribe or a consortium of Indian Tribes; c. State, county, city, or other political subdivision of a State, including a special purpose unit of a State or local government engaged in economic or infrastructure development activities, or a consortium of political subdivisions; d. Institution of higher education or a consortium of Institutions of higher education; e. Public or private non-profit Organization or association acting in cooperation with officials of a political subdivision of a State; f. A private individual org. For-profit Organization.

Beneficiary Eligibility: Description of the technical assistance that will be provided to stakeholders; Description of how the proposed project increases the economic development capacity of individuals, firms, or communities; Discussion of how the project will stimulate economic development in distressed regions; and; Explanation of how the proposed project supports EDA's mission to lead the Federal economic development agenda by promoting innovation and competitiveness, preparing and supporting American regions for growth and success in the global economy.

Award Range/Average: In recent years, the average size of R&E and NTA investments has been approximately $350,000, and investments generally range from $200,000 to $500,000. Historically, EDA has funded approximately five R&E projects per year and three NTA projects. EDA anticipates making similar awards in FY 2018-2020, subject to availability of funds.

Funding: (Project Grants) FY 18 est $1,000,000.00; FY 19 est $9,500,000; FY 20 est Estimate Not Available

HQ: 1401 Constitution Avenue NW, Room 71030, Washington, DC 20230
Phone: 202-482-0529 | Email: dives@eda.gov
http://www.eda.gov

DOC11.307 | ECONOMIC ADJUSTMENT ASSISTANCE
"Economic Adjustment"

Award: Project Grants

Purpose: The EAA supports a wide range of construction and non-construction activities. It provides resources to help communities by advancing economic development, job creation, foster collaboration, attract investment, support the construction of a publicly owned multi-tenant business, and support the regions that have been negatively impacted by changes in the coal economy.

Applicant Eligibility: EDA is not authorized to provide grants or cooperative agreements under its Public Works or EAA Programs to individuals or to for-profit entities. Requests from such entities will not be considered for funding. Pursuant to Section 3 of PWEDA (42 U.S.C. 3122) and 13 C. F. R. 300. 3, eligible applicants for EDA financial assistance under the Public Works and EAA Programs include a(n): (i) District Organization of an EDA-designated Economic Development District; (ii) Indian Tribe or a consortium of Indian Tribes; (iii) State, county, city, or other political subdivision of a State, including a special purpose unit of a State or local government engaged in economic or infrastructure development activities, or a consortium of political subdivisions; (iv) institution of higher education or a consortium of Institutions of higher education; or (v) public or private non-profit Organization or association acting in cooperation with officials of a political subdivision of a State.

Beneficiary Eligibility: Beneficiaries of investments made under Economic Adjustment are those communities who satisfy one or more of the economic distress and/or "Special Need" criteria set forth in 13 C.F.R. 301.3(a) and 13 C.F.R. 300.3 to revitalize, expand, or upgrade their economic development assets to attract new industry, encourage business expansion, diversify their local economies, and generate or retain long-term private sector jobs and capital investments. Investments are intended to alleviate long-term deterioration and sudden and severe economic dislocation in distressed communities and regions.

Award Range/Average: The average size of an EAA investment has been approximately $650,000, and investments generally range from $150,000 to $1,000,000. Historically, EDA has awarded funds for between 70 and 140 EAA projects a year.

Funding: (Project Grants (Cooperative Agreements)) FY 18 $37,000,000.00; FY 19 est $37,000,000.00; FY 20 est Estimate Not Available

HQ: 1401 Constitution Avenue NW, Room 71030, Washington, DC 20230
Phone: 202-400-0662 | Email: psaputo@eda.gov
http://www.eda.gov

Programs Administered by Regional - State - Local Offices

DOC11.312 | RESEARCH AND EVALUATION PROGRAM

Award: Project Grants

Purpose: The R&E program supports the development of tools, recommendations, and resources that shape Federal economic development policies to implement economic development throughout the country. EDA also regularly evaluates the impacts and outcomes of its various programs.

Applicant Eligibility: Pursuant to PWEDA, eligible applicants for and eligible recipients of EDA investment assistance under this NOFO include a(n): a. District Organization; b. Indian Tribe or a consortium of Indian Tribes; c. State, county, city, or other political subdivision of a State, including a special purpose unit of a State or local government engaged in economic or infrastructure development activities, or a consortium of political subdivisions; d. Institution of higher education or a consortium of Institutions of higher education; e. Public or private non-profit Organization or association acting in cooperation with officials of a political subdivision of a State; f. A private individual org. For-profit Organization.

Beneficiary Eligibility: Research and Evaluation investments are designed to finance projects for research into techniques that promote competitiveness and innovation in urban and rural regions throughout the United States.

Award Range/Average: In recent years, the average size of R&E and NTA investments has been approximately $350,000, and investments generally range from $200,000 to $500,000. Historically, EDA has funded approximately five R&E projects per year.

Funding: (Project Grants (Cooperative Agreements)) FY 18 $1,500,000.00; FY 19 est $1,500,000.00; FY 20 est Estimate Not Available

HQ: 1401 Constitution Avenue NW, Room 71030, Washington, DC 20230
Phone: 202-482-1464 | Email: rsmith2@eda.gov
http://www.eda.gov

DOC11.313 | TRADE ADJUSTMENT ASSISTANCE FOR FIRMS

Award: Cooperative Agreements

Purpose: The Trade Adjustment Assistance for Firms program assists economically distressed U.S. business in building strategies to increase exports.

Applicant Eligibility: Section 253 of the Trade Act (19 U.S.C. 2343(b)) provides that grants may be awarded to "intermediary Organizations (including Trade Adjustment Assistance Centers)" to provide assistance to trade-injured firms. For an industry association or other Organizations to be eligible for industry assistance under section 265 of the Trade Act (19 U.S.C. 2355(a)), the applicant must submit evidence demonstrating that the industry faces import competition and includes a substantial number of Trade Act-certified firms or worker groups.

Beneficiary Eligibility: Only firms certified by EDA on behalf of the Secretary of Commerce are eligible for assistance under the TAAF program. Industries that can demonstrate they have been injured by imports and have a substantial number of Trade Act certified firm or worker groups may also benefit. The principal benefit is cost-shared technical assistance: the TAA program pays up to one-half of the cost of assistance by private-sector consultants and contractors for operational improvements at certified firms.

Award Range/Average: Awards range between $1M- $1.6M.

Funding: (Cooperative Agreements) FY 18 $13,000,000.00; FY 19 est $13,000,000.00; FY 20 est Estimate Not Available

HQ: 1401 Constitution Avenue NW, Suite 71030, Washington, DC 20230
Phone: 202-482-0556 | Email: mkearse@eda.gov
http://www.eda.gov

EMPLOYEE BENEFITS SECURITY ADMINISTRATION
Regional – State – Local Offices

California

Crisanta Johnson, Director | 1055 E Colorado Boulevard Suite 200, Pasadena, CA 91106 626-229-1000

Jean Ackerman, Director | 90 7th Street Suite 11-300, San Francisco, CA 94105 415-625-2481

Florida

Norman Rivera, Supervisor | 1000 S Pine Island Road Suite 100, Plantation, FL 33324 954-424-4022

Georgia

Isabel Colon | 61 Forsyth Street SW Suite 7 B54, Atlanta, GA 30303 404-302-3900

Illinois

Donna Seermon, Acting Director | John C Kluczynski Federal Building 230 S Dearborn Street Ste 2160, Chicago, IL 60604 312-353-0900

Kentucky

Joe Rivers, Director | 1885 Dixie Highway Suite 210, Fort Wright, KY 41011-2664 859-578-4680

Maryland

Elizabeth Bond, Supervisor | 1335 E W Highway Suite 200, Silver Spring, MD 20910-3225 202-693-8700

Massachusetts

Susan Hensley, Director | JFK Building 15 New Sudbury Street Suite 575, Boston, MA 02203 617-565-9600

Michigan

211 W Fort Street Suite 1310, Detroit, MI 48226-3211 313-226-7450

Missouri

Frank Wilson, Acting Supervisor | Robert A Young Federal Building 1222 Spruce Street Suite 6310, Saint Louis, MO 63103-2818 314-539-2693

James Purcell, Director | 2300 Main Street Suite 1100, Kansas City, MO 64108 816-285-1800

New York

Jonathan Kay, Director | 33 Whitehall Street Suite 1200, New York, NY 10004 212-607-8600

Pennsylvania

Marc Machiz, Director | 170 S Independence Mall W Suite 870, Philadelphia, PA 19106-3317 215-861-5300

Texas

Deborah Perry, Director | 525 S Griffin Street Suite 900, Dallas, TX 75202-5025 972-850-4500

Washington

Judy Owen, Supervisor | 300 5th Avenue Suite 1110, Seattle, WA 98101-3212 206-757-6781

DOL17.201 | REGISTERED APPRENTICESHIP "Fitzgerald Act"

Award: Project Grants; Advisory Services and Counseling; Training

Purpose: To assist industry in the development and improvement of Registered Apprenticeship and ensure equal employment opportunities.

Applicant Eligibility: Employers, unions, and other workforce intermediaries can be eligible to start and maintain Registered Apprenticeship Programs. The vast majority of Programs are not funded by Federal grant funds. The OA and SAAs provide technical assistance. OA also administers two grant Programs, as follows: I. Women in Apprenticeship and Non-Traditional Occupations (WANTO) grants fund innovative projects to community-based Organizations (CBOs) that are designed to improve women's participation in Registered Apprenticeship Programs for nontraditional occupations in a broad range of industries. WANTO grants were awarded for Program Year (PY) 2015 and PY 2016 to three CBOs to establish regional/multi-state Technical Resource Centers to assist Registered Apprenticeship Program sponsors to improve the recruitment, hiring, training, employment, and retention of women in apprenticeships. PY 2013 and PY 2014 funds were similarly awarded to three CBOs for the same purposes. Future funding was not requested for PY 2017. These grants are jointly administered by the Department of Labor's Women's Bureau and the Employment and Training Administration. See http://www.doleta.gov/grants/grants_awarded. cfm. II. Apprenticeship USA State Accelerator Grants/State Expansion Grants Registered Apprenticeship has made available $60 million in grants to help state Governments integrate apprenticeship into their education and workforce systems; engage industry and other partners at scale to expand apprenticeship to new sectors and new populations; support state capacity to conduct outreach and work with employers to start new Programs; provide support to promote greater inclusion and diversity in apprenticeship, and implement state innovations, incentives and system Reforms. By investing in state strategies for growing Registered Apprenticeship opportunities, these funds will help strengthen the foundation for the rapid and sustained expansion of quality apprenticeship nationwide. These grants are covered under CFDA 17.285.

Beneficiary Eligibility: Registered Apprenticeship program sponsors identify the minimum qualifications to apply into their apprenticeship programs. Individuals applying for acceptance into an apprenticeship program must be at least 16 years old. To be an apprentice in a hazardous occupation, the individual must usually be 18 years. Program sponsors may also identify additional minimum qualifications and credentials to apply, e.g., education, ability to physically perform the essential functions of the occupation, ability to complete the related technical instruction, proof of age. Along with the completed application form, each prospective apprentice may be required by the program sponsor to submit a transcript of school subjects and grades, proof of age, an honourable military discharge (if applicable), and a high-school diploma or equivalence certificate (if applicable). References from all previous employers may be required.

Award Range/Average: Not Applicable.

Funding: (Salaries and Expenses) FY 17 $36,000,000.00; FY 18 est $36,000,000.00; FY 19 est $36,000,000.00

HQ: 200 Constitution Avenue NW C-5311, Washington, DC 20210

Phone: 202-693-3748 | Email: jordan.alexander@dol.gov

http://www.doleta.gov/oa

Programs Administered by Regional - State - Local Offices

DOL17.207 | EMPLOYMENT SERVICE/WAGNER-PEYSER FUNDED ACTIVITIES
"Wagner- Peyser Act of 1933"

Award: Formula Grants; Project Grants

Purpose: The Employment Service program provides a variety of services including labor exchange services, job search assistance, workforce information, referrals to employment, and other assistance to obtain qualified employment.

Applicant Eligibility: For Wagner-Peyser Employment Service grants and Labor Market Information grants, eligible applicants include all 50 States, the District of Columbia, the Virgin Islands, Puerto Rico, and Guam.

Beneficiary Eligibility: The system affords universal access to all job seekers. In addition, services are available to employers seeking to hire workers. Priority of service is given to veterans and other covered persons. These individuals receive priority referral to jobs, as well as specialized employment services and assistance.

Award Range/Average: Wagner-Peyser Formula Grants vary by year. Funding is published annually in the Federal Register.

Funding: (Formula Grants) FY 17 $701,000,000.00; FY 18 est $695,000,000.00; FY 19 est $446,000,000.00; (Project Grants) FY 17 $31,000,000.00; FY 18 est $32,000,000.00; FY 19 est $36,000,000.00

HQ: 200 Constitution Avenue NW, Room S-4203, Washington, DC 20210

Phone: 202-693-3937 | Email: kight.robert@dol.gov

http://www.doleta.gov

DOL17.225 | UNEMPLOYMENT INSURANCE
"UI"

Award: Formula Grants; Direct Payments With Unrestricted Use

Purpose: To assist eligible workers with unemployment compensation for federal employees or ex-service members, Disaster Unemployment Assistance through Trade Adjustment Assistance programs.

Applicant Eligibility: State workforce agencies, including those in the District of Columbia, Puerto Rico and Virgin Islands. The Workforce Innovation and Opportunity Act (WIOA) (Pub. L. 113-128) was passed on July 22, 2014. It supersedes titles I and II of the Workforce Investment Act of 1998, and amends the Wagner-Peyser Act and the Rehabilitation Act of 1973. The law went into effect on July 1, 2015. Also, unless otherwise stipulated, recipients are subject to Uniform Administrative Requirements, Cost Principles, and Audit Requirements for Federal Awards; Final Rule on December 26, 2013 and found at 2 CFR Part 200 along with the OMB approved exceptions for DOL at 2 CFR Part 2900 published on December 19, 2014 in the Federal Register.

Beneficiary Eligibility: All workers whose wages are subject to state unemployment insurance laws, federal civilian employees, ex-service members, and workers whose unemployment is caused by a presidentially declared disaster under the Robert T. Stafford Disaster Relief and Emergency Assistance Act, are eligible if they are involuntarily unemployed, able to work, available for work, meet the eligibility and qualifying requirements of the state law, and are free from disqualifications. Some states provide Short Time Compensation or Self Employment Assistance for eligible individuals. Workers who became unemployed or underemployed because of the adverse effect of increased imports or because of shifts in production outside the U.S. may be eligible for Trade Readjustment Allowance, Alternative Trade Adjustment Assistance or Reemployment Adjustment Assistance and other types of Trade Adjustment Assistance (see program 57.001). Individual state information on eligibility requirements is available from local American Job Centers or at http://www.servicelocator.org/.

Award Range/Average: FY 2016, estimate for the minimum award is $1.7 million and the estimated maximum award is $380 million. The estimated average award is $52 million. FY 2017, the minimum award is $1.7 million and the maximum award is $368 million. The estimated average award is $51 million. FY 2018, the estimated minimum grant award is $1.7 million and the maximum award is $338 million. The estimated average award is $47 million

Funding: (Direct Payments with Unrestricted Use) FY 17 $30,664,000,000.00; FY 18 est $29,591,000,000.00; FY 19 est $29,434,000,000.00; (Formula Grants) FY 17 $2,707,000,000.00; FY 18 est $2,734,000,000.00; FY 19 est $2,555,000,000.00

HQ: 200 Constitution Avenue NW, Room S4524, Washington, DC 20210

Phone: 202-693-3029 | Email: gilbert.gay@dol.gov

http://ows.doleta.gov/unemploy

DOL17.235 | SENIOR COMMUNITY SERVICE EMPLOYMENT PROGRAM "SCSEP"

Award: Formula Grants; Project Grants

Purpose: To provide low-income persons with training at community service employment to gain work experience for self-sufficiency.

Applicant Eligibility: The following types of Organizations are eligible to receive grants: (1) States; (2) U.S. territories; (3) Public and nonprofit private agency and Organizations; and (4) Public or nonprofit national Indian aging Organizations and public or nonprofit Pacific Island and Asian American aging Organizations. Unless otherwise stipulated, entities carrying out the project are subject to Uniform Administrative Requirements, Cost Principles, and Audit Requirements for Federal Awards found at 2 CFR Part 200 along with the OMB approved exceptions for DOL at 2 CFR Part 2900 published on December 19, 2014 in the Federal Register; Older Americans Act Reauthorization Act of 2016 published April 22, 2016; Interim Final Rule published December 1, 2017); Final Rule published December 26, 2010; and Training and Employment Guidance Letters available via https://www.doleta.gov/Seniors/html_docs/TechAssist. cfm.

Beneficiary Eligibility: SCSEP applicants must be unemployed adults 55 years or older with a family income that is not more than 125 percent of the Department of Health and Human Services (DHHS) poverty level. Prospective participants must provide documentation relevant to age and income, which is required to determine whether the individual is program eligible. With certain exceptions, the Census Bureau's Current Population Survey definition of income governs the determination of SCSEP applicants' income eligibility. Section 518 (a)(3)(A) of the OAA-2016 specifies that any income that is unemployment compensation, a benefit received under title XVI of the Social Security Act; a payment made to or on behalf of veterans or former members of the Armed Forces under the laws administered by the Secretary of Veterans Affairs, or 25 percent of a benefit received under title II of the Social Security Act, is excluded from SCSEP income eligibility determinations.

Award Range/Average: For Program Year 2013, grants ranged from $318,604 to $82.8M. For Program Year 2014, grants ranged from $324,965 to $84.2M.

Funding: (Formula Grants) FY 17 $565,000,000.00; FY 18 est $401,000,000.00; FY 19 est $0.00

HQ: 200 Constitution Avenue NW, Room C 4510, Washington, DC 20210

   Phone: 202-693-3356 | Email: chapman.lamia@dol.gov

   http://www.doleta.gov/seniors

DOL17.245 | TRADE ADJUSTMENT ASSISTANCE

Award: Formula Grants

Purpose: The Trade Adjustment Assistance for Workers Program provides employment-related benefits and services.

Applicant Eligibility: For a worker to be eligible to apply for TAA, the worker must be part of a group of workers that are the subject of a petition filed with the Department. Three workers of a company, a company official, a union or other duly authorized representative, or an AJC operator or partner may file that petition with the Department. In response to the filing, the Department initiates an investigation to determine whether foreign trade was an important cause of the workers job loss or threat of job loss. If the Department determines that the workers meet the statutory criteria for group certification of eligibility for the workers in the group to apply for TAA, the Department grants the petition and issues a certification.

Beneficiary Eligibility: Once a member of a worker group is covered by a certification for eligibility to apply for TAA, the workers individually apply for benefits and services through the American Job Centers. TAA benefits and services have specific individual eligibility criteria that must be met, such as previous work history, unemployment insurance eligibility, and individual skill levels. The TAA program currently offers the following benefits and services to eligible individuals: training, weekly income support in the form of TRA, out-of-area job search and relocation allowances, case management and employment services, and wage supplement for qualified older workers through RTAA.

Award Range/Average: This amount is published yearly in the Report to the Committee on Finance of the Senate and Committee on Ways and Means of the House of Representatives, which can be found on the program website at www.doleta.gov/tradeact.

Funding: (Formula Grants) FY 17 $391,000,000.00; FY 18 est $398,000,000.00; FY 19 est $450,000,000.00

HQ: 200 Constitution Avenue NW, Washington, DC 20210

   Phone: 202-693-3628 | Email: herrmann.erica@dol.gov

   http://www.doleta.gov/tradeact

Programs Administered by Regional - State - Local Offices

DOL17.258 | WIOA ADULT PROGRAM
"Workforce Innovation and Opportunity Act (WIOA), Adult Programs"

Award: Formula Grants

Purpose: The Adult Program serves individuals and helps employers meet their workforce needs and provides them with job search assistance and training opportunities. It also assists low-income individuals and disabled persons with employment.

Applicant Eligibility: Under WIOA, the entities eligible to receive funding from the Department are the 50 States, Puerto Rico, the District of Columbia and the outlying areas. Funds are allotted based on a statutory formula. The states in turn allocate funds to local workforce development boards which are responsible for operating American Job Centers (approximately 2, 400 nationwide).

Beneficiary Eligibility: All adults 18 years of age and older are eligible to receive career services. Several populations receive priority, with States and local areas being responsible for establishing procedures for applying the priority requirements. Priority of service is given to veterans and other covered persons. Priority for career and training services must be given to public assistance recipients, other low income populations, and low-skilled individuals.

Award Range/Average: WIOA formula grant amounts vary annually and are published in the Federal Register.

Funding: (Formula Grants) FY 17 $813,000,000.00; FY 18 est $843,000,000.00; FY 19 est $811,000,000.00

HQ: 200 Constitution Avenue NW, Room S 4203, Washington, DC 20210

Phone: 202-693-3937 | Email: kight.robert@dol.gov
http://www.doleta.gov

DOL17.259 | WIOA YOUTH ACTIVITIES
"WIOA Formula Youth"

Award: Formula Grants

Purpose: To assist low-income youth to acquire the educational and occupational skills and successfully transition into careers and productive adulthood.

Applicant Eligibility: Under WIOA, 50 states, Puerto Rico, the District of Columbia, and the outlying areas are identified as the recipients of youth training activities funds. For a state to be eligible to receive youth funds, the governor of the state will submit a Unified or Combined State Plan to the Secretary of DOL that outlines a 4-year strategy for the State's workforce development system.

Beneficiary Eligibility: To be eligible to participate in the WIOA youth program, an individual must be an Out-of-School Youth or an In-School Youth. Under WIOA, an out-of-school youth is an individual who is: (a) Not attending any school (as defined under State law); (b) Not younger than age 16 or older than age 24 at time of enrollment. Because age eligibility is based on age at enrollment, participants may continue to receive services beyond the age of 24 once they are enrolled in the program; and (c) One or more of the following: (1) A school dropout; (2) A youth who is within the age of compulsory school attendance, but has not attended school for at least the most recent complete school year calendar quarter. School year calendar quarter is based on how a local school district defines its school year quarters. In cases where schools do not use quarters, local programs must use calendar year quarters; (3) A recipient of a secondary school diploma or its recognized equivalent who is a low-income individual and is either basic skills deficient or an English language learner; (4) An offender; (5) A homeless individual aged 16 to 24 who meets the criteria defined in sec. 41403(6) of the Violence Against Women Act of 1994 (42 U.S.C. 14043e-2(6)), a homeless child or youth aged 16 to 24 who meets the criteria defined in sec. 725(2) of the McKinney-Vento Homeless Assistance Act (42 U.S.C. 11434a(2)) or a runaway; (6) An individual in foster care or who has aged out of the foster care system or who has attained 16 years of age and left foster care for kinship guardianship or adoption, a child eligible for assistance under sec. 477 of the Social Security Act (42 U.S.C. 677), or in an out-of-home placement; (7) An individual who is pregnant or parenting; (8) An individual with a disability; or (9) A low-income individual who requires additional assistance to enter or complete an educational program or to secure or hold employment Under WIOA, An in-school youth (ISY) is an individual who is:(a) Attending school (as defined by State law), including secondary and postsecondary school; (b) Not younger than age 14 or (unless an individual with a disability who is attending school under State law) older than age 21 at time of enrollment. Because age eligibility is based on age at enrollment, participants may continue to receive services beyond the age of 21 once they are enrolled in the program; (c) A low-income individual; and (d) One or more of the following: (1) Basic skills deficient; (2) An English language learner; (3) An offender; (4) A homeless individual aged 14 to 21 who meets the criteria defined in sec. 41403(6) of the Violence Against Women Act of 1994 (42 U.S.C. 14043e-2(6))), a homeless child or youth aged 14 to 21 who meets the criteria defined in sec. 725(2) of the McKinney-Vento Homeless Assistance Act (42 U.S.C. 11434a(2))), or a runaway; (5) An individual in foster care or who has aged out of the foster care system or who has attained 16 years of age and left foster care for kinship guardianship or adoption, a child eligible for assistance under sec. 477 of the Social Security Act (42 U.S.C. 677), or in an out-of-home placement; (6) An individual who is pregnant or parenting; (7) An individual with a disability; or (8) An individual who requires additional assistance to complete an educational program or to secure or hold employment.

Award Range/Average: Formula grant award amounts vary annually and are published in the Federal Register.

Funding: (Formula Grants) FY 17 $853,000,000.00; FY 18 est $886,000,000.00; FY 19 est $514,000,000.00

HQ: 200 Constitution Avenue NW, Washington, DC 20210

Phone: 202-693-3377 | Email: kemp.jennifer.n@dol.gov

http://www.doleta.gov/youth_services

DOL17.261 | WIOA PILOTS, DEMONSTRATIONS, AND RESEARCH PROJECTS "PDR (including WDQI)"

Award: Project Grants

Purpose: To address national employment and training issues for continuous improvement of the public workforce system.

Applicant Eligibility: State and local Governments, Federal agencies, private non-profit and for-profit Organizations, including faith-based and community-based Organizations, and educational Institutions. Note: Applicant eligibility may be restricted to one or more applicant classes under the particular announcement or solicitation. Only states and U.S. territories are eligible to apply for WDQI grants. These funds are used to develop, or enhance, state IT systems established as longitudinal administrative databases for the long-term analysis of individual data from pre-K through the workforce to determine the effectiveness of education and training Programs.

Beneficiary Eligibility: Generally limited to the economically disadvantaged and those who are underemployed, unemployed, need to upgrade their skills in order to retain jobs, at-risk youth, and/or to those who have barriers to employ ability. With WDQI funding, states are required to develop a scorecard, using their longitudinal administrative database, that will display information in a consumer-friendly manner. These scorecards will help inform consumer-choice when selecting workforce training providers.

Award Range/Average: Grant amounts vary and are influenced by the complexity of the initiative being studied. A general range of grant amounts would be $200,000 to $1 million and an average $500,000. WDQI grant award amounts are influenced by the total amount available funding as determined by the appropriation.

Funding: (Project Grants) FY 17 $6,000,000.00; FY 18 est $6,000,000.00; FY 19 est $6,000,000.00

HQ: 200 Constitution Avenue NW, Room N 5641, Washington, DC 20210

Phone: 202-693-2746 | Email: leonetti.ann@dol.gov

http://www.doleta.gov

DOL17.264 | NATIONAL FARMWORKER JOBS PROGRAM "NFJP"

Award: Formula Grants

Purpose: To assist individuals and their dependents in agricultural and fish farming labor and provide housing assistance and other related assistance.

Applicant Eligibility: The provisions of WIOA, Section 167(b), describe entities eligible to receive a grant as those that have: 1) an understanding of the problems of eligible migrant and seasonal farmworkers (including their dependents); 2) a familiarity with the area to be served; and 3) the ability to demonstrate a capacity to administer and deliver effectively a diversified Program of workforce investment activities (including youth workforce investment activities) and related assistance for eligible migrant and seasonal farmworkers. Entities such as state government agencies, state workforce investment boards, local government agencies, local workforce investment boards, faith-based and community-based Organizations, Institutions of higher learning, and other entities are examples of Organizations that could be eligible to apply for NFJP grants.

Beneficiary Eligibility: Beneficiaries are low-income individuals and their dependents who, for 12 consecutive months out of the 24 months prior to application for the program, have been primarily employed in agricultural or fish farming labour that is characterized by chronic unemployment or underemployment, and who face multiple barriers to economic self-sufficiency. Male NFJP Participants must not have violated section 3 of the Military Selective Service Act (50 U.S.C. App. 453).

Award Range/Average: The range and average varies by year according to appropriation levels. State allocations are published annually in the Federal Register.

Funding: (Formula Grants) FY 17 $81,000,000.00; FY 18 est $88,000,000.00; FY 19 est $0.00

HQ: 200 Constitution Avenue NW, Room C 4510, Washington, DC 20210-0001

Phone: 202-693-3912 | Email: rietzke.steven@dol.gov

http://www.doleta.gov/Farmworker/html/NFJP.cfm

Programs Administered by Regional - State - Local Offices

DOL17.265 | NATIVE AMERICAN EMPLOYMENT AND TRAINING
"WIA / WIOA, Section 166, Native American Employment and Training Program"

Award: Formula Grants

Purpose: To support employment and training services for Native Americans to develop more fully in academic, occupational, and literacy skills achieve academic and employment success and transition to careers and productive adulthood.

Applicant Eligibility: Federally-recognized Indian Tribal Governments, bands or groups, Alaska Native villages or groups (as defined in the Alaska Native Claims Settlement Act, 43 U.S.C. 1602(b)), Native Hawaiian Organizations meeting the eligibility criteria, and Native American Organizations (public bodies or private nonprofit agencies) are selected by the Secretary on a competitive basis. Tribes, bands, and groups may also form consortia in order to qualify for designation as a grantee. Detailed requirements for consortium grantee applicants are set forth in the WIOA Final Rule at 684. 200(e). Supplemental funding is automatically awarded to Federal Recognized Tribes and Tribal consortiums selected through the competitive process. However, there a few exceptions in which non-profit entities receive youth funds. Youth funds are also based on a funding formula and is restricted to Native American, Alaska Native and Native Hawaiian youth living on or near reservations, OTSA areas in Oklahoma, Alaskan villages and the state of Hawaii.

Beneficiary Eligibility: Eligibility requirements for the adult program are provided in the WIOA Final Rule at 684.300. To be eligible for services under the adult program, Individuals must meet the definition of an Indian, as determined by a policy of the Native American grantee. American Indians are generally considered members (or descendants) of federally- recognized Indian tribes, bands, and groups or members of well-established state recognized tribes such as, but not limited to, the Houma Indians in Louisiana and the Lumbee Indians in North Carolina. Applicants must also be low-income according to HHS poverty income guidelines or unemployed, or underemployed or the recipient of a bona fide lay-off notice or an individual who is employed, but is determined by the grantee to be in need of employment and training services to obtain or retain employment that allows for self-sufficiency. Eligibility requirements for the youth program are provided in the WIOA Final Rule at 684.430. To be eligible for services under the youth program, individuals must meet the definition of an Indian, as determined by a policy of the Native American grantee and must be between the ages of 14 and 24 and live on or near a reservation or in OTSA areas of Oklahoma or Alaska Native Villages or ANRC areas in Alaska, or the State of Hawaii and are low income. 684.130 of the Final Rule for WIOA provides the definition of a "high-poverty" area. If applicable Section 129(a)(2)) of WIOA allows youth living in a "high poverty" area to be considered, male applicants also must register or be registered for the Selective Service in order to be eligible for the adult or the youth program. WIOA provides for an exception that allows up to five percent of the youth participants during a program year to be placed on the youth program and not have to meet the low-income requirement.

Award Range/Average: The range and average of financial assistance varies by year. Amounts are published annually in a Training Employment Guidance Letter (TEGL) Grant awards range from $1,000 to $5,000,000. Funding is based on a formula which is based on the percentage of low-income and unemployed Native Americans living in a geographic service area requested by the applicant in the competitive proposal. Federally Recognized tribes are typically awarded funds based on their reservation area (land base) but may also apply for "off-reservation" areas.

Funding: (Formula Grants) FY 17 $63,000,000.00; FY 18 est $67,000,000.00; FY 19 est $8,000,000.00

HQ: 200 Constitution Avenue NW, Room S 4209, Washington, DC 20210
Phone: 972-850-4637 | Email: hall.duane@dol.gov
http://www.doleta.gov/dinap

DOL17.267 | INCENTIVE GRANTS-WIA SECTION 503
"WIA Incentive Grants"

Award: Project Grants

Purpose: To compensate for programs consistent with the purposes of Title I of Workforce Investment Systems, Title II of WIA Adult Education and Family Literacy Act.

Applicant Eligibility: A listing of States eligible to receive incentive grants for Program Year 2013 performance was published in the Federal Register on May 1, 2015. This is the last year that incentive grants will be awarded to states. WIOA does not authorize these grants. Under WIA, to qualify for a grant, a State must have exceed performance levels agreed to by the Secretary of education, the Secretary of Labor, the Governor, and the State education Officer, for outcomes in Titles I and II of the Workforce Investment Act (WIA) and the American education and Family Literacy Act (AEFLA), which include placement after training, retention in employment, and improvement in literacy levels, among other measures.

Beneficiary Eligibility: Regulations at 20 CFR 666.210 authorize the state to use its incentive grant award to carry out an innovative program consistent with the requirements of any one or more of the programs within Title IB or Title II of WIA or the Perkins Act. See Training and Employment Guidance Letter (TEGL) 20-01, Change 13 for additional information (http://wdr.doleta.gov/directives/attach/TEGL/TEGL%2020-01,Change%2013_Acc.pdf).

Award Range/Average: For PY13 awards, each eligible state received $3,000,000.

HQ: 200 Constitution Avenue NW, Room N-5641 Frances Perkins Building, Washington, DC 20210

Phone: 202-693-3733 | Email: murren.luke@dol.gov

http://www.doleta.gov/performance

DOL17.268 | H-1B JOB TRAINING GRANTS

Award: Project Grants

Purpose: The H-1B Job Training Grant Program funds projects to provide training and related activities to workers in gaining the skills and competencies to work in economic sectors.

Applicant Eligibility: Grants may be awarded to a partnership of private and public sector entities as defined in the American Competitiveness and Workforce Improvement Act (ACWIA). Applicants may generally be public and non-profit Organizations. See the Funding Opportunity Announcement (FOA) for specific requirements.

Beneficiary Eligibility: The scope of potential trainees under these programs can be very broad. Please review the Funding Opportunity Announcement (FOA) for specific requirements. Training may be targeted to a wide variety of populations including unemployed individuals and incumbent workers.

Award Range/Average: Awards generally range from $1,000,000 to $5,000,000. Please review specific Funding Opportunity Announcements (FOAs) for specific details.

Funding: (Project Grants) FY 17 $115,000,000.00; FY 18 est $0.00; FY 19 est $150,000,000.00

HQ: 200 Constitution Avenue NW, Room C 4518, Washington, DC 20210

Phone: 202-693-2822 | Email: baird.megan@dol.gov

http://www.doleta.gov

DOL17.270 | REENTRY EMPLOYMENT OPPORTUNITIES
"Prisoner Re-entry"

Award: Project Grants

Purpose: To compensate for youth who are involved in crime and violence. It prevents school youth from dropping out of school and provides employment.

Applicant Eligibility: Eligible applicants for Reentry Employment Opportunities (REO) grants are community-based Organizations (CBOs) that are located in, or have a staff presence in the community being served. Eligible applicants for youth focused grants vary depending on the solicitation. Examples of possible eligible applicants include community-based Organizations, school districts, state and local government juvenile justice agencies, tribal entities, and entities carrying out activities under WIOA, such as local Workforce Investment Boards or American Job Centers. Eligible applicants for adult focused grants vary depending on the solicitation.

Beneficiary Eligibility: Re-entry Employment Opportunities (REO) Adult grants serve individuals, 18 years old and older, who have been convicted as an adult and have been imprisoned for violating a state or federal law, and who have never been convicted of a sex-related offense. Depending on the solicitation, enrollment may be limited based on whether the presenting offense was violent or whether the individual has previously committed a violent crime. Eligible applicants for youth focused grants vary depending on the solicitation.

Award Range/Average: The range and average of financial assistance varies by grant announcement. Adult focused grants have recently varied from $680,000 to $1.4 million for two years of operation. Youth offender grants have recently varied from $800,000 to $5 million for two years of operation.

Funding: (Project Grants) FY 17 $78,000,000.00; FY 18 est $84,000,000.00; FY 19 est $85,000,000.00

HQ: 200 Constitution Avenue NW, Room N-4511, Washington, DC 20210

Phone: 202-693-3603 | Email: morris.richard@dol.gov

http://www.doleta.gov

DOL17.271 | WORK OPPORTUNITY TAX CREDIT PROGRAM (WOTC)
"WOTC"

Award: Formula Grants

Purpose: The federal tax helps individuals to face significant barriers and gain self-sufficiency to claim tax credits against the wages paid during the first year of employment.

Programs Administered by Regional - State - Local Offices

Applicant Eligibility: States (not individuals), the District of Columbia, the Virgin Islands, and Puerto Rico.

Beneficiary Eligibility: Beneficiaries are all employers seeking WOTC target group workers and members of those target groups seeking employment. The members of the different target groups have statutory definitions (per Public Law 104-188, as amended) with specific eligibility requirements that must be verified by the State Workforce Agencies before a new hire certification can be issued to an employer or his/her representative. Participating employers and their representatives must file their certification requests with State Workforce Agencies using IRS Form 8850 and ETA Form 9061 or 9062 within 28 days after the employment start day of the new hires.

Award Range/Average: FY 2016 grants to states ranged from $66,000 to $2,518,373

Funding: (Formula Grants) FY 17 $18,000,000.00; FY 18 est $18,000,000.00; FY 19 est $18,000,000.00

HQ: 200 Constitution Avenue NW, Room C 4510, Washington, DC 20210-0001

   Phone: 202-693-3912 | Email: rietzke.steven@dol.gov

   http://www.doleta.gov/wotc

DOL17.272 | PERMANENT LABOR CERTIFICATION FOR FOREIGN WORKERS

Award: Provision of Specialized Services

Purpose: To ensure that the admission of foreign labor does not adversely affect the wages and employment opportunities for the U.S. workers.

Applicant Eligibility: Under Section 212 (a)(5)(A) of the Immigration and Nationality Act, foreign workers who seek to immigrate to the United States for employment shall be excluded from admission unless the Secretary of Labor determines and certifies to the Secretary of State and Secretary of Homeland Security that there are not sufficient U.S. workers available for the position and that the employment of such foreign workers will not adversely affect the wages and working conditions of similarly-employed U.S. workers. The certified employer must hire the foreign worker as a full-time employee; there must be a bona fide job opening available to U.S. workers; and job requirements must adhere to what is customarily required for the occupation in the U.S. and may not be tailored to the foreign worker's qualifications. In addition, the employer shall document that the job opportunity has been and is being described without unduly restrictive job requirements, unless adequately documented as arising from business necessity. The employer must pay at least the prevailing wage for the occupation in the area of intended employment.

Beneficiary Eligibility: Any employer who is unable to find qualified U.S. workers to meet his or her needs and seeks to hire a foreign worker to fill a given job vacancy on a permanent basis is eligible to file an application for permanent labour certification with the Department of Labor. An employer who seeks to employ a foreign worker whose category of employment is included in the Department of Labor, Schedule A list of pre-certified occupations contained in Part 656, Title 20, Code of Federal Regulations is eligible to file an application directly with the appropriate U.S. Citizenship and Immigration Services Office.

Funding: (Salaries and Expenses) FY 17 $12,000,000.00; FY 18 est $12,000,000.00; FY 19 est $12,000,000.00

HQ: 200 Constitution Avenue NW, Washington, DC 20210

   Phone: 202-513-7350 | Email: ake.john@dol.gov

   http://www.foreignlaborcert.doleta.gov

DOL17.273 | TEMPORARY LABOR CERTIFICATION FOR FOREIGN WORKERS

Award: Formula Grants; Provision of Specialized Services; Federal Employment

Purpose: To ensure adequate working and living conditions are provided for foreign and domestic workers and to assist U.S. employers seeking to hire temporary foreign workers.

Applicant Eligibility: H-2A Program: An agricultural employer who anticipates a shortage of U.S. workers needed to perform agricultural labor or services of a temporary or seasonal nature may apply to the Department of Labor under the H-2A Program. The employer may be an individual proprietorship, a partnership, or a corporation. An association of agricultural producers may file as a sole employer, a joint employer with its members, or as an agent of its members. An authorized agent or attorney, whether an individual or an entity (e.g., an association), may file an application on behalf of an employer. Associations may file master applications on behalf of their members. H-2B Program: The job and the employer's need must be one-time, seasonal, peak load or intermittent; the job must be for less than one year; and there must be no qualified and willing U.S. workers available for the job. An employer must file an application for employment certification with the Department of Labor. The National Prevailing Wage Center issues prevailing wage determinations to employers considering whether or not to hire foreign workers on a temporary or permanent basis.

Beneficiary Eligibility: N/A

Funding: (Provision of Specialized Services) FY 17 $36,000,000.00; FY 18 est $36,000,000.00; FY 19 est $36,000,000.00; (Formula Grants) FY 17 $14,000,000.00; FY 18 est $14,000,000.00; FY 19 est $14,000,000.00

HQ: 200 Constitution Avenue NW, PO Box 12-200, Washington, DC 20210

Phone: 202-513-7350 | Email: ake.john@dol.gov

http://www.foreignlaborcert.doleta.gov

DOL17.274 | YOUTHBUILD

Award: Project Grants

Purpose: To compensate for the disadvantaged youth with education and employment skills to achieve self-sufficiency.

Applicant Eligibility: Eligible applicants for these grants are public or private nonprofit agency or Organization (including a consortium of such agencies or Organizations), including: a community-based Organization; a faith-based Organization; an entity carrying out activities under this title, such as a local board; a community action agency; a State or local housing development agency; an Indian tribe or other agency primarily serving Indians; a community development corporation; a State or local youth service or conservation corps; and any other entity eligible to provide education or employment training under a Federal Program other than Youth Build.

Beneficiary Eligibility: Under WIOA, an eligible youth is an individual who is (i) not less than age 16 and not more than age 24 on the date of enrollment; (ii) a member of a low-income family, a youth in foster care (including youth aging out of foster care), a youth offender, a youth who is an individual with a disability, a child of incarcerated parents, or a migrant youth; and (iii) a school dropout or an individual who was a school dropout and has subsequently re-enrolled. Up to (but not more than) 25 percent of the participants in the program may be youth who do not meet the education and disadvantaged criteria above but who are: (1) basic skills deficient, despite attainment of a secondary school diploma or its recognized equivalent (including recognized certificates of attendance or similar documents for individuals with disabilities); or (2) have been referred by a local secondary school for participation in a Youth Build program leading to the attainment of a secondary school diploma.

Award Range/Average: Grants range from $700,000 to $1.1 million.

Funding: (Project Grants) FY 17 $80,000,000.00; FY 18 est $85,000,000.00; FY 19 est $56,000,000.00

HQ: 200 Constitution Avenue NW, Room N 4508, Washington, DC 20210

Phone: 202-693-3597 | Email: smith.jenn@dol.gov

http://www.doleta.gov

DOL17.276 | HEALTH CARE TAX CREDIT (HCTC) NATIONAL EMERGENCY GRANTS (NEGS)

"HCTC Infrastructure National Dislocated Worker Grants (NDWG) (formerly called HCTC NEGs)"

Award: Project Grants

Purpose: To provide health insurance and related services through Trade Adjustment Assistance.

Applicant Eligibility: N/A

Beneficiary Eligibility: N/A

Award Range/Average: Grant amounts awarded in FY 2017 ranged from $45,422 - $500,000. The average was $217,083

Funding: (Project Grants) FY 17 $1,000,000.00; FY 18 est $0.00; FY 19 est $0.00

HQ: 200 Constitution Avenue NW, Washington, DC 20210

Phone: 202-693-3401 | Email: donvan.dominica@dol.gov

http://www.doleta.gov/tradeact

DOL17.277 | WIOA NATIONAL DISLOCATED WORKER GRANTS/WIA NATIONAL EMERGENCY GRANTS

"National Dislocated Worker Grants"

Award: Project Grants

Purpose: To temporarily expand service capacity at the state and local levels by providing time-limited funding assistance in response to significant dislocation events.

Applicant Eligibility: Entities that are generally eligible to receive a National Dislocated Worker Grant include: designated state Workforce Innovation and Opportunity Act (WIOA) Program grantee agencies; a Local Workforce Investment Area; a consortium of local boards for adjoining local areas; a designated Organization receiving WIOA funding through the Native

Programs Administered by Regional - State - Local Offices

American Program provisions of WIOA; and a consortium of states. Funds can be used to provide employment and training services (including some supportive services) to eligible participants.

Beneficiary Eligibility: Individuals who are eligible for assistance vary by type of National Dislocated Worker Grant project; however, they must meet the criteria provided in the Workforce Investment Act: National Emergency Grants - Application Procedures, 69 Federal Register (April 27, 2004).

Award Range/Average: Grant amounts awarded PY2016/FY2017 ranged from $500,000 - $12,000,000. The average was $2,559.552. Grant amounts awarded PY2017/FY2018 ranged from $210,000 - $12,000,000.

Funding: (Project Grants) FY 17 $120,000,000.00; FY 18 est $161,000,000.00; FY 19 est $177,000,000.00

HQ: 200 Constitution Avenue NW, Room C 4526, Washington, DC 20210

Phone: 202-693-3937 | Email: kight.robert@dol.gov

http://www.doleta.gov/DWGs

DOL17.278 | WIOA DISLOCATED WORKER FORMULA GRANTS
"Workforce Innovation and Opportunity Act (WIOA) Dislocated Worker Program"

Award: Formula Grants

Purpose: The purpose of the WIOA Dislocated Worker program is to help dislocated workers become reemployed.

Applicant Eligibility: Under WIOA, the entities eligible to receive formula-based funding from the Department are the 50 states, Puerto Rico, the District of Columbia and the outlying areas. Funds are allotted based on a statutory formula and states, in turn, allocate funds to local workforce development boards (approximately 600), which are responsible for operating comprehensive American Job Centers (approximately 2, 400 nationwide).

Beneficiary Eligibility: Individuals eligible for assistance through the Act are workers who have lost their jobs, including those dislocated as a result of plant closings or mass layoffs, and are unlikely to return to their previous industry or occupation; formerly self-employed individuals; and displaced homemakers who depend on income of another family member, but are no longer supported by that income. Priority of Service is given to veterans and other covered persons.

Award Range/Average: WIOA formula grants vary annually and are published in the Federal Register.

Funding: (Formula Grants) FY 17 $1,020,000,000.00; FY 18 est $1,041,000,000.00; FY 19 est $1,020,000,000.00

HQ: 200 Constitution Avenue NW, Room S 4203, Washington, DC 20210

Phone: 202-693-3937 | Email: kight.robert@dol.gov

http://www.doleta.gov

DOL17.280 | WIOA DISLOCATED WORKER NATIONAL RESERVE DEMONSTRATION GRANTS
"Workforce Innovation and Opportunity Act (WIOA) Dislocated Worker National Reserve Demonstration Grants"

Award: Project Grants

Purpose: To carry out demonstration and pilot projects for the purpose of developing and implementing techniques and approaches and demonstrating the effectiveness of specialized methods.

Applicant Eligibility: Eligible applicants include: State and local Governments, Federal agencies, private non-profit and for profit Organizations, including faith-based and community-based Organizations, and educational Institutions. Note: Applicant eligibility may be restricted to one or more applicant classes under the particular announcement or solicitation.

Beneficiary Eligibility: Project participants are dislocated workers and incumbent workers.

Award Range/Average: Six grants were awarded for this CFDA number. The grant award range $1,975,085 - $5,000,000. The average award is $3,670,516.

Funding: (Project Grants) FY 17 $0.00; FY 18 est $22,000,000.00; FY 19 est $22,000,000.00

HQ: 200 Constitution Avenue NW, Washington, DC 20210

Phone: 202-693-3937 | Email: kight.robert@dol.gov

http://www.doleta.gov

DOL17.281 | WIOA DISLOCATED WORKER NATIONAL RESERVE TECHNICAL ASSISTANCE AND TRAINING

Award: Project Grants

Purpose: To support the coordination, development, and provision of appropriate training, technical assistance, staff development, and other activities, including assistance in replicating programs of demonstrated effectiveness to States, local areas, and other entities.

Applicant Eligibility: Eligible applicants include: State and local Governments, Federal agencies, private non-profit and for profit Organizations, including faith-based and community-based Organizations, and educational Institutions. Note: Applicant eligibility may be restricted to one or more applicant classes under the particular announcement or solicitation.

Beneficiary Eligibility: Funds are used to promote the continuous improvement of assistance provided to dislocated workers.

Award Range/Average: The total grant awards/cooperative agreements for PY2016/FY2017 ranged from $79,525 to $3.5 millionThe total grant awards/cooperative agreements for PY2017/FY2018 ranged from $55,000 to $2.3 million

Funding: (Project Grants) FY 17 $10,000,000.00; FY 18 est $9,000,000.00; FY 19 est $10,000,000.00

HQ: 200 Constitution Avenue NW, Room C 4526, Washington, DC 20210

Phone: 202-693-3937 | Email: kight.robert@dol.gov

http://www.doleta.gov

DOL17.282 | TRADE ADJUSTMENT ASSISTANCE COMMUNITY COLLEGE AND CAREER TRAINING (TAACCCT) GRANTS

Award: Project Grants

Purpose: The TAACCCT program seeks to increase the number of workers who attain certificates, degrees, and other industry-recognized credentials, helping to meet the college graduation goal of increasing the percentage of adults with a post-secondary credential by 2020.

Applicant Eligibility: See Uses Section Above.

Beneficiary Eligibility: See Information Above.

Award Range/Average: There are currently no new awards being made for this program.

HQ: 200 Constitution Avenue NW, Room C 4518, Washington, DC 20210

Phone: 202-693-3644 | Email: martin.cheryl.l@dol.gov

http://www.doleta.gov/taaccct

DOL17.283 | WORKFORCE INNOVATION FUND

Award: Project Grants

Purpose: Funds projects that demonstrate innovative strategies or replicate effective evidence-based strategies that align and strengthen the workforce investment system in order to improve program delivery and education and employment outcomes for program beneficiaries.

Applicant Eligibility: Eligible Institutions are: (i) State Workforce Agencies; (ii) Local Workforce Investment Boards; (iii) entities eligible to apply for WIA Section 166 grants; (iv) consortia of State Workforce Agencies; (v) consortia of Local Workforce Investment Boards; and (vi) consortia of entities eligible to apply for WIA Section 166 grants (Tribal entities).

Beneficiary Eligibility: The scope of potential beneficiaries under these programs can be very broad. Please review the Solicitations for Grant Application for specific requirements.

Award Range/Average: See SGAs.

HQ: 200 Constitution Avenue NW, Washington, DC 20210

Phone: 202-693-2618 | Email: havenstrite.wendy@dol.gov

http://www.doleta.gov/workforce_innovation

DOL17.285 | APPRENTICESHIP USA GRANTS

"Apprenticeship USA Expansion and Innovation Grants"

Award: Project Grants

Purpose: The objectives for grant funding are to make registered apprenticeship a mainstream education and career pathway option, one that can help each state, and the country as a whole, maintain its prominence in building the strongest, most adaptable, and most credentialed workforce in the world.

Programs Administered by Regional - State - Local Offices

Applicant Eligibility: Apprenticeship USA State Expansion (i.e., development of new Registered Apprenticeship Programs) - Statewide Promotion and Outreach to engage industry and business partners in Registered Apprenticeship - State Alignment of Registered Apprenticeship, Workforce (WIOA), education and Economic Development - Increased Employer Demand through Incentives - Job Training and supportive services - Apprenticeship USA pilots and demonstrations to increase diversity in Registered Apprenticeship - Modernized Apprenticeship Data Collection and Reporting - Program Administration - Program Evaluation.

Beneficiary Eligibility: States and US Territories are the recipients of this funding.

Award Range/Average: Average grant will be approximately $1.55 million with a range of $700,000 - $3,000,000 depending on a combination of factors including but not limited to state size and level of commitment to innovate and expand Registered Apprenticeship in the State.

Funding: (Project Grants (Discretionary)) FY 17 $51,000,000.00; FY 18 est $49,000,000.00; FY 19 est $0.00

HQ: 200 Constitution Avenue NW, Room C 5321, Washington, DC 20210

    Phone: 202-693-2796 | Email: velez.anna@dol.gov

    http://www.dol.gov/apprenticeship

DOL17.286 | HURRICANES AND WILDFIRES OF 2017 SUPPLEMENTAL-NATIONAL DISLOCATED WORKER GRANTS
"Hurricanes and Wildfires Supplemental- NDWG"

Award: Project Grants (for Specified Projects)

Purpose: The purpose of the National Dislocated Worker Grant program is to temporarily expand service capacity at the state and local levels by providing time-limited funding assistance in response to significant dislocation events.

Applicant Eligibility: Entities that are eligible to receive a Disaster Recovery National Dislocated Worker Grant include: designated state Workforce Innovation and Opportunity Act (WIOA) Program grantee agencies; and a designated Organization receiving WIOA funding through the Native American Program provisions of WIOA. Funds can be used to provide disaster relief employment as well as employment and training services (including some supportive services) to eligible participants. Individuals who are eligible for assistance vary by type of National Dislocated Worker Grant project; however, they must meet the criteria provided in the Training and Employment Guidance Letter No. 2-15.

Beneficiary Eligibility: N/A

Award Range/Average: Operational Guidance for National Dislocated Worker Grants, pursuant to the Workforce Innovation and Opportunity Act (WIOA or Opportunity Act)

Funding: (Project Grants (for specified projects)) FY 17 $0.00; FY 18 est $40,000,000.00; FY 19 est $60,000,000.00

HQ: 200 Constitution Avenue NW, Room C 4526, Washington, DC 20210

    Phone: 202-693-3937 | Email: kight.robert@dol.gov

    http://www.dol.gov

ENVIRONMENTAL PROTECTION AGENCY
Regional – State – Local Offices

Alaska, Idaho, Oregon, Washington
Deborah Flood, Manager | Grants Administration Unit 1200 6th Avenue, Seattle, WA 98101 206-553-2722

Arizona, California, Hawaii, Nevada, America Samoa, Guam, Trust Territories of Pacific Islands, Wake Island
Melinda Taplin, Chief | 75 Hawthorne Street Grants & Finance Branch, San Francisco, CA 94105 415-744-1693

Arkansas, Louisiana, New Mexico, Oklahoma, Texas
Brenda Durden, Chief | 1445 Ross Avenue Grants Audit Section (6M-PG) Management Division, Dallas, TX 75202-2733 214-665-6510

Colorado, Montana, North Dakota, South Dakota, Utah, Wyoming
Wayne Anthofer, Grants Administration Branch | 8PM-GFM 999 18th Street Suite 500, Denver, CO 80202-2466 303-312-6305

Delaware, District of Columbia, Maryland, Pennsylvania, Virginia, West Virginia
Robert G. Reed, Grants Management Section | Office of the Comptroller (3PM70) 1650 Arch Street, Philadelphia, PA 19103-2029 215-814-5410

District of Columbia
Jill Young | 1300 Pennsylvania Avenue NW M/C-3903-R, Washington, DC 20460 202-564-1342

Programs Administered by Regional - State - Local Offices

Grants and IAG Management Division EPA
Mike Osinski | 1300 Pennsylvania Avenue 3903 R, Washington, DC 20460 202-564-3792

Grants EPA - Lenexa, KS
Debbie Titus | 11201 Renner Boulevard M/C – PLMGGRMS, Lenexa, KS 66219 913-551-7712

Grants EPA - LVFC
Dany Levergne | 4220 S Maryland Parkway Building C - Suite 503 M/C – LVFC, Las Vegas, NV 89119 702-798-2483

Grants EPA - New England
Cheryll Scott | 5 Post Office Square M/C - OARM05-5, Boston, MA 03109-3912 617-981-1174

Grants EPA - Region II
Rudnell O'Neal | 290 Broadway M/C-27th FL, New York, NY 10007-1866 212-637-3427

Grants EPA - Region III
Lisa White | 1650 Arch Street M/C - 3PM70, Philadelphia, PA 19103-2029 215-814-2391

Grants EPA - Region IV
Keva Lloyd | 61 Forsyth Street M/C-9T 25, Atlanta, GA 30303-8960 404-562-8420

Grants EPA - Region V
Cheryll Scott | 1 Congress Street Suite 1100 PO Box MGM, Boston, MA 02114-2023 617-918-1972

Grants EPA - Region VI
Donna Miller | 1445 Ross Avenue Suite 1200 M/C - 6, Dallas, TX 75202-2733 214-665-8093

Grants EPA - Region VIII
James Hageman | 1595 Wynkoop Street M/C-R08-OTMS, Denver, CO 80202-1129 303-312-6005

Grants EPA - Region IX
Craig Wills | 75 Hawthorne Street, San Francisco, CA 94105 415-972-3663

Grants EPA - Region X
Paula VanHaagen | M/C-OMP-173, Seattle, WA 98101 206-553-6977

Grants Fellowships
Tony Fournier | 1300 Pennsylvania Avenue NW M/C-3903-R, Washington, DC 20460 202-564-1021

Grants(Illinois, Indiana, Michigan, Minnesota, Ohio, Wisconsin)
Sharon Green | Acquisition & Assistance Branch (MC-10J) 77 W Jackson Boulevard, Chicago, IL 60604-3507 312-886-2400

Iowa, Kansas, Missouri, Nebraska
Debbie Titus | 901 N 5th Street Grants Administration Branch, Kansas City, KS 66101 913-551-7346

New Jersey, New York, Puerto Rico, Virgin Islands
Donna Vivian-McCabe, Chief | Grants Administration Branch (OPM-GRA) 290 Broadway, New York, NY 10007-1866 212-637-3402

Washington
Michael Gearhead, Director | Office of Environmental Clean-up 1200 6th Avenue, Seattle, WA 98101 206-553-7151

EPA66.001 | AIR POLLUTION CONTROL PROGRAM SUPPORT

Award: Project Grants

Purpose: To assist State, Tribal, Municipal, Intermunicipal, and Interstate agencies in planning, developing, establishing, improving, and maintaining adequate programs for the continuing prevention and control of air pollution and/or in the implementation of national primary and secondary air quality standards.

Applicant Eligibility: Municipal, Intermunicipal, State, Federally Recognized Indian Tribe, or Interstate or Intertribal with legal responsibility for appropriate air pollution planning, development, establishment, implementation, and maintenance of Clean Air Act air pollution control activities, including management of grant support for those activities, provided such Organization furnishes funds for the current year that are equal to or in excess of its recurrent expenditures for the previous year for its approved section 105 air pollution Program. The determination of expenditures is subject to decisions based on provisions of the Clean Air Act and applicable grant regulations. This Program is available to each State, territory and possession of the U.S., including the District of Columbia. For certain competitive funding opportunities under this CFDA Assistance Listing description, the Agency may limit eligibility to compete to a number or subset of eligible applicants consistent with the Agency's Assistance Agreement Competition Policy.

Beneficiary Eligibility: Municipalities (local governments), Inter municipalities, States, Federally Recognized Indian Tribes, and Interstate and Intertribal agencies.

Award Range/Average: From approximately $50,000 to $6,500,000 per recipient; average approximately $1,400,000

Funding: (Project Grants) FY 18 Actual Not Available; FY 19 est $161,500,000.00; FY 20 est $104,000,000.00; (Formula Grants Total) FY 18 $163,600,000.00; FY 19 est Estimate Not Available; FY 20 est Estimate Not Available

HQ: Office of Air and Radiation Office of Air Quality Planning and Standards 109 TW Alexander Drive, PO Box C404-02, Research Triangle Park, NC 27709
Phone: 919-541-5523 | Email: whitlow.jeff@epa.gov

Programs Administered by Regional - State - Local Offices

EPA66.032 | STATE INDOOR RADON GRANTS
"SIRG"

Award: Project Grants

Purpose: To assist States and federally Recognized Indian Tribes to provide radon risk reduction through activities that will result in increased radon testing, mitigation and radon resistant new construction.

Applicant Eligibility: Eligible entities include States (including District of Columbia (DC)), Puerto Rico, the Virgin Islands, Guam, the Canal Zone, American Samoa, the Northern Mariana Islands, Federally recognized Indian Tribes and Tribal consortia, or any other U.S. Territory or possession.

Beneficiary Eligibility: State agencies: local, municipal, district, or area wide governments and organizations; U.S. territories or possessions, Federally Recognized Indian Tribes, colleges, universities, multi-state agencies, nonprofit organizations, low-income individuals, homeowners, and the general public.

Award Range/Average: Federal funding in FY 2019 may range from $15,000 to a maximum of $805,100 (by law 10% of the annual appropriation amount) per State/Tribal applicant. (See FY 2019 regional allotments at https://www.epa.gov/radon/state-indoor-radon-grant-sirg-program).

Funding: (Project Grants) FY 18 est $7,867,000.00; FY 19 est $7,789,000.00; FY 20 est Estimate Not Available

HQ: 1200 Pennsylvania Avenue NW, PO Box 6202A, Washington, DC 20460

    Phone: 202-564-2984 | Email: hesla.kirsten@epa.gov

    http://www.epa.gov/radon/state-indoor-radon-grant-sirg-program

EPA66.033 | OZONE TRANSPORT COMMISSION
"OTC"

Award: Project Grants

Purpose: To develop or recommend air quality implementation plans for air quality control regions designated pursuant to Section 106 (interstate pollution) or Section 111 (interstate ozone pollution) of the Clean Air Act of 1990.

Applicant Eligibility: An agency or commission designated by the Governors of the affected States, which is capable of recommending to those Governors' plans for implementation of national primary and secondary ambient air quality standards and which includes representation from the States and the appropriate political subdivisions within the affected air quality control region. For certain competitive funding opportunities under this CFDA description, the Agency may limit eligibility to compete to a number or subset of eligible applicants consistent with the Agency's Assistance Agreement Competition Policy.

Beneficiary Eligibility: Municipalities, inter municipalities, States, interstate agencies or commissions, and Federally recognized Indian tribes.

Award Range/Average: There is only one cooperative agreement awarded under this program. The cooperative agreement will range from $600,000 to $650,000/fiscal year with an average award of $639,000.

Funding: (Project Grants (Cooperative Agreements)) FY 17 $639,000.00; FY 18 est $639,000.00; FY 19 est $639,000.00

HQ: 1200 Pennsylvania Avenue NW, Washington, DC 20460

    Phone: 202-564-1668 | Email: jefferson.catrice@epa.gov

    http://otcair.org

EPA66.034 | SURVEYS, STUDIES, RESEARCH, INVESTIGATIONS, DEMONSTRATIONS, AND SPECIAL PURPOSE ACTIVITIES RELATING TO THE CLEAN AIR ACT

Award: Project Grants

Purpose: To support Surveys, Studies, Research, Investigations, Demonstrations and Special Purpose assistance relating to the causes, effects (including health and welfare effects), extent, prevention, and control of air pollution.

Applicant Eligibility: Assistance under this Program is generally available to States, local Governments, territories, Indian Tribes, and possessions of the U.S., including the District of Columbia, international Organizations, public and private universities and colleges, hospitals, laboratories, other public or private nonprofit Institutions, which submit applications proposing projects with significant technical merit and relevance to EPA's Office of Air and Radiation's mission. Eligibility for projects awarded or competed exclusively with State and Tribal Assistance Grant (STAG) funds is limited to air pollution control agencies, as defined in section 302(b) of the Clean Air Act that are also eligible to receive grants under section 105 of the Clean Air Act, and/or federally recognized Tribes and inter-tribal consortia, consisting of federally recognized tribe members. For certain competitive funding opportunities under this CFDA assistance listing description, the Agency may limit eligibility to compete to a number or subset of eligible applicants consistent with the Agency's Assistance Agreement Competition Policy.

Beneficiary Eligibility: State and local governments, U.S. territories and possessions, Indian Tribes, universities and colleges, hospitals, laboratories, and other public and private nonprofit institutions.

Award Range/Average: EPA generally award grants ranging in value from $5,000 to $750,000 per fiscal year. The average value of each grant is $150,000 per fiscal year.

Funding: (Cooperative Agreements (Discretionary Grants)) FY 17 $53,809,688.00; FY 18 est $52,014,743.00; FY 19 est $46,455,000.00

HQ: 1200 Pennsylvania Avenue NW, PO Box 6102A, Washington, DC 20460

Phone: 202-564-0890 | Email: geer.eric@epa.gov

http://www.epa.gov/grants/air-grants-and-funding

EPA66.037 | INTERNSHIPS, TRAINING AND WORKSHOPS FOR THE OFFICE OF AIR AND RADIATION

Award: Project Grants

Purpose: To provide, Internships, Training, Workshops, and Technical Monitoring in support of the Clean Air Act.

Applicant Eligibility: Assistance under this Program is generally available to States, local Governments, territories, Indian Tribes, and possessions of the U.S., including the Federally Recognized Indian Tribal Government, District of Columbia and possessions of the U.S., international Organizations, public and private universities and colleges, hospitals, laboratories, other public or private nonprofit Institutions, which submit applications proposing projects with significant technical merit and relevance to EPA's Office of Air and Radiation's mission. For certain competitive funding opportunities under this CFDA description, the Agency may limit eligibility to compete to a number or subset of eligible applicants consistent with the Agency's Assistance Agreement Competition Policy.

Beneficiary Eligibility: State and local governments, U.S. territories and possessions, universities and colleges, hospitals, laboratories, other public and private nonprofit institutions, and Federally Recognized Indian Tribal Governments.

Award Range/Average: EPA generally awards grants ranging in value from $100,000 to $300,000 per fiscal year. The average amount is $250,000.

Funding: (Project Grants) FY 17 $2,000,000.00; FY 18 est $1,860,000.00; FY 19 $1,900,000.00

HQ: 1200 Pennsylvania Avenue NW, PO Box 6102A, Washington, DC 20460

Phone: 202-564-1082 | Email: geer.eric@epa.gov

http://www.epa.gov

EPA66.038 | TRAINING, INVESTIGATIONS, AND SPECIAL PURPOSE ACTIVITIES OF FEDERALLY-RECOGNIZED INDIAN TRIBES CONSISTENT WITH THE CLEAN AIR ACT (CAA), TRIBAL SOVEREIGNTY AND THE PROTECTION AND MANAGEMENT OF AIR QUALITY

"Tribal CAA 103 Project Grants"

Award: Project Grants

Purpose: To support federally recognized Indian Tribes' efforts to understand, assess and characterize air quality; design methods and plans to protect and improve air quality on tribal lands through surveys, studies, research, training, investigations, and special purpose activities.

Applicant Eligibility: Assistance under this Program is generally available to Federally-recognized Indian Tribes and Intertribal Consortia, which submit applications proposing projects with significant technical merit and relevance to EPA's Office of Air and Radiation's mission. Tribal CAA 103 Project Grants have been determined by the Agency as exempt from competition under EPA Order 5700. 5A1.

Beneficiary Eligibility: Federally-recognized Indian Tribes and Intertribal Consortia.

Award Range/Average: There is no minimum amount of assistance; the maximum is $7,750,000. The general range of the amount of assistance is $25,000 to $500,000. The average is $75,000.

Funding: (Cooperative Agreements (Discretionary Grants)) FY 17 $11,545,000.00; FY 18 est $12,000,000.00; FY 19 est $11,545,000.00

HQ: Ariel Rios Building 1200 Pennsylvania Avenue NW, PO Box 6103A, Washington, DC 20460

Phone: 202-564-1082 | Email: childers.pat@epa.gov

http://www.epa.gov/tribal-air

Programs Administered by Regional - State - Local Offices

EPA66.039 | NATIONAL CLEAN DIESEL EMISSIONS REDUCTION PROGRAM
"DERA Clean Diesel Funding Assistance Program"

Award: Project Grants

Purpose: To award grants, rebates and low-cost revolving loans to eligible entities to fund the costs of a retrofit technology that significantly reduces emissions.

Applicant Eligibility: Eligible applicants are: A regional, State, local or tribal agency or port authority with jurisdiction over transportation or air quality; and a nonprofit Organization or institution that represents or provides pollution reduction or educational services to persons or Organizations that own or operate diesel fleets; or has, as its principal purpose, the promotion of transportation or air quality are eligible for assistance under this Program. City, county, or municipal agencies, school districts, and metropolitan planning Organizations (MPOs) that have jurisdiction over transportation or air quality are all eligible entities under this Program to the extent that they fall within the definition above. For certain competitive funding opportunities under this CFDA description, the Agency may limit eligibility to compete to a number or subset of eligible applicants consistent with the Agency's Assistance Agreement Competition Policy.

Beneficiary Eligibility: Owners of eligible diesel powered vehicles and equipment. Both public owned fleets and privately owned fleets may benefit.

Award Range/Average: Smaller grants typically range from $100,000 - $300,000 with an average award of $125,000. Larger grants typically range from $500,000 - $2 million with an average award of $650,000. Recovery Act Funding awarded under the National Clean Diesel Emissions Reduction Program totaled $205,800,000.

Funding: (Project Grants) FY 17 $34,000,000.00; FY 18 est $42,000,000.00; FY 19 est $7,000,000.00

HQ: 1200 Pennsylvania Avenue NW, Washington, DC 20460

Phone: 202-343-9541 | Email: keller.jennifer@epa.gov

http://www.epa.gov/cleandiesel

EPA66.040 | STATE CLEAN DIESEL GRANT PROGRAM
"DERA State Program"

Award: Formula Grants

Purpose: To award assistance agreements to States to develop and implement such grant, rebates, and low-cost revolving loan programs in the State as are appropriate to meet State needs and goals relating to the reduction of diesel emissions.

Applicant Eligibility: Assistance under this Program is available to the 50 states and the District of Columbia, Puerto Rico, the Virgin Islands, American Samoa, Guam, and the Northern Mariana Islands.

Beneficiary Eligibility: Owners of eligible diesel powered vehicles and equipment. Both public owned fleets and privately owned fleets may benefit.

Award Range/Average: For FY 2018, the range is estimated from $68,000 (Territory Base Amount) to $273,000 (State Base Amount, including Puerto Rico and the District of Columbia). In addition, a bonus of 50% of the Base Amount is available to states and territories that match the Base Amount dollar for dollar. The average funding amount for FY 2018, including Base Amount and Bonus, is approximately $372,000.

Funding: (Formula Grants) FY 17 $15,300,000.00; FY 18 est $20,100,000.00; FY 19 est $3,000,000.00

HQ: 1200 Pennsylvania Avenue NW, PO Box 6405J, Washington, DC 20460

Phone: 202-343-9541 | Email: keller.jennifer@epa.gov

https://www.epa.gov/cleandiesel

EPA66.041 | CLIMATE SHOWCASE COMMUNITIES GRANT PROGRAM

Award: Project Grants

Purpose: To award competitive grants to communities to develop plans and demonstrate and implement projects which reduce greenhouse gas emissions.

Applicant Eligibility: Local Governments - a county, municipality, city, town, township, local public authority (including any public and Indian housing agency) school district, special district, intrastate district, council of Governments, any other regional or interstate government entity, or any agency or instrumentality of a local government. Federally recognized Indian tribal Governments - the governing body or a governmental agency of any Indian tribe, band, nation, or other organized group or community (including Native villages) certified by the Secretary of the Interior as eligible for the special Programs and services provided by him through the Bureau of Indian Affairs. Intertribal Consortia - a partnership between two or more Tribes that is authorized by the governing bodies of those Tribes to apply for and receive assistance under this Program. Intertribal Consortia are eligible to receive grants under this Program only if the Consortium demonstrates that all members of the Consortium meet the eligibility requirements for the grant and authorize the Consortium to apply for and receive assistance by submitted to EPA documentation of (1) the existence of the partnership between Indian Tribal Governments, and (2) Authorization of the Consortium by all its members to apply for and receive the grant(s) for which the Consortium has applied. For certain competitive funding opportunities under this CFDA description, the Agency may limit eligibility to compete to a number or subset of eligible applicants consistent with the Agency's Assistance Agreement Competition Policy.

Beneficiary Eligibility: Local Governments and Federally-recognized Indian Tribes, Intertribal Consortia, General Public.

Award Range/Average: There is no minimum amount of assistance. $500,000 is the maximum.

HQ: 1200 Pennsylvania Avenue NW, PO Box 6102A, Washington, DC 20460

Phone: 202-564-0890 | Email: geer.eric@epa.gov

http://www.epa.gov/statelocalenergy

EPA66.042 | TEMPORALLY INTEGRATED MONITORING OF ECOSYSTEMS (TIME) AND LONG-TERM MONITORING (LTM) PROGRAM
"TIME/LTM"

Award: Project Grants

Purpose: To conduct and promote the coordination and acceleration of research, investigations, experiments, demonstrations, surveys, and studies relating to the causes, effects, extent, prevention and control of air pollution.

Applicant Eligibility: Assistance under this Program is generally available to States, local Governments, territories, Indian Tribes, and possessions of the U.S. (including the District of Columbia); public and private universities and colleges; hospitals; laboratories; public or private nonprofit Institutions; intertribal consortia; and individuals. Nonprofit Organizations described in Section 501(c)(4) of the Internal Revenue Code that engage in lobbying activities as defined in Section 3 of the Lobbying Disclosure Act of 1995 are not eligible to apply. An intertribal consortium must meet the definition of eligibility in the Environmental Program Grants for Tribes Final Rule, at 40 CFR 35. 504 (66 FR 3782. January 16, 2001) (FRL-6929-5) and be a non-profit Organization within the meaning of OMB Circular A-122, found at Uniform Grants Guidance 2 CFR 230. For certain competitive funding opportunities under this CFDA description, the Agency may limit eligibility to compete to a number or subset of eligible applicants consistent with the Agency's Assistance Agreement Competition Policy.

Beneficiary Eligibility: State and local governments in acid-sensitive regions of the U.S., institutions of higher education, scientific research community, general public.

Award Range/Average: There is no minimum amount of assistance. EPA anticipates annual awards ranging in value of $100,000 to $205,000, with an average award of $150,000.

Funding: (Project Grants (Cooperative Agreements)) FY 17 $130,000.00; FY 18 est $130,000.00; FY 19 est $130,000.00

HQ: 1200 Pennsylvania Avenue NW, PO Box 6204M, Washington, DC 20460

Phone: 202-343-9257 | Email: lynch.jason@epa.gov

https://www.epa.gov/airmarkets/clean-air-markets-monitoring-surface-water-chemistry

EPA66.110 | HEALTHY COMMUNITIES GRANT PROGRAM
"Healthy Communities"

Award: Project Grants

Purpose: Grants are awarded to support projects that meet two criterias: 1) They must be located in and directly benefit one or more Target Investment Areas and 2) They must achieve measurable environmental and public health results in one or more of the Target Program Areas.

Applicant Eligibility: Assistance under this Program is available to State, Local, public nonprofit Institutions /Organizations, private nonprofit Institutions /Organizations, quasi-public nonprofit Institutions /Organizations, Federally Recognized Indian Tribal Governments, K-12 schools or school districts; and non-profit Organizations (e.g. grassroots and/or community-based Organizations). Funding will be considered for a college or University to support a project with substantial community involvement. Private businesses, federal agencies, and individuals are not eligible to be grant recipients; however, they are encouraged to work in partnership with eligible applicants on projects. Applicants need not be located within the boundaries of the EPA regional office to be eligible to apply for funding but must propose projects that affect the States, Tribes, and Territories within their Region. For certain competitive funding opportunities under this CFDA description, the Agency may limit eligibility to compete to a number or subset of eligible applicants consistent with the Agency's Assistance Agreement Competition Policy.

Programs Administered by Regional - State - Local Offices

Beneficiary Eligibility: State, Local, Federally Recognized Indian Tribal Governments, public nonprofit institutions/ organizations, private nonprofit institutions/organizations, quasi-public nonprofit institutions/organizations, Anyone/General public.

Award Range/Average: $15,000 to $25,000/fiscal year; $22,754/fiscal year.

Funding: (Project Grants (Discretionary)) FY 17 $299,643.00; FY 18 est $0.00; FY 19 est $0.00

HQ: U.S. EPA Region I 1 Congress Street CPT, Suite 100, Boston, MA 02114

Phone: 617-918-1797 | Email: brownell.sandra@epa.gov

http://www3.epa.gov/region1/eco/uep

EPA66.121 | PUGET SOUND PROTECTION AND RESTORATION: TRIBAL IMPLEMENTATION ASSISTANCE PROGRAM

Award: Cooperative Agreements

Purpose: To attain and maintain water quality in designated estuaries that would assure protection of public water supplies and the protection and propagation of a balanced, indigenous population of shellfish, fish and wildlife and allows recreational activities in and on the water.

Applicant Eligibility: All federally recognized Indian Tribes located within the greater Puget Sound basin, and any consortium of these eligible Tribes, may apply for funding under the Program. The greater Puget Sound basin is defined as all watersheds draining to the U.S. waters of Puget Sound, southern Georgia Basin, and the Strait of Juan de Fuca. An eligible Intertribal consortium is one that demonstrates that: 1) a majority of its members meet the eligibility requirements for this Program; 2) all members that meet the eligibility requirements authorize the consortium to apply for and receive the grant; and 3) only members that meet the eligibility requirements will benefit directly from the grant project and the consortium agrees to a grant condition to that effect. Federal and state agencies, Institutions of higher learning, units of local government, special purpose districts, conservation districts, watershed planning units organized pursuant to RCW 90. 82. 040 and 060, local management boards organized pursuant to RCW 90. 88. 030, salmon recovery lead entities organized pursuant to RCW 77. 85. 050, regional fisheries enhancement group organized pursuant to RCW 77. 95. 060 and nongovernmental entities are not eligible to directly receive financial assistance awards under this announcement. Business enterprises and individuals or families will also not be eligible applicants. However, EPA strongly encourages eligible applicants to solicit participation from these types of entities as local collaborators. All of these types of entities are eligible to apply for sub-awards or subcontracts from a successful award recipient. For certain competitive funding opportunities under this CFDA description, the Agency may limit eligibility to compete to a number or subset of eligible applicants consistent with the Agency's Assistance Agreement Competition Policy.

Beneficiary Eligibility: The beneficiary of this assistance under this program would be the Federally recognized Indian Tribes or the consortia of these Tribes that receive the assistance. Ultimate beneficiaries would include the tribal members and the general public (due to the general public's interest in restoring and protecting the resources of Puget Sound).

Award Range/Average: In past years, the average capacity award for individual tribes and consortia has been approximately $150,000. For the Tribal Lead Organization grant, the funding has ranged from $2.490M to $5.48M.

Funding: (Cooperative Agreements (Discretionary Grants)) FY 17 $7,750,000.00; FY 18 est $7,700,000.00; FY 19 est $7,700,000.00

HQ: Region 10 Office of Water and Watersheds 1200 6th Avenue, PO Box OWW-193, Seattle, WA 98101

Phone: 206-553-0332 | Email: adams.angela@epa.gov

http://www.epa.gov/puget-sound

EPA66.123 | PUGET SOUND ACTION AGENDA: TECHNICAL INVESTIGATIONS AND IMPLEMENTATION ASSISTANCE PROGRAM

Award: Cooperative Agreements

Purpose: To attain and maintain water quality in designated estuaries that would assure protection of public water supplies and the protection and propagation of a balanced, indigenous population of shellfish, fish and wildlife and allows recreational activities in and on the water.

Applicant Eligibility: Federal government agencies and Washington State government agencies are eligible to apply under this Program. Public and private Institutions of higher education located in the United States are eligible to apply under this Program. Units of local government organized under Washington State law and located within the Greater Puget Sound basin are eligible to apply. Also eligible to apply are special purpose districts, as defined by Washington State law at R. C. W. 36. 93. 020, including but not limited to, irrigation districts, and water and sewer districts that are located in or govern land and water resources within the greater Puget Sound basin. Conservation districts located in or governing land and water resources within the greater Puget Sound Basin are also eligible to apply for assistance under this Program. Watershed planning units formed under RCW 90. 82. 040 and RCW 90. 82. 060, local management boards organized under RCW 90. 88. 030, salmon recovery lead entities organized pursuant to RCW 77. 85. 050, regional fisheries enhancement groups organized pursuant to RCW 77. 95. 060 and Marine Resource Committees organized pursuant to RCW 36. 125. 010 and RCW 36. 125. 020 are eligible to apply if they are located within or their jurisdictions include waters and/or lands within the Greater Puget Sound basin. -Intrastate Organizations such as associations of cities, counties or conservation districts in the Greater Puget Sound basin are also eligible to apply. Nonprofit nongovernmental entities are also eligible to apply. Federally recognized Indian Tribes located within the greater Puget Sound basin and any consortium of these eligible Tribes are also eligible to apply. The greater Puget Sound basin is defined as all watersheds draining to the U.S. waters of Puget Sound, southern Georgia Basin, and the Strait of Juan de Fuca. For profit business entities, private individuals and families are not eligible to apply. However, all of these types of entities could partner with an eligible applicant as a sub-awardee. For certain competitive funding opportunities under this CFDA description, the Agency may limit eligibility to compete to a number or subset of eligible applicants consistent with the Agency's Assistance Agreement Competition Policy.

Beneficiary Eligibility: The direct beneficiaries would be the entities receiving the assistance. Due to the fact that the program is designed and intended to assist in the restoration and protection of the Puget Sound estuary, the ultimate beneficiaries will be the residents of the greater Puget Sound region.

Award Range/Average: The EPA made awards for scientific and technical studies in the range of $200,000 - $700,000. Awards for implementation assistance and for managing and monitoring the implementation of the CCMP ranged from $200,000 to $6,000,000 each. Funding for the Strategic Initiative leads and the Management Conference Support for Implementation Lead will range from $2.490M to $5.500M.

Funding: (Project Grants (Cooperative Agreements)) FY 17 $17,500,000.00; FY 18 est $18,000,000.00; FY 19 est $18,000,000.00

HQ: Region 10 Office of Water and Watersheds 1200 6th Avenue, Suite 900 OWW-193, Seattle, WA 98101
Phone: 206-553-0332 | Email: adams.angela@epa.gov
https://www.epa.gov/puget-sound

EPA66.124 | COASTAL WETLANDS PLANNING PROTECTION AND RESTORATION ACT
"CWPPRA also known as The Breaux Act"

Award: Cooperative Agreements

Purpose: To assist the State, local government, college or university in planning and implementing projects that create, protect, restore and enhance wetlands in coastal Louisiana.

Applicant Eligibility: Eligible applicants for assistance include State and local Governments, including their universities and colleges. For certain competitive funding opportunities under this CFDA description, the Agency may limit eligibility to compete to a number or subset of eligible applicants consistent with the Agency's Assistance Agreement Competition Policy.

Beneficiary Eligibility: State and local governments, including their universities and colleges involved in administering coastal wetlands protection, restoration and/or management programs or programs related to or that complement coastal wetlands protection programs.

Award Range/Average: $100,000 to $30,000,000. If a Phase I (E&D) project is selected for funding, the estimated amount could be from $1- $6 million. If it is a Phase II (construction) project, the estimate could be up to $30 million.

Funding: (Cooperative Agreements (Discretionary Grants)) FY 17 $0.00; FY 18 est $34,200,000.00; FY 19 est $0.00

HQ: USEPA Region 6 6WQ-AT 1445 Ross Avenue, Dallas, TX 75202
Phone: 214-665-7187
https://www.epa.gov/wetlands/coastal-wetlands

EPA66.125 | LAKE PONTCHARTRAIN BASIN RESTORATION PROGRAM (PRP)
"Lake Pontchartrain Restoration Program"

Award: Cooperative Agreements

Purpose: To restore the ecological health of the Basin by developing and funding restoration projects and related scientific and public education projects.

Applicant Eligibility: The grants for this Program are awarded to the Management Conference, also know as the PRP, for restoration projects, studies and public education projects. Eligible sub-grantees for this Program include the Parishes and Cities within the 16 parish area of the Lake Pontchartrain Basin Watershed and the Lake Pontchartrain Basin Foundation.

Programs Administered by Regional - State - Local Offices

Local, nonprofits (includes State-designated Indian Tribes, excludes Institutions of higher education and hospitals). For certain competitive funding opportunities under this CFDA description, the Agency may limit eligibility to compete to a number or subset of eligible applicants consistent with the Agency's Assistance Agreement Competition Policy.

Beneficiary Eligibility: Eligible applicants for assistance include the Parishes and Cities within the Lake Pontchartrain Basin Watershed and the Lake Pontchartrain Basin Foundation.

Award Range/Average: The range of funding for the projects for FY 2017 for fifteen (15) projects was $20,000 to $300,000. The average including all sixteen (15) projects was $62,698. The range for FY 2016, for fourteen (14) projects was $25,000 to $327,680. The average including all fourteen (14) projects was $47,500.

Funding: (Cooperative Agreements (Discretionary Grants)) FY 17 $947,000.00; FY 18 Estimate Not Available FY 19 Estimate Not Available

HQ: 1445 Ross Avenue (6WQ AT) Dallas, Dallas, TX 75202
Phone: 214-665-2773 | Email: rauscher.leslie@epa.gov
https://www.epa.gov/aboutepa/epa-region-6-south-central

EPA66.126 | THE SAN FRANCISCO BAY WATER QUALITY IMPROVEMENT FUND "SF Bay Grant Program"

Award: Project Grants

Purpose: To improve water quality and restore aquatic habitat (i.e. wetlands) in the San Francisco Bay and its watersheds. Funded projects will reduce polluted run-off, restore impaired waters and enhance aquatic habitat.

Applicant Eligibility: State, local government agencies, districts, and councils; regional water pollution control agencies and entities; State coastal zone management agencies; and public and private universities and colleges, public or private non-governmental, non-profit Institutions are eligible to apply, unless restricted by the authorizing statutes. Non-profit Organizations must have documentation of non-profit status from the U.S. Internal Revenue Service or their state of incorporation, except that non-profits Organizations as defined in Section 501(c)(4) of the Internal Revenue Code that engage in lobbying as defined in Section 3 of the Lobbying Disclosure Act of 1995 or superseding legislation are ineligible. For certain competitive funding opportunities under this assistance listing (CFDA) description, the Agency may limit eligibility to compete to a number or subset of eligible applicants consistent with the Agency's Assistance Agreement Competition Policy.

Beneficiary Eligibility: The outcomes from the SF Bay grant program will ultimately benefit the urban resident and business populations of the nine county San Francisco Bay Area, as well as the State of California in general.

Award Range/Average: Since the beginning of the program in 2008, projects have been funded from a low of $200,000 to a high of $5,000,000. In the last few years of the RFP, the funding range has shifted to approximately $800,000 to $2mil. The average award is now at about $1mil each.

Funding: (Project Grants (Discretionary)) FY 18 est $3,585,000.00; FY 19 est $4,387,000.00; FY 20 est Estimate Not Available

HQ: 75 Hawthorne Street, San Francisco, CA 94105
Phone: 415-972-3400 | Email: valiela.luisa@epa.gov
http://www.epa.gov/sfbay-delta/san-francisco-bay-water-quality-improvement-fund

EPA66.129 | SOUTHEAST NEW ENGLAND COASTAL WATERSHED RESTORATION "SNEP"

Award: Cooperative Agreements

Purpose: To develop and support the Southeast New England Program (SNEP) for coastal watershed restoration. SNEP is a geographically-based program intended to serve as a collaborative framework for advancing ecosystem resiliency, protecting and restoring water quality, habitat, and ecosystem function, and developing and applying innovative policy, science, and technology to environmental management in southeast coastal New England.

Applicant Eligibility: Assistance under SNEP is available to state, local, territorial, and Tribal Governments; Institutions of higher education; nonprofit Institutions and Organizations; intertribal consortia; and interstate agencies. Private businesses, federal agencies, and individuals are not eligible to be grant recipients; however, they are encouraged to work in partnership with eligible applicants on projects. Applicants are not limited to the geographic area of southeastern coastal New England, however, those applying from outside the specified region must carry out their projects and have at least one local partner from within the geographic area specified in the competitive funding announcement. Organizations must be capable of undertaking and managing activities that advance SNEP priorities, including managing potentially complex fiscal and administrative requirements. Non-profit Organizations described in Section 501(c)(4) of the Internal Revenue Code that engage in lobbying activities as defined in Section 3 of the Lobbying Disclosure Act of 1995 are not eligible to apply; the term interstate agency is defined in Clean Water Act Section 502 as an agency of two or more States established by or pursuant to an agreement or compact approved by the Congress, or any other agency of two or more States, having substantial powers or duties pertaining to the control of pollution as determined and approved by the Administrator. Intertribal consortia must meet the requirements of 40 CFR Section 35. 504. For certain competitive funding opportunities under this CFDA assistance listing description, the Agency may limit eligibility to compete to a number or subset of eligible applicants consistent with the Agency's Assistance Agreement Competition Policy.

Beneficiary Eligibility: Eligible beneficiaries who may benefit from this assistance are the same as those listed under "Applicant Eligibility".

Award Range/Average: Range: $2,000,000 - $5,000,000/fiscal year Average: $3,500,000/year (estimated).

Funding: (Cooperative Agreements (Discretionary Grants)) FY 17 $4,510,000.00; FY 18 est $4,200,000.00; FY 19 est Estimate Not Available

HQ: 5 Post Office Square, Suite 100, Boston, MA 02109

Phone: 617-918-1672 | Email: simpson.karen@epa.gov

http://www.epa.gov/snecwrp

EPA66.202 | CONGRESSIONALLY MANDATED PROJECTS
"Congressional Earmarks"

Award: Cooperative Agreements; Project Grants

Purpose: To implement special Congressionally directed projects or programs identified in EPA's annual appropriations act, committee reports incorporated by reference into the annual appropriation act, and other statutes mandating that EPA provide financial assistance agreements to designated recipients for projects or programs.

Applicant Eligibility: Eligible applicants are specified in the statute authorizing the earmark. Examples of recipients that may receive assistance under this Program include local, state, intrastate, interstate, U.S. territories or possessions, public or nonprofit Institutions /Organizations, public/private nonprofit Institutions /Organizations, quasi-public nonprofit Institutions /Organizations, Institutions of higher education, Federally Recognized Indian Tribal Governments, Native American Organizations, and international Organizations.

Beneficiary Eligibility: Beneficiaries vary with the project Congress has directed EPA to fund. For example, an earmark for a wastewater treatment plant or sewer system would benefit the community in which the project is constructed. An earmark for a training project would benefit the individuals receiving the training under the assistance agreement.

Award Range/Average: No range; since no appropriated funds were enacted in FY 2017 and FY 2018 for Congressionally designated projects and programs.

HQ: USEPA Headquarters 1200 Pennsylvania Avenue NW, Washington, DC 20460

Phone: 202-564-2835 | Email: humes.hamilton@epa.gov

http://www.epa.gov/aboutepa/about-office-chief-financial-officer-ocfo

EPA66.203 | ENVIRONMENTAL FINANCE CENTER GRANTS
"EFC Grant Program"

Award: Cooperative Agreements; Project Grants

Purpose: To support Environmental Finance Centers (EFCs) that provide multi-media environmental finance expertise and outreach to the regulated communities.

Applicant Eligibility: Assistance under this Program is available to public and private non-profit universities and colleges and to nonprofit Organizations. For certain competitive funding opportunities under this CFDA description, the Agency may limit eligibility to compete to a number or subset of eligible applicants consistent with the Agency's Assistance Agreement Competition Policy.

Beneficiary Eligibility: States, tribes, local governments, businesses and community organizations and the general public are the beneficiaries of this program.

Award Range/Average: Range: $60,000 to $190,000 per fiscal year Average: $138,000 per fiscal year.

Funding: (Cooperative Agreements (Discretionary Grants)) FY 18 $639,370.00; FY 19 est $740,000.00; FY 20 est $600,000.00

HQ: 1200 Pennsylvania Avenue NW, PO Box 4201T, Washington, DC 20460

Phone: 202-564-4996 | Email: mcprouty.timothy@epa.gov

http://www.epa.gov/waterfinancecente

Programs Administered by Regional - State - Local Offices

EPA66.204 | MULTIPURPOSE GRANTS TO STATES AND TRIBES

Award: Formula Grants

Purpose: To implement high priority activities, including the processing of permits, which complement programs under established environmental statutes.

Applicant Eligibility: Assistance under this Program is generally available to states, the District of Columbia, the Commonwealth of Puerto Rico, the Virgin Islands, Guam, American Samoa, the Commonwealth of the Northern Marianas, and Tribes qualified under Clean Water Act Section 518(e) that have received authorization (TAS) for WQS. Applicable grant guidance may further limit applicant eligibility.

Beneficiary Eligibility: States, the District of Columbia, the Commonwealth of Puerto Rico, the Virgin Islands, Guam, American Samoa, the Commonwealth of the Northern Marianas, and tribes qualified under Clean Water Act Section 518(e) with TAS for WQS.

Award Range/Average: Range: $15,000 to $900,000 per fiscal year. Average: $275,000 (estimated)

Funding: (Project Grants) FY 17 $162,900.00; FY 18 est $9,800,000.00; FY 19 est Estimate Not Available

HQ: 1200 Pennsylvania Avenue NW, Washington, DC 20460

Phone: 202-564-2835 | Email: humes.hamilton@epa.gov

http://www.epa.gov/grants/specific-epa-grant-programs

EPA66.305 | COMPLIANCE ASSISTANCE SUPPORT FOR SERVICES TO THE REGULATED COMMUNITY AND OTHER ASSISTANCE PROVIDERS
"Compliance Assistance Centers"

Award: Project Grants

Purpose: The EPA has sponsored partnerships with industry, academic institutions, environmental groups, and other agencies to launch sector-specific Compliance Assistance Centers. The Compliance Assistance Center addresses real world issues in language that is used by the regulated entities.

Applicant Eligibility: Applicants must be nonprofit Organizations as that term is defined in Section 4(6) of the Federal Financial Assistance Management Improvement Act of 1999, Public Law 96-107, 31 U.S.C. 6101 Note. Colleges, universities, and community colleges are eligible to apply. EPA will also accept applications from state, tribal and local Governments. However, nonprofit Organizations described in Section 501(c)(4) of the Internal Revenue Code that engage in lobbying activities as defined in Section 3 of the Lobbying Disclosure Act of 1995 are not eligible to apply. For certain competitive funding opportunities under this CFDA description, the Agency may limit eligibility to compete to a number or subset of eligible applicants consistent with the Agency's Assistance Agreement Competition Policy. Additionally, for certain funding opportunities under this CFDA, applicants may have to demonstrate how they meet the following factors for threshold eligibility purposes: 1) That they have an indirect cost rate that has been approved or is pending approval by a federal agency or has a cost allocation system that meets the requirements in the applicable OMB Circular; 2) That they have had a previous working relationship(s) with experts and national Organizations devoted to the relevant industrial, commercial or governmental sector, or intends to partner with an Organization with such expertise; 3) An understanding of the environmental needs of the relevant industrial, commercial or governmental sector through past activities, or intends to partner with an Organization with such expertise; 4) That they, or a partnering Organization, has familiarity with applicable federal, state and local environmental regulations and experience in developing tools (e.g., training, plain-language guides, fact-sheets, Agency contact locators, etc.) to improve the audiences' understanding of their regulatory obligations; 5) Previous experience (or intends to partner with an Organization with experience) in developing and maintaining web-based services.

Beneficiary Eligibility: The primary beneficiaries are small businesses, local governments and colleges/universities that are being serviced by the grantees. Other beneficiaries include state, local, general public, and the regulated business community.

Award Range/Average: $5,000/year - $110,000/year. Generally, individual Centers will receive between $5,000 - $10,000 this fiscal year to continue maintenance and operation of the Web site. An approximate average of the annual financial assistance awards that will be made this current fiscal year is $27,000.

Funding: (Project Grants (Discretionary)) FY 17 $220,000.00; FY 18 est $350,000.00; FY 19 est Estimate Not Available

HQ: Office of Enforcement and Compliance Assurance 1200 Pennsylvania Avenue NW, PO Box 2227A, Washington, DC 20460

Phone: 202-564-7076 | Email: back.tracy@epa.gov

https://www.epa.gov/compliance/compliance-assistance-centers

EPA66.306 | ENVIRONMENTAL JUSTICE COLLABORATIVE PROBLEM-SOLVING COOPERATIVE AGREEMENT PROGRAM
"EJCPS"

Award: Cooperative Agreements

Purpose: The Environmental Justice Collaborative Problem-Solving Cooperative Agreement Program provides funding to support community-based organizations in their efforts to collaborate and partner with local stakeholder groups as they develop and implement solutions that address environmental and/or public health issues for underserved communities.

Applicant Eligibility: An eligible applicant must be one of the following: incorporated non-profit Organizations including, but not limited to, environmental justice networks, faith based Organizations and those affiliated with religious Institutions; federally recognized tribal Governments including Alaska Native Villages; OR tribal Organizations. Applicant Organizations claiming non-profit status must include documentation that shows the Organization is either a 501(c) (3) non-profit Organization as designated by the Internal Revenue Service; OR a non-profit Organization recognized by the state, territory, commonwealth or tribe in which it is located. For the latter, documentation must be on official state government letterhead. Applicants must be located within the same state, territory, commonwealth, or tribe in which the proposed project is located. This means that an applicant's registered address of record (i.e. the address designated on their IRS or State-sanctioned documentation) must be in the same state, territory, commonwealth or tribe as the location of the proposed project. The following entities are INELIGIBLE to receive an award, but we encourage applicants to partner with these Organizations, as appropriate: colleges and universities; hospitals; state and local Governments and their entities; quasi-governmental entities (e.g., water districts, utilities); national Organizations and chapters of the aforementioned Organizations; non-profit Organizations supporting lobbying activities as defined in Section 3 of the Lobbying Disclosure Act of 1995. Generally, a quasi-governmental entity is one that: (1) has a close association with the government agency, but is not considered a part of the government agency; (2) was created by the government agency, but is exempt from certain legal and administrative requirements imposed on government agencies; or (3) was not created by the government agency but performs a public purpose and is significantly supported financially by the government agency. National Organizations are defined as comprising of one centralized headquarters or principal place of business that creates and controls the mission, structure and work carried out by its chapters or affiliates. For certain competitive funding opportunities under this CFDA description, the Agency may limit eligibility to compete to a number or subset of eligible applicants consistent with the Agency's Assistance Agreement Competition Policy.

Beneficiary Eligibility: Eligible beneficiaries are the Non-Profit Community Groups as described under "Applicant Eligibility", and the residents of the communities they serve. List selected is not all inclusive.

Award Range/Average: Individual awards in the past range from $100,000 to $300,000; average awards in the past and current fiscal years is $120,000. The total funding nationwide is estimated to be $1,200,000. 10 awards will be issued nationwide, one per each of the 10 EPA regions.

HQ: Office of Environmental Justice 1200 Pennsylvania Avenue NW, PO Box 2202A, Washington, DC 20460
Phone: 202-564-0152 | Email: burney.jacob@epa.gov
http://www.epa.gov/environmentaljustice

EPA66.309 | SURVEYS, STUDIES, INVESTIGATIONS, TRAINING AND SPECIAL PURPOSE ACTIVITIES RELATING TO ENVIRONMENTAL JUSTICE
"EJSS"

Award: Cooperative Agreements

Purpose: The program provides funding in support of surveys, studies and investigations, and special purpose assistance programs as they relate to environmental and/or public health issues, with a particular emphasis on environmental justice.

Applicant Eligibility: Assistance under this Program is generally available to States, territories, Indian Tribes, intertribal consortia, and possessions of the U.S., including the District of Columbia, public and private universities and colleges, hospitals, laboratories, and other public or private nonprofit Institutions which submit applications proposing projects concerning environmental justice issues with significant technical merit and relevance to EPA's mission. Some of EPA's statutes may limit assistance to specific types of interested applications. See "Authorization" listed above. For certain competitive funding opportunities under this CFDA description, the Agency may limit eligibility to compete to a number or subset of eligible applicants consistent with the Agency's Assistance Agreement Competition Policy.

Beneficiary Eligibility: States, territories, Indian Tribes, and possessions of the U.S., including the District of Columbia, public and private universities and colleges, hospitals, laboratories, and other public or private nonprofit institutions and the communities they serve.

Programs Administered by Regional - State - Local Offices

Award Range/Average: $15,000 to $35,000/fiscal year; $20,000. This program was not funded in 2017 or in 2018.
HQ: 1200 Pennsylvania Avenue NW, PO Box 2202A, Washington, DC 20460
   Phone: 202-564-2907 | Email: burney.jacob@epa.gov
   https://www.epa.gov/environmentaljustice

EPA66.310 | CAPACITY BUILDING GRANTS AND COOPERATIVE AGREEMENTS FOR COMPLIANCE ASSURANCE AND ENFORCEMENT ACTIVITIES IN INDIAN COUNTRY AND OTHER TRIBAL AREAS

Award: Project Grants
Purpose: The funds provide financial resources to build and improve the compliance assurance and enforcement capacity of federally recognized Indian tribes, inter-tribal consortia, or tribal organizations.
Applicant Eligibility: Tribal Organizations, Inter-tribal Consortia, and Federal Organizations, Colleges and universities, and non-for-profit Organizations; eligible applicants must also have enforcement and compliance assurance responsibilities in Indian country and/or other tribal areas or provide support for enforcement and compliance assurance projects in Indian country and/or other tribal areas. EPA may also limit eligibility for certain competitive funding opportunities under this CFDA assistance listing to: (1) Tribes and intertribal consortia located in the Region where a project is going to be performed; and/or (2) applicants that have access to Indian country or other tribal areas.
Beneficiary Eligibility: Federally Recognized Indian Tribal Governments; Inter-tribal Consortia and Tribal Organizations; Federal, State, and Multi-jurisdictional State Organizations; colleges and universities; and non-for-profit organizations.
Award Range/Average: $3000 to $30,000/fiscal year
Funding: (Project Grants (Discretionary)) FY 17 $140,000.00; FY 18 est $60,000.00; FY 19 est $0.00; FY 2016 $129,000; FY 2017 $140,000; FY 2018 Estimate: $60,000
HQ: Office of Enforcement and Compliance Assurance 1200 Pennsylvania Avenue NW, PO Box 2221A, Washington, DC 20460
   Phone: 202-564-2516 | Email: binder.jonathan@epa.gov
   http://www.epa.gov/compliance

EPA66.418 | CONSTRUCTION GRANTS FOR WASTEWATER TREATMENT WORKS

Award: Project Grants
Purpose: Assists and serves as an incentive in construction of municipal wastewater treatment works which are required to meet State and/or Federal water quality standards and improve the water quality in the waters of the United States.
Applicant Eligibility: Funding for this construction grants Program is for American Samoa, Commonwealth of Northern Mariana Islands, Guam, Virgin Islands, and the District of Columbia because they are exempt by the U.S. Congress from establishing a State Revolving Fund (SRF). Grants are awarded to only these territories and the District of Columbia from the SRF funds (Title VI grants), which are awarded as Title II grants. Funding requests for construction of wastewater treatment facilities are now to be made to the SRF representative of the State in which the construction is proposed.
Beneficiary Eligibility: Anyone/General public. Anyone to be served by a wastewater treatment works assisted by this program.
Award Range/Average: CWA Title II grants Range: $100,000 to $10,000,000/fiscal year; Average: $5,000,000/fiscal year.
Funding: (Project Grants) FY 18 $31,791,000.00; FY 19 est $31,470,000.00; FY 20 est Not Separately Identifiable
HQ: 1200 Pennsylvania Avenue NW, Washington, DC 20460
   Phone: 202-564-0634 | Email: singh.gajindar@epa.gov
   https://water.epa.gov/grants_funding

EPA66.419 | WATER POLLUTION CONTROL STATE, INTERSTATE, AND TRIBAL PROGRAM SUPPORT
"Section 106 Grants"

Award: Formula Grants
Purpose: Assists States and interstate agencies in establishing and maintaining adequate measures for prevention and control of surface and ground water pollution from both point and nonpoint sources.
Applicant Eligibility: Eligible entities include States (including the District of Columbia and territories), interstate water pollution control agencies as defined in the Federal Water Pollution Control Act, and Indian Tribes qualified under CWA Section 518(e). Agencies making application for funds must annually submit their pollution-control Program to the

appropriate EPA Regional Administrator for approval. Requirements of the Program are based on Section 106 of the Act, 2 CFR 200 and 1500 as applicable, and 40 CFR Parts 35 and 130.

Beneficiary Eligibility: States (including the District of Columbia), Territories, interstate water pollution control agencies and Indian tribes qualified under Section 518(e) of the Clean Water Act (CWA).

Award Range/Average: Range: $30,000 to $11,700,000/fiscal year; Average: $4,000,000/fiscal year.

Funding: (Formula Grants) FY 17 $227,150,000.00; FY 18 est $225,525,000.00; FY 19 est $153,683,000.00

HQ: 1200 Pennsylvania Avenue NW, Washington, DC 20460

   Phone: 202-564-3880 | Email: delehanty.robyn@epa.gov

   https://www.epa.gov/water-pollution-control-section-106-grants

EPA66.424 | SURVEYS, STUDIES, INVESTIGATIONS, DEMONSTRATIONS, AND TRAINING GRANTS-SECTION 1442 OF THE SAFE DRINKING WATER ACT

Award: Project Grants

Purpose: Supports surveys, studies, investigations, demonstrations, and training associated with source water and drinking water; to develop and expand capabilities of programs to carry out the purposes of the Safe Drinking Water Act.

Applicant Eligibility: Assistance under this Program is generally available to States, local Governments, territories, Indian Tribes, and possessions of the U.S. (including the District of Columbia); public and private universities and colleges; hospitals; laboratories; public or private nonprofit Institutions; and individuals. Nonprofit Organizations described in Section 501(c)(4) of the Internal Revenue Code that engage in lobbying activities as defined in Section 3 of the Lobbying Disclosure Act of 1995 are not eligible to apply. For certain competitive funding opportunities under this CFDA description, the Agency may limit eligibility to compete to a number or subset of eligible applicants consistent with the Agency's Assistance Agreement Competition Policy.

Beneficiary Eligibility: State and local governments, U.S. territories and possessions, Indian Tribes, universities and colleges, hospitals, laboratories, and other public and private nonprofit institutions and individuals.

Award Range/Average: Range: $10,000 to $6,900,000/fiscal year; Average: $1,150,000/fiscal year.

Funding: (Cooperative Agreements (Discretionary Grants)) FY 18 $22,260,000.00; FY 19 est $1,050,000.00; FY 20 est Not Separately Identifiable

HQ: 1200 Pennsylvania Avenue NW, Washington, DC 20460

   Phone: 202-564-3817 | Email: jackson.joe-a@epa.gov

   https://www.epa.gov/ground-water-and-drinking-water

EPA66.432 | STATE PUBLIC WATER SYSTEM SUPERVISION

Award: Formula Grants

Purpose: The objective of the grant is to provide financial assistance to eligible States and Tribes for the Public Water System Supervision Program, for implementation and enforcement of the requirements of the Safe Drinking Water Act that apply to public water systems.

Applicant Eligibility: Eligibility is limited to the Governments of the fifty States; the District of Columbia; the Commonwealth of Puerto Rico; the Northern Mariana Islands; the Virgin Islands; Guam; American Samoa; and federally recognized Tribes, that have either assumed primary enforcement responsibility for the PWSS Program or that want to develop a Program that will allow them to seek delegation for a PWSS Program. EPA may also use funds allotted for a State or Tribal Program, if the State or Tribe does not have, or is not developing, primary enforcement responsibility, or EPA may use all or part of the funds to support the PWSS Program in absence of an acceptable State Program. Eligibility is also limited to a single agency within each State, Territory, or Tribe - an agency that has been designated by the jurisdiction's Governor or Chief Executive Officer. Primary Enforcement Responsibility for the Public Water System Supervision Program is provided for in 40 CFR 142.

Beneficiary Eligibility: The beneficiaries are the agencies within the fifty States; the District of Columbia; the Commonwealth of Puerto Rico; the Northern Mariana Islands; the Virgin Islands; Guam; American Samoa; and federally recognized Tribes, that have been designated by the jurisdiction's Governor or Chief Executive Officer as being responsible for the supervision of water supplies within the State, Territory, or Tribe.

Award Range/Average: Range of $116,000 to $6,570,000/fiscal year; Average of $1,509,606/fiscal year.

Funding: (Formula Grants) FY 18 $98,978,800.00; FY 19 est $98,642,000.00; FY 19 est Not Separately Identifiable

HQ: Office of Ground Water and Drinking Water 1200 Pennsylvania Avenue NW, PO Box 4606M, Washington, DC 20460

   Phone: 202-564-4588 | Email: roland.kevin@epa.gov

   http://www.epa.gov/ground-water-and-drinking-water

Programs Administered by Regional - State - Local Offices

EPA66.433 | STATE UNDERGROUND WATER SOURCE PROTECTION "UIC"

Award: Formula Grants

Purpose: Fosters development and implementation of underground injection control programs under the Safe Drinking Water Act. The objective of the grant program is to provide financial assistance, to eligible States and Tribes, for the implementation of their UIC Program.

Applicant Eligibility: States, U.S. Territories and possessions, and Indian Tribes that qualify as Programs that have delegated primary Enforcement Authority pursuant to SDWA amendments of 1986.

Beneficiary Eligibility: States, U.S. Territories, and Indian Tribes.

Award Range/Average: $5,000 to $939,000/fiscal year; $180,000/fiscal year.

Funding: (Formula Grants) FY 18 est $10,130,300.00; FY 19 est $10,164,000.00; FY 20 est Not Separately Identifiable

HQ: Office of Ground Water and Drinking Water Office of Water 1200 Pennsylvania Avenue NW, Washington, DC 20460

Phone: 202-564-3149 | Email: dyroff.colin@epa.gov

http://www.epa.gov/uic

EPA66.436 | SURVEYS, STUDIES, INVESTIGATIONS, DEMONSTRATIONS, AND TRAINING GRANTS AND COOPERATIVE AGREEMENTS-SECTION 104(B)(3) OF THE CLEAN WATER ACT

Award: Project Grants

Purpose: Supports the coordination and acceleration of research, investigations, experiments, training, demonstrations, surveys, and studies relating to the causes, effects, extent, prevention, reduction, and elimination of water pollution.

Applicant Eligibility: Assistance under this Program is generally available to States, local Governments, territories, Indian Tribes, and possessions of the U.S. (including the District of Columbia); public and private universities and colleges; hospitals; laboratories; public or private nonprofit Institutions; intertribal consortia; and individuals. Nonprofit Organizations described in Section 501(c)(4) of the Internal Revenue Code that engage in lobbying activities as defined in Section 3 of the Lobbying Disclosure Act of 1995 are not eligible to apply. An intertribal consortium must meet the definition of eligibility in the Environmental Program Grants for Tribes Final Rule, at 40 CFR 35. 504 (66 FR 3782. January 16, 2001) (FRL-6929-5) and be a non-profit Organization within the meaning of 2 CFR 200. For certain competitive funding opportunities under this CFDA description, the Agency may limit eligibility to compete to a number or subset of eligible applicants consistent with the Agency's Assistance Agreement Competition Policy.

Beneficiary Eligibility: State and local governments, U.S. territories and possessions, Indian Tribes, universities and colleges, hospitals, laboratories, other public and private nonprofit institutions, and individuals.

Award Range/Average: Range: $10,000 to $580,000/fiscal year; Average: $295,000/fiscal year.

Funding: (Project Grants (Discretionary)) FY 18 $6,342,800.00; FY 19 est $1,500,000.00; FY 20 est Not Separately Identifiable

HQ: 1200 Pennsylvania Avenue NW, PO Box 3903R, Washington, DC 20460

Phone: 202-564-0783 | Email: miller.tracey@epa.gov

http://www.epa.gov/environmental-topics/water-topics

EPA66.437 | LONG ISLAND SOUND PROGRAM "Long Island Sound Study (LISS)"

Award: Project Grants

Purpose: Implements the Long Island Sound Study Comprehensive Conservation and Management Plan and assists the states of Connecticut and New York and other public or nonprofit entities in implementation, research, planning, and citizen involvement and education related to reducing pollution and improving the quality of the environment to sustain living resources in the Long Island Sound.

Applicant Eligibility: State, interstate, and regional water pollution control agencies, and other public or nonprofit private agencies, Institutions, and Organizations are eligible. Private profit-making entities, and individuals, are not eligible. For certain competitive funding opportunities under this CFDA description, the Agency may limit eligibility to compete to a number or subset of eligible applicants consistent with the Agency's Assistance Agreement Competition Policy.

Beneficiary Eligibility: Assistance under this program generally benefits state, interstate, and regional water pollution control agencies and other public or nonprofit private agencies, institutions, and organizations. The general public and Long Island

Sound user groups such as swimmers, beach goers, sport and commercial fishermen, boaters, and shellfishes, benefit from the results of the program through cleaner water, restored and protected habitat, and preserved and enhanced ecosystems.

Award Range/Average: Range: $20,000 to $2,000,000/fiscal year; Average: $438,611/fiscal year

Funding: (Project Grants (Discretionary)) FY 17 $8,000,000.00; FY 18 est $12,000,000.00; FY 19 Estimate Not Available

HQ: 1200 Pennsylvania Avenue NW, Washington, DC 20460

　　Phone: 202-564-3833 | Email: shah.surabhi@epa.gov

　　http://longislandsoundstudy.net

EPA66.440 | URBAN WATERS SMALL GRANTS

Award: Project Grants

Purpose: The objective of the Urban Waters Program is to protect and restore America's urban waterways. The funding priority is to achieve the goals and commitments established in the Agency's Urban Waters Strategic Framework.

Applicant Eligibility: Assistance under the Urban Waters Small Grants is generally available to States, local Governments, Indian Tribes, public and private universities and colleges, public or private nonprofit Institutions /Organizations, intertribal consortia, and interstate agencies. Nonprofit Organizations described in Section 501(c)(4) of the Internal Revenue Code that engage in lobbying activities as defined in Section 3 of the Lobbying Disclosure Act of 1995 are not eligible to apply. An intertribal consortium must meet the definition of eligibility in the Environmental Program Grants for Tribes Final Rule, at 40 CFR 35. 504 (66 FR 3782. January 16, 2001) (FRL-6929-5) and be a non-profit Organization within the meaning of 2 CFR 200. Indian Tribes (or "federally recognized Indian tribe"), as defined in 2 CFR 200. 54, is any Indian tribe, band, nation, or other organized group or community, including any Alaska Native village or regional or village corporation as defined in or established pursuant to the Alaska Native Claims Settlement Act (43 U.S.C. Chapter 33), which is recognized as eligible for the special Programs and services provided by the United States to Indians because of their status as Indians (25 U.S.C. 450b(e)). See annually published Bureau of Indian Affairs list of Indian Entities Recognized and Eligible to Receive Services. State, as defined in 2 CFR 200. 90, is defined as any state of the United States, the District of Columbia, the Commonwealth of Puerto Rico, U.S. Virgin Islands, Guam, American Samoa, the Commonwealth of the Northern Mariana Islands, and any agency or instrumentality thereof exclusive of local Governments. For certain competitive funding opportunities under this CFDA assistance listing description, the Agency may limit eligibility to compete to a number or subset of eligible applicants consistent with the Agency's Assistance Agreement Competition Policy.

Beneficiary Eligibility: Residents of urban areas adversely impacted by water pollution, State and local governments, Indian Tribes, other public and private nonprofit institutions, intertribal consortia, and interstate agencies.

Award Range/Average: Range: $40,000 to $60,000/fiscal year; Average: $50,000/fiscal year

Funding: (Project Grants) FY 18 $155,000.00; FY 19 est Not Separately Identifiable; FY 20 est Not Separately Identifiable

HQ: 1200 Pennsylvania Avenue NW, PO Box 4601M, Washington, DC 20460

　　Phone: 202-564-0430 | Email: orvin.chris@epa.gov

　　http://www.epa.gov/urbanwaters

EPA66.441 | HEALTHY WATERSHEDS CONSORTIUM GRANT PROGRAM

Award: Cooperative Agreements

Purpose: Supports strategically protecting healthy watersheds across the country. The program's focus is to protect freshwater ecosystems and their watersheds.

Applicant Eligibility: Universities, colleges and Institutions of higher education and hospitals are not eligible under this announcement. Non-profit, non-governmental Organizations, interstate agencies, and intertribal consortia which are capable of undertaking activities that advance watershed protection Programs are eligible to compete in this Program. The term "interstate agency" is defined in CWA Section 502 as "an agency of two or more States established by or pursuant to an agreement or compact approved by the Congress, or any other agency of two or more States, having substantial powers or duties pertaining to the control of pollution as determined and approved by the Administrator. " Intertribal consortia must meet the requirements of 40 CFR Part 35. 504. For certain competitive funding opportunities under this CFDA description, the Agency may limit eligibility to compete to a number or subset of eligible applicants consistent with the Agency's Assistance Agreement Competition Policy.

Beneficiary Eligibility: Public and private nonprofit institutions/ organizations, federally recognized Indian tribal governments, states, local governments, U.S. territories and interstate agencies.

Award Range/Average: $3,750,000 every six years. Average: $625,000/fiscal year.

Funding: (Project Grants (Discretionary)) FY 18 $655,000.00; FY 19 est $183,000.00; FY 20 est $0.00

Programs Administered by Regional - State - Local Offices

HQ: Environmental Protection Agency Nonpoint Source Management Branch Office of Oceans Wetlands and Watersheds 1200 Pennsylvania Avenue NW, Washington, DC 20460

Phone: 202-566-1202 | Email: solloway.chris@epa.gov

http://www.epa.gov/hwp

EPA66.454 | WATER QUALITY MANAGEMENT PLANNING
"205(j)(2) or 604(b)"

Award: Formula Grants
Purpose: To assist States, Regional Public Comprehensive Planning Organizations, and Interstate Organizations in carrying out water quality management planning.
Applicant Eligibility: State Water Quality Management Agencies.
Beneficiary Eligibility: Same as Applicant Eligibility.
Award Range/Average: Range: $100,000 to $1,478,000/fiscal year; Average: $251,000/fiscal year.
Funding: (Formula Grants) FY 17 $14,047,000.00; FY 18 est $16,608,000.00; FY 19 est $16,608,000.00
HQ: 1200 Pennsylvania Avenue NW, PO Box 4503T, Washington, DC 20460

Phone: 202-566-1202 | Email: solloway.chris@epa.gov

http://www.epa.gov

EPA66.456 | NATIONAL ESTUARY PROGRAM
"NEP"

Award: Project Grants
Purpose: The National Estuary Program's goal is to protect and restore the water quality and estuarine resources of estuaries and associated watersheds designated by the EPA Administrator as estuaries of national significance.
Applicant Eligibility: Assistance agreements are issued only to those estuaries designated by the Administrator. The Administrator is authorized to make grants to State, interstate, and regional water pollution control agencies and entities; State coastal zone management agencies; interstate agencies; and other public and private nonprofit agencies, Institutions, Organizations, and individuals (Section 320(g)(l)). Profit making Organizations are not eligible for grants. For certain competitive funding opportunities under this CFDA description, the Agency may limit eligibility to compete to a number or subset of eligible applicants consistent with the Agency's Assistance Agreement Competition Policy.
Beneficiary Eligibility: Anyone/General public.
Award Range/Average: The NEPs generally receive base funding in the amount of $600,000. For FY 18, each of the NEPs received base funding in the amount of $600,000.
Funding: (Project Grants (Discretionary)) FY 18 $16,800,000.00; FY 19 est $16,800,000.00; FY 20 est $0.00
HQ: 1200 Pennsylvania Avenue NW, PO Box 4504T, Washington, DC 20460

Phone: 202-566-2954 | Email: benson.robert@epa.gov

http://www.epa.gov/nep

EPA66.458 | CAPITALIZATION GRANTS FOR CLEAN WATER STATE REVOLVING FUNDS
"CW State Revolving Fund"

Award: Formula Grants
Purpose: Creates State Revolving Funds through a program of capitalization grants to States which will provide a long term source of State financing for construction of wastewater treatment facilities and implementation of other water quality management activities.
Applicant Eligibility: States and Puerto Rico are eligible to receive capitalization grants under Title VI. Indian Tribes are eligible to receive grants from Title VI for the construction of municipal wastewater facilities. The District of Columbia, territories, possessions of the U.S. are eligible to receive grants from Title VI for the construction of municipal wastewater facilities (see CFDA 66. 418).
Beneficiary Eligibility: For loans and other financial assistance (but not grants) for wastewater treatment facilities: local communities, intermunicipal, State, interstate agencies, and Indian tribes. For nonpoint source management programs and estuary activities in approved State Nonpoint Source Management Programs and Comprehensive Conservation and Management Plans: the public agencies listed above, individuals, and programs.

Award Range/Average: State Revolving Fund capitilization awards to the states in FY 2019 range from $7,879,000 to $177,146,000. Awards are also made to Indian Tribes and U.S. Territories.

Funding: (Formula Grants) FY 18 $1,569,200,000.00; FY 19 est $1,694,800,000.00; FY 20 est $1,119,800,000.00; FY 16 $1,319,293,600; FY 17 est. $1,369,202,000; and FY 18 est. $1,393,387,000; Total funds appropriated for Clean Water State Revolving Fund in Disaster Relief Act,2019.

HQ: Office of Wastewater Management State Revolving Fund Branch 1200 Pennsylvania Avenue NW Room 7309 WJE, PO Box 4204M, Washington, DC 20460

    Phone: 202-564-0686 | Email: platt.sheila@epa.gov

    https://www.epa.gov/cwsrf

EPA66.460 | NONPOINT SOURCE IMPLEMENTATION GRANTS
"319 Program"

Award: Formula Grants

Purpose: Assists States, the District of Columbia, American Samoa, Guam, Northern Marianas, Puerto Rico, Virgin Islands, and qualified Indian Tribes and intertribal consortia in implementing EPA-approved Section 319 nonpoint source management programs. EPA's funding priority is to award grants that implement a grant recipient's nonpoint source management program plan, particularly the development and implementation of watershed-based plans, focusing on watersheds with water quality impairments caused by nonpoint sources, which result in improved water quality in impaired waters.

Applicant Eligibility: Eligible entities include States and qualified Indian Tribes and intertribal consortia who have approved nonpoint source assessment reports and management plans. To be qualified, Tribes must have treatment in a manner similar to a state (TAS) status for the 319 Program. Grants to States are awarded by formula. The State allotment is awarded to the agency in each State designated by the chief executive as the lead nonpoint source agency. The lead nonpoint source agency may distribute grant funds to other Organizations in accordance with its work Program, which is approved by EPA. Eligible Tribes are allocated a base allotment by formula; the remaining Tribal portion of the 319(h) appropriation is competed among qualified Indian Tribes and intertribal consortia.

Beneficiary Eligibility: State and local governments; interstate and intrastate agencies; federally recognized Indian tribal governments; intertribal consortia; the following US territory or possessions: the District of Columbia, American Samoa, Guam, Northern Marianas, Puerto Rico, Virgin Islands; public and private nonprofit organizations and institutions. The lead nonpoint source agency may distribute grant funds to other organizations in accordance with a work program which is approved by EPA. Eligible Tribes are allocated a base allotment by formula; the remaining Tribal portion of the 319(h) appropriation is competed among qualified Indian Tribes and intertribal consortia. For certain competitive funding opportunities under this CFDA description, the Agency may limit eligibility to compete to a number or subset of eligible applicants consistent with the Agency's Assistance Agreement Competition Policy.

Award Range/Average: States/Territories: $424,000 to $8,391,800; $2,800,000. Indian Tribes: base grants $30,000 to $50,000; competitive grants up to $100,000. Ranges vary year-to-year based on size of appropriation (and also varies depending on number of applicants for grants to Indian Tribes or intertribal consortia).

Funding: (Formula Grants) FY 18 FY $167,592,800.00; 19 est $165,348,000.00; FY 20 est $0.00

HQ: 1200 Pennsylvania Avenue NW, Washington, DC 20460

    Phone: 202-566-0340 | Email: curtis.cynthia@epa.gov

    http://www.epa.gov/nps

EPA66.461 | REGIONAL WETLAND PROGRAM DEVELOPMENT GRANTS

Award: Cooperative Agreements

Purpose: Assists state, tribal, local government agencies, and interstate/intertribal entities in building programs which protect, manage, and restore wetlands. The primary focus of the grants is to build state and tribal wetland programs. A secondary focus is to build local e.g. county or municipal programs.

Applicant Eligibility: States, Tribes, local government agencies, interstate agencies, and intertribal consortia are eligible to apply to the Regions. Past recipients include, but are not limited to, wetland regulatory agencies, water quality agencies (Section 401 water quality certification), planning offices, wild and scenic rivers agencies, departments of transportation, fish and wildlife or natural resources agencies, agriculture departments, forestry agencies, coastal zone management agencies, park and recreation agencies, non-point source or storm water agencies, and city or county and other S/T/LG governmental agencies that conduct wetland-related activities. In order to be eligible for WPDG funds, Tribes must be federally recognized, although "Treatment as a State" status is not a requirement. The term "interstate agency" is defined in CWA Section 502 as "an agency of two or more States established by or pursuant to an agreement or compact approved by the Congress, or any other agency of two or more States, having substantial powers or duties pertaining to the control of pollution as determined and approved by the Administrator. " Intertribal consortia that meet the requirements of 40 CFR Part 35. 504 are eligible for direct funding. Intertribal consortia projects must be broad in scope and encompass more than one State, Tribe, or local government. universities that are agencies of a State government are eligible to receive funds through these competitions. universities must include documentation showing that they are chartered as a part of a State government in their proposal. For certain competitive funding opportunities under this CFDA assistance listing description, the Agency may limit eligibility to compete to a number or subset of eligible applicants consistent with the Agency's Assistance Agreement Competition Policy. Applicants need not be located within the boundaries of the EPA regional office to be eligible to apply for funding but must propose projects that affect the States, Tribes, and Territories within the Region.

Beneficiary Eligibility: State, Tribal, and local governments involved in administering wetlands protection, restoration and/or management programs, or programs related to or that complement wetlands protection programs.

Award Range/Average: Range: $20,000 to $600,000/fiscal year; Average: $250,000/fiscal year.

Funding: (Cooperative Agreements (Discretionary Grants)) FY 18 $13,590,016.00; FY 19 est $13,433,000.00; FY 20 est $9,362,000.00

HQ: Office of Oceans Wetlands and Watersheds Office of Water 1200 Pennsylvania Avenue NW, PO Box 4502T, Washington, DC 20460

    Phone: 202-566-1225 | Email: price.myra@epa.gov

    http://www.epa.gov/wetlands/wetland-program-development-grants

EPA66.462 | NATIONAL WETLAND PROGRAM DEVELOPMENT GRANTS AND FIVE-STAR RESTORATION TRAINING GRANT

Award: Cooperative Agreements

Purpose: Assists state, tribal, and local government agencies, and interstate/intertribal entities in building programs which protect, manage, and restore wetlands.

Applicant Eligibility: Non-profit, non-governmental Organizations, Interstate agencies, and Intertribal consortia which are capable of undertaking activities that advance wetland Programs on a national basis are eligible to compete in this Program. The term "interstate agency" is defined in CWA Section 502 as "an agency of two or more States established by or pursuant to an agreement or compact approved by the Congress, or any other agency of two or more States, having substantial powers or duties pertaining to the control of pollution as determined and approved by the Administrator. " Intertribal consortia must meet the requirements of 40 CFR Part 35. 504. For certain competitive funding opportunities under this CFDA description, the Agency may limit eligibility to compete to a number or subset of eligible applicants consistent with the Agency's Assistance Agreement Competition Policy.

Beneficiary Eligibility: State, Tribal, and local governments involved in administering wetlands protection, restoration, and/or management programs or programs related to or complement wetlands protection programs.

Award Range/Average: National Wetlands Program Development Grants: $75,000 to $200,000/every two years; $160,500/ every two years; Five-Star Restoration Training Grant: $1,000,000 every four years

Funding: (Cooperative Agreements (Discretionary Grants)) FY 18 $788,451.00; FY 19 est $775,000.00; FY 20 est $400,000.00

HQ: 1200 Pennsylvania Avenue NW, PO Box 4502T, Washington, DC 20460

    Phone: 202-566-1225 | Email: price.myra@epa.gov

    https://www.epa.gov/wetlands/wetland-program-development-grants

EPA66.466 | CHESAPEAKE BAY PROGRAM

Award: Project Grants

Purpose: The EPA's Chesapeake Bay Program awards annual grants to states, local governments, and non-governmental organizations to reduce and prevent pollution and to improve the living resources in the Chesapeake Bay. Grants are awarded for implementation projects, as well as for research, monitoring, environmental education, and other related activities.

Applicant Eligibility: Under section 117(d), funds are available for technical and general assistance grants to nonprofit Organizations, State and local Governments, colleges, universities, and interstate agencies; under section 117(e)(1)(A) and 117e(1)(B), respectively, funds are available for implementation, regulatory and accountability, and monitoring grants to signatory jurisdictions; and under section 117(g)(2), funds are available for technical assistance and assistance grants under the Small Watershed Grants Program to local Governments and nonprofit Organizations and individuals in the Chesapeake Bay region. For certain competitive funding opportunities under this CFDA assistance listing, the Agency may limit eligibility to compete to a number or subset of eligible applicants consistent with the Agency's Assistance Agreement Competition Policy.

Beneficiary Eligibility: Same as Applicant Eligibility.

Award Range/Average: $50,000 to $6,000,000 per fiscal year; $350,000 per fiscal year average.
Funding: (Project Grants (Discretionary)) FY 17 $53,652,760.00; FY 18 est $54,223,000.00; FY 19 est $7,300,000.00
HQ: 410 Severn Avenue, Suite 112, Annapolis, MD 21403
    Phone: 410-267-5743 | Email: hargett.james@epa.gov
    http://www.epa.gov/restoration-chesapeake-bay/chesapeake-bay-program-grant-guidance

EPA66.468 | CAPITALIZATION GRANTS FOR DRINKING WATER STATE REVOLVING FUNDS
"Drinking Water State Revolving Fund"

Award: Formula Grants
Purpose: Grants are made to States to capitalize their Drinking Water State Revolving Funds which will provide a long-term source of financing for the costs of drinking water infrastructure.
Applicant Eligibility: States, the District of Columbia, U.S. Territories or Possessions (the Commonwealth of Puerto Rico, Virgin Islands, Mariana Islands American Samoa, and Guam), and Federally Recognized Indian Tribal Governments are eligible for grants from the Program. For certain competitive funding opportunities under this CFDA description, the Agency may limit eligibility to compete to a number or subset of eligible applicants consistent with the Agency's Assistance Agreement Competition Policy.
Beneficiary Eligibility: States, U.S. Territories or Possessions (the Commonwealth of Puerto Rico, Virgin Islands, Mariana Islands American Samoa, and Guam), Federally Recognized Indian Tribal Governments, local, and intrastate.
Award Range/Average: States: $8,787,000 to $97,000,000/fiscal year; $16,318,800/fiscal year. Tribes: $6,000 to $2,400,000/fiscal year; $480,000/fiscal year. Territories: $1,532,000 to $8,787,000/fiscal year; $4,189,000/fiscal year. Recovery Act funds - States: $19,500,000 to $160,000,000/fiscal year. Territories: $500,000 to $2,100,000/fiscal year. Tribes: $15,600 to $3,200,000/fiscal year.
Funding: (Formula Grants) FY 17 $844,255,000.00; FY 18 est $1,136,657,000.00; FY 19 est $863,000,000.00
HQ: Drinking Water Protection Division Office of Ground Water and Drinking Water Office of Water 1200 Pennsylvania Avenue NW, PO Box 4606M, Washington, DC 20460
    Phone: 202-564-6239 | Email: fort.felecia@epa.gov
    https://www.epa.gov/drinkingwatersrf

EPA66.469 | GREAT LAKES PROGRAM
"Great Lakes Restoration Initiative (GLRI)"

Award: Project Grants; Use of Property, Facilities, and Equipment; Dissemination of Technical Information
Purpose: Helps to restore and maintain the chemical, physical, and biological integrity of the Great Lakes Basin Ecosystem.
Applicant Eligibility: Qualified non-federal entities eligible to apply for grants include non-federal governmental entities, nonprofit Organizations, and Institutions. This includes state agencies; any agency or instrumentality of local government; interstate agencies; federally-recognized Tribes and tribal Organizations; colleges and universities; non-profit Organizations; and other public or non-profit private agencies, Institutions, and Organizations. Non-profit Organization means any corporation, trust, association, cooperative, or other Organization which: (1) is operated primarily for scientific, educational, service, charitable, or similar purposes in the public interest; (2) is not organized primarily for profit; and (3) uses its net proceeds to maintain, improve, and/or expand its operations. Non-profit Organizations described in Section 501(c)(4) of the Internal Revenue Code that engage in lobbying activities as defined in Section 3 of the Lobbying Disclosure Act of 1995 are not eligible applicants. "For profit" Organizations, federal agencies, and individuals are not eligible applicants. "For profit" Organizations, federal agencies, and individuals are not eligible applicants. For certain competitive funding opportunities under this CFDA assistance listing, the Agency may limit eligibility to compete to a number or subset of eligible applicants consistent with the Agency's Assistance Agreement Competition Policy.
Beneficiary Eligibility: Beneficiaries include non-federal governmental entities, nonprofit organizations, and institutions. This includes state agencies; any agency or instrumentality of local government; interstate agencies; federally-recognized tribes and tribal organizations; colleges and universities; non-profit organizations; and other public or non-profit private agencies, institutions, and organizations. Non-profit organization means any corporation, trust, association, cooperative, or other organization which: (1) is operated primarily for scientific, educational, service, charitable, or similar purposes in the public interest; (2) is not organized primarily for profit; and (3) uses its net proceeds to maintain, improve, and/or expand its operations. Non-profit organizations described in Section 501(c)(4) of the Internal Revenue Code that engage in lobbying activities as defined in Section 3 of the Lobbying Disclosure Act of 1995 are not eligible applicants. "For profit" organizations

and individuals are not eligible applicants. For certain competitive funding opportunities under this CFDA description, the Agency may limit eligibility to compete to a number or subset of eligible applicants consistent with the Agency's Assistance Agreement Competition Policy.

Award Range/Average: Some awards are fully funded at award and others are funded incrementally over several years. Representative Award Range: $30,000/fiscal year to $5,000,000/fiscal year.

Funding: (Project Grants (Discretionary)) FY 17 $88,840,023.00; FY 18 est $65,000,000.00; FY 19 est Estimate Not Available

HQ: USEPA Great Lakes National Program Office (G-17J) 77 W Jackson Boulevard, Chicago, IL 60604

Phone: 312-353-4513 | Email: mosier.bart@epa.gov

http://www.epa.gov/greatlakes

EPA66.472 | BEACH MONITORING AND NOTIFICATION PROGRAM IMPLEMENTATION GRANTS
"BEACH Act Program"

Award: Formula Grants

Purpose: To assist Coastal and Great Lakes States and Tribes in developing and implementing programs for monitoring and notification for coastal recreation waters adjacent to beaches or similar points of access that are used by the public.

Applicant Eligibility: Coastal and Great Lakes States, territories (Puerto Rico, the U.S. Virgin Islands, Guam, American Samoa, and the Commonwealth of the Northern Mariana Islands), and Tribes eligible under Section 518(e) of the Clean Water Act, as amended. The Administrator may make a grant to a local government under this subsection for implementation of a monitoring and notification Program only if, after the one-year period beginning on the date of publication of performance criteria under Section 406 (a)(1), the Administrator determines that the State is not implementing a Program that meets the requirements of Section 406(a)(1), regardless of whether the State has received a grant under Section 406(a)(1). Interstate agencies and intertribal consortia are not eligible for Beach grants.

Beneficiary Eligibility: States, U.S. territories, Federally recognized Indian Tribal Governments, environmental and public health agencies, and local governments involved in implementing monitoring and notification programs.

Award Range/Average: $150,000 to $432,000/fiscal year for states and territories; average award was $239,300. Tribes typically receive $50,000 each.

Funding: (Formula Grants) FY 17 $9,540,300.00; FY 18 est $9,331,000.00; FY 19 est $0.00

HQ: USEPA Office of Water Standards and Health Protection Division 1200 Pennsylvania Avenue NW, PO Box 4305T, Washington, DC 20460

Phone: 202-566-1017 | Email: larimer.lisa@epa.gov

http://www.epa.gov/waterscience/beaches

EPA66.473 | DIRECT IMPLEMENTATION TRIBAL COOPERATIVE AGREEMENTS
"DITCA"

Award: Project Grants

Purpose: Direct Implementation Tribal Cooperative Agreements enables EPA to award cooperative agreements to federally recognized Indian tribes and eligible intertribal consortia to help carry out the Agency's function to directly implement Federal environmental programs required or authorized by law in the absence of an authorized or delegated tribal program, notwithstanding the Federal Grant and Cooperative Agreement Act.

Applicant Eligibility: DITCAs may be awarded to: (1) Federally Recognized Indian Tribal Government, and (2) intertribal consortia consistent with applicable provisions. In order for an intertribal consortium to be eligible to receive cooperative agreements under this authority, an intertribal consortium should be consistent with the provisions in 40 C. F. R. Part 35. See Notice of Guidance Issuance: Direct Implementation Tribal Cooperative Agreements (DITCAs) Guidance, 70 Fed. Reg 1440 (2005).

Beneficiary Eligibility: Federally Recognized Indian Tribal Government and intertribal consortia consistent with applicable provisions.

Award Range/Average: Cooperative agreement amounts range between $10,000 and $100,000/fiscal year; Average: $55,000/fiscal year.

Funding: (Project Grants) FY 17 $350,000.00; FY 18 est $350,000.00; FY 19 est $350,000.00

HQ: Indian Environmental Office (2690M) U.S. Environmental Protection Agency 1200 Pennsylvania Avenue NW, Washington, DC 20460

Phone: 202-564-4368 | Email: jones.david@epa.gov

http://www.epa.gov/tribal

EPA66.474 | WATER PROTECTION GRANTS TO THE STATES

Award: Formula Grants

Purpose: Assists states, territories, and possessions of the United States with critical water infrastructure protection.

Applicant Eligibility: Assistance under this Program is available to States, Tribes, Territories, and possessions of the United States.

Beneficiary Eligibility: Water programs of States, Territories, and possessions of the United States.

Award Range/Average: Funds are awarded by each Regional Office. The range of financial assistance available to States varies according to program and fiscal year. Contact the Grants Management Office of the pertinent EPA Regional Office, listed in Appendix IV of the Catalog, to determine the amount for which applicants are eligible. The range and average of financial assistance provided is: FY 09 - $16,700 to $380,300/fiscal year; $198,500/fiscal year.

HQ: 1200 Pennsylvania Avenue NW, Washington, DC 20460

Phone: 202-564-2106 | Email: goldbloom-helzner.david@epa.gov

http://www.epa.gov

EPA66.475 | GULF OF MEXICO PROGRAM

Award: Cooperative Agreements

Purpose: Assists States, Indian Tribes, interstate agencies, and other public or nonprofit organizations in developing, implementing, and demonstrating innovative approaches relating to the causes, effects, extent, prevention, reduction, and elimination of water pollution.

Applicant Eligibility: Funds are available to State and local Governments, interstate agencies, Tribes, colleges and universities, and other public or nonprofit Organizations. For certain competitive funding opportunities under this CFDA assistance listing, the Agency may limit eligibility to compete to a number or subset of eligible applicants consistent with the Agency's Assistance Agreement Competition Policy.

Beneficiary Eligibility: State and local governments, interstate agencies, Tribes, colleges and universities, and other public or nonprofit organizations.

Award Range/Average: FY17: $25,000 - $1,000,000, Average $330,000 FY18 (est.): $25,000 - $1,000,000, Average $430,000

Funding: (Cooperative Agreements (Discretionary Grants)) FY 17 $6,401,500.00; FY 18 est $9,500,000.00; FY 19 est $9,500,000.00

HQ: EPA/Gulf of Mexico Program Office 2510 14th Street, Suite 1212, Gulfport, MS 39501

Phone: 228-304-7441 | Email: houge.rachel@epa.gov

http://www.epa.gov/gulfofmexico

EPA66.481 | LAKE CHAMPLAIN BASIN PROGRAM
"Lake Champlain Program"

Award: Project Grants

Purpose: To implement the Lake Champlain Basin Management Plan, Opportunities for Action: An Evolving Plan for the Future of the Lake Champlain Basin 2017, and to assist the states of New York and Vermont in protecting, restoring and preserving the Lake Champlain ecosystem.

Applicant Eligibility: In accordance with Section 120 of the Clean Water Act, EPA may provide funding to the states of Vermont and New York and the New England Interstate Water Pollution Control Commission for the implementation of the Lake Champlain Basin Program. In addition, EPA may choose to solicit applications from other state, interstate, and regional water pollution control agencies, and public or nonprofit agencies, Institutions, and Organizations that are eligible to receive grants from EPA through this Program. For certain competitive funding opportunities under this CFDA assistance listing, the Agency may limit eligibility to compete to a number or subset of eligible applicants consistent with the Agency's Assistance Agreement Competition Policy.

Beneficiary Eligibility: Assistance under this program generally benefits State environmental, health, and agriculture agencies; interstate water pollution control agencies; public nonprofit institutions and organizations; sponsored organizations; Federal agencies; local agencies; intrastate agencies; public and private nonprofit institutions and organizations; private organizations; small businesses; and quasi-public nonprofit institutions.

Award Range/Average: Range: $365,000 to $3,504,022/fiscal year; Average: $1,465,000/fiscal year

Funding: (Project Grants (Discretionary)) FY 17 $4,395,000.00; FY 18 est Estimate Not Available; FY 19 est Estimate Not Available

HQ: 5 Post Office Square Suite 100, PO Box OEP 6 1, Boston, MA 02109

Phone: 617-918-1211 | Email: dore.bryan@epa.gov

http://www.epa.gov

Programs Administered by Regional - State - Local Offices

EPA66.482 | DISASTER RELIEF APPROPRIATIONS ACT (DRAA) HURRICANE SANDY CAPITALIZATION GRANTS FOR CLEAN WATER STATE REVOLVING FUNDS
"Clean Water State Revolving Fund Hurricane Sandy Supplemental Appropriation"

Award: Formula Grants

Purpose: The funding priority established by the Hurricane Sandy Supplemental Appropriation is to fund projects at wastewater facilities that will improve the resiliency of those facilities against future disasters. Only facilities that were impacted by Hurricane Sandy in the States of New York and New Jersey are eligible.

Applicant Eligibility: The States of New York and New Jersey.

Beneficiary Eligibility: The States of New York and New Jersey and wastewater treatment facilities funding resiliency projects that were impacted by Hurricane Sandy.

Award Range/Average: $191,136,855 to $283,148,135/fiscal year; $237,142,500/fiscal year.

HQ: State Revolving Fund Branch Municipal Support Division Office of Water 1200 Pennsylvania Avenue NW, PO Box 4204M, Washington, DC 20460

> Phone: 202-564-0686 | Email: platt.sheila@epa.gov
> https://www.epa.gov/cwsrf

EPA66.483 | DISASTER RELIEF APPROPRIATIONS ACT (DRAA) HURRICANE SANDY CAPITALIZATION GRANTS FOR DRINKING WATER STATE REVOLVING FUNDS
"Drinking Water State Revolving Fund Hurricane Sandy Supplemental Appropriation"

Award: Formula Grants

Purpose: The funding priority established by the Hurricane Sandy Supplemental Appropriation is to fund projects at drinking water facilities that will improve the resiliency of those facilities against future disasters. Only facilities that were impacted by Hurricane Sandy in the States of New York and New Jersey are eligible. No additional awards are anticipated in FY 2019.

Applicant Eligibility: The States of New York and New Jersey.

Beneficiary Eligibility: The States of New York and New Jersey and drinking water facilities funding resiliency projects that were impacted by Hurricane Sandy.

Award Range/Average: $38,189,000 to $56,572,000/fiscal year; $47,381,000/fiscal year.

HQ: Drinking Water Protection Division Office of Ground Water and Drinking Water Office of Water 1200 Pennsylvania Avenue NW, PO Box 4606M, Washington, DC 20460

> Phone: 202-564-6239 | Email: fort.felecia@epa.gov
> http://www.epa.gov/drinkingwatersrf

EPA66.508 | SENIOR ENVIRONMENTAL EMPLOYMENT PROGRAM
"SEE"

Award: Cooperative Agreements

Purpose: Uses the talents of Americans 55 years of age or older to provide technical assistance to Federal, State, and local environmental agencies for projects of pollution prevention, abatement, and control to achieve the Agency's goals of clean air; clean and safe water; land preservation and restoration; healthy communities and ecosystems; and compliance and environmental stewardship.

Applicant Eligibility: Private, nonprofit Organizations designated by the Secretary of Labor under Title V of the Older Americans Act of 1965.

Beneficiary Eligibility: Federal, State, and local environmental agencies and individuals 55 years old or older.

Award Range/Average: New awards and amendments: $1,000 to $750,000/FY 2017; Average $69,276/FY 2017; $332 to $837,500/FY2018; Average $30,635/FY2018. Estimates of $1,000 to $750,000/FY 2019; Average $60,000/FY 2019.

Funding: (Cooperative Agreements (Discretionary Grants)) FY 18 $40,950,198.00; FY 19 est $50,000,000.00; FY 20 est Not Separately Identifiable

Programs Administered by Regional - State - Local Offices

HQ: Office of Administration and Resources Management Office of Human Resources 1200 Pennsylvania Avenue NW, Washington, DC 20460

Phone: 202-564-4390 | Email: hughes.angela@epa.gov

https://www.epa.gov/careers/senior-environmental-employment-see-program

EPA66.509 | SCIENCE TO ACHIEVE RESULTS (STAR) RESEARCH PROGRAM

Award: Project Grants

Purpose: The Science to Achieve Results Program's goal is to stimulate and support scientific and engineering research that advances EPA's mission to protect human health and the environment.

Applicant Eligibility: Public and private nonprofit Institutions /Organizations, public and private Institutions of higher education, and hospitals located in the U.S., state and local Governments, Federally Recognized Indian Tribal Governments, and U.S. territories or possessions are eligible to apply. Profit-making firms and individuals are not eligible to apply. Non-profit Organization, as defined by 2 CFR Part 200, means any corporation, trust, association, cooperative or other Organization that: (1) is operated primarily for scientific, educational, service, charitable or similar purposes in the public interest; (2) is not organized primarily for profit; and (3) uses its net proceeds to maintain, improve and/or expand its operations. Note that 2 CFR Part 200 specifically excludes the following types of Organizations from the definition of non-profit Organization because they are separately defined in the regulation: (i) Institutions of higher education; and (ii) state, local and federally-recognized Indian tribal Governments. While not considered to be a non-profit Organization (s) as defined by 2 CFR Part 200, Institutions of Higher education and state, local and federally-recognized Indian tribal Governments are, nevertheless, eligible to submit applications under this Program. Hospitals operated by state, tribal, or local Governments or that meet the definition of nonprofit at 2 CFR 200. 70 are also eligible to apply. For-profit colleges, universities, trade schools, and hospitals are ineligible. Nonprofit Organizations described in Section 501(c) (4) of the Internal Revenue Code that lobby are not eligible to apply. Foreign Governments, international Organizations, and non-governmental international Organizations /Institutions are not eligible to apply. National laboratories funded by Federal Agencies (Federally-Funded Research and Development Centers, FFRDC) may not apply. FFRDC employees may cooperate or collaborate with eligible applicants within the limits imposed by applicable legislation and regulations. They may participate in planning, conducting, and analyzing the research directed by the applicant, but may not direct projects on behalf of the applicant Organization. The institution, Organization, or governance receiving the award may provide funds through its assistance agreement from the EPA to an FFRDC for research personnel, supplies, equipment, and other expenses directly related to the research. However, salaries for permanent FFRDC employees may not be provided through this mechanism. Federal Agencies may not apply. Federal employees are not eligible to serve in a principal leadership role on an assistance agreement. Federal employees may not receive salaries or augment their agency's appropriations through awards made under this Program unless authorized by law to receive such funding. The applicant institution may enter into an agreement with a Federal Agency to purchase or utilize unique supplies or services unavailable in the private sector to the extent authorized by law. Examples are purchase of satellite data, chemical reference standards, analyses, or use of instrumentation or other facilities not available elsewhere. A written justification for federal involvement must be included in the application. In addition, an appropriate form of assurance that documents the commitment, such as a letter of intent from the Federal Agency involved, should be included. Certain competitions may allow for early career awards. The following requirements in addition to the requirements listed above apply to early career awards. The early career awards will support research performed by PIs with outstanding promise at the Assistant Professor or equivalent level. Principal investigators from applicant Institutions applying for the early career portion of the RFA must meet the following additional eligibility requirements: 1. Hold a doctoral degree in a field related to the research being solicited by the closing date of the RFA; 2. Be untenured at the closing date of the RFA; 3. By the award date, be employed in a tenure-track position (or tenure-track-equivalent position) as an assistant professor (or equivalent title) at an institution in the U.S., its territories, or possessions. Note: For a position to be considered a tenure-track-equivalent position, it must meet all of the following requirements: (1) the employing department or Organization does not offer tenure; (2) the appointment is a continuing appointment; (3) the appointment has substantial educational responsibilities; and (4) the proposed project relates to the employee's career goals and job responsibilities as well as to the goals of the department/ Organization. Senior researchers may collaborate in a supporting role for early career awards. Early career applications should not propose significant resources for senior researchers and may not list senior researchers as co-PIs. Applicants will be asked to verify their early career status. See RFAs at: https://www.epa.gov/research-grants for additional information pertaining to eligibility requirements. For certain competitive funding opportunities under this CFDA assistance listing, the Agency may limit eligibility to compete to a number or subset of eligible applicants consistent with the Agency's Assistance Agreement Competition Policy.

Beneficiary Eligibility: Public nonprofit institutions/organizations and private nonprofit institutions/organizations located in the U.S; state and local governments; Federally Recognized Indian Tribal Governments; U.S. territories or possessions; Anyone/ General Public, Education Professional, Student/Trainee, Graduate Student, Scientists/Researchers.

Programs Administered by Regional - State - Local Offices

Award Range/Average: New awards range from $399,000 to $2,996,426 total per grant. Average awards total $500,000.
Funding: (Project Grants (Discretionary)) FY 17 $28,180,686.00; FY 18 est $28,500,000.00; FY 19 est $0.00
HQ: 1200 Pennsylvania Avenue NW, PO Box 8725R, Washington, DC 20460
  Phone: 202-564-7823 | Email: josephson.ron@epa.gov
  http://www.epa.gov/research-grants

EPA66.510 | SURVEYS, STUDIES, INVESTIGATIONS AND SPECIAL PURPOSE GRANTS WITHIN THE OFFICE OF RESEARCH AND DEVELOPMENT

Award: Project Grants
Purpose: Supports surveys, studies and investigations and special purpose assistance to determine the environmental effects of air quality, drinking water, water quality, hazardous waste, toxic substances, and pesticides.
Applicant Eligibility: These Programs are available to each State, territory and possession, and Tribal nation of the U.S., including the District of Columbia, for public and private State universities and colleges, hospitals, laboratories, State and local government departments, other public or private nonprofit Institutions, and in some cases, individuals or foreign entities. Profit-making firms are not eligible to receive assistance agreements from the EPA under this Program. Eligible nonprofit Organizations include any Organizations: 1) Are operated primarily for scientific, educational, service, charitable or similar purposes in the public interest; 2) Are not organized primarily for profit; and 3) Use its net proceeds to maintain, improve, and/or expand its operations. However, nonprofit Organizations described in Section 501(c) (4) of the Internal Revenue Code that lobby are not eligible to apply. National laboratories funded by Federal Agencies (Federally-Funded Research and Development Centers, "FFRDCs") may not apply. FFRDC employees may cooperate or collaborate with eligible applicants within the limits imposed by applicable legislation and regulations. They may participate in planning, conducting, and analyzing the research directed by the applicant, but may not direct projects on behalf of the applicant Organization. The institution, Organization, or governance receiving the award may provide funds through its assistance agreement from the EPA to an FFRDC for research personnel, supplies, equipment, and other expenses directly related to the research. However, salaries for permanent FFRDC employees may not be provided through this mechanism. Federal Agencies may not apply. Federal employees are not eligible to serve in a principal leadership role on an assistance agreement, and may not receive salaries or augment their Agency's appropriations in other ways through awards made under this Program. The applicant institution may enter into an agreement with a Federal Agency to purchase or utilize unique supplies or services unavailable in the private sector to the extent authorized by law. Examples are purchase of satellite data, chemical reference standards, analyses, or use of instrumentation or other facilities not available elsewhere. A written justification for federal involvement must be included in the application. In addition, an appropriate form of assurance that documents the commitment, such as a letter of intent from the Federal Agency involved, should be included. For certain competitive funding opportunities under this CFDA description, the Agency may limit eligibility to compete to a number or subset of eligible applicants consistent with the Agency's Assistance Agreement Competition Policy.
Beneficiary Eligibility: Public nonprofit institutions/organizations and private nonprofit institutions/organizations; state and local governments; Federally Recognized Indian Tribal Governments; U.S. territories or possessions; anyone/general public; education professionals; students/trainees; graduate students; scientists/researchers; hospitals; foreign entities; and individuals.
Award Range/Average: New grants/cooperative agreements range from $10,000 to $170,000 and average $55,000.
Funding: (Project Grants (Discretionary)) FY 17 $800,000.00; FY 18 est $1,700,000.00; FY 19 est $800,000.00
HQ: 1200 Pennsylvania Avenue NW, PO Box 8102R, Washington, DC 20460
  Phone: 202-564-4756 | Email: nanartowicz.john@epa.gov
  http://www.epa.gov/research

EPA66.511 | OFFICE OF RESEARCH AND DEVELOPMENT CONSOLIDATED RESEARCH/TRAINING/FELLOWSHIPS

Award: Project Grants
Purpose: The Office of Research and Development supports research and development to determine the environmental effects of air quality, drinking water, water quality, hazardous waste, toxic substances, and pesticides, and identify, develop, and demonstrate effective pollution control techniques.
Applicant Eligibility: These Programs are available to each State, territory and possession, and Tribal nation of the U.S., including the District of Columbia, public and private universities and colleges, hospitals, laboratories, State and local government departments, other public or private nonprofit Institutions, and foreign entities. Profit-making firms are not eligible to receive assistance agreements from the EPA under this Program. Eligible nonprofit Organizations include any

Programs Administered by Regional - State - Local Offices

Organizations that: 1) Are operated primarily for scientific, educational, service, charitable or similar purposes in the public interest; 2) Are not organized primarily for profit; and 3) Use its net proceeds to maintain, improve, and/or expand its operations. However, nonprofit Organizations described in Section 501(c) (4) of the Internal Revenue Code that lobby are not eligible to apply. National laboratories funded by Federal Agencies (Federally-Funded Research and Development Centers, "FFRDCs") may not apply. FFRDC employees may cooperate or collaborate with eligible applicants within the limits imposed by applicable legislation and regulations. They may participate in planning, conducting, and analyzing the research directed by the applicant, but may not direct projects on behalf of the applicant Organization. The institution, Organization, or governance receiving the award may provide funds through its assistance agreement from the EPA to an FFRDC for research personnel, supplies, equipment, and other expenses directly related to the research. However, salaries for permanent FFRDC employees may not be provided through this mechanism. Federal Agencies may not apply. Federal employees are not eligible to serve in a principal leadership role on an assistance agreement, and may not receive salaries or augment their Agency's appropriations in other ways through awards made under this Program. The applicant institution may enter into an agreement with a Federal Agency to purchase or utilize unique supplies or services unavailable in the private sector to the extent authorized by law. Examples are purchase of satellite data, chemical reference standards, analyses, or use of instrumentation or other facilities not available elsewhere. A written justification for federal involvement must be included in the application. In addition, an appropriate form of assurance that documents the commitment, such as a letter of intent from the Federal Agency involved, should be included. For certain competitive funding opportunities under this CFDA description, the Agency may limit eligibility to compete to a number or subset of eligible applicants consistent with the Agency's Assistance Agreement Competition Policy.

Beneficiary Eligibility: Public nonprofit institutions/organizations and private nonprofit institutions/organizations; state and local governments; Federally Recognized Indian Tribal Governments; U.S. territories or possessions; education professionals; students/trainees; graduate students; scientists/researchers; hospitals; and foreign entities.

Award Range/Average: Awards can range for new grants/cooperative agreements from $75,000 to $1,000,000; and average $250,000. .

Funding: (Cooperative Agreements (Discretionary Grants)) FY 17 $17,500,000.00; FY 18 est $18,200,000.00; FY 19 est $8,700,000.00

HQ: 1200 Pennsylvania Avenue NW, PO Box 8102R, Washington, DC 20460
   Phone: 202-564-4756 | Email: nanartowicz.john@epa.gov
   https://www.epa.gov/research-grants

EPA66.513 | GREATER RESEARCH OPPORTUNITIES (GRO) FELLOWSHIPS FOR UNDERGRADUATE ENVIRONMENTAL STUDY

Award: Project Grants

Purpose: The National Center for Environmental Research offers undergraduate fellowships to students in environmentally related fields of study. This program is intended to strengthen the environmental research capacity of institutions of higher education that receive limited funding to build such capacity.

Applicant Eligibility: Applicants must attend a fully accredited four-year U.S. college or University (located in the U.S. or its territories) for the fellowship period. Individuals must be citizens of the U.S. or its territories or possessions, or be lawfully admitted to the U.S. for permanent residence. You must have your green card at the time of application to be eligible for this Fellowship opportunity. Do not provide the green card number with your application; however, you may be asked to provide it at a later time to verify eligibility with the U.S. Citizenship and Immigration Service of the Department of Homeland Security. The GRO Undergraduate Fellowship is intended for students entering their last two years of full time study before obtaining their first bachelor's degree. Students who have already earned one bachelor's degree and are pursuing additional degrees are not eligible. The fellowship tenure is for 2 full academic years (9 months each) with a required paid summer internship after their first year. Thus, only students who will be entering their last two years of college will be considered eligible. In order to receive the fellowship, the student must attend a fully accredited four-year U.S. institution of higher education. This school must be among those that are not highly funded for research and development capacity. For the purposes of this solicitation, students attending those Institutions receiving more than $35 million in annual federal research and development funding are ineligible to apply under this solicitation. Institutions who exceed this threshold can be identified in the National Science Foundation's publication "Federal Science and Engineering Support to universities, Colleges, and Nonprofit Institutions: FY 2012, " Page 37, Table 12, column 2. These data can be found at http://www.nsf.gov/statistics/2015/nsf15305/pdf/nsf15305.pdf. Students attending those Institutions either not listed, or listed as having received $35 million or less as designated in column 2 of Table 12 are eligible to apply. Students attending two-year Institutions, community colleges, and those not in attendance at an institution of higher education at the time of application submittal may be eligible to apply. However, in order to be eligible to receive the fellowship, students attending two-year Institutions,

Programs Administered by Regional - State - Local Offices

community colleges, or those not in attendance at the time of application will need to show evidence of having received their Associate's degree, demonstrate that they only have two years left of undergraduate studies for completion of their Bachelor's degree, and will also need to demonstrate that they have been accepted to attend an accredited eligible four-year institution. This requirement is considered satisfied if the student is transferring to an accredited eligible four-year institution which has an Articulation Agreement with the two-year institution, thus meaning that all credits will transfer towards requirements for the Bachelor's degree. An Articulation Agreement is a signed contract between a community or technical college and a four-year college or University that guarantees that a student who earns an associate's degree at a participating two-year institution can transfer all of the general education core credits to the four-year institution toward the completion of baccalaureate degree requirements. More information can usually be obtained directly from the institution's Registrar. Alternately, a student with an Associate's degree may provide a letter from the Registrar of the accredited eligible four-year institution verifying that upon matriculation, the student will only have two remaining years of undergraduate study to complete the first Bachelor's degree. Students must be pursuing a bachelor's degree in an environmentally-related field, such as biology, health, the social sciences, or engineering. Students must have two (2) years remaining from the start of the Fall semester (Fall 2015) before receiving their initial bachelor's degree. Students must have at least a "B" average overall at the time of application submittal and during the tenure of the fellowship. Applicants who currently have another federal fellowship are not eligible. However, acceptance of a fellowship under this solicitation does not necessarily preclude acceptance of another private, state, regional, local, or non-profit scholarship, fellowship, traineeship, research assistantship, teaching assistantship, or grant aid. Employees of the U.S. government may apply, but must be able to prove separation from Federal service before accepting this fellowship. Applications must be submitted by the student. Applications submitted by the institution on behalf of the student will be rejected without review. The exact term (start and end dates) of the undergraduate fellowship is negotiated with the student and covers a period of nine months for each fellowship year. Students seeking a bachelor's degree may be supported for a maximum of two academic years. EPA recognizes that scientific, technical, engineering and mathematical (STEM) competence is essential to the Nation's future well-being in terms of national security and competitive economic advantage. For instance, the health and vitality of the economy is predicated, in part, on the availability of an adequate supply of scientists, technicians, engineers and mathematicians, to develop innovative technologies and solutions. In other words, this country must engage all available minds to address the challenges it faces. Minorities, women, and persons with disabilities historically have been under-represented in the STEM fields. For this reason, EPA strongly encourages women, minorities, and persons with disabilities to apply. For certain competitive funding opportunities under this CFDA description, the Agency may limit eligibility to compete to a number or subset of eligible applicants consistent with the Agency's Assistance Agreement Competition Policy.

Beneficiary Eligibility: Individual/Family; Student/Trainee.

Award Range/Average: The undergraduate fellowship provides up to $20,700 per year of academic support and $8,600 for internship support for a combined total of up to $50,000 over the life of the fellowship. Awards average $50,000.

Funding: (Project Grants (Discretionary)) FY 17 $0.00; FY 18 est $0.00; FY 19 Estimate Not Available

HQ: Office of Research and Development/NCER 1200 Pennsylvania Avenue NW, PO Box 8725R, Washington, DC 20460

Phone: 202-564-7823 | Email: josephson.ron@epa.gov

https://www.epa.gov/research-grants

EPA66.514 | SCIENCE TO ACHIEVE RESULTS (STAR) FELLOWSHIP PROGRAM

Award: Project Grants

Purpose: The National Center for Environmental Research, as part of its Science to Achieve Results program, offers graduate fellowships for master's and doctoral level students in environmentally related fields of study.

Applicant Eligibility: Applicants must attend a fully accredited U.S. college or University (located in the U.S. or its territories) for their graduate studies. Individuals must be citizens of the U.S. or its territories or possessions, or be lawfully admitted to the U.S. for permanent residence. Resident aliens must have their green card at the time of application to be eligible for this fellowship opportunity. Do not provide the green card number with your application; however, you may be asked to provide it at a later time to verify eligibility with the U.S. Citizenship and Immigration Service of the Department of Homeland Security. Applicants do not need to be enrolled in or formally accepted into a full time graduate Program at the time they apply for a fellowship, but proof of enrollment or acceptance must be produced prior to the award of the fellowship. To be eligible for this fellowship, applicants must be pursuing a master's or doctoral degree in an environmentally-related topic area at a fully accredited U.S. college or University (based in the U.S. or its territories). Applicants who are in a graduate Program at the time of application and meet either of the following two criteria as of the solicitation closing date ARE NOT eligible to receive a fellowship: 1) have completed more than one year in their current master's Program; or 2) have completed more than four years in their current doctoral Program. However, applicants enrolled in a master's Program who intend to pursue a doctoral degree beginning in the fall of 2015 may apply for a doctoral fellowship. Applicants who currently have another federal fellowship are not eligible. However, acceptance of a fellowship under this announcement does not necessarily preclude acceptance of another private, state, regional, local, or non-profit scholarship, fellowship, traineeship, research assistantship, teaching assistantship, or grant aid. Employees of the U.S. government may apply, but must be able to prove separation from Federal service before accepting this fellowship. Applications must be submitted by the student. Applications submitted by the institution on behalf of the student will be rejected without review. EPA recognizes that scientific, technical, engineering and mathematical (STEM) competence is essential to the Nation's future well-being in terms of national security and competitive economic advantage. For instance, the health and vitality of the economy is predicated, in part, on the availability of an adequate supply of scientists, technicians, engineers and mathematicians, to develop innovative technologies and solutions. In other words, this country must engage all available minds to address the challenges it faces. Minorities, women, and persons with disabilities historically have been under-represented in the STEM fields. For this reason, EPA strongly encourages women, minorities, persons with disabilities and MAI applicants to apply. For certain competitive funding opportunities under this CFDA description, the Agency may limit eligibility to compete to a number or subset of eligible applicants consistent with the Agency's Assistance Agreement Competition Policy.

Beneficiary Eligibility: Individual/Family; Student/Trainee and Graduate Student.

Award Range/Average: A maximum of $88,000 ($44,000/year) will be provided for master's fellows (two years) and up to $132,000 (three years) for doctoral fellows. Awards range from $88,000 to $132,000 total per fellowship and average $120,000.

HQ: Office of Research and Development/NCER 1200 Pennsylvania Avenue NW, PO Box 8725R, Washington, DC 20460
Phone: 202-564-7823 | Email: josephson.ron@epa.gov
https://www.epa.gov/research-grants

EPA66.516 | P3 AWARD: NATIONAL STUDENT DESIGN COMPETITION FOR SUSTAINABILITY

"People, Prosperity and the Planet (P3) Student Design Competition"

Award: Project Grants

Purpose: The U.S. Environmental Protection Agency - as part of its People, Prosperity and the Planet Award Program - is seeking applications proposing to research, develop, design, and demonstrate solutions to real world challenges.

Applicant Eligibility: Public and private Institutions of higher education (limited to degree-granting Institutions of higher education) located in the U.S. (includes eligible Institutions of higher education located in U.S. territories and possessions) are eligible to apply to be the recipient of a grant to support teams of undergraduate and/or graduate students. Profit-making firms are not eligible to receive assistance agreements from the EPA under this Program. The students on the teams supported by the institution receiving the grant must be enrolled in the college, University, or post-secondary educational institution they will be representing at the time the proposal is submitted. Institutions are allowed to submit more than one application where each application represents a unique design concept and student team. For the purposes of grant administration, the team's faculty advisor will be designated the Principal Investigator throughout the P3 grant award and competition process. In addition to the Principal Investigator, each team selected for award will also be asked to provide contact information for a student lead. Non-profit Organization, as defined by 2 CFR Part 200, means any corporation, trust, association, cooperative or other Organization that: (1) is operated primarily for scientific, educational, service, charitable or similar purposes in the public interest; (2) is not organized primarily for profit; and (3) uses its net proceeds to maintain, improve and/or expand its operations. Note that 2 CFR Part 200 specifically excludes the following types of Organizations from the definition of non-profit Organization because they are separately defined in the regulation: (i) Institutions of higher education; and (ii) state, local and federally-recognized Indian tribal Governments. While not considered to be a non-profit Organization (s) as defined by 2 CFR Part 200, Institutions of Higher education are, nevertheless, eligible to submit applications under this Program. State, local and federally-recognized Indian tribal Governments are not eligible to submit applications under this Program. Under this competition, eligible nonprofit Organizations are limited to research institutes and foundations that are part of or affiliated with a U.S. institution of higher education. For-profit colleges, universities, trade schools, and hospitals are ineligible. Nonprofit Organizations described in Section 501(c) (4) of the Internal Revenue Code that lobby are not eligible to apply. Foreign Governments, international Organizations, and non-governmental international Organizations /Institutions are not eligible to apply. National laboratories funded by Federal Agencies (Federally-Funded Research and Development Centers, "FFRDCs") may not apply. FFRDC employees may cooperate or collaborate with eligible applicants within the limits imposed by applicable legislation and regulations. They may participate in planning, conducting, and analyzing the research directed by the applicant, but may not direct projects on behalf of the applicant Organization. The institution, Organization, or governance receiving the award may provide funds through its assistance agreement from the EPA to an FFRDC for supplies, equipment, and other expenses directly related to the research. However, salaries for permanent FFRDC employees may not be provided through this mechanism. Federal Agencies may not apply. Federal employees are not eligible to serve in a principal leadership role on an assistance agreement. Federal employees may not receive salaries or augment their agency's appropriations through awards made under this Program unless authorized by law to receive such funding. The applicant institution may enter into an agreement with a Federal Agency to purchase or utilize unique supplies or services unavailable in the private sector to the extent authorized by law. Examples are purchase of satellite data, chemical reference standards, analyses, or use of instrumentation or other facilities not available elsewhere. A written justification for federal involvement must be included in the application. In addition, an appropriate form of assurance that documents the commitment, such as a letter of intent from the Federal Agency involved, should be included. For certain competitive funding opportunities under this CFDA description, the Agency may limit eligibility to compete to a number or subset of eligible applicants consistent with the Agency's Assistance Agreement Competition Policy.

Beneficiary Eligibility: Public Nonprofit Institutions/Organizations, Private Nonprofit Institutions/Organizations, Anyone/ General Public, Education Professional, Student/Trainee, Graduate Student, Scientists/Researchers.

Award Range/Average: Phase I Awards range from $13,939 to $15,000 total per grant. Average awards total $14,750. Phase II Awards range from $40,240 to $75,000 total per grant. Average awards total $72,000.

Funding: (Project Grants (Discretionary)) FY 17 $992,076.00; FY 18 est $1,041,037.00; FY 19 est $0.00

HQ: 1200 Pennsylvania Avenue NW, Washington, DC 20460

  Phone: 202-564-7823 | Email: josephson.ron@epa.gov

  http://www.epa.gov/p3

EPA66.517 | REGIONAL APPLIED RESEARCH EFFORTS (RARE)
"Rare"

Award: Project Grants

Purpose: Support surveys, studies and investigations and special purpose assistance to determine the environmental effects of air quality, drinking water, water quality, hazardous waste, toxic substances, and pesticides.

Applicant Eligibility: NOTE: Only Regions are eligible to send applications or proposals. Federal Agencies may not apply. Federal employees are not eligible to serve in a principal leadership role on an assistance agreement. Federal employees may not receive salaries or augment their agency's appropriations through awards made under this Program unless authorized by law to receive such funding. The applicant institution may enter into an agreement with a Federal Agency to purchase or utilize unique supplies or services unavailable in the private sector to the extent authorized by law. Examples are purchase of satellite data, chemical reference standards, analyses, or use of instrumentation or other facilities not available elsewhere. A written justification for federal involvement must be included in the application. In addition, an appropriate form of assurance that documents the commitment, such as a letter of intent from the Federal Agency involved, should be included.

Beneficiary Eligibility: NOTE: Only Regions are eligible to submit proposals or applications.

Award Range/Average: New cooperative agreements shall not exceed $60,000 per Year/per Region.

Funding: (Cooperative Agreements (Discretionary Grants)) FY 17 $200,000.00; FY 18 est $200,000.00; FY 19 est $0.00

HQ: Office of Research and Development/OSP 1200 Pennsylvania Avenue NW, PO Box 8104R, Washington, DC 20460

  Phone: 202-564-1720 | Email: blank.valerie@epa.gov

  http://www.epa.gov/aboutepa/about-office-science-policy-osp

EPA66.518 | STATE SENIOR ENVIRONMENTAL EMPLOYMENT PROGRAM
"SEE"

Award: Cooperative Agreements

Purpose: Provides technical assistance to State environmental agencies for projects of pollution prevention, abatement, and control to achieve the Agency's goals of Clean Air, Clean and Safe Water, Land Preservation and Restoration, Healthy Communities and Ecosystems, and Compliance and Environmental Stewardship.

Applicant Eligibility: Private, nonprofit Organizations designated by the Secretary of Labor under Title V of the Older Americans Act of 1965.

Beneficiary Eligibility: State environmental agencies and individuals 55 years old or older.

Award Range/Average: New awards and amendments: $1,000 to $750,000/FY2017; Average $69,276/FY2017; $100,000/ FY2018; Average $100,000/FY2018.

Funding: (Cooperative Agreements) FY 18 $571,227.00; FY 19 est $500,000.00; FY 20 est Not Separately Identifiable

HQ: Office of Administration and Resources Management Office of Human Resources Program Management and Communications Staff 1200 Pennsylvania Avenue NW, PO Box 3102A, Washington, DC 20460

  Phone: 202-564-4390 | Email: hughes.angela@epa.gov

  http://www.epa.gov/careers/senior-environmental-employment-see-program

EPA66.600 | ENVIRONMENTAL PROTECTION CONSOLIDATED GRANTS FOR THE INSULAR AREAS-PROGRAM SUPPORT
"Consolidated Program Support Grants"

Award: Formula Grants

Purpose: The program support grant is an alternative assistance delivery mechanism which allows an Insular Territory responsible for continuing pollution control programs to develop an integrated approach to pollution control.

Applicant Eligibility: The Territories of Guam, American Samoa, and the Virgin Islands, and the Commonwealth of the Northern Mariana Islands are eligible to receive and administer funds for more than one environmental Program.

Beneficiary Eligibility: The Territories of Guam, American Samoa, the Virgin Islands, and the Commonwealth of the Northern Mariana Islands.

Award Range/Average: In general, financial assistance has increased annually depending on program funding that is consolidated into the grant. Financial assistance has generally ranged from $2,000,000 to $3,300,000/territory/fiscal year for environmental program assistance. The total estimated average is $8,000,000/fiscal year. For FY11 and beyond, territorial Drinking Water and Clean Water SRF grant funds are being consolidated into grants for the territories of Guam, CNMI and American Samoa. For FY11 through FY15, SRF financial assistance for the territories of Guam, CNMI and American Samoa has ranged from $7M - $9M annually per territory.

Funding: (Formula Grants (Cooperative Agreements)) FY 18 $7,800,000.00; FY 19 est $7,700,000.00; FY 20 est $7,300,000.00

HQ: Grants Management Office (PMD-7) EPA Region 9 75 Hawthorne St, San Francisco, CA 94105

Phone: 415-972-3667 | Email: espitia.alba@epa.gov

http://www2.epa.gov/aboutepa/epa-region-9-pacific-southwest

EPA66.604 | ENVIRONMENTAL JUSTICE SMALL GRANT PROGRAM
"EJSG"

Award: Project Grants

Purpose: Develops a comprehensive understanding of environmental and public health issues, identify ways to address these issues at the local level, and educate and support the community.

Applicant Eligibility: For certain competitive funding opportunities under this CFDA description, the Agency may limit eligibility to compete to a number or subset of eligible applicants consistent with the Agency's Assistance Agreement Competition Policy. An eligible applicant MUST BE: an incorporated non-profit Organization; OR a Native American tribal government (Federally recognized) (AND) located within the same, territory, commonwealth, or tribe that the proposed project will be located. In addition, an eligible applicant must be able to demonstrate that it has worked directly with the affected community. An "affected community" for the purposes of this assistance agreement Program is a community that is disproportionately impacted by environmental harms and risks and has a local environmental and public health issue that is identified in the proposal. The following entities are INELIGIBLE to receive an award, but we encourage partnerships with these Organizations for technical assistance: colleges and universities; hospitals; state Governments. their entities; quasi-governmental entities (e.g., water districts, utilities); national Organizations and chapters of the aforementioned Organizations; and non-profit Organizations that engage in lobbying activities as defined in Section 3 of the Lobbying Disclosure Act of 1995 and Organizations acting only as "fiscal agents". Generally, a quasi-governmental entity is one that: (1) has a close association with the government agency, but is not considered a part of the government agency; (2) was created by the government agency, but is exempt from certain legal and administrative requirements imposed on government agencies; or (3) was not created by the government agency but performs a public purpose and is significantly supported financially by the government agency.

Beneficiary Eligibility: Eligible beneficiaries are the Non-Profit Community Groups as described in 081 above and the residents of the communities they serve. List selected may not be all inclusive.

Award Range/Average: $20,000 to $50,000/fiscal year; average $30,000.

Funding: (Project Grants (Discretionary)) FY 17 $1,080,000.00; FY 18 est $0.00; FY 19 est $1,200,000.00

HQ: Office of Environmental Justice 1200 Pennsylvania Avenue NW, PO Box 2202A, Washington, DC 20460

Phone: 202-564-2907 | Email: burney.jacob@epa.gov

http://www.epa.gov/environmentaljustice

Programs Administered by Regional - State - Local Offices

EPA66.605 | PERFORMANCE PARTNERSHIP GRANTS
"PPGs"

Award: Formula Grants; Project Grants

Purpose: Performance Partnership Grants are the cornerstone of the National Environmental Performance Partnership System - EPA's strategy to strengthen partnerships and build a results-based management system.

Applicant Eligibility: All States, interstate agencies, U.S. territories, the District of Columbia, and federally recognized Indian Tribes eligible to receive more than one of the 20 categorical grant Programs referred to in "Uses and Use Restrictions" above are eligible to apply for PPGs. Any duly authorized State or tribal entity that currently receives or is eligible to receive EPA categorical Program grants may request a PPG for the funds it administers. This may include agencies other than environmental agencies (for example, agricultural and health agencies), where authorized by state or tribal law.

Beneficiary Eligibility: States, U.S. territories, federally recognized Indian tribal governments, and interstate agencies.

Award Range/Average: There is no low-end limit for PPG awards, which may be as small as combining two programs and thousands of dollars to Tribes, or as large as combining up to 20 categorical grants to States. PPG totals for larger States can exceed $10 million. In FY 2014, state PPGs generally contained six or seven categorical grants, with award amounts averaging around $5 million.

Funding: (Formula Grants) FY 17 $445,000,000.00; FY 18 est $445,000,000.00; FY 19 est Estimate Not Available

HQ: 1200 Pennsylvania Avenue NW, PO Box 3903R, Washington, DC 20460

Phone: 202-564-3792 | Email: osinski.michael@epa.gov

http://www.epa.gov/ocir/nepps

EPA66.608 | ENVIRONMENTAL INFORMATION EXCHANGE NETWORK GRANT PROGRAM AND RELATED ASSISTANCE
"Exchange Network Grant Program"

Award: Project Grants

Purpose: Objectives of the grant program is to facilitate sharing environmental data, especially through shared and reusable services.

Applicant Eligibility: Eligible applicants for the Exchange Network Grant Program include states, U.S. Territories (i.e., American Samoa, the Commonwealth of the Northern Mariana Islands, the District of Columbia, Guam, Palau, Puerto Rico, the U.S. Virgin Islands), federally recognized Indian Tribes and native Alaska villages, and inter-tribal consortia of federally recognized Tribes (e.g., the Northwest Indian Fisheries Commission). Other entities, such as regional air pollution control districts and some public universities may apply for assistance if they are agencies or instrumentalities of a state under applicable state laws. These entities, as well as other entities that submit applications asserting they are agencies or instrumentalities of a state, must provide with the application a letter from the appropriate state Attorney General certifying that the applicant is an agency or instrumentality of the state. EPA will not consider an application that does not contain the required documentation. EPA recognizes that the delegation for some Programs extends to local Governments, which are responsible for reporting data to EPA. Local Governments that can demonstrate that they are instrumentalities of the state by providing the documentation described in the preceding paragraph are eligible to apply for Exchange Network Grants. Most local Governments that implement EPA Programs, however, are not agencies or instrumentalities of the state (i.e., a true agency or instrumentality is under the direct control of the state and the management of a state agency or instrumentality may generally be changed by the state executive or other state officials) and, therefore, are not eligible to apply. EPA encourages such entities to partner with a state applicant to allow for their data to be reported and shared through the Exchange Network. Interstate commissions and other interstate entities, likewise, are not eligible to apply and are encouraged to partner with a state applicant. 1) National Environmental Information Exchange Network/E-Enterprise for the Environment Program support: Applications for non-competitive awards to co-regulator/co-implementer Organizations will be evaluated based on the ability of the applicant to provide the following: outreach, communications, technical assistance, and other support to states/Tribes that are participating in, or may wish to participate in, the Network; and support for state participation in the EN governance. A co-regulator/co-implementer Organization is one that represents the interests of governmental units (for example, state or regional Governments) in executing a national or regional environmental Program. The membership of such a national or regional Organization is composed of officials of the co-regulator or co-implementer entities (for example, state environmental commissioners). 2) Exchange Network Support for Federally Recognized Tribes and Intertribal consortia: Assistance under this Program is available to federally recognized Indian Tribes, public and private universities and colleges, and other public or private nonprofit Institutions. Nonprofit Organizations described in Section 501(c)(4) of the Internal Revenue Code that engage in lobbying activities as defined in Section 3 of the Lobbying Disclosure Act of

1995 are not eligible to apply. For profit Organizations are not eligible for funding. Federal Agencies may not apply. Federal employees are not eligible to serve in a principal leadership role on a grant and may not receive salaries or augment their Agency's appropriations in other ways through grants made by this Program. In addition, in order to be eligible an applicant must be an Organization that is broadly representative of federally recognized Indian Tribes with the goal of expanding tribal participation in the EN. For certain competitive funding opportunities under this assistance listing description (CFDA), the Agency may limit eligibility to compete to a number or subset of eligible applicants consistent with the Agency's Assistance Agreement Competition Policy.

Beneficiary Eligibility: Additional Information: Eligible applicants for the EN Grant Program include states, the District of Columbia, U.S. territories (American Samoa, Guam, the Commonwealth of the Northern Mariana Islands, Puerto Rico, and the U.S. Virgin Islands), federally recognized Indian tribes, and intertribal consortia of federally recognized tribes.

Award Range/Average: Grants are awarded on a single year basis with the average grant award being $50,000/fiscal year. Obligations for FY17: $8,609,000; FY18: $9,646,000; and FY19 (est): $6,422,000.

Funding: (Project Grants (Discretionary)) FY 17 $8,609,000.00; FY 18 est $9,646,000.00; FY 19 est $6,422,000.00

HQ: Office of Information Collection Office of Environmental Information 1200 Pennsylvania Avenue NW, PO Box 2824-T, Washington, DC 20460

Phone: 202-566-1709 | Email: blake-coleman.wendy@epa.gov

https://www.epa.gov/exchangenetwork/exchange-network-grant-program

EPA66.609 | PROTECTION OF CHILDREN FROM ENVIRONMENTAL HEALTH RISKS

"Children's Environmental Health"

Award: Cooperative Agreements

Purpose: Supports efforts by organizations, educational institutions, and/or State, local, and tribal governmental agencies to establish or enhance their ability to take actions that will reduce environmental risks to the health of children.

Applicant Eligibility: Assistance under this Program is generally available to States or state agencies, territories, the District of Columbia, American Indian Tribes (federally recognized), and possessions of the U.S. It is also available to public and private universities and colleges, hospitals, laboratories, other public or private nonprofit Institutions, and 501(c)(3) Organizations. Nonprofit Organizations described in Section 501(c)(4) of the Internal Revenue Code that engage in lobbying activities as defined in Section 3 of the Lobbying Disclosure Act of 1995 are not eligible to apply. For profit Organizations are generally not eligible for funding. Some of EPA's statutes may limit assistance to specific types of interested applications. See "Authorization" listed above. For certain competitive funding opportunities under this CFDA description, the Agency may limit eligibility to compete to a number or subset of eligible applicants consistent with the Agency's Assistance Agreement Competition Policy.

Beneficiary Eligibility: State agencies and local governments, U.S. territories and possessions, American Indian Tribes, universities and colleges, hospitals, laboratories, and other public and private nonprofit institutions and organizations.

Award Range/Average: Range: $10,000 to $100,000 per grant. Average: $100,000 per grant (2 year grants).

Funding: (Project Grants (Cooperative Agreements)) FY 17 $25,000.00; FY 18 est $50,000.00; FY 19 est $0.00

HQ: Office of Children's Health Protection 200 Pennsylvania Avenue NW, PO Box 1107T, Washington, DC 20460

Phone: 202-564-2711 | Email: switzer.lavonne@epa.gov

http://www.epa.gov/children

EPA66.610 | SURVEYS, STUDIES, INVESTIGATIONS AND SPECIAL PURPOSE GRANTS WITHIN THE OFFICE OF THE ADMINISTRATOR

Award: Project Grants

Purpose: Supports surveys, studies, investigations, and special purpose assistance associated with air quality, acid deposition, drinking water, water quality, hazardous waste, toxic substances and/or pesticides.

Applicant Eligibility: Assistance under this Program is generally available to State agencies, territories, the District of Columbia, Indian Tribes, and possessions of the U.S. Assistance is also available to public and private universities and colleges, hospitals, laboratories, and other public or private nonprofit Institutions. Nonprofit Organizations described in Section 501(c)(4) of the Internal Revenue Code that engage in lobbying activities as defined in Section 3 of the Lobbying Disclosure Act of 1995 are not eligible to apply. For profit Organizations are generally not eligible for funding. Some of EPA's statutes may limit assistance to specific types of interested applications. See "Authorization" listed above. For certain competitive funding opportunities under this CFDA assistance listing, the Agency may limit eligibility to compete to a number or subset of eligible applicants consistent with the Agency's Assistance Agreement Competition Policy.

Beneficiary Eligibility: State agencies and local governments, U.S. territories and possessions, Indian Tribes, universities and colleges, hospitals, laboratories, and other public and private nonprofit institutions.

Award Range/Average: Range $40,000 to $520,000 per amendment. Average amount approximately $341,000 per amendment..

Funding: (Project Grants (Discretionary)) FY 17 $1,024,035.00; FY 18 Estimate Not Available; FY 19 Estimate Not Available

HQ: 1200 Pennsylvania Avenue NW, PO Box 2732A, Washington, DC 20460

   Phone: 202-564-3227 | Email: murphy.dan@epa.gov

   https://www.epa.gov/aboutepa/about-office-policy-op

EPA66.611 | ENVIRONMENTAL POLICY AND INNOVATION GRANTS

Award: Project Grants

Purpose: The program supports analyses, studies, evaluations, workshops, conferences, and demonstration projects that lead to reduced pollutants generated and conservation of natural resources.

Applicant Eligibility: Assistance under this Program is generally available to States and local Governments, territories and possessions, foreign Governments, international Organizations, Indian Tribes, interstate Organizations, intrastate Organizations, and possessions of the U.S., including the District of Columbia, public and private universities and colleges, hospitals, laboratories, other public or private nonprofit Institutions, and individuals. Nonprofit Organizations described in Section 501(c)(4) of the Internal Revenue Code that engage in lobbying activities as defined in Section 3 of the Lobbying Disclosure Act of 1995 are not eligible to apply. For profit Organizations are generally not eligible for funding. Some of EPA's statutes may limit assistance to specific types of interested applicants. See "Authorization" listed above. National laboratories funded by Federal Agencies (Federally-Funded Research and Development Centers, "FFRDCs") may not apply. FFRDC employees may cooperate or collaborate with eligible applicants within the limits imposed by applicable legislation and regulations. They may participate in planning, conducting, and analyzing the research directed by the applicant, but may not direct projects on behalf of the applicant Organization. The institution, Organization, or governance receiving the award may provide funds through its grant from the EPA to an FFRDC for research personnel, supplies, equipment, and other expenses directly related to the research. Federal Agencies may not apply. Federal employees are not eligible to serve in a principal leadership role on a grant, and may not receive salaries or augment their Agency's appropriations in other ways through grants made by this Program. For certain competitive funding opportunities under this CFDA assistance listing, the Agency may limit eligibility to compete to a number or subset of eligible applicants consistent with the Agency's Assistance Agreement Competition Policy.

Beneficiary Eligibility: State and local governments, U.S. territories and possessions, Indian Tribes, universities and colleges, hospitals, laboratories, other public and private nonprofit institutions, individuals, and international organizations.

Award Range/Average: For most recent competitively awarded grants in the area of economics - related to Environmental Economic Workshops: range is $35,000 - $95,000, with an average award of $70,000. Related to Environmental Economics Dissertations and Early Career Research: range is $35,000 - $75,000, with an average of $60,000. Related to Environmental Economic Research: range is $75,000- $300,000, with an average of $250,000. There were no earmarks included for the period FY 2010 through FY 2018. For recent awards related to community driven environmental protection strategies, the range is from $25,000 to $200,000, with an average around $100,000.

HQ: Office of Policy Office of the Administrator 1200 Pennsylvania Avenue NW, PO Box 1809T, Washington, DC 20460

   Phone: 202-566-2261 | Email: snyder.brett@epa.gov

   http://www.epa.gov/aboutepa/about-office-policy-op

EPA66.612 | SURVEYS, STUDIES, INVESTIGATIONS, TRAINING DEMONSTRATIONS AND EDUCATIONAL OUTREACH RELATED TO ENVIRONMENTAL INFORMATION AND THE RELEASE OF TOXIC CHEMICALS

Award: Cooperative Agreements

Purpose: The program provides funding in support of surveys, studies, investigations, training/demonstrations, educational outreach and special purpose assistance as they relate to environmental information and the release of toxic chemicals. This program educates the public on how to obtain access to and effectively use environmental information, including information about toxic chemical releases and other waste management activities.

Applicant Eligibility: Assistance under this Program is generally available to states, the District of Columbia, U.S. territories (for example, American Samoa, Guam, the Commonwealth of the Northern Mariana Islands, Puerto Rico, and the U.S. Virgin Islands), federally recognized Indian Tribes, intertribal consortia of federally recognized Tribes, public and private colleges and universities, and other public or private nonprofit Organizations. Nonprofit Organizations exempt from taxation under Section 501(c)(4) of the Internal Revenue Code that lobby are not eligible for financial assistance. For certain competitive funding opportunities under this CFDA assistance listing, the Agency may limit eligibility to compete to a number or subset of eligible applicants consistent with the Agency's Assistance Agreement Competition Policy.

Beneficiary Eligibility: State, territory, city, town, county, and regional governments; federally recognized Indian tribes and intertribal consortia of federally recognized tribes; public institutions and industries subject to EPA regulatory reporting requirements; and the public.

Award Range/Average: Estimated $175,000 to $225,000 with an average of $200,000 annually.

Funding: (Cooperative Agreements (Discretionary Grants)) FY 17 $175,000.00; FY 18 est $175,000.00; FY 19 est $0.00

HQ: 1200 Pennsylvania Avenue NW, PO Box 2852T, Washington, DC 20460

Phone: 202-566-0612 | Email: kaalund.dnise@epa.gov

http://www.epa.gov/toxics-release-inventory-tri-program

EPA66.700 | CONSOLIDATED PESTICIDE ENFORCEMENT COOPERATIVE AGREEMENTS

Award: Cooperative Agreements

Purpose: The Cooperative agreement program receives funds to support and strengthen their pesticide compliance programs, including pesticide compliance monitoring, inspection and enforcement activities.

Applicant Eligibility: State agencies having pesticide compliance Program responsibilities in each state, territory and possession of the United States, including the District of Columbia and Indian Tribes.

Beneficiary Eligibility: States, Federally Recognized Indian Tribal Governments, U.S. Territories and the District of Columbia.

Award Range/Average: 32,000 (territory) to 701,000; average 245,000.

Funding: (Formula Grants (Cooperative Agreements)) FY 17 $17,737,000.00; FY 18 est $11,050,000; FY 19 est Estimate Not Available

HQ: Office of Enforcement and Compliance Assurance 1200 Pennsylvania Avenue NW, PO Box 2227A, Washington, DC 20460

Phone: 202-564-4153 | Email: yaras.michelle@epa.gov

https://www.epa.gov/compliance/federal-insecticide-fungicide-and-rodenticide-act-compliance-monitoring

EPA66.701 | TOXIC SUBSTANCES COMPLIANCE MONITORING COOPERATIVE AGREEMENTS

Award: Cooperative Agreements

Purpose: Develops and maintains compliance monitoring programs to prevent or eliminate unreasonable risks to health or the environment associated with chemical substances or mixtures in their communities, specifically with lead-based paint, asbestos, and PCB.

Applicant Eligibility: For the Lead-based paint Program, state agencies, Indian Tribes, and tribal consortiums that have toxic substance compliance responsibilities, who have the authority to enter into these cooperative agreements, and who have their own lead laws in place are eligible to apply for assistance under the TSCA Compliance Monitoring Grant. For the PCB and Asbestos Programs, Grantees should have toxic substance compliance responsibilities and be designated as the lead agency with the authority to enter into these cooperative agreements.

Beneficiary Eligibility: For the Lead-based paint, PCB, and Asbestos programs: States, including the District of Columbia, the Commonwealth of Puerto Rico, Guam, America Samoa, the Northern Marianas, the Trust Territories of the Pacific Islands, the Virgin Islands, and Indian Tribes.

Award Range/Average: The following are ranges of possible funding for: Lead: $15,000 to $23,000/year per authorized lead-based paint program and PCB and Asbestos: $52,000 to $68,000/year.

Funding: (Formula Grants (Cooperative Agreements)) FY 17 $4,834,000.00; FY 18 est $4,807,000.00; FY 19 est $3,276,000.00

HQ: 1200 Pennsylvania Avenue NW, PO Box 2227A, Washington, DC 20460

Phone: 202-564-2059 | Email: engle.kelly@epa.gov

https://www.epa.gov/compliance/toxic-substances-control-act-tsca-compliance-monitoring

EPA66.707 | TSCA TITLE IV STATE LEAD GRANTS CERTIFICATION OF LEAD-BASED PAINT PROFESSIONALS

"State Lead Certification Grants"

Award: Formula Grants

Purpose: The goal of the program is to eliminate childhood lead poisoning.

Applicant Eligibility: Eligible applicants for purposes of funding under these grant Programs include any state of the United States, the District of Columbia, the Commonwealth of Puerto Rico, U.S. Virgin Islands, Guam, American Samoa, the Commonwealth of the Northern Mariana Islands, and any agency or instrumentally thereof exclusive of local Governments (includes public Institutions of higher education and hospitals).

Beneficiary Eligibility: State any state of the United States, the District of Columbia, the Commonwealth of Puerto Rico, U.S. Virgin Islands, Guam, American Samoa, the Commonwealth of the Northern Mariana Islands, and any agency or instrumentally thereof exclusive of local governments may receive assistance under Section 404(g) of TSCA.

Award Range/Average: $16,000 to $350,000; average of $200,000.

Funding: (Formula Grants) FY 17 $14,049,000.00; FY 18 est $14,049,000.00; FY 19 Estimate Not Available

HQ: 1200 Pennsylvania Avenue NW, Washington, DC 20460

Phone: 202-566-0744 | Email: price.michelle@epa.gov

https://www.epa.gov/lead

EPA66.708 | POLLUTION PREVENTION GRANTS PROGRAM
"P2 Grant Program"

Award: Project Grants

Purpose: The P2 grant program was enacted under the Pollution Prevention Act of 1990 to provide technical assistance and/or training to businesses/facilities about source reduction techniques to help them adopt and implement source reduction approaches and to increase the development, adoption, and market penetration of greener products and sustainable manufacturing practices.

Applicant Eligibility: Eligible applicants include the 50 states, the District of Columbia, the U.S. Virgin Islands, the Commonwealth of Puerto Rico, any territory or possession of the United States, any agency or instrumentality of a state, including state colleges and universities, and federally-recognized Indian Tribes that meet the requirements for treatment in a manner similar to a state as described in 40 CFR 35. 663, and Intertribal Consortia that meet the requirements in 40 CFR 35. 504. For certain competitive funding opportunities under this CFDA description, the Agency may limit eligibility to compete to a number or subset of eligible applicants consistent with the Agency's Assistance Agreement Competition Policy.

Beneficiary Eligibility: State agencies, State colleges and universities that are instrumentalities of the State and federally-recognized Tribes are encouraged to establish partnerships with businesses and environmental assistance providers to deliver seamless P2 assistance. The most successful applicants will be those that make the most efficient use of government funding. In many cases, this has been accomplished through partnerships. As a result, those who are eligible can provide P2 benefits to the following entities: states, interstate and local agencies or organizations/universities, federally-recognized Tribes, intertribal consortia, public or private nonprofit organizations/institutions, private businesses, quasi public nonprofit organizations, and the general public.

Award Range/Average: During the FY 2018 - FY 2019 grant competition cycle, P2 grant awards may potentially be in the range of $40,000- $500,000 issued over a two-year funding period.

Funding: (Project Grants (Discretionary)) FY 17 $3,942,000.00; FY 18 est $4,690,000.00; FY 19 est $4,690,000.00

HQ: 1200 Pennsylvania Avenue NW, PO Box 7409-M, Washington, DC 20460

Phone: 202-564-8857 | Email: amhaz.michele@epa.gov

http://www.epa.gov/p2/grant-programs-pollution-prevention

EPA66.716 | RESEARCH, DEVELOPMENT, MONITORING, PUBLIC EDUCATION, OUTREACH, TRAINING, DEMONSTRATIONS, AND STUDIES
"OCSPP"

Award: Project Grants

Purpose: Grants are awarded to support Research, Development, Outreach, Demonstration, and Studies relating to the protection of public health and the environment from pesticides, and potential risk from toxic substances.

Applicant Eligibility: Eligible applicants for purposes of funding under these grant Programs include any state of the United States, the District of Columbia, Native American Organizations, the Commonwealth of Puerto Rico, U.S. Virgin Islands, Guam, American Samoa, the Commonwealth of the Northern Mariana Islands, and any agency or instrumentally thereof exclusive of local Governments (includes public Institutions of higher education and hospitals). For certain competitive funding opportunities under this CFDA description, the Agency may limit eligibility to compete to a number or subset of eligible applicants consistent with the Agency's Assistance Agreement Competition Policy.

Beneficiary Eligibility: State and local governments, U.S. territories and possessions, federally recognized Indian tribal governments and Native American Organizations, universities and colleges, hospitals, laboratories, other public and private nonprofit institutions, general public, and other Non-Governmental Organizations.

Award Range/Average: $1,000 to $1,500,000. Average: $500,000 For OPPT: $80,000 to $250,000. Average: $165,000

Funding: (Project Grants (Discretionary)) FY 17 $3,150,000.00; FY 18 est $3,150,000.00; FY 19 Estimate Not Available

HQ: 1200 Pennsylvania Avenue NW, PO Box 7401M, Washington, DC 20460

Phone: 202-564-8818 | Email: kapust.edna@epa.gov

http://www.epa.gov/aboutepa/about-office-chemical-safety-and-pollution-prevention-ocspp

EPA66.717 | SOURCE REDUCTION ASSISTANCE
"SRA Grants"

Award: Project Grants

Purpose: The SRA program's goal is to provide grants to support pollution prevention, source reduction and/or resource conservation activities.

Applicant Eligibility: Eligible applicants for purposes of funding under these grant Programs include any state of the United States, the District of Columbia, the Commonwealth of Puerto Rico, U.S. Virgin Islands, Guam, American Samoa, the Commonwealth of the Northern Mariana Islands, and any agency or instrumently thereof exclusive of local Governments (includes public Institutions of higher education and hospitals), city or township Governments, independent school district Governments, state controlled Institutions of higher education, non-profit Organizations (other than Institutions of higher education), private Institutions of higher education, community-based grassroots Organizations, and federally-recognized Tribes and intertribal consortia. For certain competitive funding opportunities under this CFDA description, the Agency may limit eligibility to compete to a number or subset of eligible applicants consistent with the Agency's Assistance Agreement Competition Policy.

Beneficiary Eligibility: Any state, federally-recognized tribal government, intertribal consortia, college/university, non-profit organization, local government or independent school district.

Award Range/Average: Federal funding amounts for individual grant awards may potentially be in the range of $20,000-$260,000 in total issued; over a two-year funding period Average award total: $110,000. As of this Assistance Listing, EPA is currently soliciting proposals for FY 2018-FY 2019 grant cycle.

Funding: (Project Grants (Discretionary)) FY 17 $1,294,000.00; FY 18 est $1,000,000.00; FY 19 est $1,000,000.00

HQ: Office of Pollution Prevention and Toxics Pollution Prevention Division 1200 Pennsylvania Avenue NW, PO Box 7409-M, Washington, DC 20460

Phone: 202-564-8857 | Email: amhaz.michele@epa.gov

http://www.epa.gov/p2/grant-programs-pollution-prevention

EPA66.801 | HAZARDOUS WASTE MANAGEMENT STATE PROGRAM SUPPORT

Award: Formula Grants

Purpose: Assists state governments in the development and implementation of authorized hazardous waste management program for the purpose of controlling the generation, transportation, treatment, storage and disposal of hazardous wastes.

Applicant Eligibility: State agencies responsible for hazardous waste management within the 50 States, the District of Columbia, the Commonwealth of Puerto Rico, the Virgin Islands, Guam, American Samoa, the Commonwealth of the Northern Mariana Islands, and interstate agencies established by the appropriate states and approved by the EPA Administrator under Section 1005 of the Solid Waste Disposal Act are eligible. Eligibility for assistance agreements with funds made available by Public Law 115-123 for hazardous waste and solid waste activities is limited to the Commonwealth of Puerto Rico and the United States Virgin Islands.

Beneficiary Eligibility: State agencies responsible for hazardous waste management within the 50 States, the District of Columbia, the Commonwealth of Puerto Rico, the Virgin Islands, Guam, American Samoa, the Commonwealth of the Northern Mariana Islands, and interstate agencies established by the appropriate states and approved by the EPA Administrator under Section 1005 of the Solid Waste Disposal Act. Eligibility for assistance agreements with funds made available by Public Law 115-123 for hazardous waste and solid waste activities is limited to the Commonwealth of Puerto Rico and the United States Virgin Islands.

Award Range/Average: Most fiscal years range $350,000 to $8,500,000; average: $2,000,000.

Funding: (Formula Grants (Cooperative Agreements)) FY 17 $99,503,000.00; FY 18 est $3,050,000.00; FY 19 est $3,000,000.00

Programs Administered by Regional - State - Local Offices

HQ: Office of Land and Emergency Management U.S. EPA Headquarters 1200 Pennsylvania Avenue NW, PO Box 5303P, Washington, DC 20460
  Phone: 703-308-8630 | Email: roepe.wayne@epa.gov
  http://www.epa.gov/epawaste

EPA66.802 | SUPERFUND STATE, POLITICAL SUBDIVISION, AND INDIAN TRIBE SITE-SPECIFIC COOPERATIVE AGREEMENTS

Award: Cooperative Agreements

Purpose: Conducts site characterization activities at potential or confirmed hazardous waste sites; and also undertakes response planning and implementation actions at sites on the National Priorities List to clean up the hazardous waste sites that are found to pose hazards to human health.

Applicant Eligibility: States (and political subdivisions thereof), Commonwealths, U.S. Territories and Possessions, and Federally Recognized Indian Tribal Governments, including intertribal consortia. For certain competitive funding opportunities under this CFDA assistance listing, the Agency may limit eligibility to compete to a number or subset of eligible applicants consistent with the Agency's Assistance Agreement Competition Policy.

Beneficiary Eligibility: States (and political subdivisions thereof), Commonwealths, U.S. Territories and Possessions, and Federally Recognized Indian Tribal Governments, including intertribal consortia.

Award Range/Average: Range: $812 to $9 million; Average: $312,746

Funding: (Cooperative Agreements) FY 16 $81,500,000.00; FY 17 est $81,500,000.00; FY 18 est Estimate Not Available; FY 15 $88.9 million, FY 16 $81.5 million, FY 17 $81.5 million (estimate)

HQ: 1200 Pennsylvania Avenue NW, Washington, DC 20460
  Phone: 703-603-8714 | Email: fine.ellyn@epa.gov
  http://www.epa.gov/superfund

EPA66.804 | UNDERGROUND STORAGE TANK PREVENTION, DETECTION AND COMPLIANCE PROGRAM
"UST Prevention, Detection and Compliance Program"

Award: Formula Grants

Purpose: To assist States, Territories, Tribes and/or Intertribal Consortia that meet the requirements at 40 CFR 35.504 in the development and implementation of underground storage tank (UST) programs and for leak prevention, compliance and other activities authorized by the Energy Policy Act (EPAct) of 2005, Public Law 105-276, and EPA's annual appropriations acts.

Applicant Eligibility: Prevention, detection and compliance assistance agreements are only available to States and Territories and to Federally-recognized Tribes and Intertribal Consortia that must meet the requirements, as described in the Federal Register Notice, Vol. 67, No. 213, pp. 67181-67183, "Update to EPA Policy on Certain Grants to Intertribal Consortia. " These assistance agreements may also be used for EPA to help States, who request it, to obtain SEE enrollees through a SEE assistance agreement to work on the State's underground storage tanks and to support direct UST implementation Programs.

Beneficiary Eligibility: States, Territories, Tribes and Intertribal Consortia.

Award Range/Average: Range for States and Territories: The STAG and LUST prevention financial assistance is based on states' needs. STAG Funding: There is no STAG distribution for Tribes. In FY 2018, estimated STAG funding - Range for States and Territories: $30,000 to $280,000 Average for States and Territories = $97,600. LUST PREVENTION Funding: In FY 2018, estimated LUST Prevention funding - Range for States and Territories: $86,377 to $1,327,934. Average for States and Territories = $427,348. Range for Tribes: $20,000 to $250,000; Average for Tribes = $75,658.

Funding: (Formula Grants) FY 17 $53,734,000.00; FY 18 est $26,833,000.00; FY 19 est Estimate Not Available

HQ: 1200 Pennsylvania Avenue NW, Washington, DC 20460
  Phone: 202-564-2182 | Email: edwards.christine@epa.gov
  http://www.epa.gov/ust

EPA66.805 | LEAKING UNDERGROUND STORAGE TANK TRUST FUND CORRECTIVE ACTION PROGRAM
"Leaking UST Corrective Action Program"

Award: Formula Grants

Purpose: To support State and Tribal corrective action programs that address releases from underground storage tanks.

Applicant Eligibility: Cooperative agreements are only available to States and Territories that have UST Programs. Additionally, these cooperative agreements are only available to Federally-recognized Tribes and Intertribal Consortia that must meet the requirements, as described in the Federal Register Notice, Vol. 67, No. 213, pp. 67181-67183, "Update to EPA Policy on Certain Grants to Intertribal Consortia. ".

Beneficiary Eligibility: States, Territories, Tribes and Intertribal Consortia and the communities and industries affected by leaks from underground storage tanks.

Award Range/Average: For FY 2018, the Range for Territories and States: $40,868 - $3,149,070; Territory Average: $120,139; State Average: $1,059,331. It is anticipated that there will be approximately 4 Tribal cooperative agreements in FY 2018 for a total of $395,000.

Funding: (Formula Grants) FY 17 $112,410,000.00; FY 18 est $103,068,000.00; FY 19 est $39,743,000; LUST Obligations - Assistance Agreements to States and Tribes (for state and tribal staff oversight of initiating and cleaning up contamination from leaking underground storage tanks): For LUST State Cooperative Agreements: FY 2016 actual: $55,049,775; FY 2017 estimate: $55,040,000; FY 2018 estimate:$38,840,000. For LUST Tribal Cooperative Agreements: FY 2016 actual: $375,000, FY 2017 estimate: 390,000; FY 2018 estimate: $200,000. (Formula Grants) FY 17 $56,980,000.00; FY 18 est $64,028,000.00; FY 19 est $39,743,000.00; 2018 Estimate: Includes supplemental hurricane appropriation of $7,000,000

HQ: 1200 Pennsylvania Avenue NW, Washington, DC 20460

Phone: 202-564-2182 | Email: edwards.christine@epa.gov

https://www.epa.gov/ust

EPA66.806 | SUPERFUND TECHNICAL ASSISTANCE GRANTS (TAG) FOR COMMUNITY GROUPS AT NATIONAL PRIORITY LIST (NPL) SITES

Award: Project Grants

Purpose: To authorizes Technical Assistance Grants to be awarded to groups of individuals affected by or threatened by a release at a Superfund site.

Applicant Eligibility: A technical assistance grant (TAG) is available to any qualified group of individuals which: may be "affected" by a release or threatened release at any facility listed on the NPL or proposed for listing under the NCP where a "response action" under CERCLA has begun; meets minimum administrative and management capability requirements found in 2 CFR 200 by demonstrating they have or will have reliable procedures for record keeping and financial accountability related to TAG management; and incorporates as a nonprofit for the specific purpose of representing "affected" individuals at the site. "Affected" means subject to an actual or potential health, economic or environmental threat. A group is ineligible if: (a) The group is a "potentially responsible party" (PRP), receives money or services from a PRP, or represents a PRP; (b) The group is affiliated with a national Organization; (c) The group is an academic institution; (d) The group is a political subdivision; (e) The group was established or is presently sustained by any of the ineligible entities listed above; or (f) The group is not incorporated as a nonprofit Organization for the specific purpose of representing affected people except as provided in 40 CFR 35. 4045.

Beneficiary Eligibility: This program benefits groups of individuals affected by Superfund hazardous waste sites. Groups should be representative of the community affected by the Superfund site, which may include homeowners, land/property owners, local businesses, as well as any other individuals in the general public who live near a site.

Award Range/Average: Initial awards for assistance agreements awarded under this CFDA number will not exceed $50,000. After the initial award, additional funding may be awarded based on the criteria detailed under 40 CFR 35.4065, and subject to the availability of funds. The average additional award is $40,000 (per agreement). Since 1988,343 TAGs have been awarded. Of these,200 grantees were awarded $50,000 or less; 95 grantees have received awards with a cumulative value between $51,000 and $150,000; 31 grantees have received awards with a cumulative value ranging between $151,000 and $250,000; and 17 grantees have received awards whose cumulative value totals of more than $250,000. The cumulative award value includes the initial award and any supplemental funding awards over the life of the agreement.

Funding: (Project Grants) FY 16 $305,000.00; FY 17 est $300,000.00; FY 18 est $200,000.00

HQ: Ariel Rios Building 1200 Pennsylvania Avenue NW, PO Box 5204P, Washington, DC 20460

Phone: 703-603-8889 | Email: margand.freya@epa.gov

http://www.epa.gov/superfund

Programs Administered by Regional - State - Local Offices

EPA66.808 | SOLID WASTE MANAGEMENT ASSISTANCE GRANTS

Award: Cooperative Agreements

Purpose: To promote use of integrated solid waste management systems to solve solid waste generation and management problems at the local, regional and national levels.

Applicant Eligibility: State (including the District of Columbia, Puerto Rico, Virgin Islands, Guam, American Samoa, and Northern Mariana Islands), local, Tribal, interstate, and intrastate government agencies and instrumentalities, and non-profit Organizations that are not 501(c)(4) Organizations that lobby, including non-profit educational Institutions and non-profit hospitals. Individuals and for-profit Organizations are not eligible. For certain competitive funding opportunities under this CFDA description, the Agency may limit eligibility to compete to a number or subset of eligible applicants consistent with the Agency's Assistance Agreement Competition Policy. Additionally, EPA may limit competition under this CFDA to Tribes and Inter-Tribal Consortia.

Beneficiary Eligibility: State and local governments, U.S. territories and possessions, the public, and interstate agencies.

Award Range/Average: $10,000 to $460,000/FY 18; $50,000/FY 19

Funding: (Cooperative Agreements) FY 16 $463,500.00; FY 17 est $500,000.00; FY 18 est $500,000.00; FY 15 $463,500; FY 16 est $500,000; FY 17 est $500,000

HQ: USEPA Headquarters Ariel Rios Building 1200 Pennsylvania Avenue NW, PO Box 5305P, Washington, DC 20460
Phone: 703-308-8460 | Email: vizzone.nick@epa.gov
http://www.epa.gov/epawaste/index.htm

EPA66.809 | SUPERFUND STATE AND INDIAN TRIBE CORE PROGRAM COOPERATIVE AGREEMENTS

Award: Cooperative Agreements

Purpose: To provide funds to conduct CERCLA activities which are not assignable to specific sites.

Applicant Eligibility: States and U.S. Territories, and Federally Recognized Indian Tribal Governments.

Beneficiary Eligibility: States, U.S. Territories and Federally Recognized Indian Tribal Governments.

Award Range/Average: $15,000 to $207,514; with an average award of $88,128.

Funding: (Cooperative Agreements) FY 16 $4,600,000.00; FY 17 est $4,600,000.00; FY 18 Estimate Not Available

HQ: Assessment and Remediation Division, PO Box 5204P EPA, Washington, DC 20460
Phone: 703-603-8714 | Email: fine.ellyn@epa.gov
http://www.epa.gov/superfund

EPA66.812 | HAZARDOUS WASTE MANAGEMENT GRANT PROGRAM FOR TRIBES
"Hazardous Waste Grants"

Award: Cooperative Agreements

Purpose: To provide assistance for the development and implementation of hazardous waste management programs; to improve and maintain regulatory compliance; and for developing solutions to address hazardous waste management issues in Indian country.

Applicant Eligibility: The following are eligible to receive financial assistance: (a) an Indian tribal government, and (b) an intertribal consortium or consortia. An Indian tribal government is any tribe, band, nation, or other organized group or community, including any Alaska Native village or regional or village corporation (as defined in or established pursuant to the Alaska Native Claims Settlement Act, 43 U.S.C. 1601, et seq.), which is recognized by the U.S. Department of the Interior as eligible for the special services provided by the United States to Indians because of their status as Indians. A consortium is a partnership between two or more Indian tribal Governments authorized by the governing bodies of those Tribes to apply for and receive assistance under this Program. For certain competitive funding opportunities under this CFDA assistance listing, the Agency may limit eligibility to compete to a number or subset of eligible applicants consistent with the Agency's Assistance Agreement Competition Policy.

Beneficiary Eligibility: Federally Recognized Indian Tribal Governments.

Award Range/Average: Range = $18,000 to $100,000; Average = $56,000.

Funding: (Cooperative Agreements (Discretionary Grants)) FY 17 $300,000.00; FY 18 est $305,000.00; FY 19 est $305,000.00

HQ: Office of Resource Conservation and Recovery 1200 Pennsylvania Avenue NW, PO Box 5303P, Washington, DC 20460
Phone: 703-308-8458 | Email: roy.denise@epa.gov
http://www.epa.gov/tribal-lands

EPA66.813 | ALTERNATIVE OR INNOVATIVE TREATMENT TECHNOLOGY RESEARCH, DEMONSTRATION, TRAINING, AND HAZARDOUS SUBSTANCE RESEARCH GRANTS

Award: Project Grants

Purpose: To support grants for alternative treatment programs that refers to new technologies and techniques for treating solid waste and sites.

Applicant Eligibility: Assistance under this Program is generally available to States, territories, Indian Tribes, and possessions of the U.S., including the District of Columbia, public and private universities and colleges, hospitals, laboratories, other public or private nonprofit Institutions, and individuals. In some instances, EPA will consider applications from profit makers, proposing projects with significant technical merit and relevance to EPA's Office of Solid Waste and Emergency Response. Nonprofit Organizations described in Section 501(c)(4) of the Internal Revenue Code that engage in lobbying activities as defined in Section 3 of the Lobbying Disclosure Act of 1995 are not eligible to apply. For certain competitive funding opportunities under this CFDA assistance listing, the Agency may limit eligibility to compete to a number or subset of eligible applicants consistent with the Agency's Assistance Agreement Competition Policy.

Beneficiary Eligibility: State and local governments, U.S. territories and possessions, Indian Tribes, universities and colleges, hospitals, laboratories, industry, and other public and private institutions and individuals.

Award Range/Average: For each fiscal year it is $50,000 - $1,000,000 Average $500,000

Funding: (Project Grants (Discretionary)) FY 17 $500,000.00; FY 18 est $0.00; FY 19 est Estimate Not Available

HQ: Office of Superfund Remediation and Technology Innovation USEPA (5202-P) 1200 Pennsylvania Avenue NW, Washington, DC 20460

Phone: 703-603-9042 | Email: mcdonough.barbara@epa.gov

https://www.epa.gov/superfund

EPA66.814 | BROWNFIELDS TRAINING, RESEARCH, AND TECHNICAL ASSISTANCE GRANTS AND COOPERATIVE AGREEMENTS
"Brownfields 104(k) (7) Grants"

Award: Cooperative Agreements

Purpose: To assist the individuals and organizations to facilitate the inventory of brownfields properties, assessments, cleanup of brownfields properties, community involvement, or site preparation.

Applicant Eligibility: CERCLA 104(k)(7) cites eligible entities as: a general purpose unit of local government; a land clearance authority or other quasi-governmental entity that operates under the supervision and control of, or as an agent of, a general purpose unit of local government; a government entity created by a State legislature; a regional council or group of general purpose units of local government; a redevelopment agency that is chartered or otherwise sanctioned by a State; a State (note CERCLA 107(27) defines term "State" to include territories or possessions over which the United States has jurisdiction); an Indian Tribe other than in Alaska; an Alaska Native Regional Corporation, Alaska Native Village Corporation and the Metlakatla Indian Community. Nonprofit Organizations are also eligible for training, research, and technical assistance grants. Nonprofit Organizations must meet the definition of that term in Section 4(6) of the Federal Financial Assistance Management Improvement Act of 1999, Public Law 96-107, 31 U.S.C. 6101 Note: Under this definition, colleges, universities, and community colleges are eligible to apply. However, nonprofit Organizations described in Section 501(c)(4) of the Internal Revenue Code that engage in lobbying activities as defined in Section 3 of the Lobbying Disclosure Act of 1995 are not eligible to apply. For profit Organizations are not eligible to apply. For certain competitive funding opportunities under this CFDA description, the Agency may limit eligibility to compete to a number or subset of eligible applicants consistent with the Agency's Assistance Agreement Competition Policy.

Beneficiary Eligibility: Cooperative agreement-funded activities will benefit the community members and local stakeholders who are proximate to brownfield sites (whether in an urban, suburban or rural setting) including local governments, non-profit organizations, quasi public nonprofits, residents, local business owners, community groups, universities and colleges, industry, other public and private institutions, individuals, states and tribes.

Award Range/Average: Historically, the Brownfields Training, Research, and Technical Assistance cooperative agreements have ranged anywhere from $200,000,000 to $2,000,000 over the entire cooperative agreement, depending on the specific focus area of solicitation and the project period of the award (typical project period is 5 years) New awards made for other research, training and technical assistance grants usually range between $200,000 and $2 million and usually incrementally funded over the project period if the award is above $200,000.

Programs Administered by Regional - State - Local Offices

Funding: (Cooperative Agreements (Discretionary Grants)) FY 17 $8,500,000.00; FY 18 est $5,000,000.00; FY 19 Estimate Not Available

HQ: Office of Brownfields and Land Revitalization Office of Land and Emergency Management U.S. EPA 1200 Pennsylvania Avenue NW, PO Box 5105T, Washington, DC 20460

  Phone: 202-566-2745 | Email: lentz.rachel@epa.gov
  https://www.epa.gov/brownfields

EPA66.815 | ENVIRONMENTAL WORKFORCE DEVELOPMENT AND JOB TRAINING COOPERATIVE AGREEMENTS
"Environmental Workforce Development and Job Training Program"

Award: Cooperative Agreements

Purpose: To recruit, train, and place unemployed and under-employed, including low-income, residents of solid and hazardous waste-impacted communities with the skills needed to obtain full-time, sustainable employment in solid and hazardous waste cleanup, wastewater treatment, chemical safety, and the environmental field at large.

Applicant Eligibility: Proposals will be accepted from either eligible governmental entities as defined in CERCLA Section 104(k)(1) or eligible nonprofit Organizations as defined in Public Law 106-107, the Federal Financial Assistance Management Improvement Act. Eligible governmental entities include a general purpose local unit of government; a land clearance authority or other quasi-governmental entity that operates under the supervision and control of, or as an agent of, a general purpose unit of government; a governmental entity created by a state legislature; a regional council or group of general purpose units of local government; a redevelopment agency that is chartered or otherwise sanctioned by a state; a state; an Indian Tribe (other than in Alaska), or an Alaskan Native Regional Corporation and an Alaska Native Village Corporation as those terms are defined in the Alaska Native Claims Settlement Act (43 U.S.C. 1601 and following); and the Metlakatla Indian Community. Intertribal consortia, except consortia comprised of ineligible Alaskan Tribes, are eligible to apply as well. Eligible nonprofit Organizations include any corporation, trust, association, cooperative, or other Organization that is operated mainly for scientific, educational, service, charitable, or similar purpose in the public interest; is not organized primarily for profit; and uses net proceeds to maintain, improve, or expand the operation of the Organization. Workforce Investment Boards that meet these criteria may be eligible nonprofit Organizations. Public and nonprofit private educational Institutions are eligible to apply. However, nonprofit Organizations described in Section 501(c)(4) of the Internal Revenue Code that engage in lobbying activities as defined in Section 3 of the Lobbying Disclosure Act of 1995 are not eligible to apply. For-profit or proprietary training Organizations or trade schools are not eligible to apply. Evidence of nonprofit status under Federal, state or tribal law must be provided at the time the proposal is submitted. Applicants are also required to demonstrate that proposed environmental job training projects do not duplicate other federally funded environmental job training projects in the target community. For certain competitive funding opportunities under this CFDA assistance listing, the Agency may limit eligibility to compete to a number or subset of eligible applicants consistent with the Agency's Assistance Agreement Competition Policy. A list of environmental workforce development and job training grants awarded in Fiscal Year 2018 can be found here: https://www.epa.gov/brownfields/applicants-selected-fy18-environmental-workforce-development-and-job-training-grants.

Beneficiary Eligibility: Environmental Workforce Development and Job Training grants will provide environmental job training unemployed and underemployed residents of solid and hazardous waste-impacted neighbourhoods and help them take advantage of job opportunities created as a result of the management, assessment, and clean-up of contaminated properties, as well as employment in wastewater, alternative energy, and chemical safety related positions.

Award Range/Average: Environmental Workforce Development and Job Training grants can be funded up to $200,000.

Funding: (Cooperative Agreements (Discretionary Grants)) FY 17 $2,700,000.00; FY 18 est $3,300,000.00; FY 19 Estimate Not Available

HQ: Office of Brownfields and Land Revitalization OSWER 200 Pennsylvania Avenue NW, PO Box 5105T, Washington, DC 20460

  Phone: 202-566-1564 | Email: congdon.rachel@epa.gov
  https://www.epa.gov/brownfields

EPA66.816 | HEADQUARTERS AND REGIONAL UNDERGROUND STORAGE TANKS PROGRAM

Award: Project Grants

Purpose: To support activities that promote the prevention, compliance, and identification of underground storage tanks, and to support activities that promote corrective action, enforcement and management of releases from underground storage tank systems.

Applicant Eligibility: These assistance agreements are only available to public authorities (State, interstate, intrastate, agencies designated by States or Territorial Governors to receive UST notifications, federally-recognized Tribes and Intertribal Consortia, and local), public agencies and Institutions; private non-profit Organizations and agencies that meet the requirements of Section 8001(a) and (b) of the Solid Waste Disposal Act. Profit-making Organizations and the general public are not eligible. For certain competitive funding opportunities under this CFDA assistance listing, the Agency may limit eligibility to compete to a number or subset of eligible applicants consistent with the Agency's Assistance Agreement Competition Policy.

Beneficiary Eligibility: State and local governments, territories and possessions, interstate agencies, Tribes, Intertribal Consortia, members of the regulated community and residents in areas impacted by federally regulated underground storage tanks.

Award Range/Average: FY 2018 Range: $85,000 - $203,143; Average: $165,322.

Funding: (Project Grants (Discretionary)) FY 17 $164,242.00; FY 18 est $661,286.00; FY 19 Estimate Not Available

HQ: 1200 Pennsylvania Avenue NW, PO Box 3803R, Washington, DC 20460

Phone: 202-564-2182 | Email: edwards.christine@epa.gov

http://www.epa.gov/ust

EPA66.817 | STATE AND TRIBAL RESPONSE PROGRAM GRANTS

Award: Formula Grants

Purpose: To provide financial support to establish and enhance the four elements of an effective state or tribal response program as specified in CERCLA Section 128.

Applicant Eligibility: States (as defined in CERCLA Section 101(27) and Tribes (as defined in CERCLA Section 101(36) are eligible for funding under Section 128(a). To be eligible to receive funding under CERCLA Section 128(a), a state or tribe must demonstrate that its response Program includes, or is taking reasonable steps to include, the four elements of a response Program. States or Tribes that are parties to voluntary response Program memoranda of agreement (MOAs) are automatically eligible for Section 128(a) funding. Additionally, states and Tribes, including those with MOAs, must maintain and make available to the public a record of sites at which response actions have been completed in the previous year and are planned to be addressed in the upcoming year in order to qualify for Section 128(a) funding.

Beneficiary Eligibility: Beneficiaries include individuals living in recipient states', territories', and tribes' jurisdiction.

Award Range/Average: Most fiscal years range from $50,000 to $1,000,000; average approximately $450,000.

Funding: (Formula Grants) FY 17 $46,917,000.00; FY 18 est $33,600,000.00; FY 19 est Estimate Not Available

HQ: Office of Brownfields and Land Revitalization 1200 Pennsylvania Avenue NW, PO Box 5105T, Washington, DC 20460

Phone: 202-566-2745 | Email: lentz.rachel@epa.gov

http://www.epa.gov/brownfields

EPA66.818 | BROWNFIELDS ASSESSMENT AND CLEANUP COOPERATIVE AGREEMENTS

Award: Cooperative Agreements

Purpose: To provide real property, the expansion, redevelopment, or reuse of which may be complicated by the presence or potential presence of a hazardous substance, pollutant, or contaminant.

Applicant Eligibility: Eligibility for Multipurpose, Assessment, Revolving Loan Fund, and Cleanup Grants: a general purpose unit of local government; a land clearance authority or other quasi-governmental entity that operates under the supervision and control of, or as an agent of, a general purpose unit of local government; a government entity created by a State legislature; a regional council or group of general purpose units of local government; a redevelopment agency that is chartered or otherwise sanctioned by a State; a State; an Indian Tribe other than in Alaska; an Alaska Native Regional Corporation, Alaska Native Village Corporation and the Metlakatla Indian Community; an Organization described in section 501(c)(3) of the Internal Revenue Code of 1986 and exempt from taxation under section 501(a) of that Code; a limited liability corporation in which all managing members are Organizations or limited liability corporations whose sole members are Organizations described in subparagraph Organization described in section 501(c)(3) of the Internal Revenue Code of 1986 and exempt from taxation under section 501(a) of that Code; a limited partnership in which all general partners are Organizations described in subparagraph (I) or limited liability corporations whose sole members are Organizations described in subparagraph Organization described in section 501(c)(3) of the Internal Revenue Code of 1986 and exempt from taxation under section 501(a) of that Code; or a qualified community development entity (as defined in section 45D(c) (1) of the Internal Revenue Code of 1986. Nonprofit Organizations must meet the definition of that term in Section 4(6) of the Federal Financial Assistance Management Improvement Act of 1999, Public Law 96-107, 31 U.S.C. 6101 (Note: Under this definition, colleges, universities, and community colleges are eligible to apply.) However, nonprofit Organizations described in Section 501(c)(4) of the Internal Revenue Code that engage in lobbying activities as defined in Section 3 of the Lobbying Disclosure Act of 1995 are not eligible to apply. For-profit Organizations are not eligible to apply for direct funding from EPA. However, for profit Organizations may apply for loans made by eligible entities with RLF capitalization grants. For certain competitive funding opportunities under this CFDA assistance listing, the Agency may limit eligibility to compete to a number or subset of eligible applicants consistent with the Agency's Assistance Agreement Competition Policy.

Beneficiary Eligibility: Generally, those eligible entities identified above will benefit from the brownfields grant actions. Specifically, individuals and commercial organizations in brownfields grant communities will benefit from brownfields assessment, cleanup, and revitalization funding. New strategies for promoting environmental clean-up lessons from these grants will provide a growing base of information and knowledge for other communities across the country seeking partnerships with stakeholders to coordinate issues related to brownfields and leverage additional opportunities for redevelopment.

Award Range/Average: (1) For community-wide assessment grants, an eligible entity may apply for up to $300,000 to address sites contaminated by hazardous substances, pollutants, or contaminants (including hazardous substances co-mingled with petroleum), and sites contaminated by petroleum. For site-specific assessment grants, an eligible entity may apply for up to $200,000 to address one site contaminated by hazardous substances, pollutants, or contaminants (including hazardous substances co-mingled with petroleum) and sites contaminated by petroleum. An entity may request a waiver of the $200,000 limit up to $350,000 based on the anticipated level of contamination, size, or ownership status of the site. These limits are mandatory under CERCLA 104(k)(5)(A). An assessment coalition of eligible entities may apply for up to $600,000 to address sites contaminated by hazardous substances or petroleum on a community-wide basis. (2) For revolving loan fund grants, an eligible entity may apply for up to $1,000,000 for an initial RLF grant. This limit is mandatory under CERCLA 104(k)(5)(A). In addition, an RLF coalition of eligible entities may apply together under one recipient for up to $1,000,000 per grant. (3) For cleanup grants, an eligible entity may apply for up to $500,000 per site. The $500,000 per site limit is mandatory under CERCLA 104(k)(3)(A) as amended by the BUILD ACT of 2018. (4) For Multipurpose grants, an eligible entity may apply for up to $800,000 to address one or more brownfield sites contaminated by hazardous substances, pollutants, or contaminants (including hazardous substances co-mingled with petroleum), and sites contaminated by petroleum.

Funding: (Cooperative Agreements (Discretionary Grants)) FY 17 $0.00; FY 18 est $54,300,000.00; FY 19 Estimate Not Available

HQ: Office of Brownfields and Land Revitalization OSWER U.S. EPA 1200 Pennsylvania Avenue NW, PO Box 5105T, Washington, DC 20460

Phone: 202-566-2777 | Email: lloyd.davidr@epa.gov

http://www.epa.gov/brownfields

EPA66.926 | INDIAN ENVIRONMENTAL GENERAL ASSISTANCE PROGRAM (GAP) "GAP Grants"

Award: Project Grants

Purpose: To provide financial and technical assistance to tribal governments and intertribal consortia to assist tribes in planning, developing, and establishing the capacity to implement federal environmental programs administered by the EPA and to assist in implementation of tribal solid and hazardous waste programs.

Applicant Eligibility: The following are eligible to receive financial assistance: Indian tribal Governments (Tribes) and intertribal consortia are eligible to receive funds under this Program. These terms are defined in 40 CFR 35. 502 as follows: An Indian tribal government (tribe), except as otherwise defined in statute or applicable Program specific regulation, is any Indian tribe, band, nation, or other organized group or community, including any Alaska Native village, which is recognized as eligible by the U.S. Department of the Interior for the special services provided by the United States to Indians because of their status as Indians. An intertribal consortium is a partnership between two or more Tribes authorized by the governing bodies of those Tribes to apply for and receive assistance under [GAP]. In accordance with GAP Grant Guiding Principle, EPA will award GAP funds to help Tribes accomplish their tribal environmental Program development goals as outlined in their EPA-Tribal Environmental Plan (ETEP). To further this principle, intertribal consortia are advised to describe how their grant proposals support the Program development goals outlined in the ETEPs developed by their GAP-eligible member Tribes.

Beneficiary Eligibility: Federally Recognized Indian Tribal Governments and eligible Intertribal Consortia.

Award Range/Average: The minimum award for the first year of the grant is $75,000/fiscal year; avg. $110,000/fiscal year.

Funding: (Project Grants (Discretionary)) FY 17 $64,880,000.00; FY 18 est $64,340,000.00; FY 19 est $45,746,000.00

HQ: 1200 Pennsylvania Avenue NW, PO Box 2690M, Washington, DC 20460

    Phone: 202-566-1387 | Email: roose.rebecca@epa.gov

    http://www.epa.gov

EPA66.931 | INTERNATIONAL FINANCIAL ASSISTANCE PROJECTS SPONSORED BY THE OFFICE OF INTERNATIONAL AND TRIBAL AFFAIRS

Award: Project Grants

Purpose: To protect human health and the environment while advancing U.S. national interests through international environmental collaboration.

Applicant Eligibility: Assistance under this Program is generally available to States and local Governments, territories and possessions, foreign Governments, international Organizations, Indian Tribes, and possessions of the U.S., including the District of Columbia, public and private universities and colleges, hospitals, laboratories, other public or private nonprofit Institutions, which submit applications proposing projects with significant technical merit and relevance to EPA's Office of International Affairs' mission. For certain competitive funding opportunities under this CFDA description, the Agency may limit eligibility to compete to a number or subset of eligible applicants consistent with the Agency's Assistance Agreement Competition Policy.

Beneficiary Eligibility: States and local governments, territories and possessions, foreign governments, international organizations, Indian Tribes, and possessions of the U.S., including the District of Columbia, public and private universities and colleges, hospitals, laboratories, other public or private nonprofit institutions.

Award Range/Average: Financial assistance for projects range: $15,000 - $300,000; Average: FY 2017 $200,000 and FY 2018 est. $150,000.

Funding: (Cooperative Agreements (Discretionary Grants)) FY 17 $4,000,000.00; FY 18 est $3,500,000.00; FY 19 est $1,500,000.00

HQ: 1200 Pennsylvania Avenue NW, Washington, DC 20460

    Phone: 202-564-5343 | Email: connell.lenore@epa.gov

    https://www.epa.gov/international-cooperation

EPA66.950 | NATIONAL ENVIRONMENTAL EDUCATION TRAINING PROGRAM
"Teacher Training Program"

Award: Cooperative Agreements

Purpose: To train education professionals in the development and delivery of environmental education and training programs and studies.

Applicant Eligibility: Assistance under this Program is available to universities, non-profit Organizations, or a consortia of such Institutions to deliver environmental education training and support for education professionals. For certain competitive funding opportunities under this CFDA assistance listing, the Agency may limit eligibility to compete to a number or subset of eligible applicants consistent with the Agency's Assistance Agreement Competition Policy.

Beneficiary Eligibility: Education (0-8), education (9-12), education (13+), nonprofit institutions.

Award Range/Average: This is a 5-year program; one recipient is selected every 5 years. The project is funded on an annual basis and the amount of the annual funding depends on Congressional appropriation. In this case, per the National Environmental Education Act,25% of the annual appropriation and average financial assistance for the full 5-year project period is approximately $10,877,500.00.

Funding: (Cooperative Agreements (Discretionary Grants)) FY 17 $2,157,500.00; FY 18 est $3,000,000.00; FY 19 est Estimate Not Available

HQ: 1200 Pennsylvania Avenue NW, Washington, DC 20460

    Phone: 202-564-0453 | Email: potter.ginger@epa.gov

    http://www.epa.gov/education

Programs Administered by Regional - State - Local Offices

EPA66.951 | ENVIRONMENTAL EDUCATION GRANTS

Award: Project Grants

Purpose: To supports projects to design, demonstrate, and/or disseminate practices, methods, or techniques related to environmental education and teacher training.

Applicant Eligibility: Assistance under this Program is generally available to local education agencies, colleges and universities, state education and environmental agencies, nonprofit Organizations described in Section 501(c)(3) of the Internal Revenue Service, and noncommercial educational broadcasting entities as defined and licensed by the Federal Communications Commission. Applicant Organizations must be located in the United States or territories and the majority of the educational activities must take place in the United States, Canada, or Mexico. "Tribal education agencies" that are eligible to apply include a school or community college which is controlled by an Indian tribe, band, or nation, which is recognized as eligible for special Programs and services provided by the United States to Indians because of their status as Indians and which is not administered by the Bureau of Indian education. Tribal Organizations do not qualify unless they meet that criteria or the environmental agency or non-profit criteria listed above. The terms for eligibility are defined in Section 3 of the Act and 40 CFR 47. 105. For certain competitive funding opportunities under this CFDA description, the Agency may limit eligibility to compete to a number or subset of eligible applicants consistent with the Agency's Assistance Agreement Competition Policy.

Beneficiary Eligibility: Education (0-8), education (9-12), education (13+), nonprofit institutions and organizations, state and local government agencies.

Award Range/Average: The dollar range stated in the FY 2016 EE Local Grants solicitation notice was no more than $91,000 per grant. In FY16 and FY17 the average amount awarded per EE grant was approximately $90,000. The FY 2018 solicitation notice listed a range of $50,000 - $100,000, and the selected proposals are expected to be awarded grants mostly in the $80,000 - $100,000 range.

Funding: (Project Grants (Discretionary)) FY 17 $3,306,600.00; FY 18 est $3,000,000.00; FY 19 est Estimate Not Available

HQ: 1200 Pennsylvania Avenue NW, PO Box 1704A, Washington, DC 20460

Phone: 202-564-2194 | Email: scott.karen@epa.gov

https://www.epa.gov/education

EPA66.956 | TARGETED AIR SHEDS GRANT PROGRAM
"Targeted Air Sheds"

Award: Project Grants

Purpose: To reduce air pollution in the nation's nonattainment areas with the highest levels of ozone and fine particulate matter (PM2.5) ambient air concentrations.

Applicant Eligibility: Entities eligible to receive targeted airshed grants are those air pollution control agencies, as defined by Section 302(b) of the Clean Air Act (CAA), that: (a) have responsibilities for development and/or implementation of a State Implementation Plan or Tribal Implementation Plan to attain and maintain national ambient air quality standards for either ozone or PM2. 5 within one or more of the top five most polluted areas relative to ozone (O3), annual average fine particulate matter (PM2. 5), or 24-hour PM2. 5 National Ambient Air Quality Standards (NAAQS); and (b) have an active air Program grant under Section 103 or 105 of the CAA to carry out those responsibilities.

Beneficiary Eligibility: Certain state, local, and tribal air pollution control agencies, as defined by Section 302(b) of the Clean Air Act (CAA).

Award Range/Average: In FY17 EPA awarded 9 targeted airshed grants. The funding amount range was $3,184,875 to $4,000,000 and the average value of each grant was $3,275,444. In FY19, EPA plans to award 6-12 grants, valued at $3,000,000 to $7,000,000 each (total $39,086,491), subject to the quality of applications received.

Funding: (Project Grants) FY 17 $29,479,000.00; FY 18 est $39,086,491.00; FY 19 est $40,000,000.00

HQ: 109 TW Alexander Drive, PO Box 304-05, Research Triangle Park, NC 27709

Phone: 919-541-3223 | Email: blais.gary@epa.gov

http://www.epa.gov/grants/air-grants-and-funding

EQUAL EMPLOYMENT OPPORTUNITY COMMISSION
Regional – State – Local Offices

Alabama

Delner Franklin-Thomas, Director | 1130 22nd Street S Suite 200, Birmingham, AL 35205 205-212-2089

Erika E. La'Cour, Director | 63 S Royal Street Suite 504, Mobile, AL 36602 251-690-3001

Programs Administered by Regional - State - Local Offices

Arizona

Elizabeth T. Cadle, Acting Director | Norwest Tower 3300 N Central Avenue Suite 690, Phoenix, AZ 85012-2504 602-640-5015

Arkansas

William A. Cash, Director | 820 Louisiana Street Suite 200, Little Rock, AR 72201 501-324-5539

California

Christopher Green, Director | 555 W Beech Street Suite 504, San Diego, CA 92101 619-557-7235

Dana C. Johnson, Director | 1301 Clay Street Suite 1170-N, Oakland, CA 94612-5217 510-637-3242

Melissa Barrios, Director | 2300 Tulare Street, Fresno, CA 93721 559-487-5793

Rosa M. Viramontes, Director | 255 E Temple Avenue 4th Floor, Los Angeles, CA 90012 213-894-1000

Terrie B. Brodie, Acting Director | 96 N 3rd Street Suite 200, San Jose, CA 95112 408-291-7447

William R. Tamayo, Director | Phillip Burton Federal Building Suite 5000 450 Golden Gate Avenue, San Francisco, CA 94102-3661 415-625-5611

Colorado

Amy Burkholder, Acting Director | 303 E 17th Avenue Suite 510, Denver, CO 80203-9634 303-866-1311

District of Columbia

Mindy Weinstein, Acting Director | 131 M Street NE, Washington, DC 20507 202-419-0711

Florida

Evangeline Hawthorne, Director | 501 E Polk Street Room 1000, Tampa, FL 33602 813-228-7953

Michael J. Farrell, Director | 100 SE 2nd Street Suite 1500, Miami, FL 33131 305-808-1740

Georgia

Darrell Graham, District Director | 100 Alabama Street Suite 4R30, Atlanta, GA 30303 404-562-6930

Omayra Padilla, Director | 7391 Hodgson Suite 200, Savannah, GA 31406-2579 912-652-4077

Hawaii

Glory A. Gervacio-Saure, Director | 300 Ala Moana Boulevard Room 7-127 PO Box 50082, Honolulu, HI 96850-0051 808-541-3118

Illinois

Julianne Bowman, Director | 500 W Madison Street Suite 2000, Chicago, IL 60661 312-869-8000

Indiana

Lloyd J. Vasquez, Acting Director | 101 W Ohio Street Suite 1900, Indianapolis, IN 46204-4203 317-226-7212

Kansas

Natascha DeGuire, Director | Gateway Tower II 400 State Avenue Suite 905, Kansas City, KS 66101 913-551-5692

Kentucky

Richard T. Burgamy, Director | U.S. Post Office & Courthouse 600 Martin Luther King Jr Place Suite 268, Louisville, KY 40202 502-582-6082

Louisiana

Keith T. Hill, Director | Hale Boggs Federal 500 Poydras Street Room 809, New Orleans, LA 70112 504-595-2826

Maryland

Rosemarie Rhodes, Director | City Crescent Building 10 S Howard Street 3rd Floor, Baltimore, MD 21201 410-209-2624

Massachusetts

Feng K. An, Director | John F Kennedy Federal Building Government Center 4th Floor 1 Congress Street Room 475, Boston, MA 02203-0506 617-565-4805

Michigan

Gail Cober, Director | McNamara Federal Building 477 Michigan Avenue Suite 865, Detroit, MI 48226-9704 313-226-4600

Minnesota

Julie Schmid, Acting Director | 330 S 2nd Avenue Suite 720, Minneapolis, MN 55401-2224 612-335-4040

Mississippi

Wilma Scott, Director | Dr A H McCoy Federal Building 100 W Capitol Street Suite 207, Jackson, MS 39269 601-948-8400

Missouri

James R. Neely, Director | Robert A Young Building 1222 Spruce Street Room 8100, Saint Louis, MO 63103 314-539-7831

Nevada

333 Las Vegas Boulevard S Suite 8112, Las Vegas, NV 89101 702-388-5013

New Jersey

John Waldinger, Director | One Newark Center 21st Floor, Newark, NJ 07102-5233 973-645-4689

New Mexico

Derrick Newton, Director | 505 Marquette Avenue NW Suite 900, Albuquerque, NM 87102-2189 505-248-5201

New York

John E. Thompson, Director | 6 Fountain Plaza Suite 350, Buffalo, NY 14202 716-551-4442

Kevin J. Berry, Director | 33 Whitehall Street 5th Floor, New York, NY 10004-2112 212-336-3705

North Carolina

Arlene M. Glover, Acting Director | 2303 W Meadowview Road Suite 201, Greensboro, NC 27407 336-547-4188

Rueben Daniels, Director | 129 W Trade Street Suite 400, Charlotte, NC 28202 704-954-6422

Thomas Colclough, Acting Director | 434 Fayetteville Street Suite 700, Raleigh, NC 27601-1701 919-856-4085

Programs Administered by Regional - State - Local Offices

Ohio

Cheryl Mabry-Thomas, Director | Anthony J Celebrezze Federal Building 1240 E 9th Street Suite 3001, Cleveland, OH 44199 216-522-7447

John W. Peck | Federal Office Building 550 Main Street Suite 10-019, Cincinnati, OH 45202-5202 513-684-3967

Oklahoma

Holly J. Cole, Director | 215 Dean A McGee Avenue Suite 524, Oklahoma City, OK 73102-2265 405-231-4356

Pennsylvania

Jamie Williamson, Director | 801 Market Street 13th Floor, Philadelphia, PA 19103 215-440-2624

Roosevelt L. Bryant, Acting Director | William S Moorhead Federal Building 1000 Liberty Avenue Suite 1112, Pittsburgh, PA 15222-4187 412-395-5902

Puerto Rico

William Sanchez, Director | Plaza Las Americas 525 FD Roosevelt Avenue Suite 1202, San Juan, PR 00918-8001 787-771-1464

South Carolina

Patricia Bynum-Fuller, Director | 301 N Main Street Suite 1402, Greenville, SC 29601 864-241-4407

Tennessee

Katharine Kores, Director | 1407 Union Avenue 9th Floor, Memphis, TN 38104 901-544-1051

Sarah Smith, Director | 220 Athens Way Suite 350, Nashville, TN 37228 615-736-5820

Texas

Lucy V. Orta, Director | 300 E Main Street Suite 500, El Paso, TX 79901 915-534-4192

Pedro Esquivel, Director | 5410 Fredericksburg Road Suite 200, San Antonio, TX 78229-3555 210-281-2550

Rayford O. Irvin, Director | Mickey Leland Federal Building 1919 Smith Street 7th Floor, Houston, TX 77002 713-651-4951

Shirley Richardson, Director | 207 S Houston Street 3rd Floor, Dallas, TX 75202-4726 214-253-4726

Virginia

Daron L. Calhoun, Director | 400 N 8th Street Suite 350, Richmond, VA 23219 804-771-2200

Norberto Rosa-Ramos, Director | Federal Building 200 Granby Street Suite 739, Norfolk, VA 23510 757-441-6678

Washington

Nancy A. Sienko, Director | Federal Office Building 909 1st Avenue Suite 400, Seattle, WA 98104-1061 206-220-6870

Wisconsin

Rosemary J. Fox, Director | Henry S Reuss Federal Plaza 310 W Wisconsin Avenue Suite 500, Milwaukee, WI 53203-2292 414-297-1112

EEOC30.001 | EMPLOYMENT DISCRIMINATION TITLE VII OF THE CIVIL RIGHTS ACT OF 1964

Award: Advisory Services and Counseling; Investigation of Complaints; Federal Employment

Purpose: To prohibit employment discrimination against applicants or employees based on race, color, religion, sex (including pregnancy, gender and sexual orientation), and national origin.

Applicant Eligibility: Any aggrieved individual, or any individual, Organization, or agency filing on behalf of an aggrieved individual, who has reason to believe that an unlawful employment practice within the meaning of Title VII, as amended, has been committed by an employer with 15 or more employees, a state or local government entity, an employment agency, labor Organization, or joint labor-management committee controlling apprenticeship or other training or retraining, including on-the-job training Programs. Any aggrieved individual who believes he or she has been retaliated against for opposing employment practices that discriminate, or who testifies, or participates in any way in an investigation, proceeding, or litigation under Title VII.

Beneficiary Eligibility: Applicants, current employees, or former employees of the named respondent(s) who have been subjected to employment practices based on race, color, religion, sex, or national origin by the named respondent(s), and/or who have been subjected to retaliation for opposing discrimination or participating in a Title VII investigation, proceeding, or litigation.

Award Range/Average: Not Applicable.

Funding: (Salaries and Expenses) FY 17 $364,500,000.00; FY 18 est $379,500,000.00; FY 19 est $363,807,000.00

HQ: Office of Communications and Legislative Affairs 131 M Street NE, Washington, DC 20507

Phone: 202-663-4191

http://www.eeoc.gov

EEOC30.005 | EMPLOYMENT DISCRIMINATION PRIVATE BAR PROGRAM

Award: Provision of Specialized Services

Purpose: To assist individuals who have filed a charge with the Commission, or on whose behalf a charge has been filed, in contacting members of the private bar.

Applicant Eligibility: Any individual who has filed a charge with the Commission, or on whose behalf a charge has been filed.
Beneficiary Eligibility: Same as Applicant Eligibility.
Award Range/Average: Not Applicable.
Funding: (Provision of Specialized Services) FY 17 $364,500,000.00; FY 18 est $379,500,000.00; FY 19 est $363,807,000.00
HQ: Office of General Counsel 131 M Street NE, Washington, DC 20507
　　Phone: 202-663-4719
　　http://www.eeoc.gov

EEOC30.008 | EMPLOYMENT DISCRIMINATION AGE DISCRIMINATION IN EMPLOYMENT

Award: Advisory Services and Counseling; Investigation of Complaints; Federal Employment
Purpose: Prohibits discrimination based on age (40 or older) with respect to any term, condition, or privilege of employment, including hiring, firing, promotion, layoff, compensation, benefits, job assignments, training and harassment.
Applicant Eligibility: Any aggrieved individuals age 40 and over, or any individual, Organization, or agency filing on behalf of an aggrieved individual who has reason to believe that a covered employer has committed an unlawful employment practice within the meaning of the ADEA, as amended.
Beneficiary Eligibility: Applicants, current employees, or former employees of the named respondent(s) who are age 40 or older and who have been subjected to unlawful employment practices based on age by the named respondent(s), and/or who have been subjected to retaliation for opposing age discrimination, filing a charge of discrimination, or participating in an ADEA investigation, proceeding, or litigation.
Award Range/Average: Not Applicable.
Funding: (Investigation of Complaints) FY 17 $364,500,000.00; FY 18 est $379,500,000.00; FY 19 est $363,807,000.00
HQ: Office of Communications and Legislative Affairs 131 M Street NE, Washington, DC 20507
　　Phone: 202-663-4191
　　http://www.eeoc.gov

EEOC30.010 | EMPLOYMENT DISCRIMINATION EQUAL PAY ACT

Award: Advisory Services and Counseling; Investigation of Complaints; Federal Employment
Purpose: Prohibits sex discrimination in the payment of wages to men and women performing jobs that require substantially equal skill, effort and responsibility, under similar working conditions within the same establishment.
Applicant Eligibility: Any aggrieved individual, or any individual, Organization, or agency filing on behalf of an aggrieved individual, who has reason to believe that a covered employer has committed an unlawful employment practice within the meaning of the EPA. An employee who believes he or she has been retaliated against for opposing compensation practices that discriminate based on sex or who files a discrimination charge, testifies, or participates in any way in an investigation, proceeding, or litigation under the EPA.
Beneficiary Eligibility: Applicants, current employees, or former employees of the named respondent (s) who have been subjected to unlawful compensation practices based on gender by the named respondent (s), and/or who have been subjected to retaliation for filing a charge of discrimination, for opposing gender-based compensation discrimination or participating in an EPA investigation, proceeding, or for litigation.
Award Range/Average: Not Applicable.
Funding: (Investigation of Complaints) FY 17 $364,500,000.00; FY 18 est $379,500,000.00; FY 19 est $363,807,000.00
HQ: 131 M Street NE, Washington, DC 20507
　　Phone: 202-663-4191
　　http://www.eeoc.gov

EEOC30.011 | EMPLOYMENT DISCRIMINATION TITLE I OF THE AMERICANS WITH DISABILITIES ACT

Award: Advisory Services and Counseling; Investigation of Complaints; Federal Employment
Purpose: Prohibits employment discrimination against applicants or employees based on disability.
Applicant Eligibility: Any aggrieved individual, or any individual, or any Organization, or agency filing on behalf of an aggrieved individual, who has reason to believe that an unlawful employment practice within the meaning of Title I of the ADA has been committed by an employer with 15 or more employees, including state or local Governments, an employment agency, labor Organization, or joint labor-management committee controlling apprenticeship or other training or retraining,

Programs Administered by Regional - State - Local Offices

including on-the-job training Programs. Any aggrieved individual who believes he or she has been retaliated against for opposing employment practices that discriminate based on disability or who files an ADA charge, testifies, or participates in any way in an investigation, proceeding, or litigation under the ADA. Federal employees are protected from disability discrimination under section 501 of the Rehabilitation Act.

Beneficiary Eligibility: Applicants, for employment, current employees, and former employees of the named respondent(s) in a charge who have been subjected to unlawful employment practices based on disability by the named respondent (s), and/or who have been subjected to retaliation for filing a charge of discrimination, for opposing disability discrimination or for participating in an ADA or Rehabilitation Act investigation, proceeding, or litigation.

Award Range/Average: Not Applicable.

Funding: (Investigation of Complaints) FY 17 $364,500,000.00; FY 18 est $379,500,000.00; FY 19 est $363,807,000.00

HQ: Office of Communications and Legislative Affairs 131 M Street NE, Washington, DC 20507
    Phone: 202-663-4191
    http://www.eeoc.gov

EEOC30.013 | EMPLOYMENT DISCRIMINATION-TITLE II OF THE GENETIC INFORMATION NONDISCRIMINATION ACT OF 2008
"GINA Title II"

Award: Advisory Services and Counseling; Investigation of Complaints; Federal Employment

Purpose: Prohibits the use of genetic information in making employment decisions, restricts employers and other entities covered by Title II from requesting, requiring or purchasing genetic information, and strictly limits the disclosure of genetic information.

Applicant Eligibility: Any aggrieved individual, or any individual, labor union, association, legal representative, or Organization filing on behalf of an aggrieved individual, who has reason to believe that an unlawful employment practice within the meaning of Title II of GINA has been committed by an employer, federal agency, an employment agency, labor Organization, or joint labor-management committee controlling apprenticeship or other training or retraining, or on-the-job training Programs. Any aggrieved individual who believes that he or she has been retaliated against for opposing employment practices that discriminate on the basis of genetic information or who files a charge of discrimination, testifies, or participates in any way in an investigation, proceeding, or litigation under Title II of GINA.

Beneficiary Eligibility: Applicants, current employees, or former employees of the named respondent(s) who have been subjected to employment practices based on genetic information by the named respondent(s), and/or who have been subjected to retaliation for filing a charge of discrimination, opposing discrimination or participating in a Title II of GINA investigation, proceeding, or litigation.

Award Range/Average: Not Applicable.

Funding: (Salaries and Expenses) FY 18 $364,500,000.00; FY 19 est $364,500,000.00; FY 20 est $363,807,086.00

HQ: Office of Communications and Legislative Affairs 131 M Street NE, Washington, DC 20507
    Phone: 202-663-4191
    http://www.eeoc.gov

FARM SERVICE AGENCY
Regional – State – Local Offices

SERVICE CENTER

Alabama
Daniel Robinson | Alabama State FSA Office PO Box 235013 4121 Carmichael Road Suite 600, Montgomery, AL 36106-5013 334-279-3500

Alaska
Karen Olson | Alaska State FSA Office 800 W Evergreen Suite 216, Palmer, AK 99645-6389 907-745-7982

Arizona
George Arrendondo | Arizona State FSA Office 77 E Thomas Road Suite 240, Phoenix, AZ 85012-3318 602-640-5200

Arkansas
Mike Dunaway | Arkansas State FSA Office Federal Building Room 5416 700 W Capitol Avenue, Little Rock, AR 72201-3225 501-301-3000

California
Valente Dolcini, State Executive Director | California State FSA Office 430 G Street Suite 4161, Davis, CA 95616-4161 530-792-5538

Colorado
Robert Eisenach | Colorado State FSA Office 655 Parfet Street Suite E305, Lakewood, CO 80215-5517 303-236-2866

Programs Administered by Regional - State - Local Offices

Connecticut
Harvey Polinsky | Connecticut State FSA Office 88 Day Hill Road, Windsor, CT 06095 860-285-8483

Delaware
William Donald Clifton II | Delaware State FSA Office 1201 College Park Drive Suite 101, Dover, DE 19904-8713 302-678-2547

Florida
Kevin L. Kelley | Florida State FSA Office 440 NW 25th Place Suite 1, Gainesville, FL 32606 352-379-4500

Georgia
Hanson Carter | Georgia State FSA Office PO Box 1907 Federal Building Room 102 355 E Hancock Avenue, Athens, GA 30603-1907 706-546-2266

Hawaii
Jo-Anna Nakata | Hawaii State FSA Office 300 Ala Moana Boulevard Room 5106 PO Box 50008, Honolulu, HI 96850 808-541-2644

Idaho
Richard R. Rush | Idaho State FSA Office 9173 W Barners Suite B, Boise, ID 83705-1511 208-378-5650

Illinois
Stephen Scates | Illinois State FSA Office PO Box 19273 3500 West Avenue, Springfield, IL 62794-9273 217-241-6600

Indiana
Robert D. Peacock | Indiana State FSA Office 5981 Lakeside Boulevard, Indianapolis, IN 46278 317-290-3030, Ext. 317

Iowa
Robert Soukup | Iowa State FSA Office 10500 Buena Vista Court, Des Moines, IA 50322 515-254-1540, Ext. 600

Kansas
Adrian J. Polansky | Kansas State FSA Office 3600 Anderson Avenue, Manhattan, KS 66502-2511 785-539-3531

Kentucky
Hampton Henton | Kentucky State FSA Office 771 Corporate Drive Suite 100, Lexington, KY 40503-5478 606-224-7601

Louisiana
Willie F. Cooper | Louisiana State FSA Office 3737 Government Street, Alexandria, LA 71302-3395 318-473-7721

Maine
G.Arnold Roach | Maine State FSA Office 444 Stillwater Avenue Suite 1 PO Box 406, Bangor, ME 04402-0406 207-990-9140

Maryland
James M. Voss | Maryland State FSA Office River Center 8335 Guilford Road Suite E, Columbia, MD 21046 410-381-4550

Massachusetts
Charles A. Costa | Massachusetts State FSA Office 445 W Street, Amherst, MA 01002-2957 413-256-0232

Michigan
Chris White | Michigan State FSA Office 3001 Coolidge Road Suite 100, East Lansing, MI 48823-6321 517-337-6659, Ext. 1201

Minnesota
Linda Hennen, State Executive Director | Minnesota State FSA Office 400 Farm Credit Service Building 375 Jackson Street, Saint Paul, MN 55101-1852 612-602-7700

Mississippi
David Warrington | Mississippi State FSA Office PO Box 14995 6310 Interstate 55 N, Jackson, MS 39211 601-965-4300

Missouri
Brad Epperson | Missouri State FSA Office 601 Business Loop 70 W Suite 225 Parkade Plaza, Columbia, MO 65203 573-876-0925

Montana
Bruce E. Nelson | Montana State FSA Office PO Box 670 10 E Babcock Street Room 557, Bozeman, MT 59715 406-587-6872

Nebraska
Mark Bowen | Nebraska State FSA Office PO Box 57975 7131 A Street, Lincoln, NE 68510-7975 402-437-5581

Nevada
Wendell K. Newman | Nevada State FSA Office 1755 E Plumb Lane Suite 202, Reno, NV 89502-3207 775-784-5411

New Hampshire
James McConaha | USDA-New Hampshire State FSA Office 22 Bridge Street 4th Floor PO Box 1388, Concord, NH 03302-1338 603-224-7941

New Jersey
Debbie Borie Holtz | New Jersey State FSA Office Mastoris Professional Plaza 163 Route 130 Building 2 Suite E, Bordentown, NJ 08505-2249 609-298-3446

New Mexico
Larry Burnett | New Mexico State FSA Office 6200 Jefferson Street NE, Albuquerque, NM 87109 505-761-4900

New York
Marc A. Smith | New York State FSA Office 441 S Salina Street Suite 356 5th Floor, Syracuse, NY 13202-2455 315-477-6303

North Carolina
Phillip Farland | N Carolina State FSA Office 4407 Bland Road Suite 175, Raleigh, NC 27609-6296 919-875-4800

North Dakota
Scott Stofferahn | N Dakota State FSA Office 1025 28th Street SW PO Box 3046, Fargo, ND 58108 701-239-5205

Ohio
Steve Maurer | Ohio State FSA Office Federal Building Room 540 200 N High Street, Columbus, OH 43215 614-469-6735

Programs Administered by Regional - State - Local Offices

Oklahoma
Terry L. Peach | Oklahoma State FSA Office 100 USDA Suite 102 Farm Road & McFarland Street, Stillwater, OK 74074-2653 405-742-1130

Oregon
Jack L. Sainsbury | Oregon State FSA Office 7620 SW Mohawk PO Box 1300, Tualatin, OR 97062-8121 503-692-6830

Pennsylvania
William H. Baumgartner | Pennsylvania State FSA Office One Credit Union Place Suite 320, Harrisburg, PA 17110-2994 717-237-2113

Puerto Rico
Heriberto J. Martinez | PO Box 11188 Fernandez Junzos Station Suite 309 Cobian's Plaza 1607 Ponce DeLeon Avenue, Santurce, PR 00909-0001 809-729-6872

Rhode Island
Paul E. Brule | Rhode Island State FSA Office 60 Quaker Lane West Bay Office Complex Room 40, Warwick, RI 02886-0111 401-828-8232

South Carolina
Laurie C. Lawson | S Carolina State FSA Office 1927 Thurmond Mall Suite 100, Columbia, SC 29201-2375 803-806-3830

South Dakota
Michael O'Connor | S Dakota State FSA Office 200 4th Street SW Room 308 Federal Building, Huron, SD 57350-2478 605-352-1160

Tennessee
David McDole | Tennessee State FSA Office 579 U.S. Courthouse 801 Broadway, Nashville, TN 37203-3816 615-736-5555

Texas
Wayland Shurley | Texas State FSA Office Commerce National Bank Building 2nd Floor 2405 Texas Avenue S 77840 PO Box 2900, College Station, TX 77841-0001 409-260-9207

Utah
James L. Humlicek | Utah State FSA Office 125 S State Street Room 4239 PO Box 11350, Salt Lake City, UT 84147-0350 801-524-5013

Vermont
Ronald Allbee | Vermont State FSA Office Executive Square Office Building 346 Shelburne Street, Burlington, VT 05401-4995 802-658-2803

Virginia
Donald Davis | Virginia State FSA Office Culpeper Building Suite 138 1606 Santa Rosa Road, Richmond, VA 23229 804-287-1500

Washington
Larry R. Albin | Washington State FSA Office Rock Pointe Tower Suite 568 316 W Boone Avenue, Spokane, WA 99201-2350 509-323-3000

West Virginia
Billy B. Burke | W Virginia State FSA Office New Federal Building 75 High Street Room 239 PO Box 1049, Morgantown, WV 26507-1049 304-291-4351

Wisconsin
Douglas J. Caruso | Wisconsin State FSA Office 6515 Watts Road Room 100, Madison, WI 53719-2797 608-276-8732, Ext. 100

Wyoming
Carl Jensen | Wyoming State FSA Office 951 Werner Court Suite 130, Casper, WY 82601-1307 307-261-5231

USDA10.053 | DAIRY INDEMNITY PROGRAM
"DIPP"

Award: Direct Payments With Unrestricted Use
Purpose: To assist the dairy farmers and manufacturers through compensation because of contamination and other toxic substances.
Applicant Eligibility: Dairy farmers whose milk has been removed from the market by a public agency because of residue of any violating substance in such milk. Manufacturers of dairy products whose product has been removed from the market by a public agency because of pesticide residue in such product. This Program is also available in Puerto Rico.
Beneficiary Eligibility: Dairy farmers whose milk has been removed from the market by a public agency because of residue of any violating substance in such milk. Manufacturers of dairy products whose product has been removed from the market by a public agency because of pesticide residue in such product. This program is available in Puerto Rico.
Award Range/Average: No Payment Limitation.
Funding: (Direct Payments with Unrestricted Use) FY 18 $173,000.00; FY 19 est $3,439,646.00; FY 20 est $500,000.00
HQ: 1400 Independence Avenue SW, Washington, DC 20250-0512
Phone: 202-720-1919 | Email: danielle.cooke@wdc.usda.gov
http://www.fsa.usda.gov/programs-and-services/price-support/index

USDA10.054 | EMERGENCY CONSERVATION PROGRAM
"ECP"

Award: Direct Payments for Specified Use

Purpose: To help out farmers to incorporate the habit of water conservation to face drought and other natural calamities.

Applicant Eligibility: Any agricultural producer who as owner, landlord, tenant, or sharecropper on a farm or ranch, including associated groups, and bears a part of the cost of an approved conservation practice in a disaster area, is eligible to apply for cost-share conservation assistance. This Program is also available in American Samoa, Guam, Commonwealth of the Northern Mariana Islands, Puerto Rico, and the Virgin Islands.

Beneficiary Eligibility: Same as Applicant Eligibility.

Funding: (Direct Payments with Unrestricted Use) FY 18 $176,461,000.00; FY 19 est $260,000,000.00; FY 20 est $200,000,000.00

HQ: 1400 Independence Avenue SW, Washington, DC 20250

Phone: 202-205-4537 | Email: martin.bomar@wdc.usda.gov

http://www.fsa.usda.gov/programs-and-services/conservation-programs/emergency-conservation/index

USDA10.055 | DIRECT AND COUNTER-CYCLICAL PAYMENTS PROGRAM
"DCP"

Award: Direct Payments for Specified Use

Purpose: To provide a stable income for covered commodity producers.

Applicant Eligibility: To be eligible for payments under DCP, owners, operators, landlords, tenants, or sharecroppers must (1) share in the risk of producing a crop on base acres on a farm enrolled in DCP, and be entitled to share in the crop available for marketing from the base acres, or would have shared had a crop been produced; (2) annually report the use of the farm's cropland acreage; (3) comply with conservation and wetland protection requirements on all of their land; (4) comply with planting flexibility requirements; (5) use the base acres for agricultural or related activities; and (5) protect all base acres from erosion, including providing sufficient cover as determined necessary by the county FSA committee, and control weeds.

Beneficiary Eligibility: DCP provides payments to eligible producers on farms enrolled for the 2008 through 2013 crop years.

USDA10.056 | FARM STORAGE FACILITY LOANS
"FSFL and SSFL"

Award: Direct Loans

Purpose: The Farm Storage Facility Loan program provides loan for farm products and cattle rearing based on the environmental evaluation and also provides loan for producers of sugarcane and raw sugar.

Applicant Eligibility: An eligible FSFL borrower is any person who, as landowner, landlord, operator, producer, tenant, leaseholder, or sharecropper: (1) Has a satisfactory credit history and demonstrates an ability to repay the debt arising under this Program using a financial statement acceptable to CCC prepared within 90 days of the date of application; (2) has no delinquent Federal debt defined by the Debt Collection Improvement Act of 1996 at the time of loan disbursement; (3) is a producer of a facility loan commodity as defined by CCC; (4) demonstrates a need for storage capacity as defined by CCC; (5) provides proof of crop insurance offered under the Federal Crop Insurance Program for crops of economic significance on all farms operated by the borrower in the county where the storage facility is located; (6) is in compliance with USDA provisions for highly erodible land and wetlands provisions according to 7 CFR Part 12; (7) demonstrates compliance with any applicable local zoning, land use, and building codes for the applicable farm storage facility structures; (8) provides proof of flood insurance if CCC determines such insurance is necessary to protect the interests of CCC, and proof of all peril structural insurance, to CCC annually; (9) demonstrates compliance with the National Environmental Policy Act regulations at 40 CFR, Parts 1500- 1508; and (10) has not been convicted under Federal or State law of a controlled substance violation under 7 CFR Part 718. An eligible producer is the owner of a part or all of the domestically-grown sugar beets or sugarcane, including share rent landowners, at both the timer of harvest and the time of delivery to the processor. A sugar beet or sugarcane processor is eligible for loans only if the processor has agreed to all the terms and conditions in the loan application, and has executed a note and security agreement, and storage agreement with the Commodity Credit Corporation (CCC). Processors must: 1) Have a satisfactory credit history; 2) Demonstrate a need for increased storage capacity; 3) Demonstrate compliance with an applicable local zoning, land use and building codes; 4) Annually provide CCC proof of all-peril insurance on the structure; 5) Demonstrate compliance with the National Environmental Policy Act; 6) Not have been convicted under federal or State law of disqualifying controlled substance violation; and 7) Be approved by CCC to

Programs Administered by Regional - State - Local Offices

store sugar either owned or pledged as security to CCC. SSFL must be approved by the local FSA state or county committee before any site preparation, construction, and/or acquisition can be started. All loan requests are subject to an environmental evaluation. Accepting delivery of equipment, starting any site preparation, or construction before loan approval, may impede the successful completion of an environmental evaluation and may adversely affect loan eligibility.

Beneficiary Eligibility: Applicants/borrowers are the direct beneficiaries when they meet all eligibility criteria. Landowners, landlords, operators, producers, tenants, leaseholders, or sharecroppers are the beneficiaries. The authorized SSFL will be used by the processor for the construction or upgrading of storage and handling facilities for raw sugars and refined sugars.

Funding: (Direct Loans) FY 18 $245,952,000.00; FY 19 est $308,500,000.00; FY 20 est $308,500,000.00

HQ: USDA-FSA-PSD 1400 Independence Avenue SW, PO Box 0512, Washington, DC 20250-0512

Phone: 202-720-2270 | Email: toni.williams@usda.gov

http://www.fsa.usda.gov/fsa/webapp?area=home&subject=prsu&topic=flp

USDA10.069 | CONSERVATION RESERVE PROGRAM
"CRP"

Award: Direct Payments for Specified Use

Purpose: To safeguard natural food, water, and improve wildlife.

Applicant Eligibility: An individual, partnership, association, Indian Tribal ventures corporation, estate, trust, other business enterprises or other legal entities and, whenever applicable, a State, a political subdivision of a State, or any agency thereof may submit an offer to enroll acreage.

Beneficiary Eligibility: If their offer is accepted for enrollment, an individual, partnership, association, Indian Tribal ventures, corporation, estate, trust, other business enterprises or other legal entities and, whenever applicable, a State, political subdivision of State, or any agency thereof may earn benefits.

Funding: (Direct Payments with Unrestricted Use) FY 18 $1,953,083,000.00; FY 19 est $2,086,496,000.00; FY 20 est $2,105,453,000.00

HQ: 1400 Independence Avenue SW, Washington, DC 20250

Phone: 202-720-9563 | Email: beverly.preston@wdc.usda.gov

http://www.fsa.usda.gov/programs-and-services/conservation-programs/conservation-reserve-program/index

USDA10.074 | COMMODITY CREDIT CORPORATION AUDIT OF FINANCIAL STATEMENTS
"CCC Audit of Financial Statements"

Award: Direct Payments With Unrestricted Use

Purpose: The program provides a contract to a private Audit Firm to conduct an audit of CCC's financial statement.

Applicant Eligibility: CCC is a government owned cooperation that will use funds to solicit the most qualified and cost effective contract within a reasonable range.

Beneficiary Eligibility: The audit firm will perform the required audit services using a firm fixed price contract. This has resulted in a reduction of total costs in the requested funding.

Award Range/Average: Not Applicable.

Funding: (Salaries and Expenses) FY 17 $1,483,931,000.00; FY 18 est $1,525,248,000.00; FY 19 est $1,187,403,000.00

HQ: 355 E Street SW Patriot Plaza III, 11th Floor, Washington, DC 20024

Phone: 202-772-6029 | Email: veronica.richardson@wdc.usda.gov

http://www.fsa.gov

USDA10.087 | BIOMASS CROP ASSISTANCE PROGRAM
"BCAP"

Award: Direct Payments With Unrestricted Use

Purpose: To promote biofuels and funds for the producers of renewable biomass products.

Applicant Eligibility: To be eligible to enter into a BCAP contract for the purposes of receiving an annual payment or establishment payments, a person or legal entity must be an owner, operator, or tenant of eligible land within a project area. Eligible land must be agricultural land or nonindustrial private forest land. Eligible agricultural land includes cropland; grassland; pastureland, rangeland, hay land, and other land on which food fiber, or other agricultural products are produced or capable of being legally produced for which a valid conservation plan exists and is implemented. Ineligible land is as follows: (1) Federal lands; (2) State-owned, municipal, or other local government-owned lands; (3) Native sod; and (4) Land that is already enrolled in CCC's CRP, Wetlands Reserve Program, or Grassland Reserve Program. Eligible crops for annual and establishment payments are renewable plant materials such as feed grains, other agricultural commodities, or other plants and trees, and algae; waste materials including vegetative waste, materials, such as woods wastes and wood residues, animal waste and byproducts, such as fats, oils, greases, and manure, food waste, and yard waste. Ineligible crops are any crop eligible to receive payments under Title I of the Food, Conservation, and Energy Act of 2008 (See 8-LP, paragraph 126 and 7-CN for Title I commodities); and any plant that is invasive or noxious or has the potential to become invasive or noxious. Eligible materials for matching payments include various types of renewable biomass collected or harvested directly from the land in accordance with an approved conservation plan, forest stewardship plan, or an equivalent plan before transport and delivery to the biomass conversion facility. Materials will only be eligible if USDA determines that there is no higher value use for that material within a reasonable distance of the biomass conversion facility. Matching payments are not available for the following products: (1) Material that is whole grain from any crop that is eligible to receive; payments under Title I of the Food, Conservation, and Energy Act of 2008 or an amendment made by that title, including, but not limited to, barley, corn, grain sorghum, oats, rice, or wheat; honey; or material that is mohair; certain oilseeds such as canola, crambe, flaxseed, mustard seed, rapeseed, safflower seed, soybeans, sesame seed, and sunflower seeds; peanuts; pulse crops such as small chickpeas, lentils, and dry peas; dairy products; sugar; wool; and cotton boll fiber; (2) Animal waste and by-products of animal waste including fats, oils, greases, and manure; (3) Food waste and yard waste; and (4) Algae. All eligible material must be harvested or collected directly from the land by the eligible material owner according to a conservation, forest stewardship, or equivalent plan and be separated from the higher value product before the point of delivery. Woody biomass harvested or collected outside of project area contracts is limited to eligible material resulting from preventative treatments to address fire fuel load reduction, insect or disease outbreaks, or restore ecosystem health. Woody biomass harvested or collected outside of project area contracts is limited to eligible materials that do not have an existing market for non-biomass use and cannot be co-mingled with higher product value materials. Eligible material owner, for purposes of the matching payment, means a person or entity having the right to collect or harvest eligible material, who has the risk of loss in the material that is delivered to an eligible facility and who has directly or by agent delivered or intends to deliver the eligible material to a qualified biomass conversion facility, including: (1) For eligible material harvested or collected from private lands, including cropland, the owner of the land, the operator or producer conducting farming operations on the land, or any other person designated by the owner of the land; and (2) For eligible material harvested or collected from public lands, a person having the right to harvest or collect eligible material pursuant to a contract or permit with the US Forest Service or other appropriate Federal agency, such as a timber sale contract, stewardship contract or agreement, service contract or permit, or related applicable Federal land permit or contract, and who has submitted a copy of the permit or contract authorizing such collection to CCC. Eligible facilities are biomass conversion facilities that convert or propose to convert renewable biomass into heat, power, bio based products, or advanced biofuels and have been approved for the BCAP Program by the CCC.

Beneficiary Eligibility: Owners and operators of agricultural and non-industrial private forest land will receive the ultimate benefits because it will provide financial assistance to establish, produce, and deliver biomass feedstocks. Eligible material owners who are the person or entity having the right to collect or harvest eligible material, who has the risk of loss in the material that is delivered to an eligible facility and who has directly or by agent delivered or intends to deliver the eligible material to a qualified biomass conversion facility.

Funding: (Direct Payments for Specified Use) FY 18 $1,308,000.00; FY 19 est $0.00; FY 20 est $0.00

HQ: 1400 Independence Avenue SW, Room 3649, Washington, DC 20250

Phone: 202-720-4053 | Email: kelly.novak@usda.gov

http://www.fsa.usda.gov/bcap

USDA10.099 | CONSERVATION LOANS

Award: Guaranteed/insured Loans

Purpose: To provide loan for the less financially established farmers for implementing conservation measures.

Applicant Eligibility: An applicant must (1) Not have caused a loss to the Agency after April 4, 1996, or received debt forgiveness on more than three occasions prior to April 4, 1996 to receive a guaranteed loan, and for a direct loan, must not have received debt forgiveness from the Agency on any direct or guaranteed loan; (2) be a U.S. citizen, non-citizen national or qualified alien; (3) posses the legal capacity to incur the obligations of the loan; (4) for a direct loan, have the necessary education and/or experience, training, and managerial ability to operate a farm; and (5) for a direct loan, fulfill the Agency's borrower training requirements. If the applicant is an entity, it must be controlled by farmers engaged primarily and directly in farming in the U.S., after the loan is made. Unlike other Agency loan Programs, Conservation Loans are not limited to applicants who are unable to obtain sufficient credit from other sources at reasonable rates and terms or to those who are the owner or operator of a not larger than family size farm. However, the applicant's operation must realistically project the ability to repay the loan.

Programs Administered by Regional - State - Local Offices

Beneficiary Eligibility: Applicants are the direct beneficiaries and must meet the applicant eligibility requirements. Families, individual, and entities who are farmers are the beneficiaries.

Award Range/Average: Maximum indebtedness for direct loans, combined; farm ownership, conservation, soil and water, and recreation $600,000. Maximum indebtedness for guaranteed loans combined: farm ownership, conservation, and soil and water loan indebtedness of $1,750,000 (for FY 2019, amount adjusted annually for inflation).

Funding: (Guaranteed/Insured Loans) FY 18 $150,000,000.00; FY 19 est $150,000,000.00; FY 20 est $150,000,000.00

HQ: 1400 Independence Avenue SW, Washington, DC 20250

    Phone: 202-690-0756 | Email: houston.bruck@usda.gov

    http://www.fsa.usda.gov/programs-and-services/farm-loan-programs/index

USDA10.102 | EMERGENCY FOREST RESTORATION PROGRAM
"EFRP"

Award: Direct Payments With Unrestricted Use

Purpose: This program assists an EFRP participant with financial assistance for the disasters caused by natural calamities.

Applicant Eligibility: To be eligible to participate in EFRP, a person or legal entity must be an owner of nonindustrial private forest land affected by a natural disaster, and must be liable for or have the expense that is the subject of the financial assistance. The owner must be a person or legal entity (including Indian Tribes) with full decision-making authority over the land, as determined by FSA, or with such waivers as may be needed from lenders or others as may be required, to undertake Program commitments. Federal agencies and States, including all agencies and political subdivisions of a State, are ineligible for EFRP. For land to be eligible, it must be nonindustrial private forest land and must, as determined by FSA. The land must have existing tree cover or have had tree cover immediately before the natural disaster and be suitable for growing trees, have damage to natural resources caused by a natural disaster, which occurred on or after January 1, 2010, that, if not treated, would impair or endanger the natural resources on the land and would materially affect future use of the land. The land must be physically located in a county in which EFRP has been implemented and is ineligible for EFRP if FSA determines that the land is owned or controlled by the United States, or owned or controlled by States, including State agencies or political subdivisions of a State. A qualifying natural disaster means wildfires, hurricanes or excessive winds, drought, ice storms or blizzards, floods, or other naturally-occurring resource impacting events as determined by FSA. For EFRP, a natural disaster also includes insect or disease infestations as determined by FSA in consultation with other Federal and State agencies as appropriate.

Beneficiary Eligibility: The owners of nonindustrial private forest land will receive the ultimate benefit.

Award Range/Average: Not Applicable.

Funding: (Direct Payments with Unrestricted Use) FY 18 $12,725,000.00; FY 19 est $15,000,000.00; FY 20 est $15,000,000.00

HQ: 1400 Independence Avenue SW, Washington, DC 20250

    Phone: 202-690-0794 | Email: james.michaels@wdc.usda.gov

    http://www.fsa.usda.gov/programs-and-services/disaster-assistance-program/emergency-forest-restoration/index

USDA10.106 | DISASTER RELIEF APPROPRIATIONS ACT, EMERGENCY FOREST RESTORATION PROGRAM
"Disaster Relief Appropriations Act, EFRP"

Award: Direct Payments for Specified Use; Direct Payments With Unrestricted Use

Purpose: This program assists an EFRP participant with financial assistance for the disasters caused by natural calamities.

Applicant Eligibility: To be eligible to participate in EFRP, a person or legal entity must be an owner of nonindustrial private forest land affected by a natural disaster, and must be liable for or have the expense that is the subject of the financial assistance. The owner must be a person or legal entity (including Indian Tribes) with full decision-making authority over the land, as determined by FSA, or with such waivers as may be needed from lenders or others as may be required, to undertake Program commitments. Federal agencies and States, including all agencies and political subdivisions of a State, are ineligible for EFRP. For land to be eligible, it must be nonindustrial private forest land and must, as determined by FSA. The land must have existing tree cover or have had tree cover immediately before the natural disaster and be suitable for growing trees, have damage to natural resources caused by a natural disaster, which occurred on or after January 1, 2010, that, if not treated, would impair or endanger the natural resources on the land and would materially affect future use of the land. The land must be physically located in a county in which EFRP has been implemented and is ineligible for EFRP if FSA determines that the land is owned or controlled by the United States, or owned or controlled by States, including State agencies or political subdivisions of a State. A qualifying natural disaster means wildfires, hurricanes or excessive winds, drought, ice storms or blizzards, floods, or other naturally-occurring resource impacting events as determined by FSA. For EFRP, a natural disaster also includes insect or disease infestations as determined by FSA in consultation with other Federal and State agencies as appropriate.

Beneficiary Eligibility: The owners of industrial private forest land will receive the ultimate benefit.

Funding: (Direct Payments with Unrestricted Use) FY 18 $5,751,000.00; FY 19 est $0.00; FY 20 est $0.00

HQ: 1400 Independence Avenue SW, Washington, DC 20250

Phone: 202-205-4537 | Email: martin.bomar@wdc.usda.gov

http://www.fsa.usda.gov/programs-and-services/disaster-assistance-program/emergency-forest-restoration/index

USDA10.108 | LIVESTOCK INDEMNITY PROGRAM-2014 FARM BILL "LIP"

Award: Direct Payments With Unrestricted Use

Purpose: To compensate those who have lost their livestock due to natural disasters.

Applicant Eligibility: To be eligible for benefits, an individual or legal entity must be a citizen of the United States (U.S.); Resident alien; Partnership of citizens of the U. S; or Corporation, limited liability corporation, or other farm Organizational structure organized under State law. An eligible livestock owner must have had legal ownership of the eligible livestock on the day the livestock died and under conditions in which no contract grower could have been eligible for benefits with respect to the animal. To be eligible an eligible owner's livestock must have died as a direct result of an eligible adverse weather event occurring on or after October 1, 2011, no later than 60 calendar days from the ending date of the applicable adverse weather event, and in the calendar year for which benefits are requested. An eligible contract grower must have had possession and control of the eligible livestock and a written agreement with the eligible livestock owner setting the specific terms, conditions and obligations of the parties involved regarding the production of livestock on the day the livestock died. An eligible livestock for a livestock owner must be alpacas, adult or non-adult dairy cattle, buffalo, beefalo, elk, emus, equine, llamas, sheep, goats, swine, poultry, deer, or reindeer. An eligible livestock for a contract grower must be poultry or swine. The eligible livestock must have been maintained for commercial use as part of a farming operation before dying and on the day the eligible livestock died. An eligible adverse weather event is defined as an extreme or abnormal damaging weather event that is not expected to occur during the loss period or which it occurred, which results in eligible livestock death losses in excess of normal mortality. This includes but not limited to earthquake, lightning, tornado, tropical storm, typhoon, vog if directly related to a volcanic eruption, winter storm that last for three consecutive days and is accompanied by high winds, freezing rain or sleet, heavy snowfall and extremely cold temperatures, hurricanes, floods, blizzards, wildfires, extreme heat, extreme cold, anthrax, and a disease if exacerbated by other eligible adverse weather event. Drought is not an eligible adverse weather event except when anthrax, which is exacerbated by drought, causes the death of eligible livestock.

Beneficiary Eligibility: The eligible livestock or contract owner will receive the ultimate benefit from LIP.

Funding: (Direct Payments with Unrestricted Use) FY 18 $36,615,000.00; FY 19 est $29,779,000.00; FY 20 est $28,300,000.00

HQ: 1400 Independence Avenue SW, PO Box 0517, Washington, DC 20250

Phone: 202-720-8954 | Email: amy.mitchell1@wdc.usda.gov

http://www.fsa.usda.gov

USDA10.109 | LIVESTOCK FORAGE PROGRAM-2014 FARM BILL "LFP"

Award: Direct Payments With Unrestricted Use

Purpose: The LFP compensates those who lost their livestock due to fire or natural calamities.

Applicant Eligibility: To be eligible for benefits, an individual or legal entity must be a citizen of the United States (U.S.); Resident alien; Partnership of citizens of the U.S.; or Corporation, limited liability corporation, or other farm organization structure organized under State law. An eligible livestock producer must own, cash or share lease, or be a contract grower of covered livestock during the 60 calendar days before the beginning date of a qualifying drought or fire; provide pastureland or grazing land for covered livestock, including cash-rented pastureland or grazing land that is either physically located in a country affected by a qualifying drought during the normal grazing period for the county, or rangeland managed by a federal agency and the eligible livestock producer is prohibited from grazing the normally permitted livestock because of a qualifying fire.

Beneficiary Eligibility: The eligible livestock or contract owner will receive the ultimate benefit from LFP.

Funding: (Direct Payments with Unrestricted Use) FY 18 $487,455,000.00; FY 19 est $801,418,000.00; FY 20 est $679,699,000.00

Programs Administered by Regional - State - Local Offices

HQ: 14th and Independence Avenue SW, PO Box 0517, Washington, DC 20250
  Phone: 202-720-7997 | Email: scotty.abbott@wdc.usda.gov
  http://www.fsa.usda.gov/programs-and-services/disaster-assistance-program/livestock-forage/index

USDA10.110 | EMERGENCY ASSISTANCE FOR LIVESTOCK, HONEYBEES AND FARM-RAISED FISH PROGRAM-2014 FARM BILL
"ELAP"

Award: Direct Payments for Specified Use
Purpose: The ELAP assists producers who have lost their livestock due to disease or other natural calamities.
Applicant Eligibility: To be eligible for benefits, an individual or legal entity must be a citizen of the United States (U.S.); Resident alien; Partnership of citizens of the U.S.; or Corporation, limited liability corporation, or other farm Organizational structure organized under State law. The eligible applicant must have legal ownership of the livestock on the day the livestock died and must be a producer or contract grower of livestock, honeybee, or farm-raised fish that assumes the production and market risks associated with the agricultural production of crops or livestock on a farm and that meet the requirements to receive ELAP payments. Starting with the 2012 Program year (October 1, 2011), an eligible livestock producer who certifies they are socially disadvantaged, limited resource, or a beginning farmer or rancher, will have their payments for livestock losses under ELAP based on a national payment factor of 90 percent.
Beneficiary Eligibility: Eligible producers of livestock, honeybees, and farm-raised fish will receive the ultimate benefits from ELAP. An eligible livestock producer, honeybee producer. and eligible farm-raised fish producer may receive payments for eligible losses based on a national payment rate.
Funding: (Direct Payments for Specified Use) FY 18 $47,064,000.00; FY 19 est $37,205,000.00; FY 20 est $32,219,000
HQ: USDA FSA Production Emergencies and Compliance Division 1400 Independence Avenue SW, PO Box 0517, Washington, DC 20250
  Phone: 202-720-8954 | Email: amy.mitchell1@wdc.usda.gov
  http://www.fsa.usda.gov/programs-and-services/disaster-assistance-program/emergency-assist-for-livestock-honey-bees-fish/index

USDA10.111 | TREE ASSISTANCE PROGRAM-2014 FARM BILL
"TAP"

Award: Direct Payments With Unrestricted Use
Purpose: TAP compensate orchardists and nursery growers for the damage caused by natural calamities.
Applicant Eligibility: To be eligible for benefits, an individual or legal entity must be a citizen of the United States (U.S.); Resident alien; Partnership of citizens of the U. S; or Corporation, limited liability corporation, or other farm Organizational structure organized under State law. An eligible orchardists is a person or legal entity that produces annual crops from trees, bushes, or vines for commercial purposes. An eligible nursery tree grower is a person or legal entity that produces nursery, ornamental, fruit, nut, or Christmas trees for commercial sale. To qualify for TAP, the eligible orchardist or nursery tree grower must have planted, continuously owned, and suffered eligible losses of trees, bushes, or vines that were planted for commercial purposes; and replaced eligible trees, bushes, and vines within 12 months from the date the application is approved. Eligible losses must be the result of a natural disaster. The stand must have sustained a mortality loss in excess of 15 percent after adjustment for normal mortality, or where applicable, damage in excess of 15 percent, adjusted for normal mortality and normal damage, that occurred in the calendar year (or loss period in the case of plant disease) for which benefits are being requested. The loss could not have been prevented through reasonable and available measures; the damage or loss must be visible and obvious to the FSA representative; and FSA may require information from a qualified expert to determine the extent of loss in the case of plant disease or insect infestation. An eligible natural disaster means plant disease, insect infestation, drought, fire, freeze, flood, earthquake, lightning, or other natural occurrence of such magnitude or severity so as to be considered disastrous.
Beneficiary Eligibility: The eligible orchardists and nursery tree grower receives the TAP benefit.
Funding: (Direct Payments for Specified Use) FY 18 $11,267,000.00; FY 19 est $30,877,000.00; FY 20 est $26,782,000.00
HQ: 14th and Independence Avenue SW, PO Box 0517, Washington, DC 20250
  Phone: 202-720-5172 | Email: steve.peterson@wdc.usda.gov
  http://www.fsa.usda.gov/programs-and-services/disaster-assistance-program/tree-assistance-program/index

USDA10.114 | COTTON TRANSITION ASSISTANCE PROGRAM "CTAP"

Award: Direct Payments With Unrestricted Use

Purpose: The CTAP provides benefits for the cotton producers.

Applicant Eligibility: An eligible producer for CTAP is required to be a person or legal entity who is actively engaged in farming and otherwise eligible to receive payment. CTAP payments in each of the 2014 and 2015 Program years are limited to $40,000 per person or legal entity, similar to the $40,000 per person or legal entity limitation to applied to DCP under The Food, Conservation, and Energy Act of 2008, P. L. 110-246. A person or legal entity is ineligible for payments if the person's or legal entity's average gross income (AGI) for the applicable compliance Program year is in excess of $900,000. If a person with an indirect interest in a legal entity has AGI in excess of $900,000, the CTAP payments subject to AGI compliance provisions to the legal entity will be reduced as calculated based on the percent interest of the person in the legal entity receiving the payment.

Beneficiary Eligibility: The Farm Service Agency (FSA) will provide adequate notice to producer about the new CTAP regulations so they will be ready to begin sign-up for CTAP. Payments will process as soon as possible after October 1, 2014, as soon as the application period closes. Therefore, to begin providing benefits to producers in a timely fashion, the final rule is effective when published in the Federal Register.

Funding: (Direct Payments for Specified Use) FY 18 $35,272.00; FY 19 est $0.00; FY 20 est $0.00

HQ: 1400 Independence Avenue SW, Room 4759-S, Washington, DC 20024

Phone: 202-720-7641 | Email: brent.orr@wdc.usda.gov

http://www.fsa.usda.gov/fsa/
newsreleases?area=newsroom&subject=landing&topic=pfs&newstype=prfactsheet&type=detail&item=pf_20150706_insup_en_ctap.html

USDA10.116 | THE MARGIN PROTECTION PROGRAM "MPP-Dairy"

Award: Direct Payments for Specified Use

Purpose: To provide compensation for the dairy producers when there is a cost reduction in the dairy products.

Applicant Eligibility: All dairy operations in the U.S. shall be eligible to participate in the MPP-Dairy Program to receive margin protection payments. A dairy operation must produce milk from cows in the U.S. and must be commercially marketing milk produced at the time of enrollment and continue to market milk for the duration of the Program. A dairy operation may participate in the MPP-Dairy Program or the Livestock Gross Margin for Dairy (LGM-Dairy) but not both. LGM-Dairy is operated by the Risk Management Agency of the U.S. Department of Agriculture (USDA). However since the MPP-Dairy Program is made available after potential applicants under MPP-Dairy have applied for coverage under LGM-Dairy, for the open enrollment period established for the 2014 and 2015 calendar year coverage only, a producer with coverage under LGM-Diary that would like to participate in the MPP-Dairy Program must register to participate in the MPP-Dairy Program during the open enrollment period established for calendar 2014 and 2015 and agree not to extend or obtain new LGM-Dairy coverage.

Beneficiary Eligibility: The ultimate benefit of the MPP-Dairy program will help protect farm equity and reduce financial losses that occur during times of low margins.

Funding: (Direct Payments for Specified Use) FY 18 $230,306,000.00; FY 19 est $1,074,000,000.00; FY 20 est $818,000,000.00

HQ: 1400 Independence Avenue SW, Washington, DC 20250-0512

Phone: 202-720-1919 | Email: danielle.cooke@wdc.usda.gov

http://www.fsa.usda.gov/programs-and-services/dairy-mpp/index

USDA10.119 | DAIRY ASSISTANCE PROGRAM FOR PUERTO RICO "DAP-PR"

Award: Direct Payments With Unrestricted Use

Purpose: To compensate for the dairy producers for marketing dairy products.

Applicant Eligibility: The eligible applicants are the licensed dairy operations in Puerto Rico for acquiring feed from feed dealers in Puerto Rico.

Programs Administered by Regional - State - Local Offices

Beneficiary Eligibility: The eligible applicants must be licensed by the Department of Agriculture of Puerto Rico. This is a one time assistance to dairy operation purchase feed.

Funding: (Direct Payments with Unrestricted Use) FY 17 $0.00; FY 18 est $7,580,135.00; FY 19 est $0.00

HQ: 355 E Street SW Patriot Plaza III, 11th Floor, Washington, DC 20024

Phone: 202-772-6029 | Email: veronica.richardson@wdc.usda.gov

http://www.fsa.gov

USDA10.120 | 2017 WILDFIRES AND HURRICANES INDEMNITY PROGRAM "2017 WHIP"

Award: Direct Payments With Unrestricted Use

Purpose: To compensate the citrus producers to repair the damages and for replanting citrus trees.

Applicant Eligibility: Agriculture producers are eligible to apply.

Beneficiary Eligibility: N/A

Award Range/Average: Producers are subject to a $125,000 payment limitation, meaning a producer can't receive more than $125,000 for losses. But a producer can receive a higher payment if three-fourths or more of their income is derived from farming or another agricultural-based business. Producers who derived 75 percent of their income in tax years 2013,2014 and 2015 will be subject to a $900,000 payment limitation.

HQ: 1400 Independence Avenue SW, Washington, DC 20250

Phone: 202-720-9882 | Email: jennifer.fiser@wdc.usda.gov

https://www.fsa.usda.gov

USDA10.122 | CONSERVATION RESERVE PROGRAM FOREST INVENTORY ANALYSIS PILOT PROGRAM "CRPFIA"

Award: Project Grants (cooperative Agreements)

Purpose: To provide grants for the bottomland hardwood tree species through the Farm Service Agency.

Applicant Eligibility: Non-profit Organizations dedicated to conservation, forestry, and wildlife habitats, that have experience in conducting forest inventory analysis through the use of remote sensing data and technology are eligible to apply. The term "non-profit Organization " means any corporation, trust, association, cooperative, or other Organization that is operated primarily for scientific educational, service, charitable, or similar purposes in the public interest. This excludes colleges and universities, unless a 501(c)(3) has been established; hospitals; state, local, and federally-recognized Indian tribal Governments.

Beneficiary Eligibility: N/A

Funding: (Project Grants (Cooperative Agreements)) FY 18 est $930,970.00; FY 19 est $1,000,000.00; FY 20 est $0.00

HQ: 1400 Independence Avenue SW, Washington, DC 20024

Phone: 202-720-5291 | Email: richard.iovanna@wdc.usda.gov

https://www.fsa.usda.gov

USDA10.404 | EMERGENCY LOANS

Award: Direct Loans

Purpose: To compensate farmers and aquaculture operators with essential needs to recover from natural disasters.

Applicant Eligibility: Requires that an applicant: (a) Not have caused a loss to the Agency after April 4, 1996, or received debt forgiveness on no more than 1 occasion prior to April 4, 1996. (b) be an established family farmer, rancher, or aquaculture operator (either tenant-operator or owner-operator), who was conducting a farming operation at the time of occurrence of the disaster either as an individual proprietorship, a partnership, a cooperative, a corporation, or a joint operation; (c) have suffered qualifying crop loss and/or physical property damage caused by a designated natural disaster; (d) be a citizen of the United States or legal resident alien, or be operated by citizens and/or resident aliens owning over a 50 percent interest of the farming entity; (e) be unable to obtain suitable credit from any other source(s) to qualify for subsidized loss loans; (f) have sufficient training or farming experience in managing and operating a farm or ranch (1 year's complete production and marketing cycle within the last 3 years immediately preceding the application); (g) be able to project a feasible and sound plan of operation; (h) be a capable manager of the farming, ranching, or aquaculture operations (in the case of a cooperative, corporation, partnership or joint operation, if members, stockholders, partners or joint operators own a majority interest and are related by blood or marriage, at least one member, stockholder, partner or joint operator must operate the family farm; if not related, the majority interest holder(s) must operate the family farm); (I) have legal capacity to contract for the loan; (j) obtain eligibility certification; (k) provide adequate collateral to secure the loan request; (l) have not been convicted of crop insurance fraud (in certain situations); (m) have crop insurance if available for affected crops comply with the highly erodible land and wetland conservation provisions of Public Law 99-198 (16 U.S.C. 3801 et seq.), (Title 12 and 13) the Food Security Act of 1985 and the Food, Agriculture, Conservation, and Trade Act of 1990. Applicants who cannot meet all of these requirements are not eligible. Assistance is available in the 50 States, the Commonwealth of Puerto Rico, the Virgin Islands of the United States, Guam, American Samoa, the Commonwealth of the Northern Mariana Islands, and, to the extent the Secretary determines it to be feasible and appropriate, the Trust Territories of the Pacific Islands, when those areas (by county) are designated.

Beneficiary Eligibility: Applicants/borrowers are the direct beneficiaries when they meet all eligibility criteria. Families, individuals and entities who are farmers, ranchers or aquaculture operators are the beneficiaries.

Award Range/Average: The maximum emergency loan amount may not exceed $500,000.

Funding: (Direct Loans) FY 18 $12,713,000.00; FY 19 est $37,668,000.00; FY 20 est $62,011,000.00

HQ: 1400 Independence Avenue SW, Washington, DC 20250

Phone: 202-690-0756 | Email: connie.holman@wdc.usda.gov

http://www.fsa.usda.gov/programs-and-services/farm-loan-programs/index

USDA10.406 | FARM OPERATING LOANS

Award: Direct Loans; Guaranteed/insured Loans

Purpose: To assist farmers in making productive use of their land and maintain operations such as farming and ranching.

Applicant Eligibility: Except for youth loans, individual applicants must: (1) Be a citizen of the United States, United States non-citizen national, or a qualified alien under applicable Federal immigration laws; (2) have the legal capacity to incur the obligations of the loan; (3) be unable to obtain credit elsewhere or unable to obtain the loan without a guarantee; (4) not have had a previous loan which resulted in a loss to the Agency (with certain conditions); (5) not be delinquent on any federal debt; (6) after the loan is closed, be an owner/tenant operator of a family farm. For an operating loan (OL), the producer must be the operator of a family farm; (7) not have been convicted of crop insurance fraud (in certain circumstances); and (8) not have any controlled substance convictions. In addition, a direct loan applicant must have sufficient education, training, or experience in managing and operating a farm or ranch that demonstrates the managerial ability to succeed in farming. Corporations, cooperatives, joint operations, and partnerships and their members/stakeholders must meet most of these same eligibility requirements, and the entity must also be authorized to operate a farm or ranch in the State where the land is located. To be eligible to obtain a direct loan, a borrower must agree to abide by any "borrower training" requirements. Applicants/borrowers requesting guaranteed loan assistance must meet all lender requirements.

Beneficiary Eligibility: Applicants/borrowers are the direct beneficiaries and must meet the applicant eligibility requirements Families, individuals, and entities who are or plan to become farmers, ranchers or aquaculture operators are the beneficiaries.

Award Range/Average: Direct Farm Operating Loans up to $300,000. ($50,000 total or less is considered a microloan);Guaranteed Farm Operating Loans up to $1,399,000. (Amount adjusted annually.)

Funding: (Guaranteed/Insured Loans) FY 18 $1,085,291,000.00; FY 19 est $1,960,000,000.00; FY 20 est $1,614,953,000.00; (Direct Loans) FY 18 $1,112,835,000; FY 19 est $1,530,000,000.00; FY 20 est $1,773,714,000.00

HQ: 1400 Independence Avenue SW, Washington, DC 20250

Phone: 202-690-0756 | Email: houston.bruck@usda.gov

http://www.fsa.usda.gov/programs-and-services/farm-loan-programs/index

USDA10.407 | FARM OWNERSHIP LOANS

Award: Direct Loans; Guaranteed/insured Loans

Purpose: The Farm Service Agency provides loan for farmers in making productive use of their land to make a standard of living.

Applicant Eligibility: An applicant must: (1) Be a citizen of the United States, United States non-citizen national, or a qualified alien under applicable Federal immigration laws; (2) have the legal capacity to incur the obligations of the loan; (3) be unable to obtain credit elsewhere or unable to obtain the loan without a guarantee; (4) not have had a previous loan which resulted in a loss to the Agency (with certain conditions); (5) not be delinquent on any federal debt; (6) after the loan is closed, be an owner/tenant operator of a family farm. For an operating loan (OL), the producer must be the operator of a family farm; (7) have participated in the business operations of a farm for at least 3 out of the 10 years prior to the application (for direct loans only); (8) not have been convicted of crop insurance fraud (in certain circumstances); and (9) not have any controlled substance convictions. In addition, a direct loan applicant must have sufficient education, training, or experience in managing and operating a farm or ranch that demonstrates the managerial ability to succeed in farming. Corporations, cooperatives, joint operations, and partnerships and their members/stakeholders must meet most of these same eligibility requirements, and the entity must also be authorized to operate a farm or ranch in the State where the land is located. To be eligible to obtain a direct loan, a borrower must agree to abide by any "borrower training" requirements. Applicants/borrowers requesting guaranteed loan assistance must meet all lender requirements.

Beneficiary Eligibility: Applicants/borrowers are the direct beneficiaries and must meet the applicant eligibility requirements. Families, individuals, and entities who are or plan to become farmers, ranchers or aquaculture operators are the beneficiaries.

Award Range/Average: Direct Farm Ownership Loans up to $300,000; Guaranteed Farm Ownership Loans up to $1,399,000.

Funding: (Guaranteed/Insured Loans) FY 18 $2,119,308,000; FY 19 est $2,750,000,000.00; FY 20 est $2,750,000,000.00; (Direct Loans) FY 18 $1,145,326,000; FY 19 est $1,500,000,000.00; FY 20 est $1,500,000,000.00

HQ: 1400 Independence Avenue SW, Washington, DC 20250

Phone: 202-690-0756 | Email: houston.bruck@usda.gov

http://www.fsa.usda.gov/programs-and-services/farm-loan-programs/index

USDA10.421 | INDIAN TRIBES AND TRIBAL CORPORATION LOANS

Award: Direct Loans

Purpose: To support Indian tribes and corporations with land situated within the tribal reservations.

Applicant Eligibility: Limited to any Indian tribe recognized by the Secretary of the Interior or tribal corporation established pursuant to the Indian Re Organization Act or community in Alaska incorporated by the Secretary of Interior pursuant to the Indian Re Organization Act which does not have adequate uncommitted funds to acquire lands within the tribe's reservation or in a community in Alaska. The tribe must be unable to obtain sufficient credit elsewhere at reasonable rates and terms and must be able to show reasonable prospects of repaying the loan as determined by an acceptable repayment plan and a satisfactory management plan for the land being acquired.

Beneficiary Eligibility: American Indian Tribe or tribal corporation recognized by the Secretary of the Interior, or a community in Alaska incorporated by the Secretary of the Interior.

Award Range/Average: Not Available.

Funding: (Direct Loans) FY 17 $0.00; FY 18 est $20,000,000.00; FY 19 est $20,000,000.00

HQ: 1400 Independence Avenue SW, Washington, DC 20250

Phone: 202-690-0756 | Email: connie.holman@wdc.usda.gov

http://fsa.usda.gov/fsa/webapp?area=home&subject=fmlp&topic=landing

USDA10.435 | STATE MEDIATION GRANTS

Award: Project Grants

Purpose: To assist the agricultural producers and creditors of producers affected by the intervention of the Department of Agriculture.

Applicant Eligibility: State Governments.

Beneficiary Eligibility: Agricultural producers, creditors of producers (as applicable) and persons directly affected by actions of the Department of Agriculture.

Funding: (Project Grants) FY 18 $3,904,000.00; FY 19 est $3,904,000.00; FY 20 est $3,228,000.00

HQ: 1400 Independence Avenue SW, PO Box 0523, Washington, DC 20250-0523

Phone: 202-720-1360 | Email: courtney.dixon@wdc.usda.gov

http://www.fsa.usda.gov/fsa/
newsreleases?area=newsroom&subject=landing&topic=pfs&newstype=prfactsheet&type=detail&item=pf_20130820_
admin_en_agmed.html

USDA10.449 | BOLL WEEVIL ERADICATION LOAN PROGRAM

Award: Direct Loans

Purpose: To support the U.S. government to eradicate boll weevils.

Applicant Eligibility: Applicants may be determined eligible if the Organization: (a) Meets the Animal and Plant Health Inspection Service (APHIS) cost-sharing requirements; (b) possesses a legal nonprofit corporate authority; (c) possesses the legal authority to enter into a contract; (d) operates in an area approved by a majority of cotton producers via referendum; (e) is unable to obtain funds elsewhere; and (f) may pledge producer assets as loan collateral.

Beneficiary Eligibility: The beneficiaries of this program include the local boll weevil organization and agricultural community as well as local, State, and national governments.

Funding: (Direct Loans) FY 18 $0.00; FY 19 est $30,000,000.00; FY 20 est $60,000,000.00

HQ: 1400 Independence Avenue SW, Washington, DC 20250
Phone: 202-690-0756 | Email: houston.bruck@usda.gov
http://fsa.usda.gov/fsa/webapp?area=home&subject=fmlp&topic=landing

FEDERAL AVIATION ADMINISTRATION
Regional – State – Local Offices

California
Federal Aviation Administration Western-Pacific Region Airports Division 15000 Aviation Boulevard Room 3012, Lawndale, CA 90261 310-725-3600
PO Box 92007 Worldway Postal Center, Los Angeles, CA 90009-2007 310-725-3608

Eastern Region
159-30 Rockaway Boulevard, Jamaica, NY 11434 718-553-3330

Georgia
1701 Columbia Avenue PO Box 20636, Atlanta, GA 30320-0631 404-305-6701
Federal Aviation Administration Southern Region Airports Division Suite 540, College Park, GA 30337 404-305-6700
Federal Aviation Administration Southern Region Atlanta ADO 1701 Columbia Avenue Campus Building 2-260, College Park, GA 30337-2747 404-305-7150

Illinois
Federal Aviation Administration Airports Division O'Hare Lake Office Center 2300 E Devon Avenue, Des Plaines, IL 60018 847-294-7272
Federal Aviation Administration Chicago Airports District Office CHI-ADO-600 O'Hare Lake Office Center 2300 E Devon Avenue, Des Plaines, IL 60018 847-294-7272

Massachusetts
12 New England Executive Park Sheila Bauer ANE-40, Burlington, MA 01803-5299 781-238-7378
Federal Aviation Administration New England Region 12 New England Executive Park, Burlington, MA 01803 617-238-7600

Missouri
601 E 12th Street, Kansas City, MO 64106-2808 816-329-2600
Federal Aviation Administration Airports Division Room 335 901 Locust, Kansas City, MO 64106-2325 816-329-2600

New Jersey
New York Airports District Office Technical Center Atlantic City International Airport, Atlantic City, NJ 08405 609-485-4000

New York
Federal Aviation Administration New York ADO 600 Old Country Road Suite 446, Garden City, NY 11530 516-227-3800

Oklahoma
PO Box 25082, Oklahoma City, OK 73135

Southwest Region
Byron K. Huffman, Division Manager | 222 W 7th Avenue M/S 14, Anchorage, AK 99513 907-271-5438

Texas
2601 Meacham Boulevard, Fort Worth, TX 76137-4298 817-222-5600

Washington
Federal Aviation Administration Northwest Mountain Region Airports Division 1601 Lind Avenue SW Suite 315, Renton, WA 98057-3356 206-227-2600

NATIONAL MINE HEALTH AND SAFETY ACADEMY

Alaska
Byron K. Huffman, Division Manager | 222 W 8th Avenue Room A36, Anchorage, AK 99513 907-271-5438

DOT20.106 | AIRPORT IMPROVEMENT PROGRAM
"AIP"

Award: Project Grants; Advisory Services and Counseling
Purpose: To assist sponsors, owners, or operators of public-use airports in the development of a nationwide system of airports adequate to meet the needs of civil aeronautics.
Applicant Eligibility: States, counties, municipalities, U.S. Territories and possessions, and other public agencies including an Indian tribe or pueblo, the Republics of the Marshall Islands and Palau, and the Federated States of Micronesia are eligible for airport development grants if the airport on which the development is required is listed in the National Plan of Integrated Airport Systems (NPIAS). Certain local government Organizations may be eligible for grants to implement noise planning and compatibility projects. Private owners of public-use reliever airports or airports having at least 2, 500 passengers boarding annually and receiving scheduled passenger aircraft service may also be eligible.
Beneficiary Eligibility: States, counties, municipalities, U.S. Territories and possessions, and other public agencies including an Indian tribe or pueblo, the Republics of the Marshall Islands and Palau, the Federated States of Micronesia, and private

owners of reliever airports or airports having at least 2,500 passenger boarding annually and receiving scheduled passenger aircraft service.

Award Range/Average: FY 2018 AIP grant awards ranged from $1,100 to $45,000,000 with an average award of $1,200,000.

Funding: (Project Grants) FY 18 $3,314,339,779.00; FY 19 est $3,451,289,997.00; FY 20 est $3,436,860,404.00

HQ: 800 Independence Avenue, Washington, DC 20591

    Phone: 202-267-8170 | Email: kay.ryder@faa.gov

    http://www.faa.gov/airports/aip

DOT20.108 | AVIATION RESEARCH GRANTS

Award: Project Grants; Use of Property, Facilities, and Equipment

Purpose: To encourage and support innovative, advanced, and applied research and development in areas of potential benefit to the growth of civil aviation.

Applicant Eligibility: The eligibility of applicants for the award of a research grant varies depending upon the nature of the proposer's Organization as well as the character of work one proposes to perform. In general, colleges, universities, and other non-profit research Institutions are eligible to qualify for research grants.

Beneficiary Eligibility: Colleges, Universities, and Non-profit research institutions are eligible to benefit from assistance.

Award Range/Average: Proposals received range from $15,000 to $5,000,0000; the average range is between $50,000 and $250,000, while larger proposals received are for multi-year research.

Funding: (Project Grants (Discretionary)) FY 18 $3,000,000.00; FY 19 est $4,000,000.00; FY 20 est $8,000,000.00

HQ: William J Hughes Technical Center Atlantic City International Airport, Atlantic City, NJ 08405

    Phone: 609-485-7483 | Email: trina.bellamy@faa.gov

DOT20.109 | AIR TRANSPORTATION CENTERS OF EXCELLENCE
"FAA Centers of Excellence"

Award: Project Grants; Use of Property, Facilities, and Equipment; Provision of Specialized Services

Purpose: To conduct long term research in critical and specific areas of aviation related technology.

Applicant Eligibility: FAA COE applicants are limited to colleges and universities with the financial resources to meet statutory requirements for matching Federal funds and maintenance of effort. Academic Institutions may partner with industry affiliates, other public and private entities, government laboratories and other interested parties. Applicants must satisfy the Congressionally mandated selection criteria as stated in an open Final Solicitation.

Beneficiary Eligibility: Recipients are limited to colleges and universities with the financial resources to meet statutory requirements for matching Federal grants and maintenance of effort. In conducting research, a Center of Excellence may contract with nonprofit research organizations and other appropriate persons.

Award Range/Average: Program started in fiscal year 1992. Grant assistance is expected to be a minimum of $500,000 per year for each Center, and may be augmented by tasks funded through IDIQ contract awards.

Funding: (Cooperative Agreements) FY 18 $11,800,000; FY 19 est $24,400,000; FY 20 est $44,700,000

HQ: Office FAA William J Hughes Technical Center, Building 300, Atlantic City International Airport, NJ 08405

    Phone: 609-485-6242 | Email: karen.s.davis@faa.gov

    http://www.faa.gov/go/coe

FEDERAL HIGHWAY ADMINISTRATION
Regional – State – Local Offices

Alabama
Joe D. Wilkerson | 500 Eastern Boulevard Suite 200, Montgomery, AL 36117-2018 334-223-7370

Alaska
David Miller | 709 W 9th Street Room 851 PO Box 21648, Juneau, AK 99802-1648 907-586-7180

Arizona
Robert E. Hollis | 234 N Central Avenue Suite 330, Phoenix, AZ 85004-2220 602-379-3646

Arkansas
Sandra L. Otto | 700 W Capitol Avenue Room 3130, Little Rock, AR 72201-3298 501-324-5625

California
Michael G. Ritchie | 980 9th Street Suite 400, Sacramento, CA 95814-2724 916-498-5001

Central Region
Larry C. Smith | 555 Zang Street, Lakewood, CO 80228-1010 303-716-2000

Programs Administered by Regional - State - Local Offices

Colorado
William C. Jones | 555 Zang Street Room 250, Lakewood, CO 80228-1097 303-969-6730, Ext. 3

Connecticut
Donald J. West | 628-2 Hebron Avenue Suite 303, Glastonbury, CT 06033-5007 860-659-6703, Ext. 3009

Delaware
Tommy D. Myers | 300 S New Street Room 2101, Dover, DE 19904-0726 302-734-5323

District of Columbia
Gary L. Henderson | Union Center Plaza 820 1st Street NE Suite 750, Washington, DC 20002-4205 202-523-0163

Eastern Region
Melisa L. Ridenour | 21400 Ridgetop Circle Loudoun Technical Center, Sterling, VA 20166-6511 703-404-6201

Florida
James E. | 227 N Bronough Street Room 2015, Tallahassee, FL 32301-1330 850-942-9650

Georgia
Larry Dreihaup | 61 Forsyth Street SW Suite 17T100, Atlanta, GA 30303-3104 404-562-3630

Hawaii
Abraham Y. Wong Prince Jonah Kuhio | Kalanianaole Federal Building 300 Ala Moana Boulevard PO Box 50206 Room 3-306, Honolulu, HI 96850-5000 808-541-2700, Ext. 312

Idaho
Stephen Moreno | 3050 Lake Harbor Lane Suite 126, Boise, ID 83703-6243 208-334-9180

Illinois
Norman R. Stoner | 3250 Executive Park Drive, Springfield, IL 62703-4514 217-492-4640

Indiana
Robert F. Talley Jr., | 575 N Pennsylvania Street Room 254, Indianapolis, IN 46204-1576 317-226-7475

Iowa
Phil Barnes | 105 6th Street, Ames, IA 50010-6337 515-233-7300

Kansas
J. Michael Bowen | 3300 S Topeka Boulevard Suite 1, Topeka, KS 66611-2237 785-267-7281

Kentucky
John C. Watts | Federal Building 330 W Broadway, Frankfort, KY 40601-1922 502-223-6720

Louisiana
William A. Sussmann | 5304 Flanders Drive Suite A, Baton Rouge, LA 70808-4348 225-757-7600

Maine
Jonathan McDade | Edmund S Muskie Federal Building 40 Western Avenue Room 614, Augusta, ME 04330-6394 207-622-8487, Ext. 19

Maryland
Nelson Castellanos | 711 W 40th Street Suite 220, Baltimore, MD 21211 410-962-4440

Massachusetts
Stanley Gee | 55 Broadway 10th Floor, Cambridge, MA 02142-1093 617-494-3657

Michigan
James J. Steele | Federal Building Room 207 315 W Allegan Street Room 207, Lansing, MI 48933-1528 517-377-1844

Minnesota
Alan R Steger Galtier Plaza PO Box 75 380 Jackson Street Suite 500, Saint Paul, MN 55101-2904 651-291-6100

Mississippi
Andrew H. Hughes | 666 N Street Suite 105, Jackson, MS 39202-3199 601-965-4215

Missouri
Allen Masuda | 209 Adams Street, Jefferson City, MO 65101-3203 573-636-7104

Montana
Janice W. Brown | 2880 Skyway Drive, Helena, MT 59602-1230 406-449-5303, Ext. 235

Nebraska
William Brownell | Federal Building Room 220 100 Centennial Mall N, Lincoln, NE 68508-3851 402-437-5765

Nevada
Susan Kelepar | 705 N Plaza Street Suite 220, Carson City, NV 89701-0602 775-687-1204

New Hampshire
Kathleen O. Laffey | 279 Pleasant Street Suite 204, Concord, NH 03301-7502 603-228-0417

New Jersey
Dennis L. Merida | 840 Bear Tavern Road Suite 310, West Trenton, NJ 08628-1019 609-637-4200

New Mexico
J. Don Martinez | 604 W San Mateo Road, Santa Fe, NM 87505-3920 505-820-2021

New York
Robert E. Arnold | Leo W O'Brien Federal Building Room 719 Clinton Avenue & N Pearl Street, Albany, NY 12207 518-431-4125

North Carolina
John Sullivan | 310 New Bern Avenue Suite 410, Raleigh, NC 27601-1441 919-856-4346

North Dakota
Al Radliff | 1471 Interstate Loop, Bismarck, ND 58503-0567 701-250-4204

Ohio
Dennis Decker | 200 N High Street Room 328, Columbus, OH 43215 614-280-6896

Programs Administered by Regional - State - Local Offices

Oklahoma
Walter J. Kudzia | 300 N Meridian Suite 105S, Oklahoma City, OK 73107-6560 405-605-6011

Oregon
David O. Cox | The Equitable Center 530 Center Street NE Suite 100, Salem, OR 97301-3740 503-399-5749

Pennsylvania
James A. Cheatham | 228 Walnut Street Room 558, Harrisburg, PA 17101-1720 717-221-3461

Puerto Rico
Lubin M. Quipones | Federico Degetau Federal Building 330 Carlos Chardon Avenue Room 210, San Juan, PR 00916 787-766-5600, Ext. 223

Rhode Island
Lucy Garliauskos | 380 Westminster Mall 5th Floor, Providence, RI 02903 401-528-4560

South Carolina
Robert L. Lee | Strom Thurmond Federal Building 1835 Assembly Street Suite 1270, Columbia, SC 29201-2483 803-765-5411

South Dakota
John Rohlf | 116 E Dakota Avenue, Pierre, SD 57501-3110 605-224-8033

Tennessee
Bobby Blackmon | 640 Grassmere Park Road Suite 112, Nashville, TN 37211-3658 615-781-5770

Texas
Curtis Dan Reagan | Federal Office Building 300 E 8th Street Room 826, Austin, TX 78701-3233 512-536-5900

Utah
David Gibbs | 2520 W 4700 S Suite 9A, Salt Lake City, UT 84118-1847 801-963-0182

Vermont
Charles E. Basner | Federal Building 87 State Street PO Box 568, Montpelier, VT 05601-0568 802-828-4423

Virginia
Roberto Fonseca Martinez | 400 N 8th Street Room 750 PO Box 10249, Richmond, VA 23240-0249 804-775-3320

Washington
Daniel M. Mathis | Evergreen Plaza 711 S Capitol Way Suite 501, Olympia, WA 98501-1284 360-753-9480

West Virginia
Thomas J. Smith | Geary Plaza 700 Washington Street E Suite 200, Charleston, WV 25301-1604 304-347-5928

Western Region
Ronald W. Carmichael | 610 E 5th Street, Vancouver, WA 98661-3801 360-619-7700

Wisconsin
Bruce E. Matzke | Highpoint Office Park 567 D'Onofrio Drive, Madison, WI 53719-2814 608-829-7500

Wyoming
Philip E. Miller | 2617 E Lincolnway Suite D, Cheyenne, WY 82001-5662 307-772-2101, Ext. 40

DOT20.200 | HIGHWAY RESEARCH AND DEVELOPMENT PROGRAM
"Highway Research and Development Program Surface Transportation Research, Development, and Technology"

Award: Project Grants
Purpose: To carry out the highway research and development program as authorized by the FAST Act and conduct research needed to maintain and improve our vital transportation infrastructure.
Applicant Eligibility: Varies by project. See individual project NOFO for details. (NOFOs issued at www.Grants.gov.).
Beneficiary Eligibility: State Departments of Transportation, Local Governments, General Public.
Award Range/Average: Varies by project. See individual project NOFO for details. (NOFOs issued at www.Grants.gov.)
Funding: (Cooperative Agreements) FY 17 $81,334,227.00; FY 19 est $100,000,000.00; FY 20 est $100,000,000.00
HQ: 1200 New Jersey Avenue SE, Washington, DC 20590
  Phone: 202-366-4211 | Email: aimee.drewry@dot.gov
  http://www.fhwa.dot.gov

DOT20.205 | HIGHWAY PLANNING AND CONSTRUCTION
"Federal-Aid Highway Program, Federal Lands Highway Program"

Award: Formula Grants; Project Grants
Purpose: This Assistance Listing encompasses several transportation programs such as the Federal-aid Highway Program, The Federal Lands Highway Program, The FAST Act established two new freight programs, The Highway Infrastructure Programs in the Department of Transportation Appropriations Act, 2018.

Applicant Eligibility: By law, the Federal-aid highway Program is a federally assisted State administered Program that requires each State to have a suitably equipped and organized transportation department. Therefore, most projects are administered by or through State transportation departments (State DOTs). projects to be funded under the Federal-aid highway Program are generally selected by State DOTs or MPOs, in cooperation with appropriate local officials, as specified in 23 U.S.C. and implementing regulations. Territorial highway projects are funded in the similar manner as other Federal aid highway projects, with the territorial transportation agency functioning in a manner similar to a State transportation department. Most FLTP projects are administered by the FHWA Office of Federal Lands Highway and its Divisions or by the various FLMAs.

Beneficiary Eligibility: State transportation departments, and in some instances, Federal agencies, other State agencies, local agencies, and private, community-based organizations.

Award Range/Average: Federal-aid highway funds are provided to States on an annual basis, by a combination of statutory formula and discretionary allocation. The most recent authorization act is the Fixing America's Surface Transportation Act (FAST Act).

Funding: (Salaries and Expenses) FY 18 $43,090,835,692.00; FY 19 est $43,000,000,000.00; FY 20 est $43,000,000,000.00

HQ: 1200 New Jersey Avenue SE, Washington, DC 20590

Phone: 202-366-0027

http://www.fhwa.dot.gov

DOT20.215 | HIGHWAY TRAINING AND EDUCATION

Award: Cooperative Agreements; Training

Purpose: Encompasses several transportation training and education programs.

Applicant Eligibility: Depends on the Program: 1) NHI Training Program: Employees of State and local transportation agencies, private sector transportation company employees are eligible to participate in NHI courses. 2) DDETFP: Undergraduate (juniors and seniors at Minority Institutes of Higher education (MIHE)) and graduate students matriculating full-time at a U.S. University or college in a transportation-related discipline participate. 3) TEDP: Supports Region Workforce Centers that identify and facilitate implementation of successful transportation training and education Programs for students and transportation professionals at all levels of education; K-12, community colleges, technical schools, universities and incumbent transportation professionals. 4) GAMTTEP: Provides information about transportation curriculum and education Programs with a focus on the STEM disciplines and outreach to women and minorities.

Beneficiary Eligibility: N/A

Award Range/Average: Not Applicable.

Funding: (Project Grants (Cooperative Agreements)) FY 18 $7,760,480.00; FY 19 est $8,000,000.00; FY 20 est $8,000,000

HQ: 1310 N Courthouse Road, Suite 300, Arlington, VA 22201

Phone: 703-235-1263 | Email: virginia.tsu@dot.gov

http://www.fhwa.dot.gov/innovativeprograms/centers/workforce_dev/professionals.aspx

DOT20.219 | RECREATIONAL TRAILS PROGRAM

Award: Formula Grants

Purpose: The purpose of this program is to provide funds to the States to develop and maintain recreational trails and trail-related facilities for both nonmotorized and motorized recreational trail uses.

Applicant Eligibility: The FHWA may enter into contracts with for-profit Organizations or contracts, partnerships, or cooperative agreements with other government agencies, Institutions of higher learning, or nonprofit Organizations using its administrative funds. For funds available to the States: the Governor of each State must designate the State agency or agencies responsible for administering this Program. The State must have a State recreational trail advisory committee that represents both motorized and nonmotorized recreational trail users, which shall meet not less than once per fiscal year. If the State Recreational Trail Advisory Committee does not meet in a fiscal year, or does not have required representation, the State becomes ineligible for an apportionment. The State agency may accept project proposals from private Organizations, or from municipal, county, State, or Federal government entities, and other government entities. The projects must satisfy one or more of the permissible uses. States may provide subgrants to Federal, State, and local government entities and to private entities, at the discretion of the State.

Beneficiary Eligibility: The FHWA may enter into contracts with for-profit organizations or contracts, partnerships, or cooperative agreements with other government agencies, institutions of higher learning, or nonprofit organizations using its administrative funds. The State agency designated by the Governor. A State may opt out of the Recreational Trails Program if the Governor of the State notifies the Secretary not later than 30 days prior to apportionments being made for any fiscal year.

Award Range/Average: Apportionments to the States are based on statutory formula. All 50 States and the District of Columbia are eligible to receive apportionments. For FY 2016: $83,318,400 was potentially available (after the 1% return); $82,365,802

Programs Administered by Regional - State - Local Offices

was apportioned (Connecticut opted out for FY 2016). Awards ranged from $816,847 to $5,698,627; the average was $1,647,316.

Funding: (Formula Grants (Apportionments)) FY 18 $74,827,204.00; FY 19 est $82,000,000.00; FY 20 est $82,000,000.00
HQ: 1200 New Jersey Avenue SE, Washington, DC 20590

Phone: 202-366-5013 | Email: christopher.douwes@dot.gov
http://www.fhwa.dot.gov/environment/recreational_trails

DOT20.223 | TRANSPORTATION INFRASTRUCTURE FINANCE AND INNOVATION ACT (TIFIA) PROGRAM
"TIFIA Credit Program"

Award: Direct Loans; Guaranteed/insured Loans
Purpose: To finance projects of national or regional significance by filling market gaps and leveraging substantial non-Federal and private co-investment.
Applicant Eligibility: Public or private entities seeking to finance, design, construct, own, or operate an eligible surface transportation project may apply for TIFIA assistance. Examples of such entities include state departments of transportation; local Governments; transit agencies; special authorities; special districts; railroad companies; and private firms or consortia that may include companies specializing in engineering, construction, materials, and/or the operation of transportation facilities.
Beneficiary Eligibility: Public or private entities seeking to finance, design, construct, own, or operate an eligible surface transportation project. Examples include state departments of transportation; local governments; transit agencies; special authorities; special districts; railroad companies; and private firms or consortia that may include companies specializing in engineering, construction, materials, and/or the operation of transportation facilities.
Funding: (Direct Loans) FY 18 $1,235,863,164.00; FY 19 est $1,150,000,000.00; FY 20 est $2,000,000,000.00
HQ: 1200 New Jersey Avenue SE, Room E, Washington, DC 20590

Phone: 202-366-1059 | Email: dimitri.kombolias@dot.gov
http://www.transportation.gov/buildamerica/programs-services/tifia

DOT20.224 | FEDERAL LANDS ACCESS PROGRAM
"Access Program or FLAP"

Award: Formula Grants; Project Grants
Purpose: The goal of the Federal Lands Access Program is to improve transportation facilities that provide access to, are adjacent to, or are located within Federal lands.
Applicant Eligibility: Only the owner of the affected transportation asset or assets may submit an application.
Beneficiary Eligibility: State transportation departments, other State agencies, local agencies, and Federal agencies.
Funding: (Formula Grants) FY 18 $229,795,962.00; FY 19 est $217,600,000.00; FY 20 est $226,200,000.00
HQ: 1200 New Jersey Avenue SE, Washington, DC 20590

Phone: 202-493-0271 | Email: frances.ramirez@dot.gov
http://flh.fhwa.dot.gov/programs/flap/reports

DOT20.240 | FUEL TAX EVASION-INTERGOVERNMENTAL ENFORCEMENT EFFORT
"Fuel Tax Evasion"

Award: Project Grants
Purpose: The purpose of this program is to increase intergovernmental activities and enforcement efforts among public agencies to reduce Federal and State fuel tax evasion.
Applicant Eligibility: States, and the District of Columbia, .
Beneficiary Eligibility: Same as Applicant Eligibility.
Award Range/Average: Minimum: $10,000; Maximum $250,000
Funding: (Project Grants) FY 18 $38,384; FY 19 est $40,000; FY 20 est $40,000; -The source of funds for this program is a deduction (set-aside) of not more than $4 million per year from the funds authorized for FHWA administrative expenses.

Programs Administered by Regional - State - Local Offices

Of the amount set-aside, $2 million must be reserved to make grants for intergovernmental enforcement efforts, including research and training.

HQ: Office of Highway Policy Information (HPPI) 1200 New Jersey Avenue SE, Washington, DC 20590
Phone: 202-366-9234 | Email: michael.dougherty@dot.gov
http://www.fhwa.dot.gov/policy/otps/fueltax.htm

FEDERAL MOTOR CARRIER SAFETY ADMINISTRATION
Regional – State – Local Offices

Alabama
Judy VanLuchene | 500 Eastern Boulevard Suite 200, Montgomery, AL 36117-2018 334-223-7244

Alaska
John Quartuccio | 605 W 4th Avenue Room 249 Historic Federal Building, Anchorage, AK 99501 907-271-4068

Arizona
Eric Ice | 234 N Central Avenue Suite 305, Phoenix, AZ 85004-2002 602-379-6851

Arkansas
J. Mark Westmoreland | 700 W Capitol Avenue Room 3130, Little Rock, AR 72201-3298 501-324-5050

California
Richard Brennan | 980 9th Street, Sacramento, CA 95814-2724 916-498-5050

Colorado
William Copley | 555 Zang Street Room 264, Lakewood, CO 80228-1097 303-969-6748

Connecticut
Jeffrey Cimahosky | 628-2 Hebron Avenue Suite 303, Glastonbury, CT 06033-5007 860-659-6700

Delaware
Veron Kirkendoll | 300 S New Street Room 2101, Dover, DE 19904-0726 302-734-8173

District of Columbia
Taft Kelly | Union Center Plaza 820 1st Street NE Suite 750, Washington, DC 20002-4205 202-523-0178

Florida
James Gregg | 227 N Bronough Street Room 2060, Tallahassee, FL 32301-1330 850-942-9338

Georgia
Tom Marlow | 61 Forsyth Street SW Suite 17T85, Atlanta, GA 30303-3104 404-562-3620

Hawaii
Wendy Burke Prince Jonah Kuhio | Kalanianaole Federal Building 300 Ala Moana Boulevard Room 3-243 PO Box 50206, Honolulu, HI 96850-5000 808-541-2700

Idaho
John Francis | 3050 Lake Harbor Lane Suite 126, Boise, ID 83703-6243 208-334-1842

Illinois
John Mulcare | 3250 Executive Park Drive, Springfield, IL 62703-4514 217-492-4608

Indiana
Kenneth Stickland | 575 N Pennsylvania Street Room 261, Indianapolis, IN 46204-1570 317-226-7474

Iowa
Kent Fleming | 105 6th Street, Ames, IA 50010-6337 515-233-7400

Kansas
Teri Graham | 3300 S Topeka Boulevard Suite 1, Topeka, KS 66611-2237 785-267-7288

Kentucky
Buddy Yount | 330 W Broadway, Frankfort, KY 40601-1922 502-223-6779

Louisiana
Sterlin Williams | 5304 Flanders Drive Suite A, Baton Rouge, LA 70808-4348 225-757-7640

Maine
Gerald Amato | 40 Western Avenue Room 601, Augusta, ME 04330-6394 207-622-8358

Maryland
Terry Runge-Erle | 711 W 40th Street Suite 220, Baltimore, MD 21211 410-962-2889

Massachusetts
Richard Bates | 55 Broadway Room I-35, Cambridge, MA 02142-1093 617-494-2770

Michigan
Patrick Muinich | 315 W Allegan Street Room 205, Lansing, MI 48933-1528 517-377-1866

Minnesota
Daniel Drexler Galtier Plaza PO Box 75 175 E 5th Street Suite 500, Saint Paul, MN 55101-2904 651-291-6150

Mississippi
Benny Wood | 666 N Street Suite 103, Jackson, MS 39202-3199 601-965-4219

Missouri
Joseph Boyd | 209 Adams Street, Jefferson City, MO 65101-3203 573-636-3246

Programs Administered by Regional - State - Local Offices

Montana
Kristin Phillipps | 2880 Skyway Drive, Helena, MT 59602-1230 406-449-5304

Nebraska
Elyse Mueller | 100 Centennial Mall N Room 220, Lincoln, NE 68508-3851 402-437-5986

Nevada
Bill Bensmiller | 705 N Plaza Street Suite 220, Carson City, NV 89701-0602 775-687-5335

New Hampshire
Timothy Cotter | 279 Pleasant Street Room 202 Federal Building, Concord, NH 03301-7502 603-228-3112

New Jersey
Christopher Rotondo | 840 Bear Tavern Road Suite 310, West Trenton, NJ 08628-1019 609-637-4222

New Mexico
Martha Brooks | 2400 Louisiana Boulevard NE AFC-5 Suite 520, Albuquerque, NM 87110 505-346-7858

New York
Brian Temperine | Leo W O'Brien Federal Building Room 719 Clinton Avenue & N Pearl Street, Albany, NY 12207 518-431-4145

North Carolina
Christopher Harley | 310 New Bern Avenue Suite 468, Raleigh, NC 27601-1441 919-856-4378

North Dakota
Jeffrey Jensen | 1471 Interstate Loop, Bismarck, ND 58503-0567 701-250-4346

Ohio
Steven Mattioli | 200 N High Street Room 328, Columbus, OH 43215 614-280-5657

Oklahoma
Mac Kirk | 300 N Meridian Suite 106-S, Oklahoma City, OK 73107-6560 405-605-6047

Oregon
Andrew Eno | 530 Center Street NE Suite 100, Salem, OR 97301-3740 503-399-5775

Pennsylvania
Patrick Quigley | 228 Walnut Street Room 536, Harrisburg, PA 17101-1720 717-221-4443

Puerto Rico
Enid Martinez | US Courthouse & Federal Building Carlos Chardon Street Room 329, Hato Rey, PR 00918 787-766-5985

Rhode Island
Robert Molla | 380 Westminster Mall Room 547, Providence, RI 02903-3246 401-528-4578

South Carolina
Curtis Thomas | 1835 Assembly Street Suite 1253, Columbia, SC 29201-2430 803-765-5414

South Dakota
Mark Gilmore | 116 E Dakota Street, Pierre, SD 57501-3110 605-224-8202

Tennessee
Richard Gobbell | 640 Grassmere Park Road Suite 111, Nashville, TN 37211 615-781-5781

Texas
David Martin | Federal Office Building 300 E 8th Street Room 826, Austin, TX 78701-3233 512-536-5980

Utah
Robert Kelleher | 2520 W 4700 S Suite 9B, Salt Lake City, UT 84118-1847 801-963-0096

Vermont
Gerard Amato | 87 State Street Room 216, Montpelier, VT 05602-2954 802-828-4480

Virginia
Craig Feister | 400 N 8th Street Room 750, Richmond, VA 23240 804-775-3322

Washington
Roger Kraft | Evergreen Plaza 711 S Capitol Way Suite 501, Olympia, WA 98501-1284 360-753-9875

West Virginia
Michael Myers | 700 Washington Street E Suite 205, Charleston, WV 25301-1604 304-347-5935

Wisconsin
William Vickery | 567 D'Onofrio Drive Suite 101, Madison, WI 53719-2814 608-829-7534

Wyoming
Gary Lowe | 1916 Evans Avenue, Cheyenne, WY 82001-3764 307-772-2305

DOT20.218 | MOTOR CARRIER SAFETY ASSISTANCE "MCSAP "

Award: Formula Grants

Purpose: Provides financial assistance to States to reduce the number and severity of crashes and hazardous materials incidents involving commercial motor vehicles (CMV).

Applicant Eligibility: All States, the District of Columbia, the Commonwealth of Puerto Rico, the Commonwealth of the Northern Mariana Islands, American Samoa, Guam, and the U.S. Virgin Islands, are eligible for MCSAP. The MCSAP grants are provided annually to the State's MCSAP lead agency. A MCSAP lead agency is designated by the Governor as the State motor vehicle safety agency responsible for administering the Commercial Vehicle Safety Plan (CVSP) within the State. The

CVSP is also known in statute and regulation as the Plan and serves as the MCSAP grant Program application, project plan, and budget.

Beneficiary Eligibility: Under the Basic and Incentive grant programs, a State lead MCSAP agency, as designated by its Governor, is eligible to apply for Basic and Incentive grant funding by submitting a commercial vehicle safety plan (CVSP), in accordance with the provisions of Title 49 of the Code of Federal Regulations (CFR) Part 350.201 and 205.

Award Range/Average: Formula Grant calculation based on statutory and regulatory funding factors.

Funding: (Formula Grants) FY 18 $294,416,500.00; FY 19 est $299,735,500.00; FY 20 est $353,000,000.00

HQ: 1200 New Jersey Avenue SE, Washington, DC 20590
  Phone: 202-366-0621
  https://www.fmcsa.dot.gov/mission/grants

DOT20.231 | PERFORMANCE AND REGISTRATION INFORMATION SYSTEMS MANAGEMENT
"PRISM"

Award: Project Grants

Purpose: To determine the safety fitness of a motor carrier or registrant when applying for registration or while the registration is in effect.

Applicant Eligibility: The FMCSA may award these grants to the agencies of States, the District of Columbia, the Commonwealth of Puerto Rico, the Commonwealth of the Northern Mariana Islands, American Samoa, Guam, and the U.S. Virgin Islands. According to 49 U.S.C. 31106(d), FMCSA may use PRISM to fund other Federal departments, agencies, and instrumentalities, or by making grants to, and entering into contracts and cooperative agreements with, States, local Governments, associations, Institutions, corporations, and other persons.

Beneficiary Eligibility: Eligible applicants include State agencies located in one of the fifty States, the District of Columbia, Puerto Rico, Northern Mariana Islands, American Samoa, Guam, and the U.S. Virgin Islands. Applicants must work on highway traffic safety activities and must demonstrate a capacity to work with highway traffic safety stakeholders.

Award Range/Average: Awards can range from $100,000.00 to $750,000.00

HQ: 1200 New Jersey Avenue SE W66-443, Washington, DC 20590
  Phone: 202-366-1736 | Email: lisa.ensley@dot.gov
  http://www.fmcsa.dot.gov/safety-security/prism/prism.htm

DOT20.232 | COMMERCIAL DRIVER'S LICENSE PROGRAM IMPLEMENTATION GRANT
"CDLPI"

Award: Cooperative Agreements; Project Grants

Purpose: To assist States in complying with CDL requirements and dedicate funding to priority activities for research, development and testing, demonstration projects, public education, and other special activities and projects relating to commercial drivers licensing.

Applicant Eligibility: States may receive grant funds to comply with the requirements of section 31311 of SAFETEA-LU or if making good faith efforts toward substantial compliance with the requirements of section 31311 and 31313 receive grant funds to improve implementation of the commercial driver's license Program. States, local Governments, and other persons for projects involving research, development, demonstration projects, public education, and other special activities and projects relating to commercial driver licensing and motor vehicle safety that are of benefit to all jurisdictions of the United States or are designed to address national safety concerns and circumstances. States, local Governments, and other persons may use grant funds to address emerging issues relating to commercial driver's license improvements.

Beneficiary Eligibility: 14 - State (includes District of Columbia, public institutions of higher education and hospitals) 15 - Local (includes State-designated Indian Tribes, excludes institutions of higher education and hospitals)20 - Public nonprofit institution/organization38 - other private institutions/organizations39 - Anyone/General public.

Award Range/Average: $20,000 - $1,500,000

Funding: (Project Grants) FY 18 $31,323,000.00; FY 19 est $32,000,000.00; FY 20 est $32,700,000.00

HQ: FMCSA Grants Management Office 1200 New Jersey Avenue SE, Washington, DC 20590
  Phone: 202-366-0621
  https://www.fmcsa.dot.gov/mission/grants

Programs Administered by Regional - State - Local Offices

DOT20.233 | BORDER ENFORCEMENT GRANTS

Award: Project Grants

Purpose: To ensure motor carriers operating commercial vehicles entering the United States from a foreign country are in compliance with commercial vehicle safety standards and regulations, financial responsibility regulations and registration requirements of the United States, and to ensure drivers of those vehicles are qualified and properly licenses to operate the commercial vehicle.

Applicant Eligibility: Entities and States that share a land border with a foreign country.

Beneficiary Eligibility: States that share a land border with a foreign country (Entities and Accredited public institutions of higher education). The States of Alaska, Arizona, California, Idaho, Maine, Michigan, Minnesota, Montana, New Hampshire, New Mexico, New York, North Dakota, Texas, Vermont and Washington, and entities and local governments within these enumerated States are eligible to receive funding.

Award Range/Average: For Border Enforcement awards ranged from $22,000.00 to $18,000,000.00.

HQ: 1200 New Jersey Avenue SE W66-443, Washington, DC 20590
  Phone: 202-366-1736 | Email: lisa.ensley@dot.gov
  http://www.fmcsa.dot.gov

DOT20.234 | SAFETY DATA IMPROVEMENT PROGRAM
"SaDIP"

Award: Project Grants

Purpose: To fund State programs designed to improve the overall quality of commercial motor vehicle (CMV) data in accordance with the FMCSA State Safety Data Quality (SSDQ) measures, specifically to increase the timeliness, efficiency, accuracy and completeness of processes and systems related to the collection and analysis of large truck and bus crash and inspection data.

Applicant Eligibility: A State shall be eligible for a grant under this section in a fiscal year if the Secretary determines that the State has (1) conducted a comprehensive audit of its commercial motor vehicle safety data system within the preceding 2 years; (2) developed a plan that identifies and prioritizes its commercial motor vehicle safety data needs and goals; and (3) identified performance-based measures to determine progress toward those goals. Eligible applicants include State Departments of Public Safety, Departments of Transportation, or State Law Enforcement Agencies in any of the several States of the United States, the District of Columbia, and the Commonwealth of Puerto Rico, any territory or possession of the United States, or any agency or instrumentality of a State exclusive of local Governments. The term does not include any public and Indian housing agency under United States Housing Act of 1937.

Beneficiary Eligibility: Any of the several States of the United States, the District of Columbia, the Commonwealth of Puerto Rico, any territory or possession of the United States, or any agency or instrumentality of a State exclusive of local governments. The term does not include any public and Indian housing agency under United States Housing Act of 1937.

Award Range/Average: Range $5,000 - $500,000; Average award $250,000

HQ: 1200 New Jersey Avenue SE W66-443, Washington, DC 20590
  Phone: 202-366-1736 | Email: lisa.ensley@dot.gov

DOT20.235 | COMMERCIAL MOTOR VEHICLE OPERATOR SAFETY TRAINING GRANTS
"CMVOST"

Award: Project Grants

Purpose: To help reduce the severity and number of crashes on U.S. roads involving commercial motor vehicles, as defined in 49 U.S.C. 31301, and to assist current or former members of the U.S. Armed Forces, including National Guard and Reservists to obtain a CDL.

Applicant Eligibility: Eligible applicants must be accredited by a government Organization such as the Department of education.

Beneficiary Eligibility: Same as Applicant Eligibility.

Award Range/Average: Fiscal Year 2017: The average award was $110,000. Fiscal Year 2018: The average award was $100,000.

Funding: (Project Grants (Discretionary)) FY 18 $1,000,000.00; FY 19 est $2,000,000.00; FY 20 est $0.00

HQ: FMCSA Grants Management Office 1200 New Jersey Avenue SE, Washington, DC 20590
  Phone: 202-366-0621 | Email: rikita.jarrett@dot.gov
  http://www.fmcsa.dot.gov/mission/grants/fy2018-cmvost-nofo

DOT20.237 | MOTOR CARRIER SAFETY ASSISTANCE HIGH PRIORITY ACTIVITIES GRANTS AND COOPERATIVE AGREEMENTS
"High Priority (HP) Grant"

Award: Project Grants

Purpose: To support, enrich, and augment Commercial Motor Vehicle (CMV) safety programs through partnerships with States, local governments, federally recognized Indian tribes, other political jurisdictions, and other persons to carry out high priority activities and projects.

Applicant Eligibility: HP grants are eligible to any State agency, local government (including county, city, township, special district, and Federally-recognized Native American tribal Governments), Institutions of higher education (public, private, and State-controlled), non-profit Organizations with or without having a 501(c)(3) status with the Internal Revenue Service, for-profit entities (including small businesses), and other persons. Other persons is defined as an entity not included above and may not be an individual, foreign entity, hospital, public/Indian housing authority, or Federal institution. ITD grants are eligible to States, the District of Columbia, the Commonwealth of Puerto Rico, the Commonwealth of the Northern Mariana Islands, American Samoa, Guam, and the U.S. Virgin Islands to deploy, operate, and maintain elements of their ITD Programs. The FMCSA may award ITD funds to agencies of States, the District of Columbia, or U.S. territories that have an approved plan as outlined in the FAST Act. Individuals and businesses are not eligible to apply.

Beneficiary Eligibility: FMCSA may award these grants to the agencies of States, the District of Columbia, the Commonwealth of Puerto Rico, the Commonwealth of the Northern Mariana Islands, American Samoa, Guam, and the U.S. Virgin Islands.

Award Range/Average: Awards range from $50,000 to $1,000,000.

Funding: (Project Grants) FY 18 $42,424,178.00; FY 19 est $43,340,000.00; FY 20 est $0.00

HQ: 1200 New Jersey Avenue SE, Washington, DC 20590

  Phone: 202-366-0621

  http://www.fmcsa.dot.gov/mission/grants

FEDERAL RAILROAD ADMINISTRATION
Regional – State – Local Offices

Region I (Northeastern)
Mark H. McKeon, Regional Administrator | 55 Broadway Room 1077, Cambridge, MA 02142 617-494-2302

Region II (Eastern)
David R. Myers, Regional Administrator | 2 International Plaza Suite 550, Philadelphia, PA 19113 610-521-8200

Region III (Southern)
L.F. Dennin II, Regional Administrator | Atlanta Federal Center Suite 16T20 61 Forsyth Street SW, Atlanta, GA 30303-3104 404-562-3800

Region IV (Central)
Hiram J. Walker, Regional Administrator | 111 N Canal Street Suite 655, Chicago, IL 60606 312-353-6203

Region V (Southwestern)
John F. Megary, Regional Administrator | 8701 Bedford Euless Road Suite 425, Hurst, TX 76053 817-284-8142

Region VI (Midwestern)
Darrell J. Tisor, Regional Administrator | 901 Locust Street Suite 464, Kansas City, MO 64106-2095 816-329-3840

Region VII (Western)
Alvin Settje, Regional Administrator | 801 I Street Suite 466, Sacramento, CA 95814-2559 916-498-6540

Region VIII (Northwestern)
Dick Clairmont, Regional Administrator | Murdock Executive Plaza Suite 650 703 Broadway, Vancouver, WA 98660 360-696-7536

DOT20.301 | RAILROAD SAFETY

Award: Project Grants

Purpose: Reduces railroad-related casualties and accidents.

Applicant Eligibility: Local, Private nonprofit institution/Organization (includes Institutions of higher education), Other public institution/Organization, Profit Organization.

Beneficiary Eligibility: General public.

Award Range/Average: Range for FY18 was $4,000 to $3,567,500, and the average was $747,035.

Funding: (Project Grants) FY 18 $9,302,967.00; FY 19 est $8,578,994.00; FY 20 est $4,103,357.00

Programs Administered by Regional - State - Local Offices

HQ: 1200 New Jersey Avenue SE, Washington, DC 20590
  Phone: 202-493-6441 | Email: felicia.young@dot.gov
  http://www.fra.dot.gov

DOT20.313 | RAILROAD RESEARCH AND DEVELOPMENT
Award: Project Grants
Purpose: To foster long-range enhancement of the Federal Railroad Administration's program of research in support of rail safety by developing cooperative research relationships.
Applicant Eligibility: Applicants can be major academic and industry research Institutions with backgrounds in the rail transportation arena. A minimum of 5 years of railroad or railroad related research experience is typically required.
Beneficiary Eligibility: No restrictions.
Award Range/Average: Range for FY 2018 was $100,000 to $2,400,000 with an average of $762,500.
Funding: (Cooperative Agreements) FY 18 $2,900,000.00; FY 19 est $2,950,000.00; FY 20 est $2,950,000.00
HQ: 1200 New Jersey Avenue SE, Washington, DC 20590
  Phone: 202-493-6441 | Email: felicia.young@dot.gov
  http://www.fra.dot.gov

DOT20.314 | RAILROAD DEVELOPMENT
Award: Project Grants
Purpose: To provide financial assistance for: planning and developing railroad corridors (including environmental studies), purchasing rail equipment, rail line relocation and improvement projects, construction projects that improve rail lines, enhance service, and add capacity to the national rail system.
Applicant Eligibility: State Governments (includes District of Columbia); Regional and Local Governments (excludes Institutions of higher education and hospitals); For-profit Organizations, such as railroads.
Beneficiary Eligibility: State governments Regional and local governments For-profit organizations, such as railroads.
Award Range/Average: Range for FY18 from $595,200 to $40,200,000 with an average of $11,547,818.
Funding: (Cooperative Agreements) FY 18 $57,739,092.00; FY 19 est $3,100,000.00; FY 20 $3,811,690.00
HQ: 1200 New Jersey Avenue SE, Washington, DC 20590
  Phone: 202-493-6441 | Email: felicia.young@dot.gov
  http://www.fra.dot.gov

DOT20.315 | NATIONAL RAILROAD PASSENGER CORPORATION GRANTS
"Amtrak Grants"

Award: Project Grants
Purpose: To provide financial assistance to support the operation of and capital investment in intercity passenger rail service.
Applicant Eligibility: As directed by authorizing and appropriating statute, assistance is available only to the National Railroad Passenger Corporation.
Beneficiary Eligibility: Same as Applicant Eligibility.
Award Range/Average: Awards under this program ranged from $1,500,000 to $1,220,051,136 in FY 2018 and depend on the amount and break down of assistance made available through specific appropriation laws.
Funding: (Project Grants (Cooperative Agreements)) FY 18 $1,865,347,239.00; FY 19 est $1,931,062,000.00; FY 20 est $924,783,670.00
HQ: 1200 New Jersey Avenue SE, Washington, DC 20590
  Phone: 202-493-6441 | Email: felicia.young@dot.gov
  http://www.fra.dot.gov

DOT20.316 | RAILROAD REHABILITATION AND IMPROVEMENT FINANCING PROGRAM
"RRIF Loan Program"

Award: Direct Loans; Guaranteed/insured Loans

Purpose: Provides direct loans and loan guarantees to State and local governments, interstate compacts consented to by Congress under section 410(a) of the Amtrak Reform and Accountability Act of 1997 (49 U.S.C. 24101).

Applicant Eligibility: Eligible borrowers include railroads, state and local Governments, government-sponsored authorities and corporations, joint ventures that include at least one railroad, and limited option freight shippers who intend to construct a new rail connection.

Beneficiary Eligibility: The beneficiaries of the Program will be the State or local government organizations, railroad, joint ventures that include a railroad, and limited option freight shippers that will receive the financial assistance to permit them to complete the specified projects.

Award Range/Average: One new loan was issued in FY 2018 for $220,000,000. Two loans were issued in FY 2019 for $5,949,999 and $908,000,000.

Funding: (Direct Loans) FY 18 $220,088,000.00; FY 19 est $923,427,813.00; FY 20 est $600,000,000.00

HQ: 1200 New Jersey Avenue SE W12-426, Washington, DC 20590

Phone: 202-366-2300 | Email: duane.callendar@dot.gov

http://www.transportation.gov/buildamerica/programs-services/rrif

DOT20.317 | CAPITAL ASSISTANCE TO STATES-INTERCITY PASSENGER RAIL SERVICE
"IPR Program"

Award: Project Grants

Purpose: To provide financial assistance to fund capital improvements necessary to support improved or new intercity passenger rail service.

Applicant Eligibility: To be eligible for this assistance, States must include intercity passenger rail service as an integral part of statewide transportation planning as required under section 135 of title 23, United States Code. To be eligible for capital assistance, the specific project must be on the Statewide Transportation Improvement Plan at the time of the application to qualify.

Beneficiary Eligibility: To be eligible for this assistance, States must include intercity passenger rail service as an integral part of statewide transportation planning as required under section 135 of title 23, United States Code. To be eligible for capital assistance, the specific project must be on the Statewide Transportation Improvement Plan at the time of the application to qualify. State departments of transportation and other public agencies, although private transportation companies may participate through contractual arrangements with a State department of transportation.

Award Range/Average: No awards were made in FY 2018 or anticipated in the future.

HQ: Management Division 1200 New Jersey Avenue SE, Washington, DC 20590

Phone: 202-493-6441 | Email: felicia.young@dot.gov

http://www.fra.dot.gov

DOT20.318 | MAGLEV PROJECT SELECTION PROGRAM-SAFETEA-LU

Award: Cooperative Agreements

Purpose: Provides financial assistance for a demonstration magnetic levitation transportation project.

Applicant Eligibility: Only for existing Maglev projects.

Beneficiary Eligibility: State governments.

Award Range/Average: No obligations were made in FY 2018. One additional obligation beyond FY 2020 is planned for $13,800,000.

HQ: Office of Program Delivery 1200 New Jersey Avenue SE, Washington, DC 20590

Phone: 202-493-6441 | Email: felicia.young@dot.gov

http://www.fra.dot.gov

Programs Administered by Regional - State - Local Offices

DOT20.319 | HIGH-SPEED RAIL CORRIDORS AND INTERCITY PASSENGER RAIL SERVICE-CAPITAL ASSISTANCE GRANTS
"HSR/IPR Program"

Award: Cooperative Agreements; Project Grants

Purpose: To assist in financing the capital costs of facilities, infrastructure, and equipment necessary to provide or improve high-speed rail and intercity passenger rail service.

Applicant Eligibility: States (including the District of Columbia), groups of states, interstate compacts, public agencies established by one or more states and having responsibility for providing intercity passenger rail service or high-speed passenger rail service, Amtrak, Amtrak in cooperation with states.

Beneficiary Eligibility: The general public, both users and non-users of intercity passenger rail service. State departments of transportation and other public agencies, although private transportation companies may participate through contractual arrangements with a State department of transportation.

Award Range/Average: There were no awards in FY 2018.

Funding: (Project Grants) FY 18 $0.00; FY 19 est $3,391,372.00; FY 20 est $2,174,161.00

HQ: Office of Program Delivery 1200 New Jersey Avenue SE, Washington, DC 20590

    Phone: 202-493-6441 | Email: felicia.young@dot.gov
    http://www.fra.dot.gov

DOT20.320 | RAIL LINE RELOCATION AND IMPROVEMENT
"Rail Line Relocation"

Award: Project Grants

Purpose: Provides financial assistance for rail line relocation and improvement projects.

Applicant Eligibility: States, Political Subdivisions of States, and the District of Columbia.

Beneficiary Eligibility: Same as Applicant Eligibility.

Award Range/Average: No awards were made in FY 2017.

Funding: (Project Grants (Cooperative Agreements)) FY 18 $0.00; FY 19 est $1,742,240.00; FY 20 est $5,166,334.00

HQ: 1200 New Jersey Avenue SE, Washington, DC 20590

    Phone: 202-493-6441 | Email: felicia.young@dot.gov
    http://www.fra.dot.gov

DOT20.321 | RAILROAD SAFETY TECHNOLOGY GRANTS

Award: Project Grants

Purpose: To facilitate the deployment of train control technologies, train control component technologies, processor-based technologies, electronically controlled pneumatic brakes, rail integrity inspection systems, rail integrity warning systems, switch position indicators and monitors.

Applicant Eligibility: N/A

Beneficiary Eligibility: Passenger and freight railroad carriers; Railroad suppliers; and State and local governments for projects that have a public benefit of improved safety and network efficiency. To be eligible for assistance, the above entities subject to 49 U.S.C. 20157(a) must have submitted a revised Positive Train Control Implementation Plan (PTCIP) to FRA as required by 49 U.S.C. 20157(a). FRA considers the development and submission of a revised PTCIP under 49 U.S.C. 20157(a) to meet the eligibility requirement related to submitting a plan required under 49 U.S.C. 20156(e)(2) containing an analysis of the impact, feasibility, costs and benefits of implementing PTC system technology. FRA believes that any submission connected to sec. 20156(e)(2), which has yet to be incorporated into a Federal regulation, would merely be duplicative of what a railroad analyzed when it developed and submitted a revised PTCIP. Thus, FRA considers the submission of a revised PTCIP to meet the eligibility requirements in 49 U.S.C. 20158(b)(3) for purposes of this NOFO. If an applicant is not required to comply with either sec. 20157(a) or sec. 20156(e)(2), the applicant must demonstrate that to FRA's satisfaction in its NOFO application Individuals are not eligible for these awards.

Award Range/Average: The range was between $771,070 to $3,000,000, and the average was $2,465,178 in FY 2018.

Funding: (Project Grants) FY 18 $14,791,070.00; FY 19 est $0.00; FY 20 est $67,347.00

HQ: 1200 New Jersey Avenue SE, Washington, DC 20590

    Phone: 202-493-6441 | Email: felicia.young@dot.gov
    http://www.fra.dot.gov

DOT20.323 | FISCAL YEAR 2013 HURRICANE SANDY DISASTER RELIEF GRANTS TO THE NATIONAL RAILROAD PASSENGER CORPORATION

Award: Project Grants

Purpose: Provides supplemental assistance to the National Passenger Railroad Corporation for disaster assistance related to Hurricane Sandy.

Applicant Eligibility: As directed by authorizing and appropriating statute, assistance is available only to the National Railroad Passenger Corporation.

Beneficiary Eligibility: Same as Applicant Eligibility.

Award Range/Average: There were no awards in FY 2018. Future awards are expected to range from $13,479,978 to $21,300,000 with an average of $14,926,659.

Funding: (Project Grants) FY 18 est $0.00; FY 19 est $13,479,978.00; FY 20 est $31,291,500.00

HQ: Office of Program Delivery 1200 New Jersey Avenue SE, Washington, DC 20590

   Phone: 202-493-6377 | Email: michael.longley@dot.gov

   http://www.fra.dot.gov

DOT20.324 | RESTORATION AND ENHANCEMENT

Award: Project Grants

Purpose: Provides operating assistance grants for the purpose of initiating, restoring, or enhancing intercity rail passenger transportation.

Applicant Eligibility: Interstate, State (includes District of Columbia), Local, Profit Organization, State (1) a State, including the District of Columbia; (2) a group of States; (3) an Interstate Compact; (4) a public agency or publicly chartered authority established by 1 or more States; (5) a political subdivision of a State; (6) Amtrak or another rail carrier that provides intercity rail passenger transportation; (7) Any rail carrier in partnership with at least 1 of the entities described in (1) through (5); and (8) any combination of the entities described in paragraphs (1) through (7).

Beneficiary Eligibility: Interstate, State Profit organization, State, Local, Public nonprofit institution/organization (1) a State, including the District of Columbia; (2) a group of States; (3) an Interstate Compact; (4) a public agency or publicly chartered authority established by 1 or more States; (5) a political subdivision of a State; (6) Amtrak or another rail carrier that provides intercity rail passenger transportation; (7) Any rail carrier in partnership with at least 1 of the entities described in paragraphs (1) through (5); and (8) any combination of the entities described in (1) through (7).

Award Range/Average: No grants were awarded in FY 2018.

Funding: (Project Grants) FY 18 $0.00; FY 19 est $86,501.00; FY 20 est $24,663,500.00

HQ: Office of Program Delivery 1200 New Jersey Avenue SE, Washington, DC 20590

   Phone: 202-493-6441 | Email: felicia.young@dot.gov

   http://www.fra.dot.gov

DOT20.325 | CONSOLIDATED RAIL INFRASTRUCTURE AND SAFETY IMPROVEMENTS
"CRISI"

Award: Project Grants

Purpose: Assists in financing the cost of improving passenger and freight rail transportation systems in terms of safety, efficiency, or reliability.

Applicant Eligibility: Interstate, Public nonprofit institution/Organization (includes Institutions of higher education), Other public institution/Organization, Profit Organization, State (1) A State. (2) A group of States. (3) An Interstate Compact. (4) A public agency or publicly chartered authority established by 1 or more States. (5) A political subdivision of a State. (6) Amtrak or another rail carrier that provides intercity rail passenger transportation (7) A Class II railroad or Class III railroad (8) Any rail carrier or rail equipment manufacturer in partnership with at least 1 of the entities in (1) through (5). (9) The Transportation Research Board and any entity with which it contracts in the development of rail-related research, including cooperative research Programs. (10) A University transportation center engaged in rail-related research. (11) A non-profit labor Organization representing a class or craft of employees of rail carriers or rail carrier contractors.

Beneficiary Eligibility: (1) A State.(2) A group of States.(3) An Interstate Compact.(4) A public agency or publicly chartered authority established by 1 or more States.(5) A political subdivision of a State.(6) Amtrak or another rail carrier that provides intercity rail passenger transportation (7) A Class II railroad or Class III railroad(8) Any rail carrier or rail equipment manufacturer in partnership with at least 1 of the entities in (1) through (5).(9) The Transportation Research Board and any

Programs Administered by Regional - State - Local Offices

entity with which it contracts in the development of rail-related research, including cooperative research programs.(10) A University transportation center engaged in rail-related research.

Award Range/Average: The range was between $1,767,665 and $8,081,222 with an average of $3,943,990 in first half of FY 2019.

Funding: (Project Grants) FY 18 $0.00; FY 19 est $194,170,709.00; FY 20 est $233,298,899.00

HQ: Office of Program Delivery 1200 New Jersey Avenue SE, Washington, DC 20590

Phone: 202-493-6441 | Email: felicia.young@dot.gov

http://www.fra.dot.gov

DOT20.326 | FEDERAL-STATE PARTNERSHIP FOR STATE OF GOOD REPAIR

Award: Project Grants

Purpose: Funds capital projects that reduce the state of good repair backlog with respect to qualified railroad assets.

Applicant Eligibility: (A) a State (including the District of Columbia); (B) a group of States; (C) an Interstate Compact; (D) a public agency or publicly chartered authority established by 1 or more States; (E) a political subdivision of a State; (F) Amtrak, acting on its own behalf or under a cooperative agreement with 1 or more States; or (G) any combination of the entities described in (A) through (F).

Beneficiary Eligibility: Profit organization, Interstate, State, Local (A) a State (including the District of Columbia); (B) a group of States; (C) an Interstate Compact; (D) a public agency or publicly chartered authority established by 1 or more States; (E) a political subdivision of a State; (F) Amtrak, acting on its own behalf or under a cooperative agreement with 1 or more States; or (G) any combination of the entities described in subparagraphs (A) through (F).

Award Range/Average: No grants were awarded in FY 2018.

Funding: (Project Grants) FY 18 $0.00; FY 19 est $0.00; FY 20 est $136,125,000

HQ: Office of Program Delivery 1200 New Jersey Avenue SE, Washington, DC 20590

Phone: 202-493-6441 | Email: felicia.young@dot.gov

http://www.fra.dot.gov

FEDERAL TRANSIT ADMINISTRATION
Regional – State – Local Offices

Region I
Mary Beth Mello, Regional Administrator for Region I | 55 Broadway Suite 921, Cambridge, MA 02142-1093 617-494-2055

Region II
Marilyn Shazor | Region II - New York NY 1 Bowling Green Suite 429, New York, NY 10004-1415 212-668-2170

Region III
Brigid Hynes-Cherin, Regional Administrator for Region III | 1760 Market Street Suite 500, Philadelphia, PA 19103-4124 215-656-7100

Region IV
Yvette G. Taylor, Regional Administrator for Region IV | 230 Peachtree Street NW Suite 800, Atlanta, GA 30303-8917 404-865-5600

Region V
Marisol Simon, Regional Administrator Region for V | 200 W Adams Street Suite 320, Chicago, IL 60606-5232 312-353-2789

Region VI
Robert C. Patrick, Regional Administrator | Fritz Lanham Federal Building 819 Taylor Street Suite 8A36, Fort Worth, TX 76102 817-978-0550

Region VII
Mokhtee Ahmad, Regional Administrator | 901 Locust Street Room 404, Kansas City, MO 64106 816-329-3920

Region VIII
Linda Gehrke, Regional Administrator for Region | 8 12300 W Dakota Avenue Suite 310, Lakewood, CO 80228-2583 720-963-3300

Region IX
Leslie Rogers, Regional Administrator | 201 Mission Street Suite 2210, San Francisco, CA 94105-1926 415-744-3133

Region X
Rick Krochalis, Regional Administrator for Region X | Jackson Federal Building 915 2nd Avenue Suite 3142, Seattle, WA 98174-1002 206-220-7954

DOT20.500 | FEDERAL TRANSIT CAPITAL INVESTMENT GRANTS
"New Starts, Small Starts, and Core Capacity"

Award: Formula Grants; Project Grants

Purpose: Provides funding for fixed guideway investments such as new and expanded heavy rail, commuter rail, light rail, streetcar, bus rapid transit, and ferries as well as corridor-based bus rapid transit investments that emulate the features of rail.

Applicant Eligibility: Public agencies, including States; municipalities and other subdivisions of States; public agencies and instrumentalities of one or more States; and public corporations, boards, and commissions established under State law. Applicant must have legal, financial, and technical capacity to carry out proposed project, including safety and security aspects, and maintain facilities and equipment purchased with Federal assistance. Private non-profit Organizations are not eligible direct recipients.

Beneficiary Eligibility: Same as Applicant Eligibility.

Funding: (Project Grants) FY 18 $1,840,669,856.00; FY 19 est $2,527,170,000.00; FY 20 est $1,490,138,100.00

HQ: 1200 New Jersey Avenue SE, Washington, DC 20590

    Phone: 202-366-5159 | Email: elizabeth.day@dot.gov

    http://www.fta.dot.gov

DOT20.505 | METROPOLITAN TRANSPORTATION PLANNING AND STATE AND NON-METROPOLITAN PLANNING AND RESEARCH

Award: Formula Grants

Purpose: To assist in development of metropolitan and state transportation improvement programs, long-range transportation plans, and other technical studies in a program for a unified and officially coordinated Statewide Transportation system and Metropolitan Transportation system(s) within the state.

Applicant Eligibility: Apportionments are made to the States for 1) statewide planning and 2) formula distribution to the Metropolitan Planning Organizations designated for the urbanized areas within each State for planning within urbanized areas.

Beneficiary Eligibility: Apportionments for metropolitan planning and for state planning and research are made to the States. Funds for metropolitan planning are distributed by formula to the Metropolitan Planning Organizations (MPOs) designated for the urbanized areas within each State.

Award Range/Average: Range and Average of Financial Assistance $20,000 to $5,000,000.

Funding: (Formula Grants) FY 18 $152,806,428.00; FY 19 est $138,392,318.00; FY 20 est $141,326,235.00

HQ: 1200 New Jersey Avenue SE, Washington, DC 20590

    Phone: 202-366-2996 | Email: victor.austin@dot.gov

    http://www.fta.dot.gov

DOT20.507 | FEDERAL TRANSIT FORMULA GRANTS
"Urbanized Area Formula Program; Section 5307"

Award: Formula Grants

Purpose: To support public transportation services in urbanized areas.

Applicant Eligibility: Funds will be made available to urbanized areas (as defined by the U.S. Census Bureau) through designated recipients, which must be public entities and have the legal capacity to receive and dispense federal funds. The Governor, responsible local officials, and publicly owned operators of mass transportation services must jointly select the designated recipient(s) for an urbanized area with a population of 200,000 or more. The Governor or his designee acts as the designated recipient for an urbanized area with a population of 50,000 to 199, 999. Recipients must submit a Program of projects to FTA; submit a Program application to FTA; enter into formal agreements with FTA; and certify that public notification has been conducted.

Beneficiary Eligibility: The general public, both users and non-users, and publicly owned operators of public transportation services.

Award Range/Average: Varies according to local programming of available formula funds and the level of operating expenses incurred.

Funding: (Formula Grants) FY 18 $6,583,267,878.00; FY 19 est $4,766,778,636.00; FY 20 est $4,867,834,343.00

HQ: 1200 New Jersey Avenue SE, Washington, DC 20590

    Phone: 202-366-2623 | Email: tara.clark@dot.gov

    http://www.transit.dot.gov

Programs Administered by Regional - State - Local Offices

DOT20.509 | FORMULA GRANTS FOR RURAL AREAS AND TRIBAL TRANSIT PROGRAM
"Rural Area Program"

Award: Formula Grants

Purpose: To improve, initiate, or continue public transportation service in nonurbanized areas and to provide technical assistance for rural transportation providers.

Applicant Eligibility: Only designated State agencies and Indian Tribes may apply directly to FTA for grants. Eligible sub-recipients may include State agencies, local public bodies and agencies thereof, nonprofit Organizations, Indian Tribes, and operators of public transportation services, including intercity bus service, in rural and small urban areas. Private for-profit operators of transit or paratransit services may participate in the Program only through contracts with eligible recipients. Private intercity bus operators may participate as subrecipients or through contracts. Urbanized areas, as defined by the Bureau of the Census, are not eligible.

Beneficiary Eligibility: The general public, both users and nonusers, and private and public providers of public transportation in nonurbanized areas.

Award Range/Average: In 2018, the average award for a formula grant received under the Public Transportation on Indian Reservations Program was $247,934, ranging from $1,572 to $1,321,904. The average award for the competitive grant program was $138,834, ranging from $25,000 to $300,000. In 2019, the average award under the Formula Grants for Rural Areas was approximately $13,600,000, ranging from approximately $300,000 to $30,000,000.

Funding: (Formula Grants) FY 18 $665,576,907.00; FY 19 est $656,025,420.00; FY 20 est $669,933,159

HQ: 1200 New Jersey Avenue SE, Washington, DC 20590
  Phone: 202-366-3800 | Email: elan.flippin@dot.gov
  http://www.fta.dot.gov

DOT20.513 | ENHANCED MOBILITY OF SENIORS AND INDIVIDUALS WITH DISABILITIES

Award: Formula Grants; Project Grants

Purpose: To provide financial assistance in meeting the transportation needs of seniors and individuals with disabilities where public transportation services are unavailable, insufficient or inappropriate.

Applicant Eligibility: Eligible sub-recipients include private nonprofit Organizations, public bodies approved by the State to coordinate services for elderly persons and individuals with disabilities and public bodies which certify that no nonprofit Organizations or associations are readily available in an area to provide the service.

Beneficiary Eligibility: Seniors and persons with disabilities.

Funding: (Formula Grants (Apportionments)) FY 18 $343,595,997.00; FY 19 est $278,247,957.00; FY 20 est $284,146,814.00

HQ: 1200 New Jersey Avenue SE, Washington, DC 20590
  Phone: 202-366-3102 | Email: kelly.tyler@dot.gov
  http://www.fta.dot.gov

DOT20.514 | PUBLIC TRANSPORTATION RESEARCH, TECHNICAL ASSISTANCE, AND TRAINING
"National Research Programs"

Award: Project Grants; Direct Payments for Specified Use; Dissemination of Technical Information; Training

Purpose: To seek to develop solutions that improve public transportation. Its primary goals are to increase transit ridership, improve safety and emergency preparedness, improve operating efficiencies, protect the environment, promote energy independence, and provide transit research leadership.

Applicant Eligibility: Applicants may include State and local DOT's, nonprofit Institutions, universities, and legally constituted public agencies and operators of public transportation services, and private for-profit Organizations. Also, urban and rural transit agencies, Indian Tribes, public 4-year degree-granting Institutions of higher education as defined in section 101(a) of the Higher education Act of 1965 (20 U.S.C. 1001(a)) in order to carry out the duties of the NTI.

Beneficiary Eligibility: N/A

Award Range/Average: Not Available.

Funding: (Project Grants (Contracts)) FY 18 $2,179,076.00; FY 19 est $0.00; FY 20 est $0.00

HQ: 1200 New Jersey Avenue SE, Washington, DC 20590
Phone: 202-366-0671 | Email: edwin.rodriguez@dot.gov
http://www.transit.dot.gov/research

DOT20.516 | JOB ACCESS AND REVERSE COMMUTE PROGRAM "JARC"

Award: Project Grants
Purpose: Offers grants to local governments, nonprofit organizations, and designated recipients of Federal transit funding to develop transportation services to connect welfare recipients and low- income persons to employment and support services.
Applicant Eligibility: State and local government agencies, nonprofit agencies, and transit providers.
Beneficiary Eligibility: Low income individuals; individuals traveling to suburban work places.
Award Range/Average: $10,890 to $1,293,611. Average: $180,588
HQ: 1200 New Jersey Avenue SE, 4th Floor E Building, Washington, DC 20590
Phone: 202-366-3800 | Email: elan.flippin@dot.gov
http://www.fta.dot.gov/funding/grants/grants_financing_3550.html

DOT20.518 | CAPITAL AND TRAINING ASSISTANCE PROGRAM FOR OVER-THE-ROAD BUS ACCESSIBILITY

Award: Project Grants
Purpose: To make funds available to private operators of over-the-road buses to finance the incremental capital and training costs of complying with requirements of the Department of Transportation's Over-the-Road Bus Accessibility regulation, "Transportation for Individuals with Disabilities" (49 CFR Part 37, Subpart H).
Applicant Eligibility: Private operators of over-the-road buses that provide intercity fixed route bus service and other providers, including operators of over-the-road buses of local fixed-route service, commuter service and charter or tour service.
Beneficiary Eligibility: Persons with disabilities.
Award Range/Average: $25,000 to $ 180,000. Average: $25,000.
HQ: Office of Program Management 1200 New Jersey Avenue SE, Washington, DC 20590
Phone: 202-366-3800 | Email: elan.flippin@dot.gov
http://www.fta.dot.gov

DOT20.519 | CLEAN FUELS

Award: Project Grants
Purpose: To assist in financing the acquisition of clean fuel vehicles and related facilities for agencies providing public transportation and operating in an urbanized and non-urbanized area designated as a non-attainment or maintenance area for ozone or carbon monoxide.
Applicant Eligibility: Public agencies, including States; municipalities and other subdivisions of States; public agencies and instrumentalities of one or more States; and public corporations, boards, and commissions established under State law. Applicant had legal, financial, and technical capacity to carry out proposed project and maintain facilities and equipment purchased with Federal assistance. Applicant also operated in an urbanized area designated as a non-attainment or maintenance area for ozone or carbon monoxide. If the urbanized area is less than 200,000 in population, the State in which the area is located acted as the recipient.
Beneficiary Eligibility: The general public, both users and non-users of public transportation.
Award Range/Average: $69,720 - $5,000,000. Average approx. $2,165,596
Funding: (Project Grants) FY 18 $96,577.00; FY 19 est $0.00; FY 20 est Estimate Not Available
HQ: Department of Transportation Federal Transit Administration1200 New Jersey Avenue SE, Washington, DC 20590
Phone: 202-366-4818 | Email: vanessa.williams@dot.gov
http://www.fta.dot.gov

Programs Administered by Regional - State - Local Offices

DOT20.520 | PAUL S. SARBANES TRANSIT IN THE PARKS
"Transit in the Parks"

Award: Cooperative Agreements; Project Grants

Purpose: It addresses the challenge of increasing vehicle congestion in and around our national parks and other federal lands.

Applicant Eligibility: Eligible applicants are: (1) The following Federal land management agencies: The National Park Service, the Fish and Wildlife Service, the Bureau of Land management, the Forest Service, and the Bureau of Reclamation; and (2) State, tribal and local Governments with jurisdiction over land in the vicinity of an eligible area acting with the consent of a Federal land management agency, alone or in partnership with a Federal land management agency or other governmental or non-governmental participant.

Beneficiary Eligibility: N/A

Award Range/Average: No one project could receive more than 25 percent of funds.

HQ: 1200 New Jersey Avenue SE, Washington, DC 20590

Phone: 202-366-4818 | Email: vanessa.williams@dot.gov

http://www.fta.dot.gov

DOT20.521 | NEW FREEDOM PROGRAM

Award: Formula Grants

Purpose: The New Freedom program (Section 5317) provided grants for new capital and operating projects aimed at reducing, beyond the requirements of the Americans with Disabilities Act of 1990, transportation barriers faced by individuals with disabilities to expand mobility through transportation, including transportation to and from jobs and employment support services.

Applicant Eligibility: The chief executive officer of each State or an official designee must designate a public entity to be the recipient for New Freedom funds. In urbanized areas with populations less than 200,000 and in non-urbanized areas, the State is the designated recipient. For these areas, the chief executive officer of a State designates a State agency responsible for administering the New Freedom Program, and officially notifies the appropriate Federal Transit Administration (FTA) regional office in writing of that designation. The chief executive officer of a State may designate the State agency that receives Other Than Urbanized Area (Non-urbanized Area, Section 5311) and/or the Elderly Individuals and Individuals with Disabilities (Section 5310) Program funds to be the New Freedom recipient, or the chief executive officer of a State may designate a different agency. In urbanized areas over 200,000 in population, the recipient charged with administering the New Freedom Program must be officially designated through a process consistent with 49 U.S.C. 5307(a)(2): an entity designated in accordance with the planning process under Sections 5303, 5304, and 5306, by the chief executive officer of a State, responsible local officials, and publicly owned operators of public transportation, to receive and apportion amounts under Section 5336 that are attributable to transportation management areas identified under Section 5303.

Beneficiary Eligibility: Individuals with Disabilities.

Award Range/Average: Project funding varied based on competitive selection process at State or urbanized area level. Urbanized area apportionments range from $111 to $2.2 M. for an average of $150K. State apportionments for small urbanized areas range from $644 to $1.5 M for an average of $115K, and for rural areas from $459 to $701K for an average of 160K.

HQ: 1200 New Jersey Avenue SE, Washington, DC 20590

Phone: 202-366-2160 | Email: kelly.tyler@dot.gov

http://www.fta.dot.gov/funding/grants/grants_financing_3549.html

DOT20.522 | ALTERNATIVES ANALYSIS

Award: Project Grants

Purpose: Assisted in financing the evaluation of all reasonable modal and multimodal alternatives and general alignment options for identified transportation needs.

Applicant Eligibility: Public agencies, including States; municipalities and other subdivisions of States; public agencies and instrumentalities of one or more States; and public corporations, boards, and commissions established under State law. Applicant must have legal, financial, and technical capacity to carry out proposed project and maintain facilities and equipment purchased with Federal assistance. Private non-profit Organizations are not directly eligible recipients.

Beneficiary Eligibility: The general public, both users and non-users of public transportation and public agencies. Private consultants may participate through contractual arrangements with a public agency grantee.

Award Range/Average: In FY 2006 Congressional designations ranged from $300,000 to $2,500,000.

HQ: FTA Office of Planning and Environment 1200 New Jersey Avenue SE, Washington, DC 20590
    Phone: 202-366-1636 | Email: maurice.foushee@dot.gov
    http://www.fta.dot.gov

DOT20.523 | CAPITAL ASSISTANCE PROGRAM FOR REDUCING ENERGY CONSUMPTION AND GREENHOUSE GAS EMISSIONS
"Transit Investments for Greenhouse Gas and Energy Reduction or "TIGGER" Grants"

Award: Project Grants
Purpose: Assists public agencies that provide transit service in financing the acquisition of capital assets to reduce energy consumption or greenhouse gas emissions.
Applicant Eligibility: Only public transportation agencies are eligible recipients.
Beneficiary Eligibility: Same as Applicant Eligibility.
Award Range/Average: Not Available.
HQ: Department of Transportation 1200 New Jersey Avenue SE, Washington, DC 20590
    Phone: 202-366-0725 | Email: marcel.belanger@dot.gov
    http://www.transit.dot.gov/research

DOT20.524 | PASSENGER RAIL INVESTMENT AND IMPROVEMENT (PRIIA) PROJECTS FOR WASHINGTON METROPOLITAN AREA TRANSIT AUTHORITY (WMATA)
"PRIIA - WMATA"

Award: Project Grants
Purpose: To assist in financing part of the capital and preventive maintenance projects included in the Capital Improvement Program approved by the Board of Directors of the Washington Metropolitan Area Transit Authority.
Applicant Eligibility: This Program is only for the Washington Metropolitan Area Transit Authority (Public Law 110-432, Section 601 of the Passenger Rail Investment and Improvement Act of 2008) for construction, renewal, and rehabilitation.
Beneficiary Eligibility: WMATA, transit riders, and general public.
Funding: (Project Grants) FY 18 $148,500,000; FY 19 est $148,500,000; FY 20 est $148,500,000
HQ: 1200 New Jersey Avenue SE, Washington, DC 20590
    Phone: 202-366-0870 | Email: eric.hu@dot.gov

DOT20.525 | STATE OF GOOD REPAIR GRANTS PROGRAM

Award: Formula Grants
Purpose: To assist in financing capital projects to maintain public transportation systems in a state of good repair and to ensure public transit operates safely, efficiently, reliably, and sustainably.
Applicant Eligibility: Eligible applicants are state and local governmental authorities in urbanized areas. FTA will apportion funds to designated recipients in the urbanized areas with fixed guideway and high intensity motorbus transportation systems operating at least 7 years. The designated recipients will then allocate funds as appropriate to recipients that are state and local governmental authorities in the urbanized areas.
Beneficiary Eligibility: The general public, both users and non-users of public transportation. Public agencies, although private transportation companies may participate through contractual arrangements with public agency grantee.
Funding: (Formula Grants) FY 18 $3,222,555,568.00; FY 19 est $2,872,353,190.00; FY 20 est $2,904,460,385.00
HQ: 1200 New Jersey Avenue SE, Washington, DC 20590
    Phone: 202-366-0870 | Email: eric.hu@dot.gov

Programs Administered by Regional - State - Local Offices

DOT20.526 | BUSES AND BUS FACILITIES FORMULA, COMPETITIVE, AND LOW OR NO EMISSIONS PROGRAMS
"Bus Program"

Award: Formula Grants; Project Grants

Purpose: Provides capital funding to replace, rehabilitate, purchase, or lease buses and bus related equipment and to rehabilitate, purchase, construct, or lease bus-related facilities.

Applicant Eligibility: Beneficiaries of funding include states and direct recipients. After allocation of funds, fixed-route bus operators, the general public, both users and non-users of public transportation, public agencies, and private transportation companies may benefit.

Beneficiary Eligibility: Beneficiaries of funding include states and designated recipients. After allocation of funds, fixed-route bus operators, the general public, both users and non-users of public transportation, public agencies, and private transportation companies may benefit.

Award Range/Average: Current year: $165,000 - $40,000,000.

Funding: (Formula Grants) FY 18 $310,024,293.00; FY 19 est $610,352,255.00; FY 20 est $461,125,163.00

HQ: 1200 New Jersey Avenue SE, Washington, DC 20590

Phone: 202-366-9955 | Email: mark.bathrick@dot.gov

http://www.transit.dot.gov

DOT20.527 | PUBLIC TRANSPORTATION EMERGENCY RELIEF PROGRAM
"Transit Emergency Relief Program (ER Program)"

Award: Project Grants

Purpose: To provide operating assistance and capital funding to aid recipients and sub-recipients in restoring public transportation service, and in repairing and reconstructing public transportation assets to a state of good repair, as expeditiously as possible following an emergency or major disaster.

Applicant Eligibility: An entity that operates public transportation service in an area impacted by an emergency or major disaster, as defined by a gubernatorial or presidential declaration of such an emergency or disaster, and that receives federal transit funds directly from FTA.

Beneficiary Eligibility: Beneficiaries of funding include public transportation operators and the general public in areas for which an emergency or major disaster has been declared as defined under section 5324.

Award Range/Average: Future obligations will be made in response to assessed needs and subject to the availability of program funds.

Funding: (Project Grants) FY 18 $1,256,503,966.00; FY 19 est $1,214,382,654.00; FY 20 est $648,356,936.00

HQ: 1200 New Jersey Avenue SE, Washington, DC 20590

Phone: 202-366-9091 | Email: john.bodnar@dot.gov

http://www.transit.dot.gov/funding/grant-programs/emergency-relief-program/emergency-relief-program

DOT20.528 | RAIL FIXED GUIDEWAY PUBLIC TRANSPORTATION SYSTEM STATE SAFETY OVERSIGHT FORMULA GRANT PROGRAM
"State Safety Oversight Formula Grant Program"

Award: Formula Grants

Purpose: To improve public transportation safety by assisting States with the financing of safety oversight of rail fixed guideway public transportation systems in the jurisdiction of the state not regulated by the Federal Railroad Administration.

Applicant Eligibility: Eligible States are those with a rail fixed guideway public transportation system within the jurisdiction of the State that is not subject to regulation by the Federal Railroad Administration; or a rail fixed guideway public transportation system in the engineering or construction phase of development within the jurisdiction of the State that will not be subject to regulation by the Federal Railroad Administration. Subrecipients must be public agencies that are eligible to become Federal Transit Administration recipients.

Beneficiary Eligibility: Same as Applicant Eligibility.

Funding: (Project Grants (Contracts)) FY 18 $14,459,903.00; FY 19 est $24,135,588.00; FY 20 est $24,647,262.00

HQ: 1200 New Jersey Avenue SE, Washington, DC 20590

Phone: 202-366-5922 | Email: maria1.wright@dot.gov

DOT20.529 | BUS TESTING FACILITY
"FTA Bus Testing Program"

Award: Project Grants

Purpose: To provide assistance for the operation and maintenance of one facility capable of testing new transit bus models and reporting on their maintainability, reliability, safety, performance (including braking performance), structural integrity, fuel economy, emissions, and noise performance characteristics.

Applicant Eligibility: Applicants may include: local, anyone/general public.

Beneficiary Eligibility: N/A

Award Range/Average: 3000000

Funding: (Project Grants) FY 18 $4,278,842.00; FY 19 est $4,000,000.00; FY 20 est $3,000,000.00

HQ: Office of Mobility Innovation TRI-12 1200 New Jersey Avenue SE, Room E43-465 E Building 4th Floor, Washington, DC 20590

Phone: 202-366-0725 | Email: marcel.belanger@dot.gov

http://www.transit.dot.gov/about/12351_4584.html

DOT20.530 | PUBLIC TRANSPORTATION INNOVATION
"5312 Research Program"

Award: Project Grants; Direct Payments for Specified Use; Dissemination of Technical Information; Training

Purpose: The objectives of Public Transportation Innovation Projects are to provide various transportation services such as services to seniors, low-income individuals, performance management and operating efficiencies, advancement in vehicle technology, and safety measures. It also supports other innovative projects that improve public transportation. It also assists in the evaluation of low or no emission vehicles.

Applicant Eligibility: Federal Government departments, agencies, and instrumentalities of the Government, including Federal laboratories; State and local governmental entities; providers of public transportation; private or non-profit Organizations; Institutions of higher education; and technical and community colleges.

Beneficiary Eligibility: 14 - State, 15 - Local, 20 - Public nonprofit institution/organization, 36 - Private nonprofit institution/organization.

Award Range/Average: $50,000 to $1,000,000

Funding: (Project Grants (Cooperative Agreements or Contracts)) FY 18 $7,180,000.00; FY 19 est $28,000,000.00; FY 20 est $28,000,000.00

HQ: 1200 New Jersey Avenue SE, Washington, DC 20590

Phone: 202-366-2204 | Email: mary.leary@dot.gov

http://www.transit.dot.gov/research

DOT20.531 | TECHNICAL ASSISTANCE AND WORKFORCE DEVELOPMENT

Award: Project Grants; Direct Payments for Specified Use; Dissemination of Technical Information; Training

Purpose: The program encourage States to adopt effective programs to reduce highway deaths and injuries resulting from individuals riding unrestrained or improperly restrained in motor vehicles.

Applicant Eligibility: Federal Government departments, agencies, and instrumentalities of the Government; Metropolitan Planning Organizations; State and local governmental entities; providers of public transportation; and national non-profit Organizations (that have the appropriate demonstrated capacity to provide public transportation-related technical assistance); public four-year degree-granting Institutions of higher education, as defined in section 101(a) of the Higher education Act of 1965 (20 U.S.C. 1001(a)) to carry-out the duties of the institute.

Beneficiary Eligibility: State, Local, Public nonprofit institution/organization and Private nonprofit institution/organization. Specific applicant eligibility may vary with different program areas within this section.

Award Range/Average: $200,000 to $2,000,000.

Funding: (Project Grants (Cooperative Agreements or Contracts)) FY 18 $5,000,000.00; FY 19 est $9,000,000.00; FY 20 est $9,000,000.00

HQ: 1200 New Jersey Avenue SE, Washington, DC 20590

Phone: 202-366-2204 | Email: mary.leary@dot.gov

http://www.transit.dot.gov/research

Programs Administered by Regional - State - Local Offices

FOOD AND NUTRITION SERVICE
Regional – State – Local Offices

REGIONAL OFFICES

California

Dick Montoya | 550 Kearny Street Room 400, San Francisco, CA 94108 415-705-1310

Colorado

Craig Forman | 1244 Speer Boulevard Suite 903, Denver, CO 80204 303-844-0300

Georgia

Jerry Redding | 1st Floor Martin Luther King Jr Federal Annex 77 Forsythe Street SW Suite 112, Atlanta, GA 30303 404-730-2565

Illinois

Lawrence Rudmann | 77 W Jackson Boulevard 20th Floor, Chicago, IL 60604-3507 312-353-6664

Massachusetts

Charles DeJulius | 10 Causeway Street Room 501, Boston, MA 02222-1068 617-565-6370

New Jersey

Walt Haake | Mercer Corporate Park Corporate Boulevard CN 02150, Trenton, NJ 08650 609-259-5025

Texas

Judy Snow | 1100 Commerce Street Room 5-C-30, Dallas, TX 75242 214-767-0222

USDA10.533 | SNAP-ED TOOLKIT

Award: Cooperative Agreements

Purpose: The Supplemental Nutrition Education Toolkit provides educators with evaluation tools such as evaluation framework, training the guides implementation, evidence-based nutrition programs. These programs are apt for low-income audiences.

Applicant Eligibility: N/A

Beneficiary Eligibility: N/A

Award Range/Average: An award was made to the University of North Carolina at Chapel Hill in the amount of $140,836 for FY 2019. An award is proposed and awaiting approval for $160,091 to the University of North Carolina at Chapel Hill for FY 2020.

Funding: (Cooperative Agreements) FY 18 Actual Not Available; FY 19 est $140,836.00; FY 20 est $160,091.00

HQ: 3301 Park Center Drive, Alexandria, VA 22304
   Phone: 703-457-7762 | Email: lisa.mays@fns.usda.gov

USDA10.534 | CACFP MEAL SERVICE TRAINING GRANTS
"Child and Adult Care Food Program"

Award: Formula Grants

Purpose: The CACFP program provides training for technical assistance in childcare centers, group homes, afterschool programs, day care centers, etc., to ensure that the meals are in based on the standards of CACFP patterns.

Applicant Eligibility: State Agencies that administer the CACFP.

Beneficiary Eligibility: These are non-competitive grants for State agencies to provide Child and Adult Care Food Program (CACFP) meal service training to CACFP operators.

Funding: (Formula Grants (Apportionments)) FY 17 $0.00; FY 18 est $3,715,609.00; FY 19 est $0.00

HQ: 3101 Park Center Drive, Alexandria, VA 22302
   Phone: 703-457-7768 | Email: franciel.ikeji@fns.usda.gov

USDA10.535 | SNAP RECIPIENT INTEGRITY EDUCATION GRANT

Award: Project Grants

Purpose: To support SNAP that provides awareness programs on fraud prevention, trafficking, and other technical assistance.

Applicant Eligibility: This grant opportunity is open to the 53 State agencies that administer SNAP. FNS will consider only one application per State agency. There is no State matching requirement for this grant Program.

Beneficiary Eligibility: Agreements are established between State agencies and FNS. Grants funds can be used for projects educating recipients on eligibility fraud as well as trafficking and misuse of benefits.

Award Range/Average: On July 16,2019, nine State agencies were awarded FY 2019 SNAP Fraud Framework Implementation grants. The awards ranged from just over $300,000 to almost $745,000. The median award was just over $475,000.

Funding: (Project Grants) FY 18 Actual Not Available; FY 19 est $4,604,723; FY 20 est Estimate Not Available

Programs Administered by Regional - State - Local Offices

HQ: 3101 Park Center Drive, Room 818, Alexandria, VA 22302
Phone: 703-605-4385 | Email: jane.duffield@fns.usda.gov

USDA10.536 | CACFP TRAINING GRANTS
"Child and Adult Care Food Program competitive grants and cooperative agreements"

Award: Cooperative Agreements; Project Grants
Purpose: To develop and promote training program that provides knowledge and skills to CACFP operators to effectively operate their institutions such as childcare centers, day care homes, and other facilities of CACFP.
Applicant Eligibility: This is an announcement of the availability of funds for one new cooperative agreement for a 2-year time-frame (September 2017 - August 2019) with an accredited public or private Academic Institute of Higher Learning, a Research, or Training Institution (i.e. entity that provides training such as a corporation or non-profit). Special consideration will be given to applicants who have expertise in CACFP and/or have successfully implemented training initiatives with a child nutrition focus.
Beneficiary Eligibility: Selected applicant is to plan, develop, design, promote, and ultimately execute and evaluate a training program that uses a tiered approach to equip State agencies with the knowledge and skills necessary to train their CACFP program operators (including CACFP institutions such as sponsoring organizations and/or independent centers as well as CACFP facilities including child care centers and day care homes) to effectively operate the CACFP at the local-level.
Funding: (Project Grants (Cooperative Agreements)) FY 17 $3,000,000.00; FY 18 est $0.00; FY 19 est $0.00
HQ: 3101 Park Center Drive, Alexandria, VA 22302
Phone: 703-605-0784 | Email: barbara.smith@fns.usda.gov
https://www.fns.usda.gov/cacfp/child-and-adult-care-food-program

USDA10.537 | SUPPLEMENTAL NUTRITION ASSISTANCE PROGRAM (SNAP) EMPLOYMENT AND TRAINING (E&T) DATA AND TECHNICAL ASSISTANCE GRANTS
"SNAP E&T DATA Grants"

Award: Project Grants
Purpose: To provide support through the Food and Nutrition Act for agencies like SNAP and E and T with funds and technical assistance to become effective in their services.
Applicant Eligibility: This grant opportunity is open to the 53 State agencies that administer SNAP. There is no State matching requirement for this grant Program.
Beneficiary Eligibility: Agreements are established between State agencies and FNS. State agencies will use funds to develop and analyze outcome reporting systems.
Award Range/Average: The range is from $371,736 to $1,000,000. The average grant award is $714,799.
Funding: (Salaries and Expenses) FY 17 $5,718,393.00; FY 18 est $0.00; FY 19 est $0.00
HQ: 3101 Park Center Drive, 8th Floor, Alexandria, VA 22302
Phone: 703-305-2515 | Email: moira.johnston@fns.usda.gov
http://www.fns.usda.gov/snap

USDA10.539 | CNMI NUTRITION ASSISTANCE
"Commonwealth of the Northern Mariana Islands Nutrition Assistance Program"

Award: Direct Payments for Specified Use
Purpose: The Nutrition Assistance Program provides an allowance for certain foods to eligible residents of the CNMI.
Applicant Eligibility: Eligibility criteria are determined by the Commonwealth of the Northern Mariana Islands.
Beneficiary Eligibility: Low-income individuals and households are eligible for benefits as determined by the Commonwealth of the Northern Mariana Islands.
Funding: (Salaries and Expenses) FY 17 $20,648,000.00; FY 18 est $12,148,000.00; FY 19 est $12,148,000.00
HQ: 3101 Park Center Drive, Alexandria, VA 22302
Phone: 703-305-4397 | Email: sarah.goldberg@fns.usda.gov

Programs Administered by Regional - State - Local Offices

USDA10.540 | PARTICIPANT RESEARCH INNOVATION LABORATORY FOR ENHANCING WIC SERVICES

Award: Cooperative Agreements; Project Grants

Purpose: To support PRIL that develops interactive tools, technical resources, and innovative solutions to improve the services in WIC clinics and to improve retention for eligible children in WIC. It also supports the projects that are promoted for those eligible for WIC services.

Applicant Eligibility: The grant is to be used to establish a cooperative agreement to identify, develop and undertake projects to meet Food and Nutrition Service (FNS) Program needs and the food, nutrition, and health needs of WIC eligible participants.

Beneficiary Eligibility: All Accredited Colleges/Universities, and Private or Public Research Institutions are eligible to apply to this opportunity. This is a requirement for the selected recipient of the grants and cooperative agreements, not the sub-grantees. The recipient of the cooperative agreement is to award sub-grants to local WIC agencies aimed at identifying, developing, and evaluating interventions and innovative approaches to strengthen child retention in WIC.

Funding: (Salaries and Expenses) FY 17 Not Separately Identifiable; FY 18 est Not Separately Identifiable; FY 19 est $2,000,000.00

HQ: 3101 Park Center Drive, Room 1014, Alexandria, VA 22302
   Phone: 703-305-2309 | Email: anthony.panzera@fns.usda.gov

USDA10.541 | CHILD NUTRITION-TECHNOLOGY INNOVATION GRANT "TIG"

Award: Project Grants

Purpose: To promote funds for Child Nutrition Programs that promote innovative technology for performance measurement and to identify error-prone areas in the State and local educational agencies.

Applicant Eligibility: Grants are only available to State agencies administering the Child Nutrition Programs. The grants must relate to technology solutions for planning and implementation.

Beneficiary Eligibility: State agencies (and the local organizations that have agreements with the State agencies) administering the Child Nutrition Programs benefit from funded technology solutions.

Award Range/Average: CN TIG Planning Grant: 0- $100,000 CN TIG Implementation Grant: 0- $2,000,000 For FY 2017: Nine (9) grants were awarded with a range of $93,222 - $1,942,547 The average grant amount was $745,694

Funding: (Project Grants) FY 18 est $0.00; FY 19 est $12,765,347; FY 20 est $20,000,000

HQ: 3101 Park Center Drive, Room 628, Alexandria, VA 22302
   Phone: 703-305-2590 | Email: cindy.long@fns.usda.gov
   https://www.grants.gov/search-grants.html?cfda=10.541

USDA10.543 | HEALTHIER U.S. SCHOOL CHALLENGE: SMARTER LUNCHROOMS "HUSSC"

Award: Direct Payments for Specified Use

Purpose: The HUSSC is a voluntary certification that recognizes schools that participate in the National School Lunch Program and School Breakfast Program and provides healthier surroundings, smart lunchrooms, nutrition education, and physical activity.

Applicant Eligibility: N/A

Beneficiary Eligibility: School decision makers, school food service staff, teachers, children, parents, other educators.

Award Range/Average: Schools are awarded monetary incentive based on the applied award level:Bronze - $500 Silver - $1000 Gold - $1500 Gold Award of Distinction - $2000

Funding: (Direct Payments for Specified Use) FY 17 $1,500,000.00; FY 18 est $1,500,000.00; FY 19 est $0.00

HQ: 3101 Park Center Drive, Alexandria, VA 22302
   Phone: 703-305-2893 | Email: sheldon.gordon@fns.usda.gov
   http://www.fns.usda.gov/hussc/healthierus-school-challenge-smarter-lunchrooms

USDA10.544 | HEALTHY BODY HEALTHY SPIRIT

Award: Cooperative Agreements

Purpose: The SNAP compensates to improve nutrition and to avoid obesity.

Applicant Eligibility: To help the SNAP-Ed target audience establish healthy eating habits and an active lifestyle.

Beneficiary Eligibility: Same as Applicant Eligibility.

HQ: 3101 Park Center Drive, Alexandria, VA 22302

    Phone: 703-305-2397 | Email: usha.kalro@fns.usda.gov

    http://www.fns.usda.gov/snap/supplemental-nutrition-assistance-program-snap

USDA10.547 | PROFESSIONAL STANDARDS FOR SCHOOL NUTRITION EMPLOYEES

Award: Project Grants

Purpose: The Healthy Hunger-Free Kids Act of 2010 provides standards for nutrition employees managing National School Lunch and School Breakfast programs to ensure nutritious and enjoyable meals are provided in the school premises.

Applicant Eligibility: The State agency applies for and signs an agreement to receive Federal fund for disbursement. The State agency enters into an agreement with each sponsor that has been approved for participation.

Beneficiary Eligibility: Agreements are between USDA-FNS and State agencies.

Award Range/Average: Each State can apply for up to 150,000 for this grant

HQ: 3101 Park Center Drive, Alexandria, VA 22302

    Phone: 703-605-4437 | Email: julie.maxwell@fns.usda.gov

    http://www.fns.usda.gov/school-meals/child-nutrition-programs

USDA10.549 | RURAL CHILD POVERTY NUTRITION CENTER
"Child Nutrition Program Coordination in Rural Counties"

Award: Cooperative Agreements

Purpose: The USDA Rural Child Poverty Nutrition Center develops and administers sub-grants, supports researchers, implementing strategies and evaluation findings, reduces food insecurity, and focuses the services for rural areas.

Applicant Eligibility: The grant is to be used to establish grants and cooperative agreements to identify, develop and undertake projects to meet Food and Nutrition Service (FNS) Program needs and the food, nutrition, and health needs of Program eligible participants.

Beneficiary Eligibility: Cooperative agreements are awarded to State and local governments, hospitals, non-profit organizations and accredited colleges/universities. This is a requirement for the selected recipient of the grants and cooperative agreements, not the sub-grantees. Cooperative agreement recipients are to award sub-grants aimed at identifying, developing, and evaluating interventions and innovative approaches to strengthen the impact of Food and Nutrition Service programs on the food, nutrition, and health of program eligible participants.

Award Range/Average: Grant and sub-grant funds will be made available on a competitive basis, subject to availability of federal funds. This grant was funded at approximately $2.5 million; $1,275,500 of which will be distributed as sub-grants with a maximum award amount of $100,000 per sub-grantee.

Funding: (Salaries and Expenses) FY 17 $529,306.00; FY 18 est $580,000.00; FY 19 est $550,000.00

HQ: 3101 Park Center Drive, Alexandria, VA 22302

    Phone: 703-305-2698 | Email: danielle.berman@fns.usda.gov

USDA10.551 | SUPPLEMENTAL NUTRITION ASSISTANCE PROGRAM
"SNAP"

Award: Direct Payments for Specified Use

Purpose: SNAP improves nutrition and provides nutrition assistance for low-income people and also provides monthly benefits to increase the purchase of healthy foods.

Applicant Eligibility: SNAP Benefits: SNAP is a Federal Program administered by the States. The State or U.S. Territory agency responsible for Federally aided public assistance Programs submits requests for funding to USDA's Food and Nutrition Service. Contingency Fund: Placed in reserve for use only in such amounts and at such times as may be necessary to carry out Program operations. Enables the Program to react to shifts in Program need that we not anticipated at the time of a budget request. ARRA: This project ended in FY14. Healthy Incentive Pilot: This project ended in FY14. The purpose was to determine if incentives provided to SNAP recipients at the point-of-sale increase the purchase of fruits, vegetables or other healthful foods.

Beneficiary Eligibility: Applications for SNAP are made through a local social services agency which determines eligibility and benefit amount. Eligibility is based on household size, income, and expenses. Eligibility is also based on assets, citizenship or legal immigration status, and other factors. A gross income test is based on 130 percent of the poverty line, and the net

Programs Administered by Regional - State - Local Offices

income (after expenses) test is based on 100 percent of the poverty line. Households with elderly and disabled members need only meet the net income test. The resource limit is $2,250 ($3,250 for a household with an elderly or disabled member). A total of 42 States use broad-based categorical eligibility to align the resource limits and gross income limits with other mean tested programs. Able-bodied adults with certain limited exceptions must meet a work requirement or face time limits on participation.

Award Range/Average: Varies by income and household size. The average benefit for a household of 4 in FY15 was $257.73

Funding: (Salaries and Expenses) FY 17 $5,000,000,000.00; FY 18 est $3,000,000,000.00; FY 19 est $0.00

HQ: 3101 Park Center Drive, Alexandria, VA 22302

   Phone: 703-305-2022 | Email: jessica.shahin@fns.usda.gov
   http://www.fns.usda.gov/snap

USDA10.553 | SCHOOL BREAKFAST PROGRAM
"SBP"

Award: Formula Grants

Purpose: To compensate States through food donations for providing nutritious meals to school children.

Applicant Eligibility: States, including the District of Columbia and U.S. Territories, as applicable, may apply to administer the SBP and work in collaboration with public and nonprofit private schools and other Institutions for children, such as public and nonprofit private residential childcare Institutions. All participating schools and Institutions must agree to serve free and reduced price meals to eligible children, and operate a nonprofit meal service that is available to all children regardless of race, sex, color, national origin, age, or disability.

Beneficiary Eligibility: All children attending schools where this program is operating may receive nutrition benefits, which are determined based on the household income and size. Breakfast is served free to children who are determined by the local education agency to have household income levels at or below 130 percent, and at a reduced price to children from households with incomes higher than 130 but at or below 185 percent of the Federal poverty line. Paid breakfast is served to children who are not eligible for free and reduced-price meals. The Secretary prescribes the income eligibility guidelines for free and reduced-price meals by July 1. These guidelines are revised annually according to the Federal Income Poverty Guidelines. Children from households certified to receive benefits through the Supplemental Nutrition Assistance Program (SNAP), Food Distribution Program on Indian Reservations, or Temporary Assistance for Needy Families, and children in Head Start programs are automatically eligible for free meals. Homeless children, children in certain runaway and homeless youth grant programs, migrant children, and foster children are automatically eligible for free meals. All reimbursable meals served under the SBP at the free, reduced-price, and paid categories get cash assistance.

Funding: (Formula Grants) FY 18 $4,807,380,000.00; FY 19 est $4,816,238,000.00; FY 20 est $4,929,291,000.00

HQ: 3101 Park Center Drive, Alexandria, VA 22302

   Phone: 703-305-2590 | Email: cindy.long@fns.usda.gov
   http://www.fns.usda.gov

USDA10.555 | NATIONAL SCHOOL LUNCH PROGRAM
"School Lunch"

Award: Formula Grants

Purpose: To compensate States through food donations for providing nutritious agricultural commodities to school children.

Applicant Eligibility: States, including the District of Columbia and U.S. Territories, as applicable, may apply to administer the National School Lunch Program and work in collaboration with public and nonprofit private schools and other Institutions, such as residential childcare Institutions, to provide nutritious lunches for children. All participating schools and Institutions must agree to operate a nonprofit food service that is available to all children regardless of race, sex, color, national origin, age, or disability.

Beneficiary Eligibility: All children enrolled in schools where this program is operating may receive a lunch daily. Eligibility for free, reduced-price, or paid lunches is determined based on the household income and size. Lunch is available free to children who are determined by the local education agency to have household income levels at or below 130 percent, and at a reduced price rate to children from households with incomes higher than 130 but at or below 185 percent of the Federal poverty line. Lunch is available at the paid rate to children who are not eligible for free and reduced-price meals. The Secretary prescribes the income eligibility guidelines for free and reduced-price meals by July 1. These guidelines are revised annually according to the Federal Income Poverty Guidelines. Children from households certified to receive benefits through the Supplemental Nutrition Assistance Program (SNAP), Food Distribution Program on Indian Reservations, or

Temporary Assistance for Needy Families, and children in Head Start programs are automatically eligible for free meals. Homeless children, children in certain runaway and homeless youth grant programs, migrant children, and foster children are automatically eligible for free meals. All reimbursable meals served at the free, reduced-price, and paid categories get cash assistance.

Award Range/Average: State grants vary according to participation in this program.

Funding: (Formula Grants) FY 18 $13,133,155,000.00; FY 19 est $12,091,834,000.00; FY 20 est $12,726,216,000.00

HQ: 3101 Park Center Drive, Alexandria, VA 22302

    Phone: 703-305-2590 | Email: cindy.long@fns.usda.gov

    http://www.fns.usda.gov

USDA10.556 | SPECIAL MILK PROGRAM FOR CHILDREN
"SMP"

Award: Formula Grants

Purpose: To assist school children with subsidies and promote milk consumption.

Applicant Eligibility: The State, including the District of Columbia, or U.S. Territory as applicable, administers this Program. Public and nonprofit private school of high school grade or under, and public and private nonprofit residential and nonresidential childcare Institutions, except Job Corps centers, may participate in this Program upon request if they do not participate in a meal service Program authorized under the Richard B. Russell National School Lunch Act or the Child Nutrition Act of 1966. This generally includes nonprofit nursery schools, childcare centers, settlement houses and summer camps. Schools with split session kindergarten and pre-kindergarten Programs can receive subsidies for milk served to children in the split session kindergartens and pre-kindergartens that do not have access to another meal service Program operating in the school. All schools and childcare Institutions that participate must agree to operate this Program on a nonprofit basis for all children without regard to race, sex, color, national origin, age or disability.

Beneficiary Eligibility: All children enrolled in participating schools and institutions who do not have access to other Child Nutrition Programs, may participate in this program.

Award Range/Average: State grants vary according to participation in this program.

Funding: (Formula Grants) FY 18 $8,767,000.00; FY 19 est $8,065,00000; FY 20 est $7,185,000.00

HQ: 3101 Park Center Drive, Alexandria, VA 22302

    Phone: 703-305-2590 | Email: cindy.long@fns.usda.gov

    http://www.fns.usda.gov

USDA10.557 | WIC SPECIAL SUPPLEMENTAL NUTRITION PROGRAM FOR WOMEN, INFANTS, AND CHILDREN
"WIC Program"

Award: Formula Grants; Project Grants

Purpose: To assist breastfeeding, postpartum women, infants, and children below five with nutritious food and provide free health services. WIC also supports this cause and it provides awareness on substance abuse and healthy living habits. WIC also encourages and supports breastfeeding mothers and provides essential health and nutrition services.

Applicant Eligibility: A local agency is eligible to apply to deliver locally the services of the WIC Program, provided that: (1) it serves a population of low-income women, infants, and children at nutritional risk; and (2) it is a public or private nonprofit health or human service agency. All local agencies must apply through the responsible State, Indian Tribal Organization or U.S. Territory agency. The WIC Breastfeeding Support grant is available to small businesses, nonprofits having a 501(c)(3) status with the IRS, Institutions of higher education and for profit Organizations other than small businesses, public and State controlled Institutions of higher education and private Institutions of higher education. All applications must be submitted via the Grants.gov portal.

Beneficiary Eligibility: Pregnant, breastfeeding and postpartum women, infants, and children up to 5 years of age are eligible if: (1) they are individually determined by a competent professional to be in need of the special supplemental foods supplied by the program because of nutritional risk; and (2) meet an income standard, or receive or have certain family members that receive benefits under the Supplemental Nutrition Assistance, Medicaid or Temporary Assistance for Needy Families Programs. They must also reside in the State in which benefits are received.

Award Range/Average: For fiscal year 2017, FNS approved the operation of the WIC Program in 90 State agencies. This figure includes 50 States,34 Indian agencies, Puerto Rico, the Virgin Islands, Guam, American Samoa, the Commonwealth of the Northern Marianas and the District of Columbia. During fiscal year 2017, an average of approximately 7,286,161 women,

Programs Administered by Regional - State - Local Offices

infants and children received WIC benefits every month. Although food package costs varied widely among the States, the monthly average food package cost for fiscal year 2017 was approximately $41.23 per person.

Funding: (Formula Grants) FY 17 $6,512,698,000.00; FY 18 est $6,501,000,000.00; FY 19 est $5,660,000,000.00; FY 17 Administrative costs -$2,084,063,000; Food costs - $4,428,635,000 FY 18 Administrative costs - $2,080,320,000; Food costs - $4,420,680,000 (estimated) FY 19 Administrative costs - $1,811,200,000; Food costs - $3,848,800,000

HQ: Supplemental Food Programs Division 3101 Park Center Drive, Alexandria, VA 22302
Phone: 703-305-2746 | Email: sarah.widor@fns.usda.gov
http://www.fns.usda.gov/wic

USDA10.558 | CHILD AND ADULT CARE FOOD PROGRAM
"CACFP"

Award: Formula Grants

Purpose: To support nonprofit food service programs that assist children, elderly, or impaired at daycare centers, low-income areas, shelters by providing nutritious foods and all kinds of assistance for the differently abled.

Applicant Eligibility: The State or U.S. Territory agency applies for and signs an agreement to receive Federal funds for disbursement. The State agency enters into an agreement with each institution that has been approved for participation. The agreement is permanent and may be amended as necessary to ensure compliance with all Federal requirements. Institutions must agree to operate a nonprofit food service that is available to all eligible children and adult participants regardless of race, sex, color, national origin, age, or disability.

Beneficiary Eligibility: Approved institutions providing non residential day care services may participate in CACFP. Eligible public and nonprofit private organizations may include day care centers, outside-school-hours care centers, family day care homes, and Head Start programs. Private for-profit centers may also participate if at least 25 percent of the children in care (enrolled or licensed capacity, whichever is less) are eligible for free or reduced price school meals or receive benefits under Title XX of the Social Security Act. Also eligible for participation are nonprofit centers which provide non residential adult day care, and private for-profit centers if the center receives compensation under Title XIX of the Social Security Act or Title XX, and at least 25 percent of the adults enrolled in the center receive benefits under Title XIX, Title XX, or a combination of both. Emergency shelters which provide shelter and meals to children experiencing homelessness and at-risk after school care programs in low-income areas are also eligible. Any eligible institution may participate in CACFP upon request with State agency approval.

Funding: (Formula Grants) FY 18 $3,832,748,000.00; FY 19 est $3,815,328,000.00; FY 20 est $3,839,675,000.00

HQ: 3101 Park Center Drive, Room 628, Alexandria, VA 22302
Phone: 703-305-2590 | Email: Cindy.Long@usda.gov
http://fns.usda.gov

USDA10.559 | SUMMER FOOD SERVICE PROGRAM FOR CHILDREN
"SFSP"

Award: Formula Grants

Purpose: To support nonprofit food service programs that assist children and USDA and other local organizations that initiate to provide meals to eligible children at apt times.

Applicant Eligibility: The State or U.S. Territory agency applies for and signs an agreement to receive Federal funds for disbursement. The State agency enters into an agreement with each sponsor that has been approved for participation. The agreement is permanent and may be amended as necessary to ensure compliance with all Federal requirements. Sponsors must agree to operate a nonprofit food service that is available to all eligible children regardless of race, sex, color, national origin, age, or disability.

Beneficiary Eligibility: A service institution that conducts a regularly scheduled program for children from areas in which poor economic conditions exist is eligible to participate as a sponsor in this program. Sponsors include public or private nonprofit school food authorities; public or private nonprofit colleges or universities operating the National Youth Sports Program during the months of May to September; units of local, municipal, county, or State governments; and other faith or community-based private nonprofit organizations. Public or private nonprofit residential or non residential summer camps may also participate. However, at camps, reimbursement will only be paid for meals served to enrolled children who are individually determined to be eligible for free and reduced price school meals under USDA Income Eligibility Guidelines.

Funding: (Formula Grants) FY 18 $563,817,000.00; FY 19 est $519,456,000.00; FY 20 est $551,928,000.00

HQ: 3101 Park Center Drive, Room 628, Alexandria, VA 22302
  Phone: 703-305-2590 | Email: Cindy.Long@usda.gov
  http://fns.usda.gov

USDA10.560 | STATE ADMINISTRATIVE EXPENSES FOR CHILD NUTRITION
"State Administrative Expense (SAE) Funds"

Award: Formula Grants
Purpose: To compensate State agencies for providing technical assistance and nutrition programs for schools and adult care centers.
Applicant Eligibility: State agencies responsible for the administration of the Child Nutrition Programs and agencies responsible for the distribution of USDA Foods to schools and child or adult care Institutions, including agencies in the U.S. Territories, may apply.
Beneficiary Eligibility: N/A
Award Range/Average: FY2018:Range is $375,533 - $35,742,589 Average is $5,533,912 (50 States, DC, PR, GU, VI)
  FY2017:Range is $371,295 - $33,655,506 Average is $5,230,874 (50 States, DC, PR, GU, VI)
Funding: (Formula Grants) FY 18 est $298,847,210.00; FY 19 est $299,277,239.00; FY 20 est $300,000,000.00
HQ: 3101 Park Center Drive, Room 628, Alexandria, VA 22302
  Phone: 703-305-2590 | Email: cindy.long@fns.usda.gov
  http://www.fns.usda.gov

USDA10.561 | STATE ADMINISTRATIVE MATCHING GRANTS FOR THE SUPPLEMENTAL NUTRITION ASSISTANCE PROGRAM
"Supplemental Nutrition Assistance Program (State Administrative Match)"

Award: Formula Grants
Purpose: SNAP assists State agencies and E and T programs to provide employment oriented activities. USDA also provides reimbursement for transportation for those who participate in E and T programs. The Nutrition Education and Obesity Prevention education program assists low-income people.
Applicant Eligibility: SNAP SAE, E&T, and SNAP Ed: Agreements are between USDA-FNS and State cooperators. (U.S. Territories qualify as States for grant purposes.).
Beneficiary Eligibility: Same as Applicant Eligibility.
Award Range/Average: Unavailable
Funding: (Salaries and Expenses) FY 17 $4,644,843,000; FY 18 est $5,381,117,000; FY 19 est $5,519,070,000
HQ: 3101 Park Center Drive, Alexandria, VA 22302
  Phone: 703-305-2026 | Email: jessica.shahin@fns.usda.gov
  http://www.fns.usda.gov/fsp

USDA10.565 | COMMODITY SUPPLEMENTAL FOOD PROGRAM
Award: Formula Grants; Sale, Exchange, Or Donation of Property and Goods
Purpose: To maximize the supply of nutritious USDA foods for low-income and elderly persons and assist children with CSFP benefits as long as they are eligible.
Applicant Eligibility: Agreements are made between USDA and the State agency or an ITO recognized by the Department of the Interior or the appropriate area office of the Indian Health Service of the Department of Health and Human Services.
Beneficiary Eligibility: To be certified as eligible to receive USDA Foods through the program, individuals must be at least 60 years of age. As required by the Agricultural Act of 2014 (P.L. 113-79), women, infants, and children who apply to participate in CSFP on February 7, 2014, or later cannot be certified to participate in the program. Such individuals may be eligible for the Special Supplemental Nutrition Program for Women, Infants, and Children (WIC), the Supplemental Nutrition Assistance Program (SNAP), and other nutrition assistance programs. States also establish income guidelines to determine program eligibility for all participants. For elderly persons, income guidelines must be set at or below 130 percent of Federal poverty income guidelines. For women, infants, and children who were certified and receiving benefits as of February 6, 2014, and whose enrollment has continued without interruption, separate income and adjunctive income eligibility standards continue to apply, based on program regulations. States may require that participants be at nutritional risk, as determined by a physician or local agency staff. States may also require that an individual reside within the service area of the local agency at the time

Programs Administered by Regional - State - Local Offices

of application for program benefits. However, States may not require that the individual reside within the area for any fixed period of time.

Award Range/Average: On average, $1,016,169 in appropriated administrative funding was allocated to each State for FY18. Funding ranged from $6,395 to $7,442,023 per State. For FY18, States received $76.12 in administrative funding per assigned caseload slot.

Funding: (Salaries and Expenses) FY 18 $54,873,125.00; FY 19 est $57,683,727.00; FY 20 est $57,683,727.00

HQ: 3101 Park Center Drive, Alexandria, VA 22302

Phone: 703-305-2680 | Email: erica.antonson@fns.usda.gov

http://www.fns.usda.gov/csfp/commodity-supplemental-food-program-csfp

USDA10.566 | NUTRITION ASSISTANCE FOR PUERTO RICO
"NAP"

Award: Direct Payments for Specified Use

Purpose: To support needy people with healthy food residing in the Commonwealth of Puerto Rico.

Applicant Eligibility: The Commonwealth of Puerto Rico alone is eligible.

Beneficiary Eligibility: Low-income individuals and households are eligible for benefits as determined by the Commonwealth.

Funding: (Salaries and Expenses) FY 17 $1,949,001,000.00; FY 18 est $1,929,646,000.00; FY 19 est $1,961,927,000.00

HQ: 300 Corporate Boulevard, Robbinsville, NJ 08691

Phone: 609-259-5025 | Email: patricia.dombroski@fns.usda.gov

http://www.fns.usda.gov

USDA10.567 | FOOD DISTRIBUTION PROGRAM ON INDIAN RESERVATIONS
"FDPIR"

Award: Project Grants; Sale, Exchange, Or Donation of Property and Goods

Purpose: The Food Distribution Program on Indian Reservations provides nutrition assistance and nutrition education to the Indian Tribal and funds are provided for these activities.

Applicant Eligibility: The administration of FDPIR is limited to ITOs or to SAs that assume administration on behalf of/at the request of a Tribe(s).

Beneficiary Eligibility: FDPIR eligibility is limited to income-eligible households residing on participating reservations or income-eligible Indian Tribal Households (see definition at 7 CFR 253.2) residing in approved areas near a reservation or in approved service areas in Oklahoma. The ITOs/SAs are responsible for certifying households based on national eligibility criteria. The income standards vary by household size and are based on 100% of the Federal Poverty Guidelines adjusted by the applicable SNAP standard deduction.

Award Range/Average: In FY 2019, the monthly per person food package was approximately $70.97. Federal administrative funding to the ITOs and SAs varies based on number of persons served in each program and the unique operational needs of each program.

Funding: (Direct Payments for Specified Use) FY 18 $48,024,000.00; FY 19 est $ 49,762,000.00; FY 20 est $51,455,000.00; (Project Grants) FY 18 $104,976,000.00; FY 19 est $ 103,238,000.00; FY 20 est $78,545,000.00

HQ: 3101 Park Center Drive, 5th Floor, Alexandria, VA 22302

Phone: 703-305-2680 | Email: erica.antonson@fns.usda.gov

http://www.fns.usda.gov/fdpir/food-distribution-program-indian-reservations-fdpir

USDA10.568 | EMERGENCY FOOD ASSISTANCE PROGRAM (ADMINISTRATIVE COSTS)
"TEFAP"

Award: Formula Grants

Purpose: To provide assistance to needy people through State agencies and organizations such as food pantries, food banks, and other food providing organizations.

Applicant Eligibility: State agencies that are designated as distributing agencies by the Governor or other appropriate State executive authority may receive these administrative funds to support the distribution of USDA Foods to low-income persons.

Beneficiary Eligibility: Public or private non-profit organizations, such as food banks, food pantries, and soup kitchens, which provide food assistance to low-income persons.

Award Range/Average: In Fiscal Year 2018, the range for assistance to State agencies was from $34,572 to $12,570,848, after conversions and recoveries; the average amount of assistance was $1,648,701.

Funding: (Formula Grants) FY 18 $90,678,541.00; FY 19 est $109,630,000.00; FY 20 est $54,401,000; FY 2018 administrative funds include $64,401,000 in appropriated funds and an additional $26,341,755 after conversions and recoveries.

HQ: 3101 Park Center Drive, Alexandria, VA 22302

   Phone: 703-305-2680 | Email: erica.antonson@fns.usda.gov

   http://www.fns.usda.gov/tefap/emergency-food-assistance-program

USDA10.569 | EMERGENCY FOOD ASSISTANCE PROGRAM (FOOD COMMODITIES)
"TEFAP, USDA Foods, Commodities"

Award: Formula Grants

Purpose: To supply USDA foods through food agencies for low-income persons.

Applicant Eligibility: State agencies that are designated as distributing agencies by the Governor or other appropriate State executive authority may receive and distribute USDA Foods. States can distribute these foods to eligible recipient agencies, such as food banks, food pantries, soup kitchens, and other eligible agencies, including faith-based Organizations.

Beneficiary Eligibility: Low-income and needy individuals, including persons that are homeless, unemployed, underemployed, or receiving public assistance. The State agency must establish income-based eligibility criteria to ensure USDA Foods are provided to the needy. Persons interested in receiving TEFAP should contact their State agency (http://www.fns.usda.gov/fdd/contacts/SdaContacts.htm) for more information on how to access the program.

Award Range/Average: In Fiscal Year 2018, the range of awards was from $185,511 to $43,379,835, after conversions; the average award was $6,419,514.

Funding: (Formula Grants) FY 18 $353,073,267.00; FY 19 est $306,083,000.00; FY 20 $320,750,000.00

HQ: 3101 Park Center Drive, Alexandria, VA 22302

   Phone: 703-305-2680 | Email: erica.antonson@fns.usda.gov

   http://www.fns.usda.gov/tefap/emergency-food-assistance-program-tefap

USDA10.572 | WIC FARMERS' MARKET NUTRITION PROGRAM (FMNP)

Award: Formula Grants

Purpose: The WIC Farmers' Market Nutrition Program provides nutritious foods for women, infants, and children and it also expands income at farmer's markets.

Applicant Eligibility: Each State agency desiring to administer the FMNP shall annually submit a State Plan of Operations and enter into a written agreement with FNS for administration of the Program in the jurisdiction of the State agency. New State agencies are selected based on the availability of funds, after base grants for currently participating State agencies. Local FMNP agencies are selected by participating State agencies based on concentration of eligible WIC participants and access to farmers' markets.

Beneficiary Eligibility: Women, infants (over 4 months old) and children (ages 1 year up to age 5) who have been certified to receive WIC program benefits, or who are on a waiting list for WIC certification, are eligible to participate in the FMNP. State agencies may serve some or all of these categories.

Award Range/Average: FY 2018 grants ranged from $6,337 to $3,985,456. (actual) FY 2019 grants range from $6,337 to $3,871,070. (estimated)

Funding: (Formula Grants) FY 18 $18,548,000.00; FY 19 est $18,548,000; FY 20 est $ 0.00

HQ: 3101 Park Center Drive, Alexandria, VA 22302

   Phone: 703-305-2746 | Email: sarah.widor@fns.usda.gov

   http://www.fns.usda.gov/fmnp/wic-farmers-market-nutrition-program-fmnp

Programs Administered by Regional - State - Local Offices

USDA10.574 | TEAM NUTRITION GRANTS
"Team Nutrition Training Grants"

Award: Project Grants

Purpose: Team Nutrition support child nutrition programs. It compensates for the school meals implemented by USDA nutrition program. It promotes a fat-free diet. It implements the most recent Dietary Guidelines. Provides technical assistance to maintain childcare environment. The FY 2016 Team Nutrition Training Grant Objectives are to assist students in participating School Breakfast Program, improve nutritional content, administer schools in providing nutritious meals, and promotes healthy eating.

Applicant Eligibility: State agencies that administer the Child Nutrition Programs (e.g., NSLP, SBP, CACFP) may apply for a Team Nutrition Training Grant. States agencies must apply individually, and only one agency per State may apply each year.

Beneficiary Eligibility: School decision makers, school food service staff, students, parents, teachers, childcare professionals, and educators.

Award Range/Average: FY 2015 (Competitive) Team Nutrition Training GrantsIn FY 2015, State agencies could apply for up to $350,000 in competitive grants, and competitive awards ranged from $141,054 to $349,984. Average award per State agency was $297,017.05. FY 2016 (Competitive) Team Nutrition Training GrantsIn FY 2016, State agencies could apply for up to $500,000 in competitive grants. Awards have been accepted by States. FY 2017 (Competitive) Team Nutrition Training GrantsIn FY 2017, State agencies could apply for up to $500,000 in competitive grants. Awards have been accepted by States.

Funding: (Salaries and Expenses) FY 17 $5,311,436.00; FY 18 est $0.00; FY 19 Estimate Not Available

HQ: Division of Food and Nutrition Service 3101 Park Center Drive, Room 6th Floor, Alexandria, VA 22302
Phone: 703-305-2590 | Email: cindy.long@fns.usda.gov
http://www.fns.usda.gov/tn/team-nutrition-training-grants

USDA10.575 | FARM TO SCHOOL GRANT PROGRAM
"USDA Farm to School Grant Program"

Award: Cooperative Agreements; Project Grants; Dissemination of Technical Information; Training

Purpose: To support Farm to School program to provide local foods in eligible schools.

Applicant Eligibility: State Agencies, local agencies, Indian Tribal Organizations, small- and medium-sized agricultural/groups of agricultural producers, schools/school districts, and non-profit entities.

Beneficiary Eligibility: Eligible entities, and therefore beneficiaries, include schools/school districts, Indian Tribal Organizations, non profit organizations, schools, producer and producer groups and State and local agencies.

Award Range/Average: Planning grants will range from $20,000 - $50,000 while Implementation grants will range from $50,000 - $100,000. Training grants range $20,000 - $50,000.

Funding: (Cooperative Agreements) FY 17 $4,900,000.00; FY 18 est $5,000,000.00; FY 19 est $7,500,000.00; FY 16 $4,887,067.00; This obligation represents the planning, implementation and support service grants. FY 2017: Planning - $.5 million; Implementation - $1.7 million; Support service - $2.6 million; Training - $.1 millionFY 2018: Planning - $1.5 million; Implementation - $3.0 million; Training - $.5 million FY 2019: Planning - $2 million; Implementation - $4.5 million; Training - $1 million

HQ: 3101 Park Center Drive, Alexandria, VA 22302
Phone: 703-305-2163 | Email: mieka.sanderson@fns.usda.gov
http://www.fns.usda.gov/farmtoschool/farm-school

USDA10.576 | SENIOR FARMERS MARKET NUTRITION PROGRAM
"SFMNP"

Award: Formula Grants

Purpose: The Senior Farmer's Market Nutrition Program promotes fresh agricultural commodities, expands domestic farmer's market, aides and supports community supported agriculture.

Applicant Eligibility: State means any of the 50 States, the District of Columbia, and U.S. Territories. State agencies include State Agriculture Department, Agency on Aging, or Health Department, and Indian Tribal Organizations (ITOs). Local agencies are nonprofit entities or local government agencies which certify eligible participants, issue SFMNP coupons, arrange for distribution of eligible foods through CSA Programs, and/or provide nutrition education. Each State agency desiring to administer the SFMNP shall annually submit a State Plan of Operations and enter into a written agreement with FNS for administration of the Program in the jurisdiction of the State agency. New State agencies are selected based on the availability of funds, after base grants, for currently participating State agencies. Local SFMNP agencies are selected by participating State agencies based on concentration of eligible senior participants and access to farmers' markets.

Beneficiary Eligibility: Persons eligible for the program are low-income seniors, generally defined as individuals who are at least 60 years old and who have household incomes of not more than 185 percent of the federal poverty income guidelines published each year by the Department of Health and Human Services. Some State agencies accept proof of participation or enrollment in another means-tested program, such as the Commodity Supplemental Food Program (CSFP) or Supplemental Nutrition Assistance Program (SNAP), for SFMNP eligibility. Individual participants apply for SFMNP benefits at authorized SFMNP local agencies.

Award Range/Average: FY 2018 grants ranged from $9,925 to $1,788,983 (actual). FY 2019 grants range from $9,925 to $1,776,067 (estimated).

Funding: (Formula Grants) FY 18 $20,600,000.00; FY 19 est $20,600,000.00; FY 20 est $20,600,000.00

HQ: 3101 Park Center Drive, Alexandria, VA 22302

Phone: 703-305-2746 | Email: sarah.widor@fns.usda.gov

http://www.fns.usda.gov/sfmnp/senior-farmers-market-nutrition-program-sfmnp

USDA10.578 | WIC GRANTS TO STATES (WGS)

Award: Cooperative Agreements; Project Grants

Purpose: To assist WIC State agencies to support the implementation of projects, develops MIS system for management plans, compensates for State Agency Model amendments, encounters challenges of EBT implementation, supports Breastfeeding Peer Counseling program, and assists Maternal Nutrition Intensive Course.

Applicant Eligibility: State agencies that administer the WIC Program are eligible to apply for WIC Grant to States funds. States may apply individually or as a coalition of States for WIC technology funds. States may apply individually for WIC Breastfeeding Peer Counseling and Infrastructure grants. Disaster infrastructure grants are available to the Puerto Rico WIC and the U.S. Virgin Islands WIC to assist in the repair and restoration of buildings, equipment, technology, and other infrastructure damaged as a consequence of Hurricanes Irma and Maria.

Beneficiary Eligibility: WIC participants will be the ultimate beneficiary in that improved technology will allow for more efficient and effective clinic operations. Additionally, the WIC Program is moving towards the issuance of benefits through electronic benefit transfer. This will enhance their shopping experience and allow for greater flexibility in benefit delivery. Pregnant and breastfeeding women participating in the WIC Program are encouraged to initiate and sustain breastfeeding by peer counselors funded by Breastfeeding Peer Counselling grants. Program improvements resulting from Infrastructure Grants benefit all WIC participants. Disaster Infrastructure Grants will allow Puerto Rico WIC and Virgin Islands WIC to repair and restore buildings, equipment, technology, and other infrastructure damaged as a consequence of Hurricanes Irma and Maria.

Award Range/Average: In FY 2017,79 Breastfeeding Peer Counseling grants totaling $59,900,000 were awarded. Grants ranged from $21,000 to $8,731,149 The remaining $100,000 in Breastfeeding Peer Counseling funds were awarded as Breastfeeding Performance Bonus awards to 3 large (>1000 participants) and 3 small (<1000 participants) State agencies shown to have greatest percentage increase of the number of fully breastfed infants than in the previous fiscal year. Awards ranged from $1,217 to $60,195. 18 General Infrastructure grants ranging from $18,000 to $750,000 and four Special Project Grants focusing on improving the delivery of WIC services; the grant amounts totaled $1,128,749

Funding: (Project Grants (Cooperative Agreements)) FY 17 $0.00; FY 18 est $20,000,000.00; FY 19 est Estimate Not Available

HQ: Supplemental Food Programs Division 3101 Park Center Drive, Alexandria, VA 22302

Phone: 703-305-2746 | Email: sarah.widor@fns.usda.gov

http://www.fns.usda.gov/wic/women-infants-and-children-wic

USDA10.579 | CHILD NUTRITION DISCRETIONARY GRANTS LIMITED AVAILABILITY

Award: Project Grants

Purpose: The National School Lunch Program assists food authorities with grants and provides certification and evaluates meal counting. The State agencies conduct administrative reviews receive grants. The Electronic Benefits Transfer develop methods for addressing the nutritional status of children. Grants are provided to the State agencies that look into the health and wellness of children.

Applicant Eligibility: Determined by the legislation authorizing the grants.

Beneficiary Eligibility: Same as Applicant Eligibility.

Award Range/Average: For FY 2018, the National School Lunch Program (NSLP) Equipment Assistance Grants ranged from

Programs Administered by Regional - State - Local Offices

$37,410 to $3,662,051. Grant average was $555,556.For FY 2018, there were three Direct Certification Grants awarded ranging from $86,160 to $970,580. Grant average was $670,475.For Summer 2018, $1.2 million was awarded in late FY2017 to two additional Summer EBT for Children Grants in addition to $30.3 million awarded to seven grants in March 2017. Grants ranged from $800,000 to $12.3 million.There is no information to report for FY 2018 Administrative Review and Training Grants since the FY 2018 grant funding will be combined with previous FY 2017 grant funding in a FY 2019 RFA to be released on a future date.

Funding: (Project Grants (Discretionary)) FY 17 $59,181,000.00; FY 18 est $58,855,426.00; FY 19 est $26,957,000.00
HQ: 3101 Park Center Drive, Room 628, Alexandria, VA 22302

Phone: 703-305-2590 | Email: cindy.long@fns.usda.gov
http://www.fns.usda.gov

USDA10.580 | SUPPLEMENTAL NUTRITION ASSISTANCE PROGRAM, PROCESS AND TECHNOLOGY IMPROVEMENT GRANTS
"PTIG"

Award: Project Grants
Purpose: The process and Technology Improvement Grants support State agencies to implement SNAP and capable systems and improves the processes in the SNAP office.
Applicant Eligibility: State agencies that administer the SNAP, State or local Governments; agencies that provide health or welfare services; public health or educational entities and private nonprofit entities such as community-based or faith-based Organizations, food banks, or other emergency feeding Organizations.
Beneficiary Eligibility: The entities eligible to receive grants under this competition are:- The 53 State agencies that administer the SNAP;- State or local governments;- Agencies providing health or welfare services;- Public health or educational entities; and- Private non-profit entities such as community-based or faith-based organizations, food banks, or other emergency feeding organizations.(1) State agencies and State and local governments should have the necessary approvals of state officials (such as councils or legislatures) of funding prior to submitting the application. Applicants should also acknowledge in their application that all necessary approvals for funding have been obtained.(2) Non-profit organizations are required to submit a copy of the IRS Determination Letter, form 501(c)(3) or proof of application for exempt status under section 501(c) (3) of the Internal Revenue Code, a list of their Board of Directors if applicable, and their most recent audited financial statements signed by the Treasurer or the Treasurer of the board. Educational entities are also required to submit their most recent financial statements signed by the Treasurer or Treasurer of the board. Applications submitted without these will be considered non-responsive and eliminated from consideration. All corporations, including non-profit corporations are required to complete the attached representation regarding felony convictions and tax delinquency. Agreements are established between State Agencies and FNS. States use funds to improve service to SNAP applicants and recipients.
Award Range/Average: FY 2018-snap-process-and-technology-improvement-grantsFNS anticipates awarding between 6 and 11 awards annually.
Funding: (Salaries and Expenses) FY 18 $5,000,000.00; FY 19 est $5,000,000.00; FY 20 est $5,000,000.00
HQ: 3101 Park Center Drive, 8th Floor, Alexandria, VA 22302

Phone: 703-305-2803 | Email: maryrose.conroy@usda.gov
https://www.fns.usda.gov/grant-opportunities

USDA10.582 | FRESH FRUIT AND VEGETABLE PROGRAM
"FFVP"

Award: Project Grants
Purpose: To support States in supplying agricultural commodities to elementary schools and deduct meal price.
Applicant Eligibility: In order to be eligible to participate in the FFVP, the school must be a low-income public or nonprofit private elementary school, and must participate in the National School Lunch Program.
Beneficiary Eligibility: All elementary school children enrolled in schools participating in the Fresh Fruit and Vegetable Program receive free fresh fruits and vegetables outside of the National School Lunch and School Breakfast Programs.
Award Range/Average: FFVP funds are allocated at a level of $50 to $75 per student per school year. Funding is allocated among States based on a funding formula, which is adjusted every July 1 to reflect changes in the Consumer Price Index. The minimum grant to each of the 50 States and the District of Columbia will equal one percent of the funds made available to carry out this program for the school year. Additional funding will be allocated to all States, the District of Columbia, Guam, Puerto Rico and the Virgin Islands, on the basis of population.

Funding: (Project Grants) FY 18 $297,000,000.00; FY 19 est $176,000,000.00; FY 20 est $180,000,000.00
HQ: 3101 Park Center Drive, Alexandria, VA 22302
   Phone: 703-305-2590 | Email: cindy.long@fns.usda.gov
   http://www.fns.usda.gov

USDA10.585 | FNS FOOD SAFETY GRANTS

Award: Cooperative Agreements; Project Grants
Purpose: The Food and Nutrition Service's provide funds to the U.S. Department of Agriculture, Food and Nutrition Service. The FNS promotes child nutrition programs, food safety education programs, and supports the National Academies of Sciences Food Forum that works in the various disciplines of food aspects.
Applicant Eligibility: Assistance may be used to conduct research or perform other tasks to benefit FNS nutrition assistance Programs in the area of food safety.
Beneficiary Eligibility: FNS nutrition assistance program decision makers, FNS nutrition assistance program providers, and FNS nutrition assistance program recipients.
Award Range/Average: $15,000 - $1.8 million
Funding: (Cooperative Agreements (Discretionary Grants)) FY 17 $800,000.00; FY 18 est $600,000.00; FY 19 est $600,000.00; (Project Grants (Discretionary)) FY 17 $15,000.00; FY 18 est $15,000.00; FY 19 est $0.00; FY 16 $15,000.00; (Cooperative Agreements) FY 17 $168,000.00; FY 18 est $300,000.00; FY 19 est $300,000.00; FY 16 $300,000.00
HQ: 3101 Park Center Drive, Alexandria, VA 22302
   Phone: 703-457-6798 | Email: katie.delrosario@fns.usda.gov
   http://www.fns.usda.gov

USDA10.587 | NATIONAL FOOD SERVICE MANAGEMENT INSTITUTE ADMINISTRATION AND STAFFING GRANT
"ICN"

Award: Cooperative Agreements; Project Grants
Purpose: The National Institute of Child Nutrition Programs provides education, research, educational resources, training and technical assistance for child nutritional professionals.
Applicant Eligibility: Non-competitive. Appropriated by Congress to provide financial and other assistance to the University of Mississippi, in cooperation with the University of Southern Mississippi, to establish and maintain a food service management institute.
Beneficiary Eligibility: FNS nutrition assistance program decision makers, FNS nutrition assistance program providers, and children and teachers.
Award Range/Average: Available Administration and Staffing Grant (non-competitive) - $5,000,000.Available General Education Cooperative Agreement (non-competitive) - $800,000 -. $2,000,000
Funding: (Cooperative Agreements) FY 17 $1,170,045.00; FY 18 est $4,183,000.00; FY 19 est $800,000.00; (Salaries and Expenses) FY 17 $5,000,000.00; FY 18 est $5,000,000.00; FY 19 est $5,000,000.00
HQ: 3101 Park Center Drive, Room 628, Alexandria, VA 22302
   Phone: 703-305-2590 | Email: cindy.long@fns.usda.gov
   http://www.fns.usda.gov

USDA10.592 | HEALTHY, HUNGER-FREE KIDS ACT OF 2010 CHILDHOOD HUNGER RESEARCH AND DEMONSTRATION PROJECTS
"Demonstration Projects to End Childhood Hunger Healthy, Hunger-Free Kids Act (HHFKA) of 2010"

Award: Cooperative Agreements
Purpose: To provide strategies to end childhood hunger and promote food security. The Healthy Hunger-Free Kids Act provides $ 40 million to conduct and evaluate projects to End Childhood Hunger.
Applicant Eligibility: N/A
Beneficiary Eligibility: N/A

Programs Administered by Regional - State - Local Offices

Award Range/Average: Chickasaw: 9.7 millionKentucky: 3.6 millionNavajo Nation: 2.4 millionNevada: 3.1 millionVirginia: 8.8 millionTotal: 27.6 millionAverage: 5.52 million
HQ: 3101 Park Center Drive, Room 1014, Alexandria, VA 22302
   Phone: 703-305-4369 | Email: michael.burke@fns.usda.gov

USDA10.593 | BILL EMERSON NATIONAL HUNGER FELLOWS AND MICKEY LELAND INTERNATIONAL HUNGER FELLOWS PROGRAMS
"Bill Emerson and Mickey Leland Fellows Programs"

Award: Project Grants
Purpose: The Bill Emerson Hunger Fellowship Program addresses hunger and poverty in the United States. It encourages leaders in public service, understands the needs of low-income people, supports people in need, and increases awareness on humanitarian services.
Applicant Eligibility: N/A
Beneficiary Eligibility: N/A
Award Range/Average: Congressional Hunger Center (CHC) $2,000,000 (non-competitive)
Funding: (Project Grants (Fellowships)) FY 18 $2,000,000.00; FY 19 est $2,000,000.00; FY 20 est $2,000,000.00
HQ: 3101 Park Center Drive, Room 732, Alexandria, VA 22302
   Phone: 703-305-2048 | Email: lael.lubing@fns.usda.gov

USDA10.594 | FOOD DISTRIBUTION PROGRAM ON INDIAN RESERVATIONS NUTRITION EDUCATION GRANTS
"Food Distribution Program Nutrition Education Grants"

Award: Project Grants
Purpose: The Food Distribution Program Nutrition Education compensates $1 million to Indian Tribal Organizations for nutrition assistance and provides nutrition knowledge.
Applicant Eligibility: A current FDPIR allowance holder must submit the application. Applicants must propose projects that result in the delivery of nutrition education activities to FDPIR participants.
Beneficiary Eligibility: Applicant ITO/SDA administrators must provide services to FDPIR participants or FDPIR-eligible participants only.
Award Range/Average: Awards range from $2,000 to $214,000.
Funding: (Project Grants) FY 17 $972,504.00; FY 18 est $991,950.00; FY 19 est $0.00
HQ: 3101 Park Center Drive, Alexandria, VA 22302
   Phone: 703-305-2833 | Email: lindsay.williams@fns.usda.gov
   http://www.fns.usda.gov/fdpir/fdpir-nutrition-education-grant-awards

USDA10.596 | PILOT PROJECTS TO REDUCE DEPENDENCY AND INCREASE WORK REQUIREMENTS AND WORK EFFORT UNDER SNAP
"SNAP Employment and Training Pilots"

Award: Cooperative Agreements
Purpose: Pilot projects increase work and efforts under SNAP. It develops methods to increase workforce and maximizes the income of the workforce and provide public assistance.
Applicant Eligibility: Only State agencies that currently administer the Supplemental Nutrition Assistance Program (SNAP) Employment and Training (E&T) Program are eligible for these grants.
Beneficiary Eligibility: Same as Applicant Eligibility.
Award Range/Average: The range is $8,959,379 to $22,329,952. The grant average is approximately $17,509,239.
HQ: 3101 Park Center Drive, 8th Floor, Alexandria, VA 22302
   Phone: 703-305-2022 | Email: moira.johnston@fns.usda.gov
   http://www.fns.usda.gov/snap

USDA10.597 | SCHOOL WELLNESS POLICY COOPERATIVE AGREEMENT
"Local Wellness Policy Grant"

Award: Cooperative Agreements
Purpose: The local wellness policy surveillance system monitors state law and policy data and their effects on student health outcomes. The major national surveillance systems provide School Nutrition Dietary Assessment to analyze data on school meals and environment, meal cost, wastage of meals, the nutritional quality of school meals. The National Cancer Institute's Classification of Laws is a policy to evaluate nutrition and physical education in schools, information about obesity and other cancer-related behaviors. School Health Policies and Practices Study is a national, comprehensive survey conducted to assess school wellness in all areas. Surveys cover health education, physical education, and health services.
Applicant Eligibility: N/A
Beneficiary Eligibility: N/A
Award Range/Average: Award amount = $1,699,985
Funding: (Cooperative Agreements) FY 18 $321,423.00; FY 19 est $285,205.00; FY 20 est $0.00
HQ: 3101 Park Center Drive, Alexandria, VA 22302
　　Phone: 703-305-2105 | Email: holly.figueroa@fns.usda.gov

FOOD SAFETY AND INSPECTION SERVICE
Regional – State – Local Offices

REGIONAL OFFICES

Arkansas
Paul Kiecker, District Manager | Country Club Center 4700 S Thompson Building B Suite 201, Springdale, AR 72764 479-751-8412

California
Dr. Yudhbir Sharma, District Manager | 620 Central Avenue Building 2C, Alameda, CA 94501 510-337-5000

Colorado
Dr. Ron Nelson, District Manager | Denver Federal Center PO Box 25387 Building 45, Denver, CO 80225 303-236-9800

Georgia
Dr. Phyllis Adams, District Manager | 100 Alabama Street SW Building 1924 Suite 3R90, Atlanta, GA 30303 404-562-5900

Illinois
Paul Wolseley, District Manager | 1919 S Highland Avenue Suite 115C, Lombard, IL 60148 630-620-7474

Iowa
Dr. Dawn Sprouts, District Manager | Room 985 Federal Building 210 Walnut Street, Des Moines, IA 50309 515-727-8960

Mississippi
Dr. Paul Resweber, District Manager | 713 S Pear Orchard Road Suite 402, Ridgeland, MS 39157 601-965-4312

North Carolina
Dr. Steve Lalicker, District Manager | 6020 6 Forks Road, Raleigh, NC 27609 919-844-8400

Pennsylvania
Jan Behney, District Manager | U.S. Department of Agriculture Mellon Independence Center 701 Market Street Suite 4100A, Philadelphia, PA 19106 215-597-4219

Texas
Dr. Jennifer Beasley-McKean, District Manager | 1100 Commerce Room 516, Dallas, TX 75242 214-767-9116

USDA10.475 | COOPERATIVE AGREEMENTS WITH STATES FOR INTRASTATE MEAT AND POULTRY INSPECTION
"Meat and Poultry Inspection State Programs"

Award: Project Grants
Purpose: To assist Federal agencies to inspect meat and poultry producers to ensure that the products are qualified and properly labeled.
Applicant Eligibility: An appropriate State or U.S. Territory agency administering State or Territorial meat or poultry inspection Programs under laws equal to the Federal Meat and Poultry Products Inspection Acts.
Beneficiary Eligibility: General Public.
Award Range/Average: Not Applicable.
Funding: (Salaries and Expenses) FY 18 $54,000,000.00; FY 19 est $54,000,000.00; FY 20 est $59,000,000.00

Programs Administered by Regional - State - Local Offices

HQ: Outreach and Partnership Division Office of Outreach Employee Education and Training 355 E Street Patriot Plaza, III Building Room 9-256, Washington, DC 20024
   Phone: 202-418-8897 | Email: dean.norman@fsis.usda.gov
   http://www.fsis.usda.gov

USDA10.477 | MEAT, POULTRY, AND EGG PRODUCTS INSPECTION

Award: Provision of Specialized Services
Purpose: To ensure that meat, poultry, and egg products are inspected by the federal for safety, proper labeling, and shipped carefully.
Applicant Eligibility: Any meat or poultry plant planning to engage in slaughtering or processing meat and poultry products, and all egg products processing plants for shipment in commerce. This Program is available in the U.S. and its Territories.
Beneficiary Eligibility: General public (meat, poultry, and egg products.).
Award Range/Average: Not Applicable.
Funding: (Salaries and Expenses) FY 18 $1,058,000,000.00; FY 19 est $1,065,000,000.00; FY 20 est $1,045,000,000.00
HQ: 344 E Jamie Whitten Building, Washington, DC 20250-3700
   Phone: 202-720-8803 | Email: william.smith@fsis.usda.gov

USDA10.479 | FOOD SAFETY COOPERATIVE AGREEMENTS

Award: Project Grants
Purpose: To minimize illnesses associated with meat, poultry, and egg products. The FSIS conducts educational programs to ensure the safety of these products and directs the Food Emergency Response Network to carry out qualified food supply.
Applicant Eligibility: State, local and tribal government agencies; academic Institutions and non-profit Organizations.
Beneficiary Eligibility: General public.
Funding: (Cooperative Agreements) FY 18 est $3,000,000.00; FY 19 est $3,000,000.00; FY 20 est $1,000,000.00
HQ: U.S. Department of Agriculture FERN Staff 950 College Station Road, Athens, GA 30605
   Phone: 706-546-2349 | Email: robert.phillips@fsis.usda.gov
   http://www.fsis.usda.gov

FOREST SERVICE
Regional – State – Local Offices

REGIONAL OFFICES

Alaska
709 W 9th Street, Juneau, AK 99801-1807 907-586-8806

Colorado
740 Simms Street PO Box 25127, Golden, CO 80401-4720 303-275-5741

Georgia
1720 Peachtree Road NW, Atlanta, GA 30309 404-347-7486

Montana
Federal Building 200 E Broadway PO Box 7669, Missoula, MT 59807-7669 406-329-3511

New Mexico
333 Broadway Boulevard SE, Santa Fe, NM 87102-3407 505-842-3292

Oregon
333 SW 1st Street PO Box 3623, Portland, OR 97208-3623 503-808-2204

Pennsylvania
11 Campus Boulevard Suite 200, Newtown Square, PA 19073-3200 610-557-4103

Puerto Rico
Jardin Botanico Sur 1201 Calle Ceiba, San Juan, PR 00926-1119 787-766-5335

Utah
Federal Office Building 324 25th Street, Ogden, UT 84401-2300 801-625-5239

Wisconsin
626 E Wisconsin Avenue Suite 800, Milwaukee, WI 53202-4616 414-297-3600

RESEARCH HEADQUARTERS

California
1323 Club Drive, Vallejo, CA 95492-1110 707-562-8737
800 Buchanan Street W Annex Building, Albany, CA 94701-0245 510-559-6300

Colorado
2150 Centre Avenue Building A, Fort Collins, CO 80526-1891 303-275-5350

North Carolina
200 W T Weaver Boulevard, Asheville, NC 28804-3454 704-257-4301

Oregon

333 SW 1st Avenue, Portland, OR 97204 503-808-2592

Pennsylvania

11 Campus Boulevard Suite 200, Newtown Square, PA 19073-3200 610-557-4023

Utah

Denver P. Burns | 324 25th Street, Ogden, UT 84401 801-625-5421

Wisconsin

One Gifford Pinchot Drive, Madison, WI 53726-2398 608-231-9200

USDA10.652 | FORESTRY RESEARCH
"Research Grants & Cooperative Agreements"

Award: Cooperative Agreements; Project Grants

Purpose: To promote research activities of the Forest Service and award grants to the educational institutions and organizations engaged in renewable resources research.

Applicant Eligibility: Grants and cooperative agreements for basic or applied research may be made to State Agricultural Experiment Stations, universities and colleges, State and local Governments, U.S. Territories, nonprofit research Institutions or Organizations, international Organizations, individuals, and for-profit Organizations.

Beneficiary Eligibility: Organizations and scientists involved in basic and applied research activities related to forest and rangeland renewable resources.

Award Range/Average: $2,000 to $300,000. Average: $35,000.

Funding: (Project Grants) FY 18 $1,357,076.00; FY 19 est $2,499,472.00 FY 20 est Estimate Not Available

HQ: 201 14th Street SW 2 NW, Washington, DC 20250

Phone: 202-205-1665 | Email: crodriguezfranco@fs.fed.us

http://www.fs.fed.us/links/research.html

USDA10.664 | COOPERATIVE FORESTRY ASSISTANCE

Award: Formula Grants; Project Grants

Purpose: To promote forest resources management and conservation, control insects and diseases affecting trees and forests, avoid accidental fires, recycle biomass, maintenance of fish and wildlife habitat, and to encourage educational, technical, and financial assistance programs to assist owners of non-Federal forest lands.

Applicant Eligibility: State Forestry or equivalent State agencies, Tribes, non-profits, and municipalities are eligible. All States, the District of Columbia, the Commonwealth of Puerto Rico, the Virgin Islands of the United States, the Commonwealth of the Northern Mariana Islands, the Federated States of Micronesia, the Republic of the Marshall Islands, the Republic of Palau, and the territories and possessions of the United States are eligible.

Beneficiary Eligibility: Landowners of nonfederal lands; rural community fire fighting forces; urban and municipal governments, non-profit organizations, Tribes and other State, local, and private agencies acting through State Foresters, equivalent State officials, or other official representatives.

Award Range/Average: $25,000 to $6,000,000. Average $1,000,000

Funding: (Project Grants) FY 18 $125,721,415.00; FY 19 est $120,000,000.00 FY 20 est Not Separately Identifiable

HQ: 1400 Independence Avenue SW, PO Box 1109, Washington, DC 20250

Phone: 202-205-1657 | Email: phirami@fs.fed.us

http://www.fs.fed.us/spf

USDA10.665 | SCHOOLS AND ROADS-GRANTS TO STATES
"Payments to States"

Award: Formula Grants

Purpose: To assist the National Forests and supplemental mandatory appropriations.

Applicant Eligibility: Title I payments are made to States or territories of the United States to be allocated to counties in which national forests are situated. Title II project funds are reserved in special account in the U.S. Treasury and may be used by the Secretary of Agriculture for the purpose of entering into and implementing cooperative agreements with willing Federal agencies, State and local Governments, private and nonprofit entities, and landowners. (16 U.S. C 7122). Title III funds are paid to respective states to be passed-through to participating counties.

Programs Administered by Regional - State - Local Offices

Beneficiary Eligibility: A beneficiary of title II special project funds is a person or entity that receives a grant or enters into a cooperative agreement with the Secretary of Agriculture to carry out a project for protection, restoration, and enhancement of fish and wildlife habitat, and other resource objectives consistent with the purposes of the Secure Rural Schools Act on national forests and on non-national forest land where projects would benefit the resources on national forests. (16 U.S.C. 7122) A beneficiary of title III funds is a participating county in which a national forest is situated that has elected to allocate a portion of its State payments for title III county projects.

Award Range/Average: 25% 7 yr. average: $2 to $1,397,323 - average: $151,756 (19 states) Title I: $1 to $9,587,418 - average $366,907: (42 states) Title II: $1,922 to $1,294,931 - average: $98,145 (31 states) Title III: $1,682 to $789,552 - average: $54,134 (31 states)

Funding: (Cooperative Agreements) FY 18 $5,199,200.00; FY 19 est Not Separately Identifiable; FY 20 est Estimate Not Available

HQ: 201 14th Street SW, Suite 4 NW, Washington, DC 20250

Phone: 202-649-1177 | Email: leanne.veldhuis@usda.gov

http://www.fs.usda.gov/main/pts/home

USDA10.666 | SCHOOLS AND ROADS-GRANTS TO COUNTIES
"Direct payments to States"

Award: Direct Payments for Specified Use

Purpose: To assist the National Grasslands and Land Utilization Projects with the Counties.

Applicant Eligibility: Eligible applicants are counties of the United States containing National Grassland or a LUP.

Beneficiary Eligibility: Counties within the United States.

Funding: (Direct Payments for Specified Use) FY 17 Not Separately Identifiable FY 18 est Not Separately Identifiable FY 19 est Not Separately Identifiable

HQ: 201 14th Street SW, Suite 4 NW, Washington, DC 20250

Phone: 202-649-1177 | Email: lveldhuis@fs.fed.us

http://www.fs.fed.us/srs

USDA10.672 | RURAL DEVELOPMENT, FORESTRY, AND COMMUNITIES
"Rural Development Through Forestry"

Award: Project Grants

Purpose: To assist rural areas in assessing forest resource opportunities to develop and expand the diversify communities' economic base.

Applicant Eligibility: Tribal nations, State and Federal agencies, State Foresters, local Governments, not-for-profit Organizations, and others working in support of community identified goals.

Beneficiary Eligibility: Tribal nations, State and Federal agencies, State Foresters, local governments, not-for-profit organizations, and others. Forest Service Regions/Areas/Institutes are encouraged to further define program policies that focus resources to meet the regional, State and local needs of communities.

HQ: 201 14th Street SW, Washington, DC 20024

Phone: 202-205-1380 | Email: smarshall@fs.fed.us

USDA10.674 | WOOD UTILIZATION ASSISTANCE
"State and Private Forestry Technology, Marketing Assistance Program"

Award: Cooperative Agreements; Project Grants

Purpose: To provide technical assistance to Forest Service, tribes, and private organizations with technologies to effectively manage forests. The State & Private Forestry staff provides awareness of forest products utilization and biofuels conservation.

Applicant Eligibility: Entities eligible include: Non-profits, local, state, and Tribal Governments, business, companies, corporations (for Profit), Institutions of higher education, and special purpose districts, (public utilities districts, fire districts, conservation districts, or ports).

Beneficiary Eligibility: N/A

Award Range/Average: Typical awards are $250,000 per award. Exceptions may be made for special circumstances.

Funding: (Project Grants) FY 18 est $12,387,227.00; FY 19 est $15,000,000.00; FY 20 est Not Separately Identifiable

HQ: 201 14th Street SW, Washington, DC 20250
  Phone: 703-605-5346 | Email: melissaljenkins@fs.fed.us
  http://www.na.fs.fed.us/werc

USDA10.675 | URBAN AND COMMUNITY FORESTRY PROGRAM
Award: Project Grants
Purpose: To protect forests and related natural resources in cities and towns. The urban and community forestry program promotes ecosystem services.
Applicant Eligibility: State Foresters or equivalent State agencies, Tribal nations, interested members of the public, private non-profit Organizations and others. All States, as well as the District of Columbia, Puerto Rico, the United States Virgin Islands, the Commonwealth of the Northern Mariana Islands, American Samoa and Guam, and other territories and possessions of the United States are eligible.
Beneficiary Eligibility: State Foresters or equivalent State agencies, local governments, tribes, and non-profit organizations, and other State, local and private agencies acting through State Foresters, equivalent State agencies or other official representatives as agreed by the State Forester, equivalent State agency, and the Secretary.(082a) Projects are to be national or multi-state in scope and benefit the nation as a whole or a multi-state region. Results are to benefit, but not limited to, State Foresters or equivalent State agencies, local governments, Tribal Nations, applicable non-profit organizations, and other State, local, and applicable private agencies.
Funding: (Project Grants) FY 18 $11,362,657; FY 19 est $10,000,000; FY 20 est Not Separately Identifiable
HQ: 1400 Independence Avenue SW, PO Box 1151, Washington, DC 20250
  Phone: 202-401-4416 | Email: jkdavis@fs.fed.us
  http://www.fs.fed.us/ucf/contact_regional.shtml

USDA10.676 | FOREST LEGACY PROGRAM
"FLP"
Award: Project Grants
Purpose: The Forest Legacy Program promotes conservation of forests and forest services that includes utilization of forest products in a positive manner.
Applicant Eligibility: Projects are evaluated and prioritized by State lead agencies, in consultation with the State Forest Stewardship Coordinating Committees. All States and territories participate except North Dakota, the Commonwealth of the Northern Mariana Islands, and Guam.
Beneficiary Eligibility: State agency, landowners of private forest lands, and land trust organizations.
Award Range/Average: Not Applicable.
Funding: (Project Grants) FY 18 $62,268,593.00; FY 19 est $60,000,000.00; FY 20 est Not Separately Identifiable
HQ: 1400 Independence Avenue SW, PO Box 1123, Washington, DC 20228
  Phone: 202-205-1618 | Email: sstewart@fs.fed.us
  http://www.fs.fed.us/spf/coop/programs/loa/flp.shtml

USDA10.678 | FOREST STEWARDSHIP PROGRAM
"FSP"
Award: Project Grants
Purpose: To encourage the long-term active management of non-industrial private and non-federal forest land to preserve the multiple values and uses.
Applicant Eligibility: State forestry or equivalent State agencies, Tribes, non-profits, and municipalities are eligible. All States, the District of Columbia, Puerto Rico, the United States Virgin Islands, the Commonwealth of the Northern Mariana Islands, American Samoa, Guam, the Trust Territory of the Pacific Islands, and territories and possessions of the United States may be eligible.
Beneficiary Eligibility: Landowners of non-federal lands, non-profit organizations, tribes and other State, local, and private agencies acting through State Foresters, equivalent State officials, or other official representatives are eligible. Landowners seeking assistance through the Forest Stewardship Program should contact their state forest agency directly. Program guidelines differ from state to state.
Award Range/Average: $50,000 to $400,000
Funding: (Project Grants) FY 18 $ 9,082,072.00; FY 19 $9,000,000.00; FY 20 Not Separately Identifiable

Programs Administered by Regional - State - Local Offices

HQ: 1400 Independence Avenue SW, Washington, DC 20250
   Phone: 202-205-0929 | Email: lschoonhoven@fs.fed.us
   https://www.fs.fed.us/managing-land/private-land/forest-stewardship

USDA10.679 | COLLABORATIVE FOREST RESTORATION "CFRP"

Award: Project Grants
Purpose: To promote watersheds to control high-intensity wildfires, insect infestation, protect wildlife biodiversity, improve communication in restoring the diversity and productivity of forested watersheds, and encourage forest restoration techniques in New Mexico.
Applicant Eligibility: Local and tribal Governments, educational Institutions, landowners, conservation Organizations, and other interested public and private entities. Grant proponents must include a diverse and balanced group of stakeholders as well as appropriate Federal, Tribal, State, County, and Municipal government representatives in the design and implementation of the project. The projects may be entirely on, or on any combination of, Federal, Tribal, State, County, Land Grant, or Municipal forestlands. Processing facilities may be located on private land if they are associated with restoration activities on public land.
Beneficiary Eligibility: See Applicant Eligibility.
Award Range/Average: $66,361.00- $360,000.00
Funding: (Project Grants) FY 18 $2,901,023.00; FY 19 est $3,000,000.00; FY 20 est Not Separately Identifiable
HQ: 333 Broadway Boulevard SE, Albuquerque, NM 87102
   Phone: 505-842-3425 | Email: wdunn@fs.fed.us
   http://www.fs.usda.gov/goto/r3/cfrp

USDA10.680 | FOREST HEALTH PROTECTION

Award: Formula Grants; Project Grants
Purpose: To protect non-Federal forest and tree resources from insects, diseases, and invasive plants and to improve forest health protection technologies to safeguard forests.
Applicant Eligibility: State Forestry, State Agriculture or equivalent State agencies, subdivisions of states, Alaska native corporations and tribal Governments (for lands not held in trust), Institutions (public and private), Organizations (profit and non-profit), and municipalities are eligible. All States, the District of Columbia, Puerto Rico, the Virgin Islands, the Northern Mariana Islands, the Trust Territory of the Pacific Islands, and the territories and possessions of the United States are eligible.
Beneficiary Eligibility: State Foresters, State Plant Regulatory Officials, equivalent State officials or other official representatives, tribes, subdivisions of states, agencies, institutions (public and private), organizations (profit or nonprofit), and individuals on non-Federal lands.
Funding: (Project Grants) FY 18 $20,559,573.00; FY 19 est $20,000,000; FY 20 est Not Separately Identifiable
HQ: 1400 Independence Avenue SW, PO Box 1110, Washington, DC 20250
   Phone: 703-605-5340 | Email: rcooksey@fs.fed.us
   http://www.fs.fed.us/spf/foresthealth

USDA10.681 | WOOD EDUCATION AND RESOURCE CENTER (WERC) "WERC"

Award: Cooperative Agreements; Project Grants
Purpose: To compensate with technical assistance for projects to sustain forest products, maintain the health of forests, technologies to improve profitability and promote green buildings, knowledge on sanitizing wood packaging materials, and promoting the use of woody biomass to reduce hazardous fuels.
Applicant Eligibility: Nonfederal agencies; public and private agencies including State, local and tribal Governments; Institutions of higher education; non-profit Organizations; for-profit Organizations; corporations; businesses; and others.
Beneficiary Eligibility: Nonfederal agencies; public and private agencies including State, local and tribal governments; institutions of higher education; non-profit organizations; for-profit organizations; corporations; businesses.
Award Range/Average: Range varies from $10,000 to $80,000. Average grant award is approximately $50,000.
Funding: (Project Grants (Discretionary)) FY 18 $50,000.00; FY 19 est $50,000.00; FY 20 est Not Separately Identifiable

HQ: 1400 Independence Avenue SW, Washington, DC 20250
   Phone: 202-205-1380 | Email: smarshall@fs.fed.us
   http://www.na.fs.fed.us/werc

USDA10.682 | NATIONAL FOREST FOUNDATION
"NFF"

Award: Direct Payments for Specified Use
Purpose: The National Forest Foundation encourages the activities and services of the Forest Service of the Department of Agriculture. It promotes educational, technical, and other assistance that support the programs conducted by the Forest Service.
Applicant Eligibility: Program is authorized for the National Forest Foundation under National Forest Foundation Act, Public Law 101-593 as amended by Public Law 103-106.
Beneficiary Eligibility: Potential beneficiaries include non-governmental, nonprofit 501(c)(3) and for profit organizations, state and local governments and Native American tribes working on or adjacent to National Forests and Grasslands throughout the United States.
Award Range/Average: Not Applicable.
Funding: (Direct Payments for Specified Use) FY 18 $3,000,000.00; FY 19 est $3,000,000.00; FY 20 est $3,000,000.00
HQ: 201 14th Street SW, Suite 4NW, Washington, DC 20250
   Phone: 202-649-1177 | Email: leanne.veldhuis@usda.gov
   http://www.nationalforests.org

USDA10.683 | NATIONAL FISH AND WILDLIFE FOUNDATION
"NFWF"

Award: Direct Payments for Specified Use
Purpose: National Fish and Wildlife Foundation directs public conservation dollars to the environmental needs. The Foundation's method is simple and effective to work for conservation challenges.
Applicant Eligibility: Program authorized for the National Fish and Wildlife Foundation (NFWF) only.
Beneficiary Eligibility: N/A
Award Range/Average: Not Applicable.
Funding: (Direct Payments for Specified Use) FY 18 $3,000,000.00; FY 19 est Not Separately Identifiable; FY 20 est $3,020,000.00
HQ: 201 14th Street NW 3SE, Washington, DC 20024
   Phone: 202-205-1671 | Email: robert.harper@usda.gov
   http://www.nfwf.org

USDA10.684 | INTERNATIONAL FORESTRY PROGRAMS

Award: Cooperative Agreements; Project Grants
Purpose: Forest Service efforts improve forest policies and practices and assists forest-dependent peoples by compensating into cooperative agreements with nonprofit organizations and governments engaged in forest conservation and management.
Applicant Eligibility: Potential applicants include U.S. and international Organizations, educational Institutions, government entities, and individuals. International applicants must be from countries sanctioned by the State Department.
Beneficiary Eligibility: Potential beneficiaries include host-country forest management agencies, non-profit organizations, forest landowners in the target countries, forest-dependent communities and peoples in the targeted countries, and U.S. landowners and organizations involved in or concerned with invasive species mitigation, migratory species conservation, legal trade in forest products, and the impact of climate change on forests.
Award Range/Average: Not Applicable.
Funding: (Project Grants) FY 18 $3,557,236.00; FY 19 est $11,620,699.00; FY 20 est Estimate Not Available
HQ: 1 Thomas Circle NW, Suite 400, Washington, DC 20005
   Phone: 202-644-4613 | Email: vanessa.pinkney@usda.gov
   http://www.fs.fed.us

Programs Administered by Regional - State - Local Offices

USDA10.689 | COMMUNITY FOREST AND OPEN SPACE CONSERVATION PROGRAM (CFP)
"CFP"

Award: Project Grants

Purpose: The purpose of CFP is to provide financial assistance to local governments, Indian tribes, and nonprofit organizations; to encourage economic benefits through forest management; to promote natural resource conservation; to provide public access to the forests to enhance health, and to provide technical assistance for implementing forest projects.

Applicant Eligibility: Project grants are awarded to local Governments, Indian Tribes, or nonprofit Organizations qualified to acquire land and with the authority to manage land.

Beneficiary Eligibility: N/A

Award Range/Average: Individual grant applications may not exceed $600,000 in program financial assistance. Range is from $86,150 to $400,000, with an average of $304,283.

Funding: (Project Grants (Discretionary)) FY 18 $4,410,000.00; FY 19 $2,000,000.00; FY est Not Separately Identifiable

HQ: 1400 Independence Avenue SW, PO Box 1123, Washington, DC 20228

Phone: 202-205-1618 | Email: sstewart@fs.fed.us

https://www.fs.fed.us/managing-land/private-land/community-forest/program

USDA10.690 | LAKE TAHOE EROSION CONTROL GRANT PROGRAM

Award: Cooperative Agreements; Project Grants

Purpose: To fund for research projects for land management in the Tahoe Basin. To promote relevant research to address natural resource management needs, to protect the natural environment and maintain public health, to safeguard water quality and wildlife, and to maintain soil conservation and vegetation.

Applicant Eligibility: Eligible applicants for National Forest System awards includes State Forestry or equivalent agencies, Tribes, non-profits, and municipalities in the local governing bodies of political subdivisions in the Lake Tahoe basin. Eligible applicants for competitive research awards includes State Agricultural Experiment Stations, universities and colleges, State and local Governments, U.S. Territories, nonprofit research Institutions or Organizations, international Organizations, individuals, and for-profit Organizations.

Beneficiary Eligibility: Beneficiary eligibility for National Forest System awards include governing bodies of each of the political subdivisions (including public utilities) located in the Lake Tahoe Basin. Beneficiary eligibility for competitive research awards include organizations and scientists involved in basic and applied research activities related to forest and rangeland renewable resources.

Funding: (Project Grants (Discretionary)) FY 17 $263,000.00; FY 18 est $611,350.00; FY 19 est Not Separately Identifiable

HQ: 35 College Drive, South Lake Tahoe, CA 96150

Phone: 530-543-2657

http://www.fs.fed.us/r5/ltbmu/ecgp/index.shtml

USDA10.691 | GOOD NEIGHBOR AUTHORITY
"Good Neighbor"

Award: Cooperative Agreements

Purpose: To promote restoration and protection services on Federal land.

Applicant Eligibility: State includes state agencies that are part of a State University system. State universities are not eligible. State includes the Commonwealth of Puerto Rico.

Beneficiary Eligibility: Program authorized for states containing or affected by National Forest System Land, including the Commonwealth of Puerto Rico.

Award Range/Average: Variable. Projects may range from $5,000 - $1,000,000

Funding: (Cooperative Agreements) FY 18 $23,711,893.00; FY 19 est $25,000,000.00 FY 20 est Not Separately Identifiable

HQ: 201 14th Street SW, Washington, DC 20250

Phone: 202-205-1495 | Email: jwcrockett@fs.fed.us

USDA10.693 | WATERSHED RESTORATION AND ENHANCEMENT AGREEMENT AUTHORITY
"Wyden Amendment"

Award: Cooperative Agreements

Purpose: To promote cooperative agreements for the protection, restoration, and enhancement of wildlife habitat and reduction of risk from natural disaster where public safety is threatened.

Applicant Eligibility: Private landowners, State, local or Tribal Governments or other public entities, educational Institutions or private nonprofit entities.

Beneficiary Eligibility: Projects must be located in the same watershed where the public resource benefits will occur.

Award Range/Average: Varies by type of project and funding available.

Funding: (Cooperative Agreements (Discretionary Grants)) FY 17 $4,590,515.00; FY 18 est $1,098,493.00; FY 19 FY est Not Separately Identifiable

HQ: 201 14th Street NW, Room 3SE, Washington, DC 20024

   Phone: 202-205-1671

USDA10.694 | SOUTHWEST FOREST HEALTH AND WILDFIRE PREVENTION

Award: Direct Payments for Specified Use

Purpose: To enhance restoration treatments that will reduce the risk of wildfires, to improve the health of the dry forest, to implement forest and woodland restoration, to use ecological restoration and wildfire treatments, to assist land managers in new management technologies, and to assist Federal and non-Federal land managers in the role of fire management.

Applicant Eligibility: N/A

Beneficiary Eligibility: One (1) Institute each of (A) the State of Arizona, to be located at Northern Arizona University; (B) the State of New Mexico, to be located at New Mexico Highlands University, while engaging the full resources of the consortium of universities represented in the Institute of Natural Resource Analysis and Management (INRAM); and (C) the State of Colorado, to be located at Colorado State University.

Award Range/Average: Range of assistance is $150,000 - $1,500,000

Funding: (Direct Payments for Specified Use) FY 18 est $2,230,000.00; FY 19 est $1,500,000.00; FY 20 est Not Separately Identifiable

HQ: 333 Broadway Boulevard SE, Albuquerque, NM 87102

   Phone: 505-842-3425 | Email: wdunn@fs.fed.us

   http://www.fs.usda.gov/goto/r3/sweri

USDA10.697 | STATE & PRIVATE FORESTRY HAZARDOUS FUEL REDUCTION PROGRAM
"S&PF Hazardous Fuels Program"

Award: Cooperative Agreements; Project Grants

Purpose: To reduce wildfires, minimize the use of hazardous fuels, and to safeguard communities from wildfires.

Applicant Eligibility: Hazardous fuel reduction projects on non-Federal land.

Beneficiary Eligibility: Program supports activities on non-Federal land.

Funding: (Project Grants (Discretionary)) FY 17 $15,000,000.00; FY 18 est $15,000,000.00; FY 19 Estimate Not Available

HQ: 201 14th Street SW, Washington, DC 20250

   Phone: 202-205-1129 | Email: ffay@fs.fed.us

USDA10.698 | STATE & PRIVATE FORESTRY COOPERATIVE FIRE ASSISTANCE
"Cooperative Fire Assistance"

Award: Project Grants

Purpose: To assist in the control of rural fires, to develop new and improved fire prevention and fire technologies, to promote efficient fire mitigation and protection, to assist local rural firefighting forces.

Applicant Eligibility: Primary recipients are State Forestry agencies. Other non-profit Organizations, tribal Organizations, and educational Institutions.

Programs Administered by Regional - State - Local Offices

Beneficiary Eligibility: N/A
Funding: (Project Grants) FY 18 est $8,952,500.00; FY 19 est $15,000,000.00; FY 20 est Not Separately Identifiable
HQ: 201 14th Street SW, Washington, DC 20250
    Phone: 202-205-1504 | Email: jfortner@fs.fed.us

USDA10.699 | PARTNERSHIP AGREEMENTS
Award: Direct Payments for Specified Use
Purpose: To increase participation in forest service related programs and activities.
Applicant Eligibility: The Forest Service partners with non-profits; for-profit; Institutions of higher education; federal, state, local, and Native American tribe Governments; individuals; foreign Governments and Organizations.
Beneficiary Eligibility: The Forest Service has partnership authorities to enter into agreements and cooperative arrangements with willing members of the public, which include but are not limited to, for profit; non-profits; institutions of higher education; federal, state, local, and Native American tribe governments; foreign governments and organizations.
Funding: (Direct Payments for Specified Use) FY 18 $74,769,656.00; FY 19 est $109,285,783.00; FY 20 est Estimate Not Available
HQ: 1400 Independence Avenue SW, PO Box 1138, Washington, DC 20250
    Phone: 202-205-2254 | Email: jacqueline.emanuel@usda.gov
    http://www.fs.fed.us/working-with-us/partnerships

USDA10.701 | STEWARDSHIP AGREEMENTS
"Stewardship End Result Contracting"

Award: Cooperative Agreements
Purpose: To assist in achieving land management goals and rural community needs, including contributing to the sustainability of rural communities and providing a continuing source of local income and employment.
Applicant Eligibility: The Forest Service may enter into stewardship agreements with any entity that has the ability to either perform the work or contract it out. This can include, state and local Governments, Federally recognized Tribes and non-profit Organizations. Appropriate Stewardship Activities include (but are not limited to): Road and trail maintenance or obliteration to restore or maintain water quality; Soil productivity, habitat for wildlife and fisheries or other resource values; Setting of prescribed fires to reduce wildfire hazards, improve the composition, structure, condition, and health of forest stands, or to improve wildlife habitat; Removing vegetation or other activities to promote healthy forest stands, reduce wildfire hazards, or achieve other land management objectives; Watershed restoration and maintenance; Restoration and maintenance of wildlife and fish habitat; Control of noxious and exotic weeds and reestablishment of native plant species.
Beneficiary Eligibility: Stewardship Agreements should not be used for: Forest Service overhead costs; Forest Service salaries for contract/agreement development, preparation, or administration; Project planning or environmental analysis; Construction of administrative facilities or major developed facilities; Utilization of forage within an allotment that could be authorized through a grazing permit; Protection, operation, or maintenance of improvements resulting from stewardship projects; Research; Preparation and planning of administrative studies; Land Acquisition.
Funding: (Cooperative Agreements) FY 18 $5,625,052.00; FY 19 est $10,986,892.00; FY 20 est Estimate Not Available
HQ: 1400 Independence Avenue SW, PO Box 1138, Washington, DC 20250
    Phone: 202-205-1495 | Email: john.crockett@usda.gov

USDA10.702 | ALASKA NATIONAL INTEREST LANDS CONSERVATION ACT (ANILCA) AGREEMENTS
"ANILCA Agreements"

Award: Direct Payments for Specified Use
Purpose: This multidisciplinary collaborative program sustains fisheries and wildlife management on public lands, conservation of healthy populations of fish and wildlife and other renewable resources to rural Alaskans.
Applicant Eligibility: The U.S. Forest Service's mission is to sustain the health, diversity, and productivity of the Nation's forests and grasslands to meet the needs of present and future generations. The agency manages 193 million acres of public land, provides assistance to state and private landowners, and maintains the largest forestry research Organization in the world. To accomplish this mission, the U.S. Forest Service partners with non-profits; for-profit; Institutions of higher

education; federal, state, local, Alaska Native and Native American tribal Governments, or Alaska Native Corporations (as defined in the Alaska Native Claims Settlement Act); individuals; and Organizations.

Beneficiary Eligibility: An individual/Family, profit organization, other private institution/organization, public nonprofit institution/organization; an officer, employee, agent, department, or instrumentality of the Federal government, of the State of Alaska, municipality or political subdivision of the State of Alaska.

HQ: 161 E 1st Street Avenue Door 8, Anchorage, AK 99501

Phone: 907-743-9500 | Email: twhitford@fs.fed.us

http://www.fs.usda.gov/r10

USDA10.703 | COOPERATIVE FIRE PROTECTION AGREEMENT

Award: Direct Payments for Specified Use

Purpose: To provide reciprocal furnishing for fire protection and compensate for sustaining wildland fire management activities, including suppression and post-fire restoration.

Applicant Eligibility: The Forest Service may enter into Cooperative Fire Protection Agreements with a fire Organization. The term fire Organization means any governmental entity or public or private corporation or association maintaining fire protection facilities within the United States, its Territories and possessions, and any governmental entity or public or private corporation or association which maintains fire protection facilities in any foreign country in the vicinity of any installation of the United States. The Forest Service is charged with the duty of providing fire protection for any property of the United States and is authorized to enter into a reciprocal agreement, with any fire Organization maintaining fire protection facilities in the vicinity of such property, for mutual aid in furnishing fire protection for such property and for other property for which such Organization normally provides fire protection.

Beneficiary Eligibility: Forest Service enters into non-assistance cooperative agreements with willing fire organizations for the purpose of cooperation in the performance of wildland fire protection projects and during wildfires, emergencies and/or disasters.

Funding: (Cooperative Agreements (Discretionary Grants)) FY 18 $1,100,910.00; FY 19 est $1,610,656.00; FY 20 est Estimate Not Available

HQ: 1400 Independence Avenue SW, PO Box 1138, Washington, DC 20250

Phone: 208-387-5100 | Email: timothy.melchert@usda.gov

USDA10.704 | LAW ENFORCEMENT AGREEMENTS

Award: Cooperative Agreements

Purpose: To implement the enforcement of laws on lands within the unit of the National Forest System and to increase the protection of persons and their property to carry out specific responsibilities related to the National Forest System.

Applicant Eligibility: Cooperators include any State or political subdivision (that is, local Governments). Cooperative Law Enforcement Agreements are most commonly entered into with county Governments.

Beneficiary Eligibility: Agreements must comply with requirements in FSM 5360, Law Enforcement.

Funding: (Cooperative Agreements) FY 18 $1,024,448.00; FY 19 est $3,934,529.00; FY 20 est Estimate Not Available

HQ: 201 14th Street SW, Washington, DC 20024

Phone: 202-205-1664 | Email: tracie.wilkinson@usda.gov

USDA10.705 | COOPERATIVE FOREST ROAD AGREEMENTS

Award: Cooperative Agreements

Purpose: To encourage Forest Service to cooperate with State, county, or road authorities for the construction, improvement, and maintenance of certain forest roads.

Applicant Eligibility: State, county or local public road authorities.

Beneficiary Eligibility: Other Requirements. a. Direction regarding jurisdiction over forest transportation facilities is found in FSM 7703.3.b. Direction regarding common transportation interests with local public road authorities is found in FSM 7703.4.

Funding: (Cooperative Agreements) FY 18 $4,579,586.00; FY 19 est $3,798,798.00; FY 20 est Estimate Not Available

HQ: 201 14th Street SW, Suite 3C, Washington, DC 20024

Phone: 202-205-0963 | Email: david.b.payne@usda.gov

Programs Administered by Regional - State - Local Offices

USDA10.707 | RESEARCH JOINT VENTURE AND COST REIMBURSABLE AGREEMENTS

Award: Direct Payments for Specified Use

Purpose: To increase participation in Agricultural and forestry research activities.

Applicant Eligibility: Joint Venture Agreements: State cooperative institution, State department of agriculture, college, University, other research or educational institution or Organization, Federal or private agency or Organization, individual, or any other party Cost Reimbursable Agreements: State cooperative Institutions or other colleges and universities Forestry and Rangeland Research Institutions.

Beneficiary Eligibility: The Forest Service has partnership authorities to enter into agreements and cooperative arrangements with willing members of the public, which include but are not limited to, for profit; non-profits; institutions of higher education; federal, state, local, and Native American tribe governments; foreign governments and organizations.

Funding: (Direct Payments for Specified Use) FY 17 $70,997,322.6; FY 18 est $51,653,417.43; FY 19 Not Separately Identifiable

HQ: 1400 Independence Avenue SW, Washington, DC 20250
Phone: 703-605-4776 | Email: jacquelinehenry@fs.fed.us
https://www.fs.fed.us/research

INTERNATIONAL TRADE ADMINISTRATION
Regional – State – Local Offices

RESEARCH HEADQUARTERS

Alabama
George Norton, Director | Medical Forum Building Room 707 950 22nd Street N, Birmingham, AL 35203 205-731-1331

Alaska
Charles Becker, Director | 550 W 7th Avenue Suite 1770, Anchorage, AK 99501 907-271-6237

Arizona
Eric Nielsen, Manager | 166 W Alameda, Tucson, AZ 85701 520-670-5540

Frank Woods, Director | 2901 N Central Avenue Suite 970, Phoenix, AZ 85012 602-640-2513

Arkansas
Lon J. Hardin, Director | 425 W Capitol Avenue Suite 700, Little Rock, AR 72201 501-324-5794

California
530 Water Street Suite 740, Oakland, CA 94607 510-273-7350

Dale Wright, Manager | 917 7th Street 2nd Floor, Sacramento, CA 95814 916-498-5155

Eduardo Torres, Manager | 390-B Fir Avenue, Clovis, CA 93611 559-325-1619

Elizabeth Krauth, Manager | 330 Ignacio Boulevard Suite 102, Novato, CA 94949 415-883-1966

Fred Latuperissa, Manager | Inland Empire Export Assistance Center 2940 Inland Empire Boulevard Suite 121, Ontario, CA 91764 909-466-4134

Greg Mignano, Director | 101 Park Center Plaza Suite 1001, San Jose, CA 95113 408-271-7300

JoAllyn Scott | 101 Park Center Plaza Suite 1001, San Jose, CA 95113 408-998-7402

Julie Anne Hennessy, Acting Manager | 350 S Figueroa Street Suite 509, Los Angeles, CA 90071 213-894-4022

Julie Anne Hennessy, Manager | 11150 Olympic Boulevard Suite 975, Los Angeles, CA 90064 310-235-7104

Mark A. Weaver, Manager | c/o Monterey Institute of International Studies 411 Pacific Street Suite 320, Monterey, CA 93940 831-641-9850

Mary Boscia, Director | One World Trade Center Suite 1670, Long Beach, CA 90831 562-980-4550

Matt Andersen, Director | 6363 Greenwich Drive Suite 230, San Diego, CA 92122 619-557-5395

Michael Hoffman | 3300 Irvine Avenue Suite 345, Newport Beach, CA 92660-3198 714-660-0144

Paul Tambakis, Director | Orange County Export Assistance Center 3300 Irvine Avenue Suite 305, Newport Beach, CA 92660 949-660-1688

R.J. Donovan, Manager | 5201 Great America Parkway Suite 456, Santa Clara, CA 95054 408-970-4610

Stephen Crawford, Manager | 250 Montgomery Street 14th Floor, San Francisco, CA 94104 415-705-2300

Colorado
Isabella Cascarano, Acting Director | 1625 Broadway Suite 680, Denver, CO 80202 303-844-6623

Connecticut
Carl Jacobsen, Director | 213 Court Street Suite 903, Middletown, CT 06457-3346 860-638-6950

Florida
George L. Martinez, Manager | 1130 Cleveland Street, Clearwater, FL 33755 727-893-3738

John McCartney, Director Miami, USEAC | 200 E Las Olas Boulevard Suite 1600, Fort Lauderdale, FL 33301 954-356-6640

John McCartney, Director Miami, USEAC | 777 N W 72nd Avenue PO Box 3L2, Miami, FL 33126-3009 305-526-7425

Michael E. Higgins, Manager | 325 John Knox Road Suite 201, Tallahassee, FL 32303 850-942-9635

Philip A. Ouzts, Manager | Eola Park Centre 200 E Robinson Street Suite 1270, Orlando, FL 32801 407-648-6235

Georgia

Barbara Myrick, Manager | 6001 Chatham Center Drive Suite 100, Savannah, GA 31405 912-652-4204

Samuel P. Troy, Director | 285 Peachtree Center Avenue NE Suite 200, Atlanta, GA 30303-1229 404-657-1900

Hawaii

1001 Bishop Street Bishop Square Pacific Tower PO Box 50026 Suite 1140, Honolulu, HI 96813 808-522-8040

Idaho (Portland, Oregon District)

James Hellwig, Manager | 700 W State Street 2nd Floor, Boise, ID 83720 208-334-3857

Illinois

James Mied, Manager | 515 N Court Street PO Box 1747, Rockford, IL 61103 815-987-8123

Mary N. Joyce, Director | Chicago USEAC Xerox Center 55 W Monroe Street Room 2440, Chicago, IL 60603 312-353-8045

Robin F. Mugford, Manager | 610 Central Avenue Suite 150, Highland Park, IL 60035 847-681-8010

Indiana

Dan Swart, Manager | Indianapolis Export Assistance Center Pennwood 1 Suite 106 11405 N Pennsylvania Street, Carmel, IN 46032 317-582-2300

Iowa

Allen Patch, Director | 700 Locust Street Suite 100, Des Moines, IA 50309-3739 515-288-8614

Kansas (Kansas City, Missouri District)

George D. Lavid, Manager | 209 E William Suite 300, Wichita, KS 67202-4012 316-263-4067

Kentucky

2292 S Highway 27 Suite 240, Somerset, KY 42501 606-677-6160

John Autin, Director | 601 W Broadway Room 634B, Louisville, KY 40202 502-582-5066

Louisiana

Donald Van de Werken, Director | Delta Export Assistance Center 365 Canal Street Suite 1170, New Orleans, LA 70130 504-589-6546

Patricia Holt, Manager | 7100 W Park Drive, Shreveport, LA 71129 318-676-3064

Maine (Boston, Massachusetts District)

Jeffrey Porter, Manager | 511 Congress Street, Portland, ME 04101 207-541-7400

Maryland

Thomas Cox, Director | Baltimore USEAC World Trade Center Suite 2432 401 E Pratt Street, Baltimore, MD 21202 410-962-4539

Massachusetts

Frank J. O'Connor, Director | 164 Northern Avenue Suite 307 World Trade Center, Boston, MA 02210-2071 617-424-5990

Michigan

Neil Hesse, Director | 211 W Fort Street Suite 2220, Detroit, MI 48226 313-226-3650

Paul Litton, Manager | 425 S Main Street Suite 103, Ann Arbor, MI 48104 734-741-2430

Richard Corson, Manager | Oakland Pointe Office Building Suite 1300 W 250 Elizabeth Lake Road, Pontiac, MI 48341 248-975-9600

Thomas J. Maquire, Manager | 301 W Fulton Street Suite 718-S, Grand Rapids, MI 49504 616-458-3564

Minnesota

Ronald E. Kramer, Director | 45 S 7th Street Suite 2240, Minneapolis, MN 55402 612-348-1638

Mississippi

Harrison Ford, Director | 704 E Main Street, Raymond, MS 39154 601-857-0128

Missouri

Frank Spector, Acting Director | 2345 Grand Suite 650, Kansas City, MO 64108 816-410-9201

Randall J. LaBounty, Director | 8182 Maryland Avenue Suite 303, Saint Louis, MO 63105 314-425-3302

Montana

Mark Peters, Manager | c/o Montana World Trade Center Gallagher Business Building Suite 257, Missoula, MT 59812 406-243-2098

Nebraska

Meredith Bond, Manager | 11135 O Street, Omaha, NE 68137 402-221-3664

Nevada

Jere Dabbs, Manager | 1755 E Plumb Lane Suite 152, Reno, NV 89502 775-784-5203

New Hampshire (Boston, Massachusetts District)

Susan Berry, Manager | 17 New Hampshire Avenue, Portsmouth, NH 03801-2838 603-334-6074

New Jersey

Rod Stuart, Director | 3131 Princeton Pike Building 4 Suite 105, Trenton, NJ 08648 609-989-2100

William Spitler, Director | One Gateway Center 9th Floor, Newark, NJ 07102 973-645-4682

New Mexico (Dallas, Texas District)

Sandy Necessary, Manager | c/o New Mexico Department of Economic Development 1100 Saint Francis Drive, Santa Fe, NM 87503 505-827-0350

New York

George Soteros, Manager | Long Island Export Assistance Center 1550 Franklin Avenue Room 207, Mineola, NY 11501 516-739-1765

James Mariano, Director | 111 W Huron Street Room 1304, Buffalo, NY 14202 716-551-4191

Programs Administered by Regional - State - Local Offices

Joan Kanlian, Manager | Westchester Export Assistance Center 707 Westchester Avenue Suite 209, White Plains, NY 10604 914-682-6712

John Lavelle, Acting Director | 6 World Trade Center Room 635, New York, NY 10048 212-466-5222

K.L. Fredericks, Manager | Harlem Export Assistance Center 163 W 125th Street Suite 904, New York, NY 10027 212-860-6200

North Carolina

Roger Fortner, Director | 400 W Market Street Suite 102, Greensboro, NC 27401 336-333-5345

Roger Fortner, Director | 521 E Morehead Street Suite 435, Charlotte, NC 28202 704-333-4886

Northern Virginia

Ellen Moore, Acting Manager | 1911 N Fort Myer Drive Suite 601, Arlington, VA 22209 703-524-2885

Ohio

Dao Le, Director | 36 E 7th Street Suite 2650, Cincinnati, OH 45202 513-684-2944

Mary Beth Double, Manager | Two Nationwide Plaza Suite 1400, Columbus, OH 43215 614-365-9510

Michael Miller, Director | Bank One Center 600 Superior Avenue E Suite 700, Cleveland, OH 44114 216-522-4750

Robert Abrahams, Manager | 300 Madison Avenue, Toledo, OH 43604 419-241-0683

Oklahoma

Jimmy Williams, Manager | 700 N Greenwood Avenue Suite 1400, Tulsa, OK 74106 918-581-7650

Ronald L. Wilson, Director | 301 NW 63rd Street Suite 330, Oklahoma City, OK 73116 405-608-5302

Oregon

John O'Connell, Manager | 1401 Willamette Street, Eugene, OR 97401-4003 541-465-6575

Scott Goddin, Director | One World Trade Center Suite 242 121 SW Salmon Street, Portland, OR 97204 503-326-3001

Pennsylvania

Deborah Doherty, Manager | One Commerce Square 228 Walnut Street Suite 850 PO Box 11698, Harrisburg, PA 17108-1698 717-221-4510

Edward Burton, Director | The Curtis Center Suite 580 W Independence Square W, Philadelphia, PA 19106 215-597-6101

Ted Arnn, Manager | Federal Building Room 2002 1000 Liberty Avenue, Pittsburgh, PA 15222 412-395-5050

Puerto Rico (Hato Rey)

525 F D Roosevelt Avenue Suite 905, San Juan, PR 00918 787-766-5555

Rhode Island (Hartford Connecticut District)

Keith Yatsuhashi, Manager | One W Exchange Street, Providence, RI 02903 401-528-5104

South Carolina

5300 International Boulevard Suite 201-C, North Charleston, SC 29418 843-760-3794

Ann Watts, Director | Strom Thurmond Federal Building Suite 172 1835 Assembly Street, Columbia, SC 29201 803-765-5345

Denis Csizmedia, Manager | Upstate Export Assistance Center Park Central Office Park Building 1 Suite 109 555 N Pleasantburg Drive, Greenville, SC 29607 864-271-1976

South Dakota

Cinnamon King, Manager | Siouxland Export Assistance Center Augustana College 2001 S Summit Avenue Room 122, Sioux Falls, SD 57197 605-330-4264

Tennessee

George Frank, Manager | Old Historic City Hall 601 W Summit Hill Drive Suite 300, Knoxville, TN 37902-2011 865-545-4637

Michael Speck, Director | 211 Commerce Street 3rd Floor Suite 100, Nashville, TN 37201 615-736-5161

Ree Russell, Manager | c/o Centre For Enterprise Buckman Hall 3rd Floor 650 E Parkway S Suite 348, Memphis, TN 38104 901-323-1543

Texas

Daniel G. Rodriguez, Manager | 203 S Saint Mary Street Suite 360, San Antonio, TX 78205 210-228-9878

James D. Cook, Director | 500 Dallas Suite 1160, Houston, TX 77002 713-718-3062

Karen Parker, Manager | 1700 Congress 2nd Floor PO Box 12728, Austin, TX 78701 512-916-5939

Loree Silloway, Director | PO Box 420069 2050 N Stemmons Freeway Suite 170, Dallas, TX 75207 214-767-0542

Vavie Sellschopp, Manager | 711 Houston Street, Fort Worth, TX 76102 817-212-2673

Utah

Stanley Rees, Director | 324 S State Street Suite 221, Salt Lake City, UT 84111 801-524-5116

Vermont

Susan Murray, Manager | National Life Building PO Box 20 6th Floor, Montpelier, VT 05620-0501 802-828-4508

Virginia

Helen D. Lee Hwang, Director | 400 N 8th Street Suite 540 PO Box 10026, Richmond, VA 23240 804-771-2246

Washington

950 Pacific Avenue Suite 410, Tacoma, WA 98402 253-593-6736

David Spann, Director | 2001 6th Avenue Suite 650, Seattle, WA 98121 206-553-5615

Janet Dauble | 801 W Riverside Avenue Suite 400, Spokane, WA 99201 509-353-2625

West Virginia

David Kotler, Manager | Wheeling Jesuit University/NTTC 316 Washington Avenue, Wheeling, WV 26003 304-243-5493

Harvey Timberlake, Director | 405 Capitol Street Suite 807, Charleston, WV 25301 304-347-5123

Wisconsin

Paul D. Churchill, Director | 517 E Wisconsin Avenue Room 596, Milwaukee, WI 53202 414-297-3473

DOC11.112 | MARKET DEVELOPMENT COOPERATOR PROGRAM "MDCP"

Award: Project Grants

Purpose: The Market Development Cooperator Program develops and expands foreign markets for nonagricultural goods and services produced in the United States.

Applicant Eligibility: Applicants are found to be eligible in one of three categories. 1. Nonprofit industry Organizations (includes small business development centers, World Trade Centers, and 501(c)nonprofits such as chambers of commerce, international trade centers, port authorities, economic development Organizations, and other business interest groups). 2. Trade associations. 3. State departments of trade and their regional associations. The Statute stipulates that private industry firms or groups of firms may be found eligible in cases where no entity described above represents that industry. However, since the Program began operating in 1993, no private firm has been able to demonstrate that an Organization in one of the first three categories did not represent its interests.

Beneficiary Eligibility: U.S. firms that sell non-agricultural goods or services. (While private firms benefit from MDCP project activity, as noted above, they are generally not eligible to apply for MDCP funds.) See trade.gov/mdcp for more information.

Award Range/Average: Individual awards may not exceed $300,000.

Funding: (Cooperative Agreements (Discretionary Grants)) FY 18 $0.00; FY 19 est $0.00; FY 20 est $1,500,000.00

HQ: 14th Street and Constitution Avenue NW, Room 2872, Washington, DC 20230

Phone: 202-482-2969 | Email: brad.hess@trade.gov

http://www.export.gov/mdcp

MARITIME ADMINISTRATION
Regional – State – Local Offices

California
John Hummer | US Department of Transportation Maritime Administration Northern California Gateway Office 201 Mission Street Suite 1800, San Francisco, CA 94105 415-744-2924

Florida
Lauren Brand, DIRECTOR | 51 SW 1st Avenue Suite 1305, Miami, FL 33130 305-530-6420

Gateway (Houston): (Colorado, New Mexico, Oklahoma, Texas)
James Murphy | US Department of Transportation Maritime Administration Eastern Gulf/Lower Mississippi Gateway Office 500 Poydras Street Room 1223, New Orleans, LA 70130-3394 504-589-2000, Ext. 229

Illinois
Floyd Miras | US Department of Transportation Maritime Administration Great Lakes Gateway Office 1701 E Woodfield Road Suite 203, Schaumburg, IL 60173 847-995-0122

Missouri
Robert Goodwin | US Department of Transportation Maritime Administration Upper Mississippi Office 1222 Spruce Street Suite 2.202F, Saint Louis, MO 63103-2818 314-539-6783

New York
Shashi N. Kumar | United States Merchant Marine Academy, Kings Point, NY 11024-1699 516-773-5000

North Atlantic Gateway (New York)
Maritime Administration 1 Bowling Green Room 418, New York, NY 10004-1415 212-668-3330

Southern California
Alan Hicks | US Department of Transportation Maritime Administration Southern California Gateway Office Glenn M Anderson Federal Building 501 W Ocean Boulevard Room 5190, Long Beach, CA 90802 562-628-0246

Virginia
Frank Mach | US Department of Transportation Maritime Administration Mid Atlantic Gateway Office 7737 Hampton Boulevard Building 19 Suite 300, Norfolk, VA 23505-1204 757-322-5800

Washington
Randy Rogers | US Department of Transportation Maritime Administration Pacific Northwest Gateway Office Henry M Jackson Federal Building 915 2nd Avenue 31st Floor Room 3196, Seattle, WA 98174 206-220-7717

Programs Administered by Regional - State - Local Offices

DOT20.802 | FEDERAL SHIP FINANCING GUARANTEES

Award: Guaranteed/insured Loans

Purpose: To provide competitive financing through the issuance of guarantees of debt issued for the purpose of financing or refinancing the construction, reconstruction or reconditioning of vessels built in United States shipyards.

Applicant Eligibility: An individual with the ability, experience, financial resources, and other qualifications necessary for the adequate operation and maintenance of a vessel or an eligible shipyard.

Beneficiary Eligibility: U.S. and foreign shipowners, or eligible U.S. shipyards.

Award Range/Average: Historically projects have ranged from less than $1 million to several hundred million. (Average is not entered, because it would not be typical of the breadth of the program.)

Funding: (Guaranteed/Insured Loans) FY 18 $0.00; FY 19 est $365,000,000.00; FY 20 est $0.00

HQ: 1200 New Jersey Avenue SE, Washington, DC 20590

    Phone: 202-366-2118 | Email: david.gilmore@dot.gov

    http://www.marad.dot.gov

DOT20.803 | MARITIME WAR RISK INSURANCE
"Title XII, MMA, 1936"

Award: Insurance

Purpose: Provides war risk insurance to U.S.-flag and foreign vessels whenever it appears to the Secretary of Transportation that adequate insurance for waterborne commerce cannot be obtained on reasonable terms and conditions from commercial companies.

Applicant Eligibility: All U.S. flag vessels, and certain foreign flag vessels meeting specific criteria as determined by the Maritime Administrator.

Beneficiary Eligibility: Covered beneficiaries include vessel owners, third party liabilities, merchant mariners, and certain designated beneficiaries of deceased mariners.

Award Range/Average: Applicable only in designated combat areas, subject to terms of the binder.

Funding: (Insurance) FY 18 $100,000.00; FY 19 est $100,000.00; FY 20 est $100,000.00

HQ: 1200 New Jersey Avenue SE, Washington, DC 20590

    Phone: 202-366-1915 | Email: michael.yarrington@dot.gov

    http://www.dot.gov

DOT20.806 | STATE MARITIME SCHOOLS
"SMA"

Award: Cooperative Agreements; Direct Payments for Specified Use; Use of Property, Facilities, and Equipment; Training

Purpose: To educate and train future merchant marine officers at the State Maritime Academies (SMA).

Applicant Eligibility: State Institutions of higher education. Assistance is limited to one maritime academy in any one State.

Beneficiary Eligibility: Students, meeting eligibility requirements.

Award Range/Average: Annual assistance payment of $500,000 to each regional school provided State matches funds and admits eligible out-of-state student. A subsistence of $8,000 per academic year, not to exceed 4 years, paid to selected students in good standing in the Student Incentive Payment (SIP) Program, NTE a total of 300 students.

Funding: (Direct Payments for Specified Use) FY 18 $1,000,00.00; FY 19 est $6,000,000.00; FY 20 est $6,000,000.00

HQ: Office of Maritime Labor and Training (MAR-650) 1200 New Jersey Avenue SE, Washington, DC 20590

    Phone: 202-366-5469 | Email: christopher.wahler@dot.gov

    http://www.dot.gov

DOT20.807 | U.S. MERCHANT MARINE ACADEMY
"Kings Point"

Award: Training

Purpose: Educates and trains merchant marine officers.

Applicant Eligibility: High school graduates who are U.S. citizens and international students in accordance with legislation. In general, criteria are similar to those generally used for college admission.

Beneficiary Eligibility: High school graduates who are U.S. citizens and eligible international students.

Award Range/Average: Annual assistance payment of $400,000 to each regional school provided State matches funds and admits eligible out-of-state student. An allowance of $48,000 per academic year, not to exceed 5 years, payment to selected students in good standing in the student incentive payment program.

Funding: (Training) FY 18 $28,000.00; FY 19 est $90,000.00; FY 20 est $80,000.00

HQ: 300 Steamboat Road, Kings Point, NY 11024

   Phone: 516-726-5641 | Email: michael.bedryk@usmma.edu

   http://www.dot.gov

DOT20.808 | CAPITAL CONSTRUCTION FUND
"CCF"

Award: Direct Payments for Specified Use

Purpose: Provides for replacement vessels, additional vessels or reconstructed vessels, built and documented under the laws of the United States for operation in the United States foreign, Great Lakes, Marine Highways or noncontiguous domestic trades.

Applicant Eligibility: An applicant must be a U.S. citizen, own or lease one or more eligible vessels, have a Program for the acquisition, construction or reconstruction of a qualified vessel and demonstrate the financial capabilities to accomplish the Program.

Beneficiary Eligibility: N/A

Award Range/Average: Applicant receives tax benefits for depositing assets in accordance with the program.

HQ: Office of Financial Approvals 1200 New Jersey Avenue SE, Washington, DC 20590

   Phone: 202-366-1859 | Email: daniel.ladd@dot.gov

   http://www.dot.gov

DOT20.812 | CONSTRUCTION RESERVE FUND
"CRF"

Award: Direct Payments for Specified Use

Purpose: To promote the construction, reconstruction, reconditioning, or acquisition of merchant vessels built and documented under the laws of the United States for purposes of national defense.

Applicant Eligibility: A Construction Reserve Fund (CRF) may be established by any citizen of the United States who owns, in whole or in part, a vessel or vessels operating in the foreign or domestic commerce of the U.S., or in the fisheries. Additionally, any citizen who is operating such vessel or vessels owned by another individual may establish a CRF.

Beneficiary Eligibility: Any citizen of the United States who owns, in whole or in part, a vessel or vessels operating in the foreign or domestic commerce of the U.S. or in the fisheries. Additionally, any citizen who is operating such vessel or vessels owned by another individual.

Award Range/Average: Defer tax on gains by depositing the gains attributable to the sale of or indemnification for loss of vessels in accordance with the program.

HQ: Office of Financial Approvals 1200 New Jersey Avenue SE, Washington, DC 20590

   Phone: 202-366-1859 | Email: daniel.ladd@dot.gov

   http://www.marad.dot.gov

DOT20.813 | MARITIME SECURITY FLEET PROGRAM OR SHIP OPERATIONS COOPERATION PROGRAM
"Maritime Security Program"

Award: Direct Payments for Specified Use

Purpose: The MSP helps sustain a fleet of 60 active, commercially viable, militarily useful, privately-owned vessels operating under U.S. registry to meet national defense and other security requirements.

Applicant Eligibility: U.S. citizens and operators of U.S. flag vessels.

Beneficiary Eligibility: Ownership and operation of vessels and facilities useful to the United States in time of war or national emergency.

Award Range/Average: Authorized $3.1 million per vessel per year (FY 2012-2015); $3.5 million (FY 2016); $4.999 (FY2017); $5.0 million (FY 2018-20); $5.23 million (FY 2021); and $3.7 million (FY2022-2025)

Programs Administered by Regional - State - Local Offices

Funding: (Direct Payments for Specified Use) FY 18 $300,000,000.00; FY 19 est $300,000,000.00; FY 20 Estimate Not Available; (Direct payments) FY 16 $3.5mil per ship/annually = $210,000.00 annual; FY 17 $ $4,999,950.00 per ship/annually = $299,997.00mil annual; FY 2018 $5,000,000.00 per ship/annually = $300,000.00 mil annual; FY 19 $5,000,000.00 per ship/annually = $300,000.00 mil annual
HQ: 1200 New Jersey Avenue SE, Washington, DC 20590
  Phone: 202-366-5076 | Email: william.mcdonald@dot.gov
  http://www.marad.dot.gov

DOT20.814 | ASSISTANCE TO SMALL SHIPYARDS
"Small Shipyard Grants"

Award: Direct Payments for Specified Use
Purpose: Awards grants for capital improvements and related infrastructure improvements at qualified shipyards that will facilitate the efficiency, cost effectiveness, and quality of domestic ship construction for commercial and Federal Government use.
Applicant Eligibility: Either a shipyard or a State or local government on behalf of a shipyard can apply. The shipyard must be one in a single geographical location, located in or near a maritime community, that (1) is a small business concern within the meaning of section 3 of the Small Business Act (15 U.S.C. 632); and (2) does not have more than 600 production employees. Other factors taken into account when grants are awarded will be (a) the economic circumstances and conditions of the maritime community near to which a shipyard is located; and (B) the local, State and regional economy in which such community is located.
Beneficiary Eligibility: N/A
Award Range/Average: Awards can be in any amount up to $19,600,000.
Funding: (Project Grants) FY 18 $19,600,000.00; FY 19 est $19,600,000.00; FY 20 Estimate Not Available
HQ: Office of Shipyards and Marine Engineering 1200 New Jersey Avenue SE, Room W21-318, Washington, DC 20590
  Phone: 202-366-5737 | Email: david.heller@dot.gov
  http://www.marad.dot.gov

DOT20.816 | AMERICA'S MARINE HIGHWAY GRANTS
"Marine Highway Program"

Award: Cooperative Agreements; Project Grants
Purpose: Mitigates landside congestion, expand transportation options, and realize public benefit and external cost savings by awarding Marine Highway grants to qualified applicants to implement designated Marine Highway projects.
Applicant Eligibility: Grant applicants must be public agencies at the state, regional or local level including, but not limited to, Metropolitan Planning Organizations, State Governments (including State Departments of Transportation) and port authorities. They must also have had their projects for which they are requesting funds be designated as Marine Highway projects by the Secretary of Transportation under America's Marine Highway Program (110th Congress, Public Law 110-140). In order to receive a grant under this Program, applicants must submit an application to the Secretary and demonstrate that the project is financially viable, the funds will be spent efficiently and effectively, and that a market exists for the services of the proposed project as evidenced by contracts or written statements of intent from potential customers. An applicant shall provide at least 20 percent of the project costs from non-Federal sources. In awarding grants under the Program, the Secretary shall give a preference to those projects or components that present the most financially viable transportation services and require the lowest percentage Federal share of the costs. '' Eligible applicants include those entities defined within OMB 2 CFR 200 excluding Federal agencies due to matching-fund regulatory requirements.
Beneficiary Eligibility: Eligible beneficiaries include those entities defined in OMB 2CFR 200.
Funding: (Project Grants (Cooperative Agreements)) FY 18 $4,500,000.00; FY 19 est $6,790,000.00; FY 20 est Estimate Not Available
HQ: Office of Marine Highways and Passenger Services 1200 Pennsylvania Avenue NW, PO Box 201, Washington, DC 20590
  Phone: 202-366-0951 | Email: scott.davies@dot.gov
  http://marad.dot.gov/ships

DOT20.817 | AIR EMISSIONS AND ENERGY INITIATIVE
Award: Cooperative Agreements
Purpose: MARAD will use projects results and data for a variety of purposes including further support of air emissions reduction research, demonstration, and pilot projects.

Applicant Eligibility: Eligible applicants include vessel owners, operators, or public sponsors. Shore side equipment upgrade or shore power projects are not eligible for funding.

Beneficiary Eligibility: The benefit of this project will be for the federal government as well as anyone in the general public and research organizations.

HQ: Department of Transportation/Maritime Administration 1200 New Jersey Avenue SE, Washington, DC 20590
   Phone: 202-366-0714 | Email: daniel.yuska@dot.gov

DOT20.818 | GREAT SHIPS INITIATIVE
"Great Waters Research Collaberative (GWRC)"

Award: Cooperative Agreements

Purpose: The Great Waters Research Collaborative (GWRC) is a collaboration whose objective is to end the problem of ship-mediated invasive species in the Great Lakes-St. Lawrence Seaway System.

Applicant Eligibility: Applicants must have the following capabilities and resources: A current EPA-approved Quality Management Plan (QMP). The facilities and equipment for conducting biological analyses to determine concentrations of living organisms in three size-classes (less than 10 microns, between 10 and 50 microns, greater than 50 microns) at the levels of the proposed USCG discharge standard. A mix of personnel available for engineering support and for conducting biological analyses according to standard protocols. The ability to write and follow a rigorous quality assurance plan that maximizes the production of credible results.

Beneficiary Eligibility: Eligible beneficiaries include those entities defined in OMB A-102 and OMB Circular A-122.

Award Range/Average: N/A

Funding: (Salaries and Expenses) FY 18 $660,000; FY 19 est $800,000; FY 20 est $1,000,000;-Beyond years estimates are not available. Future funding is subject to availability of funds.

HQ: Office of Environmental1200 New Jersey Avenue SE, Washington, DC 20590
   Phone: 202-366-1920 | Email: carolyn.junneman@dot.gov

DOT20.819 | BALLAST WATER TREATMENT TECHNOLOGIES

Award: Cooperative Agreements

Purpose: MARAD will use the projects results and data for a variety of purposes.

Applicant Eligibility: The assistance will be used to support the Evaluation and Verification of Ballast Water Treatment Technologies and other Green Shipping Initiatives. Applicants must be able to provide technical services, equipment and to support the testing, evaluation, and demonstration of treatment methods, practices, systems and equipment. Technical efforts will be primarily directed towards the evaluation of the effectiveness of ballast water treatment technologies and systems at shipboard/barge-based and shore side facilities fabricated to simulate the in-tank configuration(s) and flow requirements typical of commercial vessels.

Beneficiary Eligibility: Beneficiary eligibility include State, Public nonprofit institution/organization, other public institution/organization, Private nonprofit institution/organization, and Education Professional.

Award Range/Average: Past Fiscal Year: 2017 - $1,000,000 Projection: Current Fiscal Year: 2018 - $0 Budget Fiscal Year: 2019 - $0

Funding: (Salaries and Expenses) FY 18 $1,000,000.00; FY 19 est $780,000.00; FY 20 est $500,000.00

HQ: Office of Environmental 1200 New Jersey Avenue SE, Room W26-418, Washington, DC 20590
   Phone: 202-366-1920 | Email: carolyn.junemann@dot.gov

DOT20.820 | MARITIME STUDIES AND INNOVATIONS

Award: Cooperative Agreements

Purpose: The purpose of this program is to provide assistance for projects involving studies and innovations related to shipping, vessel operations, shipyards, maritime financing and insurance.

Applicant Eligibility: The assistance must be used for projects involving studies and innovations related to shipping, vessel operations, shipyards, maritime financing and insurance, and all other maritime activities in support of the policy of the United States Government to encourage and aid the development and maintenance of a merchant marine. Limitations on applicant eligibility for a specific project, if any, will be explained and included in any Notice of Funding Opportunity posted on grants.gov.

Beneficiary Eligibility: The ultimate beneficiaries of the projects will be the United States Government and the general public.

Award Range/Average: The range of funding depends on funds available during the fiscal year.

Programs Administered by Regional - State - Local Offices

Funding: (Cooperative Agreements) FY 18 $5,000; FY 19 est Estimate Not Available; FY 20 est Estimate Not Available
HQ: 1200 New Jersey Avenue SE, Washington, DC 20590
    Phone: 202-366-2526 | Email: todd.ripley@dot.gov

DOT20.821 | WOMEN ON THE WATER (WOW)
"WOW Conference"

Award: Cooperative Agreements
Purpose: The purpose of the WOW program is to promote diversity in the maritime industry.
Applicant Eligibility: Eligible applicants for financial assistance for WOW Program activities are the six State Maritime Academies, regional maritime academies, and the U.S. Merchant Marine Academy.
Beneficiary Eligibility: Beneficiaries are individuals attending the State Maritime Academies and the U.S. Merchant Marine Academy.
Award Range/Average: FY-2017 - $15,000
Funding: (Cooperative Agreements) FY 18 $15,000.00; FY 19 est Estimate Not Available; FY 20 est Estimate Not Available
HQ: 1200 New Jersey Avenue SE, Washington, DC 20590
    Phone: 202-366-5469 | Email: christopher.wahler@dot.gov
    http://www.marad.dot.gov

DOT20.822 | PORT OF GUAM IMPROVEMENT ENTERPRISE PROGRAM

Award: Cooperative Agreements
Purpose: The purpose of this program is to provide financial assistance for the planning, design, and construction of projects for the Port of Guam.
Applicant Eligibility: Port of Guam or any subdivision, instrumentality, or agent thereof.
Beneficiary Eligibility: Same as Applicant Eligibility.
Award Range/Average: No financial assistance awards made in any prior years.
HQ: 1200 New Jersey Avenue SE, Washington, DC 20590
    Phone: 202-366-5076 | Email: robert.bouchard@dot.gov
    http://www.portofguam.com

MINE SAFETY AND HEALTH ADMINISTRATION
Regional – State – Local Offices

Colorado
PO Box 25367 DFC, Denver, CO 80225-0367 303-231-5458

Indiana
A. Simms | 2300 Willow Street Suite 200, Vincennes, IN 47591 812-882-7617

Kentucky
G. Page | 100 Fae Ramsey Lane, Pikeville, KY 41501-3211 606-432-0943

Irvin T. hooker | 3837 S U.S. Highway 25, Barbourville, KY 40906 606-546-5123

Jim W. Langley | 100 YMCA Drive, Madisonville, KY 42431-9019 270-821-4180

Pennsylvania
The Stegmaier Building Suite 034 7 N Wilkes-Barre Boulevard, Wilkes-Barre, PA 18702 570-826-6321

Thomas Light | Paladin Professional Center 631 Excel Drive Suite 100, Mount Pleasant, PA 15666 724-925-5150

Virginia
Gregory Meikle | PO Box 560, Norton, VA 24273 540-679-0230

West Virginia
Bob Cornett | 604 Cheat Road, Morgantown, WV 26508 304-225-6800

David S. Mandeville | 100 Bluestone Road, Mount Hope, WV 25880 304-877-3900

Timothy Watkins | 1301 Airport Road, Beaver, WV 25813-9426 304-253-5237

COAL MINE SAFETY AND HEALTH

Alabama
Richard Gates | 135 Gemini Circle Suite 213, Birmingham, AL 35209 205-290-7300

DOL17.600 | MINE HEALTH AND SAFETY GRANTS

Award: Project Grants
Purpose: Assists States in providing safety and health training and develop programs to improve mine health and safety conditions.
Applicant Eligibility: Any mining State of the United States.
Beneficiary Eligibility: N/A
Award Range/Average: From $31,493 to $689,756. Average: $233,912.
Funding: (Project Grants) FY 18 $10,537,000.00; FY 19 est $10,537,000.00; FY 20 est $10,537,000.00
HQ: 201 12th Street S, Arlington, VA 22202

    Phone: 202-693-9594 | Email: burns.kevin@dol.gov
    http://www.msha.gov

DOL17.601 | MINE HEALTH AND SAFETY COUNSELING AND TECHNICAL ASSISTANCE

Award: Advisory Services and Counseling; Dissemination of Technical Information
Purpose: Improves conditions of health and safety in and around coal, metal and nonmetallic mines and mineral processing facilities through technical advice, special studies, investigations, and development of mine health and safety programs.
Applicant Eligibility: Applicants should be authorized by their individual Organization to request assistance, and should work cooperatively with mine management to facilitate communications with MSHA representatives.
Beneficiary Eligibility: Representatives of state and local government agencies, professional and labour organizations, and mine operators.
Funding: (Salaries and Expenses) FY 18 FY $248,573,000.00; 19 est $29,818,000.00; FY 20 est $29,818,000.00
HQ: 201 12th Street S 4W210, Arlington, VA 22202

    Phone: 202-693-9470 | Email: francart.william@dol.gov
    http://www.msha.gov

DOL17.602 | MINE HEALTH AND SAFETY EDUCATION AND TRAINING

Award: Training
Purpose: Provides technical training for Federal Mine Inspectors and representatives of the mining industry.
Applicant Eligibility: Any mine operator, miner or their agent can request training or training materials.
Beneficiary Eligibility: Mine operators, miners or their agent, organizations and individuals.
Award Range/Average: N/A
Funding: (Salaries and Expenses) FY 17 $16,869,000.00; FY 18 est $16,011,000.00; FY 19 est $16,011,000.00
HQ: 201 12th Street S, Arlington, VA 22202

    Phone: 202-693-9594 | Email: burns.kevin@dol.gov
    http://www.msha.gov

DOL17.603 | BROOKWOOD-SAGO GRANT

Award: Project Grants
Purpose: To provide mine safety and health training and education programs for workers and mine operators, to better identify, avoid, and prevent unsafe working conditions in and around mines.
Applicant Eligibility: Any mining State of the United States, nonprofit public and private Organizations.
Beneficiary Eligibility: Mine operators and any organization employing miners or creating training materials.
Award Range/Average: At a minimum, $50,000, depending on the project needs as detailed in the solicitation for grant application and availability of funds.
Funding: (Project Grants) FY 18 $250,000.00; FY 19 est $400,000.00; FY 20 est $400,000.00
HQ: 201 12th Street S, Arlington, VA 22202

    Phone: 202-693-9570 | Email: oates.janice@dol.gov
    http://www.msha.gov

DOL17.604 | SAFETY AND HEALTH GRANTS

Award: Project Grants
Purpose: To provide mine safety and health training and education to miners, mine operators, and other individuals who may work at a mine; and to develop training and other programs to improve health and safety conditions at mines.

Programs Administered by Regional - State - Local Offices

Applicant Eligibility: Any mining State of the United States, non-profit public and private Organizations, commercial entity, or the legislatively mandated entity.

Beneficiary Eligibility: Individuals employed in workplaces covered by the Mine Act, as amended by Miner Act that receive training and/or educational services and owners and employers covered by the Mine Act receiving the benefits of the health and safety project under these grants.

HQ: 201 12th Street S, Arlington, VA 22202
  Phone: 202-693-9594 | Email: burns.kevin@dol.gov
  http://www.msha.gov

MINORITY BUSINESS DEVELOPMENT AGENCY
Regional – State – Local Offices

California

Melda Cabrera, Director | 221 Main Street Room 1280, San Francisco, CA 94105 415-744-3001

Rudy Guerra, District Officer | 9660 Flair Drive Suite 455, El Monte, CA 91731 818-453-8636

Florida

Rudy Suarez, District Officer | Federal Building Room 1314 51 SW 1st Avenue PO Box 25, Miami, FL 33130 305-536-5054

Georgia

Robert M. Henderson, Director | 401 W Peachtree Street NW Room 1715, Atlanta, GA 30308-3516 404-730-3300

Illinois

Carlos Guzman, Director | 55 E Monroe Street Suite 1406, Chicago, IL 60603 312-353-0182

Massachusetts

R. K. Schwartz, District Officer | 10 Causeway Street Room 418, Boston, MA 02222-1041 617-565-6850

New York

Heyward Davenport, Director | 26 Federal Plaza Room 3720, New York, NY 10278 212-264-3262

Pennsylvania

Alfonso Jackson, District Officer | Federal Office Building 600 Arch Street Room 10128, Philadelphia, PA 19106 215-597-9236

Texas

John F. Iglehart, Director | 1100 Commerce Street Room 7B23, Dallas, TX 75242 214-767-8001

DOC11.802 | MINORITY BUSINESS RESOURCE DEVELOPMENT

Award: Cooperative Agreements; Project Grants

Purpose: To provide financial assistance for minority business enterprises and assist in the development of competitiveness of MBEs through the administration and demonstration projects.

Applicant Eligibility: Applicants eligible to provide services under pilot or demonstration projects are nonprofit Organizations, for-profit firms, State and local Governments, Native American Tribal entities, and educational Institutions. Applicants for congressionally mandated projects are those specifically identified in applicable legislation.

Beneficiary Eligibility: Congressionally mandated award beneficiaries are members of the minority business community. Pilot or demonstration project beneficiaries are minority business enterprises.

Award Range/Average: Not Applicable.

Funding: (Project Grants) FY 18 $10,101,473.00; FY 19 est $4,510,000.00; FY 20 est $6,000,000.00

HQ: 1401 Constitution Avenue NW, Washington, DC 20230
  Phone: 202-482-0065 | Email: nchambers@mbda.gov
  http://www.mbda.gov

DOC11.804 | MBDA BUSINESS CENTER-AMERICAN INDIAN AND ALASKA NATIVE

Award: Cooperative Agreements

Purpose: The MBDA Business Center - American Indian and Alaska Native program provides a strategic deal for business consulting services to eligible American Indian and Alaska Native Minority Business Enterprises. It also supports the competitiveness of U.S. businesses that are minority-owned and secures private sectors.

Applicant Eligibility: Applicants eligible to operate an MBDA Business Center are nonprofit Organizations, for-profit firms, State and local Governments, Native American Tribal entities, and educational Institutions.

Beneficiary Eligibility: The MBDA Business Center program serves all eligible minority business enterprises through direct services or through strategic partner referral. Eligible beneficiaries of this program are: Native Americans and Alaska Natives (including Alaska Natives, Alaska Native Corporations and Tribal entities), African Americans, Hispanic Americans, Asian and Pacific Islander Americans, Asian Indians and Hasidic Jews. See 15 C.F.R. 1400.1-.2 and Executive Order 11625.

Award Range/Average: $199,999 to $600,000.

Funding: (Cooperative Agreements) FY 18 $3,190,490.00; FY 19 est $3,597,276.00; FY 20 est $3,597,275.00

HQ: 1401 Constitution Avenue NW, Washington, DC 20230

   Phone: 202-482-0065 | Email: nchambers@mbda.gov

   http://www.mbda.gov

DOC11.805 | MBDA BUSINESS CENTER
"Business Center Program"

Award: Cooperative Agreements

Purpose: The MBDA Business Center program provides strategies for business. It supports the Agency that supports the growth of U.S. businesses. It assists in minority business development, private contracts, job creation, and retention.

Applicant Eligibility: Applicants eligible to operate MBC projects are nonprofit Organizations, for-profit firms, State and local Governments, Native American Tribal entities, and educational Institutions.

Beneficiary Eligibility: The Minority Business Center program serves all eligible minority business enterprises through direct services or through strategic partner referral. Eligible beneficiaries of this program are: African Americans, Hispanic Americans, Asian and Pacific Islander Americans, Native Americans (including Alaska Natives, Alaska Native Corporations and Tribal entities), Asian Indians and Hasidic Jews. See 15 C.F.R. 1400.1-.2 and Executive Order 11625.

Award Range/Average: $225,000 to $1,000,000.

Funding: (Cooperative Agreements) FY 18 $18,230,588.00; FY 19 est $26,616,760.00; FY 20 est $26,616,758.00

HQ: 1401 Constitution Avenue NW, Washington, DC 20230

   Phone: 202-482-0065 | Email: nchambers@mbda.gov

   http://www.mbda.gov

NATIONAL AGRICULTURAL STATISTICS SERVICE
Regional – State – Local Offices

REGIONAL OFFICES

Arkansas, Delta Region
10800 Financial Centre Parkway Suite 110, Little Rock, AR 72211 501-228-9926

California, Pacific Region
650 Capitol Mall Suite 6-100 PO Box 1258, Sacramento, CA 95814 916-498-5161

Colorado, Mountain Region
1 Denver Federal Center Building 67 Room 630 PO Box 150969, Denver, CO 80225 720-787-3150

Georgia, Southern Region
Ste 100 355 E Hancock Avenue Stephens Federal Building, Athens, GA 30601 706-546-2236

Iowa, Upper Midwest Region
Federal Building 210 Walnut Street Suite 833, Des Moines, IA 50309 515-284-4340

Kentucky, Eastern Mountain Region
Gene Snyder & Courthouse Building 601 W Broadway Room 645 PO Box 1120, Louisville, KY 40202 502-582-5293

Michigan, Great Lakes Region
3001 Coolidge Road Suite 400 PO Box 30239 Lansing, East Lansing, MI 48909-7739 517-324-5300

Missouri, Heartland Region
601 Business Loop 70 W Suite 213E, Columbia, MO 65203 573-876-0950

Nebraska, Northern Plains Region
Room 263 Federal Building 100 Centennial Mall N PO Box 81069, Lincoln, NE 68508 402-437-5541

Pennsylvania, Northeastern Region
4050 Crums Mill Road Suite 203 PO Box 60607, Harrisburg, PA 17112-2875 717-787-3904

Texas, Southern Plains Region
300 E 8th Street Room 500 Federal Building PO Box 70, Austin, TX 78701 512-916-5581

Washington, Northwest Region
112 Henry Street NE Suite 202 PO Box 609, Olympia, WA 98506 360-709-2400

Programs Administered by Regional - State - Local Offices

USDA10.950 | AGRICULTURAL STATISTICS REPORTS
"Agricultural Estimates"

Award: Dissemination of Technical Information

Purpose: The National Agricultural Statistics Agency is to provide timely, accurate, and useful statistics in service to the U.S. agriculture economy and makes marketing decisions on a wide range of agricultural commodities. It also develops and administers programs for collecting statistics related to agriculture, resources, and rural communities. It assists rural communities and ensures national forests and private working lands are conserved and restored so that all of America's children have access to safe and nutritious meals.

Applicant Eligibility: Farmers and agricultural producers, marketing and processing groups, transportation and handler groups, consumers, state and local Governments, educational Institutions, and the general public including those located in the U.S. Territories. The type of assistance NASS provides is: Dissemination of Technical Information: specifically Agricultural Statistics.

Beneficiary Eligibility: Same as Applicant Eligibility.

Award Range/Average: USDA National Agricultural Statistics Service (NASS) does not award grants. The federal domestic assistance type NASS provides is: Dissemination of Technical Information: Agricultural Statistics and the Census of Agriculture.

Funding: (Dissemination of Technical Information) FY 18 $196,851,000.00; FY 19 est $174,517,000.00; FY 20 est $163,000,000.00

HQ: 1400 Independence Avenue SW, Room 5041A S Agriculture Building, Washington, DC 20250

Phone: 202-690-0919 | Email: ann.johnson@nass.usda.gov

http://www.nass.usda.gov

NATIONAL GUARD BUREAU
Regional – State – Local Offices

ANG Environmental
Elaine Magdivec | 3500 Fetchet Avenue, Andrews Air Force Base, MD 20762-5157 301-836-8904

ANG Facilities
Tony Latuff | 3500 Fetchet Avenue, Andrews Air Force Base, MD 20762-5157 301-836-8194

ANG Fire Protection
Steve Waldelich | 3500 Fetchet Avenue, Andrews Air Force Base, MD 20762-5157 301-278-8170

ANG Logistics Facilities
Robert Sinclair | 3500 Fetchet Avenue, Andrews Air Force Base, MD 20762-5157 301-836-8338

ANG Natural & Cultural Resources Mgt
Melissa Mettz | 3500 Fetchet Avenue, Andrews Air Force Base, MD 20762-5157 301-836-8427

ANG Security Guard
Kevin Leavy | 3500 Fetchet Avenue, Andrews Air Force Base, MD 20762-5157 301-836-7809

ANG Services Resources Mgt
MAJ Gerald Cullens | 3500 Fetchet Avenue, Andrews Air Force Base, MD 20762-5157 301-836-8162

ARNG Admin Services
Cindy Kadin | ARNG Readiness Center 111 S George Mason Drive, Arlington, VA 22204 703-607-7056

ARNG Anti - Terrorism Program
Dean Connors | ARNG Readiness Center 111 S George Mason Drive, Arlington, VA 22204 703-607-9198

ARNG Aviation Operations
Bob Fleming | ARNG Readiness Center 111 S George Mason Drive, Arlington, VA 22204 703-607-7752

ARNG Distributive Learning Program
MAJ Leslie Myers | ARNG Readiness Center 111 S George Mason Drive, Arlington, VA 22204 703-601-9869

ARNG Electronic Security System
Mark Brown | ARNG Readiness Center 111 S George Mason Drive, Arlington, VA 22204 703-607-7956

ARNG Environmental Resources Management
MAJ Anthony Bryant | ARNG Readiness Center 111 S George Mason Drive, Arlington, VA 22204 703-607-7340

ARNG Full Time Dining Facility Operations
Stanley Jung | ARNG Readiness Center 111 S George Mason Drive, Arlington, VA 22204 703-607-7344

ARNG Real Property
MAJ Paul Crigler | ARNG Readiness Center 111 S George Mason Drive, Arlington, VA 22204 703-607-7916

ARNG Reimbursable Maintenance Operations
MAJ David Cooper | ARNG Readiness Center 111 S George Mason Drive, Arlington, VA 22204 703-607-7721

ARNG Security Guard Activities
Deidra Wallace | ARNG Readiness Center 111 S George Mason Drive, Arlington, VA 22204 703-607-7353

ARNG Sustainable Range Program
Nick Long | ARNG Readiness Center 111 S George Mason Drive, Arlington, VA 22204 703-607-7884

ARNG Telecommunications
Freida Parks | ARNG Readiness Center 111 S George Mason Drive, Arlington, VA 22204 703-607-7654

State Family Program Activities
Joyce Wallace | 1411 Jefferson Davis Highway, Alexandria, VA 22202-3231 703-607-0882

DOD12.400 | MILITARY CONSTRUCTION, NATIONAL GUARD

Award: Cooperative Agreements

Purpose: For the acquisition of facilities essential for the training and administration of Army National Guard (ARNG) units in the 50 states, the District of Columbia, the Commonwealth of Puerto Rico, the Virgin Islands and Guam, by purchase, transfer, construction, expansion, rehabilitation or conversion.

Applicant Eligibility: The 50 States, the District of Columbia, the Commonwealth of Puerto Rico, Guam, and the territories. The State National Guard unit must be federally recognized. States must provide real estate for armory projects.

Beneficiary Eligibility: Same as Applicant Eligibility.

Award Range/Average: $300,000 and higher.

Funding: (Cooperative Agreements) FY 18 $430,498,752.00; FY 19 est 208,134,190.00; FY 20 est 435,000,000.00

> **HQ:** LTC 111 S George Mason Drive, Arlington, VA 22204 | Email: elver.crow@us.army.mil
> http://www.ngb.dtic.mil/indexshtm

DOD12.404 | NATIONAL GUARD CHALLENGE PROGRAM

Award: Formula Grants

Purpose: To conduct a National Guard civilian youth opportunities program to use the National Guard to provide military-based training, including supervised work experience in community service and conservation projects, to civilian youth who cease to attend secondary school after graduating so as to improve the life skills and employment potential of such youth.

Applicant Eligibility: The Secretary of Defense shall provide for the conduct of the National Guard Challenge Program in such States and U.S. territories and possession as the Secretary considers to be appropriate, except that Federal expenditures under the Program may not exceed $62.5 M for fiscal year 01.

Beneficiary Eligibility: Same as Applicant Eligibility.

Funding: (Formula Grants) FY 17 Actual Not Available; FY 18 est Estimate Not Available; FY 19 est $98,015,310.00

HQ: 4800 Mark Center Drive, Alexandria, VA 22311

> Phone: 571-372-8415 | Email: barbara.j.orlando.civ@mail.mil
> http://www.ngb.dtic.mil/indexstm

NATIONAL HIGHWAY TRAFFIC SAFETY ADMINISTRATION
Regional – State – Local Offices

Region I
George A. Luciano, Regional Administrator | Transportation System Center Kendall Square-Code 903, Cambridge, MA 02142 617-494-3427

Region II
Thomas M. Louizou, Regional Administrator | 222 Mamaroneck Avenue Suite 204, White Plains, NY 10605 914-682-6162

Region III
Elizabeth A. Baker, Regional Administrator | The Crescent Building 10 S Howard Street Suite 4000, Baltimore, MD 21201 410-962-0077

Region IV
Troy Ayers, Regional Administrator | 61 Forsyth Street SW Suite 17T30, Atlanta, GA 30303-3104 404-562-3739

Region V
Donald J. McNamara, Regional Administrator | 19900 Governors Drive Suite 201, Olympia Fields, IL 60461 708-503-8822

Region VI
Georgia S. Chakiris, Regional Administrator | 819 Taylor Street Room 8A38, Fort Worth, TX 76102-6177 817-978-3653

Region VII
PO Box 412515, Kansas City, MO 64141 816-822-7233

Programs Administered by Regional - State - Local Offices

Region VIII
Louis R. DeCarolis, Regional Administrator | 555 Zang Street
Room 430, Lakewood, CO 80228 303-969-6917

Region IX
David Manning, Acting Regional Administrator | 201 Mission
Street Suite 2230, San Francisco, CA 94105 415-744-3089

Region X
Curtis A. Winston, Regional Administrator | 3140Jackson
Federal Building 915 2nd Avenue, Seattle, WA 98174
206-220-7640

DOT20.600 | STATE AND COMMUNITY HIGHWAY SAFETY
Award: Formula Grants
Purpose: Provides a coordinated national highway safety program to reduce traffic crashes, deaths, injuries, and property damage.
Applicant Eligibility: States, federally recognized Indian Tribes, the District of Columbia, Puerto Rico, American Samoa, Guam, Northern Marianas, and the Virgin Islands.
Beneficiary Eligibility: Political subdivisions, through the State Highway Safety Agencies.
Award Range/Average: FY 2018 $646,425 - $23,687,928
Funding: (Formula Grants (Apportionments)) FY 18 $539,497,649.00; FY 19 est $538,169,999.00; FY 20 est $559,600,000.00
HQ: Regional Operations and Program Delivery 1200 New Jersey Avenue SE NRO-010, Washington, DC 20590
Phone: 202-366-5424 | Email: jamie.pfister@dot.gov
http://www.nhtsa.whatsup/fedassist/index.html

DOT20.601 | ALCOHOL IMPAIRED DRIVING COUNTERMEASURES INCENTIVE GRANTS I
Award: Project Grants
Purpose: Encourages States to adopt programs to reduce crashes resulting from persons driving while under the influence of alcohol.
Applicant Eligibility: States, Puerto Rico, the Virgin Islands, Guam, American Samoa, and the Commonwealth of the Northern Mariana Islands. States are provided with two alternative means to qualify for a Section 410 grant. Under the first alternative, States may qualify as a low fatality rate State if they have an alcohol-related fatality rate of 0. 5 or less per 100 million vehicle miles traveled (VMT). Under the second alternative, States may qualify as a Programmatic State if they demonstrate that they meet three of eight grant criteria for fiscal year 2006, four of eight grant criteria for fiscal year 2007, and five of eight grant criteria for fiscal years 2008, 2009 And for the remainder of the current authorization. Qualifying under both alternatives would not entitle the State to receive additional grant funds. SAFETEA-LU directs that States with low alcohol-related fatality rates, based on the agency's Fatality Analysis Reporting System (FARS), be awarded grants without the need to satisfy any of these Programmatic criteria. There is also an additional Section 410 grant available to assist the 10 States with the highest impaired driving related fatalities as determined by the most recent FARS data. A High fatality rate State may also apply as a Programmatic State.
Beneficiary Eligibility: State Highway Safety Agency.
Award Range/Average: $972,388 to $17,973,219
Funding: (Project Grants (with Formula Distribution)) FY 18 $0.00; FY 19 est $0.00; FY 20 est Estimate Not Available
HQ: Regional Operations and Program Delivery 1200 New Jersey Avenue SE NRO-010, Washington, DC 20590
Phone: 202-366-5424 | Email: jamie.pfister@dot.gov
http://www.nhtsa.gov/impaired

DOT20.602 | OCCUPANT PROTECTION INCENTIVE GRANTS
Award: Project Grants
Purpose: Encourages States to adopt effective programs to reduce highway deaths and injuries resulting from individuals riding unrestrained or improperly restrained in motor vehicles.
Applicant Eligibility: States, the District of Columbia, Puerto Rico, American Samoa, Guam, Northern Marianas, Virgin Islands, and the Bureau of Indian Affairs.
Beneficiary Eligibility: State Highway Safety agencies.
Award Range/Average: The range is $ 74,843 - 3,109,419.
HQ: 1200 New Jersey Avenue SE, Washington, DC 20590
Phone: 202-366-5424 | Email: jamie.pfister@dot.gov
http://www.nhtsa.gov

DOT20.607 | ALCOHOL OPEN CONTAINER REQUIREMENTS

Award: Project Grants
Purpose: Public transportation.
Applicant Eligibility: States, the District of Columbia, and Puerto Rico.
Beneficiary Eligibility: State Highway Safety agencies.
Award Range/Average: Varies.
Funding: (Formula Grants (Apportionments)) FY 18 $42,058,790.00; FY 19 est $42,058,790.00; FY 20 Estimate Not Available
HQ: Regional Operations and Program Delivery 1200 New Jersey Avenue SE NRO-010, Washington, DC 20590
    Phone: 202-366-5424 | Email: jamie.pfister@dot.gov
    http://www.nhtsa/whatsup/fedassist/index.html

DOT20.608 | MINIMUM PENALTIES FOR REPEAT OFFENDERS FOR DRIVING WHILE INTOXICATED

Award: Project Grants
Purpose: Encourages States to enact and enforce Repeat Intoxicated Offender laws.
Applicant Eligibility: States, the District of Columbia, and Puerto Rico.
Beneficiary Eligibility: State Highway Safety agencies.
Award Range/Average: The grants range were from $2,489,000 - $54,546,000.
Funding: (Project Grants) FY 18 $124,415,286.00; FY 19 est $124,415,286.00; FY 20 est Estimate Not Available
HQ: 1200 New Jersey Avenue SE NTI 200, Washington, DC 20590
    Phone: 202-366-5424 | Email: jamie.pfister@dot.gov
    http://www.nhtsa/whatsup/fedassist/index.html

DOT20.609 | SAFETY BELT PERFORMANCE GRANTS

Award: Project Grants
Purpose: Successful research ideas can result in innovation and development projects that improve public transportation systems nationwide to provide more efficient and effective delivery of public transportation services.
Applicant Eligibility: The 50 States, District of Columbia, Puerto Rico, American Samoa, the Commonwealth of the Northern Mariana Islands, Guam and the Virgin Islands are eligible to apply for a grant.
Beneficiary Eligibility: State Highway Safety Agencies.
Award Range/Average: States are spending down their SAFETEA-LU grant awards.
HQ: Regional Operations and Program Delivery 1200 New Jersey Avenue SE NRO-010, Washington, DC 20590
    Phone: 202-366-5424 | Email: jamie.pfister@dot.gov
    http://www.nhtsa.gov

DOT20.610 | STATE TRAFFIC SAFETY INFORMATION SYSTEM IMPROVEMENT GRANTS

Award: Project Grants
Purpose: Encourages States to adopt and implement effective programs to improve the timeliness, accuracy, completeness, uniformity, integration and accessibility of State data.
Applicant Eligibility: To qualify for a first-year grant, a State demonstrated that it has an established multi-disciplinary highway safety data and traffic records coordinating committee; a developed multi-year safety data and traffic records strategic plan, approved by the coordinating committee and containing performance-based measures; certify that the State has adopted and is using the model data elements determined by the Secretary to be useful, or certify that grant funds will be used toward adopting and using the most elements practicable. To qualify for a subsequent-year grant, a State must certify that an assessment or audit of the State traffic records system has been conducted or updated within the preceding 5 years; certify that the coordinating committee continues to operate and supports the multi-year plan; specify how the grant funds and any other funds of the State will support the multi-year strategic plan; demonstrate measurable progress toward achieving the goals and objectives identified in the multi-year plan; and submit a report, showing measurable progress in the implementation of the multi-year plan. The 50 States, District of Columbia, Puerto Rico, the Virgin Islands, Guam, American Samoa, the

Programs Administered by Regional - State - Local Offices

Commonwealth of the Northern Mariana Islands and Indian Tribes through the Bureau of Indian Affairs are eligible to apply for a grant.

Beneficiary Eligibility: State Highway Safety Agencies.

Award Range/Average: The ranges were $500.00- $2,344,000

HQ: Regional Operations and Program Delivery 1200 New Jersey Avenue SE NRO-010, Washington, DC 20590

Phone: 202-366-5424 | Email: jamie.pfister@dot.gov

http://www.nhtsa.gov

DOT20.611 | INCENTIVE GRANT PROGRAM TO PROHIBIT RACIAL PROFILING
"Section 1906"

Award: Formula Grants

Purpose: Encourages States to enact and enforce laws that prohibit the use of racial profiling in the enforcement of traffic laws on Federal-aid highways, and to maintain and allow public inspection of statistics on motor vehicle stops.

Applicant Eligibility: This Grant is available to the 50 states, the District of Columbia, Puerto Rico, the Virgin Islands, Guam American Samoa, and the Commonwealth of the Northern Mariana Islands.

Beneficiary Eligibility: State Highway Safety agencies.

Award Range/Average: Grant award ranged from $885,460- $454,170. Average grant was for $668,544

Funding: (Formula Grants) FY 18 $2,625,000.00; FY 19 est $1,500,000.00; FY 20 est $2,250,00.00

HQ: 1200 New Jersey Avenue SE NRO-100, Washington, DC 20590

Phone: 202-366-5424 | Email: jamie.pfister@dot.gov

http://www.nhtsa.gov

DOT20.612 | INCENTIVE GRANT PROGRAM TO INCREASE MOTORCYCLIST SAFETY
"Section 2010"

Award: Formula Grants

Purpose: Encourages States to adopt and implement effective programs to reduce the number of single and multi-vehicle crashes involving motorcyclists.

Applicant Eligibility: This Grant was available to the 50 states, the District of Columbia, and Puerto Rico.

Beneficiary Eligibility: State Highway Safety Agencies.

Award Range/Average: The range for these grants is: $100,000 - $482,959.

HQ: 1200 New Jersey Avenue SE NRO-100, Washington, DC 20590

Phone: 202-366-5424 | Email: jamie.pfister@dot.gov

http://www.nhtsa.gov

DOT20.613 | CHILD SAFETY AND CHILD BOOSTER SEATS INCENTIVE GRANTS
"Section 2011"

Award: Project Grants

Purpose: Encourages States to enact and enforce a child restraint law that requires children up to 65 pounds and under 8 years of age to be properly restrained in a child restraint, unless they are 4' 9' tall.

Applicant Eligibility: The grant Program was available to the 50 States, the District of Columbia and Puerto Rico.

Beneficiary Eligibility: State Highway Safety Agencies.

Award Range/Average: The range was normally $100,000 - $700,000.

HQ: 1200 New Jersey Avenue SE NRO-100, Washington, DC 20590

Phone: 202-366-5424 | Email: jamie.pfister@dot.gov

http://nhtsa.dot.gov

DOT20.614 | NATIONAL HIGHWAY TRAFFIC SAFETY ADMINISTRATION (NHTSA) DISCRETIONARY SAFETY GRANTS AND COOPERATIVE AGREEMENTS
"NHTSA Section 403 Discretionary Grants and Cooperative Agreements"

Award: Cooperative Agreements; Project Grants

Purpose: To provide technical and financial assistance to State and local government agencies, for-profit and non-profit organizations, educational institutions, hospitals, and other persons (as defined in Title 1 USC Chapter (1)) in support of highway safety research and development, special studies, educational and public awareness projects.

Applicant Eligibility: Eligibility requirements will be specified on a project-by-project basis. Generally speaking, and historically, projects have been made available to the following types of Organizations: Intrastate, Local, Sponsored Organization, Public nonprofit institution/Organization, Other public institution/Organization, Federally Recognized Indian Tribal Government, U.S. territory or possession, Specialized Group, Small Business, Profit Organization, Private nonprofit institution/Organization, Quasi-public nonprofit institution/Organization, Other private institution/Organization, Native American Organization, .

Beneficiary Eligibility: Intrastate, State, Local, Sponsored Organization, Public Nonprofit Institution/Organization, Other Public Institution/organization, Federally Recognized Indian Tribal Government, U.S. territory or possession, Specialized Group, Small Business, Profit Organization, Private nonprofit institution/organization, Quasi-public nonprofit institution/organization, Other private institution/organization, Native American Organization, Anyone/General Public, Health Professional, Scientist/Researcher, Consumer, Minority Group, Handicapped, Youth, Senior Citizen.

Award Range/Average: The range for these grants are $100,000 - $482,959.

HQ: 1200 New Jersey Avenue SE, W51-125, Washington, DC 20590

Phone: 202-366-3989 | Email: anita.barber@dot.gov

DOT20.615 | E-911 GRANT PROGRAM
"911 Grant Program"

Award: Formula Grants

Purpose: To provide federal financial assistance for the implementation and operation of 911 services, E-911 services, migration to an IP-enabled emergency network, and adoption and operation of NG911 services and applications.

Applicant Eligibility: States, U.S. Territories, and Tribal 911 agencies.

Beneficiary Eligibility: States, U. S. Territories and Tribes.

Award Range/Average: $13,191 to $11,399,076. Average: $1,957,078

Funding: (Formula Grants) FY 18 $0.00; FY 19 est $109,250.00; FY 20 $0.00

HQ: National 911 Implementation Coordination Office 1200 New Jersey Avenue SE NPD-400, Washington, DC 20590

Phone: 202-366-2705

https://www.911.gov

DOT20.616 | NATIONAL PRIORITY SAFETY PROGRAMS

Award: Formula Grants

Purpose: To encourage States to address national priorities for reducing highway deaths and injuries through occupant protection programs.

Applicant Eligibility: With the exception of the Motorcyclist Safety Program, the 50 States, District of Columbia, Puerto Rico, U.S. territories (American Samoa, Guam, Northern Marianas, and Virgin Islands) are eligible for funding. Under the Motorcyclist Safety Program, the 50 States, District of Columbia, and Puerto Rico are eligible for grant awards.

Beneficiary Eligibility: Funding is provided to State Highway Safety agencies.

Award Range/Average: $33,125 - $8,046,147.33

Funding: (Formula Grants) FY 18 $277,324,992.00; FY 19 est $255,400,000.00; FY 20 est $255,000,000.00

HQ: 1200 New Jersey Avenue SE, Washington, DC 20590

Phone: 202-366-2121 | Email: maggi.gunnels@dot.gov

http://nhtsa.dot.gov

Programs Administered by Regional - State - Local Offices

NATIONAL OCEANIC AND ATMOSPHERIC ADMINISTRATION
Regional – State – Local Offices

Northeast Region
Patricia Kurkul, Acting Regional Administrator | One Blackburn Drive, Gloucester, MA 01930 978-281-9250

Northwest Region
William Stelle Jr., Regional Administrator | 7600 Sand Point Way NE, Seattle, WA 98115 206-526-6150

Southeast Region
William T. Hogarth, Regional Administrator | 9721 Executive Center Drive N Suite 201, Saint Petersburg, FL 33702 727-570-5301

Southwest Fisheries Science Center
Dr. Michael F. Tillman, Science Director | PO Box 271, La Jolla, CA 92038-0271 619-546-7081

Southwest Region
Rodney R. McInnis, Acting Regional Administrator | 501 W Ocean Boulevard Suite 4200, Long Beach, CA 90802-4213 562-980-4001

Steven Pennoyer, Regional Administrator | PO Box 21668, Juneau, AK 99802-1668 907-586-7221

Virginia
Nicholas A. Prahl, Director | 439 W York Street, Norfolk, VA 23510-1114 757-441-6776

Washington
Nicholas A. Prahl | 1801 Fairview Avenue E, Seattle, WA 98102 206-553-7656

DOC11.015 | BROAD AGENCY ANNOUNCEMENT
"BAA"

Award: Cooperative Agreements; Project Grants
Purpose: The BAA is a mechanism to encourage educational research and innovative projects.
Applicant Eligibility: N/A
Beneficiary Eligibility: N/A
Award Range/Average: $5,000 - $4.2 million
Funding: (Project Grants) FY 17 Not Separately Identifiable; FY 18 est Not Separately Identifiable FY 19 est Not Separately Identifiable
HQ: 1325 E W Highway, 9th Floor Building 2, Silver Spring, MD 20910
  Phone: 301-628-1308 | Email: lamar.revis@noaa.gov
  http://www.noaa.gov/index.html

DOC11.021 | NOAA SMALL BUSINESS INNOVATION RESEARCH (SBIR) PROGRAM
"NOAA SBIR Program"

Award: Project Grants
Purpose: The Small Business Innovation Research stimulates technological innovation in the private sector, strengthens the role of small businesses, and encourages participation by women-owned and socially disadvantaged small business firms in technological innovation.
Applicant Eligibility: Applicant Eligibility (1) is organized for profit, with a place of business located in the United States, which operates primarily within the United States, or which makes a significant contribution to the United States economy through the payment of taxes or use of American products, materials or labor; (2) is in the legal form of an individual proprietorship, partnership, limited liability company, corporation, joint venture, association, trust or cooperative, except that where the form is a joint venture, there can be no more than 49 percent participation by foreign business entities in the joint venture; (3) is at least 51 percent owned and controlled by one or more individuals who are citizens of, or permanent resident aliens in, the United States, except in the case of a joint venture, where each entity in the venture must be 51 percent owned and controlled by one or more individuals who are citizens of, or permanent resident aliens in the United States; and (4) has, including its affiliates, not more than 500 employees. The term "affiliates" is defined in greater detail in 13 CFR 121. 103. The term "number of employees" is defined in 13 CFR 121. 106.
Beneficiary Eligibility: Each year, NOAA sets aside a portion of its extramural R&D budget to fund research from small science and technology-based firms. The NOAA SBIR Program supports innovative research projects that fall within NOAA's core mission of science, service, and stewardship.

Award Range/Average: Maximum allowable amounts are as follows:Phase I grants: $120,000 eachPhase II grants: $400,000 each

Funding: (Project Grants) FY 17 $0.00; FY 18 est $0.00; FY 19 est $9,000,000.00

HQ: 1315 E W Highway, Room 11460 HQ /R /OM61 11th Floor, Silver Spring, MD 20910

    Phone: 301-734-1174 | Email: brenda.alford@noaa.gov

    http://techpartnerships.noaa.gov/sbir.aspx

DOC11.022 | BIPARTISAN BUDGET ACT OF 2018

Award: Cooperative Agreements; Project Grants

Purpose: To identify risks related to disasters, issuing payments for disaster relief, and ensuring the funds are expended.

Applicant Eligibility: N/A

Beneficiary Eligibility: Entities affected by hurricanes, wildfires, and other disasters.

HQ: 1315 E W Highway, Room 9314 Building 2 9th Floor, Silver Spring, MD 20910

    Phone: 301-628-1310 | Email: alan.p.conway@noaa.gov

    http://www.noaa.gov

DOC11.467 | METEOROLOGIC AND HYDROLOGIC MODERNIZATION DEVELOPMENT
"Hydrometeorological Development"

Award: Project Grants; Direct Payments With Unrestricted Use; Dissemination of Technical Information; Training

Purpose: To foster Federal partnerships and provide training, education, and professional development to minimize tsunamis through hazard assessment, warning guidance, and mitigation.

Applicant Eligibility: Eligible applicants are accredited Federally recognized Institutions of higher learning, consortia of these Institutions, agencies of State or local Governments including school systems, quasi-public Institutions, consultants, and companies involved in using and developing meteorological or hydrologic forecasts or forecast methodology. In addition, the National Tsunami Hazard Mitigation Program (NTHMP) funding provides resources to reduce the impact of tsunamis through hazard assessment, warning guidance, and mitigation.

Beneficiary Eligibility: The benefits of the overall program are for reduction in loss of life and damage which the general public can realize from improvement in weather forecasts, watches, and warnings of hazardous weather and resultant flooding. For the improvements from the modernization of the Nation's weather and hydrologic services to be realized, there must be significant involvement of the entire hydrometeorological community. Thus, benefits will accrue to: (1) General public through higher quality weather products and information; (2) State and local agencies responsible for the planning and implementation of emergency services, fire prevention, allocation and control of water resources, and those agencies who project economic conditions based on weather and water resource availability; (3) educational institutions (0-13+) which need to incorporate the information which will result from modernization of the weather services into their curricula; (4) scientists and developers who will be using the new information to enhance the State of the knowledge of the atmosphere and improve present system safety and reliability; and academic institutions which are funded for programs dealing with studies of the atmospheric and hydrologic science. In addition, the National Tsunami Hazard Mitigation Program (NTHMP) funding provides resources to reduce the impact of tsunamis through hazard assessment, warning guidance, and mitigation.

Award Range/Average: $6,000 to $5,814,360 Average: $400,000

Funding: (Project Grants) FY 17 $6,011,612.00; FY 18 est $6,184,257.00; FY 19 Estimate Not Available

HQ: 1315 E W Highway, Silver Spring, MD 20910

    Phone: 301-427-9322 | Email: leroy.spayd@noaa.gov

    http://www.noaa.gov

DOC11.468 | APPLIED METEOROLOGICAL RESEARCH

Award: Project Grants

Purpose: The Collaborative Science, Technology, and Applied Research program compensate for highly collaborative research for the transition from basic and applied research. The Hurricane Forecast Improvement funds to the university to provide guidance for hurricane track and forecasts. The Next Generation Global Prediction System program funds to the university for developing a unified global modeling system to improve weather forecasting.

Applicant Eligibility: Institutions of higher education, federally funded educational Institutions, and in some cases private Organizations (profit and non-profit).

Programs Administered by Regional - State - Local Offices

Beneficiary Eligibility: Same as Applicant Eligibility.
Award Range/Average: $75,000 to $250,000 Average: $180,000
Funding: (Cooperative Agreements) FY 17 Actual Not Available; FY 18 est $5,200,000.00; FY 19 est $5,200,000.00
HQ: 1325 E W Highway SSMC2 Room 3348, PO Box W/OPS17, Silver Spring, MD 20910
   Phone: 301-427-9242
   http://www.noaa.nws.gov

DOC11.481 | EDUCATIONAL PARTNERSHIP PROGRAM
"Educational Partnership Program (EPP) with Minority Serving Institutions (MSI)"

Award: Cooperative Agreements
Purpose: To continue the development of education and natural resource management programs aimed at increasing education and graduation rates in NOAA mission.
Applicant Eligibility: Applicants are designated as minority serving Institutions by the United States Department of education list of minority serving Institutions. Non-minority Institutions may also participate in this Program when partnered with a minority serving institution. Lead Institutions applying to become Cooperative Science Center must have a Ph.D. degree Program in the science or technology disciplines (ocean, marine and environmental sciences and remote sensing technology) that directly supports NOAA mission.
Beneficiary Eligibility: The benefits to the Nation are an increased number of academic institutions capable of providing services and products in support of the agency's mission to describe and predict changes in the environment, and to conserve and manage the nation's coastal and marine resources to ensure sustainable economic opportunities. Collaboration among NOAA and academic institutions will increase the number of trained professionals in NOAA-related sciences and will also lead to a larger number of institutions participating in collaborative research and co-management of the nation's natural resources with State, local and tribal governments.
Award Range/Average: $45 K - Undergraduate Scholarship award $3.0 - $3.2M annually to Cooperative Science Centers
Funding: (Formula Grants (Cooperative Agreements)) FY 17 $12,000,000.00; FY 18 est $13,200,000.00; FY 19 est $12,000,000.00
HQ: Office of Education 1315 E W Highway SSMC 3, 10th Floor, Silver Spring, MD 20910
   Phone: 301-628-2905 | Email: jacqueline.j.rousseau@noaa.gov
   http://www.epp.noaa.gov

NATIONAL PARK SERVICE
Regional – State – Local Offices

National Park Service
1849 C Street NW, Washington, DC 20240 202-208-3264

REGIONAL OFFICES

Alaska Support Office
Robert D. Barbee, Regional Director | 2525 Gambell Street, Anchorage, AK 99503-2892 907-257-2690

Intermountain Region
Karen Wade | Intermountain Region 12795 W Alameda Parkway PO Box 25287, Denver, CO 80225-0287 303-969-2503

Midwest Region
Alan M. Hutchings, Associate Regional Director Professional Services and Legislation | National Park Service 1709 Jackson Street, Omaha, NE 68102 402-221-3084

National Capital Region
David Linderman, Chief Finance Management Officer | 1100 Ohio Drive SW, Washington, DC 20242 202-619-7160

Northeast Region
Marie Rust, Director National Park Service | U.S. Custom House 200 Chestnut Street 3rd Floor, Philadelphia, PA 19106 215-597-7013

Pacific West Region
Resources Stewardship & Partnership 111 Jackson Street Suite 700, Oakland, CA 94607 415-427-1321

Southeast Region
Jerry Belson, Director National Park Service | Atlanta Federal Center 1924 Building 100 Alabama Street SW, Atlanta, GA 30303 404-562-3100

Programs Administered by Regional - State - Local Offices

DOI15.406 | NATIONAL PARK SERVICE CENTENNIAL CHALLENGE

Award: Cooperative Agreements

Purpose: An effort to prepare national parks for another century of conservation, preservation, and public enjoyment. Project efforts will improve parks and serve all Americans.

Applicant Eligibility: Non-federal partners may include state agencies, Tribes, local Governments, non-governmental Organizations, private companies, and private individuals. Non-federal partners are expected to match NPS Centennial Challenge Cost Share funds at or above 1: 1 for their respective projects.

Beneficiary Eligibility: State and local governments, private, public, profit, nonprofit organizations and institutions who are positioned to contribute at least 50 percent of the value of projects included in the list of approved Centennial Challenge projects.

Award Range/Average: The smallest was $26,000 and largest was $1.5 million.

Funding: (Project Grants (Cooperative Agreements)) FY 18 $1,500,000.00; FY 19 est $85,000.00; FY 20 est $85,000.00

HQ: 1849 C Street NW, Washington, DC 20240

Phone: 202-513-7218 | Email: lori_bianchet@nps.gov

http://www.nps.gov/subjects/centennial/nps-centennial-challenge-projects.htm

DOI15.407 | KEWEENAW NATIONAL HISTORICAL PARK (NHP) PRESERVATION GRANTS

"Keweenaw Heritage Grants"

Award: Cooperative Agreements

Purpose: Program intends to offer annual ONPS base funding to the Keweenaw NHP Advisory Commission to aid in the fulfillment of their legislated duties: to carry out historical, educational, or cultural programs which enhance understanding and preservation of the historic and cultural resources in the park and surrounding area on Michigan's Keweenaw Peninsula.

Applicant Eligibility: Eligibility for these funds include the Keweenaw NHP Advisory Commission and owners or operators of nationally significant, or potentially significant, properties on the Keweenaw Peninsula located: within the boundaries of Keweenaw NHP; affiliated with an existing Keweenaw Heritage Site; at the Cliff Mine in Keweenaw County, along Torch Lake in Houghton County, or within the community of Painesdale in Houghton County.

Beneficiary Eligibility: Beneficiaries may include: Public Nonprofit Institution/Organization: Keweenaw NHP Advisory Commission; Keweenaw NHP Heritage Sites; local or regional units of government; academic institutions, or federally recognized Indian tribes.

Award Range/Average: RANGE: $115,000 to $300,000, AVERAGE: $250,000

Funding: (Project Grants (Discretionary)) FY 17 $206,909.00; FY 18 est $252,000.00; FY 19 est $25,200.00

HQ: 25970 Red Jacket Road, Calumet, MI 49913

http://www.nps.gov/kewe/index.htm

DOI15.904 | HISTORIC PRESERVATION FUND GRANTS-IN-AID

"HPF"

Award: Formula Grants; Project Grants

Purpose: To provide FORMULA grants eligible grantees to assist in the identification, evaluation, and protection of historic properties by such means as education, survey, planning, technical assistance, preservation, documentation, and financial incentives like grants and tax credits available for historic properties. And, to provide PROJECT grants to eligible grantees to provide for the identification, evaluation, and protection of historic properties as defined by Congress.

Applicant Eligibility: FORMULA grants: States, Territories and Tribes as defined in the 54 USC 301 et seq (commonly known as the National Historic Preservation Act), operate Programs administered by a State Historic Preservation Officer or Tribal Historic Preservation Officer appointed by the Governor, Tribal government or according to State or Tribal law, and which are otherwise in compliance with the requirements of the Act. PROJECT grants: Eligible tribal applicants include Federally recognized Indian Tribes, Alaska Native Corporations, and Native Hawaiian Organizations. Other project grants follow eligibility as defined by Congress and stated in statue or committee language.

Beneficiary Eligibility: FORMULA grants: State, Tribal and local governments, public and private nonprofit organizations, and individuals. According to their own priorities and plans, States and Tribes select their own projects and may sub-grant to public and private parties, including local governments, nonprofit and for-profit organizations, and/or individuals to accomplish program objectives. At least ten percent of each State's annual appropriation must be sub-granted to local

Programs Administered by Regional - State - Local Offices

governments certified as eligible to carry out preservation functions according to 36 CFR 61.PROJECT grants: State, Tribal, Local governments, public and private nonprofits, and federal agencies as defined by Congress.

Award Range/Average: Range $50,000.00 - $1,4000,000.00 Average $290,000.000

Funding: (Project Grants) FY 17 $13,500,000; FY 18 est $20,500,000; FY 19 est $70,500,000; -Project Grants (Mandatory): FY17 $13,500,000; FY18 $20,500,000; FY19 $70,500,000; (Formula Grants) FY 17 $56,309,039; FY 18 est $58,410,000; FY 19 est $58,000,000; -Formula Grants (Mandatory): FY17 $56,309,039; FY18 $58,410,000; FY19 $58,000,000

HQ: Department of Interior 1849 C Street NW, PO Box 7360, Washington, DC 20005
Phone: 202-354-2020
http://www.nps.gov/stlpg

DOI15.912 | NATIONAL HISTORIC LANDMARK

Award: Advisory Services and Counseling

Purpose: To preserve for public use historic sites, buildings, and objects of national significance, to make a survey of historic and archaeologic sites, buildings, and objects, to make necessary investigations and researches in the United States relating to particular sites, buildings, or objects, and to erect and maintain tablets to mark or commemorate historic or prehistoric places and events of national historical or archaeological significance.

Applicant Eligibility: Property owners and general public.

Beneficiary Eligibility: Anyone may suggest that a property be considered for inclusion in an appropriate National Historic Landmark theme study, provided the property has a high degree of historic integrity and potential national significance with relation to some broad facet of American history. The owner of the property may be an individual, government, or corporate body. Properties of only State or local significance do not qualify.

Award Range/Average: Range $20,000.00 to $100,000.00 in nonmonetary support. Average $50,000.00 on non-monetary support.

HQ: 1849 C Street NW, PO Box 7228, Washington, DC 20240
Phone: 202-354-2246 | Email: christopher_hetzel@nps.gov
http://www.nps.gov/nhl

DOI15.914 | NATIONAL REGISTER OF HISTORIC PLACES
"The National Register"

Award: Advisory Services and Counseling

Purpose: To expand and maintain the National Register of Historic Places, to make the information on districts, sites, buildings, structures and objects of historical, architectural, archeological, engineering and cultural significance more accessible to the public, and to promote greater appreciation of America's heritage.

Applicant Eligibility: Eligible applicants are the States and territories as defined in the National Historic Preservation Act, operating under Programs administered by State Historic Preservation Officers appointed by the Governors (listed in Appendix IV of the Catalog); or the Tribal Preservation Officers; Federal agencies required to nominate and consider historic properties within their jurisdiction or as a result of the National Environmental Policy Act of 1969 and Executive Order 11593, and the National Historic Preservation Act operating under Programs administered by representatives (listed in Appendix IV of the Catalog) appointed by the heads of the agencies; and, in States without approved State Historic Preservation Programs, persons and local Governments. Applicants eligible for Federal Tax benefits include owners of individually listed properties and properties certified by the Secretary of Interior as being historic and in a district certified as historic.

Beneficiary Eligibility: Public and private owners of historic properties listed in the National Register of Historic Places or of properties certified by the Secretary of Interior as being historic and in a district certified as historic.

Award Range/Average: Range $20,000.00 - $111,000.00 Non-monetary assistance through consultation with NPS staff Average $71,000.00.

HQ: 1849 C Street NW, Washington, DC 20240
Phone: 202-208-7625 | Email: joy_beasley@nps.gov
http://www.nps.gov/nr

DOI15.915 | TECHNICAL PRESERVATION SERVICES

Award: Dissemination of Technical Information

Purpose: The Technical Preservation Services office provides standards and technical preservation assistance on rehabilitating historic buildings that are used by federal, state, and local government agencies, and other general property owners.

Applicant Eligibility: Anyone/general public can use this Program.

Beneficiary Eligibility: Same as Applicant Eligibility.

Award Range/Average: Range: NAAverage: NA

HQ: 1849 C Street NW, PO Box 7243, Washington, DC 20240

    Phone: 202-354-2033

    http://www.nps.gov/tps

DOI15.916 | OUTDOOR RECREATION ACQUISITION, DEVELOPMENT AND PLANNING

"Land and Water Conservation Fund Grants"

Award: Formula Grants; Project Grants

Purpose: To give financial assistance to the States and their political subdivisions project that are included in Statewide Comprehensive Outdoor Recreation Plans (SCORPs) to meet current and future needs.

Applicant Eligibility: For planning grants, only the State agency formally designated by the Governor or State law as responsible for the preparation and maintenance of the SCORP is eligible to apply. (Treated as States for this purpose are the District of Columbia, Puerto Rico, the Virgin Islands, American Samoa, the Northern Mariana Islands, and Guam.) For acquisition and development grants, the above designated agency may apply for assistance for itself, or on behalf of other State agencies or political subdivisions, such as cities, counties, and park districts. Additionally, Indian Tribes that are organized to govern themselves and perform the functions of a general purpose unit of government qualify for assistance. Individuals, nonprofit Organizations, and private Organizations are not eligible. The general public. For planning grants, same as Applicant Eligibility. The State Liaison Officer (SLO), who is appointed by the Governor or designated in State legislation to administer the Program in the State or Territory, must provide assurance that the project is consistent with the SCORP; i.e., that it meets high priority recreation needs shown in the action Program portion of the Plan. The State must have a sufficient balance of LWCF funding and the required match available for the project. The sponsoring agency must permanently dedicate the project to public outdoor recreation and assume responsibility for its operation and maintenance. SCORPs must cite the State's legal authority to participate in the Land and Water Conservation Fund Program. 2 CFR, Part 200, 43 CFR, OMB Circulars, standard forms, and Program information.

Beneficiary Eligibility: The general public. For planning grants, same as Applicant Eligibility.

Award Range/Average: Range: $5,000.00 - $2,000,000.00 Average: $200,000.00

Funding: (Project Grants) FY 19 est $65,000,000.00; FY 18 est $65,000,000.00; FY 17 $75,932,422.00

HQ: 1849 C Street NW, PO Box 1353, Washington, DC 20240

    Phone: 202-354-6905 | Email: joel_lynch@nps.gov

    http://www.nps.gov/ncrc/programs/lwcf/contact_list.html

DOI15.918 | DISPOSAL OF FEDERAL SURPLUS REAL PROPERTY FOR PARKS, RECREATION, AND HISTORIC MONUMENTS

"Federal Lands to Parks Program (FLP); Historic Surplus Property Program (HSPP)"

Award: Sale, Exchange, Or Donation of Property and Goods

Purpose: FLP: To transfer surplus Federal real property for state and local public park and recreation use. HSPP: To transfer Federal historic real property to state and local governments for historic preservation purposes.

Applicant Eligibility: FLP: Only State or local units of government and territories are eligible to apply for surplus real property for public parks and recreation. Recipients must agree to manage the property in the public interest and for public recreational use. HSPP: Only State or local units of government and territories are eligible to apply for surplus real property for historic preservation purposes. A recipient must agree to preserve and maintain the property in perpetuity and may accomplish this goal by leasing the property to a non-profit or for-profit entity. Additionally, a property may be used for revenue-producing activities to support it, and such activities may be eligible for Federal Historic Preservation Tax Incentives (see 15. 915, Technical Preservation Services).

Beneficiary Eligibility: General public.

Programs Administered by Regional - State - Local Offices

Award Range/Average: Range: FLP: None. Value varies by the value of the available real property. HSPP: None Average: NA
Funding: (Sale, Exchange, or Donation of Property and Goods) FY 17 $0.00; FY 18 est $589,000.00; FY 19 est $0.00
HQ: 1849 C Street NW, PO Box 1353, Washington, DC 20005
   Phone: 202-354-6905 | Email: joel_lynch@nps.gov
   http://www.nps.gov/ncrc/programs/lwcf/contact_list.html

DOI15.921 | RIVERS, TRAILS AND CONSERVATION ASSISTANCE
"Rivers and Trails; RTCA"

Award: Cooperative Agreements; Advisory Services and Counseling
Purpose: To implement the natural resource conservation and outdoor recreation mission of the National Park Service in communities across America.
Applicant Eligibility: Private nonprofit Organizations and Federal, State and local government agencies.
Beneficiary Eligibility: Same as Applicant Eligibility.
Award Range/Average: This is a non-monetary program.
HQ: 1849 C Street NW ORG CODE 2240, Washington, DC 20240
   Phone: 202-354-6922 | Email: stephan_nofield@nps.gov
   http://www.nps.gov/rtca

DOI15.922 | NATIVE AMERICAN GRAVES PROTECTION AND REPATRIATION ACT
"NAGPRA"

Award: Project Grants
Purpose: Providing grants to museums to assist in the consultation on and documentation of Native American human remains and cultural items, to Indian tribes and Native Hawaiian organizations to assist in identifying human remains and cultural items, and to museums, Indian tribes and Native Hawaiian organizations to assist in the repatriation of human remains and cultural items.
Applicant Eligibility: An eligible applicant is: A museum that has control of Native American human remains, funerary objects, sacred objects, or objects of cultural patrimony and has received Federal funds. The term Museum includes state or local government agencies, private Institutions, and Institutions of higher learning that have received Federal funds. An Indian tribe, Alaska Native village, or Native Hawaiian Organization. An "Indian tribe" means any tribe, band, nation, or other organized group or community of Indians, including any Alaska Native village (as defined in, or established pursuant to, the Alaska Native Claims Settlement Act), which is recognized as eligible for the special Programs and services provided by the United States to Indians because of their status as Indians. The Department of the Interior has interpreted this definition as applying to over 560 Indian Tribes and Alaska Native villages that are recognized by the United States Government. This list does not include Alaska regional or village corporations, although Alaska Native villages may subcontract work under grants to such corporations. A Native Hawaiian Organization includes any Organization that: a) serves and represents the interests of Native Hawaiians; b) has as a primary and stated purpose the provision of services to Native Hawaiians; and c) has expertise in Native Hawaiian Affairs. NAGPRA states that such Native Hawaiian Organizations shall include the Office of Hawaiian Affairs.
Beneficiary Eligibility: State, local, public nonprofit institution/organization, other public institution/organization, Federally Recognized Indian Tribal Government, Native American organization, American Indian.
Award Range/Average: Range: $1,000.00.00 - $90,000.00 Average: $25,000.00
Funding: (Project Grants (Discretionary)) FY 18 $1,657,000.00 FY 19 est $1,657,000.00; FY 20 est $1,657,000.00
HQ: 1849 C Street NW, PO Box 7360, Washington, DC 20240
   Phone: 202-354-2201
   http://www.nps.gov/nagpra

DOI15.923 | NATIONAL CENTER FOR PRESERVATION TECHNOLOGY AND TRAINING
"NCPTT"

Award: Project Grants
Purpose: To develop and distribute preservation and conservation skills and technologies; to develop and facilitate training for Federal, State, and local resource preservation professionals, cultural resource managers, maintenance personnel, and others

working in the preservation field; to take steps to apply preservation technology benefits from ongoing research by other agencies and institutions; to facilitate the transfer of preservation technology among Federal agencies, State and local governments, universities, international organizations, and the private sector; and to cooperate with related international organizations.

Applicant Eligibility: U.S. universities and two and four year colleges; U.S. private nonprofit institution/Organizations and quasi-public nonprofit institution/Organizations that are directly associated with educational or research activity; Federal, State, local government agencies, Federally recognized Indian Tribal Governments and their Tribal Historic Preservation Offices; For-profit Organizations and private individuals may submit proposals only in partnership with an eligible U.S. Organization.

Beneficiary Eligibility: Anyone/General public.

Award Range/Average: $15,000 to $500,000; The average funding for a grant or cooperative agreement is $40,000.

Funding: (Project Grants (Discretionary)) FY 17 $1,112,247.00; FY 18 est $764,600.00; FY 19 est $695,600.00

HQ: 645 University Parkway, Natchitoches, LA 71457

Phone: 318-356-7444 | Email: mary_striegel@nps.gov

http://www.ncptt.nps.gov

DOI15.925 | NATIONAL MARITIME HERITAGE GRANTS
"Maritime Heritage Grants"

Award: Project Grants

Purpose: To provide matching grants for preservation or education projects and to help State, Tribal, and local governments and private nonprofit organizations preserve and interpret their maritime heritage.

Applicant Eligibility: State, local, tribal Governments and private nonprofit Institutions /Organizations are eligible to apply. Individuals are not eligible applicants.

Beneficiary Eligibility: Any State or local government or private non-profit institution/organization will benefit directly from grant funds. It is intended that the general public will ultimately benefit from the information conveyed by the funded projects.

Award Range/Average: Range: $15,000 to $200,000 Average: $66,000.00

Funding: (Project Grants) FY 18 $2,535,826.00; FY 19 est $0.00; FY 20 est $0.00

HQ: 1849 C Street NW, PO Box 7508, Washington, DC 20240

Phone: 202-354-2266 | Email: kelly_spradley-kurowski@nps.gov

http://www.nps.gov/maritime/grants/intro.htm

DOI15.926 | AMERICAN BATTLEFIELD PROTECTION
"Planning Grants"

Award: Cooperative Agreements

Purpose: To fund nonacquisition preservation methods such as planning, education, survey, and inventory to promote the protection and preservation of battlefield lands on American soil.

Applicant Eligibility: Applicant may be Federal, intrastate, interstate, State and local agencies, public or private nonprofit Institutions /Organizations, federally recognized Indian tribal Governments, U.S. territory and possessions, Native American Organizations, State colleges and universities, public and private colleges and universities. Multi-Organizational applications are encouraged.

Beneficiary Eligibility: Federal, intrastate, interstate, State and local agencies, public and private nonprofit institutions/ organizations, Federally recognized Indian tribal governments, U.S. territories and possessions, Native American organizations, State college or universities, public and private colleges and universities.

Award Range/Average: Range: $5,000.00 to $122,000.00 Average: $40,000.00

Funding: (Project Grants (Discretionary)) FY 18 $1,198,000.00; FY 19 est $1,198,000.00; FY 20 est $1,198,000.00

HQ: American Battlefield Protection Program 1849 C Street NW, Room 7221, Washington, DC 20240

Phone: 202-354-2071 | Email: jenifer_eggleston@nps.gov

https://www.nps.gov/subjects/battlefields/american-battlefield-protection-program-grants.htm

Programs Administered by Regional - State - Local Offices

DOI15.927 | HYDROPOWER RECREATION ASSISTANCE
"FERC Hydropower Licensing"

Award: Advisory Services and Counseling

Purpose: To support government, industry, and nonprofit partnerships in ongoing consultations and negotiations about applications for hydropower licensing; to meet present and future outdoor recreation and river conservation needs; and to maintain and improve a project's riparian areas.

Applicant Eligibility: Private nonprofit Organizations, Federal, State, and Local government agencies and hydropower licensing applicants.

Beneficiary Eligibility: Private nonprofit organizations, Federal, State, and Local government agencies and hydropower licensing applicants, as well as the general public.

Award Range/Average: Non-monetary program

HQ: 1849 C Street NW, Washington, DC 20240

Phone: 202-220-4121 | Email: susan_rosebrough@nps.gov

http://www.nps.gov/hydro

DOI15.928 | BATTLEFIELD LAND ACQUISITION GRANTS
"BLAGs"

Award: Project Grants

Purpose: To aid States and local communities acquire and preserve threatened battlefield lands from the Revolutionary War, War of 1812, and Civil War.

Applicant Eligibility: State and local Governments. Private nonprofit Organizations seeking to acquire battlefield land or easements must apply in partnership with the State or local government agency that has jurisdiction over the proposed parcel. The government agency may then sub-grant the Federal funds to the nonprofit Organization.

Beneficiary Eligibility: State and local governments (local communities, nonprofits, and battlefield landowners) benefit.

Award Range/Average: Range: $1,000.00 to $2,000,000.00 Average: $250,000.00

Funding: (Project Grants (Discretionary)) FY 18 $10,601,415.00; FY 19 est $10,000,000.00; FY 20 est $10,000,000.00

HQ: 1849 C Street NW, Room 7228, Washington, DC 20240

Phone: 202-354-2071 | Email: jenifer_eggleston@nps.gov

https://www.nps.gov/subjects/battlefields/american-battlefield-protection-program-grants.htm

DOI15.929 | SAVE AMERICA'S TREASURES

Award: Project Grants

Purpose: To provide matching grants for preservation or conservation work on nationally significant: intellectual and cultural artifacts and historic structures and sites.

Applicant Eligibility: State and Local agencies, Public or Private nonprofit Institutions /Organizations, State Colleges and universities, Public and Private Colleges and universities, and Federally Recognized Indian Tribes. Individuals are not eligible applicants. Properties receiving Save America's Treasures (SAT) grant assistance must be listed in the National Register of Historic Places for National significance.

Beneficiary Eligibility: Any Federal, Intrastate, Interstate, State and local agencies, Public or Private nonprofit institution/organization, State Colleges or University, Public and Private College or University, or Federally recognized Indian tribes.

Award Range/Average: FY17: $125,000 to $500,000 (for preservation), $25,000 to $500,000 (for collections); FY18: similar to FY17. FY17 average: not available yet. FY18 average: not available yet.

Funding: (Project Grants) FY 17 $0.00; FY 18 est $13,000,000.00; FY 19 est Estimate Not Available; (PROJECT GRANTS (Discretionary)) FY17 $0.00; FY18 $13,000,000; FY19 est Estimate Not Available.

HQ: State Tribal Local Plans and Grants Division 1849 C Street NW, PO Box 7360, Washington, DC 20240

Phone: 202-354-2020

http://www.nps.gov/stlpg

DOI15.930 | CHESAPEAKE BAY GATEWAYS NETWORK
"Chesapeake Bay Gateways and Trails"

Award: Cooperative Agreements

Purpose: To increase access to the Chesapeake and rivers, to preserve important landscapes and resources, to promote tourism and local economies, to engage youth in meaningful work and placed-based education, to improve recreational opportunities, and to interpret the natural and cultural resources of the Chesapeake region.

Applicant Eligibility: Recipients must either be a non-profit Organization qualified as such under section 501(c) of the Internal Revenue Code or a state or local government. NPS Chesapeake technical and financial assistance strategically supports projects and Programs that meet DOI's key responsibilities in the Chesapeake Bay watershed. The Chesapeake Bay Initiative Act authorizes the NPS to: identify, conserve, restore, and interpret natural, recreational, historical, and cultural resources within the Chesapeake Bay Watershed; identify and utilize the collective resources sites for enhancing public education of and access to the Chesapeake Bay; link sites with trails, tour roads, scenic byways, and other connections; develop and establish water trails comprising water routes and connections to sites and other land resources within the Chesapeake Bay Watershed; and create a network of sites and water trails. Other specific plans and strategies which guide NPS -Chesapeake implementation include: Chesapeake Bay Watershed Agreement and implementing management strategies and work plans, including the Chesapeake Bay Watershed Public Access Plan Captain John Smith Chesapeake NHT planning documents, including: Comprehensive Management Plan, Interpretive Plan, Conservation Strategy and segment plans for the James, Potomac and Lower Susquehanna rivers.

Beneficiary Eligibility: General Public.

Award Range/Average: Range: $60,000 - 650,000 Average: $170,000

Funding: (Project Grants (Cooperative Agreements)) FY 18 $1,717,821; FY 19 est$1,599,427; FY 20 est$1,600,000;-FY20 TBD (subject to appropriation)

HQ: Department of the Interior U.S. Custom House 200 Chestnut Street, 3rd Floor, Philadelphia, PA 19106
Phone: 215-597-9153 | Email: jamie_cupples@nps.gov
http://www.nps.gov/chba/learn/management/financial-assistance-for-partners.htm

DOI15.931 | CONSERVATION ACTIVITIES BY YOUTH SERVICE ORGANIZATIONS
"21st Century Conservation Service Corps Program"

Award: Cooperative Agreements

Purpose: To employ qualified nonprofit youth and young adult serving organizations to carry out natural and cultural resource conservation, education, volunteer service, and education projects on Department of the Interior lands through authorized NPS programs.

Applicant Eligibility: Private non-profit Institutions and Organizations; public and private non-profit academic Institutions; state and local government agencies; quasi-public non-profit Institutions and Organizations that support youth and young adult career training and development, and education in the areas of natural and/or cultural resource conservation and management.

Beneficiary Eligibility: Private non-profit institutions and organizations; public and private non-profit academic institutions; state and local government agencies; quasi-public non-profit institutions and organizations that support youth and young adult career training and development, and education in the areas of natural and/or cultural resource conservation and management. Individuals/families; students; and the general public will receive a benefit from the development and execution of these programs and projects.

Award Range/Average: Range: $5,000 - $900,000

Funding: (Cooperative Agreements (Discretionary Grants)) FY 17 $37,078,851.00; FY 18 est Not Separately Identifiable; FY 19 est Estimate Not Available

HQ: 1849 C Street NW, Washington, DC 20240
Phone: 202-513-7146 | Email: george_mcdonald@nps.gov
http://www.nps.gov/subjects/youthprograms/index.htm

Programs Administered by Regional - State - Local Offices

DOI15.933 | PRESERVATION OF JAPANESE AMERICAN CONFINEMENT SITES
"Japanese American Confinement Sites Grant Program"

Award: Project Grants

Purpose: To encourage projects that identify, research, evaluate, interpret, protect, restore, repair, and acquire historic confinement sites so that the present and future generations may learn and gain inspiration from these sites since they demonstrate the Nation's commitment to equal justice under the law.

Applicant Eligibility: Applicant may be State and local agencies, public or private nonprofit Institutions /Organizations, Federally recognized Indian tribal Governments, State colleges and universities, public and private colleges and universities.

Beneficiary Eligibility: Providing present and future generations of Americans learning opportunities about the nation's commitment to equal justice under the law.

Award Range/Average: Range: $16,000.00 - $250,000.00 Average: $150,000.00

Funding: (Project Grants (Discretionary)) FY 18 $2,904,999.00; FY 19 est $2,800,000.00; FY 20 est $1,000,000.00

HQ: 12795 W Alameda Parkway, Lakewood, CO 80228

Phone: 303-969-2885 | Email: kara_miyagishima@nps.gov

http://www.nps.gov/jacs

DOI15.935 | NATIONAL TRAILS SYSTEM PROJECTS

Award: Cooperative Agreements

Purpose: To preserve, protect, and develop the elements of the National Trails System.

Applicant Eligibility: States or their political subdivisions, landowners, private Organizations, or individuals.

Beneficiary Eligibility: General public, and States or their political subdivisions, landowners, private organizations, or individuals.

Award Range/Average: Range: $7,000.00 - $821,000.00 Average: $100,000.00

Funding: (Project Grants) FY 17 $38,928,877.00; FY 18 est $4,000,000.00; FY 19 est $4,000,000.00

HQ: 1849 C Street NW, Washington, DC 20240

Phone: 202-354-6900 | Email: stephan_nofield@nps.gov

http://www.nps.gov.nts

DOI15.937 | REDWOOD NATIONAL PARK COOPERATIVE MANAGEMENT WITH THE STATE OF CALIFORNIA

Award: Cooperative Agreements; Sale, Exchange, Or Donation of Property and Goods; Use of Property, Facilities, and Equipment; Advisory Services and Counseling; Dissemination of Technical Information; Training

Purpose: To develop joint operating procedures and standards to assure effective accomplishment of park activities.

Applicant Eligibility: Agencies within the State of California Government.

Beneficiary Eligibility: General Public and the State of California.

Award Range/Average: Range: $15,000.00 - $35,000.00 Average: $18,000.00

Funding: (Cooperative Agreements (Discretionary Grants)) FY 17 $78,620.00; FY 18 est $65,000.00; FY 19 est $75,000.00

HQ: 1849 C Street NW, Washington, DC 20240

Phone: 202-208-3100 | Email: steven_mietz@nps.gov

http://www.nps.gov/redw

DOI15.938 | BOSTON AFRICAN-AMERICAN NATIONAL HISTORIC SITE
"Rehab African Meetinghouse"

Award: Cooperative Agreements

Purpose: To rehabilitate the African Meetinghouse in Boston, MA.

Applicant Eligibility: Museum of African-American History.

Beneficiary Eligibility: Museum of African-American History and the General public.

Award Range/Average: Range: $37,000.00 - $225,000.00 Average: $40,000.00

Funding: (Project Grants (Cooperative Agreements)) FY 18 $129,558.00; FY 19 est $60,000.00; FY 20 est $60,000.00

HQ: 15 State Street, 9th Floor, Boston, MA 02109

Phone: 617-242-5644 | Email: michael_creasey@nps.gov

http://www.nps.gov.boaf

DOI15.939 | NATIONAL HERITAGE AREA FEDERAL FINANCIAL ASSISTANCE
"National Heritage Area Preservation and Conservation Assistance"

Award: Cooperative Agreements

Purpose: To preserve and interpret for the educational and inspirational benefit of present and future generations, to encourage a broad range of economic opportunities, and to provide a management framework to help state/local government entities, nonprofits, and others in developing policies and programs.

Applicant Eligibility: State, local, or tribal government or other public entity, an educational institution, or a private nonprofit Organization.

Beneficiary Eligibility: General public, states, their political subdivisions, non-profits, private entities, the heritage area management/coordinating entity.

Award Range/Average: Range: $150,000 - $710,000 Average: $411,000

Funding: (Cooperative Agreements) FY 18 $19,300,000.00; FY 19 est $19,300,000.00; FY 20 est $0.00

HQ: 1849 C Street NW, PO Box 7508, Washington, DC 20240

Phone: 202-354-2222 | Email: martha_raymond@nps.gov

https://www.nps.gov/subjects/heritageareas/index.htm

DOI15.940 | NEW BEDFORD WHALING NATIONAL HISTORIC PARK COOPERATIVE MANAGEMENT

Award: Cooperative Agreements

Purpose: To provide for visitor understanding, appreciation, and enjoyment by collaborating with the interested entities and individuals.

Applicant Eligibility: State, local and tribal Governments, other public entities, education Institutions, and private nonprofit Organizations.

Beneficiary Eligibility: General Public.

Award Range/Average: Range: $2,500.00 - $122,500 Average: $7,500.00

Funding: (Cooperative Agreements) FY 17 $0.00; FY 18 est $15,000.00; FY 19 est $15,000.00

HQ: 33 William Street, New Bedford, MA 02740 | Email: meghan_kish@nps.gov

http://www.nps.gov/nebe

DOI15.941 | MISSISSIPPI NATIONAL RIVER AND RECREATION AREA STATE AND LOCAL ASSISTANCE

Award: Cooperative Agreements; Advisory Services and Counseling

Purpose: To assist or fund to improve partner planning for and interpretation of non-Federal publicly owned lands within the area.

Applicant Eligibility: The State of Minnesota or its political subdivisions, counties, cities, non-profits.

Beneficiary Eligibility: Same as Applicant Eligibility.

Award Range/Average: Range: $18,000.00 - $170,000.00 Average: $25,000.00

Funding: (Project Grants (Cooperative Agreements)) FY 17 $761,898.00; FY 18 est Estimate Not Available; FY 19 est Estimate Not Available

HQ: 111 E Kellogg Boulevard, Suite 105, Saint Paul, MN 55101

Phone: 651-290-3030 | Email: denise_st_marie@nps.gov

http://www.nps.gov/miss

DOI15.942 | ENVIRONMENTAL EDUCATION AND CONSERVATION-NORTH CASCADES

Award: Cooperative Agreements

Purpose: To provide programs of public education, youth engagement, involvement in conservation, natural science, history and related fields of study, and conduct interpretive activities about the Skagit River and the North Cascades bioregion.

Applicant Eligibility: State, local, or tribal government or other public entity, an educational institution, or a private nonprofit Organization.

Beneficiary Eligibility: General public.

Award Range/Average: Range: $0 Average: $0

Programs Administered by Regional - State - Local Offices

HQ: North Cascades National Park Service Complex Denise Shultz 810 State Route 20, Sedro Woolley, WA 98284
　　Phone: 360-854-7302 | Email: denise_m_shultz@nps.gov
　　https://Nps.gov/noca

DOI15.943 | CHALLENGE COST SHARE
"National Park Service Challenge Cost Share"

Award: Cooperative Agreements; Direct Payments for Specified Use
Purpose: To increase participation by qualified partners in the preservation and improvement of NPS natural, cultural, and recreational resources in all authorized programs and activities.
Applicant Eligibility: State, local, or tribal government or other public entity, an educational institution, or a private nonprofit Organization.
Beneficiary Eligibility: General public, trail system users, and organizations with conservation missions.
Award Range/Average: Range: $1,0000.00 - $25,000.00 (subawards) Average: $20,000.00
Funding: (Direct Payments for Specified Use) FY 17 $409,399.00; FY 18 est $300,000.00; FY 19 est $300,000.00
HQ: 1201 Eye Street NW, 9th Floor, Washington, DC 20005
　　Phone: 202-354-6907 | Email: charlie_stockman@nps.gov
　　http://www.nps.gov/ccsp

DOI15.944 | NATURAL RESOURCE STEWARDSHIP

Award: Cooperative Agreements
Purpose: To evaluate and improve the health of watersheds, landscapes, and marine and coastal resources; to sustain biological communities on the lands and waters in parks; and to improve the resiliency of these natural resources and adapt them to the effects of climate change.
Applicant Eligibility: State, local, or tribal Governments, other Federal agencies, other public entities, educational Institutions, private nonprofit Organizations.
Beneficiary Eligibility: General public.
Award Range/Average: Range: $4,000.00 - $185,000.00 Average: $55,000.00
Funding: (Cooperative Agreements) FY 17 $13,645,377.00; FY 18 est $8,000,000.00; FY 19 est $8,000,000.00
HQ: 1201 Eye Street NW, Washington, DC 20024
　　Phone: 202-513-7204 | Email: karel_morales@nps.gov
　　http://www.nature.nps.gov

DOI15.945 | COOPERATIVE RESEARCH AND TRAINING PROGRAMS-RESOURCES OF THE NATIONAL PARK SYSTEM
"Cooperative Ecosystem Studies Units (CESU) Network"

Award: Cooperative Agreements
Purpose: To support coordinated cooperative research, technical assistance, education and training, and usable knowledge development to inform science-based management of the National Park System and to establish and maintain cooperative study units.
Applicant Eligibility: State and local Governments, federally recognized Indian tribal Governments, public/private nonprofit Organizations, nonprofit Institutions of higher education, and individuals.
Beneficiary Eligibility: State and local governments, federally recognized Indian tribal governments, public/private nonprofit organizations, nonprofit institutions of higher education, and individuals (including members of the general public).
Award Range/Average: Range: $5,000.00 - $970,000.00 Average: $48,500.00
Funding: (Cooperative Agreements (Discretionary Grants)) FY 17 $52,778,345.00; FY 18 est $40,000,000.00; FY 19 est $40,000,000.00
HQ: Network National Program Office 1849 C Street NW, Room 2649, Washington, DC 20240
　　Phone: 202-354-1825 | Email: tom_fish@nps.gov
　　http://www.cesu.org

DOI15.946 | CULTURAL RESOURCES MANAGEMENT

Award: Cooperative Agreements

Purpose: To conduct cultural resource stewardship largely at the park level. To carry out and further this stewardship responsibility, the Service implements programs that cover a broad range of research, operational, and educational activities.

Applicant Eligibility: State, local, or tribal government or other public entity, an educational institution, or a private nonprofit Organization.

Beneficiary Eligibility: State and local governments, Federally recognized Indian Tribal governments, nonprofit organizations, educational or scientific institutions, associations, individuals.

Award Range/Average: Range: $1,000.00 - $5,500,000.00 Average: $192,000.00

Funding: (Cooperative Agreements) FY 17 $7,951,735.00; FY 18 est $15,000,000.00; FY 19 est $15,000,000.00

HQ: U.S. Department of the Interior 1849 C Street NW, Room 2737, Washington, DC 20240

    Phone: 202-208-7625 | Email: joy_beasley@nps.gov

    http://www.nps.gov/history

DOI15.947 | BOSTON HARBOR ISLANDS PARTNERSHIP

Award: Cooperative Agreements; Direct Payments for Specified Use

Purpose: To acquire from and provide to the partners goods and services for cooperative management of lands within the Park and to provide for safe visitor access, public information, youth programs, resource management, and citizen science and scholarly research.

Applicant Eligibility: The Commonwealth of Massachusetts, members of the Boston Harbor Islands Partnership, and other public entities, education Institutions, and private nonprofit Organizations.

Beneficiary Eligibility: General Public.

Award Range/Average: $10,000 - $600,000 Average = $140,000

Funding: (Cooperative Agreements (Discretionary Grants)) FY 18 $550,000; FY 19 est $450,000; FY 20 est $450,000;-FY19 and 20 are estimates based on previous year funding only.

HQ: Boston Harbor Islands National Recreation Area 15 State Street, 9th Floor, Boston, MA 02109

    Phone: 617-242-5644 | Email: michael_creasey@nps.gov

    http://www.nps.gov/boha

DOI15.948 | NATIONAL FIRE PLAN-WILDLAND URBAN INTERFACE COMMUNITY FIRE ASSISTANCE

Award: Cooperative Agreements; Use of Property, Facilities, and Equipment; Provision of Specialized Services; Advisory Services and Counseling; Dissemination of Technical Information

Purpose: To enforce the National Fire Plan and assist communities at risk from catastrophic wildland fires.

Applicant Eligibility: States and local Governments at risk as published in the Federal Register or as determined by the state, Indian Tribes, public and private education Institutions, nonprofit Organizations.

Beneficiary Eligibility: Same as Applicant Eligibility.

Award Range/Average: Range: $300,000 - $600,000 Average: $450,000.00

Funding: (Cooperative Agreements (Discretionary Grants)) FY 18 $578,000.00; FY 19 est $328,000.00; FY 20 est $328,000.00

HQ: 3833 S Development Avenue, Boise, ID 83705

    Phone: 208-387-5090 | Email: mark_koontz@nps.gov

    http://www.forestsandrangelands.gov

DOI15.954 | NATIONAL PARK SERVICE CONSERVATION, PROTECTION, OUTREACH, AND EDUCATION

Award: Cooperative Agreements

Purpose: To assist projects complementary to National Park Service (NPS) program endeavors in resource conservation and protection, historical preservation, and environmental sustainability.

Applicant Eligibility: State, local and tribal Governments, educational Institutions, and nonprofit Organizations.

Beneficiary Eligibility: Profit organizations, public nonprofit institutions/organizations, private nonprofit institutions/organizations, and State, local and tribal governments, industry and public decision makers, research scientists, engineers, and the general public.

Award Range/Average: Range: $2,000.00 - $925,000.00 Average: $67,000.00

Programs Administered by Regional - State - Local Offices

Funding: (Cooperative Agreements) FY 17 $23,656,912.00; FY 18 est $20,000,000.00; FY 19 est $20,000,000.00
HQ: 12795 W Alameda Parkway, Lakewood, CO 80228
    Phone: 303-969-2065 | Email: heidi_sage@nps.gov
    http://www.nps.gov

DOI15.955 | MARTIN LUTHER KING JUNIOR NATIONAL HISTORIC SITE AND PRESERVATION DISTRICT

Award: Cooperative Agreements
Purpose: To protect and interpret for the benefit, inspiration, and education of present and future generations the places where Martin Luther King, Junior, was born, where he lived, worked, and worshipped, and where he is buried.
Applicant Eligibility: Owners of properties of historical or cultural significance within the District, State, local, or tribal government or other public entity, an educational institution, or a private nonprofit Organizations.
Beneficiary Eligibility: State, local and tribal governments, public non profit institutions/organizations, private non profit institutions/organizations, general public, institutions of higher education will ultimately benefit from knowledge gained under this program.
Award Range/Average: Range: $100,000.00 to $800,000.00 Average: $600,000.00
Funding: (Cooperative Agreements) FY 17 $971,000.00; FY 18 est $800,000.00; FY 19 est $800,000.00
HQ: MLK NHS 450 Auburn Avenue NE, Atlanta, GA 30303
    Phone: 404-331-2022 | Email: judy_forte@nps.gov
    http://www.nps.gov

DOI15.956 | COOPERATIVE MANAGEMENT OF EBEY'S LANDING NATIONAL HISTORICAL RESERVE.

Award: Direct Payments for Specified Use; Provision of Specialized Services
Purpose: To manage the Reserve; administer and protect sites acquired by the NPS; administer programs within the scope of the Reserve purposes; participate in the land use review process; cooperate with Town and County departments and staff to assure awareness and protection of resources of the Reserve; and enter into contracts with individuals, private organizations and local community and governmental bodies to protect, research enhance document, and interpret the resources of the Reserve.
Applicant Eligibility: The authorizing legislation for Ebey's Landing National Historical Reserve states that the Secretary of Interior is authorized to transfer management and administration of the Reserve to an appropriate unit of local government. A joint administrative board called the Ebey's Landing National Historical Reserve Trust Board (Trust Board), was created in accordance with the provision of RCW 39. 34. 030. The Trust Board consists of nine members: Three representatives of Island County, residing in the Reserve, three representatives from the Town of Coupeville, one [Washington] State Park representative, and one National Park Service representative. The Trust Board complies with the Open Public Meeting Act Chapter 42. 30 RCW and members of the Trust Board are enrolled as Volunteers in Parks (VIP).
Beneficiary Eligibility: Other Public Institution/organization.
Award Range/Average: Range: $1,000 - $50,000 Average: $45,000
Funding: (Cooperative Agreements) FY 18 Actual Not Available; FY 19 est Estimate Not Available; FY 20 est $ 39,998
HQ: Pacific W Regional Office 909 1st Avenue, Suite 500, Seattle, WA 98104
    Phone: 206-220-4000 | Email: roy_zipp@nps.gov

DOI15.957 | EMERGENCY SUPPLEMENTAL HISTORIC PRESERVATION FUND
"HPF Hurricane Sandy Relief Grant Program"

Award: Formula Grants; Project Grants
Purpose: To assist the historic resources within a major disaster declaration area that are listed in or determined eligible for the National Register.
Applicant Eligibility: Eligible applicants are State and Tribal Historic Preservation Offices located within areas receiving major disaster declarations from FEMA.
Beneficiary Eligibility: States and Tribes.
Award Range/Average: Range: $500,000.000 to $10,000,000.00 Average: $5,000,000.00.
Funding: (Formula Grants) FY 17 $0.00; FY 18 est $47,500,000.00; FY 19 est Estimate Not Available; (Project Grants) FY 17 $0.00; FY 18 est $1,000,000.00; FY 19 Estimate Not Available

HQ: 1849 C Street NW, PO Box 7360, Washington, DC 20240
   Phone: 202-354-2062 | Email: megan_brown@nps.gov
   http://www.nps.gov/stlpg

DOI15.958 | ROUTE 66 CORRIDOR PRESERVATION

Award: Cooperative Agreements

Purpose: To preserve the cultural resources of the Route 66 corridor and to authorize the Secretary of the Interior to give assistance.

Applicant Eligibility: Interstate, intrastate, state, local, sponsored Organizations, public nonprofit institution/Organizations, other public institution/Organizations, Federally recognized tribal Governments, individual/family, minority groups, specialized groups, small businesses, profit Organizations, private nonprofit institution/Organizations, quasi-public nonprofit institution/Organization, other private institution/Organizations, anyone/general public, native American Organizations.

Beneficiary Eligibility: Interstate, Intrastate, State, Local, Sponsored Organization, Public Nonprofit Institution/Organization, Other Public Institution/organization, Federally Recognized Indian Tribal Government, Individual/Family, Minority Group, Specialized Group, Small Business, Profit Organization, Private Organization, Quasi-Public Nonprofit Organization, Other Private Institution/organization, Anyone/General Public, Native American Organization, Health Professional, Education Professional, Student/Trainee. Graduate Student, Scientists/Researcher, Artist/Humanist, Engineer/Architect. Builder/Contractor/Developer. Farmer/Rancher/Agriculture Producer, Industrialist/Business Person, Small Business Person, Consumer, Land/Property Owner, Black American. American Indian, Spanish Origin, Oriental, Other Non-white, U.S. Citizen, Women, Handicapped (Deaf, Blind, Crippled), Preschool, School, Child (6-15), Youth (16-21), Senior Citizen (60+), Moderate Income, Low Income, Major Metropolis (over 250,000), Other urban, Suburban, Rural, Education (0-8), Education (9-12), Education (13+).

Award Range/Average: Range: $5,000- $30,000

Funding: (Project Grants (Discretionary)) FY 17 $174,551.00; FY 18 est $90,000.00; FY 19 est $90,000.00

HQ: 1100 Old Santa Fe Trail, PO Box 728, Santa Fe, NM 87505
   Phone: 505-988-6701 | Email: kaisa_barthuli@nps.gov
   http://www.nps.gov/rt66/grnts

DOI15.961 | FEDERAL HISTORIC PRESERVATION TAX INCENTIVE
"Historic Tax Credit"

Award: Advisory Services and Counseling

Purpose: To promote historic preservation and community improvement through the private investment in the rehabilitation of historic buildings.

Applicant Eligibility: For the rehabilitation tax credit: private owners of commercial and other income-producing historic buildings held for investment purposes. For the conservation easement deduction; private owners of historic buildings proposed as the subject of charitable easement donations.

Beneficiary Eligibility: For the rehabilitation tax credit: private owners of historic buildings held for investment purposes. For the income tax deduction for the donation of conservation easements: private owners of buildings.

Award Range/Average: Not Available.

HQ: Technical Preservation Services 1849 C Street NW, PO Box 7243, Washington, DC 20240
   Phone: 202-354-2033
   http://www.nps.gov/tps/tax-incentives.htm

DOI15.962 | NATIONAL WILD AND SCENIC RIVERS SYSTEM
"Partnership Wild and Scenic Rivers"

Award: Cooperative Agreements

Purpose: To plan, protect, and manage river resources associated with those rivers designated into the National Wild and Scenic River system whereas the Department of Interior will act as the federal administrator.

Applicant Eligibility: States or their political subdivisions, landowners, private non-profit Organizations, other federal agencies or duly authorized by a river's enabling legislation wild and scenic river management councils or committees.

Beneficiary Eligibility: Same as Applicant Eligibility.

Award Range/Average: Range: $20,000.00 - $350,000.00 Average: $85,000.00

Funding: (Project Grants (Cooperative Agreements)) FY 18 est $974,000.00; FY 19 est $974,000.00; FY 20 est $974,000.00

Programs Administered by Regional - State - Local Offices

HQ: 1849 C Street NW, Washington, DC 20240
  Phone: 202-354-6908 | Email: corita_waters@nps.gov
  http://www.nps.gov/pwsr

NATURAL RESOURCES CONSERVATION SERVICE
Regional – State – Local Offices

LONGSHORE AND HARBOR WORKERS' COMPEN-SATION

District of Columbia
Maurice Mausbach, Director | Soil Quality Institute 14th & Independence Avenue NW, Washington, DC 20250 202-720-4525

Wildon Fontenot, Co-Director | PO Box 2890, Washington, DC 20013-2890 202-720-4909

Iowa
Dean M. Thompson, Director | NRI&A Institute Statistical Laboratory 202 Snedecor Hall Iowa State University, Ames, IA 50011 515-294-8177

Louisiana
Scott Peterson, Director | National Plant Data Center PO Box 74490, Baton Rouge, LA 70874 504-775-6280

Maryland
Billy Teels, Director | Wetlands Science Institute Snowden Hall 11400 American Holy Drive, Laurel, MD 20708-4014 301-497-5911

Nebraska
Dennis Lytle, Chairman | National Soil Survey Center Federal Building Room 152 100 Centennial Mall N, Lincoln, NE 68508-3866 402-437-5499

Phillip Jones, Head | National Soil Mechanics Center Federal Building Room 152 100 Centennial Mall N, Lincoln, NE 68508-3866 402-437-5318

North Carolina
Frank Clearfield, Director | Social Sciences Institute North Carolina A&T State University Applied Survey Research Laboratory Beech & Lindsay Streets, Greensboro, NC 27411 202-720-1511

Oregon
Carolyn Adams, Director | Watershed Sciences Institute 101 SW Main Street Suite 1700, Portland, OR 97204-3225 502-414-3001

John Werner, Co-Director | National Water & Climate Center 101 SW Main Street, Portland, OR 97204-3225 503-414-3107

Texas
National Employee Development Center 501 Felix Street Building 23, Fort Worth, TX 76115

Rhett Johnson, Director | Grazing Lands Institute 501 Felix Street Building 23 PO Box 6567, Fort Worth, TX 76115 817-334-5282, Ext. 3510

Richard Folsche, Director | National Carto & Geospatial Database Center 501 Felix Street Building 23, Fort Worth, TX 76115 817-334-5292, Ext. 3031

REGIONAL OFFICES

California
Rosendo Trevino III | W Regional Office 650 Capitol Mall Room 6072, Sacramento, CA 95814 916-498-5284

Georgia
Charles Adams, Director | SE Regional Office 1720 Peachtree Road NW Suite 716-N, Atlanta, GA 30367 404-347-6105

Nebraska
Jeffery Vonk | Northern Plains Regional Office 100 Centennial Mall N Room 152, Lincoln, NE 68508 402-437-5315

Texas
Judy Johnson | S Central Regional Office 501 W Felix Street Building 23 PO Box 6459, Fort Worth, TX 76115 817-334-5224, Ext. 3700

Virginia
Diane Gelburd | East Regional Office 1400 Wilson Boulevard Suite 1100, Arlington, VA 22209 703-312-7282

Wisconsin
Charles Whitmore | Midwest Regional Office One Gifford Pinchot Drive Room 204, Madison, WI 53705-3210 608-264-5281

SERVICE CENTER

Alabama
Ronnie D. Murphy | 3381 Skyway Drive, Auburn, AL 36830 334-887-4500

Alaska
Robert N. Jones | 800 W Evergreen Avenue Suite 100, Palmer, AK 99645 907-761-7760

Arizona
Michael Somerville | 3003 N Central Avenue Suite 800, Phoenix, AZ 85012-2945 602-280-8808

Arkansas
Kalvin L. Trice | 700 W Capitol Avenue Federal Building Room 5404 PO Box 2323, Little Rock, AR 72201-3228 501-324-5445

California
Henry Wyman | 2121-C 2nd Street Suite 102, Davis, CA 95616-5475 916-757-8215

Programs Administered by Regional - State - Local Offices

Colorado
Leroy Stokes, Resource Planning Specialist | 655 Parfet Street Room E200C, Lakewood, CO 80215-5517 303-236-2886, Ext. 202

Connecticut
Margo L. Wallace | 16 Professional Park Road, Storrs, CT 06268-1299 203-487-4014

Delaware
Elesa K. Cottrell | 1203 College Park Drive Suite 101, Dover, DE 19904-8713 302-678-4160

Florida
T. Niles Glasgow | 2614 NW 43rd Street PO Box 141510, Gainesville, FL 32606-6611 904-338-9500

Georgia
Earl Cosby | Federal Building PO Box 13 355 E Hancock Avenue, Athens, GA 30601-2769 706-546-2272

Hawaii
Kenneth M. Kaneshiro | 300 Ala Moana Boulevard Room 4316 PO Box 50004, Honolulu, HI 96850-0002 808-541-2601

Idaho
Luana E. Kiger | 3244 Elder Street Room 124, Boise, ID 83705-4711 208-378-5700

Illinois
William J. Gradle | 1902 Fox Drive, Champaign, IL 61820-7335 217-398-5267

Indiana
Robert L. Eddleman | 6013 Lakeside Boulevard, Indianapolis, IN 46278-2933 317-290-3200

Iowa
LeRoy Brown | 210 Walnut Street Suite 693 Federal Building, Des Moines, IA 50309-2180 515-284-6655

Kansas
Tomas M. Dominguez | 760 S Broadway, Salina, KS 67401 913-823-4565

Kentucky
David G. Sawyer | 771 Corporate Drive Suite 110, Lexington, KY 40503-5479 606-224-7350

Louisiana
Kevin Norton | 3737 Government Street, Alexandria, LA 71302-3727 318-473-7751

Maine
Darrel Dominick | 5 Godfrey Drive, Orono, ME 04473 207-866-7241

Maryland
David P. Doss | John Hansen Business Center Suite 301 339 Busch's Frontage Road, Annapolis, MD 21401-5534 410-757-0861

Massachusetts
Chris Clarke | 451 W Street, Amherst, MA 01002-2995 413-253-4351

Michigan
Jane E. Hardisty | 1405 S Harrison Road Room 101, East Lansing, MI 48823-5243 517-337-6701, Ext. 1201

Minnesota
William Hunt | 600 Farm Credit Building 375 Jackson Street, Saint Paul, MN 55101-1854 612-290-3675

Mississippi
Homer L. Wilkes | Suite 1321 Federal Building 100 W Capital Street, Jackson, MS 39269-1399 601-965-5205

Missouri
Roger A. Hansen | Parkade Center Suite 250 601 Business Loop 70 W, Columbia, MO 65203-2546 573-876-0901

Montana
Shirley Gammon | Federal Building Room 443 10 E Babcock Street, Bozeman, MT 59715-4704 406-587-6813

Nebraska
Stephen K. Chick | Federal Building Room 152 100 Centennial Mall N, Lincoln, NE 68508-3866 402-437-5327

Nevada
William D. Goddard | 5301 Longley Lane Building F Suite 201, Reno, NV 89511-1805 702-784-5863

New Hampshire
Dawn W. Genes | Federal Building 2 Madbury Road, Durham, NH 03824-1499 603-433-0505

New Jersey
Wayne Maresch | 1370 Hamilton Street, Somerset, NJ 08873-3157 908-246-1205

New Mexico
Dennis Alexander | 6200 Jefferson NE Room 305, Albuquerque, NM 87109-3734 505-761-4400

New York
Richard D. Swenson | 441 S Salina Street Suite 354 Room 520, Syracuse, NY 13202-2450 315-477-6504

North Carolina
Mary T. Kollstedt | 4405 Bland Road Suite 205, Raleigh, NC 27609-6293 919-873-2102

North Dakota
Scott Hoag Jr., | Federal Building PO Box 1458 220 E Rosser Avenue & 3rd Street Room 270, Bismarck, ND 58502-1458 701-250-4421

Ohio
Terry J. Cosby | Federal Building 200 N High Street Room 522, Columbus, OH 43215-2478 614-255-2472

Oklahoma
Ronnie L. Clarke | 100 USDA Suite 203, Stillwater, OK 74074-2624 405-742-1204

Oregon
Robert J. Graham | Federal Building 16th Floor 101 SW Main Street Suite 1300, Portland, OR 97204-3221 503-414-3201

Programs Administered by Regional - State - Local Offices

Pacific Basin Area
Joan B. Perry | Suite 301 FHB Building 400 Route 9, Guam, GU 96927 9-011-671-472-7490

Pennsylvania
Janet L. Oertly | One Credit Union Place Suite 340, Harrisburg, PA 17110-2993 717-782-2202

Puerto Rico
Juan Martinez, Director | IBM Building Suite 604 654 Munoz Rivera Avenue, Hato Rey, PR 00918-4123

Rhode Island
Denis G. Nickel | 60 Quaker Lane Suite 46, Warwick, RI 02886-0111 401-828-1300

South Carolina
Mark W. Berkland | Strom Thurmond Federal Building 1835 Assembly Street Room 950, Columbia, SC 29201-2489 803-765-5681

South Dakota
Dean F. Fisher | Federal Building 200 4th Street SW, Huron, SD 57350-2475 605-352-1200

Tennessee
James W. Ford | 801 Broadway 675 U.S. Courthouse, Nashville, TN 37203-3878 615-736-5471

Texas
John P. Burt | W R Poage Federal Building 101 S Main Street, Temple, TX 76501-7682 817-774-1214

Utah
Phillip J. Nelson Jr., | Wallace F Bennett Federal Building 125 S State Street Room 4402, Salt Lake City, UT 84147 801-524-5050

Vermont
John C. Titchner | 69 Union Street, Winooski, VT 05404-1999 802-951-6795

Virginia
M. Denise Doetzer | Culpeper Building 1606 Santa Rosa Road Suite 209, Richmond, VA 23229-5014 804-287-1691

Washington
Lynn A. Brown | USDA Natural Resources Conservation Service W 316 Boone Avenue Suite 450, Spokane, WA 99201-2348 509-323-2900

West Virginia
William J. Hartman | 75 High Street Room 301, Morgantown, WV 26505 304-291-4153

Wisconsin
Patricia S. Leavenworth | 6515 Watts Road Suite 200, Madison, WI 53719-2726 608-264-5577

Wyoming
Lincoln E. Burton | Federal Office Building 100 E B Street Room 3124, Casper, WY 82601 307-261-5201-1911

USDA10.072 | WETLANDS RESERVE PROGRAM "WRP"

Award: Cooperative Agreements
Purpose: To safeguard wetlands and to understand the advantages of wildlife.
Applicant Eligibility: An individual landowner, partnership, association, corporation, estate, trust, other business or other legal entities and Indian Tribe. This Program was repealed by the Agricultural Act of 2014 (2014 Farm Bill), effective February 7, 2014. Therefore, no new enrollments are authorized for this Program after that date. Implementation of contracts entered into prior to that date will continue.
Beneficiary Eligibility: An individual landowner, partnership, association, corporation, estate, trust, other business enterprises or other legal entities and Indian Tribe. This program was repealed by the Agricultural Act of 2014 (2014 Farm Bill), effective February 7, 2014. Therefore, no new enrollments are authorized for this program after that date. Implementation of contracts entered into prior to that date will continue.
Award Range/Average: Not Applicable.
Funding: (Cooperative Agreements) FY 18 $122,328,000.00; FY 19 est $23,994,000.00; FY 20 est $0.00;- (Salaries and Expenses) FY 18 $30,646,000.00; FY 19 est $7,006,000.00; FY 20 est $0.00
HQ: 1400 Independence Avenue SW, Washington, DC 20250
Phone: 202-690-1905 | Email: andrew.james@usda.gov
http://www.nrcs.usda.gov/wps/portal/nrcs/main/national/programs/easements/wetlands

USDA10.093 | VOLUNTARY PUBLIC ACCESS AND HABITAT INCENTIVE PROGRAM
"VPA-HIP"

Award: Formula Grants

Purpose: The VPA-HIP program provides access to the public on private farms and lands for recreational purposes.

Applicant Eligibility: Only States and Tribal Governments are eligible for VPA-HIP. An eligible State government means any State or local government, including State, city, town, or county government. An eligible Tribal Government means any Federally-recognized Indian tribe, band, nation, or other organized group, or community, including pueblos, rancherias, colonies and any Alaska Native Village, or regional or village corporation as defined in or established pursuant to the Alaska Native Claims Settlement Act (43 U.S. C 1601-1629H), which is recognized as eligible for the special Programs and services provided by the United States to Indians because of their status as Indians.

Beneficiary Eligibility: The beneficiary eligibility is extended to the public for the purposes of expanding existing public access programs or create new public access programs or provide incentives to improve habitat on enrolled program lands. Proposals for grant money should be submitted to the local State or Tribal governments by owners and operators of privately-held farm, ranch, and forest land. An eligible owner is one who has legal ownership of farmland, ranch land, or forestland. An eligible operator (individual, entity, or joint operation) is one who is determined by the FSA county committee to be in control of the farming, ranching, or silvicultural operations on the farm. For the purposes of receiving grant money, an appropriate wildlife habitat should be suitable or proper, as determined by the applicable State or tribal government, to support fish and wildlife populations in the area. An eligible farmland or ranch land means the sum of the Direct and Counter-Cyclical (DCP) cropland, forest, acreage planted to an eligible crop acreage and other land on the farm. Eligible forest land is at least 120 feet wide and one acre in size with at least 10 percent cover (or equivalent stocking) by live trees of any size, including land that formerly had such tree cover and that will be naturally or artificially regenerated. Forest land includes transition zones, such as areas between forest and non-forest lands that have at least 10 percent cover (or equivalent stocking) with live trees and forest areas adjacent to urban and built-up lands. Roadside, streamside, and shelterbelt strips of trees must have a crown width of at least 120 feet and continuous length of at least 363 feet to qualify as forest land. Unimproved roads and trails, streams, and clearings in forest areas are classified as forest if they are less than 120 feet wide or an acre in size. Tree-covered areas in agricultural production settings, such as fruit orchards, or tree-covered areas in urban settings, such as s city parks, are not considered forest land. Eligible privately-held land means farm, ranch, or forest land that is owned or operated by an individual or entity that is not an entity of any government unit or Tribe.

Funding: (Project Grants) FY 18 $0.00; FY 19 est $9,000,000.00; FY 20 est $14,000,000.00;- (Salaries and Expenses) FY 18 $0.00; FY 19 est $1,000,000.00; FY 20 est $4,000,000.00

HQ: 1400 Independence Avenue SW, Room 5237-S, Washington, DC 20250
Phone: 202-720-1844 | Email: maggie.rhodes@wdc.usda.gov
http://www.nrcs.usda.gov

USDA10.902 | SOIL AND WATER CONSERVATION

Award: Advisory Services and Counseling

Purpose: To provide technical assistance in conserving, improving and sustaining natural resources and environment to local landowners.

Applicant Eligibility: The CTA Program is delivered to private individuals, groups of decision makers, Tribes, units of Governments, and non-governmental Organizations in all 50 States, the District of Columbia, Puerto Rico, U.S. Virgin Islands, Guam, American Samoa, the Commonwealth of the Northern Mariana Islands, the Federated States of Micronesia, the Republic of Palau, and the Marshall Islands.

Beneficiary Eligibility: General public, State governments, and local governments.

Award Range/Average: Not Applicable.

Funding: (Salaries and Expenses) FY 18 $735,694,000; FY 19 est $837,462,000; FY 20 est $661,152,000

HQ: 1400 Independence Avenue SW, Washington, DC 20250
Phone: 202-260-9230 | Email: aaron.lauster@usda.gov
http://www.nrcs.usda.gov/wps/portal/nrcs/site/national/home

Programs Administered by Regional - State - Local Offices

USDA10.903 | SOIL SURVEY

Award: Dissemination of Technical Information

Purpose: To provide soil survey information of the United States to assist interested agencies, organizations, and individuals to make use of this information.

Applicant Eligibility: All individuals and groups that have a need for soil survey information can access it on the Web Soil Survey at websoilsurvey.nrcs.usda.gov or by contacting the local Natural Resources Conservation Service Office.

Beneficiary Eligibility: All individuals and groups that have a need for soil survey information are eligible to receive assistance.

Award Range/Average: Not Applicable.

Funding: (Salaries and Expenses) FY 18 $77,556,000.00; FY 19 est $82,442,000.00; FY 20 est $74,987,000

HQ: 1400 Independence Avenue SW, Washington, DC 20250

   Phone: 202-205-4211 | Email: pam.thomas@wdc.usda.gov

   http://www.nrcs.usda.gov/wps/portal/nrcs/site/national/home

USDA10.904 | WATERSHED PROTECTION AND FLOOD PREVENTION
"Watershed Program; Public Law 566 Operations Phase"

Award: Project Grants; Advisory Services and Counseling

Purpose: To assist in technical and financial assistance in the development and utilization of land and water resources.

Applicant Eligibility: Any State agency, county or groups of counties, municipality, town or township, soil and water conservation district, flood prevention or flood control district, Indian tribe or tribal Organization, or any other nonprofit agency with authority under State law to levy taxes, condemnation authority, and to carry out maintenance, and operate watershed works of improvement may apply for assistance. This Program is available in Puerto Rico, the Virgin Islands, Guam, American Samoa, the Mariana Islands and the Trust Territories of the Pacific Islands.

Beneficiary Eligibility: N/A

Award Range/Average: (per State) $0 to $2,164,000; $650,000.

Funding: (Salaries and Expenses) FY 18 $26,493,000.00; FY 19 est $72,737,000.00; FY 20 est $0.00; (Project Grants (Cooperative Agreements)) FY 18 $106,480,000.00; FY 19 est $201,201,000.00; FY 20 est $0.00

HQ: 1400 Independence Avenue SW, Washington, DC 20113

   Phone: 202-720-3413 | Email: kevin.farmer@usda.gov

   http://www.nrcs.usda.gov

USDA10.905 | PLANT MATERIALS FOR CONSERVATION

Award: Provision of Specialized Services

Purpose: To promote the use of soil, water, and related resource conservation and to develop technology for land management and restoration with plant materials.

Applicant Eligibility: Cooperating State and Federal agencies and cooperators of conservation districts where structured evaluations are conducted and commercial seed growers and nurserymen interested in the commercial production of selected plant materials. Applicants are also eligible in Puerto Rico and the Virgin Islands. The general public is not eligible to participate in this Program.

Beneficiary Eligibility: Cooperating State and Federal agencies and co-operators of conservation districts and commercial seed growers and nurserymen interested in the production of selected plant materials. Applicants are also eligible in Puerto Rico and the Virgin Islands.

Award Range/Average: Not Applicable.

Funding: (Salaries and Expenses) FY 18 $8,703,000.00; FY 19 est $11,062,000.00; FY 19 est $9,481,000.00

HQ: 1400 Independence Avenue SW, PO Box 2890, Washington, DC 20113

   Phone: 202-720-0536 | Email: john.englert@wdc.usda.gov

   http://plant-materials.nrcs.usda.gov

USDA10.907 | SNOW SURVEY AND WATER SUPPLY FORECASTING
"Snow Surveys"

Award: Dissemination of Technical Information

Purpose: To support NRCS conservation by providing timely and accurate forecasts of surface water supply to water managers and information on snow, water, climate, and hydrologic conditions.

Programs Administered by Regional - State - Local Offices

Applicant Eligibility: General public, including those located in the U.S. Territories.
Beneficiary Eligibility: Same as Applicant Eligibility.
Award Range/Average: Not Applicable.
Funding: (Salaries and Expenses) FY 18 $8,939,000.00; FY 19 est $10,105,000.00; FY 20 est $9,380,000.00
HQ: National Water and Climate Center Natural Resources Conservation Service Department of Agriculture, PO Box 2890, Washington, DC 20013
  Phone: 503-414-3055 | Email: michael.strobel@por.usda.gov
  http://www.nrcs.usda.gov

USDA10.912 | ENVIRONMENTAL QUALITY INCENTIVES PROGRAM "EQIP"

Award: Direct Payments for Specified Use
Purpose: To promote agricultural production, forest management, environmental benefits, and implementation of structural vegetative land management practices on eligible lands through Commodity Credit Corporation.
Applicant Eligibility: Agricultural producers who face serious threats to soil, water, and related natural resources, or who need assistance with complying with Federal and State environment laws. A participant may be an owner, landlord, operator, or tenant of eligible agricultural lands or non-industrial forestlands. Limited resource producers, small-scale producers, social disadvantaged individuals, federally recognized Indian tribal Governments, Alaska natives, and Pacific Islanders are encouraged to apply.
Beneficiary Eligibility: To be eligible the agricultural producers must be in compliance with highly erodible land and wetland conservation provisions and in compliance with the Adjusted Gross Income (AGI) payment limitations.
Award Range/Average: Total EQIP conservation payments are limited to $450,000 in financial assistance per person or legal entity for contracts entered into between fiscal years 2019 through 2023, regardless of the number of contracts. Average contract payments are estimated to be $23,000.
Funding: (Salaries and Expenses) FY 18 $463,599,000.00; FY 19 est $444,190,000.00; FY 20 est $491,101,000.00; (Direct Payments for Specified Use) FY 18 $1,395,449,000.00; FY 19 est $1,492,072,000.00; FY 20 est $1,320,656,000.00
HQ: Financial Assistance Programs Division Natural Resources Conservation Service 1400 Independence Avenue SW, Room 5231-S, Washington, DC 20250
  Phone: 202-690-2621 | Email: jeffrey.white2@usda.gov
  http://www.nrcs.usda.gov

USDA10.913 | FARM AND RANCH LANDS PROTECTION PROGRAM "FRPP"

Award: Direct Payments for Specified Use
Purpose: To compensate for eligible agricultural lands that possess important soils and archaeological resources from converting into non-agricultural farms and preserve them using conservation methods.
Applicant Eligibility: An eligible entity was any local or State agency, county or groups of counties, municipality, town or township, soil and water conservation district, or Indian tribe or tribal Organization, that has a farmland protection Program that purchases conservation easements for the purpose of protecting agricultural use and related conservation values by limiting conversion to non- agricultural uses of land, and that has pending offers. This Program was available in all 50 States, Puerto Rico, the Virgin Islands, Guam, American Samoa, the Mariana Islands, and the Trust Territories of the Pacific Islands. The Program was repealed by the Agricultural Act of 2014 effective February 7, 2014. No new enrollments are authorized after that date.
Beneficiary Eligibility: Landowners must be in compliance with the Wetland Compliance (WC) and Highly Erodible Land (HEL) provisions of the Farm Bill and met the Adjusted Gross Income (AGI) limitations in the Farm Bill.
Award Range/Average: $2,700 to $1,000,000 per landowner. Average: $97,000.
Funding: (Direct Payments for Specified Use) FY 18 $1,000.00; FY 19 est $1,896,000.00; FY 20 $0.00
HQ: 1400 and Independence Avenue SW, Washington, DC 20250
  Phone: 202-690-1905 | Email: jerome.faulkner@usda.gov
  http://www.nrcs.usda.gov

Programs Administered by Regional - State - Local Offices

USDA10.914 | WILDLIFE HABITAT INCENTIVE PROGRAM "WHIP"

Award: Direct Payments for Specified Use

Purpose: To assist those protecting wildlife, wetland, endangered species, and fisheries.

Applicant Eligibility: Applicant must meet Highly Erodible Land and Wetland Conservation (HEL/WC) requirements, Adjusted Gross Income (AGI) requirements, verification that applicant will be in control of land for the duration of a contract.

Beneficiary Eligibility: A participant may be an owner, landlord, operator, or tenant of eligible lands. Limited resource producers, small-scale producers, producers of minority groups, Federally Recognized Indian Tribal Governments, Alaska natives, and Pacific Islanders are encouraged to apply.

Award Range/Average: Average contract payments are estimated to be $4,500.

Funding: (Direct Payments for Specified Use) FY 18 $73,000.00; FY 19 est $1,980,000.00; FY 20 $0.00; (Salaries and Expenses) FY 18 $5,327,000.00; FY 19 est $7,020,000.00; FY 20 est $0.00

HQ: 1400 Independence Avenue SW, Room 5231-S, Washington, DC 20250

Phone: 202-720-4265 | Email: jeffrey.white2@usda.gov

http://www.nrcs.usda.gov

USDA10.916 | WATERSHED REHABILITATION PROGRAM "Watershed Rehabilitation; PL-566 Watershed Program"

Award: Advisory Services and Counseling

Purpose: To provide technical and financial assistance to dams that are in bad condition and which are constructed with the assistance of USDA Watershed Programs.

Applicant Eligibility: Sponsoring local Organizations for existing watershed projects that include dams that were originally constructed with assistance from one of the following water resource Programs: Public Law 78-534, Section 13 of the Flood Control Act of 1944; Public Law 156-67, the pilot watershed Program authorized under the heading Flood Prevention of the Department of Agriculture Appropriation Act of 1954; Public Law 83-566, the Watershed Protection and Flood Prevention Act of 1954; and Subtitle H of Title XV of the Agriculture and Flood Act of 1981, commonly known as the Resource Conservation and Development Program.

Beneficiary Eligibility: Any State agency, county or groups of counties, municipality, town or township, soil and water conservation district, flood prevention or flood control district, Indian tribe or tribal organization, or any other nonprofit agency with authority under State law to carry out, maintain, and operate watershed works of improvement may become a sponsoring local organization for a watershed rehabilitation project.

Award Range/Average: $0 to $6,451,000; $770,000 average per state.

Funding: (Salaries and Expenses) FY 18 $10,375,000.00; FY 19 est $10,618,000.00; FY 20 est Estimate Not Available; (Cooperative Agreements (Discretionary Grants)) FY 18 $5,380,000.00; FY 19 est $7,132,000.00; FY 20 est Estimate Not Available; (Direct Payments for Specified Use) FY 18 $39,638,000.00; FY 19 est $10,255,000.00; FY 20 est Estimate Not Available.

HQ: 1400 Independence Avenue SW Room 6015-S, PO Box 2890, Washington, DC 20250

Phone: 202-720-3414 | Email: kevin.farmer@usda.gov

http://www.nrcs.usda.gov

USDA10.917 | AGRICULTURAL MANAGEMENT ASSISTANCE

Award: Direct Payments for Specified Use

Purpose: To assist producers in private lands to improve water management structures to improve water quality, maximize conservation practices, soil erosion control, pest management, etc.

Applicant Eligibility: The land must be in one of the 16 following eligible states: Connecticut, Delaware, Hawaii, Maine, Maryland, Massachusetts, Nevada, New Hampshire, New Jersey, New York, Pennsylvania, Rhode Island, Utah, Vermont, West Virginia, and Wyoming.

Beneficiary Eligibility: Applicants must have control of the land for the length of the contract which may not be more than 10 years.

Funding: (Salaries and Expenses) FY 18 est $749,000.00; FY 19 est $938,000.00; FY 20 $1,000,000.00; (Direct Payments for Specified Use) FY 18 est 3,473,000.00; FY 19 est $3,752,000.00; FY 20 $4,000,000.00

HQ: 1400 Independence Avenue SW, Room 5231-S, Washington, DC 20250
 Phone: 202-720-4265 | Email: jeffrey.white2@usda.gov
 http://www.nrcs.usda.gov

USDA10.920 | GRASSLAND RESERVE PROGRAM
"GRP"

Award: Direct Payments for Specified Use

Purpose: To assist landowners in protecting eligible grazing lands and other lands through rental contracts and easements.

Applicant Eligibility: GRP is available on privately owned lands. Eligible land includes grassland, land that contains forbs, or shrubs, including rangeland and pasture land; or land that is located in an area that has historically been dominated by grassland, forbs, and shrubs; and has potential to provide habitat for animal or plant populations of significant ecological value. Incidental lands, in conjunction with eligible land, may also be considered for enrollment to allow for the efficient administration of an easement or rental contract.

Beneficiary Eligibility: Only landowners may submit applications for easements; landowners and others who have general control of the acreage may submit applications for rental contracts. Easements may also be acquired by eligible entities based on a 50 percent cost-share with the Federal government. Eligible entities are defined as units of State, local or Tribal government or nongovernmental organizations that have a charter describing a commitment to conserving ranch land, agricultural land, or grassland for grazing and conservation purposes. All participants are subject to the Adjusted Gross Income Provision set forth in 7 CFR Part 1400.

Award Range/Average: The 5 year average estimated cost per acre for easement acquisition was approximately $400, ranging from $65 per acre to over $30,000 per acre. The average estimated cost per acre for rental contracts was $134 per acre over the life of the rental contract. Over 250 GRP easements were acquired on over 117,000 acres.

Funding: (Direct Payments for Specified Use) FY 18 $1,000.00; FY 19 est $5,175,000.00; FY 20 est $5,980,000.00; (Salaries and Expenses) FY 18 $1,461,000.00; FY 19 est $9,825,000.00; FY 20 est $11,353,000.00

HQ: 1400 and Independence Avenue SW, Room 5234-S, Washington, DC 20250
 Phone: 202-690-1905 | Email: jerome.faulkner@usda.gov
 http://www.nrcs.usda.gov

USDA10.921 | CONSERVATION SECURITY PROGRAM
"CSP"

Award: Direct Payments for Specified Use

Purpose: The CSP assists for conservation and improvement of soil, water, air, energy, plant and animal life, on Tribal and private lands. It rewards those farmers and ranchers for maintaining and enhancing natural resources.

Applicant Eligibility: Applicants must have applied prior to Oct. 1, 2008. An individual producer, partnership, association, corporation, estate, trust, other business or other legal entities controlling eligible lands. The term producer means an owner, operator, landlord, tenant or sharecropper that shares in the risk of producing any crop or livestock; and must be entitled to share in the crop or livestock available for marketing from an agricultural operation. An applicant must be in compliance with highly erodible land and wetland conservation provisions, and average adjusted gross income requirements. Lands enrolled in the Conservation Reserve Program, Wetlands Reserve Program, the Grassland Reserve Program pursuant to 16 U.S.C. 3838n, public land including land owned by a Federal, State or local unit of government are not eligible for enrollment in CSP and may not receive CSP payments.

Beneficiary Eligibility: An individual producer, partnership, association, corporation, estate, trust, other business or other legal entities controlling eligible lands. The term producer means and owner, operator, landlord, tenant or sharecropper that shares in the risk of producing any crop or livestock; and must be entitled to share in the crop or livestock available for marketing from an agricultural operation. A participant must be in compliance with highly erodible land and wetland conservation provisions, and average adjusted gross income requirements. Lands enrolled in the Conservation Reserve Program, Wetlands Reserve Program, the Grassland Reserve Program pursuant to 16 U.S.C. 3838n, public land including land owned by a Federal, State or local unit of government are not eligible for enrollment in CSP and may not receive CSP payments.

Award Range/Average: Not Applicable.

Funding: (Salaries and Expenses) FY 18 $4,000.00; FY 19 est $0.00; FY 20 est $0.00

HQ: 1400 Independence Avenue SW, Room 5247-S, Washington, DC 20250
 Phone: 202-690-2621 | Email: jeffrey.white2@usda.gov
 http://www.nrcs.usda.gov

Programs Administered by Regional - State - Local Offices

USDA10.922 | HEALTHY FORESTS RESERVE PROGRAM (HFRP)

Award: Direct Payments for Specified Use

Purpose: To assist landowners in enhancing forest ecosystems, safeguard endangered species, improve biodiversity, etc.

Applicant Eligibility: To be eligible to enroll an easement or restoration agreement in the HFRP, a person must: be the landowner of eligible private land for which enrollment is sought; agree to provide such information to the Natural Resources Conservation Service (NRCS) as the Agency deems necessary or desirable to assist in its determination of eligibility for Program benefits and for other Program implementation purposes.

Beneficiary Eligibility: Only landowners.

Award Range/Average: The average estimated cost per acre for easement acquisition was approximately $1,048. Congressional authorization of funds for HFRP is discretionary. Currently funds for HFRP are only available under the Regional Conservationist Partnership Program (RCPP).

Funding: (Salaries and Expenses) FY 18 $23,000.00; FY 19 est $1,016,000.00; FY 20 est $0.00; (Direct Payments for Specified Use) FY 18 $47,000.00; FY 19 est $6,684,000.00; FY 20 est $0.00

HQ: 1400 and Independence Avenue SW, Washington, DC 20250

   Phone: 202-690-1905 | Email: jerome.faulkner@usda.gov

   http://www.nrcs.usda.gov

USDA10.923 | EMERGENCY WATERSHED PROTECTION PROGRAM "EWP"

Award: Project Grants

Purpose: The EWP Program assists landowners and operators in implementing emergency recovery measures to prevent erosion and safeguard methods from natural disaster.

Applicant Eligibility: Public and private landowners are eligible for assistance but must be represented by a project sponsor. Project sponsor means a State government or a State agency or a legal subdivision thereof, local unit of government, or any Native American tribe or tribal Organization as defined in section 4 of the Indian Self-Determination and education Assistance Act (25 U.S.C. 450b), with a legal interest in or responsibility for the values threatened by a watershed emergency; is capable of obtaining necessary land rights, and permits; and is capable of carrying out any operation and maintenance responsibilities that may be required. Sponsors are also responsible for furnishing the local cost share and for accomplishing the installation of work. Work can be done either through Federal or local contracts. Emergency watershed protection is authorized in the 50 States, the District of Columbia, the Commonwealth of Puerto Rico, the U.S. Virgin Islands, Guam, the Commonwealth of the Northern Mariana Islands, and American Samoa.

Beneficiary Eligibility: N/A

Funding: (Salaries and Expenses) FY 18 est $22,295,839.00; FY 19 est 121,342,750.00; FY 20 est $0.00; (Cooperative Agreements (Discretionary Grants)) FY 18 $181,198,198.00; FY 19 est 387,545,681.00; FY 20 est $0.00

HQ: Watershed Programs Branch USDA NRCS 1400 Independence Ave, PO Box 2890, Washington, DC 20250

   Phone: 202-720-3413 | Email: kevin.farmer@usda.gov

   http://www.nrcs.usda.gov/programs/ewp

USDA10.924 | CONSERVATION STEWARDSHIP PROGRAM "CSP"

Award: Cooperative Agreements

Purpose: The CSP and NRCS provide financial and technical assistance to conserve soil, water, air, and related natural resources on their land. CSP encourages to improve conservation performance on agricultural lands and nonindustrial private forest lands.

Applicant Eligibility: The Program provides equitable access to all producers, regardless of operation size, crops produced, or geographic location. Individual producers, legal entities, corporations, and Indian Tribes may be eligible for the Program. Eligible lands include cropland, grassland, prairie land, improved pastureland, rangeland, nonindustrial private forest land, and agricultural land under the jurisdiction of an Indian tribe. As stated in the Federal Register, 1470. 6a, Applicants must be the operator of record in the USDA farm records management system for the eligible land being offered for enrollment; have documented control of the land for the term of the proposed contract; include the eligible land in their entire operation as represented for other USDA Programs; and be in compliance with the highly erodible land and wetland conservation provisions of 7 CFR Part 12, and adjusted gross income provisions of 7 CFR part 1400. The applicants operation must also meet a stewardship threshold.

Beneficiary Eligibility: Same as Applicant Eligibility.

Award Range/Average: CSP payments to a person or legal entity may not exceed $40,000 in any year and $200,000 during any 5-year period. Each CSP contract will be limited to $200,000 over the term of the initial contract period. The above limitations exclude funding arrangements with federally recognized Indian tribes or Alaska Native corporations as described in 1470.24. The program shall have a national average rate of $18 per acre.

Funding: (Cooperative Agreements) FY 18 $949,353,000; FY 19 est $1,491,689,000; FY 20 est $1,340,515,000; (Salaries and Expenses Total) FY 18 $247,941,000; FY 19 est $380,193,000; FY 20 est $342,492,000

HQ: 1400 Independence Avenue SW, Room 5241-S, Washington, DC 20250

Phone: 202-690-2621 | Email: jeffrey.white2@usda.gov

http://www.nrcs.usda.gov/wps/portal/nrcs/main/national/programs/financial/csp

USDA10.925 | AGRICULTURAL WATER ENHANCEMENT PROGRAM "AWEP"

Award: Direct Payments for Specified Use

Purpose: AWEP promotes ground and surface water conservation on agricultural lands and to improve water quality on eligible agricultural lands.

Applicant Eligibility: Partners representing agricultural producers who face serious threats to soil, water, and related natural resources, or who need assistance with complying with Federal and State environment laws. A participant may be an owner, landlord, operator, or tenant of eligible agricultural lands or non-industrial forestlands. Limited resource producers, small-scale producers, socially disadvantaged individuals, federally recognized Indian tribal Governments, Alaska natives, and Pacific Islanders are encouraged to apply. Eligible partners include: Federally recognized Indian Tribes, States, units of local government, agricultural or silvicultural associations or other groups of such producers, or other nongovernmental Organization with experience working with agricultural producers.

Beneficiary Eligibility: To be eligible the agricultural producers must be in compliance with highly erodible land and wetland conservation provisions and in compliance with the Adjusted Gross Income (AGI) payment limitations.

Award Range/Average: Conservation payments are limited to a maximum payment limitation per producer of $300,000 for the life of the 2008 Farm Bill. Average contracts are estimated to be $40,841. This program was repealed by the Agricultural Act of 2014 (2014 Farm Bill), effective February 7,2014. Therefore, no new enrollments are authorized for this program after that date.

Funding: (Salaries and Expenses) FY 18 $1,227,000.00; FY 19 est $5,100,000.00; FY 20 est $0.00; (Direct Payments for Specified Use) FY 18 $20,000.00; FY 19 est $900,000.00; FY 20 est $0.00

HQ: 1400 Independence Avenue SW, Room 5231-S, Washington, DC 20250

Phone: 202-690-2621 | Email: jeffrey.white2@usda.gov

http://www.nrcs.usda.gov/wps/portal/nrcs/main/national/programs/financial/awep

USDA10.926 | CHESAPEAKE BAY WATERSHED PROGRAM "CBWP"

Award: Direct Payments for Specified Use

Purpose: The Chesapeake Bay Watershed Program assists producers in improving water quality and quantity, preserve soil, air, and related resources through the implementation of conservation practices.

Applicant Eligibility: Only agricultural producers owning or operating within the Chesapeake Bay Watershed are eligible to participate in CBWP. In addition, NRCS applies the eligibility requirements of the particular natural resource Program used to implement CBWP (e.g., the Environmental Quality Incentives Program (EQIP) (16 U.S.C. 3839aa et seq.), the Wildlife Habitat Incentives Program (WHIP) (16 U.S.C. 3839bb-1)). Limited resource producers, small-scale producers, beginning farmers and ranchers, socially-disadvantaged producers, and federally recognized Indian Tribes are encouraged to apply.

Beneficiary Eligibility: To be eligible, the agricultural producers must be in compliance with highly erodible land and wetland conservation provisions at 7 CFR part 12, and in compliance with the Adjusted Gross Income (AGI) payment limitations at 7 CFR part 1400.

Award Range/Average: Conservation payments are limited to the rules for the particular natural resource program used to implement CBWP (e.g., EQIP, WHIP).

Funding: (Direct Payments for Specified Use) FY 18 $438,000.00; FY 19 est $5,049,000.00; FY 20 est $0.00; (Salaries and Expenses) FY 18 $1,392,000.00; FY 19 est $3,951,000.00; FY 20 est $0.00

Programs Administered by Regional - State - Local Offices

HQ: 1400 Independence Avenue SW, Room 5231-S, Washington, DC 20250
Phone: 202-690-2621 | Email: jeffrey.white2@usda.gov
http://www.nrcs.usda.gov/wps/portal/nrcs/detailfull/national/programs/initiatives/?cid=stelprdb1047323

USDA10.927 | EMERGENCY WATERSHED PROTECTION PROGRAM-DISASTER RELIEF APPROPRIATIONS ACT
"EWP - Disaster Relief (Hurricane Sandy)"

Award: Project Grants
Purpose: The EWP Program is to assist sponsors, landowners, and operators in implementing emergency recovery measures to prevent erosion and safeguard methods from a natural disaster that causes a sudden watershed.
Applicant Eligibility: For this appropriation, only applicants affected by Hurricane Sandy and only in those areas declared as a major disaster are eligible for assistance through the EWP Program. Public and private landowners are eligible for assistance but must be represented by a project sponsor. Project sponsor means a State government or a State agency or a legal subdivision thereof, local unit of government, or any Native American tribe or tribal Organization as defined in section 4 of the Indian Self-Determination and education Assistance Act (25 U.S.C. 450b), with a legal interest in or responsibility for the values threatened by a watershed emergency; is capable of obtaining necessary land rights, and permits; and is capable of carrying out any operation and maintenance responsibilities that may be required. Sponsors are also responsible for furnishing the local cost share and for accomplishing the installation of work. Work can be done either through Federal or local contracts.
Beneficiary Eligibility: N/A
Award Range/Average: N/A
Funding: (Salaries and Expenses) FY 18 $84,942.00; FY 19 est $4,671,025.00; FY 20 est $0.00; - Project Grants (Cooperative Agreements or Contracts) FY 18 $0.00; FY 19 est $12,388,452.00; FY 20 est $0.00
HQ: 1400 Independence Avenue SW, Washington, DC 20250
Phone: 202-720-3413 | Email: kevin.farmer@usda.gov

USDA10.928 | EMERGENCY WATERSHED PROTECTION PROGRAM-FLOODPLAIN EASEMENTS-DISASTER RELIEF APPROPRIATIONS ACT
"EWP-FPE Hurricane Sandy"

Award: Direct Payments for Specified Use
Purpose: The Emergency Watershed Protection-Floodplain Easement Program provides an alternative measure to restore the flood storage, erosion control, and improve the practical management of the easement.
Applicant Eligibility: For this appropriation, only applicants affected by Hurricane Sandy and only in those areas declared as a major disaster are eligible for assistance through the EWP-FPE Program. Pursuant to 7 CFR 624. 10(b)(2), NRCS may determine land is eligible under for EWP-FPE if any of the following apply: 1) The floodplain lands were damaged by flooding at least once within the previous calendar year or have been subject to flood damage at least twice within the previous 10 years. 2) Other lands within the floodplain are eligible, provided the lands would contribute to the restoration of the flood storage and flow, provide for control of erosion, or that would improve the practical management of the floodplain easement. 3) Lands would be inundated or adversely impacted as a result of a dam breach. NRCS may determine that land is ineligible under this section if any of the following apply: 1) Implementation of restoration practices would be futile due to onsite or offsite conditions. 2) The land is subject to an existing easement or deed restriction that provides sufficient protection or restoration, as determined by the Chief of NRCS, of the floodplain's functions and values. 3) The purchase of an easement would not meet the purposes of this part.
Beneficiary Eligibility: Private and non-federal landowners are eligible for EWP-FPE. To be eligible for FPE, the NRCS will require participating landowners to-1) Comply with the terms of the easement.2) Comply with all terms and conditions of any associated agreement.3) Convey title to the easement that is acceptable to NRCS and warrant that the easement is superior to the rights of all others, except for exceptions to the title that are deemed acceptable by NRCS. For projects that include parcels with residential dwellings or other structures on non-agricultural lands (such as flood mitigation efforts intended to assist families in moving from flood-prone areas as part of EWP recovery efforts), a local sponsor will be identified and serve as the local cooperating entity for these efforts. A sponsor will be a local or State unit of government (city, county, conservation district, watershed conservancy district, or State agency) that has a local presence and staff available to assist in the implementation of the program.

Award Range/Average: N/A

Funding: (Direct Payments for Specified Use) FY 18 $1,835,333.00; FY 19 est $69,796,257.00; FY 20 est $0.00; (Salaries and Expenses) FY 18 $479,073.00; FY 19 est $20,189,112.00; FY 20 est $0.00

HQ: 1400 and Independence Avenue SW, Room 5234-S, Washington, DC 20250

    Phone: 202-690-1905 | Email: jerome.faulkner@wdc.usda.gov

    http://www.nrcs.usda.gov/programs/ewp

USDA10.929 | WATER BANK PROGRAM

Award: Direct Payments for Specified Use

Purpose: To preserve wetlands habitat, wildlife, conserve waters, reduce soil and wind erosion, flood control, improve water quality, etc.

Applicant Eligibility: N/A

Beneficiary Eligibility: Landowners and operators of specified types of wetlands in designated important migratory waterfowl nesting, breeding and feeding areas.

Award Range/Average: $20 to $50 per acre. Average: $35.

Funding: (Project Grants (Cooperative Agreements or Contracts)) FY 18 $4,064,000.00; FY 19 est $4,198,000.00; FY 20 est $0.00; (Salaries and Expenses) FY 18 $192,000.00; FY 19 est $196,000.00; FY 20 est $0.00

HQ: 1400 Independence Avenue SW, Room 5237-S, Washington, DC 20250

    Phone: 202-690-2621 | Email: jeffrey.white2@usda.gov

    http://www.nrcs.usda.gov

USDA10.931 | AGRICULTURAL CONSERVATION EASEMENT PROGRAM "ACEP"

Award: Cooperative Agreements

Purpose: The Agricultural Conservation Easement Program compensates to eligible entities to purchase conservation easements to protect the agricultural lands and to reduce nonagricultural uses of the land and to enhance wetlands.

Applicant Eligibility: For ACEP-ALE an eligible entity that is an Indian Tribe, State government, local government, or a nongovernmental Organization which has a farmland or grassland protection Program that purchases agricultural land easements for the purpose of protecting agriculture use and related conservation values, including grazing uses and related conservation values, by limiting conversion to nonagricultural uses of the land, and that has pending offers may apply for funds. This Program is available in all 50 States, Puerto Rico, the Virgin Islands, Guam, American Samoa, the Mariana Islands, and the Trust Territories of the Pacific Islands. Individual landowners must apply through the local agency or Organization that handles the farmland or grassland protection Program. For ACEP-WRE, private landowners, including individual landowners, partnerships, associations, corporations, estates, trusts, and other business or legal entities, and Indian Tribes are eligible to apply.

Beneficiary Eligibility: All landowners applying for ACEP must be in compliance with the Wetland Compliance (WC) and Highly Erodible Land (HEL) provisions of the Farm Bill and, within the exception of FY2014, meet the Adjusted Gross Income (AGI) limitations in the Farm Bill. For ACEP-ALE, applications are submitted by an eligible entity who will be the participant in the program. For ACEP-WRE, only private landowners, partnerships, associations, corporations, estates, trusts, other business or legal entities and, Indian tribes may submit applications for easements.

Award Range/Average: Under ACEP-ALE, cost-share provided by NRCS for the purchase of an agricultural land easement ranges from $216 per acre for grassland easements to $13,670 per acre for cropland easements. The average per acre cost-share amount provided by NRCS is $2,790 per acre.Under ACEP-WRE, easement compensation amounts provided directly to eligible landowners ranges from $1,200 per acre to $13,000 per acre, with an average cost of $2,600 per acre.

Funding: (Cooperative Agreements) FY 18 $250,637,000.00; FY 19 est $$367,240,000.00; FY 20 est $310,350,000.00; (Salaries and Expenses) FY 18 $86,792,000.00; FY 19 est $187,504,000.00; FY 20 est $158,457,000.00

HQ: 1400 and Independence Avenue SW, Washington, DC 20250

    Phone: 202-690-1905 | Email: jerome.faulkner@usda.gov

    http://www.nrcs.usda.gov/wps/portal/nrcs/main/national/programs/easements/acep

Programs Administered by Regional - State - Local Offices

USDA10.932 | REGIONAL CONSERVATION PARTNERSHIP PROGRAM "RCPP"

Award: Cooperative Agreements

Purpose: To further the conservation of soil, water, wildlife, related natural resources on eligible land; avoid local natural resource regulatory requirements; and encourage the four former conservation programs partners to understand the conservation needs.

Applicant Eligibility: Eligible partners include advocate groups for conservation and those interested in assisting agricultural producers who face serious threats to soil, water, and related natural resources, or who need assistance with complying with Federal and State environment laws. Eligible partnering Organizations include: An agricultural or silvicultural producer association or other group of producers; A State or unit of local government; An Indian Tribe; A farmer cooperative; A water district, irrigation district, rural water district or association, or other Organization with specific water delivery authority to producers on agricultural land; A municipal water or wastewater treatment entity; An institution of higher education; An Organization or entity with an established history of working cooperatively with producers on agricultural land; Conservation driven nongovernmental Organizations.

Beneficiary Eligibility: To be eligible the agricultural producers participating within an approved project area must be in compliance with highly erodible land and wetland conservation provisions and in compliance with the Adjusted Gross Income (AGI) payment limitations. Conservation payments for the Conservation Stewardship Program are limited to a maximum payment limitation per producer of $200,000 for the life of the 2014 Farm Bill. Conservation payments for the Environmental Quality Incentives Program are limited to a maximum payment limitation per producer of $450,000 for the life of the 2014 Farm Bill.

Award Range/Average: There is no minimum amount and the maximum amount for any fiscal year will be established by the Chief of NRCS.

Funding: (Salaries and Expenses) FY 18 $30,950,000.00; FY 19 est $117,703,000.00; FY 20 est $123,654,000.00; (Cooperative Agreements) FY 18 $41,903,000.00; FY 19 est $274,639,000.00; FY 20 est $288,527,000.00

HQ: 1400 Independence Avenue SW, Washington, DC 20250

Phone: 202-720-6037 | Email: kari.cohen@usda.gov

http://www.nrcs.usda.gov/wps/portal/nrcs/main/national/programs/farmbill/rcpp

USDA10.933 | WETLANDS MITIGATION BANKING PROGRAM

Award: Cooperative Agreements; Project Grants

Purpose: The Wetlands Mitigation Banking Program helps producers with wetland conservation to maintain eligibility for the Federal crop insurance premium subsidy.

Applicant Eligibility: Eligible entities that may submit applications include Tribal Nations, State, and local units of government, and nongovernmental Organizations (NGOs), including for profit NGOs. NRCS will accept proposals for the development and establishment of mitigation banks submitted under this notice by eligible applicants from all 50 States, the District of Columbia, the Caribbean Area (Puerto Rico and the U.S. Virgin Islands), and the Pacific Islands Area (Guam, American Samoa, and the Commonwealth of the Northern Mariana Islands). Applications will also be accepted from existing banks with established credits that meet the described needs of the Program.

Beneficiary Eligibility: Mitigation banks established through this program are for the explicit and sole purpose of assisting agricultural producers with wetland conservation compliance, also known as Swamp buster compliance.

Award Range/Average: This is a one-time direct appropriation provided in FY 2014, and the funds are available until expended. Up to $9 million will be available for awards.

Funding: (Cooperative Agreements) FY 18 $0.00; FY 19 est $750,000.00; FY 20 est $0.00; (Salaries and Expenses) FY 18 $603,000.00; FY 19 est $750,000.00; FY 19 est $0.00; FY 20 est $0.00

HQ: 8000 S15th Street, Lincoln, NE 68508

Phone: 402-560-1309 | Email: shaun.vickers@usda.gov

https://www.nrcs.usda.gov/wps/portal/nrcs/detail/national/programs/farmbill/?cid=nrcseprd362686

OCCUPATIONAL SAFETY AND HEALTH ADMINISTRATION
Regional – State – Local Offices

Alabama

3737 Government Boulevard Suite 100, Mobile, AL 36693-4309 251-441-6131

Todd Mall 2047 Canyon Road, Birmingham, AL 35216-1981
205-731-1534, Ext. 133

Programs Administered by Regional - State - Local Offices

Alaska
301 W Northern Lights Boulevard Room 407, Anchorage, AK 99503-7571 907-271-5152

Alaska, Idaho, Oregon, Washington
Richard Terrill, Regional Administrator | Department of Labor OSHA 1111 3rd Avenue Suite 715, Seattle, WA 98101-3212 206-553-5930

Arizona
3221 N 16th Street Suite 100, Phoenix, AZ 85016 602-640-2007

Arkansas
TCBY Building Suite 450 425 W Capitol Avenue, Little Rock, AR 72201 501-324-6291

California
101 El Camino Boulevard Suite 105, Sacramento, CA 95815 916-566-7470

5675 Ruffin Road Suite 330, San Diego, CA 92123 619-557-5904

71 Stevenson Street Suite 420, San Francisco, CA 94105 415-975-4316

Colorado
1391 Speer Boulevard Suite 210, Denver, CO 80204-2552 303-844-5285

7935 E Prentice Avenue Suite 209, Englewood, CO 80111-2714 303-843-4500

Connecticut
Clark Building 1057 Broad Street 4th Floor, Bridgeport, CT 06604 203-579-5581

Federal Office Building 450 Main Street Room 613, Hartford, CT 06103 860-240-3152

Delaware
Caleb Boggs Federal Building 844 King Street Room 2209, Wilmington, DE 19801 302-573-6518

Florida
5807 Breckenridge Parkway Suite A, Tampa, FL 33610 813-626-1177

Building H100 8040 Peters Road, Fort Lauderdale, FL 33324 954-424-0242

Ribault Building Suite 227 1851 Executive Center Drive, Jacksonville, FL 32207 904-232-2895

Georgia
2400 Herodian Way Suite 250, Smyrna, GA 30080-2968 770-984-8700

450 Mall Boulevard Suite J, Savannah, GA 31406-1418 912-652-4393

Building 7 Suite 110 2183 N Lake Parkway La Vista Perimeter Office Park, Tucker, GA 30084-4154 770-493-6644

Hawaii
300 Ala Moana Boulevard Suite 5-146, Honolulu, HI 96850 808-541-2685

Idaho
1150 N Curtis Road Suite 201, Boise, ID 83703 208-321-2960

Illinois
11 Executive Drive Suite 11, Fairview Heights, IL 62208 618-632-8612

1600 167th Street Suite 12, Calumet City, IL 60409 708-891-3800

2918 W Willow Knolls Road, Peoria, IL 61614 309-671-7033

365 Smoke Tree Plaza N, Aurora, IL 60542 630-896-8700

701 Lee Street Suite 950, Des Plaines, IL 60016 847-803-4800

Indiana
U.S. Post Office & Courthouse 46 E Ohio Street Room 423, Indianapolis, IN 46204 317-226-7290

Iowa
210 Walnut Street Room 815, Des Moines, IA 50309 515-284-4794

Kansas
271 W 3rd Street Room 400, Wichita, KS 67202 316-269-6644

8600 Farley Suite 105, Overland Park, KS 66212-4677 913-385-7380

Kentucky
U.S. Department of Labor-OSHA John C. Watts Federal Building 330 W Broadway Room 108, Frankfort, KY 40601-1922 502-227-7024

Louisiana
9100 Bluebonnet Centre Boulevard Suite 201, Baton Rouge, LA 70809 225-389-0474

Maine
202 Harlow Street Room 211, Bangor, ME 04401-4906 207-941-8177

Edmund S Muskie Federal Building 40 Western Avenue Room G26, Augusta, ME 04330 207-626-9160

Maryland
1099 Winterson Road Suite 140, Linthicum, MD 21090 410-865-2055, 2056

Massachusetts
1441 Main Street Room 550, Springfield, MA 01103-1493 413-785-0123

639 Granite Street 4th Floor, Braintree, MA 02184 617-565-6924

Valley Office Park 13 Branch Street 1st Floor, Methuen, MA 01844 617-565-8110

Michigan
801 S Waverly Road Suite 306, Lansing, MI 48917-4200 517-327-0904

Minnesota
300 S 4th Street Suite 1205, Minneapolis, MN 55415 612-664-5460

Mississippi
3780 Interstate 55 N Suite 210, Jackson, MS 39211-6323 601-965-4606

Missouri
6200 Connecticut Avenue Suite 100, Kansas City, MO 64120 816-483-9531

Programs Administered by Regional - State - Local Offices

U.S. Department of Labor-OSHA 911 Washington Avenue Room 420, Saint Louis, MO 63101 314-425-4249

Montana
2900 4th Avenue N Suite 303, Billings, MT 59101 406-247-7494

Nebraska
Overland-Wolf Building Room 100 6910 Pacific Street, Omaha, NE 68106 402-221-3182

Nevada
Federal Building Room 204 705 N Plaza, Carson City, NV 89701 775-885-6963

New Hampshire
55 Pleasant Street Room 3901, Concord, NH 03301 603-225-1629

New Jersey
299 Cherry Hill Road Suite 304, Parsippany, NJ 07054 973-263-1003
500 Route 17 S 2nd Floor, Hasbrouck Heights, NJ 07604 201-288-1700
Marlton Executive Park 701 Route 73 S Building 2 Suite 120, Marlton, NJ 08053 856-757-5181
Plaza 35 Suite 205 1030 Saint Georges Avenue, Avenel, NJ 07001 732-750-3270

New Mexico
Western Bank Building 505 Marquette Avenue NW Suite 820, Albuquerque, NM 87102 505-248-5302

New York
1400 Old Country Road Suite 208, Westbury, NY 11590 516-334-3344
201 Varick Street Room 905, New York, NY 10014 212-620-3200
3300 Vickery Road, North Syracuse, NY 13212 315-451-0808
42-40 Bell Boulevard, Bayside, NY 11361 718-279-9060
5360 Genesee Street, Bowmansville, NY 14026 716-684-3891
660 White Plains Road 4th Floor, Tarrytown, NY 10591-5107 914-524-7510
John Tomich Federal Building 401 New Karner Road Suite 300, Albany, NY 12205-3809 518-464-4338

North Carolina
Century Station Federal Building Room 438 300 Fayetteville Mall, Raleigh, NC 27601-9998 919-856-4770

North Dakota
Federal Office Building 1640 E Capitol Avenue, Bismarck, ND 58501 701-250-4521

Ohio
Federal Office Building 200 N High Street Room 620, Columbus, OH 43215 614-469-5582
Federal Office Building Room 4028 36 Triangle Park Drive, Cincinnati, OH 45246 513-841-4132
Federal Office Building Room 899 1240 E 9th Street, Cleveland, OH 44199 216-522-3818
Ohio Building 420 Madison Avenue Suite 600, Toledo, OH 43604 419-259-7542

Oklahoma
55 N Robinson Suite 315, Oklahoma City, OK 73102 405-278-9560

Oregon
1220 SW 3rd Avenue Room 640, Portland, OR 97204 503-326-2251

Pennsylvania
3939 W Ridge Road Suite B-12, Erie, PA 16506 814-833-5758
49 N Progress Avenue Progress Plaza, Harrisburg, PA 17109 717-782-3902
7 N Wilkes-Barre Boulevard Suite 410, Wilkes-Barre, PA 18702 570-826-6538
850 N 5th Street, Allentown, PA 18102 610-776-0592
Federal Building Room 1428 1000 Liberty Avenue, Pittsburgh, PA 15522-4101 412-395-4903
U.S. Customs House Room 242 2nd & Chestnut Streets, Philadelphia, PA 19106 215-597-4955

Puerto Rico
BBV Plaza Building 1510 FD Roosevelt Avenue Suite 5 B, Guaynabo, PR 00968 787-277-1560

Region I
Marthe Kent, Regional Administrator | Department of Labor OSHA JFK Federal Building Low Rise Building Room E-340, Boston, MA 02114 617-565-9860

Region II
Robert Kulick, Regional Administrator | Department of Labor OSHA 201 Varick Street Room 670, New York, NY 10014 212-337-2378

Region III
John Hermanson, Regional Administrator | The Curtis Center – Suite 740 W 170 Independence Mall W, Philadelphia, PA 19106-3309 215-861-4900

Region IV
Cindy Coe, Regional Administrator | 61 Forsyth Street SW Room 6 T50, Atlanta, GA 30303 404-562-2300

Region V
Michael Connors, Regional Administrator | Department of Labor OSHA 230 S Dearborn Street 32nd Floor Room 3244, Chicago, IL 60604 312-353-2220

Region VI
Dean McDaniel, Regional Administrator | Department of Labor OSHA 525 Griffin Street Room 602, Dallas, TX 75202 214-767-4731

Region VII
Charles E. Adkins, Regional Administrator | Department of Labor OSHA City Center Square 1100 Main Street Suite 800, Kansas City, MO 64105 816-426-5861

Region VIII
Greg Baxter, Regional Administrator | Department of Labor OSHA 1999 Broadway Street Room 1690, Denver, CO 80202-5716 303-844-1600

Region IX

Ken Atha, Regional Administrator | Department of Labor OSHA 71 Stevenson Street Room 420, San Francisco, CA 94105 415-975-4310

Rhode Island

380 Westminster Mall Room 243, Providence, RI 02903 401-528-4669

South Carolina

1835 Assembly Street Room 1468, Columbia, SC 29201 803-765-5904

Tennessee

2002 Richard Jones Road Suite C-205, Nashville, TN 37215-2809 615-781-5423

Texas

17625 El Camino Real Suite 400, Houston, TX 77058 281-286-0583

507 N Sam Houston Parkway E Suite 400, Houston, TX 77060 281-591-2438

700 E San Antonio Street Room C-408, El Paso, TX 79901 915-534-6251

8344 E R L Thornton Freeway Suite 420, Dallas, TX 75228 214-320-2400

903 San Jacinto Boulevard Suite 319, Austin, TX 78701 512-916-5783

Corpus Christi Area Office U.S. Department of Labor OSHA Wilson Plaza W 606 N Carancahua Suite 700, Corpus Christi, TX 78476 361-888-3420

Federal Building Room 806 1205 Texas Avenue, Lubbock, TX 79401 806-472-7681

N Star II Suite 302 8713 Airport Freeway, Fort Worth, TX 76180-7610 817-428-2470

Utah

1781 S 300 W PO Box 65200, Salt Lake City, UT 84165-0200 801-487-0521

Virginia

200 Granby Street Room 614, Norfolk, VA 23510 757-441-3820

Washington

505 106th Avenue NE Suite 302, Bellevue, WA 98004 206-553-7520

West Virginia

405 Capitol Street Suite 407, Charleston, WV 25301 304-347-5937

Wisconsin

1310 W Clairmont Avenue, Eau Claire, WI 54701 715-832-9019

1648 Tri Park Way, Appleton, WI 54914 920-734-4521

4802 E Broadway, Madison, WI 53716 608-441-5388

Henry S Reuss Building 310 Wisconsin Avenue Suite 1180, Milwaukee, WI 53203 414-297-3315

DOL17.502 | OCCUPATIONAL SAFETY AND HEALTH SUSAN HARWOOD TRAINING GRANTS
"Susan Harwood Training Grants"

Award: Project Grants

Purpose: To provide occupational safety and health training and education to employees and employers, particularly in the recognition, avoidance and abatement of workplace hazards.

Applicant Eligibility: Non-profit Organizations including qualifying labor unions, community-based and faith-based Organizations, employer associations that are not an agency of a state or local government, state or local government-supported Institutions of higher education, Indian Tribes, tribal Organizations, Alaska Native entities, Indian-controlled Organizations serving Indians, and Native Hawaiian Organizations may apply.

Beneficiary Eligibility: Individuals employed in workplaces that receive training and/or educational services under grants.

Award Range/Average: Fiscal Year 2018 grants ranged from $35,000 to $285,000.

Funding: (Training) FY 18 $10,537,000.00; FY 19 est $10,537,000.00; FY 20 est Estimate Not Available

HQ: 200 Constitution Avenue NW, Washington, DC 20210

Phone: 847-759-7769 | Email: robertson.donna@dol.gov

http://www.osha.gov

DOL17.503 | OCCUPATIONAL SAFETY AND HEALTH STATE PROGRAM
"State Plan Grant Awards"

Award: Project Grants

Purpose: Funds federally approved comprehensive State occupational safety and health programs that are "at least as effective" as the Federal program.

Applicant Eligibility: Designated State agencies which have federally approved occupational safety and health plans.

Beneficiary Eligibility: Any employer, worker or their representative from a business engaged in interstate commerce except those under jurisdiction of other Federal agencies.

Programs Administered by Regional - State - Local Offices

Award Range/Average: Fiscal year 2019 grants ranged from $215,000 to $29,078,000. These awards represent approximately 50 percent of the total program cost.

Funding: (Salaries and Expenses) FY 18 $100,850,000.00; FY 19 est $102,350,000.00; FY 20 est $102,350,000.00

HQ: 200 Constitution Avenue NW, Washington, DC 20210

> Phone: 202-693-2423 | Email: krivitskiy.aleks@dol.gov
> http://www.osha.gov

DOL17.504 | CONSULTATION AGREEMENTS
"Consultation Grant Program"

Award: Cooperative Agreements

Purpose: Funds consultative workplace safety and health services, targeting smaller employers with more hazardous operations.

Applicant Eligibility: Designated State agencies which have been authorized by the Governor to enter into a Cooperative Agreement with full power to perform the obligations funded therein and to expend Federal funds as well as State funds as required.

Beneficiary Eligibility: Any private employer operating within a State, with priority given to smaller employers with the more hazardous operations.

Award Range/Average: Fiscal year 2019 grants ranged from $246,000 to $5,527,000. These awards represent approximately 90 percent of total program costs.

Funding: (Salaries and Expenses) FY 18 $59,500,000.00; FY 19 est $59,500,000.00; FY 20 est $59,500,000.00

HQ: 200 Constitution Avenue NW N-3419, Washington, DC 20210

> Phone: 202-693-2423 | Email: krivitskiy.aleks@dol.gov
> http://www.osha.gov

OFFICE OF LABOR-MANAGEMENT STANDARDS
Regional – State – Local Offices

California
915 Wilshire Boulevard Suite 910, Los Angeles, CA 90017 213-534-6405

District of Columbia
375 E Street SW, Washington, DC 20024 202-513-7300

Georgia
Atlanta Federal Building Room 8B85 61 Forsyth Street SW, Atlanta, GA 30303-2219 404-562-2083

Illinois
Federal Office Building Suite 774 230 S Dearborn Street, Chicago, IL 60604-1505 312-596-7160

Louisiana
600 S Maestri Place Room 604, New Orleans, LA 70130 504-589-6174

Massachusetts
JFK Federal Building Room E-365, Boston, MA 02203-0002 617-624-6690

Michigan
211 W Fort Street Suite 1313, Detroit, MI 48226-3237 313-226-6200

Missouri
1222 Spruce Street Suite 9 109E, Saint Louis, MO 63103-2830 314-539-2667

New York
130 S Elmwood Street Room 510, Buffalo, NY 14202-2465 716-842-2900

201 Varick Street Suite 878, New York, NY 10014 646-264-3190

Ohio
Federal Office Building Suite 831 1240 E 9th Street, Cleveland, OH 44199-2053 216-357-5455

Pennsylvania
Federal Office Building Room 1411 1000 Liberty Avenue, Pittsburgh, PA 15222-4004 412-395-6925

The Curtis Center 170 S Independence Mall W Room 760W, Philadelphia, PA 19106-3310 215-861-4818

Tennessee
233 Cumberland Bend Drive Suite 110, Nashville, TN 37228-1809 615-736-5906

Texas
A Maceo Smith Federal Building Suite 300 525 Griffin Street, Dallas, TX 75202-5007 972-850-2500

REGIONAL OFFICES

California
90 7th Street Room 2825, San Francisco, CA 94103-6701 415-625-2661

Colorado
1244 Speer Boulevard Room 415, Denver, CO 80204
720-264-3232

District of Columbia
375 E Street SW, Washington, DC 20024 202-513-7300

Ohio
36 E 7th Street Room 2550, Cincinnati, OH 45202-3168
513-684-6840

Washington
300 5th Avenue Room 1290, Seattle, WA 98104-3308
206-398-8099

Wisconsin
310 W Wisconsin Avenue Room 1160 W, Milwaukee, WI
53203-2213 414-297-1504

DOL17.309 | LABOR ORGANIZATION REPORTS
"Labor-Management Reporting and Disclosure Act (LMRDA)"

Award: Advisory Services and Counseling; Dissemination of Technical Information; Investigation of Complaints

Purpose: To provide for the reporting and disclosure of financial transactions and administrative practices of labor organizations, employers, labor consultants and others required to report under the Labor-Management Reporting and Disclosure Act (LMRDA).

Applicant Eligibility: Officers of unions may obtain assistance in preparing reports or otherwise complying with the Act. Union members or union Organizations may request assistance in investigating alleged violations. All reports required to be filed are available for inspection and disclosure to the general public.

Beneficiary Eligibility: Union officers, union members, union organizations. All reports required to be filed are available for inspection and disclosure to the general public.

Award Range/Average: Not Applicable.

Funding: (Salaries and Expenses) FY 17 $39,332.00; FY 18 est $41,392.00; FY 19 est $46,634.00

HQ: OLMS 200 Constitution Avenue NW, Room N 5119, Washington, DC 20011
Phone: 202-693-1182 | Email: willertz.stephen@dol.gov
http://www.dol.gov/olms

OFFICE OF SURFACE MINING, RECLAMATION AND ENFORCEMENT
Regional – State – Local Offices

Alabama
Birmingham Field Office 135 Gemini Circle Suite 215, Homewood, AL 35209 205-290-7282

Colorado
U.S. Department of the Interior Western Regional Coordinating Center 1999 Broadway Suite 3320, Denver, CO 80202-5733 303-844-1401

District of Columbia
U.S. Department of the Interior 1951 Constitution Avenue NW, Washington, DC 20240 202-208-4006

Illinois
U.S. Department of the Interior 501 Belle Street Room 216, Alton, IL 62002 618-463-6460

Kentucky
Lexington Field Office 2675 Regency Road, Lexington, KY 40503-2922 859-233-2494

New Mexico
Albuquerque Field Office 505 Marquette Avenue NW Suite 1200, Albuquerque, NM 87102 505-248-5070

Office of Surface Mining
Indianapolis Field Office 575 N Pennsylvania Street Room 301, Indianapolis, IN 46204 317-226-6700

Oklahoma
Tulsa Field Office 5100 E Skelly Drive Suite 470, Tulsa, OK 74135 918-581-6431

Pennsylvania
Harrisburg Field Office 415 Market Street Suite 3C Harrisburg Transportation Center, Harrisburg, PA 17101 717-782-4036
U.S. Department of the Interior Appalachian Regional Coordinating Center Three Parkway Center, Pittsburgh, PA 15220 412-937-2828

Tennessee
Knoxville Field Office 530 Gay Street SW Suite 500, Knoxville, TN 37902 423-545-4103

Virginia
Big Stone Gap Field Office Powell Valley Square Shopping Center 1941 Neeley Road Suite 201 Compartment 116, Big Stone Gap, VA 24219 540-523-4303

Programs Administered by Regional - State - Local Offices

West Virginia
Charleston Field Office 1027 Virginia Street E, Charleston, WV 25301 304-347-7162

Wyoming
Casper Field Office Federal Building 100 E B Street Room 2128, Casper, WY 82601-1918 307-261-6555

DOI15.250 | REGULATION OF SURFACE COAL MINING AND SURFACE EFFECTS OF UNDERGROUND COAL MINING
"Regulatory Grant Program"

Award: Project Grants; Direct Payments for Specified Use

Purpose: To aid the States and Tribes with active coal mining in administering approved regulatory programs.

Applicant Eligibility: The State must have an approved Program to regulate surface coal mining and a designated State agency to receive and administer grants.

Beneficiary Eligibility: State agencies responsible for regulation, reclamation and enforcement of provisions protecting the environment from negative effects of coal mining operations.

Award Range/Average: $38,343 to $3,034,757; $615,988. (FY 2017 final distribution not yet awarded.)

Funding: (Project Grants) FY 18 $68,590,000.00; FY 19 est $68,590,000.00; FY 20 est $68,590,000.00

HQ: Department of the Interior 1849 C Street NW, Room 4545, Washington, DC 20240
   Phone: 202-208-2868 | Email: ynorman@osmre.gov
   http://www.osmre.gov

DOI15.252 | ABANDONED MINE LAND RECLAMATION (AMLR)
"Abandoned Mine Lands (AML) Program"

Award: Formula Grants; Project Grants

Purpose: The key aspect is to protect the public, health, safety and general welfare, and restore land, water and environmental resources affected by coal and non-coal mining practices.

Applicant Eligibility: The AML Program is restricted to states with (1) an approved coal mining regulatory Program, (2) lands eligible for reclamation, and (3) active coal mining operations within their borders that are paying coal reclamation fees into the Abandoned Mine Reclamation Fund; and to Federally-recognized Indian Tribes with (4) eligible lands, and (5) active mining operations paying fees into the Fund. An eligible state or Indian tribe may submit a reclamation plan to the Office of Surface Mining Reclamation and Enforcement (OSMRE) for approval. The AML Pilot Program is restricted to six Appalachian states with the highest amount of inventoried priority coal problems as described in paragraphs (1) and (2) of section 403(a) of SMCRA. In addition AML Pilot funds are also available to Federally recognized Indian Tribes without regards for their certified or uncertified status under SMCRA.

Beneficiary Eligibility: Citizens and the general public are protected from physical hazards and benefit from the reclamation of abandoned mine lands and polluted waters by reducing exposure to safety and health risks.

Award Range/Average: The range of financial assistance is $126,440 to $97,794,527; $11,499

Funding: (Project Grants) FY 17 $321,979,595.00; FY 18 est $327,600,000.00; FY 19 Estimate Not Available

HQ: Division of Reclamation Support Department of the Interior 1849 C Street NW, Washington, DC 20240
   Phone: 202-208-2868
   http://www.osmre.gov

DOI15.253 | NOT-FOR-PROFIT AMD RECLAMATION
"Watershed Cooperative Agreement Program (WCAP)"

Award: Cooperative Agreements

Purpose: It seeks applications from eligible applicants to restore streams affected by Acid Mine Drainage (AMD) to a level that will support a diverse biological community and provide recreational opportunities for the community.

Applicant Eligibility: Recipients must be not-for-profit IRS 501(c) (3) status Organizations. Federal, state, local Governments, colleges, and universities are not eligible to receive direct funding.

Beneficiary Eligibility: Communities impacted by streams polluted by AMD will benefit from this program.

Award Range/Average: The approximate average amount of the financial assistance is $100,000

Funding: (Cooperative Agreements) FY 18 $942,953.00; FY 19 est $$3,500,000.00; FY 20 est Estimate Not Available

HQ: Department of the Interior 1849 C Street NW, Washington, DC 20240
    Phone: 202-208-2868 | Email: ynorman@osmre.gov
    http://www.osmre.gov

DOI15.254 | OSM/VISTA AMERICORPS
"OSMRE/AmeriCorps Program; OSMRE/VISTA Program; OSMRE Semester Internship Program"

Award: Cooperative Agreements

Purpose: The purpose is to promote and stimulate public purposes such as education, job training, development of responsible citizenship and productive community involvement. The program is designed to further the understanding and appreciation of natural and cultural resources through the involvement of youth and young adults. It is also designed to continue the longstanding efforts of OSMRE to provide opportunities for public service, youth employment, minority youth development, training, and participation of young adults in accomplishing environmental-related work.

Applicant Eligibility: The not-for-profit sponsor Organization will be responsible for the daily operation of the OSMRE/ VISTA Program, working closely with OSMRE to ensure the Program aligns with the mission of the Bureau. Eligible sponsor Organizations will have, at minimum, the following to be considered eligible: Have a 501(c)(3) status Have access to AmeriCorps positions through partnership with the Corporation for National and Community Service, or other intermediary Organization Have the Organizational capacity to oversee participants in the field and across the country.

Beneficiary Eligibility: Youth and local communities that benefit from reclamation of abandoned mine lands; Youth interested in gaining experience in a Federal agency.

Award Range/Average: Range and Average of Financial Assistance for OSMRE's Youth Program is $80,000 - $625K OSMRE/ VISTA Program: Est. Average of $200,000 OSMRE Semester Internship Program: Est. Average of $90,350.76 OSMRE/ AmeriCorps Program: Est. Average of $491,250

Funding: (Direct Payments for Specified Use) FY 18 $638,201.00; FY 19 est $925,000.00; FY 20 est Estimate Not Available

HQ: 1849 C Street NW, Room 4545 Main Interior Building, Washington, DC 20240
    Phone: 202-208-2585 | Email: ynorman@osmre.gov
    http://www.osmre.gov

DOI15.255 | SCIENCE AND TECHNOLOGY PROJECTS RELATED TO COAL MINING AND RECLAMATION
"Technology Development and Transfer Program"

Award: Cooperative Agreements

Purpose: Supports applied Science projects that develop and demonstrate improved technologies to address public safety and environmental issues related to coal mining and reclamation of abandoned mined lands and polluted waters.

Applicant Eligibility: Applied Science projects: Recipients may be any of the following: public, private, or non-profit entities; Federal, state, local or tribal Governments; and colleges and universities located in the United States. Underground Mine Map projects: Recipients may be any state or Indian tribe where coal mining or reclamation activities authorized under SMCRA are occurring. Mine Drainage Technology Initiative projects: Recipients may be any of the following: public, private, or non-profit entities; Federal, state, local or tribal Governments; and colleges and universities located in the United States.

Beneficiary Eligibility: Communities impacted by coal mining and reclamation of the land after mining.

Award Range/Average: Award amounts ranges from $116K to $200K.

HQ: 1849 C Street NW, PO Box 4550, Washington, DC 20240
    Phone: 202-208-2895 | Email: hpayne@osmre.gov
    http://www.osmre.gov

Programs Administered by Regional - State - Local Offices

RISK MANAGEMENT AGENCY
Regional – State – Local Offices

REGIONAL OFFICES

Billings
Doug Hagel, Director | 3490 Gabel Road Suite 100, Billings, MT 59102-6440 406-657-6447

Central Region
Alvin Gilmore, Director | 6501 Beacon Drive, Kansas City, MO 64131 816-926-7963

Davis
Jeff Yasui, Director | 430 G Street Suite 4168, Davis, CA 95616-4168 530-792-5871

Eastern Region
Jessica Dedrick, Director | 4405 Bland Road Suite 165, Raleigh, NC 27609 919-875-4930

Jackson
Rock Davis, Director | 803 Liberty Road, Jackson, MS 39232 601-965-4771

Midwest Region
Ronie Griffin, Director | 6045 Lakeside Boulevard, Indianapolis, IN 46278 317-290-3050

Northern Region
Scott Tincher, Director | 3440 Federal Drive Suite 200, Eagan, MN 55122-3500 651-452-1688, Ext. 222

Oklahoma
Debra J. Bouziden, Director | 205 NW 63rd Street Suite 170, Oklahoma City, OK 73116-8209 405-879-2710

Raleigh
Scott Lucas, Director | 4405 Bland Road Suite 160, Raleigh, NC 27609 919-875-4880

Saint Paul
Duane Voy, Director | 30 7th Street E Suite 1890, Saint Paul, MN 55101-4901 651-290-3304, Ext. 233

Southern Region
Billy M. Pryor, Director | 1111 W Mockingbird Lane Suite 280, Dallas, TX 75247-5016 214-767-7700

Spokane
Dave Paul, Director | 11707 E Sprague Avenue, Spokane Valley, WA 99206-6125 509-228-6322

Springfield
Brain Frieden, Director | 3500 Wabash Avenue, Springfield, IL 62711 217-241-6600, Ext. 113

Topeka
Rebecca Davis, Director | 2651 SW Wanamaker Road Suite 201, Topeka, KS 66614-4971 785-228-5512

Valdosta
Diane Amera, Director | 106 S Patterson Street Suite 250, Valdosta, GA 31601-5673 912-242-3044

Western Region
Susan Choy, Director | 430 G Street Suite 4167, Davis, CA 95616-4167 530-792-5850

USDA10.450 | CROP INSURANCE

Award: Insurance
Purpose: The Risk Management Agency provides risk-management strategies to America's agricultural producers and strengthens the economic stability of agricultural producers and rural communities.
Applicant Eligibility: Unless otherwise restricted by the insurance policy, owners or operators of farmland, who have an insurable interest in a crop in a county where insurance is offered on that crop, are eligible for insurance.
Beneficiary Eligibility: This program is excluded from coverage under OMB Circular No. A-87.
Award Range/Average: Level of assistance varies according to policy, crop and indemnities paid.
Funding: (Insurance) FY 18 $10,165,923,642.00; FY 19 est $10,954,000,000.00; FY 20 est $12,505,000,000.00
HQ: PO Box 419205, Stop 0801, Kansas City, MO 64141-6205
   Phone: 816-926-6142 | Email: david.zanoni@usda.gov
   http://www.rma.usda.gov

USDA10.458 | CROP INSURANCE EDUCATION IN TARGETED STATES
"Targeted States"

Award: Cooperative Agreements
Purpose: To provide crop insurance education and information to U.S. agricultural producers to the Targeted States of U.S. such as Alaska, Connecticut, Delaware, Hawaii, Vermont, West Virginia, etc.
Applicant Eligibility: Eligible applicants include State departments of agriculture, universities, non-profit agricultural Organizations, and other public or private Organizations with the capacity to lead a local Program of crop insurance education for farmers and ranchers in a Targeted State. Individuals are eligible applicants. Although an applicant may be eligible to

compete for an award based on its status as an eligible entity, other factors may exclude an applicant from receiving federal assistance under this Program (e.g. debarment and suspension; a determination of non-performance on a prior contract, cooperative agreement, grant or partnership; a determination of a violation of applicable ethical standards).

Beneficiary Eligibility: The ultimate beneficiaries of this education program are agricultural producers in the Targeted States. Applicants receiving awards will ensure that such producers receive effective crop insurance education and information either directly or through agribusiness professionals that can impart crop insurance information to producers.

Award Range/Average: $0 to $613,000 per agreement as announced in the Request for Applications. Average $207,716

Funding: (Cooperative Agreements) FY 18 $4,557,000.00; FY 19 est $0.00; FY 20 est $0.00

HQ: 1400 Independence Avenue SW, Room 6717-S USDA S Building, Washington, DC 20250-0808

Phone: 202-720-1416 | Email: young.kim@rma.usda.gov

http://www.rma.usda.gov

USDA10.460 | RISK MANAGEMENT EDUCATION PARTNERSHIPS

Award: Cooperative Agreements

Purpose: To provide training and activities in the management of production, marketing, financial to the U.S. agricultural producers, especially for those not insured with Federal crop insurance.

Applicant Eligibility: Eligible applicants include State departments of agriculture, universities, non-profit agricultural Organization and other public or private Organizations with the capacity to lead a local Program of risk management education for farmers and ranchers in an RMA Region. Individuals are not eligible applicants. Although an applicant may be eligible to compete for an award based on its status as an eligible entity, other factors may exclude an applicant from receiving Federal assistance under this Program (e.g. debarment and suspension; a determination of non-performance on a prior contract, cooperative agreement, grant, or partnership; a determination of a violation of applicable ethical standards.

Beneficiary Eligibility: The ultimate beneficiaries of this education program are agricultural producers with a priority of producers of crops not insurable by Federal crop insurance, specialty crops, and undeserved commodities. Applicants receiving awards will ensure that such producers receive effective risk management education, information and outreach activities that can impact the risk management decision making.

Award Range/Average: Fiscal year 2018, RMA awarded approximately 56 cooperative agreements with an average of $109,051 (the lowest amount being $16,045 and the highest award at $290,430).

Funding: (Cooperative Agreements) FY 18 $6,106,852.00; FY 19 est $0.00; FY 20 est $0.00

HQ: 1400 Independence Avenue SW, Room 6717-S USDA S Building, Washington, DC 20250-0808

Phone: 202-720-1416 | Email: young.kim@rma.usda.gov

http://www.rma.usda.gov

SSA96.006 | SUPPLEMENTAL SECURITY INCOME

Award: Direct Payments for Specified Use; Direct Payments With Unrestricted Use

Purpose: The program ensures that physically-challenged people aged 65 and above receive a better income when it is below the specified level.

Applicant Eligibility: To be found disabled for SSI purposes: an individual age 18 or older must be unable to perform any substantial gainful activity by reason of any medically determinable physical or mental impairment which can be expected to result in death or which has lasted or can be expected to last for a continuous period of at least 12 months; an individual under age 18 must have a medically determinable physical or mental impairment or combination of impairments that causes marked and severe functional limitations, and that can be expected to cause death or that has lasted or can be expected to last for a continuous period of at least 12 months. An individual under age 18 who files a new application for benefits and is engaging in substantial gainful activity will not be considered disabled. To be found blind for SSI purposes, an individual of any age must be "statutorily blind. " This means central visual acuity of 20/200 or less in the better eye with use of a correcting lens. The eligibility of an individual who has attained age 65 or who is blind or disabled is determined on the basis of an assessment of the individual's monthly income and resources, citizenship or alien status, U.S. residency, and certain other eligibility requirements. In determining a month's income, the first $20 of Social Security or other unearned income is not counted. An additional $65 of earned income ($85 if the person had no unearned income) received in a month plus one-half of the remainder above $65 (or $85) also is not counted. If, after these (and other) exclusions, an individual's countable income, effective January 2018, is less than $750 per month ($1,125 for a couple, both of whom are aged, blind or disabled) and countable resources are less than $2,000 ($3,000 for a couple), the individual may be eligible for payments. The values of household goods, personal effects, an automobile, life insurance, and property needed for self support are, if within limits set out in regulations, excluded in determining value of resources. Burial spaces for an individual and immediate family and

Programs Administered by Regional - State - Local Offices

burial funds, up to $1,500 each for an individual and spouse, are excluded from resources. The value of a home which serves as the principal place of residence is also excluded in resource valuation.

Beneficiary Eligibility: Individuals who have attained age 65 or are blind or disabled, who continue to meet the income and resources tests, citizenship/qualified alien status, U.S. residence, and certain other requirements. Eligibility may continue for beneficiaries who engage in substantial gainful activity despite disabling physical or mental impairments.

Award Range/Average: Monthly Federal cash payments range from $1 to $750 for an aged, blind, or disabled individual who does not have an eligible spouse, and from $1 to $1,125 for an aged, blind, or disabled individual and an eligible spouse. These rates became effective January 2018. The average Federal monthly benefit payment for January 2018 was $536.

Funding: (Direct Payments with Unrestricted Use) FY 17 $54,600,000,000.00; FY 18 est Estimate Not Available FY 19 est Estimate Not Available

HQ: 6401 Security Boulevard, Baltimore, MD 21235

　　Phone: 800-772-1213

　　http://www.socialsecurity.gov

SSA96.007 | SOCIAL SECURITY RESEARCH AND DEMONSTRATION
"SSA Research and Demonstration"

Award: Project Grants

Purpose: The program's purpose is to conduct research on social, economic and demographic topics related to the Social Security Old Age, Survivors and Disability Insurance and Supplemental Security Income programs while focusing on the current and future well-being of their beneficiaries. It also conducts research on rehabilitating beneficiaries and encouraging them to return to work.

Applicant Eligibility: Applicants applying for grant funds may include research Organizations, associations of research Organizations, State and local Governments, educational Institutions, hospitals, public and private Organizations, and nonprofit and profit Organizations. Private individuals are not eligible to apply. Profit Organizations may apply with the understanding that no grant funds may be paid as profit to grant recipients. Profit is considered any amount in excess of the allowable costs of the grant recipient. A profit Organization is a corporation or other legal entity that is organized or operated for the profit or benefit of its shareholders or other owners and must be distinguishable or legally separable from that of an individual acting on his/her own behalf.

Beneficiary Eligibility: State agencies, local governments, educational institutions, hospitals, nonprofit organizations, and profit organizations are eligible to apply for grant funding.

Award Range/Average: Range: $275,000 to $2,065,938 and Average $3,300,000.

Funding: (Salaries and Expenses) FY 17 $11,293,230.00; FY 18 est $11,293,230.00; FY 19 est $10,695,000.00

HQ: Social Security Administration Office of Acquisition and Grants 6401 Security Boulevard, 1540 Robert M Ball Building, Baltimore, MD 21235

　　Phone: 410-965-9534 | Email: dionne.mitchell@ssa.gov

　　http://www.ssa.gov

SSA96.008 | SOCIAL SECURITY-WORK INCENTIVES PLANNING AND ASSISTANCE PROGRAM
"SSA Work Incentives Planning and Assistance (WIPA) Program or Work Incentives Outreach Progra"

Award: Project Grants

Purpose: The Work Incentives Planning and Assistance Program complies with the Ticket-to-Work and Work Incentives Improvement Act of 1999 and Social Security Protection Act of 2004 to support beneficiaries who want to return to work to make a successful and profitable transition to the workforce. It also acts as a repository for information about benefits counseling and work incentive services.

Applicant Eligibility: Applicants applying for cooperative agreement funds may include State or local Governments (excluding any State administering the State Medicaid Program), public or private Organizations, or nonprofit or for-profit Organizations (for-profit Organizations may apply with the understanding that no cooperative agreement funds may be paid as profit to any awardee), as well as Native American tribal Organizations that the Commissioner determines is qualified to provide work incentives planning and assistance to all SSDI and SSI beneficiaries with disabilities, within the targeted geographic area. These may include Centers for Independent Living established under Title VII of the Rehabilitation Act of 1973, protection and advocacy Organizations, Native American tribal entities, client assistance Programs established in accordance with Section 112 of the Rehabilitation Act of 1973, State Developmental Disabilities Councils established in accordance with Section 124 of the Developmental Disabilities Assistance and Bill of Rights Act, and State agencies administering the State Program funded under Part A of Title IV of the Act. The Commissioner may also award a cooperative agreement to a State or local Workforce Investment Board, a Department of Labor (DOL) One-Stop Career Center System established under the Workforce Improvement Act of 1998, or a State Vocational Rehabilitation agency. Cooperative agreements may not be awarded to any individual, the Social Security Administration Field Offices, any State agency administrating the State Medicaid Program under Title XIX of the Act, any entity that the Commissioner determines would have a conflict of interest if the entity were to receive a cooperative agreement under the Work Incentives Planning and Assistance (WIPA) Program or any Organization described in Section 501(c)(4) of the Internal Revenue Code of 1968 that engages in lobbying (in accordance with Section 18 of the Lobbying Disclosure Act of 1995, 2 U.S.C. 1611).

Beneficiary Eligibility: WIPA projects serve beneficiaries who are age 14 and older, and receive any of the following benefits based on their own disabilities: Social Security Disability Insurance Benefits; Childhood Disability Benefits; Disabled Widow(er)s Benefits; SSI based on blindness or disability; Medicare under the Extended Period of Medicare Coverage (for former disability beneficiaries performing substantial work); Medicaid under Section 1619(b) of the Social Security Act (for SSI beneficiaries ineligible for payment due to work income); A State supplementary SSI payment (even if the beneficiary is not due a Federal SSI payment); or; Medicare coverage based on disability and Medicare qualified government employment.

Award Range/Average: Range $100,000 to $300,000, average $235,940

Funding: (Salaries and Expenses) FY 17 $19,583,013.00; FY 18 est $19,583,013.00; FY 19 est $19,583,013.00

HQ: Social Security Administration Office of Acquisition and Grants 6401 Security Boulevard, 1540 Robert M Ball Building, Baltimore, MD 21235

Phone: 410-965-9534 | Email: dionne.mitchell@ssa.gov

http://www.ssa.gov

SSA96.009 | SOCIAL SECURITY STATE GRANTS FOR WORK INCENTIVES ASSISTANCE TO DISABLED BENEFICIARIES
"Protection and Advocacy (P&A) Systems: PABSS and SPSSB"

Award: Project Grants

Purpose: The Protection and Advocacy for Beneficiaries of Social Security provide information and legal support to help people resolve their disability employment-related concerns, while the Strengthening Protections of Social Security Beneficiaries program pays for performance reviews and monitoring the representative payees.

Applicant Eligibility: Applicants applying for grant funds are limited to State protection and advocacy systems established pursuant to Part C of Title I of the Developmental Disabilities Assistance and Bill of Rights Act.

Beneficiary Eligibility: All individuals within the State who are entitled to SSDI or eligible for SSI benefits based on disability or blindness.

Award Range/Average: PABSS Range: $50,000 to $319,000 average $107,496.SPSSB Range: $30,000 to $2,200,000 average $431,138.

Funding: (Project Grants) FY 17 $6,725,001.00; FY 18 est $31,725,001.00; FY 19 est $31,725,001.00

HQ: 6401 Security Boulevard, 1540 Robert M Ball Building, Baltimore, MD 21235

Phone: 410-965-9534 | Email: dionne.mitchell@ssa.gov

http://www.ssa.gov

SSA96.020 | SPECIAL BENEFITS FOR CERTAIN WORLD WAR II VETERANS
"Special Veterans Benefits; SVB"

Award: Direct Payments With Unrestricted Use

Purpose: The program pays special privileges for World War II veterans who are eligible for Supplemental Security Income benefits while meeting other criteria when residing outside of the United States.

Applicant Eligibility: Be age 65 or older on December 14, 1999, be a World War II veteran (includes Filipino veterans of World War II or organized guerrilla forces under the auspices of the U.S. military); be eligible for SSI benefits for December 1999 and for the month that the application for SVB was filed; and, have other benefit income that is less than 75 percent of the SSI Federal benefit rate. For 2018, 75 percent of the SSI Federal benefit rate is $562.50.

Beneficiary Eligibility: Benefits are paid to certain World War II veterans meeting the criteria specified under Applicant Eligibility. Credentials/Documentation.

Programs Administered by Regional - State - Local Offices

Funding: (Direct Payments with Unrestricted Use) FY 16 $2,906,072.00; FY 17 est $2,388,885.00; FY 18 Estimate Not Available

HQ: OISP 6401 Security Boulevard, Robert M Ball Building, Baltimore, MD 21235

  Phone: 410-965-3549 | Email: phyllis.mathers@ssa.gov

  http://www.socialsecurity.gov

U.S. CENSUS BUREAU
Regional – State – Local Offices

California
Julie Lam, Regional Director | 15350 Sherman Way Suite 300, Van Nuys, CA 91406-4224 818-904-6393

Colorado
Susan A. Lavin, Regional Director, Census Bureau | 6900 W Jefferson Avenue Suite 100, Denver, CO 80235-2032 303-969-6750

Georgia
George Grandy Jr., Regional Director | 101 Marietta Street NW Suite 3200, Atlanta, GA 30303-2700 404-730-3832

Illinois
Stanley D. Moore, Regional Director, Census Bureau | 2255 Enterprise Drive Suite 5501, Westchester, IL 60154-5800 708-562-1376

Indiana
Jean Ann Banet, Technical Services Supervisor | Bureau of the Census PO Box 1545, Jeffersonville, IN 47131 812-218-3046

Kansas
Henry Palacios, Regional Director, Census Bureau | 1211 N 8th Street, Kansas City, KS 66101-2129 913-551-6728

Massachusetts
Arthur G. Dukakis, Regional Director, Census Bureau | 2 Copley Place Suite 301 PO Box 9108, Boston, MA 02117-9108 617-424-0500

Michigan
Dwight P. Dean, Regional Director, Census Bureau | 1395 Brewery Park Boulevard, Detroit, MI 48207-5405 313-259-1158

New York
Lester A. Farthing, Regional Director, Census Bureau | 395 Hudson Street Suite 800, New York, NY 10014 212-264-3860

North Carolina
Susan B. Hardy, Regional Director, Census Bureau | 901 Center Park Drive Suite 106, Charlotte, NC 28217-2935 704-344-6142

Pennsylvania
Fernando E. Armstrong, Regional Director, Census Bureau | 1601 Market Street 21st Floor, Philadelphia, PA 19103-2395 215-656-7550

Texas
Alfonso E. Mirabal, Regional Director, Census Bureau | 8585 N Stemmons Freeway Suite 800S, Dallas, TX 75247-3841 214-640-4400

Washington
Ralph J. Lee, Regional Director, Census Bureau | Key Tower 700 5th Avenue Suite 5100, Seattle, WA 98104-5018 206-553-5837

DOC11.016 | STATISTICAL, RESEARCH, AND METHODOLOGY ASSISTANCE

Award: Cooperative Agreements

Purpose: To make awards to cooperative agreements, Federal, State, or local governmental unit and to analyze information for program and policy considerations for undertaking special research.

Applicant Eligibility: Activities under this Program must relate to the Census Bureau's mission to serve as the leading source of quality data about the nation's people and economy that honors privacy, protects confidentiality, and is guided by scientific objectivity, and research-based innovation.

Beneficiary Eligibility: Eligible respondents include any appropriate entities, including but not restricted to Federal, State, or local governmental unit, or institution of higher education.

Award Range/Average: $300,000 - $1,000,000

Funding: (Cooperative Agreements) FY 16 est $1,000,000.00; FY 17 est $5,000,000.00

HQ: 4600 Silver Hill Road, Suitland, MD 20746

  Phone: 301-763-4628

  http://www.census.gov

U.S. FISH AND WILDLIFE SERVICE
Regional – State – Local Offices

California, Nevada
Judy Frye | 2800 Cottage Way Suite W2606, Sacramento, CA 95825 916-414-6486

Region I
Dave Allen | 911 NE 11th Avenue, Portland, OR 97232 503-872-2716

Region II
PO Box 1306 500 Gold Avenue SW Room 3018, Albuquerque, NM 87103 505-248-6910

Region III
Robyn Thorson | Federal Building 1 Federal Drive, Fort Snelling, MN 55111 612-713-5284

Region IV
Sam Hamilton | 1875 Century Boulevard, Atlanta, GA 30345 404-679-4006

Region V
Marvin Moriarty | 300 Westgate Center Drive, Hadley, MA 01035 413-253-8308

Region VI
Ralph O. Morgenweck | PO Box 25486 Denver Federal Center, Denver, CO 80025 303-236-7920

Region VII: Alaska
Rowan Gould | 1011 E Tudor Road, Anchorage, AK 99503 907-786-3306

DOI15.605 | SPORT FISH RESTORATION
"Dingell-Johnson Sport Fish Restoration Program"

Award: Formula Grants

Purpose: Supports activities designed to restore, conserve, manage, or enhance sport fish populations; the public use and benefits from these resources; and activities that provide boat access to public waters.

Applicant Eligibility: Agencies from the 50 States, the District of Columbia, the Commonwealths of Puerto Rico and the Northern Mariana Islands, and the territories of Guam, the U.S. Virgin Islands, and American Samoa with primary responsibility for fish and wildlife conservation may submit grant proposals to the U.S. Fish and Wildlife Service. To be eligible, they must pass assent legislation to the provisions of the Act for the conservation of sport fish that includes a prohibition against the diversion of license fees paid by anglers for any purpose other than the administration of the fish and wildlife agency.

Beneficiary Eligibility: General Public (While direct participation is limited to fish and wildlife agencies, the public will ultimately benefit from these fishery conservation measures.).

Award Range/Average: Range is $900,000 to $14,700,000; Average $5,200,000.

Funding: (Formula Grants) FY 18 $351,900,000.00; FY 19 est $365,400,000.00; FY 20 est $357,000,000.00

HQ: Wildlife and Sport Fish Restoration Program Policy and Programs Division 5275 Leesburg Pike, PO Box WSFR, Falls Church, VA 22041

Phone: 703-358-2156

http://wsfrprograms.fws.gov

DOI15.608 | FISH AND WILDLIFE MANAGEMENT ASSISTANCE

Award: Project Grants

Purpose: Provides technical and financial assistance to other federal agencies, states, local governments, native American tribes, non-governmental organizations, citizen groups, and landowners on the conservation and management of fish and wildlife resources.

Applicant Eligibility: Applicants may be other federal agencies, state agencies, local Governments, native American Organizations, interstate, intrastate, public nonprofit institution/Organization, other public institution/Organization, nonprofit/Organization, private landowners, or any other Organization subject to the jurisdiction of the United States with interests that support the mission of the U.S. Fish and Wildlife Service on a cost recoverable basis. Applicants applying for State/Interstate ANS Management Plan funds must be a State or Interstate Organization with an ANS Task Force approved plan.

Beneficiary Eligibility: Federal agencies, state agencies, local governments, Native Americans, Interstate, Intrastate, public nonprofit institution/organization, other public institution/organization, private nonprofit/organization, or any other organization subject to the jurisdiction of the United States with interests that support the mission of the Service on a cost recoverable basis.

Programs Administered by Regional - State - Local Offices

Award Range/Average: Range is $1,000 to $750,000; Average $75,000.

Funding: (Project Grants (Discretionary)) FY 18 $19,964,000.00; FY 19 est $19,964,000.00; FY 20 est $19,964,000.00

HQ: Fish and Aquatic Conservation Department of the Interior 5275 Leesburg Pike, PO Box FAC, Falls Church, VA 22041-3803

Phone: 703-358-2373 | Email: julie_jackson@fws.gov

http://www.fws.gov/fisheries

DOI15.611 | WILDLIFE RESTORATION AND BASIC HUNTER EDUCATION
"Pittman-Robertson Wildlife Restoration Program"

Award: Formula Grants

Purpose: Provides grants to State, Commonwealth, and territorial fish and wildlife agencies for projects to restore, conserve, manage, and enhance wild birds and mammals and their habitat.

Applicant Eligibility: Agencies from the 50 States, the Commonwealths of Puerto Rico and the Northern Mariana Islands, and the territories of Guam, the U.S. Virgin Islands, and American Samoa with primary responsibility for fish and wildlife conservation may submit grant proposals to the Fish and Wildlife Service. To be eligible, they must pass assent legislation to the provisions of the Act for conservation of wildlife that includes a prohibition against the diversion of license fees paid by hunters for any other purpose than the administration of the fish and wildlife agency.

Beneficiary Eligibility: General Public (While direct participation is limited to fish and wildlife agencies, the general public will ultimately benefit from these wildlife conservation measures.).

Award Range/Average: Range is $268,000 to $7,187,000; Average $2,750,000.

Funding: (Formula Grants) FY 18 $797,200,000.00; FY 19 est $673,600,000.00; FY 20 est $744,000,000.00

HQ: Policy and Programs Division 5275 Leesburg Pike, PO Box WSFR, Falls Church, VA 22041

Phone: 703-358-2156

http://wsfrprograms.fws.gov

DOI15.614 | COASTAL WETLANDS PLANNING, PROTECTION AND RESTORATION
"National Coastal Wetlands Grants"

Award: Project Grants

Purpose: Provides competitive matching grants to coastal States for coastal wetlands conservation projects.

Applicant Eligibility: Eligible applicants include any agency or agencies designated by the Governor of a coastal State. It is usually a State natural resource or fish and wildlife agency. Eligible coastal States are States bordering the Great Lakes (Illinois, Michigan, Minnesota, New York, Ohio, Pennsylvania, and Wisconsin); States bordering the Atlantic, Gulf (except Louisiana), and Pacific coasts (Alabama, Alaska, California, Connecticut, Delaware, Florida, Georgia, Hawaii, Maine, Maryland, Massachusetts, Mississippi, New Hampshire, New Jersey, New York, North Carolina, Oregon, Rhode Island, South Carolina, Texas, Virginia, and Washington); and American Samoa, Commonwealth of the Northern Mariana Islands, Guam, Puerto Rico, and the Virgin Islands.

Beneficiary Eligibility: States, Commonwealths, or territories as designated in the applicant eligibility section.

Award Range/Average: Range: $125,000 - $1,000,000; Average: $575,000

Funding: (Project Grants (Discretionary)) FY 18 $17,000,000.00; FY 19 est $17,000,000.00; FY 20 est $17,000,000.00

HQ: The National Refuge System - Division of Natural Resources and Conservation Planning 5275 Leesburg Pike, PO Box NWRS, Falls Church, VA 22041-3803

Phone: 703-358-1849 | Email: chris_darnell@fws.gov

https://wsfrprograms.fws.gov/subpages/grantprograms/CW/CW.htm

DOI15.615 | COOPERATIVE ENDANGERED SPECIES CONSERVATION FUND

Award: Project Grants

Purpose: Provides federal financial assistance through its appropriate State or territorial agency, to assist in the development of programs for the conservation of endangered and threatened species.

Applicant Eligibility: Participation limited to State agencies that have a cooperative agreement with the Secretary of the Interior. The annual Notice of Funding Opportunity (NOFO), announced through www.grants.gov and posted to the U.S. Fish and Wildlife Service Web site at http://www.fws.gov/endangered/grants/index. html, describes the criteria that must be satisfied for an application to be eligible for funding.

Beneficiary Eligibility: All States that have entered into a cooperative agreement with the Secretary of the Interior.

Award Range/Average: Varies by program element.

Funding: (Project Grants (Discretionary)) FY 17 $11,141,000.00; FY 18 est $0.00; FY 19 est $0.00
HQ: 5279 Leesburg Pike, PO Box ES, Falls Church, VA 22041
    Phone: 703-358-2171
    http://www.fws.gov/endangered/grants/index.html

DOI15.616 | CLEAN VESSEL ACT
"CVA"

Award: Project Grants
Purpose: Program provides funding to States, the District of Columbia, Commonwealths, and territories for the construction, renovation, operation, and maintenance of sewage pump out stations, waste reception facilities, and pump out boats for recreational boaters.
Applicant Eligibility: Agencies from the 50 States, the District of Columbia, the Commonwealths of Puerto Rico and the Northern Mariana Islands, and the territories of Guam, the U.S. Virgin Islands, and American Samoa may submit grant proposals to the U.S. Fish and Wildlife Service.
Beneficiary Eligibility: General public, recreational boaters, municipalities, and private marinas within eligible States, the District of Columbia, Commonwealths, and territories.
Award Range/Average: Maximum Federal award is $1,500,000. The average award is approximately $350,000.
Funding: (Project Grants (Discretionary)) FY 18 $14,515,203.00; FY 19 est $17,800,000.00; FY 20 est $15,000,000.00
HQ: Wildlife and Sport Fish Restoration Program Policy and Programs Division 5275 Leesburg Pike, PO Box WSFR, Falls Church, VA 22041-3803
    Phone: 703-358-2156
    https://wsfrprograms.fws.gov/subpages/grantprograms/CVA/CVA.htm

DOI15.619 | RHINOCEROS AND TIGER CONSERVATION FUND

Award: Project Grants
Purpose: Provides financial assistance for projects for the effective long-term conservation of rhinoceros and tigers. This program supports projects that focuses on enhanced protection of at-risk rhinoceros and tiger populations; protected area/reserve management in important rhinoceros and tiger range.
Applicant Eligibility: Applications may be submitted by any government agency responsible for the conservation and protection of rhinoceroses and/or tigers and any other Organization, multi-national secretariat or individual with demonstrated experience in rhinoceros and/or tiger conservation may submit proposals to this Fund. U.S. non-profit, non-governmental Organizations must submit documentary evidence of their Section 501(c)(3) non-profit status.
Beneficiary Eligibility: Any government agency responsible for conservation and protection of rhinoceros and/or tigers and any other organization or individual with demonstrated experience in rhinoceros or tiger conservation.
Award Range/Average: Variable amounts. Largely $50,000 or less. Higher amounts may be requested.
Funding: (Project Grants (Discretionary)) FY 18 $3,540,000; FY 19 est $4,000,000; FY 20 est $4,000,000
HQ: Department of the Interior 5275 Leesburg Pike, PO Box IA, Falls Church, VA 22041-3803
    Phone: 703-358-1754
    http://www.fws.gov/international/wildlife-without-borders/rhino-and-tiger-conservation-fund.html

DOI15.620 | AFRICAN ELEPHANT CONSERVATION FUND

Award: Project Grants
Purpose: Provides financial assistance to support projects that will enhance sustainable conservation programs to ensure effective, long-term conservation of African elephants. The African Elephant Conservation fund supports projects that promote conservation through applied research on elephant populations and their habitat, including surveys and monitoring; development and execution of elephant conservation management plans.
Applicant Eligibility: Applications may be submitted by any African government agency responsible for African elephant conservation and protection and any other Organization or individual with demonstrated experience in African elephant conservation.
Beneficiary Eligibility: Any African government agency responsible for African elephant conservation and protection and any other organization or individual with demonstrated experience in African elephant conservation.
Award Range/Average: Variable amounts. Generally $50,000 or less. Higher amounts may be requested
Funding: (Project Grants (Discretionary)) FY 18 $3,190,000.00; FY 19 est $3,000,000.00; FY 20 est $3,000,000.00

Programs Administered by Regional - State - Local Offices

HQ: Department of the Interior 5275 Leesburg Pike, PO Box IA, Falls Church, VA 22041-3803
  Phone: 703-358-1754
  http://www.fws.gov/international/wildlife-without-borders/african-elephant-conservation-fund.html

DOI15.621 | ASIAN ELEPHANT CONSERVATION FUND

Award: Project Grants
Purpose: To support the conservation of Asian elephants, to promote research and monitoring of laws that prohibit trade of Asian elephant, to regulate conservation education and management plans, to reduce human-elephant conflicts, to inspect wildlife and law enforcement.
Applicant Eligibility: Applications may be submitted by any Asian government agency responsible for Asian elephant conservation and protection, and any other Organization or individual with demonstrated experience in Asian elephant conservation.
Beneficiary Eligibility: Any Asian government agency responsible for Asian elephant conservation and protection, and any other organization or individual with demonstrated experience in Asian elephant conservation.
Award Range/Average: Variable amounts. Generally $50,000 or less. Higher amounts may be requested.
Funding: (Project Grants (Discretionary)) FY 18 $1,804,898.00; FY 19 est $1,800,000.00; FY 20 est $1,800,000.00
HQ: Department of the Interior 5276 Leesburg Pike, PO Box IA, Falls Church, VA 22041-3803
  Phone: 703-358-1754
  http://www.fws.gov/international/wildlife-without-borders/asian-elephant-conservation-fund.html

DOI15.622 | SPORTFISHING AND BOATING SAFETY ACT

Award: Project Grants
Purpose: To fund to States of Columbia and territories for renovation and maintenance of docking and other facilities for recreational purposes.
Applicant Eligibility: Agencies from the 50 States, the District of Columbia, the Commonwealths of Puerto Rico and the Northern Mariana Islands, and the territories of Guam, the U.S. Virgin Islands, and American Samoa may submit grant proposals to the U.S. Fish and Wildlife Service.
Beneficiary Eligibility: General Public, specifically owners and/or users of transient, recreational boats 26 feet or greater in length, and municipalities and private marinas within those eligible States, the District of Columbia, Commonwealths, and territories.
Award Range/Average: Tier 1 grants average $179,000; Tier 2 range from $100,000 to $1,500,000; Average $954,000.
Funding: (Project Grants (Discretionary)) FY 18 $13,921,275.00; FY 19 est $20,000,000.00; FY 20 $15,000,000.00
HQ: Wildlife and Sport Fish Restoration Program Policy and Programs Division 5275 Leesburg Pike, PO Box WSFR, Falls Church, VA 22041
  Phone: 703-358-2156
  https://wsfrprograms.fws.gov/subpages/grantprograms/BIG/BIG.htm

DOI15.623 | NORTH AMERICAN WETLANDS CONSERVATION FUND "NAWCF"

Award: Project Grants
Purpose: To compensate for conservation projects in the United States, Canada, and Mexico.
Applicant Eligibility: Available to private or public Organizations or to individuals who have developed partnerships to carry out wetlands conservation projects in the U.S., Canada, and Mexico.
Beneficiary Eligibility: Available to any private or public organization or individual.
Award Range/Average: Range is $0 to $75,000 for Small Grants; over $75,000 to $1,000,000 for U.S. Standard Grants. Average award is approximately $42,000 and $710,000 for Small Grants and U.S. Standard Grants, respectively.
Funding: (Project Grants (Discretionary)) FY 18 $65,000,000.00; FY 19 est $85,000,000.00; FY 20 est $ 70,000,000
HQ: Division of Bird Habitat Conservation 5275 Leesburg Pike, PO Box MB, Falls Church, VA 22041-3803
  Phone: 703-358-1784
  http://www.fws.gov/birds/grants/north-american-wetland-conservation-act.php

DOI15.626 | ENHANCED HUNTER EDUCATION AND SAFETY

Award: Formula Grants

Purpose: To fund for archery education programs and construction of firearm shooting and archery ranges.

Applicant Eligibility: Agencies from the 50 States, the Commonwealths of Puerto Rico and the Northern Mariana Islands, and the territories of Guam, the U.S. Virgin Islands, and American Samoa with primary responsibility for fish and wildlife conservation may submit grant proposals to the Fish and Wildlife Service. To be eligible, they must pass assent legislation to the provisions of the Act for the conservation of wildlife that include a prohibition against the diversion of license fees paid by hunters for any other purpose than the administration of the fish and wildlife agency.

Beneficiary Eligibility: General Public (While direct participation is limited to fish and wildlife agencies, the general public will ultimately benefit from these wildlife conservation measures).

Award Range/Average: Range is $13,300 to $240,000; Average $145,000.

Funding: (Formula Grants) FY 18 est $8,000,000.00; FY 19 est $8,000,000.00; FY 20 est $8,000,000.00

HQ: Wildlife and Sport Fish Restoration Program Policy and Programs Division 5275 Leesburg Pike, PO Box WSFR, Falls Church, VA 22041-3803

Phone: 703-358-2156

http://wsfrprograms.fws.gov

DOI15.628 | MULTISTATE CONSERVATION GRANT

Award: Project Grants

Purpose: To fund for fish and wildlife restoration projects.

Applicant Eligibility: Eligibility is limited to: 1) Agencies with lead management responsibility for fish and wildlife resources in each of the 50 States, the District of Columbia, Commonwealths of Puerto Rico and the Northern Mariana Islands, and the territories of American Samoa, Guam, and the U.S. Virgin Islands, or a group of these agencies; 2) The Service, only for the purpose of carrying out the National Survey; or 3) Non-governmental Organizations (NGOs) with and without 501(c) status. United States non-profit NGOs with 501(c) Internal Revenue Service (IRS) status must provide a copy of their Section 501(c) status determination letter received from the IRS. In addition, NGOs including educational Institutions that are invited to submit full proposals must submit a certification that their Organization will not use grant funds to fund, in whole or in part, any activity that promotes or encourages opposition to the regulated hunting or trapping of wildlife or the regulated taking of fish in their application. Only projects that propose benefits to sport fish, wild birds and/or mammals are eligible. Proposed projects must also benefit: 1) At least 26 States or; 2) A majority of the States in a Service Region; or 3) A regional association of State fish and wildlife agencies. Federal law mandates that all entities applying for Federal financial assistance must have a valid Dun & Bradstreet Data Universal Numbering System (DUNS) number and have a current registration in the System for Award Management (SAM). See Title 2 of the Code of Federal Regulations (CFR), Part 25 for more information.

Beneficiary Eligibility: Projects must benefit at least 26 States, a majority of States in a Region of the U.S. Fish and Wildlife Service, or a Regional association of State fish and game departments.

Award Range/Average: The range based on FY 2017 awards was $50,000 to $560,000; Average $150,000.

Funding: (Project Grants (Discretionary)) FY 18 $6,000,000.00; FY 19 est $6,000,000.00; FY 20 est $6,000,000.00

HQ: 5275 Leesburg Pike, PO Box WSFR, Falls Church, VA 22041-3803

Phone: 703-358-2156

http://wsfrprograms.fws.gov

DOI15.629 | GREAT APES CONSERVATION FUND

Award: Project Grants

Purpose: To assist for the conservation of great apes and their habitats, to promote ape conservation management plans; to implement laws that prohibit trade of ape, to encourage conservation education, to decrease human-ape conflicts, to inspect wildlife and law enforcement for protecting apes.

Applicant Eligibility: Applications may be submitted by any government agency responsible for conservation and protection of apes and any other Organization or individual with demonstrated experience in ape conservation.

Beneficiary Eligibility: Any government agency responsible for conservation and protection of apes and any other organization or individual with demonstrated experience in ape conservation.

Award Range/Average: Variable amounts. Generally $50,000 or less. Higher amounts may be requested.

Funding: (Project Grants (Discretionary)) FY 18 est $5,200,000.00; FY 19 est $5,000,000.00; FY 20 est $5,000,000.00

HQ: Department of the Interior 5275 Leesburg Pike, PO Box IA, Falls Church, VA 22041-3803

Phone: 703-358-1754

http://www.fws.gov/international/wildlife-without-borders/great-ape-conservation-fund.html

Programs Administered by Regional - State - Local Offices

DOI15.630 | COASTAL

Award: Cooperative Agreements

Purpose: To assist in protecting and improving habitats for fish and wildlife.

Applicant Eligibility: Federal, State, interstate and intrastate agencies; local and tribal Governments; public nonprofit institutes and Organizations (such as conservation Organizations, watershed councils, land trusts, schools and Institutions of higher learning); U.S. territories and possessions; private landowners including individuals and businesses.

Beneficiary Eligibility: Federal, state, interstate and intrastate agencies, tribes, local governments; public nongovernmental organizations (such as conservation organizations, watershed councils, land trusts, schools and universities); U.S. territories and possessions; private landowners, including individuals and businesses.

Award Range/Average: Range is $5,000 to $50,000.

Funding: (Cooperative Agreements (Discretionary Grants)) FY 18 $13,000,000.00; FY 19 est $13,000,000.00; FY 20 est $13,000,000.00

HQ: Department of the Interior 5278 Leesburg Pike, PO Box NWRS, Falls Church, VA 22041-3803
Phone: 703-358-2332 | Email: samantha_brooke@fws.gov
http://www.fws.gov/coastal

DOI15.631 | PARTNERS FOR FISH AND WILDLIFE

Award: Project Grants

Purpose: To provide financial assistance to landowners, States, and Tribes in restoring habitats for fish and wildlife on their lands.

Applicant Eligibility: Private landowners, tribal Governments, local and state Governments, educational, for-profit, and non-profit Institutions and Organizations are eligible for financial and technical assistance from Partners for Fish and Wildlife Program. projects must be located on private lands. Private land is defined by the Partners for Fish and Wildlife Act of 2006, 16 U.S.C. 3771-3774, as any land that is not owned by the Federal Government or a State. Private land includes tribal land and Hawaiian homeland.

Beneficiary Eligibility: Same as Applicant Eligibility.

Award Range/Average: Cost-share range per project is from $200 to $25,000. The average cost per project is $5,400.

Funding: (Cooperative Agreements) FY 18 $52,000,000.00; FY 19 est $52,000,000.00; FY 20 est $52,000,000.00

HQ: Department of the Interior 5278 Leesburg Pike, PO Box NWRS, Falls Church, VA 22041-3803
Phone: 703-358-2011 | Email: matthew_filsinger@fws.gov
http://www.fws.gov/partners

DOI15.633 | LANDOWNER INCENTIVE
"LIP"

Award: Project Grants

Purpose: To provide financial assistance to landowners and States in managing habitats and protecting species and other endangered species.

Applicant Eligibility: Agencies from the 50 States, the District of Columbia, the Commonwealths of Puerto Rico and the Northern Mariana Islands, and the territories of Guam, the U.S. Virgin Islands, and American Samoa with primary responsibility for fish and wildlife conservation may submit grant proposals to the U.S. Fish and Wildlife Service.

Beneficiary Eligibility: Private landowners and the public (While direct participation is limited to State, the District of Columbia, Commonwealth, or territorial fish and wildlife agencies, private landowners will directly benefit from financial and technical assistance and the public will ultimately benefit from these wildlife conservation measures implemented on private lands).

Award Range/Average: Not Applicable.

HQ: Department of the Interior 5278 Leesburg Pike, PO Box WSFR, Falls Church, VA 22041-3803
Phone: 703-358-2231
http://wsfrprograms.fws.gov

DOI15.634 | STATE WILDLIFE GRANTS
"SWG"

Award: Formula Grants; Project Grants

Purpose: To fund for the development and implementation of conservation projects for the benefit of fish and wildlife habitats and other endangered species.

Applicant Eligibility: Agencies from the 50 States, the District of Columbia, the Commonwealths of Puerto Rico and the Northern Mariana Islands, and the territories of Guam, the U.S. Virgin Islands, and American Samoa with primary responsibility for fish and wildlife conservation may submit grant proposals for formula or competitive project grants to the U.S. Fish and Wildlife Service if they maintain a current, Service-approved Comprehensive Wildlife State Wildlife Action Plan. The four regional Associations of Fish and Wildlife Agencies (NEAFWA, SEAFWA, MAFWA, and WAFWA) are eligible for competitive project grants at the discretion of recipient State fish and wildlife agencies.

Beneficiary Eligibility: General Public (While direct participation is limited to fish and wildlife agencies, the public will ultimately benefit from these wildlife conservation measures.).

Award Range/Average: Range is $30,000 to $3,000,000; Average $500,000.

Funding: (Formula Grants) FY 18 $53,000,000.00; FY 19 est $54,000,000.00; FY 20 est $55,000,000.00; PROJECT GRANTS (Discretionary) FY18 $6,300,000.00; FY19 est $6,300,000.00; FY20 est $6,300,000.00

HQ: Division of Policy and Programs 5275 Leesburg Pike, PO Box WSFR, Falls Church, VA 22041-3803
Phone: 703-358-2231
https://wsfrprograms.fws.gov/subpages/grantprograms/swg/swg.htm

DOI15.635 | NEOTROPICAL MIGRATORY BIRD CONSERVATION

Award: Project Grants

Purpose: To fund for the conservation of migrating birds.

Applicant Eligibility: An individual, corporation, partnership, trust, association, or other private entity; an officer, employee, agent, department, or instrumentality of the Federal Government, of any State, municipality, or political subdivision of a State, or of any foreign government; a State municipality, or political subdivision of a State; or any other entity subject to the jurisdiction of the United States or of any foreign country; or international Organization with an interest in neotropical migratory bird conservation.

Beneficiary Eligibility: An individual, profit organization, other private institution/organization, public nonprofit institution/organization, an officer, employee, agent, department, or instrumentality of the Federal Government, of any State, municipality, or political subdivision of a State, or of any foreign government; a State municipality, or political subdivision of a State; or any other entity subject to the jurisdiction of the United States or of any foreign country; or international organization with an interest in neotropical migratory bird conservation.

Award Range/Average: Ranged from $2,000 to $200,000, with an average of $100,000.

Funding: (Project Grants (Discretionary)) FY 18 $3,792,700.00; FY 19 est $3,793,000.00; FY 20 est $3,793,000

HQ: Division of Bird Habitat Conservation 5275 Leesburg Pike, PO Box MB, Falls Church, VA 22041-3803
Phone: 703-358-1784
http://www.fws.gov/birds/grants/neotropical-migratory-bird-conservation-act.php

DOI15.636 | ALASKA SUBSISTENCE MANAGEMENT

Award: Cooperative Agreements

Purpose: To sustain fisheries and wildlife management on Federal public lands. The Fisheries Resource Monitoring Program funds to manage Federal fisheries. The Partners for Fisheries Monitoring Program strengthens Alaska Native and rural areas in fisheries management and research.

Applicant Eligibility: An individual/family, profit Organization, other private institution/Organization, public nonprofit institution/Organization; an officer, employee, agent, department or instrumentality of the Federal government, of the State of Alaska, municipality or political subdivision of the State of Alaska; Federally recognized Indian Tribal Government (including any Native village as defined in the Alaska Native Claims Settlement Act).

Beneficiary Eligibility: An individual/Family, profit organization, other private institution/organization, public nonprofit institution/organization; an officer, employee, agent, department, or instrumentality of the Federal government, of the State of Alaska, municipality or political subdivision of the State of Alaska, or of any foreign government.

Award Range/Average: Variable amounts. Monitoring Program: Awards range from $60,000 to $860,000 for up to a 4-year project period. Partners Program: Awards range from $120,000 to $680,000 over a 4- year period.

Funding: (Cooperative Agreements (Discretionary Grants)) FY 18 $3,531,430; FY 19 est $3,470,262; FY 20 est $4,328,861

Programs Administered by Regional - State - Local Offices

HQ: Office of Subsistence Management 1011 E Tudor Road, PO Box 121, Anchorage, AK 99503
   Phone: 907-786-3387 | Email: karie_crow@fws.gov
   http://www.doi.gov/subsistence

DOI15.637 | MIGRATORY BIRD JOINT VENTURES

Award: Project Grants

Purpose: To assist in the conservation of migratory birds.

Applicant Eligibility: Federal, State and local government agencies, Federally recognized Indian Tribal Governments, private nonprofit Institutions /Organizations; public nonprofit Institutions /Organizations; profit Organizations, interstate and intrastate entities, and individuals or families who are also private landowners.

Beneficiary Eligibility: General Public.

Award Range/Average: Range is $2,400 to $900,000; Average $225,000.

Funding: (Project Grants (Discretionary)): FY18 $4,413,405.00; FY19 est $5,000,000.00 FY20 est $5,000,000.00

HQ: 5275 Leesburg Pike, PO Box MBSP, Falls Church, VA 22041-3803
   Phone: 703-358-1784
   http://www.fws.gov

DOI15.639 | TRIBAL WILDLIFE GRANTS
"TWG"

Award: Project Grants

Purpose: To assist in the protection of wildlife habitat and other endangered species.

Applicant Eligibility: Participation is limited to Federally recognized Indian tribal Governments.

Beneficiary Eligibility: Anyone/General Public (While direct participation is limited to Federally recognized Indian tribal governments, the general public will ultimately benefit from these wildlife conservation measures).

Award Range/Average: Range $0 - $200,000; Average $167,000.

Funding: (Project Grants (Discretionary)) FY 18 $4,209,000.00; FY 19 est $4,209,000.00; FY 20 est Estimate Not Available

HQ: 1211 SE Cardinal Court, Suite 100, Vancouver, WA 98683
   Phone: 360-604-2531 | Email: scott_aikin@fws.gov
   http://www.fws.gov/nativeamerican

DOI15.640 | LATIN AMERICA AND CARIBBEAN REGIONAL

Award: Project Grants

Purpose: To assist in innovative training programs in Latin America and the Caribbean that will train future generations to adapt to modern society and the landscapes on which the society depends.

Applicant Eligibility: Participation is limited to Federal, State and local Governments, non-profit, non-governmental Organizations; public and private Institutions of higher education; and any other Organization or individual with demonstrated experience deemed necessary to carry out the proposed project.

Beneficiary Eligibility: Federal, State and local government agencies; non-profit, non-governmental organizations; public and private institutions of higher education; and any other organization or individual with demonstrated experience deemed necessary to carry out the proposed project.

Award Range/Average: Variable amounts. Generally $50,000 or less. Higher amounts may be requested

Funding: (Project Grants (Discretionary)) FY 18 $2,283,851.00; FY 19 est $2,100,000.00; FY 20 est $1,200,000.00

HQ: Wildlife Service Division of International Conservation 5275 Leesburg Pike, PO Box IA, Falls Church, VA 22041
   Phone: 703-358-1754
   http://www.fws.gov/international/wildlife-without-borders/western-hemisphere

DOI15.641 | WILDLIFE WITHOUT BORDERS-MEXICO

Award: Project Grants

Purpose: To assist in creating innovative nature of training on the conservation of biodiversity management in Mexico.

Applicant Eligibility: Participation is limited to Federal, State and local Governments, non-profit, non-governmental Organizations; public and private Institutions of higher education; and any other Organization or individual with demonstrated experience deemed necessary to carry out the proposed project.

Beneficiary Eligibility: Federal, State and local government; public nonprofit institution/organizations; public and private institutions of higher education; and any other organization or individual with demonstrated experience deemed necessary to carry out the proposed project.

Award Range/Average: Variable amounts. The average grant amount is $35,000.

HQ: Division of International Conservation 5275 Leesburg Pike, PO Box IA, Falls Church, VA 22041-3803
Phone: 703-358-1754
http://www.fws.gov/international/wildlife-without-borders/mexico/index.html

DOI15.642 | CHALLENGE COST SHARE
"CCS"

Award: Project Grants

Purpose: To promote partnerships with nonfederal governments, organizations, educational institutions, and businesses to protect fish, wildlife, and plants for the benefit of the U.S. citizens.

Applicant Eligibility: Applicants may be an individual/family, minority group, specialized group, small business, profit Organization, private nonprofit/Organization, quasi-public nonprofit institution/Organization, native American, Federal, Interstate, Intrastate, State, Local, Sponsored Organization, public nonprofit institution/Organization, other public institution/Organization, U.S. territory, or any Organization with interests which support the mission of the Service. This Program requires the cooperator(s) to provide a minimum of 50 percent of cost share from non-Federal sources, for local Programs on National Wildlife Refuges, or benefitting other Service lands.

Beneficiary Eligibility: The Challenge Cost Share program is not a grant program, although they do use cooperative agreements for donations to these field projects. Service field station managers are encouraged to form partnerships and to secure project cost-sharing for projects initiated at that refuge or field station. By Service policy, the matching 50% cost share is provided by non-Federal sources, state/local governments, private individuals/organizations, business enterprises, and philanthropic and charitable groups.

Award Range/Average: Not Available.

HQ: Department of the Interior 5275 Leesburg Pike, PO Box NWRS, Falls Church, VA 22041-3803
Phone: 703-358-2248
http://www.fws.gov

DOI15.643 | ALASKA MIGRATORY BIRD CO-MANAGEMENT COUNCIL
"AMBCC"

Award: Project Grants

Purpose: To facilitate and administer regional programs to involve hunters of migratory birds in the management and regulation of migratory birds.

Applicant Eligibility: Native American Organizations, Public nonprofit Institutions /Organizations, other public Institutions / Organizations, Federally Recognized Indian Tribal Governments, and Local Governments.

Beneficiary Eligibility: Native American Organizations, Public nonprofit institutions/organizations, Federally recognized Indian Tribal Governments, local governments, and Alaska Native American Indians.

Award Range/Average: Range is $14,800 to $129,400.

Funding: (Project Grants (Discretionary)) FY 18 $430,064.00; FY 19 est $430,064.00; FY 20 est $430,064.00

HQ: 1011 E Tudor Road, Anchorage, AK 99503
Phone: 907-786-3887 | Email: cheryl_graves@fws.gov
http://Alaska.fws.gov/ambcc/index.htm

DOI15.644 | FEDERAL JUNIOR DUCK STAMP CONSERVATION AND DESIGN
"Junior Duck Stamp Contest"

Award: Cooperative Agreements

Purpose: To make use of visual arts programs and a nation-wide art contest to teach school students environmental science, wildlife management, wetlands ecology, and the importance of habitat conservation.

Applicant Eligibility: Federal, State and Local Governments, Non-profit Organizations both with and without 501(c)(3) IRS status, Private Institutions of Higher education, Public and State controlled Institutions of Higher education.

Programs Administered by Regional - State - Local Offices

Beneficiary Eligibility: Individual/Family, Student/Trainee, Artist/Humanist, U.S. citizens, resident aliens, or nationals who are in kindergarten through twelfth grades at a public, private, or home school in the United States or U.S. territories.

Award Range/Average: Each award may range from $500 to $2,500. Awards are based on previous year participation numbers and base funding of $500.

Funding: (Project Grants) FY 18 FY $3,300.00; 19 est $1,700.00; FY 20 est $4,000.00

HQ: Federal Duck Stamp Office Department of the Interior 5275 Leesburg Pike, PO Box MBSP, Falls Church, VA 22041-3803
   Phone: 703-358-1784
   http://www.fws.gov/juniorduck

DOI15.645 | MARINE TURTLE CONSERVATION FUND

Award: Project Grants

Purpose: To help conserve marine turtles and their nesting habitats in foreign countries by supporting and providing financial resources.

Applicant Eligibility: Applications may be submitted by any government agency responsible for conservation and protection of marine turtles and any other Organization or individual with demonstrated experience in marine turtle conservation.

Beneficiary Eligibility: Same as Applicant Eligibility.

Award Range/Average: Variable amounts. Generally $50,000 or less. Higher amounts may be requested.

Funding: (Project Grants (Discretionary)) FY 18 $2,341,095.00; FY 19 est $2,000,000.00; FY 20 est $2,000,000.00

HQ: 5275 Leesburg Pike, PO Box IA, Falls Church, VA 22041-3803
   Phone: 703-358-1754
   http://www.fws.gov/international/wildlife-without-borders/marine-turtle-conservation-fund.html

DOI15.647 | MIGRATORY BIRD CONSERVATION

Award: Project Grants

Purpose: To maintain and enhance populations and habitats of migratory bird species found in the Upper Midwest (IL, IN, IA, MI, MN, MO, OH, and WI).

Applicant Eligibility: Federal, State and local government agencies; Federally-recognized Indian Tribal Governments; private nonprofit Institutions /Organizations; and public nonprofit Institutions /Organizations.

Beneficiary Eligibility: Federal, State and local government agencies; Federally-recognized Indian Tribal governments; private nonprofit institutions/organizations; public nonprofit institutions/organizations; and general public.

Award Range/Average: Range $15,000 to $79,606; average $43,218 in FY16.

Funding: (Project Grants (Discretionary)) FY 18 $313,195.00; FY 19 est $220,000.00; FY 20 est $200,000.00

HQ: 5600 American Boulevard W, Suite 990, Bloomington, MN 55437
   Phone: 612-713-5362
   http://www.fws.gov/midwest/midwestbird

DOI15.648 | CENTRAL VALLEY PROJECT IMPROVEMENT ACT (CVPIA) "CVPIA"

Award: Project Grants

Purpose: To protect, restore, and enhance fish, wildlife, and associated habitats in the Central Valley and Trinity River basins of California; to address impacts of the Central Valley Project on fish, wildlife, and associated habitats; to improve the operational flexibility of the Central Valley Project; to increase water-related benefits; to achieve a reasonable balance among competing demands for use of Central Valley Project water.

Applicant Eligibility: Applicants may be State, local Governments, Native American Organizations, other public nonprofit Institutions /Organizations, private nonprofit/Organizations, or for profit Organizations. No other Federal agency may apply.

Beneficiary Eligibility: General public.

Funding: (Project Grants (Discretionary)) FY 18 $2,170,154.00; FY 19 est $5,000,000.00; FY 20 est $5,000,000.00

HQ: 2800 Cottage Way, Suite W2606, Sacramento, CA 95825
   Phone: 916-414-6464 | Email: paul_souza@fws.gov
   http://www.fws.gov/lodi/anadromous_fish_restoration/afrp_index.htm

DOI15.649 | SERVICE TRAINING AND TECHNICAL ASSISTANCE (GENERIC TRAINING)

Award: Project Grants

Purpose: To support and provide financial resources for training, meetings, workshops and conferences to promote the public's conservation awareness.

Applicant Eligibility: Federal, State and local government agencies; Federally-recognized Tribal Governments; private nonprofit Institutions /Organizations; public nonprofit Institutions / Organizations; for profit Organizations.

Beneficiary Eligibility: Federal, State and local government agencies; Federally-recognized Tribal governments; private nonprofit institutions/organizations; public nonprofit institutions/ organizations; general public.

Award Range/Average: Range and average varies by program activity.

Funding: (Project Grants (Discretionary)) FY 18 $358,721.00; FY 19 est $0.00; FY 20 est $0.00

HQ: Policy Branch Financial Assistance Support and Oversight Division Chief Wildlife and Sport Fish Restoration Program 5275 Leesburg Pike, PO Box WSFR, Falls Church, VA 22041-3803

    Phone: 703-358-2701

    http://www.fws.gov

DOI15.650 | RESEARCH GRANTS (GENERIC)

Award: Project Grants

Purpose: To provide financial assistance for land management, research, and data collection/analysis to further the conservation of natural resources.

Applicant Eligibility: Federal, State and local government agencies; Federally-recognized Tribal Governments; private nonprofit Institutions /Organizations; public nonprofit Institutions / Organizations; for profit Organizations.

Beneficiary Eligibility: N/A

Award Range/Average: Range and average varies by program activity.

Funding: (Project Grants (Discretionary)) FY 18 $101,354.00; FY 19 est $0.00; FY 20 est $0.00

HQ: 5275 Leesburg Pike, PO Box WSFR, Falls Church, VA 22041-3803

    Phone: 703-358-2701

    http://www.fws.gov

DOI15.651 | CENTRAL AFRICA REGIONAL

Award: Project Grants

Purpose: Wildlife Without Borders-Africa funds projects that reduce threats to key wildlife populations and undertakes long-term conservation programs.

Applicant Eligibility: Federal, State and local government agencies; non-profit, non-governmental Organizations; and public and private Institutions of higher education, or any of the stated associate entities on behalf of an eligible individual.

Beneficiary Eligibility: Federal, State and local government. agencies; nonprofit, non-governmental organizations; and public and private institutions of higher education. All recipients, both individual and institutional, must have a bank account and have the ability to receive funds directly.

Award Range/Average: Variable amounts. Generally $50,000 or less. Higher amounts may be requested.

Funding: (Project Grants (Discretionary)) FY 18 $15,028,276.00; FY 19 est $15,000,000.00; FY 20 est $15,000,000

HQ: Division of International Conservation 5275 Leesburg Pike, PO Box IA, Falls Church, VA 22041-3803

    Phone: 703-358-1754

    http://www.fws.gov/international/wildlife-without-borders/africa/index.html

DOI15.652 | INVASIVE SPECIES

Award: Project Grants

Purpose: To encourage coordination and integration of endeavors between the U.S. Fish and Wildlife Service (USFWS) and interested parties to accomplish successful prevention or management of invasive species.

Applicant Eligibility: Applicants may be State and local Governments, educational Institutions, private and public nonprofit Organizations, and Institutions and private individuals which support the mission of the Service.

Beneficiary Eligibility: State and local governments; private and public nonprofit organizations; other private and public organizations; and private individuals who support the mission of the Service.

Award Range/Average: Range: $9,000 - $200,000 Average: $45,000

Programs Administered by Regional - State - Local Offices

Funding: (Project Grants (Discretionary)) FY 18 $226,965; FY 19 est $350,000; FY 20 est $350,000
HQ: 5275 Leesburg Pike, PO Box NWRS, Falls Church, VA 22041
  Phone: 703-358-1744
  http://www.fws.gov

DOI15.653 | NATIONAL OUTREACH AND COMMUNICATION
"NOC "

Award: Cooperative Agreements
Purpose: To improve communications with anglers, boaters, and the public to reduce obstacles to participate in these activities; to advance adoption of fishing and boating practices; to promote conservation and the responsible use of the nation's aquatic resources; and to further safety in fishing and boating.
Applicant Eligibility: N/A
Beneficiary Eligibility: N/A
Funding: (Cooperative Agreements (Discretionary)): FY 18 $12,263,000.00; FY19 est $12,599,000.00; FY20 est $13,294,000.00
HQ: 5275 Leesburg Pike, PO Box FAC, Falls Church, VA 22041
  Phone: 703-358-2056
  http://www.fws.gov

DOI15.654 | NATIONAL WILDLIFE REFUGE SYSTEM ENHANCEMENTS
"Refuges and WIldlife"

Award: Cooperative Agreements
Purpose: To provide technical and financial assistance; deliver public access and high-quality outdoor recreational opportunities; build a volunteer cadre; and inspire the next generation of hunters, anglers. and wildlife enthusiasts.
Applicant Eligibility: Applicants may be State and local Governments, private, public, nonprofit Organizations, Institutions and private individuals, which support the mission of the Service.
Beneficiary Eligibility: State and local governments; private and public nonprofit organizations; other private and public organizations; and private individuals who support the mission of the Service.
Award Range/Average: $1,000 to $1,000,000, or greater.
Funding: (Cooperative Agreements (Discretionary Grants)) FY 18 $4,100,000.00; FY 19 est $3,900,000.00; FY 20 est $3,900,000.00
HQ: 5275 Leesburg Pike, PO Box NWRS, Falls Church, VA 22041
  Phone: 703-358-1744
  http://www.fws.gov

DOI15.655 | MIGRATORY BIRD MONITORING, ASSESSMENT AND CONSERVATION
"Migratory Bird"

Award: Project Grants
Purpose: To conserve, enhance, and understand the ecology and habitats of migratory bird species.
Applicant Eligibility: Federal; Interstate; Intrastate; State; Local; including Tribal Government; Public Nonprofit Institution/Organization; Other Public Institution/Organization; Federally Recognized Tribal Government; U.S. Territory or Possession; Institutions of Higher education including Public Private, State College, University, Junior, and Community College; Individual/Family; Specialized Group; Small Business; Profit Organization; Private Nonprofit Institution/Organization; Quasi-Public Nonprofit Institution/Organization; Other Private Institution/Organization; or Native American Organization.
Beneficiary Eligibility: Federal; Interstate; Intrastate; State; Local; including Tribal Government; Public Nonprofit Institution/Organization; Other Public Institution/Organization; Federally Recognized Tribal Government; U.S. Territory or Possession; Institutions of Higher Education including Public Private, State College, University, Junior, and Community College; Individual/Family; Specialized Group; Small Business; Profit Organization; Private Nonprofit Institution/Organization; Quasi-Public Nonprofit Institution/Organization; Other Private Institution/Organization.
Award Range/Average: Not Available.

Funding: (Project Grants (Discretionary)) FY 18 $800,000.00; FY 19 est $1,000,000.00; FY 20 est $1,000,000.00
HQ: 5275 Leesburg Pike, PO Box MB, Falls Church, VA 22041-3803
    Phone: 703-358-1757
    http://www.fws.gov/migratorybirds

DOI15.656 | RECOVERY ACT FUNDS-HABITAT ENHANCEMENT, RESTORATION AND IMPROVEMENT.
"ARRA"

Award: Cooperative Agreements
Purpose: To provide technical and financial assistance to identify, protect, conserve, manage, enhance, or restore habitat or species on both public and private lands.
Applicant Eligibility: N/A
Beneficiary Eligibility: N/A
Award Range/Average: Not Applicable.
HQ: Department of the Interior 1849 C Street NW, Washington, DC 20240
    Phone: 202-208-6394
    http://www.fws.gov

DOI15.657 | ENDANGERED SPECIES CONSERVATION-RECOVERY IMPLEMENTATION FUNDS

Award: Project Grants
Purpose: To provide federal financial assistance to secure endangered or threatened species information, undertake restoration actions that will lead to delisting of a species, help prevent extinction of a species, or aid in the recovery of species.
Applicant Eligibility: State and local government agencies. Institutions of higher education, including public, private state colleges and universities, nonprofits that have 501(c)(3) status with the IRS, Native American tribal Organizations (other than recognized tribal Governments), city, county or township Governments, individuals, Native American tribal Governments (federally-recognized), for-profit Organizations, and small businesses.
Beneficiary Eligibility: Same as Applicant Eligibility.
Award Range/Average: Varies by Region
Funding: (Project Grants (Discretionary)) FY 18 $10,000,000.00; FY 19 est $10,000,000.00; FY 20 est Estimate Not Available
HQ: Division of Restoration and Recovery 5275 Leesburg Pike, PO Box ES, Falls Church, VA 20241
    Phone: 703-358-2171
    http://www.fws.gov/endangered

DOI15.658 | NATURAL RESOURCE DAMAGE ASSESSMENT AND RESTORATION
"NRDAR"

Award: Project Grants
Purpose: To restore natural resources injured by oil spills or hazardous substance releases. The purpose of the Natural Resource Damage Assessment and Restoration (NRDAR) Program is to restore natural resources and their services that have been injured by an oil spill or hazardous substance release for the benefit of the American people.
Applicant Eligibility: Anyone/general public. Use of assistance is primarily for natural resources but also can be for public education and recreation.
Beneficiary Eligibility: Anyone/General public.
Award Range/Average: Projects may range from $1,000 to $1,000,000 or greater.
Funding: (Project Grants (Discretionary)) FY 18 $3,787,318.00; FY 19 est $2,713,323.00; FY 20 est $4,000,000.00
HQ: 5275 Leesburg Pike, PO Box ES, Falls Church, VA 20241
    Phone: 703-358-2171
    https://www.fws.gov/ecological-services/habitat-conservation/NRDAR.html

Programs Administered by Regional - State - Local Offices

DOI15.659 | NATIONAL WILDLIFE REFUGE FUND
"Refuge Revenue Sharing"

Award: Direct Payments With Unrestricted Use
Purpose: The USFWS makes revenue-sharing payments to counties for the lands that are administered.
Applicant Eligibility: No functional Application/Unlimited Application of any local unit of government where fee owned
NWRS lands are located automatically receive payments based on legislated formulas.
Beneficiary Eligibility: Same as Applicant Eligibility.
HQ: Division of Realty U.S. Fish and Wildlife Service Department of the Interior 5275 Leesburg Pike, PO Box NWRS, Falls
Church, VA 22041-3803
　　Phone: 703-358-1713
　　http://www.fws.gov/refuges/realty/rrs.html

DOI15.660 | ENDANGERED SPECIES-CANDIDATE CONSERVATION ACTION FUNDS

Award: Project Grants
Purpose: To provide a means by which the ecosystems upon which candidate and at-risk species depend may be conserved.
Applicant Eligibility: Anyone except Federal Agencies.
Beneficiary Eligibility: Anyone/General public.
Award Range/Average: Varies by Region
Funding: (Cooperative Agreements (Discretionary Grants)) FY 18 $339,507.00; FY 19 est $410,000.00; FY 20 est $410,000.00
HQ: Branch of Communications and Candidate Conservation 5275 Leesburg Pike, PO Box ES, Falls Church, VA 20241
　　Phone: 703-358-2171
　　https://www.fws.gov/grants

DOI15.661 | LOWER SNAKE RIVER COMPENSATION PLAN
"LSRCP"

Award: Cooperative Agreements
Purpose: To mitigate for the losses of fish and wildlife caused by the U.S. Army Corps of Engineers while constructing four
hydroelectric dams on the lower Snake River.
Applicant Eligibility: N/A
Beneficiary Eligibility: N/A
Award Range/Average: Range $274,268 to $5,609,594
Funding: (Cooperative Agreements (Discretionary Grants)) FY 18 $33,483,000.00; FY 19 est $30,483,000.00; FY 20 est
$31,000,000.00
HQ: 911 NE 11th Avenue, Portland, OR 97232-4181
　　Phone: 503-231-2763
　　http://www.fws.gov/lsnakecomplan

DOI15.662 | GREAT LAKES RESTORATION
"Great Lakes Restoration Initiative; Great Lakes Restoration Program"

Award: Project Grants
Purpose: To provide technical and financial aid to enforce the highest priority actions in order to protect and restore the Great
Lakes.
Applicant Eligibility: Program -specific.
Beneficiary Eligibility: Same as Applicant Eligibility.
Award Range/Average: Projects may range from $1,000 to $1,000,000, or greater.
Funding: (Project Grants (Discretionary)) FY 18 $51,902,000.00; FY 19 est $45,800,000.00; FY 20 est $40,000,000.00
HQ: Department of the Interior 1849 C Street NW, Washington, DC 20240
　　Phone: 202-208-6394
　　http://www.fws.gov/glri

DOI15.663 | NFWF-USFWS CONSERVATION PARTNERSHIP
"NFWF"

Award: Project Grants

Purpose: National Fish and Wildlife Foundation provides grants to recipients who work to conserve and protect fish and wildlife species and their habitats.

Applicant Eligibility: Specified in the National Fish and Wildlife Foundation Establishment Act.

Beneficiary Eligibility: Beneficiaries include fish, wildlife and their habitats, the American people and, where applicable, international partners, wildlife and natural resources.

Award Range/Average: Not Applicable.

Funding: (Project Grants) FY 18 $6,825,600.00; FY 19 est $6,000,000.00; FY 20 est Estimate Not Available

HQ: 5275 Leesburg Pike, PO Box WSFR, Falls Church, VA 20241

    Phone: 703-358-2214

    http://www.nfwf.org

DOI15.664 | FISH AND WILDLIFE COORDINATION AND ASSISTANCE
"FWCA"

Award: Project Grants

Purpose: To implement legislation mandating specific conservation and/or environmental project activity(ies), including, but not limited to, financial assistance funding for special appropriations projects to a designated recipient(s); and/or unfunded Congressional mandates.

Applicant Eligibility: Eligibility varies by opportunity and is limited to entity(ies) designated by the authorizing legislation.

Beneficiary Eligibility: The general public benefits from the conservation and environmental efforts as identified by the authorizing legislation.

Award Range/Average: Range and average varies by program activity.

Funding: (Project Grants (Discretionary)) FY 18 $1,280,748.00; FY 19 est $5,000,000.00; FY 20 est $5,000,000.00

HQ: Policy Branch Financial Assistance Support and Oversight Division 5275 Leesburg Pike, PO Box WSFR, Falls Church, VA 22041-3803

    Phone: 703-358-2701

DOI15.665 | NATIONAL WETLANDS INVENTORY
"NWI"

Award: Project Grants

Purpose: For mapping wetlands of the nation, digitizing the maps, archiving and distributing the data, and producing a ten-year national wetlands status and trends report to the Congress.

Applicant Eligibility: Organizations receiving financial assistance must be experienced in image-interpretation for wetlands and for arid western riparian for targeted ecosystems using National standards (Cowardin et al. 1979 and Wetlands Mapping Standard 2009); in wetlands mapping or delivery research or technologies, or in supporting activities (e.g. mapping standards training or analysis) for wetlands mapping; or have the project-specific imagery or ancillary data needed for wetlands mapping. Based on Agency need, financial assistance, in general, is available to qualified Americans, profit or nonprofit corporations or Institutions, domestic Organizations, and Federal, State, Tribal, Territorial, and local agencies.

Beneficiary Eligibility: The American public, and Federal, State, Tribal, Territorial, and local agencies, profit and nonprofit corporations or institutions benefit from having wetlands geospatial data to help inform decision making for clean water, fish and wildlife conservation, wetlands conservation, landscape-level planning, green infrastructure, and urban, rural, infrastructure, and energy development.

Award Range/Average: $30,000- $532,000

Funding: (Project Grants (Discretionary)) FY 18 $996,000.00; FY 19 est $862,000.00; FY 20 est Estimate Not Available

HQ: 5275 Leesburg Pike, PO Box ES, Falls Church, VA 22041-3803

    Phone: 703-358-2171

    http://www.fws.gov/wetlands

Programs Administered by Regional - State - Local Offices

DOI15.666 | ENDANGERED SPECIES CONSERVATION-WOLF LIVESTOCK LOSS COMPENSATION AND PREVENTION
"Wolf Livestock Demonstration Project Grant Program"

Award: Project Grants

Purpose: To reduce the risk of livestock loss due to wolf attacks, and to compensate livestock manufacturers for the losses due to such predation.

Applicant Eligibility: State Governments /agencies Indian Tribes as defined in Public Law111-11.

Beneficiary Eligibility: Individual/ Family Small Business Profit Organization Private Organization Anyone/ General Public Farmer/ Rancher/ Agricultural Producer Small Business Person Land/ Property Owner.

Award Range/Average: $9,000 - $100,000. Average grant award amount is $50,000

Funding: (Project Grants (Discretionary)) FY 18 $900,000; FY 19 est $900,000; FY 20 est $900,000

HQ: Division of Restoration and Recovery 5275 Leesburg Pike, PO Box ES, Falls Church, VA 20241

Phone: 703-358-2171

http://www.fws.gov/endangered/grants/index.html

DOI15.667 | HIGHLANDS CONSERVATION

Award: Project Grants

Purpose: To preserve and protect high-priority conservation land in the Highland regions by conserving priority lands and natural resources and recognizing the importance of the water, forest, agricultural, wildlife, recreational, and cultural resources.

Applicant Eligibility: Any state or state agency with authority to own and manage land located within the Highlands region for conservation purposes may apply by identifying the source of non-Federal funds, describing the management objectives for the project land, identifying the purpose of the use of the land, and providing that the land will not be converted, used or disposed of for a purpose inconsistent with land conservation.

Beneficiary Eligibility: Beneficiaries are states or state agencies with authority to own and manage land within the Highlands region for conservation purposes, including the Palisades Interstate Park Commission.

Award Range/Average: Range : $646,600 to $1,940,000; Average $970,000

Funding: (Project Grants (Discretionary)) FY 18 $9,680,000.00; FY 19 est $19,680,000.00; FY 20 est $9,680,000.00

HQ: Wildlife and Sport Fish Restoration 300 W Gate Center Drive, Hadley, MA 01035

Phone: 413-253-8501 | Email: colleen_sculley@fws.gov

https://www.fws.gov/northeast/highlands-conservation-act/index.html

DOI15.668 | COASTAL IMPACT ASSISTANCE
"CIAP"

Award: Formula Grants

Purpose: To disburse funding to entitled producing States and coastal political subdivisions for the purpose of conservation, protection, or restoration of coastal areas.

Applicant Eligibility: States eligible to receive funding are Alabama, Alaska, California, Louisiana, Mississippi, and Texas and 67 coastal political subdivisions among the six States.

Beneficiary Eligibility: The producing coastal states, their eligible coastal political subdivisions, and the public will ultimately benefit from the program.

Award Range/Average: $20,000 - $20,000,000; average $1,000,000

HQ: 5275 Leesburg Pike, PO Box WSFR, Falls Church, VA 22041-3803

Phone: 703-358-2156

http://wsfrprograms.fws.gov

DOI15.669 | COOPERATIVE LANDSCAPE CONSERVATION
"Landscape Conservation Cooperatives (LCCs)"

Award: Project Grants

Purpose: No awards anticipated.

Applicant Eligibility: N/A

Beneficiary Eligibility: N/A

Award Range/Average: Range is $1,000 - $1,000,000. Average award amount varies by project type and duration.
Funding: (Project Grants (Discretionary)) FY 18 $14,500.00; FY 19 est $0.00; FY 20 est $0.00
HQ: Science Applications U.S. Fish and Wildlife Service Department of the Interior 5275 Leesburg Pike, PO Box SA, Falls Church, VA 22041-3803

Phone: 703-358-1881 | Email: anna-marie_york@fws.gov
http://lccnetwork.org

DOI15.670 | ADAPTIVE SCIENCE

Award: Project Grants
Purpose: Strategic Habitat Conservation is based on the principles of adaptive management and uses population and habitat data, ecological models, and focused monitoring and assessment efforts to develop and utilize strategies that result in measurable fish and wildlife population outcomes. It uses the best available scientific information to predict how fish and wildlife populations will respond to changes in the environment.
Applicant Eligibility: N/A
Beneficiary Eligibility: N/A
Award Range/Average: Range is $1,000 - $1,000,000. Average award amount varies by project type and duration.
Funding: (Project Grants (Discretionary)) FY 18 $2,007,000.00; FY 19 est $2,500,000.00; FY 20 est $2,500,000.00
HQ: Department of the Interior 5275 Leesburg Pike, PO Box SA, Falls Church, VA 22041-3803

Phone: 703-358-1881 | Email: anna-marie_york@fws.gov
http://www.fws.gov/science

DOI15.671 | YUKON RIVER SALMON RESEARCH AND MANAGEMENT ASSISTANCE
"R&M Fund"

Award: Project Grants
Purpose: Yukon River Salmon Research and Management Assistance funds projects that increase/improve the understanding of research and management of Yukon River salmon.
Applicant Eligibility: The intended result of this funding is to improve the understanding of the biology and management of Yukon River salmon species.
Beneficiary Eligibility: Projects that are awarded money from this source will ultimately benefit the rural and urban American and Canadian public that subsist off of the salmon resources of the Yukon River.
Award Range/Average: Range: $3,000-220,456; Average: $40,756
Funding: (Project Grants (Discretionary)) FY 18 $251,091.00; FY 19 est $290,000.00; FY 20 est $300,000
HQ: 1011 E Tudor Road, Anchorage, AK 99503

Phone: 907-786-3523
http://alaska.fws.gov/fisheries/fieldoffice/fairbanks/index.htm

DOI15.672 | WILDLIFE WITHOUT BORDERS-AMPHIBIANS IN DECLINE

Award: Project Grants
Purpose: To provide funding for specific conservation actions to amphibian species facing imminent threat of extinction.
Applicant Eligibility: Applications may be submitted by any non-domestic (outside of the United States) government agency responsible for amphibian conservation and any other U.S. -based or non-domestic public or private Organization or institution or individual with demonstrated experience in amphibian conservation.
Beneficiary Eligibility: Non-domestic (outside of the United States) government agencies responsible for amphibian conservation and any other U.S.-based or non-domestic public or private non-governmental organization or institution or individual with demonstrated experience in amphibian conservation.
Award Range/Average: Not Applicable.
HQ: Division of International Conservation 5275 Leesburg Pike, PO Box IA, Falls Church, VA 22041-3803

Phone: 703-358-1754
http://www.fws.gov/international/wildlife-without-borders/amphibians-in-decline.html

Programs Administered by Regional - State - Local Offices

DOI15.673 | WILDLIFE WITHOUT BORDERS-CRITICALLY ENDANGERED ANIMAL CONSERVATION FUND

Award: Project Grants

Purpose: To reduce threats to highly endangered wildlife in their natural habitat. The proposals should identify specific conservation actions that have a high likelihood of creating durable benefits.

Applicant Eligibility: Applications may be submitted by any non-domestic (outside of the United States) government agency responsible for endangered species conservation and any other U.S.-based or non-domestic public or private Organization or institution or individual with demonstrated experience in endangered species conservation.

Beneficiary Eligibility: Non-domestic (outside of the United States) government agencies responsible for endangered species conservation and any other U.S.-based or non-domestic public or private non-governmental organization or institution or individual with demonstrated experience in endangered species conservation.

Award Range/Average: Not Applicable.

HQ: Division of International Conservation 5275 Leesburg Pike, PO Box IA, Falls Church, VA 22041-3803
Phone: 703-358-1754
http://www.fws.gov/international/wildlife-without-borders/critically-endangered-animals-conservation-fund.html

DOI15.674 | NATIONAL FIRE PLAN-WILDLAND URBAN INTERFACE COMMUNITY FIRE ASSISTANCE

Award: Cooperative Agreements; Use of Property, Facilities, and Equipment; Provision of Specialized Services; Advisory Services and Counseling; Dissemination of Technical Information; Training

Purpose: To utilize the National Cohesive Wildland Fire Management Strategy and aid communities at risk from catastrophic wildland fires.

Applicant Eligibility: State and local Governments and communities at risk and communities of interest, as published in the Federal Register/Vol. 66, No. 160 / Friday, August 17, 2001 or updated Governor-signed list, Indian Tribes, private land owners, public and private education Institutions, and nonprofit Organizations that manage lands. All selectees must be identified as significant to FWS, deemed by a cooperative agreement, memorandum of understanding, and/or part of an interagency agreement that serves as a clearinghouse for HFR assistance monies. Federal law mandates that all Organizations applying for Federal financial assistance must have a valid Dun & Bradstreet Data Universal Number System (DUNS) number and have a current registration in the Central Contractor Registry (CCR). Individuals submitting an application on their own behalf and not on behalf of a company, state, local or tribal government, academia or other type of Organization are exempt from the DUNS number and CCR requirements.

Beneficiary Eligibility: State and local governments and communities at risk and communities of interest, as published in the Federal Register or updated Governor-signed list, Indian Tribes, private land owners, public and private education institutions, and nonprofit organizations that manage lands. All selectees must be identified as significant to FWS. For mitigation activities (projects that are removing hazardous fuels) all work funded must be identified from a signed CWPP or CWPP/E or will be signed by expected funding date.

Funding: (Cooperative Agreements (Discretionary Grants)) FY 18 $0.00; FY 19 est $300,000.00; FY 20 est $200,000.00

HQ: 3833 S Development Avenue, Boise, ID 83705
Phone: 208-387-5941 | Email: tate_fischer@fws.gov
http://www.fws.gov/fire

DOI15.676 | YOUTH ENGAGEMENT, EDUCATION, AND EMPLOYMENT "YEEEP"

Award: Project Grants

Purpose: To provide experiential, education, and employment program opportunities for youth to participate in conservation activities conducted by the U.S. Fish and Wildlife Service, and/or in collaboration with other Department of the Interior bureaus, and thereby promoting intra-agency and external partnership and employment opportunities.

Applicant Eligibility: Applicants may be state agencies, local Governments, Tribal Organizations, interstate, Intrastate, public nonprofit institution/Organization, other public institution/Organization, private nonprofit/Organization, or any other Organization subject to the jurisdiction of the United States with interests that support the mission of the Service.

Beneficiary Eligibility: Same as Applicant Eligibility.

Award Range/Average: $750.00 - $200,000

Funding: (Cooperative Agreements (Discretionary Grants)) FY 18 $6,229,792.00; FY 19 est $8,900,000.00; FY 20 est $8,900,000.00
HQ: 5275 Leesburg Pike, Falls Church, VA 22041-3803
Phone: 703-358-2386 | Email: deborah_moore@fws.gov
http://www.fws.gov

DOI15.677 | HURRICANE SANDY DISASTER RELIEF ACTIVITIES-FWS

Award: Project Grants
Purpose: To provide technical and financial assistance to identify, protect, conserve, manage, improve, or reconstruct habitat and structures on both public and private lands that have been impacted by Hurricane Sandy.
Applicant Eligibility: Awards may be made to State/Local Governments, Indian Tribal Governments, Non-Profits, Institutes of Higher education, Hospitals and For-Profit companies.
Beneficiary Eligibility: These projects will directly benefit the public as a whole.
Funding: (Project Grants (Discretionary)) FY 18 $4,820,000.00; FY 19 est $820,000.00; FY 20 est $0.00
HQ: 300 W Gate Center Drive, Hadley, MA 01035
Phone: 413-253-8528

DOI15.678 | COOPERATIVE ECOSYSTEM STUDIES UNITS
"CESU"

Award: Cooperative Agreements
Purpose: To provide scientific research, technical assistance, and education on natural and cultural resource issues to federal land management, environmental, and research agencies.
Applicant Eligibility: N/A
Beneficiary Eligibility: University faculty; federal employees by accessing increased opportunities for interdisciplinary, multi-agency research projects related to federal resource management issues; any entity which may, will, or can benefit from the contemplated activity; students, researchers, experts, and instructors as members of the general public.
Award Range/Average: $20,000 - $150,000 ($85,000)
Funding: (Project Grants (Discretionary)) FY 18 $4,635,714.00; FY 19 est $3,800,000.00; FY 20 est $4,000,000.00
HQ: 5275 Leesburg Pike, PO Box SA, Falls Church, VA 22041-3803
Phone: 703-358-1881 | Email: anna-marie_york@fws.gov
http://www.fws.gov/science/cesu.html

DOI15.679 | COMBATING WILDLIFE TRAFFICKING

Award: Project Grants
Purpose: Combating Wildlife Trafficking program funds projects that helps to advance counter-wildlife trafficking activities.
Applicant Eligibility: N/A
Beneficiary Eligibility: Non-domestic (outside of the United States) government agencies responsible for combating wildlife trafficking and any other U.S.- based or non-domestic public or private non-governmental organization or institution or individual with demonstrated experience in the activities proposed.
Award Range/Average: We anticipate issuing 10 awards for $100,000 or less each to be used for projects lasting one year.
Funding: (Project Grants (Discretionary)) FY 18 $3,257,723.00; FY 19 est $4,500,000.00; FY 20 est $4,500,000.00
HQ: Headquarters Office Division of International Conservation 5275 Leesburg Pike, PO Box IA, Falls Church, VA 22041
Phone: 703-358-2134
http://www.fws.gov/international/grants-and-reporting/how-to-apply.html

DOI15.680 | MEXICAN WOLF RECOVERY

Award: Project Grants
Purpose: To provide federal financial assistance to secure Mexican Wolf information, initiate actions that will lead to delisting of the Mexican Wolf and help prevent extinction or aid in the recovery of the Mexican Wolf.
Applicant Eligibility: State and local government agencies; Institutions of higher education, including public, private state colleges and universities; nonprofits that have 501(c)(3) status with the IRS; Native American tribal Organizations (other than recognized tribal Governments); city, county or township Governments; individuals; Native American tribal Governments (federally-recognized); for-profit Organizations; and small businesses.

Programs Administered by Regional - State - Local Offices

Beneficiary Eligibility: Same as Applicant Eligibility.

Award Range/Average: 0 to $250,000; Average $78,571.00

Funding: (Project Grants (Discretionary)) FY 18 $580,000.00; FY 19 est Estimate Not Available; FY 20 est Estimate Not Available

HQ: 500 Gold Avenue SW, Albuquerque, NM 87102

Phone: 505-248-6477 | Email: janet_huff@fws.gov

http://www.fws.gov/southwest/es/mexicanwolf

DOI15.681 | COOPERATIVE AGRICULTURE

Award: Use of Property, Facilities, and Equipment

Purpose: To produce or modify specific cover types and/or growing methods to meet the life history requirements of species and produce foods for wildlife species.

Applicant Eligibility: Applicants must be private individuals or small business entities.

Beneficiary Eligibility: Selected co-operators who conduct cooperative agriculture on NWRS lands under this program, excluding coordination areas (which are areas managed by the Service in coordination with the States).

Award Range/Average: $0. This is a nonfinancial assistance program.

HQ: National Wildlife Refuge System Headquarters, Falls Church, VA 22041-3803

Phone: 703-358-2678 | Email: aaron_mize@fws.gov

https://www.fws.gov/refuges/whm/cooperativeAgriculture.html

U.S. GEOLOGICAL SURVEY
Regional – State – Local Offices

California

Alan M. Mikuni | 345 Middlefield Road PO Box 531, Menlo Park, CA 94025-3591 415-329-4254

T. John Conomos, Regional Hydrologist | 345 Middlefield Road PO Box 470, Menlo Park, CA 94025-3591 415-329-4414

Colorado

CR Federal Center PO Box 911, Denver, CO 80225 303-236-5435

Dave J. Lystrom, Regional Hydrologist | Mail Stop 406 PO Box 25046 Denver Federal Center Building 25, Lakewood, CO 80225-0046 303-236-5950

Dr. J. Larry Ludke, Regional Chief Biologist | DFC Building 020 Room A1419 PO Box 25046 PO Box 300, Denver, CO 80225 303-236-2739, Ext. 238

Randle W. Olsen | Denver Federal Center Building 810 Mail Stop 508 PO Box 25046, Denver, CO 80225-0046 303-202-4040

Georgia

Wanda C. Meeks, Regional Hydrologist | Spalding Woods Office Park Suite 160 3850 Holcomb Bridge Road, Norcross, GA 30092-2202 404-409-7701

Missouri

Max Ethridge | 1400 Independence Road Mail Stop 300, Rolla, MO 65401 573-308-3800

South Dakota

Donald T. Lauer | Mundt Federal Building, Sioux Falls, SD 57198 605-594-6123

Virginia

953 National Center, Reston, VA 20192 703-648-6662

Gregory Smith, Acting Regional Chief Biologist | National Center Room 4A100 12201 Sunrise Valley Drive PO Box 300, Reston, VA 20192 703-648-4060

Pat Dunham | National Center PO Box 567, Reston, VA 20192 703-648-6002

William Carswell Jr., Regional Hydrologist | 433 National Center Mail Stop 433, Reston, VA 22092 703-648-5813

Washington

Dr. John D. Buffington, Regional Chief Biologist | 909 1st Avenue Suite 800, Seattle, WA 98104 206-220-4600

REGIONAL OFFICES

California

345 Middlefield Road PO Box 919, Menlo Park, CA 94025 415-650-5102

DOI15.805 | ASSISTANCE TO STATE WATER RESOURCES RESEARCH INSTITUTES
"Water Research Institute Program"

Award: Formula Grants; Project Grants

Purpose: Providing financial assistance to Water Resources Research Institutes located at designated State universities.

Applicant Eligibility: One University Water Research Institute is authorized in each State and other jurisdictions specified in Section 104. Other colleges and universities within a State are encouraged to participate in the Program in cooperation with the designated Institute.

Beneficiary Eligibility: Researchers at qualified universities and colleges in the State through the designated Institute for the State.

Award Range/Average: (Formula Grants) $92,335 to $277,005; average $95,755. (Competitive Grants) $140,162 to $249,949; average $212,950.

Funding: (Cooperative Agreements (Discretionary Grants)) FY 18 $1,000,000.00; FY 19 est $1,000,000.00; FY 20 est $1,000,000.00; (Formula Grants Total) FY 18 $5,200,000.00; FY 19 est $5,200,000.00; FY 20 est $5,200,000.00

HQ: Department of the Interior Office of External Research 5522 Research Park Drive, Baltimore, MD 21228

Phone: 443-498-5505 | Email: eagreene@usgs.gov

http://water.usgs.gov/wrri/

DOI15.807 | EARTHQUAKE HAZARDS PROGRAM ASSISTANCE
"Earthquake Hazards Program Grants"

Award: Project Grants

Purpose: To support earthquake hazards research and monitoring and develop information, knowledge, and methods relevant to the major Earthquake Hazards Program elements.

Applicant Eligibility: Public and private colleges and universities; Non-profit, non-academic Organizations; For-profit Organizations; State and Local Governments; and unaffiliated scientists.

Beneficiary Eligibility: Research scientists, engineers, and the general public will ultimately benefit from the program.

Award Range/Average: $6,000 to $1,340,000; average $74,000.

Funding: (Cooperative Agreements (Discretionary Grants)) FY 18 $28,500,000.00; FY 19 est $28,500,000.00; FY 20 est $28,500,000.00

HQ: Department of the Interior National Center 12201 Sunrise Valley Drive, PO Box 905, Reston, VA 20192

Phone: 703-648-6716 | Email: jfranks@usgs.gov

http://earthquake.usgs.gov/research/external/

DOI15.808 | U.S. GEOLOGICAL SURVEY RESEARCH AND DATA COLLECTION

Award: Cooperative Agreements

Purpose: To support research in classification of the public lands and examination of the geological structure, water, mineral, and biological resources, and products of the national domain.

Applicant Eligibility: Profit Organizations, public nonprofit Institutions /Organizations, private nonprofit Institutions / Organizations, and State and local Governments may make application for support by a named principal investigator. Due to limited availability of funds to support new external projects, consultation with USGS is strongly recommended prior to submission of applications.

Beneficiary Eligibility: Profit organizations, public nonprofit institutions/organizations, private nonprofit institutions/ organizations, and State and local governments, industry and public decision makers, research scientists, engineers, and the general public will ultimately benefit from knowledge gained under the program.

Award Range/Average: Range is 1,000 to $625,000; average $77,940

Funding: (Cooperative Agreements (Discretionary Grants)) FY 18 $13,778,721.00; FY 19 est $14,000,000.00; FY 20 est $14,000,000.00

HQ: Reston, VA 20192

Phone: 703-648-4582

http://www.usgs.gov/contracts

Programs Administered by Regional - State - Local Offices

DOI15.810 | NATIONAL COOPERATIVE GEOLOGIC MAPPING
"StateMap and EdMap"

Award: Cooperative Agreements
Purpose: To create geologic maps of areas where the knowledge of geology is important to the economic, social, or scientific welfare of individual states.
Applicant Eligibility: State Map Program is restricted by statue to State geological surveys. Where State surveys are organized under a State University system, an application may be submitted by a State college or University on behalf of the State geological survey. Ed Map Program is restricted to universities with geoscience or related departments or Programs.
Beneficiary Eligibility: State geological surveys participating in this program and the general public will ultimately benefit from this program.
Award Range/Average: StateMap: $8,000 to $364,442; proposal average $115,064. EdMap: $5,572 to $10,948 per student; average per student $7,971. The maximum award allowed per graduate student is $17,500 and $10,000 per undergraduate student.
Funding: (Cooperative Agreements) FY 18 $5,982,437.00; FY 19 est $5,982,437.00; FY 20 est $5,982,437.00
HQ: 12201 Sunrise Valley Drive, Reston, VA 20192
Phone: 703-648-6973 | Email: dmcphee@usgs.gov
http://www.ncgmp.usgs.gov

DOI15.811 | GAP ANALYSIS
"GAP"

Award: Cooperative Agreements
Purpose: To document where native animal species and natural plant communities occur and identify gaps in their representation to assist preservation of diverseness.
Applicant Eligibility: Profit Organizations, public nonprofit Institutions /Organizations, private nonprofit Institutions / Organizations, and State and local Governments may make application for support by a named principal investigator.
Beneficiary Eligibility: Profit organizations, public nonprofit institutions/organizations, private nonprofit institutions/ organizations, State and local governments, as well as the general public will ultimately benefit from this program.
Award Range/Average: Range: $50,000 to $250,000; average $125,000
Funding: (Cooperative Agreements (Discretionary Grants)) FY 18 $350,000.00; FY 19 est $350,000.00; FY 20 est $350,000
HQ: Forest and Rangeland Ecosystem Science Center - Snake River Field Station 970 Lusk Avenue, Boise, ID 83706
Phone: 208-426-5219 | Email: gergely@usgs.gov
http://gapanalysis.usgs.gov

DOI15.812 | COOPERATIVE RESEARCH UNITS
"CRUP"

Award: Cooperative Agreements
Purpose: To work in partnership with States and universities to address the information requirements of local, state, and federal fish, wildlife, and natural resource agencies via research, technical assistance, and education.
Applicant Eligibility: Universities hosting Cooperative Fish and Wildlife Research Units established under authority of the Cooperative Research Units Act of 1960.
Beneficiary Eligibility: Federal, State and local governments, industry and public decision makers, research scientists, State institutions of higher education, and the general public will ultimately benefit from the program.
Award Range/Average: $5,000 to $721,603; average $52,081.
Funding: (Cooperative Agreements (Discretionary Grants)) FY 18 $13,191,682.00; FY 19 est $14,000,000.00; FY 20 est $14,000,000.00
HQ: Cooperative Research Units 12201 Sunrise Valley Drive, PO Box 303, Reston, VA 20192
Phone: 703-648-4262 | Email: jthompson@usgs.gov
http://www.coopunits.org

DOI15.814 | NATIONAL GEOLOGICAL AND GEOPHYSICAL DATA PRESERVATION

Award: Project Grants

Purpose: To preserve and provide access to geological, geophysical, and engineering samples extracted from the earth to inform science and decision-making.

Applicant Eligibility: State geological surveys are eligible to apply. For State geological surveys organized under a State University system, such universities may submit a proposal on behalf of or through the State geological survey.

Beneficiary Eligibility: Research scientists, engineers, and the general public will ultimately benefit from the program.

Award Range/Average: For FY 15, the most recent year for which totals are available: range is $3,132 to $63,320; average is $24,291.For FY16, the most recent year for which totals are available: range of financial assistance is $10,209 to $79,472; average is $37,042.

Funding: (Project Grants (Discretionary)) FY 18 $1,029,690.00; FY 19 est $2,109,839.00

HQ: Denver Federal Center Core Science Systems, PO Box 25046, Denver, CO 80225

   Phone: 302-202-4828 | Email: lpowers@usgs.gov

   http://datapreservation.usgs.gov/index.shtml

DOI15.815 | NATIONAL LAND REMOTE SENSING EDUCATION OUTREACH AND RESEARCH

"National Cooperative Geographic Information System"

Award: Project Grants

Purpose: To encourage the uses of space-based land remote sensing data and technologies through educational activity and outreach.

Applicant Eligibility: Nonprofit Organizations, Public and Private colleges and universities, and State and local Governments may make an application for support by a named principal investigator.

Beneficiary Eligibility: States, research scientists, engineers, education (0-13+) and the general public will ultimately benefit from the program.

Award Range/Average: $1,217,400 to $1,217,400; average $1,217,400.

Funding: (Project Grants (Discretionary)) FY 18 $1,250,000.00; FY 19 est $1,215,000.00; FY 20 est Estimate Not Available; FY18 actual $1,250,000; FY19 estimated $1,215,000; FY19 is subject to the availability of funds. A final FY20 budget is yet to be determined

HQ: 516 National Center, Reston, VA 20192

   Phone: 703-648-5551 | Email: tcecere@usgs.gov

   http://www.usgs.gov

DOI15.817 | NATIONAL GEOSPATIAL PROGRAM: BUILDING THE NATIONAL MAP

"The National Map"

Award: Cooperative Agreements

Purpose: To encourage the uses of space-based land remote sensing data and technologies through educational activity and outreach.

Applicant Eligibility: Proposals from State, Local, Interstate, Federally or State recognized Indian Tribal Governments, US Territories and Possessions, Institutions of Higher education, Private Foundations, and Nonprofit Organizations are invited. Due to limited availability of funding to support new external projects, consultation with the U.S. Geological Survey (USGS) is strongly recommended prior to submission of applications.

Beneficiary Eligibility: Interstate, State, intrastate, and local government agencies, educational institutions, private firms, private foundations, nonprofit organizations, Federally-acknowledged or state-recognized Native American tribes or groups, U.S. territories and possessions, public decision makers, research scientists, engineers, graduate students, students/trainees, and the general public will ultimately benefit from knowledge gained under the program.

Award Range/Average: $25,000 to $770,500; average $134,682.

Funding: (Cooperative Agreements (Discretionary Grants)) FY 17 $2,350,000.00; FY 18 est $3,563,000.00; FY 19 est $0.00

HQ: PO Box 25046, Reston, VA 20192

   Phone: 703-648-5519

   http://www.nationalmap.gov

Programs Administered by Regional - State - Local Offices

DOI15.818 | VOLCANO HAZARDS PROGRAM RESEARCH AND MONITORING
"Volcano Hazards Program"

Award: Cooperative Agreements
Purpose: To improve the scientific understanding of volcanic processes and to decrease the harmful impacts of volcanic activity. The Volcano Hazards Program (VHP) provides domestic assistance to expand the expertise and capabilities applied to fulfilling its mission.
Applicant Eligibility: N/A
Beneficiary Eligibility: N/A
Award Range/Average: $20,000 to $2,000,000; average $250,000.
Funding: (Cooperative Agreements) FY 18 $2,632,491.00; FY 19 est $3,500,000.00; FY 20 est $3,500,000.00
HQ: 3A204 National Center, Reston, VA 20192
   Phone: 703-648-4773 | Email: cmandeville@usgs.gov
   http://volcanoes.usgs.gov

DOI15.819 | ENERGY COOPERATIVES TO SUPPORT THE NATIONAL ENERGY RESOURCES DATA SYSTEM
"NCRDS"

Award: Cooperative Agreements
Purpose: To collect, interpret, correlate, and assess energy-related data that support USGS Energy Resources Program research initiatives, to build and maintain national energy databases of, to conduct energy-related research and conduct resource assessments within the United States.
Applicant Eligibility: Applicants can be affiliated (but are not required to be affiliated) with State agencies, universities, Tribal Governments or Organizations. Applications must have the ability to conduct research consistent with the Energy Resources Program goals. Applicants must not be employed by a U.S. Federal agency.
Beneficiary Eligibility: Research scientists, their agencies, and ultimately the general public will benefit from the program.
Award Range/Average: $15,000- $26,000; average $15,190.
Funding: (Cooperative Agreements (Discretionary Grants)) FY 18 $15,000.00; FY 19 est $15,000.00; FY 20 est $15,000.00
HQ: Department of the Interior National Center 12201 Sunrise Valley Drive, PO Box 956, Reston, VA 20192
   Phone: 703-648-6450 | Email: jeast@usgs.gov
   http://energy.er.usgs.gov/coal_quality/state_coops

DOI15.820 | NATIONAL AND REGIONAL CLIMATE ADAPTATION SCIENCE CENTERS
"NRCASC"

Award: Cooperative Agreements
Purpose: To provide national and regional habitat and population modeling and forecasting tools, integrating physical climate models with ecological models, assessing vulnerabilities and forecasting changes, and developing standardized approaches.
Applicant Eligibility: There are eight (8) DOI CSCs; each CSC has a single "Host Institution" that is eligible to apply on behalf of themselves and members of the CSC University consortium: Alaska CSC: University of Alaska, Fairbanks; Southeast CSC: North Carolina State University, Raleigh; Northwest CSC: Oregon State University, Corvallis; Southwest CSC: University of Arizona, Tucson; North Central CSC: Colorado State University, Ft. Collins; South Central CSC: Oklahoma University, Norman; Northeast CSC: University of Massachusetts, Amherst; Pacific Islands CSC: University of Hawaii, Manoa.
Beneficiary Eligibility: Research scientists, policy makers, natural resource managers, educators, and the general public will benefit from the program.
Award Range/Average: The range for individual NRCASC financial assistance awards (individual projects) is up to $1,000,000 in FY 2019.
Funding: (Cooperative Agreements (Discretionary Grants)) FY 18 $6,000,000.00; FY 19 est $6,500,000.00; FY 20 est $6,500,000.00
HQ: 12201 Sunrise Valley Drive, Reston, VA 20192
   Phone: 703-648-4607 | Email: nhartke@usgs.gov
   http://nccwsc.usgs.gov

DOI15.978 | UPPER MISSISSIPPI RIVER RESTORATION LONG TERM RESOURCE MONITORING
"LTRM"

Award: Cooperative Agreements

Purpose: To supply decision makers with information needed to maintain the Upper Mississippi River System (UMRS) as a sustainable large-river ecosystem.

Applicant Eligibility: State agencies stipulated in the Water Resources Development Act of 1986 (Public Law 99-662) are eligible to apply.

Beneficiary Eligibility: UMRS State, Federal, and private natural resource managers, users, and the general public.

Award Range/Average: $389,475 to $785,628 average $455,294.

Funding: (Cooperative Agreements (Discretionary Grants)) FY 18 $3,200,000.00; FY 19 est $3,500,000.00; FY 20 est $3,500,000.00

HQ: WI 54603

Phone: 608-783-6451 | Email: jsauer@usgs.gov

http://www.usgs.gov/ltrmp.html

DOI15.979 | HURRICANE SANDY

Award: Cooperative Agreements

Purpose: To support research and data collection complementary to continued USGS activities supporting recovery and restoration efforts related to the Hurricane Sandy.

Applicant Eligibility: Proposals from State, Local, Interstate, Federally or State recognized Indian Tribal Governments, US Territories and Possessions, Institutions of Higher education, Private Foundations, and Nonprofit Organizations are invited. Due to limited availability of funding to support new external projects, consultation with the Geological Survey is strongly recommended prior to submission of applications.

Beneficiary Eligibility: Federal, State and local governments, Federally or State recognized Indian Tribal Governments, industry and public decision makers, research scientists, State institutions of higher education, private firms, private foundations, nonprofit organizations, and the general public will ultimately benefit from the program.

Award Range/Average: Not Applicable.

HQ: 12201 Sunrise Valley Drive, Reston, VA 20192

Phone: 703-715-7020 | Email: hsweyers@usgs.gov

http://www.usgs.gov/contracts

DOI15.980 | NATIONAL GROUND-WATER MONITORING NETWORK

Award: Cooperative Agreements

Purpose: To provide support to multi-state, State, Tribal, or local Water-Resource agencies that collect groundwater data to serve as data providers for the National Ground-Water Monitoring Network.

Applicant Eligibility: Proposals will be accepted from interstate, State, U.S. territory or possession, local, public nonprofit water-resource agencies/Organizations which collect and maintain groundwater-level or groundwater-quality data. Various elements of the data which are required for the National Ground-Water Monitoring Network are often available from different agencies within a state. Each agency within a state which wishes to participate in the Network can submit a proposal for their part of the work. States may also submit a single proposal that covers the work of multiple state agencies. Coordination of agencies within a state is strongly encouraged.

Beneficiary Eligibility: Federal, State, Federally recognized Indian Tribal, and local governments, public nonprofit institutions/ organizations, private nonprofit institutions/organizations, profit organizations, industry and public decision makers, research scientists, engineers, and the general public will ultimately benefit from data made available through the program.

Award Range/Average: $15,000 to $150,000 per year for each of two years; average $55,000 per year.

Funding: (Cooperative Agreements (Discretionary Grants)) FY 17 $1,150,000.00; FY 18 est $1,800,000.00; FY 19 est $1,800,000.00

HQ: 411 National Center 12201 Sunrise Valley Drive, Reston, VA 20192

Phone: 703-648-5005 | Email: wcunning@usgs.gov

http://www.usgs.gov/contracts

Programs Administered by Regional - State - Local Offices

DOI15.981 | WATER USE AND DATA RESEARCH

Award: Cooperative Agreements

Purpose: To provide support to State water resource agencies in developing water use and availability datasets maintained by the USGS.

Applicant Eligibility: Proposals will be accepted from state agencies that collect and maintain water use data and databases. Various elements of the data that are required for the Water Use Data and Research (WUDR) Program are often available from different agencies within a state; however only one agency is eligible to submit a proposal for the Program. We ask that State agencies collaborate in this instance, and States may submit a single proposal that covers the work of multiple state agencies. Coordination of agencies within a state is strongly encouraged to avoid proposals that overlap.

Beneficiary Eligibility: State, Federally recognized Indian Tribal, and local governments, public nonprofit institutions/ organizations, private nonprofit institutions/organizations, profit organizations, industry and public decision makers, research scientists, engineers, and the general public will ultimately benefit from data made available through the program.

Award Range/Average: $24,000 to $125,000; average $75,000.

Funding: (Cooperative Agreements (Discretionary Grants)); FY 18 $1,500,000.00; FY 19 est $1,500,000.00; FY 20 est $1,500,000

HQ: Reston, VA 20192

　　Phone: 770-283-9728 | Email: msdalton@usgs.gov
　　http://www.usgs.gov/contracts

DOL17.801 | DISABLED VETERANS' OUTREACH PROGRAM (DVOP) "DVOP"

Award: Formula Grants

Purpose: To provide individualized career services to meet the employment needs of disabled and other eligible veterans identified by the Secretary of Labor with maximum emphasis in meeting the employment needs of those who are economically or educationally disadvantaged.

Applicant Eligibility: The state administrative entity designated by each Governor.

Beneficiary Eligibility: Veterans and eligible persons with emphasis on service-connected special disabled veterans, other disabled veterans, economically or educationally disadvantaged veterans, homeless veterans and veterans with other significant barriers to employment.

Award Range/Average: FY 2016, range from $115,000 to $13,524,029 and average assistance: $2,055,404 (rounded). FY 2017, range from $136,620 - $13,376,652 and average assistance: $2,156,223

Funding: (Formula Grants) FY 17 $116,436,068.00; FY 18 est $115,078,724.00; FY 19 est $115,078,724.00;-Estimated obligations by are determined by aggregating requests for funding from States.

HQ: 200 Constitution Avenue NW, Room S-1325, Washington, DC 20210

　　Phone: 202-693-4706 | Email: temiquel.maria@dol.gov
　　http://www.dol.gov/vets

DOL17.804 | LOCAL VETERANS' EMPLOYMENT REPRESENTATIVE PROGRAM "LVER Program"

Award: Formula Grants

Purpose: Perform outreach to employers including conducting seminars for employers, job search workshops and establishing job finding clubs; and facilitates employment, training, and placement services furnished to veterans in a state under the applicable State employment service.

Applicant Eligibility: The state administrative entity designated by each Governor.

Beneficiary Eligibility: Veterans, transitioning service members and eligible persons; business associations, businesses and other employers.

Award Range/Average: FY 2016, ranges from $0 to $5,958,324 and the average assistance: $1,071,745 (rounded). FY 2017, ranges from $0 to $4,677,738 and the average assistance: $1,004,468 (rounded)

HQ: 200 Constitution Avenue NW, Room S 1325, Washington, DC 20210

　　Phone: 202-693-4706 | Email: temiquel.maria@dol.gov
　　http://www.dol.gov/vets

DOL17.805 | HOMELESS VETERANS REINTEGRATION PROGRAM "HVRP"

Award: Project Grants

Purpose: Provide services to assist in reintegrating homeless veterans into meaningful employment within the labor force; and to stimulate the development of effective service delivery systems that will address the complex problems facing homeless veterans.

Applicant Eligibility: State and Local Workforce Investment Boards, State and State Agencies, local public agencies, Native American tribal Governments (federally recognized), Native American tribal Organizations, non-profit Organizations (including faith-based and community Organizations) and for-profit/commercial entities, and for-profit commercial entities. Potential jurisdictions are metropolitan areas of the largest U.S. cities or Non-Urban areas in need, as announced in the latest solicitation for grant applications (SGA).

Beneficiary Eligibility: Individuals who are homeless veterans. The term "homeless" or "homeless individual" includes: (1) An individual who lacks a fixed, regular, and adequate night-time residence; and (2) an individual who has a primary night-time residence that is: (a) a supervised publicly or privately operated shelter designed to provide temporary living accommodations including welfare hotels, congregate shelters, and transitional housing for the mentally ill; (b) an institution that provides a temporary institutionalized; or (c) a public or private place not designed for, or ordinarily used as, a regular sleeping accommodations for human beings (Reference: 42 U.S.C. 1302), and (3) an individual or family who - (a) will imminently lose their housing, including housing they own, rent, or live in without paying rent, are sharing with others, and rooms in hotels or motels not paid for by Federal, State, or local government programs for low-income individuals or by charitable organizations, as evidenced by - (i) a court order resulting from an eviction action that notifies the individual or family that they must leave within 14 days; (ii) the individual or family having a primary night time residence that is a room in a hotel or motel and where they lack the resources necessary to reside there for more than 14 days; or (iii) credible evidence indicating that the owner or renter of the housing will not allow the individual or family to stay for more than 14 days, and any oral statement from an individual or family seeking homeless assistance that is found to be credible shall be considered credible evidence for purposes of this clause; (b) has no subsequent residence identified; and (c) lacks the resources or support networks needed to obtain other permanent housing. A "veteran" is an individual who served in the activity military, naval, or air service, and who was discharged or released there from under conditions other than dishonorable. (Reference: 33 U.S.C. 101 (2).).

Award Range/Average: In PY 2016, there were 153 grant awards, ranging from $100,000 to $300,000 for an average of $236,737. In PY 2017,155 grants awarded, ranging from $100,000 to $500,000 for an average of $279,763.

Funding: (Project Grants) FY 17 $45,000,000.00; FY 18 est $50,000,000.00; FY 19 est $50,000,000.00

HQ: 200 Constitution Avenue NW, Room S-1325, Washington, DC 20210

Phone: 202-693-4706 | Email: temiquel.maria@dol.gov

http://www.dol.gov/dol/vets

AGENCY INDEX

Agency Index

AGENCY FOR INTERNATIONAL DEVELOPMENT 98.001 - 98.012

The agency for international development is a federal government agency that provides assistance to neighboring countries in the course of development. It serves at providing disaster relief, socioeconomic development, technical assistance, financial assistance, assistance in the management of offices, health and family planning, providing new employment opportunities, global development issues, faces challenges regarding development, etc.

Agency For international Development 98.001 - 98.012

APPALACHIAN REGIONAL COMMISSION 23.001 - 23.011

The Appalachian Regional Commission is a development agency. It builds community and promotes economic growth in Appalachia. It works at building a sustainable economic future for the Region. It helps at creating jobs, invests on projects, provides education and training, develops telecommunications, promotes health care programs for the people of Appalachia, and many other services.

Appalachian Regional Commission 23.001 - 23.011

BARRY GOLDWATER SCHOLARSHIP AND EXCELLENCE IN EDUCATION FUND 85.200 - 85.200

This foundation was established by the Congress of U.S. state government. The scholarship is provided for natural sciences, engineering, and mathematics. It is a scholarship for undergraduates and junior students. It supports the students pursuing research in the above-mentioned categories of studies.

Barry Goldwater Scholarship and Excellence in Education Fund 85.200 - 85.200

BROADCASTING BOARD OF GOVERNORS 90.500 - 90.500

The broadcasting board of governors serves at providing information and engaging people to support democracy. It provides guidance for technical, professional, and administrative support. The Broadcasting Board of Governors is an international broadcasting, including the Voice of America and other broadcasts. BBG broadcasts programs in 61 languages via radio, TV, internet and other media. The BBG provides news, information, and relevant discussion.

Broadcasting Board of Governors 90.500 - 90.500

CENTERS FOR DISEASE CONTROL AND PREVENTION 93.061 - 93.998

The Centers for Disease Control and Prevention provides information and tools for people and communities to protect their health through prevention of disease and other health threats.

Centers For Disease Control and Prevention 93.061 - 93.998

CONSUMER PRODUCT SAFETY COMMISSION 87.002 - 87.002

The Consumer Product Safety Commission protects the public from consumer products that deliver unreasonable risks of serious injury or death. CPSC works at detecting hazardous materials in the consumer products. It evaluates the industries to produce standard products, bans products that contain hazardous materials, conducts investigations on products with potential hazards, responds to consumer queries regarding certain products, and creates awareness on specific products that are harmful.

Consumer Product Safety Commission 87.002 - 87.002

CORPORATION FOR NATIONAL AND COMMUNITY SERVICE 94.002 - 94.027

The corporation for national and community service help at improving the lives of U.S. citizens. It meets the community needs throughout the localities of America. It provides services related to education, economic development, and disaster recovery services. Other services include building houses for the homeless, provides computer skills to youth, health services, small business development, promotes leadership programs, etc.

Corporation For National and Community Service 94.002 - 94.027

DELTA REGIONAL AUTHORITY 90.200 - 90.204

The Delta Regional Authority is a federal government agency. The DRA makes investments to boost economic development. DRA creates economic development through local and regional leadership, builds communities, addresses social challenges, strengthens the lives of those live delta regions, makes strategic investments for improving infrastructures, etc.

Delta Regional Authority 90.200 - 90.204

DENALI COMMISSION 90.100 - 90.199

The Denali Commission serves the federal government in an effective manner. The Commission provides job training and other economic development services in rural communities and especially in Alaska. It promotes rural development, power generation, transition facilities, modern communication systems, water and sewer systems and other infrastructures. The Commission plans and constructs health care facilities and water transportation projects.

Denali Commission 90.100 - 90.199

DEPARTMENT OF AGRICULTURE 10.001 - 10.962

Department of agriculture is the federal department of U.S. government. It is also a part of U.S. executive department. It is responsible for creating laws regarding farming, forestry, and food. It works at meeting the needs of the farmers, promotes agricultural trade and production, assures food safety, ensures to protect natural resources, etc.

Agricultural Marketing Service 10.153 - 10.178
Agricultural Research Service 10.001 - 10.700
Animal and Plant Health inspection Service 10.025 - 10.030
Economic Research Service 10.250 - 10.255
Farm Service Agency 10.051 - 10.451
Food and Nutrition Service 10.528 - 10.597
Food Safety and inspection Service 10.475 - 10.479
Foreign Agricultural Service 10.600 - 10.962
Forest Service 10.652 - 10.707
National Agricultural Statistics Service 10.950 - 10.950
National institute of Food and Agriculture 10.200 - 10.525
Natural Resources Conservation Service 10.072 - 10.934
Risk Management Agency 10.450 - 10.460
Rural Business Cooperative Service 10.350 - 10.890
Rural Housing Service 10.405 - 10.766
Rural Utilities Service 10.751 - 10.886
USDA, Assistant Secretary For Departmental Management 10.443 - 10.464
USDA, office of The Chief Economist 10.290 - 10.291

DEPARTMENT OF COMMERCE 11.008 - 11.999

The Department of Commerce serves at increasing the exports and imports of the country in many other commodities. The main purpose of this department is the development and promotion of international trade. The other services of the department include promoting commercial relationships with other countries, increasing economic zones, developing trading facilitation, regulation of industries, providing job opportunities, etc.

Bureau of industry and Security 11.150 - 11.150
Economic Development Administration 11.313 - 11.020
International Trade Administration 11.112 - 11.112
Minority Business Development Agency 11.802 - 11.805
National institute of Standards and Technology 11.013 - 11.620
National Oceanic and Atmospheric Administration 11.008 - 11.999

Agency Index

National Telecommunications and information Administration 11.549 - 11.557
U.S. Census Bureau 11.016 - 11.016

DEPARTMENT OF DEFENSE 12.002 - 12.987

The Department of Defense is to provide the security of a country. The military defends the homeland and builds security. The defense is prepared to fight against any adversaries. The Department is not only in charge of the military but also employs civilian workforce. The Department of Defense is the backbone for national security. The department also provides training and programs for joining the Department of Defense.

Advanced Research Projects Agency 12.910 - 12.910
Defense intelligence Agency (DIA) 12.598 - 12.598
Defense Logistics Agency (DLA) 12.002 - 12.002
Defense Pow/Mia Accounting Agency (DPAA) 12.740 - 12.740
Defense Threat Reduction Agency 12.351 - 12.501
Department of Defense 12.551 - 12.620
Department of Air Force 12.800 - 12.840
Department of Army 12.004 - 12.987
Department of Navy 12.300 - 12.369
Immediate office of The Secretary of Defense 12.219 - 12.700
National Guard Bureau 12.400 - 12.404
National Security Agency 12.900 - 12.905
Office of Economic Adjustment 12.003 - 12.618
Office of The Secretary of Defense 12.355 - 12.888
Office of The Secretary of Defense, Logistics and Material Readiness, Maintenance Policy & Programs 12.225 - 12.225
Uniformed Services University of The Health Sciences (USUHS) 12.750 - 12.750

DEPARTMENT OF EDUCATION 84.002 - 84.938

The department of education promotes education and looks into issues that affect education. The department of education works under the administration of secretary of education. It provides assistance to education by collecting data on schools that have been established in the U.S. It also ensures proper education for all, especially the homeless. It supports the education system through funds and monitors that the funds are accessed for the right purpose and ensures equal education access without discrimination.

Department of Education 84.165 - 84.938
Institute of Education Sciences 84.305 - 84.372
Office of Career, Technical, and Adult Education 84.002 - 84.259
Office of Elementary and Secondary Education 84.004 - 84.415
Office of Federal Student Aid 84.007 - 84.408
Office of Human Resources and Administration 84.145 - 84.145
Office of Postsecondary Education 84.015 - 84.414
Office of Special Education and Rehabilitative Services 84.027 - 84.380

DEPARTMENT OF ENERGY 81.005 - 81.250

The department of energy provides awareness regarding handling nuclear material. It is responsible for creating awareness of nuclear weapons. The DOE works under the administration of U.S. Secretary of Energy. It serves at supporting research for projects related to physical sciences. It provides programs based on science and innovation, clean energy, energy efficiency, nuclear security, saving natural energies such as electricity and fuel, etc.

Department of Energy 81.005 - 81.250

DEPARTMENT OF HEALTH AND HUMAN SERVICES 93.001 - 93.998

The U.S. Department of Health and Human Services protects the health and services for U.S. citizens. It serves at enhancing public health and social services. It strengthens the nation's healthcare system, protects the health of Americans, enhances social well-being, promotes effective management in stewardship, grants healthcare policies, etc.

Administration for Children and Families 93.060 - 93.872
Administration for Community Living (ACL) 93.041 - 93.873
Agency for Healthcare Research and Quality 93.225 - 93.226
Agency for Toxic Substances and Disease Registry 93.161 - 93.534
CDC National Center for Chronic Disease Prevention and Health Promotion 93.792 - 93.792
Centers for Disease Control and Prevention 93.061 - 93.998
Centers for Medicare and Medicaid Services 93.332 - 93.986
CMS Center for Medicare and Medicaid Innovation 93.381 - 93.381
Food and Drug Administration 93.103 - 93.876
Health Resources and Services Administration 93.011 - 93.976
Immed Office of the Secretary of Health and Human Services 93.001 - 93.983
Indian Health Service 93.123 - 93.972
National Institutes of Health 93.077 - 93.989
Office of Disease Prevention and Health Promotion 93.990 - 93.990
Office of Minority Health 93.004 - 93.910
Office of Population Affairs 93.217 - 93.974
Office of the Assistant Secretary for Administration (ASA) 93.291 - 93.291
Office of the National Coordinator for Health Information Technology (ONC) 93.345 - 93.347
President's Council on Fitness, Sports, and Nutrition 93.289 - 93.289
Substance Abuse and Mental Health Services Administration 93.104 - 93.997

DEPARTMENT OF HOMELAND SECURITY 97.005 - 97.134

The Department of Homeland Security works at providing security for the nation. The Department secures the nation from many threats. The DHS enhances security by preventing terrorism, administering laws, securing borders, protecting cyberspace, disaster recovery plans, etc. It also strengthens homeland security enterprises.

Domestic Nuclear Detection Office 97.077 - 97.130
Federal Emergency Management Agency 97.005 - 97.134
National Protection and Programs Directorate 97.120 - 97.128
Office of Health Affairs 97.091 - 97.122
Science and Technology 97.061 - 97.108
U.S. Citizenship and Immigration Services 97.009 - 97.010
U.S. Coast Guard 97.012 - 97.012
U.S. Immigration and Customs Enforcement 97.076 - 97.076

DEPARTMENT OF HOUSING AND URBAN DEVELOPMENT 14.008 - 14.92

The Department of Housing and Urban Development creates shelter and facilities for the citizens. The Department also builds discrimination-free environment. Creating inclusive communities, affordable homes, protecting people, strengthening housing market, boosting the economy, etc., are some of the services that the Department of Housing and Urban Development is involved in.

Assistant Secretary for Community Planning and Development 14.231 - 14.279
Assistant Secretary for Fair Housing and Equal Opportunity 14.400 - 14.418
Assistant Secretary for Policy Development and Research 14.008 - 14.536
Assistant Secretary for Public and Indian Housing 14.856 - 14.899
Asst Secretary for Housing Federal Housing Commissioner 14.103 - 14.329
Department of Housing and Urban Development 14.897 - 14.920

Agency Index

Office of Housing-Federal Housing Commissioner 14.175 - 14.198
Office of Lead Hazard Control and Healthy Homes 14.900 - 14.914
Office of Public and Indian Housing 14.850 - 14.850

DEPARTMENT OF THE INTERIOR 15.011 - 15.981

The Department of the Interior serves at protecting natural resources, heritage, cultures and traditions, tribal communities, etc. The Department also works at building external and internal affairs, land management, energy management, natural resources management, wildlife management, address societal challenges, fights natural hazards, etc.

Bureau of Indian Affairs and Bureau of Indian Education 15.020 - 15.960
Bureau of Land Management 15.214 - 15.247
Bureau of Ocean Energy Management 15.408 - 15.444
Bureau of Reclamation 15.504 - 15.567
Bureau of Safety and Environmental Enforcement 15.441 - 15.442
Department of Interior 15.154 - 15.568
Insular Affairs 15.875 - 15.875
National Park Service 15.011 - 15.962
Office of Surface Mining, Reclamation and Enforcement 15.250 - 15.255
Office of the Secretary of the Interior 15.152 - 15.535
U.S. Fish and Wildlife Service 15.605 - 15.683
U.S. Geological Survey 15.805 - 15.981

DEPARTMENT OF JUSTICE 16.001 - 16.922

The Department of Justice is to enforce the law and defend the public against threats. The Department works at preventing and controlling crime. Right punishment for those found guilty, fair and impartial administration of justice, protecting the civil rights, administering justice for the victims and offenders, instituting law enforcement academies, etc., are some of the areas the Department is involved in.

Department of Justice 16.843 - 16.843
Drug Enforcement Administration 16.001 - 16.004
Federal Bureau of Investigation 16.300 - 16.309
Federal Prison System / Bureau of Prisons 16.601 - 16.603
Office of Justice Programs 16.015 - 16.922
Office on Violence Against Women (OVW) 16.016 - 16.889
OJP Bureau of Justice Assistance 16.844 - 16.844

DEPARTMENT OF LABOR 17.002 - 17.807

The Department of Labor provides information on jobs and training and work-related benefits. The DOL works for the welfare of the workforce. The Department of Labor works at resolving issues impacting employees, programs for employers and employees, employment training services, information of labor market information, safety and regulations, the welfare of the wage earners, work-related benefits and rights, etc.

Bureau of International Labor Affairs 17.007 - 17.401
Bureau of Labor Statistics 17.002 - 17.005
Department of Labor 17.701 - 17.701
Department of Labor Womens Bureau (WB) 17.700 - 17.700
Departmental Management 17.791 - 17.791
Employee Benefits Security Administration 17.150 - 17.286
Employment and Training Administration 17.287 - 17.287
Mine Safety and Health Administration 17.600 - 17.604
Occupational Safety and Health Administration 17.502 - 17.504
Office of Disability Employment Policy 17.720 - 17.720

Office of Labor-Management Standards 17.309 - 17.309
Office of Workers Compensation Program 17.302 - 17.310
Veteran's Employment and Training Service 17.801 - 17.807

DEPARTMENT OF STATE 19.009 - 19.979

The Department of State promotes democratic values and develops economic prosperity. It implements various operations in and around a state. The state department's services include initiating foreign policy, makes agreements with neighboring countries, promotes the economic welfare of the country, boosts the country's development in various aspects, etc.

Bureau of African Affairs 19.979 - 19.979
Bureau of Democracy, Human Rights and Labor 19.345 - 19.345
Bureau of East Asian and Pacific Affairs 19.124 - 19.124
Bureau of Economic and Business Affairs 19.322 - 19.322
Bureau of Educational and Cultural Affairs 19.009 - 19.452
Bureau of European and Eurasian Affairs 19.878 - 19.878
Bureau of International Information Programs 19.440 - 19.441
Bureau of Population, Refugees and Migration 19.018 - 19.523
Department of State 19.013 - 19.901
Office of Overseas Schools 19.023 - 19.023
Office of the Coordinator for Cyber Issues 19.035 - 19.035
Office of the Coordinator of U.S. Assistance to Europe and Eurasia 19.900 - 19.900
Office of the Under Secretary for Public Diplomacy and Public Affairs 19.040 - 19.040
Office of U.S. Global Aids Coordinator 19.029 - 19.029
Office to Monitor and Combat Trafficking In Persons 19.019 - 19.019
Political Military Affairs/ Weapons Removal and Abatement 19.800 - 19.800
Secretary Office Representative to Muslim Communities 19.032 - 19.032
Secretary's Office of Global Women's Issues 19.801 - 19.801
U.S. Permanent Mission to the Organization of American States 19.948 - 19.948

DEPARTMENT OF TRANSPORTATION 20.106 - 20.934

The Department of Transportation is a separate entity that plays a major role in the development of a country. It serves at providing safe and secure travel for the citizens. The DOT serves at providing infrastructure for a proper transportation. Its other administrations include aviation, highway, traffic safety, motor carrier safety, railroad, hazardous material safety, etc.

Federal Aviation Administration 20.106 - 20.109
Federal Highway Administration 20.200 - 20.240
Federal Motor Carrier Safety Administration 20.218 - 20.237
Federal Railroad Administration 20.301 - 20.326
Federal Transit Administration 20.500 - 20.531
Maritime Administration 20.802 - 20.823
National Highway Traffic Safety Administration 20.600 - 20.616
Office of the Secretary 20.701 - 20.934
Pipeline and Hazardous Materials Safety Administraton 20.700 - 20.725

DEPARTMENT OF THE TREASURY 21.004 - 21.021

The Treasury Department promotes economic growth. The Department takes care of all economic and financial issues. It fosters governance in a critical financial situation. It maintains financial infrastructure, produces currency, works with neighboring governments, promotes economic growth, provides shelter for a living, fights financial crises, provides national security, etc.

Community Development Financial Institutions 21.011 - 21.021

Agency Index

Department of Treasury 21.009 - 21.016
Departmental Offices 21.017 - 21.017
Internal Revenue Service 21.004 - 21.008

DEPARTMENT OF VETERANS AFFAIRS 64.005 - 64.203

The department of veterans affairs provides benefits for veterans and their family members. The department was launched to benefit the veterans in as many aspects as possible. It provides non-healthcare benefits, rehabilitation services, education, loans, insurance for life, burial and memorial benefits, etc.

Department of Veterans Affairs 64.034 - 64.052
National Cemetery System 64.203 - 64.203
VA Health Administration Center 64.005 - 64.054
Veterans Benefits Administration 64.027 - 64.128

ELECTION ASSISTANCE COMMISSION 90.401 - 90.404

The U.S. Election Assistance Commission was established to provide guidelines for the voting system. It also provides information on election administration. It also maintains the national mail voter registration form. It certifies voting system, reports the effects of elections, administers funds to State as per requirements, develops innovative election technology, delivers strategies for effective administration, implements election law and procedures, etc.

Election Assistance Commission 90.401 - 90.404

ENVIRONMENTAL PROTECTION AGENCY 66.001 - 66.956

The Environmental Protection is an agency of the U.S. government. It has implemented various environmental laws. It serves by protecting endangered species, food quality and protection, water pollution, etc. Its principal implementation of laws includes Clean Air Act, Environmental Response Act, Emergency Planning and Recovery Act, Insecticide and Fungicide Act, Conservation Act, Toxic Substances Control Act, Safe Drinking Water Act, etc.

Environmental Protection Agency 66.001 - 66.956

EQUAL EMPLOYMENT OPPORTUNITY COMMISSION 30.001 - 30.013

The Equal Employment Opportunity Commission enforces federal laws. It investigates into issues of discrimination on the basis of race, color, religion, and gender. The EEOC promotes equal employment opportunity, provides technical assistance, monitors and evaluates federal agencies, ensures affirmative employment programs, conducts training for stakeholders, etc.

Equal Employment Opportunity Commission 30.001 - 30.013

EXECUTIVE OFFICE OF THE PRESIDENT 95.001 - 95.009

The Executive Office of the President consists of several agencies and administrations. It supports the works of the president. Some of the agencies are as follows: office of president and vice-president, council of economic advisers, national security council, national drug control policy, science and technology policy. The executive office looks into overall administration works and implementations in the United States.

Executive Office of the President 95.001 - 95.009

EXPORT-IMPORT BANK OF THE U.S. 31.007 - 31.007

The Export-Import Bank of the United States helps in dealing with the finance of U.S. It serves at sustaining U.S. export-related jobs. EXIM Bank provides loans to businesses, supports all kinds of jobs in the U.S, provides financial support to private sectors, creates good-paying U.S. jobs, etc.

Export-Import Bank of the U.S. 31.007 - 31.007

THE FEDERAL COUNCIL ON THE ARTS AND HUMANITIES 45.201 - 45.201

The Federal Council on the Arts and Humanities helps to minimize the costs of insuring international exhibitions. The organization covers for works of art owned by U.S. entities while on exhibition in the United States. It provides advice and consultation to the National Endowment for the Arts, the National Endowment for the Humanities on major problems and the Institute of Museum and Library Services that includes joint support of activities. Other services include planning and coordinating programs, activities and participation in major and historic national events. Conduct studies and prepare reports that address the state of arts and humanities in the country, especially with their economic problems and needs.

Federal Council on the Arts and Humanities 45.201 - 45.201

FEDERAL MEDIATION AND CONCILIATION SERVICE 34.002 - 34.002

The federal mediation and conciliation service is to promote peace and cooperation. It provides strategies to resolve conflicts in communities and government agencies. Its services include resolving labor-management disputes, fosters partnership building among the labors, persuades on effective communications, provides skills development training, provides conference and workshops on various technological information, etc.

Federal Mediation and Conciliation Service 34.002 - 34.002

GENERAL SERVICES ADMINISTRATION 39.002 - 39.007

The General Services Administration helps and supports federal agencies. The GSA serves the U.S. government offices and handles other management tasks. GSA promotes business and aides the private sectors, delivers real estate services, regulates effective policies, helps small businesses, provides education on modern technologies, etc.

General Services Administration 39.002 - 39.007

GULF COAST ECOSYSTEM RESTORATION COUNCIL 87.051 - 87.052

The gulf coast ecosystem restoration council was established to restore the natural ecosystem and economy of the gulf coast. The gulf coast ecosystem restoration task force enacts certain functions for restoration purposes. The functions of the task force are as follows; It implements restoration steps to improve the government efforts, it supports the relevant departments responsible for restoration actions, engages public, communities, and stakeholders to develop restoration strategies, etc.

Gulf Coast Ecosystem Restoration Council 87.051 - 87.052

INSTITUTE OF MUSEUM AND LIBRARY 45.301 - 45.313

Institute of museum and library is a space where a lot of innovative ideas of different people is kept safely. It provides information on science, technology, engineering, and math. The institute of museum and library delivers access to content and historical collections, helps to develop community and economy, provides information on digital content and related services, and engages learners of all ages and capabilities.

Institute of Museum and Library 45.301 - 45.313

INTER-AMERICAN FOUNDATION 85.750 - 85.750

The Inter-American Foundation is a department that funds projects undertaken by non-governmental organizations and other groups. The IAF provides economic opportunities for individual development. The IAF strengthens the relationship with people of the hemisphere by providing business opportunities, develops and encourages partnership with government and various community organizations, assists people who are in the development process, and many other services.

Inter-American Foundation 85.750 - 85.750

Agency Index

JAPAN-U.S. FRIENDSHIP COMMISSION 90.300 - 90.300

The Japan-U.S. friendship commission is a U.S. government agency established to develop the relationship between the United States and Japan. The commission supports Japanese engaged in graduate studies, in doctorates, in the sciences, engineering, mathematics, medical sciences, and technology. It supports non-profit organizations, U.S.-Japan training centers, research and exchange programs, etc.

Japan-U.S. Friendship Commission 90.300 - 90.300

MILLENIUM CHALLENGE CORPORATION 85.002 - 85.002

The millennium challenge corporation works at providing economic assistance. It serves at dealing with factors affecting economic growth. It looks into policies matter that affects economic growth. It addresses the projects that are cost-effective and directly affects positive development. MCC makes a partnership with other countries to develop investments that could sustain countries strength in various other factors for development.

Millenium Challenge Corporation 85.002 - 85.002

MORRIS K. UDALL SCHOLARSHIP AND EXCELLENCE IN NATIONAL ENVIRONMENTAL POLICY FOUNDATION 85.400 - 85.402

This foundation was established by the Congress of U.S. state government. It is a scholarship for undergraduates and junior students. It aides at providing funds for environmental-related studies. It supports the institutions that conduct research on environmental policies, health care issues, and issues that affect the tribal policies. The foundation also assists parties that look into concerns such as resolving environmental conflicts, natural resources conflict, public land issues, etc.

Morris K. Udall Scholarship and Excellence in National Environmental Policy Foundation 85.400 - 85.402

NATIONAL AERONAUTICS AND SPACE ADMINISTRATION 43.001 - 43.012

The National Aeronautics and Space Administration is an individual working body. The federal government takes care of aeronautics space research. NASA has explored into space a number of times, unfolding mysteries. Space exploration, scientific research in the space, exploring the neighboring planets, developing innovative machines and rockets, studying the critical challenges that the planet earth is facing, etc., are some of the day today missions of NASA.

National Aeronautics and Space Administration 43.001 - 43.012

NATIONAL ARCHIVES AND RECORDS ADMINISTRATION 89.001 - 89.003

The National Archives and Records Administration is a U.S. government agency that keeps a record of all materials and documents of business conducted in the U.S. The task of NARA is to maintain public records of men and women who fought for the U.S. The records assist at claiming the rights of citizens in the U.S. It also preserves, manages, and provides access to government electronic records. It also assists non-federal institutions. It identifies records with permanent value and discards temporary records.

National Archives and Records Administration 89.001 - 89.003

NATIONAL COUNCIL ON DISABILITY 92.002 - 92.002

The National Council of disability is a federal agency that serves at advising other agencies regarding policies, practices, and procedures that affect people with disabilities. It enhances equal opportunity by gathering and analyzing information, influences debates and agendas for disabled people, provides solutions for challenges faced by disabled people, implements effective tools to help disabled people, etc.

National Council on Disability 92.002 - 92.002

NATIONAL CREDIT UNION ADMINISTRATION 44.002 - 44.002

The national credit union administration is a U.S. federal agency. It fosters governance in a critical financial situation. It maintains financial infrastructure, works with neighboring governments, promotes economic growth, provides shelter for a living, fights financial crises, provides national security, etc.

National Credit Union Administration 44.002 - 44.002

NATIONAL ENDOWMENT FOR THE ARTS 45.024 - 45.025

The Federal Council on the Arts and Humanities helps to minimize the costs of insuring international exhibitions. The organization covers for works of art owned by U.S. entities while on exhibition in the United States. It provides advice and consultation to the National Endowment for the Arts, the National Endowment for the Humanities on major problems and the Institute of Museum and Library Services that includes joint support of activities. Other services include planning and coordinating programs, activities and participation in major and historic national events. Conduct studies and prepare reports that address the state of arts and humanities in the country, especially with their economic problems and needs.

National Endowment for the Arts 45.024 - 45.025

NATIONAL ENDOWMENT FOR THE HUMANITIES 45.129 - 45.169

The Federal Council on the Arts and Humanities helps to minimize the costs of insuring international exhibitions. The organization covers for works of art owned by U.S. entities while on exhibition in the United States. It provides advice and consultation to the National Endowment for the Arts, the National Endowment for the Humanities on major problems and the Institute of Museum and Library Services that includes joint support of activities. Other services include planning and coordinating programs, activities and participation in major and historic national events. Conduct studies and prepare reports that address the state of arts and humanities in the country, especially with their economic problems and needs.

National Endowment for the Humanities 45.129 - 45.169

NATIONAL SCIENCE FOUNDATION 47.041 - 47.083

The National Science Foundation is an agency of the U.S. government. The NSF works for the welfare of national health and national defense. It organizes research and education through various disciplines such as biological sciences, technological information science and engineering, mathematical and physical sciences, behavior and economic sciences, etc.

National Science Foundation 47.041 - 47.083

NORTHERN BORDER REGIONAL COMMISSION 90.601 - 90.601

The Northern Border Regional commission works for economic development. The NBRC serves at developing the transportation, water, sewer, energy, and telecommunications infrastructure.

Northern Border Regional Commission 90.601 - 90.601

NUCLEAR REGULATORY COMMISSION 77.006 - 77.009

The Nuclear Regulatory Commission is a U.S. government agency. It safeguards public health from radioactive materials and protects the environment. The responsibilities of the NRC include promotes safety and security of the public, certification of nuclear reactors that are standardized, provides materials that are radioactive for industrial use, aides at researching test reactors, etc.

Nuclear Regulatory Commission 77.006 - 77.009

Agency Index

OVERSEAS PRIVATE INVESTMENT CORPORATION 70.002 - 70.003

The overseas private investment corporation is the U.S. Government's finance institution. It serves at improving U.S. government's foreign policy. It provides strategies to fight challenges regarding development, helps the private sectors in U.S, funds businesses of any size, creates job opportunities in U.S, provides certain benefits for the U.S. taxpayers, helps to expand small enterprises, etc.

Overseas Private Investment Corporation 70.002 - 70.003

PEACE CORPS 45.400 - 45.400

The peace corps is a U.S. government program. The program fosters peace among the neighboring countries. The corps deliver a variety of programs which include effective ways for farming, things that could be recycled, education on environment, how to manage a park tidy, protected areas management, forest management, etc.

Peace Corps 45.400 - 45.400

PENSION BENEFIT GUARANTY CORPORATION 86.001 - 86.001

The pension benefit guaranty corporation protects and provides pensions, retirement benefits, and financial assistance. The PBGC encourages private sectors with pension plans. The revenue department of tax funds the PBGC. The pension benefit plans assured by PBGC is guided by law and adjusted on a yearly basis. It supports the employees by collecting the insurance premium and ensures appropriate pension settlements.

Pension Benefit Guaranty Corporation 86.001 - 86.001

RAILROAD RETIREMENT BOARD 57.001 - 57.001

The Railroad Retirement Board is an agency that provides retirement benefits. It supports the workers and their families under the railroad retirement plan and administers social insurance for the workers.

Railroad Retirement Board 57.001 - 57.001

SMALL BUSINESS ADMINISTRATION 59.006 - 59.069

The Small Business Administration helps small businesses in the United States. It provides suggestions for business development. The SBA provides practical guidelines for risk management, disaster assistance, promotes equal employment opportunity and civil rights, international trade, increasing performance of the business, effective communication, etc.

Small Business Administration 59.006 - 59.069

SOCIAL SECURITY ADMINISTRATION 96.001 - 96.020

The Social Security Administration is a U.S. government agency that serves at providing retirement benefits and Social Security awareness. It provides citizenship eligibility, Medicare programs, provides Social Security numbers, Social Security benefits, death and survivorship benefits, insurance coverage, etc.

Social Security Administration 96.001 - 96.020

UNITED STATES INSTITUTE OF PEACE 91.005 - 91.005

The United States Institute of Peace works at resolving conflicts. It promotes national security, supports groups that oppose extremism, and helps countries to resolve conflicts in a peaceful manner. It provides individuals with research, analysis, mediation, and other peace-building measures. It works on peace information services to promote international peace. It operates programs in conflict areas, operates a training academy, conducts conferences and workshops for building peace.

United States Institute of Peace 91.005 - 91.005

VIETNAM EDUCATION FOUNDATION 85.801 - 85.803

The Vietnam Education Foundation is a U.S. government agency established to develop the relationship between the United States and Vietnam. The VEF supports Vietnamese engaged in graduate studies, in doctorates, in the sciences, engineering, mathematics, medical sciences, and technology. It also assists Vietnamese pursuing research projects at U.S. universities and U.S. professors teaching at Vietnamese universities.

Vietnam Education Foundation 85.801 - 85.803

FEDERAL HEADQUARTERS INDEX

Federal Headquarters Index

Federal Headquarters Index

Federal Headquarters Index

Federal Headquarters Index

Federal Headquarters Index

Federal Headquarters Index

Federal Headquarters Index

Federal Headquarters Index

Federal Headquarters Index

Federal Headquarters Index

Federal Headquarters Index

Federal Headquarters Index

Federal Headquarters Index

Federal Headquarters Index

Federal Headquarters Index

Federal Headquarters Index

Federal Headquarters Index

Federal Headquarters Index

Federal Headquarters Index

Federal Headquarters Index

Federal Headquarters Index

REGIONAL-STATE-LOCAL OFFICES
INDEX

Regional-State-Local Offices Index

Agency Abbreviation	Federal Agency	Program Range	Page
DOD	ADVANCED RESEARCH PROJECTS AGENCY	12.910 - 12.910	574
USDA	AGRICULTURAL MARKETING SERVICE	10.153 - 10.178	574
USDA	AGRICULTURAL RESEARCH SERVICE	10.001 - 10.700	582
USDA	ANIMAL AND PLANT HEALTH INSPECTION SERVICE	10.025 - 10.030	583
DOI	BUREAU OF INDIAN AFFAIRS AND BUREAU OF INDIAN EDUCATION	15.020 - 15.960	584
DOL	BUREAU OF LABOR STATISTICS	17.002 - 17.005	602
DOI	BUREAU OF LAND MANAGEMENT	15.214 - 15.247	604
DOI	BUREAU OF RECLAMATION	15.504 - 15.567	611
CNCS	CORPORATION FOR NATIONAL AND COMMUNITY SERVICE	94.002 - 94.027	629
ED	DEPARTMENT OF EDUCATION	84.165 - 84.938	634
DOC	ECONOMIC DEVELOPMENT ADMINISTRATION	11.313 - 11.020	651
DOL	EMPLOYEE BENEFITS SECURITY ADMINISTRATION	17.150 - 17.286	654
EPA	ENVIRONMENTAL PROTECTION AGENCY	66.001 - 66.956	666
EEOC	EQUAL EMPLOYMENT OPPORTUNITY COMMISSION	30.001 - 30.013	710
USDA	FARM SERVICE AGENCY	10.051 - 10.451	714
DOT	FEDERAL AVIATION ADMINISTRATION	20.106 - 20.109	727
DOT	FEDERAL HIGHWAY ADMINISTRATION	20.200 - 20.240	728
DOT	FEDERAL MOTOR CARRIER SAFETY ADMINISTRATION	20.218 - 20.237	733
DOT	FEDERAL RAILROAD ADMINISTRATION	20.301 - 20.326	737
DOT	FEDERAL TRANSIT ADMINISTRATION	20.500 - 20.531	742
USDA	FOOD AND NUTRITION SERVICE	10.528 - 10.597	750
USDA	FOOD SAFETY AND INSPECTION SERVICE	10.475 - 10.479	765
USDA	FOREST SERVICE	10.652 - 10.707	766
DOC	INTERNATIONAL TRADE ADMINISTRATION	11.112 - 11.112	776
DOT	MARITIME ADMINISTRATION	20.802 - 20.823	779
DOL	MINE SAFETY AND HEALTH ADMINISTRATION	17.600 - 17.604	784
DOC	MINORITY BUSINESS DEVELOPMENT AGENCY	11.802 - 11.805	786
USDA	NATIONAL AGRICULTURAL STATISTICS SERVICE	10.950 - 10.950	787
DOD	NATIONAL GUARD BUREAU	12.400 - 12.404	788
DOT	NATIONAL HIGHWAY TRAFFIC SAFETY ADMINISTRATION	20.600 - 20.616	789
DOC	NATIONAL OCEANIC AND ATMOSPHERIC ADMINISTRATION	11.008 - 11.999	794
DOI	NATIONAL PARK SERVICE	15.011 - 15.962	796